MODERN MICROECONOMICS

THEORY AND APPLICATIONS

Nineteenth Edition

Based on UGC New Model Syllabi for B.A. (Hons.) Economics, B.Com. (Hons.) and B.A. (Hons.) Business Economics under Choice-Based Credit System (CBCS)

H.L. AHUJA
M.A., Ph.D. (DSE)
Former Senior Reader in Economics
Zakir Husain Delhi College
University of Delhi, Delhi

S Chand And Company Limited
(ISO 9001 Certified Company)

S Chand And Company Limited

(ISO 9001 Certified Company)

Head Office: Block B-1, House No. D-1, Ground Floor, Mohan Co-operative Industrial Estate, New Delhi – 110 044 | Phone: 011-66672000

Registered Office: A-27, 2nd Floor, Mohan Co-operative Industrial Estate, New Delhi – 110 044 Phone: 011-49731800

www.**schandpublishing.com**; e-mail: **info@schandpublishing.com**

Branches

Chennai	:	Ph: 23632120; chennai@schandpublishing.com
Guwahati	:	Ph: 2738811, 2735640; guwahati@schandpublishing.com
Hyderabad	:	Ph: 40186018; hyderabad@schandpublishing.com
Jalandhar	:	Ph: 4645630; jalandhar@schandpublishing.com
Kolkata	:	Ph: 23357458, 23353914; kolkata@schandpublishing.com
Lucknow	:	Ph: 4003633; lucknow@schandpublishing.com
Mumbai	:	Ph: 25000297; mumbai@schandpublishing.com
Patna	:	Ph: 2260011; patna@schandpublishing.com

First Edition 1983
Subsequent Editions and Reprints 1988, 89, 90, 92, 93, 95, 96, 97, 98, 2000, 2001, 2002, 2004, 2006, 2008, 2009, 2010, 2011, 2012, 2013, 2014
Nineteenth Edition 2016
Reprints 2018 (Twice), 2019 (Twice), 2020, 2021 (Twice)

LPSPE 2022

ISBN: 978-93-550-1101-5 **Product Code:** H5MEC41ECON10ENAA21L

PRINTED IN INDIA

By Vikas Publishing House Private Limited, Plot 20/4, Site-IV, Industrial Area Sahibabad, Ghaziabad – 201 010 and Published by S Chand And Company Limited, A-27, 2nd Floor, Mohan Co-operative Industrial Estate, New Delhi - 110 044.

PREFACE TO THE NINETEENTH EDITION

It gives me immense pleasure to bring out the nineteenth edition of the book with significant changes in some parts. My efforts have been to incorporate fully the latest changes in the syllabi of B.A.(Hons.) Economics and B.Com. (Hons.) of the universities. Besides, revising the book for nineteenth edition has given me an opportunity to incorporate the various topics of UGC new syllabi of B.A. (Hons.) Economics, B.Com. (Hons.) and B.A. (Hons.) Business Economics under the '*Choice Based Credit System*' (CBCS) which is to be adopted by all India Universities with making up to 30 per cent changes in them, if they so desire. On the important suggestion of the fellow colleagues from Delhi and other Indian universities, I incorporated in a previous edition a new comprehensive chapter (given as Appendix to Chapter 3) on ***"The Use of Mathematical Concepts, Graphs and Other Techniques in Economics."*** In it, I have explained the use of graphs in economics, various types of curves and measurement of their slopes, the concept of function, both linear and power functions, the concept of derivatives and the use of differential calculus as optimising technique for solving the problems of maximisation and minimisation in economics. I hope the study of this appendix will enable the students to understand various economic theories better as economics in recent years has become increasingly mathematical.

A general misconception about economics is that it is an uninteresting subject dealing with abstract issues. This is however not correct. Economics is concerned with very relevant and interesting subjects which are important for everyday economic life of the people. In fact, Marshall, a great British economist of the twentieth century, had defined economics as "*a study of mankind in the ordinary business of life.*" The revisions of this book and addition of new topics explained show that the study of economics is a highly useful and interesting subject that has great relevance for the everyday life of the people. The following topics have either been added or substially revised in the present nineteenth edition of the book.

First, in Chapter 5, I have added the explanation of ***Basic Competitive Model and its Essential Features.*** It may be noted that ***market-friendly new economic reforms*** carried out in India since 1991 are based on the assumed economic efficiency of this basic competitive model. I have critically examined this basic competitive model in Part-I of this book.

Secondly, the government intervention in the economy through the means of price control and rationing, rent control, agricultural minimum support prices (MSP) has been explained with demand-supply model. Besides, phenomenon of ***'poverty amidst plenty'*** in the contest of farmers' income; why did OPEC could not keep the price of petrol at a high level for long, distribution of burden of indirect taxes, fight against illegal drugs have been explained through demand-supply analysis.

In Part II, I have discussed the nature of ***'preferences'*** of the individuals on which indifference curve analysis and revealed preference theory of demand is based. It may be noted that indifference curves are used not only to explain consumer's behaviour but also other important issues such as whether ***subsidy in kind*** **(*e.g.*, food stamp programme) or** ***cash subsidy*** **(*i.e.*, direct cash transfer)** is better and further that whether direct or indirect taxes are better with regard to their impact on individuals' welfare. All these important issues are explained in this book. Similarly, important topics of decision by individuals regarding supply of labour (i.e., *work-leisure choice*) and supply of savings by the people which involves *intertemporal choice by the individuals* have also been explained using indifference curve technique in Chapter 11A.

In Chapter 14, dealing with the theory of consumer surplus, I have added the study of very useful concepts of ***compensating variation in income*** **and** ***equivalent variation in income*** with which we measure ***change in welfare in money terms*** of changes in prices of goods.

A new Chapter 7B has been added which explains the assumed **economic efficiency of perfectly competitive market economy in terms of consumer surplus and producer surplus.** In subsequent chapters concerning monopoly, oligopoly, monopolistic competition, we study how in the real world in which monopolies, oligopolies prevail they cause misallocation of resources of the economy and cause loss of economic efficiency. In the analysis of price determination, in addition to profit-maximising model, I have critically examined **sales-maximisation model and Game theory and competitive price strategy.**

Another important addition is the ***Hicksian analysis of wage-determination under collective bargaining in terms of employer's concession curve and labour union's resistance*** curve in Chapter 33A. Further, the study of an important topic of ***common property resources*** and how they lead to their overuse, which is usually called ***tragedy of commons***, has been incorporated. It may be further noted that I have withrawn the last three chapters, namely, Borrowing-bending Equilibrium, Investment Decision Analysis and Choice under Risk and Uncertainty as they have been deleted under the UGC's new CBCS syllabi.

It is worth mentioning that trends in recent years in question papers of Delhi and other Indian universities are that the Questions on Numerical/Mathematical Problems are asked to test the understanding of economic concepts and theories by the students. Accordingly, in various chapters, I have explained the mathematical derivations of various microeconomic concepts and theories and numerical problems based on them.

With the above changes I hope the students of **B.A. (Hons.) Economics, B.Com. (Hons.) and B.A. (Hons.) Business Economics of Indian universities** will find the present edition of the book more useful and instructive for them. This book will also be of immense use for professional courses such as **Business Economics, BBA, CA, ICWA** and for the candidates preparing for all India and State level competitive examinations such as IAS, IES and allied services. Suggestions for the further improvement of the book from fellow teachers will be heartily welcomed. In this connection, the author can be approached at e-mail drhlahuja@gmail.com.

H.L. AHUJA

69, Vaishali
Pitampura
Delhi—110 034

UGC New CBCS SYLLABUS of B.A. (Hons.) Economics

Course – 1, Semester – I

Introductory Microeconomics

COURSE OUTLINE

1. Exploring the Subject matter of Economics

Why study economics ? The scope and method of economics; scarcity and choice; questions of what, how and for whom to produce and how to distribute output; the basic competitive model; prices, property rights and profits; incentives and information; rationing; opportunity sets; economic systems; reading and working with graphs.

Reference : Modern Microeconomics, Chapters 1, 2, 3, 5, 6

2. Supply and Demand : How Markets Work, Markets and Welfare

Individual demand and supply schedules and the derivation of market demand and supply; shifts in demand and supply curves; the role of prices in resources allocation; the concept of elasticity and its application; consumer and producer surplus; taxes and their efficiency costs.

Reference* : *Modern Microeconomics, Chapters 6, 7, 7A, 7B, 13, 20

3. Households

The consumption decision : preferences and their representation with indifference curves; budget constraint; a consumer's optimum choice; income and substitution effects; labour supply and savings decisions.

Reference* : *Modern Microeconomics; Chapters, 9 Appendix B to Chapter 9, Chapter 11A

4. Firms and Perfect Market Structure

Behaviour of profit-maximizing firms and the production process, short-run costs and output decision: costs and output in the long run.

Reference : Modern Microeconomics, Chapters 18, 19, 23

5. Imperfect Market Structure

Monopoly and anti-trust policy; government policies towards competition; imperfect competition.

Reference : Modern Microeconomics, Chapters 26, 26A, 28

6. Input Market

Labour and land markets; concepts of derived demand, Input productivity, Marginal Productivity of labour marginal revenue product demand curve for labour and input demand curves and shifts in them competitive Labour markets and public policy.

Reference : Modern Microeconomics, Parts of Chapters 32, 33, 34

Course – 6, Semester – II

Intermediate Microeconomics – 1

Consumer Theory

Preference, utility, budget constraint; choice; demand; Slutsky equation; buying and selling; choice under risk and intertemporal choice; revealed preference.

Reference : Modern Microeconomics; Chapters; 9, Appendices A & B to Chapter 9, 12.

2. Production, Costs and Perfect Competition

Technology; isoquants; production with one and more variable inputs; returns to scale; short run and long run costs; cost curves in the short run and long run; review of perfect competition.

Reference : Modern Microeconomics, Chapters 16, 17, 18, 19, 23, 7B.

Course – 7, Semester – IV :

Intermediate Microeconomics – II

1. General Equilibrium, Efficiency and Welfare

Equilibrium and efficiency under pure exchange and production; overall efficiency and welfare economics.

Reading : Modern Microeconomics Chapters, 37, 38, 39

2. Market Structure and Game Theory

Monopoly; pricing with market power; price discrimination; peak-load pricing; two part tariff; monopolistic competition and oligopoly; game theory and competitive strategy.

Reading **:** ***Modern Microeconomics***; Chapters, 26, 27, Appendix to Chapter 27, 28, 29, 31

3. Market Failure

Externalities; public goods and markets with asymmetric information.

Reading : *Modern Microeconomics*. Chapters 40, 43.

Note. ***It is hereby clarified that the university has recommended different books as Readings. We have given the chapter numbers of our book Modern Microeconomics : Theory and Applications for students, reference.***

CBCS Syllabus B.Com. (Hons.)
Semester – I, Paper – 1.4
Microeconomics

Duration : 3 hrs. **Lectures : 65**

Objective: Objective of the course is to acquaint the students with the concepts of microeconomics dealing with consumer behaviour. The course also makes the students understand the supply side of the market through the production and cost behaviour of firms.

Learning Outcomes: The students would be able to apply tools of consumer behaviour and firm theory to business situations.

Course Contents

Unit – I: Demand and Consumer Behaviour **Lectures : 13**

Concepts of revenue: marginal and average: Revenue under conditions of perfect and imperfect competition Elasticity of demand: price, income and cross.

Consumer Behaviour: Indifference curve analysis of consumer behaviour; .Consumer's equilibrium (necessary and sufficient conditions). Price elasticity and price consumption curve, income consumption curve and Engel curve, price change and income and substitution effects. Indifference curves as an analytical tool (cash subsidy vs. kind subsidy). Revealed Preference Theory.

Unit II: Production and Cost **Lectures : 13**

Production isoquants, marginal rate of technical substitution, economic region of production, optimal combination of resources, the expansion path, isoclines, returns to scale using isoquants.

Cost of Production: Social and private costs of production, long run and short run costs of production. Economies and diseconomies of scale and the shape of the long run average cost curve, Learning Curve and economies of scope.

Unit III: Perfect Competition **Lectures : 13**

Perfect competition: Assumptions. Equilibrium of the firm and the industry in the short and the long runs, including industry's long run supply curve. Measuring producer surplus under perfect competition. Stability Analysis – Walrasian and Marshallian. Demand – supply analysis including impact of taxes and subsidy.

Unit – IV: Monopoly **Lectures : 13**

Monopoly: short run and long run equilibrium. Shifts is demand curve and the absence of the supply curve. Measurement of monopoly power and the rule of thumb for pricing. Horizontal and vertical integration of firms. The social costs of monopoly power including deadweight loss. Degrees of price discrimination.

Unit – V: Imperfect Competition **Lectures : 13**

Monopolistic Competition and Oligopoly: Monopolistic competition : price and output decision-equilibrium. Monopolistic competition and economic efficiency Oligopoly and Interdependence – Cournot's duopoly model, Stackelberg model, Kinked demand model. Prisoner's dilemma, collusive oligopoly – price-leadership model-dominant firm, cartels, sales maximization, Contestable markets theory. Pricing of Public Utilities.

B.A. (Hons.) Business Economics: CBCS Programme

Course – 1, Semester – I
Microeconomics and Applications – I

Unit-1: Basic Concepts **Lectures : 12**

Scarcity and choice; Production possibility frontier, Positive and normative economics; constructing a model, scientific method; concepts of opportunity cost, rate of growth, and of total, average and marginal functions.

Demand and supply: Market demand, elasticity, shifts and movements, Applications of demand, supply and elasticity. Revenue and Expenditure, elasticity and marginal revenue; income elasticity of demand; consumer surplus.

Unit-2: Consumer Choice **Lectures : 18**

Cardinal theory, derivation of demand in case of one or more goods; Ordinal theory: Budget sets and Preferences under different situations. Indifference curves; the rate and elasticity of substitution. Consumer equilibrium; effects of change in prices and income; Engel's curve. Derivation of demand curve. Income and substitution effects: Hicks and Slutsky. Applications of indifference curves to other economic problems.

Revealed preference theory: WARP; SARP and the derivation of demand curve.

Unit-3: Production **Lectures : 10**

Production functions: single variable – average and marginal product, variable proportions, stages of production. Two variables - isoquants, returns to scale and to a factor; factor prices; cost minimisation and output maximisation; Elasticity of substitution. Expansion path and the cost function.

Unit-4: Cost **Lectures : 10**

Concept of economic cost; short-run and long-run cost curves; increasing and decreasing cost industries; envelope curve; L-shaped cost curves; economies of scale. Prices as parameters: Firm's equilibrium and profit; short and long-run supply function; taxes and subsidies.

Unit-5: Forms of Market **Lectures : 15**

Perfect competition: Equilibrium of the market. Long-run industry supply: producer and consumer surplus. Applications: Effects of taxes and subsidies.

Monopoly: Equilibrium, supply; multiplant firm; monopoly power; deadweight loss; price discrimination; dumping; two-part tariffs. Monopolistic Competition: Product differentiation; equilibrium of the firm in the industry-with entry of new firms and with price competition. Comparison with pure competition.

Course – 3, Semester – II
Microeconomics and Applications – II

Unit-1: Oligopoly and Game Theory **Lectures : 12**

Cournot model and reaction curves; Stackelberg's model, Bertrand model; Quantity leadership; Price leadership; Non-collusive stable equilibrium; simultaneous quantity setting; collusion; cartels; Concepts of Game Theory: Dominant strategies and Nash Equilibrium; Mixed strategies; Prisoner's Dilemma. Specification of oligopoly models in game theoretic terms. Repeated Games and Entry Deterrence.

Unit-2: Factor Markets **Lectures : 12**

Factor pricing in the case of single and many variable factors; demand for labour in a product market with perfect competition and monopoly. Monopsony, bilateral monopoly and role of labour unions. Economic rent and quasi rent.

Unit-3: General Equilibrium **Lectures : 15**

Edgeworth box: 2 good, 2 factor, 2 consumer analysis and Pareto optimality conditions; market trade; Walras Law; Relative prices; Equilibrium and efficiency; Grand Utility possibility frontier. Implication of first and second welfare theorem.

Unit-4: Welfare Failure **Lectures : 11**

Social welfare function: welfare maximization; Fair allocation; Envy and equity. Arrow's Impossibility Theorem.

Unit-5: Market Failure **Lectures : 15**

Externalities: Environment and its impact on market, Common property resources and public goods, Asymmetric Information and Signaling, Joint production and consumption.

CONTENTS

PART I

SCOPE AND METHODOLOGY OF ECONOMICS

PART II

THE THEORY OF DEMAND

PART III

THE THEORY OF PRODUCTION AND COST

PART IV

THE THEORY OF FIRM AND PRICING IN VARIOUS MARKET STRUCTURES

PART V

THE THEORY OF DISTRIBUTION

PART VI

GENERAL EQUILIBRIUM ANALYSIS WELFARE ECONOMICS AND MARKETS WITH ASYMMETRIC INFORMATION

PART - I

THE SCOPE AND METHODOLOGY OF ECONOMICS

- The Economic Problem : Scarcity and Choice
- The Scope of Economics : Micro and Macro-Economics
- The Use of Mathematical Concepts, Graphs and other Techniques
- The Methodology of Economics
- Economic Statics and Dynamics
- Central Problems of an Economy
- Market Economy : Role of Price Mechanism
- Alternative Economic Systems : Command Economy and Mixed Economic System

CHAPTER 1

THE ECONOMIC PROBLEM : SCARCITY AND CHOICE

Introduction

Knowledge has many branches and economics is an important and useful branch of knowledge. In recent years, the science of economics has assumed greater significance in view of the fact that knowledge of economics is being used for initiating and accelerating growth in the economics of the world and thus for eradicating want, poverty and unemployment from the human race. Besides, the nature of so many other problems such as inflation, food, stagnation and recession, population explosion, adverse balance of payments and so on that confront the economies of today cannot be understood and solution for them cannot be provided without the adequate knowledge of the science of economics.

The science of economics in the form in which we have it today is just two hundred years old.[1] It has made a remarkable progress during this period. In this book we shall explain the principles of modern economics, that is, economics in the form in which we have it today. But before we start the study of the principles of modern economics, it will be desirable to explain to the students what economics is about or what we study in economics, or, in other words, what is the subject matter of economics. Every science or a branch of knowledge is concerned with a particular subject. Thus, the science of physics deals with the properties of matter and energy, the science of chemistry deals with the constitution or composition of matter. Political science studies the nature of State and Government. In biology, we study the constituion and evolution of living organisms. Therefore, the question which a beginner is likely to ask is: "What is the subject matter of economics ?"Therefore, economists have also tried to define the subject matter of economics. By defining the subject matter of economics they have tried to distinguish it from other branches of knowledge.

Perhaps there is no other science or a body of knowledge in regard to which there has been such a great controversy about its subject matter or its proper definition as about economics. J.N. Keynes is right when he says that "Political Economy is said to have strangled itself with definitions."[2] Economics has been variously defined by different economists from time to time. This is partly because "*economics is an unfinished science*."[3] With the passage of time there have been significant developments in economic theory and new subjects have been included in it. It is still in the process of growth and development. Therefore, the old definitions of economics have become irrelevant. The definition of a science or a body of knowledge delimits its subject matter that is already in existence. But in a science like economics that is growing and developing, its correct and satisfactory definition can be given only after it has sufficiently developed and grown. Now that the science of economics has sufficiently developed, we can provide an adequate and satisfactory definition of economics.

Changing Perspectives of Economics

Economics as a Study of Wealth. Adam Smith in his well-known book '*Wealth of Nations*'

1. Adam Smith who is generally known as father of economics brought out his famous book "*The Nature and Causes of Wealth of Nations*" in the year 1776. Before Adam Smith, there were other writers who expressed important economic ideas but economics as a distinct branch of knowledge started with Adam Smith's *Wealth of Nations*. It is worth noting that in the beginning the name of economics was "*Political Economy*."
2. J. N. Keynes *Scope and Method of Political Economy* p. 153.
3. F. Zuethen, *Economic Theory and Method* (1953), p. 3.

defined economics as '*an enquiry into the wealth of nations*. Thus Adam Smith laid emphasis on the expansion of wealth and riches of a society as a subject matter of economics. Another classical economist David Ricardo shifted the emphasis from the expansion of wealth to the *distribution of wealth*. Ricardo writes, "The produce of the earth all that is derived from its surface by the united application of labour, machinery and capital is divided among three classes of the economy namely, the proprietor of the land, the owner of the stock of capital necessary for its cultivation and the labourers by whose industry it is cultivated". He further writes, "*To determine the laws which regulate this distribution is the principle problem in political economy*".

That economics is a science of production and distribution of wealth has been severely criticised by men of letters, especially Carlyle and Ruskin who prompted by emphasis on wealth in economics called it as 'Gospel of Mammon' and a dismal science. They alleged that economists had ignored the higher values of life and sought to enquire how to increase the material wealth and riches of the people and a nation. In our view this interpretation of wealth by Carlyle and Ruskin is not correct. Wealth consists of material goods and not gold and diamond and these goods satisfy the wants of the people. To achieve maximum satisfaction of wants of the people to promote their welfare is the ultimate objective of economics. However, the view that economics is a science of wealth suffers from two main shortcomings. First, in the concept of wealth, Adam Smith and Ricardo included only the *material goods* and ignored the importance of services such as education, health and several others which also satisfy human wants. Several modern economists, especially Prof. Amartya Sen, a Nobel Prize winner in economics, have emphasised the role of education, health and good administration and have shown that they greatly raise the productivity of man and promote economic growth of the nations. In view of their vital importance in raising production and productivity, good health, education and skills have in fact been called *human capital* by modern economists and investment in human capital or investment in man is as important as investment in physical capital.

Economics as a Science of Material Welfare of Man

Another drawback in making economics a "science of wealth" by classical economists may be noted. By laying conspicuous emphasis on wealth and put man to the secondary place in economic studies they did not lay adequate stress on *man's behaviour* in relation to wealth. Nor did they emphasise the end or ultimate objective of economics which is the promotion of human and social welfare. As a matter of fact, wealth is only a means to an end, the end being the welfare of man and society. To regard wealth as the be-all and the end-all of economic science is to make the means as the end. The credit goes to Alfred Marshall, a prominent English economist, for shifting the emphasis from wealth to man and also from wealth to welfare. According to him, economics is "*on the one side a study of wealth; and on the other; and more important side, a part of the study of man*".[6] He further writes, economics examines that part of individual and social action which is most closely connected with the attainment and with the use of material requisites of well-being".[7]

Economics as a Study of Allocation of Scarce Resources

However, a leading British economist Lionel Robbins in the early thirties put forward an alternative view of economics. He pointed out that the economic problem arises because of scarcity of resources in relation to human wants. The scarcity of resources and unlimited wants of the people necessitates choice regarding what wants to be satisfied and, therefore, the particular allocation of scarce resources among various goods and services. He thus writes, Economics is the science which studied human behaviour as a relationship between ends and scarce means which have alternative uses". Thus Robbins lays stress on three facts, namely (1) human wants are unlimited, (2) the resources to satisfy these wants are scarce, and (3) the scarce resources have alternative uses.

4. Daved Ricardo, "*Preface to his Principles of Economics*"
5. *Op. cit.*
6. Alfred Marshall, *Principles of Economics*, 8th ed. p.1
7. L. Robbins, *The Nature and Significance of Economic Science*. p.2

Thus, according to Robbins, economics is a science of choice. It deals with how the resources of a society are allocated to the satisfaction of various human wants. Whenever, the resources which help to produce goods and services are scarce and wants for them are unlimited, the question of choice arises. The man has to choose which wants are to be satisfied with the limited resources. Thus Robbins writes, "when time and means for achieving ends are limited and capable of alternative application and the ends are capable of being distinguished in order of preference, the behaviour necessarily assumes the form of choice".

In recent years even Robbins view has been challenged we shall critically examine Robbins definition of economics in detail later in this chapter. Robbins has not only ignored normative aspects of economics but his view regarding economics does not cover important problems such as unemployment of resources, especially of labour, distribution of output or income among the population and economic stability. It was J.M. Keynes who explained the problems of unemployment of resources and economic stability and laid the foundations of what is now called macroeconomics. Besides, **Robbins' view does not cover the important problem of economic growth** which explains how through raising the rate of investment or capital formation and technological progress, national output and income can be increased. Later in this chapter we shall give some modern definitions of economics which cover these important issues and problems.

THE ECONOMIC PROBLEM : SCARCITY AND CHOICE

Economics is mainly concerned with the achievement and use of material requirements to satisfy human wants. Human wants are unlimited and productive resources such as land and other natural resources, skilled labour, raw materials, capital equipment with which to produce goods and services to satisfy those wants are scarce or limited. Thus, goods and services which satisfy human wants are scarce because productive resources with which to produce goods and services are scarce. The problem of scarcity of resources is felt not only by individuals but also by the society as a whole. With wants being unlimited and resources scarce, we individually as well as collectively cannot satisfy all our wants. This gives rise to the problem of how to use scarce resources to attain maximum possible satisfaction of the people. This is generally called '*the economic problem*' as it lies at the root of all economic problems faced by the society. Every economic system, be it capitalist, socialist or mixed, has to contend with this central problem of scarcity of resources relative to wants for them.

Thus the economic problem derives from the scarcity of resources relative to human wants This gives rise to the struggle of man for existence and efforts by him to increase his well-being. That the scarcity of resources in relation to human wants is the fundamental economic problem can be easily understood in the context of poor and developing countries like India where quite a large number of population lives at a bare subsistence level. The struggle for existence due to the scarcity of resources is too obvious in them to need any elaborate explanation. However, to say that the developed countries such as U.S.A. where affluence and prosperity have been brought about also confront the scarcity problem raises some doubts. But the *fact is that*, despite of their affluence and riches, developed societies too face the problem of scarcity. Of course, their possession of goods and services has enormously increased, but so has their wants. Indeed, their wants for goods and services has been multiplying during the course of economic growth so that their present wants still remain ahead of their resources and capacity to produce.

Unlimited Wants. As has been said above, the economic problem arises not merely due to the limited resources and capacity to produce alone but also due to unlimited human wants. Most of us want better food, more and better clothing, more education and health care, good houses, new TV sets, computers and so many other goods. So long as human wants for goods and services remain ahead of the resources, both natural and acquired, the economic problem of scarcity would be there.

8. Op. cit. p.14.

If Americans today, for example, were to content to live at the level of the Indian middle class people, all their wants would be fully satisifed with their available resources and capacity to produce. In that situation they would face little or no scarcity and economic problem for them would disappear. However, the affluent and developed countries of the U.S.A. and Western Europe face the problem of scarcity even today as their present wants remain ahead of their increased resources and capability to produce.

Scarcity of Resources and the Problem of Choice

Whereas wants of the people are unlimited means to satisfy those wants are limited or scarce. It is due to the scarcity of resources that even a richest society like that of the USA can produce only a limited quantity of the goods and services that people would want to consume if these things were free. Now, the goods and services are scarce because the resources to produce them are searce. The scarcity of resources to satisfy human wants gives rise to the basic economic problem of choice. If we cannot have all the goods and services we would like to have we must choose what goods and services are produced to satisfy the wants of the people and what wants be left unsatisfied. Scarcity of resources requires that efficient and optimum use of resources be made so that we should get most out of them and maximum possible satisfaction of the people is achieved. Further, since all wants cannot be satisfied due to scarcity of resources we face *the problem of choice* — choice among multiple wants which are to be satisfied. If it is decided to use more resources in one line of production, then some resources must be withdrawn from another commodity. Thus, the problem of choice from the viewpoint of the society as a whole refers to which goods and in what quantities are to be produced and how productive resources allocated for their production accordingly so as to achieve the greatest possible satisfaction of the people. An eminent English economist Lord Robbins defines economics in terms of this basic economic problem. According to him, "*Economic is a science which studies human behaviour as a relationship between ends and scarce resources which have alternative uses.*" Ends refer to wants which are considered to be unlimited. The use and allocation of scarce resources to produce goods and services has to be such as would maximise satisfaction. This applies both to the behaviour of the individual as well as to that of the society as a whole.

Kinds of Resources

There are various kinds of resources which help us in producing goods and services. They are also called factors of production. Economists traditionally classify productive resources into four types; land, labour, capital and enterprise (or entrepreneurship). These resources provide the energy and materials that are combined through technology to produce goods and services. We explain them below in some detail.

Labour. Labour represents all physical and mental abilities which people can make available for production of goods and services. Labour is usually measured by the time spent in working during a period.

Land. In economics, land includes all natural resources which are free gift of nature. Thus, by land economists do not mean only agricultural soil but also other natural resources such as minerals, water, climate and forests.

Capital. Capital refers to man-made resources of production. Capital includes equipment, factory-buildings, all sorts of tools, machines, roads, dams, transport buses, trucks etc. These are often called capital goods which help in the production of further goods and services. Since these capital goods are man-made, they can be produced more every year. In this way capital formation every year adds to the stock of capital and increases our capacity to produce goods and services. Capital formation in a year is also called *real investment*.

It is important to note that money, shares and bonds are also often called capital. But they do not represent physical or real capital which helps in further production of goods and resources. Since with money or shares and bonds, we can purchase capital goods or other resources, they are called *money capital or financial capital.* Thus, real capital is different from money capital.

Entrepreneurship. Entrepreneurship represents a special human resource which provides his entrepreneurial ability or what is also called enterprise. Entrepreneur plays a crucial role in a free market economy. It is he who initiates and organises the production process by combining other resources such as labour, capital and land. Entrepreneur takes various business-policy decisions and bears risk of loss from his venture. Another important task of an entrepreneur is to introduce innovations such as the use of new and better techniques of production, launching of new products.

All economic resources, labour, land, capital and entrepreneurial ability are scarce or limited in supply. Arable land, mineral resources, labour-time, capital equipment required for the production of goods and services are available in limited quantities. Thus scarce or limited resources put a constraint on the amount of goods and services that can be produced.

Types of Output

Just as there are different kinds of resources, there are different types of output. There are mainly four types of output : (1) Consumer goods and services. The consumer goods are tangible commodities such as foodgrains, cloth, cars, shoes which are produced with resources. There are *single-use consumer goods* such as food, Coca Cola, milk which are used up in a single act of consumption. There are *durable-use consumer goods* such as a car, a house, computer which are used over and over again for a long period of time.

The second types of output is services which are intangible such as education provided by a teacher, health services given by a doctor, telephone calls etc. They also provide direct satisfaction to the people. Thirdly, there are *capital goods* which are not used for direct satisfaction of wants of the people but, as mentioned above, they are used for producing other goods. Finally, there are *raw materials*, and *intermediate goods* such as steel, cement, fertilizers. The intermediate goods are also not used for direct for satisfaction of the wants of the consumers but can be used for the production of either consumer goods and services or capital goods.

The process by which resources are transformed into goods and services is called production. It may be noted that the market value of all final goods and services produced in a year in a country is called gross domestic product (GDP).

CENTRAL PROBLEMS OF AN ECONOMY

As stated above, the scarcity of resources relative to human wants gives rise to various *basic problems, issues* or *questions* which have to be solved by an economy if it is to fulfil its purpose. These basic economic problems are also called central problems of the economy. All these problems involve choice to be made by the society. These problems are ;

1. *What* to produce
2. *How* to produce
3. *For Whom* to produce
4. *What Provision* (if any) be made for economic growth.

We explain below these central problems in some detail.

What to Produce ?

This means that what goods and in what quantities are produced by a society, 'Guns or butter' has been the popular way of describing this dilemma of choice posed by the scarcity of resources. But this choice between war goods and goods for civilian consumption is not the only problem of choice faced by the society. The society has to choose among thousands of consumer goods themselves and decide about allocation of resources between them. Of special mention in this regard is the choice between necessities and luxuries. For example, how much necessities such as foodgrains and clothing and how many luxury cars and air conditioners are to be produced and resources allocated accordingly. Further, an important choice about the production of goods and resource allocation is to decide about what amounts of consumer goods and capital goods are to be produced. As shall be made clear later, this decision about the allocation of resources between consumer goods and capital goods is of crucial importance from the point of view of economic growth.

More generally, in answering the question what goods shall be produced, society would have to choose somehow or other among scores of goods such as cars, hospitals, schools, houses, radios, televisions, nuclear bombs, wheat , rice, cloth, machinery, steel, soap, lipsticks, terylene, nylon, etc. But this decision is only half the story. Once society has decided which goods shall be produced, it must then give proper weights to each of the good it selects to produce. The fact that resources are scarce means that society cannot produce unlimited amounts of even these selected goods. Therefore, society must decide how much wheat, how many hospitals, how many schools and how many metres of cloth are to be produced. In fact, most of the goods in the above list will be decided to be produced Only the question of what quantity of each of the goods is to be produced would have to be decided. Thus, scarcity of resources forces us to make a choice what goods and in what quantities are to be produced. This will determine the allocation of scarce resources among them.

In a free market economy the choice of what goods and in what quantities are made is decided by the interaction between private firms who organise production on the one hand and consumers whose wants are to be satisfied by producing goods and services on the other. We will explain in a later chapter how prices play a critical role in determining what goods and in what quantities are produced in a free market economy. However, in a free market economy today government also influences the choice of goods to be produced.

How to Produce : Choice of a Production Technique

This means with what methods or techniques a society will decide to produce goods. A combination of resources (or factors) implies a technique of production. Usually, there are various alternative techniques of producing a commodity and the society has to choose among them, each technique using a different combination of resources like labour and capital. For instance, cotton cloth can be produced with either handlooms, or automatic looms (as used in modern textile mills). Production with technique of handlooms involves the use of more labour relatively to capital and therefore represents a labour-intensive technique. On the other hand, the production of cloth with automatic looms of the modern textile mills involves use of more capital relative to labour and hence represents a capital-intensive technique of production. Likewise, alternative techniques involving different degrees of capital and labour intensity are available for producing other commodities. With use of better or technologically advanced machines productivity is higher but they require less labour. In the choice of a technique of production prices of different factors play an important role. However, government in a market economy today affects the choice of methods for producing goods through its fiscal and monetary policies. Obviously, the choice between different techniques would depend on the available supplies of different factors of production and their relative prices.

Scarcity of resources demands that goods should be produced with the most efficient method. If the economy uses its resources inefficiently, the output would be smaller and there would be unnecessarily sacrifice of goods that otherwise would have been available. Therefore, it is in society's interest that those techniques of production are used that make greater use of relatively abundant factors and economise as much as possible on those factors which are relatively scarce.

For Whom to Produce : How is Output Distributed ?

For whom to produce means who will get how much for consumption. In other words, it means how the national product is to be distributed among the members of the society. Productive resources and the resulting output being scarce, we cannot satisfy all wants of all the people. Therefore, a society has to decide who should get how much from the total output of goods and services. This is, as it were, sharing of national cake among the people constituting a society. Obviously, in a free market economy who would get how much of national output depends on his money income. The greater the money income a person enjoys, the greater the amount of goods he would be able to buy from the market. Therefore, the greater the inequalities in the distribution of money incomes, the greater the inequalities in the distribution of national output. Therefore, this raises the question as to how a free market economy decides about the distribution of money incomes.

Money income can be obtained in two ways. First, it can be obtained through work, that is, selling one's labour services. Wages (and salaries) represent the incomes from work. Differences in wages earned by various people arise due to differences in production- activities, skill, education as well as due to the bargain-ing powers of various social classes and a host of social and institutional factors. Second, income can be made from property such as land, factories and other forms of capital. Rent, interest and profits are the examples of income from property. Differences in the ownership of property in a free market economy cause differences in incomes from proper-ty. Thus, money incomes of the people made in these ways go to determine the distribution of national output. Therefore, in order to explain the distribution of output, we have to explain how distribution of income, that is, wages of labour, rent of land, interest on capital and profits of enterprise are determined. However, in the market economies government also influences the incomes of the people through imposition of taxes, grant of subsidies and various government expenditure programmes aimed at redistributing incomes.

How the national income is to be distributed has been a burning topic not only in the field of economics but also in politics. There is perhaps no topic in the whole of economics on which discussion has been so hot and furious as the distribution of national product and income. Some have argued with a good deal of justification that all people should get equal incomes and hence equal shares from the national product. According to Karl Marx, the distribution of national income should be on the basis of "*from each according to his ability, to each according to his needs*". Another important view has been that *each individual should get income equal to the contribution he makes to the national production.*

What Provision Should be Made for Economic Growth ?

Both an individual and a society would not like to use all its scarce resources for current consumption only. This is because if all resources are used for producing consumer goods only and no provision in terms of allocating some resources for investment, that is, for production of capital goods, is made, the resources or productive capacity would not increase in future. This implies that incomes or standards of living of the people would remain stagnant. Indeed, if no provision is made for investment, the future productive capacity and hence the levels of living may decline. For, in the absence of this provision, the stock of capital would fall due to depreciation as a result of its use for producing consumer goods in a period. This is better expressed by quoting an old Chinese saying which states. "*He who cannot see beyond the dawn will have much good wine to drink at noon, much green wine to cure his headache at dusk and only rain water to drink for the rest of days.*" Therefore, a wise individual or a society could like to provide for its growth of productive capacity.

The objective to promote growth so as to raise the living standards of the people requires that a part of its resources should be devoted to the production of capital goods and for promotion of research and development activity which would bring about technological progress. The capital accumulation and technological progress achieved in this way would enable the society to produce more of consumer goods in the future and ensure higher living standards for its people. It follows that provision for capital accumulation and technological progress implies the sacrifice of some current consumption. In fact, the sacrifice of current consumption to produce more capital goods and devote resources to research and development to promote progress in technology is called *cost of growth.* Therefore, a society has to decide how much saving and investment (that is, how much sacrifice of current consumption) should be made for future economic progress. The pangs of the sacrifice of some current consumption for promoting economic growth are greatly felt in less developed countries like India where not only the *present consumption levels* are very low (and there-fore any sacrifice of current consumption is *hard hitting*) but also the need for economic growth is very pressing.

What, How and For Whom: Subject Matter of Microeconomics

We have explained above the four basic problems which have been the concern of economists. The function and purpose of all economic systems is to solve these problems. It is noteworthy that the analysis of first three problems, namely, what, how and for whom to produce are discussed in what is now called microeconomics. Microeconomics studies behaviour of individual consumers as to what they will consume and demand, of producers or firms as to what and how they will produce, of individual industries as to how demand for their products and the supply by them will determine their prices. It is demand for and prices of various products that determine the allocation of resources among them.

Besides, microeconomics studies how prices of factors such as wages of labour, rent of land, interest on capital and profits of enterprise are determined. It is these factor prices that, on the one hand, determine the incomes of various individuals and hence the demand for various products and, on the other, determine the cost of products It is the money incomes of the various people that determine who would get how much from national output.

It may be noted that not only does microeconomics explain the mechanism through which the above three problems are solved but also analyses the implications of alternative choices made in this regard for welfare of the society. We will explain the subject matter of microeconomics in detail in the next chapter.

Macroeconomics: Whether Resources are Fully Utilised ?

Now, the pertinent question is which of the above problems are studied by what is now called macroeconomics. This requires some elaboration. Despite the fact that not enough resources are available to satisfy all human wants, in a free market economic system it so happens that they are not fully utilised. This goes contrary to the view held by the Classical and Neo-Classical economists who believed in the existence of full employment of resources. A noted English economist challenged this viewpoint during nineteen thirties during which a severe depression overtook the capitalist economies. At this time, strange phenomenon of a large number of workers (human resources) were rendered unemployed and a good deal of the factories and capital equipment installed in then remained idle or under-utilised. Keynes in his well known work "*General Theory of Interest, Money and Employment*" explained that despite the scarcity of resources, the unemployment may be caused due to the lack of effective demand. Thus the level at which employment of labour and (non-human resources will be used and hence the level of national income will be determined depends on effective demand. Keynesian analysis greatly improved our understanding of the working of the capitalist system which cause involuntary unemployment of human and capital resources due to lack of effective demand. Macroeconomics is concerned with explaining how the employment of resources and hence the level of national income is determined and what causes fluctuations and growth in them.

HOW ARE THE CENTRAL PROBLEMS SOLVED

We have explained above the four central problems of an economy which must be solved somehow or other by an economy. Now, the important thing to know is how an economy solves these central problems which are essential to its functioning. There are two main methods to solve these central problems. The first method is to solve these problems through *market or price mechanism*. That is, what goods are to be produced and what quantities, which methods for production are to be employed for the production of goods and how the output is to be distributed, should be decided by the free play of the forces of demand and supply. In such an economic system, capital and other means of production are the private property of the individuals and private entrepreneurs who undertake the work of production. Consumers have freedom to buy the goods they want. In such a system, those goods are produced more for which there is greater demand and those goods are produced less for which there is less demand. The demand for and supply of various goods determine the prices and quantities produced of various goods. Besides, the prices of factors such as labour capital, land *i.e.*, wages, interest, rent also depend upon their demand and supply and these factor prices determine the incomes of the owners of these factors and it is these incomes which determine the distribution of goods among the various individuals in a society.

Given the prices of the factors, entrepreneur decides which technique of production is to be employed (that is, which combination of factors or resources is to be used) for production of goods. This method of solving these central problems through market mechanism, that is, through forces of demand and supply is used by a free-enterprise capitalist economy.

The second method which can be employed to solve the central problems is the adoption of *economic planning*. In this method, the solution of the various basic problems is not achieved through the free working of demand for and supply of goods and factors. But to solve these problems, Government sets up a central planning authority which has been called by several names, such as planning commission, planning ministry or planning board. What goods should be produced and in what quantities, bow should they be produced, how should they be distributed among the population and how much should be invested to bring about economic growth are all decided by the central planning authority. This method of solving the central problems through the use of economic planning had been adopted in the former communist countries such as Soviet Russia, Poland, etc. In such an economic system, the capital and property are collectively owned by the society and work of production is organised by the Government. In this system, private entrepreneurs have no right to undertake the work of production and consumers lose their freedom to choose and consume the goods of their choice.

It is worth noting that there is no any country in the world today, which allows the solution of these central problems through unfettered market mechanism: In capitalist countries such as England, the U.S.A., France, Governments intervene in the economy and regulate the market mechanism, directly or indirectly. In this way, in these capitalist countries also, Government plays an active role in the solution of the various central problems, regarding production, distribution and investment. In the so-called capitalist countries, Government interferes in the economy and affects the solution of these problems through the adoption of proper monetary policy (in which the policies regarding supply of money, bank credit and rate of interest are included), fiscal policy (which is concerned with the Government expenditure and taxation policies) and direct controls, such as industrial licencing policies, control on prices, imports and exports.

The Government interferes in the working of the capitalist economy through these various policy instruments because it has now been realised that the unfettered functioning of the market mechanism or the forces of demand and supply, results in wide economic fluctuations, price instability and unemployment and lack of economic growth. In other words, with the free working of the market mechanism, the achievement of the objectives of economic stability, full employment and rapid economic , growth is not possible. During 1929-33, when in all the capitalist countries, there occurred a great depression which resulted in widespread unemployment among the population, then famous economist J.M. Keynes laid stress on the adoption of appropriate fiscal and monetary policies so as to achieve the objective of full employment. After Keynes main problem of the capitalist countries has been of inflation *i.e.* a severe rise in general level of prices. Besides inflation, these countries also desire more rapid economic growth and the problem is how to ensure steady rate of economic growth. Therefore, after Keynes, economists have laid stress on the intervention by the Government to tackle the problem of inflation and also to ensure steady rate of economic growth. As a matter of fact, the Governments of these countries have taken active steps to hold the price line and to promote steady growth. Therefore, economists such as Paul Samuelson, Hansen, Galbraith, call these so-called capitalist countries as *mixed capitalist enterprise system* or simply *mixed economies*. This is because in these countries, now-a-days, market or price mechanism does not work freely to solve the central problems and instead the Government plays an active role through the adoption of appropriate policy instruments to regulate these economies.

It is worth noting here that the nature of mixed economy of India is different from that of the mixed economies of America and England. In India, Government not only regulates and controls the private enterprise and market mechanism through monetary and fiscal measures and direct controls but also itself undertakes the work of production. Various important industrial and power projects have been set up in the public sector, the working of which does not depend upon market and price mechanism. Besides, in India public enterprises and other economic activities of the Government are conducted according to the policies laid down in Five-Year Plans. Thus, in the mixed economy of India, direct participation of the Government *i.e.*, public enterprise and economic planning have an important place in the working of Indian economy. So far as private sector is concerned, its working primarily depends upon the market or price mechanism. But Government tries to regulate and control the activities of the private sector through appropriate direct controls, monetary and fiscal policies. As regards public sector, the decisions regarding what to produce, how to produce and how much to invest are taken by the Government and Planning Commission.

We have only indicated here that there are two main methods of solving the central problems. How these central problems are solved by a capitalist economy and a centrally planned socialist economy will be explained in detail in a later chapter.

ROBBINS' DEFINITION: ECONOMICS IS A SCIENCE OF SCARCITY AND CHOICE

Robbins not only criticised Marshall's definition and other welfare definitions of economics but also provided a new definition which he considered to be more scientific and correct. He has given this definition in his famous book, "*An Essay on the Nature and Significance of Economic Science*," which he brought out in 1931. According to Robbins, economics studies the problems which have arisen because of the scarcity of resources. Nature has not provided mankind sufficient resources to satisfy all its wants. Therefore, the people have to choose for which ends or for which wants the resources are to be utilised. Thus, according to Robbins, economics is the science of scarcity and it studied how the scarce resources are allocated among their different uses. Thus he has given the following definition: "*Economics is the science which studied human behaviour as a relationship between ends and scarce means which have alternative uses.*" This definition is based upon the following three facts :

1. **Unlimited wants.** The first fact on which Robbins' definition is based is that man's wants are unlimited. In his definition 'ends' implies wants and for statisfying wants the man uses resources. That man's wants are unlimited is a very important and fundamental fact of economic life of the people. If man's wants were limited, then no economic problem would have arisen. But in the real life of the people there is no limit to their wants; when one want is satisfied, another want crops up. An important things to know about wants is that they are not of equal intensity; some are more intense than others. It is because of the different intensities of the wants that people are able to allocate the resources to satisfy their different wants.

2. **Scarce means.** The second element which gives rise to economic problem is that resources

9. Lionel Robbins, *An Essay on The Nature and Significance of Economic Science*, 1935.

are scarce in relation to wants. If the resources like wants were unlimited, no economic problem would have arisen because in that case all wants could have been satisfied and there would have been no problem of choosing between the wants and allocating the resources between them. Because the resources are scarce, all wants cannot be satisfied. Therefore, human beings have to decide for the satisfaction of which wants the resources should be used and which wants should be left unfulfilled. It should be noted that means or resources here refer to natural productive resources, man-made capital goods, consumer goods, money and time available with men, *etc*. If the means or resources were unlimited, then we would have obtained goods in the desired quantities because in that state of affairs goods would have been free goods. But in the real life we cannot obtain goods free or without price; we have to pay price for them and make efforts to obtain them.

3. **Alternative uses of means.** The third fact on which Robbins' definition is based is that resources or means have various alternative uses. In other words, the resources can be put to various uses. For instance, coal can be used as a fuel for the production of industrial goods, it can be used for running trains, it can be used for domestic cooking purposes and for so many other purposes. Likewise, monetary resources can be utilised for the production of essential consumer goods, for the production of capital goods and so many other goods. It has to be decided how the resources have to be allocated among different uses. The man or society has, therefore, to choose the uses for which resources have to be employed. If the resources would have a single use only, the question of choice would not have arisen at all. In the case of single use of resources, they would have been employed for the uses which they have. It is because of the various alternative uses of the resources that we have to decide about the best allocation of resources.

We thus see that Robbins' definition stands on the above-mentioned three facts, namely, unlimited wants, scarce resources and alternative uses of the resources. According to him, economics studies human behaviour regarding how he satisfies his wants with the scarce resources. According to him, economics is a human science and not a mere social science. It studies man in society or without society when he is confronted with the problem of allocating scarce resources to satisfy his unlimited wants. An important thing to note about Robbins' definition is that Robbins does not distinguish between material and non-material, between welfare and non-welfare. According to him, economics studies man's activities in regard to all goods and services, whether they are material or immaterial, provided they satisfy the wants of the people.

Economics is neutral between ends

Besides, whether the goods and services are conducive to human welfare or not, economics should study them if they satisfy the wants of some men. It is also worth noting that in view of Robbins, economics does not deal with the question as to what ends should be achieved, that is, what wants should be satisfied and what not, because in this regard man himself has to decide. Economics itself does not make a choice. Economist only tells in what ways the given ends or wants can be achieved with the minimum possible resources. What ends or wants should be selected for satisfaction is not the concern of economists. Whether the ends chosen by man are good or bad, noble or ignoble, economics should study them, because the task of economist is not to praise or condemn but only to analyse and explain. To decide about the desirability or otherwise of a thing is beyond the scope of economics. Therefore, *according to Robbins, economics is neutral between ends.*

Economics as a Science of Choice

It follows from the definition of Robbins that economics is a *science of choice*. It deals with how the resources of society should be allocated to the satisfaction of different wants. Whenever the resources are scarce and the wants are many, the question of choice arises. The man has to choose between the wants to which resources are to be allocated. Thus, Professor Robbins remarks, "***When time and means for achieving ends are limited and capable of alternative application and the ends are capable of being distinguished in order of importance, then behaviour necessarily assumes the*** *form of choice*."[10] It is thus clear that economics is the science of choice.

Like Robbins many other economists have defined economics in terms of scarcity of resources and choice. Thus, Professor Wicksteed says that economics is a "study of those principles on which the resources of a community should be so regulated and administered as to secure social ends without waste."[11] Likewise, Professor Stigler defines economics in the following words: "*Economics is the study of the principles of governing the allocation of scarce means among competing ends when the objective of allocation is to maximise the attainment of the ends*."[12] Similarly, Scitovosky says, "Economics is a social science concerned with the administration of scarce resources."[13] Professor Erich Roll has also defined economics in terms of scarcity of resources and the choice. Thus, according to him, "The economic problem is essentially a problem arising from the necessity of choice; choice of the manner in which limited resources with the alternative uses are disposed of. It is the problem of the husbandry of resources.... economics studies the activity of husbandry."[14]

It is thus clear that after Robbins economics has assumed the character of science which is concerned with the scarcity of resources and the problem of choice which arises because of the scarcity. Robbins' definition has been claimed to be more scientific. It has broadened the scope of economics whereas the material welfare definitions had narrowed down the scope of economic study.

With this definition of economics which lays a stress on scarcity of resources and the problem of choice, economics can no longer be called dismal science. Economics has no responsibility about the choice of ends; ends may be good or bad, economics has no concern with it. When the ends are many and resources scarce, the science of economics is required to study this problem.

Critical Evaluation of Robbins' Definition

No doubt, Robbins has made economics a scientific study and his definition has become very popular among the economists. This definition brings to light the basic economic problem which confronts the society. But Robbins' definition has also been criticised on several grounds. The main charge against Robbins is that he has made economics quite impersonal, colourless and devoid of any normative element. He says equilibrium is just an equilibrium. He does not seek to make economics as study of human welfare. Therefore, many economists like Durbin, Fraser, Beveridge and Wootton have tried to defend Marshall's idea about the true scope of economics and its objective of the promotion of social welfare. Thus Wootton has said that "It is very difficult for economists to divest their discussions completely of all normative significance." We give below the various criticisms which have been levelled against Robbins' definition.

1. Firstly, Robbins' definition has been criticised on the ground that it is not justified on the part of Robbins to oppose making economics as an engine of social welfare. In fact it has been contended that even in Robbins' definition the idea of welfare is present. If we closely analyse Robbins' definition we would come to the conclusion that it says that economics is concerned with how a man and society uses its scarce resources so as to achieve maximum possible satisfaction of its wants. But this maximum satisfaction of wants is nothing else but maximum welfare. Robbins' definition implies that allocation of resources has to be made in such a way that maximum satisfaction is achieved. Thus, without the satisfaction or welfare being brought into consideration the question of allocation of scarce resources does not arise.

2. Secondly, Robbins has been criticised on the ground that he has made economics neutral between ends. Many economists are of the view that if economics has to play an important role in

10. Lionel Robbins, *Nature and Significance of Economic Science,* p.14.
11. Wicksteed, *Commonsense of Political Economy*.
12. G.J. Stigler, *The Theory of Price*, 1949, p.12.
13. Tibor Scitovosky, *Welfare and Competition*, 1952, p. 3.
14. Erich Roll, *The Elements of Economic Theory*, 1950, p. 16.

promoting social welfare and economic growth, it has to give its decision regarding what is good and what is bad to achieve these ends. That is, if economics is to serve as an engine of social betterment, it would have to abandon the neutrally between ends or objectives. Economist would have to tell what is good or bad for welfare and progress and whether efforts should be made to attain some given ends or not. Professor Thomas rightly remarks, "the *function of the economist is not only to explain and explore but also to praise and condemn.*"[15]

3. A serious objection against Robbins' definition is that it has reduced economics to a mere value theory, i.e., the theory of product and factor pricing. In other words, according to him, economics should study only the allocation of resources among the production of various goods and consequently how the prices of goods and factors are determined. But the scope of economics is wider than the allocation of resources and the price theory. These days the importance of macro-economics has increased in which we study how the national income of a country and its total employment are determined. But the determination of national income and employment does not fall within the purview of Robbins' definition which only lays stress on the allocation of resources. The history of Western economies has revealed that there has been great instability in them. There has been periodic occurrence of mass unemployment and depression. Referring to Robbins book "*Eassy on the Nature and Significance of Economic Science*' wherein he described economics as the subject that deals with the allocation of scarce means between alternative uses. Joan Robinson writes, "By the time the book came out there were 3 million workers unemployed in Great Britain and satistical measure of GNP in USA had recently fallen to half its former level. It was just a coincidence that the book appeared when means for any economic had rarely been less scarce".[16] On the other hand, at other times, these economies have witnessed periods of boom and inflation. It is the basic task of economics to explain this instability and to prescribe policies for removing fluctuations in the levels of income, output and employment. But Robbins' definition leaves this issue untouched. It is thus clear that macro-economics which has become more important these days does not come within the purview of economics as defined by Robbins.

4. Robbins' definition is also criticised on the ground that it does not cover the theory of economic growth and development. The theory of economic growth and development studies how the national income and per capita income of a country increase over a long period of time and what factors cause such increases. With economic growth productive capacity of the country expands which brings about increases in national income, per capita income and the level of employment. While Robbins takes the resources as given and talks about their allocation, the theory of economic growth is concerned with *reducing the scarcity of resources* through raising the level of national income and accumulating more capital and wealth. In developing countries the question of economic growth is of vital importance because these countries are making efforts to remove poverty of their people and to raise their living standards through economic growth. In the recent years, many theories regarding how to initiate and accelerate economic growth in developing countries have been propounded. The theory of economic growth has now become the core of the science of economics both in developed and developing countries. Robbins' definition is defective because it does not cover an important subject like economic growth.

5. Even the problem of unemployment which is being faced by both the developing and developed countries of the world is not covered by Robbins' definition. As has been said above, Robbins' definition deals with the problem of scarcity, however the problem of unemployment is not the problem of scarcity but one of abundance of manpower in relation to demand for it. As is well known, labour or manpower is an important factor of production and its unemployment implies that it is abundant and not scarce. It is the task of economists to study the causes of the problem of unemployment and surplus labour and to suggest means to solve it.

---

15. S.E. Thomas, *Elements of Economics.*

16. Joan Robinson, The Second Crisis of Economic Theory, printed in her *Selected Economic Writings*, Oxford University Press, 1974, p. 237.

6. Robbins' definition has also been attacked for its making our economics a human science instead of social science. In one sense the scope of economics has been unnecessarily widened by Robbins. In accordance with Robbins' views, economist would also study a *sadhu*, who lives in a cave of Himalaya, because that *sadhu* would also be faced with the problem of how to distribute his time between various ends. That is, a *sadhu* has also to face the problem of choice and therefore comes within the purview of Robbins' definition. But many economists are of the view that economics is a social science and it should study the problem of choice when it has a social aspect, that is, when a man's choice affects other members of the society. Therefore, many economists though laying stress on the scarcity of resources and the problem of choice consider economics as a social science and not a human science as Robbins does. Thus Scitovsky defines economics as "a social science concerned with the administration of scarce resources." According to Cairncross, "Economics is a social science studying how people attempt to accommodate scarcity to their wants and how these attempts interact through exchange." It is thus clear that, contrary to the views of Robbins, economics has been regarded by many economists as a social science; economics studies the problem of choice if it has social repercussions, that is, when an individual's choice affects other members of the society.

SOME RECENT DEFINITIONS OF ECONOMICS

For a long time Robbins' definition was accepted as a proper one but these days it is felt that Robbins'definition does not indicate adequately the scope and the subject matter of economics. As has been pointed out above, Robbins' definition does not cover the theory of income and employment determination as well as the theory of economic growth. According to Professor Schultze of the University of Maryland, Robbins'definition of economics is misleading, "in particular it does not fully reflect two of the major concerns of modern economics, growth and instability."[17] Therefore, some modern economists have tried to give new definitions of economics which cover the theory of income and employment determination as well as of economic growth.

Professor Henry Smith has given a more correct definition of economics. According to him, economics is "*the study of how in a civilised society one obtains the share of what other people have produced and of how the total product of society changes and is determined.*"[18] By civilised society it is meant that there are some legal institutions as well as rights of property and other things in the society.

This definition of economics contains three main subjects and problems of economics. First, it contains the problem of distribution of income among the various members of the society since it incorporates in it 'the study of how a person obtains share of what other people have produced'. Secondly, it includes how total national income and employment are determined because it states that "how the total product of society... is determined". It should be remembered that the level of employment in a country depends to a great extent upon the level of national product or income. Other things remaining the same, when more is produced more people have to be employed. Thus, the greater the level of national production, the greater the level of employment. Thirdly, Professor Smith's definition also incorporates the theory of economic growth since it explicitly states that economics enquires into "how the total product of society changes." This means economists should explain the factors which determine economic growth of the country which implies the increase in the national product over a long period of time. It is thus clear that all the three important subjects of economics, namely, the distribution of national income and output, determination of national income and employment and theory of economic growth are incorporated in Henry Smith's definition of economics. It is, therefore, more adequate definition. But this definition has neglected the problem of allocation of resources and pricing of products which has been the concern of economics for a long time.

17. Charles L. Schultze, *National Income Analysis* (Foundations of Modern Economic Theory), 1965, p.2.
18. Henry Smith, *A Prospect of Political Economy* (1968), p. 20.

Prof. Samuelson, a Nobel Laureate in economics, defines economics as '*the study of how societies use scarce resources to provide valuable commodities and distribute them among different people*". Prof. Samuelson in his definition lays stress on the scarcity of resources and choice and also distribution of national product among people of a society. He also does not explicitly mention the problems of economic instability and economic growth whch in recent yars have been the chief concern of economists.

In our view, however, the subject matter of the science of economics has grown so wide and vast that it is extremely difficult to put it in a "nutshell" of a definition. It is because of this fact that modern economists have now stopped discussing the proper way of defining economics. In fact, they think any attempt to define economics is a useless and futile exercise. They are of the view that what economics is about can bc better explained by pointing out the various issues and questions with which economists are concerned. It is because of the difficulties in putting the whole subject-matter of economics in a definition of a few words that Jacob Viner has given a pragmatic definition of economics. According to him, "*Economics is what economists do.*" In other words, what economics is, can be better understood from what economists do and what they have been doing. That is to say, what type of questions economists ask and have been asking and what answers they have provided for them. Thus what economics is about or, in other words, what is the subject matter of economics can be better known by spelling out the questions economists ask and have been asking.

QUESTIONS FOR REVIEW

1. "Economics is a science of wealth which enquires into the nature and causes of wealth of nations". Who gave this definition of economics and make your comments on it?
2. According to Marshall, economics is a science of material welfare of man. Critically examine this. How is it different from Robbin's definition?
3. According to Marshall, "economics is a study of mankind in the ordinary business of life". Explain and critically examine this.
4. Define '*The Economic Problem*'. How does it give rise to central economic problems faced by an economy.
5. Scarcity is the mother of all economic problems. Do you agree ? If so, how ?
6. What are the central problems of an economy ? Explain them briefly.
7. (*a*) Explain the following basic problems of the economy.
   1. What to produce ?
   2. How to produce ?
   3. For whom to produce ?

   (*b*) How do they arise from the problem of scarcity ?
8. What are the basic problems of an economic system ? Which of these constitute the subject-matter of micro-economic analysis ? Discuss briefly.
9. An eminent British economist J.M. Keynes explained that at times of depression, there was unemployment and surplus of both labour and capital resources. Is it not inconsistent with the problem of scarcity ?
10. Explain the problem of economic growth. How is it related to the problem of scarcity ? On what factors does economic growth depend ?
11. Explain Robbin's definition of economics. How is it based on unlimited wants and scarce means? Critically examine it. Are subjects of unemployment and economic growth covered in it ?
12. "Economics is a science which studies human behaviour as a relationship between ends and scarce means which have alternative uses". Discuss.
13. "Economics is a science of choice". Discuss.
14. What is meant by scarcity in economics? Scarcity is mother of all economic problem. Discuss.
15. Economics is neutral between ends. Explain and critically examine this view point.
16. The task of an economist is not to praise and condemn but only to analyse and explain.

CHAPTER 2

PRODUCTION POSSIBILITY CURVE, CHOICE AND OPPORTUNITY COST

Introduction

An important subject of study in economics is how individuals and firms in a society allocate scarce resources to make them as well off as possible. In fact, microeconomics has been defined as the study of how individuals and firms decide to allocate scarce resources to satisfy human wants. For this decision of allocation of scarce resources, the concepts of production possibility curve and the opportunity cost are extensively used in modern economics. As shall be explained below a production possibility curve (or which is also called production possibility frontier) graphically represents the various possible combinations of two goods that can be produced with the given limited resources. Choice has to be made regarding which combination of goods to be produced and resources allocated accordingly. Besides, when more resources are allocated to the increase the production of a good, some resources have to be withdrawn from the other goods. That is, for producing one good more, some amount of other goods has to be sacrificed. That is, there is opportunity cost of producing one good more.

CHOICE AND OPPORTUNITY COST

People want goods and services for the satisfaction of their wants. Since the resources are scarce, no economy can produce enough goods and services to satisfy all wants of the people. As explained above, scarcity of resources in relation to the wants of the people gives rise to the problem of choice. A society has therefore to make a choice about what goods and services and in what quantities should be produced with the given resources. Every individual has a given income in a period to spend on goods and services. Suppose with a given money income you are considering to see a movie in a cinema hall with your two friends. The cost of seeing a movie is generally measured as the money cost which you spend on the tickets. But a more important way of looking at the cost you incur for seeing a movie is in terms of what other good you must forego in order to obtain the tickets for seeing a movie. Suppose the next best thing you give up in order to buy the tickets is a book on economics. Then, the real cost of buying three tickets to see a movie in a cinema hall is the book on economics which you could have purchased with the same amount but had to forego for seeing a movie along with your friends. Then, a book on economics is called opportunity cost of three tickets to see a movie. *Thus, the opportunity cost of anything is the next best alternative that is given up for it.* Thus, in view of the scarcity of resources (money income in case of our individual), we cannot have every thing we want. If we have one thing more, we have to forego some thing else. There is no such thing as a free lunch in economics.

What applies in case of an individual also applies to the economy as a whole. In view of the scarcity of resources, the economy must make a choice among alternative goods and services it can produce with its limited resources. *The opportunity cost of a good or service is the value of the next best alternative good or service that is given up for it.* While making a choice, a rational decision maker, be it a consumer, a producer or government must decide on the basis of the opportunity cost calculations. For example, given its budgetary resources, if government of a country decides to increase its defence expenditure to provide or produce guns and other armaments for its defence forces, it will have to curtail its expenditure on agriculture, education and health care. Guns or butter is a popular way of describing the choice facing a society.

PRODUCTION POSSIBILITY CURVE

The issue of choice when resources are scarce and the opportunity cost of this choice and the nature of some basic economic problems can be better understood with the aid of an important graphic tool of modem economics known as production possibility curve. Production possibility curve is also called *production possibility frontier.* We shall explain below the concept of production possibility curve and bring out its relation with the basic economic problems stated above.

Production possibility curve (frontier) represents graphically alternative production possibilities facing an economy. In fact, the production possibility curve represents what economists call the **opportunity set**. *An opportunity set is the group of options available in view of the given constraints.* As will be explained below, the scarce resources and the given technology are the constraints of the economy for producing goods and services. As the total productive resources of the economy are limited, the economy has to choose between different goods. The productive resources can be employed for the production of various alternative goods. It has, therefore, to be decided which goods to be produced more and which ones less. In deciding what amounts of various goods are to be produced, society would in fact be deciding about the allocation of resources among different possible goods. How much labour and capital should go into raising wheat on the farms and how much should be employed for manufacturing cloth ? How many factories should produce arms for the army and how many should produce consumer goods for the civilians ? In order to simplify our analysis we shall assume that two types of goods–wheat and cloth–are to be produced, assuming that the production of other goods and services remain constant. We shall explain the production possibilities of these two goods but the analysis made will equally apply to the choice between any other two goods.

Let us assume that there is a *given amount of productive resources* for the production of two goods, namely, wheat and cloth, they remain fixed. Although resources are fixed in quantity, yet they can be shifted from the production of one good to another. Further, we assume that the given resources are being used fully and with utmost efficiency. In other words, we assume that resources are neither unemployed nor underemployed. This means that economy is working at the level of full-employment and using its productive capacity fully. We also assume that technology does not undergo any change. In other words, we rule out any progress in technology. In short, we assume fixed resources, full employment of resources, economic efficiency in the use and allocation of the given resources and a given technology. All these assumptions imply that we are looking at our economy at some particular point in time or over a very short period of time. This is because it will be very unrealistic to rule out progress in technology and growth in the supply of resources over a long period of time.

With the given amount of resources and a given technology, we have constructed the following table showing various production possibilities between wheat and cloth. If all the given resources are employed for the production of wheat, it is supposed that 15 thousand quintals of wheat are produced. On the other hand, if all resources are devoted to the production of cloth, 5 thousand metres of cloth are made. But these are the two extreme production possibilities. In between these two, there will be many other production possibilities such as *B*, *C*, *D* and *E*.

With production possibility *B*, the economy can produce, with given resources, 14 thousand quintals of wheat and one thousand metres of cloth, and with production possibility *C*, the economy, can have 12 thousand quintals of wheat, and 2 thousand metres of cloth and so on. As we move from possibility *A* towards *F*, we draw away some resources from the production of wheat and devote them to the production of cloth. In other words, we give up some units of wheat in order to have some more units of cloth. As we move from alternative *A* to *B*, we sacrifice one thousand quintals of

Table 2.1 : Alternative Production Possibilities

Production Possibilities	*Cloth (in thousand metres)*	*Wheat (in thousand quintals)*
A	0	15
B	1	14
C	2	12
D	3	9
E	4	5
F	5	0

wheat for the sake of one thousand metres of cloth. That is, one thousand quintals of wheat is the opportunity cost of one thousand meters of cloth Again, our movement from alternative B to C involves the sacrifice of two thousand quintals of wheat for the sake of one thousand more metres of cloth. Thus, the opportunity cost of one thousand metres of cloth has now gone up to 2 thousand metres of cloth. A look at the table will show that our sacrifice of wheat (i.e. opportunity cost of cloth) goes on increasing as we move further from *C* towards *F*. It is, therefore, clear that in a full-employment economy which is working with productive efficiency more of one good can be obtained only by cutting down the production of another good. Thus, we conclude that *with full-employment and working with production efficiency, an economy must always give up something of one good to obtain some more of another*. The basic fact that resources are limited and fully employed prevents an economy from having more of both the goods.

The alternative production possibilities can be illustrated graphically by plotting the data of the Table 2.1 on a graph paper. The curve *AF* in Figure 2.1 is obtained when the data of the table are plotted, This curve *AF* is called the *production possibility curve which shows the various combina-*

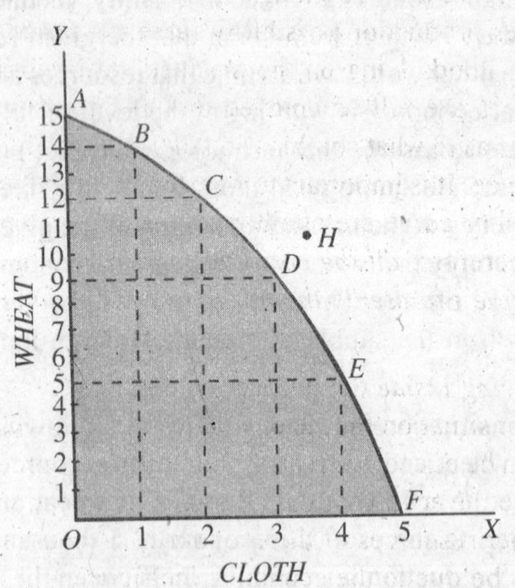

Fig. 2.1. *Production Possibility Curve and Opportunity Set*

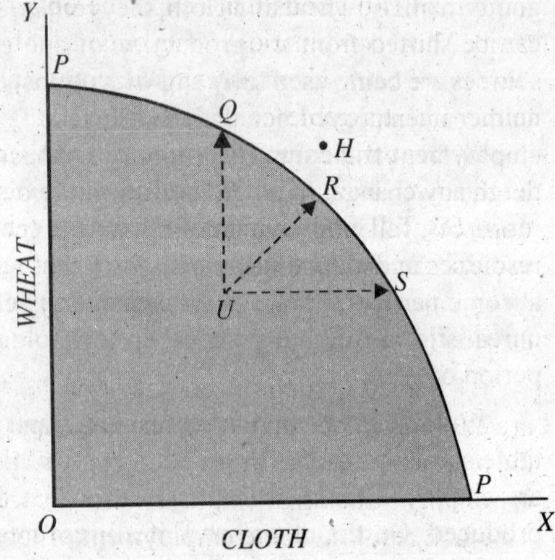

Fig. 2.2. *The Problem of Unemployment and Production Inefficiency*

tions of two goods which the economy can produce with a given amount of resources and a given technology, and working with production efficiency. This production possibility curve *AF* like the Table 2.1 illustrates that in a full-employment economy and with a given technology, an increase in the amount of cloth necessitates a decrease in the amount of wheat. As we move from *A* towards *F* on the production possibility curve we sacrifice some units of wheat for having more of cloth. On the other hand, if we move up from F towards A, we will be giving up some amount of cloth for the sake of more of wheat.

The problem of choice regarding what quantities of the two goods should be produced means at waht point on the given production possibility curve the economy should produce. If the economy chooses point C on the production possibility curve AF, it means it will be producing 2 thousand metres of cloth and 12 thousand quintals of wheat. On the other hand, if it chooses to produce at point E on the given production possibility curve, it will be producing 4 thousand metres of cloth and five thousand quintals of wheat. It is worth mentioning that alternative points of choice for production on the given production possibility curve indicate different allocation of the given resources between the two commodities. The production possibility curve is also called *transformation curve* because in moving from one point to another on it, one good is 'transformed' into another, not physically but by transferring resources from one use to the other. With the given resources being fully employed and efficiently used, the combination of two goods produced can lie anywhere on the production possibility curve *AF* but not inside or outside it. For example, the combined output of two goods can neither lie at *U*, nor at *H* in Fig. 2.2. This is so because at point *U* the economy would not be utilising its resources fully, and the output of two goods represented by point *H*, given the productive resources, would lie beyond the capacity of the economy to produce.

When there is inefficiency either in use of resources or when there is unemployment of resources, output combination of two products can lie below the economy's production possibility frontier, such as at a point like *U* in Fig. 2.2, where the economy can produce more of both the goods or more of either of the two goods (as indicated by arrows) by putting idle resources to work. As shown in Fig. 2.2 if the economy is working at *U*, *then by using its idle resources fully and most efficiently, it can move from* U to *Q*, or to *R*, or to *S* on the production possibility curve *PP*.

The points outside the production possibility curve such as point *H* in Figure 2.2 show combinations of two goods that cannot be obtained because there are not enough resources to produce them. Thus, combinations lying outside or beyond a given production possibility curve are *unattainable combinations of goods*. The combinations of two goods lying on the production possibility curve are attainable combinations if the given resources are fully employed and also used with productive efficiency. The economy has to make a choice as to what combination of two goods lying on the given production possibility curve it should produce. It is important to note that the combinations of two goods lying *inside* the production possibility curve are attaible combinations as the society can produce them with the given resources. Therefore, *all the combinations of two goods lying on or inside the given production possibility curve represents the* **opportunity set** *for the economy*.

However, though the combinations of two goods *lying inside* the production possibility curve are attainable, they do not represent a happy or desirable situation for the economy. This is because the production inside the production possibility curve can be due to two reasons. First, if the economy is not fully utilising or employing its resources, it will not be achieving its full production potential. This will result in some employment of labour and other resources of the economy. Secondly, the production inside the production possibility curve may be due to the economic inefficiency in the use of the given resources of the society. We will explain both these reasons in detail in later sections.

The Law of Increasing Opportunity Cost

The production possibility frontier *AF* in Figure 2.1 shows an important principle of economics. That principle is the law of increasing opportunity cost. From looking at the Table 2.1 it will be clear that as we move from possibility *A* to possibility *B*, we have to give up one thousand quintals of wheat in order to have one thousand metres of cloth. It means, in other words, that a first thousand metres of cloth has the opportunity cost of one thousand quintals of wheat to the society. But as we step up the production of cloth and move further from *B* to *C*, extra two thousand quintals of wheat have to be forgone for producing extra one thousand metres of cloth. Thus, in moving from *B* to *C* one thousand metres of cloth involves the opportunity cost of two thousand quintals of wheat. As we move further from *C* to *D*, *D* to *E* and *E* to *F*, the sacrifice in terms of wheat which we have to make for having extra one thousand metres of cloth goes on increasing. In other words, opportunity cost goes on increasing as we have more of cloth and less of wheat. The cost of extra one thousand metres of cloth as we move from *C* to *D*, *D* to *E* and *E* to *F* is 3 thousand, 4 thousand and 5 thousand quintals of wheat respectively. It is this *principle of increasing opportunity cost that makes the production possibility curve concave to the origin.*

But the question now arises: Why does the sacrifice of wheat or the opportunity cost increases as we produce more of cloth. A simple answer to this question is that the economic resources are not completely suited or adaptable to alternative uses. This is known as *specificity of resources*: one resource is more suited to the production of one good than another. Thus, land is more suited to the production of wheat than cloth. The production of wheat requires relatively larger use of land than cloth. As we increase the production of cloth, resources which are less and less adaptable or productive in the production of cloth would have to be pushed in that line of production. As we move from *A* towards *F*, we will first transfer those resources which are more productive in making cloth. As we move further from *B* to *C*, *C* to *D* and so forth, we will have to transfer those resources to the production of cloth which are more productive for producing wheat but less productive for making cloth. It is, therefore, obvious that as the resources which are more suited to the production of wheat are withdrawn, extra loss of wheat for the sake of producing extra one thousand metres of cloth will go on increasing. This law equally holds good if we move from *F* towards *A*; more and more amount of cloth would have to be given up for the sake of a given extra increase in the amount of wheat.

USES OF PRODUCTION POSSIBILITY CURVE

Choice and Opportunity Cost

A production possibility curve illustrates three basic economic concepts, namely, (1) scarcity of resources (2) choice by a society from the opportunity set and (3) opportunity cost. Scarcity is depicited by the boundary of the production possibility curve beyond which the economy cannot produce goods and services. That is why the production possibility curve is also called **production possibility frontier**. Given the resources and the state of technology, the economy has to operate either on the production possibility curve or inside it.

The issue of choice arises because when the resources are fully employed and efficiently used and allocated and also the technology remains the same we cannot have more of both the goods represented by a production possibility curve. *Given these constraints of resources and technology, a society has to make a choice at what point on the production possibility curve it should operate to produce goods and services. Thus, a society has to make a constrained choice.*

As explained above, when nation's given resources are fully employed and are being used most efficiently, and therefore, the economy is working at *a point* on the given production production possibility curve, *then more of one good can be produced only by taking away resources from the other good.* However, operating at a point on the production possibility curve does not necessarily mean that it is achieving *overall economic efficiency*. Overall economic efficiency implies not only that resources are being fully used and goods are being produced efficiently (that is, with minimum social cost) but also that *those goods are produced that people want.* In other words, along with full-employment and production efficiency, *product-mix must also be efficient*. That is, the quantities of goods must also be in accordance with the preferences or wants of the people.

The concept of opportunity cost can be illustrated with the use of a production possibility curve. As we more along a production possibility curve we give up or sacrifice some units of a commodity to obtain a unit of the other commodity. That is, there is trade-off between the two commodities; more of one commodity is obtained at the cost of less of the other commodity. The amount of one commodity which is forgone to obtain a unit of the other commodity is the opportunity cost of the latter. Thus, when we move from point *B* to point *C* we forgo 2 thousand quintals of wheat to obtain one thousand metres of cloth. Therefore, the opportunity cost of one thousand metres of cloth is here equal to 2 thousand quintals of wheat.

Unemployment of Resources

As mentioned above, it is not necessary that the economy must be operating at a point on the production possibility curve. If some of labour, capital and other resources are unemployed or lying idle, as happens when there is a recession or depression in the economy, it works below the production possibility curve as at point *U* in Figure 2.2. When the economy is working inside the production possible curve such as point *U*, then it is possible to produce one good more without the reduction in the quantity of the other good or more of both can be produced. During the Great Depression of the 1930s, 25 per cent of labour force in the United States was rendered unemployed and the GNP in 1933 was 93 billion dollars less as compared to the year 1929. Similarly, millions of workers were rendered unemployed during the Great Depression in other capitalist or free market economies. Not only a large number of workers remained unemployed for a prolonged period but also a good amount of the industrial plant and capital remained idle. Thanks to J.M. Keynes who in his path breaking work. '*The General Theory of Employment, Interest and Money*' convencingly explained that the economy could be in equilibrium when there is a lot of unemployment of labour and capital due to the fall in aggregate demand. That is, when aggregate demand is not large enough to buy the output of goods obtained by working on a production possibility curve the involuntary unemployment will emerge. As a result, the economy will be operating at a point below the given production possible curve.

Inefficiency in Production

Another important reason for the economy to find itself operating inside the production possibility curve is when it is using its resources inefficiently. We achieve production efficiency in the use of resources if with the given resources and technology, more of one good cannot be produced without the reduction in the output of the other. If the resources are not being used efficiently, then the production of both the goods could be increased or the production of one good can be increased without producing less of the other. For example, if land of a village which is better suited for the production of wheat is wrongly employed for the production of cotton, the economy will not be using its resources efficiently which will result in loss of output. This will make the economy work below or inside the production possibility curve. Similarly, if we employ textile engineers who have skills to perform a specialised job in the production of cotton cloth for the production of wheat, we will not be maximising output from our given resources. We could get more wheat and more cloth if we employ the workers and engineers for the tasks that closely match their skills.

Take another example, if managers of firms lack incentives to maximise output from the given resources (or to minimise cost to produce a given output, economy will not be making optimum use of its resources resulting in loss of output. As a consequence, the economy will be operating below the production possible curve. This applies both to the managers of public sector and private corporate sector. It is claimed by some that it is the lack of incentives on the part of managers in the former Communist Soviet Russia and in the various public enterprises in India which are incurring heavy losses that is responsible for low productivity and poor performance of public enterprises.

Economic Growth

Let us turn to the question of economic growth and see what happens to the production possibility curve when the economy's productive capacity increases over time. As already pointed out, the production possibility curve is drawn with a given amount of productive resources like land, labour and capital equipment. Now, if these productive resources increase, the production possibility curve will shift outward and to the right showing that more of both goods can be produced than before.

Further, when the economy makes progress in technology, that is, when the scientists and engineers discover new and better ways of doing things, the production possibility curve will shift to the right and will indicate the possibility of producing more of both the goods. Technological progress by improving productive efficiency allows the society to produce more of both the goods with a given and fixed amount of resources.

From above it follows that when the supplies of resources increase or an improvement in technology occurs, the production possibility curve shifts outward such as from *PP* to *P′P′*, in Fig. 2.3. On production possibility curve *P′P′*, the economy can produce more goods than on the production possibility curve *PP*. The increase in the amount of capital, natural and human resources and the progress in technology are determinants of economic growth. Thus with the growth of the economy production possibility curve shifts outward.

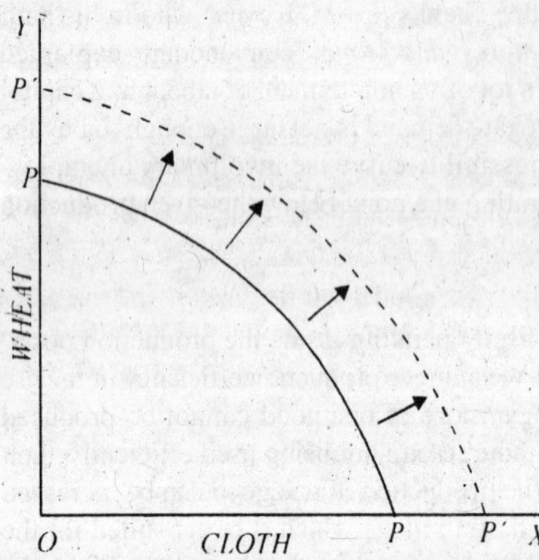

Fig. 2.3. *Shift in Production Possibility Curve due to Economic Growth*

It is very important to understand the distinction between (*i*) the movement of the economy from a point inside the production possibility curve to a point on it, such as from point *U* to point *Q* in Fig. 2.2 and (*ii*) the movement of the economy from one production possibility curve to another. In both these cases national product or output of goods and services will increase. But the former involves fuller employment of the given resources while the latter involves the increase in resources or productive capacity. While the first type of movement is dealt with by the short–run macroeconomic theory, the latter is dealt with by the theory of economic growth. The fact that in both these movements of the economy the national product or income increases they are likely to be confused with each other. But the two movements are of quite different nature and different types of measures are required to bring them about. When the economy is working at a point below its production possibility curve due to the lack of aggregate demand as it happens in times of depression in free-market economies then those policy measures should be adopted which raise the level of aggregate demand. The increase in aggregate demand under such circumstances will bring about a shift of the economy from a point below the production possibility curve to a point on it. This will mean full employment or full utilisation of available labour and capital resources and as a result the levels of national income, output and employment will rise and the existing unemployment and under-utilisation of productive capacity will be removed.

On the other hand, when the economy is fully utilising its given resources and is, therefore, working at a point on the production possibility curve, the increase in national output and employment cannot be achieved by simply raising aggregate demand. Under such circumstances, national income and employment can be increased by adopting measures which generate economic growth. These measures aimed at generating economic growth involve stepping up of rate of capital accumulation and making a progress in technology.

Capital Formation and Economic Growth. Economic growth depends on several factors. But the two most important factors that determine rate of economic growth are capital accumulation and technological progress. For poor developing countries capital accumulation is essential for accelerating rate of economic growth. They need to build roads, factory buildings, machines and tools, tractors, means of irrigation, communication networks and transportation system. To produce more capital goods and build infrastructure, a society has to sacrifice some of its current consumption. The same is true of making technological progress. Technological changes come from research and development that also require resources. The resources that have to be used for building up capital and making technological advances have to come from cutting the current production of consumer goods In fact, the cut in current consumption is the opportunity cost of increase in future consumption.

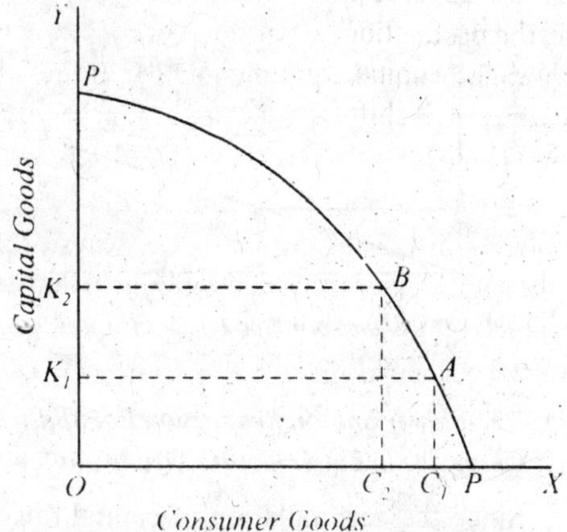

Fig. 2.4. *Resource Allocation between Consumer and Capital Goods*

In order to explain the problem of capital formation we have to construct such a production possibility curve in which on one axis capital goods and on the other axis consumer goods are measured. This has been done in Figure 2.4 in which along the *X*-axis consumer goods and along the *Y*-axis, capital goods are measured. If the economy is allocating the available resources between capital and consumer goods in such a way that it operates at point *A* on the production possibility curve *PP*, it will be producing OC_1 of consumer goods and OK_1 of capital goods. Now, suppose that the society decides to produce more of capital goods. To implement this decision, society will have to withdraw some resources from the production of consumer goods and use them for the production of capital goods. As a result, the production of consumer goods will decline. It is clear from Figure 2.4, that if the economy reallocates its resources between consumer and capital goods and shifts from point *A* to point *B* on the production possibility curve *PP*, it will now produce OK_2 of capital goods and OC_2 of consumer goods. That is, K_1K_2 amount of capital goods will be produced more and C_1C_2 amount of consumer goods will be produced less than before. We, therefore, conclude that in order to step up the rate of capital formation the production of consumer goods and therefore consumption has to be reduced.

For poor developing countries where a large part of population is very poor, it is difficult to reduce the production of consumer goods such food and clothing to devote the resources so released for the capital accumulation and making technological progress. Thus, **the poor developing countries face the dilemma**. While there is a urgent need to accelerate capital formation and technological progress, they are too poor to release resources by curtailing consumption.

However, the evidence of the last half a century shows that with active role of government for in raising resources through taxes and other means and also through getting foreign aid and investment some developing countries have in fact succeeded in accelerating capital formation and achieving a higher rate of economic growth.

But it is worth noting that when the rate of capital formation is raised, this does not mean that amount of consumption is reduced for ever. The accumulation of more capital enables economy to increase its production of consumer goods in the future. That is, the accumulation of capital raises the productive capacity of the economy and enables the economy to produce more consumer goods in the future. Thus, capital accumulation implies that "*less jam today for more jam tomorrow.*"

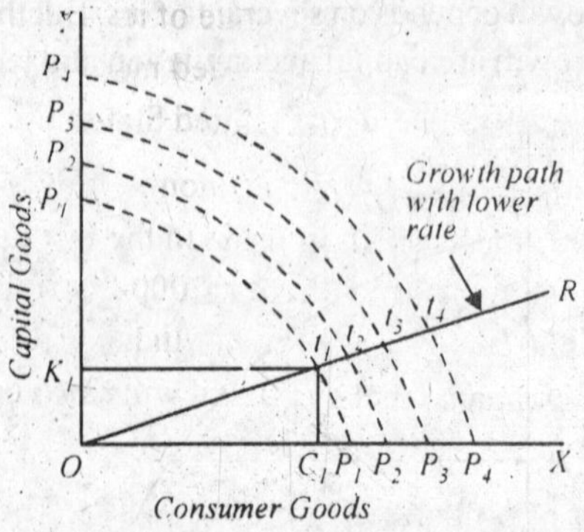

Fig. 2.5. *Slower Shift in Production Possibility Curve due to Lower Capital Accumulation Rate*

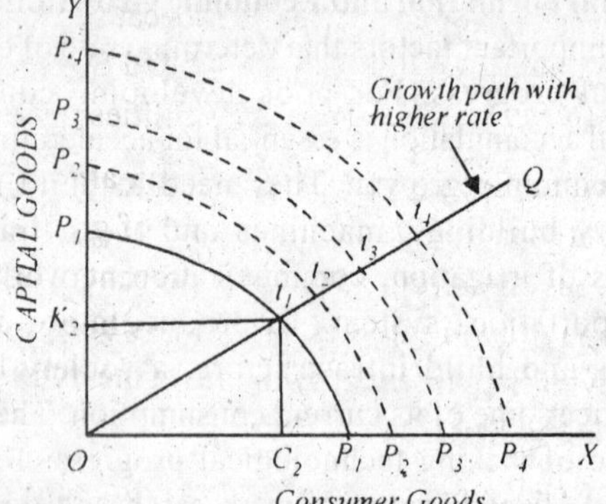

Fig. 2.6. *Rapid Shift in Production Possibility Curve due to Higher Capital Accumulation Rate*

Since the accumulation of capital raises the productive capacity, national production will increase, that is, economic growth will take place. As a result, the economy will not remain on the same production possibility curve and its production possibility curve will shift outward which indicates that the economy will be able to produce more than before. The greater the rate of capital formation, the greater the extent of shift in the production possibility curve, and the greater the rate of economic growth. Consider Figure 2.5 in which in the beginning the economy is producing OC_1 of consumer goods and OK_1 of capital goods on the production possibility curve P_1P_1. If the economy maintains this rate of capital formation, then the production possibility curve will go on shifting and the economy will be growing annually at a certain rate. It should be noted that in Figure 2.5, as a result of low rate of capital formation, production possibility curve shifts outward at a relatively slow speed. Thus growth path *OR* in Fig. 2.5 represents a lower rate of economic growth.

If the society wants to obtain a higher rate of economic growth, it will have to raise its rate of capital formation. This is shown in Fig. 2.6 in which the economy is producing at point t_1 on the production possibility curve P_1P_1, with OK_2 of capital goods and OC_2 of consumer goods. If the economy maintains this rate of capital formation, production possibility curve will go on shifting outward to a greater extent than in Figure 2.5. This means that the rate of economic growth will now be relatively greater than in Figure 2.5. In the two Figures 2.5 and 2.6, it will be noticed that, in the beginning in Fig. 2.6; the production of consumer goods is less than in Figure 2.5, but when as a result of higher rate of economic growth, production possibility curves reach their position P_4 P_4 at time t_4, it will be producing more consumer goods in Fig. 2.6 exhibiting higher rate of economic growth than in Figure 2.5, where the rate of capital formation and therefore the rate of economic growth is relatively less.

We have explained above economic growth which has been brought about by capital formation. Besides capital formation, there are other factors which determine rate of economic growth. Progress in technology and expansion in education also favourably affect rate of economic growth and cause production possibility curve to shift outward.

It may be noted that several developing countries prominent among which are Hong Kong Singapore, South Korea, Taiwan, popularly called *Asian Tigers* in the last 50 years or so, have in fact achieved a high rate of economic growth through accelerating capital formation, technological progress, promoting education (*i.e.* human capital). For example, in 1960, the production possibilities per person in Hong Kong were one-fourth of the United States. Since 1960, both countries have achieved economic growth. But because Hong-Kong devoted a much higher rate of its resources to accumulating capital than the United States, its production possibilities expanded more rapidly so that in 1997 its production possibilities per person reached the level of the United States.

More recently, India and China are also experiencing higher rates of economic growth. And again it is more due to higher rate of gross domestic investment which in India in the last over 10 years has risen from 25% to 36 percent of national income. In the last 10 years (2000-2010) India's average growth rate per annum has been more than 8 per cent per annum. If India succeeds in achieving 10 percent growth rate in the future years, it is estimated that by 2050 it will catch up with the United States.

We have explained above only some important uses of production possibility curve. There are several other uses of production possibility curve. The concept of production possibility curve has also been extensively used in welfare economics and in the theory of international trade. In the modern economic theory gains from international trade have also been explained with the aid of production possibility curve.

QUESTIONS FOR REVIEW

1. What is production possibility curve ? What assumptions are made while drawing it ? Why is it generally concave towards the origin ?
2. How would you explain the following problems with the help of production possibility curve?
   (*i*) The choice between the production of basic consumer goods and luxuries.
   (*ii*) The problem of unemployment
   (*iii*) The problem of economic growth
   (*iv*) The production inefficiency
3. What is opportunity cost ? How does it affect social choice ?
4. What is opportunity cost of a commodity ? Why does it increase when more of a commodity is produced ?
5. What is meant by economic growth ? On what factors does it depend ? How does economic growth affect the production possibility curve of the economy ?
6. Explain the law of increasing opportunity with the help of production possibility curve.
7. What is opportunity set ? Explain opportunity set for a society with a production possibilit curve.
8. What is meant by economic efficiency ? Does all points on a production possibility curv represent overall economic efficiency ?
9. Explain the reasons that make an economy work below its production possibility curve.

CHAPTER 3
THE SCOPE OF ECONOMICS

Micro and Macro-economics

The scope of economics refers to what is the subject matter of economics, that is, what are the various issues and questions that are analysed in it. Besides, in the scope of economics we deal with the issues of positive and normative economics. In what follows we shall discuss the subjects of microeconomics and macroeconomics as well as positive and normative economics.

The subject-matter of economics has been divided into two parts : Microeconomics and Macro-economics. These terms were first coined and used by Ragnar Frisch and have now been adopted by economists all the world over. *Nowadays one can hardly come across a text-book on modern economic analysis which does not divide its analysis into two parts, one dealing with microeconomics and the other with macroeconomics*. The term microeconomics is derived from the Greek word *mikros*, meaning "small" and the term macroeconomics is derived from the Greek word *makros*, meaning "large." Thus microeconomics deals with the analysis of small individual units of the economy such as individual consumers, individual firms and small aggregates or groups of individual units such as various industries and markets. On the other hand, macro-economics concerns itself with the analysis of the economy as a whole and its large aggregates such as total national output and income, total employment, total consumption, aggregate investment. Thus, according to K. E. Boulding, "Microeconomics is the study of particular firms, particular house-holds, individual prices, wages, incomes, individual industries, particular commodities."[1] About macroeconomics he writes, "Macroeconomics deals not with individual quantities as such but with aggregates of these quantities; not with individual incomes but with national income; not with individual prices but with price levels; not with individual outputs but with the national output."[2]

MICROECONOMICS

As stated above, microeconomics studies the economic actions and behaviour of *individual units* and *small groups* of individual units. In microeconomic theory we discuss how the various cells of economic organism, that is, the various units of the economy such as thousands of consumers, thousands of producers or firms, thousands of workers and resource suppliers in the economy do their economic activities and reach their equilibrium states. In other words, in microeconomics we make a *microscopic study* of the economy. But it should be remembered that microeconomics does not study the economy in *its totality*. Instead, in microeconomics we discuss equilibrium of innumerable units of the economy *piece meal* and their inter-relationship to each other. Thus, micro-economics consists of looking at the economy through a microscope, as it were, to see how the millions of cells in the economy —the individuals or households as consumers, and the individuals firms as producers— play their part in the working of the whole economic organisation. For instance, in microeconomic analysis we study the demand of an individual consumer for a good and from there go on to derive the *market demand* for the good (that is, demand of a group of individuals consuming a particular good) Likewise, microeconomic theory studies the behaviour of the individual

1. K. E. Boulding, *A Reconstruction of Economics*, (1950), p. 3.
2. K. E. Boulding, *Economic Analysis*, p. 25.

firms in regard to the fixation of price and output and their reactions to the changes in the demand and supply conditions. From there we go on to establish price-output fixation by an industry (Industry means a group of firms producing the same product).

Thus, microeconomic theory seeks to determine the mechanism by which the different economic units attain the position of equilibrium, proceeding from the individual units to a *narrowly defined group*. Microeconomic analysis concerns itself with narrowly defined groups since it does not study the *totality of behaviour* of all units in the economy . In other words, the study of economic system or economy as a whole lies outside the domain of microeconomic analysis.

Microeconomics and Allocation of Resources

Microeconomic theory takes the total quantity of resources as given and *seeks to explain how they are allocated to the production of various goods*. It is the allocation of resources that determines what goods shall be produced and how they shall be produced. The allocation of resources to the production of various goods in a free-market economy depends upon prices of the various goods and prices of the various resources or factors of production. Therefore, to explain how the allocation of resources is determined, microeconomics proceeds to analyse how relative prices of goods and factors are determined. Thus the theory of product pricing and the theory of factor pricing (or the theory of distribution) fall within the domain of microeconomics. The theory of product pricing explains how relative prices of cotton cloth, foodgrains, jute, kerosene oil, *Vanaspti ghee* and thousands of other goods are determined. The theory of distribution explains how *wages* (price for the use of labour), *rent* (payment for the use of land), *interest* (price for the use of capital) and *profits* (the reward for the entrepreneur) are determined. Thus, the theory of product pricing and the theory of factor pricing are the branches of microeconomic theory.

Prices of products depend upon the forces of demand and supply. The demand for goods depends upon the consumers' behaviour pattern, and the supply of goods depends upon the conditions of production and cost and the behaviour pattern of the firms or entrepreneurs. Thus the demand and supply sides have to be analysed in order to explain the determination of prices of goods and factors. Thus the theory of demand and the theory of production are two subdivisions of the theory of pricing.

Microeconomics and Economic Efficiency.

Besides analysing the pricing of products and factors and the allocation of resources based upon the price mechanism, microeconomics also seeks to explain whether the allocation of resources determined is *efficient*. Efficiency in the allocation of resources is attained when the resources are so allocated that maximises the satisfaction of the people. Economic efficiency involves three efficiencies; *efficiency in production, efficiency in distribution* of goods among the people (This is also called *efficiency in consumption*) and *allocative economic efficiency*, that is, efficiency in the *direction of production*. Microeconomic theory shows under what conditions these efficiencies are achieved. Microeconomics also shows what factors cause departure from these efficiencies and result in the decline of satisfaction from the maximum possible level.

Efficiency in production involve producing the maximum possible amount of various goods from the given available amount of resources. When such productive efficiency is attained, then it is no longer possible by any reallocation of the productive resources or factors among the production of various goods and services to increase the output of any good without a reduction in the output of some other good. Efficiency in consumption consists of distributing the given amount of produced goods and services among millions of the people for consumption in such a way as to maximise the total satisfaction of the society. When such an efficiency is achieved it is no longer possible — by any redistribution of goods among the people — to make some people better off [3]

3. Making some people *better off* means increasing their satisfaction.

without making some other ones worse off.[4] Allocative economic efficiency or optimum direction of production consists of producing those goods which are most desired by the people, that is, when the amounts of different goods produced is such that maximises the satisfaction of the people.

In other words, allocative economic efficiency implies that pattern of production (*i.e.* amounts of the various goods and services produced) should correspond to the desired pattern of consumption of the people. Even if efficiencies in consumption and production of goods are present, it may be that the goods which are produced and distributed for consumption may not be those preferred by the people. There may be some goods which are more preferred by the people but which have not been produced and vice versa. To sum up, *allocative efficiency (optimum direction of production) is achieved when the resources are so allocated to the production of various goods that the maximum possible satisfaction of the people is obtained.* Once this is achieved, then by producing some goods more and others less by any rearrangement of the resources will mean loss of satisfaction or efficiency. The question of economic efficiency is the subject matter of theoretical *welfare economics* which is an important branch of microeconomic theory.

That microeconomic theory is intimately concerned with the question of efficiency and welfare is evident from the following remarks of A. P. Lerner, a noted American economist. "In microeconomics we are more concerned with the avoidance or elimination of waste, or with inefficiency arising from the fact that production is not organised in the most efficient possible manner. Such inefficiency means that it is possible, by rearranging the different ways in which products are being produced and consumed, to get more of something that is scarce without giving up any part of any other scarce item, or to replace something by something else that is preferred. Microeconomic theory spells out the conditions of efficiency (*i.e.*, for the elimination of all kinds of inefficiency) and suggests how they might be achieved. These conditions (called Pareto-optimal conditions) can be of the greatest help in raising the standard of living of the population."[5]

The four basic economic questions namely, (1) what goods shall be produced and in what quantities, (2) how they shall be produced, (3) how the goods and services produced shall be distributed among the people and (4) whether the production of goods and their distribution for consumption is efficient fall within the domain of micro-economics. The whole content of microeconomic theory is presented in the following chart :

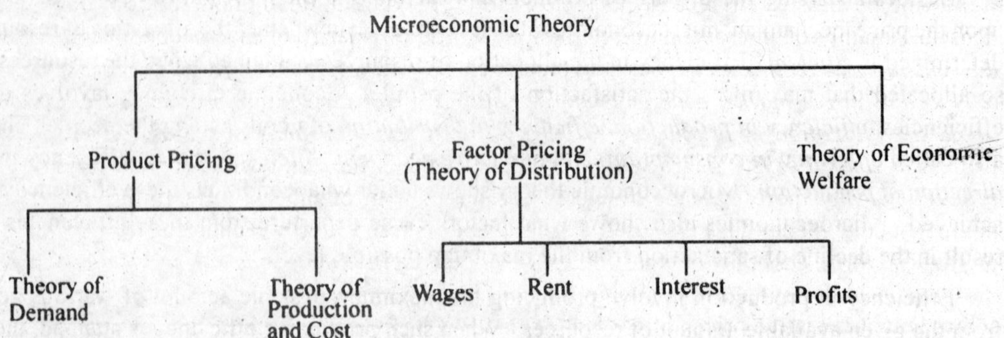

Microeconomics as a Microscopic Study of the Economy

It is generally understood that microeconomics does not concern itself with the economy as a whole and an impression is created that microeconomics differs from macroeconomics in that whereas

4. Making some people *worse off* means reducing their satisfaction.
5. Abba P. Lerner, Microeconomic Theory, printed in *Perspectives in Economics*, edited by Brown, Neuberger and Palmatier (Preliminary edition, 1968), p. 50.

the latter examines the economy as a whole, the former is not concerned with it. But this is not correct. That microeconomics is concerned with the economy as a whole is quite evident from its discussing the problem of allocation of resources in the society and judging the efficiency of the same. Both microeconomics and macroeconomics analyse the economy as a whole but with two different ways or approaches. Microeconomics examines the economy as a whole, so to say *microscopically*, that is, it analyses the behaviour of individual economic units of the economy, their inter-relationships and equilibrium adjustment to each other which determine the allocation of resources in the society. This is known as *general equilibrium analysis*.

No doubt, microeconomic theory mainly makes particular or partial equilibrium analysis, that is the analysis of the equilibrium of the individual economic units, taking other things remaining the same. But microeconomic theory, as stated above, also concerns itself with general equilibrium analysis of the economy wherein it is explained how all the economic units, various product markets, various factor markets, money and capital markets are inter-related and interdependent to each other and how through various adjustments and readjustments to the changes in them, they reach a general equilibrium, that is, equilibrium of each of them individually as well as collectively to each other. Professor A. P. Lerner rightly points out, "Actually microeconomics is much more intimately concerned with the economy as a whole than is macroeconomics, and can even be said *to examine the whole economy microscopically*. We have seen how economic efficiency is obtained when the "cells" of the economic organism, the households and firms, have adjusted their behaviour to the prices of what they buy and sell. Each cell is then said to be 'in equilibrium.' But these adjustments in turn affect the quantities supplied and demanded and therefore also their prices. This means that the adjusted cells then have to readjust themselves. This in turn upsets the adjustment of others again and so on. An important part of microeconomics is to examine whether and how *all* the different cells get adjusted at the same time. This is called *general equilibrium analysis* in contrast with *particular equilibrium* or *partial equilibrium analysis*. General equilibrium analysis is the microscopic examination of the inter-relationships of parts within the economy as a whole. Overall economic efficiency is only a special aspect of this analysis."[6]

Importance and Uses of Microeconomics

Microeconomics occupies a vital place in economics and it has both theoretical and practical importance. It is highly helpful in the formulation of economic policies that will promote the welfare of the masses. Till recently, especially before Keynesian Revolution, the body of economics consisted mainly of microeconomics. In spite of the popularity of macroeconomics these days, microeconomics retains its importance, theoretical as well as practical. It is *microeconomics that tells us how a free-market economy with its millions of consumers and producers work to decide about the allocation of productive resources among the thousands* of goods and services. As Professor Watson says, "microeconomic theory explains the composition or allocation of total production, why more of some things are produced than of others."[7] He further remarks that microeconomic theory has many uses. The greatest of these is depth in understanding of how a free private enterprise economy operates."[8] Further, it tells us *how the goods and services produced are distributed among the various people for consumption through price or market mechanism*. It shows how the relative prices of various products and factors are formed, that is, why the price of cloth is what it is and why the wages of an engineer are what they are and so on.

Moreover, as described above, microeconomic theory *explains the conditions of efficiency in consumption and production* and highlights the factors which are responsible for the departure from the efficiency or economic optimum. On the basis of this microeconomic theory *suggests suitable*

6. Abba P. Lerner, *op. cit.*, pp. 36-37.
7. D. S. Watson, *Price Theory and its Uses* (1963), p. 5.
8. *Ibid.*, p. 11.

policies to promote economic efficiency and welfare of the people. Thus, not only does microeconomic theory describe the actual operation of the economy, it has also a normative role in that it suggests policies to eradicate "inefficiency" from the economic system so as to maximise the satisfaction or welfare of the people. The usefulness and importance of microeconomics has been nicely stated by Professor Lerner. He writes, "Microeconomic theory facilitates the understanding of what would be a hopelessly complicated confusion of billions of facts by constructing simplified models of behaviour which are sufficiently similar to the actual phenomena to be of help in understanding them. These models at the same time enable economists to explain the degree to which the actual phenomena depart from certain ideal constructions that would most completely achieve individual and social objectives. They thus help not only *to describe* the actual economic situation but to *suggest policies* that would most successfully and most efficiently bring about desired results and to predict the outcomes of such policies and other events. Economics thus has descriptive, normative and predictive aspects."[9]

We have noted above that microeconomics reveals how a decentralised system of a free private enterprise economy functions without any central control. It also brings to light the fact that the functioning of a completely centrally directed economy with efficiency is impossible. Modern economy is so complex that a central planning authority will find it too difficult to get all the information required for the optimum allocation of resources and to give directions to thousands of production units with various peculiar problems of their own so as to ensure efficiency in the use of resources. To quote Professor Lerner again, "Microeconomics teaches us that completely 'direct' running of the economy is impossible — that a modern economy is so complex that no central planning body can obtain all the information and give out all the directives necessary for its efficient operation. These would have to include directives for adjusting to continual changes in the availabilities of millions of productive resources and intermediate products, in the known methods of producing every thing everywhere, and in the quantities and qualities of the many items to be consumed or to be added to society's productive equipment. The vast task can be achieved, and in the past has been achieved, only by the development of a decentralised system whereby the millions of producers and consumers are induced to act in the general interest without the intervention of anybody at the centre with instructions as to what one should make and how and what one should consume."[10]

Microeconomic theory shows that welfare optimum or economic efficiency is achieved when there prevails perfect competition in the product and factor markets. Perfect competition is said to exist when there are so many sellers and buyers in the market that no individual seller or buyer is in a position to influence the price of a product or factor. Departure from perfect competition leads to a lower level of welfare, that is, involves loss of economic efficiency. It is in this context that a large part of microeconomic theory is concerned with showing the nature of departures from perfect competition and therefore from welfare optimum (economic efficiency). The power of giant firms or a combination of firms over the output and price of a product constitutes the problem of monopoly. Microeconomics shows how monopoly leads to misallocation of resources and therefore involves loss of economic efficiency or welfare. It also makes important and useful policy recommendations to regulate monopoly so as to attain economic efficiency or maximum welfare. Like monopoly, *monopsony* (that is, when a large buyer or a combination of buyers exercises control over the price) also leads to the loss of welfare and therefore needs to be controlled. Similarly, microeconomics brings out the welfare implications of oligopoly (or oligopsony) whose main characteristic is that individual sellers (or buyers) have to take into account, while deciding upon their course of action, how their rivals react to their moves regarding changes in price, product and advertising policy.

9. A. P. Lerner, *op cit.*, p. 29.
10. A. P. Lerner, *op. cit.*, p. 33.

Another class of departure from welfare optimum is the problem of *externalities*. Externalities are said to exist when the production or consumption of a commodity *affects other people* than those who produce, sell or buy it. These externalities may be in the form of either *external economies* or *external diseconomies*. External economies prevail when the production or consumption of a commodity by an individual benefits other individuals and external diseconomies prevail when the production or consumption of a commodity by him *harms other individuals*. Microeconomic theory reveals that when the externalities exist, free working of the price mechanism fails to achieve economic efficiency since it does not take into account the benefits or harms made to those external to the individual producers and the consumers. The existence of these externalities requires government intervention for correcting imperfections in the price mechanism in order to achieve maximum social welfare.

Microeconomic analysis is also usefully applied to the various applied branches of economics such as Public Finance, International Economics. It is the microeconomic analysis which is used to explain the factors which determine the distribution of the *incidence or burden* of a commodity tax between producers or sellers on the one hand and the consumers on the other. Further, microeconomic analysis is applied to show the *damage* done to the social welfare or economic efficiency by the imposition of a tax. If it is assumed that resources are optimally allocated or maximum social welfare prevails before the imposition of a tax, it can be demonstrated by microeconomic analysis that what amount of the damage will be caused to the social welfare. The imposition of a tax on a commodity (*i.e.*, indirect tax) will lead to the loss of social welfare by causing deviation from the optimum allocation of resources, the imposition of a direct tax (for example, income tax) will not disturb the optimum resource allocation and therefore will not result in loss of social welfare. Further, microeconomic analysis is applied to show the *gain from international trade* and to explain the factors which determine the distribution of this gain among the participant countries. Besides, microeconomics finds application in the various problems of international economics. Whether devaluation will succeed in correcting the disequilibrium in the balance of payments depends upon the elasticities of demand and supply of exports and imports. Furthermore, the determination of the foreign exchange rate of a currency, if it is free to vary, depends upon the demand for and supply of that currency.

We thus see that microeconomic analysis is a very useful and important branch of modern economic theory.

MACROECONOMICS

We now turn to explain the approach and content of macroeconomics. As said above, word macro is derived from the Greek word '*makros*' meaning '*large*' and therefore macroeconomics is concerned with the economic activity *in the large*. Macroeconomics analyses the behaviour of the whole economic system in totality or entirety. In other words, macroeconomics studies the behaviour of the large aggregates such as total employment, the national product or income, the general price level of the economy. Therefore, macroeconomics is also known as *aggregative economics*. Macroeconomics analyses and establishes the functional relationship between these large aggregates. Thus Professor Boulding says, "Macroeconomics deals not with individual quantities as such but with the aggregates of these quantities; not with individual incomes but with the national income; not with individual prices but with the price level; not with individual output but with the national output.[11]

In his other famous work, "*Economic Analysis*", he similarly remarks, "Macroeconomics, then, is that part of the subject which deals with large aggregates and averages of the system rather than

11. K. E. Boulding, "*A Reconstruction of Economics*" (1950), p. 3.

with particular items in it and attempts to define these aggregates in a useful manner and to examine their relationships."[12] Professor Gardner Ackley makes the distinction between the two types more clear and specific when he says, "macroeconomics concerns itself with such variables as the aggregate volume of output in an economy, with the extent to which its resources are employed, with the size of the national income, with the "general price level". Microeconomics, on the other hand, deals with the *division* of total output among industries, products and firms and the allocation of resources among competing uses. It considers problems of income distribution. Its interest is in relative prices of particular goods and services.[13]

Macroeconomics should be carefully distinguished from microeconomics. It should be noted that microeconomics also does deals with some "aggregates" but not of the type with which macroeconomics is concerned. Microeconomics examines the behaviour of the industry in regard to the determination of its product price, output and employment, and the industry is an *aggregate of the various firms* producing the same or similar product. Likewise, micro-economic theory seeks to explain the determination of price of a product through the interaction of market demand and market supply for a product. Market demand for a product is the aggregate of individual demands of all consumers wishing to buy the product and the market supply of a product is the aggregate of the productions of many firms producing that product. Similarly, demand for and supply of labour in an industry of a city through which microeconomics explains wage determination are aggregative concepts.

But the aggregates with which macroeconomics is concerned are of somewhat different variety. Macroeconomics concerns itself with these *aggregates which relate to the whole economy.* Macroeconomics also discusses the sub-aggregates of the large aggregates relating to the whole economy, but these sub-aggregates of macroeconomics, unlike the aggregates of microeconomics which examines aggregates relating to a particular product, a particular industry or a particular market, cut across various products and industries. For example, the total production of consumer goods (*i.e.*, total consumption) and the total production of capital goods (*i.e.*, total investment) are two important sub-aggregates dealt with in macroeconomics but these aggregates are not confined to a single product or a single industry but instead they refer to all industries producing consumer goods and all industries producing capital goods. Moreover, the sub-aggregates, discussed in macroeconomics, add up to an aggregate for the whole economy. For instance, total consumption and total investment, two important sub-aggregates in macroeconomics, together constitute the total national product. Likewise, the total wage income (*i.e.*, total share of labour) and total profits (defined as total property income) add up to the national income. Professor Ackley thus says, Macroeconomics also *uses* aggregates smaller than for the whole economy but only in a context which makes them sub-divisions of an economy wide total. Microeconomics also uses aggregates, but not in a context which relates them to *an economy-wide* total."[14]

Macroeconomics as a Study of Determination of Income and Employment

As we said above, the subject matter of microeconomics consists in explaining the determination of relative prices of products and factors and the allocation of resources based upon them. On the other hand, the subject matter of macroeconomic analysis is to explain what determines the *level of national income and employment*, and what causes *fluctuations* in the level of national income, output and employment. Further, it also explains the *growth* of national income over a long period of time. In other words, macroeconomics examines the determination of the level, fluctuations (cycles) and trends (growth) in the overall economic activity (*i.e.*, national income, output and employment).

It is worth mentioning that neo-classical economics, in which writings of Pigou and Marshall predominate, is mainly micro-analysis. Neo-classical writers assumed that full-employment of

12. K. E. Boulding, "*Economic Analysis* . p. 259.
13. Gardner Ackley, *Macroeconomic Theory*, 1961, p. 4.
14. *Op. cit.*, p. 5.

resources prevailed in the economy and concentrated mainly upon showing how the resources were allocated to the production of various goods and how the relative prices of products and factors were determined. It is mainly because of their full-employment assumption and their preoccupation with the problem of determination of prices, outputs and resource employments in individual industries that they could not explain the existence of involuntary unemployment and under-utilisation of the productive capacity at times of depression in private-enterprise capitalist countries. They thus could not provide adequate explanation of the occurrence of the trade cycles in a private enterprise economy. What is worse, the classical writers tried to apply the economic generalisations valid in the case of an individual industry to the behaviour of the whole economic system and to macro-economic variables.

For instance, Pigou asserted that involuntary unemployment existing at the time of depression could be eliminated and employment expanded by cutting down the wages. This is quite incorrect. While a cut in wages may expand employment in an individual industry, the reduction in wages throughout the economy will mean a fall in incomes of the working classes which will result in the decrease in level of aggregate demand. The fall in aggregate demand will tend to lower the level of employment rather than expand it.

There were no doubt pre-Keynesian theories of business cycles and the general price level which were "macro" in nature but it was late Lord J. M. Keynes who laid great stress on macro-economic analysis and put forward a general theory of income and employment in his revolutionary book, "*A General Theory of Employment, Interest and Money*" published in 1936. Keynes' theory made a genuine break from the classical economics and produced such a fundamental and drastic change in economic thinking that his macro-economic analysis has earned the names "*Keynesian Revolution*" and "*New Economics*". Keynes in his analysis made a frontal attack on the classical "*Say's Law of Markets*" which was the basis of full-employment assumption of classical economics and challenged the classical dictum that involuntary unemployment could not prevail in a free private enterprise economy. He showed how the equilibrium level of national income and employment was determined by aggregate demand and aggregate supply and further that this equilibrium level of income and employment may well be established at a far less than full employment level in a free private enterprise economy and thereby causing involuntary unemployment of labour on the one hand and excess productive capacity (*i.e.*, under-utilization of the existing capital) on the other. His macro-economic model reveales how consumption function, investment function, liquidity preference function, conceived in aggregative terms, interact to determine national income, employment, interest and the general price level.

Therefore, before showing how a level of income and employment is determined, we have to study the determinants of consumption function and investment function. The analysis of consumption function and investment function are the important subjects of macroeconomic theory. It is the total consumption demand and total investment demand taken together that constitute the level of aggregate demand which is the crucial determinant of the level of income and employment in the country.

Macroeconomics and Inflation

Besides studying how a level of income and employment is determined in the economy, macro-economics also concerns itself with showing how the general level of prices is determined. Keynes made a significant improvement over the Quantity Theory of Money by showing that the increase in the supply of money does not always bring about rise in prices. Important topic in this field is to explain the causes of inflation. Keynes, who before the Second World War showed that involuntary unemployment and depression were due to deficiency of aggregate demand, during the war period when prices rose very high he explained in a booklet entitled "*How to Pay for War*" that just as unemployment and depression were caused by deficiency of aggregate demand, inflation was due to excessive aggregate demand. Since Keynes' theory of inflation has been further developed and many types of inflation depending upon various causes have been pointed out. The problem of inflation is a serious problem faced these days, both by the developed and developing countries of the world. Theory of inflation is an important subject of macroeconomics.

Macroeconomics and Theory of Economic Growth

Another distinct and more important branch of macroeconomics that has been developed recently is the *theory of economic growth*, or what is briefly called *growth economics*. The problem of growth is a long-run problem and Keynes did not deal with it. In fact, Keynes is said to have once remarked that "in the long run we are all dead". From this remark of Keynes it should not be understood that he thought long run to be quite unimportant. By this remark he simply emphasised the importance of short-run problem of fluctuations in the level of economic activity (involuntary cyclical unemployment, depression, inflation). It was Harrod[15] and Domar[16] who extended the Keynesian analysis to the long-run problem of growth with stability. They pointed out the dual role of investment one of income generating, which Keynes considered, and the second of increasing capacity which Keynes ignored because of his pre-occupation with the short run. In view of the fact that an investment adds to the productive capacity (*i.e.*, capital stock), then if growth with stability (*i.e.* without secular stagnation or secular inflation) is to be achieved, income or demand must be increasing at a rate sufficient enough to ensure the full utilisation of the increasing capacity. Thus, macroeconomic models of Harrod and Domar have revealed the rate of growth of income that must take place if steady growth of the economy is to be achieved. These days growth economics has been further developed and extended a good deal. Though a general growth theory applies to both the developed and developing economies, special theories which explain the causes of under-development and poverty in developing countries and which also suggest strategies for initiating and accelerating growth in them have been propounded. These special growth theories relating to developing countries are generally known as *Economics of Development*.

Macroeconomics and Relative Income Shares

Still another important subject of macroeconomic theory is to explain what determines the *relative shares* in the total national income of the various classes, especially workers and capitalists, in the society. The interest in this subject goes back to Ricardo who not only emphasised that how the produce of earth was distributed among the three social classes landlords, workers and capitalists was the principal problem in economics but also propounded a theory explaining the determination of relative shares of rent, wages and profits in the total national income. Like Ricardo, Marx also showed a deep interest in this problem of determination of relative shares in a capitalist economy. But after Marx interest in this subject declined very much and the theory of distribution came to be discussed mostly in micro-terms, that is, the theory of distribution merely assumed the role of explaining the determination of *factor prices* rather than the relative aggregative shares of the social classes. Thanks to the efforts of M. Kalecki and Nicholas Kaldor, the interest in this macro-

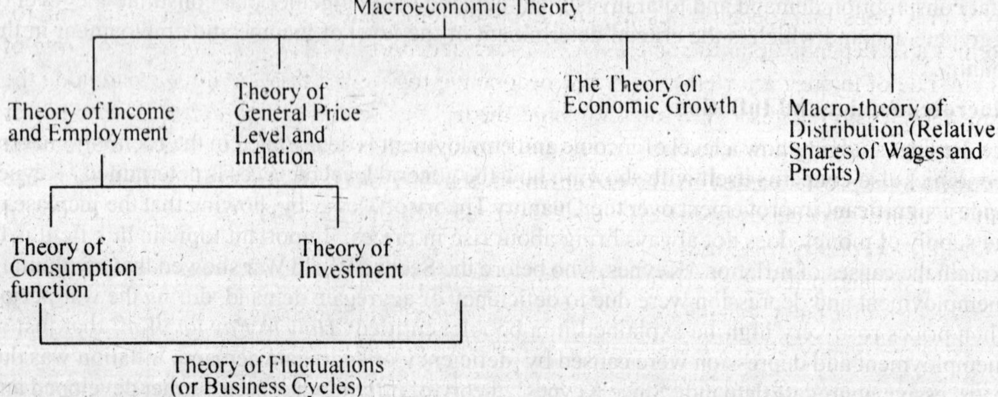

15. R. F. Harrod, *Towards a Dynamic Economics* (1948).
16. E. D. Domar, Expansion and Employment, *American Economic Review* (March 1947).

theory of distribution has again been revived. Kalecki advanced the view that the relative shares of wages and profits in the national income are governed by the degree of monopoly in the economy. On the other hand, Kaldor has applied the Keynesian analysis and has shown that the relative shares of wages and profits in the national income depend upon the ratio of investment to national income.

We have now stated, in brief, all aspects of macroeconomic theory. These various aspects of macroeconomic theory are shown in the following above chart :

INTERDEPENDENCE BETWEEN MICRO AND MACRO ECONOMICS

Actually micro and macro-economics are interdependent. The theories regarding the behaviour of some macroeconomic aggregates (but not all) are derived from theories of individual behaviour. For instance, the theory of investment, which is a part and parcel of the microeconomic theory, is derived from the behaviour of individual entrepreneur. According to this theory, an individual entrepreneur in his investment activity is governed by the expected rate of profit on the one hand and rate of interest on the other. And so is the aggregate investment function. Similarly, the theory of aggregate consumption function is based upon the behaviour patterns of individual consumers. It should be noted that we are able to derive aggregate investment function and aggregate consumption function from individual functions because in this respect the behaviour of the aggregate is in no way different from the behaviour patterns of individual components. Moreover, we can derive the behaviour of these aggregates only if either the composition of aggregates is constant or the composition changes in some regular way as the size of aggregates changes. From this it should not be understood that behaviour of all macroeconomic relationships is in conformity with behaviour patterns of individuals composing them. As we saw above, saving-investment relationship and wage-employment relationship for the economic system as a whole are quite different from the corresponding relationships found in case of individual parts.

Microeconomic theory contributes to macroeconomic theory in another way also. The theory of relative prices of products and factors is essential in the explanation of the determination of general price level. Even Keynes used microeconomic theory to explain rise in the price level as a result of increase in the money supply in the economy. According to Keynes, when as a result of the increase in money supply, aggregate demand in the economy increases and more output is produced, the cost of production rises. With the rise in the cost of production, the price level rises. According to Keynes, cost of production rises because of (1) the law of diminishing returns operates and (2) wages and prices of raw materials may rise as the economy approaches full-employment level. Now, the influence of cost of production, diminishing returns, etc., on the determination of prices are parts of microeconomics.

Not only does macroeconomics depend upon to some extent on microeconomics, microeconomics also depends upon to some extent on macroeconomics. The determination of rate of profit and rate of interest are well-known microeconomic topics, but they greatly depend upon the macroeconomic aggregates. In microeconomic theory, the profits are regarded as reward for uncertainty bearing but microeconomic theory fails to show the economic forces which determine the magnitude of profits earned by the entrepreneur and why there are fluctuations in them. The magnitude of profits depends upon the level of aggregate demand, national income, and the general price level in the country. We know that at times of depression when the levels of aggregate demand, national income and price level are low, entrepreneurs in the various fields of the economy suffer losses. On the other hand, when aggregate demand, incomes of the people, the general price level go up and conditions of boom prevail, entrepreneurs earn huge profits.

Now, take the case of the rate of interest. Strictly speaking the theory of the rate of interest has now become a subject of macroeconomic theory. Partial equilibrium theory of interest which belongs to microeconomic theory does not reveal all the forces which take part in the determination of the rate of interest. Keynes showed that the rate of interest was determined by the liquidity preference function and the stock (or supply) of money in the economy. The liquidity preference function and the stock of money in the economy are macroeconomic concepts. No doubt, the Keynesian theory of interest has also been shown to be indeterminate, but in the modern theory of interest Keynesian aggregative concepts of liquidity preference and stock of money play an important role in the determination of rate of interest. Moreover, in the modern interest theory (intersection of LM and IS curves), along with liquidity preference and supply of money, the other two forces which are used to explain the determination of interest are saving and investment functions which are also conceived in aggregative or macro terms.

It is thus clear from above that the determination of the profits and rate of interest cannot be explained without the tools and concepts of macroeconomics. It follows that though microeconomics and macroeconomics deal with different subjects, there is great interdependence between them. In the explanation of many economic phenomena, both micro and macro economic tools and concepts have to be applied. About interdependence between microeconomics and macroeconomics, Professor Ackley's remarks are worth quoting. He says, "The relationship between macroeconomics and theory of individual behaviour is a two-way street. On the one hand, microeconomic theory should provide the building blocks for our aggregate theories. But macroeconomics may also contribute to microeconomic understanding. If we discover, for example, empirically stable macroeconomic generalisations which appear inconsistent with microeconomic theories, or which relate to aspects of behaviour which microeconomics has neglected, macroeconomics may permit us to improve our understanding of individual behaviour."[17]

POSITIVE ECONOMICS AND NORMATIVE ECONOMICS

It is important to know the difference between positive economics and normative economics. Positive economics is concerned with explaining '*what it is,*' that is, it describes theories and laws to explain observed economic phenomena, whereas normative economics is concerned with '*what should be*' or '*what ought to be*' the things. J.N. Keynes drew the distinction between the two types of economics in the following manner: "A positive science may be defined as a body of systematised knowledge concerning what it is; normative science or a regulative science as a body of systematised knowledge relating to criteria of what ought to be, and concerned with the ideal as distinguished from the actual.... The objective of a positive science is the establishment of uniformities (*that is, scientific laws*); of a normative science, the determination of the ideals."[18] Thus, in positive economics we derive propositions, theories and laws about the actual behaviour of consumers, producers, investors, workers in their decision making about consumption, production, investment and supply of labour. Besides, in positive economics we explain how the economy as a whole works to determine level of national income and employment, inflation and exchange rate following certain rules of logic and observations of facts (*i.e.*, empirical evidence). These theories, laws and propositions explain the cause and effect relationship between economic variables. In positive microeconomics, we are broadly concerned with explaining the determination of relative prices of goods and factors of production and the allocation of resources between different commodities.

In positive macroeconomics, we are broadly concerned with how the level of national income and employment, aggregate consumption and investment and the general level of prices and rate of inflation are determined. In these parts of positive economics, what should be the prices, what should be the saving rate, what should be the allocation of resources, and what should be the distribution of

---

17. Gardner Ackley, *op. cit.*
18. J.N. Keynes, *Scope and Method of Political Economy,* MacMillan, London, 1930, p. 46., (italics added)

income among people are not discussed. These questions of what should be and what ought to be, fall within the purview of normative economics. Thus, given the profit maximization assumption, positive economics states that monopolist will fix a price which will equate marginal cost with marginal revenue. The question what price should or ought to be fixed so that maximum social welfare is achieved lies outside the purview of positive economics. Similarly, given the monopsony in the labour market, positive economics explains how actual wage rate is determined. It does not go into the question what is the just wage rate that should be paid to the labourer so that they should not be exploited. Likewise, how national income between different individuals is distributed falls within the domain of positive economics. But positive economics is not concerned with the question how national income *should be* distributed, how much labour the workers should supply, how much investment in social infrastructure the producers should be made etc. are outside the domain of positive economics as such advices depend on the personal opinions or ethical beliefs of the economists giving such advices.

On the other hand, normative economics is concerned with describing what should be the things. It is, therefore, also called *prescriptive economics*. What price for a product should be fixed, what wage rate should be paid, how income should be distributed, *etc.*, fall within the purview of normative economics. When economists advise that Governments should provide subsidies on foodgrains, Kerosene oil, cooking gas to reduce poverty, start employment guarantee programmes to reduce unemployment, they are giving normative advises. Besides, the economists those days are advocating for prevention of degradation and pollution of environment to promote well being not only of present generation but also of future generation. This is also normative prescription. It may however be noted that when economists advise that unemployment can be reduced if Government steps up its expenditure on infrastructure projects, this is based on conclusion of positive economics and well not therefore be a normative advice.

However, an important difference between positive economics and normative economics may be noted. *The propositions or laws of positive economics are derived from a set of axioms or assumptions. Whereas the propositions or laws so derived are capable of being tested and verified by observations of the facts in the real world, the propositions of welfare economics cannot be so tested and verified because we cannot know whether welfare has actually increased or not.* This is because welfare is not an observable quantity like price or quantities of goods; "it is a bird of another sort."[19] We cannot measure welfare in cardinal terms. Being subjective, welfare or satisfaction resides in the mind of an individual and, therefore, it is not capable of being measured in quantitative terms. Further, there are still more difficulties in testing a proposition regarding social welfare because propositions regarding social welfare generally involve value judgements of some sort. Therefore, to judge the validity of the welfare propositions we must test its assumptions or premises which invariably involve value judgements. Professor Graff rightly writes, "*in positive economics, the proof of the pudding is indeed in the eating. The welfare cake, on the other hand, is so hard to taste, that we must sample its ingredients before baking.*"[20]

Normative Economics and Value Judgements

It should be noted that, normative economics involves *value judgements* or what are simply known as *values*. By value judgements or values, we mean the conceptions of the people about what is good or bad. These conceptions regarding values of the people are based on the ethical, political, philosophical and religious beliefs of the people and are not based upon any scientific logic or law Because normative economics involves value judgements eminent economist Professor Robbins contended that economics should not become normative in character. [21] He opined that it was unscientific to include the value judgements in the economic analysis. To quote him, "the role of the economist is more and more conceived of as that of the expert, who can say what consequences are

19. J. De V. Graff, *Theorectical Welfare Economics*, Combridge University Press, 2nd Edition, 1957, p.2
20. *Ibid*, p.2.
21. L. Robbins, *"Nature and Significance of Economic Science."* MacMillan, London, 2nd Edition, 1938

likely to follow certain actions, but who cannot judge as an economist the desirability of ends."[22] While drawing difference between economics and ethics he further writes, "economics deals with ascertainable facts, ethics with valuations and obligations. The two fields of inquiry are not on the same plane of discourse. Between the generalisations of positive and normative economics, there is a logical gulf fixed which no ingenuity can disguise and no juxtaposition in space or time bridge over. Propositions involving the verb 'ought' are different in kind from propositions involving the verb 'is'.[23]

Value judgements of various individuals differ and their rightness or wrongness cannot be decided on the basis of scientific logic or laws. Therefore, in our view, positive economics should be kept separate and distinct from normative economics. However, because normative economics involves value judgements, it does not mean that it should be considered as useless or not meaningful and should not be the concern of economics. As a matter of fact, many vital issues concerning economic welfare of the society necessarily involve some value judgements. If economics is to become an 'engine for social betterment', it has to adopt certain norms, ideals or criteria with which to evaluate economic issues and pass judgements on what is good and what is bad from the viewpoint of social welfare. We agree with Professor A.C. Pigou, "*Our impulse is not the philosopher's impulse, knowledge for the sake of knowledge but rather the physiologist's knowledge for the healing that knowledge may help to bring.*"[24] The economist should not refrain from making value judgements if there is a wide consensus about them among the community. Using his knowledge of economics and these value judgements he should comment upon the desirability or otherwise of certain policies and issues. Professor Paul Streeten rightly says, "*Economists cannot and should not refrain from making value judgements if their studies are to be more than a purely formal technique of reasoning, an algebra of choice. The technique, the algebra is important and ought to be as scientific as possible, but it is significant only as a means to study of wealth and welfare and of the ways to improve them.*"[25]

As is clear from above, normative ecnomics is concerned with welfare propositions, since what is good or what is bad ultimately depends upon its effect on the welfare of the individual and the society. In recent years, a branch of economics, known as *welfare economics*, has been developed. This welfare economics seeks to evaluate the social desirability of alternative social states or economic policies. Thus, Professor Scitovsky writes, " welfare economics is that branch of economic analysis which is concerned primarily with establishment of criteria that can provide a positive basis for adopting policies which are likely to maximise social welfare."[26] In short, the subject of welfare economics is to prescribe criteria or norms with which to judge the social desirability of certain economic re-organisations and prescribe policies on the basis of these criteria.

It should be noted that as far as the welfare of individual is concerned, through difficult to measure in cardinal terms, economists can measure it in ordinal terms and by observing the act of choice of the individual. For instance, if an individual chooses A rather than B , it shows that his welfare is greater in A than in B. Thus, choice by an individual is an objective test for knowing and comparing his welfare in different economic states. Therefore, what promotes individual welfare or not can be tested and verified. However, when welfare economics has to judge the social welfare or group welfare, it encounters difficulties, because the measurement of social welfare is not an easy task and contains value judgements and interpersonal comparisons of utility This is because the society or group whose welfare we have to judge cannot be regarded as an organic whole, having its own mind. Therefore, social welfare, unlike individual welfare, is not something which resides in the mind of the society. We cannot derive propositions of social welfare from choices of individuals

22. *Ibid.*
23. *Ibid.*
24. A C. Pigou, *Economics of Welfare*. 4th Edition, MacMillan, London, 1932, p.5.
25. Paul Streeten, Economics and Value Judgements, *Quarterly Journal of Economics*, 1950, p. 595.
26. Tibor Scitovsky, *Papers on Welfare and Growth*, 1962. p. 174.

comprising the society because various individuals choose differently and therefore, there is no unanimous social choice. Individual choices differ because various individuals have different tastes, preferences and ethical beliefs and therefore different value judgements. The vital issues in welfare economics are concerned with social welfare and devising certain criteria to judge social welfare. Therefore, welfare economics cannot be purely objective or free from value judgements.

Thus, according to several modern economists such as Paul Samuelson, I.M.D. Little. K.E. Boulding welfare economics cannot be purged of value judgements. In fact the study of welfare economics has been developed to make policy recommendations to promote social welfare. And for doing so economists cannot escape from introducing ethical norms or value judgements since we all take interest in the questions concerning happiness and welfare of the society "*Welfare economics and ethics cannot, then, be separated.... They are inseparable. Getting rid of value judgements would be throwing the baby away with the bath-water.* The subject is one about which nothing interesting can be said without value judgements, for the reason that we take a moral interest in welfare and happiness.[27]

It should not be understood from above that the explicit introduction of value judgements makes the study of normative economics unscientific. In spite of the explicit introduction of value judgements in welfare studies, the economist's approach can still be scientific in the sense that he scientifically deduces the welfare propositions from the given value judgements.

QUESTIONS FOR REVIEW

1. Distinguish between microeconomics and macroeconomics.

2. What is micro-economics ? Explain the subjects which are studied in microeconomics.

3. What is meant by economic efficiency ? In which branch of economics, the subject of economic efficiency is studied ? Explain the following concepts of economic efficiency :

(*i*) Production efficiency
(*ii*) Efficiency in distribution
(*iii*) Efficiency in resource allocation.

4. Microeconomic theory is intimately concerned with the question of efficiency and welfare. Explain.

5. Microeconomics is a microscopic study of the economy. Explain.

6. Explain the importance of microeconomic theory and describe the fields of economics in which it has been usefully applied.

7. What is macroeconomics ? Explain important issues which form the subject matter of macroeconomics .

8. Macroeconomics is a study of economic aggregates Discuss.

9. Why is there a need for a separate study of macroeconomics ? Explain giving some examples of *macroeconomic paradoxes*.

10. Distinguish between Micro and Macroeconomics. Show how the two are interdependent.

11. Which of the following subjects fall under microeconomics and which ones under macroeconomics?

(1) Determination of wage rate
(2) Determination of the level of employment in the economy
(3) How is general price level determined ?

---

27. I.M.D. Little, *A Critique of Welfare Economics*, Oxford University Press, 2nd Edition, 1957.

(4) Determination of price of wheat
(5) How is national income determined ?
(6) What determines rate of economic growth of a country ?

12. Tick the correct answer. Macroeconomics is concerned with:
(*a*) The level of output of goods and sources.
(*b*) The determination of the level of employment and unemployment.
(*c*) The general level of prices and inflation.
(*d*) The growth of real output.
(*e*) All the above.

13. The study of which of the following problems fall within the purview of microeconomics:
(1) Allocation of resources
(2) How to produce
(3) For whom to produce
(4) Unemployment of labour
(5) Economic efficiency in resource allocation
(6) Economic growth of a country.
(7) The level of national income.

14. Tick which of the following topics fall within the purview of macroeconomics:
(1) Inflation in the economy
(2) Price of steel
(3) Level of national income
(4) Output of cotton fabrics
(5) Income from film industry
(6) Unemployment in the economy
(7) Growth of the economy
(8) Per capita income of a country
(9) Cement production in a year.

15. Distinguish between positive economics and normative economics. Explain the questions which are discussed in each of them.

16. What are value judgements ? Explain their role in economics.

Appendix to Chapter 3
THE USE OF MATHEMATICAL CONCEPTS, GRAPHS AND OTHER TECHNIQUES

Introduction

In recent years economics has become increasingly mathematical as in the economic analysis various mathematical concepts such as functions, optimising techniques of differential calculus, maxima and minima are being extensively used. Besides, graphs are being used to represent and interpret economic data and see whether there is any causal relationship between changes in two variables. In what follows we shall first study how economists use and work with graphs and then explain the use of mathematical concepts of functions and differential calculus in economics.

However, it is worth noting that economics is not about graphs and functions in abstract, it is concerned with how people behave and make choices in the use of scarce resources to satisfy their wants or fulfil their objectives. It is to represent this people's behaviour that mathematical graphs and functions are used. As a social science economics makes a scientific analysis of how people work to overcome the universal problem of scarcity.

Working With Graphs

Economists use graphs to interpret the data and illustrate the theories they have developed about people's economic behaviour in order to make vivid and easier to understand economic concepts and theories. The graphs are important learning aid to illustrate economic laws and theories as well as to interpret economic data. It is difficult to understand any data from '*numbers*' but easy to understand it, when shown by graphs.

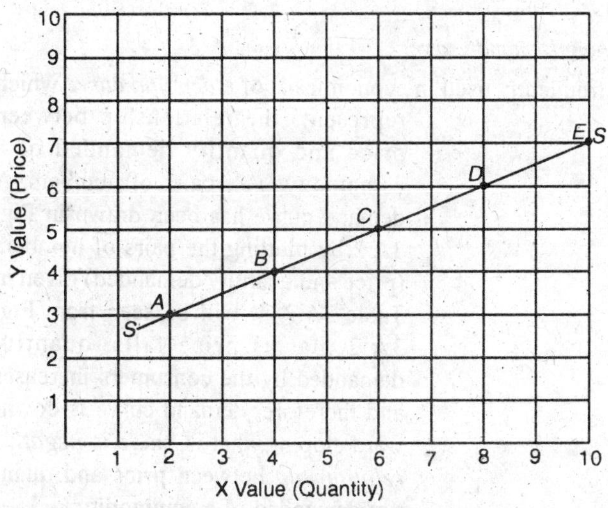

Fig. 3A.1. *Upward Sloping Supply Curve*

Table 3A.1. Pairs of Numbers : Supply Schedule

	Y Price	*X* Quantity
A	3	2
B	4	4
C	5	6
D	6	8
E	7	10

An important use of graphs is to represent a pair of numbers and to know what is the relationship between them. In Table 3A.1 we have shown six pairs of two numbers *Y* (price) and *X* (quantity supplied). We represent these six pairs of numbers by a graph by plotting them in a space between coordinate axes in Fig. 3A.1. We measure the variable price on the horizontal axis (also called *Y*-axis) and the variable quantity supplied on the vertical axis (also called *X*-axis). We plot point *A* representing price Rs. 3 and quantity supplied equal to 2, plot point *B* representing price Rs. 4 and quantity equal to 4, plot point *C* depicting price Rs. 5 and quantity equal to 6, point *D* depicting price Rs. 6 and quantity equal to 8, and lastly point *E* representing price equal to 7 and quantity supplied equal to 10. We join the points *A, B, C, D* and *E* representing pairs of numbers representing price and quantity supplied to get a straight line curve *SS*. This supply curve *SS* depicts the relationship between price and quantity supplied by producers. Thus, this graph represents the supply curve which is a graphic representation of an economic theory according to which there is a *positive relationship* between price and quantity supplied.

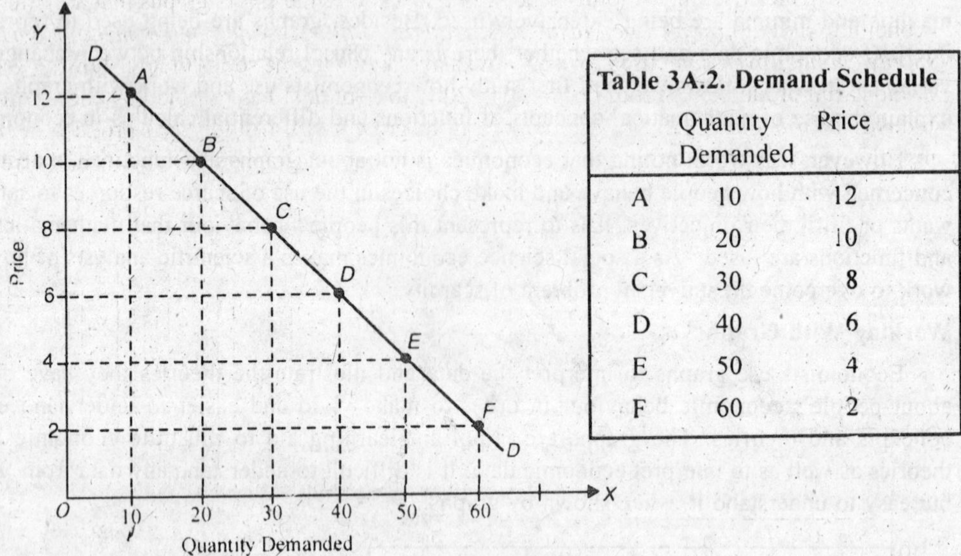

Table 3A.2. Demand Schedule

	Quantity Demanded	Price
A	10	12
B	20	10
C	30	8
D	40	6
E	50	4
F	60	2

Fig. 3A.2. *Negatively Sloping Demand Curve*

Another important graph that is very frequently used in economics is of a *demand curve* which represents the relationship between price and quantity demanded of a commodity (*i.e.*, pairs of numbers. A demand curve has been drawn in Fig. 3A.2 by plotting the pairs of numbers (price and quantity demanded) given in Table 3A.2 It will be seen from Fig. 3A.2 that as price falls, quantity demanded by the consumers increases and therefore, demand curve is downward sloping, that is, there is *negative relationship* between price and quantity demanded of a commodity.

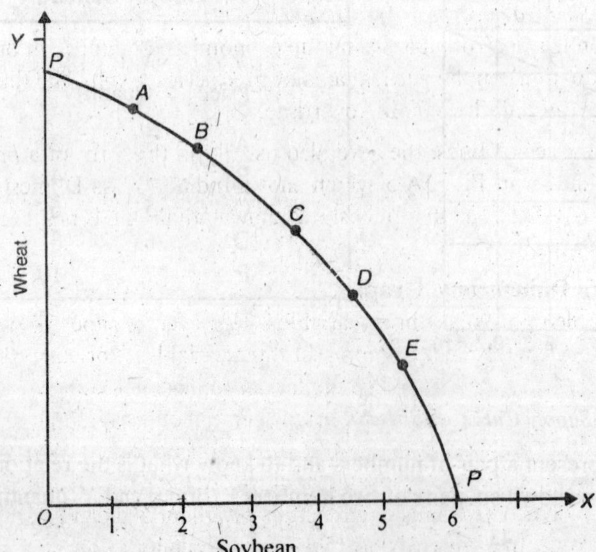

Fig. 3A.3. *Production Possibility Curve*

Another important economic graph used in economics is that of *production possibility curve* which has been explained in the previous chapter. A typical graph of a production possibility curve *PP* between wheat and soybean has been drawn in Fig. 3A.3. This production possibility curve has *a negative slope and is generally concave to the origin.* As explained in the previous chapter, a production possibility curve depicts the various combinations of two goods (wheat and soybean) in Fig. 3A.3, such as *A*, *B*, *C* and *D*) which can be produced with a given limited *amount of resources* assuming that they are *fully employed* and used *most efficiently* with the *given state of technology*.

The production possibility curve is negatively sloped as when one good is produced more (say, soybean), some amount of the other good (wheat in the present case) has to be given up. Besides, its concave shape indicates that *the opportunity cost in terms of another good foregone for producing an additional unit of a good goes on increasing*. This is because all given resources are not equally suitable or productive for the production of various goods.

Time Series Graphs. Another type of graphs called time-series graphs that are often used in economics show that *how one variable, say output, inflation rate, employment, exports, money supply changes over time*. In Figure 3A.4 we have drawn a time series graph, showing growth rate of industrial production in India from Sept. 2009 to Sept. 2010 as revealed by change in Index of Industrial Production (IIP). It will be seen from growth rate in industrial production in various months, year-on-year basis, has been changing over the years. In the time series graph,

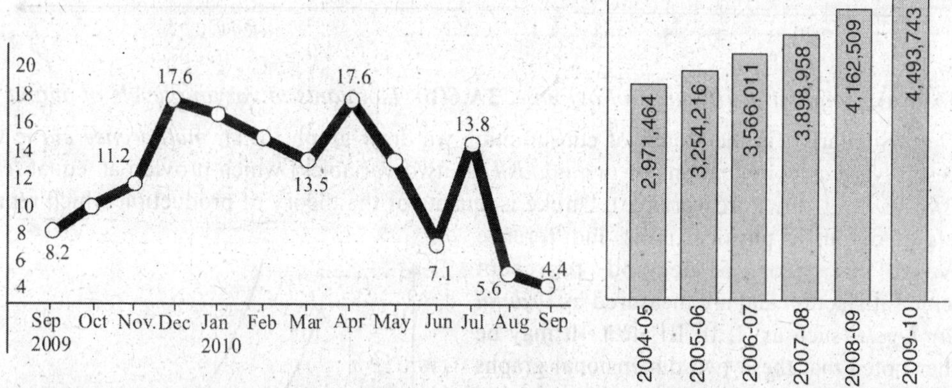

Fig. 3A.4. *Growth Rate of Industrial Production in India From Sept. 2009 to Sept. 2010*

Fig. 3A.5. *Gross Domestic Product of India at Factor Cost (Rs. crore)*

years or months (*i.e.*, time) are shown on the horizontal axis and the economic magnitude (in our Fig. 3A. 4 growth rate of Industrial Production) on the vertical axis of time series graph. The time series graph gives a good idea about the *trend* of the variable overtime.

Graphs are not only of the type of curves or lines, they are also usually in the form of a *bar diagram*. Such a bar-diagram graph is shown in Fig. 3A.5 which shows India's Gross Domestic Product (GDP) from 2004-05 to 2009-10. This bar diagram shows how India's GDP has been growing over the years (2004-05 to 2009-10).

Representing Three Variables in a Two Dimensional Graph

In economics some important problems involve three variables. However, a paper is two dimensional and therefore it requires a special technique to represent three variables. For example, in decision-making by a firm involves three variables, namely, the labour (man-hours) employed, capital (machine hours) used to produce a third variable *output*. Various combinations of labour and capital can be used to produce a given level of output. The economists use a concept called *isoquant* (or equal product curve) to represent a given level of output (say 100 units. We have drawn a graph of such an isoquant in Figure 3A.6 (a) which show various combinations of labour and capital such as *A*, *B*, *C*, *D* to produce 100 units of output. In Figure 3A.6(b) we have shown an *isoquant map* showing three isoquants Q_1, Q_2, Q_3 representing combinations of two inputs to produce 100, 120, 140 units of output respectively.

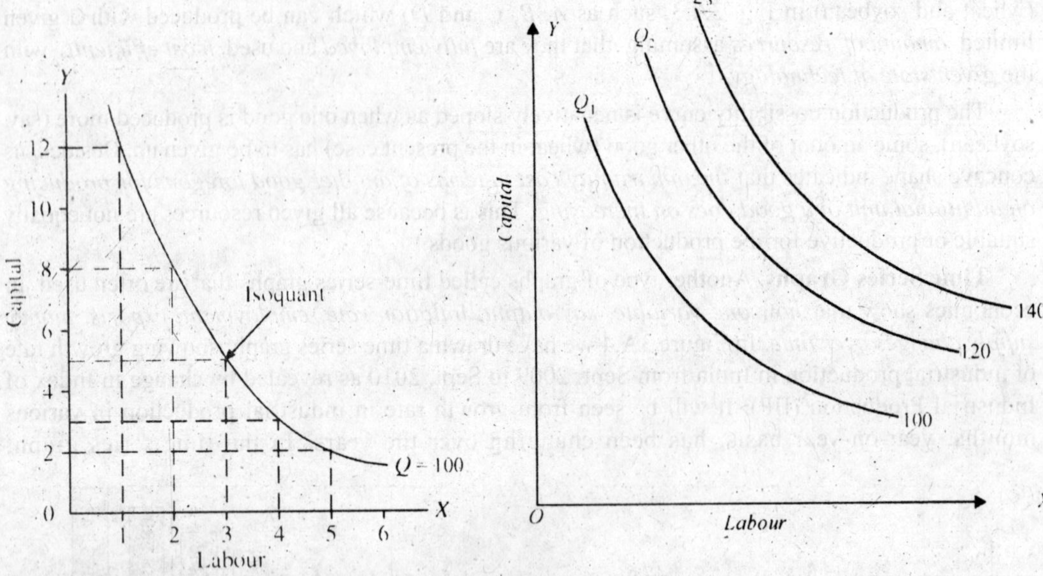

3A.6(a). *Isoquant of 100 units of output* **3A.6(b).** *Isoquants of varying levels of output*

Similarly, in the theory of consumption we draw graph of an *indifference curve* which represent various combinations of *two goods* (*i.e.,* two variables) which provide an equal *level of satisfaction* (*i.e.,* the third variable). Unlike isoquants of the theory of production which represent levels of output in physical units, indifference curves of the theory of demand represent psychic satisfaction and are measured by *ordinal utility levels* (such as I, II, III etc.). It may be further noted that these two dimensional graphs representing three dimensions are like *contour lines map.* A contour line represents the places which have *equal height above the sea level.*

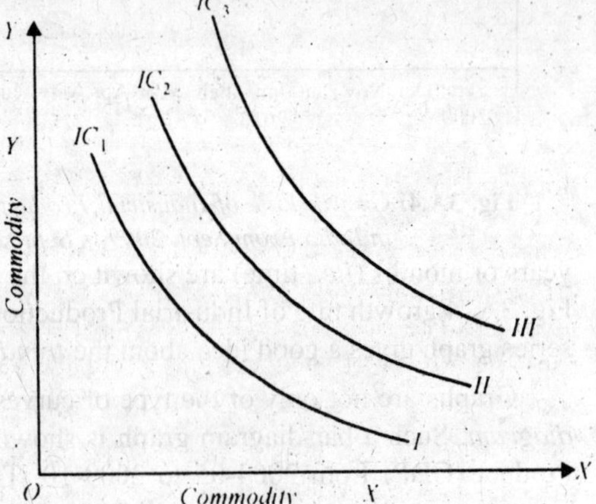

Fig. 3A.7. *A Set of Indifference Curves*

Slope of a Curve

An important feature of the graph of a line or curve is its slope. *The slope of a line or curve indicates whether the relationship between the two variables represented on the two axes is positive or negative.* A positive slope of a curve indicates that when the value of variable Y increases, the value of variable X also increases. On the other hand, the negative slope indicates the increase in the value of Y is associated with the decrease in value of X. The slope also indicates the *extent of response* of a variable X to the change in value of Y. Let X and Y are the two variables which are represented by a straight line such as shown in Fig. 3A.8. The slope of a straight line or curve depicting the two variables X and Y is the change in the value of a variable Y to the change in the value of the variable X. The slope of a straight line is the ratio of the vertical change (*i.e.,* change in the value of Y) to the horizontal change (*i.e.,* change in the value of X) as we move from left to right along a line or curve. In other words, slope of a

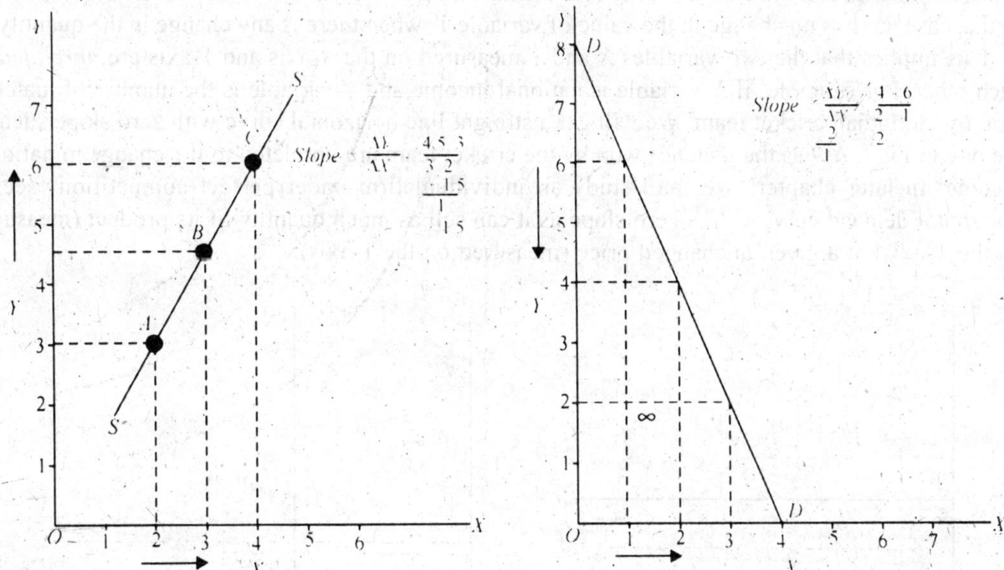

Fig. 3A.8(a) *A Curve with a Positive Slope* Fig. 3A.8(b) *Curve with Negative Slope*

curve is the ratio of '*rise*' to the '*run*'. Consider Figure 3A.8(a) where an upward sloping curve *SS* has been drawn. When we move to the right from point *A* to *B*, the value of variable *Y* rises by 3 to 4.5 the value of variable *X* increases from 2 to 3. The slope is therefore equal to $\frac{4.5-3}{3-2} = \frac{+1.5}{1} = +1.5$. To put in general terms, slope $= \frac{\Delta Y}{\Delta X} = \frac{Y_2 - Y_1}{X_2 - X_1}$.

It will be seen from Fig. 3A.8 (a) the increase in *Y* is associated with the increase in *X*, that is, slope or $\frac{\Delta Y}{\Delta X}$ is a positive number. That is, there is a positive relationship between *Y* and *X* in the upward sloping curve *SS* of Figure 3A.8(a). Such positive relationship occurs in case of supply curve of a commodity which depicts relationship between price of a commodity and the quantity supplied. The positive relationship also occurs between income and consumption and therefore consumption function curve depicting the relationship between income and consumption is up-ward-sloping. The slope of *SS* line in Fig. 3A.8(a), is positive and equal to +1.5.

In Fig. 3A.8(b) a line *DD* has been drawn where when the value of variable *Y* falls, the value of variable *X* increases. There is therefore *negative relationship* between *Y* and *X* in Fig. 3A.8(b). For example, when the value of *Y* falls, from 6 to 4, the quantity of *X* increases from 1 to 2. That is, slope is here equal to $\frac{4-6}{2-1} = \frac{-2}{1} = -2$. Such negative relationship occurs in case of demand curve for a commodity which depicts *negative relationship* between price and quantity demanded of a commodity. Such negative relationship is also found in case of production possibil-ity curve in the theory of production, indifference curve in the theory of consumption and isoquant in the theory of production as all these are negatively sloping .

Curves with Zero Slope and Infinite Slope. There are two special cases of slope of lines or curves. In Fig. 3A.9, we have drawn a horizontal straight line *AB* whose slope is zero (slope = 0). In this case there is no change in the value of variable *Y*, when there is any change in the quantity of *X*. This implies that the two variables *X* and *Y* measured on the *X*-axis and *Y*-axis are *unrelated* to each other. For example, if *X*-variable is national income and *Y*-variable is the number of matches won by the Indian cricket team. We will get a straight line horizontal curve with zero slope such as the one in Fig. 3A.9 as the matches won by the cricket team are unrelated to the change in national income. In later chapters we shall study an individual firm under perfect competition faces a horizontal demand curve with a zero slope as it can sell as much quantity of its product (measured on the *X*-axis) at a given unchanged price (measured on the *Y*-axis).

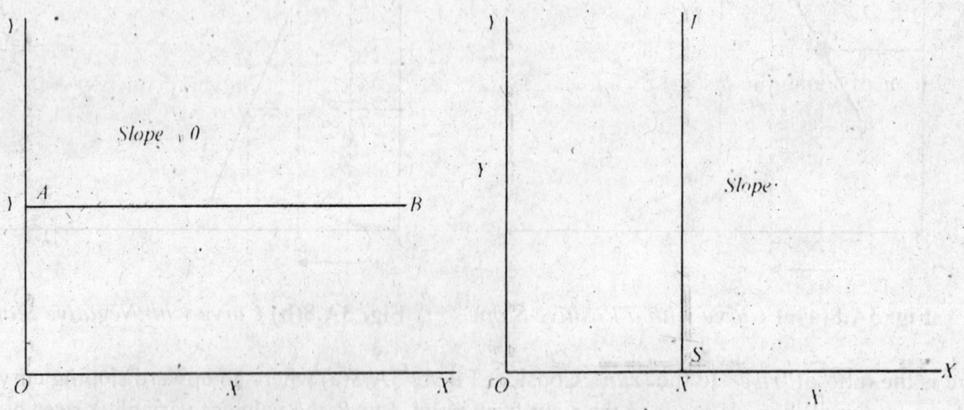

Fig. 3A.9. *Line with a zero Slope* **Fig. 3A.10.** *Line with infinite Slope*

On the other hand in Fig. 3A.10 a vertical straight line *SL* has been drawn whose slope is infinite as in this case when the value of *Y* variable increases, there is no change at all in the variable *X*. In this case also the two variables *X* and *Y* are *unrelated* to each other. In economics such a zero response case in a variable is found in case of *supply of land for the society as a whole which remains the same irrespective of any rise in rent (measured on the Y-axis).*

The Slope of a Curved Line

Now we shall explain how to measure slope at a point on a curved line such as shown in Fig. 3A.11 by the indifference curve *IC*. The slope of a curved line at a point is found out by *measuring the slope of tangent drawn to the curve at that point*. In Fig. 3A.11 the slope of *IC* curve at point *A* can be obtained by drawing a tangent *tt* at that point. By applying the definition of slope explained above

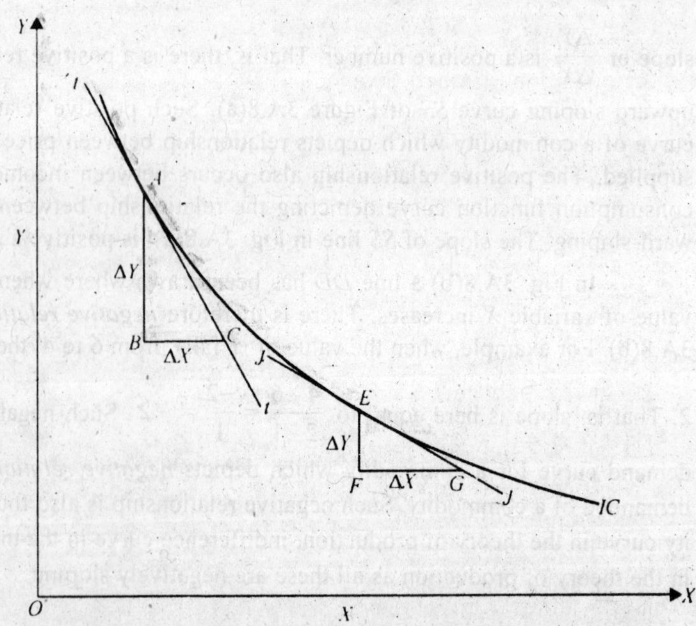

Fig. 3A.11. *Measuring Slope at a Point on a Curved Line*

slope of *IC* curve in Fig. 3A.11 at point *A* is given by :

$$\frac{\Delta Y}{\Delta X} = \frac{\text{distance } AB}{\text{distance } BC}$$

If the distance *AB* equals 3 and distance *BC* equals 2, then slope of *IC* at point *A* is $\frac{-3}{2} = -1.5$. It is a negative number because when the value of the variable *Y* falls, the variable *X* increases.

Now, in Fig. 3A.11 at point *E* on the curved line *IC*, the slope is given by the slope of tangent *JJ* drawn at this point. It will be seen from this figure that slope of tangent *JJ* at point *E* on the given *IC* curve, though negative, is less than that at point *A* on it. That is, slope of *IC* curve is falling as we move along the curve to the right.

Now consider the upward-sloping curved line *CD* in Figure 3A.12 which is concave upward. Slopes of tangents drawn at points *A* and *B* to this curve are positive but as will be seen from the figure that as we move to the right, slope is increasing. Such a curve with an increasing

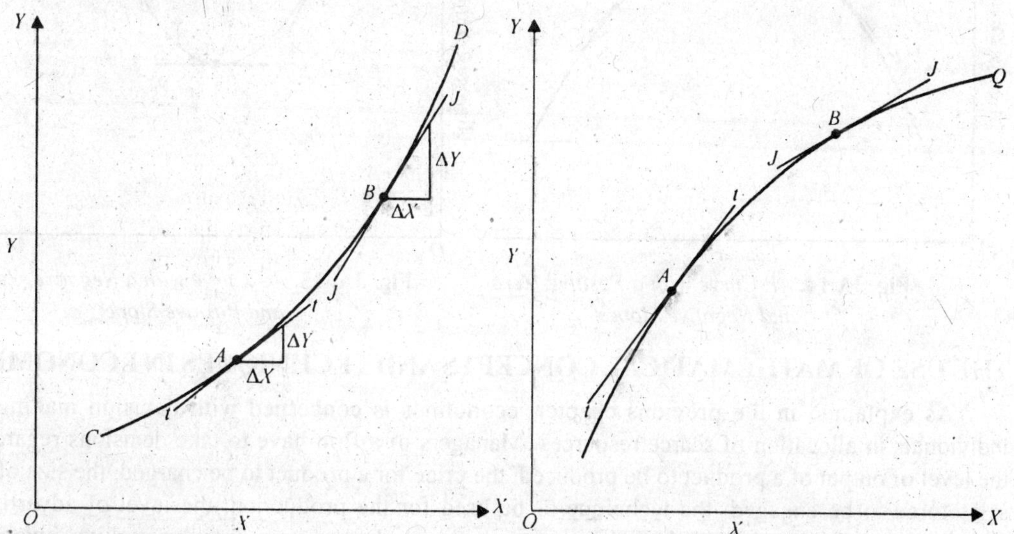

Fig. 3A.12. *Slope is positive but increasing* **Fig. 3A.13.** *Slope is positive but declining*

slope is found in economics in case of total cost curve of a product whose slope measures marginal cost (*MC*) which usually rises as more output of a product is produced.

Now, consider Fig. 3A.13 where an upward-sloping curved line has been drawn which is convex upward. In such a curve slope is positive but declines as we move to the right. This can be known as we draw tangents at points *A* and *B* on it. It will be seen that the slope of the tangent drawn at point *B* is less than that at point A. This type of curve in economics we get in case of total product curve with one factor, say labour, as variable, keeping capital and technology as fixed. The slope of a total product curve indicates marginal product (*MP*) of labour which decreases as more of labour is employed due to the operation of diminishing returns.

Curves with Positive and Negative Slopes

In economics we find relationship between two variables, (for example, (1) between average product of labour and the quantity of labour used , (2) between average cost and level of output) when a curve has both positive and negative slopes in different regions. In Figure 3A.14 we have drawn the curve of average product of labour. In this as labour is increased, the average product curve has a positive slope in the beginning but declines till it reaches at zero slope at point *B* beyond which its slope is negative.

In Fig. 3A.15, the opposite case occurs where we have first negative slope, then zero slope and as we move further to the right *AC* curve assumes positive slope.

It follows from the above discussion of graphs of curves that while reading and working with graphs, students should understand the implications of the slopes of the lines and curves they are using. Whether a curve representing any economic phenomenon, concept or theory has a positive slope, zero slope or negative has an important economic implications. Therefore, graphs must be interpreted carefully.

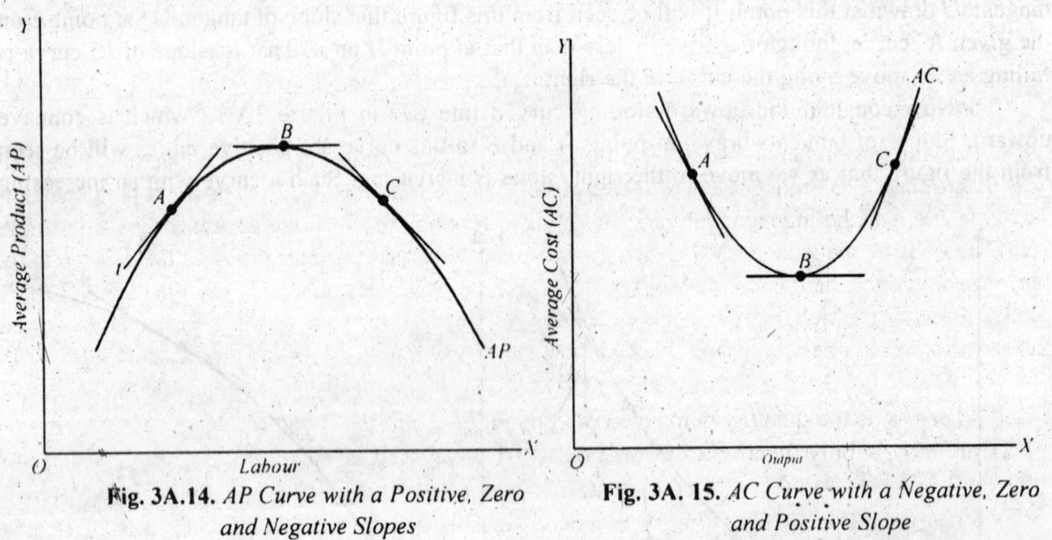

Fig. 3A.14. *AP Curve with a Positive, Zero and Negative Slopes*

Fig. 3A. 15. *AC Curve with a Negative, Zero and Positive Slope*

THE USE OF MATHEMATICAL CONCEPTS AND TECHNIQUES IN ECONOMICS

As explained in the previous chapter, economics is concerned with decision making by individuals in allocation of scarce resources. Managers of a firm have to take decisions regarding the level of output of a product to be produced, the price for a product to be charged, the size of the sales force to be engaged, the technique to be used for the production, the level of advertising expenditure to be incurred and many other such things. In business decision making given the resources a large number of options are open to a manager from which he has to make a choice. Obviously, a manager will try to make a best choice from among different options available to him. *A best or optimum choice is one that best achieves the desired goal or objective of the firm.* It is generally assumed in economies that an entrepreneur or manager of a firm will try to maximise profits. Similarly, he may be considering to choose among the various combinations of factors or inputs that can be used for producing a level of output. To maximise profits he will choose the combination of inputs that minimises cost for producing a given level of output. Evidently, this is a minimisation problem which he has to solve. Given his scarce resources, (for example, with his given limited income), a consumer also tries to maximise his satisfaction.

Decision making that involves solving of maximisation and minimisation problems is called optimisation. Therefore, for making efficient decision it is necessary to learn the techniques of optimisation. It may however be on noted that popular techniques of optimisation are mathematical in nature. In recent years the use of analytical models of decision making has increased the importance of the knowledge of techniques of optimisation for the students of economics. Mathematical formulations of these analytical models of decision-making are expressed in terms of functions which describe economic relationship between various variables. Therefore, to begin with we will explain the concept of a function and its various important types. Besides, optimisation techniques involve the use of differential calculus and its concepts of derivatives. Therefore, after studying the concept of function and its various types we will proceed to explain the concept of a derivative and rules of differentiation. At the end of this chapter we will give some examples of how differential calculus is used for optimisation problems in economics.

FUNCTIONS

A function describes the relation between two or more than two variables. That is, a function expresses dependence of one variable on one or more other variables. Thus, if the value of a variable Y depends on the value of another variable X, we may write

$$Y = f(X) \qquad \ldots(1)$$

Where f stands for function.

This expression (1) is read as 'Y is function of X'. This implies that every value of the variable Y is determined by a unique value of the variable X. In the function (1), Y is known as the dependent variable and X is the independent variable. Thus in function (1) Y is the dependent variable and its value depends on the value of X. Further, the independent variable is interpreted as the cause and the dependent variable as the effect. An important function which is extensively used in economics is a demand function which expresses that quantity demanded of a commodity is a function of its price, other factors being held constant. Thus, demand for a commodity X is described as under :

$$D_x = f(P_x)$$

Where D_x is the quantity demanded of commodity X and P_x is its price.

Similarly, supply function of a commodity X is expressed as

$$S_x = f(P_x)$$

When the value of the variable Y depends on more than two variables $X_1, X_2 \ldots\ldots\ldots X_n$ this function is written in general form as :

$$Y = f(X_1, X_2, X_3, X_4 \ldots\ldots\ldots\ldots\ldots\ldots X_n)$$

This shows the variable Y depends on several independent variables $X_1, X_2, \ldots\ldots\ldots\ldots X_n$ where n is the number of independent variables. Again note that in economics we write '*causes*' as the independent variables and '*effect*' as the dependent variable.

For example, demand for a product is generally considered to be a function of its own price, prices of other commodities (which may be substitutes or complements), income of the consumers, tastes and preferences of the consumers and advertising expenditure made by a firm to promote its product. Thus,

$$D_x = f(P_x, P_y, M, T, A)$$

Where

D_x = demand for the commodity X

P_x = price of the commodity X.

P_y = price of a substitute product Y.

M = income of the consumers

T = tastes and preferences of the consumer for the product.

A = advertising expenditure incurred by the firm.

The exact nature of relation of dependent variable with the independent variables can be known from the *specific form* of the function. The specific form of a function can take a variety of mathematical forms. We explain below some specific types of functions.

Linear and Power Functions

A widely used mathematical form of a function is a *linear function*. A linear function can be stated in the following general form :

$$Y = a + bX$$

Where a and b are positive constants and are called *parameters* of the function. Note that parameters of a function are variables that are fixed and given in a specific function. The values of constants a and b determine the specific nature of a linear function. The linear demand function with price as the only independent variable is written as

$$Q_d = a - bP$$

The minus sign before coefficient b indicates that quantity demanded of a commodity is negatively related with price of the commodity. That is, if price of a commodity falls, its quantity demanded increases and vice versa. If a equals 7 and b equals 0.5, the linear demand function can be expressed in the following specific form :

$$Q_d = 7 - 0.5\,P$$

The above specific demand function shows that a unit fall in price of the commodity will cause 0.5 units increase in the quantity demanded of the commodity. If price (P) is zero, the second term ($0.5P$) in the demand function drops out and the quantity demanded is equal to 7.

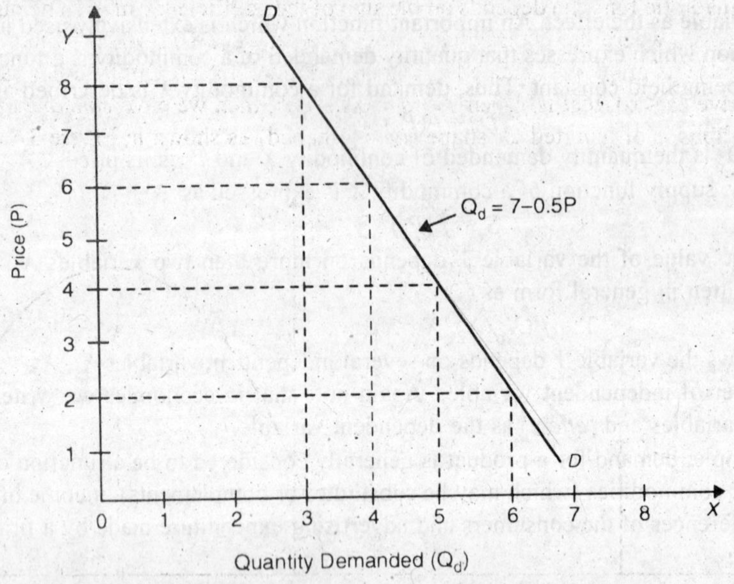

Fig. 3A.16. *Graph of a Linear Demand Function* ($Q_d = 7 - 0.5P$)

We can take various values of P and find out different quantities (Q_d) of a commodity demanded at them. In Figure 3A.16 we have plotted these price-quantity combinations on a graph and have obtained demand curve DD of the commodity representing the given demand function ($Q_d = 7 - 0.5P$).

It should be noted that, contrary to mathematical practice, by *convention* in economics to represent a function we show the independent variable (price in the above case of demand function) on the Y-axis and the dependent variable (the quantity demanded in the present case) on the X-axis. Graph of linear demand function is shown in Figure 3A.16. It is worth noting that slope of the demand function curve in Figure 3A.16 will represent $\frac{\Delta P}{\Delta Q}$. However, if we represent quantity demanded (Q_d) on the Y-axis, and price (P_x) on the X-axis; the slope of the demand curve so drawn would be equal to $\frac{\Delta Q}{\Delta P}$.

Power Functions

The linear functions stated above are known as *first degree functions* where the independent variables X_1, X_2, X_3, etc are raised to the first power only. We now turn to explain power functions. In economics power functions of the quadratic and cubic forms are also extensively used.

Quadratic Functions : In quadratic function one or more of the independent variables are squared, that is, raised to the second power. Note that power is also referred to as *exponent.* A quadratic function may be written as

$$Y = a + bX + cX^2$$

This implies that value of the dependent variable Y depends on the constant a plus the coefficient b times the value of the independent variable X plus the coefficient c times the square of the variable X. Suppose $a = 4$, $b = 3$ and $c = 2$ then quadratic function takes the following specific form :

$$Y = 4 + 3X + 2X^2$$

We can obtain the different values of Y for taking different values of the independent variable X. Quadratic functions are of two types : convex quadratic functions and concave quadratic functions. The form of quadratic function depends on the sign of the coefficient c of X^2. The quadratic function, $Y = a + bX + cX^2$, where the coefficient c of X^2 is positive (i.e. $c > 0$) is called *convex* quadratic function, because its graph is U-shaped as shown in Figure 3A.17. On the other hand, if coefficient of X^2 is negative ($c < 0$), that is, when $Y = a + bX - cX^2$, then we have *concave* quadratic function because its graphs is of inverted U- shape (*i.e.* ∩-shaped) as shown in Figure 3A.17.

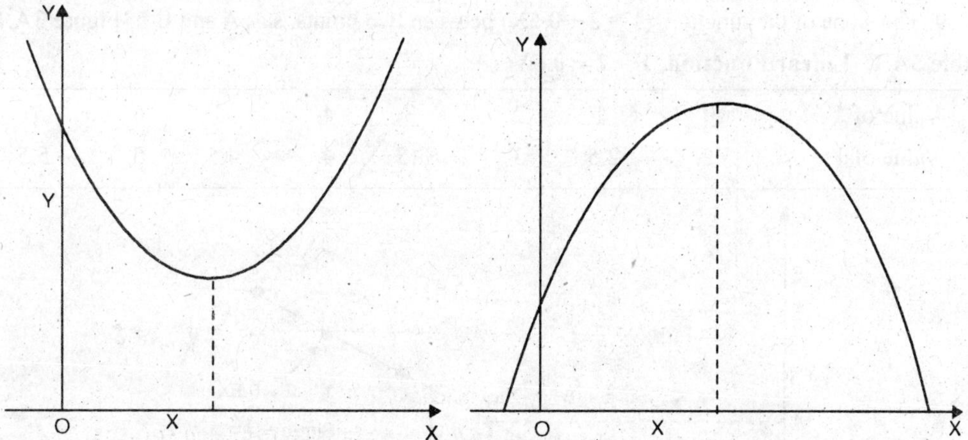

Fig. 3A.17. *Convex Quadratic function* **Fig. 3A.18.** *Concave Quadratic Function*

It is worth noting that slope of the curve of convex quadratic functions as is evident from U-shaped graph in this case where coefficient of X^2 is positive, slope is increasing every where. On the other hand, in case of concave quadratic function where coefficient of X^2 is negative ($c < O$), slope of its graph is decreasing every where. It should be further noted that in analytical geometry it is proved that graph of any quadratic function is a *parabola* which may be be either convex or concave. *A parabola is a curve which has a turning point and unlike the curve of a linear function, its slope is changing at different values of X.*

Cubic Function. A cubic function is a power function in which there is a *third degree term* relating to an independent variable. Thus, a cubic functions may have first degree, second degree and third degree terms. A cubic function may have the following form :

$$Y = a + bX + cX^2 + dX^3$$

a is the intercept term, the dependent variable X has the first degree, second degree and third degree terms. When the signs of all the coefficients a, b, c and d are positive, then the values of Y will increase by progressively larger increments as the value of X increases. However, when the *signs* of various coefficients differ in the cubic function, that is, some have positive signs and some have negative signs, then the graph of the function may have both convex and concave segments depending on the values of the coefficients. Such a cubic function where signs of the coefficients of variables differ may be expressed as follows :

$$Y = a + bX - cX^2 + dX^3$$

in which the sign of the coefficient c of variable X^2 is negative whereas the coefficients of others are positive.

SLOPES OF FUNCTIONS

In economics it is important to know *the rate at which a variable changes* in response to a change in another variable; the slope of a variable measures this rate. For example, it is important to know the rate at which quantity demanded of a commodity changes in response to a change in price of a commodity. In the field of economics we find both linear and non-linear functions. Let us first take the slope of a linear function.

Consider the following linear function.

$$Y = f(X) = 2 + 0.5\,X$$

In Table 2A.1 we have calculated the values of the variable Y *by* taking different values of X such as 1, 2, 3, 4 etc. Further, we have plotted the different values of Table 2A.1 on a graph shown in Fig. 3A.19. The slope of the function. ($Y = 2 + 0.5X$) between two points, say, A and B in Figure 3A.19 is

Table 3A.1. Linear Function, $Y = 2 + 0.5X$

Value of X	0	1	2	3	4	5	6	7
Value of Y	2	2.5	3	3.5	4	4.5	5	5.5

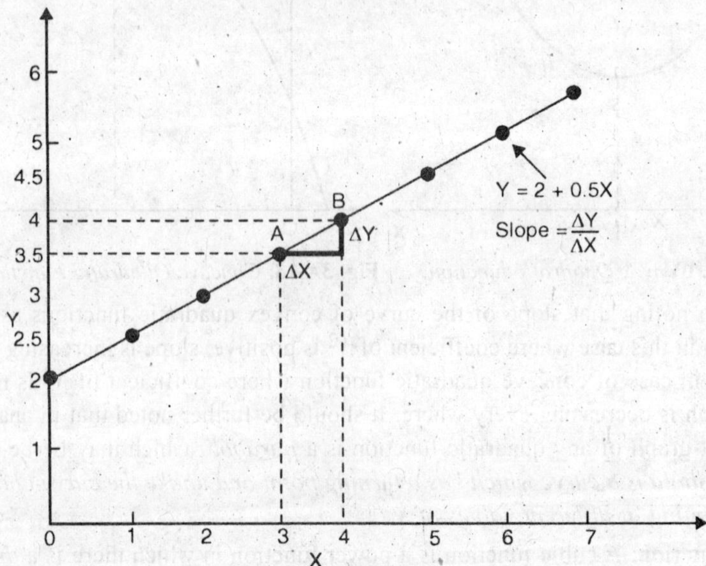

Fig. 3A.19. *Graph of $Y = 2 + 0.5X$*

given by the ratio of change in Y to the change in X. That is, slope $= \dfrac{\Delta Y}{\Delta X}$. For example, at point A of the given function value of variable X is 3 and corresponding to it the value of variable Y is 3.5.

When value of X rises from 3 to 4, value of Y increases from 3.5 to 4. Thus, the slope of the function ($Y = 2 + 0.5Y$) is :

$$\frac{\Delta Y}{\Delta X} = \frac{4 - 3.5}{4 - 3} = \frac{0.5}{1} = +0.5$$

This implies that value of Y increases by 0.5 when value of X increases by 1. It should be noted that slope of a linear function is constant throughout.

However, the slope of a linear function can be directly known from the linear function itself and for that purpose there is no need to plot the data. Consider the following linear function

$$Y = a + bX$$

It will be seen from this linear function that when the value of X is zero, the value of Y will be equal to a. Thus a is Y *intercept*. Further, in this function b is the coefficient of X and measures change in Y due to change in X, that is, $\frac{\Delta Y}{\Delta X}$. Thus, b represents the slope of the linear function. In linear function $Y = 2 + 0.5X$, 2 is the Y-intercept, that is, value of Y when X is zero, 0.5 is the b coefficient which measures the slope $\frac{\Delta Y}{\Delta X}$ of the linear function.

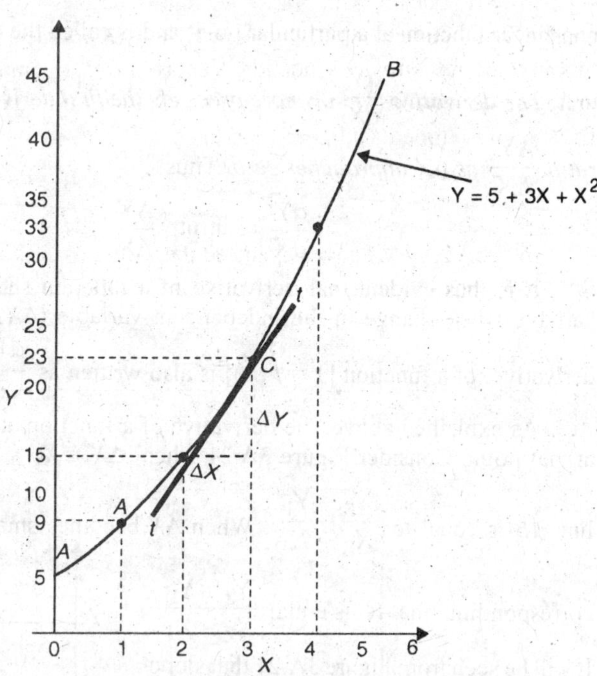

Fig. 3A.20. *Slope of a Quadratic Function*

Slope of a Non-linear Function

We now turn to explain how slope of a non-linear function, say, a quadratic function ($Y = a + bX + cX^2$) can be measured. On plotting the non-linear function in a graph, we get a non-linear curve. Let us take the following specific quadratic function :

$$Y = 5 + 3X + X^2$$

In Table 3A.2 we have calculated the various values of Y by taking different values of X (0, 1, 2, 3, etc).

Table 3A.2. Quadratic Function : $Y = 5 + 3X + X^2$

Value of X	0	1	2	3	4	5	6
Value of Y	5	9	15	23	33	45	59

The data so obtained have been plotted to get a curve in Figure 2A.20.

As explained above, *the slope at a point on the non-linear function curve can be measured by the slope of a tangent drawn to the curve at that point*. Thus slope of AB curve in Fig. 3A.20 can be measured by drawing a tangent *tt* at point C and measuring its slope.

OPTIMISATION TECHNIQUES : DIFFERENTIAL CALCULUS

Optimisation techniques are an important set of tools required for efficient use of resources. In what follows we will focus on the use of differential calculus to solve certain types of optimisation problems.

Differential Calculus : The Concept of a Derivative

In a continuous and smooth *non-linear curve* when a change in the independent variable, that is, ΔX gets smaller and approaches zero, $\frac{\Delta Y}{\Delta X}$ becomes better approximation of the slope the function, $Y = f(X)$, at a particular point. Thus, if ΔX is infinitesimally small, $\frac{\Delta Y}{\Delta X}$ measures the slope of the non-linear function at a particular point and is called the derivative $\frac{dY}{dX}$ of the function with respect to X. *The derivative* $\frac{dY}{dX}$ *or more precisely the first derivative of a function is defined as limit of the ratio* $\frac{\Delta Y}{\Delta X}$ *as* ΔX *approaches zero.* Thus

$$\frac{dY}{dX} = \lim_{\Delta x \to 0} \frac{\Delta Y}{\Delta X}$$

It is thus evident that derivative of a function shows the change in value of the dependent variable when change in the independent variable (ΔX) becomes infinitesimally small. Note that derivative of a function $[Y = f(X)]$ is also written as $\frac{d(fX)}{dX}$ or $f'(X)$.

As explained above, the derivative of a function at a point measures the slope of the tangent at that point. Consider Figure 3A.21 when $\Delta X = X_3 - X_1$, the slope of the corresponding straight line AB is equal to $\frac{Y_3 - Y_1}{X_3 - X_1}$. When ΔX becomes smaller and is equal to $X_2 - X_1$, slope of the corresponding line AC is equal $\frac{Y_2 - Y_1}{X_2 - X_1}$.

It will be seen from Figure 3A.21 that slope of line AC is more near to the slope of the tangent tt drawn at point A to the function curve. Similarly, if ΔX is reduced further, slope of the straight line between the two corresponding points will go on becoming closer and closer to the slope of the tangent tt drawn at point A to the curve. At the limit of $\frac{\Delta Y}{\Delta X}$ *when* ΔX *approaches zero, slope of the tangent such as tt at a point on a function becomes the derivative* $\frac{dY}{dX}$ *of the function with respect to X.*

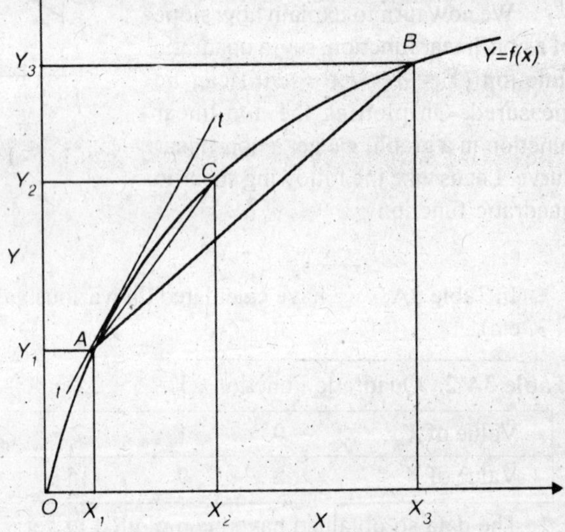

Fig 3A.21. *Finding Derivative of a Function (Y = f(X) at a Point*

Thus, derivative $\frac{dY}{dX}$ is slope of a

function whether it is linear or non-linear and represents a change in the dependent variable due to a small change in the independent variable. The concept of a derivative is extensively used in economics and eonomic decision making, especially in solving the problems of optimisation such as those of profit maximisation, cost minimisation, output and revenue maximisation.

There are various types of functions and for them there are different rules for finding the derivatives. We will explain below the basic rules of finding derivatives of the various types of functions.

RULES OF DIFFERENTIATION

Process of finding the derivative of a function is called **differentiation.** As stated above, derivative of a function represents the change in the dependent variable due to a infinitesimally small change in the independent variable and is written as $\frac{dY}{dX}$ for a function $Y = f(X)$. A series of rules have been derived for differentiating various types of functions. We describe below these rules of differentiation.

Derivative of a Constant Function. A constant function is expressed as

$$Y = f(X) = a$$

Where 'a' is constant. The constant 'a' implies that Y does not vary as X varies, that is, Y is independent of X. Therefore, the derivative of a constant function is equal to zero. Thus, in this constant function

$$\frac{dY}{dX} = 0$$

For example, let the constant function be

$$Y = 2.5$$

This is graphed in Figure 3A.22. It will be seen that a constant function is a horizontal straight line (having a zero slope) which shows that irrespective of the value of the variable X, the value of Y does not change at all. Therefore, in this case derivative $\frac{dY}{dX} = 0$.

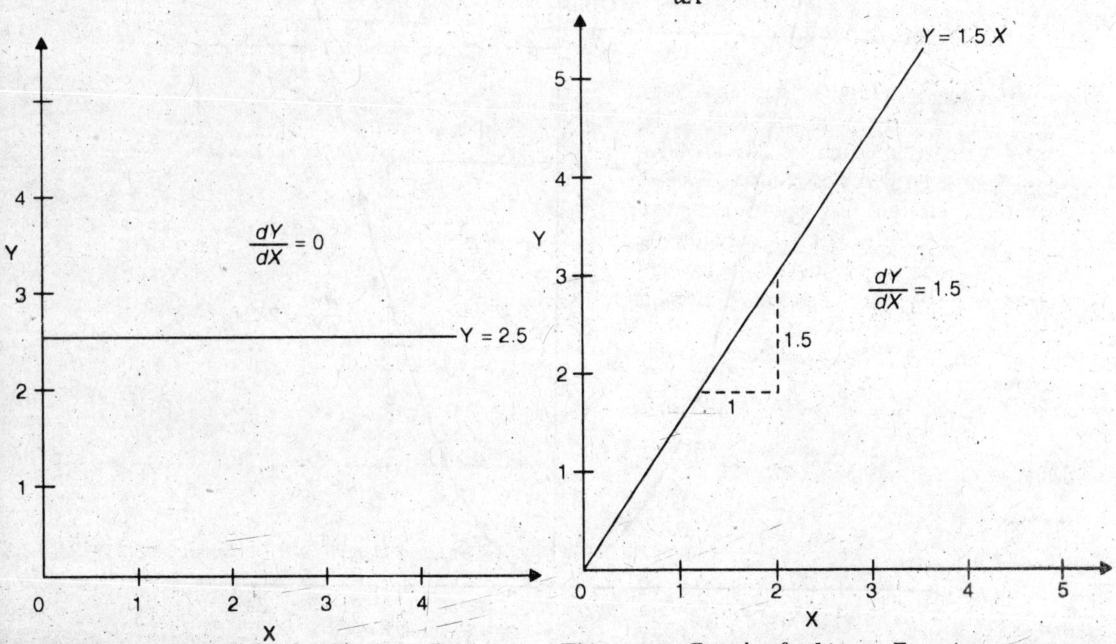

Fig. 3A.22. *Graph of a Constant Function* **Fig. 3A.23.** *Graph of a Linear Function*

Derivative of a Power Function

A power function takes the following form :

$$Y = aX^b$$

Where a and b are constants. Here a is the coefficient of the X term and the variable X is raised to the power b. The derivative of this power function is equal to the power b multiplied by the coefficient a times the variable X raised to the power $b - 1$. Thus rule for the derivative of power function ($Y = a X^b$) is

$$\frac{dY}{dX} = b.a.X^{b-1}$$

Let us take some examples of determining the derivative of a power function.

First, take the following power function :

$$Y = 1.5\,X$$

In this function 1.5 is the coefficient of variable X, that is, a and the power b of X is 1 (implicit). Using the above rule for the derivative of a power function we have

$$\frac{dY}{dX} = 1 \times 1.5\,X^{1-1} = 1 \times 1.5\,X^0 = 1.5$$

This is graphically shown in Figure 3A.23. It will be seen from this figure that slope of the linear function ($Y = 1.5\,X$) is constant and is equal to 1.5 over any range of the values of the variables X.

Quadratic Power Function. Let us take the following example of a power function which is of quadratic type.

$$Y = X^2$$

$$\text{Its derivative,} \quad \frac{dy}{dx} = 2X^{2-1} = 2X^1 = 2X$$

To illustrate it we have calculated the values of Y, associated with different values of X such as 1, 2, 2.5 and −1, −2, −2.5 and have been shown in Table 3A.3.

Table 3A.3. Quardratic Power Function $Y = X^2$

Value of X	−2.5	−2	−1	+1	+2	+2.5
Value of Y	−6.25	−4	−1	+1	+4	+6.25

Fig. 3A.24. *Graph of a Quadratic function*

We have plotted the values of X and corresponding values of Y to get a U-shaped parabolic curve in Figure 3A.24. It will be seen that derivative $\frac{dY}{dX}$ or, in other words, slope of this quadratic function is changing at different values of X. Some other examples of power function and their derivatives are :

For power function,

$$Y = 3X^2$$

$$\frac{dy}{dx} = 2 \times 3.X^{2-1} = 6X$$

For power function; $Y = X^5$

$$\frac{dY}{dX} = 5 \times 1.X^{5-1} = 5X^4$$

For power function; $Y = X$

$$\frac{dY}{dX} = 1 \times 1\,X^{1-1} = 1 \times 1.X^0 = 1$$

It should be noted that *any variable raised to the zero power (as in our example X^0) is equal to 1*

For power function, $Y = 3X^{-2}$

$$\frac{dY}{dX} = -2 \times 3.X^{-2-1} = -6X^{-3}$$

Derivative of a Sum or Difference of Two Functions

The derivative of a sum of the two functions is equal to the *sum* of the derivatives obtained separately of the two functions.

Suppose, $Y = f(X) + g(X)$

Where $f(X)$ and $g(X)$ are the two unspecified functions and Y is the sum of the two functions. The derivative of their sum is

$$\frac{dY}{dX} = \frac{df(X)}{dX} + \frac{dg(X)}{dX}$$

Likewise, the derivative of the difference of the two or more different functions is the difference of their separate derivatives. Thus, if

$$Y = f(X) - g(X)$$

then

$$\frac{dY}{dX} = \frac{df(X)}{dX} - \frac{dg(X)}{dX}$$

To illustrate, we take some examples.

If, $Y = 4X^2 + 5X$

then $\frac{dY}{dX} = 2 \times 4X^{2-1} + 1 \times 5X^{1-1} = 8X + 5$

If $Y = 5X^2 - 2X^5$

$$\frac{dY}{dX} = 10X - 10X^4$$

Now, consider the following profit function where each of the three terms represents a function

$$\pi = -40 + 140Q - 10Q^2$$

Where π stands for profit and Q for level of output. Then, derivative of profit (π) with respect to output (Q) is

$$\frac{d\pi}{dQ} = 0 + 140 - 20\,Q$$

$$= 140 - 20\,Q$$

Note that derivative of a constant (–40) is zero, derivative of 140 Q is 140 and derivative $10\,Q^2 = 20\,Q$.

Derivative of a Product of the Two Functions

Suppose Y is the product of the two separate functions $f(X)$ and $g(X)$.

$$Y = f(X).\,g(X)$$

The derivative of the product of these two functions is equal to the first function multiplied by the derivative of the second function plus the second function multiplied by the derivative of the first function. Thus,

$$\frac{dY}{dX} = f(X).\frac{dg(X)}{dX} + g(X).\frac{df(X)}{dX}$$

For example, take the following function

$$Y = 5X^2\,(2X + 3)$$

$f(X) = 5X^2$ and $g(X) = (2X + 3)$ are the two functions. Then, derivative of the product of these two functions,

$$\frac{dY}{dX} = 5X^2.\frac{d\,(2X+3)}{dX} + (2X+3).\frac{d(5X^2)}{dX}$$

$$\frac{dY}{dX} = 5X^2.2 + (2X + 3).10X$$

$$= 10X^2 + 20X^2 + 30X$$

$$= 30X^2 + 30X$$

$$= 30\,(X^2 + X)$$

Take another example of the product rule. Let

$$Y = (X^3 + X^2 + 5)\,(2X^2 + 3)$$

then, $$\frac{dY}{dX} = (X^3 + X^2 + 5)\,.\,\frac{d\,(2X^2+3)}{dX} + (2X^2 + 3)\,.\,\frac{d\,(X^3+X^2+5)}{dX}$$

$$= (X^3 + X^2 + 5)\,.\,4X + (2X^2 + 3)\,.\,(3X^2 + 2X)$$

$$= (4X^4 + 4X^3 + 20X) + 6X^4 + 9X^2 + 4X^3 + 6X$$

$$= 10X^4 + 8X^3 + 9X^2 + 26X$$

SUMMARY OF SOME RULES OF DIFFERENTIATION

	Function	*Derivative*
1.	**Constant Function :** $y = f(x) = a$	$\frac{dy}{dx} = 0$
2.	**Power Function :** $y = ax^b$	$\frac{dy}{dx} = b.a.\,x^{b-1}$
3.	**Sum of functions :** $y = f(x) + g(x)$	$\frac{dy}{dx} = \frac{df(x)}{dx} + \frac{dg(x)}{dx}$
4.	**Product of two Function :** $y = f(x).\,g(x)$	$\frac{dy}{dx} = f(x).\,\frac{dg(x)}{dx} + g(x).\,\frac{df(x)}{dx}$

DIFFERENTIATION OF FUNCTIONS WITH TWO OR MORE THAN TWO INDEPENDENT VARIABLES

Partial Derivatives

So far we have been concerned with the differentiation of functions with one independent variable. However, in economics relations contain two or more than two independent variables about whose use firms have to take decisions. For example, demands for the product of a firm depends on its price, income of the consumers, price of its substitute, advertising outlay made by the firm to promote the sales of its product and some others. Further, output of a product depends on the amounts of labour, capital, raw materials etc used for the production of a commodity. Other examples of functions from economics and business with two or more independent variables can be given.

When a function has two or more independent variables and each of them has an effect on the value of the dependent variable, we use the concept of a partial derivative. It is called partial derivative because in this the effect of only a part of influences on the dependent variable is examined. *A partial derivative of a function measures the marginal effect of a change in one variable on the value of the dependent variable, holding constant all other variables.* Thus, in a function, $y = f(x_1, x_2, x_3)$, partial derivative of y with respect to x_1, will show the marginal effect of a very small change in x_1 on Y, keeping constant x_2, x_3. By convention and to distinguish it from derivative of a function with one independent variable, for partial derivative we use lower case delta (∂) instead of lower case d. However, rules of differentiation in finding partial derivatives are the same as explained above in case of derivative of a function with a single independent variable.

It is worth nothing that in multivariable function, *the partial derivative of one independent variable depends on the values at which other independent variables are held constant.* That is why the expression for partial derivative of profit function of a multi-product firm with two independent variables, products x and y, indicates that $\frac{\partial \pi}{\partial x}$ depends on the level at which the other independent variable y is held constant. Similarly, the partial derivative of the profit function with respect to y, indicates that it depends on the value of the variable x which is held constant. The economic reasoning for this will become clear if we take a two factor production function $q = f(L, K)$. In this partial derivative of production function with respect to labour (L), that is, $\frac{\partial q}{\partial L}$ implies marginal product of labour. Now, as is well known, marginal product of labour depends not only on its own skill and efficiency, but also on with how much capital (K) he has to work with. Generally, the greater the amount of capital with which a worker works, the higher will be marginal productivity of labour, the other things remaining the same.

To illustrate the concept of partial derivative we take the example of profit function with sales of two products as independent variables

$$\pi = f(x, y) = 50x - 3x^2 - xy - 4y^2 + 60Y$$

where π represents profits, x and y are the sales of the two products being produced by a firm. The function represents that profits of a firm depend on the sales of two products produced by it.

Determining the partial derivative of profit (π) function with respect to sales of the product x treating sales of y as constant from the above profit function we obtain

$$\frac{\partial \pi}{\partial x} = 50 - 6x - y$$

Thus, with partial derivative we are able to isolate the marginal effect on profit (π) of the change in the sales of the product x, keeping the sales of products y as constant.

Note that in finding partial derivative of the profit function with respect to x, fourth and fifth terms in the profit function are not considered because they do not contain the variable x.

Likewise through partial derivative we can separate the marginal effect of the variation in sales of the product y on profit (π) while holding x constant.

Thus, partial derivative of profit (π) function with respect to y is

$$\frac{\partial \pi}{\partial y} = -x - 8y + 60.$$

APPLICATIONS OF DIFFERENTIAL CALCULUS (DERIVATIVES) TO OPTIMISATION PROBLEMS

We have explained above the concept of a derivative and rules for its differentiation in different types of functions because they are widely used in solving the problems of optimisation in economics and business management. *The process of optimisation often requires us to determine the maximum or minimum value of a function.* For a function to be a maximum (or minimum) its first derivative is zero. As explained above, derivative of a function measures its slope. Therefore, maximization of a function occurs where its derivative is equal to zero, Thus, an important optimisation problem facing a firm is to produce a level of output which maximises firm's profits. Similarly, optimum use of resources requires that cost be minimised for producing a given level of output. These problems of maximisation and minimisation can be solved with the use of the concept of derivative.

Use in Profit Maximisation

For example, consider the following profit function :

$$\pi = -100 + 160Q - 10Q^2$$

where π = profits and Q is units of output.

For the profit (π) function to be maximum, its first derivative must be equal to zero.

Therefore, to find the profit-maximising level of output we find the derivative of the given profit function and set it equal to zero. Thus

$$\frac{d\pi}{dQ} = 160 - 20Q.$$

Setting it equal to zero.

$$\frac{d\pi}{dQ} = 160 - 20\,Q = 0$$

$$20Q = 160$$

$$Q = \frac{160}{20} = 8$$

At 8 units of output profits will be maximum. Maximisation of profits through the use of derivative is graphically shown in Figure 3A.25. It will be seen that profit maximisation curve reaches its maximum point at point H. Therefore, at point H, the slope of the tangent (which measures the value of the first derivative $\frac{d\pi}{dQ}$) drawn to the profit curve at this point is equal to zero. It will be seen that corresponding to maximum profit point H on the profit function level of output is 8 units.

Total profits made at 8 units of output can be obtained by substituting 8 for Q in the given profit function. Thus

$$\pi = -100 + 160 \times 8 - 10\,(8)^2$$
$$= 1280 - 740 = 540$$

Thus at output level of 8 units profits are equal to 540.

Graphical analysis *cannot tell us easily* exactly at what level of output, profits will be maximum, for it takes time to draw a graph and conclude from it. However, it is easier to use differential calculus to find the profit-maximising output. For this we simply find the first derivative of the profit function and set it equal to zero.

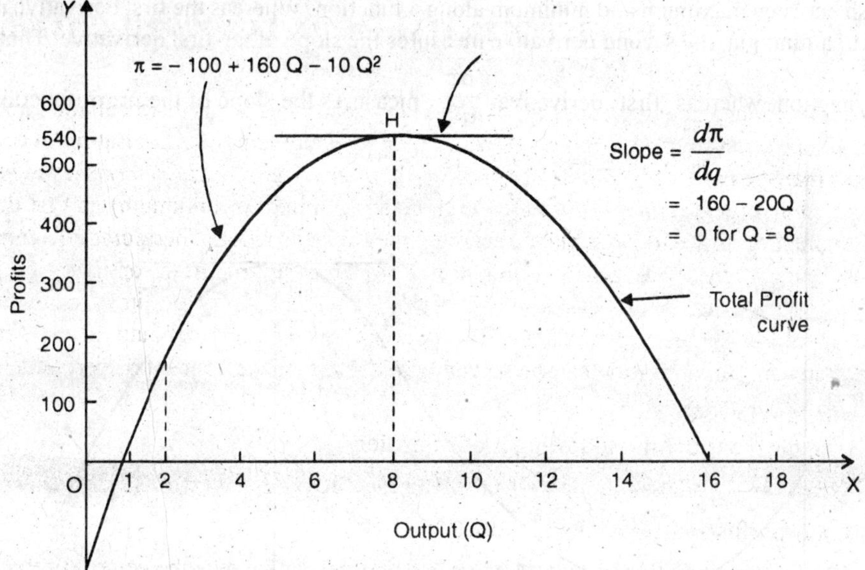

Fig. 3A.25. *Profit Maximisastion is reached at output level where* $\frac{d\pi}{dQ} = 0$

Second Derivative and Second Order Condition for Optimisation

A problem arises when we use the first derivative of a function to determine its maximum or minimum value. For setting the first derivative of a function equal to zero and solving the resulting equation for the optimum value of the independent variable does not guarantee that optimum value (maximum or minimum as the case may be) will in fact he obtained. For the optimum value, the first derivative being equal to zero is a necessary condition for maximum or minimum, but it is not a sufficient condition : For example, in a profit function, first derivative is equal to zero, both at maximum and minimum profit levels. To ensure that the derivative is zero at the profit maximising level of the decision variable (*i.e.,* output in the present case), we require to apply the second order condition. *According to the second order condition, for profit maximisation, the second derivative of the profit function must be negative, that is,* $\frac{d^2\pi}{dQ^2} < 0$. Thus, if optimisation requires maximisation of function say, $y = f(x)$, then the second derivative, which is written as $\frac{d^2y}{dx^2}$, must be negative.

It should be noted that the second derivative of a function is obtained by differenting the first derivative with respect to the independent variable. In case optimisation requires minimisation of a function as in case of minimisation of cost for producing a given level of output, the second derivative must be positive, that is, $\frac{d^2y}{dx^2} > 0$.

Consider again the case of profit maximisation explained above. A profit function curve such as the one drawn in Figure 3A.26 may have both minimum point and maximum points. It will be seen from Figure 3A.26 that point L represents the minimum point and H represents the maximum point of the profit curve. Important thing to note is that at both minimum point L and maximum point H, first order condition, that is, first derivative $\frac{d\pi}{dQ}$ be zero is satisfied at both points, L and H, corresponding to OQ_1 and OQ_2 levels of output. However, at point L profits are minimum and at point H profits are maximum. It is with the help of the second derivative of a function that we can distinguish between maximum and minimum along a function. Whereas the first derivative measures the slope of a function, the second derivative measures the slope of the first derivative. Thus, in case of profit function, whereas first derivative, $\frac{d\pi}{dQ}$, measures the slope of the profit function curve,

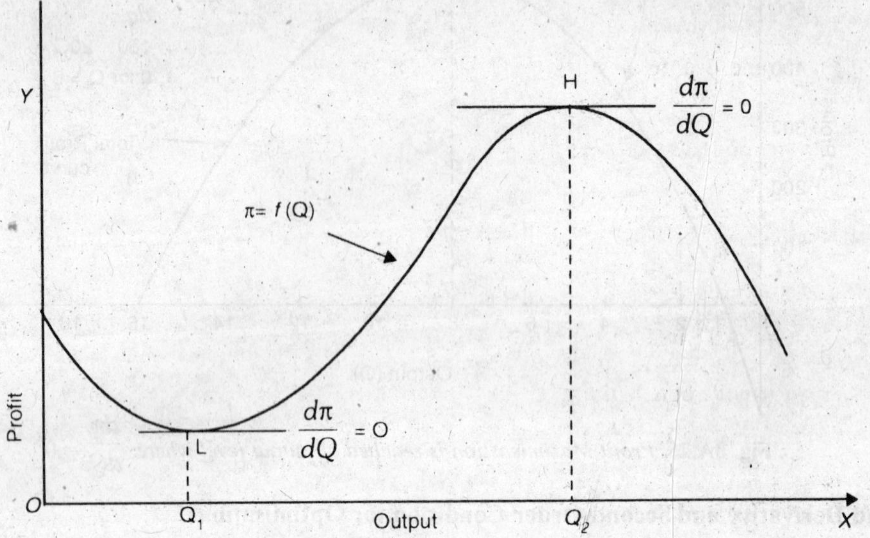

Fig. 3A.26. *Second Order Condition for Optimisation*

that is, marginal profit, its second derivative, $\frac{d^2\pi}{dQ^2}$, measures slope of the marginal profit function curve.

Since the second derivative of a function when measured at the maximisation level is always negative and when measured at the minimisation level is always positive, it can be used to distinguish between points of maximum and minimum. For example, if the second derivative in our profit function curve is negative, it implies that profits are maximum at the level where first derivative is equal to zero. On the other hand, if the second derivative at a point on a profit function where first derivative is zero is positive, it shows profits are in fact minimum rather than maximum. It can be easily known from having a look at Figure 3A.26. It will be seen from this figure that up to point L, marginal profit $\left(\frac{d\pi}{dQ}\right)$, that is, slope of the total profit curve, is negative and has been causing the total profits to fall. At point L, marginal profit $\left(\frac{d\pi}{dQ}\right)$ becomes zero and thereafter it becomes positive and therefore it will causes the total profit to increase. Hence, point L beyond which the second derivative (*i.e.* the slope of the first derivative) is positive, and therefore profits will be increasing, cannot be point of maximum profits.

Now consider point H on the total profit corresponding to output level OQ_2. At point H, first derivative $\left(\frac{d\pi}{dQ}\right)$ is again equal to zero but after that marginal profit $\frac{d\pi}{dQ}$ becomes negative as the slope of total profit curve is negative as output is expanded beyond Q_2. This causes the total profits to fall. This shows that point H at which first derivative, $\frac{d\pi}{dQ}$ is zero and also beyond which second derivative $\left(\frac{d^2\pi}{dQ^2}\right)$, that is, slope of the first derivative becomes negative is indeed the point of maximum profit.

To conclude, we get a following general test for maximum and minimum.

(1) If the second derivative $\frac{d^2y}{dx^2}$ of a function is negative (< 0) at the point where first derivative $\left(\frac{dy}{dx}\right)$ is zero, it will represent a point of maximum.

(2) If the second derivative $\left(\frac{d^2y}{dx^2}\right)$ of a function is positive (> 0) at the point where first derivative is zero, it will represent a point of minimum.

Coming back to our profit function (p · 100 + 160 Q 10 Q^2) in which case the first derivative is zero at 8 units of output, we test for the sign of second derivative. Thus,

The first derivative, $\frac{d\pi}{dQ} = 160 - 20Q$

The second derivative, $\frac{d^2\pi}{dQ^2}$ 20.

Thus, we find that at 8 units of output profits will in fact be maximum.

Minimisation Problem

In some decision making problems the objective of a firm is to minimise the objective function. For example, efficiency in the use of resources requires that a firm should produce at the minimum possible cost per unit of output. For example, the following average cost function of a firm is given :

$$AC \quad 25{,}000 \quad 180Q + 0.50Q^2$$

A firm is interested to find what level of output it will minimise its average cost. This can be obtained by differentiating the AC function with respect to output (Q) and setting it equal to zero, Thus

$$\frac{d(AC)}{dQ} \quad 180 + 1.0Q$$

Setting it equal to zero and solving for Q we have

$$-180 + 1.0\,Q = 0$$
$$Q = 180$$

Applying the second order condition to ensure whether it is really minimum we take the second derivative of AC function

$$\frac{d^2 AC}{dQ^2} = +1.0$$

Since second derivative of AC function is positive, $\frac{d^2 AC}{dQ^2} > 0$, output of 180 units of output is one that minimises average cost of production.

QUESTIONS FOR REVIEW

1. What is meant by optimisation ? Explain its significance in managerial decision making.
2. Define the following terms
   (*i*) Function
   (*ii*) Dependent Variable
   (*iii*) Independent Variable
   (*iv*) Constant
   (*v*) Intercept
3. (*a*) What is a linear function ? What factors determine a specific form of a linear function ? How does its graph look like ?
   (2) (a) Write a linear demand function with a single independent variable.
   (*b*) Give an example of a specific linear demand function with a single independent variable.
   (*c*) How will you interpret the coefficient of the independent variable in a linear demand function ?
4. (*a*) Write a multivariable linear demand function ? How will you interpret the coefficients of various independent variables ?
   (*b*) How is the effect of non-price variables on demand for a commodity depicted in economics?
5. What is a quadratic function ? Distinguish between a convex and concave quadratic functions. How will their graphs look like ? Show them with diagrams.
6. Write a quadratic function with two independent variables. How will its graph look like ?
7. What is a cubic function ? Write a general form of a cubic function. Can a cubic function contain first degree, second degree and third degree terms in it ?
8. What does slope of a function indicate ? Plot the following linear function and measure its slope.

$$y = 5 + 0.8x$$

9. Draw a curve representing a quadratic function : How will you measure slope at a point on it? Does slope of a quadratic function remain constant along it ?
10. (a) Explain the concept of a derivative of a function. Explain the logic of using the derivative of a function to find the maximum or minimum of that function.
    (b) What is the significance of the concept of derivative in business applications ?

11. Why is derivative of a constant function equal to zero? Draw a graph of a constant function.
12. You are given the following linear supply function :

$$Q = 2 + 1.5P$$

Draw its graph and show the value of its derivative.
13. Describe the following rules of differentiation
    (1) Power rule of differentiation
    (2) Function of a function rule of differentiation
    (3) Chain rule of differentiation
    (4) Product rule of differentiation
14. What is a partial derivative of a function ? In which type of function the concept of a partial derivative is applied ? What is the assumption that underlies the interpretation of any one variable?
15. What is a second derivative ? How is the second derivative used in distinguishing between a maximium and minimum point ?
16. Find the first and second derivatives of the following total revenue (*TR*) and total cost (*TC*) functions. Find the values of these derivatives at the level of output of 10 units. Also interpret the values of the first and second derivatives so obtained
    1. $TR = 40\,Q - 2Q^2$
    2. $TR = 150 + 25Q + 10Q^2$
    3. $TC = 300 + 15Q$
    4. $TC = 150 + 7Q - 3Q^2 + Q^3$
17. You are given the following production functions where *Q* stands for output, *L* and *K* for units of labour and capital respectively used in the production process. Find the first and second derivatives of these functions with respect to labour and explain what these derivatives imply :
    1. $Q = 3L^2 + 2\,LK - 5K^2$
    2. $Q = 5L^2 + 10\,LK + 2K$
    3. $Q = 100L^{0.5}\,K^{0.5}$
18. Consider the following demand function of a product facing a firm

$$P = 25 - Q$$

Where P = price and Q = quantity demand of the product measured in units
    (*a*) Express the total revenue function
    (*b*) Express the marginal revenue function
    (*c*) At what quantity demanded total. revenue will be maximised.
19. How does the manager of a business firm determine the profit maximising level of output ? Use concept of derivatives.
20. Suppose objective function of a firm is to maximise its sales. How will it determine sales-maximisation level of output ?

(**Hints.** Sales is considered in value terms. Thus sales mean total revenue received from the output produced and sold) Take inverse demand function (that is, price expressed as a function of quantity demanded (*Q*) and multiply it with *Q* to get total revenue. Then use the concept of derivatives to determine sales maximisation level of output).
21. What is meant by a partial derivative ? How is it obtained ? Can the partial derivative of a function with respect to one independent variable depend also on the value of the other independent variable ? If so, why ?

CHAPTER 4

SCIENCE OF ECONOMICS AND ITS METHODOLOGY

THE SCIENCE OF ECONOMICS

Every science derives hypotheses, generalisations, principles, laws and theories which explain the behaviour of phenomena it studies. For deriving generalisations and theories it has to adopt a certain methodology. One of the controversies in economics relates to the kind of methods to be adopted to discover generalisations and theories about the relationship between economic facts. Economists have in fact adopted both deductive and inductive methods of reasoning. Recently econometrics, that is, application of statistical methods to test economic hypotheses have gained much popularity among economists. These different methods will be explained below.

Economics is a social science. It studies the problem of scarcity of resources and choice of resource allocation with a scientific approach. The economics being a science is based on a systematic explanation of the problem of choice. Therefore, being a systematic study, economics involves the formulation of theories and testing them by empirical evidence and judging whether the predictions made on the basis of a theory prove to be correct. In what follows we first explain what is meant by a scientific approach. We will then explain how economists derive economic theories and construct economic models. At the end we will explain the role of making experiments in economics.

Nature of a Scientific Theory

A scientific theory sets up a relationship between facts or, in other words, it describes cause and effect relationship between various variables. The variables with which economists are concerned are prices, quantities demanded and supplied, the money supply, national income, employment, wages, profits, etc. Every theory is based upon a set of assumptions, often called premises or postulates. It is worth mentioning that some assumptions are taken merely to simplify the analysis, though they may not be entirely realistic. In economics, these assumptions may be behavioural, that is, relating to the behaviour of economic variables or they may be technological pertaining to the production technology and the availability of productive factors. From the assumptions or postulates taken implications or conclusions are deduced through logical process of reasoning. The process of logical deduction to discover relevant conclusions from a set of definitions and assumptions is carried out either in words or in the language of symbolic logic or it may be done with the aid of geometry or more formal mathematics. It is these conclusions drawn from the assumptions through deductive logic which are called hypotheses.

It is worth noting that a **scientific hypothesis or a theory** *states the proposition about relationship between facts or variables in a form that is testable or falsifiable, that is, proposition which is capable of being refuted.* If the predictions based on a hypothesis are refuted by the direct observation of actual facts or through the statistical methods of interpreting actual facts, a hypothesis stands rejected. If on testing the predictions based on a given hypothesis are proved correct, it stands established as a scientific theory. For instance, the quantity demanded varies inversely with price is one of the important economic hypotheses established in economics. If a sales tax is imposed on a commodity and as a result the price of the commodity rises, the prediction will be that the quantity demanded will decline, other things remaining constant. This has not been falsified and in fact has been corroborated by the facts of the real world. So the law of demand stating that there is inverse relationship between price and quantity demanded is a scientific economic law. Likewise, the generalisation regarding the direct relationship between price and quantity supplied, that is, the higher the price, the greater will be the quantity supplied, other factors held constant, has also been found to be consistent with facts in several cases.

Further, the Keynesian theory that under conditions of less than full-employment of resources, levels of national income and employment are determined by the magnitude of aggregate effective demand is also a well established economic hypothesis regarding the developed capitalist economies. The predictions based on the above Keynesian hypothesis that the increase in aggregate demand through deficit budgeting by the Government under conditions of less than full-employment will lead to the rise in national income and employment has been found to be consistent with facts. Therefore, Keynesian principle of effective demand is a very important hypothesis about the advanced capitalist economies which has been proved to be valid by empirical evidence.

If the predictions based on a hypothesis are falsified by the facts of the real world, either some error would have been committed during the process of logical deduction or the assumptions made would have been too unrealistic, wrong or irrelevant to the subject of economic enquiry. Thus, in order to establish scientific economic hypotheses, error in logic and mistake of making unrealistic assumptions be avoided. It is worth emphasising that *every hypothesis or theory is based upon some simplifying assumptions which are not quite realistic*, that is, a theory is an abstraction from reality. But good hypotheses and theories abstract from reality in a useful and significant way. Indeed, if we do not abstract from reality we would merely duplicate the real world in a camera like manner and will not gain any understanding of it. The crucial test of a theory is that whether predictions which follow from it are falsified or not by the empirical evidence, that is, by the facts in the real world. If the predictions of a hypothesis or theory are found to be consistent with the facts, its assumptions would be justified even if they are unrealistic. Thus, an economic hypothesis or theory should not be criticised simply because assumptions it makes are unrealistic, if its predictions are found to be consistent with the facts.

ECONOMIC THEORIES

Economic theory is a statement which explains certain economic phenomenon and establishes cause and effect retationship between variables. A theory is based on a set of assumptions and conclusions are derived from these assumptions about the relations between the variables which have a bearing on the phenomenon in question. As explained above, economic theories are derived through using logical deductive approach. If the assumptions and deductive reasoning arc correct, then the conclusions derived will be correct. Therefore, an economic theory is used to predict what will happen if certain change in an independent variable changes. One of the oldest theories is *law of demand* which was clearly stated by English economist, Alfred Marshall in 1890. According to law of demand, if price of a commodity rises, its quantity demanded by the people will tend to fall and if price of the commodity falls, its quantity demanded by people tend to increase. Thus this theory of demand is used to predict that if an excise duty on a commodity is raised, it will lead to the rise in price of a commodity and reduction in its output.

The generalisations of economics, like the laws of other sciences, state cause and effect relationships between variables and describe those economic hypotheses which have been found consistent with facts or, in other words, have been found to be true by empirical evidence. But a distinction may be drawn between a *generalisation (law) and a theory*. A law or generalisation *just describes* the relationship between variables; it does not provide any explanation of the described relation. On the other hand, *a theory provides an explanation of the stated relation between the variables, that is, it brings out the logical basis of the generalisation.* An economic theory or a model derives a generalisation through process of logical reasoning and explains the conditions under which the stated generalisation will hold true.

Economic theories can be derived by using formal quantitative data but it can also be derived by collecting observations of people's behaviour and their responses or reactions to certain changes in the variable.

Economic Theories and Variables

Variables are basic elements of an economic theory. A variable is a magnitude whose value varies from time to time and from one observation to another. Thus, a variable has different values for different individuals and for same individual at different times. In the theory of demand, quantity demanded of a good, price of a good, incomes of individuals, prices of related goods, tastes, and preferences of individuals, the number of individuals consuming a commodity are the relevant variables. It is important to note the distinction between the *dependent variable and independent variables* in an economic theory. The variables that cause changes in another variable are independent variables and the variable whose value is determined or affected by changes in the independent variables is called the dependent variable. In the theory of demand referred to above, the quantity demanded of a good is the dependent variable whose value is determined or caused by the price of the good, income of the individuals, prices of related goods which are independent variables in this case.

Distinction is also made between *endogenous variables* and *exogenous variables*. An endogenous variable is a variable whose value is determined and explained within a theory or a model whereas exogenous variable are determined by forces outside a theory or a model. The exogenous variables affect the values of endogeneous variables. For example, the quantity demanded of such goods as ice cream, air conditioners also depends on weather. If in a week or a month such as December and January there is very cold, the demand for ice cream and airconditiones is very much affected. Thus weather is an exogenous variable which works from outside to determine demand for goods like ice cream and air conditioners.

METHODS OF SCIENCE OF ECONOMICS

After having explained the scientific nature of economic theory we are now in a position to explain in detail how the generalisations in economics are derived and to clearly bring out the nature of economic reasoning. Economic generalisations describe the *laws* or *statements of tendencies* in various branches of economics such as production, consumption, exchange and distribution of income. In the view of Robbins, economic generalisations or laws are statements of uniformities which describe human behaviour in the allocation of scarce resources between alternative ends. The generalisations of economics, like the laws of other sciences, state cause and effect relationships between variables and describe those economic hypotheses which have been found consistent with facts or, in other words, have been found to be true by empirical evidence. But a distinction may be drawn between a generalisation (law) and a theory. A law or generalisation *just describes* the relationship between variables; it does not provide any explanation of the described relation. On the other hand, a theory provides an explanation of the stated relation between the variables, that is, it brings out the logical basis of the generalisation. An economic theory or a model derives a generalisation through process of logical reasoning and explains the conditions under which the stated generalisation will hold true.

Deductive Method

Theories in economics have been derived in two ways: (1) *Deductive Method*, (2) *Inductive Method*. We shall first explain the deductive method of deriving economic generalisations. The deductive method is also called *abstract, analytical* and *a priori* method and represents an abstract approach to the derivation of economic generalisations and theories. The principal steps in the process of deriving economic generalisations through deductive logic are: (*a*) perception of the problem to be enquired into; (*b*) defining precisely the technical terms and making appropriate assumptions, often called postulates or premises; (*c*) deducing hypotheses, that is, deriving conclusions from the premises through the process of logical reasoning; and (*d*) testing of hypothesis deduced.

(*a*) **Perception of the Problem.** In any scientific enquiry, the analyst or theorist must have a clear idea of the problem to be enquired into. He must know the significant variables regarding whose behaviour and interrelationship he wants to derive generalisations. The perception of the problem is by no means an easy task.

(*b*) **Definition of Technical Terms and Making of Assumptions.** The next step in the process of deriving economic generalisations is to define precisely and unambiguously the various technical terms to be used in the analysis as well as to state clearly the assumptions he makes to derive generalisations. As mentioned above, assumptions may be behavioural pertaining to the behaviour of the economic variables or they may be technological relating to the state of technology and the factor endowments. The crucial assumptions are made on the basis of observations or introspection. A crucial assumption that has been taken in economics is that consumers try to maximise their satisfaction and producers try to maximise their profits. Likewise, it is assumed that investors try to minimise their risk and maximise the expected rate of their profits. Some of the assumptions are made merely to simplify the analysis and may not be quite realistic. The actual economic world is quite complex and full of details in which numerous factors play a part and act and interact on each other. The introduction of simplifying assumptions is quite necessary in order to bring out the importance of really significant factors having a bearing on the problem under investigation. According to Prof. Boulding, economic theory represents just a 'map' of real world phenomenon and not a perfect picture of it. To quote him, "Just as we do not expect a map to show every tree, every blade of grass in a landscape, so we should not expect economic analysis to take into account every detail and quirk of real economic behaviour."[1]

It, therefore, follows that each and every assumption made by a theory may not be realistic. The crucial factor in building up a valid theory is whether its predictions are corroborated by the facts in the world. A correct scientific theory or generalisation must be expressed in the form of a hypothesis that is conceivably refutable. As mentioned above, Professor Friedman in his now well-known article, "*The Methodology of Positive Economics*" has expressed the view that undue importance should not be given to the 'realism' of assumptions. What matters most from the viewpoint of scientific theory, according to him, is whether it enables us to predict things accurately.

(*c*) **Deducing Hypotheses through Logical Deduction.** The next step in deriving generalisations through deductive logic is deducing hypotheses from the assumptions or premises taken. A hypothesis describes relationship between factors affecting a phenomenon; it establishes the cause and effect relationship between the variables having a bearing on the phenomenon. Then, through logical process, hypothesis is deduced from the assumptions made. This logical reasoning may be carried out verbally or it may be conducted in symbolic terms using the language of what is known as symbolic logic. The geometric or graphic technique is also usually employed to deduce the hypotheses about the relationship between factors. Besides, the process of logical deduction may be done with the help of more formal mathematics. These days in almost all branches of modern economics, mathematics as tool of analysis for deriving economic theories and generalisations is being increasingly used. The use of mathematics in economic analysis proves extremely useful where geometrical methods make the analysis more complicated to comprehend. Besides, the use of mathematical method makes the derivation of economic hypotheses more rigorous and exact.

1.K. E. Boulding, *Economic Analysis*, Hamish Hamilton, New York, 1956, p. 11.

It is worthwhile to note that in deriving analytically sound hypotheses, one should guard against committing *logical fallacy* in the process of logical deduction. For instance, it is inappropriate to conclude that A must be the cause of B, if A happens to precede B. Further, it is logically fallacious to argue that since there exists a high degree of correlation between the two factors, say between the supply of money and the general price level, the former must be the cause of the latter, unless the causation must be logically developed.

(*d*) **Testing or Verification of Hypotheses.** Hypotheses obtained above have to be verified before they are established as generalisations or principles of economics. For the verification of hypotheses, economists cannot make controlled experiments, because they have to discover uniformities in behaviour patterns of man. We cannot make experiments with man under controlled conditions, such as in laboratories as physical scientists make experiments with inanimate objects of nature and biologists make these with animals and plants. Therefore, economists have to rely on uncontrolled experience and observations. The informations regarding uncontrolled experience about the behaviour patterns concerning variables about man and the economy are quite amply available. The reliance by economists on uncontrolled experiences, however, does increase the number of observations required to verify the hypotheses or to establish the generalisations. Besides, the need to rely on uncontrolled experiences complicates the analysis and requires that facts must be carefully interpreted to discover successfully the significant relationship between relevant economic variables. Prof. Baur rightly remarks, "The need to rely on uncontrolled experiences does, however, increase the number of observations required, and also complicates their successful analysis and interpretation, before we can discern successfully the significant uniformities and ascertain their limits."[2]

It may, however, be pointed out that in spite of the complexities and difficulties involved in verifying economic hypotheses through successful analysis and proper interpretation of uncontrolled experiences and observations, several useful and significant generalisations have been established in economics. In the field of microeconomics, the well-established generalisations relate to the inverse relationship between price and quantity demanded, the direct relation between price and quantity supplied, the tendency of the price of the product to be equal to the marginal cost under conditions of perfect competition, and the tendency for the wages to be equal to the value of marginal product under conditions of perfect competition and several others. In the field of macroeconomics, established generalisations relate to the determination of the level of national income by aggregate demand and aggregate supply in a capitalist economy, the multiple increase in income and employment as a result of a given initial increase in investment depending upon the size of marginal propensity to consume, the dependence of the amount of investment on the marginal efficiency of capital and the rate of interest and several others.

It is worth noting that the absence of controlled experiments in economics affects the exactness of economic laws and generalisations.[3] This means that the generalisations in economics are not as exact as those of physical sciences and they are therefore not universally applicable under all circumstances. Because of the absence of controlled experiments economic generalisations lack in firmness, they are not easily accepted by all and even generalisations that are refuted by empirical evidence are not abandoned for good by all. Prof. Baur rightly points out, the absence of the vivid and dramatic evidence provided by the controlled experiments adds greatly to the difficulty of securing acceptance for generalisations which are amply justified by the analysis of the available evidence."[4] Likewise, absence of controlled experiments, according to Friedman, renders the weeding out of unsuccessful hypotheses slow and difficult. They are seldom downed for good and are

2. P. T. Baur, *Economic Analysis and Policy in Under-developed Countries*, Routledge and Kegan Paul Ltd., 1957, p. 8.
3. P. T. Baur, *op. cit.*, p. 9.
4. *Ibid*, p. 9.

always cropping up again.[5]

In regard to framing and testing of economic generalisations; two related distinctions must be borne in mind. First, functional relationship between economic variables and a historically sequence of events must be distinguished. For instance, the law of demand stating inverse relationship between price and quantity demanded does not become invalid in view of the fact that both prices and quantities sold of many commodities increase during boom periods. This is because certain other forces such as a rise in aggregate investment demand operates which causes increase in both the price and quantity sold during a boom period. Second, prediction of a generalisation to show its validity must be carefully differentiated from the forecasting of future events; actual events may not exactly come about as predicted by a generalisation and yet that generalisation may be correct. This is because, as mentioned above, the actual course of events is governed by several other factors assumed by a generalisation which remains constant under the qualification "other things remaining the same". Thus, "even if the prediction that producers of a particular crop respond to a higher price by producing more is correct, this prediction does not enable us to forecast accurately next year's output (still less the harvest in the more distant future) which in the event will be affected by many factors besides changes in price."

In the absence of controlled experiments, for the verification of their theories economists have to rely on the direct observations of events in the real world. By direct observations we mean "gathering of information personally or reliance on comparatively unprocessed material such as files of business firms and government departments, locally published reports, proceedings of representative assemblies, newspapers, advertisements, market reports, auction notices and the like." In order to prove the validity of hypotheses and therefore to establish laws or generalisations, importance of direct observations cannot be underrated. Thus Prof. Baur correctly assets, "The depth and significance of economic generalisations depend on the quality of the underlying observations and analysis."[6]

Testing of Economic Hypotheses through Statistical Methods

In recent years a very useful method to test economic hypothesis has been developed. This is the *statistical method* or what is now popularly called *econometric method.* The statistical[7] or econometric method to verify and establish the theoretical generalisations occupies an important place because of the limited applicability of controlled experimentation in economics. The various statistical methods such as regression analysis have been developed to empirically test the economic hypotheses on the basis of collected economic data. The merit of econometrics is that the degree of functional relationship between relevant economic variables in precise quantitative terms is obtained by it and also the level of significance of the results can also be estimated. Recently, econometric method has been used to establish the precise relationships between money supply and the price level, quantity of money and the national income, consumption and income, capital accumulation and rate of economic growth and so forth.

It may, however, be pointed out that statistical analysis or econometrics alone cannot be used to derive and establish economic principles and theories. Economic hypotheses or theories must be developed logically before we can meaningfully use statistical analysis to test and verify them. Indeed, a theory or hypothesis is needed beforehand for selecting the relevant facts and data regarding relevant variables which can be subjected to empirical testing through the methods of econometrics. Prof. Myrdal is quite right, when he says, "theory, therefore, must always be *a prior* to the empirical observation of facts. Facts come to mean something only as ascertained and

5. Milton Friedman, *Essays in Positive Economics*, Chicago, 1953, p. 11.
6. P. T. Baur, *Economic Analysis and Policy in Under-developed Countries*, 1957, pp. 10-11.
7. *Ibid*, p. 9.
8. Gunnar Myrdal, *Value in Social Theory*, Routledge and Kegan Paul Ltd., London, 1958, p. 233.

organised in the frame of a theory. Indeed, facts as part of scientific knowledge have no existence outside such a frame. Questions must be asked before answers can be obtained and, in order to make sense, the questions must be part of a logical co-ordinated attempt to understand social reality as a whole. A non-theoretical approach is, in strict logic, unthinkable."[8]

Principal steps followed in formulation of economic theories and generalisations through deductive method can be summarised as given below.

Various Steps in Deductive Method

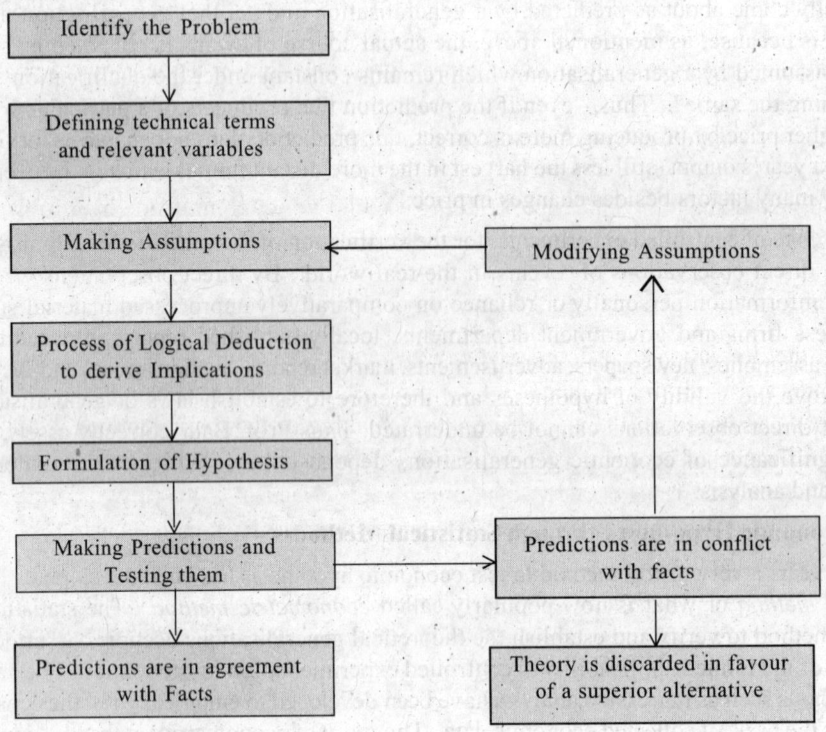

Fig. 1.

Merits and Demerits of Deductive Method

The deductive approach to establish economic generalisations was extensively used by Classical and Neo-Classical economists such as Ricardo, Malthus, Senior, J. S. Mill, Marx, Marshall and Pigou. It still remains popular with modern economists as it has several merits. First, useful mathematical techniques can be employed to derive laws and theories of economics. With the aid of rigorous mathematical logic, economic theories can be developed through the process of deduction which can successfully explain economic phenomena. Secondly, through deductive logic useful economic theories can be derived without the tenuous and detailed collection and analysis of data which are required under the inductive method. Thus, as compared to inductive method, deduction is less time-consuming and less expensive. Thirdly, in view of the limited scope for controlled experimentation in economics, the method of deduction is extremely useful method of constructing economic theories. This is because several forces act simultaneously on an economic phenomenon and it is not possible to eliminate some of these by means of a controlled experiment. This indicates the crucial importance of deductive logic for building up economic principles or theories. Fourthly, the use of sophisticated mathematical methods in the deductive approach enables the economists to introduce accuracy and exactness in economic principles and theories.

In spite of the above-mentioned merits, shortcomings of the deductive approach should not be overlooked. The use of deductive method in deriving economic generalisations requires the use of a high-level competence in logic and theoretical abstraction. A good deal of care and objectivity is needed to avoid bad logic or faulty economic reasoning. Prof. Blaug rightly opines, "It is perfectly true that economists have often deceived themselves and their readers by engaging in what Leontief once called "implicit theorising" presenting tautologies in the guise of substantive contributions to economic knowledge." Besides, most economists have preconceived notions or biases on several economic issues. If sound and valid economic generalisations are to be established, economists must dissociate themselves from normative preconceptions and biases in their logical process of deducing economic generalisations. Further, a great demerit of deductive approach is that with it highly sophisticated theoretical models based on highly unrealistic assumptions may be developed which do not have any operational significance. Indeed, such highly irrelevant analytical models with little empirical content and incapable of being used for policy formulation have in fact been developed by economists. Such models are no more than mere "intellectual toys". If economics is to serve as an instrument of social betterment, building of such theoretical models having no operational use should be avoided.

Lastly, in the derivation of economic hypotheses and conclusions through deductive logic, assumptions play a crucial role. If the assumptions made are such that when on removing them, economic hypothesis based on them is refuted, then making of these assumptions is not valid. Thus, one who uses deductive approach should always keep in mind to what extent the validity of generalisations derived depends on the assumptions made. For instance, the Keynesian macroeconomic analysis is based upon the assumption of a depression-ridden capitalist economy with a lot of excess productive capacity. Therefore, a positive harm has been done in applying the Keynesian theories in the context of developing countries such as ours where the assumptions made by Keynes do not hold good. Hence, mere "deductive arm-chair analysis" should be avoided, if the scientific character of economics is to be maintained.

Inductive Method

The inductive method which is also called empirical method derives economic generalisations on the basis of experience and observations. In this method detailed data are collected with regard to a certain economic phenomenon and effort is then made to arrive at certain generalisations which follow from the observations collected. But, it is worth mentioning that the number of observations has to be large if it can yield a valid economic generalisation. One should not generalise on the basis of a very few observations. There are three ways which can be used for deriving economic principles and theories. They are: (*a*) experimentation, (*b*) observations, (*c*) statistical or econometric method. As has been mentioned above, the experimentation, that is, the use of contrived experiments is of limited applicability in economics. First, unlike natural sciences which are concerned with analysing the behaviour of either inanimate objects or obedient animals such as rats and rabbits under the influence of chloroform, economics deals with the behaviour of man who is quite fickle, wayward and unmanageable. Besides, man cannot tolerate the idea of being experimented upon, either individually or collectively. Secondly, an economic phenomenon is the result of multiplicity of factors and causes acting and interacting upon each other. Therefore, economic phenomenon does not repeat itself in the same uniform pattern. Numerous factors acting on an economic phenomenon 'disturb' it and make its exact repetition unlikely. Thus, as compared with the natural phenomena, economic phenomena are of less uniform pattern, less repetitive and more variable.

Thirdly, economists study the economic phenomena in which pressure groups such as employers' associations, trade unions, farming lobby, political parties with their different ideologies play a crucial part and their activities render it difficult to make controlled experiments in the economic world. However, in spite of these difficulties, experimental method can be used in some fields. For instance, experiments have been conducted to find out which law of production is valid, that is, whether law of diminishing returns, law of constant returns or law of increasing returns operates in the real world. Besides, public undertakings or big industrial firms often try to assess the effect of the changes in the prices of their products on the demand for it and thus find out the demand elasticity of their products.

Various Steps in Inductive Method

Various steps are gone through in developing economic theories through inductive method. The first step, as in the deductive approach, is to *identify the problem.* The second step is *defining technical terms and variables related to the problem.* It is the next step which is peculiar to the inductive method, namely, the *collection of data* about the variables related to the problem and doing some preliminary thinking about the possible functional relationships between the relevant variables.

The next important step in the construction of economic theories in this method is the *processing of data* collected and finding out what relations between the variables actually hold good. From this, a theory is developed which can be further refined and tested through statistical methods. Once the theory has been developed one can make predictions on its basis, as is done in the deductive approach. If predictions of theory are in agreement with the facts and actual behaviour of the economy, then a new reliable theory has been developed. If a *new theory explains "how things work" better than the existing ones, it replaces them.*

However, if predictions are in conflict with actual facts and behaviour of the economy, either the theory is discarded or fresh efforts are made to *modify and refine it by collecting more data and processing them.* The various steps in the construction and development of economic theories through inductive method are illustrated in Figure 2.

Various Steps in Inductive Method

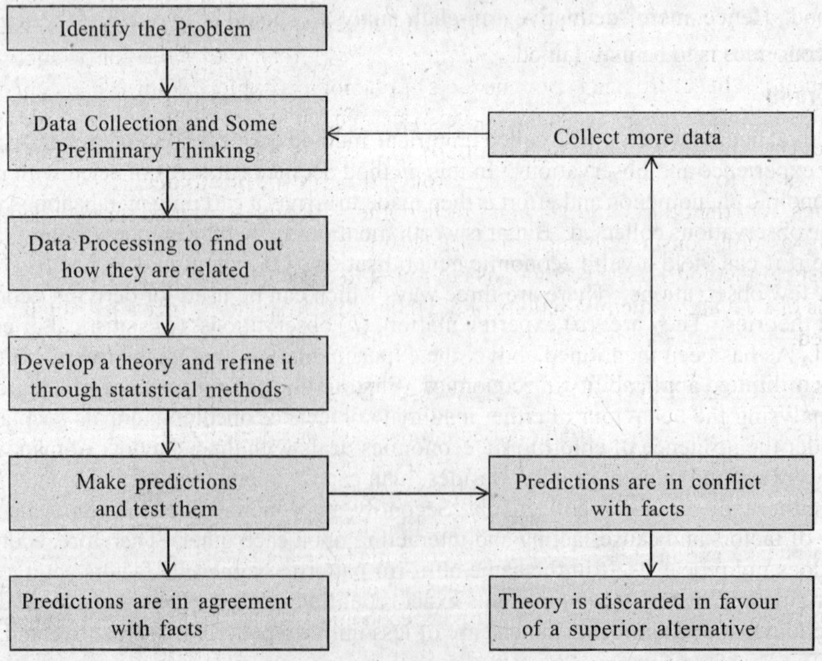

Fig. 2

Evaluation of Inductive Method

As has been explained above, observations of facts through collection of detailed data and the use of statistical methods to arrive at economic generalisations establishing relationship between facts are being increasingly made. Some of the recent researches in the field of macroeconomics, such as the nature of consumption function describing the relation between income and consumption, the principle of acceleration describing the factors which determine investment in the economy have been obtained through the use of mainly inductive method.

However, it needs to be emphasised again that the use of induction or empirical method is not of much value if it is not supported by the economic hypothesis or theory developed by deductive logic. The inductive method can at best be used to empirically test the theory or hypothesis as to whether it is consistent with or refuted by facts. The inductive method has another limitation in that there is a great risk of conclusions being drawn from insufficient data. To obtain generalisations through inductive method, one should take care that sufficient number of observations or data has been taken into account. Besides, the collection of data itself is also not an easy task. And a researcher who wants to employ the inductive method to arrive at generalisations must have good knowledge of statistical methods, that is, he must know the art of collecting, processing and interpreting data. It is obvious that as compared with the deductive method, the inductive method is time-consuming and expensive.

Conclusion : Integration of Two Methods

Now, the controversy which existed among the earlier economists as to whether deductive or inductive approach is more appropriate in developing economic theories and principles has been resolved. The modern viewpoint in this regard is that both are needed for the proper development of scientific economic theories. Indeed, the two are complementary rather than competitive. The modern economists first derive economic hypotheses through the process of logical deduction and then empirically test them through statistical or econometric methods. Marshall rightly pointed out, "*induction and deduction are both needed for scientific thought as the right and left foot are both needed for walking*."[9] Empirical studies made through statistical or inductive method without a theoretical hypothesis to serve as a guide for the selection of data are quite useless. The derivation of economic generalisations through the approach of deductive logic without empirically testing them through inductive method is also not quite proper. Empirical studies made in inductive approach also bring to light significant economic facts or phenomena which require analytical explanation through deductive logic. For instance, Farm Management Studies in India in the mid- fifties led to the discovery of a fact that output per acre on the small-sized farms is higher than that on large farms. This led to the various theoretical explanations of the phenomenon observed in the empirical studies. On the other hand, a theory or hypothesis is first developed through deductive logic from some assumptions and then predictions based on the hypothesis are tested through inductive or statistical method. If the predictions are found to be constant with facts, the hypothesis or theory stands proved and if the predictions of the theory are found to be inconsistent with facts, it stands rejected.

NATURE OF ECONOMIC LAWS AND GENERALISATIONS

We have discussed the subject matter of economics and have seen that it is very wide and comprehensive. Economics is a science and like other sciences it also has its laws. Economic laws are also known as *generalisations, principles and uniformities*. The economic laws describe how a man behaves as a producer and a consumer. The economic laws are also concerned with how the economic system works and operates. Man in his economic life produces wealth, consumes wealth, exchanges it with others. Therefore, economic laws have been framed which govern production, consumption and exchange of wealth by men. Besides, economic laws are also concerned with how the

10. Alfred Marshall, *Principles of Economics*, 8th edition.

national product produced is distributed and how the level of income and employment are determined. Lastly, economic laws also describe growth of the economy as well as international trade between the various countries of the world. In fact, economic laws have been framed in all fields of the subject matter of economics, namely, consumption, production, price determination, determination of income and employment, growth of the economy, foreign trade, etc. Among the important laws of economics, mention may be made of Law of Demand, Law of Diminishing Marginal Utility, Law of Variable Proportions or Diminishing Returns, Keynesian Psychological Law of Consumption, the Principles of Multiplier and Accelerator, Malthusian Law of Population , Law of comparative Advantage.

According to Marshall, "economic laws are these social laws which relate to branches of conduct in which the strength of the motives chiefly concerned can be measured by money price."[10] By this Marshall means that economists have framed laws and theories which explain the conduct or behaviour of man who tries to maximise some things or seek to fulfil his objectives, and these things and objectives must be measurable in terms of money. What is not measurable in terms of money does not come within the purview of economics. However, this is a very narrow view about economic laws. Therefore, Robbins broadened the scope of economic laws and brought out that whether any objective or conduct of man is concerned with money or not, it can come within purview of laws of economics if it is concerned with the problem of choice, that is, allocation of scarce resources among unlimited wants. According to Robbins, economic laws are statements of tendencies which govern human behaviour concerning the utilisation of scarce resources for the achievement of unlimited wants. In other words, when resources are scarce and wants are unlimited and therefore the problem of choice arises, economists have to frame the laws of choice, whether or not variables and objectives involved in it are measurable with money.

Economic Laws as Statements of Tendencies

The nature of economic laws has been a subject of controversy. Marshall thought that the laws of economics are not exact and definite; they are mere *statements of tendencies*. According to him, this is unlike the laws of physical sciences which are quite exact, precise and definite. Because of the exactness and definiteness, the laws of physical sciences can predict the course of events. But laws of economics lack this predictive value. Laws of economics are conditional and are associated with a number of qualifications and assumptions and these assumptions and qualifications are generally contained in the phrase "other things remaining the same, "or *Ceteris Paribus* which is attached to every law and theory of economics. But, in the real world, these other things generally do not remain the same because the economic world is dynamic and ever-changing. For example, according to the law of demand when price of a commodity rises, its quantity demanded by the consumer will fall. But if along with the rise in price of the commodity, income of the consumer increases, then the consumer may demand more of the commodity even at the higher price. This seems to be contrary to the law of demand but in fact this is not so because the law of demand assumes that other things, such as income, tastes and prices of the related goods remain the same, and in our case this qualification has not been fulfilled because income of the consumer has increased. Law of demand will hold good only if other things such as income, tastes and preferences, the prices of related goods remain constant and unchanged.

Likewise, according to the law of diminishing returns, when amount of labour to a given piece of land is increased, marginal product of labourer would diminish beyond a certain stage. But again in actual practice this may not happened so. It may happen that when the use of labour is increased on a given piece of land, improved and more productive technology is employed, then the marginal product of labour may increase rather than decline. Actually this has happened in the present-day developed countries where along with the growth of population and labour force on land, marginal product of labour has increased and this is due to the fact that there has been rapid progress in agricultural technology in these countries due to which marginal productivity has increased. But this also does not prove that law of diminishing returns is invalid. This is because law of diminishing returns also assumes that other things such as technology amount of capital *etc*. remain unchanged.

It is worth mentioning that laws of economics are not like those of the legal laws passed by the Government or Parliament. These legal laws are made by the Government or the Parliament in order to maintain law and order in the country, and it is compulsory for the citizens to obey those laws. If any man violates these legal laws he invites punishment from the government. On the other hand, economic laws tell us how a rational man behaves in his economic life.

Scientific Nature of Economic Laws

Laws of economics are of scientific nature. All scientific laws establish relationship between cause and effect. Economic laws also establish relationship between cause and effect about economic behaviour of man and economic phenomena. If we observe man in using his scarce resources to satisfy his unlimited wants, then we will see that he behaves in a particular manner. By observing the behaviour of several people, economists have established certain generalisations or general principles which are called economic laws. Therefore, these economic laws are general tendencies of man's behaviour in his economic life. Therefore economic laws are related to economic life of man. In his economic life, man produces wealth and consumes it. Besides, the distribution and exchange of wealth also affect the economic life of man. Economists have made several laws regarding production, consumption, distribution and exchange of wealth. Like other scientific laws, economic laws also establish relationship between cause and effect. For example, according to the law of demand, when price of a commodity falls, its quantity demanded increases, other things remaining the same. Here the fall in the price is the cause, and the rise in quantity demanded is the effect. Law of Diminishing Marginal Utility describes that as a man has more units of a commodity, its marginal utility goes on diminishing. Here, the increase in the quantity of the commodity is the cause and the fall in marginal utility is the effect. This holds goods in case of other economic laws also.

It is thus clear that *economic laws are hypothetical and conditional*. But this does not mean that economic laws are not scientific or that they are useless. As a matter of fact, all scientific laws are conditional. The famous scientific law of gravitation is also conditional. According to the law of gravitation, when any commodity is thrown in the air, then it falls down to the ground. This is because the earth has the power to attract and pull other things to itself. But this famous scientific law also depends upon the fulfilment of certain conditions. The condition for the law of gravitation to apply is that no opposing forces obstruct the commodity from falling to the ground. We often see that aeroplanes, birds, balloons, etc. fly in the air and don't fall to the ground. This is because some opposing forces are at work which prevent these things from falling to the ground. Due to the working of these opposing forces, law of gravitation does not apply in these cases. Therefore, law of gravitation also applies when the opposing forces do not operate. Take another example of a scientific law from the science of chemistry. According to a well-known law of chemistry, water is formed if two atoms of hydrogen are mixed with one atom of oxygen: but this law will also apply under specific conditions. Water will be formed with two atoms of hydrogen and one atom of oxygen under certain conditions of temperature and pressure. Thus, all scientific laws hold good under certain conditions. Therefore, the fact that economic laws are conditional and hypothetical is not a unique thing. Nor does this conditional and hypothetical nature destroy the scientific nature of economic laws. Economic laws are, therefore, as important and useful as the laws of physical sciences.

Economic Laws are Less Exact and Definite than Laws of Physical Sciences

But it is worth mentioning that laws of economics are less exact and definite than the laws of physical sciences. Law of gravitation which we have mentioned above is so exact and definite that

11. Alfred Marshall, *Principles of Economics*, 8th edition, p. 26.

we can calculate and measure exactly the movements of the solar system and we can predict their exact position at a particular time. But this is not true in case of economic laws. As said above, economic laws are not so exact and definite; we cannot say with certainty how a man would behave under certain conditions and, therefore, cannot exactly predict his behaviour. We can only say that a man would tend to behave in a particular manner. But because of ignorance, habit, blind faith, emotion, it is quite possible that he behaves contrary to a relevant economic law. That is why, Marshall said that "*the laws of economics are to be compared with the laws of tides, rather than with the simple and exact law of gravitation.*" [11] Laws of tides tell us that how tides rise and fall twice in a day. Besides, they tell us that the height of the tides is maximum on a full-moon day. In other words, on a full-moon day tides are most furious. We can know from these laws of tides that what would be the length of these tides at a certain place on a certain day. But all this we cannot say with definiteness and certainty because tides are affected by external conditions such as air, weather, rain and storm. It cannot be said that what these external conditions will be at a particular place and time. Therefore, how much tides rise at a particular date and time cannot be predicted with certainty. We can say only this much that if these other conditions remain the same, what will be the height of these tides at a certain place and time. Thus, like economic laws, laws of tides are also statements of tendencies.

Now the question arises why economic laws are less definite and exact than those of natural sciences. This is because the object of economic study is such that economic laws cannot be completely definite and exact. The object of economic study is man with a free will and with certain wants and resources. The behaviour of man is governed by several external forces which are beyond his control. Economic behaviour of man is affected by his tastes, fashions, social conditions and customs, family conditions, etc. and all these go on changing. Therefore, economic laws framed by establishing relation between cause and effect in regard to human behaviour cannot be exact and definite. Man's tastes and other external conditions often change and, therefore, man may behave contrary to the established laws of economics. On the other hand, the objects of physical sciences are inert things which lack free will and whose nature always remain the same. Therefore, the laws of physical sciences are more exact and definite. Besides the laws of physical sciences are formulated by making controlled experiments.

By controlling many factors the functional relationship between physical variables are established, but it is not possible to make such controlled experiments regarding human behaviour. We cannot shut a man in a laboratory and keep many things constant and study his attitude and reactions to a particular change and thus establish relationship between relevant economic variables. In order to establish economic laws regarding human behaviour, we have to observe man's actions and reactions in the actual world. Empirical observations are an important way of establishing laws of economics. Another way to formulate laws of economics is the *use of introspective or psychological method.* Economists by knowing their reactions to a certain economic phenomenon also think that others too would behave in the same way, human nature being the same. Thus, by their own psychological reactions they derive generalisations about economic behaviour of the people.

Although laws of economics are less exact and definite than the laws of physical sciences, yet they are more exact and definite than the laws of other social sciences. Economics is fortunate enough to have a measure of money with which we can assess the motives or objectives as well as the results. Such a measure is not available to other social sciences.

Role of Assumptions in Economics : Friedman's View

As has been pointed out above, every law and generalisation of economics is based upon some assumptions. Now, the question is whether for the formulation of proper economic laws these assumptions should be realistic or not. One view is that laws of economics if they are to be

12. See his book "*Essays on Positive Economics.*"
13. Milton Friedman, *op. cit.*

valid and unseful must be based upon assumptions which are realistic. Thus, according to this view, making unrealistic assumptions and establishing laws on their basis will make these laws invalid. However, a contrary view has been put forward by Prof. Milton Friedman of Chicago University in his now well-known article, "*The Methodology of Positive Economics*."[12] In this context Prof. Friedman draws a distinction between positive economics and normative economics. According to Prof. Friedman, positive economics explains "a system of generalisations that can be used to make correct predictions about the consequences of any change in circumstances."[13] Because the predictions of this positive economics have to be tested with the empirical evidence it is as much a science as any other physical science even though the assumptions made may be unrealistic. The crucial point is whether the predictions based on economic laws of positive economics are confirmed by the facts and empirical evidence. According to Friedman, assumptions cannot be realistic; since they are made merely to simplify the analysis. However, it may be pointed out that while drawing conclusions from economic theories and laws regarding economic policies it must be known whether the assumptions made do not make the policy conclusions invalid if these assumptions are removed. Dr. K. N. Raj has rightly said, "some of the differences between economists regarding policy questions can be traced to the assumptions they choose to make when faced with the problems of this kind."[14] He further adds, "it is, however, essential in the interest of clarity and intellectual honesty that economists state clearly the assumptions on which one set of policies and programmes is advanced in preference to another and the reasons for making these assumptions"[15]

QUESTIONS FOR REVIEW

1. What is a scientific theory ?
2. Differentiate between deductive and inductive methods of constructing economic theories. Explain their merits and demrits.
3. What is deductive method? How economic theories are established through deductive method?
4. How economists test or verify their theories ? What happens if predictions of a theory are found to be in conflict with facts.
5. Explain the various steps in formulating economic theories through deductive method.
6. What is inductive method? How is inductive method used for constructing an economic theory?
7. Explain the various steps of constructing economic theories through inductive method.
8. "Induction and deduction are both needed for scientific thought as the right and left foot are both needed for walking." Do you agree? Discuss.
9. Explain why there is limited scope for making controlled experiments in economics.
10. Explain and illustrate the role of deductive and inductive methods in economics.
11. Explain Deductive and Inductive methods of economic analysis.
12. Explain the nature of economic laws and compare them with laws of physical sciences.
13. Laws of economics have been compared to the complex laws of tides rather than to simple laws of gravitation. Why ?
14. Economic laws are mere statements of tendencies. Do you agree? Discuss.
15. Are economic laws universal ? Give some examples of economic laws which though valid for developed countries are not applicable to the developing countries.
16. Economic laws are unscientific because they are based on unrealistic assumptions. Do you agree ? Discuss referring to Prof. Milton Friedman's views in this regard.
17. Name five laws of economics. Explain them briefly.
18. Economists must make realistic assumptions to derive economic laws and theories. Discuss ?

14. See his Presidential Address to the 55th Annual Conference of the Indian Economic Association, held at Bodh Gaya, Magadh University, Dec. 1972, reprinted in *The Indian Economic Journal.* Vol. XX, No. 3.
15. *Ibid*.

CHAPTER 5

BASIC COMPETITIVE MODEL AND ROLE OF PRICE MECHANISM

Introduction

We have explained in the earlier chapters the basic issues, problems which the economists study. What goods and services are produced, how they are produced, how the output of goods and services produced are distributed among the people of a country and what provision is made for promoting economic growth are the main problems analysed in economics. We have also explained that these basic problems arise due to the scarcity of resources in relation to human wants. Now, the important questions is who make these choices of what, how and for whom to produce and how much resources be allocated to capital accumulation and bringing about technological progress for promoting economic growth. The present chapter is devoted to answer who and how the above mentioned social choices are made. It is important to note that economics has been evolved and developed in framework of a free market economy in which the resources of a society are owned by individuals and firms. Thus, a market economy recognises and protects *property rights*, that is, the rights that govern the ownership, use and disposal of resources and the goods and services produced with their help. Historically, such a social arrangement in which resources are privately owned and consumers (i.e. individuals or households) and producing firms interact to determine the choices regarding production and distribution of goods and services has been called capitalism. Thus, according to W.N. Loucks, "*Capitalism is a system of economic organisation featured by the private ownership of and the use of man-made and nature-made capital*"[1].

Since the term capitalism has been associated with exploitation of man by man, we will avoid using the term capitalism or capitalist economy and prefer to use the term '*market economy*'. In the basic model of a market economy we also assume that competitive markets prevail in a market economy in which no individual consumer and firm exercises any control over the prices of product and resources. Hence we call this model of a market economy as ***basic competitive model.*** In what follows we will first explain the essential features of a competitive market economy and the basic competitive model and then analyse how the basic units of the economy — individual households and firms — make choices when they are faced with scarcity of resources in relation to their needs or wants. Besides, we will study how the interaction of these units determine social choices regarding how the scarce resources are used and allocated. It is important to mention here that for determining the social choices of what to produce, how to produce and for whom prices play a crucial role. Therefore, in the discussion of basic competitive model we will study the role of price mechanism in making the above social choices.

THE BASIC COMPETITIVE MODEL : ESSENTIAL FEATURES

We will study the salient features of a free-market economy in the next section. However, we must note basic ingredients of the basic competitive model of a market economy which we will primarily use to explain how *constrained choices* are made by individuals and firms, that is, choices made by them when they confront the problem of scarcity. There are three main assumptions of this

1. W. N. Loucks, *Comparative Economic Systems.*

basic model. They are (1) rational, self-interested consumers, (2) profit-maximising firms and (3) the existence of competitive markets. This simple and basic model ignores the role of government that intervenes to influence the choices made by the consumers and firms. This analysis of a market economy will show how an economy without any intervention by government might work to determine the constrained social choices. We briefly explain them below.

1. Rational Self-interested Consumers. In the analysis of consumers' behaviour economists assume that subject to their budget constraint consumers make a *rational choice*. By rational behaviour or choice we mean the consumers try to maximise their satisfaction, or act in a consistent manner given the budget constraint. Given their budget constraint, there will be an **opportunity set** of goods and services. *By opportunity set we mean the combinations of goods and services that consumers can buy with the given money income and prices of goods and services.* Rational behaviour on the part of consumers requires that they will choose a combination of goods and services which maximise their satisfaction or they will choose a combination of them which they prefer most. Thus, rationality assumption about the behaviour of consumers implies that they will make choices to promote their self-interest. Different individuals have different desires and preferences. One individual may like to live in a good house equiped will air conditioners, the other may prefer to have costly cars Economists make no judgement about whether preferences of one individual are better than those of others. We are concerned how these different preferences and tastes about goods and services affect their rational choice while they pursue their respective self-interest.

2. Profit-Maximising Firms. Similarly in the case of firms, economists assume that they will also pursue their self interest in making choices. Generally, rational behaviour on the part of the firms means that in their choices of what goods will be produced and in what quantities, how they will be produced, they are guided by the motive of maximisation of profits. A firm makes a constrained choice as it also faces the problem of limited resources. In other words, for them also there is opportunity set of goods and services among which they have to make a rational choice, and also an opportunity set of various methods (*i.e.* the ways in which resources are combined) available to produce goods and services. From the opportunity sets open to the firms, the economists assume that they will make a choice that maximise their profits.

3. Competitive Markets. In ordinary speech the word *market* means a place where buyers and sellers meet to buy and sell goods. In economics, market has a wider meaning and is interpreted to mean any arrangement that enables buyers and sellers to exchange things; they may contact each other through telephone, fax or direct computer link to negotiate prices of goods they buy and sell. In our above example, rational and self-interested consumers and profit-maximising firms contact each other through any media and buy and sell things on the negotiated price.

The self-interested consumers are interested in low prices of goods they buy and, on the other hand, the profit-maximising firms will be interested in charging a higher price of the goods they produce and offer for sale in the market. However, through their interaction they may agree to buy and sell goods at the agreed price.

In the basic competitive model, it is assumed that neither the consumers, nor the firms have any market power to influence the prices of the goods and services they want to buy and sell. In fact, the economists generally assume that *perfect competition* prevails in the market. Under perfect competition, there are a large number of firms producing a good and since no one is in a position to influence the price, they take prices of goods as given and constant, that is, each firm is a *price taker*. Each firm must accept the price prevailing in the market. This prevailing price is determined by the interaction of *all* firms and buyers. We will see in a later chapter how demand for a good by all the consumers who want to buy the goods and supply by all the firms who produce and supply a good together determine the market price of the goods. Suffice it to say here, if a firm in this perfectly competitive market charges a higher than the prevailing price, it will not be able to sell any quantity of the goods because his customers will switch to other firms producing and supplying the same good.

Similarly, in such a perfectly competitive market since each consumer cannot influence the market price, it must accept it as given and make a choice about how much to buy the various goods and services, given his budget constraint and preferences for different goods. Thus, in the basic competitive model of a market economy, rational and self-interested consumers and profit-maximising firms interact to determine prices of goods and resources. As will be explained later, these prices play a crucial role in determining social choices regarding what, how and for whom to produce.

The Basic Competitive Model and Economic Efficiency

The basic competitive model has a very important property which is that it ensures economic efficiency in the functioning of the market economy. As we shall prove in a later chapter, the working of a perfectly competitive market economy produces such results that it is not possible to produce more of one good without producing less of another. Besides, working of this model yields such results that it is not possible to make any one better off without making someone else worse off. This economic efficiency of a perfectly competitive economy is achieved without intervention by the government.

However, most of the economists recognise that the real world is not characterised by the competitive model. **In the actual market economies it is monopolies, oligopolies and monopolistic competitions that prevail,** where the firms exercise a large market power and influence the prices of the products they produce. We will study in later chapters how inefficiencies arise in a market economy where such forms of market exist.

Besides, economists recognise that even when perfect competition prevails in the market economy, inefficiencies in production and distribution of goods and allocation of resources can exist. This happens when there are **externalities, negative or positive** of the activities of firms and consumers. For example, negative externalities arise when the productive activities of firms impose costs on others such as when they cause pollution of environment for which they do not have to pay. These externalities *cause difference between private cost and social cost*. The firms which aim at maximising their private profits do not take into account these costs or harmful external effects of their productive activities. This results in economic inefficiency, though there may be a perfectly competitive market for selling and buying of goods. We will explain in detail in a later chapter how these cause obstructions for the achievement of economic efficiency or maximum social welfare.

It follows from above that actual market economies may not be *perfectly* described by our basic competitive model, but it is still used as a convenient benchmark. We will see in later chapters the important difference between the predictions based on our competitive model and the actually observed outcomes in some cases and in those cases we use different models to explain the facts. However, the economists recognise that though perfectly competitive model may not provide good descriptions of the actual situations in some cases, it still makes fairly correct predictions, though not perfectly correct ones, of the actual outcomes.

CHIEF FEATURES OF A FREE MARKET ECONOMY

The efficient working of a free market economy requires that the producer firms must have incentives to work hard and produce goods and services at the lowest possible cost per unit of output Market economies provide incentives to the firms and individuals by recognising and enforcing the property rights of the individuals and firms to own the resources and goods and services produced by using them. It also allows the individuals and firms to use the resources owned by them for making profits. *Earning of profits from using resources owned by them also provides incentives to the firms and individuals to produce goods and services efficiently*. Profits depend on cost per unit incurred and price charged of goods and services produced. The prices of goods and resources provide information to the individuals and firms about the relative scarcity of different goods and services. Thus property rights, profits, prices and incentives play a crucial role in the functioning of a market economy. We briefly explain them below.

Property Rights

Property rights are social institutions that govern the ownership, use and disposal of resources, goods and services. There are different types of property which individuals and firms can privately own. (1) *Real property* which includes land, buildings, durable goods such as plant, capital equipment etc. (2) *Financial property* which includes shares and bonds, bank deposits, money kept at home. (3) *Intellectual property*, which is the latest addition to the list of property, represents the products of creative effort and includes books written, audio and video material, computer programmes. It is interesting to note here that Bill Gates have become the richest man of the world by possessing intellectual property in the form of computer programmes such as windows, Miscrosoft Office.

The right of private property is a fundamental feature of a market economy. The right of private property means that productive resources such as land, factories, machinery, mines, etc. are under the private ownership. In other words, an individual has a right to acquire and to use the means of production. Besides, the owner is free to sell or dispose of his property in any way he likes. Because of this right of private property, goods like land, factories, mines, machinery, houses, and other producer and consumer goods are privately owned by the people. They use these means of production for their individual benefit. Moreover, the right of private property includes in itself the **right of inheritance**. The right of inheritance means that on the death of a person, his sons or daughters or some relatives become the owners of his property. No doubt, there are always some restrictions on the right to private property imposed by the Government for social harmony and benefit. But, except for some restrictions capitalist economic system tries to protect and enforce the right of private property.

The two attributes of property rights, namely, *the right of the owner to use the property as he likes and the right to sell it provide incentives to the owners to use their property efficiently*. For example, the owner of a factory building will try to make most profitable use of it by producing a commodity which yields him maximum profits. If he makes a wrong decision and produces a commodity for which there is insufficient demand he will incur losses. This gives him incentive to think carefully and try to obtain adequate information before making a decision about what to produce and in what quantity. The owners of the property would also try to *maintain it* properly so that when in future he wants to sell it he can do so at a good price.

It is important that government should enforce the property rights. If property rights are not enforced, then the incentives to use the property efficiently is weakened and the potential gain from its efficient use will be lost. *Enforcing intellectual property rights is proving to be a big challenge these days* in view of the modern technologies that make it relatively easy to copy books, audio and video material and computer programmes.

Freedom of Private Enterprise

Allied to the property rights is freedom of enterprise which is another basic feature of a market economy. Freedom of enterprise means that everybody is free to engage in whatever economic activity he pleases. In other words, he is free to choose to work in any industry he likes or adopts any occupation or trade he desires. More specifically, freedom of enterprise means that an entrepreneur is free to set up any firm or business unit to produce goods or make investment in shares or bonds of corporate sector. True , he may not have enough capital to invest in business or a productive unit like factory or he may not have enough ability or training to follow certain occupations. But subject to these limitations and to the laws passed by the Government in public interest, an individual or firm is free to engage in any economic activity he feels most desirable or profitable. In India before 1991, there was a *system of industrial licensing* which restricted the freedom of enterprise. For setting up industrial units in various industries, the private sector firms had to obtain licenses which were not easily available. Similarly, for procuring necessary raw materials and inputs such as steel, cement, businessmen had to get *permits* from the government to purchase these products and to get permits businessmen had to bribe the government officials. This license-permit system greatly restricted the freedom of enterprise of the private sector firms. This not only caused allocative inefficiency but also obstructed economic growth of the country. Under the structural economic reforms initiated in 1991 by Dr. Manmohan Singh who was then Finance Minister ,industrial licensing has been largely abolished and the system of permits has been done away with. Grant of licenses to import goods, machines and raw materials has been greatly liberalised and custom duties have been drastically reduced. As a result, private sector now enjoys greater freedom to invest in industries they think it profitable and diversify their productive capacity by producing multiple products.

Abolition of industrial licensing system and liberalisation of imports and ending of permit system has tended to promote competition in the Indian economy. The greater competition has helped to keep inflation under check and to achieve higher industrial growth rate.

Profits and Prices : Incentives and Information

No individuals would work and save if adequate incentives are not provided to them in the form of wages and interest respectively. Similarly, the firms will not produce goods and services and bear risk of losing money if sufficient incentives are not given to them. Profits are earned from undertaking the task of producing goods and services and introducing new products and new techniques of production. Profits earned by the firm depend on prices of goods and services produced and cost incurred. As seen above, in a perfectly competitive market firms are price takers, that is they take price of a product or service as given. With a given price, firm's profits will be larger, if cost per unit of output is smaller. Therefore, in order to maximise profits, firms try to minimise cost for producing a given level of output. *Thus profits serve as incentive for the firm to produce efficiently*.

The working of price system ensures that those individuals and firms will get goods who are willing and able to pay for them. Prices of goods and services indicate how much money individuals are prepared to pay for them. In other words, *prices convey information to the firms about how individuals value different goods and services*. The goods and resources which are relatively more scarce, will have higher prices in the market. On the other hands, the goods and resources which are relatively less scarce will have low market prices. The profit motive induces firms to respond to the prices of different goods. The firms will earn more profits if they produce goods which people want most efficiently, that is, economise the use of scarce resources and use relatively more those resources which are relatively less scarce in supply. Thus, by producing efficiently the firms are able to increase profits. It is important to note that for profit motive to be effective the firms must be allowed to keep a good part of the profits earned by them and not taxed away by government. As seen above, this is implied by property rights enjoyed by the firms. Similarly, if incentives to individuals or households have to be provided to work hard and acquire skills and training, they should be permitted to retain a good amount of what they earn from their work or what they receive as a return on their investments.

Importance of Information and Incentives. It follows from above that *for market economies to solve its basic economic problems and work efficiently individuals and firms must have adequate information and have incentives to act on the available information*. In market economies it is prices through which individuals and firms get information about the relative scarcity of goods and resources. Relatively more scarce goods and resources tend to have higher prices than the relatively less scarce resources. Further, in market economies incentives play a crucial role for the working of individuals and firms. Professor Stiglitz, a Nobel laureate in economics writes, "*incentives can be viewed as being at the heart of economics. Without incentives, why would individuals go to work in* *the morning? Who would undertake the risks of bringing out new products ? Who would put aside savings for a rainy day*?"[2] Emphasising the importance of incentives he further writes, "Providing appropriate incentives is a fundamental economic problem. In modern market economies, profits provide incentives for firms to produce the goods individuals want and wages provide incentives for individuals to work, property rights also provide people with important incentives not only to invest and to save but also to put their assets to the best possible use."[3]

It follows from above that property rights are important features of market economies and play a significant role in their efficient working.

Incentives vs. Inequality. While incentives play a significant role in market economies for their working efficiently to solve the basic problems of what to produce, how to produce, for whom to produce and how much to invest for bringing about economic growth, but they involve a cost which must be taken into account. *The cost of providing incentives is the inequality in the economy they cause*. Any system of incentives must provide compensation to individuals and firms in terms of higher wages, larger profits, higher return on investment for better performance or higher efficiency. If pay for work, return on investment is tied to performance etc. then since performances differ, the compensation for them too will differ and this will bring about inequality in incomes. This raises the question how much incentives should be given for better performance or higher efficiency so that inequality of incomes is not much higher. Since the greater the incentives given, the greater will be the inequality of incomes, there is *incentive -inequality trade-off.* If a society provides greater incentives to promote efficiency and growth, there is likely to be more inequality of incomes.

It may be noted that one basic problem facing governments of market economies is to devise a tax system (*i.e.* kinds of taxes and rates of taxes) that tends to reduce incentives on the one hand but provide revenue to finance welfare programmes for those who have low incomes. Thus, providing incentives to earn higher wages or return and profits encounters serious problem of increasing inequalities of income in a society.

Competitive Markets

In ordinary speech the word *market* means a place where buyers and sellers meet to buy and sell goods. In economics, market has a wider meaning and is interpreted to mean any arrangement that enables buyers and sellers to exchange things; they may contact each other through telephone, fax or direct computer link to negotiate prices of goods they buy and sell. In our above example, rational and self-interested consumers and profit-maximising firms contact each other through any media and buy and sell things on the negotiated price.

The self-interested consumers are interested in low prices of goods they buy and, on the other hand, the profit-maximising firms will be interested in charging a higher price of the goods they produce and offer for sale in the market. However, through their interaction they may agree to buy and sell goods at the agreed price.

In the basic competitive model of a market economy, it is assumed that neither the consumers, nor the firms have any market power to influence the prices of the goods and services they want to buy and sell. In fact, the economists generally assume that *perfect competition* prevails in the market. Under perfect competition, there are a large number of firms producing a good and since no one is in a position to influence the price, they take prices of goods as given and constant, that is, each firm is a *price taker*. Each firm must accept the price prevailing in the market. This prevailing price is determined by the interaction of *all* firms and buyers. We will see in a later chapter how demand for a good by all the consumers who want to buy the goods and supply by all the firms who produce and supply a good together determine the market price of the goods. Suffice it to say here,

2. Joseph Stiglitz. *Principles of Economics,* p.25.
3. *Op. cit.,* p. 26.

if a firm in this perfectly competitive market charges a higher than the prevailing price, it will not be able to sell any quantity of the goods because his customers will switch to other firms producing and supplying the same good.

Similarly, in such a perfectly competitive market since each consumer cannot influence the market price, it must accept it as given and make a choice about how much to buy the various goods and services, given his budget constraint and preferences for different goods. Thus, in the basic competitive model of a market economy, rational and self-interested consumers and profit-maximising firms interact to determine prices of goods and resources. As will be explained later, these prices play a crucial role in determining social choices regarding what, how and for whom to produce.

Consumer Sovereignty

In a free market economy there is a freedom of choice for the consumers to buy goods and services which suit their tastes and preferences. In a market economy only those goods and services are produced if the firms producing and supplying them are able to sell them at a profit. Now, profits are made if goods or services produced are sold for more than what it costs to produce them. Therefore, firms cannot expect to make profits, if they do not make goods or services which are not in accordance with the preferences and demands of the consumers and also for which consumers are not willing to pay adequate price. Since firms are guided by profit motive, they will produce those goods which ensure greater profits to them. Therefore, in what goods and in what quantities will be produced by firms is dictated ultimately by the tastes and preferences of consumers who in a way '*vote*' for the goods they buy. This is generally called the principle of *consumer sovereignty*. This means in a market economy the consumers are just like a king or sovereign who dictate what goods and services and what quantities of them are produced.

ROLE OF PRICE MECHANISM IN THE FUNCTIONING OF THE FREE–MARKET ECONOMIY

A market economy has no central planning commission or bureau to decide what and how goods are to be produced and how the total national product is to be distributed among the consumers. In a free market or capitalist economy there is a freedom of enterprise and choice. Consumers are free to buy whatever they like. Businessmen are free to produce and sell what they choose and suppliers of factors of production are free to supply their material and human resources to whatever occupations they prefer. Now, in the absence of any central co-ordinating body it looks like a miracle as to how such an economy functions and is able to take decisions regarding what, how and for whom to produce? If consumers want cloth, producers choose to make motor cars and resource suppliers wish to give their services for making bread, there will be complete confusion and chaos because of the inconsistency of such choices. So there must be some co-ordinating and organising mechanism to prevent such confusion and chaos posed by the freedom of enterprise and choice. But if there is no central planning authority to make the fundamental economic decisions and thus to allocate productive resources among various competing uses, how can then a free-enterprise economy solve its central problems ? The answer is that a free market economy uses the impersonal forces of market to solve its central problems and thus determine the allocation of its resources. Market forces are reflected in price changes and prices determine what goods are to be produced, how they are to be produced, and for whom they are to be produced. Thus price mechanism plays a vital role in the working of a free-enterprise market economy.

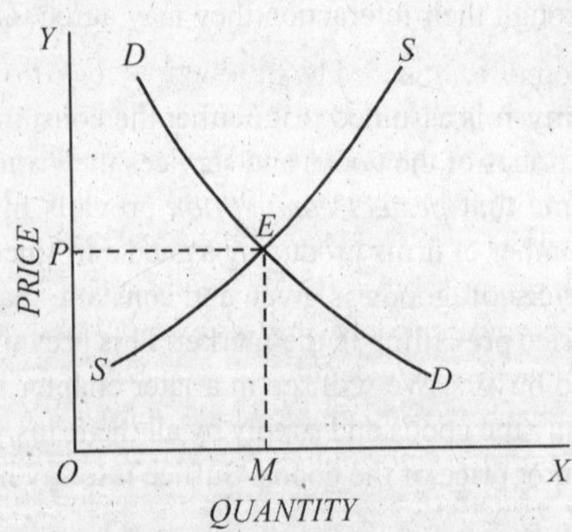

Fig. 5.1. *Market mechanism determining price*

Now the question is what does market mechanism or price mechanism mean? Market stands for the contact between buyers and sellers of goods through which the buyers get goods in exchange for the price they pay for them. The buyers bring the demand for the goods and the sellers offer supply of the goods to meet the wants of the buyers. The interaction of demand for and supply of goods determine their prices. Thus the market stands for the forces of demand and supply of goods. How price is determined by market mechanism, that is, through demand and supply is shown in Figure 5.1. The price at which the demand and supply curves intersect each other will come to stay in the market. In Figure 5.1, *OP* price is determined at which *OM* quantity of the good is demanded and sold. The productive resources will be allocated to the production of the good to the extent that *OM* quantity of the good is produced.

How Does Price Mechanism Allocate Resources ?

Now, how does price mechanism allocate resources among goods in a market economy. It is worth noting that competition among the sellers or producers and among the buyers of goods is essential for the working of a market economy. Production of goods requires resources such as labour, capital (mechanies, etc), raw materials, fuel or power for their production. In any economic system, scarce resources are allocated among various goods and services. A market economy relies on demand for and supply of goods and services for allocating resources among goods and services. Demand for and supply of goods and services determine their prices. *Prices are signals that direct the allocation of resources among production of goods and services.* Since a firm is driven by profit motive, it will produce, what is profitable to produce. If a firm can sell a product at a price which is more than the cost per unit incurred on it, the firm is likely to produce it. In a free market system resources flow towards the production of those goods which yield profits to the firms. Higher prices of certain goods mean higher profit opportunities in the production those of goods. As a result, firms will devote more resources to the production of products whose prices are relatively higher and therefore prospects of making profits in the production of these products is greater.

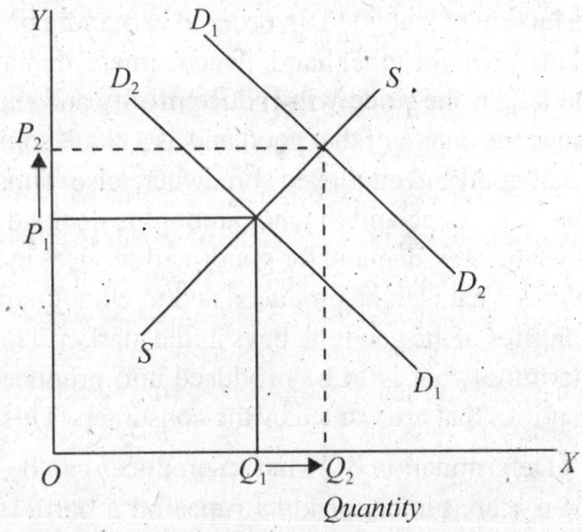

Fig. 5.2. *Allocation of Resources to the Production of Cars*

It is worth mentioning that *demand curve of a product represents what people are willing to pay*. If people's preferences or income change, the demand for different goods will change causing changes in their prices and therefore change in profit opportunities in the production of different goods. As a result, there will be reallocation of resources among different goods and services. To illustrate how resource are allocated consider Figure 5.2 where as a result of change in preferences of individuals or increase in their incomes, demand curve for cars increases and as a result demand for cars shifts to the right from D_1D_1 to D_2D_2. It will be seen from Fig. 5.2 that shift in demand curve of cars from D_1D_1 to D_2D_2 causes price of cars to go up from P_1 to P_2. Rise in price of cars relative to any increase in average cost of producing cars makes it profitable to produce more cars. Towards that end, the existing firms will expand their capacity by buying more capital (*i.e.* installing new machines), procure new buildings to install these machines and employ more labour and raw materials to produce more cars. Besides, to avail of the profit opportunities in car production new firms will enter the business of car manufacturing. As a result of all these, more resources will be allocated to the production of cars.

Invisible Hand and Resource Allocation

We have seen above how through changes in prices resulting from changes in demand for and supply of goods and services market economy automatically functions, as if through an invisible hand. There is no any central visible authority that directs the working of a free market economy. It is claimed that market economy not only works without any regulation by government or any other authority, it works and performs well to promote social welfare and achieve economic efficiency. More than 200 years ago Adam Smith emphasised the self-regulatory nature of market economy. He pointed out that each individual in a market economy is guided by his own interests but by pursuing his own interest he promotes the interest of society. He is led by invisible hand to promote an end which was no part of his intention.[4]

We shall now explain in detail how the central problems of an economy are solved through price or market mechanism in a free-market capitalist economy. In other words, we shall describe below at length what role price mechanism plays in the functioning of the capitalist economy.

Deciding What to Produce

In a free market economy, there are thousands of entrepreneurs or businessmen to produce goods for the society. The aim of entrepreneurs or businessmen is to earn as much money profits as possible. The desire for profits causes businessmen to compete with one another to produce those goods which consumers wish to buy. For instance, when the consumers raise their demand for a particular good, price of that good will rise. A rise in price of that good, cost remaining the same, will lead to more profits. The increase in profits will attract more productive resources into the production of that good. In order to earn more profits businessmen will produce that good in a larger quantity. On the other hand, if consumers' demand for a good decreases, price of the good will fall. The fall in the price will reduce profits and may cause losses. The businessmen will, therefore, reduce the output of that good and as a result some resources will be withdrawn from the production of that good and employed somewhere else. Thus in a free market economy, the question regarding what to produce and in what amount is decided ultimately by the preferences of the consumers as shown by their demand for goods and services in the market. The consumer is, so to say, a king, who decides what is to be produced and in what quantity by making his wishes known by the types and quantities of the goods he buys in the market. Thus, in a free enterprise economic system consumers determine what is to be produced and producers only act and produce such goods and in such quantities that are wanted by the consumers. This is known as the principle of consumer sovereignty.

Determination of 'what to produce' can be better understood by comparing it to an election. When a consumer spends a rupee on a particular good, it is as if he was casting a vote for the production of that good. Various goods will be produced in proportion to the number of 'rupee votes' cast for them. That good will be produced in a larger quantity for which the 'rupee votes' cast are greater. But the economic election is not democratic because every consumer does not have equal number of votes to cast. The greater the income of a consumer, the greater the number of his money-votes. Therefore, in a capitalist economy while luxuries are produced for the rich people who have got enough purchasing power or ability to pay for such goods, the necessities are not produced in sufficient quantities for the poor people because they do not have much ability to pay. Thus, capitalist economic system may work in such a way that while the poor people are unable to feed milk to their children, the rich people feed milk to their dogs. The market mechanism arranges things in such a manner that milk or anything else goes to anyone in whatever quantity he wishes so long as he is able and willing to pay for it.

Deciding How to Produce

The entrepreneurs who produce goods in capitalist economies are in search of profits. In fact,

4. Adam Smith, *The Wealth of Nations* (New York, Random House, 37), p.456.

they aim at maximising their money profits. Profits are the difference between the revenue earned and the cost of production incurred. Now, given the level of output, profits can be maximised by minimising the cost of production. Therefore, an entrepreneur will produce a given level of output with that combination of resources or he will employ that technique of production which renders his cost of production minimum. In other words, producers will produce with the least-cost combination of resources or with the most efficient technique of production. If labour is relatively cheaper than capital, labour-intensive methods of production will be used. On the other hand, if capital is cheaper than labour, capital-intensive technique will be employed for production. Which combination of resources is the least cost one depends upon the prices of the various factors of production. In the least-cost combination of resources the quantity of that productive factor will be larger whose price is relatively lower. In order to minimise cost, the producers will use various factors of production in such a proportion that marginal products of factors are proportional to their prices.

In a free market economy the factor of competition and the motive of profit force all businessmen to produce goods with least-cost combination of factors and with most efficient technique. The inefficient firms who fail to employ the least-cost method of production will have to go out of the field because of competition. The maximum efficiency in production or least-cost production is very desirable from the viewpoint of the society because it ensures that the scarce resources of the society are being used to produce largest possible output of goods desired by the consuming public.

Deciding for Whom to Produce: Distribution of National Product

Who gets the goods and how much depends upon the money income one has to spend on goods? Distribution of total output of goods and services depends upon the distribution of national income. More unequal the distribution of national income, more uneven will be the distribution of national product. There are thus two steps in the process of distribution.

The first is the distribution of money income. Incomes can be earned either by doing work or by lending the services of one's property such as land, capital and houses. Thus, there are two sources of getting money income: first, income from work; and second, income from property. The forces of competition in a free-enterprise economy force the entrepreneurs to pay the workers according to the contribution made to production by them. Therefore, a worker gets income or wage equal to the value of their marginal products in the production of the goods he helps to produce. Similarly, in a capitalist economy, the owners of the land, that is landlords, and the owners of capital, that is, capitalists, get rent and interest respectively according to the value of the marginal products of the services of their respective resources. And the entrepreneurs or businessmen earn profits by setting up business and bearing the risks of production. Wages, rent, interest and profits are respectively the prices of factors of production, labour, land, capital and enterprise. Just as there are markets for goods, similarly there are markets for the factors of production. Demand and supply for the different factors determine their market prices. These factor prices constitute the incomes of the owners of the factors. It is thus clear that price mechanism (*i.e.*, demand and supply of the factors and their prices) work to determine the incomes of the various individuals and hence their shares of output.

How much income an individual will be able to make depends not only on the amount of work he does and the prices of the factors he owns but also on how much property in the form of land and capital he owns. A person who owns a large amount of property will be enjoying a higher income. In a capitalist economy, because of the large inequalities in the ownership of property, there are glaring inequalities of incomes.

Next step in the distribution process is the sharing of goods and services between different individuals or consumers. As in a free-enterprise capitalist economy, incomes of different individuals as determined by price mechanism and ownership of property are very much unequal, the distribution of total output of goods and services is also very much unequal. People with low incomes receive small shares from the national product. Poor people cannot obtain high-priced goods because incomes being small their ability to pay is limited. They may not even get necessities in sufficient quantities. Whom some goods are in short supply, their prices are bid up and goods are delivered to those who are able and willing to pay the most for them. Not only the prices of factors but also the prices of goods also determine the share of each individual in the national output. Suppose an individual has earned income of ₹ 4,000 as determined by the price and the amount of factors he owns; Now, how much amount of the goods he will be able to get with ₹ 4,000 from the market depends upon the prices of the goods as determined by their demand and supply. The higher the prices of the goods, the smaller the amount of goods he will be able to obtain.

We thus see that just as prices determine what goods are produced, in what quantities, and by what methods, so, under free private enterprise, these also determine the .share of each individual in the national output.

Deciding about Rate of Economic Growth

Rate of economic growth depends on rate of saving and investment. In solving this problem also a free market or capitalist economy depends largely on the freedom of choice between consumption and saving by the consumers and free decisions regarding investment by private entrepreneurs. Money and capital market play an important role in carrying out the decisions by the consumers and entrepreneurs. Each individual decides how much of his income he wants to save. His saving is governed by the rate of interest prevailing in the money market. Rate of interest is the price for the use of money. Thus, we see that the price governs the savings made by the individuals. Investment decisions made by entrepreneurs depend upon the profit opportunities in making various types of capital goods. In other words, investment depends upon the rate of return on capital. The greater the profit expectations, that is, the larger the rate of return on capital, the greater will be the amount of investment made by the entrepreneur. Thus we see that it is the price system – the rate of interest on savings and rate of return on capital – which regulates the amount of savings and investment in a free-market economy.

It may, however, be pointed out that this is the problem where a free market economy has often run into trouble. If the aggregate investment planned by entrepreneurs is equal to the aggregate savings made by the households and individuals, then the free market economy will run smoothly. But there is no guarantee that planned savings and planned investment will be equal. This is because savings and investments are made by two different groups of people. Whereas savings are largely made by households, the investment is made by entrepreneurs. When planned investment exceeds planned saving, income and employment will tend to rise and there may arise conditions of boom and inflation. And when planned investment falls short of planned savings, income and employment will tend to fall resulting in depression and unemployment. Thus, the fluctuations in economic activity, or what are called business cycles, are inherent in the working of a free market economy.

Solving All the Problems Simultaneously

We have discussed above the solutions of basic problems by a free market economy separately. But it is worth mentioning that in the actual working of the free market economy, these decisions are not made separately. All of the four problems are solved simultaneously. Solutions of all the four problems are completely interdependent. Economic system is in fact a huge inter-connected set of markets each with buyers and sellers. The problems are simultaneously solved by the millions of decisions made by consumers, workers, entrepreneurs, bankers, etc., who constitute buyers and sellers in various markets. In fact, the solution of the problem in the free market economy is like that of solving a set of simultaneous equations in mathematics. The various interdependent decisions and markets represent a sort of simultaneous equations.

The working of free-market capitalist economy through price and market mechanism can be more easily understood with the help of a flow diagram depicted in Figure 5.3. In the upper part of this diagram a rectangle is constructed to show the working of product markets in which demand and supply of various goods and services determine their prices. On the right hand side of this diagram, a rectangle representing the households has been made. These households which represent the whole population of the society serve two functions in an economy. Firstly, these households repre sent the consumers of the society who provide demand for goods and services. Secondly,

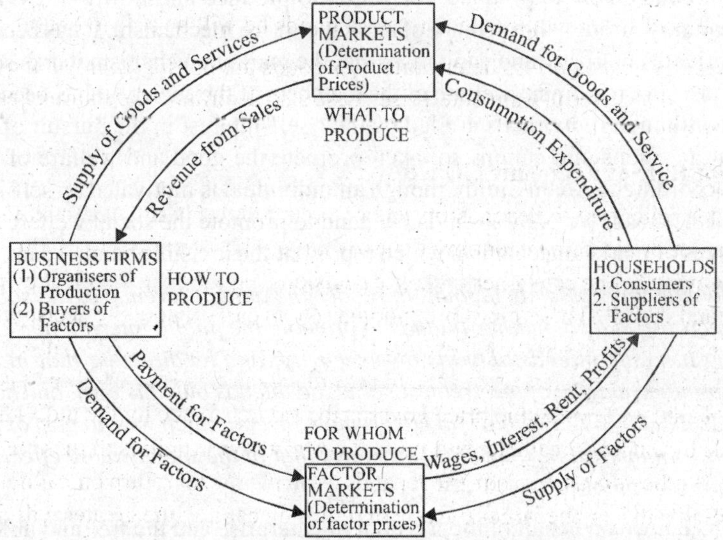

Fig. 5.3. *Functioning of a Free-Market Capitalist Economy*

these households are suppliers of the various resources or factors such as labour, land, capital and entrepreneurial ability. On the left hand side is shown a rectangle representing the businesses or productive firms which are organisers of production for the society as well as the sellers who supply goods and services in the product markets. For their function of organising production, business firms have to obtain the factors of production from the households through factor markets shown at the bottom of the diagram. In the factor markets demand for factors by the business firms and the supply of these factors by the households interact to determine their prices, such as wages of labour, rent of land, interest on capital, etc.

It is shown by arrow marks in the diagram who supply the goods and services and who demand them in the product markets. Likewise in the factor markets also, it is shown by arrow marks who supply and who demand the factors in the factor markets. Along with these supply and demand for goods and factors, money flows are also shown. Thus, with the determination of prices of goods in the product markets, the money will be spent by the households, which will become the revenue receipts of the business firms. It is transactions in these product markets where demand and supply interact to determine prices of goods and services that decide what goods shall be produced and in what quantities. In other words, it is the forces of demand and supply working in the product markets that decide the allocation of resources between the production of various goods.

Equally important in the working of a free market economy is factor markets through which the flow of money expenditure returns to the households in the form of wages, interest, rent and profits. It is here in the factor markets that the problem for whom to produce, that is, the distribution of income (and therefore the shares in the. total output) is determined. Lastly, there are the business firms themselves who organise the production work of the society by combining the factors. It is here that the problem of 'how to produce', that is, the methods or techniques of production to produce goods and services are decided.

It is thus evident from this flow diagram as to how a free-market capitalist economy works through market mechanism.

CRITICAL EVALUATION OF THE EFFICIENCY OF MARKET ECONOMY AND PRICE MECHANISM

Invisible Hand Theorem. We have studied above how a free-market capitalist economy decides what to produce, how to produce, for whom to produce and how to provide for economic growth of the country through the medium of market or price mechanism. It has been claimed by the supporters of private enterprise and capitalism that the market mechanism works so efficiently and effectively as to ensure maximum welfare of the members of the society. It has been asserted that in such a system, although individuals are led by their self-interest in the pursuit of their economic activities, their decisions and actions so taken promote the good and welfare of the society as a whole. Thus, according to Adam Smith, though an individual is motivated by self-interest and personal gain, he is led, as it were, by an invisible hand to promote the social welfare as well. It is the impersonal forces of market mechanism which represent the invisible hand. Adam Smith writes.

"*Every individual necessarily labours to render the annual revenue of the society as great as he can. He generally, indeed, neither intends to promote the public interest, nor knows how much he is promoting it ..... he intends only his own security; and by directing that industry in such a manner as its produce may be of the greatest value, he intends only his own, and he is in this, as in many other cases, led by an invisible hand to promote an end which was no part of his intention..... By pursuing his own interest he frequently promotes that of the society more effectively than when he really intends to promote it*"[4]

It has been claimed on behalf of the freedom of enterprise and the free and unfettered working of price mechanism that it is the one and only way in which people can achieve the maximum satisfaction of their wants with a minimum sacrifice. It is contended that we can always trust the free private enterprise and market mechanism to decide about what goods shall be produced, how they shall be produced, and how they shall be distributed among the members of the society, better than any other method. The case for freedom of enterprise and free functioning of market mechanism that they ensure maximum satisfaction of the people with minimum cost has been ably summed up by Professor Slicher in the following words:

"The reasoning in support of the belief that freedom of enterprise ensures the maximum of satisfaction at the minimum of cost is very simple. Each individual, it is said, is better able than anyone else to judge his own interests. If men are at liberty to spend their money as they choose, they will naturally purchase those things that will yield them most satisfaction. Consequently, the very commodities which give consumers the greatest pleasure are the most profitable for business enterprises to produce. Likewise, if men are free to use such methods of production as they wish, they will select those which involve the least cost per unit of output. With the goods which give the greatest gratification being made by the methods which are least costly, it follows, according to the theory, that there will be the maximum surplus of satisfaction over sacrifice."[5]

But in the modern times it is generally believed that free enterprise and unfettered working of price mechanism does not work so effectively and efficiently as to ensure maximum satisfaction of the society at the minimum social cost. The free and unfettered working of market system has led to so many evils that even in capitalist countries the governments regulate and control it through various measures such as physical controls, monetary and fiscal measures. We discuss below why and in what ways market mechanism fails to function effectively and efficiently so as to achieve maximum satisfaction of the people at the least social cost.

---

4. Adam Smith, *The Wealth of Nations* Book IV.
5. Sumner H. Slicher, Free Private Enterprise, published in ***Readings in Economics*, edited by Paul A. Samuelson, 6th edition, 1970.**

1. Free market system does not ensure maximum social satisfaction at minimum social cost. We have described above how a free private -enterprise economy decides about what and for whom goods are to be produced. Maximum social satisfaction can result only if goods produced go to those consumers who will derive the greatest satisfaction from them. We have further seen that in such a system goods go into the hands of those people who can offer best prices for them. In other words, goods are distributed according to the ability to pay of the people rather than their needs and desires.

Now, it has been rightly pointed out by critics that the distribution of goods in accordance with the ability to pay of the people does not ensure maximum satisfaction of the members of the society. The people who are willing and able to pay most for goods are not generally those who will derive greatest satisfaction from consuming them. In that case, it is possible to "increase the satisfaction of the society as a whole by getting goods distributed according to the needs or wants rather than ability to pay for them. Professor Slicher rightly remarks: "*We have no way of comparing the amount of pleasure which two persons derive from consuming an article. And yet it seems ridiculous to assert that ability to derive satisfaction from goods is proportionate to ability to pay for them.* Assume that *A* and *B* each wish a pair of shoes, A, who is well-to-do, is willing to pay $ 12; B, who is poor, will offer only $ 7. Obviously A will get the shoes. But because he is rich and well supplied with shoes, an additional pair is only a slight convenience to him. *B*, poor and scantily supplied, has urgent need for another pair. It seems clear that the sum total of satisfaction would be greater if *B* obtained the shoes and yet it seems equally clear that under freedom of enterprise they will go to A."[6]

The free market system may work in such a way that while poor people are unable to feed milk to their children, the rich people feed milk to their dogs. Thus, the market mechanism distributes goods in such a manner that milk or anything else goes to anyone, in whatever quantity he wants, who is able and willing to pay for it. Likewise, in a market system while luxuries are produced for the rich people who have got enough purchasing power or ability to pay for such goods, the necessities or wage-goods as they are called these days which are consumed most by the poor people are not produced in adequate quantities for the poor because they have not much ability to pay. Total satisfaction of the community can be increased by withdrawing productive resources from the production of luxuries and devoting them to the production of necessities. But this is not possible under free market mechanism where production is governed by market prices rather than basic human needs and wants. Market prices of goods do not accurately measure human needs and wants; they merely indicate the ability to pay for them.

Nor is the claim of the advocates of free-market mechanism that it distributes various jobs of producing goods among the members so as to result in a minimum sacrifice for each unit of output is valid. To achieve minimum sacrifice in the production of goods it is necessary that the jobs or tasks of producing goods must be assigned to those who can perform them with least sacrifice for each unit of output. But there is no guarantee that this will actually be the case in a free-market system. In a free-market system, a job will be assigned to those persons who will be prepared and willing to do a work at a less price than others. Now, the fact that an individual *A* is willing to do a work at a price less than that at which individual *B* is willing to do does not necessarily mean that, for individual *A*, the particular work is less onerous or unpleasant than *B* and sacrifice or cost of the society is less. It may be that individual A may have a more urgent need for money and is, therefore, willing to work at a less price in order to get it. To quote Professor Slicher, "*In face of the fact that ability to derive pleasure from goods does not appear to correspond to capacity to pay for them and that jobs are not necessarily given to the men who can do them with least sacrifice for each unit of*

---

6. Slicher, *op.cit.* p.34 (*italics added*).

product, how can it be asserted that industrial liberty results in a maximum of satisfaction over sacrifice?"[7]

It may, however, be pointed out that advocates of free enterprise and market mechanism try to answer the above criticism by pointing out that any interference in the working of market mechanism by distributing goods according to the needs rather than ability to pay and assigning various jobs to those who can do them with the least sacrifice might increase the satisfaction of the society and reduce its total sacrifice in the short run, but any such measure will be reducing the total satisfaction in the long run by adversely affecting the total production. People have incentive to produce more and work more for the purpose of earning more so that they have larger ability to pay and hence a larger share from the national output. If the national output is distributed according to the needs and not according to the ability to pay, then people will lose incentive to produce more which will result in reduction in total production. Fall in total production will mean fall in social welfare. Any attempt to distribute the 'Cake' according to the needs of the people will lead to the reduction in its size. They assert that the Marxian principle, "*from each according to his capacity, to each according to his needs*", will not work.

The argument regarding the role of incentives in promoting production' has a great force in it, but large inequalities in incomes and shares in national output as exist in the real-world market economies of the capitalist countries cannot be justified on the basis of incentives. No doubt some incentives are necessary to promote production, hard work and efficiency, but the prevailing much of inequalities in incomes in free market economies such as the US are not of functional type as they are not needed to serve any incentive to work hard, save, invest and produce more. They are the result of highly skewed ownership of capital assets and property and monopolistic exploitation by corporate business firm. To qute Nobel Laureate Joseph E. Stiglitz, " *Inequality is bad for economy, democracy and society. Much of the inequality in the US arises out of rent-seeking monopoly exploitative practices by banks and corporate exploitation of public resources*".[7a] There is nothing in the market mechanism that guarantees an equitable distribution of income in a society. It is also wrong on the part of advocates of market system to argue that capacity to derive satisfaction from the goods is proportionate to the ability to pay, *i.e.* incomes of the people.

2. Principle of consumer sovereignty is no longer valid. We have seen above that a distinguishing feature of a market system is that, in it, the consumer ultimately directs and controls the pattern of production or allocation of resources among the various goods. It is the desires of consumers that decide which goods shall be produced and in what quantities, and not the desires of society's sellers and producers. It is because of this that consumers are said to be sovereign or king in a free market economy. It is because of this sovereignty and the existence of competition among the sellers or producers to sell their products to the consumers that they are able to get the products at the lowest possible prices. While individual producers might wish to make large profits from the consumers but the consumers are protected from the exploitation of producers because of the prevalence of competition among the producers. Thus, the existence of competition and consumer sovereignty force down the price to the minimum possible level.

But the actual world has travelled far away from this ideal situation. The growth of giant corporations, big businesses and monopolies have radically changed the whole situation. Corporations or big businesses predominate the economies of the present-day capitalist countries and have greatly weakened the force of competition and restricted the-sovereignty of the consumers. The *giant corporations or big producers today do not merely "satisfy or fill" the wants of consumers, they themselves try to create these wants by massive expenditure an advertisement and propaganda to influence the public to buy the products they manufacture*. Thus while the

7. *Op. cit.*
7a. Joseph E. Stiglitz, '*Price of Inequality*'.

consumers still decide the allocation of resources among the goods to satisfy their "wants", these wants are themselves increasingly influenced by the producers. The advertisement expenditure by the producers or sellers has enormously increased in market economies. For example, in U.S.A. in 1968, $ 15 billion were spent on advertising their products by businesses. Thus expenditure on advertisement in U.S.A. to influence the consumers to buy their products is much greater than the government's expenditure on elementary and secondary education.

Most of the economists now agree that consumer sovereignty in a market economy is a myth. To quote Professor Galbraith, a famous American economist, "*the initiative in deciding what is to be produced comes not from the sovereign consumer who, through the market, issues the instructions that bend the productive mechanism to its own ultimate will. Rather it comes forward from the great producing organisation which reaches forward to control the markets that it is presumed to serve and, beyond, to bend customer to its needs.*"[8]

3. Failure of Market System to ensure economic stability and full employment. Another serious shortcoming of market mechanism is that it does not ensure a high and stable level of employment. Nor does it guarantee stability of the price level. As a result of the free working of market mechanism, there take place cyclical fluctuations in levels of economic activity with ups and downs in the levels of employment and prices. In these cyclical fluctuations, business booms are followed by business depression. These alternating periods of booms and depressions are generally called business or trade cycles in economics. Both depressions and booms (inflation) are bad and cause great suffering to the people. The depression causes huge unemployment and a lot of human suffering. The depression of nineteen thirties in the Western capitalist countries caused so much unemployment and human suffering that the revolutions were feared to take place there. Similarly, the period of inflation is also quite harmful. The consumers, especially the people having fixed incomes, are hit hard by inflation.

During the early thirties (1929-33) there was severe economic depression in the free-market capitalist economies which caused huge losses in output and employment. Such was severity of this depression that rate of unemployment in the US shot up to 25% of labour force causing a lot of human suffering. This led to the loss of faith in the smooth and efficient working of free-market capitalist system and many economists turned to socialism as preached by Karl Marx. However, British economist J.M. Keynes rescued capitalism by advocating intervention by the government through adoption of expansionary fiscal policy to get the economy out of depression.

That the free market system does not guarantee economic stability and full employment has been proved by the **recent global financial crisis (2007-09)** which started in the US and spread to other countries (including India) through global linkages of free trade and capital flows and caused global slowdown. The financial crisis started with the burst of sub-prime housing bubble as a result of manipulative practices of banks and other financial institutions causing widespread mortgage defaults and large losses to the banks and other financial institutions. Due to heavy losses causing lack of liquidity and risk of default banks stopped giving loans to the corporate sector for investment. The decline in investment resulted in recession in the American economy which through global linkages of foreign trade and capital flows affected other countries causing world-wide economic slowdown.

But the important point to note is that market system which was believed by the classical economists, monetarists led by Milton Friedman and new classical economists led by Robert Lucas to correct itself automatically and recover from the crisis failed to deliver. As a result, there were loud protests about the failure of free market capitalist system to ensure economic stability and full employment. Again it was Keynesian thought which came to the rescue of the US and other

8. J.K. Galbraith, *The New Industrial State*

countries which adopted Keynesian expansionary fiscal and monetary policies to give stimulus to the economies so as to get out of recessionary conditions. These stimulus packages worked successfully and in economies of the US, European economies, Japan, China and India economic recovery started and it was expected that these economies would return to growth path soon.

4. It does not ensure rapid growth in developing countries. An important problem in developing countries like India is to promote growth so as to raise the standards of living of the people and to eradicate poverty and unemployment. In these countries market mechanism and free private enterprise cannot guarantee rapid and sustained economic growth. There is nothing in the market mehanism that will direct adequate resources away from consumption to capital accumulation which is needed to achieve higher level of income and consumption in the future. Left to the market forces, these countries will remain caught up in the vicious circle of poverty. This is because an important factor that determines economic growth is capital accumulation which in turn depends upon the rate of saving and investment in the economy. In a free market system, the rate of investment in developing countries will remain very small because of the limited profit prospects due to the low incomes of the people of the develping countries. Moreover, *private enterprise guided by market forces will not invest adequately in economic infrastructure such as power, communication, roads, highways, ports, large irrigation works and transport system which are vital for growth of the economy*. Professor Galbraith aptly remarks, "*there is much that the market can usefully encourage and accomplish. But the market cannot reach forward to take great strides when these are called for. As it cannot put a man into space so it cannot bring quickly into existence a steel industry where there was little or no steel making capacity before. Nor can it quickly create an integrated industrial plant. Above all, no one can be certain that it will do so in countries where development has lagged and where there is not only a need for development but an urgent demand that it should occur promptly. To trust the market is to take an unacceptable risk that nothing, or too little, will happen.*"[9]

Economic growth in developing countries is also inhibited by lack of social infrastructure such as education and health care in which private sector guided as it is by market prices will not invest adequately in them because *they create positive* or *beneficial externalies* because market prices do not reflect their social benefits.

It is because of the ineffectiveness of free private enterprise guided by market mechanism to ensure economic growth that in developing countries planning has been adopted to initiate and accelerate the process of economic growth and the governments of these countries play a vital role in the development of their economies.

5. Decline of Competition and its Adverse Effect on the Working of the Price System. We saw above in the discussion of the working of private-enterprise market system that the existence of perfect competition among the producers or sellers of the products was essential for the achievement of production and sale of goods at minimum possible prices and the attainment of efficient allocation of resources. Thus competition is thought to be the controlling mechanism through which a free market system realises its ideal of maximum satisfaction of the people with the most efficient use of scarce resources. But in the real world, competition has greatly weakened. What we actually find is the world of oligopolies and monopolies so that industries are dominated by a small number of firms. Two factors have been responsible for the decline of competition. Firstly, producers in order to get rid of the irksome competition try to restrict competition through merger and by elimination of rivals through cut-throat competition and higher productive efficiency. Secondly, technological progress which has taken place has contributed a good deal to the decline of competition. Modern technology requires (1) the use of extremely large amount of capital equipment, (2) large markets, (3) complex and huge managerial set-up and (4) large and reliable sources of raw materials.

9. J.K. Galbraith, *op. cit.*

This requires operation of firms on a very large scale not only in the absolute sense but also in relation to the size of the market. Thus, the achievement of maximum productive efficiency through the employment of the modern technology often requires the existence of a few large firms rather than a large number of small firms.

As a result of the decline of competition and the emergence of oligopolies and monopolies, prices charged from the consumers are considerably higher than they would be under competitive conditions. The pricing power or market power enjoyed by the oligopolistic or monopolistic business firms goes against the public interest and violates the principle of consumer sovereignty. "*To the degree that competition declines, the price system will be weakened as a mechanism for efficiently allocating resources. Producers and resource suppliers will be less subject to the will of consumers, the sovereignty of producers and resource suppliers will then challenge and weaken the sovereignty of consumers.*"[10]

We thus see that with the decline of competition and the predominance of oligopolies and monopolies in the business world price system does not provide the goods most wanted by the society, that is, has become less efficient in allocating resources in accordance with the wishes of consumers.

6. **Concentration of Wealth and Income as a result of the Free Working of the Price System.** Another defect of the free working of the private-enterprise market system has been that the more efficient, more cunning entrepreneurs as well as those who enjoy large monopolistic power have been able to accumulate large amounts of wealth and property. These inequalities of wealth and property have further increased through time by the right of inheritance. The concentration of wealth and property in the hands of a few has led to the extremely large inequalities in money incomes in free market economies. Owing to the large inequalities of money incomes, the people differ in their abilities to express their wants in the market; the rich have more "rupee votes" than poor and are, accordingly, in a better position to get goods produced for them. We have already noted above the effect of the unequal distribution of income on the production of luxuries and necessities in a free market economy. In order to reduce inequity in income distribution the Government body.

Is there an Effective Countervailing Power ?

We have discussed above the various defects that result from the free working of market mechanism. There have been two forces at work to correct these defects of the market system. First, there has emerged what Professor Galbraith has called "*countervailing power*" to check the monopolistic power of the giant firms and its evils. By countervailing power, Galbraith means that the growth of giant and monopolistic firms on one side of the market has also led to the growth of powerful firms on the opposite side of the market. The decline of competition and emergence of strong economic power on each side of the market has, therefore, been neutralised to some extent by the growth of equally strong power on the opposite side of the market. This has prevented to some extent the evils of decline of competition and the growth of monopoly power in the free-market economy. "*To-day powerful corporate sellers often face equally powerful corporate buyers. The giant raw materials producer who faces little or no competition within his industry must sell to the giant chemical or other processing plant; the giant steel mill to the giant auto firm; the giant canner to the giant supermarket chain. Not least important, the large firm no longer bargains with the individual employee, but with the large and powerful unions.*"[11] However, in our view, the growth of such countervailing power is not fully effective in every market and in every situation and do not work as powerful restraining force on the unhindered exercise of monopoly power.

A second force, according to Galbraith, that has tended to maintain competition is the existence of competition among different products. "Even if all steel prices are kept at "administered" levels,

10. Robert, L. Heilbroner, *The Economic Problem*, First Edition, p.126.
11. J.K. Galbraith, *op, cit.*

steel as a whole must compete with aluminium. Nor does the competition ends here. What we find, indeed, is an immense chain of interproduct competition steel against aluminium, aluminium against glass, glass against plastics, plastics against wood, wood against concrete, concrete against steel. And this competition is without doubt effective." [12] How far such competition is effective in protecting consumers from exploitation by the monopolistic producers is doutful.

QUESTIONS FOR REVIEW

1. Explain the essential elements of capitalism, or a free-market economy.
2. Why government policy to make the distribution of income more equitable might lead to less efficiency.
3. Explain how information and incentives play a crucial role for the efficient working of market economies.
4. Examine the role of prices, property rights and profits for the efficient working of the market economy.
5. What is a free market economy? Explain its important features.
6. Explain the role of price mechanism in solving the basic economic problems in a free-market economy.
7. Explain the main characteristics of a free market economy. How does it solve its central economic problems ?
8. What is meant by '*invisible hand*' ? How does a free market economy function through it ?
9. What are the functions performed by price mechanism ? How does a free-market system determine the following :
   1. Rationing or distribution of goods 2. Allocation of resources 3. Choice of production techniques
10. Who controls the functioning of a free market economy ? Consumer or producers.
11. It is said in a free-market (capitalist) economy, consumer is a king who directs its functioning? Is this valid in free market economies of the world today ? Explain.
12. A free market economic system ensures maximum social welfare at minimum social cost. Do you agree? Discuss
13. What is meant by '*Countervailing power*'? How has it affected the working of a capitalist economy?
14. Explain the factors which led to the collapse of command economy system in Soviet Russia and other socialist countries.
15. Profit motive and private property rights provide incentives for rational individuals and firms to work hard and efficiently. Analyse. *(D.U. B.A (Hons) Economics 2009)*
16. Discuss the role and limitations of market in developing countries. Why is regulation of market in both developed and developing countries being emphasized ? What is even after the adoption of market system under the new economic policy of liberalisation, privatisation and globalisation, the role of Government in the developing countries is said to be of crucial importance in promoting economic growth ?

---

12. *Ibid.*

CHAPTER 6
ALTERNATIVE ECONOMIC SYSTEMS AND NEW MARKET-FRIENDLY ECONOMIC REFORMS

Introduction

Having discussed the working of a free-market economy and its failures we now turn to explain alternative economic systems, namely, socialism and mixed economy that have been tried. After revolution in 1917, Russia adopted socialism (or its extreme form, communism) on the basis of which the soviet economy was proposed to be governed. From the economic viewpoint, Soviet style socialism was based on centralised planning which decided resource allocation in the economy and determine distribution of incomes. Socialism prevailed not only in soviet Russia but also in some East European Countries such as Hungary, Poland, Yugoslavia, North Korea and China. Initially for about 50 years, socialism achieved a high rate of growth. But in the eighties its flaws came into lime light. Growth slowed down substantially, unemployment rose, essential goods were not available. As a result, in the eighties authoritarian socialism collapsed in Soviet Russia, China and East European Countries and gave way to free-market economy.

After independence India avoided both capitalism and socialism and adopted a middle path of mixed economy which was supposed to function in a planned democratic framework with consumers enjoying freedom to choose. At the end of nineteen eighties serious problems of falling economic growth and macroeconomic imbalances arose in India also which compelled us to introduce new economic reforms which are based on the adoption of the free-market economy and greater role to the private sector. In what follows we will first discuss both socialism and mixed economy and then critically examine market-friendly new economic reforms.

SOCIALISM OR COMMAND ECONOMY

In the previous chapter we have explained how the free-market economic system which is historically called *capitalism* works and what are its merits and drawbacks. We have also studied how at present in the market economies government plays a role in improving the functioning of market economic system. Now, an important question is if there is any altenative economic system that can solve the basic economic problem faced by the nations. In fact an alternative economic system known as authoritarian socialist system or *command economy* was adopted in erstwhile Soviet Russia, China, East European countries such as Poland, Czechoslovakia. In this authoritarian socialist system or command economy basic economic problem of what, how and for whom to produce etc. are resolved through a combination of state ownership of productive enterprises and centralised planning. It is government or any central authority set up by it that decides output targets for each public enterprise, allocates resources to them and fixes prices of various goods and services and incomes (wages, salaries) of various types of workers.

In a centrally planned socialist economy, there exists a central planning authority, which organises and regulates the various economic activities. Thus it is the central planning authority which determines what the various production units shall produce, what the various individuals shall obtain for consumption and as a result what shall be left for investment. Further, it decides what type of investment shall be made.

It should be realised that the organization of the various economic activities by one planning authority is full of administrative and economic difficulties. The authority is faced with the political and administrative problems of getting their decisions implemented. In other words, there are problems of governance, that is, putting the various decisions into effect. Moreover, the planning authority is faced with an overall economic problem, namely, how to use the limited productive resources for achieving the best possible results. The particulars purposes for which resources are to be used have to be decided. In other words, allocation of resources as between various kinds of consumer goods, and as between consumer goods and capital goods, and as between civilian goods and war goods, has to be decided. Taking of all these decisions is indeed a very difficult task. Besides, decisions have to be taken about the particular techniques with which various products are to be produced and about distributing goods among the people.

It may be noted that planning of actual production of various products is greatly difficult due to the fact that technical relations between different kinds of products are very much complicated. For example, to build ships it apparently seems that only steel and other materials which make up ships are required. But little more thinking will reveal that arrangements for the complicated process of production of steel and other materials have to be made before steel and other materials become available for use in ship building. Moreover, various types of machinery would have to be made for converting iron ore into steel as well as converting steel into ships. Further, the arrangements for coal, electricity and transport have to be made if the production of steel and ships is to become possible. Thus, technical relations between different kinds of output are so complicated that for carrying out the decision to produce more of one kind of product, adjustments on several other lines have to be made.

Collapse of the Command Economy or Authoritarian Socialist System

It is obvious from what has been said above that the planning of productvie activities by one central authority is a very difficult task. The planning authority in the centrally planned economies like those of erstwhile Soviet Russia and East European countries which used to plan production with the aid of several technical experts before the system broke down in the late eighties. In the late eighties the socialist countries, Soviet Russia and countries of Eastern Europe such as Poland, Czechoslovakia had to face severe economic problems which led to the collapse of Soviet-type authoritarian socialism or what is called command economy. *In its place the market system has been introduced and this is proclaimed as victory of capitalism over socialism.*

There is more than one reason for the collapse of the command economy in Soviet Russia and Eastern Europe. The important reason for the collapse of socialism and centralised planning *was* ***lack of efficiency in resource allocation.*** It was found that for a central planning authority consisting of bureaucrats it was difficult to make right decisions to allocate scarce resources according to the wants and preferences of the people. As result, shortage in some goods and surplus in others emerged. These could not be easily corrected due to corrupt, inefficient and unresponsive government officials. This caused a lot of wastage of national resources. The most glaring example of inefficiency in allocation of resources in Soviet Russia and the command economies was the emergence of ***acute scarcity of essential consumer goods.*** This led to *long-queues* of the people at the consumer stores to get these goods.

This acute scarcity of consumer goods led to the lack of faith in socialism to deliver the goods. Indeed, it was said that Soviet-type authoritarian socialism promised bread at the expense of liberty of the people. But in actual practice people got neither bread nor liberty. Since by the late nineteen eighties the then Soviet President Mickhail Gorbachev had introduced some freedom for the people, the wide expression of resentment about the scarcity of consumer goods could not be suppressed. This led to the collapse of authoritarian socialism and introduction of reforms aimed at introduction of private enterprise and the market system.

The other important reason for the failure of centralised planning was that the **managers of public enterprises** ***lacked incentives to improve productivity and efficiency.*** This was due to the absence of profit motive on the part of managers of public enterprises. This caused inefficiency in the use and allocatiion of scarce resources.

The most important economic problem faced by these socialist countries was ***slowdown in economic growth*** in these countries. In Soviet Russia the growth rate which in the post-war period averaged about 7 per cent in 1950s and about 5 per cent in 1960s slipped into 3 per cent range during the 1970s and was nearly zero in the 1980s. Similar experience of slowdown in economic growth rate was observed in other socialist countries of Eastern Europe. Now, when growth rate in them was higher, more employment opportunities were increasing and more goods were forthcoming which enabled people to improve their levels of living. However, when there was sharp slowdown in economic growth, to satisfy the ever-rising wants of the people for goods became difficult and a strong need was felt to make a switch over to the market system to speed up the rate of economic growth.

Lastly, *problems of centralised planning with its inflexibility and inefficiency* have been present throughout in the post-revolution period in Soviet Russia. Lacking profit-motive the managers of productive enterprises do not have sufficient incentives to produce the right type of goods in the most efficient way. This causes inefficiency in the use and allocation of resources which accounted for *low productivity and efficiency* in the socialist countries. Owing to lack of incentives managers of productive enterprises were more concerned with fulfilling the quotas assigned to them (which they succeeded in achieving them by deliberately setting them at lower levels) rather than improving efficiency. But still deeper problem posed by the absence of profit motive was *managers of state enterprises lacked incentives to introduce innovations and undertake risks* which caused inefficiency and slow economic growth and ultimately stagnation.

To conclude, the above problems led to the downfall of authoritarian socialism or command economy system in Soviet Russia and other socialist countries. This led to the process of liberalisation of Soviet Russia and other socialist countries. It is because of these problems of economic inefficiency and slowdown in economic growth that even China and India introduced economic reforms which lay stress on privatisation and greater role of market mechanism for solving the economic problems. It may be noted here tha India has adopted the path of a mixed economy. In India's mixed economy both private sector and economic planning by the Government play roles in the working of the Indian economy.

MIXED ECONOMIC SYSTEM

In the real word today a pure free-market economy and pure command economy or a centrally planned economic system is not found. Almost all economies have now become mixed economic system in which government plays an important role in allocation of resources and distribution of income. Thus mixed economy or mixed economic system refers to an economic system in which both free market and Government have significant roles in the working of the economy. In a mixed economy elements of both free market system and control or regulation by the Government are present. The proportion of free market working and Government regulation varies from country to country.

Many economies of the present-day world are examples of mixed economy. Mixed economy functions through private enterprise as well as the Government. The Government interferes with or regulates the private enterprise in various ways. It has now been realised that the free and unfettered functioning of the private enterprise gives rise to many evils. As a result of free working of the private enterprise, there are violent fluctuations in economic activities, sometimes the conditions of depression and unemployment are created and sometimes the conditions of boom and inflation emerge. Thus a free-market economy suffers from what are called business cycles, with all their consequent evils. Besides, as a result of free functioning of the private enterprise and price mechanism, extreme inequalities of income and wealth are produced. The following of *'Laissez Fair'* policy by the Government, weaker sections of the society are not protected. On the other hand, the command economic system in which resource allocation and income distribution is decided through centralised planning collapsed due to various deficiencies and failures as explained above. Therefore, in both Russia and China free-market economic system along with some government control has been adopted.

In has also been realised that in a developing country like India, desired rate of economic growth cannot be achieved under free private enterprise. Therefore, in order to avoid the above-mentioned evils of the free private enterprise and free functioning of the market mechanism and to achieve the desired rate of economic growth the Government takes an active part in the functioning of the economic system in most economies of the world. Today all the capitalist economies have become mixed form of economies, because in all of them economic role of the Government has greatly increased. '*Laissez Fair*' policy advocated by Adam Smith and other classical economists has now been given up because of its several shortcomings and evils. Therefore, the economies of the United States of America and Britain have also become mixed systems. Paul Samuelson and A.H. Hansen, eminent American economists, have called the economies of America, Britain and France as '*Mixed Capitalist System*' or '*Mixed Enterprise System*', because in them the Government now interferes in the economic activities and takes active part in the functioning of the economic system and regulates and controls the private enterprise by various methods.

Two Forms of Mixed Economic Systems

It is worth noting that mixed economies can be classified into two forms. One form of mixed economy is that in which means of production are in the ownership of private sector and the Government regulates and controls the activities of private enterprise through direct controls (such as price control, licensing system, control over imports, etc.) as well as through monetary and fiscal policies. In such a type of economy, the government does not take over the means of production, and if it does, it does so relatively on a small scale. That is why such a type of 'mixed system' has been called *Mixed Capitalist System* because such an economic system is basically capitalist and the Government regulates and controls the economic activities through various types of direct controls and various measures of monetary and fiscal policies so that the various evils of the free working of the private enterprise and the price mechanism are avoided and the economic system is directed towards the desired goals. In such a type of 'mixed economy,' Government itself does not undertake the work of production on a large scale. Government's production work is merely confined to the production of equipments and materials for the army and the working of the public utility services. Such a type of mixed economic system is also called *controlled capitalism*.

Indian Economy as a Mixed Economic System

The second form of a mixed economy is that in which the Government not only regulates and controls the private enterprise through various types of direct controls and appropriate monetary and fiscal policies, *it also directly participates in the production of various goods and services*. In such a type of mixed economy, various basic industries and infrastructure industries are in the ownership of the public sector and it is the government which organises and runs them. The remaining industries are in the ownership of private enterprise and it is the private enterprise which is assigned the task of production in them. But it is worth remembering that the government regulates and controls the private enterprise in such industries also through direct control and appropriate monetary and fiscal measures.

The economies of the United States of America and Britain have also become mixed economies. But, the nature of mixed economy of India is quite different from them, because in the mixed economy of India the public enterprise takes more active, more important and more extensive part in the working and growth of the economy. Whereas the mixed economies of the U.S.A. and England are biased towards capitalism, **the mixed economy of India is biased towards socialism.**

Functioning of a Mixed Economy

A mixed economy functions through both price mechanism and planning by the Government. So far as the industries in the public sector are concerned the price, output and investment decisions are taken by the government or the authorities appointed by the government according to the strategy and policy frame of the development plans. But the private sector of the mixed economy is governed and regulated by the price and market mechanism and therefore in regard to the industries in the private sectors, the decisions regarding price, output and investment are taken by the private entrepreneurs or the industrialists with a view to making profits and these decisions are mainly based on price mechanism. The private sector in the mixed economy is, however, influenced, regulated and controlled by the government through monetary and fiscal measures as well as through direct or physical controls.

Prior to 1991 in India, the government had a 'licensing system' according to which to start and establish factories in certain industries, the government's permission or licence was necessary. However, under the economic reforms initiated since 1991 in India, licensing and permit system has been done away with and private sector has been given a lot of freedom for deciding about production and expansion in their enterprises. Even foreign investment by multinational companies have been allowed to make investment in India and repatriate the profits to their home states. However the government also regulates and controls the investment and production in the private sector through appropriate monetary and fiscal measures. By providing concessions in taxation, and by making available cheap credit facilities, the government provides incentives to private entrepreneurs for investment in the desired lines of production decided in development plans.

Role of Government in a Mixed Economic Systems

As noted above, in the mixed economic system the Government plays a significant role in allocation of scarce resources and distribution of income. However, despite the important role of Government, the people and private enterprises are free to make economic transactions. They voluntarily decide whether or not to transact, have the right to buy and sell what they want. Workers are free to accept or refuse any work they do not want to do, free to move to different places for employment of their choice. *The right to own property and freedom of contract are maintained by the Government*. The Government makes laws which provide right to ownership of property and freedom of contract and courts are set up by it to enforce these laws. Besides, the Government maintains law and order to protect life and liberty of the people and to enforce property rights of the people. It also makes arrangements for defence of the country against foreign aggression.

Besides the above basic functions, Government intervenes in the economy to correct what are called ***market failures.*** These are the situations in which free market does not work efficiently. For example, natural resources such as forests, mines, common pastures tend to be overexploited resulting in their destruction under free market conditions. Further, some goods, called *public goods* such as defence, law and order are not produced at all by private enterprises which are driven by profit motive. This is because once produced the people who do not even pay for them cannot be prevented from using them.

Moreover, private enterprises while producing goods often impose costs that are called ***detrimental externalities*** on others by their economic activities. For example, the production of goods in factories *pollute air and water* surrounding them. This *environment pollution* causes a lot of harm to the people but the private enterprises do not have to pay for the harms they do to others. Nor do they take into account these externalities into account while making their investment decisions. As a result, there is overproduction of such goods whose production pollute environment and impose costs on others and this causes misallocation of resources. The Government can prevent them by imposing taxes on private enterprises which pollute environment.

Above all, the Government in modern mixed economic systems takes fiscal and monetary policies to *stabilise the economy* against fluctuations in national income, employment and prices. Recession causes huge unemployment which deprives people of their livelihood. On the other hand when there is inflation, cost of living of the people rises and as result there is a lot of human suffering. Inflation is a tax that hurts the poor people most. Following J.M. Keynes the Government adopts for discretionary fiscal and monetary policies to lift the economy out of recession. For example, recently in 2007-09 when due to global financial crisis originated in the US due to bursting of sub-prime housing loan bubble which caused global recession and meltdown, the Governments in the US, Britain, Japan, France and India too increased public expenditure and cut taxes to revive their economies. In the US and other free market economies the Government even helped private banks with funds to bail them out of the turmoil. In India the Government borrowed heavily in 2008-09 and 2009-10 to increase its expenditure and also to cut taxes to prevent slowdown of the Indian economy due to the impact of global financial crisis. Similarly, when there is inflation the Central Bank of a country adopts tight monetary policy and contractionary fiscal policy to control rising prices.

Last but not the least, it is a vital function of the modern Government to promote economic growth. Economic growth requires capital accumulation, progress in technology and investment in social sectors such as education and health. Besides, in developing countries like India the Government has to adopt measures to eradicate poverty that prevails on a large scale in these countries. For example, the Indian Government has started Mahatma Gandhi national rural employment guarantee scheme (MNREGS) under which it provides guaranteed employment to the poor households. Further, to help the poor the Government in India has begun Public Distribution System under which it provides subsidised foodgrains to the poor households. Just as there are *market failures*, there are *Government failures too*. Mixed economy concept has been adopted a middle path between a purely free-market economy and purely command economy to avoid both market failures and government failures.

NEW MARKET-FRIENDLY ECONOMIC REFORMS IN DEVELOPING COUNTRIES SINCE 1980

Since 1980s there has been a *neoclassical counter revolution* in economic policy in both the developed countries such as United States, Britain, Canada, West Germany and developing countries of Latin America and Asian Countries such as India, Pakistan, Bangladesh. Under this there has been a change from public ownership of enterprises in various sectors of the economy to dismanting of public ownership, and also to the dilution of the role of government and public sector in the economy. As a result, market economy has been allowed to work freely without much controls by government over it. Besides, under this new policy framework, *supply-side macroeconomic policies* have been given dominant role in promoting economic growth in place of *demand-management policies* adopted under the influence of J.M. Keynes.

Many developing countries (including India) after independence did not completely do away with market system of production, exchange and distribution by private sector on the basis of profit motive. In fact, India and also some other developing countries adopted '*mixed economy model*' where both the public and private sectors were allowed to work and grow in their respective fields. In India, Industrial Policy Resolution 1956 demarcated the respective fields in which the public and private sectors were conceived to work and grow with crucial sectors such as basic heavy industries, power generation, making arms and ammunition, atomic energy having been reserved for the public sector. The almost all consumer goods industries were left to the private sector for production, exchange and distribution on the basis of free play of market forces. However, the role of centralised planning and public sector was given a dominant role in providing or producing goods, especially in which private sector was not attracted to invest. In India for almost four decades from 1950 to 1990 this mixed economy system of coexistence of public and private sectors *with public sector occupying commodity heights of the economy prevailed.*

However, the actual experience with the mixed economy model though seemed to work well for some time, it had its shortcomings too. Economic growth rate in India in the first four five year plans (1951-1974) achieved was on an average 3.5 per cent per annum which was hardly sufficient to make dent into the problems of poverty and unemployment in view of rapid population growth of around 2% per annum and requirement of 1% of GDP for increase in investment per year in the economy. As a result, the magnitudes of poverty and unemployment remained very high. Given a very modest poverty line (₹ 49.1 per capita per month for rural India and ₹ 56.6 per capita per month at 1973-74 prices), 54.9 per cent of population was found to be living below the poverty line in 1973 which fell to 51.36 per cent of population in 1977-78 and to around 40 per cent in 1983 for All India (both rural and urban areas put together). Likewise, in India in 1983 a high 9 per cent of labour force was found to be unemployed on daily status basis.

However, as a result of relaxation of certain industrial controls over the private sector and adoption of some measures to promote exports during the eighties and pick-up in public sector investment in the later part of the eighties, the growth rate of GDP rose to 5.6 per cent per annum during the highties. However, the period of eighties in India was characterised by large-scale borrowing from abroad which led to the large increase in India's foreign debt and its annual service charges. This ultimately resulted in balance of payments crisis in 1990-91 and sharp rise in inflation rate in India. Thus in the overall period of four decade (1951-91) reliance on centralised planning and important role given to the public sector for accelerating economic growth seemed to be not successful. It was realised that as there are market failures, there are government failures too. Thus the apparent failures of economic planning and the macroeconomic imbalances as reflected in balance of payments crisis on the one hand and high inflation on the other in India and other developing countries, the role of government and planning in economic growth began to be called into question. This called for revision of the role of government and planning in economic development.

Why Market-Friendly New Economic Reforms were Adopted ?

Due to failures of Government in the late eighties it was felt that importance given to the public sector in the strategy of industrial development and stiff controls over the working and expansion of the private sector were obstructing economic growth and *promoting inefficiency.* Further, in 1991, India experienced serious problems of a *high rate of inflation* on the one hand and *huge deficit in the balance of payments* on the other. To overcome these problems some economists such as I.M.D. Little, Jagdish Bhagwati, Bela Balassa who had been advisors of World Bank and IMF argued for the adoption of the policy of economic liberalisation by India and other developing countries to promote growth, check inflation and solve the problem of balance of payments. They advocated that *free markets and greater role of private sector (including foreign investors) would ensure efficiency by encouraging competition.*

As explained above, the experiment of a mixed economy as described in the Industrial Policy Resolution of 1956 and later amendments made in it wherein public sector was given a prominent role in industrial development of the Indian economy seemed to be a success in the beginning. It was through public sector investment a lot of infrastructure such as irrigation, transport, power was developed. Many basic and basic heavy industries such as steel, fertilizers, machine-making industries were built by the public sector. But during the eighties several shortcomings of the working of public sector were observed. First, the *public sector which was expected to generate adequate resources* for the growth of the economy not only failed to do so but *in fact was incurring huge losses* which raised the expenditure of the Government. The losses of the public sector were said to be due to the inefficiency of the public sector enterprises. Secondly, the *problem of macroeconomic imbalances,* both in the internal and external sectors, emerged and assumed serious proportions in 1990-91. The huge budget deficits of the Government and expansion in money supply led to the serious problem of inflation. On the external front, higher commercial borrowing from abroad at higher rates of interest resulted in the serious problem of persistent deficit in the balance of payments. This caused a *sharp decline in the foreign exchange reserves*. The foreign exchange reserves fell to such a meagre amount that it could meet the payments for imports only for 15 days. This compelled the Government to approach IMF, and World Bank for necessary help to tide over the foreign exchange crisis. IMF and World Bank agreed to help only if policy of economic liberalisation was adopted and accordingly greater role be assigned to the private sector in boosting industrial investment and production in a competitive environment. *It was believed that market competition would ensure efficiency and stimulate economic growth.* The objective of new industrial policy based on liberalisation, privatisation and globalisation was to improve the efficiency of the economic system by eliminating the regulatory mechanism that involved various licenses and permits which reduced competition in the market and planning in the late eighties switched back to the market system which led to the policy of liberalisation and privatization in many developing countries under the guidance and direction of World Bank and IMF. Dr. C. Rangarajan, Chairman of the Advisory Council to the Prime Minister of India writes, "*The thrust of the new economic policy was towards creating competitive environment in the economy as a means to improving the productivity and efficiency of the system. This is to be achieved by removing the barriers to entry and restrictions on growth of the firm. While the industrial policy seeks to bring about a greater competitive environment domestically, the trade policy seeks to improve international competitiveness subject to the protection offerred by tariffs which are coming down.*"[13]

We explain below these structural adjustment reforms, with special reference to India. After independence, India avoided the extremes of both capitalism and socialism and opted for a mixed economy where planning and the public sector played an important role in the economic development of the country. The experiment of a mixed economy as evolved in India seemed to be a success in the beginning but during the seventies and eighties several shortcomings of its working had been noticed.

Inefficient Working of Public Enterprises. First, the public sector which was expected to generate adequate resources for the growth of the economy not only failed to do so but in fact was incurring huge losses which raised the expenditure of the Government. The losses of the public sector were said to be due to the *inefficiency in the working of public enterprises*. Secondly, the problem of *macroeconomic imbalances*, both in the internal and external sectors, emerged and assumed serious proportions in 1990-91. The huge deficits in the successive budgets of the government due to internal imbalance of Government expenditure and revenue led to the creation of more money supply which created the serious problem of rising prices, so much so that rate of inflation went up to about 17 per cent per annum during August 1991. This compelled the newly elected Congress government to reduce Government expenditure and fiscal deficit for stabilising prices.

Balance of Payments Crisis. In the external sector, *the huge deficits in the balance of payments due to the rising imports and sluggish exports persisted for a long time and, to meet this deficit, the Government resorted to commercial borrowing from abroad at higher market rates of interest*. As a result of persistent deficits on the current account, the foreign exchange reserves declined to a very small sum in June 1991 which could last for payments for necessary imports only for about few weeks. This compelled the Government to approach IMF (International Monetary Fund) for loans to make necessary payments and enhance the foreign exchange reserves.

Thirdly, though the annual growth of national income *during the eighties* went up to over 5 per cent and of the industrial sector to 8 per cent, which was considered to be a good performance, but due to macro-economic imbalances which emerged in the economy they could no longer be sustained any more. In the external sector, the situation became so worse in 1991 that India came to the brink of default. To avoid the default and to win over the confidence of international business

---

13. C.N. Rangarajan, Growth and Challenges, *Survey of Indian Industry* 2011, The Hindu, pp. 9-10.

community, the Government had to sell a part of its gold reserves and a certain amount of gold was even pledged with Bank of England to obtain the foreign exchange reserves to meet its obligations. Further, it had to approach the IMF for loans to tide over the foreign exchange crisis.

Excessive Government Controls over Private Sector. Besides, excessive Government regulation and control over the private sector proved to be counter-productive. The following drawbacks of excessive regulation of the private sector were emphasised and case for liberalisation of private sector was built up, especially by Jagdish Bhagwati and T.N. Srinivasan, the two economists associated with World Bank and International Monetary Fund. The following arguments were given in favour of dereguation of the private sector and assigning to it a greater role in economic growth of the Indian economy.

1. The industrial licensing and controls had degenerated into arbitrary bureaucratic controls on the allocation of resources in competing industries. The licenses were issued to make investment in those industries which bureaucrats chose in tune with the policies they administered. This licensing system replaced the efficient market system of resource allocation by personal system of resource allocation. Thus excessive regulation of the private sector, according to the advocates of economic reforms, had resulted in the sub-optimal resource allocation in industries. Hence, there was a need for liberalisation.

2. The Industrial licensing system had stiffled private initiative and enterprise because this system had left no scope for private initiatives in investment planning and investment decisions. In fact, the industrial licensing system did not allow the competitive economic environment to operate. As a result of this, the entrepreneurs had become attuned to secure *monopoly rent*, rather than to earn profits through enterprise and skills. Jagdish Bhagwati and T.N. Srinivasan identified

licensing and control regime as the causative factor responsible for low productivity and high capital-output ratio. Hence, industrial liberalisation became an imperative condition for the growth of forces of competition to ensure high efficiency and productivity in Indian industries.

3. Under the regime of licensing, the industrial units which tried to increase output by making full utilisation of *installed capacity*, were penalised on the ground that their production exceeded the *licensed capacity* even if goods produced were much needed and were in short supply. Hence, industrial liberalisation became essential from the point of view of promoting industrial growth by the creation of additional productive capacity and its optimal utilisation.

4. The industrial licensing policy had failed to achieve its objectives of balanced regional industrial development and prevention of concentration of economic power. In fact, during licensing regime, the regional industrial imbalances and concentration of economic power had got intensified. Hence, there was a strong case for scrapping licensing system and switching over to market system.

WASHINGTON CONSENSUS, DEVELOPMENT POLICY AND STRUCTURAL ADJUSTMENT ECONOMIC REFORMS

Before explaining the economic reforms initiated in 1991 under the pressure of IMF and World Bank, it may be mentioned that these reforms mainly constituted what is now labelled as *Washington Consensus*. This consensus was formulated by John Williamson, with the other officials of World Bank, IMF and key US government agencies. This consensus contains 10 elements of development policy which were suggested to promote economic growth in the developing countries and also help them solve their problems of indebtedness, balance of payments difficulties and high rate of inflation. It is noteworthy that this Washington Consensus followed a free market approach to development and, contrary to the views of many development economists, it did not emphasise elimination of poverty and reducing inequalities to achieve real development, as it is now widely understood. The Washington Consensus and fiscal and structural reforms it envisages views that poverty will be automatically removed if rapid economic growth is achieved. Its message is 'take care of growth, poverty will take care of itself'.

Let us list below the various elements of Washington Consensus.

1. **Fiscal Adjustment.** This means that developing countries should take steps to reduce fiscal deficit through curtailing Government expenditure by drastically reducing explicit and implicit subsidies provided by the Government of developing countries.

2. **Tax Reforms.** It was suggested that tax rates should be cut substantially to promote saving and private investment. This will promote investment and ensure a higher rate of economic growth. This was in line with supply-side economics. In fact, Jagdish Bhagwati and T.N. Srinivasan invoked ***Laffer Curve*** Concept of supply-side economics to argue that reduction in rates of taxes would cause not only greater private saving and investment but will lead to greater revenue for the government.

Besides, it was suggested to broaden the tax base by withdrawing exemptions and plugging the loopholes in taxes.

3. **Deregulation.** This was most significant policy measure under which it was recommended that industrial licensing controls be abolished but also such measures as Monopolistic and Restrictive Trade Practices Commission (MRTPC) and FERA (Foreign Exchange Regulation Act) be done away with so that private sector should grow without any obstructions.

4. **Privatisation.** This is another significant measure of development policy under which it was proposed that there should be disinvestment of public sector enterprises and accordingly either they should be sold outrightly to the private sector or Government stake should be reduced and its shares sold or transferred to private enterprises.

5. **Trade Liberalisation.** Under this it was suggested that tariffs on imports should be drastically reduced *to promote free trade*. Besides, all quantitative restrictions on imports were also to be eliminated to permit free trade.

6. **Competitive Exchange Rate.** Under this it was recommended that developing countries like India should devalue their over-valued currencies and ultimately adopt flexible exchange rate system. Besides, it was suggested to make the currency convertible so that obstacles to growth of free trade and capital mobility be removed.

7. **Removal of Barriers to Foreign Investment.** It was stressed that economic growth in developing countries could be accelerated through larger foreign direct investment (FDI). Therefore, all barriers put up by developing countries should be eliminated to attract foreign investment in their countries. To facilitate foreign investment it was also suggested to adopt *Convertivibility of currency on current account as well as on capital account*.

8. **Financial Reforms.** They involve reforms in the banking and insurance system and also in capital market.

9. **Protection of Property Rights.** According to this, suitable legislative measures should be taken to protect property rights. Besides, labour law should be amended so that it becomes easy for *private enterprise to enter and exit* the industries. In this, *freedom to exit* was emphasised and it was recommended that labour laws be made flexible so that it should be easy to retrench workers.

10. **Redirection of Public Sector Investment.** Lastly, it was emphasised that public sector investment should be redirected towards education, health and infrastructure only and also leave these and other fields open to private sector operation.

Various Reforms Under New Market-Friendly Economic Policy : Liberalisation, Privatisation and Globalisation

However, to evolve a long-term solution to promote price stability, to bring about equilibrium in balance of payments and, above all, to ensure higher rate of economic growth, the newly elected Congress Government with Dr. Manmohan Singh as Finance Minister adopted in 1991 what is popularly called *New Economic Policy* on the advice of IMF and World Bank. According to this policy, the Government was to prune down its expenditure so as to *recue budget deficits for achieving price stability. But more important element of new economic policy is the adoption of what are called Structural Adjustment Reforms* which sought to change the nature of Indian economic system by ultimately establishing *a free market economy*. Under this structural adjustment programme, the role of public sector in economic development had been diluted and that of private sector enhanced and expanded.

It may be noted that the policy of free-market economy also got strong stimulus due to the collapse of socialist system in Soviet Russia and other centrally planned socialist economies in the Eastern Europe. Accordingly, under the new economic policy, the idea of the predominant role of the public sector was abandoned and the private sector was given a greater role in promoting economic growth through competition and efficiency. Instead of being directed by the planning and licencing, the private sector would now be governed by the market forces, that is, by the free play of demand and supply of commodities and factors. We describe below the new economic reforms undertaken in India since 1991 under the *New Economic Policy or Structural Adjustment Programme.*

De-reservation of Industries of the Public Sector. The new industrial policy 1991 has been adopted under which far-reaching structural reforms have been initiated to lift excess direct controls and regultions on industries and to ensure a free-market oriented economic system. The list of industries reserved for the public sector has been pruned. Now, only 6 industries remain reserved for the public sector. Among the industries reserved earlier for the public sector were many core industries like iron and steel, electricity, air transport, ship building, heavy machinery industries such as heavy chemical plants and telecommunication cables and instruments. The new industrial policy of 1991 threw open all these industries for the private sector for investment and growth. Thus the new policy indicates the Government's intention to invite a greater degree of participation by the private sector in important areas of the economy. The six industries which continue to be reserved for the public sector are in areas where security and strategic considerations predominate. According to the new policy, the resources in the public sector will now be used for the development of strategic, high-technology industries and essential infrastructure areas and for social sectors such as education, public health and poverty alleviation programmes.

Liberalisation: Abolition of Industrial Licensing System. Until 1991 the Indian industrial sector had functioned under a system of tight controls and regulations represented by industrial licencing which meant to allocate the scarce resources towards building the industrial base of the economy. By the year 1991 the Indian industrial economy had a quite wide and diversified base, the new policy abolished all industrial licencing irrespective of the level of investment except for 15 industries for which licence was still required. These industries are those which are essential for security and safety purposes and for protection of environment. For granting of licence for even these 15 industries procedure has been greatly simplified. For getting licences only certain locational guidelines are to be fulfilled so that polluting industries should not cluster around the major urban centres. Besides, restrictions by Monopolistic and Restrictive Act (MRTPA) for expansion of big firms were also relaxed.

Privatisation of Public Sector Enterprises. An important aspect of new industrial policy of the Government is that it should not operate commercial enterprises. With that end in view the Government decided to disinvest the public enterprises. The Government can sell its enterprises completely to the private sector or disinvest a part of its equity capital held by it to the private sector companies or in the open market. Therefore *this policy of public sector disinvestment has also been called the policy of privatisation.* Through disinvestment or privatisation, the Government can mop up a good amount of resources which can be used for various purposes. The released resources can be used to restructure and strengthen the public sector enterprises which are potentially viable. These resources can also be used to pay back a part of public debt. These resources can also be used to finance budget deficits.

What are the reasons for the policy of privatisation or public sector disinvestment. First, resources available with the Government are scarce. The Government needs resources to reduce its budget deficit. The Government urgently requires resources to make investment in infrastructure, education, public health and for poverty alleviation programmes. Resources released through disinvestment can be used for investment in these crucial sectors. Second, a good number of existing public enterprises are working inefficiently and incurring huge losses.

Accordingly, a part of the economic reforms policy, the Government started reforms in public sector enterprises. The main elements of Government policy towards Public Sector Enterprises (PSU) are:

(1) Disinvestment of Government equity in all *non-strategic* Public Sector Undertakings (PSU) to 26 per cent or lower if necessary.

(2) Those public sector enterprises which are potentially viable have to be restructured and revived.

(3) Those Public Sector Undertakings (PSU) which cannot be revived would be closed down.

Globalisation

The following measures for globalisation of the Indian economy were taken.

Welcoming Private Foreign Investment and Foreign Technology . Till 1991, foreign investment and import of foreign technology was regulated tightly in India. In the case of foreign technology agreements sought by Indian firms as well as foreign investment, it was necessary to obtain specific prior approval from the government for each project. This involved delays and hampered business decision making in the import of technology by Indian firms. Under the new economic policy for a selected list of high technology and high investment priority industries, firms receive *automatic approval* to make foreign technology agreements within certain guidelines. This policy measure is expected to remove the delay and uncertainty which earlier clouded the relationships between Indian and foreign firms.

Further, the government has *liberalised its policy regarding foreign investment*. To attract private foreign investment,it has been decided to grant *automatic permission to private*

foreign investors to invest up to 51 per cent of the total equity shares in 34 high priority industries if certain norms are fulfilled. This facility will be available to those firms which are able to finance their capital equipment imports through their foreign equity. This is a major departure from the previous policies which required case-by-case approval of foreign investment normally limited to 40 per cent equity participation. The priority sector includes power generation and petroleum refining. Further, the government has given a guarantee of 16 per cent return on foreign investment in priority sectors. There is also proposal to allow automatic clearance for foreign *financial* and technical collaboration with Indian firms.

Trade Liberalisation. In a bid to open up the economy, under the new economic policy *quantitiave restrictions*, that is, import licencing for imports of goods have been removed. Further, to promote competitiveness, efficiency and globalisation of the Indian economy import duties have been reduced to the 20 per cent (excluding agricultural and dairy products) with effect from Jan. 9, 2004. The new thinking is that with the cheapening of imported goods, the Indian firms will try to increase their efficiency and reduce costs so that their products can compete with the foreign products. In this way they will be able to expand their exports.

Currency Convertibility and Floating of Indian Rupee. Another major step taken towards libralisation of the Indian economy has been to make the Indian rupee fully convertible on current account since March 1993. This implies that for the purpose of foreign trade and travel you can convert the rupees into dollars and dollars into rupees in the foreign exchange market at the market determined exchange rate. That is, the foreign exchange rate of rupee is now not fixed but liable to change as demand for and supply of foreign exchange change. In July 1991, the Indian rupee was devalued by about 20 per cent. But now with market-determined exchange rate, the Indian rupee can depreciate or appreciate depending upon demand and supply conditions.

A CRITICAL EVALUATION OF MARKET-FRIENDLY NEW ECONOMIC REFORMS

It is evident from the reforms introduced in the Indian economy that from a planned economy it has moved towards a free-market economy. Though we still have mixed economy with both the public and private sectors coexisting but the role of private sector which is governed by market forces has been greatly increased and that of the public sector greatly diluted. So we now have a mixed economy with greater orientation towards a free market and private sector.

More than two decades have passed when we initiated economic reforms in 1991 laying greater emphasis on liberalisation and privatisation. Now, the pertinent question is whether these economic reforms have ensured higher and sustained economic growth which the supporters of these reforms argued that they would, whether these reforms have led to a higher growth rate and to the greater reduction of poverty and unemployment which was expected of them.

Emergence of Market Failures

Now, from 2008 onwards as a result of financial crisis which shattered the US and European countries and through the greater integration of the world economy through trade and international capital flows the developing countries (including India) could not remain unaffected. Financial crisis in the US occurred because banks and other financial institutions in their financial market operations clubbed sub-prime housing loans securities into the new derivatives in a non-transparent manner and sold them in the market. This whole financial market system collapsed when people started defaulting in paying their housing loans. In India as in other developing countries, which adopted the free market system under directions of World Bank and IMF which insisted on the adoption of policy of liberalisation, privatisation, globalisation as a pre-condition to bail them out of the balance of payments crisis and tough fiscal situation have witnessed again in recent years the failures of market system to ensure growth with stability. The most important reason is that in developing countries markets are characterised by widespread imperfections due to which they failed to work with efficiency and rationality. Joseph E. Stiglitz argues that *"markets are not necessarily either efficient or stable or that our economy is not well described by the standard model of competitive equilibrium used by a majority of economists"*[14]

Impact of Imperfections on the Working of the Market Economy. The markets in developing countries are in fact characterised by widespread imperfections. The product markets are *characterised by widespread imperfections. The product markets are characterised by monopolies, oligopoly and other forms of imperfect markets.* Prices in these market do not reflect their social values and are set above the marginal cost of production and leads to less than socially optimum output. There is need for government to regulate the prices of goods, especially those of essential products such as drugs, milk soaps, washing powder, cement, steel, petroleum products such as petrol, diesel, LPG etc. Besides, the competition commission should ensure that mergers do not lead to the emergence of monopolies or formation of cartels. Further, *imperfect factor markets* prevail in developing countries due to which factor prices determined do not reflect the social opportunity

14. Joseph E. Stiglitz, 'Let a hundred theories bloom', in *The Economic Times*, Aug. 2012.

cost. Under the pressure of trade unions, labour is overvalued and paid higher wages than its productivity. On the other hand, to provide incentives to investors, capital is undervalued compared to its scarcity value by providing various tax breaks, lower interest rate policy of the Central Bank of the developing countries. The overvaluation of labour and undervaluation of capital lead to the use of capital-intensive techniques of production which cause increase in unemployment of labour. Likewise, foreign exchange rate of the national currency of a developing country may be overvalued which discourages exports and encourages imports and causes difficulties of balance of payments of a country.

It is evident from above that imperfections in product, factor and foreign exchange markets of developing countries would lead to economic inefficiency or pareto non-optimality and would therefore be unable to achieve maximum social value. There is therefore a case *for government intervention to remove these factors price distortions* if the goal of economic efficiency is to be achieved.

Impact of Externalities on Resourse Allocation and Production. Even when perfect competition prevails in the markets there is no guarantee that social optimum levels of certain important goods *which generate substantial positive externalities* would be produced. The most important examples of such goods are education and health care facilities which have substantcial positive externalities and *should be provided below their cost of production or even free*. It is the government which can provide them *in adequate quantities*. The private sector, guided as it is by profit motive would not produce them free or below their cost of production. It is quite well known that so called public schools in India not only charge high tuition fees from the students but also huge capitation fees from them for admission. The engineering and medical institutes run by private sector trusts demand several lakhs of rupees as capitation fee for admission in them. Obviously, the general public or common men cannot get their children and boys admitted in these private institutions for education. Likewise, in private hospitals such as Apollo, Fortis, Max charges are so high that only the rich can get treatment in them while common man is deprived of proper treatment to maintain their health. Because of generating positive externalities education and health services have a high social value which is not reflected in market prices. In modern economic thinking education and health services are called ***human capital*** because of their crucial importance for economic growth but the private sector guided by market forces do not make adequate investment in these sectors.

Therefore, to accelerate economic growth and provide social justice, it is of paramount importance that government should make adequate investment in them. The government intervention in these manpower resources (i.e., education and health) will not only quicken the process of economic growth but will also help in eradicating poverty. Todaro and Smith write, "*Because such goods, such as education and health services must be valued at a price below their cost or even free, the private sector has no incentive to produce them. Thus the government often be responsible for providing these goods in order to ensure a minimum of welfare. In view of the population growth and poverty that characterize many developing countries it is likely that public sector activity in this area will continue to expand.*"[15]

Besides social capital represented by education and health services, the ***physical infrastructure*** **such** as power generation, coal and gas, transport facilities (including roads and highways), posts also create positive externalities and are a major bottlenecks to accelerate economic growth the private sector has no incentive to make adequate investment in them as much of their benefits *accrue to others*. Therefore, it is now well-recognised that in developing countries the government should make adequate investment in them to achieve higher rate of economic growth.

Impact of Imperfect Information on the Working of Market. Another important imperfec-

15. Todaro & Smith, *Economic Development*, Pearson Education. Asia (Singapore) Pvt. Ltd. Eighth Edition, 2003, p. 700.

tion in developing countries is *lack information and the presence of uncertainty* that are faced by both producers and consumers. Joseph E. Stiglitz rightly emphasizes that even if markets are competitive, *they are almost never efficient when information is imperfect or asymmetric.* By asymmetric information it is meant that of the two parties in the market while one party has complete information about the good, service or financial security which is being sold, the other party lacks the necessary information about this. Writing about the financial crisis arising out of bursting of housing bubble in 2008, he says that investors in the tainted securities did not have the same information about the quality of the securities as the banks or investment institutions issuing them. According to Stiglitz, this asymmetric information played a crucial role in bringing about financial crisis in the US in 2008 when the sub-priming housing bubble burst.

Stiglitz also brings out flaws in so called ***rational expectations model*** of Lucas according to which investors are rational and their behaviour will ensure stability in the market. Referring to the financial crisis of 2008 in the US he writes, "A long line of research has shown that even using the models of the so called "*rational expectations*" school of economics, markets might not behave stably and that there can be price bubbles. *The crisis has indeed provided ample evidence that expectations are far from rational*, but the flaws in the rational expectations line of reasoning, namely, hidden assumption such as that all investors have the same information had been exposed well before the crisis"[16].

He further adds, "Just as the crisis has *reinvigorated thinking about the need for regulations*, so it has given new impetus to the exploration of alternative strands of throught that would provide better insights into how our complex economic system functions".[17] Similarly, speaking about the situations prevailing in developing countries Todaro and Smith write, "in many developing countries producers are often unsure about the size of local market, the presence of other producers, and the availability of inputs, both domestic and imported. Consumers may be unsure about the quality and availability of products and their substitutes. Moreover, in contrast to their counterparts in developed countries, producers and consumers usually lack the tools to ferret out this information because little is done by way of marketing. *Under such circumstances profit and utility maximising behaviour may be based on wrong information and hence does not lead to an efficient allocation of resources*. The government may attempt to provide this information or may decide to intervene in the market by guiding producers and consumers".

Accelerating Capital Formation. Further, it is worth noting that even if market under competitive conditions work well in attaining efficiency in allocating current resources at a given point of time, it may not however ***operate efficiently in allocating resources over time***, that is, it may not ensure adequate rate of investment which is required to bring about rapid capital accumulation so as to raise the levels of production and consumption in the future.[18] This also shows that the government needs to intervene in the market for allocating resources over time. Capital formation is a pre-requiste for economic growth. Though there are large inequalities in income distribution in developing countries that should ensure higher rate of private saving. But due to the conspicous consumption by the rich and the working of its demonstration effect on the upper middle class and middle class people, the private saving rate determined by market mechanism is not large enough to meet the needs of higher rate of investment or capital formation. Therefore, it is through appropriate fiscal and monetary policy measures that can raise the total saving and capital accumulation to accelerate economic growth. In this connection, investment in infrastructure, both physical and

16. Joseph E. Stiglitz (coauthered by George Aberlop), "Let a hundred theories bloom", *The Economic Times*. August 2012 (italics added).
17. *Ibid*.
18. Todaro and Smith, *op.cit*., p.700

social, is of crucial importance. Private sector, as explained may have neither any incentive nor sufficient funds to make adequate investment in them.

Further, it is important to note that economic development is a *process of structural change.* The market may perform well in allocating resources at the margin by developing some industries further and allow others to decline but is generally ineffective in structural transformation of the developing economy that requires a broad and long-term view of the growth process. Therefore, active role in making a desired structural change of the economy is essential. Todaro and Smith rightly wirte, "the market may be ineffective in producing *large discontinuous change in the economic structure*, changes that may be crucial to the country's long-term development. The government may therefore have to intervene in sectors crucial to the country's development to ensure that they change over time and flourish".[19]

It is evident from above that due to widespread imperfections and the special requirements for eradicating absolute poverty and chronic unemployment and bringing about structural changes the market mechanism fails to deliver and therefore active government intervention is needed to achieve the desired results. Besides, as seen above, the free working of market mechanism without regulation by the government may produce income distribution that is highly unequal that can pose dangers to the social and economic stability. However, this should not mean that government should do everything and put stringent controls on the private sector and on the working of market mechanism. In fact as there are market failures, there are government failures too. What is needed is the ***judicious mix of roles of private sector and Government*** to bring about not only rapid economic growth but also to ensure equitable distribution of income and eradication of poverty and unemployment. To conclude in the words of Professors Todaro and Smith, "No Central Planning agency is capable of regulating the vast array of different goods and services, nor this would be desirable. Rather it means greater and more effective *cooperation between the public and private sectors*. It also means that governments must seek to determine in which areas the market can most efficiently operate and in which areas the governments itself can achieve the best results given its own limited human resources. This *public-sector-privat-sector* partnership through a proactive government industrial policy is a key lesson of the success stories of South Korea, Taiwan and Singapore"[20]

19. Todaro and Smith, *op.cit.*, p. 701
20. Todaro and Smith, *op.cit.* P. 70.

PART – II

THE THEORY OF CONSUMER'S BEHAVIOUR AND DEMAND

- Demand, Supply and Market Equilibrium and Law of Demand
- Applications of Demand and Supply Analysis
- Cardinal Utility Analysis
- Indifference Curve Analysis of Consumer Demand
- Cardinal Utility Analysis vs. Indifference Curve Analysis
- Applications and Uses of Indifference Curves
- Revealed Preference Theory of Demand
- Elasticity of Demand
- Consumer Surplus

CHAPTER 7
DEMAND, SUPPLY AND MARKET EQUILIBRIUM

People demand goods because they satisfy the wants of the people. The utility means want-satisfying power of a commodity. *It is also defined as the amount of satisfaction which a person derives from consuming a commodity*. Utility is a subjective entity and resides in the minds of men. Being subjective it varies with different persons, that is, different persons derive different amounts of utility from a given good. People know utility of goods by means of introspection. The desire for a commodity by a person depends upon the utility he expects to obtain from it. The greater the utility he expects from a commodity, the greater his desire for that commodity. It should be noted that no question of ethics or morality is involved in the use of the word 'utility' in economics. The commodity may not be useful in the ordinary sense of the term, even then it may provide utility to some people. For instance, alcohol may actually harm a person but it possesses utility for a person whose want it satisfies. Thus, the desire for alcohol may be considered immoral by some people but no such meaning is conveyed in the economic sense of the term. Thus, in economics, the concept of utility is ethically neutral.

The Meaning of Demand

It is useful to know what economists mean by the demand of the goods by consumers. The demand for a commodity is essentially consumers' attitude and reaction towards that commodity. Demand for a good is in fact a photograph or a panoramic picture of consumers' attitude towards a commodity. This consumers' attitude gives rise to actions in purchasing units of a commodity at various given prices. *Precisely stated, the demand for a commodity is the amount of it that a consumer will purchase or will be ready to take off from the market at various given prices in a period of time*. This, demand in economics implies both the desire to purchase and the ability to pay for a good. It is noteworthy that mere desire for a commodity does not constitute demand for it, if it is not backed by the ability to pay. For example, if a poor man who hardly makes both ends meet, wishes to have a car, his wish or desire for a car will not constitute the demand for the car because he cannot afford to pay for it, that is, he has no purchasing power to make his wish or desire effective in the market. Thus, in economics unless demand is backed by purchasing power or ability to pay it does not constitute demand.

Demand for a good is determined by several factors, such as, the tastes and desires of the consumer for a commodity, income of the consumer, the prices of related goods, substitutes or complements. When there is a change in any of these factors, demand of the consumer for a good changes. Individual consumer's demand and market demand for a good may be distinguished. Market demand for a good is the total sum of the demands the individual consumers who purchase the commodity in the market. We shall discuss in detail later in this chapter the various factors which determine demand for a commodity and also how a demand curve for a commodity is derived.

The Law of Demand

An important generalisation about demand is described by the law of demand. This law of demand expresses the functional relationship between price and quantity demanded. The law of demand or functional relationship between price and quantity demanded is one of the best known and most important laws of economic theory. According to the law of demand, other things being equal, *if price of a commodity falls, the quantity demanded of it will rise, and if price of the commodity rises, its quantity demanded will decline*. Thus, according to the law of demand, there is inverse relationship between price and quantity demanded, other things remaining the same. These other things which are assumed to be constant are the tastes or preferences of the consumer, the income of the consumer, and the prices of related goods. If these other factors which determine demand also undergo a change, then the inverse price-demand relationship may not hold good. Thus, the constancy of these other things is an important qualification or assumption of the law of demand.

Demand Schedule and Demand Curve

The law of demand can be illustrated through a demand schedule and a demand curve. A demand schedule is presented in Table 7.1. It will be seen from this demand schedule that when price of a commodity is ₹ 12 per unit, consumer purchases 10 units of the commodity. When price of the commodity falls to ₹ 10, he purchases 20 units of the commodity. Similarly, when price further falls, quantity demanded by him goes on rising until at price ₹ 2, the quantity demanded by him rises to 60 units. We can convert this demand schedule into a demand curve by graphically plotting the various price-quantity combinations, and this has been done in Figure 7.1, where along the X-axis, quantity demanded is measured and along the Y-axis, price of the commodity is measured. By plotting 10 units of the commodity at price ₹ 12, we get point *Q* in Figure 7.1. Likewise, by plotting 20 units of the commodity demanded at price ₹ 10, we plot point *S* in Figure 7.1. Similarly, points *S*, *T*, *U* and *V* are plotted, representing other combinations of price and quantity demanded presented in Table 7.1. By joining these various points, *Q*, *R*, *S*, *T*, *U*, and *V*, we get a curve *DD*, which is known as the demand curve. Thus, the *demand curve is a graphic statement or presentation of quantities of a good which will be demanded by the consumer at various possible prices at a given moment of time.*

Table 7.1
Demand Schedule of an Individual Consumer

Price (₹)	*Quantity Demanded*
12	10
10	20
8	30
6	40
4	50
2	60

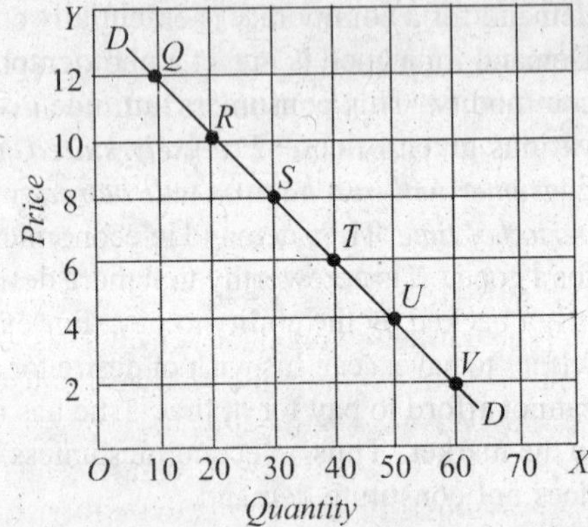

Fig. 7.1. *The Demand Curve of a Consumer*

It should be noted that a demand schedule or a demand curve does not tell us what the price is; it only tells us how much quantity of the good would be purchased by the consumer at various possible prices. Further, it will be seen both from the demand schedule and the demand curve that as price of a commodity falls, more quantity of it is purchased or demanded. Since more is demanded at a lower price and less is demanded at a higher price, the demand curve slopes downward to the right. Thus, the downward-sloping demand curve is in accordance with the law of demand which, as stated above, describes inverse price-demand relationship. It is important to note here that behind this demand curve or price-demand relationship always lie the tastes and preferences of the consumer, his income, the prices of substitutes and complementary goods, all of which are assumed to be constant in describing price-demand relationship. If any change occurs in any of these factors, the whole demand schedule or demand curve will change and a new demand schedule or demand curve will have to be drawn. In drawing a demand curve, we assume that the buyer or consumer does not exercise any influence over the price of a commodity, that is, he takes the price of the commodity as given and constant for him.

Market Demand Curve

We can add or sum up the various quantities demanded by the number of consumers in the market and by doing so we can obtain the *market demand curve* for a commodity which like the individual consumer's demand curve will slope downward to the right. How this summation is done is illustrated in Fig. 7.2. Suppose there are three individual buyers of the good in the market. In Fig. 7.2 diagrams (*a*), (*b*) and (*c*) show the demand curves of the three independent individual buyers. Now, the market demand curve can be obtained by adding together the amounts of the good which individuals wish to buy at each price. Thus, at price P_1 the individual *A* wishes to buy Oa_1 of the good; individual *B* wishes to buy Ob_1 of the good and individual *C* wishes to buy Oc_1. The total quantity of the good that all the three individuals plan to buy at price P_1 is therefore $Oa_1 + Ob_1 + Oc_1$ which is equal to *OQ* in Fig. 7.2 (*d*). Similarly, we can plot the quantity of the good that will be demanded by all the three individuals at every other price of the good. When all the points showing the amounts demanded of the good at various prices are joined together we get a market demand curve for the good. For the sake of convenience we have supposed that there are three individuals or buyers in the market for a good. Whatever be the number of individuals in the market, their demand curves can be added together, as illustrated above, to get a market demand curve for the good.

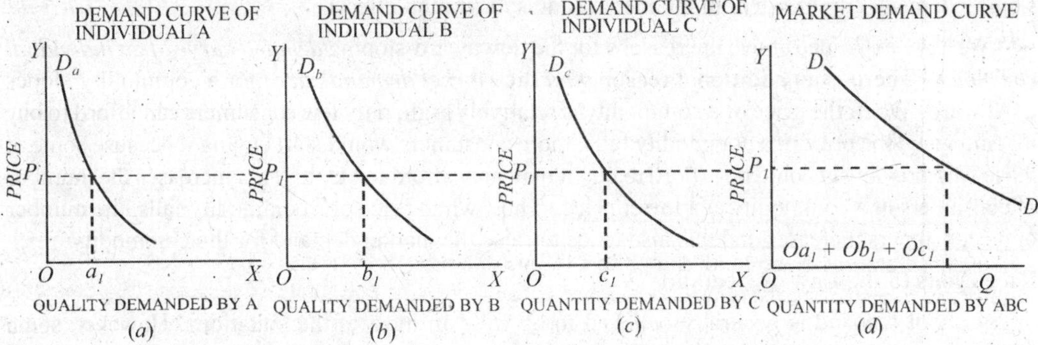

Fig. 7.2. *Derivation of Market Demand Curve*

The market demand curve will slope downward to the right since the individual demand curves, whose lateral summation gives us the market demand curve, normally slope downward to the right. Besides, as price of the good falls, it is very likely that the new buyers will enter the market and will further raise the quantity demanded of the good. This will be another reason why the market demand curve should slope downward to the right.

Reasons for the Law of Demand : Why does Demand Curve Slope Downward ?

We have explained above that when price falls the quantity demanded of a commodity rises and vice versa, other things remaining the same. It is due to this law of demand that demand curve slopes downward to the right. Now, the important question is why the demand curve slopes downward, or in other words, why the law of demand describing inverse price-demand relationship is valid. We can explain this with marginal utility analysis and also with the indifference curve analysis which we will do in the next chapters.

When price of a commodity falls, the consumer can buy more quantity of the commodity with his given income. Or, if he chooses to buy the same amount of the commodity as before, some money will be left with him because he has to spend less on the commodity due to its lower price. In other words, as a result of fall in price of the commodity, consumer's real income or purchasing power increases. This increase in real income induces the consumer to buy more of that commodity. This is called *income effect of the change in price* of the commodity. This is one reason why a consumer buys more of a commodity whose price falls. The other important reason why the quantity demanded of a commodity rises as its price falls, is the *substitution effect*. When the price of a commodity falls, it becomes relatively cheaper than other commodities. This induces the consumer to substitute the commodity whose price has fallen for other commodities which have now become relatively dearer. As a result of this substitution effect, the quantity demanded of the commodity, whose price has fallen, rises. This substitution effect is more important than the income effect. Marshall explained the downward-sloping demand curve with the aid of this substitution effect alone, since he ignored the income effect of the price change. But in some cases even the income effect is very significant and cannot be ignored. As will be discussed in a later chapter, Hicks and Allen who put forward indifference curve analysis of consumer's behaviour explain this downward-sloping demand curve with both the income and substitution effects.

We have explained above the reasons for the downward-sloping *demand curve of an individual consumer*. There is an additional reason why the *market demand curve* for a commodity slopes downward. When the price of a commodity is relatively high, only few consumers can afford to buy it. And when the price of a commodity falls, more consumers would start buying it because some of those who previously could not afford to buy it may now afford to buy it. This increases the number of consumers of a commodity at a lower price. Thus, when price of a commodity falls, the number of its consumers increases and this also tends to raise the market demand for the commodity.

Exceptions to the Law of Demand

Law of demand is generally believed to be valid in most of the situations. However, some exceptions to the law of demand have been pointed out.

Goods having Prestige Value : Veblin Effect. One exception to the law of demand is associated with the name of the economist Thorstein Veblin who propounded the doctrine of conspicuous consumption. According to Veblen, some consumers measure the utility of a commodity entirely by its price *i.e.,* for them, the greater the price of a commodity, the greater its utility. For example, diamonds are considered as prestige good in the society and for the upper strata of the society the higher the price of diamonds, the higher the prestige value of them and therefore the greater utility or desirability of them. In this case, the consumer will buy less of the diamonds at a lower price because with the fall in price its prestige value will go down. On the other hand, when price of diamonds goes up, their prestige value will go up and therefore their utility and desirability. As a result, at a higher price the quantity demanded of diamonds by a consumer will rise. This is called *Veblin effect*.

Giffin Goods. Another exception to the law of demand was pointed out by Sir Robert Giffin who observed that when the price of bread increased, the low-paid British workers in the early 19th century purchased more bread and not less of it, and this is contrary to the law of demand described above. The reason given for this is that these British workers consumed a diet of mainly bread and when the price of bread went up they were compelled to spend more on given quantity of bread. Therefore, they could not afford to purchase as much meat as before. Thus, they substituted even bread for meat in order to maintain their intake of food. After the name of Robert Giffin, such goods in whose case there is a direct price-demand relationship are called *Giffin goods*. It is *important to note that when with the rise in the price of a commodity*, its quantity demand increases and with the fall in its price its quantity demanded decreases, the demand curve will slope upward to the right and not downward.

---

1. See his book, *The Economics of Leisure Class.*

Some False Exceptions

There are some other exceptions to the law of demand which are only apparent and not genuine In other words, these exceptions to the law of demand are false. One of the false exceptions relates to the changes in the expectations of the people regarding prices of the commodities in the future. Suppose, the rainfall in India in any year does not occur in adequate quantity and there is widespread drought, the expectations of the people will be that the prices would rise in the future. Therefore, even if the prices of foodgrains are higher at the present, they would demand greater quantities since they will be expecting that the prices in the future would be still higher. This is contrary to the law of demand, but in this case applying the law of demand is not valid. This is because in this case the increase in the quantity demanded is not due to the rise in price but due to the rightward shift in the demand curve as a result of changes in the price expectations of the people.

Furthermore, statistical data regarding the quantities purchased of various goods reveal that larger amounts of them have been purchased at high prices and smaller quantities have been purchased at lower prices over the course of the business cycle. This is also apparently the violation of the law of demand but properly interpreted it does not contradict the law of demand, for this only shows that demands for many commodities increase in times of prosperity periods of the business cycles due to the increase in the incomes of the people, and the demands for the commodities decrease in times of the depression periods of the business cycles due to the fall in incomes of the people.

Another false exception to the law or demand is found when a commodity is sold under two brand names whose prices greatly differ. It is often found that some people demand high-priced brand more than the low-price one, although they are almost identical. This author has seen that some of his friends buy more of 'Supreme Lux' having a much higher price than 'Lux' having a low price even though the two are of almost the same quality. However, this is not a real exception to the law of demand. This is because those who buy more of high-priced brand *think* that the high-priced brand is different from and superior to the low-priced brand. Therefore, for analysing the nature of demand for these brands, they should be regarded as two different commodities.

DETERMINANTS OF DEMAND

We have explained above demand changes as a result of changes in price. Demand schedule and law of demand state the relationship between price and quantity demanded by assuming *"other things remaining the same"*. When there is a change in these other things, the whole demand schedule or demand curve undergoes a change. In other words, these other things determine the *position and level* of the demand curve. If these other things or the determinants of demand change, the whole demand schedule or the demand curve will change. As a result of the changes in these factors or determinants, a demand curve will shift above or below as the case may be. The following are the factors which determine demand for goods.

1. **Tastes and Preferences of the Consumers.** An important factor which determines demand for a good is the tastes and preferences of the consumers for it. A good for which consumers' tastes and preferences are greater, its demand would be large and its demand curve will lie at a higher level. People's tastes and preferences for various goods often change and as a result there is change in demand for them. The changes in demand for various goods occur due to the changes in fashion and also due to the pressure of advertisements by the manufacturers and sellers of different products. For example, a few years back when Coca Cola plant was established in New Delhi demand for it was very small. But now people's taste for Coca Cola has undergone a change and become favourable to it because of large advertisement and publicity done for it. The result of this is that the demand for Coca-Cola has increased very much. In economics we would say that the demand curve for Coca Cola has shifted upward. On the contrary when any good goes out of fashion or people's

tastes and preferences no longer remain favourable to it the demand for it decreases. In economics we say that the demand curve for these goods will shift downward.

2. **Incomes of the People.** The demand for goods also depends upon incomes of the people. The greater the incomes of the people the greater will be their demand for goods. In drawing a demand schedule or a demand curve for a good we take incomes of the people as given and constant. When as a result of the rise in incomes of the people, the demand increases, the whole of the demand curve shifts upward and *vice versa.* The greater income means the greater purchasing power. Therefore, when incomes of the people increase, they can afford to buy more. It is because of this reason that the increase in income has a positive effect on the demand for a good. When the incomes of the people fall they would demand less of the goods and as a result the demand curve will shift below. For instance, during the planning period in India the incomes of the people have greatly increased owing to the large investment expenditure on the development schemes by the Government and the private sector. As a result of this increase in incomes, demand for foodgrains has greatly increased which has resulted in rightward shift in the demand curve for them. Likewise, when because of drought in a year the agricultural production greatly falls, incomes of the farmers decline. As a result of the decline in incomes of the farmers, they demand less of cotton cloth and other manufactured products.

3. **Changes in the Prices of the Related Goods.** The demand for a good is also affected by the prices of other goods, especially those which are related to it as substitutes or complements. When we draw a demand schedule or a demand curve for a good we take the prices of the related goods as remaining constant. Therefore, when the prices of the related goods, substitutes or complements, change the whole demand curve would change its position; it will shift upward or downward as the case may be. When price of a substitute for a good falls, the demand for that good will decline and when the price of the substitute rises, the demand for that good will increase. For example, when price of the tea as well as the incomes of the people remain the same but price of the coffee falls, the consumers would demand less of tea than before. Tea and coffee are very close substitutes, therefore when coffee becomes cheaper, the consumers substitute coffee for tea and as a result the demand for tea declines. The goods which are complementary with each other, the change in the price of any of them would affect the demand of the other. For instance, if price of the milk falls, the demand for sugar would also be affected. When people would take more milk or would prepare more *khoya, burfi*, *rasgullas* with milk; the demand for sugar will also increase. Likewise, when price of cars falls, the demand for them will increase which in turn will increase the demand for petrol Cars and petrol are complementary with each other.

4. **The Number of Consumers in the Market.** We have already explained that the market demand for a good is obtained by adding up the individual demands of the present as well as prospective consumers or buyers of a good at various possible prices. The greater the number of consumers of a good, the greater the market demand for it. Now, the question arises on what factors the number of consumers of a good depends. If the consumers substitute one good for another, then the number of consumers of that good which has been substituted by the other will decline and for the good which has been used in its place, the number of consumers will increase. Besides, when the seller of a good succeeds in finding out new markets for his good and as a result the market for his good expands, the number of consumers of that good will increase. Another Important cause for the increase in the number of consumers is the growth in population. For instance, in India the demand for many essential goods, especially foodgrains, has increased because of the increase in the population of the country and the resultant increase in the number of consumers for them.

5. **Changes in Propensity to Consume.** People's propensity to consume also affects the demand for them. The income of the people remaining constant, if their propensity to consume rises, then out of the given income they would spend a greater part of it with the result that the demand for goods will increase. On the other hand, if propensity to save of the people increases, that is, if

propensity to consume declines, then the consumers would spend a smaller part of their income on goods with the result that the demand for goods will decrease. It is thus clear that with income remaining constant, change in propensity to consume of the people will bring about a change in the demand for goods.

6. **Consumers' Expectations with regard to Future Prices.** Another factor which influences the demand for goods is consumers' expectations with regard to future prices of the goods. If due to some reason, consumers expect that in the near future prices of the goods would rise, then in the present they would demand greater quantities of the goods so that in the future they should not have to pay higher prices. Similarly, when the consumers hope that in the future they will have good income, then in the present they will spend greater part of their incomes with the result that their present demand for goods will increase.

7. **Income Distribution.** Distribution of income in a society also affects the demand for goods. If distribution of income is more equal, then the propensity to consume of the society as a whole will be relatively high which means greater demand for goods. On the other hand, if distribution of income is more unequal, then propensity to consume of the society will be relatively less, for the propensity to consume of the rich people is less than that of the poor people. Consequently with more unequal distribution of income, the demand for consumer goods will be comparatively less. This is the effect of the income distribution on the propensity to consume and demand for goods. But the change in the distribution of income in the society would affect the demand for various goods differently. If progressive taxes are levied on the rich people and the money so collected is spent on providing employment to the poor people, the distribution of income would become more equal and with this there would be a transfer of purchasing power from the rich to the poor. As a result of this, the demand for those goods will increase which are generally purchased by the poor because the purchasing power of the poor people has increased and, on the other hand, the demand for those goods will decline which are usually consumed by the rich on whom progressive taxes have been levied.

Extension and Contraction in Demand

We have studied above the demand schedule, demand curve and law of demand. All these show that when price of a good falls, quantity demanded of it rises, and when its price rises, its quantity demanded falls, other things remaining the same. *When as a result of changes in price, the quantity demanded rises or falls, extension or contraction in demand is said to have taken place. Therefore, in economics, the extension and contraction in demand are used when the quantity demanded rises or falls as a result of changes in price and we move along a given demand curve.* When the quantity demanded of a good rises due to the fall in price, it is called *extension of demand* and when the quantity demanded falls due to the rise in price, it is called *contraction of demand.* For instance, suppose the price of bananas in the market at any given time is Rs.12 per dozen and a consumer buys one dozen of them at that price. Now, if other things such as tastes of the consumer, his income, prices of other goods remain the same and price of bananas falls to Rs. 8 per dozen and the consumer now buys 2 dozen bananas, then extension in demand is said to have occurred. On the contrary, if the price of bananas rises to Rs. 15 per dozen and consequently the consumer now buys half a dozen of the bananas, then contraction in demand is said to have occurred.

It should be remembered that *extension and contraction in the demand takes place as a result of changes in the price alone when other determinants of demand such as tastes, income, propensity to consume and prices of the related goods remain constant.* These other factors remaining constant means that the demand curve remains the same, that is, it does not change its position; only the consumer moves downward or upward on it.

The extension and contraction in demand is illustrated in Figure 7.3. Assuming other things such as income, tastes and fashion, prices of related goods remaining constant, a demand curve *DD* goods remaining constant, a demand curve *DD* has been drawn. It will be seen in this figure that when the price of the good is *OP*, then the quantity demanded of the good is *OM*. Now, if the price of the good falls to *OP′* the quantity demanded of the good rises to *ON*. Thus, there is extension in demand by the amount *MN*. On the other hand, if price of the good rises from *OP* to *OP″* the quantity demanded of the good falls to *OL*. Thus, there is contraction in demand by *ML*. We thus see that *as a result of changes in price of a good the consumers move along the given demand curve; the demand curve remains the same and does not change its position.*

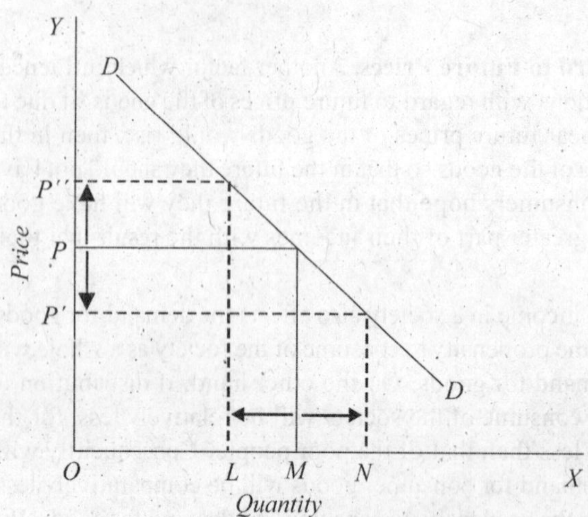

Fig. 7.3. *Extension and Contraction in Demand*

Demand and Quantity Demanded. It is important to understand the distinction between the concepts of demand and quantity demanded as they are often confused with each other. Demand represents the whole demand schedule or demand curve and shows how price of a good is related to quantity which the consumers are willing and able to buy, other factors which determine demand being held constant. On the other hand, quantity demanded refers to the quantity which the consumers buy at a *particular price*. The quantity demanded of a good varies with changes in its price; it increases when price falls and decreases when price rises. The changes in demand for a commodity occur when there is a change in the factors other than price, namely, tastes and preferences the people, incomes of the consumers, and prices of related goods.

Changes in Demand : Increase and Decrease in Demand

When demand changes due to the factors other than price, there is shift in the whole demand curve. As mentioned above, apart from price, demand for a commodity is determined by incomes of the consumers, their tastes and preferences, prices of related goods. Thus, when there is any change in these factors, it will cause a shift in demand curve. For example, if incomes of the consumers increase, say due to the hike in their wages and salaries or due to the grant of dearness allowance, they will demand more of a good, say cloth, at each price. This will cause a shift in the demand curve to the right as is shown in Figure 7.4. To being with *DD* is the demand curve. With the increase in income, the demand curve shifts to the right to *D′D′* which implies that at each price such as P_1, P_2, P_3 the consumers demand more of the commodity than before. Similarly, if preferences of the people for a commodity, say colour *TV*, become greater, their demand for colour TVs will increase, that is, the demand curve will shift to the right and, therefore, at each price demand for colour TVs will increase .

The other important factor which can cause an increase in demand for a commo-dity is the *expectations about future prices.* If people expect that price of a commodity is likely to go up in future, they will try to purchase the commodity, especially a durable one, in the current period which will boost the current demand for the good and cause a shift in the demand curve to the right.

The prices of related commodities such as substitutes and complements can also change the demand for a commodity. For example, if price of coffee rises, other factors remaining the constant, this will cause the demand for tea, a substitute for coffee, to increase and its demand curve to shift to the right.

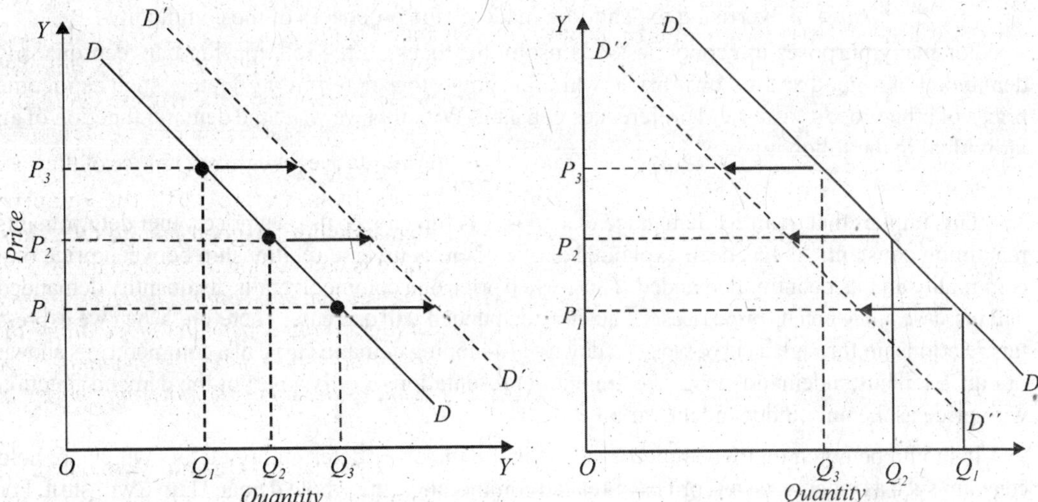

Fig. 7.4. *Increase in demand leads to the shift in the demand curve to the right.*

Fig. 7.5. *Decrease in demand leading to the shift in the demand curve to the left.*

Decrease in Demand and Shift in the Demand Curve. If there are adverse changes in the factors influencing demand; it will lead to the decrease in demand causing a shift in the demand curve to the left as shown in Figure 7.5. For example, if due to inadequate rainfall agricultural production in a year declines, this will cause a fall in the incomes of the farmers. This fall in incomes of the farmers will cause a decrease in the demand for industrial products, say cloth, and will result in a shift in the demand curve to the left as shown in Figure 7.5. It will be seen from Figure 7.5, that as a result of decrease in demand, demand curve shifts to the left to *D′′D′′* and at each price such as P_1, P_2, P_3 the farmers demand less of cloth than before. Similarly, change in preferences for commodities can also affect the demand. For example, when colour TVs came to India people's greater preference for them led to the decrease in demand for black and white TVs causing leftward shift in demand curve for these black and white TVs.

Conclusion

From the above analysis it is clear that in case of extension and contraction in demand, a consumer moves along the same demand curve. He goes up and down on it due to the changes in price of the good alone. On the other hand, in the case of increase and decrease in demand the whole demand curve changes or shifts; in case of increase in demand it shifts to the right and in case of decrease in demand it shifts to the left.

DEMAND FUNCTION AND DEMAND CURVE

Individual's demand for a commodity depends on the own price of a commodity, his income, prices of related commodities (which may be either substitutes or complements), his tastes and preferences, and advertising expenditure made by the producers for the commodity in question. Individual demand for a commodity can be expressed mathematically in the following *general functional* form :

$$Q_d = f(P_x, I, P_r, T, A) \quad \ldots (1)$$

where P_x = Own price of the commodity X

I = Income of the individual

P_r = **Prices of related commodities**

T = Tastes and preferences of the individual consumer

A = Advertising expenditure made by the producers of the commodity

For many purposes in economics, it is useful to focus on the relationship between quantity demanded of a good and its own price, while keeping other determining factors such as income prices of other goods, tastes and preferences constant. With this we write the demand function of an individual in the following way.

$$Q_d = j(P) \qquad ... (2)$$

This implies that quantity demanded of a good X is function of its own price, other determinants remaining constant. As has been explained above, there is inverse relationship between price of a commodity and its quantity demanded. Thus, when price of a commodity falls, its quantity demanded will increase and when its price rises, its quantity demanded will decrease. Therefore, when we express this relationship through a curve we get a downward-sloping demand curve of a commodity as shown in Fig. 7.1. Thus, a demand curve is a graphic representation of only a part of the demand function with price as the only independent variable.

It should be noted that when there is a change in the other determining factors which are held constant such as income, tastes, prices of related commodities, the whole demand curve will shift. For example, if income increases, the whole demand curve will shift to the right and, on the contrary, if income decreases, then the whole demand curve shifts to the left. Similarly, changes in other determining factors such as tastes, prices of related commodities, advertising cause shift in the demand curve and are therefore called *shift factors*.

The individual's demand function in (2) above is a *general* functional form and does not show how much quantity demanded of a consumer will change following a unit change in price (P_x). For the purpose of actually estimating demand for a commodity we need a specific form of the demand. function. Generally, demand function is considered to be of a *linear* form. The specific demand function of a linear form is written as

$$Q_d = a - bP_x \qquad ... (3)$$

where a is a constant intercept term on the X–axis and b is the coefficient showing the slope of the demand curve. If on estimating the demand function (3) from the information about monthly quantities demanded of sugar at its various prices by an individual consumer, we find the constant a to be equal to 12 and the constant b to be equal to 2, we can write individuals demand function as

$$Q_d = 12 - 2P_x$$

This is interpreted as *one rupee fall* in price of sugar will cause its *quantity demanded to increase by 2 units* of sugar.

Market Demand Function

A market consists of several individuals. Market demand function is obtained by summing up the demand functions of the individuals constituting the market.

Example 1

A market for a commodity consists of three individuals A, B and C whose demand functions for the commodity are given below. Find out the market demand function.

$$Q_A = 40 - 2P$$

$$Q_B = 25.5 - 0.75P$$

$$Q_C = 36.5 - 1.25P$$

When individual demand functions are expressed as *'quantity as a function of price'* as is the case in our problem stated above, market demand function can be obtained by summing up the individual demand functions. Thus, market demand function is

$$Q_M = Q_A + Q_B + Q_C$$
$$= (40 - 2P) + (25.5 - 0.75P) + (36.5 - 1.25P)$$
$$= (40 + 25.5 + 36.5) - (2 + 0.75 + 1.25)P$$
$$= 102 - 4P$$

However, note that when individual demand functions are expressed as *"price as function of quantity"*, then in order to obtain the market demand, they have to be first converted into 'quantity as function of price'.

Example 2

Suppose a market consists of three consumers, A, B and C whose inverse demand functions are given below:

(A) : $P = 35 - 0.5Q_A$

(B) : $P = 50 - 0.25Q_B$

(C) : $P = 40 - 2.00Qc$

(i) *Find out the market demand function for the commodity.*

(ii) *If the market supply function is given by $Q_S = 40 + 3.5P$, determine the equilibrium price and quantity*

Since the individual demand functions are expressed as 'price as function of quantity, that is, we are given *"inverse demand functions"* we have first to transform them into 'quantity demanded as function of price'. Transforming them yields the following demand functions:

$$Q_A = 70 - 2P$$
$$Q_B = 200 - 4P$$
$$Q_C = 20 - 0.5P$$

Market demand function :

$$Q_D = (70 - 2P) + (200 - 4P) + (20 - 0.5$$
$$Q_D = 70 + 200 + 20 - (2 + 4 + 0.5)P$$
$$= 290 - 6.5P$$

Market supply function $(Q_S) = 40 + 3.5P$

In equilibrium, $Q_D = Q_S$

$$290 - 6.5P = 40 + 3.5P.$$
$$10P = 250$$
$$P = \frac{250}{10} = 25$$

Substituting the equilibrium value of price in the demand function equation, we have

$$Q = 290 - 6.5\ (25)$$
$$= 290 - 162.5$$
$$= 127.5$$

Thus, the equilibrium price is ₹ 25 and equilibrium quantity is 127.5 units.

SUPPLY AND SUPPLY FUNCTION

As demand is defined as a schedule of the quantities of good that will be purchased at various prices, similarly the supply refers to the schedule of the quantities of a good that will be offered for sale at various prices. To be more correct, supply of a commodity is the schedule of the quantities of a commodity that would be offered for sale at all possible prices during a period of time, for example, a day, a week, a month and so on.

Supply should be carefully distinguished from **stock.** *Stock is the total volume of a commodity which can be brought into the market for sale at a short notice* and supply means the quantity which is *actually brought* in the market. For perishable commodities like fish and fruits, supply and stock are the same because whatever is in stock must be disposed of. The commodities, which are not perishable, can be held back if prices are not favourable. If the price is high, larger quantities of non-perishable commodities are offered by the sellers from their stock. And if the price is low, only small quantities are brought out for sale. In short, *stock is potential supply*.

Supply should be distinguished from the ***quantity supplied***. Whereas supply of a commodity is the entire schedule of the quantities of a commodity that would be offered for sale at all possible prices during a period of time, for example, a day, a week, a month and so on, the quantity supplied refers to the quantity of a commodity which the firms are able and willing to sell at a *particular price* of the commodity. Thus the term supply refers to the entire relationship between the price of a commodity and the quantity supplied at various possible prices and is illustrated by the entire supply curve or supply schedule as given in Figure 7.6 and Table 7.2, where the term quantity supplied refers to a *point* on a given supply curve, that is, quantity supplied at a particular price.

Two things are worth mentioning about the concept of supply. First, supply is a **flow concept,** that is, it refers to the amount of a commodity that the firms produce and offer for sale in the market per period of time, say a week, a month or a year. Without specifying the time period, supply of a commodity has a little meaning. Second, the quantity supplied of a commodity which the producers plan to produce and sell at a price is not necessarily the same as *the quantity actually sold*. Sometimes the quantity which the firms are willing to produce and sell at a price is greater than the quantity demanded, so the quantity actually bought and sold is less than the quantity supplied.

Supply Function

The quantity of a commodity that firms will be able and willing to offer for sale in the market depends on several factors. The important factors determining supply of a commodity are :

1. The price of the commodity
2. The prices of inputs (i.e. resources) used for the production of the commodity
3. The state of technology
4. The number of firms producing and selling the commodity
5. The prices of related goods produced
6. Future expectations regarding price of the commodity.

We will explain these factors determining supply of a commodity in detail in a later section. However, it may be noted that out of the above determinants of supply the own price of the commodity, the prices of inputs (i.e. resources) used to produce the commodity, and the technology are three important factors and therefore the supply function of a commodity is often written taking these factors as independent variables. *Thus supply function of a commodity is written as*

$$Q^s_x = S(P_x, F_1, F_2 ...., F_m)$$

where Q^s_x is the quantity supplied of the commodity X, P_x is it own price, $F_1, F_2 ...... F_m$ are the prices of inputs used to produce the commodity X and the state of technology determines the form of supply function S. It must be noted that *the form of the function refers to the precise quantitative relation between the independent variables* such as the own price of the commodity X, prices of factors such as F_1, F_2 etc., and the technology.

In economics when describing supply of a commodity prices of factors are assumed to remain constant and supply is expressed as a function of price of the commodity alone. Thus, supply function is generally written as

$$Q_x^S = f(P_x)$$

That is, other things remaining the same, quantity supplied of commodity *X* is a function of price of the commodity *X*.

LAW OF SUPPLY

Supply of a commodity is functionally related to its price. The law of supply relates to this functional relationship between price of a commodity and its quantity supplied. In contrast to the inverse relationship between the quantity demanded and the changes in price, the quantity supplied *of a commodity the generally varies directly with its price*. That is, the higher the price, the larger is the quantity supplied of a commodity.

Table 7.2
Supply Schedule of Wheat

Price Per Quintal (₹)	*Quantity Supplied* (*in quintals*)
500	100
510	150
520	200
530	225
540	250
550	275

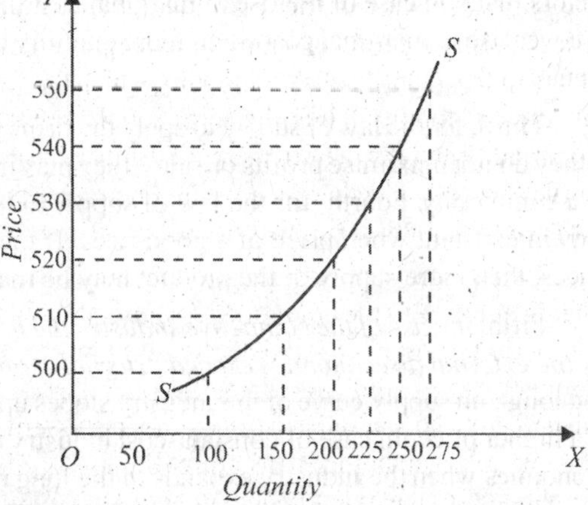

Fig. 7.6. *Supply Curve Showing Direct Relationship Between Price and Quantity Supplied*

The supply schedule and supply cruve reflect the law of supply. According to the law of supply, *when the price of a commodity rises, the quantity supplied of it in the market increases, and when the price of a commodity falls, its quantity supplied decreases, other factors determining supply remaining the same*. Thus, according to the law of supply, the quantity supplied of a commodity is directly or positively related to price. It is due to this direct relationship between price of a commodity and its quantity supplied that the supply curve of a commodity slopes upward to right as seen from supply curve *SS* in Fingure. 7.6. When price of wheat rises from ₹ 520 to ₹ 530 per quintal the qunatity supplied of wheat in the market increases from 200 quintals to 225 quintals per period.

Corresponding to the demand schedule explained in an earlier chapter, we can construct an individual's supply schedule. Also by totalling up the amount supplied at various prices by all the sellers in a market, we can obtain the supply schedule of the market. Supply schedule represents the relation between prices and the quantities that the firms are willing to produce and sell. We have given in Table 7.2 a supply schedule of wheat per day in a market.

It will be seen from the above table that when price of wheat is ₹ 500 per quintal, the 100 quintals of wheat are supplied in the market. When price of wheat rises to ₹ 510 per quintal, 150 quintals of wheat are supplied. When price of wheat goes up to ₹ 550 per quintal, its quantity supplied in the market has risen to 275 quintals. By plotting the above supply schedule of wheat on a graph paper we have obtained supply curve *SS* in Fig. 7.6. In Fig. 7.2, the quantity supplied has been measured along the *X*-axis and price of wheat has been measured along the *Y*-axis. It will be seen from this figure that supply curve slopes upward from left to right, which indicates that as the price of wheat rises, quantity supplied increases and *vice versa*. This is in a sharp contrast to the demand curve of a commodity which slopes downward from left to right.

Assumptions of Law of Supply

As stated above, according to the law of supply, there is **positive relation between price and**

quantity supplied, that is, more quantity of a good is supplied at a higher price. As in case of other laws of economics, the law of supply is also based on some assumptions. First, the law of supply assumes that firms operate in a competitive market structure and no individual firm has a monopoly over the production of the commodity. This law does not apply to the supply by the monopolist or any producer working under oligopoly and monopolistic competition as individual firms in these market structures exercise some control over the price of their products. Second, this law of supply applies when the short-run marginal cost is rising in the region where it is profitable to produce. It may be recalled that short-run marginal cost-rises due to the diminishing marginal returns to the variable factors. Only in case of the rise in marginal cost the firms would supply more at a higher price so as to cover rise in marginal cost when more quantity of output is produced by hiring additional variable inputs.

Third, for the law of supply to apply the firms should aim at maximising profits or sales revenue. If they do not maximise profits or sales, they may not produce more to increase the quantity supplied of a commodity. Fourth, for the law of supply to hold it is assumed that technology or input prices remain constant when price of a good rises. If there is improvement in technology or fall in input prices, then more supply of the product may be made by firms at the given various prices.

Fifth, *in case of the competive industry the law of supply will hold if on the expansion of industry the external diseconomies exceed external economies* so that we have an increasing-cost industry and long-run supply curve of the industry slopes upward. Therefore, in this case too more is supplied at a higher price. In case of constant-cost industry external diseconomies, if any, cancel out external economies when the industry expands in the long run by the entry of new firms, the long-run supply curve of the industry is a horizontal straight line. Therefore, in constant cost industry more is supplied at the same price in the long run and the law of supply does not apply in this case. On the other hand, if on the expansion of industry *external economies* outweigh the *external diseconomies*, the industry will be *decreasing-cost industry* and its long-run supply curve will be downward sloping. As a consequence, in case of decreasing cost industry in the long-run *more will be supplied at a lower price by the industry*. This behaviour is quite opposite of the law of supply.

Explanation of the Law of Supply: Why does Supply Curve Generally Slope Upward ?

It has been observed from the experiences in the real world that price of a product and quantity supplied of it by firms producing it are directly related with each other, that is, at a higher price more is supplied and *vice versa*, other things remaining the same. In analysing the relation between price of a commodity and the quantity supplied, given *Cetris paribus* assumption we are dealing with the supply function, $Q_x^S = f(P_x)$. This positive relationship between price and quantity supplied is an important law of economics. How do we explain it? It should be remembered that firms are driven by profit motive. The higher the price of a product, given the cost per unit of output, makes it profitable to produce more of it. The higher price of a product serves as an incentive for the producer to produce more of it. The higher the price, the greater the incentive for the firm to produce and supply more of a commodity in the market, other things remaining the same.

The basic reason behind the law of supply (that is, the positive relationship between price of a commodity and quantity supplied of it) is the way the cost per unit changes as output is expanded to offer more for sale. Further, the changes in quantity supplied of a product following changes in its price depends on the *possibilities of substitution of one product for an other*. For example, if price of wheat in the market rises, the farmers will alter the cropping pattern so as to produce more of wheat by withdrawing land and other resources from the cultivation of gram and devoting them to the production of wheat. This is because high market price for wheat relative to gram induces farmers, who aim at maximising profits, to use more resources for production of wheat and fewer resources for production of gram.

To produce more of a product, firms have to devote more resources to its production. As seen above, when production of a product is expanded by using more resources, diminishing marginal returns to variable factors occur. Due to the diminishing marginal returns average and marginal costs of production increase. This implies that more quantity of commodity would be produced and supplied in the market only at a higher price so as to cover higher cost of production.

However, if marginal cost of production does not rise with the increase in output as, for instance, happens when a commodity is being produced under conditions of *constant returns*, the more will be produced and supplied at the given constant price. That is, supply curve in this case will be a horizontal straight line. It is also worth mentioning that if a commodity is subject to increasing returns, the expansion of output of the commodity will reduce the unit cost of production. As a result of increasing returns, more will be supplied at the lower prices and the supply curve will be sloping downward. But, since it is diminishing marginal returns (that is, increasing average and marginal costs) what is merasuring average and marginal costs) which is generally the rule, *the supply curve generally slopes upward to the right*.

The Concept of Supply Curve and Perfect Competition

As 'demand' is defined as a schedule of the quantities of a good that will be purchased at different prices, the supply similarly, refers to a schedule of the quantities of a good that will be offered for sale at different prices. Supply curve is therefore, a graphic representation of what quantities of a good will be offered for sale at all possible prices. Supply curve depicts the sellers' quantity reactions to various prices. Thus the quantity supplied, like the quantity demanded, is a function of price. There is, however, an important difference between the reaction of quantity supplied and that of quantity demanded to changes in price of the good. Whereas the quantity demanded of a good generally increases with the fall in price of the good and decreases with the rise in its price, the quantity supplied decreases with the fall in price of a good and increases with the rise in its price. In other words, while the quantity demanded has a negative or inverse relation with the price, the quantity supplied bears generally a direct relation with the price. The positive relation between quantity supplied and price lies in the nature of the marginal costs of production which generally rise as more quantity of a good is produced. This is because of positive relation between price and quantity supplied that supply curve slopes upward from left to right. *While the short-run supply curve always slopes upward to right, the long-run supply curve may slope either upward or downward, or it may be of a horizontal straight line depending upon whether the industry is working under increasing cost or decreasing cost or constant cost conditions.* However, the upward-sloping supply curve showing increasing cost is a more typical case even in the long run.

It is worth nothing here that the concept of supply curve, as it is used in economic theory, is relevant only for the case of perfect or pure competition and it is quite inapplicable to the cases of imperfect competition—monopolistic competition, monopoly and oligopoly. This is because the *notion of supply curve refers to the question as to how much quantity of a commodity a firm will supply at various given prices*. In other words, notion of supply curve refers to the quantity reactions of a firm when the firm itself exercises no influence over the determination of price and takes price as given datum for it and adjusts its quantity produced or supplied. Since only in perfect or pure competition a firm exercises no influence over the price which is determined by impersonal market mechanism of demand and supply and is beyond the control of individual firms, the concept of supply curve is relevant only for perfect or pure competition. So far as short-run supply curve of the industry under perfect competition is concerned, it is a mere lateral summation of the short-run supply curves of the firms.

Under various forms of imperfect competition, an individual firm does not take the price as given and is not a mere quantity adjuster. In fact, under various forms of imperfect competition, a firm sets its own price. For a firm under imperfect competition it is not a question of adjusting output or supply at a given price but of choosing *price-output combination* which maximises its profits. Commenting on the relevance of supply curve, Prof. Baumol writes, "*The supply curve is, strictly speaking, a concept which is usually relevant only for the case of pure (or perfect) competition. The reason for this lies in its definition–the supply curve is designed to answer question of the form, 'How much will firm A supply if it encounters a price which is fixed at P dollars*'. But such a question is most relevant to the behaviour of firms that actually face prices over whose determination they exercise no influence.

CHANGES IN SUPPLY : INCREASE AND DECREASE IN SUPPLY

As stated above, the supply of a commodity in economics means the entire schedule or curve

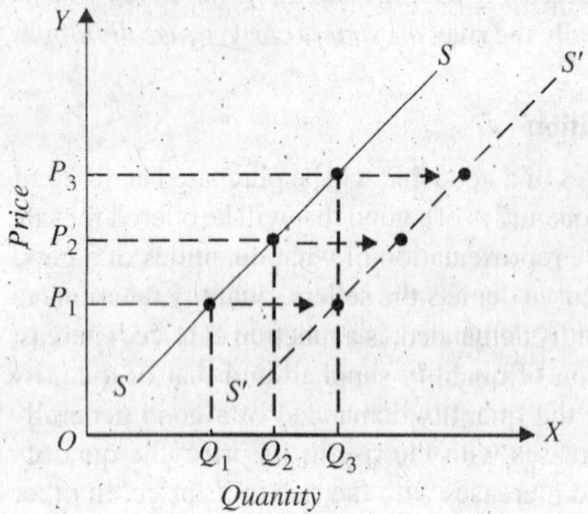

Fig. 7.7. *Increase in supply causing a rightward shift in the supply curve*

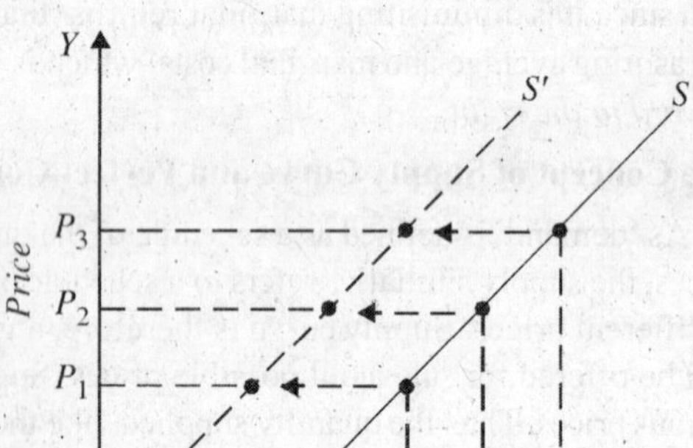

Fig. 7.8. *Decrease in supply causing a leftward shift in the supply curve*

depicting the relationship between price and quantity supplied of the commodity, given the other factors influencing supply. These other factors are the state of technology, prices of inputs (resources), prices of other related commodities, etc., which are assumed constant when the relationship between price and quantity supplied of a commodity is examined. It is the change in these factors that cause a shift in the supply curve due to the changes in factors other than price. For example, when prices of inputs such as labour and raw materials used for the production of a commodity decline, this will result in lowering the cost of production which will induce the producers to produce and make available a greater quantity of the commodity in the market at each price. This increases in supply of a commodity due to the reduction in prices of inputs will cause the entire supply curve to shift to the right as shown in Figure 7.7 where the supply curve shifts from *SS* to *S'S'*. As shown by arrow marks, at price P_1, P_2 and P_3 quantity supplied increases when supply increases causing a rightward shift in the supply curve. Similarly, progress in technology used for production of a commodity which increases productivity and reduces cost per unit will also cause the supply curve to shift to the right.

On the other hand, *decrease in supply means the reduction in quantity supplied at each price of the commodity* as shown in Figure 7.8 where as a result of decrease in supply the supply curve shifts to the left from *SS* to *S'S'*. As shown by the arrow marks, at each price such as P_1, P_2, P_3, the quantity supplied on the supply curve *S''S''* has declined as compared to the supply curve *SS*. The decrease in supply occurs when the prices of factors (inputs) used for the production of a commodity is produced at a higher cost per unit which causes a reduction in quantity supplied at each price. Similarly, the

7. W. J. Baumol, *Economic Theory and Operations Analysis,* **2nd edition, p.342.**

imposition of an excise duty or sales tax on a commodity means that each quantity will now be supplied at a higher price than before so as to cover the excise duty or sales tax per unit. This implies that quantity supplied of the commodity at each price will decrease as shown by the shift of the supply curve to the left.

Another important factor causing a decrease in supply of a commodity is the *rise in prices of other commodities* using the same factors. For example if the price of wheat resies sharply, it will become more profitable for the farmers to grow it. This will induce the farmers to reduce the cultivated area under other crops, say sugarcane, and devote it to the production of wheat. This will lead to the decrease in supply of sugarcane whose supply curve will shift to the left.

Further, agricultural production in India greatly depends on the rainfall due to Monsoon. If Monsoon comes in time and rainfall is adequate, there are bumper crops, the supply of agricultural products increases. However, in a year when Monsoon are untimely or highly inadequate, there is a sharp drop in agricultural output which cause shift in the supply curve of agricultural output to the left.

We thus see that there are several factors other than price which determine the supply of a commodity and any change in them will cause a shift in the entire supply curve.

Factors Determining Supply

It is clear from the supply schedule (Table 7.1) and the supply curve (Figure 7.1) given above that the quantity supplied varies directly with price of the product. A supply schedule and supply curve shows that the supply of a product is function of its price. However, the supply depends not only on the price of a product but on several other factors too. It should be remembered that in economic theory whereas the effect of changes in price of a product on the quantity supplied of it is depicted and explained *by movement along a given supply schedule or curve, the effect of other factors is represented by the shifts of the entire supply schedule or supply curve*. While making a supply schedule or drawing a supply curve we assume that these other factors remain the same. Thus when these other factors change, they cause a shift in the entire supply curve. The factors other than price which determine price are the following :–

(*a*) **Production Technology**–The change in technology affects the supply function by altering the cost of production. If there occurs an improvement in production technology used by the firm, the unit cost of production declines and consequently the firms would supply more than before at the given price. That is, the supply would increase implying thereby that the entire supply curve would shift to the right.

(*b*) **Prices of Inputs or Factors**– Changes in prices of factors or resources also cause a change in cost of production and consequently bring about a change in supply. For example, if either wages of labour increase or prices of raw materials and fuel go up, the unit cost of production will rise. With higher unit cost of production, less would be supplied than before at various given prices. This implies that supply curve would shift to the left.

(*c*) **Prices of other Products**–When we draw a supply curve we assume that the prices of other products remain unchanged. Now, any change in the prices of other products would influence the supply of a product by causing substitution of one product for another. For example, if the market price of wheat rises, it will lead to the reduction in the production and supply of gram by the farmers as they would withdraw land and other resources from the production of gram and devote them to the production of wheat. This will cause a leftwards shift in the supply curve of gram.

(*d*) **Objective of the Firm**—The objective of a firm also determines the supply of a product produced by it. If the firms aim to maximise sales or revenue rather than profits, the production of the product produced by them and hence its supply in the market would be larger. Similarly, if the firms seek to maximise their growth rather than short-run profits, they may produce and supply more as compared to their profit-maximising levels of output.

(*e*) **Number of Producers (or firms)**–If the number of firms producing a product increases, the market supply of the product will increase causing a rightward shift in the supply curve. When, in the short run, firms in an industry are making supper-normal profits, the new firms enter that industry in the long run and consequently the total production and supply of the product of the industry increases. On the other hand, due to losses in the short-run if some firms leave the industry, the supply of its product will decrease.

(*f*) **Future Price Expectations**–The supply of a commodity in the market at any time is also determined by sellers' expectations of future prices. If, as happens during inflationary periods, sellers expect the prices to rise in future, they would reduce supply of a product in the market at would instead hoard the commodity. The hoarding of huge quantities of goods by traders is an important factor in reducing their supplies in the market and thus causing further rise in their prices.

(*f*) **Taxes and Subsidies**– Taxes and subsidies also influence the supply of a product. If an excise duty or sales tax is levied on a product, the firms will supply the same amount of it at a higher price or less quantity of it at the same price. This implies that imposition of a sales tax or excise duty causes a leftward slift in the supply curve. The opposite happens in case of the supply of a commodity on which government decides to provide subsidy.

If follows from above that technology, prices of factors and products, expectations regarding future prices and objective of the firms are the important determinants of supply which cause rightward or leftward slift in the whole supply curve.

COMPETITIVE MARKET EQUILBRIUM

There was a dispute among earlier economists who came befroe Marshall as to whether it is supply of a good or the demand for it that determines its price. Broadly speaking, there were two schools of thought in this regard. One school of thought believed that it is cost of production, that is, the force working on the supply side, which determiens the price of the product. The other school of thought held the view that it is the utility or more precisely the marginal utility that determines the demand and therefore the price of the product. But each school of thought took one-sided view of the pricing problem. The credit of finding the true answer to the pricing problem goes to Marshall who held that both demand and supply were equally important in determining the price of a product. In other words, Marshall said that both the marginal utility of a product and the cost of producing it took part in determining price. He likened the price determination to the cutting of a piece of a paper by a pair of scissors. This famous analogy is worth quoting here. "*We might as reasonably dispute whether it is the upper or the under blade of a pair of scissors that cuts a piece of paper as whether value is governed by utility or cost of production. It is true that when one blade is held still and the cutting is effected by moving the other, we may say with careless brevity that the cutting is done by the second, but the statement is not strictly accurate and is to be excused only so long as it claims to be merely a popular and not a strictly scientific account of what happens.*"[3]

Neither the upper blade nor the lower one taken individually can cut the paper; both are required to do the work of cutting. The lower blade may be held stationary and only the upper one may be moved, yet both are indispensable for cutting the paper. Similarly, both demand and supply are essential forces for determining prices of goods. Professors Stonier and Hague rightly remark, "*The only really accurate answer to the question whether it is supply or demand which determines price is that it is both. At times it will seem that one is more important than the other, for one will be active and the other passive. For example, if demand remains constant but supply conditions vary, it is demand which is passive and supply active. But neither is more or less important than the other in determining price.*"[4]

In the chapters on theory of demand we saw that the demand curve of a commodity normally slopes downward. In other words, with the fall in price, quantity demand rises and *vice versa*. In the theory of firm we studied that the supply curve of a commodity usually slopes upward. In other

3. Alfred Marshall, *Principles of Economics*, 8th edition, p. 344
4. Stonier and Hague: *A Textbook of Economic Theory*, 4th edition, 1972, p. 155

words, an industry will offer to sell more quantity of a good at a high price than at a lower one. The level of price at which demand and supply curves intersect each other will finally come to stay in the market. In other words, the price which will come to prevail in the market is one at which quantity demanded is equal to quantity supplied. *The price at which quantity demanded equals quantitty supplied is called equilibrium price*, for at this price the two forces of demand and supply exactly balance each other. *The quantity of the good which is purchased and sold at this equilibrium price is called equilibrium amount*. Thus, the intersection of demand and supply curves determines price-quantity equilibrium.

Only at the equilibrium price wishes of both the buyers and sellers are satisfied. If prices were greater or less than the equilibrium price, the buyers' and sellers' wishes would be inconsistent; either the buyers would demand more than the amount offered by sellers, or the sellers would be ready to supply more than the amount demanded by the buyers. If price was greater than the equilibrium price, quantity supplied would exceed quantity demanded. It means some of the sellers will not be able to sell the amount of the good they wanted to supply. These unsatisfied sellers would try to dispose of the unsold amount of the good by bidding down price. The price will go on declining until the quantity demanded equals quantity supplied.

On the other hand, if price was lower than the equilibrium price, the quantity demanded would exceed quantity supplied. Some buyers would not be able to obtain the amount of the good they wanted to pruchase at the prevailing price. They will therefore bid up price in their effort to get all that they desired to buy. The price will go on rising until the quantity demanded and quantity supplied are again equal. We thus see that the price which will settle down can be neither greater than, nor less than the equilibrium price. It is the equilibrium price which will finally come to stay in the market.

We illustrate below in Table 7.3 the process of price determination with the aid of the demand and supply schedules and the curves which will make the whole thing very clear. In the table below are given demand and supply schedules relating to a woollen cloth. It will be seen there that only at a price of ₹ 40, quantity demanded is equal to quantity supplied. Therefore, price of ₹ 40 will settle down in the market. Only at this price are all buyers and sellers satisfied. Thus, price of ₹ 40 is the equilibrium price and quantity exchanged at this price is 120 thousands metres. 120 thousand metres is the equilibrium amount. Once this equilibrium price comes to prevail in the market, there will be no tendency for it to change. If price is greater or lower than ₹ 40, then it will tend to change and come to the level of ₹ 40. For instance, if the price was ₹ 50, the buyers would demand 80

Table 7.3
Equilibrium Between Demand and Supply

Price ₹	*Quantity Demanded (in thousand-metres)*	*Quantity Supplied (in thousand metres)*	*Pressure on Price*
10	240	20	↓
20	200	40	↓
30	160	80	↓
40	120	120	Equilibrium
50	80	160	↑
60	40	200	↑
70	20	240	↑

thousand metres, while the sellers will be ready to supply 160 thouand metres. Thus, the sellers would not be able to sell the whole quantity of the cloth they want to supply and would therefore compete with each other to sell the extra quantity of the cloth by bidding down the price. In this way, the price will go on falling until the equilibrium level of ₹ 40 is reached where the quantity which the buyers would demand equals the quantity which the sellers would be prepared to sell. Further, suppose the price was below the equilibrium price, say ₹ 30. At price of ₹ 30, the quantity demanded by the buyers is 160 thousand metres while the sellers are willing to supply only 80 thousand metres. The unsatisfied buyers will then bid up the price. In this way, price will go on rising till it fianlly comes to settle down at ₹ 40 where all buyers and sellers are satisfied.

In graphical terms, the equilibrium between demand and supply is depicted in Fig. 7.9 where *DD* is the demand curve sloping downward and *SS* is the supply curve sloping upward. Demand and supply are in equilibrium at point *E* where two curves intersect each other. It means that only at price *OP* (corresponding to the intersection point), the quantity demanded is equal to quantity supplied. *OM* is the equilibrium quantity which is exchanged at price *OP*, if price is greater than the equilibrium price, say *OP″*, the quantity demanded by the buyers is *P″L*, while the quantity offered to supply by the sellers is *P″K*. Thus *LK* is the excess supply which the buyers will not take off from the market at price *OP″*. In order to dispose of this excess supply, the sellers will compete with each other and in doing so they will bring down the price. Thus there will be tendency for the price to fall to the level of equilibrium price *OP*.

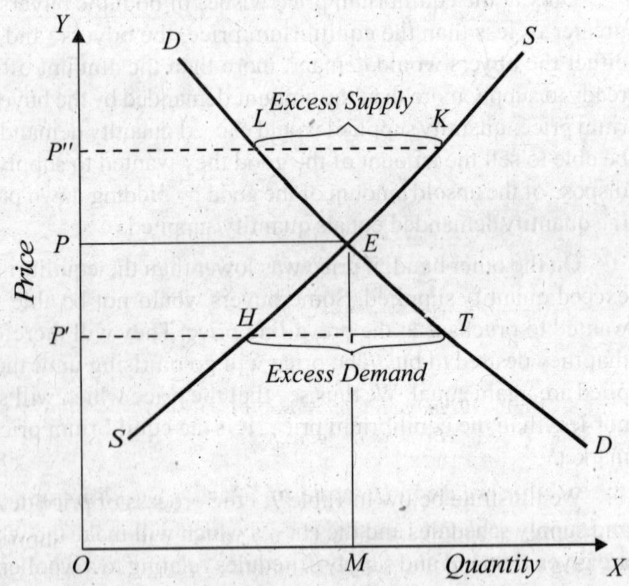

Fig. 7.9. *Determination of Price through Intersection of Demand and Supply Curves*

At price *OP′*, which is less than the equilibrium price, the buyers demand *P′T*, the sellers are prepared to supply only *P′H*. *HT* represents excess demand. The unsatisfied buyers will compete with each other to obtain the limited supply of cloth and in their effort they will bid up the price. Thus there will be tendency for the price to rise to the level of equilibrium price *OP* where all wanting to buy and all wanting to sell will be satisifed.

From above it follows that if the price is above or below the equilibrium price, certain forces in the system will operate to bring the price to the level at which there is equilibrium between demand and supply or what is often called market equilibrium. The price at which demand and supply curves intersect each other will eventually come to prevail in the market.

CHANGES IN MARKET EQUILIBRIUM

Changes in either demand or supply cause changes in market equilibrium. Several forces bringing about changes in demand and supply are constantly working which cause changes in market equilibrium, that is, equilibrium prices and quantities. In the earlier chapters we have explained the factors or forces which cause shift in demand and supply curves. The demand may increase or decrease, the supply curve remaining unchanged. This would cause a change in equilibrium price and quantity. Similarly, the increase or decrease in supply, the demand curve remaining constant, would have an impact on equilibrium price and quantity. Both supply and demand for goods may change simultaneously causing a change in market equilibrium. Supply-demand analysis is an important tool of economics with which we can make forecasts about how prices and quantities will change in response to changes in demand and supply. We explain below the impact of changes in demand and supply on equilibrium price and quantity.

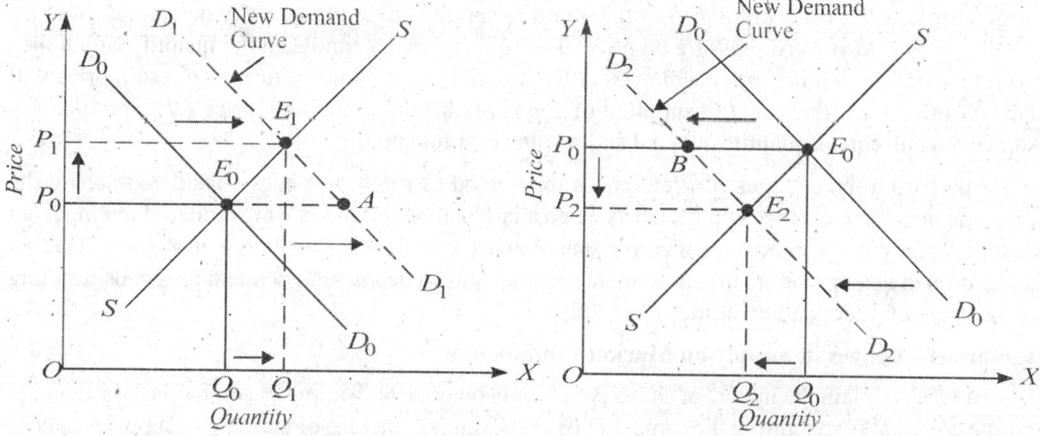

Fig. 7.10. *Impact of increase in Demand on Price and Quantity (P↑, Q↑).*

Fig. 7.11. *Impact of Decrease in Demand on Price and Quantity. (P↓, Q↓).*

Impact of Increase in Demand on Market Equilibrium

Increase in demand affect prices and quantities. Suppose there is increase in income of the working class due to the enhancement of their salaries by the Pay Commission. As a result of this increase in income, their demand for cloth for shirting will increase causing a shift in the entire demand curve for cloth to the right. This will raise the equilibrium price and quantity of cloth, the supply curve of cloth remaining unchanged as is shown in Fig. 10.10. It is important to understand the chain of causation which leads to the increase in price and quantity as a result of increase in demand. Consider Fig. 7.10, in which D_0D_0 and *SS* are the initial demand and supply curves of cloth. The increase in income causes a shift in the entire demand curve to the right to the new position D_1D_1 while the supply curve *SS* remains constant. It will be observed from Fig. 7.10, that with the shift in demand curve to D_1D_1 at the old price OP_0 excess demand of cloth equal to E_0A has emerged. This excess demand of the good exerts upward pressure on price. This will result in rise in price to OP_1 where again quantity demanded equals quantity supplied and new market equilibrium is attained and excess demand is eliminated. It is worth noting that increase in demand is the most important factor causing inflation, that is, rise in prices and is generally described as *demand-pull* inflation. Though the term inflation is used in the context of *a rise in general price level*, but it has roots at the micro level (*i.e.*, in case of individual goods). Apart from increase in income, a favourable change in consumer's preferences for a particular good, rise in price of its substitutes will also cause an increase in demand for a good.

Impact of Decrease in Demand on Market Equilibrium

Now, take the opposite case of the impact of decrease in demand on market equilibrium, the supply curve remaining the same. As explained earlier, the decrease in demand causes a shift in the entire demand curve to the left. This is graphically shown in Fig. 7.11, where originally demand curve D_0D_0 intersects the supply curve *SS* of eggs at point E_0 and determines equilibrium price equal to OP_0 and equilibrium quantity OQ_0. Now, suppose that doctors advise the people to take less eggs as it contains greater quantity of cholestrol which increases the risk of heart disease. Consequently, demand for eggs decreases causing a shift in the demand curve to the left to the new position D_2D_2. The new equilibrium between demand and supply is attained at price P_2 and quantity Q_2, which are lower than the initial equilibrium price OP_0 and quantity OQ_0. Thus, *the decrease in demand leads to the fall in both price and quantity*. How does this come about? With the decrease in demand and consequently leftward shift in the demand curve to D_2D_2, supply curve remaining unchanged, at the original price OP_0, the surplus E_0B of the quantity supplied over the quantity demanded emerges which exerts a downward pressure on price. The sellers which cannot sell the quantity which they want to sell at the original price will make offers to sell eggs at a lower price. As a result, price will fall. As price falls, the quantity supplied of eggs is reduced. At the new price OP_2, the quantity supplied again equals quantity demand and surplus is eliminated.

Apart from the changes in preferences for a good as in case of eggs considered above, the decrease in incomes of the people such as when a large number of people are rendered unemployed during depression, the reduction of crop production in agriculture due to failure of Monsoon leading to the drop in incomes of the Indian farmers can also cause a decrease in demand for goods resulting in lowering of prices and quantities of goods.

Impact of Changes in Supply on Market Equilibrium

Now, we explain the impact of changes in supply on price and output of commodity, the demand for the commodity remaining the same. Let us first examine the case of increase in supply. Suppose in a year there is good Monsoon in India yielding bumper crop of wheat. This will increase the supply of wheat in the market causing a shift in its supply curve to the right. The impact of increase

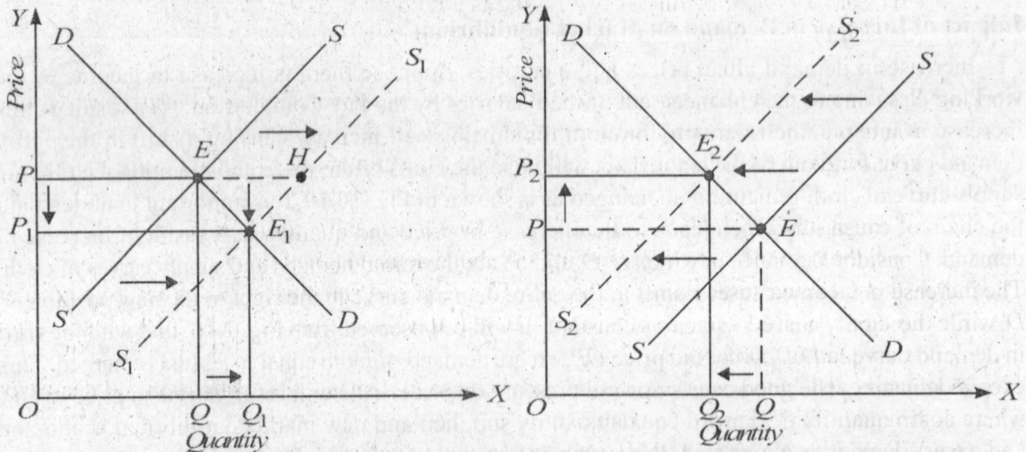

Fig. 7.12. *Increase in supply results in lowering of price and increase in quantity*

Fig. 7.13. *Decrease in supply cause rise in price and fall in quantity.*

in supply of wheat on equilibrium price and quantity is graphically depicted in Fig. 7.12. Originally, demand curve *DD* and supply curve *SS* of wheat intersect at point *E* and determine equilibrium price equal to *OP* and equilibrium quantity *OQ* exchanged between the sellers and buyers. Now, due to good monsoon resulting in bumper crop of wheat the supply curve of wheat shifts to the right from *SS* to the new position S_1S_1. The new supply curve S_1S_1 intersects the given demand curve *DD* at point E_1 at which the new lower equilibrium price OP_1 and larger quantity OQ_1 are determined. Thus, the *increase in supply leads to the fall in price and increase in equilibrium quantity*.

Improvements in technology, reduction in the prices of factors and resources used in the production of a commodity or lowering of excise duty on a commodity also leads to the increase in supply of the commodity. For example, in recent years improvements in technology in the manufacture of personal computers have served to increase the supply of personal computers causing their supply curve to shift to the right. This has resulted in lowering the prices of personal computers. A personal computer which was available at price above ₹ 60,000 a few years ago are now available at about ₹ 20,000. Similarly, in the Central Budget for 1993-94, the Finance Minister Dr. Manmohan Singh reduced excise duties on several commodities with the hope that producers it would pass it on to the consumers and result in shifting their supply curve to the right and thereby causing the drop in their prices. At lower prices, he argued, more of these commodities would be demanded and therefore it would help the industries which were facing demand recession.

Figure 7.13. illustrates the effect of decrease in supply on equilibrium price and quantity. It should be recalled in that decrease in supply can occur when prices of inputs (including labour) used in the production of a commodity rise. For example, hike in oil prices, increase in wages of labour, rise in prices of raw materials will raise the unit cost of production and cause a shift in the supply curve of a commodity to the left as shown in Figure 7.13. Similarly, hike in excise duty or sales tax or reduction in subsidely on a commodity will also lead to leftward shift in the supply curve of a commodity. It will be seen from Fig. 7.13 that decrease in supply and consequently leftward shift in the supply curve from *SS* to S_2S_2, leads to rise in equilibrium price of a commodity and fall in equilibrium quantity bought and sold.

QUESTIONS FOR REVIEW

1. Define demand for a commodity. Explain the various factors which determine demand for a commodity.
2. Demand for a commodity refers to :
   (*a*) desire for a commodity (*b*) need for a commodity
   (*c*) desire for a commodity backed by ability to pay for it.
   (*d*) ability to pay for a commodity.
3. What is meant by *Ceteris Paribus* ? What factors are covered under *Ceteris Paribus* condition in relation to demand for a commodity ?
4. You are given the following demand function for a commodity :

   $$Q_d = 20 - 2P$$

   where Q_d stands for quantity demand of a commodity and P for its price.
   Draw the demand curve representing the above demand function.
   [**Hints.** Taking some prices such as ₹ 3, 5, 7 etc. and substitute them in the given demand function to find the quantities demanded at various prices. Then plot these various price-quantity combinations.
5. Distinguish between (1) extension and increase in demand, (2) contraction and decrease in demand. Illustrate with diagrams.
6. Which of the following statements are *true* and which are *false* ?
   (*a*) The law of demand states a direct relationship between demand and price
   (*b*) Increase in demand for a commodity is due to a fall in its price
   (*c*) There is an inverse relationship between price and quantity demanded
   (*d*) Contraction in demand is the result of decrease in the number of consumers
   (*e*) Decrease in demand and contraction in demand have the same meaning
   (*f*) In a typical demand schedule quantity demanded varies directly with price
   (*g*) A change in quantity demanded as a result of a price change will mean a shift in the demand curve.
7. Distinguish between the movement along a demand curve and a shift in the demand curve.
8. State the law of demand. How would you explain it with substitution effect and income effect ? Are there any exceptions to this law ?

9. Given the following market demand function for the commodity X

$$Q_x = f(P_x, P_y, P_z, I.T.A)$$

where

P_x = Price of the commodity X

P_y = Price of a substitute commodity Y

P_z = Price of commodity Z which is complement of X

I = Level of per captia income of consumers

T = Tastes and preferences of consumers

A = Advertising expenditure by a firm producing X

How will the market demand for a commodity change ?

(*i*) if price of the commodity X rises,

(*ii*) if price of the substitute good Y rises,

(*iii*) if price of complementary commodity Z falls,

(*iv*) per capita income (I) of the consumers rises,

(*v*) the firm producing X increases its advertisement expenditure.

10. A survey shows that most people prefer Zen to Maruti 800. If this is true why do more people buy Maruti 800 than Zen ?

(**Hint** : People's demand does not depend on preferences only, but also depends on their income and prices of goods. Though more people like to have Zen Car, they do not go in for it and instead buy Maruti 800 because price of Zen is higher and their income is relatively low.)

11. Why does demand curve usually slope downward to the right ? Are there any exceptions to this ?

12. Distinguish between Giffen paradox and Veblen effect.

13. Distinguish between a demand function and demand curve. What are the factors that cause a shift in the demand curve ?

CHAPTER 7A
APPLICATIONS OF DEMAND AND SUPPLY ANALYSIS

Introduction

In the last chapter we have explained how prices of goods are determined by demand and supply. The analysis of price determination in terms of demand and supply is not merely of great theoretical significance but it has important several practical applications in economic life of a country. This analysis of demand and supply has been used to explain the implications of price control and rationing, minimum price fixation, incidence of taxes, several other economic problems and policies. In the present chapter we shall explain some of these applications of demand and supply analysis.

In the analysis of the previous chapter we have assumed that market mechanism is allowed to function without interference by the government. But government in the modern mixed economies interferes with the functioning of the market system to influence prices so as to promote social welfare when it is felt that free working of market will not produce desirable results. The government can interfere with the working of the economy in two main ways. The first government fixes the *maximum price* (often called *price ceiling*) or fix the minimum price often called floor price). *Price control* of foodgrains, rent controls are the examples of fixation of maximum price or price ceiling above which the sellers cannot charge the price. *Agricultural price support programme* is the example of fixation of minimum price to assure minimum remunerative prices to farmers so as to protect their interests.

The second way in which government interferers with the price or market system is *working through the market*. In the second way government can impose taxes on the commodities or provide subsidies. These taxes and subsidies affect the market supply or demand curves which determine prices of goods and services. Imposition of heavy excise duties on cigarettes or other drugs and providing subsidies on agricultural products are examples of interference by government through market. In what follows we will explain both types of intervention with the functioning of markets by government we begin our analysis with the imposition of price control and rationing by government.

PRICE CONTROL AND RATIONING

In times of war imposition of price control is quite common and was introduced by several countries during the Second World War. Even in peace time, price controls on essential commodities have been introduced in several countries to help the poor against inflation. *Under price control the maximum price of a good is fixed above which the sellers cannot charge from the consumers*. Price control is imposed or price ceiling is set below the equilibrium price. This is because if the price ceiling is set above the equilibrium price that balances supply and demand, it will have no effect or in other words, *it will not be binding*. Consider Fig. 7A.1 where demand and supply balance each other at price P_1. At this equilibrium price both buyers and sellers are satisfied, buyers are getting the quantity of the good they want to buy at this equilibrium price and the sellers are selling what they want to sell at this price. Therefore, the higher price P_2 than the price P_1 fixed by government will have no effect.

When it is realised that the equilibrium price of a commodity is too high and consequently some buyers go unsatisfied, for they lack the means to pay for it, the Government may pass a law through which *it fixes the maximum price of the commodity* at a level below the equilibrium price. Now, at a price lower than the equilibrium price, quantity demanded will be larger than the quantity supplied and thus *shortage* of the commodity will emerge; some consumers who are willing and able to buy at that price will go unsatisfied. Buyers would, if permitted, bid up the price to the equilibrium level.

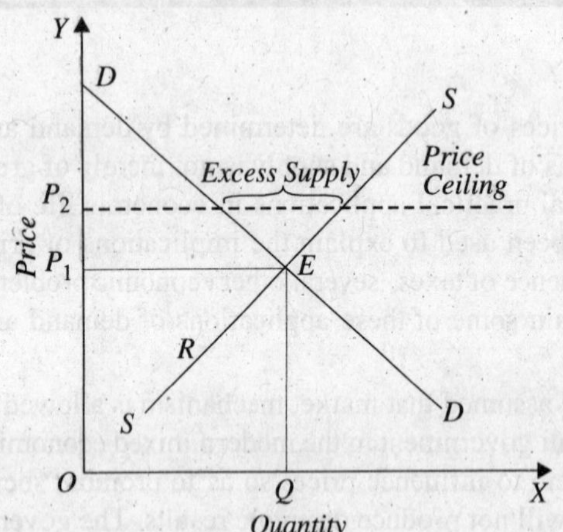

Fig. 7A.1. *Price Ceiling above the Equilibrium: Price is Not Binding and is Ineffective*

Fig. 7A.2. *Effect of Price Control (i.e., Fixing Price Ceiling below the Equilibrium Level)*

But under price control by the Government, price is not free to move to equate quantity demanded with the quantity supplied. Thus, when the Government intervenes to fix the maximum price for a commodity, price loses its important function of a rationing device.

Price control and problems raised by it are graphically illustrated in Fig. 7A.2 where demand and supply curves, *DD* and *SS* of sugar are given. As will be seen from this figure that demand and supply curves intersect at point *E* and accordingly OP_1 is the equilibrium price of sugar. Suppose that this equilibriumm price OP_1 of sugar is very high so that many poor people are not able to obtain any quantity of it. Therefore, the Government intervenes and fixes the maximum price of sugar at the level OP_0 which is below the equilibrium price OP_1. As will be seen from Fig. 7A.2 at the controlled price OP_0 quantity demanded exceeds the quantity supplied. At price OP_0, whereas the producers offer to supply P_0R quantity of sugar, the consumers are prepared to buy P_0T quantity of it. As a result, shortage of sugar equal to the amount *RT* has emerged and some consumers will go unsatisfied.

In the absence of Government intervention fixing the maximum price at OP_0 level, the excess demand equal to *RT* would have led to rise in the price to the equilibrium level OP_1 where quantity demanded is equal to quantity supplied. *But, under price control by the government, to charge a price higher than the legally fixed maximum price* OP_0 is punishable under the law. Therefore, the available supply *OM* at the fixed price OP_0 has to be somehow allocated or rationed between the consumers. The rationing can take many forms. This task of rationing the available supply *OM* may be done by the producers or sellers themselves. The sellers may adopt the principle of "*first come first served*" and distribute the available supply of sugar among those who are *first in the queue* before their shops. This system of rationing is therefore called *queue rationing*. The second method of rationing or allocating the scarce supply of the good is to distribute it on the basis of what has been called, "*allocation by sellers' preferences*". Under this, the available supply of good is sold by the sellers to certain preferred consumers at the controlled price. The sellers may sell the good at the controlled price to their regular customers. They may also adopt the policy of selling the available supply to the buyers belonging to certain caste, religion, colour etc. and not to others.

If the Government does not like the rationing of a commodity among the population on the basis of either "first come first served" or arbitrary allocation by sellers' preferences, it may introduce *coupon rationing* of the commodity. Under the coupon rationing system consumers are given ration coupons just sufficient to buy the available quantity of the commodity. The number of ration coupons issued to a family may depend on the age of its members, sex, and the number of family members or on any other criterion considered desirable.

Black Market. A point worth noting is that price control with or without rationing is likely to give rise to the *black market* in the commodity. *By black market we mean the sale of a commodity by the producers or sellers at a price higher than the controlled price.* As mentioned above, at the controlled maximum price *fixed below the equilibrium price*, the quantity demanded would exceed the quantity supplied and consequently shortage of the commodity would develop. It is thus clear that some buyers of the commodity will not be fully satisfied as they will not be able to get the quantity of the good they wish to buy at the controlled price. Therefore, they will be prepared to pay a higher price for getting more quantity of the good, but they can do so only in the black market. Sellers will also be interested in selling the commodity, at least some quantity of it, in the black market at a higher price as it will fetch them larger profits.

Even when coupon rationing is introduced there will be pressure for the black market to develop. This is because the consumers are willing to buy more quantity of the commodity than is available at the controlled price, whereas rationing only distributes the available quantity of the commodity. Therefore, the consumers who want to procure larger quantity than the rationing amount will be prepared to pay a higher price to get some quantity in the black market.

There is sufficient evidence in India and abroad to confirm the predictions based on demand and supply analysis. *When price control and rationing system for some commodities which were in shortage were introduced during the Second World War and after, black markets developed in spite of punitive measures taken by the authorities.*

RENT CONTROL

Rent controls is an other example of maximum price that Government fixes on the rental price of housing units. Under rent control, the Government fixes the rent per month per housing unit of a standard size which is *below the equibrium rent* that would otherwise prevail in the marekt. The maximum rent fixed by the Government helps the tenants, who generally belong to lower and middle income groups and intend to prevent their exploitation by rich landlords who would charge a very high market determined rates of rent. Market determined equilibrium rent rate happens to be high because demand for rental housing tend to be relatively greater than supply of it. In several important cities such a New York, London, Mumbai, Delhi. Government has imposed rent control to help the lower and middle income people by ensuring rental houses at fair rents. In Delhil under Delhi Rent Control Act, 1958 which has now been amended by the recently passed New Rent Control Act 1995. This law specifies some monthly rental rates of housing units of some standard sizes above which the landlord cannot charge rent. Besides, the landlord cannot evict the tenants easily except under some conditions laid down in the law. It is however important to understand both the short-run and long-run effects of rent control.

Economists often point out the adverse effects of rent control and hold the view that it is highly inefficient way of helping the poor and lower middle class people. The adverse effects of rent control are evident only in the long run because it always takes time to construct new housing units/ apartments and also for the tenants to adjust to the rent and housing accommodation available on rent. So the long-run effect of rent control is different from the short run. In the short run the landlords have almost a fixed number of housing units/appartments to give on rent. Therefore, the supply curve of rental units is inelastic in the short-run. On the other hand, people searching for rental-housing units are also not very responsive in the short run as it always take time for them to adjust their housing arrangements. Thus, even demand for rental housing in relatively inelastic in the short run.

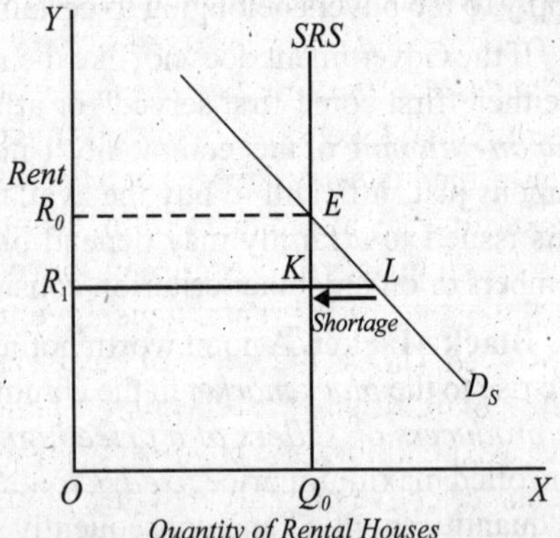

Fig. 7A.3. *Effect of Rent Control in the Short Run*

The effect of rent control in the short run is shown in Fig. 7A.3 short-run supply curve of housing units is perfectly inelastic at Q_0 number of housing units available for renting. D_S is the short-run demand curve which is also relatively inelastic. If left free to the market force, rent equal to R_0 will be determined at which there is equilibrium between demand and supply. Suppose R_0 is too high for the poor and middle class people to pay. To help them, government fixes ceiling on rent at R_1. It will seen from Fig. 7A.3 that at R_1, people demand R_1L housing units whereas supply of them remains at R_1K or OQ_0. Thus KL shortage of housing units has emerged since the demand and supply of housing units in the short run is inelastic, shortage caused by rent control is small. The main effect of rent control in the short-run is to reduce rents.

Although in the short run, landlords cannot do much to the lowering of rent through control, *further investment in constructing houses and apartments* by them will be reduced causing reduction in the supply of rental houses in the long run. In addition to this, the landlords will not spend any money *onrepairs and maintenance* of rental houses when rents are lowered. These steps will ultimately lead to the poor quality of rental houses and apartments. Thus, *in the long run, rent control has an important effect on the availability or supply of rental houses and their quantity*. It will be seen from Fig. 7A.4 that at the lower controlled rent OR_1 the quantity demanded of rental housing increases to OQ_2 and the quantity supplied of rental housing units falls to OQ_1. Thus, fixation of lower controlled rent OR_1 results in increase in the quantity demanded and decrease in the quantity supplied of rental houses and thereby leads to the emergene of the large shortage of rental houses equal to Q_1Q_2 or KL as will be see from Fig. 7A.4. *The greater the elasticity of supply and demand for rental housing in the long run, the greater will be the shortage of rental housing units as a result of imposition of rent control act.*

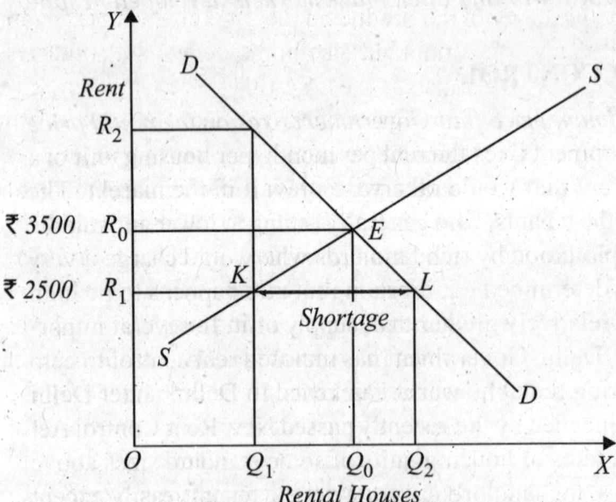

Fig. 7A.4. *Effect of Rent Control in the Long Run*

It many be noted that this shortage of rental housing represents the conditions of excess demand for rental housing. An important question is whether fixation of maximum rent which is lower than the equilibrium rent can be effectively enforced when conditions of excess demand or shortage of rental housing units emerges. Of course, no one can openly or explicitly charge a rent higher than the controlled rate. However, the emergence of the conditions of excess demand or shortage of rental housing will tend to put upward pressure on the actual rents received. Due to the excess demand conditions landlords have devised various ways to circumvent the rent control act and charge higher actual rents. Consider Fig. 7A.4 where it will be seen that at the controlled rent OR_1 of rental housing the quantity supplied of rental housing is OQ_1. Further, for OQ_1 rental housing units tenants are willing to pay rent equal to OR_2. *Under these conditions of excess demand and shortage of rental housing units, landlords tend to extract side payments from tenants, though explicitly they charge controlled rent.* For example, in Delhi and New York, two of the important world cities where rent control law operates, landlords require tenants to make a large non-refundable pay deposits or a large advance payments adjustable against monthly rents. Further, landlords may also require from tenants to make costly fittings or get expensive wood work done in the rental houses as a condition for rent and further also requiring them to pay for the repairs and maintenance of the rental housing units. All these ways of evading the rent control act have been observed. Unless the law explicity prohibits such practices, they will be operating and will have the effect of nullifying the rent control policy. That is, tenants will pay controlled rent OR_1 explicitly but extra expenditure and payments they are required to incur may add up to R_1R_0 per month so that the actual effective monthly rent may amount to the equilibrium rent OR_0.

It is evident from above that the consequence of rent control, like that of any other price control, is the emergence of shortage. However, in case of shortage of rental housing units those who are unable to get them, will make efforts to make another living arrangements. They may decide to live in other cities or satellite towns which are not covered by rent controls. Further, the disappointed seekers of rental housing may turn to the construction of their own self-occupied houses. But this requires a lot of finance which have to be arranged by them.

MINIMUM SUPPORT PRICE

In the price control we examined the case when the government fixed a *price ceiling* (that is, *maximum price*) to prevent it from rising to the equilibrium level. For many agricultural products the Government policy has been to fix a *price floor*, that is, the *minimum support price* above the equilibrium level which is considered to be low and unremunerative to the farmers. While in case of price control or fixation of price ceiling the Government simply announces the maximum price above which price cannot be charged by the producers or sellers of a product, in case of minimum support price, the Government becomes an active buyer of the product in the market. It is not only in India but also in the developed countries such as the USA that price support policy for agricultural products is adopted to provide reasonable prices to the farmers and increase their income. The effects of imposition of minimum support price for wheat, an important agricultural product, in India is illustrated in Fig. 7A.5 where demand curve *DD* and supply curve *SS* of wheat intersect at point *E*. Thus if price of wheat is allowed to be determined by the free working of demand for and supply of wheat, equilibrium price is *OP* and equilibrium quantity determined is *OQ*.

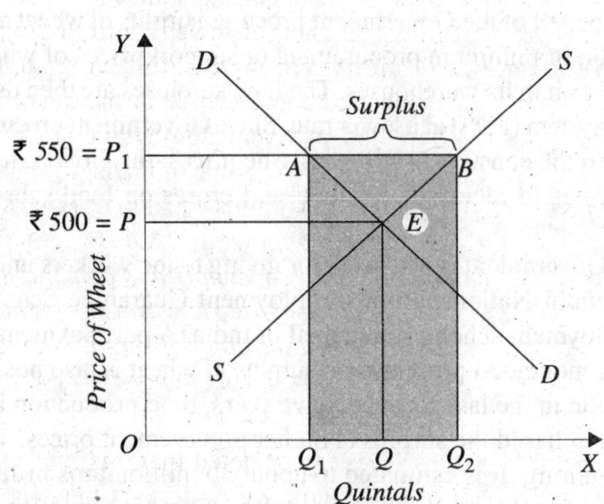

Fig. 7A.5. *Minimum Support Price for Agriculture*

Now suppose this free market determined equilibrium price *OP* (= ₹ 500 per quintal) is considered to be unremunerative which does not provide incentives to the farmers to produce wheat or expand its production. Therefore, to promote the interests of the farmers, the Government intervenes and fixes a higher minimum support price OP_1 (₹ 550 per quintal) for wheat. It will be seen from Fig. 7A.5 that at price OP_1 of wheat, the quantity demanded of wheat decreases to OQ_1 (= P_1A).

On the other hand, at higher price OP_1 farmers expand their output and supply a greater quantity OQ_2 (= P_1B) of wheat. Thus at minimum support price OP_1 the quantity of wheat supplied by the farmers exceeds the quantity demanded of it by the consumers in the market. This means that the imposition of minimum support price of wheat higher than the equilibrium price OP leads to the emergence of *surplus of wheat* equal to AB or Q_1Q_2. If the Government does not purchase this surplus this will tend to depress the price of wheat. Therefore, in order to ensure this minimum price of wheat OP_1 (= ₹ 550 per quintal) to the farmers the Government will have to purchase the entire surplus AB or Q_1Q_2 from the farmers. It should be noted that to purchase the surplus Q_1Q_2 from the farmers, the Government will have to make expenditure equal to $OP_1 \times Q_1Q_2$, that is, equal to the area Q_1ABQ_2. This expenditure on purchase of wheat surplus may be financed by taxation of the people.

It follows from above that under minimum support price OP_1 the farmers sell OQ_1 quantity of wheat in the free market and quantity Q_1Q_2 to the Government. At the free market determined equilibrium price OP and quantity OQ, the total income of the farmers will be equal to the area $OPEQ$. Now, with minimum support price equal to OP_1 and the total quantity sold equal to OQ_2, the income of the farmers has increased to OP_1BQ_2. Thus minimum support price policy has greatly benefited the farmers both in terms of price they receive for their product and the income they are able to earn.

A major problem facing the Government is how to dispose of the surplus it purchases from the farmer at the higher minimum support price. If the Government sells it in the market, the price of wheat in the market will fall which will defeat the purpose of support price policy. Alternatively, the Government may store the surplus and in this case the Government will incur storage costs. Besides, the wheat and any other foodgrains get rottoned if kept for longer time in storage bins. Thus while to produce surplus requires valuable resources such as labour, fertilizers, irrigation and other inputs, yet it is quite often left to decay in government warehouses. In America, one important way of disposing of surplus is to give them to the developing countries as food aid. But this food aid is not without problems. The American food aid to developing countries has tended to depress prices of foodgrains in these countries and therefore has harmed the interests of farmers of these developing countries.

In India Food Corporation of India on behalf of the Government procures surplus of wheat and rice production created as a result of fixation of minimum procurement or support prices of wheat and rice. Food Corporation of India then keeps it in its warehouses. The food surpluses are then used for distribution through Public Distribution System (PDS) at a lower rate. Since Government procures these food grains at a higher rate and sells to the consumers at lower issue prices, the Government subsidises the foodgrain consumption and has to incur several thousand crores on food subsidy annually.

Besides, food surplus procured by the Government is also used for giving to the workers under '*food for work*' programme, Mahatma Gandhi National Rural Employment Guarantee Scheme (MGNREGS) and other such special employment schemes launched in India. A part payment of wages is made in food and a part in form of money. At present food surplus of wheat is also posing a problem in India. Due to the good monsoon in the last six successive years, food production has been substantial and the Government has purchased the surplus at higher procurement prices. The surplus with the Government has been mounting. It is estimated to about 50 million tons in June 2003. On the other hand, off-take from public distribution system has fallen. There is a real danger of these food surpluses getting rottoned in warehouses of the Food Corporation of India. Therefore, Government of India deciding to export of wheat.

It should be noted that in Indian Government has been raising year after year the procurement or support prices for wheat and rice. This raises the food cost in every sector of the economy which must lead to higher prices all round. Thus, increase in procurement prices of wheat and rice have been an important factor that has created inflationary pressures in the Indian economy.

We summarise below the important results of price support policy:–

1. Price paid by the consumers who buy from the open market increases when the minimum support price of the agricultural product is fixed at a higher level than the equilibrium price. This is because supply of the agricultural product in the open market decreases as a result of Government purchases of it from the farmers.
2. Fixation of minimum support price (*i.e.,* price floor) leads to the emergence of wheat surplus which the Government has to purchase from the farmers. This is quite obvious from the Indian experience where fixation of higher minimum support price (*MSP*) has resulted in mountain of foodgrains with Food Corporation of India.
3. Taxpayers pay more tax money to finance the Government's wheat purchases as well as storage costs.
4. How to dispose of the surplus purchased from the farmers poses a big problem. There are several ways to dispose of the surplus procured. One way is to sell it at subsidised rate to the persons below the poverty line through public distribution system. Second, the surplus can be used to make a part payment of wages in terms of foodgrains under '*food for work*' programme. Third, food surplus can be given to other countries as foreign aid or it can be exported.
5. Incomes of the farmers increase as a result of minimum support price fixed at a higher level than the free market equilibrium price. As a result of price support, they receive higher price than that which would prevail in the free market and also they produce and sell more than before. They sell a part of their larger production in the market and a part to the Government.

INCIDENCE OF INDIRECT TAXATION

A significant application of demand-supply model is that it explains the problem of incidence of indirect taxes such as sales tax and excise duty on commodities. By incidence of taxes we mean who bear the money burden of taxes. For example, if sale tax is imposed on a commodity the question is whether the producers will bear the burden of the tax or the consumers who buy the commodity or the money burden of the sales tax would be distributed in some way between the producers and the consumers. We will confine ourselves to the explanation of incidence of indirect taxes, that is, taxes which are levied on either production or sale or purchase of commodities.

It is worthwhile to note that the price of a commodity is determined by demand and supply only when perfect competition prevails in the market. Supply curve of a commodity slopes upward as it is assumed that law of diminishing returns operates. The upward sloping supply curve implies that as the price of a commodity rises the producer would offer more quantity for sale in the market. If no tax is levied on the commodity, the seller or producer will receive the whole amount of the price. Now, if the sales tax is imposed equal to ₹ 5 per unit, then the supply price of each unit of the quantity offered for sale in the market will rise by ₹ 5. In this case, the producer would receive the market price minus the amount of the tax per unit. Thus, if the producer is to receive the same amount of price as prior to the imposition of the sales tax, then the supply price of each unit of the

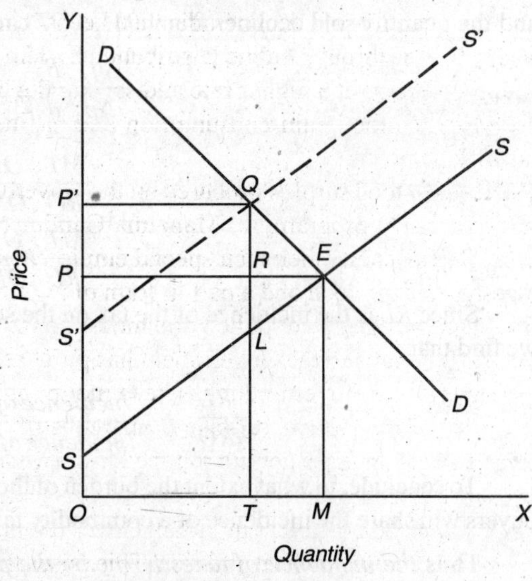

Fig. 7A.6. *Incidence of an Indirect Tax*

commodity sold will rise by the full amount of the tax. This implies that the supply curve of the commodity will now shift upward by the amount of the tax as a result of the imposition of the sales tax.

Figure 7A.6 illustrates the incidence of a sales tax under conditions of perfect competition. *DD* is the demand curve for a commodity and *SS* is its supply curve before the imposition of tax on it. Interaction of these demand and supply curves determines price *OP* of the commodity and *OM* is the quantity sold and purchased. Suppose a unit sales tax, that is, sales tax per unit of the commodity equal to *SS′* (= *LQ*) is levied by the Government on the commodity in question. This will raise the supply price of the commodity by the sellers as the unit tax *SS′* will now be included by the sellers in their supply price. As a result, the supply curve of the commodity will shift to the left by the magnitude of tax *SS′*. The new supply curve *SS′* intersects the demand curve *DD* at the point *Q* and determines the new price *OP′* and quantity exchanged *OT*. It will be seen from the Fig. 7A.6 that price has risen by *PP′ or RQ* which the buyers will bear whereas the tax per unit is *SS′* or *LQ*. It may be noted that the buyers will bear the burden of a tax to the extent that they have to pay the higher price than before. Thus the incidence of the tax borne by the buyers will be equal to *RQ*. The remaining part of the tax equal to *RL*, will be borne by the sellers. Thus of the tax *SS′* or *LQ*, *RQ* is incidence of the tax on the buyers and *RL* is the incidence on the sellers. Now, we can show that the incidence of the tax *RL* and *RQ* on the sellers and buyers respectively is equal to the ratio of the elasticity of demand and the elasticity of supply.

$$\frac{RL}{RQ} = \frac{\text{Incidence of tax on the sellers}}{\text{Incidence of tax on the buyers}}$$

$$\text{Price elasticity of demand} = \frac{\Delta q}{\Delta p} \cdot \frac{p}{q}$$

By referring to Fig. 7A.6, elasticity of demand when the price rises from *OP* to *OP′* for the buyers will be

$$e_d = \frac{\Delta q_d}{\Delta p} \cdot \frac{p}{q} = \frac{MT}{RQ} \cdot \frac{OP}{OM} \quad \text{... (i)}$$

Likewise, elasticity of supply when the price received by the sellers falls from *OP* (= *ME*) to *TL* and the quantity sold declines from *OM* to *OT* can be found out. Thus :

$$e_s = \frac{\Delta q_s}{\Delta p} \cdot \frac{P}{q} = \frac{MT}{RL} \cdot \frac{OP}{OM} \quad \text{.....(ii)}$$

$$\frac{e_d}{e_s} = \frac{\frac{MT}{RQ} \cdot \frac{OP}{OM}}{\frac{MT}{RL} \cdot \frac{OP}{OM}} = \frac{RL}{RQ}$$

Since *RL* is the incidence of the tax on the sellers and *RQ* is the incidence of tax on the buyers, we find that

$$\frac{RL}{RQ} = \frac{\textit{Incidence of tax on seller}}{\textit{Incidence of tax on buyers}} = \frac{\textit{Price elasticity of demand}}{\textit{Price elasticity of supply}}$$

To conclude, to what extent the burden of the tax will be shifted and the proportion in which the buyers will share the incidence of a commodity tax depends on the elasticities of demand and supply.

Thus *the incidence of taxes borne by the producer and the consumer will depend upon the elasticity of demand as well as elasticity of supply. The lower the elasticity of demand, the greater will be the incidence of tax borne by the consumer.*

If the demand for a commodity is perfectly inelastic the whole of the burden of the commodity tax will fall on consumer. This is shown in Fig. 7A.7. In this figure demand curve *DD* is a vertical straight line showing that demand for the commodity is completely inelastic. As a result of the intersection of the demand and supply curves, price *OP* is determined. If now the tax equal to *SS′* is imposed on the commodity, the supply curve will shift vertically upward to the dotted position *S′S′*. It will be seen that the new supply curve *S′ S′* intersects the demand curve *DD* at point *E′* and the new equilibrium price *OP′* is determined. It will be noticed from Fig. 7A.7 that in this case the price of the commodity has risen by *PP′* or *EE′* which is equal to the full amount of the tax *SS′*. It means that producers pass on the full tax to the consumers and they themselves do not bear any incidence. It, therefore, follows that *in case of perfectly inealstic demand, the whole incidence of the tax falls on the consumers*.

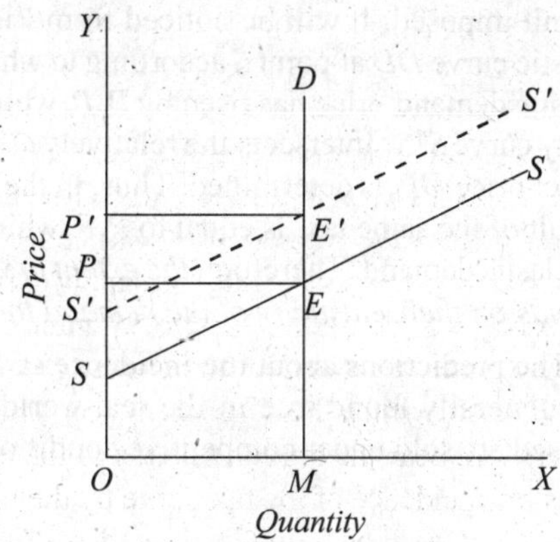

Fig. 7A.7. *Incidence of Tax in Case of Perfectly Inelastic Demand*

On the contrary, if the consumer's demand for a quantity is perfectly elastic, as is shown by *DD* curve in Fig. 7A.8 the imposition of the tax on it will not cause any rise in price. In this case, the whole burden will be borne by the manufacturers or sellers. It will be seen from Fig. 7A.8 that as a result of the indirect tax by the amount *SS′* and the resultant upward shift in supply curve to *S′ S′* the equilibrium price remains unchanged at the leve *OP*. Since the price has not risen, the consumer would not bear any burden of the tax in this case. Therefore, the whole incidence of the tax will fall on the producers or sellers in case of perfectly elastic demand.

It should be noted that the more inelastic the demand for a commodity, the greater the rise in the price paid by the consumer and the vice versa. In order to show this clearly we have drawn two demand curves—one inelastic and the other relatively more elastic in Fig. 7A.9. Supply curve *SS*

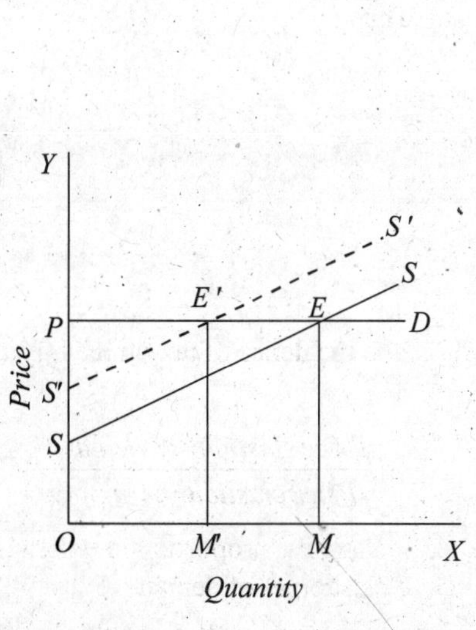

Fig. 7A.8. *Incidence of tax in case of perfectly elastic demand*

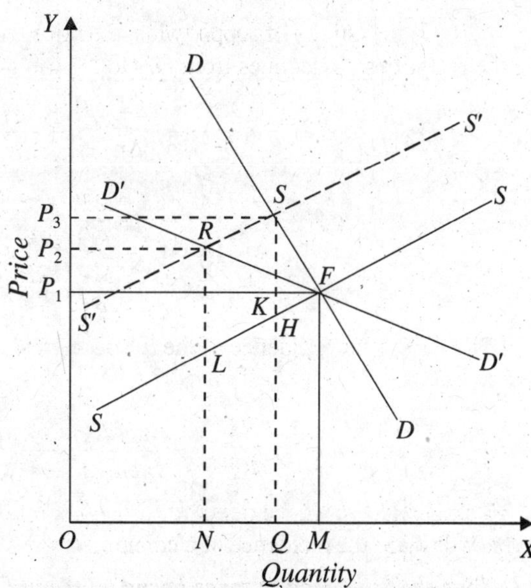

Fig. 7A.9. *Incidence of an indirect tax in case of elastic and inelastic demand*

has been drawn which intersects the two demand curves *DD* and *D′ D* at the same point *F*. Now before the imposition of any tax, the quantity sold and purchased is *OM* and the price of the commodity is OP_1. Now, if the sales tax tax is imposed, supply curve shifts upward to *S′ S′* by the amount of tax per unit imposed. It will be noticed from Fig. 7A.9 that the new supply curve *S′ S′* intersects the inelastic curve *DD* at point *S* according to which equilibrium price OP_3 is determined. In this case of inelastic demand price has risen by $P_1 P_3$ which is the burden borne by the consumers. Now, the new supply curve *S′ S′* intersects the relatively elastic demand curve *D′ D′* at point *R* according to which market price OP_2 is determined. Thus, in the case of elastic demand curve *D′ D′*, the rise in price as a result of the same tax, is equal to P_1P_2 which is smaller than $P_1 P_3$ borne by the consumer in case of inelastic demand. Therefore, *the extent to which the incidence of the tax will fall on the consumers depends on their elasticity of the demand for the commodity in question.*

The predictions about the incidence of taxes borne by the consumers and the producers have been generally found true in the real world situation when the commodities on which taxes are imposed are sold under competitive conditions.

CHAPTER 7B

CONSUMER SURPLUS, PRODUCER SURPLUS AND ECONOMIC EFFICIENCY OF PERFECTLY COMPETITIVE MARKET

Introduction

We have explained in a previous chapter how in a perfectly competitive market price and output of commodities are determined through equilibrium between demand for and supply of goods. Now, an important question is how well do the competitive markets perform to allocate society's scarce resources ? Do they use and allocate society's resources efficiently for satisfying the satisfaction of wants of the people ? In economics welfare of the people in a society is related to the efficiency with which its resources are used and allocated among the production of goods and services. *The resources of a society are efficiently used if they are so used and allocated that the consumers get the maximum possible satisfaction. When such an efficiency has been achieved, it is then not possible through any reorganisation of resources and production of goods and services to make anyone better off without making someone worse off.* Under such conditions of efficiency, the welfare or satisfaction of one individual can be increased only at the loss of welfare by another. It is important to note that efficiency in economics is not a mechanical concept. It is a concept based on the welfare of the people, that is, how people feel about the satisfaction or benefits they derive from the goods and services that are produced and the way they are distributed among them. One important way in which we can explain the issue of economic efficiency is to use the concepts of consumer surplus and producer surplus.

Consumer Surplus

In explaining the efficiency in production and distribution of goods and services we view demand and supply curves from a different angle. For example in the previous discussion we viewed demand curve as how much quantities of goods the consumers will buy at different prices of a good. *In the present discussion of issue of efficiency or welfare we look at the demand curve from the viewpoint of how much price the consumers are willing to pay for a given quantity of a commodity.* How much they will be willing to pay for an additional unit of a commodity will indicate the marginal utility or benefit received by the individual. However, *in the real world the individuals do not always have to pay the maximum price they are willing to pay.* Thus when people pay something less than they are willing to pay, they are said to obtain consumer surplus. To understand consumer surplus consider Fig. 7B.1 given where *DD* is the demand curve (or in the present context marginal benefit curve) of the commodity. It will be seen from this figure that 20th unit of the commodity the consumer is willing to pay of ₹ 85 per unit but actually he pays price *OP* = ₹ 50 which is determined by the market equilibrium. Thus he pays ₹ 35 less than he is willing to pay from 20th unit of the commodity. This implies that he derives consumer surplus from this 20th unit of the commodity. Given the market price equal to *OP*, the total consumer surplus obtained by the consumers for buying *OQ* quantity of the commodity is the area *DPE* under the demand curve *DD* and above the market price line *PE*.

At present we will use the concepts of consumer surplus and producer surplus to explain whether working of competitive markets achieve economic or allocative efficiency as defined above.

The consumer surplus obtained by the consumers from buying a product is the price that they are willing to pay over and above the market price which they actually pay for a commodity. As mentioned above, this willingness to pay for a unit of a commodity byconsumers measures the *utility or satisfaction* they hope to get from it. In economics the welfare of an individual is measured by the utility or satisfaction individuals obtain from the consumption of goods. The market demand curve of a commodity is obtained through the horizontal addition of the demand curves of individuals for the commodity. The consumer surplus obtained by all individuals is the gain in utility or well-being from consuming a good over and above the price they pay for it. Thus consumer surplus represents the *net gain* of utility or welfare individuals get from consuming a commodity. Welfare is measured by the area under the given demand curve as shown in Fig. 7B.1 where *DD'* is the demand curve of a commodity, *OP* is the market price as determined by demand for and supply of the commodity. The consumers will buy *OQ* quantity of the commodity and will pay total value equal to the *OPEQ* for the commodity while total value (equal to the money value of satisfaction they will get) is measured by what they are willing to pay for the commodity which is equal to the total area under the demand curve upto the quantity *OQ* purchased, which is equal to the area *ODEQ*. Thus, total value they are willing to pay for *OQ* quantity of the commodity, that is, *ODEQ minus* the value *OPEQ* they actually pay for it gives us the amount of consumer surplus they obtain from buying the commodity. Remember consumer surplus measures the net gain or welfare by the consumer for buying the commodity from the market.

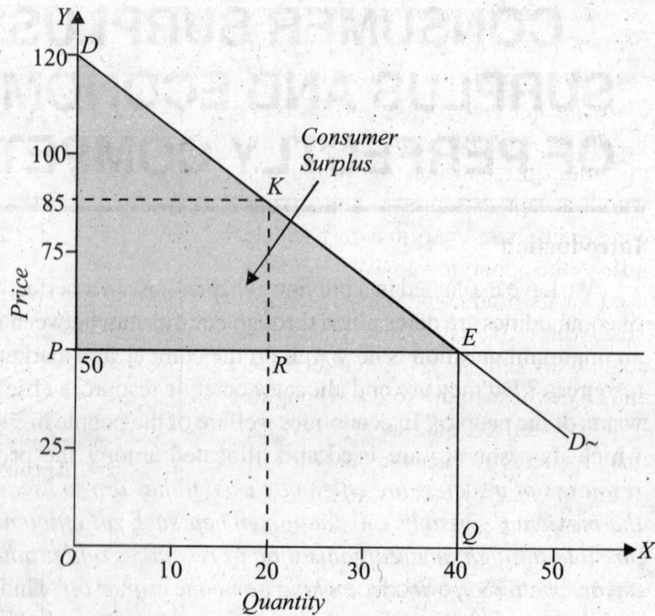

Fig. 7B.1. *Measurement of Consumer Surplus*

Producer Surplus

Producer surplus is a concept similar to consumer surplus. It relates to the cost of production incurred in supplying commodies and prices received by them. Cost of producing a commodity is in fact the *opportunity cost* of it, that is, what a producer foregoes for producing a commodity and price what a producer receives for producing and supplying a commodity. In our analysis of supply in previous chapters, we have viewed it as how much quantities of a commodity a producer will produce and supply in the market at its various prices. In the present context, while considering supply we are more concerned with how much extra revenue a producers earns over and above the opportunity cost of producing a commodity. And the *opportunity cost of producing a commodity shows the minimum price that a producers must receive to induce them to produce a certain quantity of a commodity*. The cost of producing an additional unit of a commodity is called marginal cost (more precisely, it is marginal opportunity cost), that is, the minimum that producers must receive to make it worthwhile for them to produce an extra unit of the commodity price. It is opportunity cost of production with which we are concerned in the present analysis of production and supply of a commodity by producers because to produce a commodity the producers have to forego to produce other goods.

But it is important to mention that *producers do not always receive the minimum supply price represented by the opportunity cost*. They receive the price for a commodity an determined by market demand for and supply of a commodity. If the price at which they sell a commodity exceeds the cost they incur to produce it they will earn a surplus called the producer surplus.

The producer surplus is the excess of market price at which producers sell the quantity of a commodity over and above the minimum price at which they would be willing to supply it. The minimum price which the producers would accept to supply a unit of the commodity is its marginal cost which reflects the opportunit cost of resources used for its production. Consider Fig. 7B.2 where *SS* is supply curve of a commodity and *OP* as the market price and *OQ* is the quantity sold and bought. It will be seen from the supply curve *SS* that producers produce the last *Q*th unit of the commodity at the marginal cost which is just equal to the market price *OP*. However, as is indicated by the supply curve *SS* the producers will be ready to supply the earlier successive units from zero to *Q*th unit at much less than the market price *OP*. Thus, from these earlier units the producers actually get more than their minimum acceptable supply price. The area *OSEQ* below the supply curve is indicator of the aggregate opportunity cost of *OQ* units of the commodity produced and supplied by the producers. On the other hand, the total revenue earned by them is equal to the area *OPEQ* (market price *OP* × quantity *OQ* sold). Thus, the producers earn revenue equal to the shaded area *SEP* more than the aggregate opportunity cost of production. This excess amount *SEP* over the aggregate opportunity cost of production is the aggregate producer surplus earned by the producers. The *producer surplus earned by the producers is the measure of benefits obtained by them for producing and selling the commodity.*

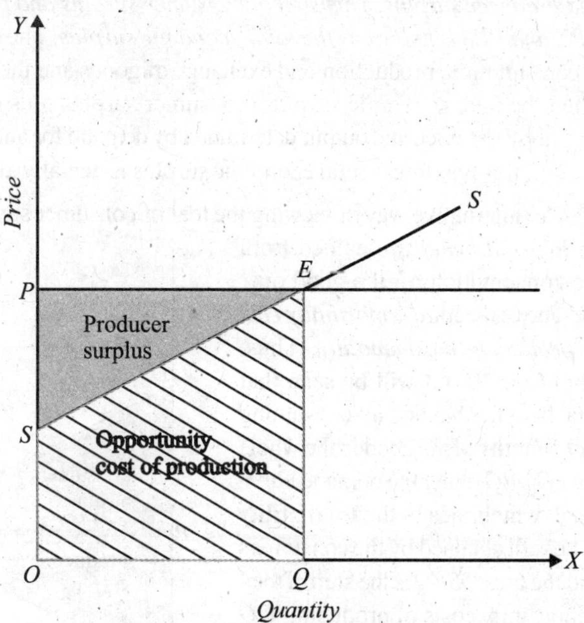

Fig. 7B.2. *The Concept of Producer Surplus*

Economic Efficiency of Perfectly Competitive Equilibrium

One of the most beneficial feature of perfectly competitive market is that it results in economic efficiency which means that it enables the use of resources for production of goods that ensures maximum welfare to the persons in a society. Allocative efficiency of perfectly competitive markets also implies the mutually beneficial exchange between consumers and producers of goods. That is, both are better off in participating in the exchange. Under conditions of perfectly competitive markets optimum production and exchange of goods takes place which ensures the achievement of maximum social welfare. This can be shown by the concept of producer surplus and consumer surplus.

Recall that consumer surplus measures the welfare gain to the consumers from buying a commodity equal to the amount which they are willing to pay (which reflects their utility derived from the commodity) over and above the market price they actually pay for the good which they buy from the producers. Consumer surplus is measured by the area under the demand curve over the market price.

Thus, in Fig. 7B.3 where demand curve *DD′* of consumers and supply curve *SS′* of consumers through their intersection at point *E* determine market price *OP* and quantity *OQ* of the good proudced and exchanged between them. Consumer surplus obtained by the consumers is equal to the area *DPE*. On the other hand, as explained above, *PES* is producer surplus obtained by the producers which measures the excess revenue obtained by them over above the sum of marginal costs (i.e. supply price) incurred by them for producing *OQ* amount of the good.

It follows from above that both the consumers and producers gain from exchange and production of goods. *From the society's point of view, the total gain is the sum of consumer surplus and producer surplus. This sum of consumer surplus and producer surplus, that is, the sum of areas DPE and PES is known as the total economic surplus.* The economic efficiency or maximum welfare in consumption, production and exchange of goods and therefore maximum social benefit is attained when the total economic surplus (consumer surplus plus producer surplus) is maximised. And, as seen above, at price and output determined by demand for and supply of goods in a perfectly competitive market, this maximum total economic surplus is actually attained.

An alternative way of viewing the toal of consumer surplus and producer surplus is to consider it as the *total benefits* obtained from the consumption of the good over and above the *total opportunity cost of producing a commodity*. Thus, from Fig. 7B.3 it will be seen that total benefit obtained by consuming *OQ* quantity of the good is the whole area *ODEQ* under the demand curve *DD'* which means the total utility or benefit obtained by the consumers and the area *OSEQ* is the sum of total opportunity costs of producing *OQ* quantity of the good. Thus, the area *DES* measures the total surplus (*i.e.* the sum of consumer surplus and producer surplus). *This sum of consumer surplus and producer surplus therefore measures the net social benefit from producing and consuming OQ quantity of the good.*

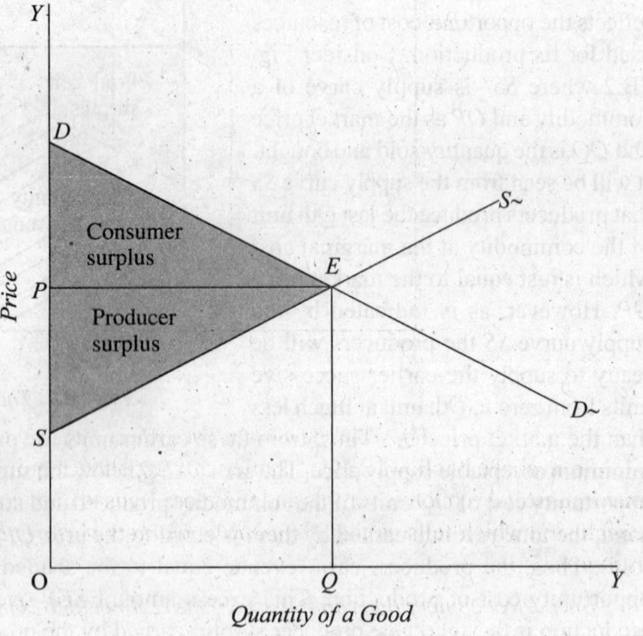

Fig. 7B.3. *Maximisation of Total Economic Surplus: Achieving Economic Efficiency*

The key question is whether the total surplus is maximised at the competitive equilibrium as determined by demand for and supply of the good. If some other production and consumption of the good (or in other words, some other resource allocation to the good in question) leads to a higher total surplus, the output *OQ* of the good determined by competitive equilibrium would not be efficient. This is because it would then be possible to make consumers and producers better off collectively. On the other hand, if there is no alternative resource allocation to the good in question which generates a higher level of total surplus, the competitive equilibrium is economically efficient.

To understand this consider Fig. 7B.4 where competitive equilibrium is attained by producing *OQ* quantity of the good. Now, suppose a smaller quantity OQ_1 of the good is produced, then as will be seen from Fig. 7B.4 the consumers and producers will suffer a loss of total ecnomic surplus equal to the area *HKE*. Likewise, any other quantity smaller than *OQ* would mean a lower total economic surplus than that obtained from producing and consuming *OQ* quantity of the good by allocating required resources to its production.

If a greater quantity than *OQ*, say OQ_2, *is produced and consumed, the consumers would get less* utility (or welfare benefit) as indicated by the demand curve in the range of quantity Q to Q_2 which is lower than the cost of producing the good as indicated by the higher level of the supply curve in this quantity range (*i.e.* Q to Q_2). Thus, the production of the greater quantity OQ_2 of the good than the competitive output OQ leads to the loss of total economic surplus equal to the area *ERT*.

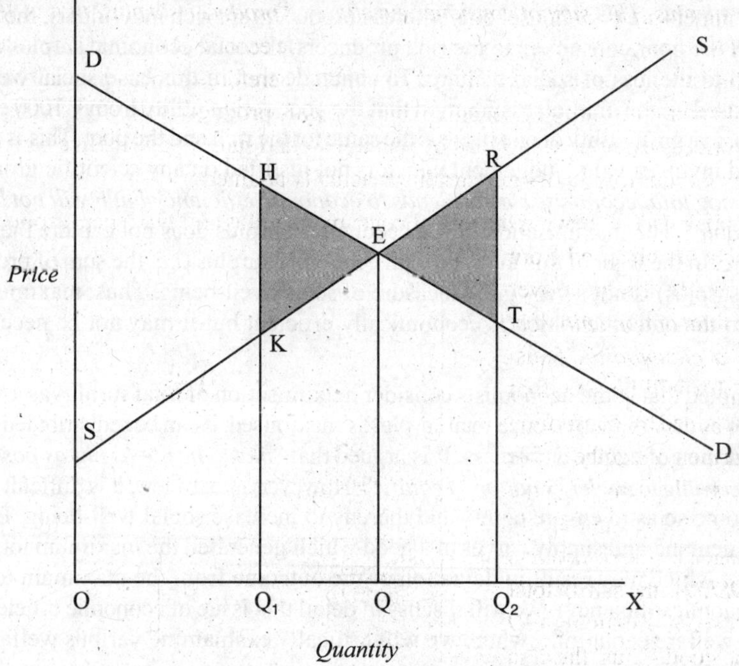

Fig. 7B.4. *Economic Efficiency of Perfectly Competitive Equilibrium*

From above it follows that production of competitive equilibrium OQ quantity of the good ensures maximum total economic surplus and therefore leads to maximum social benefit. This is an important conclusion which tells us that *competitive markets perform quite well in allocating scarce social resources.*

But perfect competition rarely exists in the real world. It is market forms of monopolies, oligopolies and monoplistic competition that exist in the real world and not perfect competition. We shall study in the next few chapters how market categories of monopolies, oligopolies and monopolistic competition create economic inefficiencies in resource allocation and hence loss of social welfare.

Further, as shall be studied in chapters on welfare economics that *economic efficiency is achieved under conditions of even perfect competition only when there do not exist any externalities, negative or positive.* The existence of externalities causes divergence between private benefit and social benefit as well as between private cost and social cost. Thus, perfectly competitive equilibrium based on private cost and private benefit would not lead to the maximum social welfare when externalities are present.

Economic Efficiency and Equity

That under conditions of perfect competition, the conclusion that welfare is maximum is based on the thinking that the total economic surplus is true measure of social welfare. To consider so is to ignore the effect of distribution of output and income on social welfare. *The equity, that is, fairness in distribution is as important as maximisation of total economic surplus.* To consider the size of total economic surplus as the sole criterion of assessment of social welfare is to implicitly make the value judgement that a rupee gives each person the same satisfaction irrespective of whether the person is consumer or producer, rich or poor. To clarify this let us consider that price of a prouduct is raised. As a result, the consumers would lose some consumer surplus and producers would gain some extra producer surplus. The criterion of total economic surplus is based on the net change in surplus in rupee terms. Suppose as a result of rise in price of a good consumers suffer a loss of consumer surplus of ₹ 1000 and producers gain extra producer surplus of ₹ 1000. Thus, the total economic surplus remains unchanged.

But, if consumers are poor households whereas producers are rich individuals, the redistribution of income from the poor consumers to the rich producers, the total economic surplus remaining the same, will lead to the loss of social welfare. To conclude that in this case social welfare remains unchanged is based on the implicit assumption that the poor derive utility from ₹ 1000 equal to that of the rich. That is, marginal utility of one rupee is the same for the rich and the poor. This is a questionable assumption and involves value judgement which is not justified on any scientific grounds. In other words, *maximising total economic surplus leads to economic efficiency but it will not be necessarily 'fair' or 'equitable'*. The maximisation of total economic surplus does not capture the equity aspect of social welfare. In the light of this fact, the total economic surplus (*i.e.* the sum of producer surplus and economic surplus) is not a very good measure of social well-being. Thus, maximisation of total surplus leads to the outcome which is economically efficient but it may not be necessarily fair or equitable.

It may be noted that some economists consider maximisation of total surplus as a valid criterion of social welfare as they think that once total surplus is maximised, it can be redistributed in accordance with society's notion of equity or fairness. It is argued that "*make the pie as big as possible and then distribute it according to society's notion of equity*." However, in our view, it is difficult to redistribute output and income so as to ensure equity and thereby to increase social well-being. Besides, in the redistribution, demand and supply curves of a good which generated the maximum total surplus, are likely to change which may result in deviation of the outcome from the maximum total economic surplus (or economic efficiency). We will discuss in detail this issue of economic efficiency vs. equity in chapters on welfare economics where we will critically examamine various welfare criteria put forward by economists to evaluate alternative resource allocations.

EFFICIENCY COSTS OF TAXES

The Concept of Efficiency in Taxation

The concept of economic efficiency is the central notion in microeconomics. *The economy is said to be operating efficiently if it has exhausted all available opportunities for use of its scarce resources for production of goods and distribution of output among individuals in a society so as to make someone better off without making someone else worse off. Conceived in this sense then almost all taxes cause inefficiencies in the economy*. This is because if taxes were withdrawn, some individuals could be made better off without making somebody else worse off. However, to compare an economy with taxes to an economy without taxes is not proper. The government, after all, levies taxes to collect revenue which is spent on providing usefull collective services. And these services provide benefits to the people of a country. Therefore, when economists are concerned with efficiency in taxation they examine the taxes that cause least amount of inefficiency.

Regarding inefficiency of taxation, it is important to understand the concept of *burden of a tax*. By burden of a tax on an individual we mean how much monetary loss he incurs on payment of a tax as compared to its absence. By levying a tax, government collects revenue. *The burden of a tax usually exceeds the revenue collected by government*. This is because when government levies a tax on a commodity, income or profits, it induces people to alter their behaviour in way that they tend to reduce or avoid tax liability. Whenever imposition of tax induces people to change their behaviour, that is, when it distorts their choices, it has an excess burden. As a result, tax revenue raised by government by levying tax is less than the burden of tax. Thus, this would become clear as we Regarding inefficiency of taxation, it is important to understand the concept of *burden of a tax*. By burden of a tax on an individual we mean how much monetary loss he incurs on payment of a tax as compared to its absence. By levying a tax, government collects revenue. *The burden of a tax usually exceeds the revenue collected by government*. This is because when government levies a tax on a commodity, income or profits, it induces people to alter their behaviour in way that they tend to reduce or avoid tax liability. Whenever imposition of tax induces people to change their behaviour, that is, when it distorts their choices, it has an excess burden. As a result, tax revenue raised by government by levying tax is less than the burden of tax. Thus, this would become clear as we discuss the effects and burden of some taxes. *Total tax burden = Revenue collected + Excess burden.*

Efficiency Cost of Excise Duties

An excise duty is a tax on the production of a commodity and is paid by the producers to the government. Consider Fig. 7B.5 where prior to imposition of excise duty demand curve *DD* and supply curve *SS* of a commodity intersect at point *A* and determine price P_0 and quantity bought and sold equal to Q_0. Suppose government levies unit excise duty equal to *AT* per unit of the commodity

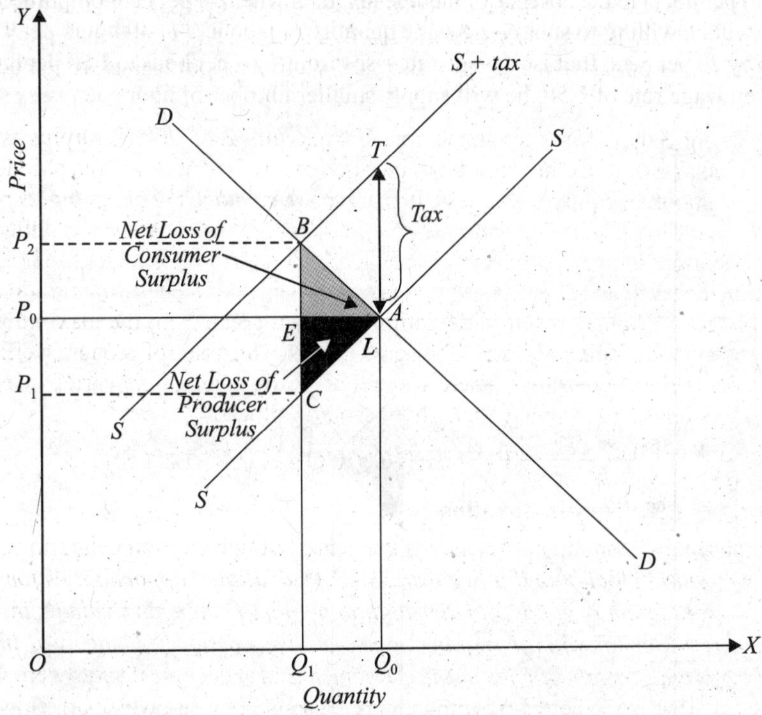

Fig. 7B.5. *Excess Burden or Dead Weight Loss of Welfare of an Excise Duty*

produced and sold. As a result of this excise tax, supply curve shifts upward by a level of *tax*. This is because in order to pass on the burden of the excise tax to the consumers, producers will be willing to sell or supply a given quantity at a price higher by the amount of the tax per unit. The consumers will also change their behaviour in purchasing the commodity at a higher price. To reduce their tax liability, they will demand a smaller quantity at a higher price than before.

It will be observed from Fig. 7B.5 that the new supply curve *S + tax* intersects the demand curve of the buyers *DD* at point *B*. Thus, price has risen from P_0 to P_2 and quantity bought and sold has fallen to Q_1. It will be seen from the Fig. 7B.5 that there is a loss of total economic surplus (*i.e.* sum of consumer surplus plus producer surplus) equal to the area P_1CABP_2 while government collects revenue equal to P_1CBP_2 which is less than the loss of total economic surplus by the shaded area *ABC*. It is thus evident that people suffer a *dead weight loss of welfare* equal to the area *ABC*; while consumers suffer a net loss of consmer surplus equal to the area *ABE*, the producers suffer a net loss of producer surplus equal to the area *AEC*, *The dead-weight loss caused by levying excise duty shows its economic inefficiency*. It is worth mentioning that dead-weight loss of excise duty will be relatively greater in case demand curve is more elastic (The students themselves should show this.)

The Efficiency Cost of Income Tax

We now examine the efficiency costs of income taxes. Income taxes are levied on incomes of the individuals and on profits of corporate firms. Income taxes may be proportional or progressive. We assume that government levies a proportional income. The effect of proportional income tax is illustrated in Fig. 7B.6. It is assumed that labour market is competitive. With no income tax on wage-income, *LD* is the demand curve of labour and *LS* is the supply curve of labour and together they determine wage equal to W_0 and each one of the workers employed work 40 hour per week in the equilibrium in the labour market. Suppose W_0 is ₹ 50 per hour and 20 per cent flat rate of income tax rate is levied by government. If workers are willing to supply 40 hours a week at wage-rate W_0 (= ₹ 50 per hour) in the absence of income tax, then when 20 per cent proportional tax is imposed, a worker will be willing to supply the same quantity of labour (*i.e.* 40 hours per week) only if wage rate rises by 20 per cent, that is, if wage rate rises from ₹ 50 per hour to ₹ 60 per hour. Alternatively, at the given wage rate of ₹ 50, he will supply smaller number of hours per week.

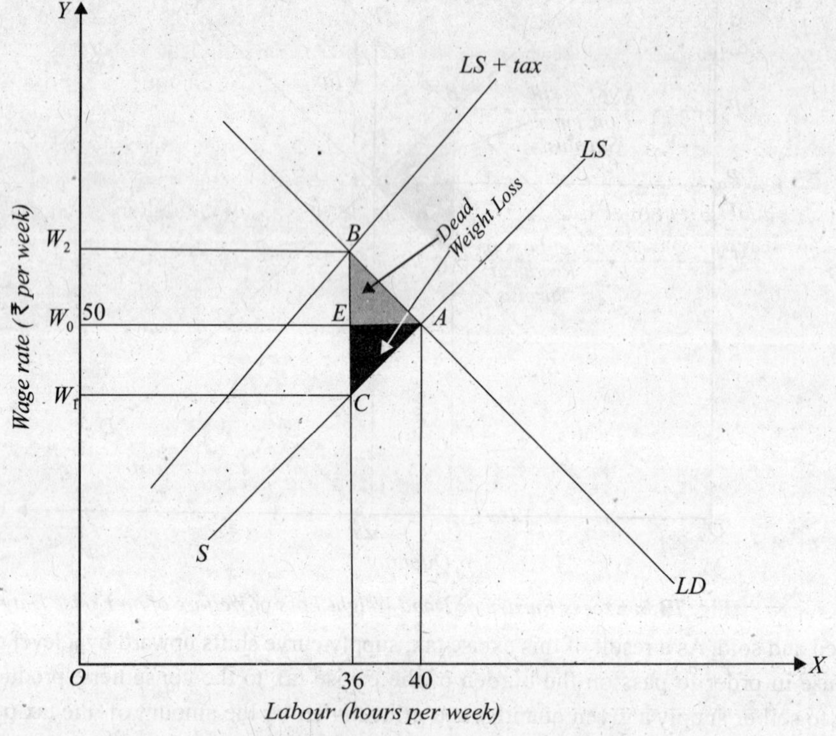

Fig. 7B.6. *Efficiency Cost of Income Tax*

Note that income tax causes a wedge between wage rate paid by the employer and that received by a worker. This implies that supply curve of labour will shift to the left to the new position *LS* + *tax* which intersects the demand curve *LD* for labour and determines a higher wage rate per hour W_2. It will be seen seen from Fig.7B.6 that whereas firm pays wage rate equal to W_2, the worker receives wage rate W_1, the difference $W_2 - W_1$ goes to government by way of income tax. Imposition of income tax on wage-income has led to the fall in employment from 40 hours per week to 36 hours per week and wage rate has risen from W_0 per week to W_2 per week. Government raises revenue from income tax equal to the area W_1CBW_2, while loss of total economic surplus suffered by workers and employers is equal to W_1CABW_2. The *shaded area ABC* is the dead-weight loss and measures the extent of inefficiency caused by income tax. This inefficiency has been caused because of change in behaviour of workers and employers to the imposition of income tax. The workers are willing to supply same labour hours per week only at a higher wage rate and this causes a change in the labour-supply curve. The firm employing labour reduces demand for labour at a higher wage rate. This causes a change in labour market equilibrium which results in loss of economic efficiency as depicted by dead-weight loss.

Effects of Corporate Profits Tax

Corporate profits tax is levied on the profits of corporations, that is, companies organised as joint stock companies. A general perception among people is that corporate profit tax is borne by the corporate companies and does not affect consumers and workers. This perception about corporate profits tax is quite wrong. The majority view among economists is that corporation tax is highly inefficient and most of its burden rests on workers and consumers. How taxing corporate profits is inefficient is explained below ?

It may be noted that corporate profits tax is misnamed. It is *only partly* a tax on economic profits. ***Actually, corporation profits tax is a tax on the income from capital.*** A corporation tax is a tax on capital because much of corporation profits tax is in fact a return on the capital invested in it. Levying tax on the income from capital works like taxing the income from labour, as explained above. However, there are one important difference. Unlike the supply of labour, supply of capital is highly elastic and the quantity of capital affects the productivity of labour and wages. As a result, though the burden of corporate profits tax seems to be borne by the firms, but it is actually borne by workers and consumers and not the owners of corporate firms – the shareholders. Who bears the burden of corporation tax, viewed as tax on capital, is shown in Fig. 7B.7. In this figure, initially demand curve *DD* for capital intersects the supply curve $S_0 S_0$ of capital and determines r_0 as the rate of interest/return on capital.

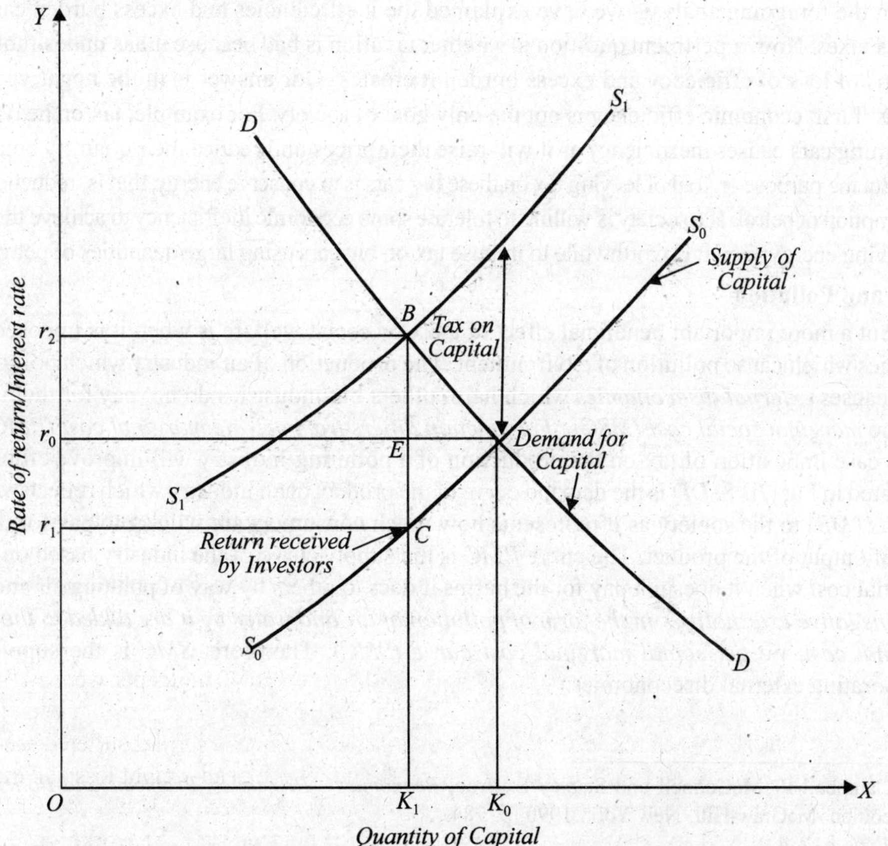

Fig. 7B.7. *Burden or Efficiency Cost of Corporate Profits Tax (Viewed as Tax on Capital)*

It will be seen that imposition of corporate profit tax (*i.e.* tax on capital) causes upward shift in the supply curve of capital to $S_1 S_1$ and as a result interest rate rises. It will be seen from Fig. 7B.7 that investors bear only a part *EC* of the burden of tax equal to *BC*. Thus, after-tax return is reduced not by the full amount of tax *BC*. If investors do not bear fully the burden of the capital tax, who bear it? It will be seen from Fig. 7B.7 that as a result of tax on corporate profits (*i.e.* on corporate capital) interest rate which firms pay increases which will raise the cost of production of the products produced by the corporate profits. *The rise in costs of production will cause prices of products to go up*. As a result, consumers will bear some burden of the higher cost and therefore of the tax imposed on the corporate profits. Besides, *if due to higher prices of products, sales of the product decrease, demand for labour will decrease and as a result wages may fall in which case workers will bear some of the burden of the tax*. In addition, the higher cost of capital will induce firms to use less capital. From Fig. 7B.7, it will be seen that capital used has fallen from K_0 to K_1 as a result of tax on corporate capital. The lower quantity of capital will affect productivity of labour which in turn will affect their wages. Further, it has been pointed out that if investors find investment in the corporate sector less profitable as a result of the corporation tax, they may shift their savings to the unincorporated sector.

It follows from above that, in partial equilibrium analysis of efficiency, cost or burden of corporate profits tax is incomplete and therefore its general equilibrium analysis is required if its full effects are to be known.[1] To quote Joseph Stiglitz a Nobel Laureate in Economics, "*Most economists agree that in the long run, most of burden of the corporation tax rests on workers and consumers, and relatively little on corporations, their shareholders or others who have lent money — contrary to popular belief*."[2].

Can Taxation improve efficiency ?

In the foregoing analysis we have explained the inefficiencies and excess burden caused by various taxes. Now, a pertinent question is whether taxation is bad because it has undesirable effect in terms of loss of efficiency and excess burden it creates. Our answer is in the negative for two reasons. First, economic efficiency is not the only goal of society. For example, tax on heavy petrol consuming cars causes inefficiency as it will raise their prices and reduce their quantity bought and sold. But the purpose or goal of levying tax on these big cars is to conserve energy, that is, reduction in the consumption of petrol. If a society is willing to tolerate some economic inefficiency to achieve the goal of conserving energy, then it is worthwhile to impose tax on big cars using large quantities of petrol.

Taxes and Pollution

But a more important beneficial effect of a tax on social welfare is when it is imposed on the activities which cause pollution of environment. The production of an industry which pollute air or water causes *external diseconomies* which harm others but industries do not pay for them. In this case the *marginal social cost (MSC) of production differs from private marginal cost (PMC)*. How in this case imposition of tax on the production of a polluting industry will improve efficiency is illustrated in Fig. 7B.8. *DD* is the demand curve of the product of an industry which reflects *marginal benefits* (*MB*) to the society as it represents how much consumers are willing to pay for different units of output of the product. The curve *PMC* is the supply curve of the industry based on private marginal cost when it does not pay for the harms it does to others by way of poluting air and water. *When negative externalities in the form of pollution of air and water by it are added to the private marginal cost, we get social marginal cost curve (SMC)*. Therefore, *SMC* is the supply curve incorporating external diseconomies.

---

1. Campbell R. McConnell and Stanley L. Brue, *Economics : Principles, Problems and Policies*, 11th edition, McGraw-Hill, New York, 1990, p. 784.
2. *Ibid.*, p. 784

Initially, prior to imposition of tax on the production of polluting industry, quantity of a product produced is Q_0 and price is P_0 at which demand curve and supply curve *PMC* intersect. Now, with the imposition of tax per unit of output produced equal to the negative externalities it causes the supply curve to shift to *SMC*. It will be seen from Fig. 7B.8 that this supply curve *SMC* intersects the demand curve *DD* at point E_1. As a result, price rises to P_1 and production of polluting industry falls to Q_1. In the new equilibrium at output Q_1 and price P_1, marginal benefit (*MB*) from production of the commodity is equal to its social marginal cost (*SMC*). Thus, imposition of tax has achieved allocative efficiency. To conclude, *taxes on industries or services which create external diseconomies may improve economic efficiency rather than cause efficiency losses.*

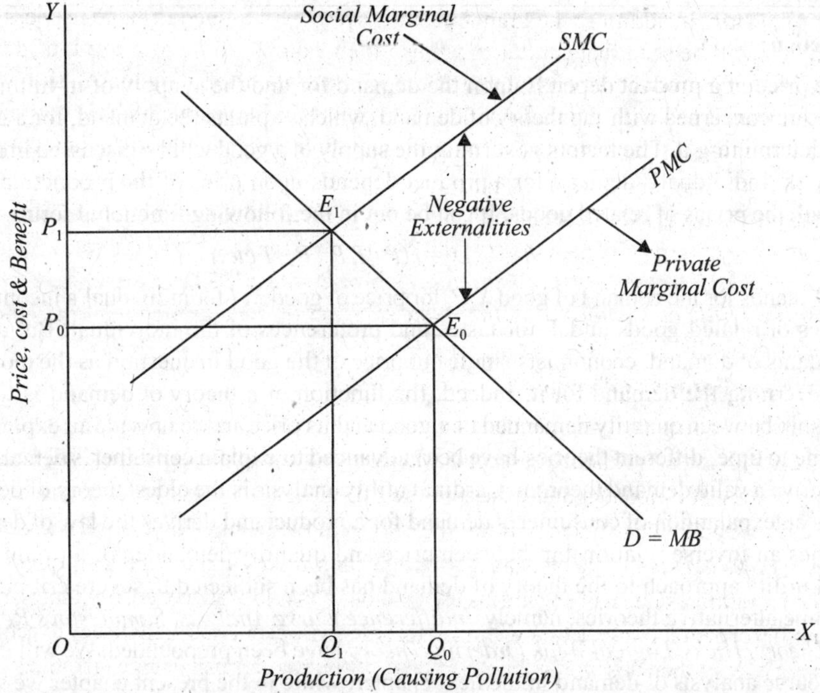

Fig. 7B.8. *Imposition of Tax on the Production of Polluting Industry to Acheive Economic Efficiency*

QUESTIONS FOR REVIEW

1. What is meant by economic efficiency ? Show with the help of consumer surplus and producer surplus that competive market model ensures the achievement of economic efficiency.
2. Show that competitive market model ensures economic efficiency but not equity in income distribution.
3. Suppose the government levies a tax on electricity. With the help of demand and supply curves show the dead weight loss and government revenue. Would the dead weight loss and government revenue be larger in the first few months or after a year ? Explain *D.U., BA (Hons.) Economics Ist Year 2006*
   (**Hints.** Loss in government revenue will be larger in the long run because demand in the long run is more elastic)
4. The government removes the entertainment tax on a movie and make it tax free. If demand and supply of movie tickets depend on price, show how the removal of this tax affects consumer surplus, tax revenue and the whole society. *D.U., B.A (Hons.) Eco. Ist Year 2008*
5. A unit tax is imposed on a product in the market. Explain the dead-weight loss of this tax. Given a normal supply curve of the product, how do elasticities of demand and supply affect the dead weight loss of the same amount of tax. *D.U., B.A. (Hons.) Eco. 2009*

CHAPTER 8

CONSUMER'S BEHAVIOUR : CARDINAL UTILITY ANALYSIS

Introduction

The price of a product depends upon the demand for and the syupply of it. In this part of the book we are concerned with the theory of demand, which explains the demand, for a good and the factors determining it. The factors governing the supply of a good will be discussed in the next part of the book. Individual's demand for a product depends upon price of the product, income of the individual, the prices of related goods. It can be put in the following functional form:

$$D_x = f(P_x, I, P_y, P_z, T\ etc.)$$

where D_x stands for the demand of good X P_x for price of good X, I for individual's income, P_y, P_z, for the prices of related goods and T for tastes and preferences of the individual. But among these determinants of demand, economists single out price of the good in question as the most important factor governing the demand for it. Indeed, the function of a theory of demand is to establish a relationship between quantity demanded of a good and its price and to provide an explanation for it. From time to time, different theories have been advanced to explain consumer's demand for a good and to derive a valid demand theorem. Cardinal utility analysis is the oldest theory of demand which provides an expalantion of consumer's demand for a product and derives the law of demand which establishes an inverse relationship between price and quantity demanded of a product. Recently, cardinal utility approach to the theory of demand has been subjected to severe criticisms and as a result some alternative theories, namely, *Indifference Curve Analysis, Samuelson's Revealed Preference Theory, Hicks' Logical Weak Ordering Theory* have been propounded. We will discuss indifference curve analysis of demand in the next chapter, while in the present chapter we shall be concerned with the cardinal utility analysis of demand. Though cardinal utility approach to the theory of demand is very old, its final shape emerged at the hands of Marshall. Therefore, it is Marshallian cardinal utility analysis of demand which has been discussed in this chapter.

Assumptions of Cardinal Utility Analysis

Cardinal utility analysis of demand is based upon certain important assumptions. Before explaining how cardinal utility analysis explains consumer's equilibrium in regard to the demand for good, it is essential to describe those basic assumptions on which the whole utility analysis rests. As we shall see later, cardinal utility analysis has been criticised because of its unrealistic assumptions. the basic assumptions or premises of utility analysis are as follows:

The Cardinal Measurability of Utility. The exponents of cardinal utility analysis regard utility to be a cardinal concept. In other words, they hold that utility is a measurable and quantifiable entity. According to them, a person can express utility or satisfaction he derives from the goods in the quantitative cardinal terms. Thus, a person can say that he derives utility equal to 10 units from the consumption of a unit of good A, and 20 units from the consumption of a unit of good B. Moreover, the cardinal measurement of utility involves that a person can compare in respect of size, that is, how much one level of utility is greater than another. A person can say that the utility he gets from the consumption of one unit of good *B* is double the utility he obtains from the consumption of one unit of good *A*.

According to Marshall, marginal utility is *actually measurable in terms of money.*[1] Money represents the general purchaing power and it can therefore be regarded as a command over alternative utility-yielding goods. Marshall argues that the amount of money which a person is prepared to pay for a unit of a good rather than he without it is a measure of the utility he derives from that good. Thus, according to him money is the measuring rod of utility. Some economists belonging to the cardinalist school measure utility in imaginary units called "utils". They assume that a consumer is capable of saying that one apple provides him utility equal to 4 utils. Further, on this ground, he can say that he gets twice as much utility from an apple as from an orange.

The Hypothesis of Independent Utilities. The second important tenet of the cardinal utility analysis is the hypothesis of *independent utilities*. On this hypothesis, the utility which a consumer derives from a good is the function of the quantity of that good and of that good only. In other words, the utility which a consumer obtains from a good does not depend upon the quantity consumed of other goods; it depends upon the quantity purchased of that good alone. On this assumption, then the total utility which a person gets from the whole collection of goods purchased by him is simply the total sum of the separate utilities of the goods. Thus, the cardinalist school regards utility as '*additive*', that is, separate utilities of different goods can be added to obtain the total sum of the utilities of all goods purchased.

Constancy of the Marginal Utility of Money. Another important assumption of the cardinal utility analysis is the constancy of the marginal utility of money. Thus, while the marginal utility analysis assumes that marginal utilities of commodities diminish as more of them are purchased or consumed, but the marginal utility of money remains constant throughout when the individual is spending money on a good and due to which the amount of money with him varies. Daniel Bernoulli first of all introduced this assumption but later Marshall adopted this in his famous book "*Principles of Economics*'. As stated above, Marshall measured marginal utilities in terms of money. But measurement of marginal utility of goods in terms of money is only possible if the marginal utility of money itself remains constant. It should be noted that the assumption of constant marginal utility of money is very crucial to the Marshallian analysis, because otherwise Marshall could not measure the marginal utilities of goods in terms of money. If the money which is the unit of measurement itself varies as one is measuring with it, it cannot then yield correct measurement of the marginal utility of the good.

When the price of a good falls and the real income of the consumer rises, the marginal utility of money to him will fall but Marshall ignored this and assumed that marginal utility of money did not change as a result of the change in price. Likewise, when the price of a good rises, the real income of the consumer will fall and his marginal utility of money will rise. But Marshall ignored this and assumed that marginal utility of money remains the same. Marshall defended this assumption on the ground that "his (the individual consumer's) expenditure on any one thing.....is only a small part of his whole expenditure."

Introspective Method. Another important hypothesis of the marginal utility analysis is the use of introspective method in judging the behaviour of marginal utility. "Introspection is the ability of the observer to reconstruct events which go on in the mind of another person with the help of self-observation. This form of comprehension may be just guesswork or intution or the result of long lasting experience."[1] Thus, the economists construct with the help of their own experience the trend of feeling which goes on in other men's mind. From his own response to certain forces and by experience and observation one gains understanding of the way other people's minds would work in similar situations. To sum up, in introspective method we attribute to another person what we know

1. Emil Kauder, *A History of Marginal Utility Theory*, (Princeton, New Jersy, 1965). p. 120.

of our own mind. That is, by looking into ourselves we see inside the heads of other individuals. So the law of diminishing marginal utility is based upon introspection. We know from our own mind that as we have more of a thing, the less utility we derive from an additional unit of it. We conclude from it that other individuals' mind will work in a similar fashion, that is, marginal utility to them of a good will diminish as they have more units of it.

With the above basic premises, the founders of marginal utility analysis have developed tow laws which occupy an important place in economic theory and have several applications and uses. These two laws are : (1) Law of Diminishing Marginal Utility and (2) Law of Equi-Marginal Utility. It is with the help of these two laws about consumers'behaviour that the exponents of utility analysis have derived the law of demand. We explain below these two laws in detail.

LAW OF DIMINISHING MARGINAL UTILITY

An important tenet of cardinal utility analysis relates to the behaviour of marginal utility. This familiar behaviour of marginal utility has been stated in the Law of Diminishing Marginal Utility according to which marginal utility of a good diminishes as an individual consumes more units of a good. In other words, as a consumer takes more units of a good, the extra utility or satisfaction that he derives from an extra unit of the good goes on falling. It should be carefully noted that it is the marginal utility and not the total utility that declines with the increase in the consumption of a good. The law of diminishing marginal utility means that the total utility increases at a decreasing rate.

Marshall who was the famous exponent of the cardinal utility analysis has stated the law of diminishing marginal utility as follows:

"The additional benefit which a person derives from a given increase of his stock of a thing diminishes with every increase in the stock that he already has."

This law is based upon two important facts. First, while the total wants of a man are virtually unlimited, each single want is satiable. Therefore, as an individual consumes more and more units of a good, intensity of his want for the good goes on falling and a point is reached where the individual no longer wants any more units of the good. That is, when saturation point is reached, marginal utility of a good becomes zero. Zero marginal utility of a good implies that the individual has all that he wants of the good in question. The second fact on which the law of diminishing marginal utility is based is that the different goods are not perfect substitutes for each other in the satisfaction of various particular wants. When an individual consumes more and more units of a good, the intensity of his particular want for the good diminishes but if the units of that good could be devoted to the satisfaction of other wants and yielded as much satisfaction as they did initially in the satisfaction of the first want, marginal utility of the good would not have diminished.

It is obvious from above that the law of diminishing marginal utility describes a familiar and fundamental tendency of human nature. This law has been arrived at by introspection and by observing how people behave.

Illustration of the Law of Diminishing Marginal Utility

Consider Table 8.1. where we have presented the total and marginal utilities derived by a person from cups of tea consumed per day. When one cup of tea is taken per day, the total utility derived by the person is 12 utils. And because this is the first cup its marginal utility is also 12. With the consumption of 2nd cup per day, the total utility rises to 22 but marginal utility falls to 10. It will be seen from the table that as the consumption of tea increases to six cups per day, marginal utility from the additional cups goes on diminishing (*i.e.* the total utility goes on increasing at a diminishing rate). However, when the cups of tea consumed per day increases to seven, then instead of giving *positive* marginal utility, the seventh cup gives *negative* marginal utility equal to – 2. This is because too many cups of tea consumed per day (say more that six for a particular individual) may cause acidity and gas trouble. Thus, the extra cups of tea beyond six to the individual in question gives him disutility rather than positive satisfaction.

Table 8.1
Diminishing Marginal Utility

Cups of Tea consumed per day	*Total Utility (utils)*	*Marginal Utility (utils)*
1	12	12
2	22	10
3	30	8
4	36	6
5	40	4
6	41	1
7	39	–2
8	34	–5

We have graphically represented the data of the above table in Figure 8.1. We have constructed rectangles representing the toal utility obtained from various numbers of cups of tea consumed per day. As will be seen from the Figure 8.1 the length of the rectangle goes on increasing up to the sixth cup of tea and beyond that length of the rectangle declines, indicating thereby that up to the sixth cup of tea total utility obtained from the increasing cups of tea goes on increasing whereas beyond the 6th cup, total utility declines. In other words, marginal utility of the additional cups up to the 6th cup is positive whereas beyond the sixth cup marginal utility is negative. The marginal utility obtained by the consumer from additional cups of tea as he increases the consumption of tea has been shaded. A glance at the figure 8.1 will show that this shaded area goes on declining which shows that marginal utility from the additional cups of tea is diminishing.

We have joined the various rectangles by a smooth curve which is the curve of total utility which rises up to a point and then declines due to negative marginal utility. Moreover, the shaded areas of the rectangle representing marginal utility of the various cups of tea have also been shown separately in the figure given at the bottom. We have joined the shaded rectangles by a smooth curve which is the curve of marginal utility. As will be seen, this marginal utility curve goes on declining throughout and even falls below the *X*-axis. Portion below the *X*-axis indicates the negative marginal utility. This downward-sloping marginal utility curve has an important implication for consumer's behaviour regarding demand for goods. We shall explain below how the demand curve is derived from marginal utility curve.

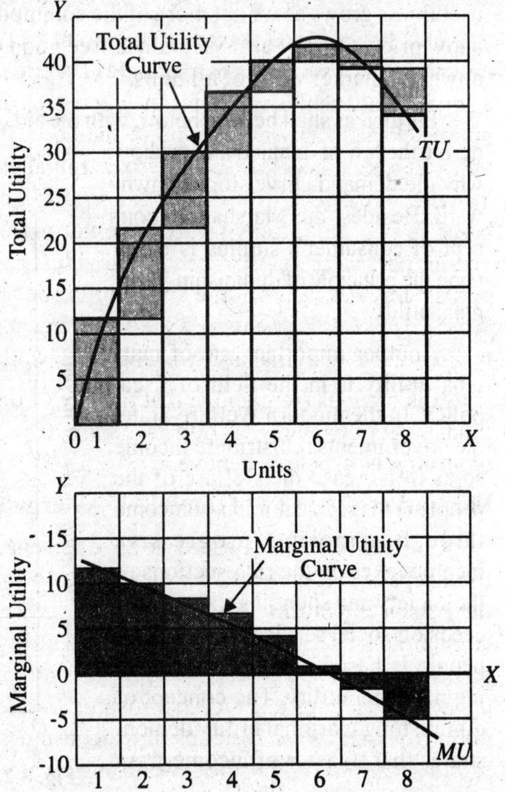

Fig. 8.1. *Diminishing Marginal Utility*

The significance of the diminishing marginal utility of a good for the theory of demand is that the quantity demanded of a good rises as the price falls and *vice versa*. Thus, it is because of the diminishing marginal utility that the demand curve slopes downward. This will be explained in detail later in this chapter. If properly understood the law of diminishing marginal utility applies to all objects of desire including money. But it is worth mentioning that marginal utility of money is generally never zero or negative. Money represents purchasing power over all other goods, that is, a man can satisfy all his material wants if he possesses enough money. Since man's total wants are practically unlimited, therefore the marginal utility of money to him never falls to zero.

Applications and Uses of Diminishing Marginal Utility

The marginal utility analysis has a good number of uses and applications in both economic theory and policy. The concept of marginal utility is of crucial significance in explaining determination of the prices of commodities. The discovery of the concept of marginal utility has helped to explain the *paradox of value* which troubled Adam Smith in *The Wealth of Nations*. Adam Smith was greatly surprised to know why water which is so very essential and useful to life has such a low price (indeed no price), which diamonds which are quite unnecessary, have such a high price. He could not resolve this water-diamond paradox. But modern economists can solve it with the aid of concept of marginal utility. According to the modern economists, the total utility of a commodity does not determine the price of a commodity and it is the marginal utility which is crucially important determinant of price. Now, the water is available in abundant quantities so that its relative marginal utility is very low or even zero. Therefore, its price is low or zero. On the other hand, the diamonds are scarce and therefore their relative marginal utility is quite high and this is the reason why their prices are high. Prof. Samuelson explains this paradox of value in the following words:—"The more there is of a commodity, the less the relative desirability of its last little unit becomes, even though its total usefulness grows as we get more of the commodity. So, it is obvious why a large amount of water has a low price. Or why air is actually a free good despite its vast usefulness. The many later units pull down the market value of all units."[2]

Further, as shall be seen below, with the aid of the law of diminishing marginal utility, we are able to derive the law of demand and to show why the demand curve slopes downward. Besides, the Marshallian concept of consumer's surplus is based upon the principle of diminishing marginal utility.

Another important use of marginal utility is in the field of fiscal policy. In the modern Welfare State, the governments redistribute income so as to increase the welfare of the people. This redistribution of income through imposing progressive income taxes on the rich sections of the society and spending the tax proceeds on social services for the poor people is based upon the diminishing marginal utility. The concept of diminishing marginal utility demonstrates that transfer of income from

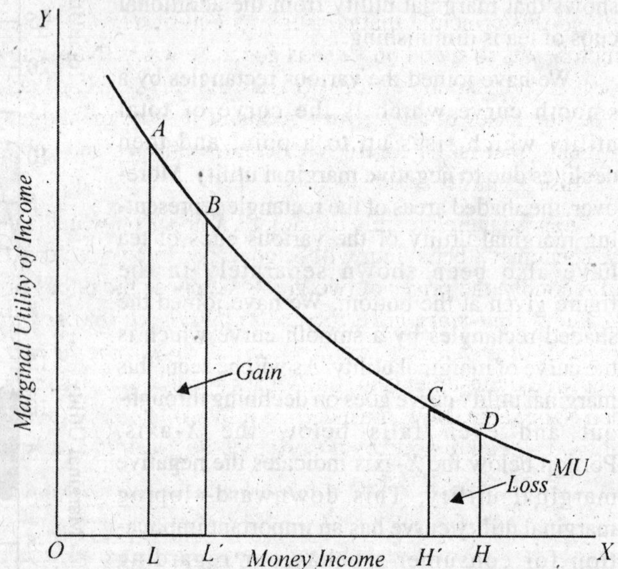

Fig. 8.2. *Redistribution of Income to Increase Social Welfare*

2. Paul Samuelson, *Economics*, McGraw Hill, 8th edition, p. 417.

the rich to the poor will increase the economic welfare of the community. As has been pointed out above, law of diminishing marginal utility also applies to the money; as the money income of a consumer increases, the marginal utility of money to him falls. How the redistribution of income will increase welfare of the community, is illustrated in Figure 8.2. In this figure, money income is measured along *X*-axis and marginal utility of income is measured along *Y*-axis. *MU* is the marginal utility curve of money which is sloping downward. Suppose *OL* is the income of a poor person and *OH* is the income of a rich person. If rich person is subjected to the income tax and amount of money equal to *HH′* is taken from him and the same amount of money *LL′* (equal to *HH′*) is given to the poor man, it can be shown that the welfare of the community will increase. As a result of this transfer of income, the income of the rich man falls by *HH′* and the income of the poor person rises by *LL′* (*HH′* = *LL′*). Now it will be seen from Figure 8.2 that the loss of satisfaction or utility of the rich man as a result of decline in his income by *HH′* is equal to the area *IIDCII′*. Further, it will bee seen that the gain in satisfaction or utility by the increase of an equivalent amount of income *LL′* of the poor man, is equal to *LABL′*.

It is thus obvious from the figure that the gain in utility of the poor person is greater than the loss of utility of the rich man. Therefore, the total utility or satisfaction of the two persons taken together will increase. Thus, on the basis of the diminishing marginal utility of money many economists and political scientists have advocated that Government must redistribute income in order to raise economic welfare of the society. However, it may be pointed out that some economists challenge the validity of such redistribution of income to promote social welfare. They point out that the above analysis of marginal utility is based upon interpersonal comparison of utility which is quite invalid and unscientific. They argue that people differ greatly in their preferences and capacity to enjoy goods and, therefore, it is difficult to know the exact shapes of the marginal utility curves of the different persons. Therefore they assert that the losses and gains of utility of the poor and the rich cannot be measured and compared.

PRINCIPLE OF EQUI-MARGINAL UTILITY : CONSUMER'S EQUILIBRIUM

Priniciple of equi-marginal utility occupies an important place in cardinal utility analysis. It is through this principle that consumer's equilibrium is explained. A consumer has a given income which he has to spend on various goods he wants. Now, the question is how he would allocate his money income among various goods, that is to say, what would be his equilibrium position in respect of the purchases of the various goods. It may be mentioned here that consumer is assumed to be 'rational', that is, he carefully calculates utilities and substitutes one good for another so as to maximise his utility or satisfaction.

Suppose there are only two goods *X* and *Y* on which a consumer has to spend a given income. The consumer's behaviour will be governed by two factors: first, the marginal utilities of the goods and secondly, the prices of two goods. Suppose the prices of the goods are given for the consumer. *The law of equi-marginal utility states that the consumer will distribute his money income between the goods in such a way that the utility derived from the last rupee spent on each good is equal.* In other words, consumer is in equilibrium position when marginal utility of money expenditure on each good is the same. Now, the marginal utility of money expenditure on a good is equal to the marginal utility of a good divided by the price of the good. In symbols,

$$MU_e = \frac{MU_x}{P_x}$$

where MU_e is marginal utility of money expenditure and MU_x is the marginal utility of *X* and P_x is the price of *X*. The law of equi-marginal utility can therefore be stated thus: the consumer will spend his money income on different goods in such a way that marginal utility of money expenditure each good is equal. That is, consumer is in equilibrium in respect of the purchases of two goods *X* and *Y* when

$$\frac{MU_x}{P_x} = \frac{MU_y}{P_y}$$

Now, if $\frac{MU_x}{P_x}$ and $\frac{MU_y}{P_y}$ are not equal and $\frac{MU_x}{P_x}$ is greater than $\frac{MU_y}{P_y}$, then the consumer will substitute good *X* for good *Y*. As a result of this substitution, the marginal utility of good *X* will fall and marginal utility of good *Y* will rise. The consumer will continue substituting good *X* for good *Y* till $\frac{MU_x}{P_x}$ becomes equal to $\frac{MU_y}{P_y}$. When $\frac{MU_x}{P_x}$ becomes equal to $\frac{MU_y}{P_y}$ the consumer will be in equilibrium.

But the equality of $\frac{MU_x}{P_x}$ with $\frac{MU_y}{P_y}$ can be achieved not only at one level but at different levels of expenditure. The question is how far does a consumer go in purchasing the goods he wants. This is determined by the size of his money income. With a given income and money expenditure a rupee has a certain utility for him: this utility is the marginal utility of money to him. Since the law of diminishing marginal utility applies to money income also, the greater the size of his money income the smaller the marginal utility of money to him. Now, the consumer will go on purchasing goods till the marginal utility of money expenditure on each good becomes equal to the marginal utility of money to him. Thus, the consumer will be in equilibrium when the following equation holds good:

$$\frac{MU_x}{P_x} = \frac{MU_y}{P_y} = MU_m$$

Where MU_m is marginal utility of money expenditure (that is, the utility of the last spent on eachy good).

If there are more than two goods on which the consumer is spending his income, the above equation must hold good for all of them.

Let us illustrate the law of equi-marginal utility with the aid of an arithmetical table given below:

Table 8.2
Marginal Utility of Goods X and Y

Units	MU_x *(Utils)*	MU_y *(Utils)*
1	20	24
2	18	21
3	16	18
4	14	15
5	12	9
6	10	3

Let the prices of goods *X* and *Y* be Rs. 2 and Rs. 3 respectively. Reconstructing the above table by dividing marginal utilities of *X* (MU_x) by Rs. 2 and marginal utilities of *Y*(MU_y) by Rs. 3 we get the Table 8.3.

Table 8.3
Marginal Utility of Money Expenditure

Units	$\frac{MU_x}{P_x}$	$\frac{MU_y}{P_y}$
1	10	8
2	9	7
3	8	6
4	7	5
5	6	3
6	5	1

Suppose a consumer has money income of Rs. 24 to spend on the two goods. It is worth noting that in order to maximise his utility the consumer will not equate *marginal utilities of the goods* because prices of the two goods are different. He will equate the marginal utility of the last rupee (*i.e.* marginal utility of money expenditure) spent on these two goods. In other words, he will equate $\frac{MU_x}{P_x}$ with $\frac{MU_y}{P_y}$ while spending his give money income on the two goods. By looking at the Table 8.3 it will become clear that $\frac{MU_x}{P_x}$ is equal to 5 utils when the consumer purchases 6 units of good *X* and $\frac{MU_y}{P_y}$ is equal to 5 utils when he buys 4 units of good *Y*. Therefore, consumer will be in equilibrium when he is buying 6 units of good *X* and 4 units of good *Y* and will be spending (Rs. 2 × 6 + Rs. 3 × 4) = Rs. 24 on them. Thus, in the equilibrium position where he maximises his utility,

$$\frac{MU_x}{P_x} = \frac{MU_y}{P_y} = MU_m$$

$$\frac{10}{2} = \frac{15}{3} = 5$$

Thus, marginal utility of the last rupee spent on each of the two goods he purchases is the same, that is, 5 utils.

Consumers' equilibrium is graphically protrayed in Fig. 8.3. Since marginal utility curves of goods slope downward, curves depicting $\frac{MU_x}{P_x}$ and $\frac{MU_y}{P_y}$ also slope downward. Thus, when the consumer is buying *OH* of *X* and *OK* of *Y*, then

$$\frac{MU_x}{P_x} = \frac{MU_y}{P_y} = MU_m$$

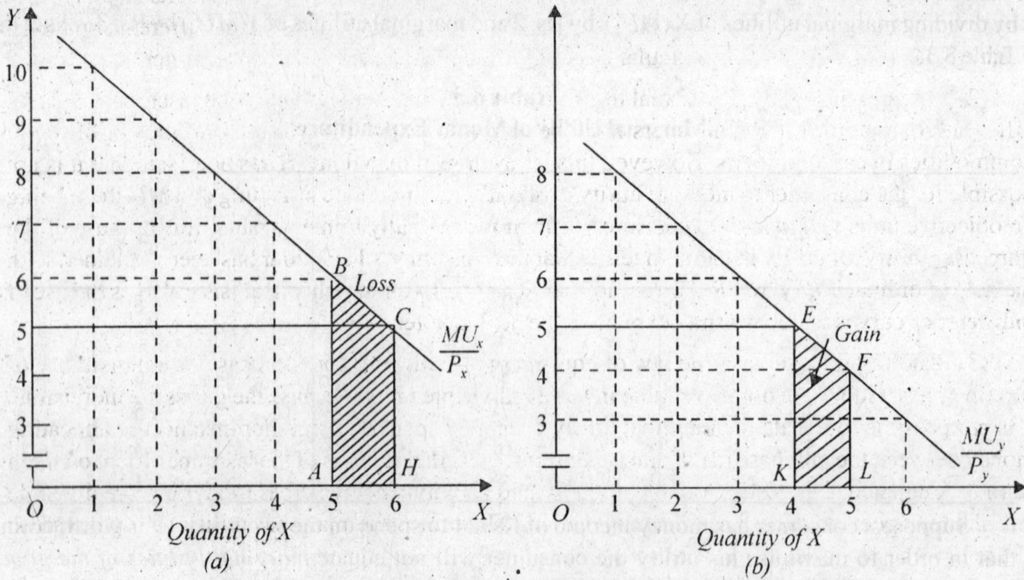

Fig. 8.3. *Equi-Marginal Principle and Consumer's Equilibrium*

Therefore, the consumer is in equilibrium when he is buying 6 units of *X* and 4 units of *Y*. No other allocation of money expenditure will yield greater utility than when he is buying 6 units of commodity X and 4 units of commodity *Y*. Suppose if the consumer buys one unit less of good *X* and one unit more of good *Y*. This will lead to the decrease in his total utility. It will be observed from Figure 8.3 (a) that the consumption of 5 units instead of 6 units of commodity *X* means a loss in satisfaction equal to the shaded area *ABCH* and from Fig. 8.3(b) it will be seen that consumption of 5 units of commodity *Y* instead of 4 units will mean gain in utility by the shaded area *KEFL*. It will be noticed that with this rearrangement of pucrchases of the two goods, the loss in utility *ABCH* exceeds gain in utility *KEFL*. Thus, his total satisfaction will fall as a result of this rearrangement of purchases. Thus when the consumer is making purchases by spending his given income in such a way that $\frac{MU_x}{P_x} = \frac{MU_y}{P_y}$, he will not like to make any further changes in the basket of goods and will therefore be in equilibrium situation by maximizing his utility.

The above equi-marginal condition for the equilibrium of the consumer will hold even when a consumer spends his money income on several goods. Thus

$$\frac{MU_x}{P_x} = \frac{MU_y}{P_y} = \dots\dots\dots = \frac{MU_n}{P_n} = MU_m$$

Limitations of the Law of Equi-Marginal Utility

Like other laws of economics, law of equimarginal utility is also subject to various limitations. This law, like other laws of economics, brings out an important tendency among the people. This is not necessary that all people exactly follow this law in the allocation of their money income and therefore all may not obtain maximum satisfaction. This is due to the following reasons:–

(1) For applying this law of equi-marginal utility in the real life, consumer must weigh in his mind the marginal utilities of different commodities. For this he has to calculate and compare the marginal utilities obtained from different commodities. But it has been pointed out that the ordinary consum-

ers are not so rational and calculating. Consumers are generally governed by habits and customs. Because of their habits and customs they spend particular amounts of money on different commodities, regardless of whetner the particular allocation maximises their satisfaction or not.

(2) For applying this law in actual life and equate the marginal utility of the last rupee spent on different commodities, the consumers must be able to measure the marginal utilities of different commodities in cardinal terms. However, this is easier said than done. It has been said that it is not possible for the consumer to measure utility cardinally. Being a state of feeling and also there being no objective units with which to measure utility, it is cardinally immeasurable. It is because of the immeasurability of utility in cardinal terms that the consumer's behaviour has been explained with the help of ordinal utility by J.R. Hicks and R.G.D. Allen. Ordinal utility analysis involves the use of indifference curves which we shall explain in the next chapter.

(3) Another limitation of the law of equi-marginal utility is found in case of indivisibility of certain goods. Goods are often available in large indivisible units. Because the goods are indivisible, it is not possible to equate the marginal utility of money spent on them. For instance, in allocating money between the purchase of car and foodgrains, marginal utilities of the last rupee spent on them cannot be equated. Car costs about Rs. 200,000 and is indivisible, whereas foodgrains are divisible and money spent on them can be easily varied. Therefore, the marginal utility of rupee varies. Therefore, the marginal utility of rupee obtained from cars cannot be equalised with that obtained from foodgrains. Thus, indivisibility of certain goods is a great obstacle in the way of equalisation of marginal utility of a rupee from different commodities.

DERIVATION OF THE DEMAND CURVE AND THE LAW OF DEMAND

We now turn to explain how the deamnd curve and the law of demand is derived in the marginal utility analysis. As stated above, the demand curve or the law of demand shows the relationship between price of a good and its quantity demanded. Marshall derived the demand curves for goods from their utility functions. It should be further noted that in his utility analysis of demand Marshall assumed the utility functions of different goods to be independent of each other. In other words, Marshallian technique of deriving demand curves for the goods from their utility functions rests on the hypothesis of *additive utility functions*, that is, utility function of each good consumed by the consumer does not depend on the quantity consumed of any other good. As has already been noted, in case of independent utilities or additive utility functions, the relations of substitution and complementarity between goods are ruled out. Further, in deriving demand curve or law of demand Marshall assumes the marginal utility of money expenditure (MU_m) to remain constant. The law of demand or the demand curve can be derived in two cases: first, in case of single commodtiy with the aid of law of diminishing marginal utility, and secondly, in case of several commodities with the help of the law of equi-marginal utility. We shall explain below these two cases.

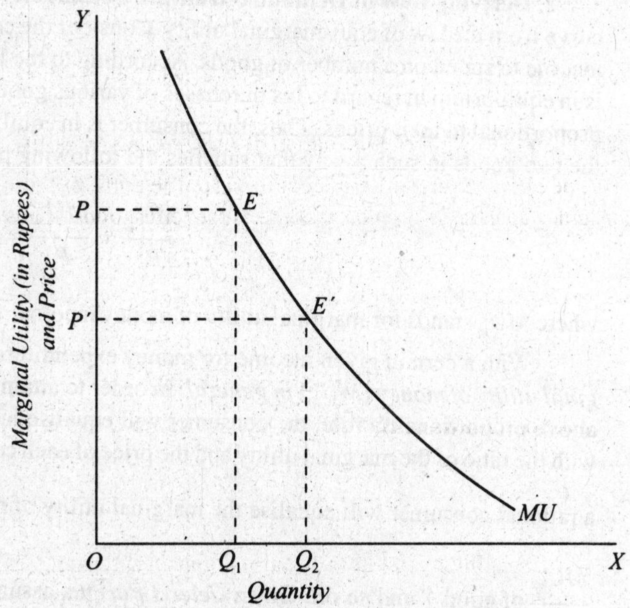

Fig. 8.4. *Diminishing Marginal Utility and Demand*

1. **Deriving Demand Curve : A Single Commodity Case.** The law of marginal utility states that as the quantity of a good with a consumer increases, marginal utility of the good to him expressed in terms of money falls. In other words, the marginal utility curve of a good is downward sloping. Now, a consumer will go on puchasing a good until the marginal utility of the good in rupees equals the market price. In other words, *the consumer will be in equilibrium in respect of the quantity of a good purchased where marginal utility of the good measured in terms of money equals its price.* His satisfaction will be maximum only when marginal utility equals price. Thus the "*marginal utility equals price*" is the condition of equilibrium. When price of a good falls, downward-sloping marginal utility curve implies that the consumers must buy more of the good so that its marginal utility falls and becomes equal to the new price. It therefore follows that the diminishing marginal utility curve implies the downward-sloping demand curve, that is, when price of the good falls, more of it will be bought. The whole argument will be more clearly understood from Fig. 8.4. In this figure the curve *MU* represents the diminishing *marginal utility of the good measured in terms of money.* Suppose price of the good is *OP*. At this price the consumer will be in equilibrium when he purchases OQ_1 quantity of the good, since at OQ_1 the marginal utility is equal to the given price *OP*. Now, if price of the good falls to *OP′*, the equality between the marginal utility of the good in rupees and the price will be disturbed. Marginal utility Q_1E at quantity OQ_1 will be greater than the new price *OP′*. In order to equate the marginal utility with the lower price *OP′*, the consumer must buy more of the good. It is evident from Fig. 8.4 that when the consumer increases the quantity purchased to OQ_2 the marginal utility (in terms of rupees) of the good falls and becomes equal to the new price *OP′*.

It is thus clear that when price of a good falls, the consumer buys more of the good so as to equate his marginal utility to the lower price. It therefore follows that the quantity demanded of a good varies inversely with price; the quantity bought rises when price falls and *vice versa*, other things remaining the same. This is the famous *Marshallian Law of Demand*. It is now quite evident that the law of demand is directly derived from the law of diminishing marginal utility. The downward-sloping marginal utility curve is transformed into the downward-sloping demand curve. In Fig. 8.4 where price is also measured on the *Y*-axis marginal utility curve *MU* becomes the demand curve. It follows therefore that the force working behind the law of demand or the downward-sloping demand curve is the force of diminishing marginal utility.

2. **Deriving Law of Demand : Multiple Commodity Case.** We now proceed to derive demand curve from the law of equi-marginal utility. Consider the case of a consumer who has a certain given income to spend on a number of goods. According to the law of equi-marginal utility, the consumer is in equilibrium in regard to his purchases of various goods when marginal utilities of the goods are proportional to their prices. Thus, the consumer is in equilibrium when he is buying the quantities of the two goods in such a way that satisfies the following proportionality rule:

$$\frac{MU_x}{P_x} = \frac{MU_y}{P_y} = MU_m$$

where MU_m stands for marginal utility of money income.

With a certain given income for money expenditure the consumer would have a certain *marginal utility of money* (MU_m) *in general*. In order to attain the equilibrium position, according to the above proportionality rule, the consumer will equalise his marginal utility of money (expenditure) with the ratio of the marginal utility and the price of each commodity he buys. It follows therefore that a rational consumer will equalise the marginal utility of money (MU_m) with $\frac{MU_x}{P_x}$ of good *x*, with $\frac{MU_y}{P_y}$ of good *Y* and so on. Given *Ceteris Paribus* assumption, suppose the price of good X falls.

With the fall in the price of good *X*, the price of good *Y*, consumer's income and tastes remaining unchanged, the equality of the $\frac{MU_x}{P_x}$ with $\frac{MU_y}{P_y}$ and MU_m in general would be disturbed. With the lower price than before $\frac{MU_x}{P_x}$ will be *greater than* $\frac{MU_y}{P_y}$ or MU_m (It is assumed of course that the marginal utility of money does not change as a result of the change in the price of one good). Then in order to restore the equality, marginal utility of *X* or MU_x must be reduced. And the marginal utility of *X* or MU_x can be reduced only by consumer's buying more of the good *X*. It is thus clear from the proportionality rule that as the price of a good falls, its quantity demanded will rise, other things remaining the same. This will make the demand curve downward sloping. How the quantity purchased of a good increases with the fall in its price and also how the demand curve is derived in the present multi-commodity case is illustrated in Fig. 8.5.

In the upper portion of the Fig. 8.5, on the *Y*-axis is shown $\frac{MU_x}{P_x}$ and on the *X*-axisis is shown the quantity demanded of good *X*. Given a certain income of the consumer , the marginal utility of money is equal to *OH*. The consumer is buying Oq_1 of good *X* when the price is Px_1 since at the quantity Oq_1 of *X*, the marginal utility of money *OH* is equal to $\frac{MU_x}{P_{x1}}$. Now, when price of good *X* falls, to Px_2 the curve will shift upward to the new position $\frac{MU_x}{P_{x2}}$. In order to equate marginal utility of money (*OH*) with the new $\frac{MU_x}{P_{x2}}$ the consumer increases the quantity demanded to Oq_2. Thus, with the fall to P_{x2}, in price of good *X* the consumer buys more of it. It should be noted that no account is taken of the increase in real income of the consumer as a result of fall in price of good *X*. This is because if the change in real income is taken into account then the marginal utility of money will also change and this would have an effect on the purchases of goods. Marginal utility of money can remain constant in two cases. Firstly, when the

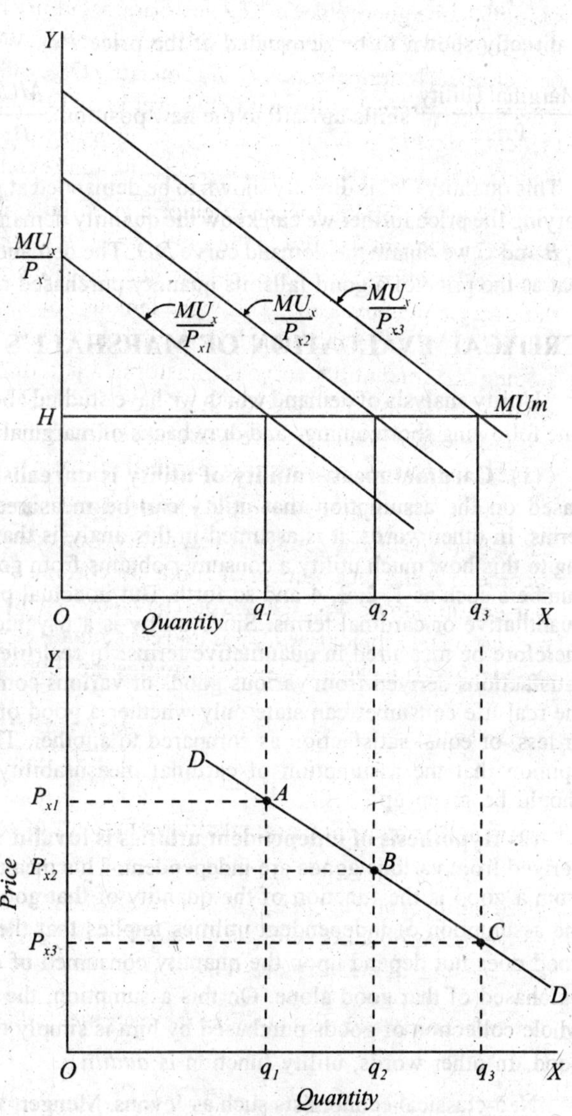

Fig. 8.5. *Derivation of Demand Curve*

constant in two cases. Firstly, when the elasticity of marginal utility curve (price elasticity of demand) is unity so that even with increase in the purchase of a commodity following the fall in price, the money expenditure made on it remains the same. Second, marginal utility of money will remain approximately constant for small changes in price of unimportant goods, that is, goods which account for negligible part of consumer's budget. In case of these unimportant goods increase in real income following the fall in price is negligible and therefore can be ignored.

At the bottom of Figure 8.5 the demand curve for X is derived. In this lower diagram, price is measured the on Y-axis. As in the upper portion, the X-axis represents quantity. When the price of good X is Px_1, the relevant curve of $\frac{\text{Marginal Utility}}{\text{Price}}$ is $\frac{MU_x}{P_{x_1}}$ which is shown in the upper portion. With $\frac{MU_x}{P_{x1}}$, as explained earlier, he boys Oq_1 of good X. Now, in the lower portion this quantity Oq_1 is directly shown to be demanded at the price Px_1. When price of X falls to Px_2, the curve of $\frac{\text{Marginal Utility}}{\text{Price}}$ shifts upward to the new position $\frac{MU_x}{P_{x_2}}$. With $\frac{MU_x}{P_{x_2}}$ the consumer buys Oq_2 of X. This quantity Oq_2 is directly shown to be demanded at price Px_2 in the lower portion. Similarly, by varying the price further we can know the quantity demanded at other prices. Thus, by joining points A, B and C we obtain the demand curve DD. The demand curve DD slopes downward which shows that as the price of a good falls, its quantity purchased rises.

CRITICAL EVALUATION OF MARSHALL'S CARDINAL UTILITY ANALYSIS

Utility analysis of demand which we have studied above has been criticised on various grounds. The following shortcomings and drawbacks of marginal utility analysis have been pointed out:

(1) **Cardinal measurability of utility is unrealistic:** Cardinal utility analysis of demand is based on the assumption that utility can be measured in absolute, objective and quantitative terms. In other words, it is assumed in this analysis that utility is cardinally measurable. According to this how much utility a consumer obtains from goods can be expressed or stated in cardinal numbers such as 1, 2, 3, 4 and so forth. But in actual practice utility cannot be measured in such quantitative or cardinal terms. Since utility is a psychic feeling and a subjective thing, it cannot therefore be measured in quantitative terms. In real life, consumers are only able to *compare* the satisfactions derived from various goods or various combinations of the goods. In other words, in the real life consumer can state only whether a good or a combination of goods gives him more, or less, or equal satisfaction as compared to another. Thus, economists like J.R. Hicks are of the opinion that the assumption of cardinal measurability of utility is unrealistic and therefore it should be given up.

(2) **Hypothesis of independent utilities is invalid :** Utility analysis also assumes that utilities derived from various goods are independent. This means that the utility which a consumer derives from a good is the function of the quantity of that good and of that good alone. In other words, the assumption of independent utilities implies that the utility which a consumer obtains from a good does not depend upon the quantity consumed of other goods; it depends upon the quantity purchased of that good alone. On this assumption, the total utility which a person gets from the whole collection of goods purchased by him is simply the total sum of the separate utilities of the good. In other words, utility function is *additive*.

Neo-classical economists such as Jevons, Menger, Walras and Marshall considered that utility ıunctions were additive. But in the real life this is not so. In actual life the utility or satisfaction derived from a good depends upon the availability of some other goods which may be either substitutes for or complementary with each other. For example, the utility derived from a pen depends upon whether ink is available or not. On the contrary, if you have *only tea*, then the utility derived from it would be greater but if along with tea you also have the coffee then the utility of tea to you would be comparatively less. Whereas pen and ink are *complements* with each other, tea and coffee are *substitutes for each other*. It is thus clear that various goods are related to each other in the sense that some are complements with each other and some are substitutes for each other. As a result of this, the utilities derived from various goods are independent, that is, they depend upon each other. Therefore, the utility obtained from a good is not the function of its quantityt alone but also depends upon the existence or consumption of other related goods (complements or substitutes). It is thus evident that the assumption of the independencc of utilities by Marshall and other supporters of marginal utility analysis is a great defect and shortcoming of their analysis. As we shall see below, the hypothesis of independent utilities along with the assumption of constant marginal utility of money reduces the validity of Marshallian demand theorem to the one-commodity model only.

(3). **Assumption of constant marginal utility of money is not valid.** An important assumption of cardinal utility analysis is that when a consumer spends varying amount on a good or various goods or when the price of a good changes, the marginal utility of money remains unchanged. But in acutal practice this is not correct. As a consumer spends his money income on the goods, money income left with him declines. With the decline in money income of the consumer as a result of increase in his expenditure on goods, the marginal utility of money to him rises. Further, when the price of a commodity changes, the real income of the consumer also changes. With this change in real income, marginal utility of money will change and this would have an effect on the demand for the good in question, even though the total money income available with the consumer remains the same. But utility analysis ignores all this and does not take cognizance of the changes in real income and its effect on demand for goods following the change in the price of a good.

As has been explained earlier, according to Marshall, utility from a good can be measured in terms of money (that is, how much money a consumer is prepared to sacrifice for a good). But, to be able to measure utility in terms of money marginal utility of money itself should remain constant. Therefore, assumption of constant marginal utility of money is very crucial in Marshallian demand analysis. But in case the consumer has to spread his money income on a number of goods, there is a necessity for revision of marginal utility of money with every change in the price of a good. In other words, in a multi-commodity model marginal utility of money does not remain invariant or constant.

(4) **Marshallian demand theorem cannot genuinely be derived except in a one commodity case.** J.R. Hicks and Tapas Majumdar have further criticised the Marshallian utility analysis on the ground that "Marshallian demand theorem cannot genuinely be derived from the marginal utility hypothesis except in a one-commodity model without contradicting the assumption of constant marginal utility of money".[3] In other words, Marshall's demand theorem and constant marginal utility of money are incompatible except in a one commodity case. As a result, Marshall's demand theorem cannot be validity derived in the case when a consumer spends his money on more than one good. In order to know the truth of this assertion consider a consumer who has a given amount of money income to spend on some goods with given prices. According to utility analysis, consumer will be in equilibrium when he is spending money on goods in such a way that ratios of marginal utilities of various goods to their prices are equal.

Let us assume that in this equilibrium position, consumer is buying q_1 quantity of a good X at a price p_1. Since the consumer is buying q_1 quantity of good X at price p_1, he will be spending p_1q_1

3. Tapas Majumdar, *Measurment of Utility*, p. 55.

amount of money on it. Suppose that the price of good X rises from p_1 to p_2 and as a result quantity demanded falls from q_1 to q_2 so that the new expenditure will be euqal to $p_2 q_2$. Now, the important thing to see is that whether his new expenditure $p_2 q_2$ on good X is equal to, smaller or greater than $p_1 q_1$. This depends upon the elasticity of marginal utility curve (*i.e.* price elasticity of demand). If elasticity of marginal utility curve of good X is unity, then the new expenditure on X (that is, $p_2 q_2$) after the rise in price of X from p_1 to p_2, will be equal to the initial expenditure $p_1 q_1$. When the monetary expenditure made on the good remains constant as a result of change in price, then the Marshallian demand theory is valid. But constant monetary expenditure on a commodity following a price change is only a rare phenomenon.

Thus, in case of more than one good, Marshallian demand theorem cannot be genuinely derived while keeping the marginal utility of money constant. If, in Marshallian demand analysis, this difficulty is avoided "by giving up the assumption of constant marginal utility of money, then money can no longer provide the measuring rod, and we can no longer express the marginal utility of a commodity in units of money[4].

(5) **Cardinal utility analysis does not split up the price effect into substitution and income effects.** The third shortcoming of the cardinal utility analysis is that *it does not distinguish between the income effect and the substitution effect of the price change.* We know that when price of a good falls, the consumer becomes better off than before, that is, a fall in price of a good brings about an increase in real income of the consumer. In other words, if with the fall in price the consumer purchases the same quantity of the good as before, then he would be left with some income. With this extra income he would be in a position to purchase more of this good as well as other goods. This is the income effect of the fall in price on the quantity demanded of the good. Besides, when price of a good falls, it becomes relatively cheaper than other goods and as a result the consumer is induced to substitute that good for others. This results in the increase in the quantity demanded of that good. This is the substitution effect of the price change on the quantity demanded of the good.

Thus, with the fall in price of a good, the quantity demanded of it rises because of income effect and substitution effect. But cardinal utility analysis does not make clear the distinction between the income and the substitution effects of the price hange by assuming the constancy of marginal utility of money. Thus, according to Tapas Majumdar, "the assumption of constant marginal utility of money obscured Marshall's insight into the truly *composite character* of the price-demand relationship."[5] Marshall explained the changes in demand as a result of change in the price of a good on the basis of substitution effect on it. Thus, marginal utility analysis does not tell us about how much quantity demanded increases due to income effect and how much due to substitution effect as a result of the fall in price of a good. J.R. Hicks rightly remarks, "*the distinction between income effect and substitution effect of a price change is accordingly left by the cardinal theory as an empty box which is crying out ot be filled*". [6]

(6) **Marshall could not explain Giffen Paradox.** By not visualising the price effect as a combination of substitution and income effects and ignoring the income effect of the price change, Marshall could not explain Giffen Paradox. He treated it merely as an exception to his law of demand. In contrast to it, indifference curve analysis has been able to explain satisfactorily the Giffen good case. According to indifference curve analysis, in case of Giffen Paradox or Giffen good negative income effect of the price change is more powerful than the substitution effect so that when the price of a of a Giffen good falls the negative income effect outweighs the substitution effect with the result

4. Tapas Majumdar, *ot.cit. p.*56.
5. Ibid, p. 57.
6. J.R. Hicks, *A Revision of Demand Theory*, Oxford University Press, 1956.

that quantity demanded of it falls. Thus, in case of a *Giffen good quantity demanded varies directly with the price and the Marshall's law of demand does not hold good.* It is because of the constant marginal utility of money and therefore the neglect of income effect of the price change that Marshall could not explain why the quantity demanded of the Giffen good falls when its price falls and rises when its price rises. This is a serious lacuna in Marshallian's utility analysis of demand.

(7) *Cardinal utility analysis assumes too much and explains too little*: Cardinal utility analysis is also criticised on the ground that it takes more assumptions and also more restrictive ones than those of ordinal utility analysis of indifference curve technique. Cardinal utility analysis assumes, among others, that utility is cardinally measurable and also that marginal utility of money remains constant. Hicks and Allen's indifference curve analysis does not take these assumptions and even then it is not only able to deduce all the theorems which cardinal utility analysis can but also deduces a *more general theorem of demand.* In other words, indifference curve analysis explains not only that much as cardinal utility analysis but even goes further and that too with fewer and less restrictive assumptions. Taking less restrictive assumption of ordinal measurement of utility and without assuming constant marginal utility of money, indifference curve analysis is able to arrive at the condition of consumer's equilibrium, namely, equality of marginal rate of substitution (MRS) with the price ratio between goods, which is similar to the proportionality rule of Marshall. Further, since indifference curve analysis does not assume constant marginal utility of money, it is able to derive a valid demand theorem in the multi-commodity case also.

Because of the above drawbacks, cardinal utility analysis has been given up in modern economic theory and demand is analysed with indifference curves which we shall explain in the next chapter.

QUESTIONS AND PROBLEMS FOR REVIEW

1. State and explain the law of diminishing marginal utility? How is law of demand related to it?
2. What is meant by consumer equilibrium ? How does a consumer maximise his satisfaction in cardinal utility analysis ?
3. Explain the Law of Equi-marginal utility ? How does it explain consumer equilibrium ?
4. You are given the following marginal utilities of goods *X* and *Y* obtained by a consumer. Given that price of *X* = Rs. 5, price of *Y* = Rs. 2 and income = Rs. 22, find out the optimal combination of goods.

Number of units consumed of a commodity	*MUx (utils)*	*MUy (utils)*
1	30	20
2	25	18
3	20	16
4	15	14
5	10	12
6	5	10
7	1	8

(**Hint**: Divide marginal utilities of goods *X* and *Y* by their prices and then compare.)

5. On what grounds Marshall's cardinal utility analysis has been criticised ?

6. Distinguish between cardinal utility and ordinal utility. Which is more realistic ?
7. Why assumption of constant marginal utility of money is essential in Marshall's cardinal utility analysis of demand. What argument Marshall gave in defence of this assumption.
8. What is Giffen Paradox ? Why Marshall could not explain it ?
9. Derive the demand curve for a commodity from Marshall's cardinal utility analysis. Explain in terms of cardinal utility theory why demand curve for a commodity slopes downward.
10. Deduce the inverse relationship between the quantity demanded of a commodity and its price in terms of Marshallian marginal utility analysis, indicating the underlying assumptions. How would you explain in terms of this analysis, the phenomenon that a fall in price of salt does not make a consumer buy more of it ? (*D.U.B.A.* (Hons.)
11. Suppose the *MU* of good *X* is 20 its price is Rs. 4 and the *MU* of good *Y* is 50 and its price is Rs. 5. The individual to whom this information applies is spending Rs. 20 on each good. Is he or she maximising satisfaction ? Why or why not ? [*D.U. B.A. (Hons.) 1997*)]

[**Hints :** $\frac{MU_x}{P_x} = \frac{20}{4} = 5$ and $\frac{MU_y}{P_y} = \frac{50}{5} = 10$

Given the prices and expenditure on each good equal to Rs. 20 the consumer is buying 5 units of *X* and 4 units of *X*. With this he will not be maximising satisfaction because as found above $\frac{MU_y}{P_y} > \frac{MU_x}{P_x}$. He will substitute *Y* for *X* until $\frac{MU_y}{P_y}$ becomes equal to $\frac{MU_x}{P_y}$. However, for knowing his exact optimum position, the complete marginal utility schedules of the consumer for the two goods are required.

12. What is value paradox? How does diminishing marginal utility explain this paradox?

CHAPTER 9

INDIFFERENCE CURVE ANALYSIS OF CONSUMER'S DEMAND

In the last chapter we explained and critically evaluated Marshall's cardinal utility analysis of demand. A popular alternative theory of consumer's demand is the Indifference Curve Analysis which forms the subject-matter of the present chapter. The technique of indifference curves was first of all invented by a classical economist Edgeworth but he used it only to show the possibilities of exchange between two persons and not to explain consumer's demand.

Two English economists, J.R. Hicks and R.G.D. Allen in their now well-known paper '*A Reconsideration of the Theory of Value*' severely criticized Marshall's cardinal utility analysis based upon cardinal measurement of utility and put forward the indifference curve approach based on the notion of ordinal utility to explain consumer's behaviour. In 1939 Hicks reproduced the indifference curve theory of consumer's demand in his book '*Value and Capital*' modifying somewhat the version of the original paper.

CONSUMER PREFERENCES

The analysis of consumer behaviour is concerned with the choice he makes among different goods or bundles of goods, given his budget constraint. It is from the choices of quantities of goods, given their prices, that consumers make that we derive demand curve for a good. In economics it is assumed that *consumers behave rationally* in the choice of goods or bundle of goods for satisfaction of their wants. To explain consumer behaviour economists assume that consumers have a set of preferences which guide them in choosing among goods for their consumption. The preferences of different individuals differ substantially. For example, some individuals prefer white shirts while others may prefer coloured shirts. Likewise, some prefer apples, others may like bananas and so on. In real life, the consumers have to make a choice among several goods but the use of two dimensional diagrams compels us to limit to two goods. However, economists use the concept of a *composite commodity* which represents all other goods and the choice is between two goods while one of them is composite good. Since money represents general purchasing power which can buy other goods, it is taken as a *composite commodity*. Thus with the help of the composite commodity, we can consider consumer choice involving many goods and still use two dimensional diagrams.

Let us explain how we explain consumer preferences. Let x_1 denote the quantity of good 1 and x_2 quantity of good 2. Thus a bundle of two goods containing x_1 of good 1 and x_2 of good 2 is generally denoted by (x_1, x_2) and is called X bundle. Similarly, the other bundle may consists of y_1 amount of good 1 and y_2 amount of the good 2 and therefore is denoted by (y_1, y_2) and is called Y bundle. In the theory of consumer preferences it is assumed that, given the two bundles of goods, (x_1, x_2) and (y_1, y_2), the *consumer is able to rank* them in order of his preference. In other words, the consumer can determine whether he ***strictly prefers*** one bundle of goods to the other one or he is indifferent between the two bundles. '*strictly prefers*' implies that he definitely likes the one over the other. This preference relation has an operational significance. If a person strictly prefers one bundle over the other, he will choose that one rather than the other if there is opportunity for him to have any of them. Thus, the consumer's choice and demand for goods will depend on whether he strictly prefers one bundle over another. Thus, if a consumer always chooses a bundle (x_1, x_2) when bundle (y_1, y_2) is available, it shows he prefers (x_1, x_2) to (y_1, y_2).

Further, if the consumer shows his *indifference* between any two bundles of goods, it means he derives the same satisfaction from consuming bundle (x_1, x_2) as the other bundle (y_1, y_2) of the goods.

There is a third case which occurs if the consumer *either prefers or is indifferent* between the two bundles of goods, it is then said that the consumer ***weakly prefers*** one basket (x_1, x_2) to the other available basket (y_1, y_2) of the two goods.

This weak preference has been used by J.R. Hicks in his revision of demand theory based on logical ordering. In his analysis of weak-ordering preference hypothesis Hicks assumes that when a person chooses one bundle of two goods from among the several bundles of two goods available to him, it means he either prefers the chosen combination over all others available or he will be indifferent between the chosen one and some others available. Thus, Hicks even in his revised demand theory does not rule out the indifference of the chosen bundle with any other bundle of the two goods available to the consumer but not chosen. Thus weakly preference implies that choice of a bundle of goods among several bundles available to the consumer means that he does not strictly prefer the bundle he chooses among the various alternative bundles available to him; it is likely, according to weakly preference hypothesis, that he may be indifferent between the chosen bundle and some other alternative bundles available to him.

Assumptions about Consumer Preferences

In analysing consumer behaviour economists usually make some crucial assumptions about the nature of consumer preferences. Some of these assumptions about consumer preferences are so fundamental that they are referred to as '*axioms*' of consumer theory. There are the following three such assumptions made about consumer preferences.

1. Completeness. According to this assumption, the consumer is *capable of ranking* alternative bundles of goods for his consumption. This implies that between two bundles of goods a consumer can rank them so that he either prefers one bundle to another or is indifferent between them. This assumption about consumer preferences rules out the possibility that the consumer cannot decide which bundle is preferable. For example, if a person is offered a choice between an apple and orange and he chooses the apple, it means he prefers the apple. If he has no preference, he would not care which fruit, apple or orange, is given to him since either of them will leave him equally satisfied (that is, he will be indifferent between the two).

2. Transitivity. The second assumption about preferences of consumers is that consumers' preference over bundles of goods is consistent. According to this, if a consumer prefers bundle *A* to an alternative bundle *B* and prefers the bundle *B* to another bundle *C*, then he will also prefer bundle A to bundle *C*. Similarly, if a consumer is indifferent between bundles *A* and *B* and between bundles *B* and *C*, then he will also be indifferent between bundles *A* and *C*. Thus, this assumption of transitivity of preferences implies that the consumer is *able to rank all available bundles of goods in a consistent manner*. In fact, transitivity principle implies that the consumer behaviour is rational.

3. More is Better. The third assumption about consumer preferences is that, all else remaining the same, more of a commodity is better than less of it, that is, more of the commodity is preferred to less of it. This implies that the person is *not already satiated* because if a person has already consumed so much of the good that he is fully satiated, then the extra amount of it would not give him more satisfaction.

It may however he noted that there are some things for which *less of them is preferred to more*. They are called ***bads*** in economics. For example, pollution, smog, germs are bads and less of them is preferred to more. However, the standard economic theory does not deal with bads and explains consumer choice with regard to desirable combinations of goods.

INDIFFERENCE CURVE APPROACH

Indifference curve method has been evolved to supersede the marginal utility analysis of demand which was discussed in the last chapter. The indifference curve method seeks to derive all rules and laws about consumer's demand that are derivable from the cardinal utility analysis. At the same time the inventors and supporters of new method contend that their analysis is based on fewer and more reasonable assumptions. The indifference curve analysis has, however, retained some of the assumptions of Marshall's cardinal utility analysis. Thus, the indifference curve approach, like the old cardinal utility approach, assumes that the *consumer possesses 'complete information'* about all the relevant aspects of economic environment in which he finds himself. For example, the prices of goods, the markets in which they are available, the satisfaction to be obtained from them etc. are all known to the consumer. Further, it is assumed that the *consumer acts rationally* in the sense that, given the prices of goods and the money income, he will choose the combination from among the various possible combinations that gives him maximum satisfaction. Moreover, the *assumption of 'continuity'* has also been retained by Hicks-Allen indifference curve method. Continuity assumption means that the consumers are capable of ordering or ranking all *conceivable combinations of goods* according to the satisfaction they yield.

The fundamental approach of indifference curve analysis is that it has abandoned the concept of cardinal utility and instead has *adopted the concept of ordinal utility*. According to the supporters of the indifference curves theory, utility is a psychic entity and it cannot therefore be measured in quantitative cardinal terms. In other words, utility being a psychological feeling is not quantifiable. The concept of cardinal utility, according to the exponents of the indifference curve theory, is therefore untenable. On the other hand, the assumption of ordinal utility, according to them, is quite reasonable and realistic. *The ordinal utility implies that the consumer is capable of simply 'comparing the different levels of satisfaction'*. In other words, according to the ordinal utility hypothesis, while the consumer may not be able to indicate the exact amounts of utilities that he derives from commodities or any combination of them, but he is capable of judging whether the satisfaction obtained from a good or a combination of goods is equal to, lower than, or higher than another.

Notions of Indifference and Preference

For deriving the theory of consumer's behaviour, it is sufficient to assume that the consumer is able to rank his preferences consistently. Thus, the basis of indifference curve analysis of demand is the *preference-indifference hypothesis*. This means that if the consumer is presented with a number of various combinations of goods, he can order or rank them in '*scale of preferences*'. If the various combinations are marked *A*, *B*, *C*, *D*, *E*, etc. the consumer can tell whether he prefers *A* to *B*, or *B* to *A*, or is indifferent between them. Similarly, he can indicate his preference or indifference between any other pair of combinations. *The concept of ordinal utility implies that the consumer cannot go beyond stating his preference or indifference*. In other words, if a consumer happens to prefer *A* to *B*, he cannot tell by how much he prefers *A* to *B*. Thus, under ordinal utility hypothesis, the consumer cannot tell the '*quantitative differences*' between various levels of satisfaction; he can simply compare them 'qualitatively', that is, he can merely judge whether one level of satisfaction is higher than, lower than or equal to another. Further, according to the supporters of indifference-curve method, by 'how much' one combination of goods is preferred to another is not even needed for deriving laws concerning consumer's behaviour. It is sufficient to assume that the consumer is able to tell whether one combination of goods gives him greater, equal, or less satisfaction than another.

It may be noted that the *consumer formulates his scale of preferences independently of the market prices of goods keeping in view only the satisfaction which he hopes to get from various combinations of goods*. In consumer's scale of preferences some combinations will occupy the same place, *i.e.*, the consumer will be indifferent among them. Combinations occupying a higher place in the scale will be preferred to the combinations occupying lower places in the scale. Moreover, the indifference curve analysis assumes that the preference and indifference relations are '*transitive*'. The transitivity of preferences or indifference relations means that if a consumer prefers *A* to *B*, and *B* to *C*, then he will also prefer *A* to *C* and likewise, if he is indifferent between *A* and *B*, and between *B* and *C*, then he will also be indifferent between *A* and *C*.

WHAT ARE INDIFFERENCE CURVES ?

The basic tool of Hicks-Allen ordinal analysis of demand is the indifference curve which represents all those combinations of goods which give same satisfaction to the consumer. Since all the combinations on an indifference curve give equal satisfaction to the consumer, he will be indifferent between them, that is, it will not matter to him which one he gets. In other words, all combinations of the goods lying on a consumer's indifference curve are equally desirable to or equally preferred by him. To understand indifference curves, it is better to start with indifference schedules. In Table 9.1, two indifference schedules are given. In each schedule the amounts of goods *X* and *Y* in each combination are so much that the consumer is indifferent among the combinations in each schedule. In schedule 1, the consumer has to start with 1 unit of *X* and 12 units of *Y*. Now, the consumer is asked to tell how much of good *Y* he will be willing to give up for the gain of an additional unit of *X* so that his level of satisfaction remains the same. If the gain of one unit of *X* compensates him fully for the loss of 4 units of *Y*, then the next combination of 2 units of *X* and 8 units of *Y* ($2X + 8Y$) will give him as much satisfaction as the initial combination ($1X + 12Y$). Similarly, by asking the consumer further how much of *Y* he will be prepared to forgo for successive increments in his stock of *X* so that his level of satisfaction remains unaltered, we get combinations $3X + 5Y$, $4X + 3Y$, and $5X + 2Y$, each of which provides same satisfaction as combination $1X + 12Y$ or $2X + 8Y$. Since his satisfaction is the same whichever combination of goods in the schedule is offered to him, he will be indifferent among the combinations of two goods included in the schedule.

Table 9.1. Two Indifference Schedules

I		*II*	
Good *X*	Good *Y*	Good *X*	Good *Y*
1	12	2	14
2	8	3	10
3	5	4	7
4	3	5	5
5	2	6	4

In schedule II, the consumer has initially 2 units of *X* and 14 units of *Y*. By asking the consumer how much of *Y* he will be prepared to abandon for the successive additions of *X* in his stock so that his satisfaction remains equal to what he derives from the initial combination ($2X + 14Y$), we get combinations $3X + 10Y$, $4X + 7Y$, $5X + 5Y$ and $6X + 4Y$. Thus, each of the combinations in schedule II will be equally desirable to the consumer and he will be indifferent among them. But it should be borne in mind that the consumer will prefer any combination in schedule II to any combination in schedule I. That is, any combination in schedule II will give him more satisfaction than any combination in shcedule I. This is because it is assumed that more of a commodity is preferable to less of it (in other words, the greater quantity of a good gives an individual more satisfaction than the smaller quantity of it), the quantities of other goods with him remaining the same. Initial combination in schedule II contains more of both the goods than the initial combination in schedule I, therefore the former will give greater satisfaction to the consumer than the latter. Now, since each of the other combinations in indifference schedule II provides the same satisfaction as the initial combination ($2X + 14Y$) of the schedule and also each of other combinations in indifference schedule I gives the same satisfaction as the initial combination ($1X + 12Y$), any combination of the schedule II will be preferred to (will yield greater satisfaction than) any combination of schedule I.

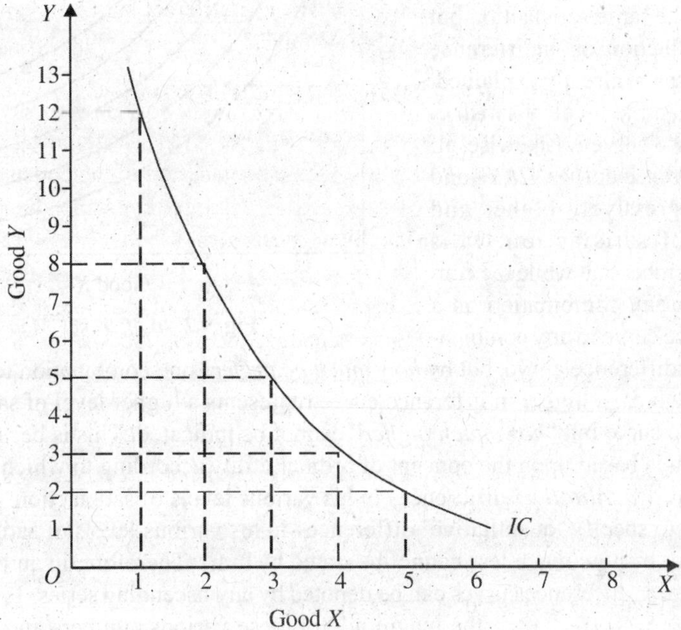

Fig. 9.1. *An Indifference Curve.*

Now, we can convert the indifference schedules into indifference curves by plotting the various combinations on a graph paper. In Fig. 9.1 an indifference curve *IC* is drawn by plotting the various combinations of the indifference schedule I. The quantity of good X is measured on the horizontal axis, and the quantity of the good *Y* is measured on the vertical axis. As in an indifference schedule, combinations lying on an indifference curve will also be equally desirable to the consumer, that is, will give him the same satisfaction. The smoothness and continuity of an indifference curve means that goods in question are assumed to be perfectly divisible. If the indifference schedule *II* is also converted into indifference curve, this will lie above the indifference curve *IC*.

Any combination on a higher indifference curve will be preferred to any combination on a lower indifference curve. It is thus clear that the indifference curve lying above and to the right of an indifference curve will indicate higher level of satisfaction than the latter. It may be noted that while an indifference curve shows all those combinations of two goods which provide equal satisfaction to the consumer, it does not indicate *exactly how much* satisfaction is derived by the consumer from those combinations. This is because the concept of ordinal utility does not involve the quantitative measurability of utility. Therefore, no attempt is made to label an indifference curve by the quantity or amount of satisfaction it represents.

Indifference Map

A complete description of consumer's tastes and preferences can be represented by an *indifference map* which consists of a set of indifference curves. Because the field in a two-dimensional diagram contains an infinite number of points each representing a combination of goods *X* and *Y*, there will be an infinite number of the indifference curves each passing through combinations of goods that are equally desirable to the consumer. In Fig. 9.2 an indifference map of a consumer is shown which consists of five indifference curves. The consumer regards all combinations on the indifference curve *I* as giving him equal satisfactions. Similarly, all the combinations lying on indifference curve *II* provide the same satisfaction but the level of satisfaction on indifference curve *II*, for the reason already explained, will be greater than the level of satisfaction on indifference curve I. Likewise, all the higher indifference curves, *III*, *IV* and *V* represent progressively higher and higher levels of satisfaction. It is importnat, to remember that while the consumer will prefer any combination on a higher indifference curve to any combination on a lower indifference curve, but by *how much he prefers* one combination to another cannot be said. In other words, a higher indifference curve represents a higher level of satisfaction than a lower indifference curve but "*how much higher*" cannot be indicated. This is because the indifference curve system is based upon the concept of ordinal utility according to which the consumer is able to sate only the '*qualitative*' differences in his various levels of satisfaction. It is not possible for the consumer to specify 'quantitative' differences in his various levels of satisfaction (*i.e.*, by how much more or by how much less cannot be stated by him). Therefore, in an indifference map successively higher indifference curves can be denoted by any ascending series, 1, 3, 7, 9...; or 1, 4, 6, 8, 13...; or 1, 2, 5, 8, 10...; etc., the magnitude of these various numbers and the quantitative differences among them having no relevance. It is more usual to label the indifference curves by ordinal numbers as *I*, *II*, *III*, *IV*, *V* as is done in Fig. 9.2.

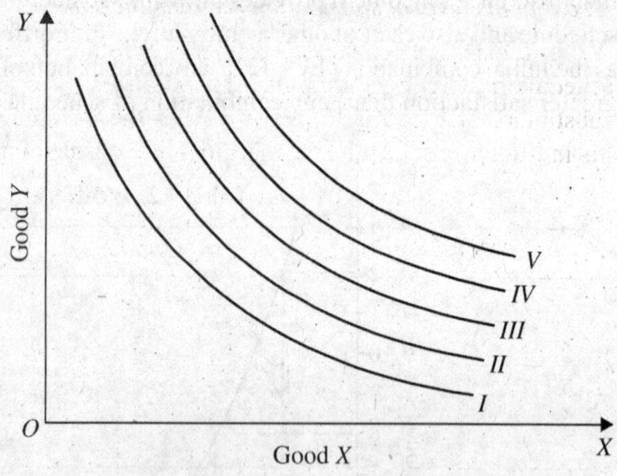

Fig. 9.2. *Indifference Map*

An indifference map of a consumer represents, as said earlier, his tastes and preferences for the two goods and his preferences between different combinations of them. In other words, *an indifference map portrays consumer's scale of preferences*. Scale of preferences of indifference curve analysis replaces Marshall's utility schedule. So long as consumer's tastes and preferences remain unchanged, the whole indifference map will remain the same. If the consumer's tastes and preferences undergo a change, then a new indifference map corresponding to new tastes and preferences will have to be drawn. If, for instance, good *Y* is eggs and good *X* is bread, and if the doctor advises our consumer to take more of eggs to overcome some diseases, the shapes of all his indifference curves will change and his indifference map will have to be redrawn. Since the doctor's advice will intensify our consumer's desire for eggs, now a smaller quantity of eggs than before will be given up by him for a given increment in bread.

MARGINAL RATE OF SUBSTITUTION

The concept of marginal rate of substitution is an important tool of indifference curve analysis of demand. The rate at which the consumer is prepared to exchange goods *X* and *Y* is known as marginal rate of substitution. In our indifference schedule I above, which is reproduced in Table 9.2, in the beginning the consumer gives up 4 units of *Y* for the gain of one additional unit of *X* and in this process his level of satisfaction remains the same. It follows that one unit gain in *X* fully compensates him for the loss of 4 units of *Y*. It means that at this stage he is prepared to exchange 4 units of *Y* for one unit of *X*. Therefore, at this stage consumer's marginal rate of substitution of *X* for *Y* is 4. Thus, *we may define the marginal rate of substitution of X for Y as the amount of Y whose loss can just be compensated by one unit gain in X*. In other words, marginal rate of substitution of *X* for *Y* represents the amount of *Y* which the consumer has to give up for the gain of one additional unit of *X so that his level of satisfaction remains the same.*

In Table 9.2, when the consumer moves from combination *B* to combination *C* on his indifference schedule he forgoes 3 units of *Y* for additional one unit gain in *X*. Hence, the marginal rate of substitution of *X* for *Y* is 3. Likewise, when the consumer moves from *C* to *D*, and then from *D* to *E* in his indifference schedule, the marginal rate of substitution of *X* for *Y* is 2 and 1 respectively.

Table 9.2. Indifference Schedule

Combination	*Good X*	*Good Y*	MRS_{xy}
A	1	12	
B	2	8	4
C	3	5	3
D	4	3	2
E	5	2	1

How to measure marginal rate of substitution on an indifference curve ? Consider Fig. 9.3 where an indifference curve is shown. When the consumer moves from point *A* to *B* on this indifference curve he gives up *AS* of *Y* and takes up *SB* of *X* and remains on the same indifference curve (or, in other words, at the same level of satisfaction). It means that the loss of satisfaction caused by giving up *AS* of *Y* equals the gain in satisfaction due to the increase in good *X* by *SB*. It follows that the consumer is prepared to exchange *AS* of *Y* for *SB* increase in *X*. In other words, marginal rate of substitution of *X* for *Y* (MRS_{xy}) is equal to $\frac{AS}{SB}$. Now, a small change in the amount *Y* such as *AS*, along an indifference curve can be written as ΔY and the change in the amount of *X* as ΔX. Thus, ΔY shows the amount which the consumer has to give up for the ΔX increase in *X* if he is to remain on the same indifference curve. Therefore, it follows that:

$$\text{Marginal rate of substitution of } X \text{ for } Y\ (MRS_{xy}) = \frac{AS}{SB} = \frac{\Delta Y}{\Delta X}$$

Now, suppose that points *A* and *B* are very close to each other so that it can be assumed that both of them lie on the same tangent *t T*. Now, in a right-angled traingle *ASB*, $\frac{AS}{SB}$ is equal to the tangent of the angle *ABS*. It therefore follows that:

$$MRS_{xy} = \frac{AS}{SB} = \frac{\Delta Y}{\Delta X} = \text{tangent of } \angle ABS$$

But in Fig. 9.3 $\angle ABS = tTO$

Hence MRS_{xy} = tangent of $\angle tTO$

But the tangent of $\angle tTO$ is equal to $\frac{Ot}{OT}$

The tangent of $\angle tTO$ indicates the slope of the tangent line *tT* drawn at point *A* or *B* on the indifference curve. In other words, the slope of the indifference curve at point *A* or *B* is equal to the tangent of $\angle tTO$. It therefore follows:

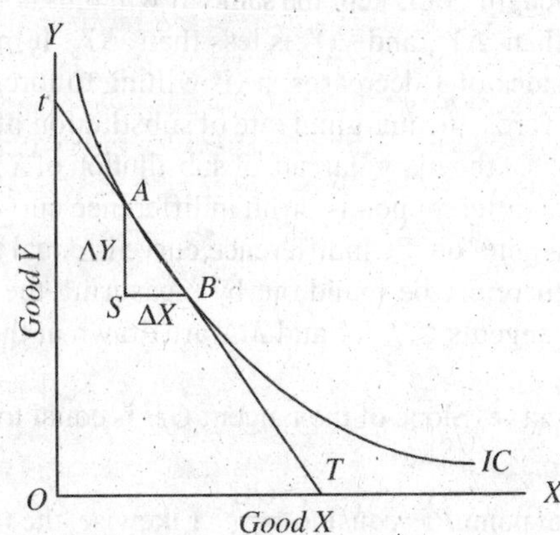

Fig. 9.3. *Graphic Illustration of the Concept of Marginal Rate of Substitution*

$$MRS_{xy} = \text{tangent of } \angle tTO = \text{slope of the indifference curve on } A \text{ or } B = \frac{Ot}{OT}$$

It is thus clear from above that if we have to find out the MRS_{xy} at a point on the indifference curve we can do so by drawing tangent at the point on the indifference curve and then measuring the slope by estimating the value of the tangent of the angle which the tangent line makes with the X-axis.

Principle of Diminishing Marginal Rate of Substitution

An important principle of economic theory is that marginal rate of substitution of X for Y diminishes as more and more of good X is substituted for good Y. In other words, as the consumer has more and more of good X, he is prepared to forego less and less of good Y. The principle of diminishing marginal rate of substitution is illustrated in Fig. 9.4. In Fig. 9.4 (a) when the consumer slides down from A to B on the indifference curve he gives up ΔY_1 of good Y for the compensating gain of ΔX of

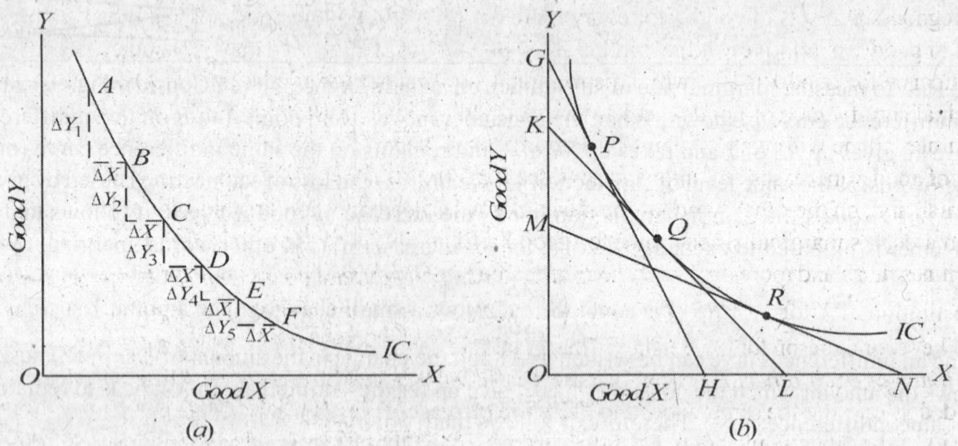

Fig. 9.4. *Diminishing Marginal Rate of Substitution*

good X. Therefore, the marginal rate of substitution (MRS_{xy}) is here equal to $\frac{\Delta Y_1}{\Delta X}$. But as the consumer further slides down on the curve, the length ΔY becomes shorter and shorter, while the length ΔX is kept the same. It will thus be seen from Fig. 9.4 (*a*) that ΔY_2 is less than ΔY_1; ΔY_3 is less than ΔY_2; and ΔY_4 is less than ΔY_3. It means that as the consumer's stock of X increases and his stock of Y decreases, he is willing to forego less and less of Y for a given increment in X. In other words, the marginal rate of substitution of X for Y falls as the consumer has more of X and less of Y. That the marginal rate of substitution of X for Y diminishes can also be known from drawing tangents at different points on an indifference curve. As explained above, the marginal rate of substitution at a point on the indifference curve is equal to the slope of the indifference curve at that point and can therefore be found out by measuring the slope of tangent drawn at a point. In Fig. 9.4 (*b*) three tangents GH, KL and MN are drawn at the points P, Q and R respectively to the given indifference curve. Slope of the tangent GH is equal to $\frac{OG}{OH}$. Hence, the marginal rate of substitution of X for Y at point P is equal to $\frac{OG}{OH}$. Likewise, the marginal rate of substitution at point Q is equal to $\frac{OK}{OL}$ and at point R it is equal to $\frac{OM}{ON}$. It will be noticed that $\frac{OK}{OL}$ is smaller than $\frac{OG}{OH}$ and $\frac{OM}{ON}$ is smaller than

$\frac{OK}{OL}$. It follows that MRS_{xy} diminishes as the consumer slides down on his indifference curve.

That the marginal rate of substitution falls is also evident from the Table 9.2. In the beginning the marginal rate of substitution of *X* for *Y* is 4 and as more and more of *X* is obtained and less and less of *Y* is left, the MRS_{xy} keeps on falling. Between *B* and *C* it is 3; between *C* and *D*, it is 2; and finally between *D* and *E*, it is 1.

Now, the question is what accounts for the diminishing marginal rate of substitution. In other words, why is it that the consumer is willing to give up less and less of *Y* for a given increment in *X* as he slides down on the curve? The following three factors are responsible for diminishing marginal rate of substitution

First, *the want for a particular good is satiable* so that as the consumer has more and more of a good the intensity of his want for that good goes on declining. It is because of this fall in the intensity of want for a good, say *X*, that when its stock increases with the consumer, he is prepared to forego less and less of good *Y* for every increment in *X*. In the beginning, when the consumer's stock of good *Y* is relatively large and his stock of good *X* is relatively small, consumer's marginal significance for good *Y* is low, while his marginal significance for good *X* is high. Owing to higher marginal significance of good *X* and lower marginal significance of good *Y* in the beginning the consumer will be willing to give up a larger amount of *Y* for one unit increase in good *X*. But as the stock of good *X* increases and intensity of desire for it falls, his marginal significance of good *X* will diminish and, on the other hand, as the stock of good *Y* decreases and the intensity of his desire for it increases, his marginal significance for good *Y* will go up. As a result, therefore, as the individual substitutes more and more of *X* for *Y*, he is prepared to give up less and less of *Y* for one unit increase in *X*.

The second reason for the decline in marginal rate of substitution is that the *goods are imperfect substitutes of each other*. If two goods are perfect substitutes of each other, then they are to be regarded as one and the same good, and therefore increase in the quantity of one and decrease in the quantity of the other would not make any difference in the marginal significance of the goods. Thus, in case of perfect substitutability of goods, the increase and decrease will be virtually in the same good which cancel out each other and therefore the marginal rate of substitution remains the same and does not decline.

Assumptions of Indifference Curves

We now turn to discuss the properties or attributes which the indifference curves normally possess. It will be userful if we first mention the assumptions about the behaviour of the consumer, which are generally made in indifference curve analysis.

1. More of a commodity is better than less. It is assumed that the consumer will always prefer a larger amount of a good to a smaller amount of that good, provided that the other goods at his disposal remains unchanged. This is a very reasonable and realistic assumption. This assumption implies that the consumer is not over-supplied with any good. When a consumer is over-supplied or over-satiated with one good, he will prefer a smaller quantity of that good to its larger quantity. It is thus assumed that the consumer has not yet reached the point of satiety in the consumption of any good. This assumption is therefore known as *non-satiety assumption.*

2. Preferences or indifferences of a consumer are transitive. Suppose there are three combinations of two goods : *A, B* and *C*. If the consumer is indifferent between *A* and *B* and also between *B* and *C*, it is then assumed that he will be indifferent between *A* and *C* too. This condition implies that consumer's tastes are quite consistent. This assumption is known as *assumption of transitivity.*

3. Diminishing marginal rate of substitution. In indifference curve analysis the principle of diminishing marginal rate of substitution is assumed. In other words, it is assumed that as more and more units of *X* are substituted for *Y*, the consumer will be willing to give up fewer and fewer units of *Y* for each additional unit of *X*, or when more and more of *Y* is substituted for *X*, he will be willing to give up successively fewer and fewer units of *X* for each additional unti of *Y*. This rule about consumer's behaviour is described as the principle of diminishing, marginal rate of substitution. As seen above, this principle follows as a matter of logical necessity from the assumption that particular wants are satiable and that various goods are not perfect substitutes for one another.

PROPERTIES OF INDIFFERENCE CURVES

We now proceed to deduce from the above-mentioned assumptions the important properties of typical indifference curves.

Property I. Indifference curves slope downward to the right.

This property implies that an indifference curve has a negative slope. This property follows from assumption I. Indifference curve being downward sloping means that when the amount of one good in the combination is increased, the amount of the other good is reduced. This must be so if the level of satisfaction is to remain the same on an indifference curve. If, for instance, the amount of good *X* is increased in the combination, while the amount of good *Y* remains unchanged, the new combination will be preferable to the original one and the two combinations will not therefore lie on the same indifference curve.

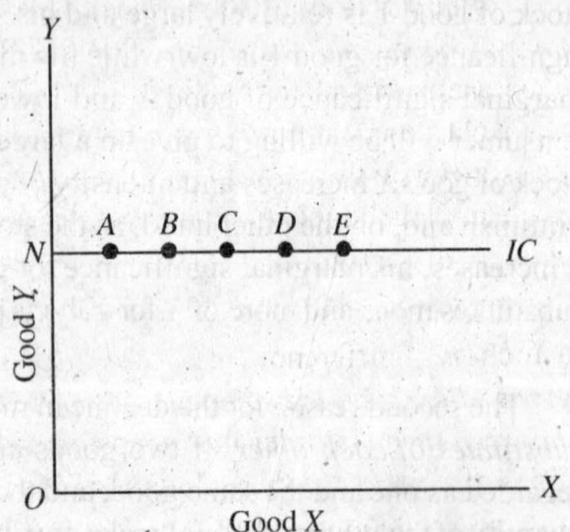

Fig. 9.5. *Indifference curve cannot be a horizontal straight line.*

A little reflection will make it clear that an indifference curve on which those combinations of two goods lie that yield the same satisfaction to the consumer cannot take a shape other than downward-sloping to the right. If the indifference curve had the shape of a horizontal straight line (parallel to the *X*-axis), as in Fig. 9.5, that would mean as the amount of the good *X* was increased, while the amount of good *Y* remained the same, the consumer would remain indifferent as between various combinations. But this cannot be so if our assumption I is to hold good. According to assumption I, the consumer always prefers a larger amount of a commodity to the smaller amount of it, other things being given. In Fig. 9.5 in various combinations such as *A*, *B*, *C* and *D* on indifference curve *IC* while the amount of good *X* is successively larger, the amount of good *Y* remains unchanged (= *ON*). If the consumer is to prefer a larger amount of good *X* to a smaller amount, then how he can be indifferent between combinations *A*, *B*, *C*, and *D* etc. It is thus concluded that indifference curve cannot be a horizontal straight line.

Likewise, indifference curve cannot be a vertical straight line becaue a vertical straight line would mean that while the amount of good *Y* in the combination increases, the amount of good *X* remains the same. Thus, in Fig. 9.6, a vertical straight line *IC* is drawn on which are shown combinations A, *B*, *C*, *D* and *E*. While all these combinations contain the same amount of *X*, the amount of *Y* is successively larger. Thus, combinations *A*, *B*, *C*, *D*, etc. would not yield the same amount of satisfaction to the consumer and therefore cannot be the points of an indifference curve. We therefore conclude that indifference curve cannot be a vertical straight line too.

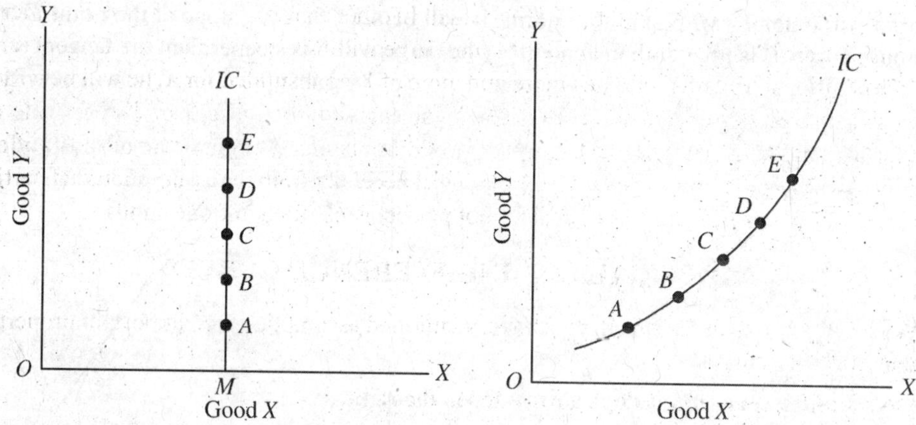

Fig. 9.6. *Indifference curve cannot be a vertical line.* **Fig. 9.7.** *Indifference curve cannot slope upward.*

A third possibility for a curve is to slope upward to the right as in Fig. 9.7. But indifference curve cannot be of this shape too. Upward-sloping curve means that the amounts of both the goods increase as one moves to the right along the curve. If the indifference curve were upward sloping to the right, it would mean that a combination which contains more of both the goods gave the same satisfaction to the consumer as the combination which had smaller amounts of both the goods. This is clearly invalid in view of our assumption I. It follows therefore that indifference curve cannot slope upward to the right.

The last possibility for the curve is that it slopes downward to the right and this is the shape which the indifference curve can reasonable take. *An indifference curve represents those combinations which give the same amount of satisfaction to the consumer and he is therefore indifferent between them.* In order that a consumer should get the same satisfaction from the various combinations of a curve and thus to maintain his indifference between them, then as the amount of good *X* is increased, the amount of good *Y* must be reduced. And this is what a downward-sloping curve indicates. A downward-sloping curve means that with every increase in the amount of good *X*, there is corresponding decrease in the amount of good *Y*. As one moves to the right on such a curve, the various combinations on it will contain successively larger amount of *X*, but successively smaller amount of *Y*. Thus, a consumer's satisfaction can remain the same and he can be indifferent between the various combinations on a curve which slopes downward. We thus conclude that indifference curve slopes downward to the right. The slope of the indifference curve at its various points will depend upon how much of good *Y* the consumer is willing to give up for an additional unit of good *X*.

Property II: Indifference curves are convex to the origin.

Another important property of indifference curves is that they are usually convex to the origin. In other words, the indifference curve is relatively flatter in its right-hand portion and relatively steeper in its left-hand portion. This property of indifference curves follows from assumption 3, which is that the marginal rate of substitution of *X* for *Y* (MRS_{xy}) diminishes as more and more of *X* is substituted for *Y*. Only a convex indifference curve can mean a diminishing marginal rate of substitution of *X* for *Y*. If indifference curve was concave to the origin it would imply that the marginal rate of substitution of *X* for *Y* increased as more and more of *X* was substituted for *Y*, as shown in Fig. 9.8 (*a*). It will be clear from Fig. 9.8 (*a*) that as more and more of *X* is acquired for each extra unit of *X*, the consumer is willing to part with more and more of *Y*, that is, MRS_{xy} increases as more and more of *X* is substituted for *Y*. That the concave indifference curve shows increasing MRS_{xy} is also evident from Fig. 9.8 (*b*). We know the slope at a point on an indifference curve shows the marginal rate of substitution of X for Y (MRS_{xy}) at that point. It will be seen that the slope at the point E on the indifference curve IC is greater than at point A (the tangent at E is steeper than the tangent at A). It

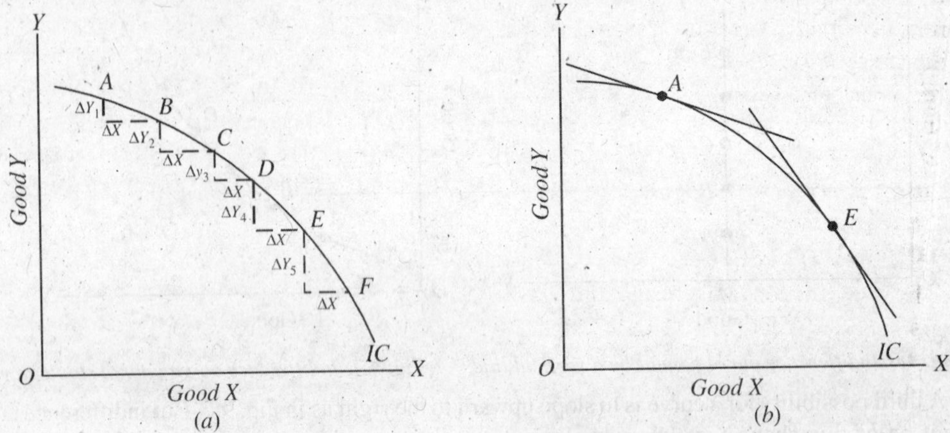

Fig. 9.8. *Indifference curve generally cannot be concave to the origin.*

therefore follows that MRS_{xy} is greater at E than at A on the indifference curve IC. In other words, as more of X has been substituted for Y, MRS_{xy} has increased.

The above Fig. 9.8 (*a*) and Fig. 9.8 (*b*) have been drawn to show that if indifference curves were concave to the origin, it would mean that the marginal rate of substitution of X for Y *increased* as the consumer obtained more and more of X in place of Y. But this clearly violates our fundamental assumption about the consumer's behaviour (assumption 3) which states that MRS_{xy} declines as consumer substitutes more and more of X for Y. If the principle of diminishing marginal rate of substitution is valid, then the indifference curve cannot be concave to the origin.

Likewise, indifference curve cannot be a straight-line, except when goods are perfect substitutes. A straight-line indifference curve would mean that MRS_{xy} remains constant as more units of X are acquired in place of Y. As shown in Fig. 9.9 that on a straight-line indifference curve the amount of Y which the consumer is willing to give up for each additional unit of X remains the same as more and more of X is substituted for Y, that is, MRS_{xy} remains constant. Since MRS_{xy} is equal to the slope of indifference curve at a point on it, and because a straight-line has the same slope throughout, therefore the straight-line indifference curve will mean the same MRS_{xy} throughout. But, as said above, MRS_{xy} cannot remain constant except when goods happen to be perfect substitutes. Normal consumer's behaviour reveals that when goods are less than perfect substitutes MRS_{xy} usually falls as more of good X is substituted for Y (Assumption 3). It is therefore concluded that indifference curve cannot normally be a straight line.

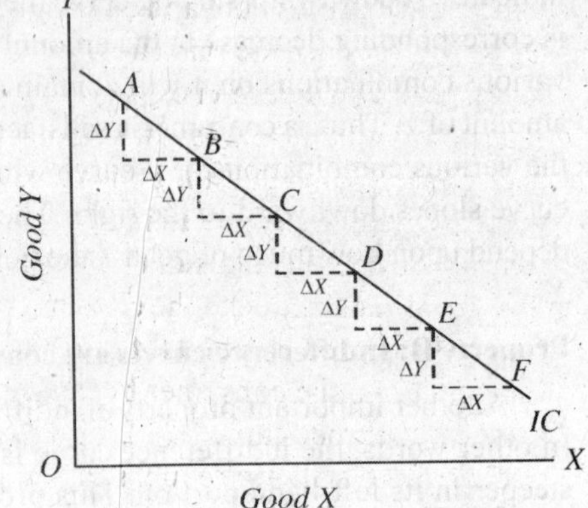

Fig. 9.9. *Except in case of perfect substitutes an indifference curve cannot be a straight line.*

The third possibility for indifference curve in this regard is that it may be convex to the origin and this is the shape which indifference curves normally possess. This is so because indifference curves being convex to the origin are consistent with the principle of diminishing marginal rate of substitution of X for Y. As shown in Fig. 9.4, when the indifference curve is convex to the origin,

MRS_{xy} diminishes as more of X is substituted for Y. We therefore conclude that indifference curves are generally convex to the origin.

Our assumption regarding diminishing MRS_{xy} and the convexity of indifference curves is based upon the observation of actual behaviour of the normal consumer. When we shall discuss consumer's equilibrium we shall see that indifference curves that are either concave or straight lines when viewed from the origin would suggest consumer's behaviour which is contrary to that which is generally observed in real life. *If indifference curves were concave or straight lines, the consumer would succumb to monomania, that is, he would buy and consume only one good.* We know that consumers in actual world do not generally buy and consume one good. It is for this reason that we reject indifference curves of concave or straight-line shapes and assume that indifference curves are normally convex to the origin.

The degree of convexity of an indifference curve depends on the rate of fall in the marginal rate of substitution of X for Y. As stated above, when two goods are perfect substitutes of each other, the indifference curve is a straight line on which marginal rate of substitution remains constant. A straight-line indifference curve of perfect substitutes is shown in Fig. 9.9. The better substitutes the two goods are for each other, the closer the indifference curve approaches to the straight line so that when the two goods are perfect substitutes, the indifference curve is a straight line.

The greater the fall in marginal rate of substitution, the greater the convexity of the indifference curve. The less the ease with which two goods can be substituted for each other, the greater will be the fall in the marginal rate of substitution. In the extreme case when two goods cannot be substituted for each other and are used in a given fixed ratio the indifference curve will be of right-angle shape. Perfect substitutes and perfect complements stand at opposite ends of the substitution scale. Between them are found most of the cases, for which indifference curves are convex to the origin.

Property III: Indifference curves cannot intersect each other.

Third important property of indifference curves is that they cannot intersect each other. In other words, only one indifference curve will pass through a point in the indifference map. This property follows from assumptions 1 and 2. This property can be easily proved by first making the two indifference curves cut each other and then showing the absurdity or self-contradictory result it leads to. In Fig. 9.10 two indifference curves are shown cutting each other at point C. Now take point A on indifference curve IC_2 and point B on indifference curve IC_1 vertically below A. Since an indifference curve represents those combinations of two commodities which give equal satisfaction to the consumer, the combinations represented by points A and C will give equal satisfaction to the consumer because both lie on the same indifference curve IC_2. Likewise, the combinations B and C will give equal satisfaction to the consumer; both being on the same indifference curve IC_1. If combination A is equal to combination C in terms of satisfaction, and combination B is equal to combination C, it follows that the combination A will be equivalent to B in terms of satisfaction. But a glance at Fig. 9.10 will show that this is absurd conclusion since combination A contains more of good Y than combination B, while the amount of good X is the same in both the combinations. Thus, the consumer will definitely prefer A to B, that is, A will give more satisfaction to the consumer than B (Assumption 1). But the two indiffference curves cutting each other lead us to an absurd conclusion

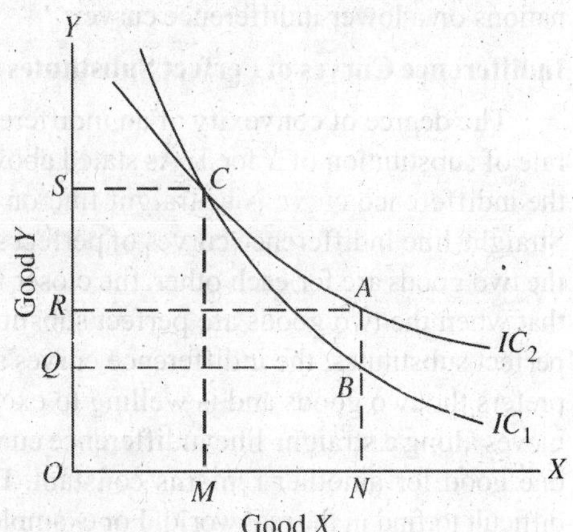

Fig. 9.10. *No two indifference curves can cut each other.*

of *A* being equal to *B* in terms of satisfaction. We therefore conclude that indifference curves cannot cut each other.

Another point which is worth mentioning in this regard is that indifference curves cannot even meet or touch each other or be tangent to each other at a point. The meeting of two indifference curves at a point, will also lead us to an absurd conclusion. The same argument holds good as developed above in the case of intersection of indifference curves.

Property IV: A higher indifference curve represents a higher level of satisfaction than a lower indifference curve.

The last property of indifference curve is that a higher indifference curve will represent a higher level of satisfaction than a lower indifference curve. In other words, the combinations which lie on a higher indifference curve will be preferred to the combinations which lie on a lower indifference curve. Consider indifference curves IC_1 and IC_2 in Fig. 9.11. IC_2 is a higher indifference curve than IC_1. Combination *Q* has been taken on a higher indifference curve IC_2 and combination S on a lower indifference curve IC_1. Combination *Q* on the higher indifference curve IC_2 will give a consumer more satisfaction than combination *S* on the lower indifference curve IC_1 because the combination *Q* contains more of both goods *X* and *Y* than the combination *S* (Assumption *I*). Hence by assumption I, the consumer must prefer *Q* to *S*. And by transitivity assumption *II*, he will prefer any other combination on IC_2 (all of which are indifferent with *Q*) to any combination on IC_1 (all of which are indifferent with *S*). We, therefore, conclude that a higher indifference curve represents a higher level of satisfaction and combinations on it will be preferred to the combinations on a lower indifference curve.

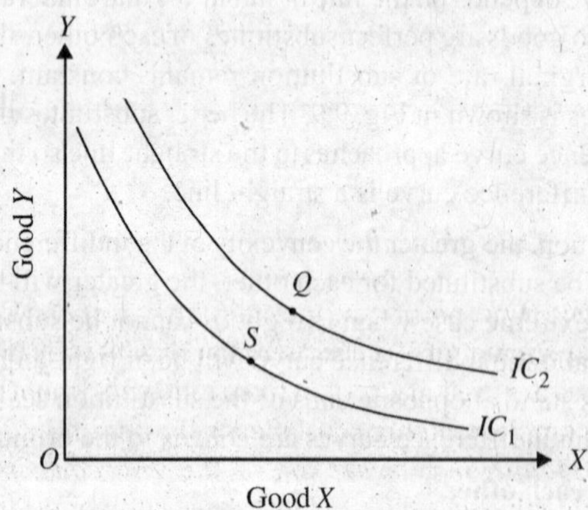

Fig. 9.11. *A higher indifference curve shows a higher level of satisfaction.*

Indifference Curves of Perfect Substitutes and Perfect Complements

The degree of convexity of an indifference curve depends upon the rate of fall in the marginal rate of substitution of *X* for *Y*. As stated above, when two goods are perfect substitutes of each other, the indifference curve is a straight line on which marginal rate of substitution remains constant. Straight-line indifference curves of perfect substitutes are shown in Fig. 9.12. The better substitutes the two goods are for each other, the closer the indifference curve approaches to the straight-line so that when the two goods are perfect substitutes, the indifference curve is a straight line. In case of perfect substitutes, the indifference curves are parallel straight lines because the consumer equally prefers the two goods and is welling to exchange one good for the other at a constant rate. As one moves along a straight-line indifference curve of perfect substitutes, marginal rate of substitution of one good for amother remains constant. Examples of goods that are perfect substitutes are not difficult to find in the real world. For example, Dalda and Rath Vanaspati, two different brands of cold drink such as Pepsi Cola and Coca Cola are generally considered to be perfect substitutes of each other.

The greater the fall in marginal rate or substitution, the greater the convexity of the indifference curve. The less the ease with which two goods can be substituted for each other, the greater will be the fall in the marginal rate of substitution. At the extreme, when two goods cannot at all be substituted for each other, that is, when the two goods are perfect complementary goods, as for example gasoline and coolant in a car, the indifference curve will consist of two straight lines with a right angle bent which is convex to the origin as shown in Fig. 9.13. perfect complementary goods are used in a certain fixed ratio. As will be seen in Fig. 9.13, the left-hand portion of an indifference curve of the perfect complementary goods is a vertical straight line which indicates that an infinite amount of *Y* is

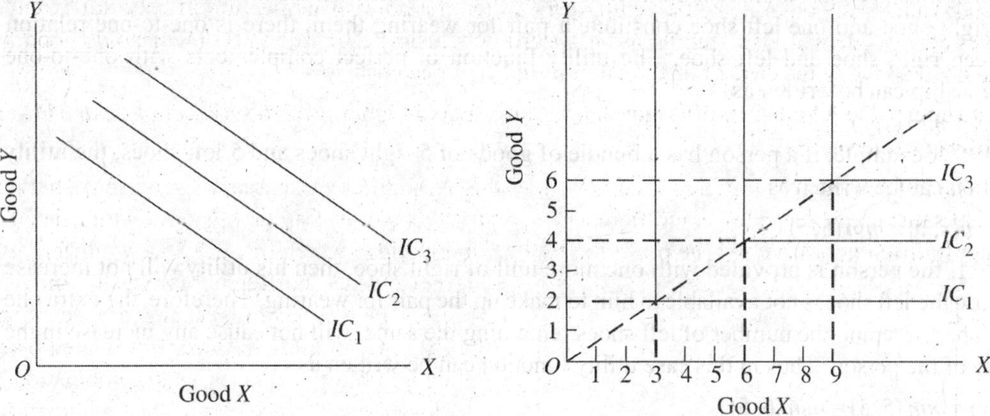

Fig. 9.12. *Indifference Curves of Perfect Substitutes*

Fig. 9.13. *Indifference Curves of Perfect Complements*

necessary to substitute one unit of *X*, and the right-hand portion of the indifference curve is a horizontal straight line which means that an infinite amount of *X* is necessary to substitute one unit of *Y*. All this means that the two perfect complements are used in a certain fixed ratio and cannot be substituted for each other. In Fig. 9.13 two perfect complements are consumed in the ratio, 3*X* : 2*Y*. *Complements are thus those goods which are used jointly in consumption so that their consumption increases or decreases simultaneously.* Pen and ink, right shoe and left shoe, automobile and petrol, sauce and hamburger, type writer and typists are some examples of perfect complements.

Utility Functions of Perfect Substitutes and Perfect Complements

Perfect Substitutes. In general utility function of perfect substitutes can be written as

$$U(x, y) = ax + by$$

where *x* and *y* are the quantities of two goods *X* and *Y* and *a* and *b* are some positive numbers that measure the values of goods to the consumer. The slope of indifference curve representing the above utility function of perfect substitutes is equal to $-\frac{a}{b}$.

If the consumer is willing to substitute good *X* and *Y* at the rate of *one-to-one*, the utility function of the perfect substitute goods can be written as

$$U(x, y) = x + y$$

The indifference curves of such substitute goods with one-to-one relationship in consumption has a slope of –1.

Further, if a consumer is willing to accept two units of good *y* to compensate him for the loss of one unit of good *X*, then utility function of these two perfect substitutes can be written as

$$U(x, y) = 2x + y$$

This means that good *X* is *twice as valuable* to the consumer than good *Y*. Now, the indifference curve representing such utility function will have a slope of –2.

Besides, the squares of the quantities of two goods in the utility function $[U(x, y) = x + y]$ of perfect substitutes will also give us the following utility function of the perfect substitutes

$$U(x, y) = (x + y)^2$$

1. The budget line has been variously named by different authors. Other names in the literature for the budget line are *price line, price opportunity line, price-income line, outlay line, budget constraint, expenditure line and consumption possibility line.*

Perfect Complements. Now, how can we describe the utility function of two perfect complements such as left shoe and right shoe. In case of two perfect complements, the consumer considers the *pairs* of shoes for wearing them. Therefore, in order to have complete pairs of shoes for wearing a person must have the *minimum* number of right shoes (call them x). Because, in the case of shoes, one right shoe and one left shoe constitute a pair for wearing them, there is one-to-one relation between right shoe and left shoe. The utility function of perfect complements with one-to-one relationship can be written as

$u(x, y) = min\,(x, y)$

For example, if a person has a bundle of goods of 5 right shoes and 5 left shoes, the utility function can be written as

$$u(x, y) = min\,(5, 5)$$

If the person is provided with one more unit of right shoe, then his utility will not increase because the left shoe is not available to him to make up the pair for wearing. Therefore, the extra one right shoe, keeping the number of left shoes remaining the same, will not cause any increase in the utility of the person. Thus in this case utility function can be written as

$u(x, y) = min\,(5, 5) = min\,(6, 5)$

The above cases of complements relate to when there is one-to-one relation of the two perfect complements. However, there are cases of perfect complements when the consumer consumes goods in proportion other than one-to-one. For example, consider a consumer who always uses two teaspoons of sugar with each cup of tea. Thus in this case appropriately sweetened cups of tea will be minimum $(x, \frac{1}{2}y)$ and in this case of perfect complements utility function can be written as $u(x, y) = min\,(x, \frac{1}{2}y)$

In general, the utility functions of two perfect complements can be written as $u(x, y) = min\,(ax + by)$

where a and b are the proporitions in which the two goods are consumed.

BUDGET LINE

The knowledge of the concept of budget line[1] is essential for understanding the theory of consumer's equilibrium. As explained above, a higher indifference curve shows a higher level of satisfaction than a lower one. Therefore, a consumer in his attempt to maximise his satisfaction will try to reach the highest possible indifference curve. But in his pursuit of buying more and more goods and thus obtaining more and more satisfaction he has to work under two constraints: first, he has to pay the prices for the goods and, secondly, he has a limited money income with which to purchase the goods. Thus, how far he would go in for his purchases depends upon the prices of the goods and the money income which he has to spend on the goods. As explained above, indifference map represents consumer's scale of preferences between two goods. Now, in order to explain consumer's equilibrium there is also the need for introducing into the indifference curve analysis the budget line which represents the prices of the goods and consumer's money income.

Suppose our consumer has got income of ₹ 50 to spend on two goods X and Y. Let price of the good X in the market be ₹ 10 per unit and that of Y ₹ 5 per unit. If the consumer spends his whole income of ₹ 50 on good X, he would buy 5 units of X; if he spends his whole income of ₹ 50 on good Y he would buy 10 units of Y. If a straight line joining $5X$ and $10Y$ is drawn, we will get what is called the price line or the budget line. *Thus budget line shows all those combinations of two goods which the consumer can buy by spending his given money income on the two goods at their given prices*. A look at Fig. 9.14 shows that with ₹ 90 and the prices of X and Y being ₹ 10 and ₹ 5 respectively the consumer can buy $10Y$ and $0X$, or 8Y and $1X$; or $6Y$ and $2X$, or $4Y$ and $3X$ etc. In other words, he can buy any combination that lies on the budget line with his given money income and given prices of the goods. It should be carefully noted that any combination of the two goods such such as H ($5Y$ and $4X$) which lies above and outside the given budget line will be beyond the reach of the consumer. But any combination lying within the budget line such as K ($2X$ and $2Y$) will be well within the reach of the consumer, but if he buys any such combination he will not be spending all his income of Rs. 50. Thus, with the assumption that whole of the given income is spent on the given goods and at given prices of them, the consumer has to choose from all those combinations which lie on the budget line.

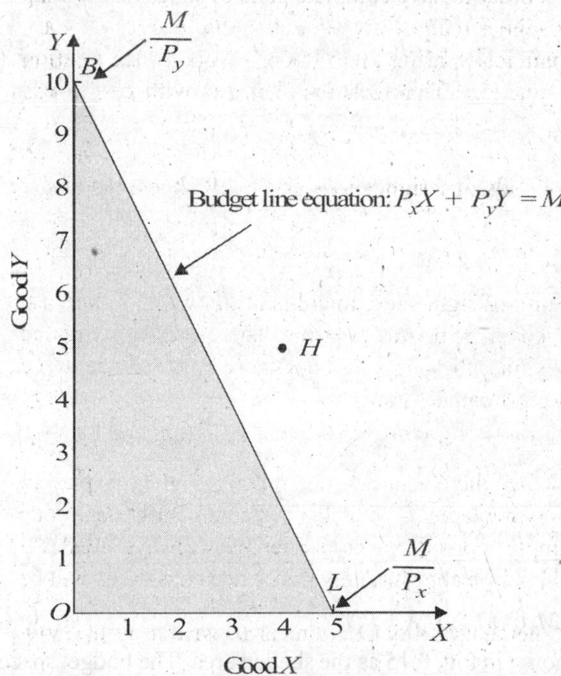

Fig. 9.14. *Budget Line*

It is clear from above that budget line graphically shows the *budget constraint*. The combinations of commodities lying to the right of the budget line are *unattainable* because income of the consumer is not sufficient to be able to buy those combinations. Given his income and prices of the two goods, the combinations of goods lying to the left of the budget line are *attainable*, that is, the consumer can buy any one of them. It is also important to remember that the intercept OB on the Y-axis in Fig. 9.14 equals the amount of his entire income divided by the price of commodity Y. That is, $OB = M/Py$. Likewise, the intercept OL on the X-axis measures the total income divided by the price of commodity X. Thus $OL = M/P_x$.

The budget line can be written algebraically as follows :

$$P_xX + P_yY = M \qquad \text{...(9.1)}$$

where P_x and P_y denote prices of goods X and Y respectively and M stands for money income:

The above budget-line equation (9.1) implies that, given the money income of the consumer and prices of the two goods, every combination lying on the budget line will cost the same amount of money and can therefore be purchased with the given income. The budget line can be defined as *a set of combinations of two commodities that can be purchased if whole of a given income is spent on them* and its slope is equal to the negative of the price ratio.

Budget Space

It should be carefully understood that the budget equation $P_xX + P_yY = M$ or $Y = M/P_y - Px/P_y.X$ depicted by the budget line in Fig. 9.14 only describes the budget line and not the budget space. *A budget space shows a set of all commodity combinations that can be purchased by spending the whole or a part of the given income*. In other words, budget space represents all those combinations of the commodities which the consumer can afford to buy, given the budget constraint. Thus, the budget space implies the set of all combinations of two goods for which income spent on good X (*i.e.*, P_xX) and income spent on good Y (*i.e.* $P_y Y$) *must not exceed* the given money income. Therefore, we can algebraically express the budget space in the following form of inequality:

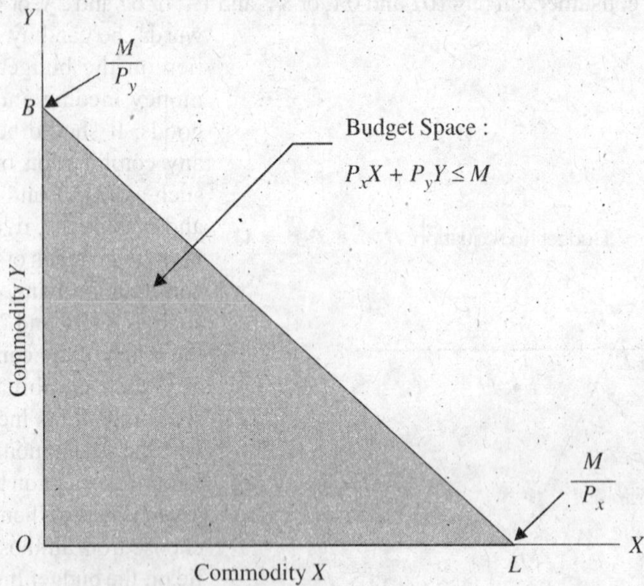

Fig. 9.15. *Budget Space*

$$P_xX + P_yY \leq M, \text{ or } M \geq P_xX + P_yY$$

The budget space has been graphically shown in Fig. 9.15 as the shaded area. The budget space is the entire area enclosed by the budget line *BL* and the two axes.

Changes in Price and Shift in Budget Line

Now, what happens to the price line if either the prices of goods change or the income changes. Let us first take the case of the changes in prices of the goods. This is illustrated in Fig. 9.16. Suppose the budget line in the beginning is *BL*, given certain prices of the goods *X* and *Y* and a certain income. Suppose price of *X* falls, the price of *Y* and income remaining unchanged. Now, with a lower price of *X* the consumer will be able to purchase more quantity of *X* than before with his given income. Let at the lower price of *X*, the given income purchases *OL′* of *X* which is greater than *OL*. Since the price of *Y* remains the same, there can be no change in the quantity purchased of good *Y* with the same given income and as a result there will be no shift in the point *B*. Thus, with the fall in the price of good *X*, the consumer's money income and the price of *Y* remaining constant, the price line will take the new position *BL′*.

Now, what will happen to the budget line (initial budget line *BL*) if the price of good *X* rises, the price of good *Y* and income remaining unaltered. With higher price of good *X*, the consumer can purchase smaller quantity of *X*, say *OL′′* than before. Thus, with the rise in price of *X* the price line will assume the new position *BL′′*.

Figure 9.17 shows the changes in the price line when price of good Y falls or rises, with the price of *X* and income remaining the same. In this the initial budget line is *BL*. With the fall in price of good *Y*, other things remaining unchanged, the consumer could buy more of *Y* with the given money income and therefore budget line will shift to *LB′*. Similarly, with the rise in price *Y*, other things being constant, the budget line will shift to *LB′′*.

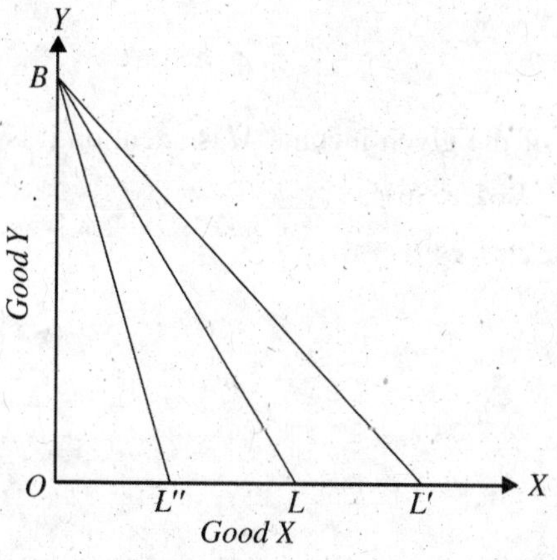

Fig. 9.16. *Changes in Budget Line as a Result of Changes in Price Good X*

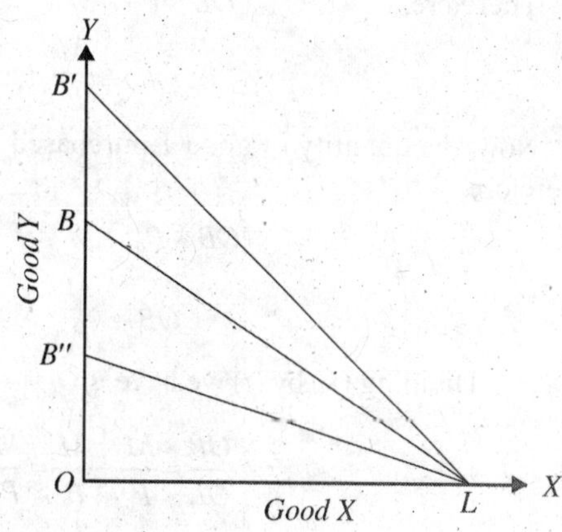

Fig. 9.17. *Changes in Price Line as a Result of Changes in Price of Good Y*

Changes in Income and Shifts in Budget line

Now, the question is what happens to the budget line if income changes, while the prices of goods remain the same. The effect of changes in income on the budget line is shown in Fig. 9.18. Let *BL* be the initial budget line, given certain prices of goods and income. If the consumer's income increases while the prices of both goods *X* and *Y* remain unaltered, the price line shifts upward (say, to *B′L′*) and is parallel to the original budget line *BL*. This is because with the increased income the consumer is able to purchase proportionately larger quantity of good *X* than before if whole of the income is spent on *X*, and proportionately greater quantity of good *Y* than before if whole of the income is spent on *Y*. On the other hand, if income of the consumer decreases, the prices of both goods *X* and *Y* remaining unchanged, the budget line shifts downward (say, to *B′L′*) but remains parallel to the original price line *BL*. This is because a lower income will purchase a proportionately smaller quantity of good *X* if the whole of the income is spent on *X* and proportionately smaller quantity of good *Y* if the whole of the income is spent on *Y*.

It is clear from above that the budget line will change if either the prices of goods change or the income of the consumer changes. Thus, the two determinants of the budget line are : (*a*) *the prices of goods, and (b) the consumer's income to be spent on the goods.*

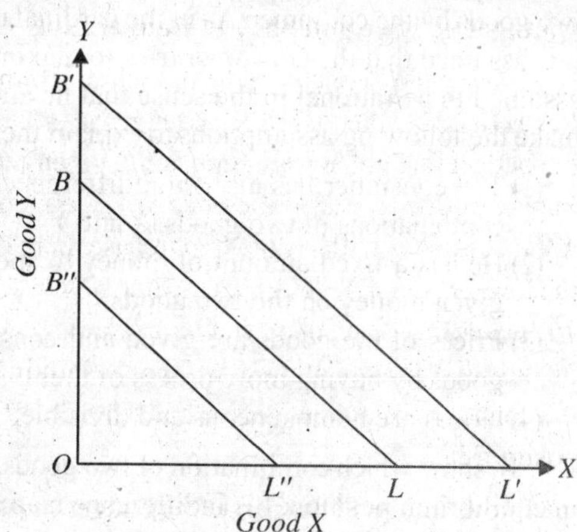

Fig. 9.18. *Shifts in Budget Line as a Result of Changes in Income*

Slope of the Budget Line and Prices of two Goods

It is also important to remember that the *slope* of the budget line is equal to the ratio of the prices of two goods. This can be proved with the aid of Fig. 9.14. Suppose the given income of the consumer is *M* and the given prices of goods *X* and *Y* are P_x and *Py* respectively. The slope of the budget line *BL* is $\frac{OB}{OL}$. We intend to prove that slope is equal to the ratio of the prices of goods *X* and *Y*.

The quantity of good *X* purchased if whole of the given income *M* is spent on it is *OL*.

Therefore, $OL \times P_x = M$

$$OL = \frac{M}{P_x} \quad ...(i)$$

Now, the quantity of good Y purchased if whole of the given income M is spent on it is OB. Therefore,

$$OB \times P_y = M$$

$$OB = \frac{M}{P_y} \quad ...(ii)$$

Dividing (*ii*) by (*i*) we have

$$\frac{OB}{OL} = \frac{M}{P_y} \div \frac{M}{P_x} = \frac{M}{P_y} \times \frac{P_x}{M} = \frac{P_x}{P_y}$$

$$\text{Thus, slope of budget line} = \frac{OB}{OL} = \frac{P_x}{P_y}$$

It is thus proved that the slope of the budget line BL represents the ratio of the prices of two goods.

CONSUMER'S EQUILIBRIUM : MAXIMISING SATISFACTION

We are now in a position to explain with the help of indifference curves how a consumer reaches equilibrium position. *A consumer is said to be in equilibrium when he is buying such a combination of goods as leaves him with no tendency to rearrange his purchases of goods.* He is then in a position of balance in regard to the allocation of his money expenditure among various goods. In the indifference curve technique the consumer's equilibrium is discussed in respect of the purchases of two goods by the consumer. As in the cardinal utility analysis, in the indifference curve analysis also it is assumed that the consumer tries to maximise his satisfaction. In other words, the consumer is assumed to be rational in the sense that he aims at maximising his satisfaction. Besides, we shall make the following assumptions to explain the equilibrium of the consumer:

(1) The consumer has a given indifference map exhibiting his scale of preferences for various combinations of two goods, X and Y.

(2) He has a fixed amount of money to spend on the two goods. He has to spend whole of his given money on the two goods.

(3) Prices of the goods are given and constant for him. He cannot influence the prices of the goods by buying more or less of them.

(4) Goods are homogeneous and divisible.

To show which combination of two goods, X and Y, the consumer will decide to buy and will be in equilibrium position, his indifference map and budget line are brought together. As seen above, while indifference map portrays consumer's scale of preferences between various possible combinations of two goods, the budget line shows the various combinations which he can afford to buy with his given money income and given prices of the two goods. Consider Fig. 9.19 in which we depict consumer's indifference map together with the budget line BL. Good X is measured on the X-axis and good Y is measured on the Y-axis. With a given money to be spent and given prices of the two goods, the consumer can buy any combination of the goods which lies on the budget line BL. Every combination on the budget line BL costs him the same amount of money. In order to maximise his satisfaction the consumer will try to reach the highest possible indifference curve which he could with a given expenditure of money and given prices of the two goods. Budget constraint forces the consumer to remain on the given budget line, that is, to choose a combination from among only those which lie on the given budget line.

It will be seen from Fig. 9.19 that the various combinations of the two goods lying on the budget line *BL* and which therefore the consumer can afford to buy do not lie on the same indifference curve; they lie on different indifference curves. The consumer will choose that combination on the budget line *BL* which lies on the highest possible indifference curve. The highest indifference curve to which the consumer can reach is the indifference curve to which the budget line *BL* is tangent. Any other possible combination of the two goods either would lie on a lower indifference curve and thus yield less satisfaction or would be unattainable.

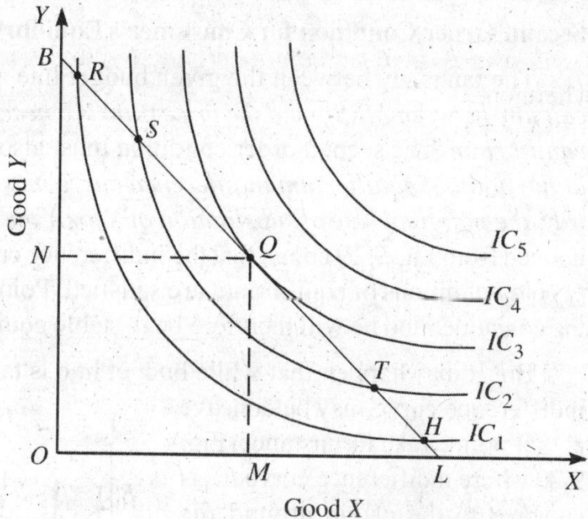

Fig. 9.19. *Consumer's Equilibrium*

In Fig. 9.19 budget line *BL* is tangent to indifference curve IC_3 at point *Q*. Since indifference curves are convex to the origin, all other points on the budget line *BL*, above or below the point *Q*, would lie on lower indifference curves. Take point *R* which also lies on the budget line *BL* and which the consumer can afford to buy. Combination of goods represented by *R* costs him the same as the combination *Q*. But, as is evident, *R* lies on the lower indifference curve IC_1 and will therefore yield less satisfaction than *Q*. Likewise, point *S* also lies on the budget line *BL* but will be rejected in favour of *Q* since S lies on the indifference curve IC_2 which is also lower than IC_3 on which *Q* lies. Similarly, *Q* will be preferred to all other points on the budget line *BL* which lies to the right of *Q* on the budget line, such as *T* and *H*. It is thus clear that of all possible combinations lying on budget line *BL*, combination *Q* lies on the highest possible indifference curve IC_3 which yields maximum possible satisfaction. Of course, combinations lying on indifference curves IC_4 and IC_5 will give greater satisfaction to the consumer than *Q*, but they are unattainable with the given money income and the given prices of the goods as represented by the budget line *BL*. It is therefore concluded that with the given money expenditure and the given prices of the goods as shown by *BL* the consumer will obtain maximum possible satisfaction and will therefore be in equilibrium position at point *Q* at which the budget line *BL* is tangent to the indifference curve IC_3. In this equilibrium position at *Q* the consumer will buy *OM* amount of good *X* and *ON* amount of good *Y*.

At the tangency point *Q*, the slopes of the budget line *BL* and indifference curve IC_3 are equal. Slope of the indifference curve shows the marginal rate of substitution of *X* for *Y* (MRS_{xy}), while the slope of the budget line indicates the ratio between the prices of two goods P_x/P_y. Thus, at the equilibrium point *Q*.

$$MRS_{xy} = \frac{\text{Price of good } X}{\text{Price of good } Y} = \frac{P_x}{P_y}$$

When the marginal rate of substitution of *X* for *Y* (MRS_{xy}) is greater or less than the price ratio between the two goods, it is advantageous for the consumer to substitute one good for the other. Thus, at points *R* and *S* in Fig. 9.19, marginal rates of substitution (MRS_{xy}) are greater than the given price ratio[2], the consumer will substitute good *X* for good *Y* and will come down along the budget line *BL*. He will continue to do so until the marginal rate of substitution becomes equal to the price ratio, that is, the given budget line *BL* becomes tangent to an indifference curve.

On the contrary, marginal rates of substitution at points *H* and *T* in Fig. 9.19 are less than the given price ratio. Therefore, it will be to the advantage of the consumer to substitute good *Y* for good *X* and accordingly move up the budget line *BL* until the MRS_{xy} rises so as to become equal to the given price ratio.

We can therefore express the condition for the equilibrium of the consumer by either saying that the given budget line must be tangent to the indifference curve, or the marginal rate of substitution of good X for good Y must be equal to the ratio between the prices of the two goods.

Second Order Condition for Consumer's Equilibrium

The tangency between the given budget line and an indifference curve or, in other words, *the equality between MRS_{xy} and the price ratio is a necessary but not a sufficient condition of consumer's equilibrium*. The second order condition must also be fulfilled. *The second order condition is that at the point of equilibrium indifference curve must be convex to the origin, or to put it in another way, the marginal rate of substitution of X for Y must be falling at the point of equilibrium.* It will be noticed from Fig. 9.19 above that the indifference curve IC_3 is convex to the origin at Q. Thus at point Q both conditions of equilibrium are satisfied. Point Q in Fig. 9.19 is the optimum or best choice for the consumer and he will therefore be in stable equilibrium at Q.

But it may happen that while budget line is tangent to an indifference curve at a point but the indifference curve may be concave at that point. Take for instance, Fig. 9.20 where indifference curve IC_1 is concave to the origin around the point J. Budget line BL is tangent to the indifference curve IC_1 at point J and MRS_{xy} is equal to the price ratio, P_x/P_y. But J cannot be a position of equilibrium because consumer's satisfaction would not be maximum there. Indifference curve IC_1 being concave at the tangency point J, there may be some points on the given budget line BL such as U and T, which will lie on an indifference curve higher than IC_1. Thus the consumer by moving along the given budget line BL can go to points such as U and T and obtain greater satisfaction than at J. We therefore conclude that for the consumer to be in equilibrium, the following two conditions are required:

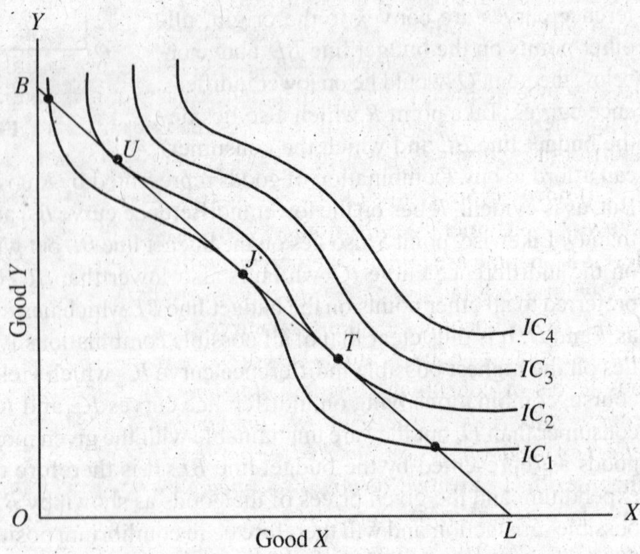

Fig. 9.20. *Second Order Condition for Consumer's Equilibrium*

1. *A given budget line must be tangent to an indifference curve, or marginal rate of substitution of X for Y (MRS_{xy}) must be equal to the price ratio of the two goods* $\frac{P_x}{P_y}$.
2. *Indifference curve must be convex to the origin at the point of tangency.*

The above explanation of consumer's equilibrium in regard to the allocation of his money expenditure on the purchases of two goods has been made *entirely in terms of the consumer's relative preferences of the various combinations of two goods*. In this indifference curve analysis of consumer's equilibrium no use of cardinal utility concept has been made which implies that satisfaction or utility obtained from the goods is measurable in the quantitative sense.

INCOME EFFECT : INCOME CONSUMPTION CURVE

With a given money income to spend on goods, given prices of the two goods and given an indifference map (which portrays given tastes and preferences of the consumers), the consumer will be in equilibrium at a point in an indifference map. We are now interested in knowing how the consumer will react in regard to his purchases of the goods when his money income changes, prices of the goods and his tastes and preferences remaining unchanged. Income effect shows this reaction of the consumer. Thus, *the income effect means the change in consumer's purchases of the goods as a result of a change in his money income.* Income effect is illustrated in Fig. 9.21.

With given prices and a given money income as indicated by the budget line P_1L_1, the consumer is initially in equilibrium at point Q_1 on the indifference curve IC_1 and is having OM_1 of X and ON_1 of Y. Now suppose that income of the consumer increases. With his increased income, he would be able to purchase larger quantities of both the goods. As a result, budget line will shift upward and will be parallel to the original budget line P_1L_1. Let us assume that the consumer's money income increases by such an amount that the new budget line is P_2L_2 (consumer's income has increased by L_1L_2 in terms of X or P_1P_2 in terms of Y). With budget line P_2L_2, the consumer is in equilibrium at point Q_2 on indifference curves IC_2 and is buying OM_2 of X and ON_2 of Y. Thus, as a result of the increase in his income the consumer buys more quantity of both the goods. Since he is on the higher indifference curve IC_2 he will be better off than before *i.e.*, his satisfaction will increase. If his income increases further so that the budget line shifts to P_3L_3, the consumer is in equilibrium at point Q_3 on indifference curve IC_3 and is having greater quantity of both the goods than at Q_2. Consequently, his satisfaction further increases. In Fig. 9.21 the consumer's equilibrium is shown at a still further higher level of income and it will be seen that the consumer is in equilibrium at Q_4 on indifference curves IC_4 when the budget line shifts to P_4L_4. As the consumer's income increases, he switches to higher indifference curves and as a consequence enjoys higher levels of satisfaction.

If now various points Q_1, Q_2, Q_3 and Q_4 showing consumer's equilibrium at various levels of income are joined together, we will get what is called *Income Consumption Curve* (*ICC*). Income consumption curve is thus the locus of equilibrium points at various levels of consumer's income. *Income consumption curve traces out the income effect on the quantity consumed of the goods.* Income effect can either be *positive or negative. Income effect for a good is said to be positive when with the increase in income of the consumer, his consumption of the good also increases.* This is the normal case. When the income effect of both the goods represented on the two axes of the figure is positive, the income consumption curve (*ICC*) will slope upward to the right as in Fig. 9.21. Only the upward-sloping income consumption curve can show rising consumption of the two goods as income increases.

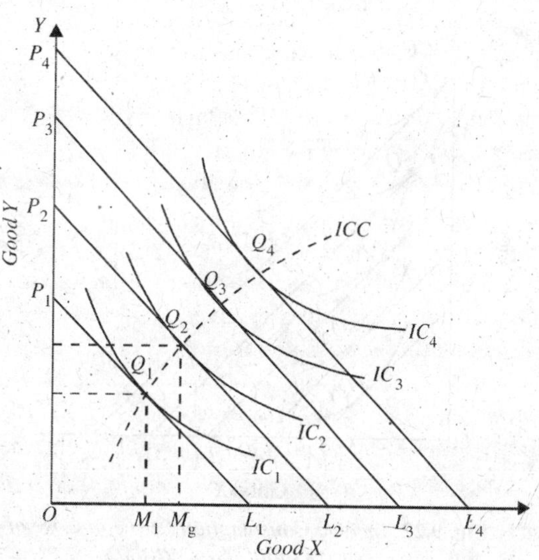

Fig. 9.21. *Income Consumption Curve: Income Effect*

However, for some goods, income effect is negative. *Income effect for a good is said to be negative when with the increases in his income, the consumer reduces his consumption of the good.* Such goods for which income effect is negative are called *Inferior Goods*. This is because the goods whose consumption falls as income of the consumer rises are considered to be some way 'inferior' by the consumer and therefore he substitutes superior goods for them when his income rises. When with the increase in his income, the consumer begins to consume superior goods, the consumption

2. Tangents drawn at point R and S on indifference curves IC_1 and IC_2 respectively have greater slopes than the given slope of the budget line BL.

or quantity purchased by him of the inferior goods falls. When the people are poor, they cannot afford to buy the superior goods which are often more expensive. Hence as they become richer and can afford to buy more expensive goods they switch to the consumption of superior and better quality goods. For instance, most of the people in India consider cheaper common foodgrains such as maize, jawar, bajra as inferior goods and therefore when their income rises, they shift to the consumption of superior varieties of foodgrains like wheat and rice. Similarly, most of the Indian people regard Vanaspati Ghee to be inferior and therefore as they become richer, they reduce its consumption and use '*Desi Ghee*' instead.

In case of inferior goods, indifference map would be such as to yield income consumption curve which either slopes backward (*i.e.*, toward the left) as in Fig. 9.22, or downward to the right as in Fig. 9.23. It would be noticed from the two figures that income effect becomes negative only after a point. It signifies that only at higher ranges of income, some goods become inferior goods and up to a point their consumption behaves like those of normal goods. In Fig. 9.22 income consumption curve (*ICC*) slopes backward *i.e.*, bends toward the *Y*-axis. This shows good *X* to be an inferior good, since beyond point Q_2, income effect is negative for good *X* and as a result its quantity demanded falls as income increases. In Fig. 9.23 income consumption curve (*ICC*) slopes downward to the right beyond point Q_2 *i.e.*, bends towards the *X*-axis. This signifies that good *Y* is an inferior good because beyond point Q_2, income effect is negative for good *Y* and as a result its quantity demanded falls as income increases. It follows from above that the income consumption curve can have various possible shapes.

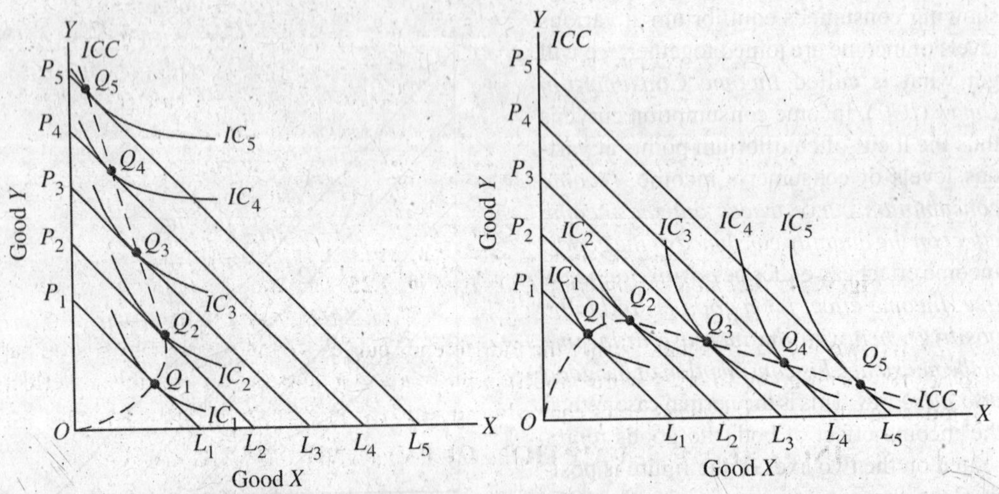

Fig. 9.22. *Income Consumption Curve in Case of Good X being Inferior Good.*

Fig. 9.23. *Income Consumption Curve in Case of Good Y being Inferior Good.*

But normal goods can be either necessities or luxuries depending upon whether the quantities purchased of the goods by the consumers increase less than or more than proportionately to the increases in his income. If the quantity purchased of a commodity rises less than proportionately to the increases in his income, the commodity is known as a *necessity*. On the other hand, if the quantity purchased of a commodity increases more than proportionately to the increases in his income, it is called a *luxury*. In Fig. 9.24, the slope of income consumption curve ICC_1 is increasing which implies that the quantity purchased of the commodity *X* increases less than proportionately to the increases in income. Therefore, in this case of ICC_1, good *X* is a necessity and good *Y* is luxury. On the other hand, the slope of income consumption curve ICC_3 is decreasing which implies that the quantity purchased of good *X* increases more than proportionately to increases in income and therefore in this case good *X* is luxury and good *Y* is necessity. It will be seen from Fig. 9.24 that the income consumption curve ICC_2 is a *linear* curve passing through the origin which implies that the increases in the quantities purchased of both the goods are rising in proportion to the increase in income and therefore neither good is a luxury or a necessity.

If income effect is positive for both the goods *X* and *Y*, the income consumption curve will slope upward to the right as in Fig. 9.21. But upward-sloping income consumption curves to the right for various goods may be of different slopes as shown in Fig. 9.24 in which income consumption curves, with varying slopes, are all sloping upward and therefore indicate both goods to be normal goods having positive income effect. *If income effect for good X is negative, income consumption curve will slope backward to the left as ICC′ in Fig. 9.25. If good Y happens to be an inferior good and income consumption curve will bend towards X-axis as shown by ICC″ in Fig. 9.25.* In Figs. 9.24 and 9.25, various possible shapes which income consumption curve can take are shown bereft of indifference curves and budget lines which yield them. It may however be pointed out that given an indifference map and a set of budget lines there will be one income consumption curve.

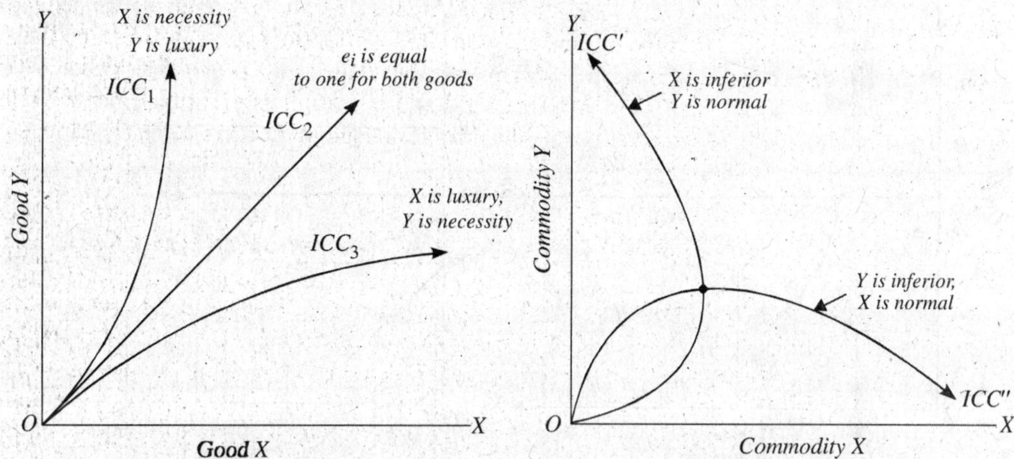

Fig. 9.24. *Income Consumption Curves of Normal Goods.* **Fig. 9.25.** *Income Consumption Curves of Inferior Goods.*

A noteworthy point is that it is not the indifference curves which explain why a good happens to be an inferior good. In other words, indifference curves do not explain why income effect for a good is negative. Indifference curves can only illustrate the inferior-good phenomenon.

INCOME CONSUMPTION CURVE AND ENGEL CURVE

As seen above, income consumption curve is the locus, in indifference curve map, of the equilibrium quantities consumed by an individual at different levels of his income. Thus, the income consumption curve (*ICC*) can be used to derive the relationship between the level of consumer's income and the quantity purchased of a commodity by him. A nineteenth century German statistician Ernet Engel (1821–1896) made an empirical study of family budgets to draw conclusions about the pattern of consumption expenditure, that is, expenditure on different goods and services by the households at different levels of income. The conslusions he arrived at are still believed to be generally valid. According to Engel's studies, as the income of a family increases, the proportion of its income spent on necessities such as food falls and that spent on luxuries (consisting of industrial goods and services) increases. In other words, the poor families spend relatively large proportion of their income on necessities, whereas rich families spend a relatively a large part of their income on luxuries. *This change in the pattern of consumption expenditure (that is, decline in the proportion of income spent on food and other necessities and increase in the proportion of income spent on luxuries) with the rise in income of the families has been called Engel's law.*

Though Engel dealt with the relationship between *income and expenditure* on different goods, in order to keep our analysis simple we will describe and explain the *relationship between income and quantities* purchased of goods. However, both types of relations will convey the same information about individual's consumption behaviour as in our analysis of Engel's curve, the prices of goods are held constant. *The curve showing the relationship between the levels of income and quantity purchased of particular commodities has therefore been called Engel curve.* In what follows we explain how an Engel curve is derived from income consumption curve. In our analysis of Engel curve we relate *quantity purchased* of a commodity, rather than *expenditure* on it, to the level of consumer's income.[3]

It is worth noting that like the demand curve depicting relationship between price and quantity purchased, other factors remaining the same, Engel curve shows relationship between income and quantity demanded, other influences on quantity purchased such as prices of goods, consumer preferences are assumed to be held constant.

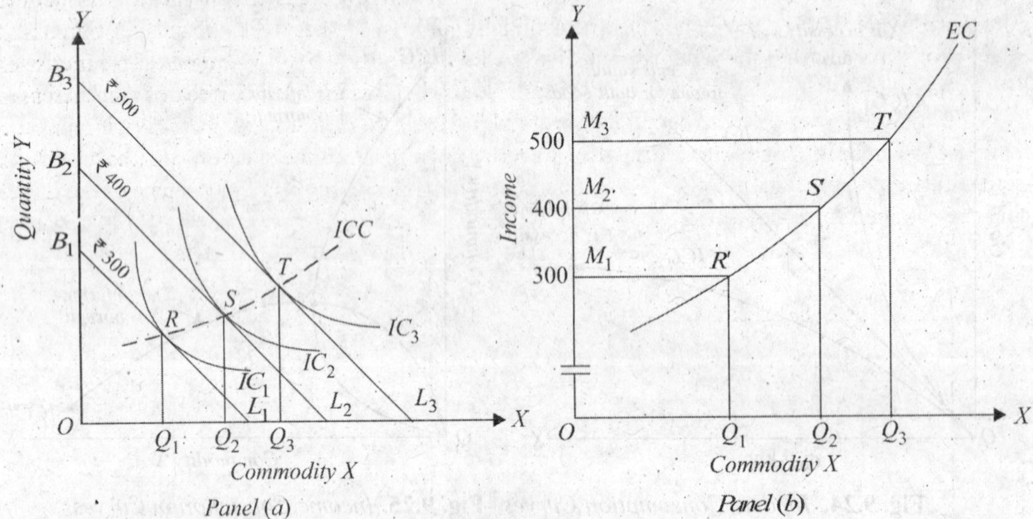

Fig. 9.26. *Deriving Engel Curve from Income Consumption Curve in Case of Necessities*

For deriving Engel curve from income consumption curve we plot level of income on the *Y*-axis and quantity purchased of a commodity on the *X*-axis. Consider panel (*a*) in Fig. 9.26. Given the indifference map representing the preferences of a consumer and the prices of two goods *X* and *Y*, *ICC* is the income consumption curve showing the equilibrium quantities purchased of a commodity by the consumer as his income increases from ₹ 300 to ₹ 400 and to ₹ 500 per day. It will be seen from panel (*a*) of Fig. 9.26 that when income is ₹ 300, given prices of goods *X* and *Y*, the consumer is buying OQ_1 quantity of the commodity.

In panel (*b*) of Fig. 9.26 in which level of income is represented on the vertical axis and quantity purchased of commodity *X* on the horizontal axis we directly plot quantity OQ_1 against income level of ₹ 300. As income increases to ₹ 400, prices of goods remaining constant, the budget line in panel (*a*) shifts outward to the left to the new position B_2L_2 with which consumer is in equilibrium at point *S* and the consumer buys OQ_2 quantity of good *X*. Thus, in panel (*b*) of Fig. 9.26 we plot quantity purchased OQ_2 of commodity *X* against income level of ₹ 400. Likewise, as income further rises to

3. It may be noted that modern economists also study the relationship between expenditure and level of income and represent this by a curve which they call Engel Expenditure Curve. When they study the relationship between income and quantity purchased and derive a curve of this relationship, they call it simply Engel Curve as we are doing in the present chapter.

₹ 500, budget line in panel (*a*) shifts to B_3L_3 and the consumer buys OQ_3 quantity of X in his new equilibrium position at T. Therefore, in panel (*b*) of Fig. 9.26, we plot OQ_3 against income of Rs. 500. Thus equilibrium points constituting the income consumption curve in consumer's indifference map have been transformed into Engel curve depicting quantity-income relationship. Each point of an Engel curve corresponds to a relevant point of income consumption curve. Thus R' of the Engel curve EC corresponds to point R on the ICC curve. As seen from panel (*b*), *Engel curve for normal goods is upward sloping which shows that as income increases, consumer buys more of a commodity.*

The slope of Engel curve EC drawn in panel (*b*) of Figure 9.26 equals $\Delta M/\Delta Q$ where ΔM stands for income and ΔQ a for change in quantity demanded of good X and has a positive sign. It is important to note that *the slope of the Engel curve in Fig. 9.26 (panel (b)) increases as income increases.* This indicates that with every equal increase in income, expansion in quantity purchased of the good successively declines. This upward-sloping Engel curve with increasing slope as income rises depicts the case of necessities, consumption of which increases relatively less as income rises. For instance, in Fig. 9.26 when income is initially ₹ 300 (= M_1) per week, the quantity purchased of the good X equals OQ_1 and when income rises by Rs. 100 to Rs. 400 (= M_2) per week he increases his consumption to OQ_2, that is, by quantity Q_1Q_2. Now, when his income per week further increases by ₹ 100 to ₹ 500 per week, the quantity consumed increases to OQ_3, that is, by Q_2Q_3 which is less than Q_1Q_2. Thus, in Engel curve drawn in panel (*b*) of Fig. 9.26 the quantity purchased of the commodity increases with the increase in income but *at a decreasing rate*. This shape of the Engel curve is obtained for *necessities*.

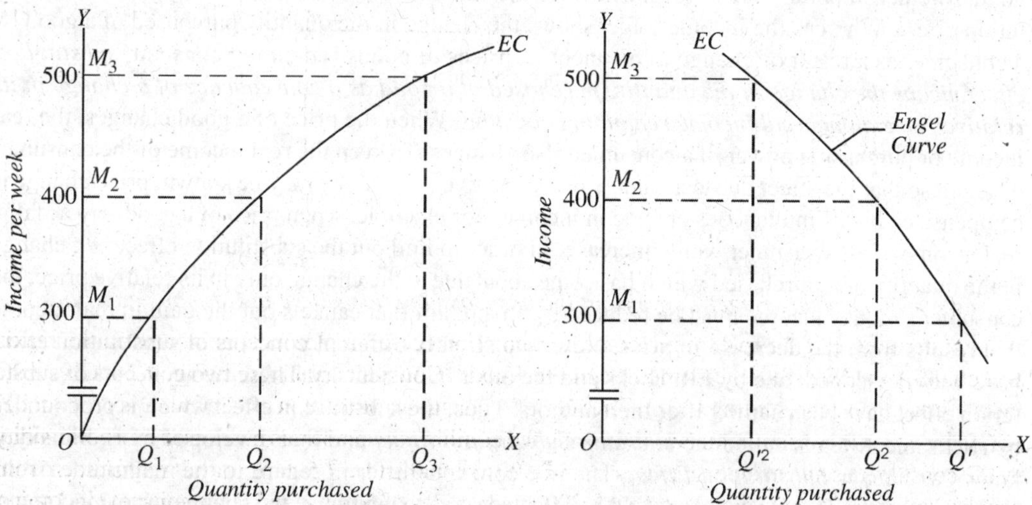

Fig. 9.27. *Engel Curve of a Luxury.*

Fig. 9.28. *Backward Bending Engel Curve of an Inferior Good.*

The Engel curve drawn in Fig. 9.27 is upward sloping but is concave. This implies that slope of the Engel curve ($\Delta M/\Delta Q$) is declining with the increase in income. That is, in the Engel curve of a commodity depicted in Fig. 9.27 the equal increments in income result in successively larger increases in the quantity purchased of the commodity. Thus, in Fig. 9.27 at income of ₹ 300 the consumer purchases OQ_1 quantity of a commodity. The increase in income by Rs. 100 to ₹ 400 results in increase in quantity purchased of the commodity equal to Q_1Q_2. With the further increase in income by the same amount of ₹ 100 to ₹ 500, the quantity purchased increases by Q_2Q_3 which is larger than Q_1Q_2. This implies that as a consumer becomes richer he purchases relatively more of the commodity. Such commodities are called luxuries. Example of luxuries are air travel, butter, costly woollen suits, air conditioners, costly fruits, etc.

In case of *inferior goods*, consumption of the commodity declines as income increases. Engel curve of an inferior good is drawn in Figure 9.28 which is backward bending indicating a fall in the quantity purchased of the good as income increases.

An extreme case of Engel curve is a vertical straight line as drawn in Fig. 9.29. This represents the case of a *neutral* commodity which is quite unresponsive to the increase in income. The Engel curve of the shape of a vertical straight line shows that a person goes on consuming the same amount of a commodity whatever the level of his income. For example, the quantity of common salt purchased by a family remains the same, determined as it is by food habits, with the increase in their income.

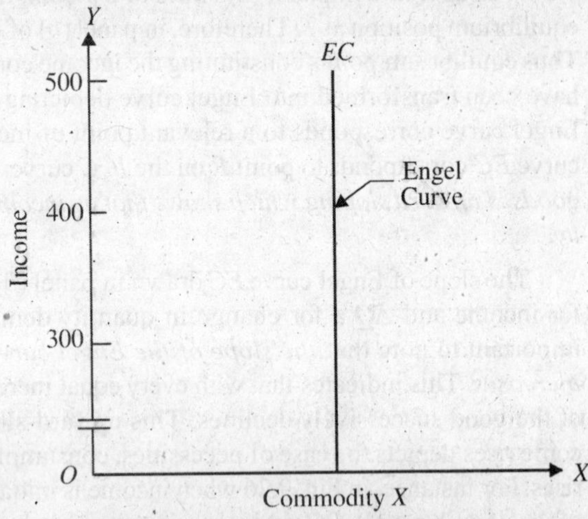

Fig. 9.29. *Engel Curve of a Neutral Good*

SUBSTITUTION EFFECT

We have explained above the effect of changes in income on purchases or consumption of a good. Another important factor responsible for the changes in consumption of a good is the substitution effect. Whereas the income effect shows the change in the quantity purchased of a good by a consumer as a result of change in his income, prices of goods remaining constant, *substitution effect means the change in the quantity purchased of a good as a consequence of a change in its relative price alone, real income remaining constant.* When the price of a good changes, the real income or purchasing power of a consumer also changes. To keep the real income of the consumer constant so that the effect due to a change in the relative price alone may be known, price change is compensated by a simultaneous change in income. For example, when price of a good, say *X*, falls, real income of the consumer would increase. In order to find out the substitution effect *i.e.*, change in the quantity of *X* purchased which has come about due to the change only in its relative price, the consumer's money income must be reduced by an amount that cancels out the gain in real income that results from the decrease in price. Now, two slightly different concepts of substitution effect have been developed; one by J.R. Hicks and the other by E. Slutsky. These two concepts of substitution effect have been named after their authors. Thus, the substitution effect which is propounded by Hicks and Allen is called the *Hicksian Substitution Effect* and that developed by E. Slutsky is known as *Slutsky Substitution Effect*. The two concepts differ in regard to the magnitude of the change in money income which should be effected so as to neutralise the change in real income of the consumer which results from a change in the price. We shall explain here the Hicksian substitution effect.

In the Hicksian substitution effect price change is accompained by a so much change in money income that the consumer is neither better off nor worse off than before. In other words, money income of the consumer is changed by an amount which keeps the consumer on the same indifference curve on which he was before the change in the price. Thus the Hicksian substitution effect takes place on the same indifference curve. *The amount by which the money income of the consumer is changed so that the consumer is neither better off nor worse off than before is called* Compensating *Variation in Income*. In other words, *compensating variation in income is a change in the income of the consumer which is just sufficient to compensate the consumer for a change in the price of a good.*

Thus, in the Hicksian type of substitution effect, income is changed by the magnitude of the *compensating variation in income*. Hicksian substitution effect is illustrated in Fig. 9.30. With a given money income and given prices of the two goods as represented by the budget line *PL*, the consumer is in equilibrium at point *Q* on the indifference curve *IC* and is purchasing *OM* of good *X* and *ON* of good *Y*. Suppose that the price of good *X* falls (price of *Y* remaining unchanged) so that the budget line now shifts to *PL'*. With this fall in price of *X*, the consumer's real income or purchasing power would increase. In order to find out the substitution effect, this gain in real income should be wiped out by reducing the money income of the consumer by such an amount that forces him to remain on the same indifference curve *IC* on which he was before the change in price of the good *X*. When some money is taken away from the consumer to cancel out the gain in real income, then the budget line which shifted to position *PL'* will now shift downward but will be parallel to *PL'*. In Fig. 9.30, a budget line *AB* parallel to *PL'* has been drawn at such a distance from *PL'* that it touches the indifference curve *IC*. It means that reduction of consumer's income by the amount *PA* (in terms of *Y*) or *L'B* (in terms of *X*) has been made so as to keep him on the same indifference curve. *PA* or *L'B* is thus just sufficient to cancel out the gain in the real income which occurred due to the fall in the price of *X*. *PA* or *L'B* is therefore compensating variation in income.

Now, budget line *AB* represents the new relative prices of goods *X* and *Y* since it is parallel to the budget line *PL'* which was obtained when the price of good *X* had fallen. In comparison to the budget line *PL*, *X* is now relatively cheaper. The consumer would therefore rearrange his purchases of *X* and *Y* and will substitute *X* for *Y*. That is, since *X* is now relatively cheaper and *Y* is now relatively dearer than before, he will buy more of *X* and less of *Y*. It will be seen from Fig. 9.30 that budget line *AB* represents the changed relative prices but a lower money income than that of *PL*, since consumer's income has been reduced by compensating variation in income.

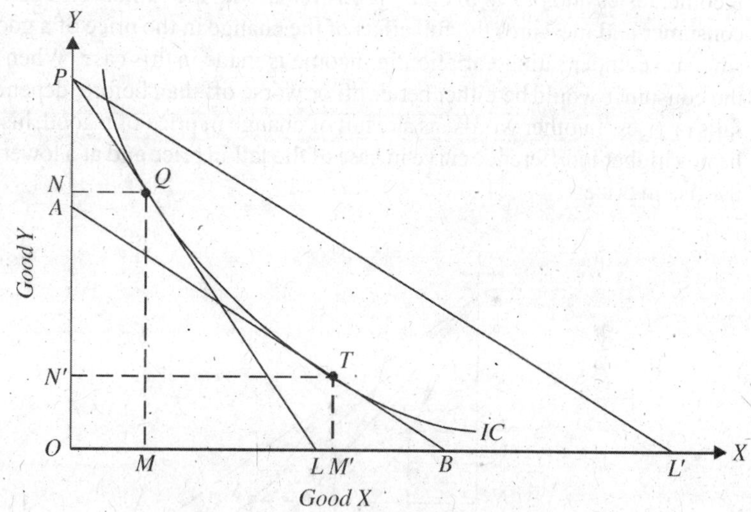

Fig. 9.30. *Hicksian Substitution Effect*

It will seen from Fig. 9.30 that with budget line *AB* the consumer is in equilibrium at point *T* and is now buying *OM'* of *X* and *ON'* of *Y*. Thus in order to buy *X* more he moves on the same indifference curve *IC* from point *Q* to point *T*. This increase in the quantity purchased of good *X* by *MM'* and the decrease in the quantity purchased of good *Y* by *NN'* is due to the change only in the relative prices of goods *X* and *Y*, since effect due to the gain in real income has been wiped out by making a simultaneous reduction in consumer's income. Therefore, movement from *Q* to *T* represents the substitution effect. Substitution effect on good *X* is the increase in its quantity purchased by *MM'* and substitution effect on *Y* is the fall in its quantity purchased by *NN'*. It is thus clear that as a result of the Hicksian substitution effect the consumer remains on the same indifference curve; he is however in equilibrium at a different point from that at which he was before the change in price of good *X*. The less the convexity of the indifference curve, the greater will be the substitution effect. As is known, the convexity of indifference curve is less in the case of those goods which are good substitutes. It is thus clear that the substitution effect in case of good substitutes will be large.

It is thus clear that, a fall in relative price of a commodity always leads to the increase in its quantity demanded due to the substitution effect, the consumer's satisfaction or indifference curve remaining the same. Thus the *substitution effect is always negative*. The negative substitution effect implies that the relative price of a commodity and its quantity demanded change in opposite direction, that is, the *decline* in relative price of a commodity always causes *increase* in its quantity demanded. This inverse relationship between relative price and quantity demanded holds good in *case the indifference curves are convex to the origin*. Given that indifference curves are convex to the origin, a fall in the relative price of a commodity causing an increase in its quantity demanded is known as *Slutsky theorem* as this proposition was originally put forward by Slutsky. It is this negative substitution effect which lies at the root of the famous law of demand stating inverse relationship between price and quantity demanded.

PRICE EFFECT: PRICE CONSUMPTION CURVE

We will now explain how the consumer reacts to charges in the price of a good, his money income, tastes and prices of other goods remaining the same. Price effect shows this reaction of the consumer and measures the full effect of the change in the price of a good on the quantity purchased since no compensating variation in income is made in this case. When the price of a good charges, the consumer would be either better off or worse off than before, depending upon whether the price falls or rises. In other words, as a result of change in price of a good, his equilibrium position would lie at a higher indifference curve in case of the fall in price and at a lower indifference curve in case of the rise in price.

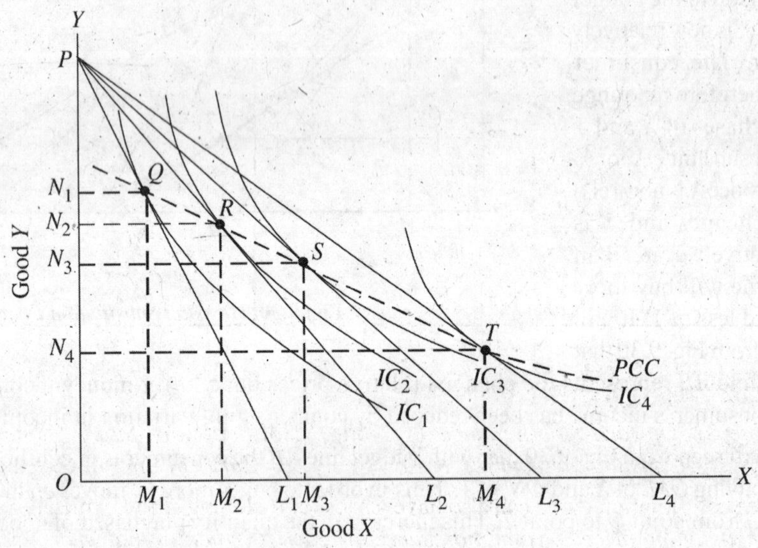

Fig. 9.31. *Downward-Sloping Price Consumption Curve*

Price effect is shown in Fig. 9.31. With given prices of goods *X* and *Y*, and a given money income as represented by the budget line PL_1, the consumer is in equilibrium at *Q* on indifference curve IC_1. In this equilibrium position at *Q*, he is buying OM_1 of *X* and ON_1 of *Y*. Let price of good *X* fall, price of *Y* and his money income remaining unchanged. As a result of this price change, budget line shifts to the position PL_2. The consumer is now in equilibrium at *R* on a higher indifference curve IC_2 and is buying OM_2 of *X* and ON_2 of *Y*. He has thus become better off, that is, his level of satisfaction has increased as a consequence of the fall in the price of good *X*. Suppose that price of *X* further falls so that PL_3 is now the relevant price line. With budget line PL_3 the consumer is in equilibrium at *S* on indifference curve IC_3 where he has OM_3 of *X* and ON_3 of *Y*. If price of good *X* falls still further so that budget line now takes the position of PL_4, the consumer now attains equilibrium at *T* on indifference curve IC_4 and has OM_4 of X and ON_4 of *Y*. When all the equilibrium points such as *Q*, *R*, *S*, and *T* are joined together, we get what is called *Price Consumption Curve* (*PCC*). *Price consumption curve traces out the price effect. It shows how the changes in price of good X will affect the consumer's purchases of X, price of Y, his tastes and money income remaining unaltered.*

In Fig. 9.31 price consumption curve (*PCC*) is sloping downward. Downward sloping price consumption curve for good *X* means that as price of good *X* falls, the consumer purchases a larger quantity of good *X* and a smaller quantity of good *Y*. This is quite evident from Fig. 9.31. As we shall discuss in detail in the chapter concerning elasticity of demand, we obtain downward-sloping price consumption curve for good *X* when demand for it is elastic (*i.e.*, price elasticity is greater than one). But downward sloping is one possible shape of price consumption curve. Price consumption curve can have other shapes also. In Fig. 9.32 upward-sloping price consumption curve is shown. *Upward-sloping price consumption curve for X means that when the price of good X falls, the quantity demanded of both goods X and Y rises.* We obtain the upward-sloping price consumption curve for good *X* when the demand for good is inelastic, (*i.e.*, price elasticity is less than one).

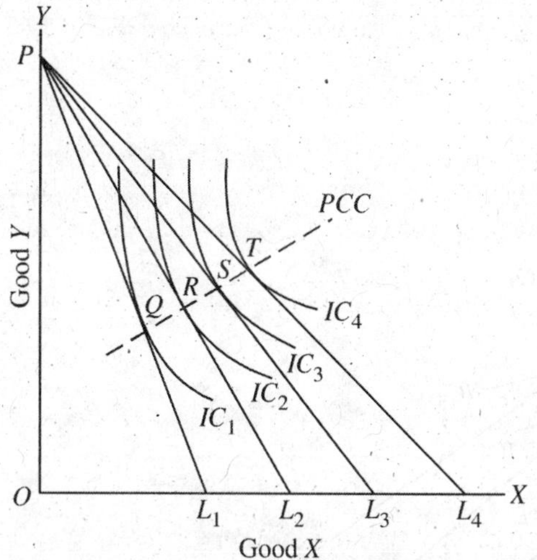

Fig. 9.32. *Upward-Sloping Price Consumption Curve*

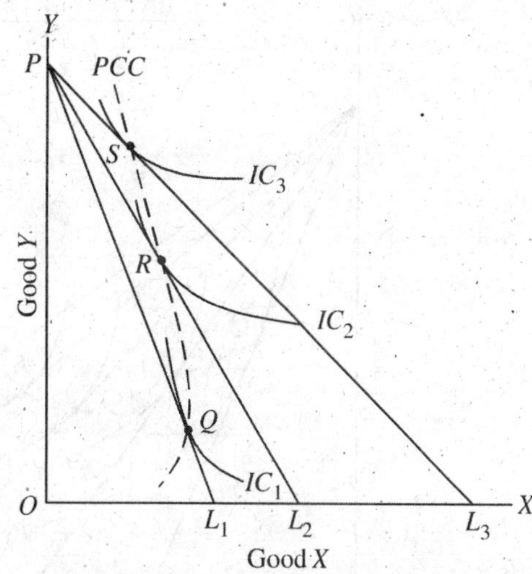

Fig. 9.33. *Backward-Sloping Price Consumption Curve in Case of Giffen Goods*

Price consumption curve can also have a backward-sloping shape, which is depicted in Fig. 9.33. *Backward-sloping price consumption curve for good X indicates that when price of X falls, after a point smaller quantity of it is demanded or purchased.* We shall see later in this chapter that this is true in case of exceptional type of goods called Giffen Goods.

Price consumption curve for a good can take horizontal shape too. It means that when the price of the good *X* declines, its quantity purchased rises proportionately but quantity purchased of *Y* remains the same. Horizontal price consumption curve is shown in Fig. 9.34. We obtain horizontal price consumption curve of good *X* when the price elasticity of demand for good *X* is equal to unity.

But it is rarely found that price consumption curve slopes downward throughout or slopes upward throughout or slopes backward throughout. More generally, price consumption curve has

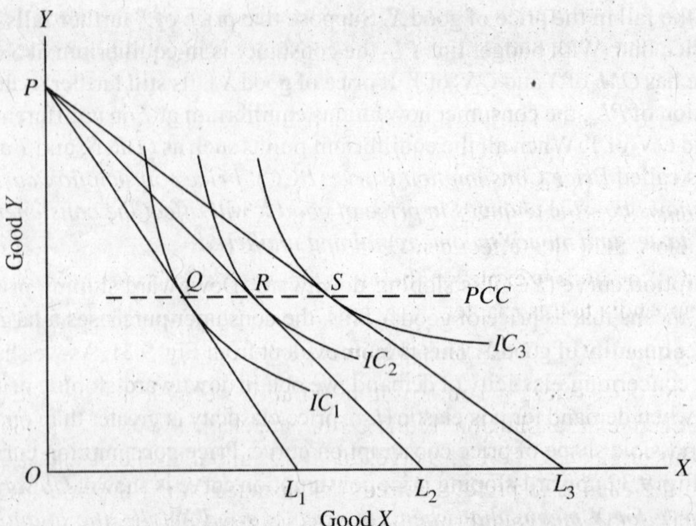

Fig. 9.34. *Horizontal Price Consumption Curve.*

different slopes at different price ranges. At higher price levels it generally slopes downward, and it may then have a horizontal shape for some price ranges but ultimately it will be sloping upward. For some price ranges it can be backward sloping as in case of Giffen goods. A price consumption curve which has different shapes or slopes at different price ranges is drawn in Fig. 9.35. We shall study in a subsequent chapter that such a type of price consumption curve means that price elasticity of demand varies at different price ranges.

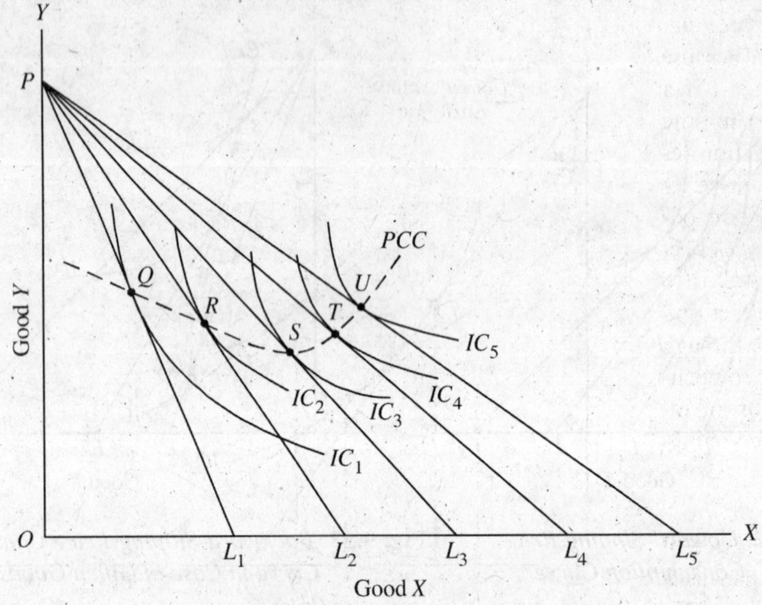

Fig. 9.35. *Price Consumption Curve with Varying Slopes*

DECOMPOSING PRICE EFFECT INTO INCOME AND SUBSTITUTION EFFECTS

It has been explained above that as price of a good *X* falls, other things remaining the same, consumer would move to a new equilibrium position at a higher indifference curve and would buy more of good *X* at the lower price unless it is a Giffen good. Thus, in the Fig. 9.36 the consumer who is initially in equilibrium at *Q* on indifference curve IC_1 moves to the point *R* on indifference curve IC_2 when the price of good *X* falls and the budget line twists from PL_1 to PL_2. The movement from *Q* to *R* represents the price effect. It is now highly important to understand that this price effect is the net result of two distinct forces, namely, substitution effect and income effect. In other words, price effect can be split up into two different parts, one being the substitution effect and the other income effect.

There are two approaches for decomposing price effect into its two parts, substitution effect and income effect. They are the Hicksian approach and Slutsky approach. Further, Hicksian approach uses two methods of splitting the price effect, namely (*i*) *Compensating variation in income* (*ii*) *Equivalent variation in income*. Slutsky uses *cost-difference method* to decompose price effect into its two component parts. How the price effect can be decomposed into income effect and substitution effect by the Hicksian methods is explained below, whereas Slutsky's cost-difference method will be explained in an appendix to this chapter.

1. Decomposing Price Effect: Compensating Variation in Income

In the method of decomposing price effect by compensating variation we adjust the income of the consumer so as to offset the change in satisfaction resulting from the change in price of a good and bring the consumer back to his original indifference curve, that is, his initial level of satisfaction which he was obtaining before the change in price occurred. For instance, when the price of a commodity falls and consumer moves to a new equilibrium position at a higher indifference curve his satisfaction increases. To offset this gain in satisfaction resulting from a fall in price of the good we must take away from the consumer enough income to force him to come back to his original indifference curve. *This required reduction in income (say, through levying a lump sum tax) to cancel out the gain in satisfaction or welfare occurred by reduction in price of a good is called compensating variation in income.* This is so called because it compensates (in a negative way) for the gain in satisfaction resulting from a price reduction of the commodity. How the price effect is decomposed into substitution effect and income effect is through the method of compensating variation in income illustrated in Fig. 9.36.

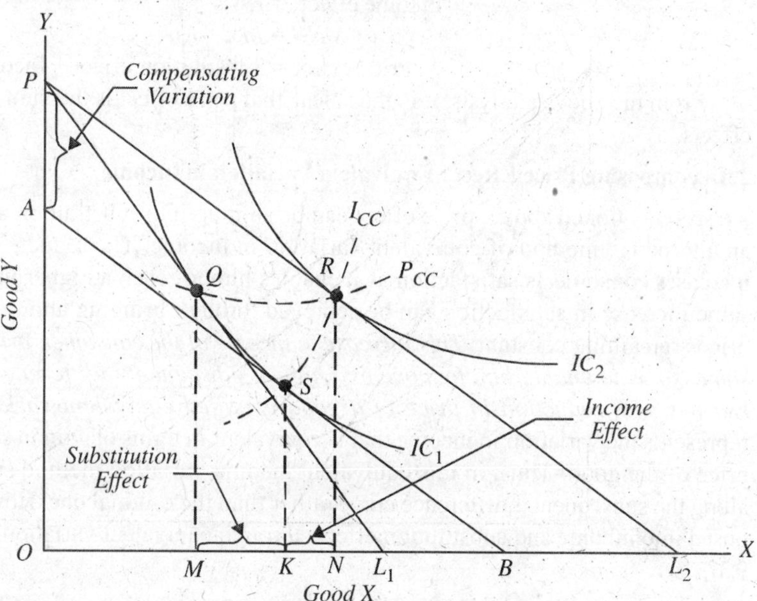

Fig. 9.36. *Price Effect Split up into Substitution and Income Effects through Compensating Variation Method*

When the price of good X falls and as a result budget line shifts to PL_2, the real income of the consumer rises, *i.e.*, he can buy more of both the goods with his given money income. That is, price reduction enlarges consumer's opportunity set of the two goods. With the new budget line PL_2 he is in equilibrium at point R on a higher indifference curve IC_2 and thus gains in satisfaction as a result of fall in price of good X. Now, if his money income is reduced by the compensating variation in income so that he is forced to come back to the indifference curve IC_1 as before, he would buy more of X since X has now become relatively cheaper than before. In Fig. 9.36 as result of the fall in price of X, price line switches to PL_2. Now, with the reduction in income by compensating variation, budget line shifts to *AB* which has been drawn parallel to PL_2 so that it just touches the indifference curve IC_1 where he was before the fall in price of *X*. Since the price line *AB* has got the same slope as PL_2, it represents the changed relative prices with *X* being relatively cheaper than before. Now, *X* being relatively cheaper than before, the consumer in order to maximise his satisfaction in the new price-income situation substitutes *X* for *Y*. Thus, when the consumer's money income is reduced by the compensating variation in income (which is equal to *PA* in terms of *Y* or L_2B in terms of *X*), the consumer moves along the same indifference curve IC_1 and substitutes *X* for *Y*. With price line *AB*, he is in equilibrium at *S* on indifference curve IC_1 and is buying *MK* more of *X* in place of *Y*. This movement from *Q* to *S* on the same indifference curve IC_1 represents the substitution effect since it occurs due to the change in relative prices alone, real income remaining constant. If the amount of money income which was taken away from him is now given back to him, he would move from *S* on indifference curve IC_1 to *R* on a higher indifference curve IC_2. The movement from *S* on a lower in difference curve to *R* on a higher in difference curve is the result of income effect. Thus the movement form *Q* to *R* due to price effect can be regarded as having been taken place into two steps : first from *Q* to *S* as a result of substitution effect and second from *S* to *R* as a result of income effect. In is thus mainfest that price effect is the combined result of a substitution effect and an income effect.

In Fig. 9.36 the various effects on the purchases of good *X* are:

$$\text{Price effect} = MN$$
$$\text{Substitution effect} = MK$$
$$\text{Income effect} = KN$$
$$MN = MK + KN$$

or

$$\text{Price effect} = \text{Substitution effect} + \text{Income effect}$$

From the above analysis, it is thus clear that price effect is the sum of income and substitution effects.

2. Decomposing Price Effect : Equivalent Variation in Income

As mentioned above, price effect can be split up into substitution and income effects through an alternative method of equivalent variation in income. The reduction in price of a commodity increases consumer's satisfaction as it enables him to reach a higher indifference curve. Now, the same increase in satisfaction can be achieved through bringing about an increase in his income, prices remaining constant. *This increase in income of the consumer, prices of goods remaining the same, so as to enable him to move to a higher subsequent indifference curve at which he in fact reaches with reduction in price of a good is called equivalent variation in income* because it represents the variation in income that is equivalent in terms of gain in satisfaction to a reduction in price of the good. Thus, in this equivalent income-variation method substitution effect is shown along the subsequent indifference curve rather than the original one. How this price effect is decomposed into income and substitution effects through equivalent variation in income is shown in Fig. 9.37.

When price of good *X* falls, the consumer can purchase more of both the goods, that is, the purchasing power of his given money income rises. It means that after the fall in price of *X*, if the consumer buys the same quantities of goods as before, then some amount of money will be left over. In other words, the fall in price of good *X* will release some amount of money. Money thus released can be spent on purchasing more of both the goods. It therefore follows that a change in price of the good produces an income effect. When the power to purchase goods rises due to the income effect of the price change, or in other words, when some amount of money is released as a result of the fall in price, the consumer has to decide how this increase in his purchasing power is to be spread over the two goods he is buying. How he will spread the released purchasing power over the two goods depends upon the nature of his income consumption curve which in turn is determined by his preferences about the two goods.

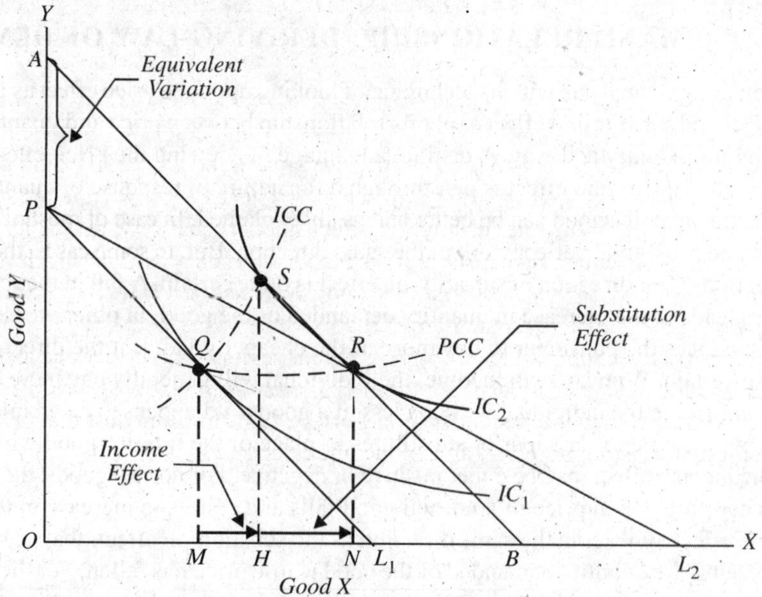

Fig. 9.37. *Price Effect Split Up into Income and Substitution Effects through Equivalent Variation Method*

From above it follows, that, as a result of the increase in his purchasing power (or real income) due to the fall in price, the consumer will move to a higher indifference curve and will become better off than before. It is as if the price had remained the same but his money income was increased. In other words, a fall in price of good *X* does to the consumer what an equivalent rise in money income would have done to him. As a result of fall in price of *X*, the consumer can therefore be imagined as moving up to a higher indifference curve along the income consumption curve as if his money income had been increased, prices of *X* and *Y* remaining unchanged. Thus, a given change in price can be thought of as an equivalent to an appropriate change in income.

It will be seen from Fig. 9.37 that with price line PL_1, the consumer is in equilibrium at *Q* on indifference curve IC_1. Suppose price of good *X* falls, price of *Y* and his money income remaining unaltered, so that budget line is now PL_2. With budget line PL_2, he is in equilibrium at *R* on indifference curve IC_2. Now, a line *AB* is drawn parallel to PL_1 so that it touches the indifference curve IC_2 at *S*. It means that the increase in real income or purchasing power of the consumer as a result of the fall in price of *X* is equal to *PA* in terms of *Y* or L_1B in terms of *X*. Movement of the consumer from *Q* on indifference curve IC_1 to *S* on the higher indifference curve IC_2 along the income consumption curve is the result of income effect of the price change. But the consumer will not be finally in equilibrium at *S*. This is because now that *X* is relatively cheaper than *Y*, he will substitute *X*, which has become relatively cheaper, for good *Y*, which has become relatively dearer. It will be a profitable thing for the consumer to do so. Thus the consumer will move along the indifference curve IC_2 from *S* to *R*. This movement from *S* to *R* has taken place because of the change in relative prices alone and therefore represents substitution effect. Thus the price effect can be broken up into income and substitution effects, showing in this case substitution along the subsequent indifference curve. In Fig 9.37 the magnitudes of the various effects are :

$$\text{Price effect} = MN$$

$$\text{Income effect} = MH$$

$$\text{Substitution effect} = HN$$

In Fig. 9.37, $MN = MH + HN$

or Price effect = Income Effect + Substitution Effect

PRICE-DEMAND RELATIONSHIP: DERIVING LAW OF DEMAND

Indifference curve analysis with its technique of looking upon the price effect as a combination of income effect and substitution effect explains relationship between price and quantity demanded in a better and more analytical way. A distinct advantage of viewing the price effect as a sum of income effect and substitution effect is that through it the nature of response of quantity purchased to a change in the price of a good can be better and easily explained. In case of most of the goods, the income effect and substitution effect work in the same direction. But, in some cases, they may pull in different directions. The direction of substitution effect is quite certain. A fall in the relative price of a good always leads to the increase in quantity demanded of the good. In other words, substitution effect always induces the consumer to buy more of the cheaper good. But the direction of income effect is not so certain. With a rise in income, the individual will generally buy more of a good. But with the rise in income the individual will buy less of a good if it happens to be an inferior good for him since he will use better or superior substitutes in place of the inferior good when his income rises. Thus the income effect may be either positive or negative. For normal goods, the income effect is positive. Therefore, when price of a normal good falls and results in increase in the purchasing power, income effect will act in the same direction as the substitution effect, that is, both will work towards increasing the quantity demanded of the good whose price has fallen. For the inferior good in which case income effect is negative, income effect of the price change will work in opposite direction to the substitution effect. The net effect of the price change will then depend upon the relative strengths of the two effects. To sum up, price effect is composed of income effect and substitution effect and further that the direction in which quantity demanded will change as a result of the fall in price will depend upon the direction and strength of the income effect on the one hand and strength of the substitution effect on the other.

Price Demand Relationship : Normal Goods

In order to understand the way in which price-demand relationship is established in indifference curve analysis, consider Fig. 9.36. Given the price of two goods and his income represented by the budget line PL_1, the consumer will be in equilibrium at Q on indifference curve IC_1. Let us suppose that, price of X falls, price of Y and his money income remaining unchanged so that budget line now shifts to PL_2. The consumer will now be in equilibrium at a point on the new budget line BL_2. If the equilibrium position on BL_2 lies to the right of Q such as at R in Fig. 9.36, it will mean that the consumer buys more quantity of good X than at Q. Now, it can be proved that in case of normal goods the *new equilibrium point on* BL_2 *will lie to the right of* Q, *meaning thereby that the quantity demanded of the good X will increase as its price falls.*

As seen above, the direction and magnitude of the change in quantity demanded as a result of the fall in price of a good depend upon the direction and strength of income effect on the one hand and substitution effect on the other. As for normal goods, the income effect is positive, it will work towards increasing the quantity demanded of good X when its price falls. The substitution effect which is always negative and operates so as to raise the quantity demanded of the good if its price falls and reduces the quantity demanded of the good if its price rises. Thus, both the income effect (when positive) and negative substitution effect works in the same direction and cause increase in the quantity purchased of good X whose price has fallen with the result that the new equilibrium point will lie to the right of the original equilibrium point Q such as point R in Fig. 9.36 above. Substitution effect causes MK increase in quantity demanded. Income effect which is positive here also leads to the increase in quantity demand by KN. Each effect therefore reinforces the other. As a result, the total effect of a fall in price of X from the level indicated by PL_1 to the level indicated by PL_2

is the rise in quantity demanded of good *X* from *OM* to *ON*, that is, quantity demanded increases by *MN* which is equal to *MK* + *KN*. To sum up, *the income effect and substitution effect in case of normal goods work in the same direction and will lead to the increase in quantity demanded of the good whose price has fallen*. In other words, quantiy purchased of a normal good will vary inversely with its price as in its case income effect is positive.

Price-Demand Relationship : Inferior Goods. In case of inferior goods the income effect will work in opposite direction to the substitution effect. When price of an inferior good falls, its negative income effect will tend to reduce the quantity purchased, while the substitution effect will tend to increase the quantity purchased. But normally it happens that negative income effect of the change in price is not large enough to outweigh the substitution effect. This is so because a consumer spends a very small proportion of his income on a single commodity and when price of the commodity falls, a very little income is released. In other words, income effect even when negative is generally too weak to outweigh the substitution effect. It follows therefore that as a result of the fall in price of a good the substitution effect which always induces the consumer to buy more of the good whose price has fallen will usually outweigh the negative income effect. Thus even in most cases of inferior goods the net result of the fall in price will be increase in its quantity demanded. It is thus

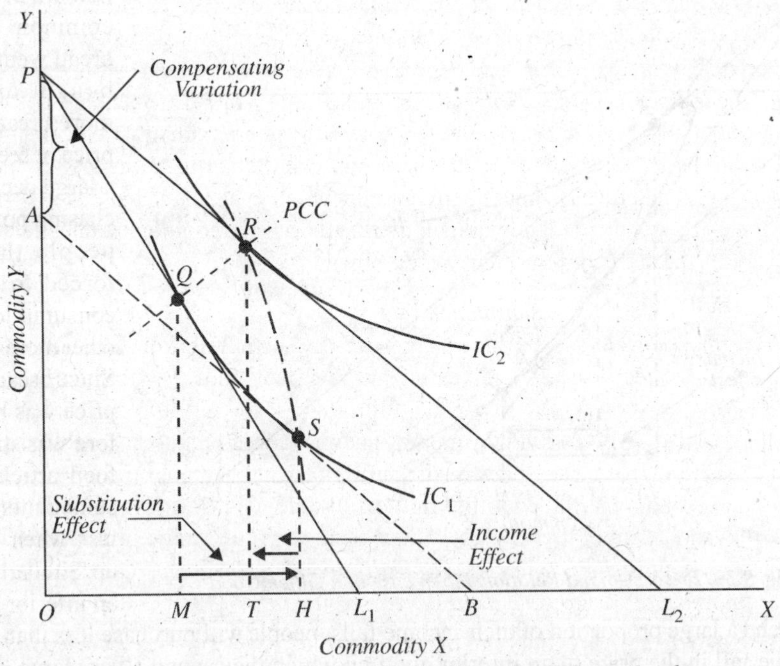

Fig. 9.38. *Price-Demand Relationship in Case of an Inferior Good.*

clear that in a majority of inferior goods quantity demanded of the good will vary inversely with price and the Marshallian Law of Demand will hold good. The price-demand relationship, in case of inferior goods having weaker income effect is illustrated in Figure 9.38. It will be seen from Fig. 9.38 that the fall in price of good *X* makes the consumer to shift from equilibrium *Q* to a new equilibrium at *R*. As a result, quantity purchased rises from *OM* to *OT*. But the income effect is negative and is equal to *HT*. If income effect alone was working, it would have caused the consumer to buy *HT* less of good *X*. But substituion effect is universally present and always induces the consumer to buy more of the relatively cheaper good. In Fig. 9.38 substitution effect is equal to *MH* and is greater than negative income effect *HT*. Therefore, the net effect of the fall in price of good *X* is the rise in quantity demanded by *MT*. Hence we conclude that *in case of inferior goods, quantity demanded varies inversely with price when negative income effect is weaker than the substitution effect.* In other words, even in case of inferior goods having weaker income effect, the demand curve will be downward sloping.

Price-Demand Relationship: Giffen Goods or Giffen Paradox. There is a third possibility. This is that there may be some inferior goods for which the negative income effect is strong or large enough to outweigh the substitution effect. In this case, quantity purchased of the good will fall as its price falls and quantity purchased of the good will rise as its price rises. In other words, quantity purchased or demanded will vary directly with price. Now, the income effect can be substantial only when the consumer is spending a very large proportion of his income on the good in question so that when price of the good falls, a good amount of income is released. If that good happens to be inferior good, the income effect will be negative as well as strong and may outweigh the substitution effect so that with the fall in price, the consumer will buy less of the good. *Such an inferior good in which case the consumer reduces its consumption when its price falls and increases its consumption when its price rises is called a Giffen good* named after the British statistician, Sir Robert Giffen, who in the mid-nineteenth century is said to have claimed that when price of cheap common foodstuff like bread went up the people bought and consumed more bread. A rise in the price of bread caused such a large decline in the purchasing power of the poor people that they were forced to cut down the consumption of meat and other more expensive food. Since bread even when its price was higher than before was still the cheapest food article, people consumed more of it and not less when its price went up. Similarly, when price of an inferior good on which people spend a large proportion of their income falls, people will purchase less than before. This is because the fall in the price of an inferior good on which they spend a very large portion of their income causes such a large increase in their purchasing power that creates a large negative income effect. They will therefore reduce the consumption of that good when its price falls since large negative income effect outweighs the substitution effect.

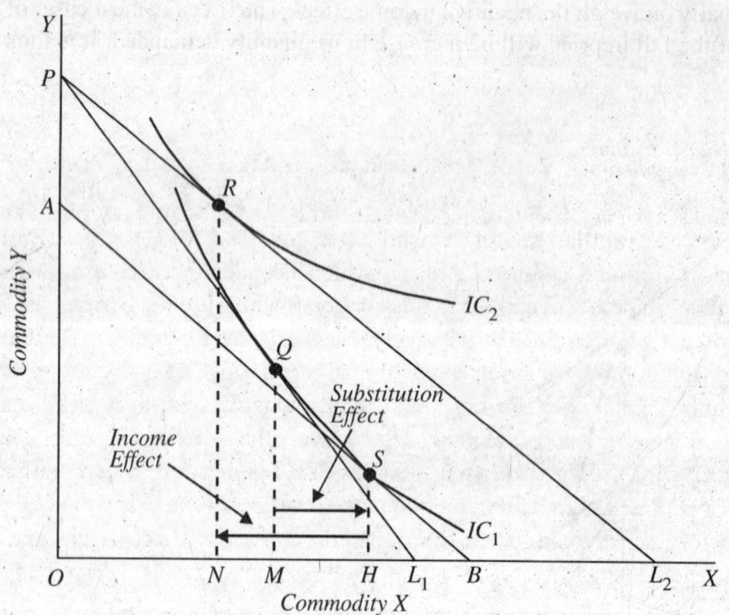

Fig. 9.39. *Price-Demand Relationship in case of a Giffen Good*

The price-demand relationship in case of a Giffen good is illustrated in Fig. 9.38. With a certain given price-income situation depicted by the budget line *PL*, the consumer is initially in equilibrium at *Q* on indifference curve IC_1. With a fall in the price of the good, the consumer shifts to point *R* on indifference Curve IC_2. It will be seen From Fig. 9.39 that with the fall in price and, as a result, the shift of the price line from PL_1 to PL_2 the consumer reduces his consumption of the good *X* from *OM* to *ON*. This is the net effect of the negative income effect which is here equal to *HN* which induces the consumer to buy less of good *X* and the substitution effect which is equal *MH* which induces the consumer to buy more of the good. Since the negative income effect *HN* is greater than the substitution effect *HM*, the net effect is the fall in quantity purchased of good *X* by *MN* with the fall in its price. Thus, *the quantity demanded of a Giffen good varies directly with price. Therefore, if a demand curve showing price-demand relationship, is drawn it will slope upward.*

Thus, *the quantity demanded of a Giffen good* varies directly with price. For a good to be a Giffen good, the following three conditions are necessary:[4]

(1) The good must be inferior good with a large negative income effect;
(2) The substitution effect must be small; and
(3) The proportion of income spent upon the inferior good must be very large.

Three Demand Theorems Based on Indifference Curve Analysis

It follows from above that, indifference curve analysis enables us to derive a more general law of demand in the following composite form, consisting of three demand theorems to which the Marshallian law of demand constitutes a special case.[5]

(*a*) The quantity demanded of a good varies inversely with price when the income effect is positive or nil.

(*b*) The quantity demanded of a good varies inversely with price when the income effect for the good is negative but is weaker than the substitution effect.

(*c*) The quantity demanded of a good *varies directly with price* when the income effect for the good is negative and this negative income effect of a change in price is larger than the substitution effect.

In the case, (*a*) and (*b*) the Marshallian law of demand holds good and we get a downward sloping demand curve. The case (*a*) applies to normal goods in which income effect and substitution effect work *in the same direction*. The case (*b*) applies to inferior goods which are not Giffen goods. When the third case occurs, we get a Giffen good of positively sloping demand curve. Marshallian law of demand does not hold true in the third case. Marshall mentioned a Giffen good case as an exception to his law of demand. Thus the indifference curve analysis is superior to Marshallian analysis in that it yields a more general law of demand which covers the Giffen-good case. The explanation for the occurrence of a Giffen good is that in its case the negative income effect outweighs the substitution effect. Since Marshall ignored the income effect of the change in price, he could not provide a satisfactory explanation for the reaction of the consumer to a change in price of a Giffen good.

However, it may be pointed out that it is very hard to satisfy the above mentioned third conditions for the occurrence of the Giffen good, namely, the consumer must be spending a very large proportion of his income on an inferior good. Therefore, although Giffen case is theoretically possible the chance of its occurrence in the actual world is almost negligible.[6] This is because consumption of the people is generally diversified so that people spend a small proportion of their income on a single commodity with the result that price-induced income effect even when negative is generally small and cannot therefore outweigh the substitution effect. As mentioned earlier, Marshall believed that quantity demanded in actual practice could vary directly with price, and, as mentioned above, Sir Robert Giffen is said to have actually observed this phenomenon. But there is a controversy about the intrepretation of this so-called Giffen good. But from our analysis it is clear that Giffen good case can occur in theory. As explained above, when negative income effect of the fall in the price of an inferior good is larger than substitution effect we get a positively-sloping demand

---

4. J.R. Hicks, *A Revision of Demand Theory*, p. 66.
5. Tapas Majumdar, *Measurement of Utility*, pp. 74-75.
6. J.R. Hicks, *op.cit*, p. 67.

curve of Giffen good. Thus Giffen good is theoretically quite possible. But, since income effect of the change in price of a single commodity in the real world is small, the negative income effect of the change in price of an inferior good is too weak to outweigh the substitution effect and therefore a Giffen good, although theoretically conceivable, rarely occurs in practice.

DERIVATION OF INDIVIDUAL'S DEMAND CURVE FROM INDIFFERENCE CURVE ANALYSIS

Price consumption curve traces the effect of a change in price on the quantity demanded of a good. But price consumption curve does not directly relate price with quantity demanded. In indifference curve diagram price is not explicitly shown on the *Y*-axis. On the other hand, demand curve directly relates price with quantity demanded, price being shown on the *Y*-axis and quantity demanded on the *X*-axis. A demand curve shows how much quantity of a good will be purchased or demanded at various prices, assuming that tastes and preferences of a consumer, his income, prices of all related goods remain constant. This demand curve showing explicit relationship between price and quantity demanded can be derived from price consumption curve of indifference curve analysis.

In Marshallian utility analysis, demand curve was derived on the assumptions that utility was cardinally measurable and marginal utility of money remained constant with the change in price of the good. In the indifference curve analysis, demand curve is derived without making these dubious assumptions.

Let us suppose that a consumer has got income of ₹ 300 to spend on goods. In Fig. 9.40 money is measured on the *Y*-axis, while the quantity of the good *X* whose demand curve is to be derived is measured on the *X*-axis. An indifference map of a consumer is drawn along with the various budget lines showing different prices of the good *X*. Budget line PL_1 shows that price of the good *X* is ₹ 15 per unit. As price of good *X* falls from ₹ 15 to ₹ 10, the budget line shifts to PL_2. Budget line PL_2 shows that price of good *X* is ₹ 10. With a further fall in price to ₹ 7.5 the budget line takes the position PL_3. Thus PL_3 shows that price of good *X* is Rs. 7.5. When price of good *X* falls to ₹ 6, PL_4 is the relevant budget line. The various budget lines obtained are shown in the column 2 of the following table. Tangency points between the various budget lines and indifference curves, which when joined together by a line constitute the price consumption curve which shows the amounts of good *X* purchased or demanded at various prices. With the budget line PL_1 the consumer is in equilibrium at point Q_1 on the price consumption curve at which the budget line PL_1 is tangent to indifference curve IC_1. In his equilibrium position at Q_1 the consumer is buying *OA* units of the good *X*. In other words, it means that the consumer demands *OA* units of good *X* at price Rs. 15. When price falls to ₹ 10 and thereby the budget line shifts to PL_2, the consumer comes to be in equilibrium at point Q_2 of the price-consumption curve where the budget line PL_2 is tangent to indifference curve IC_2. At Q_2, the consumer is buying *OB* units of good *X*. In other words, the consumer demands *OB* units of the good *X* at price ₹ 10. Likewise, with budget lines PL_3 and PL_4, the consumer is in equilibrium at points Q_3 and Q_4 of price consumption curve and is demanding *OC* units and *OD* units of good *X* at price Rs. 7.5 and ₹ 6 respectively. It is thus clear that from the price consumption curve we can get information which is required to draw the demand curve showing directly the amounts demanded of the good *X* against various prices. With the above information we draw up the demand schedule in the table given as follows:

Demand Schedule

Price of good X ₹	*Budget Line*	*Quantity Demanded*
15	PL_1	*OA*
10	PL_2	*OB*
7.5	PL_3	*OC*
6	PL_4	*OD*

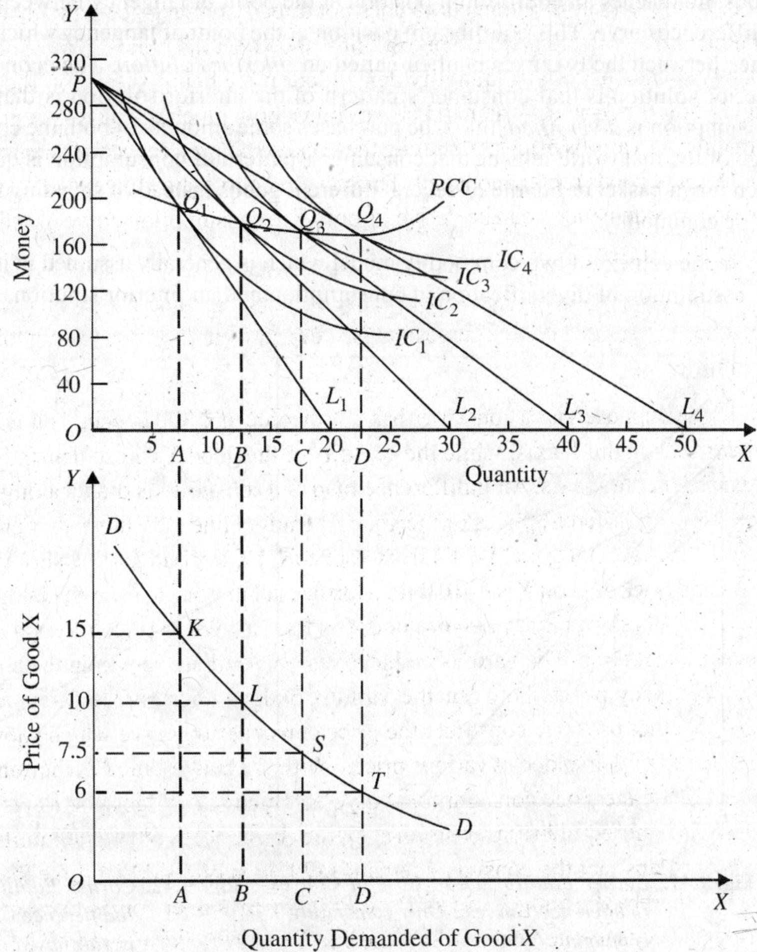

Fig. 9.40. *Derivation of Individual's Demand Curve.*

The adjoining demand schedule which has been derived from the indifference curve diagram can be easily converted into a demand curve with price shown on the *Y*-axis and quantity demanded on the *X*-axis. It is easier to understand if this demand curve is drawn rightly below the indifference curve diagram. This has been done so in Fig. 9.40. In the diagram at the bottom, on the *X*-axis the quantity demanded is shown as in indifference curves diagram in top pannel, but on the *Y*-axis in the diagram at the bottom *price per unit* of the good *X* is shown instead of total money. In order to obtain the demand curve, various points *K*, *L*, S and *T* representing the demand schedule of the above table are plotted. By joining the points *K*, *L*, *S* and *T* we get the required demand curve *DD*. In most cases the demand curve of individuals will slope downward to the right, because as the price of a good falls both the substitution effect and income effect pull together in extending the demand of the good. Even when the income effect is negative, the demand curve will slope downward to the right if the substitution effect is strong enough to overwhelm the negative income effect. Only when the negative income effect is powerful enough to outweigh the substitution effect can the demand curve slope upward to the right instead of sloping downward to the left.

Consumer's Equilibrium : Corner Solution

When a consumer's preferences are such that he likes to consume some amount of both the goods, he reaches an equilibrium position at the point of tangency between the budget line and his indifference curve. This equilibrium position at the point of tangency which lies within commodity space between the two axes is often called an *interior solution*. The economic implication of the interior solution is that consumer's pattern of the interior solution is that consumer's pattern of consumption is *diversified*, tht is, he purchases some amounts of both the commodities. Our knowledge of the real world tells us that consumer's pattern of consumption is quite diversified and they often buy a basket or bundle of several different goods instead of spending their entire income on a single commodity.

In the context of two commodity model which is generally assumed in indifference curve analysis, assumption of diversification in consumption and an interior solution, which implies that consumer purchases some amount of both goods, is correct. However, in the real world of many commodities we often find that a typical consumer does not buy positive amounts of all the goods and services available in the market. In fact, a typical consumer buys only a small number of goods available in the market. How to explain this real world phenomenon ?

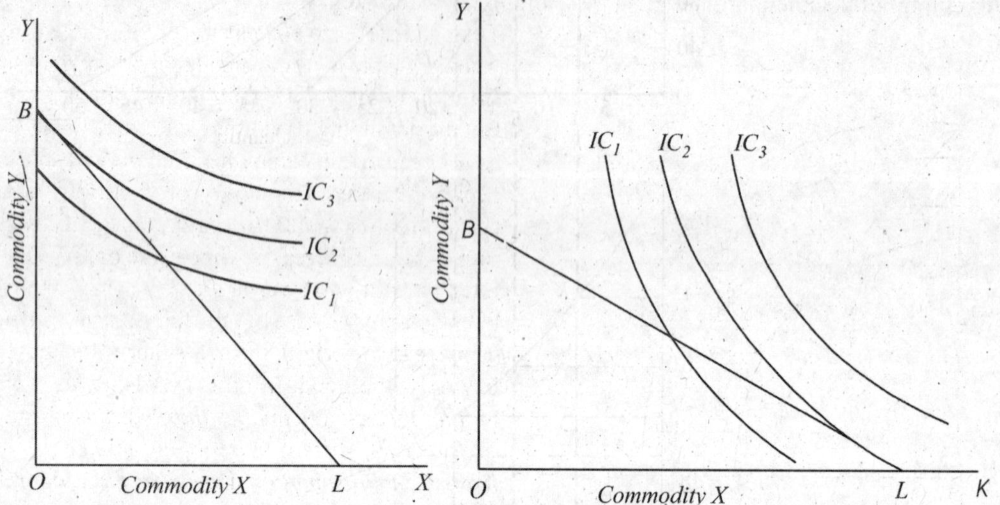

Fig. 9.41. *Corner Equilibrium in Case of Convex Indifference Curves : Only commodity Y is bought.*

Fig. 9.42. *Corner Equilibrium in Case of Convex Indifference Curves : Only commodity X is purchased.*

Convex Indifference Curves and Corner Equilibrium

The reason for not purchasing a commodity by a consumer may be that the price or opportunity cost of that particular commodity may be too high for him. One may like to have a Maruti car, air conditioner or a colour TV, but may not actually have them on account of their prices being too high. The indifference curve analysis enables us to explain even this phenomenon. Consider Figure 9.41, where indifference map between goods *X* and *Y* and budget line *BL* are such that the interior solution is not possible and consumer in its equilibrium position at point *B* will not consume any quantity of commodity *X*. This is because as seen in the Figure 9.41 the price of commodity *X* is so high that budget line is steeper than the indifference curves between the two commodities. In economic terms it means that the price or opportunity cost of commodity *X* in the market is greater than the marginal rate of substitution of *X* for *Y* which indicates willingness to pay for the commodity *X*. The price of goods *X* is so high as compared to marginal rate of substitution (willingness to pay for *X* or the marginal valuation of the first unit of the commodity *X* that the consumer does not purchase even one unit of the commodity *X* ($P_x/P_y > MRS_{xy}$). Thus the consumer maximises his satisfaction or is in equilibrium at the corner point *B* where he buys only commodity *Y* and none of commodity *X*. Thus we have a corner solution for consumer's equilibrium.

On the other hand, in Figure 9.42 the indifference map between the two goods is such that the budget line *BL* is less steep than the indiffrence curves between the two goods so that the $MRS_{xy} > P_x/P_y$ for all levels of consumption along the budget line *BL*. Therefore, he maximizes his satisfaction at the corner point *L* where the buys only commodity *X* and none of *Y*. In this case price of commodity *Y* and willingness to pay (*i.e. MRS*) for it are such that he does not consider it worth while to purchase even one unit of it.

Corner Equilibrium and Concave Indifference Curves

As said above, indifference curves are usually convex to the origin. Convexity of indifference curves implies that the marginal rate of substitution of *X* for *Y* falls as more of *X* is substituted for *Y*. Thus, indifference curves are convex to the origin when principle of diminishing marginal rate of substitution holds good which is generally the case. But the possibility of indifference curves being concave to the origin cannot be ruled out in some exceptional cases. Concavity of the indifference curves implies that the marginal rate of substitution of *X* for *Y* increases when more of *X* is substituted for *Y*. It will be clear from the analysis made below that in the case of indifference curves being concave to the origin, the consumer will choose or buy only one good. In other words, *concavity of indifference curves implies that the consumer has a distaste for variety, that is, does not like diversification in consumption*. However, distaste for variety cannot be considered a normal or model behaviour, so we regard convexity to be the general case. But when consumer have a distaste for variety and diversification the case of concave indifference curves will occur.

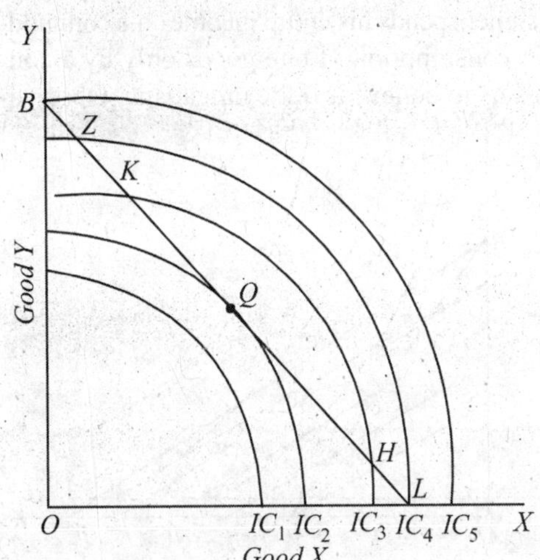

Fig. 9.43. *Consumer Equilibrium in Case of Concave Indifference Curves*

In case of concave indifference curves, the consumer will not be in equilibrium at the point of tangency between budge line and indifference curve, that is, in this case interior solution will not exist. Instead, we would have *corner solution* for consumer's equilibrium. Let us take Fig. 9.43 where indifference curves are shown to be concave. The given budget line *BL* is tangent to the indifference curve IC_2 at point *Q*. But the consumer cannot be in equilibrium at *Q* since by moving along the given budget line *BL* he can get on to higher indifference curves and obtain greater satisfaction than at *Q*. Thus, by moving to *K* on the given budget line *BL*, he will get more satisfaction than at *Q* since *K* lies on a higher indifference curve than *Q*. He can increase his satisfaction still more by moving to point *Z* on the budget line *BL*.

Thus, as he moves upward from tangency point Q on the budget line his satisfaction will go on increasing until he reaches the extremity point B. Likewise, if from Q he moves downward on the budget line, he will get on to higher indifference curves and his satisfaction will go on increasing till he reaches the other extremity point L. In these circumstances the consumer will choose only one of two goods: he will buy either X or Y depending upon whether L or B lies on the higher indifference curve. In the situation depicted in Fig. 9.43 point B lies on a higher indifference curve than point L. Therefore, the consumer will choose only Y and will buy OB of Y. It should be carefully noted that at B the budget *line is not tangent to the indifference curve* I_5 *even though the consumer is here in equilibrium*. Thus, in case of concave indifference curve, we have a corner solution to consumer's equilibrium. It is clear that when a consumer has concave indifference curves, he will succumb to monomania, that is, he will consume only one good.

Conclusion

In our analysis above, we have shown that corner solution of consumer's equilibrium is possible even when his indifference curves between goods are convex. It is worth noting that *in case of convex indifference curves, corner equilibrium is however not inevitable; it occurs only when price of a commodity is too high as compared to the marginal rate of substitution of even the first unit of the commodity. However, when the indifference curves are concave, consumer's equilibrium will inevitably be a corner solution.* This implies that more of commodity X a consumer has the more useful or significant in terms of satisfaction an extra unit of it becomes. Therefore, the concave indifference curves do not seem to be plausible or realistic. Now, as seen above, the concavity of indifference curves for a consumer implies that the consumer spends his entire income on a commodity and therefore buys only one commodity. However, consumption of one goods only by a consumer which the concavity of indifference curves leads us to believe is quite unrealistic. Observations in the real world reveal that consumers do not spend their entire income on a single commodity and in fact purchase a multitude of different goods and services. This rejects the existence of concave indifference curves.

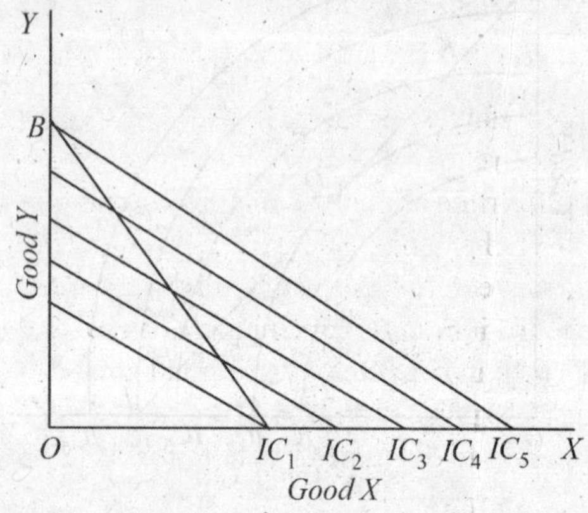

Fig. 9.44. *Corner Equilibrium in Case of Perfect Substitutes*

Our anyalsis of inevitability of corner equilibrium in case of concave indifference curves provides us an important *economic rationale for indifference curves being convex rather than concave*. If indifference curves were predominantly concave the consumers would spend their entire income on a single commodity alone and thus consume only one commodity. This is quite inconsistent with the observed behaviour of consumers. This reinforces our belief that indifference curves of consumers are generally convex.

Corner Solution in Case of Perfect Substitutes and Perfect Complements

Another case of corner solution to the consumer's equilibrium occurs in case of perfect substitutes. As seen above, indifference curves for perfect substitute are linear. In their case too, *tangency or interior solution for consumer's equilibrium is not possible since the budget line cannot be tangent to a point of the straight-line indifference curve of substitutes.* In this case budget line would cut the straight-line indifference curves. Two possibilities can be visualised: either the slope of the budget line BL can be greater than the slope of indifference curves, as in Fig. 9.44 or the slope of the budget line can be less than the slope of indifference curves, as in Fig. 9.45. If the slope of the **budget line is greater than the slope of indifference curves,** B would lie on a higher indifference curve than L and therefore the consumer will buy only Y. If the slope of the budget line is less than the slope of indifference curves as in Fig. 9.45, L would lie on a higher indifference curve than B and the consumer will buy only X. It should be noted that in these cases too, the consumer will not be in equilibrium at any point between B and L on the budget line since in case of Figure 9.44 of all the points on the given budget line extremity point B would lie on the highest possible indifference curve and in case of Figure 9.45 of all the points of the budget line extremity point L would lie on the highest possible indifference curve. It is thus manifest that *even in case of perfect substitutes, the consumer will succumb to monomania* and equilibrium will be achieved at a corner point.

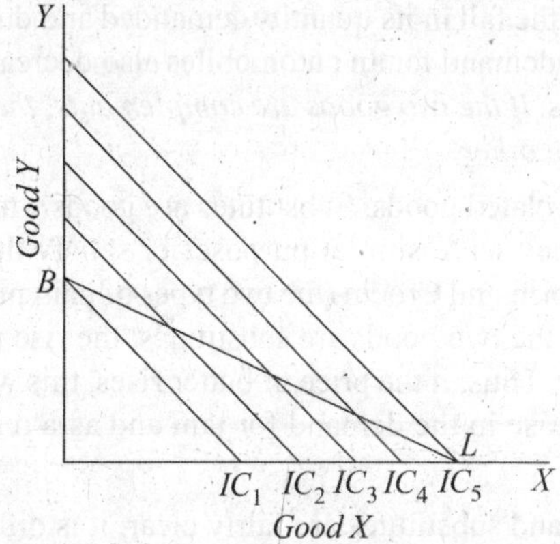

Fig. 9.45. *Corner Equilibrium in Case of Perfect Substitutes*

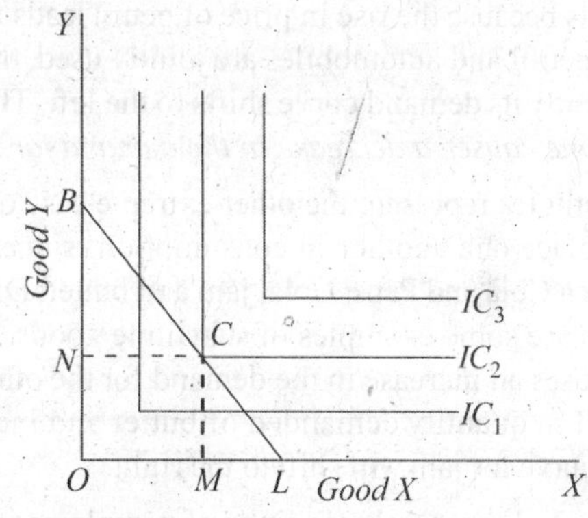

Fig. 9.46. *In case of perfect complementary equilibrium exists at the corner of an indifference curve.*

Another non-normal case is of *perfect complementary goods*, which is depicted in Figure 9.46. Indifference curves of perfect complementary goods have a right-angle shape. In such a case the equilibrium of the consumer will be determined at the corner point of the indifference curve through which the budget line passes. At no other point of the indifference curve of perfect complementary goods, equilibrium is possible. In Figure 9.46 given the budget line BL the consumer will be in equilibrium at the corner point C on indifference curve IC_2 and consumer will buy OM of X and ON of Y. It should be noted, in strict mathematical sense, point C in Fig. 9.46 is not a tangency point as slope of IC_2 at point C is not well defined. Thus, even in case of perfectly complementary goods tangency solution to consumer's equilibrium is not achieved.

EXERCISE : *Is tangency between an indifference curve and the budget line a necessary condition for a bundle to be an optimal. Substantiate your answer through the following situations*:

(1) *kinked indifference curves, and*

(2) *strictly convex preferences leading to a corner optimum.*

Tangency between an indifference curve and budget line is not a necessary condition for consumer's equilibrium. This is firstly because even in case of *convex indifference curves* a consumer *may be in equilibrium at the corner* where he buys only one commodity as we have seen in Figure 9.41 and 9.42 where the shopes of budget line are no where equal to the slopes of indifference curves in any interior combination of goods. Secondly, we have seen in case of perfect complements in whose case indifference curves are kinked, the consumer is in equilibrium at the corner or kink of the indifference curve and consumer's equilibrium is not a tangency solution as slope of a corner or kink point is not well-defined (see Fig. 9.46).

COMPLEMENTS AND SUBSTITUTES

An important use of indifference curves is to explain complements and substitutes in a better way. It will be recalled that complements and substitutes represent the case of related goods. Whenever, a demand curve for a good is drawn it is assumed that the other things such as income, consumer preferences, the prices of other goods remain constant because they also affect the demand for a particular good. Complements are those goods which are used jointly in consumption so that their consumption increases or decreases simultaneously. Pen and ink, right shoe and left shoe, automobile and petrol, typewriter and typists, sauce and hamburger are some examples of complements. If the price of petrol rises, it affects the demand for automobiles such as car, scooters etc. This is because the rise in price of petrol leads to the fall in its quantity demanded and due to the fact that petrol and automobiles are jointly used, the demand for an automobiles also decreases and consequently its demand curve shifts to the left. Thus, *if the two goods are complements, the rise in price of one causes a decrease in the demand for the other.*

Substitutes represent the other extreme case of related goods. Substitutes are goods which can easily replace one another in consumption, since they serve similar purposes or satisfy the same want. Coca Cola and Pepsi Cola, jam and butter. Disprin and Crocin (the two types of pain pills), tea and cofee are some examples of substitute goods. If the two goods are substitutes, the rise in price of one causes an increase in the demand for the other. Thus, if the price of butter rises, this will lead to the fall in quantity demanded of butter and increase in the demand for jam and as a result the demand curve for jam will shift to the right.

Though the general meanings of complements and substitutes are fairly clear, it is difficult to define them in theoretical terms in an unambiguous manner. Marshall did not give any definitions of substitute and complementary goods. However, before Marshall, Edgeworth and Pareto had provided the definitions of substitute and complementary goods in terms of marginal utility. According to Edgeworth-Pareto definitions, "*Y is a complementary with X in the consumer's budget if an* increase in the supply of *X* (*Y* constant) raises the marginal utility of *Y*; *Y* is competitive with *X* (or a substitute for *X*) if an increase in the supply of *X* (*Y* constant) lowers the marginal utility of *Y*"[7]

From above Edgeworth-Pareto definition, it follows that assuming marginal utility of money remains constant if the price of good *X* falls and consequently the quantity demanded of good *X* increases, this will bring about an increase in the marginal utility of good *Y* if goods *X* and *Y* are complementary, and will therefore bring about increase the demand for *Y*. On the contrary, if goods *X* and *Y* are substitutes, according to Edgeworth-Pareto definition, the fall in the price of good *X* and consequently the increase in the quantity demanded of *X* will lower the marginal utility of *Y* and thereby bring about a decline in the demand for *X*. Thus, it is in this way that Edgeworth and Pareto explained the demanded for inter-related goods–complementary and substitute goods.

However, J.R. Hicks, the pioneer of indifference curve analysis of demand, criticized Edgeworth-Pareto definition of complements and substitutes. According to him, Edgeworth-Pareto definition of complementary and substitute goods is based on the assumption that utility is cardinally measurable. But Pareto regarded the utility to be immeasurable in cardinal or quantitative sense. Therefore, Pareto contradicted himself by defining complementary and substitute goods, in terms of measurable utility. Thus, according to Hicks, "Edgeworth-Pareto definition sins against Pareto's own principle of the immeasurability of utility. The distinction between complemetary and competitive goods will differ according to the arbitrary measure of utility which is adopted."[8]

Hicksian Explanation of Complementary and Substitute Goods

With indifference curves analysis of demand in which price effect was split up into substitution

7. J.R. Hicks, *Value and Capital*, p. 42
8. *Op., cit.*, p.43

effect and income effect, Hicks was able to explain in a satisfactory way the cases of substitute and complementary goods. As seen above, before Hicks, substitutes and complementary goods were generally explained in terms of *total price effect.* According to Hicks, if income effect is taken into account, then even if with the fall in price of *X*, the quantity demanded of good *Y* may also increase even though the good *Y* may be substitute or competitive good. Suppose with the fall in price of good *X*, there is a large income effect which more than offsets the substitution effect. Income effect of the fall in price of good *X* tends to increase the quantity demanded of good *Y* (as also of the good *X*) and the substitution effect of the fall in price of *X* works in favour of *X* (that is, tends to increase its quantity demanded) and against good *Y* (that is, tends to reduce its quantity demanded). When this income effect for *Y* is stronger than substitution effect, then the quantity demanded of *Y* increases as a result of the fall in price of *X*, even though the two may be substitute goods. Therefore, effect for the commodity *Y* which has become relatively dearer due to the fall in price of good *X*, the purchases of both goods *X* and *Y* increase as a result of the fall in price of good *X*. Thus, on the basis of total price effect, the goods would be described as complements, even though they are in fact substitute goods. Therefore, according to Hicks, goods can be classified as substitutes or complements more accurately by reference to the substitution effect or preference function alone. Hence, *in the opinion of Hicks, we can define substitute and complementary goods correctly and precisely only in a situation when we have eliminated the income effect of the price change by making a compensating variation in income.* When with a change in price compensating variation in income is also made, the effect which remains is the substitution effect.

Since indifference curve analysis splits up the price effect into income and substitution effects, it is greatly helpful in analysing the relations of substitution and complementarily. Take two goods *X* and *Y*. If the price of good *X* falls, price of *Y* remaining constant, the quantity demanded of good *X* will increase due to the substitution effect and income effect (we suppose that good *X* is not an inferior good). Now, if after the income of the consumer is reduced by compensating variation in income so that with reduced price of good *X* he is no better off than before, the quantity demanded of *X* increases and the quantity demanded of *Y* declines, then good *Y* is a substitute for *X*. In this case due to the relative fall in its price, good *X* has been substituted for good *Y* and because of compensating variation in income, consumer is no better off than before.

Now, if the price of good *X* falls and after making compensation variation in income, the quantity demanded of *X* increases due to the substitution effect and if with it the quantity demanded of *Y* also increases, then *Y* is complement of *X*. Thus, in this case of complements, the quantity purchased of both the goods increases and *both substitute some other good.* Consumer is no better off than before, since compensating variation in income having been made, the quantities purchased of two complementary goods increase due to the substitution effect alone. In view of the above analysis, Professor Hicks defines the substitutes and complements in the following way :

"*I shall say Y is a substitute of X if a fall in the price of X leads to a fall in the consumption of Y; Y is a complement of X if a fall in the price of X leads to a rise in the consumption of Y; a compensating variation in income being made of course in each case.* Thus, a fall in the price of X, combined with a compensated variation in income, which must tend to increase the consumption of *X* itself (by the first substitution theorem), will increase the consumption of complements, but diminish the consumption of substitutes."[9]

We have been above that the type of relation of substitutability or complementarity depends on the substitution effect. To determine the substitution effect is quite simple if there are only two commodities on which the consumer has to spend his money income. We know that a fall in the price of good *X* always leads to the substitution of *X* for the other goods; and if *Y* was the only other goods available to the consumer, then the substitution effect of the fall in price of good *X* must

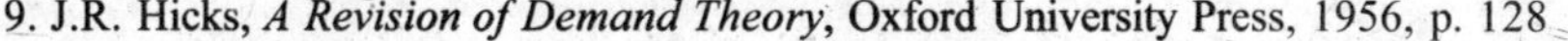

9. J.R. Hicks, *A Revision of Demand Theory*, Oxford University Press, 1956, p. 128

necessarily reduce the quantity demanded of *Y*. However, when there are more than two goods, a fall in the price of good *X* may not reduce the quantity demanded of *Y*; it may in fact increase the quantity purchased of good *Y*, if the two goods *X* and *Y* happen to be complements. Here the two goods *X* and *Y* are substituted for *some other things*.

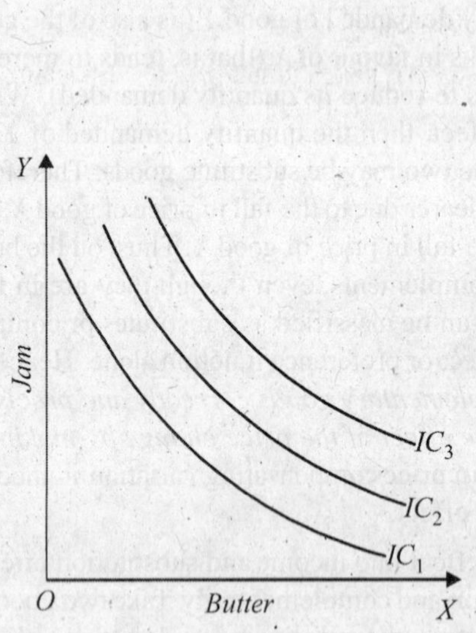

Fig. 9.47. *Close Substitutes*

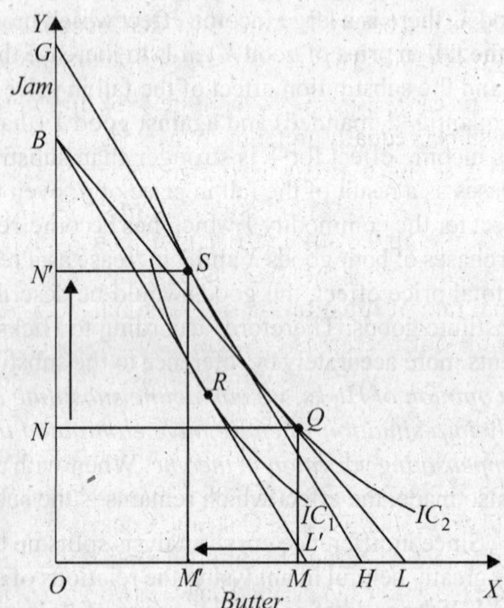

Fig. 9.48. *Close Substitutes : A large replacement of one good by another resulting from a small change in relative price.*

From the above description, it is clear that the definition and proper analysis of substitutes and complementary goods require at least three goods. That is why J.R. Hicks in his *value and Capital* defined them by taking three commodities, *X*, *Y* and money and in terms of the concept of marginal rate of substitution. It should be remembered that money stands for all other goods lumped together and is known as a *composite commodity*.

However, in order to keep our analysis simple we confine ourselves to depict and explain substitutes and complements taking two goods case which tables us to explain them with two dimensional indifference curves. We first take up substitutes for our analysis.

Analysis of Substitutes with Indifference Curve

As mentioned above, the indifference curves of substitute goods are nearly linear, that is, they have a slight convexity. Jam and butter, *HCL* computers and Wipro computers, wheat and rice, Kashmiri apples and H.P. apples are some examples of good substitutes. The indifference curves between two substituttes, jam and butter, and drawn in Figure 9.47, which are nearly linear with a very small degree of convex curvature. In this case of chose substitutes a very small change in the relative price of one good leads to a relatively large change in quantity demanded of the other. Consider Figure 9.45. Suppose to begin with, budget constraint and price ratio of two goods, jam and butter, are such that we have a budget line *BL*. As will be seen from Figure 9.48, the budget line is tangent to the indifference curve IC_2 at point *Q* and accordingly demand *OM* of butter and *ON* of jam. Now suppose that price of butter rises slightly so that the budget line rotates and attains the new position *BL'*. In order to find out the true degree of substitutability, we need to increase the income of the individual to compensate him for the rise in price (that is, to increase his income equal to compensating variation, as has been suggested by J.R. Hicks). Thus, if following the rise in price of butter, if his income is raised by *BG* in terms of jam (see Figure 9.48) so that the budget line representing new price ratio shifts from *BL'* to *GH*. With budget line *GH* he reaches in equilibrium position at point *S* indicating that with the slight rise in price of butter and after the compensating variation in income has been made the individual substitutes a large quantity *NN'* of jam for *MM'* of butter. This shows that the two goods, jam and butter, are close substitutes.

In case of perfect substitutes, the indifference curves are parallel straight lines because the consumers equally prefer the two goods and is willing to exchange one good for the other at a constant rate. As one moves along the straight-line indifference curve of perfect substitutes, marginal rate of substitution of one good for the other remains constant.

Examples of goods that are perfect substitutes are not difficult to find in the real world. For example, Dalda and Rath Vanaspati, two different brands of cold drink such as Pepsi Cola and Coca Cola, two different brands of tooth paste (such as Colgate and Binaca), two different brands of butter with equal quality and fat content. It is however worth noting that if the price ratio of the two perfect substitute goods differs from the slope of their straight-line indifference curves, there will be a *corner solution* with respect to consumer's equilibrium. That is, the consumer will consume only one good in this case, and not any combination of the two. This is illustrated in Figure 9.45 and where five parallel straight-line indifference curves between two perfect substitute goods have been drawn. If the price-ratio of the two goods *X* and *Y* is represented by the slope of the budget line *BL*, he will be in equilibrium at the corner point *L* which lies on the higher indifference curve IC_5 and will consume commodity *X* alone. On the other hand, if the price ratio of the two commodities is such that the slope of the budget line *BL* is less than the slope of the indifference curve the consumer will be in equilibrium at the corner point *B* which lies on the higher indifference curve IC_3 (as compared to point *L* which lies on lower indifference curve IC_1) and will consume commodity *Y* alone (see Fig. 9.44.

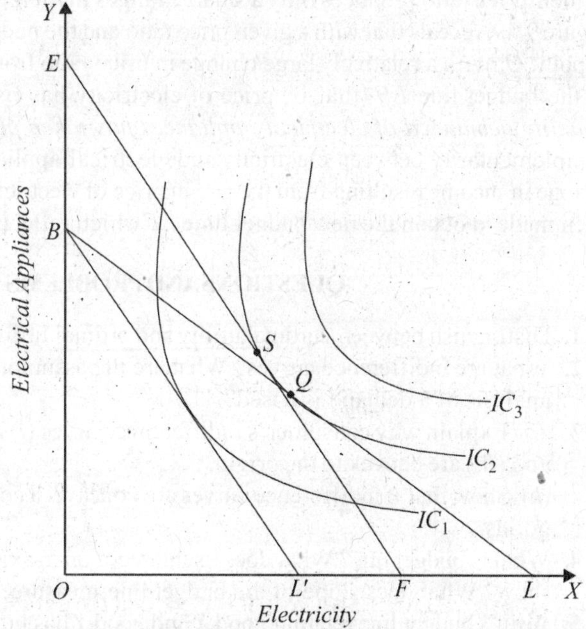

Fig. 9.49. *In case of complementary goods, a large change in price ratio causes only a small change in their quantities demanded..*

Analysis of Complements with Indifference Curves

In indifference curve analysis, the case of *perfect complements* is depicted by L-shaped or right angled indifference curves as shown in Figure 9.49. The two perfect complementary goods are used not only jointly but they are also used in a fixed ratio, that is; one is useless without the required quantity of the other. In other words, perfect complements are those jointly used goods which cannot be substituted for each other at all; the substitution effect of the change in price of one good is zero in case of perfect complements. Right and left shoes, right nd left gloves are important examples of perfect complements. However, it may be noted that as in case of perfect substitutes the perfect complements also do not have any practical significance. This is because consumers never consider right and left shoes, right and left gloves as *separate* goods. They lend to consider *pairs* of shoes or *pairs* of gloves in their demand for them.

But, of practical significances are the cases of two goods which are *strong* (but not perfect) complements. Their indifference curves have appearance as shown in Figure 9.49, where the indifference curves between electricity and electrical appliances with a very high degree of convexity have been drawn. It is worth mentioning that in case of these strong complements relatively large changes in their price ratio produces only a small changes in their quantities used or demanded. A glance at Figure 9.49, reveals that with a given price ratio and the budget constraint, consumer is in equilibrium at point Q. With a relatively large change in price ratio from the slope of budget line BL to the slope of the budget line EF (that is, price of electricity has risen very high), *only a small decline in quantity demanded of electrical appliances has taken place*. This shows the presence of strong complementarity between electricity and electrical appliances. It may be noted that to offset the change in income resulting from the rise in price of electricity, compensating variation in income has been made to obtain the new budget lime EF which reflects the new price ratio.

QUESTIONS AND PROBLEMS FOR REVIEW

1. Distinguish between cardinal utility and ordinal utility? Which is more realistic?
2. What are indifference curves? What are the assumptions on which indifference curve analysis of a demand is based?
3. (*a*) Explain why consumer's indifference curves (*i*) have negative slope, (*ii*) do not intersect and (*iii*) are convex to the origin.

   (*b*) Show that if indifference curves are concave, a consumer will consume only one of the two goods.
4. What is budget line? What does its intercept on X-axis show? What does its intercept on Y-axis show? What does slope of the budget line measure?
5. Amit's budget line relating good X and good Y has intercepts of 50 units of good X and 20 units of good Y. If the price of good X is 12, what is Amit's income? What is the price of good Y? What is the slope of the budget line ?

[**Hints :** Intercept of the budget line on X-axis $= \dfrac{M}{P_x}$ (where M = income and P_x = Price of good X)

$$50 = \frac{M}{12}, \text{ or } \quad M = 600$$

$$\text{Intercept on } Y-\text{axis} = \frac{M}{P_y}$$

$$\text{or} \qquad 20 = \frac{600}{P_y}$$

$$P_y = \frac{600}{20} = 30$$

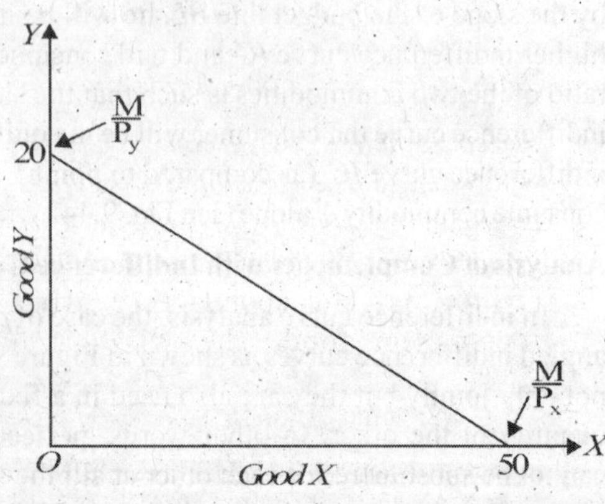

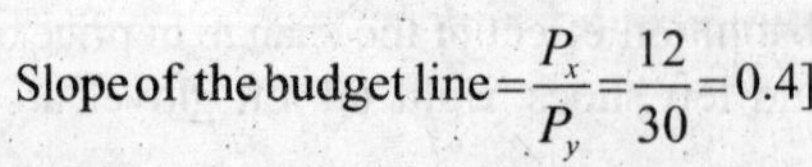

$$\text{Slope of the budget line} = \frac{P_x}{P_y} = \frac{12}{30} = 0.4]$$

6. What is marginal rate of substitution? An indifference curve of Sonia contains the following market baskets of apples and bananas. Each of these baskets gives her equal satisfaction.

Market basket	*Apples*	*Bananas*
1	2	16
2	3	11
3	4	7
4	5	4
5	6	2
6	7	1

Find out marginal rate of substitution of Sonia. How does marginal rate of substitution vary as she consumes more of apples and less of bananas? Give reasons.

7. Explain consumer's equilibrium condition with the help of indifference curve approach. How will a change in consumer's income affect his equilibrium ? *(DU,BA(H), B.Com (H).*

8. Explain why a consumer will choose a market basket so that marginal rate of substitution (*MRS*) equals price ratio.

9. A consumer spends all her income on food and clothing. At the current prices of P_f= ₹ 10 and P_c= ₹ 5, she maximises her utility by purchasing 20 units of food and 50 units of clothing.
(*a*) What is the consumer's income?
(*b*) What is the consumer's marginal rate of substitution of food for clothing at the equilibrium position ?

[**Hints:** (*a*) Income (*M*) can be obtained from budget equation :

$$M = P_f.Q_f + P_c.Q_c$$
$$= 10 \times 20 + 5 \times 50$$
$$= 200 + 250 = ₹450$$

(*b*) Consumer's marginal rate of substitution at the equilibrium point is equal to the ratio of prices of goods. Thus, $MRS_{fc} = \frac{P_f}{P_c} = \frac{10}{5} = 2$

10. *Priya spends all her monthly income of ₹ 5000 on food and clothing. Price food is ₹ 250 and price of clothing is ₹ 100 and her monthly consumption of food is 10 units and that of clothing is 1, that is, 25 units. With this consumption of the two commodities her marginal rate of substitution' of food for clothin is* $MRS_{fc} = \frac{1C}{1F}$. *Is she in equilibrium with this consumption, which commodity she will substitute for the other to reach equilibrium position? Illustrate diagrammatically with indifference curves.*

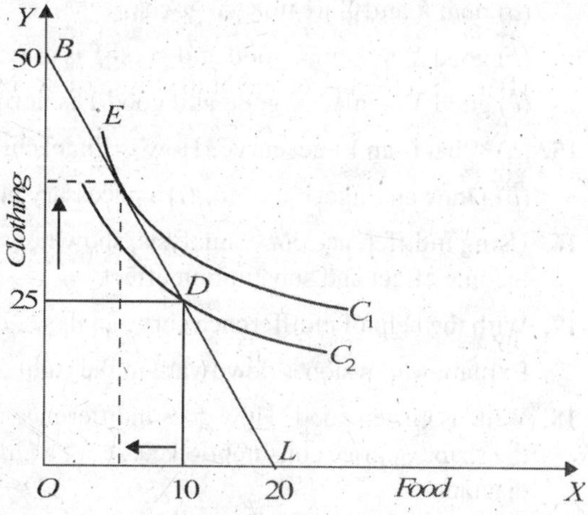

[**Hints :** If she spends for entire income on food, she will have $\frac{5000}{250} = 20$ units of food. Thus the intercept of the budget line on *X*-axis is 20. If she spends her entire income on clothing, she will have $\frac{5000}{100} = 50$ units of clothing. Thus, intercept of the budget line on the Y-axis is 50. With these intercepts we draw the budget line in Figure 2. With present consumption, she is at point like D where the indifference curve is intersecting the budget line BL.

Now, since her MRS_{FC} with present consumption of the two goods at point D is equal to $\frac{1C}{1F}$, she is willing to give up one unit of food for one unit of extra clothing, her satisfaction remaining constant. (Note that *slope of indifference curve* at point D is equal to $\frac{P_F}{P_C} = \frac{250}{100} = \frac{2.5}{1}$. that is, 2.5. Thus, with present consumption of the two commodities at point $D MRS_{FC} < \frac{P_F}{P_C}$.

Therefore, presently she is not in equilibrium position.

Now, since since in the market with the given prices of the two goods, *she can exchange* 1 *unit of food for 2.5 units of clothing* while she is willing to forego 1 unit of food for 1 unit of clothing to keep her satisfaction constant, she will be increasing her satisfaction by consuming less a food and substituting clothing for it. This is because with loss of 1 unit of food she will be having extra 2.5 units of clothing, while only one unit of clothing is sufficient to compensate her for the loss of one unit of food.

11. What is the inferior good? How is it different from normal goods? Show them with the help of indifference curves.

12. Use indifference curves to explain what happends to the demand for an inferior good as consumers's real income increases at constant relative prices. *[C.U.B. Com., (H)1999]*

13. What is price consumption curve? What is the relationship between price consumption curve and price elasticity of demand?

(*b*) Derive demand curve from Price Consumption Curve *[D.U. B.Com., (H)]*

14. What is income consumption curve. Draw indifference curve diagrams showing the income consumption curve in the following case:

(*a*) both *X* and *Y* are normal goods

(*b*) good *X* is normal good and good *Y* is inferior ,

(*c*) good *X* is inferior good and good *Y* is normal good.

15. (*a*) What is an Engel curve? How is Engel curve derived from income consumption curve?

(*b*) Draw an Engel curve for (*i*) a necessary good, (*ii*) luxury good (*iii*) neutral good.

16. Using indifference curve analysis, show how price effect of a commodity is decomposed into income effect and substitution effect. *[D.U.B. Com.(H) 2000; C.U.B. Com., 1998]*

17. With the help of indifference curve analysis, derive demand curve for a normal commodity? Explain why it slopes downward to the right.

18. What is Giffen good? How does indifference curve analysis explain Giffen Paradoix? What is the shape of price consumption curve for a Giffen good? Illustrate it with an indifference curve diagram.

19. Derive demand curve for a Giffen good. Why has it a positive slope? *(D.U.B.com (H) 1996)*

20. What is an inferior good? What is the shape of a demand curve for an inferior good which is not a Giffen good?

21. 'All Giffen' goods are inferior goods but all inferior goods are not Giffen goods." Do you agree? Give reasons. *(D.U. B.Com.(H)2001)*

22. Why is an indifference curve generally convex to the point of orgin ? When will it be :
(*i*) a straight line (*ii*) right-angled (*D.U. B.Com. (H) 2000*)

23. What is compensating variation in income ? Using the concept of compensating variation in income distinguish between income and substitution effects of a fall in price of a commodity with the help of indifference curve technique in case of (*a*) normal good, and (*b*) a Giffen good.

24. (*a*) How does Hicks define substitute and complementary goods ? How do his definitions differ from those given by Edgeworth and Pareto

(*b*) Analyse substitute and complementary goods with Hicksian indifference curve analysis of demand.

25. Differentiate between inferior goods and Giffen goods with the help of indifference curve analysis of demand.

26. An individual's marginal utilities for commodities are given by the following relations :
$MU_x = 40 - 5X$ and $MU_y = 20 - 3Y$.

What is his marginal rate of substitution in consumption at the consumption basket $X=3$, $Y=5$? If $P_x =$ ₹ 5 and $P_y =$ Re. 1, is the basket a consumption equilibrium ?(*DU. BA (H)*).

[**Hints :** $MRS_{xy} = \dfrac{MU_x}{MU_y} = \dfrac{40-5X}{20-3Y}$

Now, given that $X = 3$ and $Y = 5$ we have $MRS_{xy} = \dfrac{40-15}{20-15} = \dfrac{25}{5} = 5$

we have $\dfrac{P_x}{P_y} = \dfrac{5}{1} = 5$

Thus $MRS_{xy} = \dfrac{P_x}{P_Y}$

Thus, the given basket of consumption ($X = 3$ & $Y = 5$) is an equilibrium basket].

27. "Rajeev likes oranges better than bananas". What would be the shape of his indifference curves relating these two goods. Does it mean he will consume only oranges ?

Hint : His greater preference for oranges than bananas implies that with oranges measured on the X-axis and bananas on the Y-axis, his indifference curves will be *vertically inclined* as shown in the adjoining figure. This implies that to forego one unit of orange he requires relatively more bananas to remain on the same indifference curve. This does not mean he will eat only oranges. How many oranges and bananas will he consume depend on the prices of two goods as reflected in the slope of the budget line. If oranges are relatively cheaper than bananas as shown by budget line BL in the adjoining figure he will consume more oranges than bananas. But if oranges are relatively dearer as reflected by the budget line B_1L_1 (dotted), he will

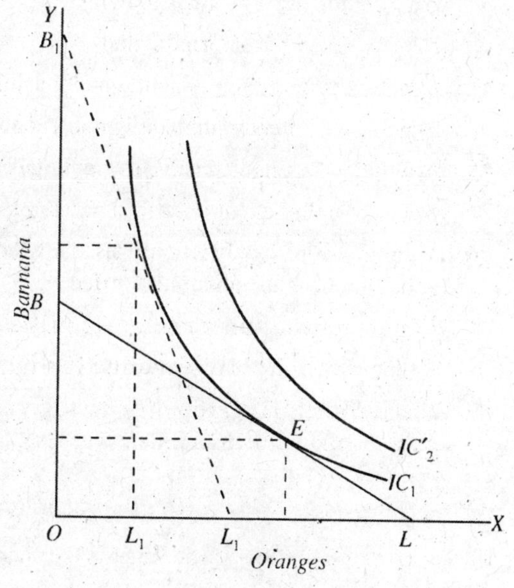

consume relatively less of oranges despite Rajeev's greater liking for them. However, it may be noted that preferences between the two goods as depicted by indifference curves and the slope of the budget line may be such that we get corner solution where he consumes only oranges (see text of the chapter for this case).

28. If we observe an individual to demand less of a good as its price falls, we may conclude that it is an inferior good for him. Do you agree ? Explain *(D.U. BA. (Hons) 1993)*

(**Hint :** When an individual demands less of a good when it price falls, this is the case of a Giffen good. All Giffen goods are inferior goods. Therefore, we can conclude that the good will be inferior good).

29. A consumer is observed to consume only one of two goods available. Illustrate and explain in terms of the indifference curve model when this can happen. Mention in particular how the usual first order condition has to be interpreted in this case. *(D.U. B.A. (Hons.) 1986)*

30. If a consumer's indifference curves are concave, will he consume both the goods in equilibrium ? Why or why not ?

31. If a consumer spends all his income on two goods, can both the goods be inferior ? Explain *D.U. B.A. (Hons) 1997*

32. Assume that consumer's income consumption curve for good *X* is a vertical line. Show that his demand curve for *X* must be downward sloping. *D.U. B.A. (Hons) 2001*

[**Hints.** Vertical income consumption curve indicates that income effect for goods *X* is zero. Since substitution effect is always negative and operates to *increase the quantity* demanded of a good whose *price falls*, the demand curve for good *X* will be downward sloping]

33. Explain using income and substitution effects why Giffen goods have demand curves that slope upward. *DU BA (Hons.) Economics Ist Year 2008*

APPENDIX A TO CHAPTER 9*

INDIFFERENCE CURVES OF GOODS AND BADS

Goods and Bads

We have drawn and explained the indifference curves of commodities which are "goods", that is, desirable objects. If a commodity is 'good', then more of it is preferred to less of it. As seen above, indifference curves between two commodities which are "goods" slope downward and are convex to the origin. However, when for a consumer a commodity is a 'bad', that is, an undesirable object, the more of it will lower his satisfaction. Thus, if a commodity which is bad, less is preferable to more. Pollution, risk, unpleasant work, and illness are some examples of bads. In the case of bads, indifference curves are of different shape. Suppose a bad (for example, pollution) is represented on the X-axis and clothing which is "good" is represented on the Y-axis, then the indifference curve will be sloping upward (that is, will have a positive slope) as displayed in Fig. 9A.1. This is because in this case a movement towards the right along an indifference curve implies more of pollution which will reduce consumer's satisfaction and, therefore, in order to keep his level of satisfaction constant, the quantity of a commodity which is "good" such as clothing will have to be increased. The direction of preference in this case is upward and to the left.

An important application of indifference curve analysis in recent years relates to the problem of *portfolio selection*. Portfolio selection by an individual means his choice of a particular distribution of his wealth among several assets such as equity shares, debentures, real estate, etc. These different

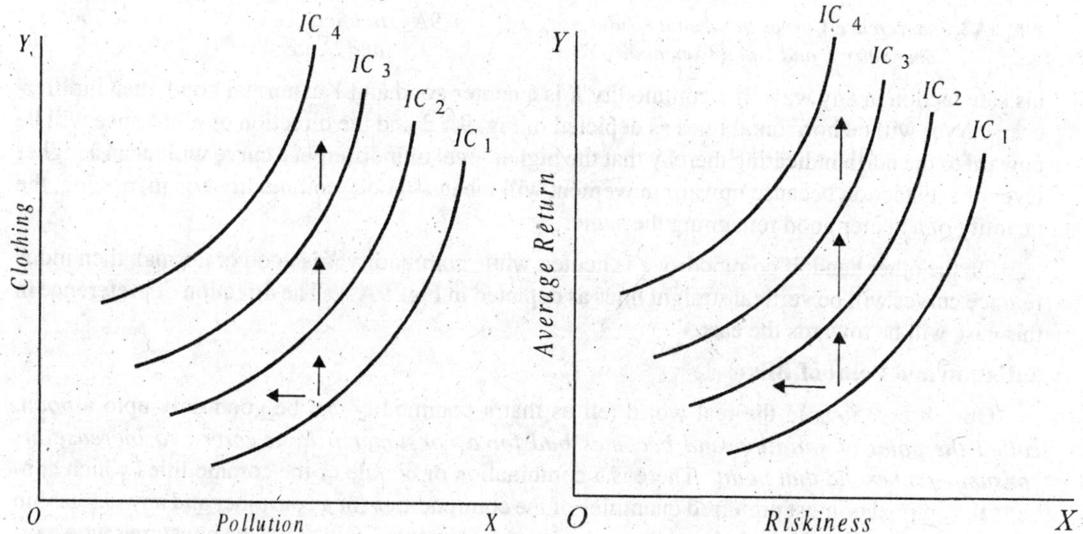

Fig. 9A1. *Indifference Curves between 'Bad' and 'Good'*

Fig. 9A2. Indifference Curves betwee Riskiness (Bad) and Average Return (Good)

assets yield different rates of return and involve varying degree of riskiness. In the analysis of portfolio selection, the *average or mean return* from a portfolio enters as a "good" or a desired object, whereas degree of risk involved enters as a bad or an undesired object. In Figure 9A.2 we depict indifference curves of an investor who wants or prefers a high average return and a low risk. The higher the average return, the higher the satisfaction of the investor; and higher the degree of risk involved in a portfolio, the lower the satisfaction of the investor. Therefore, in this case also, the indifference curve between riskiness (*i.e.*, bad) and rate of return (*i.e.*, a good) slopes upward. This is because as we move rightward satisfaction declines due to greater risk and to compensate for the decline in satisfaction due to greater risk and to keep the level of satisfaction constant, rate of return (*i.e.*, 'good') has to be increased. It may be noted that direction of preference in this case will also be northward and westward as indicated in the diagram.

Neuter. A commodity can be neuter (or a neutral good) in which case the consumer does not care whether he has more or less of that commodity. That is, more or less of a neuter does not affect

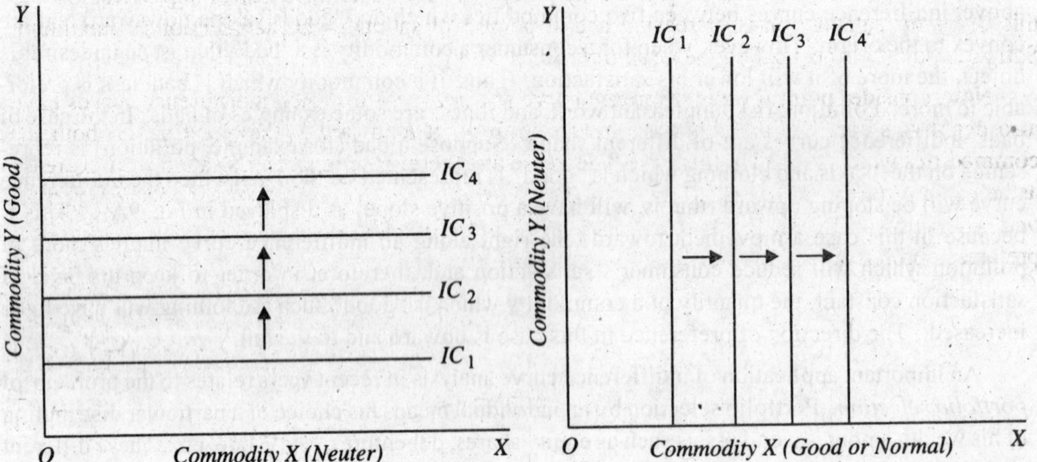

Fig. 9A3. *Indifference Curves between a Neuter Community X and Good Commodity Y*

Fig. 9A4. *Indifference Curves between Good X and Neuter Y.*

his satisfaction in any way. If a commodity *X* is a neuter good and *Y* a normal good, then indifference curves will be horizontal lines as depicted in Fig. 9A.3 and the direction of preference will be upward to the north indicating thereby that the higher level of indifference curve will mean a higher level of satisfaction because upward movement will mean a 'good' commodity *Y* is increasing, the quantity of a neuter good remaining the same.

On the other hand, if commodity *Y* is neuter, while commodity *X* is good or normal, then indifference curves will be vertical straight lines as depicted in Fig. 9A.4. The direction of preference in this case will be towards the east.

Satiation and Point of Bliss

Our observations in the real world tell us that a commodity can be good only upto a *point, called the point of satiation and becomes bad for a consumer if he is forced to increase his consumption beyond that point.* There is a combination or bundle of the commodities which contains the optimal or most preferred quantities of the commodities for a consumer and any increase in the quantity of each of them beyond that best or optimal quantity will make the consumer worse off (that is, will reduce his satisfaction), quantities of other commodities remaining the same. Too much of everything is bad. Suppose, commodity *X* becomes bad beyond the quantity X_1 and commodity *Y* becomes bad beyond the quantity Y_1. Two goods case is represented in Fig. 9A.5 where the *circular indifference curves* between the two commodities *X* and *Y* are drawn. Suppose X_1 and Y_1 are the quantities of two commodities which the consumer considers as the best or optimal quantities beyond which the two commodities become bad. Point S represents these most preferred quantities of the two commodities and is therefore the *point of satiation or bliss.* In zone 1, the portions of indifference curves between the two commodities have negative slope and, therefore, the two commodities are good in this zone.

Let us consider point A in zone 2 which contains more of Y than the quantity regarded optimal or best by our consumer. Beyodn Y_1, the commodity Y becomes bad, that is, his satisfaction from it starts declining. Therefore, in order to keep his satisfaction constant, he has to be compensated by increase in the quantity of X (Note that in zone 2 the quantity of X remains less than X_1 and increase in its quantity is therefore desirable and adds to his satisfaction. In zone 2, indifference curves have positive slope and here while commodity X is too little, the commodity Y is too much. Therefore, in zone 2, the commodity Y becomes bad while the commodity X remains good. It may be further noted that as the consumer moves toward the point S or his indifference curves approach closer to this point, his satisfaction is increasing and at point S of satiation his satisfaction is maximum. Satiation point S is also called the *point of bliss.*

Now, consider point R on indifference curve IC_1 in zone 3 in which indifference curves have also negative slope. As the consumer moves from point R toward S, the quantities of both the commodities which are bad in this zone 3 decrease and therefore counsumer's satisfaction increase as he reaches nearer to the point S of his satiation or bliss. *In this case both the commodities are bad.* The sum and substance of the whole matter is that as a consumer moves nearer to his most preferred combination S, his satisfaction increases.

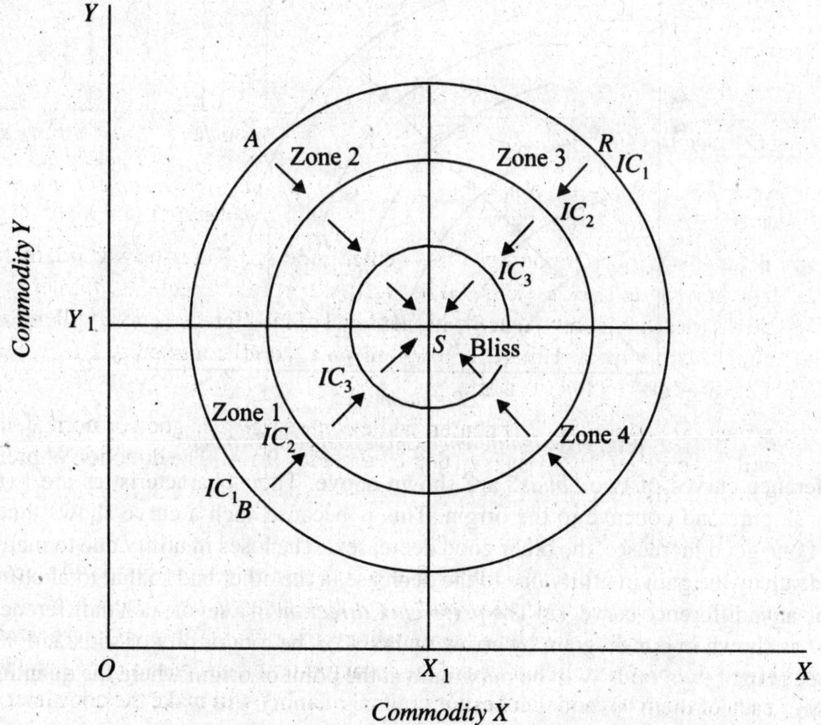

Fig. 9A5. *Difference Zones of Goodness and Badness and Point of Bliss*

In zone 4, whereas the commodity X is more than the desirable quantity X_1, (that is, commodity X becomes bad beyond X_1) commodity Y is less than its optimal quantity. Indifference curves in this region are positively sloping indicating that commodity X being bad in this region increase in its quantity has to be compensated by the increase in the quantity of *Y* which is desirable in this region to keep the level of consumer's satisfaction constant.

It follows from above that a consumer has some optimal or most preferred combination of commodities and closer he is to that combination, the better off he is. The combinations of two commodities, say chocolate and ice cream, which are nearer to the point of satiation or bliss point, lie on higher indifference curves and the combinations lying further away from the satiation point, would lie on lower indifference curves. There will be some optimal combination of chocolate and ice cream which a consumer would like to eat per week. Consumers would not voluntarily like to consume too much of them, that is, more than what they want. Thus, the interesting and relevant region for consumer's choice of commodities is where he has less than optimal quantities of both these commodities. In Fig. 9A.5 this region is represented by zone 1 in which the consumer has less of the two goods than he wants and therefore increase in the quantities of the two goods in this zone will cause an increase in his satisfaction and will move him nearer to the point of satiation.

SOME EXERCISES ON GOODS AND BADS

Exercise - 1: *Draw indifference curves between two economic bads such as pollution and risk. What are special features of such indifference curves ?*

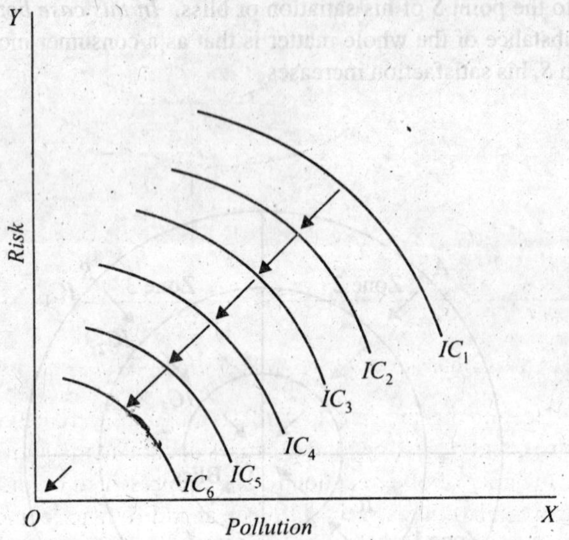

Fig. 9A6. *Indifference Curves between Two bads*

Indifference curves of two "*bads*" are shown above. Their characteristics are : (*i*) they are negatively sloping and concave to the origin. This is because such a curve shows that while the quantity of one good increases, the other good decreases. The loses in utility due to increase in one bad is made up by the gain in utility due to the decrease in the other bad so that total utility remains constant on an indifference curve. (2) The *preference direction* in a set of such indifference curves is *south-west* as shown in our diagram by arrow marks. (3) The total utility or satisfaction in case of indifference map of two '*bads*' will be maximum at the point of origin where the quantities of both bads is zero.

Exercise 2. *Suppose for a consumer, each of the two commodities X and Y is economic 'good' upto a certain level of consumption and beyond that it becomes economic 'bad'. Draw various indifference curves between such commodities. Can you give some example of such commodities ?*

Most of the commodities we consume such as food, sugar, tea, Coca-Cola are 'goods' upto a certain level of consumption, called *point of satiation* and become bad beyond that. This means beyond a limit they cause decline in satisfaction or their marginal utility become negative. The indifference curves of such a goods are shown in Fig. 9A6 given below. Commodity *X* is economic good upto *OQ* quantity which is a *satiation point*. Indifference curves are downward sloping upto

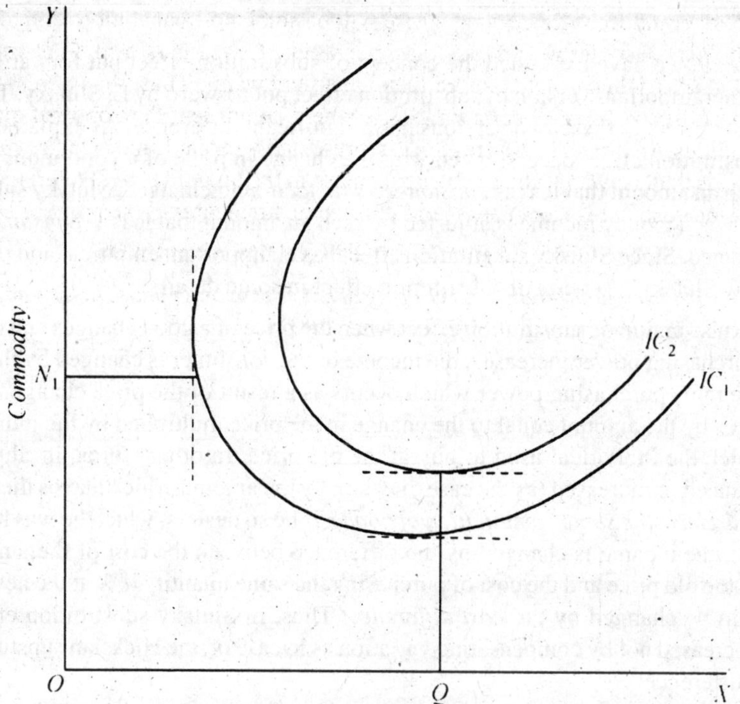

Fig. 9A6. *Both Commodities X and Y are Good up to a certain point*

this satiation quantity. Beyond this they are upward sloping. Indifference curves are upward sloping beyond point *Q* because quantity of *X* beyond *Q* causes decline in total utility which is compensated by the increase in the quantity of other economic good represented on the *Y*-axis which causes the increase in utility so that total utility or satisfaction on an indifference curve remains constant. Similarly, commodity *Y* has positive marginal utility up to *ON* quantity and beyond that it becomes bad. Too much of every thing is bad and therefore most of the goods in the real world will have indifference curves of this shape.

APPENDIX B TO CHAPTER 9*
SLUTSKY SUBSTITUTION EFFECT

In chapter 9, we have explained the concept of substitution effect put forward by J.R. Hicks. There is another important version of substitution effect put forward by E. Slutsky. The treatment of the substitution effect in these two versions has a significant difference. As explained earlier, while Hicksian substitution effect occurs, when with the change in price of a good money income is adjusted by such an amount that leaves *consumer's satisfaction* unchanged, Slutsky substitution effect comes about when money income is adjusted by such an amount that leaves *consumer's purchasing power* unchanged. Since Slutsky substitution effect has an important empirical and practical use, we explain below Slutsky's version of substitution effect in some detail.

In Slutsky's version of substitution effect when the price of a good changes and consumer's real income or purchasing power increases, the income of the consumer is changed by the amount equal to the change in its purchasing power which occurs as a result of the price change. His purchasing power changes by the amount equal to the change in the price multiplied by the :number of units of the good which the individual used to buy at the old price. In other words, in Slutsk's approach, income is reduced or increased (as the case may be), by the amount which leaves the consumer to be just able to *purchase the same combination of goods*, if he so desires, which he was having at the old price. That is, the income is changed by the difference between the cost of the amount of good *X* purchased at the old price and the cost of purchasing the same quantity if *X* at the new price. Income is then said to be changed by the *cost difference*. Thus, in Slutsky substitution effect, income is reduced or increased not by compensating variation as in case of the Hicksian substitution effect but by the cost difference.

Slutsky Substitution Effect For a Fall in Price

Slutsky substitution effect is illustrated in Fig. 9B.1 With a given money income and the given prices of two goods as represented by the price line *PL*, the consumer is in equilibrium at *Q* on the indifference curve IC_1 buying *OM* of X and *ON* of *Y*. Now suppose that price of X falls, price of *Y* and money income of the consumer remaining unchanged. As a result of this fall in price of *X*, the price line will shift to *PL′* and the real income or the purchasing power of the consumer will increase. Now, in order to find out the Slutsky substitution effect, consumer's money income must be reduced by the cost-difference or, in other words, by the amount which will leave him to be just able to purchase the old combination *Q*, if he so desires.

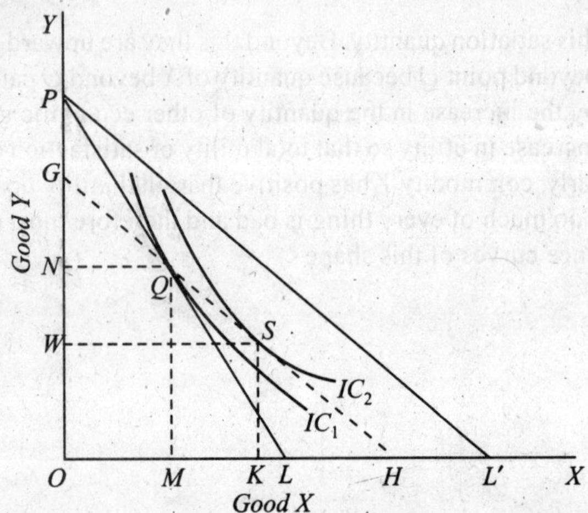

Fig. 9B.1. *Slutsky Substitution Effect (For a Fall in Price)*

* This appendix is meant for B.A (Hons.) and B.Com. (Honours) classes and should therefore be omitted by B.A. (Pass) Course students.

For this, a price line *GH* parallel to *PL′* has been drawn which passes through the point *Q*. It means that income equal to *PG* in terms of *Y* or *L′H* in terms of *X* has been taken away from the consumer and as a result he can buy the combination *Q*, if he so desires, since *Q* also lies on the price line *GH*. Actually, he will not now buy the combination *Q* since *X* has now become relatively cheaper and *Y* has become relatively dearer than before. The change in relative prices will induce the consumer to rearrange his purchases of *X* and *Y*. He will substitute *X* for *Y*. But in this Slutsky substitution effect, he will not move along the same indifference curve IC_1, since the price line *GH*, on which the consumer has to remain due to the new price-income circumstances is nowhere tangent to the indifference curve IC_1. The price line *GH* is tangent to the indifference curve IC_2 at point *S*. Therefore, the consumer will now be in equilibrium at a point *S* on a higher indifference curve IC_2. This movement from *Q* to *S* represents Slutsky substitution effect according to which the consumer moves not on the same indifference curve, but from one indifference curve to another. A noteworthy point is that movement from *Q* to *S* as a result of Slutsky substitution effect is due to the change in relative prices alone, since the effect due to the gain in the purchasing power has been eliminated by making a reduction in money income equal to the cost-difference. At *S*, the consumer is buying *OK* of *X* and *OW* of *Y*; *MK* of *X* has been substituted for *NW* of *Y*. Therefore, Slutsky substitution effect on *X* is the increase in its quantity purchased by *MK* and Slutsky substitution *effect on Y* is the decrease in its quantity purchased by *NW*.

Slutsky Substitution Effect for a Rise in Price

We have graphically explained above Slutsky substitution effect for a fall in price of good *X*. It will be instructive to explain it also for a rise in price of *X*. This is demonstrated in Fig. 9B.2. Initially, the consumer is in equilibrium at point *Q* on the indifference curve IC_1, prices of the two goods and his money income being given. Now suppose that price of good *X* rises, price of *Y* remaining unchanged. As a result of the rise in price of *X*, budget line will shift downward to *PL″* and consumer's real income or purchasing power of his given money income will fall. Further, with this price change, good *X* has become relatively dearer and good *Y* relatively cheaper than before. In order to find out Slutsky substitution effect in this present case, consumer's money income must be increased by the 'cost-difference' created by the price change to compensate him for the rise in price of *X*. In other words, his money income must be increased to the extent which is just large enough to permit him to purchase the old combination *Q*, if he so desires, which he was buying before. For this, a budget line *GH* has been drawn which passes through point *Q*. It will be evident from the figure that, *PG* (in terms of *Y*) or *L″ H* (in terms of *X*) represents 'cost difference' in this case. With budget line *GH* he can buy if he so desires the combination *Q*, which he was buying at the previous price of *X*. But actually he will not buy combination *Q*, since on budget line *GH*, *X* is relatively dearer than before, he will therefore replace some *X* by *Y* (*i.e.*, he will substitute of *Y* for *X*). As is shown Fig. 9B.2, with budget line *GH* he is in equilibrium position at *S* on a higher indifference curve of IC_2 and is buying *OK* of *X* and *OW* of *Y*. *MK* of *X* has been replaced by *NW* of *Y*. Movement from point *Q* to *S* is the result of Slutsky substitution effect; the effect due to the fall in purchasing power has been cancelled by giving him money equal to *PG* of *Y* or *L″ H* of *X*. In this present case of stipulated rise in price of *X*, Slutsky substitution effect on *X* is

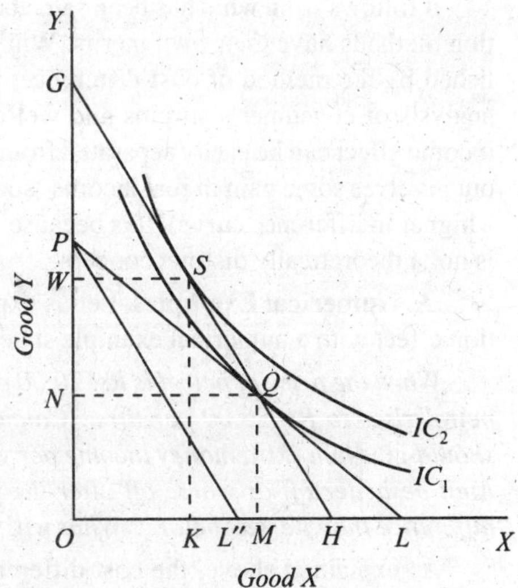

Fig. 9B.2. *Slutsky Substitution Effect (for a rise in price)*

the fall in its quantity brought by *MK* and Slutsky substitution effect an *Y* is the increase in its quantity brought by *NW*.

From the above analysis it is clear that whereas Hicks-Allen substitution effect takes place on the same indifference curve, Slutsky substitution effect involves the movement from one indifference curve to another curve, a higher one. The difference between the two versions of the substitution effect arises solely due to the magnitude of money income by which income is reduced or increased to compensate for the change in income. The Hicksian approach just restores to the consumer his initial level of satisfaction, whereas the Slutsky approach "over-compensates" the consumer by putting him on a higher indifference curve.

Merits and Demerits of Hicksian and Slutsky Methods

Prof. J.R. Hicks points out that the method of adjusting the level of money income by the compensating variation "has the merit that on this interpretation, the substitution effect measures the effect of change in relative price, *with real income constant*, the income effect measures the, effect of the change in real income. Thus the analysis which is based upon the compensating variation is a resolution of the price change into two fundamental economic 'directions', we shall not encounter a more fundamental distinction upon any other route,.[1]

But Slutsky method has a distinct advantage in that it is easier to find out the amount of income equal to the 'cost difference' by which income of the consumer is to be adjusted. On the other hand, it is not so easy to know the compensating variation in income. Thus, the cost-difference method has the advantage of being dependent on observable market data, while for knowing the amount of compensating variation in income, knowledge of indifference curves (that is, tastes and preferences) of the consumer between various combinations of goods is required.

It follows from what has been said above that both the cost-difference and compensating variation methods have their own merits. While the law of demand can be easily and adequately established by the method of cost-difference, method of compensating variation is very useful for the analysis of consumer's surplus and welfare economics. With the help of the cost-difference, the income effect can be easily separated from the substitution effect but the substitution effect so found out involves some gain in real income (since it causes movement from a lower indifference curve to a higher indifference curve). It is because of this that, on cost-difference method, substitution effect is not a theoretically distinct concept.

A. Numerical Examples. Let us explain the concept of cost-difference and Slutsky substitution effect with a numerical example stated below:

When the price of petrol is Rs. 20.00 per litre, Amit consumes 1,000 litres per year. The price of petrol rises to Rs. 25.00 per litre.. Calculate the cost difference equal to which the Government should give him extra money income per year to compensate him for the rise in price of petrol. Will Amit be better off or worse off after the price rise plus the cash compensation equal to the cost difference than he was before? What will happen to petrol consumption ?

As explained above, the cost difference is equal to $\Delta P.Q$ where ΔP stands for the change in price of a good and Q stands for the quantity of commodity he was consuming prior to the change in price. Thus, in our above example.

$$\Delta P = \text{Rs. } 25 - 20 = \text{Rs. } 5$$

$$Q = 1{,}000 \text{ litres per year}$$

$$\text{Cost-difference} = \Delta P.Q$$

$$= \text{Rs. } 5 \times 1{,}000 = \text{Rs. } 5{,}000.$$

Now, with higher price of petrol of Rs. 25.00 per litre and cash compensation of Rs. 5,000 equal to the cost difference he can buy, if he so desires, the original quantity of 1,000 litres of petrol per

1. J.R. Hicks. *A Revision of Demand Theory*; 1956 p. 62.

year. However, he may not buy this original quantity of petrol in the new price-income situation if his satisfaction is maximum at some other point. Consider Figure 9B.3. where we measure petrol on the X-axis and money income representing other goods on the Y-axis. Suppose, BL_1 is the initial budget line when price of petrol is Rs. 20.00 per litre and consumer is in equilibrium at point Q on the indifference curve IC_1 where he is consuming 1,000 litres of petrol per year. Now, with the rise in price of petrol to Rs. 25.00 per litre, suppose the budget line shifts to BL_2. Now, if to compensate for the rise in price, his, money income is raised by Rs. 5,000, that is, equal to the cost difference, the budget line shifts in a parallel manner to the left so that it reaches the position GH which passes through the original point of consumption Q. A glance at Fig. 9B.3, will reveal that the consumer with higher price of petrol and having received monetary compensation equal to the cost difference of Rs. 5,000 will not be in equilibrium at the original point Q and instead he will maximising his satisfaction in the new situation at point S on a higher indifference curve IC_2 where his consumption of petrol has decreased to ON litres (that is, the decrease in consumption of petrol by MN is the Slutsky substitution effect.) Since, with the rise in price and simultaneous increase in his income equal to the cost-difference has enabled him to attain a higher indifference curve, he has become better off than before the rise in price.

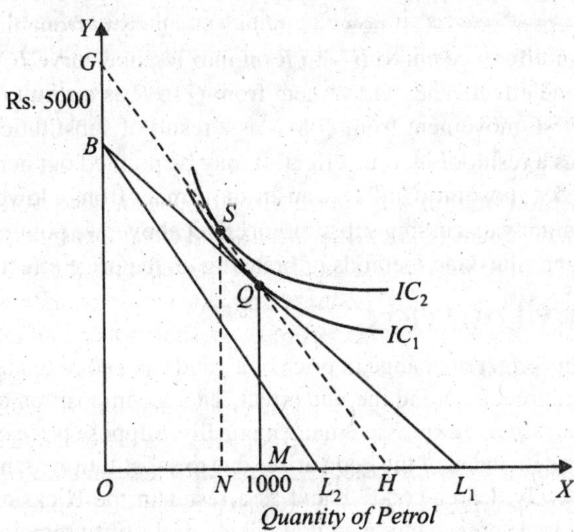

Fig.9B.3. *Cash Compensation for a Rise in Price of Petrol.*

Price Effect Broken Up into Income and Substitution Effects: Slutsky Method

In our discussion of substitution effect we explained that Slutsky presented a slightly different version of the substitution and income effects of a price change from the Hicksian one. In fact it was Slutsky who first of all divided the price effect into income and substitution effects. His way of breaking up the price effect is shown in Fig. 9B.4. With a certain price-income situation, the consumer is in equilibrium at Q on indifference curve IC_1 With a fall in price of X, other things remaining the same, budget line shifts to PL_2. With budget line PL_2, the consumer would now be in equilibrium at R on the indifference curve IC_3. This movement from Q to R represents the price effect. As a result of this he buys MN quantity of good X more than before. Now, in order to find out the substitution effect his money income be reduced by such an amount that he can buy, if he so desires, the old combination Q. Thus, a

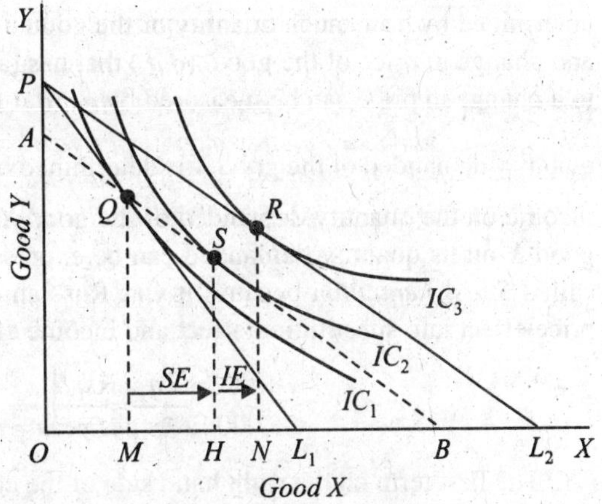

Fig. 9B4. *Price Effect is decomposed into Substitution and Income Effects with Slutsky's Cost-Difference Method.*

line AB, which is parallel to PL_2, has been so drawn that it passes through point Q. Thus PA in terms of good Y represents the cost difference. With budget line AB, the consumer can have combination Q if he so desires, but actually he will not buy combination Q because X is now relatively cheaper than before. It will pay him to substitute X for Y. With budget line AB he is in equilibrium at S on indifference curve IC_2. The movement from Q to S represents Slutsky substitution effect which induces the consumer to buy MH quantity more of good X. If now the money taken away from him is restored to him, he will move from S on indifference curve IC_2 to R on indifference curve IC_3. This movement from S to R represents income effect. Thus, movement from Q to R as a result of price effect can be divided into two steps. First, movement from Q to S as a result of substitution effect and secondly, movement from S to R as a result of income effect. It may be pointed out here again that, unlike the Hicksian method, Slutsky substitution effect causes movement from a lower indifference curve to a higher one. While separately discussing substitution effect above, we pointed out the merits and demerits of the Hicksian and Slutskian methods of breaking up the price effect.

SLUTSKY EQUATION

We have graphically shown above how the effect of change in price of a good can be broken up into its two component parts, namely, substitution effect and income effect. The decomposition of price effect into its two components can be derived and expressed mathematically. Suppose price of good X falls, its substitution effect on quantity demanded of the good arises due to substitution of the relatively cheaper good X for the now relatively dearer good Y and as a result in the Hicksian method the consumer moves along the same indifference curve so that his level of utility remains constant. The overall effect of change in its own price on the quantity demanded can be expressed as $\frac{dq_x}{dp_x}$ and the substitution effect can be expressed $\left.\frac{\partial q_x}{\partial p_x}\right|_{U=\bar{U}}$. The term $\left.\frac{\partial q_x}{\partial p_x}\right|_{U=\bar{U}}$ shows change in quantity demanded resulting from a relative change in price of X while utility or satisfaction of the consumer remains constant.

However, expressing income effect of the price change mathematically is rather a ticklish affair. Suppose a unit change in income (∂I) causes a (∂q_x) change in quantity demanded of the good. This can be written as $\frac{\partial q_x}{\partial I}$. But how much income changes due to a change in price of the good is determined by how much quantity of the good (q_x) the consumer was purchasing on the one hand and change in price of the good (∂p_x) that has taken place on the other. The change in income due to a change in price can be measured by q_x (∂p_x). How much this change in income will affect the quantity demanded of the good X is determined by $\frac{\partial q_x}{\partial I}$ which shows the effect of a unit change in income on the quantity demanded of the good X. Thus the overall effect of change in price of the good X on its quantity demanded can be expressed by the following equation which is generally called *Slutsky equation* because it was Russian economist E. Slutsky who first of all divided the price effect into substitution effect and income effect.

$$\frac{\partial q_x}{\partial p_x}=\left.\frac{\partial q_x}{\partial p_x}\right|_{u=\bar{u}}+q_x\cdot\partial p_x\frac{\partial q_x}{\partial I} \quad \ldots (i)$$

The first term on the right hand side of the equation represents the substitution affect obtained after income of the consumer has been adjusted to keep his level of utility constant. The second term on the right hand side of the equation shows the income effect of the fall in price of the good. The term $q_x \cdot \partial P_x$ measures the increase in income or purchasing power caused by the fall in price and

$\frac{\partial q_x}{\partial I}$ measures the change in quantity demanded resulting from a unit increase in income (I). Therefore, income affect of the price change is given by $q_x .\partial p_x \frac{\partial q_x}{\partial I}$.

Since the *fall* in price *increases* income or purchasing power of the consumer which in case of normal goods leads to the *increase in quantity demanded* of the good, sign of the income affect has been taken to be positive.

Further, a point needs to be clarified. In the above analysis of *Slutsky equation*, we have considered the substitution effect when with a change in price, the consumer is so compensated as to keep his real income or purchasing power constant. In obtaining Slutsky substitution effect, income of the consumer is adjusted to *keep his purchasing power (i.e. real income) constant* so that he could buy the original combination of goods if he so desires. On the other hand, in the Hicksian substitution effect, with a change in price of a good money income with the consumer is so adjusted that his *satisfaction* remains constant. In fact, Hicks interprets real income in terms of satisfaction obtained by a consumer. This difference was later emphasised by J.R. Hicks, but since it was Slutsky who first of all split up the price effect into substitution effect and income effect the above equation is popularly known as *Slutsky equation*. It is proper to call it *Slutsky-Hicks equation*.

An important result follows from the Slutsky equation. If the commodity is a normal good, then $\frac{\partial q_x}{\partial I}$ is positive by definition. It follows that a *fall* in price will lead to the *increase* in income causing *increase in quantity demanded* of the good and therefore the expression for income effect of the price change $q_x .\partial p_x \times \left(\frac{\partial q_x}{\partial I}\right)$ is taken to be positive in the Slutsky equation (i) above. Besides, since the *substitution effect is always negative*, a *fall* in the relative price of a good will cause the *increase* in its quantity demanded. Therefore, Slutsky equation tells us that *when commodity X is normal*, the price effect $\frac{dq_x}{dp_x}$ is *necessarily negative* implying that *fall* in price will cause quantity demanded of the good to *increase*. Thus, in case of normal goods both the substitution effect and income effect work in the same direction and reinforce each other. Thus in case of normal goods a fall in price of a commodity leads to the increase in quantity demanded due to both the substitution effect and income effect.

On the other hand, if price of the commodity *rises*, then due to the negative substitution effect, the consumer will buy *less* of the good, his pruchasing power remaining the same. Therefore, in case of *rise* in price of a good, the first term in the right side of Slutsky equation, namely, $\frac{\partial q_x}{\partial p_x} \mid u=\overline{u}$, will have a *negative* sign. Further, *rise in price of a good causes income of the consumer to fall*, and income effect will lead to the *decrease* in quantity demand of good and therefore, the second term $\left(q_x .\partial p_x \frac{\partial q_x}{\partial I}\right)$ on the right hand side of the equation will have a negative sign in case of normal goods. Thus, in case of rise in price of a good, both the substitution effect and also income effect (if it is a normal good) will work in the same direction to reduce the quantity demanded of the good whose price rises.

The second important conclusion which follows from Slutsky equation is that as the quantity of commodity (q_x) consumed becomes smaller and smaller, the income effect of the price change will become smaller and smaller. Thus, if the quantity consumed of a commodity is very small, then the income effect is not very significant.

QUESTIONS FOR REVIEW

1. What is Slutsky Substitution effect ? Explain Slutsky substitution effect for a rise in price of good *X* with indifference curves analysis.
2. Distinguish between Hicks' and Slutsky approach to the measurement of income and substitution effects. *(D.U.B.A (Hons)* 1990)
3. Show graphically the substitution and the real income effect by Hicks and Slutsky. What is the advantage of Slutskys measure ?
4. A consumer spends all his income on two good *X* and *Y*. When the price of goods *X* is Rs. 2. he consumes 100 units of goods *X*. If the price of good *X* increases to Rs. 3 and income is increased by Rs. 100 to enable him to purchase the original bundle, price of *Y* remaining constant, (*i*) would the level of satisfaction of the consumer change; and (*ii*) what would happen to the quantity consumed of *X* ? *D.U. B.Com (Hons)* 2002
5. State the Slutsky equation algebraically and explain each term in it. Using the equation explain. (*i*) what must be the sign and magnitude of the income effect for a downward-sloping demand curve ? (*ii*)Under what circumstances we will get a Giffen good case ? *D.U. B.A. (Hons.)* 2000.

CHAPTER 10

MARSHALL'S CARDINAL UTILITY ANALYSIS VS. INDIFFERENCE CURVE ANALYSIS

We are now in a position to compare the indifference curve analysis with Marshallian cardinal utility analysis. Barring the views of some economists like Dennis Robertson, W. E. Armstrong, F. H. Knight, it is now widely believed that indifference curve analysis makes a definite improvement upon the Marshallian cardinal utility analysis. It has been asserted that whereas Marshallian cardinal utility analysis assumes 'too much' it explains 'too little'. On the other hand, the indifference curve analysis explains more by taking fewer as well as less restrictive assumptions.

It may be noted that there are some similarities in these two theories of demand. First, both these theories assume that consumers are rational and therefore try to maximize utility or satisfaction. Second, both these theories use psychological or introspective method to explain consumer's behaviour. Thirdly, both these theories of demand assume in some form diminishing marginal utility or desire for a commodity as a consumer takes more units of the commodity. In this connection it is generally believed that the principle of diminishing marginal rate of substitution is similar to the law of diminishing marginal utility of Marshallian cardinal utility analysis.

SUPERIORITY OF INDIFFERENCE CURVE ANALYSIS

After having pointed out the similarities between the two types of analysis, we now turn to study the difference between the two and to show how far indifference curve analysis is superior to the Marshallian cardinal utility analysis.

1. **Ordinal vs. Cardinal Measurability of Utility.** In the first place, Marshall assumes utility to be *cardinally measurable*. In other words, he believes that utility is *quantifiable*, both in principle and in actual practice. According to this, the consumer is able to assign a specific amount to the utility obtained by him from the consumption of a certain amount of a good or a combination of goods. Further, the amounts of utility can be manipulated in the same manner as weights, lengths, heights, etc. In other words, the utilities can be compared and added. Suppose, for instance, utility which a consumer gets from a unit of good *A* is equal to 15, and from a unit of good *B* equal to 45. We can then say that the consumer prefers *B three times as strongly as A* and the utility obtained by the consumer from the combination containing one unit of each good is equal to 60. Likewise, even the differences between the utilities obtained from the various goods can be so compared as to enable us to say *A* is preferred to *B* twice as much as *C* is preferred to *D*.

According to the critics, the Marshallian assumption of cardinal measurement of utility is very restrictive; it demands too much from the human mind. They assert that utility is a psychological feeling and the precision in measurement of utility assumed by Marshall and others is therefore unrealistic. Critics hold that the utility possesses only ordinal magnitude and cannot be expressed in cordial terms.

According to the sponsors of the indifference curve analysis, utility is merely *orderable* and not quantitative. In other words, indifference curve technique assumes what is called '*ordinal measurement of utility*'. According to this, the consumer need not be able to assign specific amounts to the utility he derives from the consumption of a good or a combination of goods but it is assumed that he is capable of *comparing* the different utilities or satisfactions in the sense whether one level of satisfaction is equal to, lower than, or higher than another. He cannot say by *how much* one level of satisfaction is higher or lower than another. That is why the indifference curves are generally labelled by the ordinal numbers such as I, II, III, IV, etc., showing successively higher levels of satisfaction. The advocates of indifference curve technique assert that for the purpose of explaining consumer's behaviour and deriving the theorem of demand, it is quite sufficient to assume that the consumer is able to *rank his preferences consistently*.

It is obvious that the ordinal measurement of utility is a less restrictive assumption and sounds more realistic than cardinal measurement of utility. This shows that the indifference curve analysis of demand which is based upon the ordinal utility hypothesis is superior to Marshall's cardinal utility analysis.

2. **Analysis of Demand Without Assuming Constant Marginal Utility of Money.** Another distinct improvement made by indifference curve technique is that unlike Marshall it explains consumer's behaviour and derives demand theorem without the assumption of constant marginal utility of money. In indifference curve analysis, it is not necessary to assume constant marginal utility of money. As has already been seen, Marshall assumed that the marginal utility of money remained constant when there occured a change in the price of a good. It has been shown in the last chapter that the Marshallian demand analysis based upon constancy of marginal utility of money is not self-consistent. In other words, "the Marshallian demand theorem cannot genuinely be derived from the marginal utility hypothesis except in one commodity model, without contradicting the assumption of constant marginal utility of money." [1] It means that "the constancy of marginal utility of money is incompatible with a proof of the demand theorem in a situation where the consumer has more than a single good to spread his expenditure on."[2] To overcome this difficulty in Marshallian cardinal utility analysis, if the assumption of constant marginal utility of money is abandoned, then money can no longer serve as a measuring rod of utility and we can no longer measure marginal utility of a commodity in units of money.

On the other hand, indifference curve technique using ordinal utility hypothesis can validly derive the demand theorem without the assumption of constant marginal utility of money. In fact, as we shall see below, the abandonment of the assumption of constant marginal utility of money enables the indifference curve analysis to derive a *more general* demand theorem.

3. **Greater Insight into Price Effect.** The superiority of indifference curve analysis further lies in the fact that it makes greater insight into the effect of price change on the demand for a good by distinguishing between income and substitution effects. The indifference technique splits up the price effect analytically into its two component parts substitution effect and income effect. The distinction between the income effect and the substitution effect of a price change enables us to gain a better understanding of the effect of a price change on the demand for a good. The amount demanded of a good generally rises as a result of the fall in its price due to two reasons. First, real income rises as a result of the fall in price (income effect) and, secondly, because the good whose price falls becomes relatively cheaper than others and therefore the consumer substitutes it for others (substitution effect). In indifference curve technique, income effect is separated from the substitution effect of the price change by the methods of 'compensating variation in income' and 'equivalent variation in income'.

1. Tapas Majumdar, *op. cit.*, p. 55.
2. *Ibid*, p. 55–56.

But, by assuming constant marginal utility of money Marshall ignored the income effect of a price change. He failed to understand the composite character of the effect of a price change. Prof. Tapas Majumdar rightly remarks, "the assumption of constant marginal utility of money obscured Marshall's insight into the truly composite character of the unduly simplified price-demand relationship"[3]. In this context, remarks made by J. R. Hicks are worth noting, "The distinction between direct and indirect effects of a price change is accordingly left by the cardinal theory as an empty box, which is crying out to be filled."[4] Commenting on the improvement made by Hicks-Allen indifference curve approach over the Marshallian utility analysis, Prof. Tapas Majumdar says : "The efficiency and precision with which the Hicks-Allen approach can distinguish between the 'income' and 'substitution' effects of a price change really leaves the cardinalist argument in a very poor state indeed."[5]

4. **Deriving a more general and adequate 'Demand Theorem'.** A distinct advantage of the technique of dividing the effect of a price change into income and the substitution effects employed by the indifference curve analysis is that it enables us to enunciate a *more general* and a more *inclusive* theorem of demand than the Marshallian law of demand. In the case of most of the normal goods in this world, both the income effect and the substitution effect work in the same direction, that is to say, they tend to increase the amount demanded of a good when its price falls. The income effect ensures that when the price of a good falls the consumer buys more of it because he can now afford to buy more; the substitution effect ensures that he buys more of it because it has now become relatively cheaper and is, therefore, profitable for him to substitute it for others. This thus accounts for the inverse price-demand relationship (Marshallian law of demand) in the case of normal goods.

When a certain good is regarded by the consumer to be an inferior good, he will tend to reduce its consumption as a result of the increase in his income. Therefore, when price of an inferior good falls, the income effect so produced would work in the opposite direction to that of the substitution effect. But so long as the inferior good in question does not claim a very large proportion of consumer's total income, the income effect will not be strong enough to outweigh the substitution effect. In such a case therefore the net effect of the fall in price will be to raise the amount demanded of the good. It, therefore, follows that even for most of the inferior goods, the Marshallian law of demand holds good as much as for normal goods.

But it is possible that there may be inferior goods for which the income effect of a change in price is larger in magnitude than the substitution effect. This is the case of Giffen goods for which the Marshallian law of demand does not hold good. In such cases the negative income effect outweighs the substitution effect so that the net effect of the fall in price of the good is the reduction in demand for it. Thus, amount demanded of a Giffen good varies directly with price.

It is clear from above that by breaking the price effect into income effect and substitution effect, the indifference curve analysis enables us to arrive at a general and a more inclusive theorem of demand in the following composite form.[6]

(*a*) The demand for a commodity varies *inversely* with price when the income effect for that commodity is nil or positive.

(*b*) The demand for a commodity varies inversely with price when the income elasticity is negative but the income effect of the price change is smaller than the substitution effect.

(*c*) The demand for a commodity varies *directly* with price when the income effect is negative and this income effect of the price change is larger than the substitution effect.

In the case of (*a*) and (*b*) the Marshallian law of demand holds while in (*c*) we have a Giffen good

3. Tapas Majumdar, *op cit*., p. 76.
4. J. R. Hicks, *A Revision of Demand Theory*, p. 14.
5. Tapas Majumdar, *op. cit*., p. 57.
6. **Tapas Majumdar,** ***op. cit, pp*****., 74–75.**

case which is exception to the Marshallian law of demand. Marshall could not account for 'Giffen Paradox', because by assuming constant marginal utility of money, he ignored the income effect of the price change. The indifference curve technique by distinguishing between the income and substitution effects of the price change can explain the Giffen good case. According to this, the Giffen good case occurs in the case of an inferior good for which the negative income effect of the price change is so powerful that it outweighs the substitution effect, and hence when the price of a Giffen good falls, its quantity demanded also falls instead of rising. Thus, a great merit of Hicks-Allen indifference curve analysis is that it offers an explanation for the Giffen-good case, while Marshall failed to do so.

5. **Significance of a Price Change in terms of Income and Welfare Increments.** Another distinct improvement of Hicks-Allen ordinal theory is that through it the welfare consequences of a change in price can be translated into those of a change in income. As seen above, a fall in the price of a good enables the consumer to shift from a lower to a higher level of welfare (or satisfaction). Likewise, a rise in the price of the good would cause the consumer to shift down to a lower indifference curve and therefore to a lower level of welfare. This means that a fall in price of a good causes a change in consumer's welfare exactly as the rise in income would do. In other words, the consumer can be thought of reaching a higher level of welfare through an equivalent rise in income rather than the fall in price of a good. In Fig. 10.1 with the fall in price of good X from PL_1 to PL_2 the consumer shifts from indifference curve IC_1 to the indifference curve IC_2 showing an increase in the level of welfare. Now, if instead of the fall in price from PL_1 to PL_2 the consumer's income is increased by the amount equal to PA or L_1B, he will reach the indifference curve IC_2. Thus the increase in consumer's welfare due to the rise in income by PA or, L_1B is equal-to that of the change in price of X from PL_1 to PL_2. "*The equivalence of a given change in price to a suitable change in income is a major discovery of ordinal utility analysis.*"[7] This fundamental relation necessarily remains obscure in cardinal utility analysis with its single good model and the assumption of constant marginal utility of money.

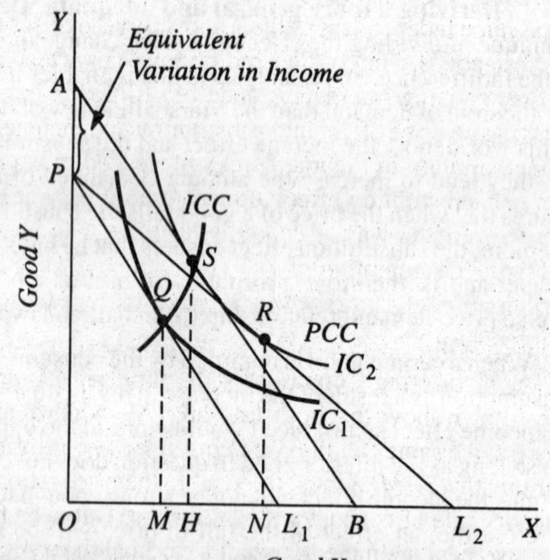

Fig. 10.1. *Income Equivalent of a Price Change*

The discovery of a suitable change in income equivalent in terms of welfare to a given change in price has enabled Hicks to extend Marshall's concept of consumer's surplus. Marshall's concept of consumer's surplus was based upon the assumption that utility was cardinally measurable and also that the marginal utility of money remained constant when the price of a good changed. Hicks has freed the concept of consumer's surplus from these dubious assumptions and by using ordinal utility hypothesis along with the discovery that the welfare effect of a price change can be translated into a suitable change in income he has not only been able to rehabilitate the concept of consumer's surplus but also to extend it further.

6. **Hypothesis of Independent Utilities Given Up.** Marshall's cardinal utility analysis is based upon the *hypothesis of independent utilities*. This means that the utility which the consumer derives from any commodity is a function of the quantity of that commodity and of that commodity alone. In other words, the utility obtained by the consumer from a commodity is independent of that derived from any other. *By assuming independent utilities Marshall completely bypassed the relation of*

7. Tapas Majumdar, op. cit., p. 72.

substitution and complementarity between commodities.

Demand analysis based upon he hypothesis of independent utilities, as shown in the last chapter, leads us to the conclusion "that in all cases a reduction in the price of one commodity only will either result in an expansion in the demand for all other commodities or in a contraction in the demands for all other commodities." But this is quite contrary to the common cases found in the real world. In the real world, it is found that as a result of the fall in price of a commodity the *demand for some commodities expands while the demand for others contracts.* We thus see that Marshall's analysis based upon `independent utilities' does not take into account the complementary and substitution relations between goods. This is a great flaw in Marshall's cardinal utility analysis.

On the other hand, this flaw is not present in Hicks-Allen indifference curve analysis which does not assume independent utilities and duly recognises the relation of substitution and complementarity between goods. Hicks-Allen indifference curve technique by taking more than one commodity model and recognising interdependence of utilities is in a better position to explain related goods. By breaking up price effect into substitution and income effects by employing the technique of compensating variation in income, Hicks succeeded in explaining complementary and substitute goods in terms of substitution effect alone. Accordingly, it can define and explain substitutes and complements in a better way. According to Hicks, *Y* is a substitute for *X* if a fall in the price of *X* leads to a fall in the consumption of *Y*; *Y* is a complement of *X* if a fall in the price of *X* leads to a rise in the consumption of *Y*, *a compensating variation in income being made in each case so as to maintain indifference*.

7. **Analysing Consumer's Demand with Less Restrictive and Fewer Assumptions.** It has been shown above that both the Hicks-Allen indifference curve theory and Marshall's cardinal theory arrive at the same condition for consumer's equilibrium. Hicks-Allen condition for consumer's equilibrium, that is, *MRS* must be equal to the price ratio amounts to the same thing as Marshall's proportionality rule of consumer's equilibrium. But even here indifference curve's ordinal approach is an improvement upon the Marshall's cardinal theory in so far as the former arrives at the same equilibrium condition with less restrictive and fewer assumptions. Dubious assumptions such as (*i*) utility is quantitatively measurable, (*ii*) marginal utility of money remains constant, and (*iii*) utilities of different goods are independent of each other, on which Marshall's cardinal theory is based, are not made in indifference-curve's ordinal utility theory.

IS INDIFFERENCE CURVE ANALYSIS "OLD WINE IN A NEW BOTTLE" ?

But superiority of indifference curve theory has been denied by some economists, foremost among them are Prof. D. H. Robertson, F. H. Knight, W. E. Armstrong. Prof. Knight remarks, "indifference curve analysis of demand is not a step forward; it is in fact a step backward." Prof. D. H. Robertson is of the view that the indifference curve technique is merely "*the old wine in a new bottle*." The indifference curve analysis, according to him, has simply substituted new concepts and equations in place of the old ones, while the essential approach of the two types of analyses is the same. Instead of the concept of `utility', the indifference curve technique has introduced the term 'preference' and scale of preferences. In place of cardinal number system of one, two, three, etc., which is supposed to measure the amount of utility derived by the consumer, the indifference curves have the ordinal number system of first, second, third, etc., to indicate the order of consumer's preferences. The concept of marginal utility has been substituted by the concept of marginal rate of substitution. And against the Marshallian 'proportionality rule' as a condition for consumer's equilibrium, indifference curve approach has advanced the condition of equality between the marginal rate of substitution and the price ratio.

Prof. Robertson's view that the concept of marginal rate of substitution of indifference curve analysis represents the reintroduction of the concept of marginal utility in demand analysis requires further consideration. Prof. Robertson says : "In his earlier book *Value and Capital* Hicks's treatment involved making an assumption about the convexity of those 'indifference curves' which appeared to some of us to involve reintroduction of marginal utility in disguise."[8] It has thus been held that the *use of marginal rate of substitution implies the presence of cardinal element in indifference curve technique.* In going from one combination to another on an indifference curve, the consumer is assumed to be able to tell what constitutes his compensation in terms of a good for the loss of a marginal unit of another good. In other words, the consumer is able to tell his marginal rate of substitution of one good for another. Now, the marginal rate of substitution has been described by Hicks and others as the ratio of the marginal utilities of two goods.

$$\left(MRS_{xy} = \frac{MU \text{ of } X}{MU \text{ of } Y} \right)$$

But ratio cannot be measured unless the two marginal utilities in question are at least measurable in principle. It has, therefore, been held that the concept of marginal rate of substitution and the idea of indifference based upon it essentially involves an admission that utility is quantifiable in principle.

Against this, Hicks contends that we need not assume measurability of marginal utilities in principle in order to know the marginal rate of substitution. He says, "All that we shall be able to measure is what the ordinal theory grants to be measurable – namely the ratio of the marginal utility of one commodity to the marginal utility of another." This means that *MRS* can be obtained without actually measuring marginal utilities. If a consumer, when asked, is prepared to give up 4 units of good *Y* for the gain of one marginal unit of *X*, *MRS* of *X* for *Y* is 4 : 1. We can thus directly derive the ratio indicating *MRS* by asking him how much quantity of good *Y* the consumer would forego for the gain of a marginal unit of *X*. The contention that the concept of marginal rate of substitution is a mere reintroduction of the marginal utility (a cardinal concept) in disguise is therefore not valid.

It has been further contended by Robertson and Armstrong that it is not possible to arrive at the Hicksian *principle of diminishing marginal rate of substitution* without making use of the concept of marginal utility and the principle of diminishing marginal utility. It is asked why *MRS* of *X* for *Y* diminishes as more and more of *X* is substituted for *Y*? The critics point out that the marginal rate of substitution (MRS_{xy}) diminishes and the indifference curve becomes convex to the origin, because as the consumer's stock of *X* increases, the marginal utility of *X* falls and that of *Y* increases. They thus hold that Hicks and Allen have not been able to derive the basic principle of diminishing marginal rate of substitution independently of the law of diminishing marginal utility. They contend that by a stroke of terminological manipulation, the concept of marginal utility has been relegated to the background, but it is there all the same. They, therefore, assert that "the principle of diminishing marginal rate of substitution is as much determinate or indeterminate as the poor law of diminishing marginal utility".

However, even this criticism of indifference curve approach advanced by the defenders of the Marshallian cardinal utility analysis is not valid. As shown above, the derivation of marginal rate of substitution does not depend upon the actual measurement of marginal utilities. While the law of diminishing marginal utility is based upon the cardinal utility hypothesis (*i.e.*, utility is quantifiable and actually measurable), the principle of marginal rate of substitution is based upon the ordinal utility hypothesis (*i.e.*, utility is mere orderable). As a consumer gets more and more units of good *X*, his strength of desire for it (though we cannot measure it in itself) will decline and therefore he will be prepared to forego less and less of *Y* for the gain of a marginal unit of *X*. It is thus clear that the principle of diminishing marginal rate of substitution is based upon purely ordinal hypothesis and is derived independently of the cardinal concept of marginal utility, though both laws reveal essentially the same phenomenon. We therefore agree with Prof. Hicks who claims that "*the replacement of the principle of diminishing marginal utility by the principle of diminishing marginal rate of substitution*

8. Sir Dennis Robertson, *Lectures on Economic Principles*, The Fontana Library Edition, 1963, p. 85.

is not a mere translation. It is a positive change in the theory of consumer demand".

It follows from what has been said above that indifference curve analysis of demand is an improvement upon the Marshallian utility analysis and the objections that the former too involves cardinal elements are groundless. It is of course true that the indifference curve analysis suffers from some drawbacks and has been criticized on various grounds, as explained below, but as far as the question of indifference curve technique versus Marshallian utility analysis is concerned, the former is deci-dedly better.

CRITIQUE OF INDIFFERENCE CURVE ANALYSIS

Indifference curve analysis has come in for criticism on several grounds. In the first place, it is argued that the indifference curve approach for avoiding the difficulty of measuring utility quantitatively is forced to *make unrealistic assumption that the consumer possesses complete knowledge of all his scale of preferences or indifference map*. The indifference curve approach, so to say, falls from the frying pan into the fire. The indifference curve analysis envisages a consumer who carries in his head innumerable possible combinations of goods and relative preferences in respect of them. It is argued: Is not this carrying into his head all his scales of preferences too formidable a task for a real human being ? Hicks himself admits this drawback. When revising his demand theory based on indifference curves, he says that "one of the most awkward of the assumptions into which the older theory appeared to be impelled by its geometrical analogy was the notion that the consumer is capable of ordering all conceivable alternatives that might possibly be presented to him – all the positions which might be represented by points on his indifference map. This assumption is so unrealistic that it was bound to be a stumbling block."[10] This is one of the reasons that Hicks gave up indifference curves in his *Revision of Demand Theory*.

Further, there is another unrealistic element present in indifference curve analysis. It is pointed out that *such curves include even the most ridiculous combinations which may be far removed from his habitual combinations*. For example, while it may be perfectly sensible to compare whether three pairs of shoes and six shirts would give a consumer as much satisfaction as two pairs of shoes and seven shirts, the consumer will be at a loss to know and compare the desirability of an absurd combination such as eight pairs of shoes and one shirt. The way the indifference curves are constructed, they include absurd combinations like the one just indicated.

A further shortcoming of the indifference curve technique is that *it can demonstrate and analyse consumer's behaviour effectively only in simple cases, especially those in which the choice is between the quantities of two goods only*. In order to demonstrate the case of three goods, three-dimensional diagrams are needed which are difficult to understand and handle. When more than three goods are involved geometry altogether fails and recourse has to be taken to the complicated mathematics which often tends to conceal the economic point of what is being done. Prof. Hicks also admits this shortcoming of indifference curve technique.

Another demerit of indifference curve analysis because of its geometrical nature is that it involves the *assumption of continuity* "a property which the geometrical field does have, but which the economic world in general does not". The real economic world exhibits discontinuity and it is quite unrealistic and analytically bad if we do not recognise it. This is why Hicks also abandoned the assumption of continuity in his later work *A Revision of Demand Theory*.

Prof. Armstrong has criticized the relation of transitivity involved in indifference curve technique. He is of the view that in most cases the consumer's indifference is due to his imperfect ability to perceive difference between alternative combinations of goods. In other words, the consumer indicates his indifference between the combinations which differ very slightly from each other not because they give him equal satisfaction but because the difference between the combinations is so

9. J.R. Hicks, *A Revision of Demand Theory*, p.20.

small that he is unable to perceive the difference between them. *If this concept of indifference is admitted, then the relation of indifference becomes non-transitive. Now, with non-transitivity of indifference-relation; the whole system of indifference curves and the demand analysis based upon it breaks down.*

It may, however, be pointed out that Prof. Armstrong's interpretation of indifference is not correct. Actually, the relation of indifference in the ordinal theory is the exact equivalent of the relation of 'equality' in the cardinal sense. In other words, the consumer is said to be indifferent between *A* and *B*, for instance, because he derives equal utility from the two combinations and not because the difference between the utilities from *A* and *B* is imperceptible. If such is the case then "the axiom of transitivity of ordinal indifference emerges automatically and is no more subject to dispute than is the axiom of transitivity of numerical equality".

Further, *indifference curve analysis has been criticised for its limited empirical nature*. Indifference curve analysis is neither based upon purely imaginary and subjective utility functions, nor is it based upon purely empirically derived indifference functions. It is because of this fact that Professor Schumpeter dubbed indifference curve analysis as 'a midway house'. It would have been quite valid if indifference curve analysis was based upon experimentally obtained quantitative data in regard to the observed market behaviour of the consumer. But, in Hicks-Allen theory, indifference curves are based upon *hypothetical experimentation*. The indifference curve theory of demand is, therefore, based upon imaginary drawn indifference curves. Commenting on Hicks-Allen theory of demand Prof. Schumpeter remarked, "If they use nothing that is not observable in principle they do use "potential" observations which so far no body has been able to make in fact : from a practical standpoint we are not much better off when drawing purely imaginary indifference curves than we are when we speak of purely imaginary utility functions."[10]

It may, however, be pointed out that attempts have recently made by some economists and psychologists to derive or measure indifference curves experimentally. But a limited success has been achieved in this regard. This is because such experiments have been made under controlled conditions which render these experiments quite unfit for drawing conclusions regarding real consumer's behaviour in 'free circumstances'. So, for all intents and purposes, indifference curves still remain imaginary.

An important criticism against Hicks-Allen ordinal theory of demand is that *it cannot formalise consumer's behaviour when uncertainty or risk is present*. In other words, consumer's behaviour cannot be explained by ordinal theory when he has to choose among alternatives involving risk or 'uncertainty of expectation'. Von Neumann and Morgenstern[12] have asserted that while cardinal utility theory can, the ordinal utility theory cannot formalise consumer's behaviour when we introduce "uncertainty of expectations with regard to the consequences of choice."

We thus find that Hicks-Allen ordinal utility system cannot formalise consumer's behaviour when there exists uncertainty of expectations with regard to the consequences of choice. On the other hand, cardinal utility theory can formalise consumer's behaviour in the presence of uncertainty of expectations since it involves quantitative estimates of utilities or preference intensities. Commenting on indifference preference hypothesis, Neumann and Morgenstern remark : "If the preferences are not all comparable, then the indifference curves do not exist. If the individual preferences are all comparable, then we can even obtain a (uniquely defined) numerical utility which renders the indifference curves superfluous."[11]

Further, Prof. *Samuelson has criticized the indifference curves approach as being predomi-*

10. J. A. Schumpeter, *History of Economic Analysis*, P. 1067
11. See their work "*The Theory of Games and Economic Behaviour*"

nantly introspective. Prof. Samuelson himself has developed a behaviourist method of deriving the theory of demand. He seeks to derive demand theorem from observed consumer's behaviour. He regards the behaviouristic approach as being 'scientific'. His theory is based upon the strong-ordering hypothesis, namely, '*choice reveals preference*'. Samuelson thinks that his theory removes the last vestiges of the psychological analysis in the explanation of consumer's demand.

QUESTIONS FOR REVIEW

1. Compare indifference curve analysis of demand with Marshallian cardinal utility analysis. Which do you think is superior ? *Punjab University, B.A. (Hons) 2000*
2. Distinguish between cardinal and ordinal measurement of utility. Which do you think is more realistic ?
3. The equivalence of a given change in price to a suitable change in income is a major discovery of ordinal utility analysis. Explain
4. "By assuming independent utilities Marshall completely bypassed the relation of substitution and complementary between comodities' Discuss
5. Indifference curve analysis is "*old wine in a new bottle*" (D.H. Robertson). Do you agree ? Discuss. *I.A.S. (Main), 1998.*
6. "The distinction between direct and indirect effects of a price change is accordingly left by cardinal utility theory as an empty box, which is crying out to be filled" (J.R. Hicks). Discuss.
7. "The replacement of the principle of diminishing marginal utility by the principle of diminishing marginal rate of substitution is not a mere translation. It is a positive change in the theory of consumer demand". (J.R. Hicks). Discuss.

CHAPTER 11

SOME IMPORTANT APPLICATIONS OF INDIFFERENCE CURVES

We have studied the indifference curve analysis of demand. But the technique of indifference curves has been used not only to explain consumer's behaviour and demand but also to analyse and explain several other economic problems. In other words, besides analysing consumer's demand, indifference curves have several other applications. Thus, indifference curves have been used to explain the concept of consumer's surplus, substitutability and complementarity of goods, supply curve of labour of an individual, several principles of welfare economics, burden of different forms of taxation, gain from foreign trade, welfare implications of subsidy granted by the Government, index number problem, mutual advantage of exchange of goods between two individuals and several other things. We shall discuss applications of indifference curves in some of the above stated fields in their relevant chapters. We shall explain below only few applications.

EFFECT OF SUBSIDIES TO CONSUMERS: PRICE SUBSIDY *VS* CASH SUBSIDY

An important application of indifference curves is to analyse with its aid the effect of subsidies to the consumers. Several kinds of subsidies are paid to the individuals these days by the Government for promoting welfare of the people. We will explain and compare the effects of two types of subsidies, price subsidy and lump sum cash grant, on consumer's welfare. It is worth noting that *price subsidity on a commodity is also generally called excise subsidy. Under price or excise subsidy the Government pays a part of the price of a good and allows the consumer to buy as many units of the good as he desires at the subsidised price*. On the other hand in case of cash subsidy the government provides a lump sum cash income to the consumer. Let us take the case of food subsidy which is given by the Government to help the needy families. Suppose that under food-subsidy programme, the needed families are entitled to purchase food at half the market price, the other half of the market price is paid by the Government as subsidy. The effect of this subsidy on consumer's welfare and money value of this subsidy to the consumer is illustrated in Figure 11.1 where the quantity of food is measured on the

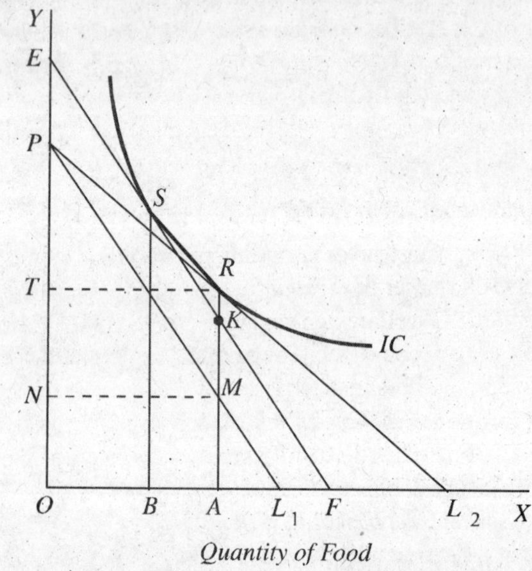

Fig. 11.1. *Effect of Subsidies to Consumers*

X-axis and money on the *Y*-axis. Let us suppose that the individual has *OP* money income. Given this money income and given the market price of food, the price line is PL_1. Since we are assuming that subsidy paid by the Government is half the market price of food, the consumer would pay half the market price. Therefore,with subsidy the individual will face the price line PL_2 where $OL_1 = L_1 L_2$. With price line PL_2, the individual is in equilibrium at point *R* on the indifference curve *IC* at which he is purchasing *OA* quantity of food. By purchasing *OA* quantity of food, the individual is spending *PT* amount of money. Now, if no food subsidy was given and therefore the price line was PL_1, then for buying *OA* quantity of food, the individual would have spent *PN* amount of money. In other words, *PN* is the market price of *OA* quantity of food. Since *PT* amount of money is paid by the individual himself, the remaining amount *TN* or *RM* (the vertical distance between the price lines PL_1 and PL_2 at *OA* amount of food) is paid by the Government as food subsidy for the individual.

Now, the important question is what is the *money value* of this price subsidy (*RM*) on food to the individual. When no price subsidy is paid, the individual faces the price line PL_1. In order to find the money value of the subsidy to the individual, draw a line *EF* parallel to PL_1 so that it touches the same indifference curve *IC* where the individual comes to be in equilibrium when subsidy is paid. It will be seen from Figure 11.1 that budget line *EF* touches the indifference curve *IC* at a point *S* and is buying *OB* quantity of food. This means that if individual is paid *PE* amount of money (say as a cash grant), he reaches the same indifference curve *IC* (same level of welfare) at which he is when price subsidy is paid by the Government on food. Thus *PE*, is money value of the subsidy to the individual. It will be seen from Figure 11.1 that *PE* is less than *RM* which is the amount of money paid by the Government as subsidy. In our Figure *PE* = *MK* (the vertical distance between two parallel lines) and *RM* is greater than *MK*. Therefore, *RM* is also greater than *PE*. It follows that *PE* is less than *RM*. If instead of giving *RM* as price subsidy on food, Government pays the individual cash money equal to *PE*, the individual will reach the same level of welfare as he does with *RM* subsidy.

Thus, the cash money equivalent of the price subsidy to the individual is less than the cost of the subsidy to the Government. "In fact, it would always be so whatever the subsidy and whatever the preferences of consumers so long as only the indifference curves remain convex and smooth. *Thus the cost of giving subsidies to consumers is always greater than the money equivalent of the subjective gain to the consumers*". Here, of course, is a special case of general principle that, apart from considerations of etiquette and sentiments, *you can make someone happier if you give him cash instead of a commodity even if the commodity is something he wants.*[1]

Lump-Sum Cash Subsidy

Now, if instead of providing price subsidy on food, the Government gives lump-sum cash grant to the consumer *equivalent to the cost of price subsidy on food*, what will be its impact on the individual's welfare and consumption of food by him. As explained above in Fig. 11.1 cost of price subsisdy on food to the Government equals *RM* amount of money. If the Government provides the consumer lump-sum cash grant of *RM* instead of price subsidy on food, this will amount to increasing the money income of the consumer by *RM* amount. With this extra cash transfer equal to *RM* (=*PC*), the budget-line will shift to the right to the position *CD* in Fig. 11.2 which passes through point R. It will be seen from Figure 11.2 that with the budget line *CD* though the individual *can buy the same market basket R, if he so desires*, which he was purchasing with price subsidy on food, he is actually in equilibrium at point *H* on higher indifference curve IC_2. Thus, the cash transfer equivalent to the cost of price subsidy has led to the greater increase in welfare or satisfaction of the individual as compared to the price subsidy. Further, as will be seen from Figure 11.2, *with a cash*

1. D. S. Watson, *Price Theory and Its Uses*, 1963, p. 94.

grant the individual buys less food and more of other goods relative to the situation under price subsidy with the equivalent monetary cost.

That the individual with cash transfer must be better off and his food consumption must be less as compared with price subsidy on food is due to the fact that indifference curves being convex, the budget line *CD* obtained with cash transfer *must intersect* the indifference curve IC_1 at point *R* reached with the equivalent price subsidy. Therefore, given that the consumer is free to spend money as he likes, with cash grant his new equilibrium position must be to the left of point *R on the budget line CD* where it will be tangent to the higher indifference curve than IC_2. This implies that in *case of lump-sum cash subsidy, the consumer will be better off and consume less food* relative to the equilibrium position under price subsidy on food

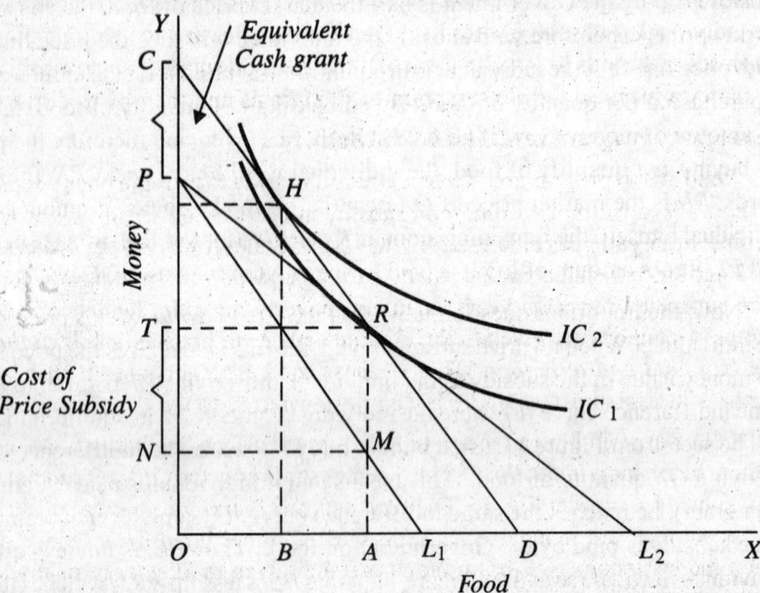

Fig. 11.2. *Lump-Sum Cash Grant is Better than Price Subsidy*

The superiority of cash grant in terms of its impact on the welfare of the individuals can be explained in a slightly different way. Though both the lump-sum cash transfer and price subsidy on a commodity produces income effect making the individual better off, under *cash grant the individual is free to buy different goods according to his own tastes and preferences which ensures a higher level of welfare as compared to the policy of price subsidy on food which imposes a certain pattern of consumption favouring food.* Besides, a lower price of food due to price subsidy on it induces the consumer to substitute food for other goods causing greater consumption of food as compared to the scheme of lump-sum cash grant which have no such substitution effect and permits free choice of goods to the individual according to his own preference. Thus, to quote Prof. Watson again, "*you can make someone happier if you give him cash instead of a commodity, even if the commodity is something he wants.*[2] Likewise, Professor Scitovsky remarks, "*one can make a man happier by giving him cash and letting him spend it as he thinks best than by forcing him to take all his relief in the form of one commodity. Hence, relief payments in cash are preferable to a food subsidy because they are economically more efficient, giving the relief receipts either a greater gain at the same cost to the Government or the same gain at a lower cost.*"[3]

But the above principle regarding the programme of subsidised food, subsidised housing etc. cannot always be validly applied to the Government subsidy programme since the above principle is based upon the *subjective benefits to the individuals* which is not always the correct criteria to judge the desirability of Government subsidy programme. For instance, the aim of Government's food subsidy programme may be that the needy families should consume more food so that their

---

2. D. S. Watson, *Price Theory and Its Uses*, 1963, p. 94.
3. Tibor Scitovsky, *Welfare and Competition*, revised edition, 1971, p. 70.

health and efficiency may be improved. It will be seen from Figure 11.2 that with food subsidy *RM*, the individual is having *OA* amount of food, whereas with equivalent cash payment of *PC* the individual purchases *OB* amount of food which is less than *OA*. Thus the food subsidy has induced the individual to consume more food than in case of cash payment. Similarly, if a country has food surpluses and wants to dispose them of, then the food subsidy to the needy families will be the ideal measure to increase the consumption of foodgrains and thereby to dispose of the food surpluses.

Food Stamp Programme : In-kind Food Subsidy

Food stamp programme is a type of food subsidy to provide poor people with adequate quantity of food. It is a form of *in-kind food subsidy* in contrast to the subsidy provided in the form of cash income, often called *cash subsidy*. In the United States it was introduced in 1964 and was amended in 1979 and since then it continues there in the amended form. In India also food stamp programme has been suggested in recent years as an anti-poverty measure. Under food stamp programme, some stamps or coupons are given to the eligible persons or households. *With these stamps, the recipient can buy food and only food.* That is, these food stamps cannot be used to buy non-food goods. Further, these stamps cannot be traded or transferred to the other people.

Let us explain how a receipt of food stamps affects the budget line, consumption of food and welfare of the individual. We will also demonstrate how the effect of food-stamp subsidy differs from cash subsidy. Consider Fig. 11.3 where along the *X*-aixs we measure quantity of food and along the *Y*-axis we measure money which represents all other goods, (*i.e.* goods other than food). With a given money income $OB_1$of an individual and given market price of food, B_1L_1 is the budget line whose slope represents the price of food (Note that price of money represented on the *Y*-axis is Re. 1., that is, price of rupee one is Re.1.). Before the receipt of food stamps the individual is in equilibrium at point E_1 on indifference curve IC_1 and is consuming OF_1 quantity of food and ON_1 quantity of other goods per week.

Now, suppose the individual is given food stamps of Rs. 200 per week which he can spend on food alone. Suppose further that price of food is Rs. 10 per kg. With stamps of Rs. 200 he can therefore buy 20 kg of food which is equal to B_1C at the given market price. Since the consumer cannot use food stamps to buy non-food items (other goods) he cannot spend more than his initial income OB_1 on other goods. Thus above the horizontal line B_1C, the combinations of other goods and food are not attainable when he is given the food stamps of Rs. 200. Since at the given market price of food, he can buy B_1C amount of food with the food stamps of Rs. 200 provided to him, while spending his entire income *OB* on other goods. *For instance, if price of food is Rs. 10 per kg., then with Rs. 200 he can buy 20 kg of food.* In this case, therefore, B_1C, will be equal to 20 kg. If the individual wants to buy more foodgrains than B_1C, then he will spend some part of his initial income to purchase additional food. Since the food stamps are in addition to his initial income OB_1 his budget line with food stamps becomes a kinked line $B_1\,CL_2$.

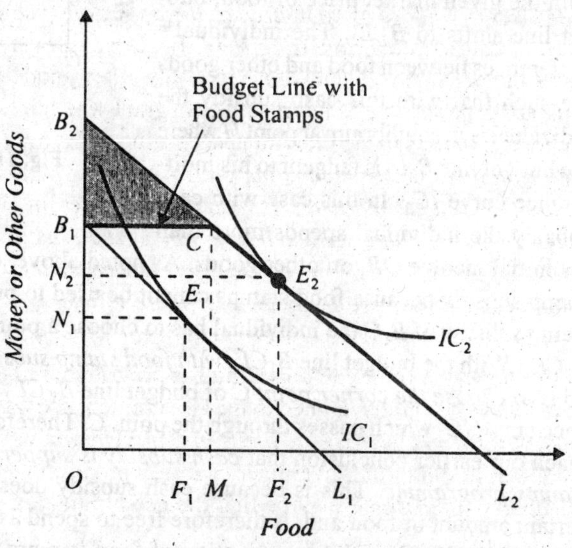

Fig. 11.3. *Effects of Food Stamp Programme on Consumption*

The food stamp programme can affect the recipient in two ways. One possibility is that with the food-stamp subsidy and resultant kinked budget line B_1CL_2, in Fig. 11.3 the individual maximises his satisfaction at point E_2 where his budget line is tangent to indifference curve IC_2 . At this new equilibrium point E_2 he is purchasing OF_2 quantity of food and ON_2 of other goods. Thus, as compared to the situation prior to food-stamp subsidy, he is on higher indifference curve showing a greater level of satisfaction or welfare and consuming greater quantities of food and other goods. Thus, *food stamps subsidy has led him to buy not only more food but also more of other goods. This means that a part of food stamp subsidy has been* indirectly *used for financing the purchases of non-food commodities.*

It is important to note that in this possible case, the effect of food stamp subsidy is exactly the same as would be the case if cash subsidy is granted to the individual. Thus, if instead of the food stamps the individual is given equivalent cash income of $B_1 B_2$ (*Note that with given market price of food, cash income of B_1B_2 can buy B_1C quantity of food and thus the two are equivalent*), the budget line will shift from $B_1 L_2$ to $B_2 L_2$. But given the preferences of the individual between food and other goods, he is in equilibrium at the same point E_2 at which his budget line B_2L_2 is tanget to the indifference curve IC_2. Thus, in this possibility, the effect of equivalent cash subsidy is exactly the same as the effect of food stamp subsidy. This happens because the preferences of the individual between food and other commodities are such that he wants to have more than B_1C quantity of food which is the quantity of food provided under the food stamp subsidy.

Another important conclusion from this possible case is that with either food stamp subsidy or cash subsidy the individual buys more of both food and other goods than he buys before the grant of subsidy. This is because food and other goods are here considered as normal goods whose quantity demanded increase with the increase in income.

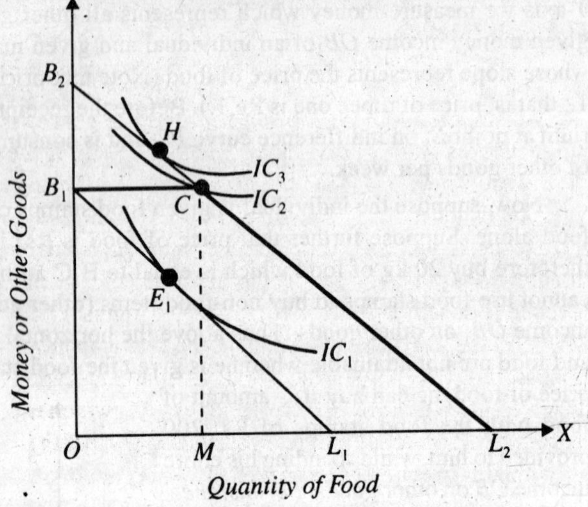

Fig. 11.4. *Effects of Food Stamp Subsidy and Cash Subsidy on Consumption and Welfare*

The second possibility of the effect of food stamp subsidy is illustrated in Fig. 11.4. Prior to grant of any subsidy, and given his budget line $B_1 L_1$ the individual is in equilibrium at point E_1 on indifference curve IC_1. Now let us assume that he is given the cash subsidy of $B_1 B_2$ so that with the given market price of food, budget line shifts to $B_2 L_2$. The individual's preferences between food and other goods are such that with this cash subsidy the individual is in equilibrium at point H where the budget line B_2L_2 is tangent to his indifference curve IC_3. In this case with cash subsidy the individual spends more than his initial income OB_1 on other goods. As noted above, combination H is not available under food stamp subsidy because food stamps cannot be used to purchase other goods. With equivalent food stamp subsidy of B_1C the individual has to choose a point which must be on the kinked budget line B_1CL_2. With the budget line B_1CL_2 *with food stamp subsidy of B_1 C, the best that the individual can do is to choose the corner point C* of budget line B_1 CL_2 which lies on the highest possible indifference curve IC_2 which passes through the point C. Therefore, from the point of individual welfare we reach our earlier conclusion that *cash subsidy is supperior to in-kind subsidy represented by food stamps programme.* This is because cash subsidy does not limit a person that he must purchase certain amount of food and is therefore free to spend as he likes. But it should be noted that in the second possible case the consumption of food is more under the food stamp subsidy programme than in case of cash subsidy. If the purpose is to increase the consumption of food and therefore provide adequate diet to the people, then food stamp subsidy is better than cash subsidy as under the former, the individual is constrained to buy at least a given quantity of food.

Another important result obtained from our above analysis is that *even with food stamps programme the individual increases the consumption of all other goods* (*i.e.* that is, non-food items) too. This shows that a part of food stamp subsidy is *indirectly* used to finance the increased consumption of other goods. This is because some part of the income which the individual was spending on food prior to food-stamp subsidy get released because of the food-stamps being used for its purchase and this released income is spent on non-food items. This increases the consumption of non-food items also. This result is of special importance because supporters of food-stamp subsidy have been emphasising that food subsidy should not be used to finance any part of non-food unnecessary items such as liquor. However, as seen above, in practice it is difficult to make a plan that will increase the consumption of subsidised food and will not affect the consumption of other goods.

Lastly, out of the two possibilities of the effects of food-stamp subsidy and cash subsidy which is the most common result, that is, the most common outcome of the two possible cases presented in Fig. 11.3 and Fig. 11.4 . However, the final result of the two types of subsidies depends on the value of food stamps relative to preferences and incomes of the individuals whom subsidies are granted. We cannot predict the specific result purely on theoretical grounds. Empirical research conducted in the USA however reveals that most recipients of food stamp porogramme represent situation depicted in Fig. 11.3. This means for most of the recipients, food stamp programme has the same effect as a cash subsidy.

DIRECT TAX VERSUS INDIRECT TAX

An important application of indifference curves is to judge the welfare effects of direct and indirect taxes on the individuals. In other words, if the Government wants to raise a given amount of revenue whether it will be better to do so by levying a direct tax or an indirect tax from the view point of welfare of the individuals[4]. We shall study below that indirect tax such as excise duty income causes excess burden on the individuals, that is, indirect tax reduces welfare more than the direct tax, say income tax when an equal amount of revenue is raised through them. Consider Figure 11.5 where on the X-axis, good X and on the Y-axis money is measured. With a given income of the individual and the given price of good X, the price line is PL_1 which is tangent to indifference curve IC_3 at point Q_3 where the individual is in equilibrium position.

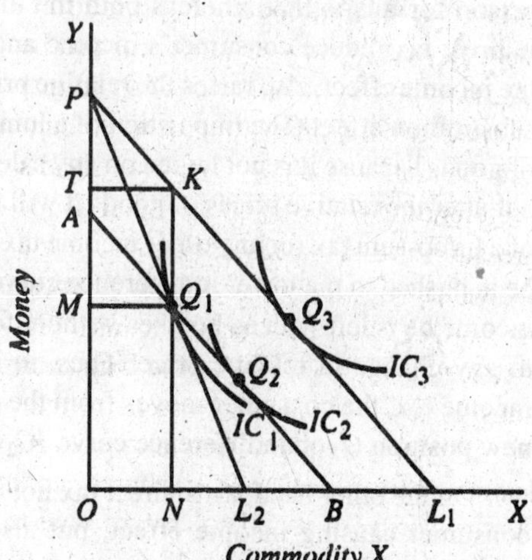

Fig. 11.5. *Indirect tax causes excess burden.*

Suppose now that Government levies an excise duty (an indirect tax) on good X. With the imposition of excise duty, the price of good X will rise. As a result of the rise in price of good X, the price line rotates to a new position PL_2 which is tangent to indifference curve IC_1 at point Q_1. It is thus clear that as a result of the imposition of excise duty, the individual has shifted from a higher indifference curve IC_3 to a lower one IC_1, that is, his level of satisfaction or welfare has declined. It is worth noting that the movement from Q_3 on indif-

4. Direct taxes are those taxes whose incidence cannot be shifted to others. Income tax, wealth tax, death duty are the examples of direct tax. On the other hand, an indirect tax is one which can be passed on or shifted to others by raising the prices of the goods. The excise duty, sales tax are the examples of indirect tax.

ference curve IC_3 to Q_1 on indifference curve IC_1 is the combined result of the income effect and substitution effect caused by the excise duty.

It should be further noted that at point Q_1 (that is, after the imposition of excise duty) the individual is purchasing *ON* amount of good *X* and has paid *PM* amount of money for it. At the old price (before the excise duty was imposed), he could purchase *ON* quantity of good *X* for *PT* amount of money. Thus, the difference *TM* (or KQ_1) between the two is the amount of money which the individual is paying as the excise duty. Direct taxes are those taxes whose incidence cannot be shifted to others. Lump sum tax, proportionate and progressive income taxes, wealth tax, death duty are the examples of direct tax. On the other hand, an indirect tax is one which can be passed on or shifted to others by raising the prices of the goods. The excise duty, sales tax are the examples of indirect tax.

Now, suppose that instead of excise duty, Government levies a direct tax of the type of lump-sum tax on the individual when the individual is initially at point Q_3 on indifference curve IC_3. With the imposition of lump sum tax, the price line will shift below but will be parallel to the original price line PL_1. Further, if the same amount of revenue is to be raised through lump-sum tax as with the excise duty, then the new price line *AB* should be drawn at such a distance from the original price line PL_1 that it passes through the point Q_1. So, it will be seen from Figure 11.5 that with the imposition of lump sum tax equivalent in terms of revenue raising to the excise duty, we have drawn the budget line *AB* which is passing through the point Q_1. However, with *AB* as the price line, individual is in equilibrium at point Q_2 on indifference curve IC_2 which lies at a higher level than IC_1. In other words, at point Q_2 individual's level of welfare is higher than at Q_1. Lump-sum tax has reduced the individual's welfare less than that by the excise duty. Thus, *indirect tax (excise duty) causes an excess burden on the individual.*[5]

Now, the important question is why an indirect tax (an excise duty or a sales tax on a commodity) causes excess burden on the consumer in terms of loss of welfare or satisfaction. The basic reason for this is that whereas both the lump-sum tax (or any other general income tax) and an indirect tax reduce consumer's income and produce income effect, the indirect tax in addition to the income effect, also raises the relative price of the good on which it is levied and therefore causes substitution effect. The imposition of a lump-sum tax (or any income tax) does not affect the prices of goods because it is not levied on any saleable goods. Since lump-sum tax or any income tax does not alter the relative prices of goods it will not result in any substitution effect. With the imposition of a lump-sum tax (or any other income tax), a certain income is taken away from the consumer and he is pushed to the lower indifference curve (or a lower level of welfare) but he is free to spend the income he is left with as he likes without forcing him to substitute one commodity for another due to any change in relative price. Thus, in Figure 11.5, imposition of an equivalent lump-sum or income tax, the consumer moves from the equilibrium position Q_3 on indifference curve IC_3 to the new position Q_2 on indifference curve IC_2 which represents the income effect.

On the other hand, an indirect tax not only reduces the purchasing power or real income of the consumer causing income effect, but also produces price-induced substitution effect and thus

---

5. This conclusion regarding excess burden of indirect tax compared to the direct tax is however based on several assumptions about initial conditions. Whether or not indirect tax reduces welfare more than direct tax depends upon so many initial conditions before the taxes are introduced. For knowing the analysis regarding welfare implications of direct and indirect taxes, see (1) I.M.D. Little, Direct Versus Indirect Taxes, *Economic Journal*, Sept. 1951. (2) Milton Friedman, The Welfare Effects of Taxes, *Essays in Positive Economics*. University of Chicago Press, 1953 and (3) R.A. Musgrave, *Theory of Public Finance*.

forcing him to purchase less of the commodity on which indirect tax has been levied and buy more of the non-taxed commodity. And this later substitution effect caused due to the price-distortion by the indirect tax further reduces his welfare. As will be seen from Figure 11.5, as a result of income effect of the indirect tax the consumer moves from point Q_3 on indifference curve IC_3 to point Q_2 on lower indifference curve IC_2 and as a result of substitution effect he is further pushed to point Q_1 on still lower indifference IC_1.

EFFECT OF RATIONING ON CONSUMER'S WELFARE

Indifference curve analysis can be used to explain under what conditions rationing of goods by the Government can act as binding or a constraint on consumer's choices and further how it affects his welfare. It may be noted that income of a consumer along with the prices of goods serves as a constraint on his choices and is often called a *budget constraint*. This budget constraint can be written as follows :

$$P_x.X + P_y.Y \leq M$$

The above inequality implies that consumer can choose a combination of goods from within or on the *market opportunity set*. With given income of the consumer and prices of the two goods we draw a budget line *BL* in Figure 11.6. The shaded region bounded by the budget line *BL* and the coordinate axes represents market opportunity set from which the consumer can make a choice of the two commodities. If now the Government introduces a rationing for commodity *X* and fixes a ration of *X* equal to OR_x (At point R_x we have shown a vertical line showing the constraint or ration limit imposed by the rationing fixed at OR_x). It will be seen that with ration limit fixed at OR_x rationing does not act as a binding at all and prove to be quite ineffective in restricting the consumption of good *X* which is the objective of the policy. However, such a situation is relevant in case of a poor family whose income is so small that it cannot buy even the rationed quantity. It is the income that serves as a binding on his consumption choice and not the ration limit.

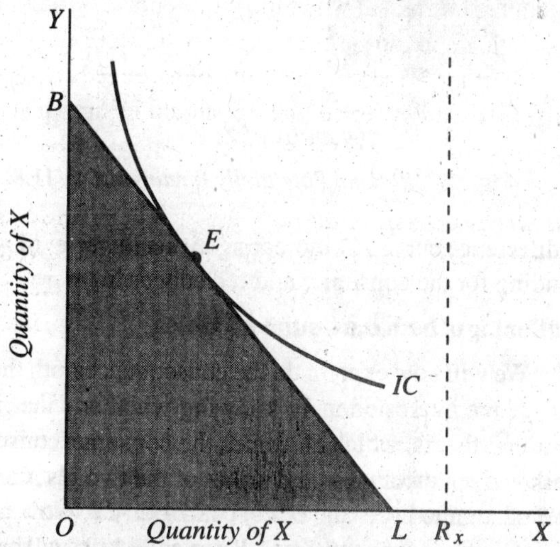

Fig. 11.6. *Ration : not Binding*

Now consider Figure 11.7 where ration limit is fixed at R_x which lies to the left of *L*. This ration limit reduces or truncates his market opportunity set (*i.e.* set of attainable combinations of two goods *X* and *Y*) as shown by the reduced shaded area in Figure 11.7 and therefore in this case the *ration limit is only potentially binding* on him. Though the consumer can buy the ration amount, that is, ration limit is attainable but he is not willing to consume good *X* as much as the ration limit permits him. He is in equilibrium at point *E* where he consumes quantity of good *X* which is smaller than the ration amount R_x. Thus, his preferences are such that rationing is not actually binding for him. Ration limit is potentially binding here because due to ration limit the consumer *cannot* buy any set of two commodities lying in the region SLR_x, if he so desires though his price-income situation permits him to do so.

However, the more important and relevant case of rationing is depicted in Figure 11.8. In this case ration limit fixed is R_x which lies to the left of his equilibrium position *E*. Without the restriction of rationing he will consume a larger amount of commodity *X* and will be at indifference curve IC_1. With the budget line *BL* and the rationed quantity R_x he will be at point *E*′ which lies at lower indifference curve IC_0. Thus ration limit serves as a binding for him and forces him to consume less of good X and more of good Y than he prefers. That is why at point K in Fig. 11.8 he is at lower

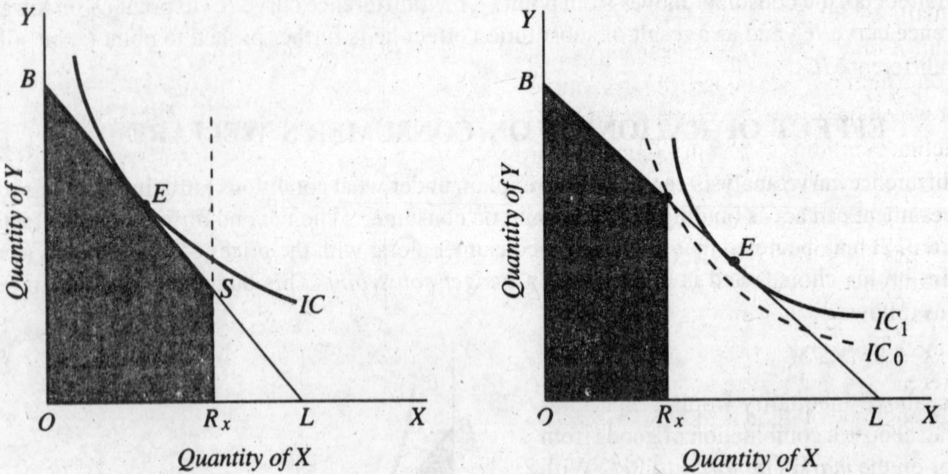

Fig. 11.7. *Ration : Potentially Binding* **Fig. 11.8.** *Ration is binding and reduces consumer's welfare.*

indifference curve IC_0 indicating his lower level of welfare. Thus, in this case, rationing is actually binding for the consumer and reduces his welfare.

Rationing of both the Commodities

We will now explain the consequences if both the commodities X and Y are rationed. In particular we are interested in knowing whether it is the ration limits or income of the consumer that is binding, that is, which forces the consumer to consume less amounts of the goods. In Figure 11.9 with a given income and prices of the two goods X and Y the consumer is in equilibrium at E buying OM of commodity X and ON of commodity Y. Now, suppose with the introduction of rationing, ration limit R is fixed for good X and R_y for good Y. It will be seen from Figure 11.9 that ration amounts of R_x and R_y of goods X and Y respectively are greater than OM and ON which the consumer is buying with his price-income situation. Therefore, the ration limits in this case are *not actually binding* since these do not any more constrain his consumption. Of course, these ration limits narrow down or truncate his market opportunity set at both ends on the X and Y axes, and in this way they are *potentially binding* but they are *not effective* in restraining his consumption. Therefore, this can be interpreted to be the case of a poor family whose optimum consumption basket of the two goods is small because of its low income and therefore remains unaffected if ration limits are set at higher levels.

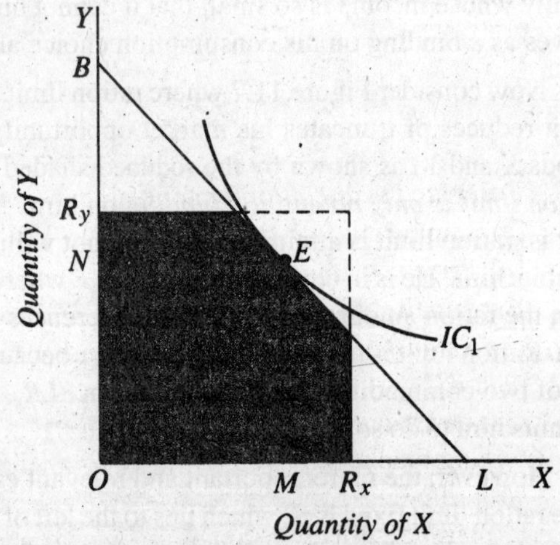

Fig. 11.9. *Ration is potentially binding*

Now, consider Figure 11.10 where it will be seen that ration limit R_y is smaller than consumer's optimum consumption of Y as indicated by combination E of the two goods on the budget line BL which has been drawn with his given income and prices of two goods. But ration limit R_x for good X is larger than his optimum or equilibrium consumption quantity of good X. It follows therefore that for good Y ration limit is actually binding as it forces the consumer to point K on a lower indifference curve IC_0 than optimum point E on indifference curve IC_1 at which he would have been without the restriction of rationing. On the other hand, in case of good X in Figure 11.10 the ration limit R_x does not seem to be effective, though it is potentially binding as it truncates his market opportunity set. It will be observed that binding by rationing lowers his level of welfare as he is forced to come to the point L on a lower indifference IC_0 where he consumes less of good Y and moe of good X than he prefers.

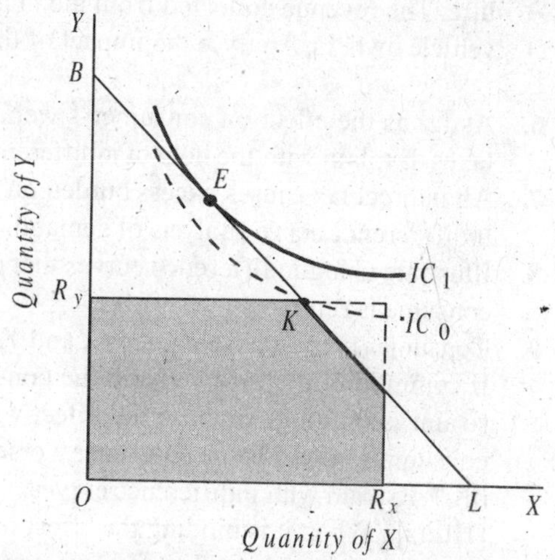

Fig. 11.10. *Y-Ration is Binding, X-Ration is Not Binding.*

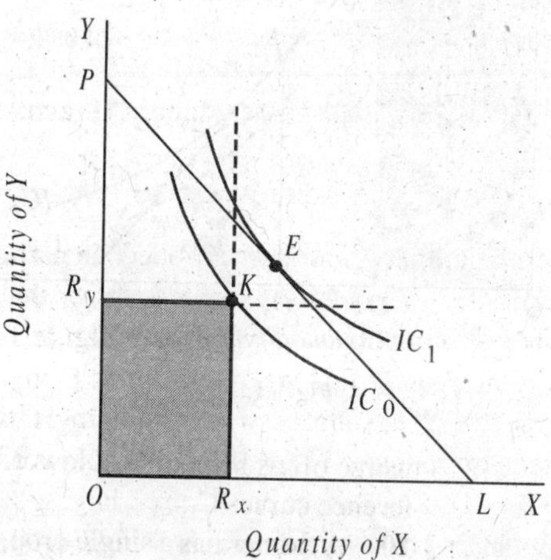

Fig. 11.11. *Both Ration Limits are Binding and reduce consumer's Welfare.*

In Figure 11.11 both ration limits R_x and R_y are actually binding and force the individual to consume less of both the commodities than he consumes at his equilibrium position E in the absence of rationing of the two commodities. Figure 11.11 depicts the case of a relatively rich person who without the binding of rationing is at point E on indifference curve IC_1 and is consuming greater quantities of the two goods than the ration amounts. Introduction of rationing limits forces him to come to point K on the lower indifference curve IC_0 and consume less amounts of both the goods than he would do without the restriction of rationing. Thus in this case rationing is actually binding on him and reduces his welfare.

QUESTIONS FOR REVIEW

1. Compare the effects of the following policies on consumer welfare.
   (*i*) Lump-sum cash transfer.
   (*ii*) Price subsidy on food
   (D.U.B. Com.(H) 2000
2. Explain the effect of a food subsidy on the welfare of consumers and compare it with an *outright cash transfer of the same cost*. What considerations determine government's policy in this regard?
   (D.U. B.A. (H) 1990)
3. One can make a man happier by giving him cash and letting him spend as he thinks best than by forcing to take all his relief in the form of one commodity (Scitovsky). Do you agree ? Discuss with reference to the effect of excise subsidy on sugar.
4. Explain the effect on consumption and welfare of food subsidiy in the form of food stamps.. Compare it with the effects of cash subsidy.

5. During the energy crisis of 1990-91 a proposal was made to increase the tax on petrol by ₹ 2.0 per litre. The revenue collected from the increased tax was to be given as a cash subsidy to motor-vehicle owners. Analyse the impact of the proposal on the consumption of the petrol.

D.U. (B.A. (Hons.)1996)

6. As far as the effect on consumer's welfare is concerned, direct taxes are superior to indirect taxes. Explain with the help of indifference curve analysis. *D.U. (B.Com.(Hons.) 1998)*

7. An indirect tax causes excess burden on the consumer. Do you agree? Explain with the help of indiffderence curve analysis of demand. *D.U. (B.Com. (Hons.) 1995)*

8. Illustrate using indifference curves that consumers become worse off when a product that they consume is rationed.

9. Consumer consumes two goods *X* and *Y*. If commodity *x* is rationed and the constraint is binding. What is the effective consumption set ? Is the consumer worse off ? Explain with indifference curves.

[Hints] : When it is binding the effect of rationing is to reduce the effective consumption set. For example, in Figure 11.21 with the budget line *BL*, a consumer is in equilibrium at point *E* on indifference curve IC_2 and consuming OQ_2 quantity of *X*. With imposition of OQ_1 of good *X* as a ration quantity the consumer is forced to shift to the position *K* on the given budget line *BL* where he is at his lower indifference curve IC_1. The effective consumption set is reduced to the shaded area OQ_1 *KB*. Rationing has made him worse off as he is now at lower indifference curve IC_1.

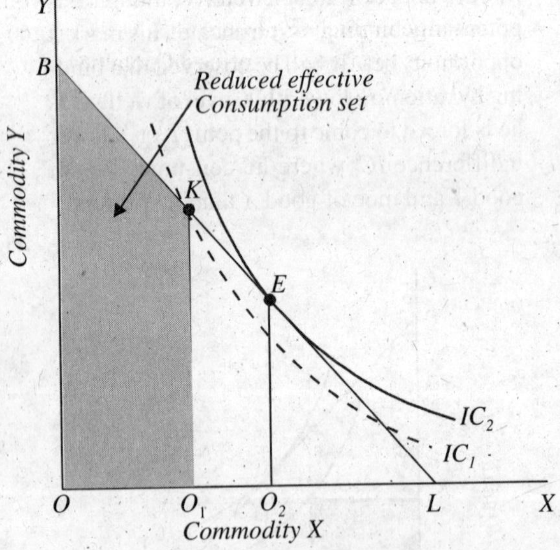

Fig. 11. 12

10. A farmer has a single crop, potatoes, for the support of his family. He consumes some and sells the remainder to obtain income to spend on other goods. Assuming a given price for potatoes and given prices for all other goods, illustrate his equilibrium position using indifference curve analysis.

What would be the impact of higher potatoes price on the quantity of potatoes consumed with all other prices remaining unchanged?

D.U.B.A. (Hons) 1995

[Hints : This is just like the case of workers selling their labour. Here, a farmer sells his potatoes produced by him. Suppose, the farmer's production of potatoes is *OB* (= 100 quintals) in Figure 11.22 . If price of potatoes is ₹ 50 per quintal, the income from the

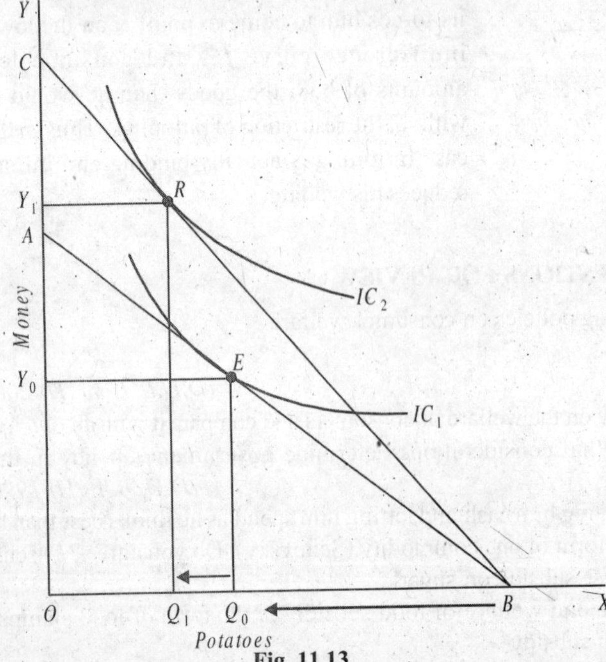

Fig. 11.13

sale of the whole quantity *OB* (*i.e.* 100 quintals) will be ₹ 5000 (= *OA*). Thus, *BA*. is the price-income line facing the farmer. He is in equilibrium at point *E* on indifference curve IC_1 drawn between potatoes and money. With equilibrium at *E* he is selling BQ_0 quantity of potatoes to earn income equal to OY_0. He is having OQ_0 potatoes left for self-consumption.

Now suppose price of potatoes rises to ₹ 55 per quintal so that price income line shifts upward to the new position *BC*. If the farmer *responds positively* to the rise in price his new equilibrium will lie to the left of point *E* showing he will sell more quantity of potatoes and consequently will have less quantity of potatoes for self-consumption. It will be seen from Figure 11.22 that with *BC* as the new price-income line he is in equilibrium at point *R* on the higher indifference curve IC_2. With this new equilibrium point *R* he has sold larger quantity BQ_1 of potatoes and therefore have smaller quantity OQ_1 left for self-consumption. Note that change in price of potatoes has both income effect and substitution effect. The response of the farmer to change in price of potatoes can be explained in terms of income and substitution effects of change in price].

CHAPTER 11A
LABOUR SUPPLY AND SAVING DECISIONS

The Household as Supplier of Labour and Savings

Labour and capital are two important factors of production. How households decide about the amount of labour supplied and the quantity of savings. Savings are required for making investment in building of capital goods. In modern economics indifference curve analysis is used to explain the decisions of individuals regarding supply of labour and capital. We have explained some important applications of indifference curve analysis in a previous chapter. In the present chapter we will analyse labour supply and saving decisions of households with indifference curve analysis.

LABOUR SUPPLY DECISION

Labour is an important factor in the process of production. The amount of a good produced depends on the amount of labour used along with capital. Therefore, increase in labour supply determines the growth of production. *The labour supply depends not only the population of a country but also on labour-force participation rate and the number of hours worked by workers.* Labour supply in various countries has changed greatly not only because of population growth but also due to change in labour-force participation rate and the number of hours per week. Thus, the average work week for an unskilled workers in Britain has declined from about 45 hours in 1947 to about 40 hours a week today. But the labour force participation of women in Britain has substantially increased. Because of this increased participation of women in labour force, average married household works more hours in a week than it did in 1900. There has been increase in part-time extra jobs in Britain and. USA today which are mostly done by women. This has tended to increase labour supply.

Choice between Consumption (Income) and Leisure.

The basic model of labour supply used by the economists is based on choice of individuals between consumption (or income) and leisure. Leisure in economics means '*not working by an individual for pay*' when he is able to do so. In the leisure-time individuals can listen to radio, watch television, take care of their children and play with them, spend time in outdoor recreation and entertainment. In economics leisure is regarded as a normal good, that is, with the increase in his income an individual would like to have more leisure.

There is trade-off between leisure and income. By foregoing some present leisure, a person earns additional income and therefore increase his consumption. On the other hand, by working fewer hours and therefore earning less income the individual scarifies some consumption in order to enjoy more leisure.

It may be noted that though a typical job requires the individuals to work for fixed hours in a day or week even then individuals can influence how many hours in a week they will work (i.e. quantity of labour supplied). The individual can change the quantity of labour supplied in a variety of ways. First, individuals can decide about whether they would work overtime or not. Second, the individuals can take second part time jobs and thus increase their work-hours in a week. Thus, even though individuals have no choice about how much to work in their primary job, they still have choices through which they can influence amount of work-hours (or labour) supplied. Lastly, it is worth mentioning that reduction in work hours in general in many countries including India has been largely due to increase in preference for leisure by individuals as the economies have grown. In this connection we can use the concept of budget constraint explained in the theory of consumer choice. In Figure 11A.1(a) we have drawn a budget constraint line *BL* of an individual who works at the hourly wage rate of ₹ 25 per hour. We suppose that an individual must sleep 8 hours in a day and

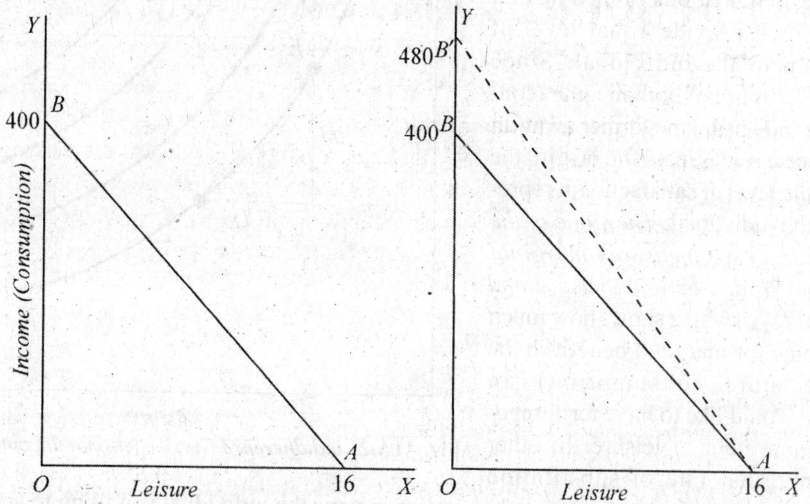

Fig. 11A.1. (a) *Budget Constraint of Workers* **Fig. 11A.1(b)** *Shift in the Budget Constraint due to Rise in Wage Rate*

the remaining 16 hours are available for either working for income (*i.e.* consumption) or spending in enjoying leisure. If he works for all 16 hours available to him in a day he will earn ₹ 400 per day. Thus, for each extra hour of work and earning ₹ 25, he foregoes one hour of leisure. Thus, if he works for all 16 hours in a day, he will have income of ₹ 400 to spend on goods and services which he can consume, but he will have no leisure. Thus, according to budget constraint shown in Fig. 11A.1(*a*), trade off is ₹ 25 per hour. The slope of the budget constraint is equal to the wage rate. It may be noted that **the budget contraint describes the opportunity set of combinations of leisure and income or consumption open to an individual from which he can choose.**

It is worth mentioning that increase in wage rate will cause the budget constraint to shift to the right. In Figure 11A.1(*b*) when the wage rate rises from ₹ 25 per hour to ₹ 30 per hour, budget constraint line shifts to right to *AB′*.

The individual will choose a point on the given budget constraint depending on his preferences between income (consumption) and leisure. Therefore, on a budget constraint different individuals will choose different points or combinations of income (or consumption) and leisure depending on their preferences between income and leisure. Indifference curve analysis can be used to explain the choice of a combination of income (consumption) and leisure on a give budget constraint. Therefore, let us first explain the indifference curves drawn between income (or consumption) and leisure. Remember that in economics leisure is regarded as a normal commodity.

Indifference Curves Between Income and Leisure

In economics leisure is regarded as a normal commodity the enjoyment of which yields satisfaction to the individual. While leisure yields satisfaction to the individual directly, income represents general purchasing power capable of being used to buy goods and services for satisfaction of various wants. Thus income provides satisfaction indirectly. Therefore, we can draw indifference curves between income and leisure both of which give satisfaction to the individual. An indifference map between income and leisure is depicted in Figure 11A.2 and have all the usual properties of indifference curves. They slope downward to the right, are convex to the origin, and do not intersect. Each indifference curve represents various alternative combinations of income and leisure, which provide equal level of satisfaction to the individual. Since people prefer more of both income (consumption) and leisure the farther away an indifference curve is from the origin, the higher is the level of satisfaction it represents for the individual. *The slope of the indifference curve measures marginal rate of substitution between leisure and income (MRS_{LM})* which shows how much extra income (or marginal benefit in the form of more consumption) an individual would like to have for foregoing one more hour of leisure. In other words, marginal rate of substitution between income and leisure measures how much income the individual is willing to accept for one hour sacrifice of leisure time. In geometric terms, it will be seen from Figure 11A.2 that on indifference curve IC_1 at point D the individual is willing to accept M income for sacrificing an hour (L) of leisure. Thus marginal rate of substitution between income and leisure at this point is, therefore, $\frac{M}{L}$. At different income-leisure levels, the marginal rate of substitution between leisure and income varies.

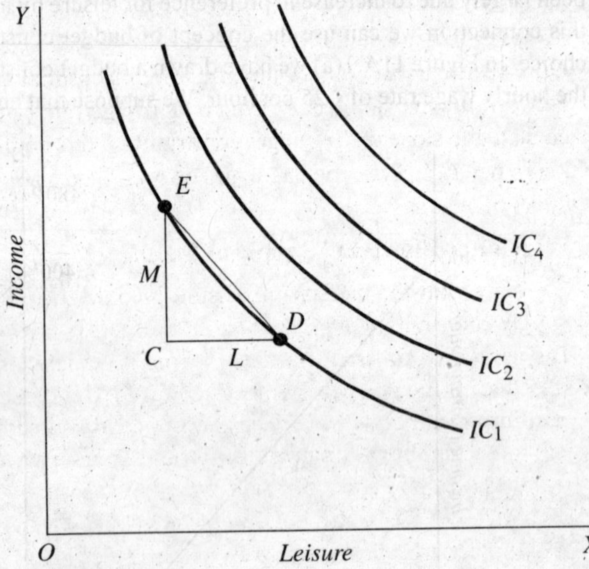

Fig. 11A.2. *Indidfference Curves between Income and Leisure*

Income-Leisure Equilibrium : Labour Supply

Now, we can bring together the indifference map showing ranking of preferences of the individual between income and leisure, and the budget constraint line to show the actual choice of leisure and income by the individual in his equilibrium position. We will further show how much work effort (*i.e.* supply of labour in terms of hours worked) he would put in this optimal situation. Our analysis is based on two assumptions. First, the individual is *free to work as many hours per day as he likes*. Second, wage rate is the same irrespective of the number of hours he chooses to work.

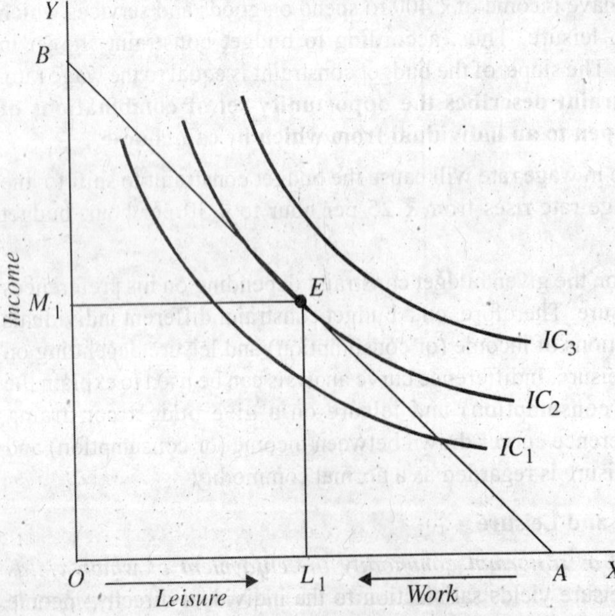

Fig. 11A.3. *Income-Leisure Equilibrium*

Figure 11A.3 displays income-leisure equilibrium of the individual. With the given wage rate, the individual will choose a combination of income and leisure lying on the given budget line that maximises his satisfaction. It will be seen from Figure 11A.3 that the given budget constraint line AB is tangent to the indifference curve IC_2 between income and leisure at point E showing choice of OL_1 of leisure and OM_1 of income. In this optimal situation, marginal rate of substitution MRS between income and leisure equals the wage rate (w), that is, the market exchange rate which is equal to the slope of the budget constraint. In this equilibrium position the individual works for AL_1 hours per day. Thus, he has worked for $\cong L_1$ hours to earn OM_1 amount of income and enjoy OL_1 hours of leisure.

Wage offer Curve and Supply of Labour

Now with the analysis of leisure-income choice, it is easy to derive supply curve of labour. Supply curve of labour shows how an individual's work effort responds to changes in the wage rate. The derivation of supply curve of labour is depicted in 11A.4. In panel (a) of this figure it will be seen that, at the wage rate w_0 ($w_0 = OB_0/OA$), budget constraint line is AB_0 and the individual is in equilibrium at point Q where he chooses OL_0 leisure time and works for AL_0 hours. That is, at wage rate w_0 he supplies AL_0 amount of labour. This supply of labour is directly shown against wage rate w_0 in panel (*b*) of Figure 11A.4. Now, when the wage rate rises to w_1, budget constraint line shifts to AB_1 ($w_1 = OB_1/OA$), the individual reduces his leisure to OL_1 and supplies AL_1 hours of work; $L_1 L_0$ more than before (see panel (*a*) in Figure 11A.4). Thus, AL_1 number of work-hours supplied is shown against w_1 in panel (*b*) of Figure 11A.4. Likewise, when the wage rate rises to w_2 (w_2, = OB_2/OA), budget constraint line shifts to AB_2, the individual chooses to have leisure time OL_2 and

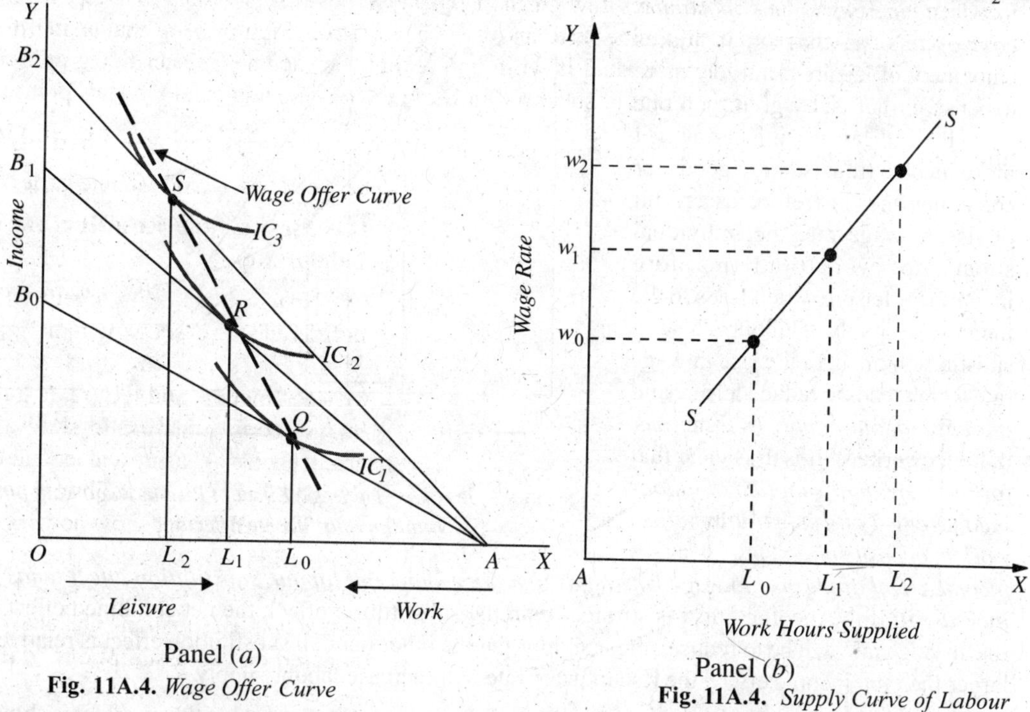

Panel (*a*)
Fig. 11A.4. *Wage Offer Curve*

Panel (*b*)
Fig. 11A.4. *Supply Curve of Labour*

supplies AL_2 work-hours. In panel (*a*) on joining points Q, R and S we get what is often called *wage-offer curve* which is similar to price-consumption curve. In panel (*b*), the information supplied by the wage-offer curve, that is, the supply of labour (work-hours) by the individual at different wage rates is shown directly as, in this panel, supply of labour (hours worked) is measured along the X-axis and wage rate along the Y-axis. A glance at panel (*b*) of Figure 14.4 will reveal that labour supply curve is upward sloping indicating that *labour supply (i.e. work hours) by an individual increases with the rise in wage rate.*

Income Effect and Substitution Effect of the Change in Wage Rate

It is important to note that the supply curve of labour does not always slope upward as is shown in Fig. 11A.4(*b*). It can slope or bend backward which implies that at a higher wage rate, the individual will supply less labour (*i.e.* will work for less hours). Under what conditions supply curve of labour (*i.e.* work-hours) slopes upward and under what circumstances it bends backward can be explained in terms of income effect and substitution effect of a change in wage rate. As in case of change in price, **rise in wage rate has both the substitution effect and income effect.** The net combined effect on the supply of labour (hours worked) depends on the magnitude of the substitution effect and income effect of the rise in wage rate. It is important to note that *leisure is a normal commodity which means that increase in income brought about by rise in wage rate will lead to the increase in leisure enjoyed (i.e. less work-hours supplied)*. This means that, income effect of the rise in wage rate on labour supply is negative, that is, it tends to *decrease labour supply* (*i.e.*, hours worked).

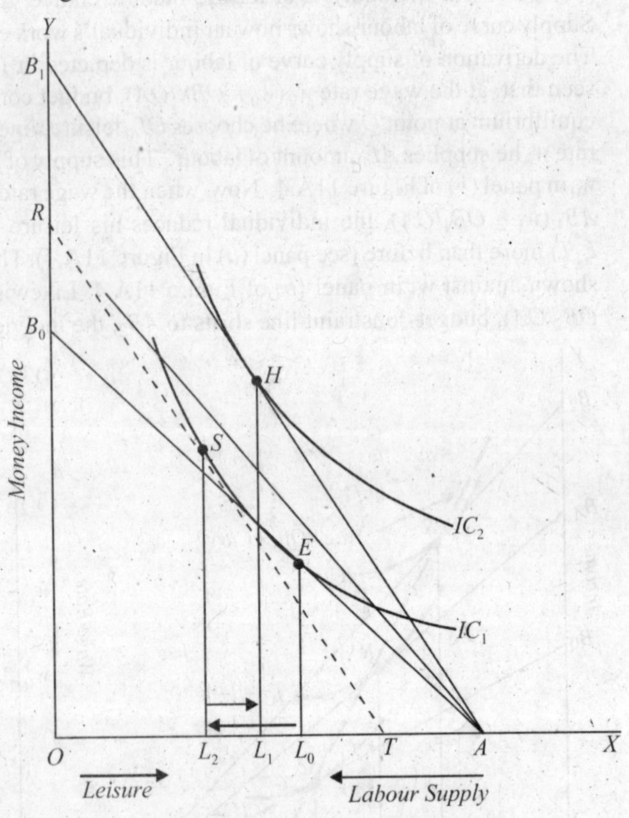

Fig. 11A.5. *Breaking Up Price Effect of Rise in Wage Rate into Substitution and Income Effects*

On the other hand, *the rise in wage rate increases the opportunity cost of leisure*, that is, it makes enjoyment of leisure relatively more expensive, that is, by giving up one more hour of leisure, it can now get more income (that is, more goods for consumption). Therefore, as a result of rise in wage rate the individual substitutes work (and therefore income) for leisure which leads to the increase in supply of labour. This is a substitution effect of the rise in wage rate which tends to reduce leisure and *increase labour supply* (*i.e.* number of hours worked). It is thus clear that *for an individual supplier of labour income effect and substitution effect work in opposite directions*[1]. *Whereas income effect of the rise in wage rate tends to reduce supply of labour, substitution effect tends to increase it*. If the income effect is stronger than the substitution effect, the net combined effect of rise in wage rate will be to reduce labour supply. On the other hand, if substitution effect is relatively larger than the income effect, the rise in wage rate will increase labour supply.

How the effect of rise in wage rate is split up into income effect and substitution effect is shown in Fig. 11A.5. In this figure we measure money income on the *Y*-axis and leisure (reading from left to right) and labour supply (reading from right to left) on the *X*-axis. Suppose to begin with the wage

---

1. Note that this is unlike the case of *price effect of normal goods* in which case substitution effect and income effect work in the *same* direction and reinforce each other.

rate is w_0 and if all the available hours OA are used to do work, OB_0 money income is earned. This gives us AB_0 as the *budget constraint* or which in the present context is also called *leisure-income* constraint. It will be seen from Figure 11A.5 that AB_0 is tangent to indifference curve IC_1 between leisure and income at point E. Thus, with wage rate w_0 the individual is in equilibrium when he enjoys OL_0 leisure and therefore he is supplying AL_0 work-hours of labour. Now, suppose that wage rate rises to w_1 with the result that budget constraint line rotates to AB_1. Now, with AB_1 as new budget constraint line, the individual is in equilibrium at point H on indifference curve IC_2 at which he supplies AL_1 work-hours of labour which are more than AL_0. Thus, with the rise in wage rate, supply of labour has increased by L_0L_1. To break up this wage effect on labour supply, we reduce his money income by compensating variation in income.

To do so we take away so much income from the individual that he comes back to the original indifference curve IC_1. RT is such line obtained after reducing his money income by compensating variation. RT is tangent to indifference curve IC_1 at point S at which he supplies AL_2 hours for work. This shows with rise in wage rate from w_0 to w_1 which makes leisure relatively more expensive, he substitutes work (*i.e.* labour supply) L_0L_2 for leisure. This is substitution effect of rise in wage rate which tends to increase labour supply by L_0L_2. Now, if the money taken from him is given back to him so that budget constraint line again shifts back to AB_1. With AB_1 he reaches his old equilibrium position at point H on indifference curve IC_2 where he supplies AL_1 work-hours. Thus, movement from point S to H and as a result the decrease in labour supply by L_2L_1 represents the income effect of the rise in wage rate. Thus, while income effect of the increase in wage rate causes decrease in labour supply by L_2L_1, its substitution effect causes increase in labour supply by L_0L_2. It will be seen from Fig. 14.5 that income effect is weaker than substitution effect so that the net result is increase in labour supply by L_0L_1 work-hours. Now, if income effect had been stronger than substitution effect, work-hours supplied would have decreased as a result of rise in wage rate and we will get backward-sloping supply curve of labour. We thus find that **if substitution effect dominates the income effect of rise in wage rate, we get upward-sloping supply curve of labour. On the other hand, if income effect of rise in wage rate dominates the substitution effect we get the backward-bending supply curve of labour.**

Backward Bending Supply Curve of Labour

It may, however, be noted that on theoretical grounds it cannot be predicted which effect will be stronger. It has, however, been empirically observed that when the wage rate is small so that the

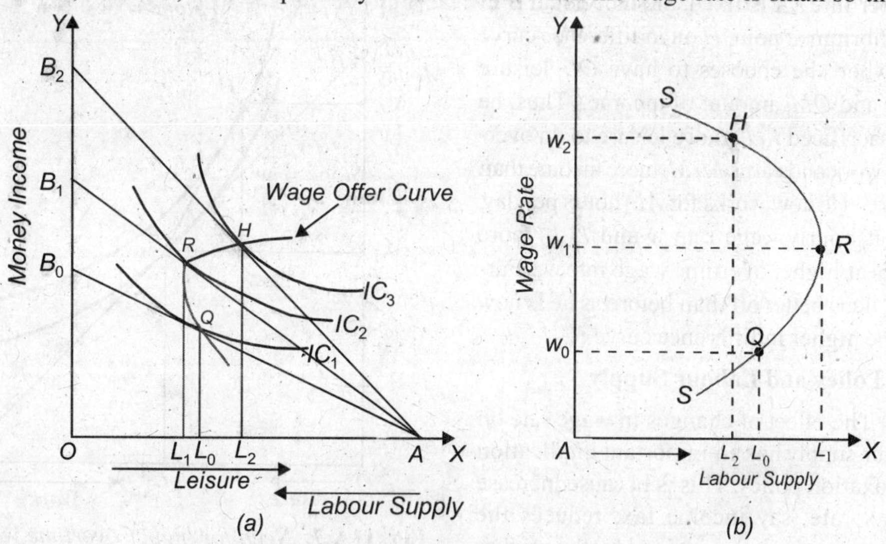

Fig. 11A.6. *Backward - Bending Supply Curve of Labour*

demand for more income to purchase goods and services for consumption is very strong, substitution effect is larger than the income effect so that the net effect of rise in wage rate will be to reduce leisure and increase the supply of labour. But when he is already supplying a large amount of labour and is earning sufficient income, further increases in wage rate may induce the individual to prefer more leisure on the margin so that income effect may outweigh the substitution effect at higher wage rates. This implies that at higher wage rates, labour supply may be reduced in response to a further rise in wage rates.

This means that up to a point substitution effect is stronger than income effect so that labour supply curve slopes upward, but beyond that at higher wage rates supply curve of labour bends backward. This is illustrated in Fig. 11A.6 where in panel (*a*) wage offer curve is shown, and in panel (*b*) supply curve of labour is drawn corresponding to leisure-work equilibrium points in panel (*a*). Thus, to start with, at wage rate w_0 (*i.e.* AB_0 as budget constraint) AL_0 amount of work-hours (labour) are supplied. This is directly plotted against the wage rate w_0 in panel (*b*) of Fig. 11A.6. When the wage rate rises to w_1 (budget constraint becomes AB_1 in panel (*a*) of Fig. 11A.6), the greater amount of labour AL_1 is supplied, which is greater than AL_0. Amount of labour AL_1 is directly plotted against higher wage rate w_1 in panel (*b*) of Fig. 11A.6. With the further increase in wage rate to w_2, the budget constraint line rotates to AB_2 and the individual is in equilibrium when he supplies AL_2 work-hours which are smaller than AL_1. Thus, with the rise in wage rate above w_1 labour supply decreases. In other words, upto wage rate w_1, labour supply curve slopes upward and beyond that it starts bending backward. This is quite evident from panel (*b*) of Fig. 11A.6.

Need for Higher Overtime Wage Rate

It will be interesting to know why there is need for paying higher wage rate than the normal wage rate for getting more or overtime work from the individuals. As explained above, with the given wage rate and given trade-off between income and leisure the individual chooses to work for AL_1 hours per day. To do overtime work, he will have to sacrifice more leisure-time and therefore to provide him incentive to forego more leisure and thus to work for more hours it is required to pay him higher wage rate. This is depicted in Figure 11.7 where at the equilibrium point *E* a steeper budget constraint line (i.e., leisure-income line) *EK* than *AT* has been drawn AL_1 is the hours worked at the wage rate *w* represented by the slope of the income-leisure line *AT*. If the higher overtime wage rate *w* ! represented by the steeper line *EK* is fixed, the individual is in equilibrium at point *H* on indifference curve IC_2 where he chooses to have OL_2 leisure time and OM_2 amount of income. Thus, he has sacrificed L_1L_2 more leisure to do overtime work and earns M_1M_2 more income than before. He now works for AL_2 hours per day, AL_1 at hourly wage rate *w* and L_1L_2 more hours at higher overtime wage rate *w* !. Further, he is better off than before as he is now on the higher indifference curve IC_2.

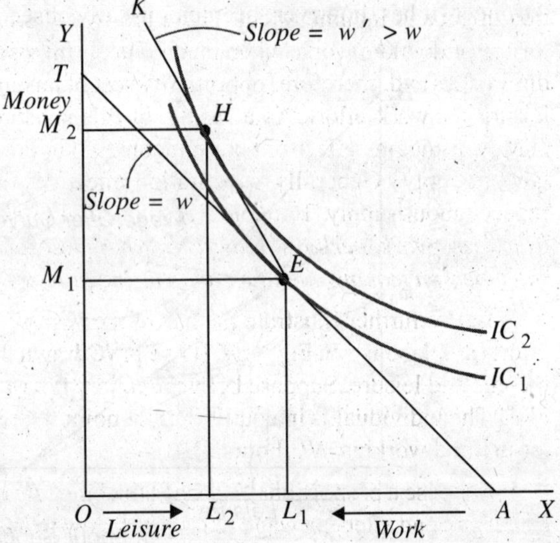

Fig. 11A.7. *Need for higher overtime wage rate.*

Tax Policy and Labour Supply

The effect of changes in wage rate on labour supply has an important implication for taxation policy. This is because increase in tax rate, say income tax, reduces the *after-tax wage rate* received by the worker and therefore it affects people's willing to provide larger productive effort. As a result, income tax by reducing after-tax wage rates, reduces labour supply as shown in Figure 11A.8 where labour supply curve *SS* is upward sloping. Imposition of income tax reduces after-tax wage rate from W_1 to W_2 which induces decrease in the quantity of labour supplied from L_1 to L_2. However, if labour supply curve is backward-bending the imposition of a tax that reduces after-tax wage rate will increase labour-supply as is shown in Figure 11A.9. where backward-bending supply curve of labour *SS* has been drawn. It will be seen from this Fig. 11A.9 that when wage rate is reduced from W_1 to W_2 by increase in the tax rate, labour supply increases from OL_1 to OL_2. However, *typical* labour supply curve is upward sloping and in this case, as seen in Figure 11A.8, increase in tax rate reduces work effort or labour supply.

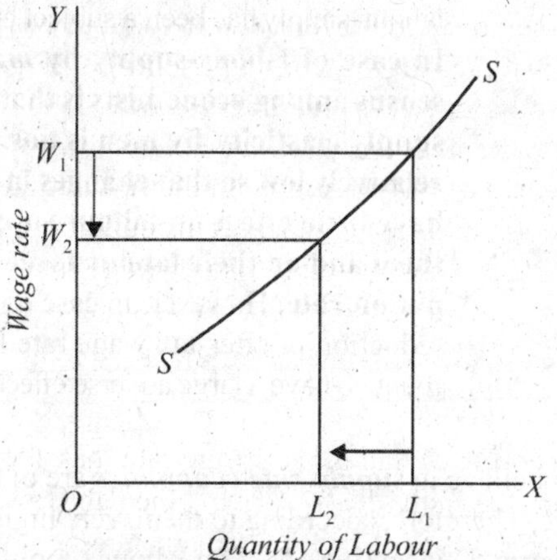

Fig. 11A.8. *Income Tax reduces Labour Supply.*

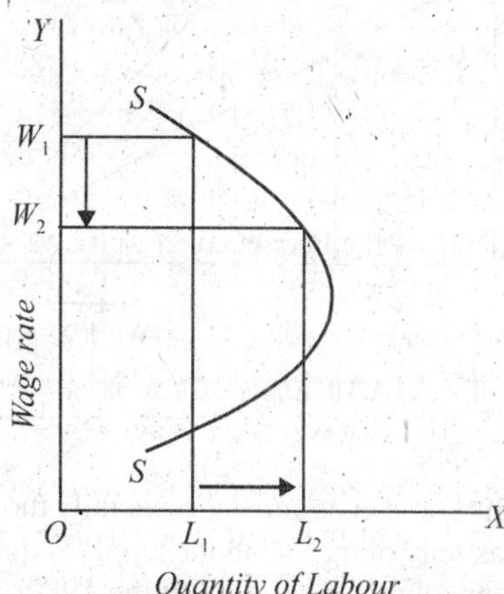

Fig. 11A.9. *Income Tax increases labour supply.*

With lesser productive effort or smaller labour supply as a result of imposition of tax economic performance of the economy is undermined and economic growth is adversely affected. In modern economics the analysis of effect of tax on labour-supply is explained in the framework of substitution effect and income effect. There are two alternatives before an individual: either enjoy more leisure or do more work. When income tax is imposed, after-tax wage rate, that is, return from work diminishes and, therefore, opportunity cost of leisure falls. This induces the individual to substitute leisure for work effort. As a results of this substitution effect, supply of work effort is reduced. However, income effect of tax on income which reduces income will reduce leisure and increase labour supply. Generally, substitution effect dominates and therefore imposition of tax tends to reduce labour supply. To quote Eckstein, "*If a worker has to pay taxes, say one half of his income from extra work, perhaps a lawyer working weekends, a doctor taking on additional patients or a sales-person making evening calls, his incentives will certainly be reduced.*"[2]

Let us further illustrate the harmful effect of a direct tax, say income tax, on supply of work effort (*i.e.*, labour). In Fig. 11A.10 we have drawn the indifference curves of an individual between income and leisure. Suppose before taxation, the wage rate is depicted by the slope of the wage line NW_1. The individual is in equilibrium at point *A* on indifference curve IC_2 where he is enjoying OL_1 leisure and working NL_1 hours.

Suppose a proportional income tax at the rate of 50% is levied. As a result, after-tax wage rate is reduced and after-tax wage line shifts below to NW_2. The individual moves to equilibrium point *B*

2. Otto, Eckstein, *Public Finance,* Prentice Hall.

on indifference curve IC_1. In this equilibrium situation B the individual has increased his leisure to OL_2 and reduced his work effort to NL_2. Thus, as a result of levying of income tax and consequently lowering of the wage rate the individual has substituted leisure for work, resulting in the decrease of labour supply (*i.e.*, work effort). In case of Figure 11A.10 substitution effect dominates the income effect. This is a normal behaviour. Of course, there are some exceptions to this normal behaviour.

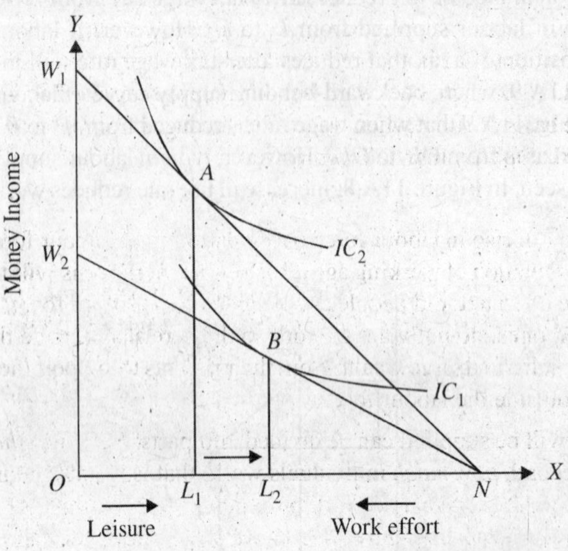

Fig. 11A.10. *Effect of Tax on Labour Supply*

Recently, the effect of tax policy on labour-supply has been a subject of debate. **In case of labour-supply by *men*, consensus among economists is that labour supply elasticity by men is positive but relatively low so that changes in tax rate have little effect on labour supplied by them and on their labour force participation rate.** However, in case of women, reduction in after-tax wage rate has been found to have a large adverse effect on their labour supply.

But some economists, especially those who believe in ***supply-side economics*** are of the view that elasticity of men's labour supply is quite large. Therefore, according to them, very high tax rate on income that prevailed until the 1980s had a large disincentive effect on labour supply. Indeed, some advocates of supply-side economics laid so much emphasis on the adverse effect of tax on labour supply that they suggested that if tax rates were reduced the high-income groups would supply so much more labour and their incomes would increase so much that government's revenue would increase even with lower rates of tax. Following this logic, income tax rates in the United States were reduced in the 1980s[3]. However, the prediction of supply-siders did not prove to be true. As mentioned above, the evidence in case of men indicates elasticity of labour supply is very small. As a result of tax cuts in the 1980s in the United States, *overall tax revenue* declined instead of increasing. However, *tax revenue from upper-income groups did increase.*[4] However, this increase in tax revenue from the rich does not seem to be the result of their putting in more work effort.

Two other explanations have been offered to explain the increase in tax revenue collected from the rich. First, the lower tax rates increase tax compliance by the rich and reduce tax evasion by them.[5] Lower tax rates not only reduced tax evasion but also "meant that the value of *avoiding taxes* through tax shelters fell and investors moved their money back into taxable activities"[6]. Second, as has been stressed by J. Stiglitz, a Nobel laureate in economics, after the tax cuts in the United States, "Wage inequality continued to increase over the period. The rich became richer not because they worked more hours but because they earned more per hour worked".[7] One important change in

3. In India too income tax rates have been greatly reduced since 1991 when Dr. Manmohan Singh became Finance Minister and initiated economic reforms.
4. See J. Stiglitz and C.E. Walsh, *The Principles of Economics*, Second Edition, 2000, p.169
5. In the case of India, a noted Cambridge economist Nicholas Kaldor argued that lower tax rates would check tax avasion and thereby increase tax compliance. Dr. Manmohan Singh as Finance Minister (1991-96) and P.C. Chitambaran later have provided this reason for reduction in income tax rates.
6. J. Stiglitz, *op*. cit., p.169

income tax system in the United States and India that has provided incentive to the married women to participate in the labour market is to the separate treatment of wife and husband for taxation purposes. Previously, married couples (that is, husband and wife) were treated as a single entity and in the context of progressive income tax, this meant that they had to pay a higher marginal tax rate since their joint income was larger. As a result of tax reforms, husband and wife are treated as two *separate individuals* liable for tax payment. Thus, at present, each has to pay lower tax rate and as a result has a greater incentive to work on the basis of substitution effect. This change in tax policy has worked to increase substantially the labour-supply by married women.

Labour Force Participation

Labour supply also increases as a result of rise in labour force participation rate. Labour force participation rate means the ratio of total population of working age which either works or is willing to work for pay. The children below the age of 15 and old people are excluded from labour force. A large number of women, especially married ones, do not want to work so they are also outside the labour force. The wealthy people who have inherited large wealth from their parents to support their families and do not want to work are also outside the labour force.

The decision about how much labour will be supplied can be divided into parts: *First, whether individuals work or are willing to work*. Second, *how much* individuals work, that is, what amount of labour they supply. The decision of individual *whether* to work or express their willingness to work is called *labour force participation decision.* In Figure 11A.11 we have drawn the labour

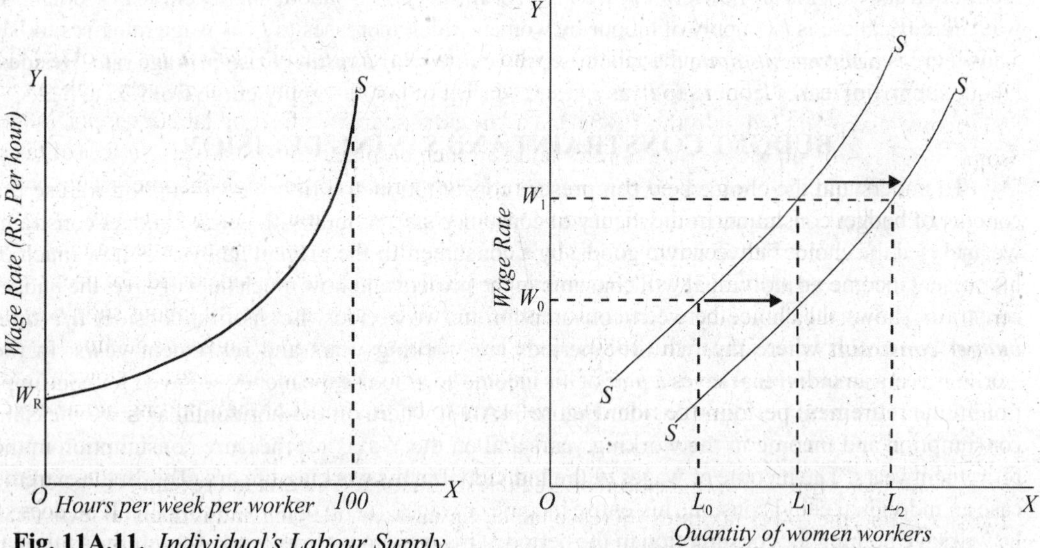

Fig. 11A.11. *Individual's Labour Supply Curve.*

Fig. 11A.12. *Labour Supply by Women*

supply curve *S* of an individual. This shows how many hours of work the individual is willing to work at each wage rate. It will be seen that below wage rate W_R, the individual will not work, that is, will not participate in the labour force. Thus W_R is the minimum wage rate at which the individual will decide to work. This, minimum wage rate below which an individual is not willing to work is known as *reservation wage rate*. As the wage rate rises above W_R, the individual supplies more work-hours per week. Suppose for more than 100 hours per week the individual will not work whatever the wage rate. Therefore, at 100 hours per week labour supply curve of labour becomes perfectly inelastic.

Men except those who are either old or very rich who have inherited large wealth from their

7. *Ibid.*

parents generally work or are willing to work. This is because they have to earn the livelihood for themselves and their families. Therefore, the minimum wage at which they offer their labour services or express their willingness to work is very low. With change in wage rate will affect men's decision as to how many however they will work. *The empirical evidence shows that elasticity of labour supply of men to changes in wage rate is quite small.*

In recent years in both the developed and developing countries women also participate in labour force. Previously, married women worked proportionately less. But in recent years even the proportion of married women in labour force has greatly increased. Even after child birth married women are returning to work more quickly and in greater numbers than before. However, *an important feature of labour supply by women is that it is more sensitive to changes in wage rates than that of men.* Therefore, labour-supply curve of women is more elastic as compared with that of men. According to empirical evidence, elasticity of labour-supply by women is equal to one. That is, one per cent change in wage rate brings about one per cent change in labour supplied by women.

Another important feature of women's labour supply is that in some developed countries such as the U.K. and the USA *while labour force participation of men has declined, women's labour force participation has risen in the recent decades*[8]. The services sector has grown rapidly since 1980 in both the developed and developing countries (including India) and it has provided more employment, opportunities to women. Thus increase in labour supply by women is due to two reasons. First, with rise in wage rate, women have offered more labour supply (*i.e.* work hours). Over time labour force supply curve of women has shifted due to operation of other factors mentioned above. This is shown in Figure 11A.12. Initially SS is labour supply curve of women. At wage rate W_0, there is L_0 supply of labour by women which increases to L_1 as wage rate rises to W_1. Thus there is a *movement along* the labour supply curve SS as a result of rise in wage rate. Besides, labour supply increases from L_1 to L_2 as a result of shift in labour supply curve from SS to $S S$.

BUDGET CONSTRAINT AND SAVING DECISION

To understand the choice between present consumption and future consumption we use the concept of budget constraint. In the theory of consumer's behaviour with help of budget constraint we analysed the choice between two goods, by a consumer. In the present analysis of how much of his present income an individual will consume in the present and how much he will save, the budget constraint shows the choice between consumption in two periods. Let us first consider ***life-time budget constraint*** where the two time periods are working years and retirement years. In the working years an individual saves a part of his income so as to use the money so saved for consumption in the retirement period. Consider Figure 11A.13. where on the horizontal axis we measure consumption and income in the working years and on the Y-axis we measure consumption in the retirement years. The income or wages of the individual in his working life are OY_0. In the extreme case an individual could consume his entire income or wages (OY_0) of his working life. If he does so he will save nothing for consumption in the period of his retirement from work. Generally, a rational individual thinks of the need for consumption in the years of his retirement.

On the other extreme case, he may save all his income or wages of the working years and consumes nothing. In this case he will earn interest on his savings which are either lended to others or kept in bank-deposits. If we denote interest by r, then in case of saving his entire income (Y_0) of the working years the individual will have income equal to $Y_0(1 + r)$ for consumption in the period of retirement. It is important to note that our analysis of saving decision is based on ***life-cycle model.*** According to this model, individuals' consumption and saving decisions during a given year depends not only on his current consumption needs but also on his future consumption requirements during the rest of his life. To simplify our analysis, we assume that *an **individual*** **lives in two**

8. See J. Stiglitz, op. cit. pp.166-167.

periods (present period and the future period). Further, the present period is the period of his *working years* and the future period is of his *retirement years*.

It is evident that by saving, that is, postponing his consumption he will he able to consume more goods in the future because he will have not only his saved money to spend but also interest earned on it. Thus, how much more consumption in future (i.e. retirement years) he will have for sacrifice of his consumption in the present (working years) depends on the rate of interest. For example if interest rate is 10 per cent, then every one hundred rupees saved by him in the present year he will have ₹ 110 in the next year. If he saves ₹ 100 in the present period, he will have 100 (1 + 0.1) to spend on goods for his consumption in the future. *The cost of more consumption in future is sacrifice of his current consumption (i.e., consumption in the working years) which he has to make for enjoying more consumption of goods in future.* It is clear from above that relative price of consumption in the present period is 1 plus rate of interest.

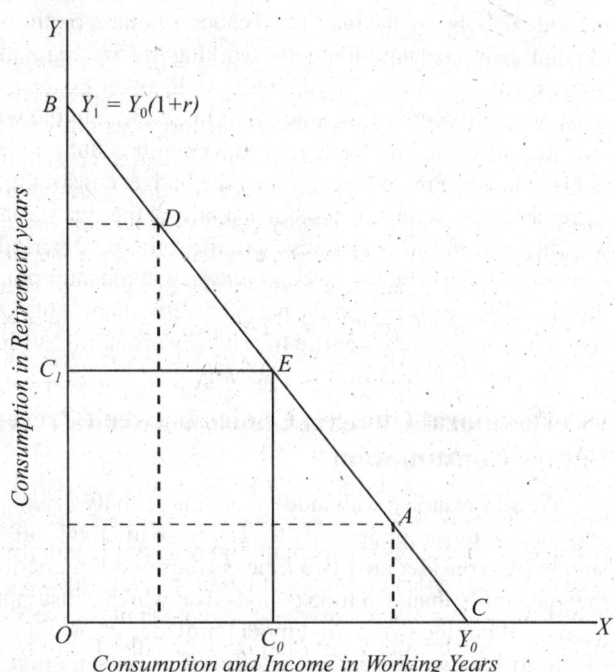

Fig. 11A.13 . *Life Time Budget Constraint*

It is worth mentioning that in deciding about consumption and saving in the working years and consumption in the retirement years an individual is guided by *real rate* of interest and not merely *money* rate of interest. The difference between money rate of interest and real rate of interest arises due to the inflation that may be taking place over the years. Real rate of interest is money rate of interest minus rate of inflation. Thus, if money rate of interest is 10 percent per annum and annual rate of inflation is 6 per cent, than real rate of interest will be 4 per cent per annum. In our example, we have divided the life span of an individual into two periods : the working years period and the retirement period. From the point of view of how much money he will have in real terms what matters is the length of time between when a person earns and saves and the time when he uses his savings for consumption in the retirement period and real rate of interest that he will earn on his savings. In deciding about his choice about consumption and saving in the working years he will also take into account the *compound* rate of interest that he will earn on his savings and not merely the amount of savings he makes in the working years. For example, if rate of interest is simple 4 per cent and not compound rate of interest, then Re. 1 saved today and kept in bank deposits at 4% simple real rate of interest for 35 years, it will earn interest of $35\,B\frac{4}{100}>$ ₹1.40. Thus, Re. 1 saved will become equal to 1 + 1.40 = ₹ 2.40 after 35 years. But if interest is 4 per cent compound interest rate, then Re. 1 saved today will earn interest in 35 years equal to $(1 + 0.04)^{35} = 2.94$ and thus 1 + 2.94 = ₹ 3.94 will be available for consumption after 35 years. This is just to illustrate the power of compound rate of interest. The slope of budget constraint is equal to 1 + *r* where *r* is rate of interest.

Now, consider the life-time budget constraint *BC* drawn in Figure 11A.13. Which point an individual will choose on this budget line depends on his preference between present consumption and future consumption. A complete analysis of his choice requires the iunclusion of his indifference curves between present consumption (*i.e.* consumption in working years) and consumption in the years of retirement. This indifference curve analysis of choice between present consumption and saving will be made in the next section. However we can consider the some possible choices by the individual. Suppose the individual chooses point A on the budget constraint line BC. With his choice of point A, his consumption in the working life will be relatively large and saving for consumption in the years of retirement will be small. At the other extreme, he may choose point D in which case he will consume a very small amount of his income in the working period and save a relatively large amount of his income for future consumption. But empirical evidence shows that a typical individual chooses a middle position on the budget constraint such as point E in between the above two extreme cases. With his choice at point E, the individual consumes C_0 and saves $Y_0 - C_0$ in the working period and consumes C_1 in the retirement period. In his choice of point E on the budget constraint, the individual has *smoothened* his consumption, that is, his consumption in the working-life period is the same as in the period of retirement. This kind of saving behaviour which smoothens consumption over one's entire life span by providing sufficient saving for consumption in the years of retirement is called *life-cycle saving.*

Intertemporal Choice : Choice between Present Consumption and Future Consumption

We now examine with indifference curve analysis how an individual will choose between present and future consumption so as to maximise his total satisfaction over time. To make our analysis simple (we consider only two time periods, working period and the retirement period). In real life there are more than two time periods over which consumption and saving decisions are made by an individual but the two period model provides us useful insights into the basic issues involved. As mentioned above, the exchange of present consumption for future consumption is done through saving and lending these savings to others or keeping them in bank deposits which yield interest.

In our analysis we denote present period income by Y_0, future period income by Y_1, current consumption by C_0, future consumption by C_1 and rate of interest by i. Given his present income Y_0 and rate of interest (r), an individual has to decide how much he will consume in the present (*i.e.* C_0) and how much he will save for consumption in the future (*i.e.* C_1). The consumer's preferences between the present consumption and future consumption are represented by a set of indifference curves such as I_1, I_2 which are downward-sloping and convex to the origin as shown in Figure 11A.14. The downward sloping feature of indifference curves implies that the individual is willing to substitute some amount of present consumption for future consumption and the rate at which he is willing to substitute present consumption for future consumption depends on the particular pattern of consumption he likes to have.

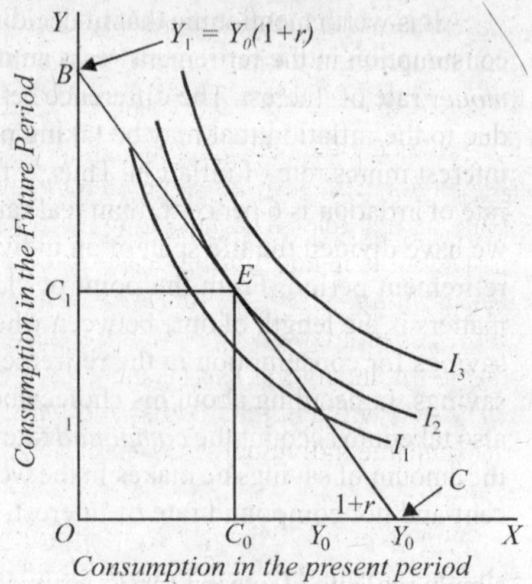

Fig. 11A.14. *Choice Between Present and Future Consumption : Life Saving Model*

The convexity of indifference curves implies that the individual would like to have some '*average*' *amount of consumption* in each period rather than extremely large consumption in the present and no or little consumption in the future or *vice versa.*

The Budget Constraint. To understand the choice, it is important to know the nature of budget constraint an individual faces in this regard. There are two possible kinds of consumption choices.

First, he consumes his entire income in present period, that is, he consumes Y_0 in the present period and saves nothing for the future (*i.e.* next period). The second possibility is that he chooses to consume less than his present income and saves some for future consumption. That is, some present consumption is exchanged for more consumption in the future. How much more future consumption he will have for sacrifice of some consumption in the present depends on the rate of interest. Thus, if market real rate of interest is 10 per cent, then if he saves ₹ 100 in the present year, he will have Rs 110 in the next year (110 = 100 + 10% of 100). In other words, he has exchanged ₹ 100 of the present consumption for consumption of ₹ 110 in the next year.

We now derive the budget constraint or what is called *intertemporal budget line* which has been shown by *BC* in Figure 11A.14. We denote the individual's income in the present period by Y_0 and the next period's income by Y_1. In order to draw the intertemporal budget constraint we have to determine what would be the future income if the individual saves all his present income equal to Y_0. Given the interest rate equal to *r*, the next period's income will be $Y_1 = Y_0(1 + r)$. We represent it by point *B*.

Thus, if the individual decides to save his entire present income Y_0 for future consumption, then his next period's consumption which we denote by Y_1 will be

$$Y_1 \quad Y_0(1 \,.r)$$

We represent Y_1 by point *B* on the vertical axis in Fig. 11A.14. If we join *B* with *C* we get the intertemporal budget line *BC* representing the budget constraint. The slope of the budget constraint line $BC = -(1+r)$. Thus the slope of the budget line depends on the rate of interest which is equal to $-(1 + r)$ where *r* is the market rate of interest. It may be noted that *rate of interest is in fact the return on saving.*

Intertemporal Choice ; Individual's Equilibrium

The pattern of individual's indifference curves depicts his preferences of present consumption over future consumption. In fact present consumption and future consumption can be regarded as two different goods. The slope of the indifference curve, that is, $\frac{\Gamma C_1}{\Gamma C_0}$ measures the marginal rate of substitution (*MRS*) between present consumption and future consumption and reflects his rate of time preference between the present and future consumption. On the other hand, as explained above, the slope of the budget line is given by $-(1 + r)$ where *r* is rate of interest.

In his choice between present and future consumption, the consumer will try to maximise his satisfaction. But, as in consumer theory, the individual will be maximising his satisfaction where the given budget line *BC* is tangent to an indifference curve. It will be seen from Figure 14.14 that the individual is in equilibrium at point *E* on the indifference curve I_2. Thus the consumer's optimal equilibrium position is point *E* on indifference curve I_2 where his present consumption is C_0 and future consumption is C_1. With his equilibrium position at *E* present his consumption C_0 is less than his present income Y_0. That is, he is saving $Y_0 - C_0$ of his present income for consumption in the next period. He will lend this saving and earn interest on it so that his consumption in the next period is C_1. Thus, the individual saves a part of his income in the present period and lends it to others to earn interest.

It may be noted that at the equilibrium point *E*, the slope of indifference curve of the individual depicting his marginal rate of substitution between present consumption and future consumption ($MRS_{C_0C_1}$) is equal to the slope of the intertemporal budget line *BC* which in absolute terms is equal to $(1 + r)$. Thus, at equilibrium or optimal point *E*,

$$MRS_{C_0C_1} \quad (1 \,.r)$$

Saving and Interest Rate

It is useful to know what will be the impact of change in the rate of interest on individual's intertemporal choice or on his savings. This is depicted in Fig. 11A.15. With the equilibrium position at E_0, suppose rate of interest rises. The rise in rate of interest will change the budget constraint. With a higher interest rate than the previous one, the new budget line $B' C'$ will be steeper than the previous budget line BC. But. It will be seen from Fig. 11A.15 the new budget line $B' C'$ representing higher rate of interest is steeper than the previous budget line BC. With this new budget line $B' C'$ the individual is in equilibrium at point E_1 on his higher intertemporal indifference curve I_2 and is therefore better off than before. Besides, it will be noticed that with the new position E_1 of intertemporal choice on indifference curve I_2, the individual's present consumption has decreased from C_0 to C_0', that is, he has saved more at the higher rate of interest to increase his consumption in the future period by C_1C_1'.

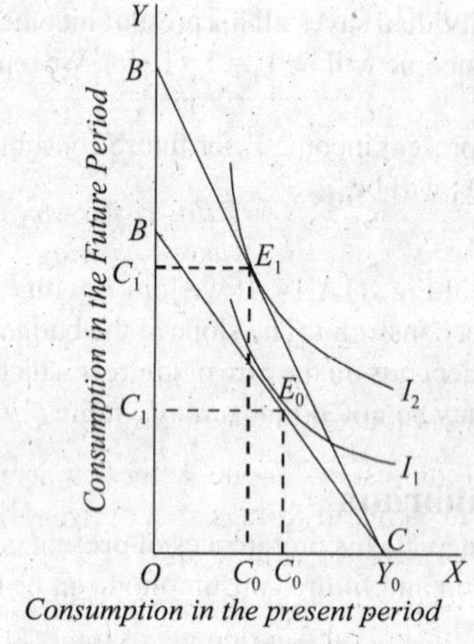

Fig. 11A.15. *Impact of Rise in Interest Rate on Savings : Substitution Effect Dominates.*

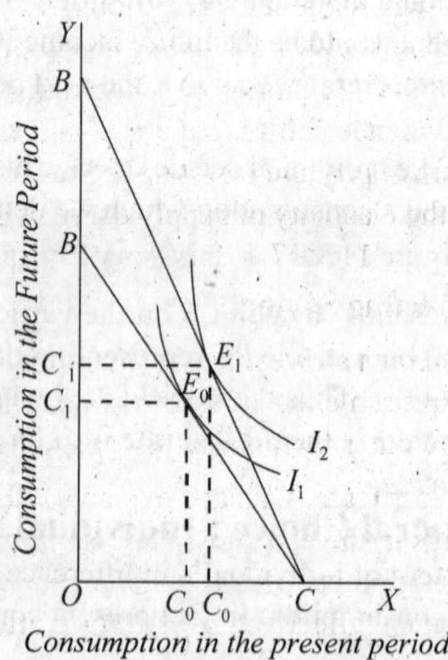

Fig. 11A.16. *Impact of Rise in Interest Rate on Savings : Income Effect Dominates.*

The effect of rise in interest rate has income effect as well as substitution effect. A rise in rate of interest increases income of the individual and therefore makes him better off. This induces him to consume more in the present. This is the income effect which tends to reduce savings. But the rise in interest rate also increases return on savings. This induces him to postpone consumption because every sacrifice of consumption (i.e. savings) will mean more consumption in the next period due to higher interest earned. This is substitution effect which tends to increase savings. Thus, the substitution effect and income effect of rise in interest rate work in opposite direction. Therefore, net effect of rise in interest rate on saving is quite uncertain. Either of the two effects may dominate. As a result, higher interest rate may cause more or less savings. In Figure 14.16 we have shown the case when income effect dominates and therefore higher interest rate results in lower savings. However, empirical evidence in the USA shows that substitution effect slightly outweights the income effect. As a result, there is a *small net positive effect* of higher interest rate on savings.[9] However, in India the empirical evidence reveals that the effect of higher interest rate on financial savings of households is quite substantial.

Supply Curve of Saving

As seen above, in Figure 14.15, a rise in the rate of interest induces the individual to save more. In this way, we can determine the saving of an individual at different rates of interest. The higher the rate of interest, the greater is the supply of saving by him. By summing up the savings of various

9. See J. E. Stiglitz and C.E. Walsh, *Principles of Economics*, 2nd Edition, 2000. p. 166.

individuals at various rates of interest we can obtain market supply curve of savings, which will slope upward showing positive relationship between rate of interest and savings. It may be noted that in case of some individuals who have a target of having a certain fixed level of income or consumption in future, a higher rate of interest will enable them to earn that fixed income by saving and lending less in this year. That is, for these individuals supply curve of saving will be backward sloping. However, those individuals who save and lend more at higher rates of interest predominate and therefore the overall supply curve of savings slopes upward, though at very high rates of interest backward-bending shape of the supply curve of saving cannot be ruled out. However, empirical evidence shows that a rise in interest rate has only a small positive effect on the rate of saving. Therefore, the elasticity of supply curve of saving as shown in Figure 11A.17 is quite small.

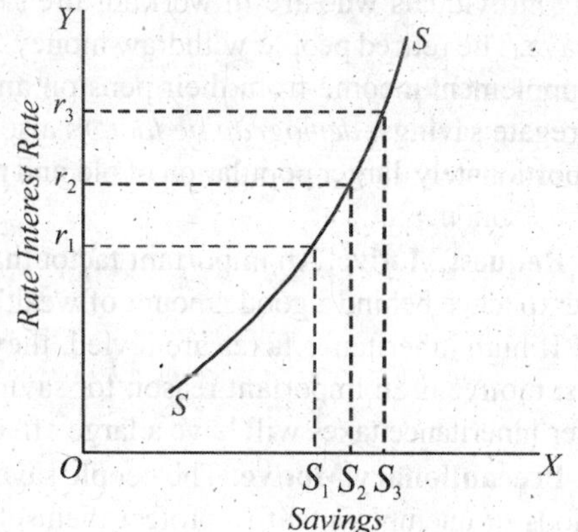

Fig. 11A.17. *Positively-sloping Supply Curve of Saving*

Factors Affecting Savings

We have seen above that people save during working years so that they can consume enough in the years of retirement. And interest rate affects the saving for retirement. In addition to interest rate rate there are other factors that affect savings. We explain below all these factors.

1. Interest Rate. We have explained above that interest rate is one factor that determines supply of savings in the economy. The rise in interest rate generally brings about increase in supply of savings, though this effect is not significant. This is because rise in interest rate gives rise to two effects – income effect and substitution effect – which work in opposite direction. While income effect of rise in wage rate tends to reduce savings and its substitution effect tends to increase it. Since substitution effect generally dominates there is a net positive effect, though a small one, of rise in interest rate on supply of savings.

2. Income. Keynes emphasised that it is level of disposable income that determines savings. As the income rises, both consumption and saving increase. However, according to Keynes, average propensity to consume declines as income increases and therefore saving rate rises at higher levels of income.

3. Social Security Provisions. Social security measures adopted by the government such as state pension, free health care lower savings. Generous pension scheme reduces the need for saving for the retirement years. Similarly, the provision of free health care through the National Health Service also reduces the need for savings to meet the medical expenses. It has been pointed by some economists that low saving rate of the UK and USA is mainly due to the comprehensive social security system in these countries.

4. Taxation System. Taxes also affect savings by individuals. In India and other countries income tax is the main direct tax levied on individuals' incomes including interest and dividend income. It has been pointed that income tax discourages saving. For people who keep their savings in bank deposits or use them for buying bonds and shares, tax on interest and dividends reduce after-tax return from them. "*The tax on interest income substantially reduces the future payoff from current saving and as a result reduces the incentives for people to save*"[10]. According to N.G. Mankiw, "*Low rate of saving in the United States is at least partly attributable to tax laws that discourage savings*"[11].

10. See J. Stiglitz, and C.E. Walsh, *op.cit p.* 176.

11. N. Gregory Mankiw, *Principles of Economics*, Second Edition, 2001, P. 566

Aggregate Savings

Savings of all individuals in a society constitute aggregate savings of the economy. At any time, some individuals who are in working life save and others who are old and leading a retired life dissave. The retired people withdraw money from their bank accounts and/or sell shares and bonds to supplement income from their pension and other social security schemes. In determination of aggregate savings, *demographic factors* also play a role. A more slowly growing population has a proportionately larger population of old and retired people and this depresses aggregate saving rate of the economy.

Bequest Motive. An important factor that determines saving of a society is bequest motive. In order to leave behind a good amount of wealth for their children some rich people save during their life. If high inheritance taxes are levied, they would discourage saving on this account. Since bequest motive is an important reason for savings by individuals, especially the wealthy people, the lower inheritance taxes will have a large effect on increasing the saving rate of the economy.

Precautionary Motive. The people save for the unforeseen contingencies such as illness and periods of unemployment to protect themselves against these emergencies for which these is no insurance coverage.

Purchasing Power of Assets. The real value, that is, purchasing power of assets such as shares, bonds, houses possessed by the people also influence savings of the people. If the prices of these assets rise, people feel better off than before. This induces them to consume more and therefore save less. It has been found that when prices of assets rise, people even get more loans from the banks and spend them for consumption purposes.

We have explained above some important factors that affect savings of a society.

QUESTIONS FOR REVIEW

1. Explain how do people decide to make a choice about the number of hours they will work ? Use indifference curve analysis to explain this choice.
2. How does rise in wage rate affect labour - supply ? Distinguish between income effect and substitution effect of rise in wage rate. How do they affect labour supply ?
3. Discuss the impact on labour supply of a worker when wage rate rises. Can there be backward-sloping labour supply curve ? Explain using indifference curves.
D.U., B.A (Hons.) Economics Ist Year 2009
4. Will increase in the wage rate always lead to an increase in the number of hours worked ? Why or why not ? *D.U., B.A. (Hons.) 2002)*
5. It is customary for the union-management contracts to lay down higher wage rates for overtime work. Does such arrangement always lead to more work on the part of workers ?
6. Supply curve of labour is backward bending because substitution effect of wage increase outweighs the income effect. Do you agree or disagree ?
D.U., B.A (Hons.) Economics Ist year 2006
7. The saving decision is a decision of when to consume, today or tomorrow. Explain ?
8. A principal motive of saving is to smooth consumption during working years and retirement years.
9. Explain the concept of budget constraint with regard to choice between consumption and saving. What is the factor that determines slope of the budget constraint in this regard ?
10. Explain with the helps of indifference curve analysis how an individual will determine how much to consume and save in the present ?
11. How will the rise in interest rate affect savings of individuals ? Distinguish between income effect and substitution effect of rise in wage rate. How do these effect influence supply of savings ?
12. When the interest rate rises, the substitution effect induces the person to save more. True or False. Explain *D.U., B.A (Hons.) Economics Ist Year 2008*

CHAPTER 12

REVEALED PREFERENCE THEORY OF DEMAND

In both the Marshallian cardinal utility theory of demand and Hicks-Allen indifference curve theory of demand introspective method has been applied to explain the consumer's behaviour. In other words, both these theories provide psychological explanation of consumer's demand; they derive laws about consumer's demand from how he would react psychologically to certain hypothetical changes in price and income. But the Revealed Preference Theory which has been put forward by Prof. Samuelson seeks to explain consumer's demand from his actual behaviour in the market in various price-income situations. Thus, in sharp contrast to psychological or introspective explanation *Prof. Samuelson's revealed preference theory provides behaviouristic explanation of consumer's demand.* Besides, revealed preference theory is based upon the concept of ordinal utility. In other words, revealed preference theory regards utilities to be merely comparable and not quantifiable. Prof. Tapas Majumdar has described Samuelson's revealed preference theory as "*Behaviourist Ordinalist.*"[1] The description "Behaviourist Ordinalist" highlights the two basic features of the revealed preference theory : first, it applies behaviouristic method, and secondly it uses the concept of ordinal utility.

PREFERENCE HYPOTHESIS AND STRONG ORDERING

Prof. Samuelson's revealed preference theory has *Preference Hypothesis* as a basis of his theory of demand. According to this hypothesis when a consumer is observed to choose a combination A out of various alternative combinations open to him, then he 'reveals', his preference for A over all other alternative combinations which he could have purchased. In other words, when a consumer chooses a combination A,it means he considers all other alternative combinations which he could have purchased to be inferior to A. Still in other words, it means he rejects all other alternative combinations open to him in favour of the chosen combination A. Thus, according to Prof. Samuelson, *choice reveals preference*. Choice of a combination A reveals his definite preference for A over all other rejected combinations. From the hypothesis of 'choice reveals preference' we can obtain definite information about the preferences of a consumer from observing his behaviour in the market. By comparing preferences of a consumer revealed in different price-income situations we can obtain certain information about his preference scale.

Let us graphically explain the preference hypothesis. Given the prices of two commodities X and Y and the income of the consumer, budget line PL is drawn in Fig. 12.1. The budget line PL, represents a given price-income situation. Given the price-income situation as represented by PL, the consumer can buy or choose any combination lying within or on the triangle OPL. In other words, all combinations lying on the line PL such as A, B,C and lying below the line PL such as D

1. Tapas Majumdar, *Measurement of Utility*, Chapter VII

E, *F* and *G* are alternative combinations open to him, from among which he has to choose any combination. If our consumer chooses combination *A* out of all those open to him in the given price-income situation, it means he reveals his preference for *A* over all other combinations such as *B*, *C*, *D*, *E* and *F* which are rejected by him. As is evident from Fig. 12.1, in his observed chosen combination *A*, the consumer is buying *OM* quantity of commodity *X* and *ON* quantity of commodity *Y*.

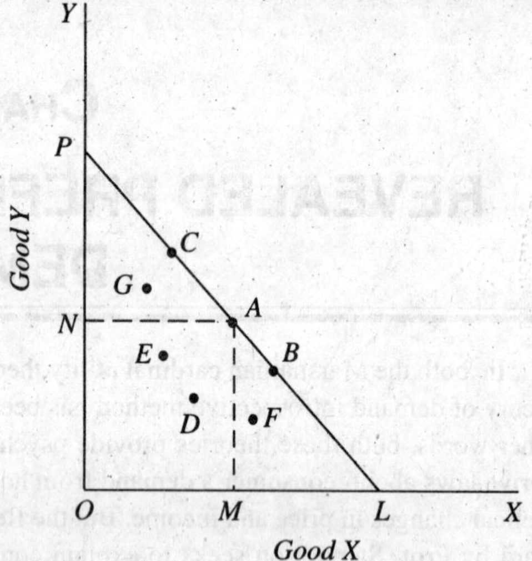

Fig. 12.1. *Choice reveals preference*

Strong Form of Preference Hypothesis

It should be carefully noted that Prof. Samuelson's revealed preference theory is based upon the strong form of preference hypothesis. In other words, in revealed preference theory, strong-ordering preference hypothesis has been applied. Strong ordering implies that there is *definite ordering* of various combinations in consumer's scale of preferences and therefore the choice of a combination by a consumer reveals his definite preference for that over all other alternatives open to him. Thus, *under strong ordering, relation of indifference between various alternative combinations is ruled out*. When in Fig. 12.1 a consumer chooses a combination *A* out of various alternative combinations open to him, it means he has a definite preference for *A* over all others, the possibility of the chosen combination *A* being indifferent to any other possible combination is ruled out by strong ordering hypothesis.

Consistency Postulate or Weak Axiom of Revealed Preference (WARP)

The revealed preference theory rests upon another basic assumption which has been called the '*consistency postulate*'. In fact, the consistency postulate is implied in strong ordering preference hypothesis. The consistency postulate can be stated thus : 'no two observations of choice behaviour are made which provide conflicting evidence to the individual's preference." In other words, *consistency postulate asserts that if an individual chooses A rather than B in one particular instance, then he cannot choose B rather than A in any other instance.* If he chooses *A* rather than *B* in one instance and chooses *B* rather than *A* in another when *A* and *B* are present in both the instances, then he is not behaving consistently. Thus, consistency postulate requires that if once *A* is revealed to be preferred to *B* by an individual, then *B* cannot be revealed to be preferred to *A* by him at any other time when *A* and *B* are present in both the cases. Since comparison here is between two situations, consistency involved in this case has been called '*two term consistency*' by J. R. Hicks.

If a person chooses a combination *A* rather than combination *B* which he could purchase with the given budget constraint, then it cannot happen that he would choose (*i.e. prefer*) *B* over *A* in some other situation in which he could have bought *A* if he so wished. This means his choices or preferences must be consistent. This is called *revealed preference axiom.* We illustrate, revealed preference axiom in Figure 12.2. Suppose with the given prices of two goods *X* and *Y* and given his money income to spend on two goods, *PL* is the budget line facing a consumer. In this budgetary situation *PL*, the consumer chooses *A* when he could have purchased *B* (note that combination *B* would have even cost him less than *A*). Thus, his choice of *A* over *B* means he prefers the combination *A* to the combination *B* of the two goods.

Now suppose that price of good *X* falls, and with some income adjustment, budget line changes to *P′L′*. Budget line *P′L′* is flatter than *PL* reflecting relatively lower price of *X* as compared to the budget line *PL*. With this new budget line *P¢L¢* if the consumer chooses combination *B* when he can purchase combination *A* (as *A* lies below the budget line *P¢L¢*in Figure 12.2), then the consumer will

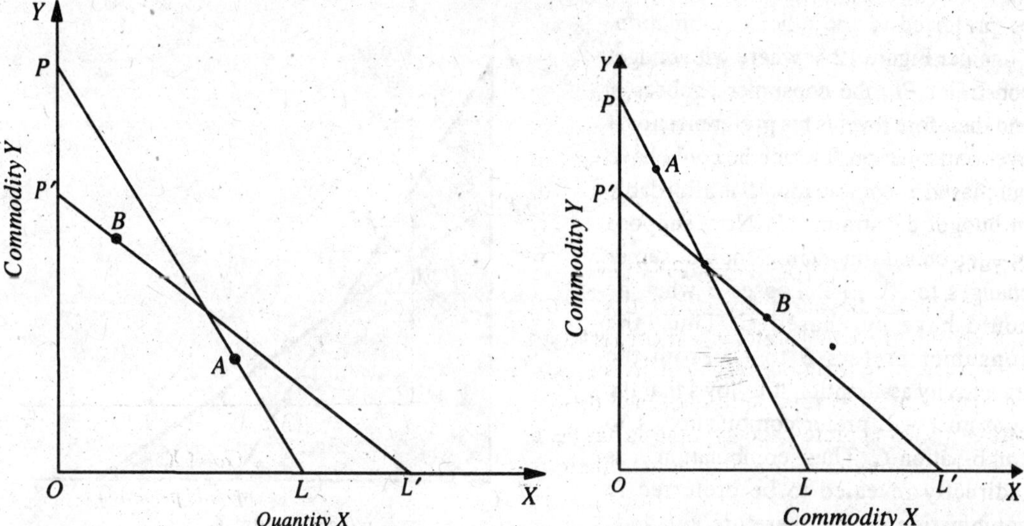

Fig. 12.2. *Consumer's Preferences are inconsistent.*

Fig. 12.3. *Consumer's choices satisfy axiom of revealed preference.*

be inconsistent in his preferences that is, he will be violating the axiom of revealed preference. Such inconsistent consumer's behaviour is ruled out in revealed preference theory based on strong ordering. This axiom of revealed preference according to which consumer's choices are consistent is also called '*Weak Axiom of revealed Preference* or simply *WARP*. To sum, up according to the axiom of revealed preference , *if combination A is directly revealed preferred to another combination B, then in any other situation, the combination B cannot be revealed to be preferred to A by the consumer when combination A is also affordable*.[2]

Now consider Figure 12.3 where to start with a consumer is facing budget line *PL* where he chooses combination *A* of two goods *X* and *Y*. Thus, consumer prefers combination *A* to all other combinations within and on the triangle *OPL*. Now suppose that budget constraint changes to *P¢L¢* and consumer purchases combination *B* on it. as combination *B* lies outside the original budget line *PL* it was not affordable when combination *A* was chosen. Therefore, choice of combination *B* with the budget line *P¢L¢*is consistent with his earlier choice *A* with the budget constraint *PL* and is in accordance with the axiom of revealed preference .

Transitivity Assumption of Revealed Preference Theory

The axiom of revealed preference described above provides us a consistency condition that must be satisfied by a rational consumer who makes an optimum choice. Apart from the axiom of revealed preference, revealed preference theory also assumes that *revealed preferences are transitive*. According to this, if an optimizing consumer prefers combination *A* to combination *B* of the goods and prefers combination *B* to combination *C* of the goods, then he will also prefer combination *A* to combination *C* of the goods. To put briefly, assumption of transitivity of preferences requires that if $A > B$ and $B > C$, then $A > C$.

2. See Hal R. Varian, *Intermediate Microeconomics*, 1990, p. 124.

In this way we say that combination A is *indirectly* revealed preferred to combination C. Thus, *if a combination A is either directly or indirectly revealed to be preferred* to another combination we say that combination A is revealed to be preferred to the other combination. Consider Figure 12.4 where with budget constraint PL, the consumer chooses A and therefore reveals his preference for A over combination B which he could have purchased as combination B is affordable in budget constraint PL. Now suppose budget constraint facing the consumer changes to $P'L'$, he chooses B when he could have purchased C. Thus, the consumer prefers B to C. From the transitivity assumption it follows that the consumer will prefer combination A to combination C. Thus, combination A is indirectly revealed to be preferred to combination C. We therefore conclude that the consumer prefers A either directly or indirectly to all those combination of the two goods lying in the shaded region in Figure 12.4.

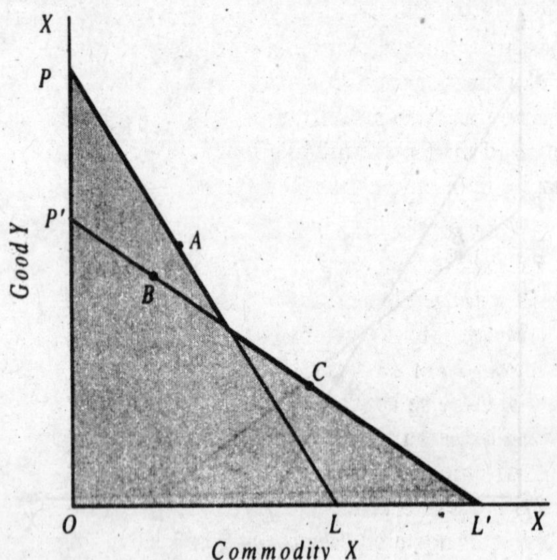

Fig. 12.4. *Revealed preferences are transitive.*

It is thus evident from above that concept of revealed preference is a very significant and powerful tool which provides a lot of information about preferences of a consumer who behaves in an optimising and consistent manner. By merely booking at the consumer's choices in different price-income situations we can get a lot of information about the underlying consumer's preferences.

DERIVING DEMAND THEOREM FROM REVEALED PREFERENCE HYPOTHESIS

Revealed preference hypothesis can be utilised to establish the demand theorem. Prof. Samuelson has derived the Marshallian law of demand from his revealed preference hypothesis. Marshallian law of demand, as is well known, states that a rise in the price of a good must, if income and other prices are held constant, results in the reduction of amount demanded of the good and *vice versa.* In other words, according to Marshall's law of demand, there is inverse relation between price and amount demanded of a good. Samuelson proceeds to establish relationship between price and demand by *assuming that income elasticity of demand is positive.* From positive income elasticity, he deduces the Marshallian inverse price-demand relationship. He states the demand theorem what he calls the *Fundamental Theorem of Consumption Theory* as under :

"Any good (simple or composite) that is known always to increase in demand when money income alone rises must definitely shrink in demand when its price alone rises".

It is clear from the above statement of Fundamental Theorem of Consumption that positive income elasticity of demand has been made a necessary qualification to the inverse price-demand relationship. The geometrical proof of the Fundamental Theorem is illustrated in Fig. 12.5. Let us suppose that the consumer spends his entire income on two goods X and Y. Further suppose that his income in terms of good X is OB, and in terms of Y is OA. Now the budget line AB represents the price-income situation confronting the consumer. All the combinations of goods X and Y lying within or on the triangle OAB are available to the consumer, from which he can buy any combination. Suppose that the consumer is observed to choose the combination Q. This means that Q is revealed to be preferred to all other combinations that lie in or on the triangle OAB.

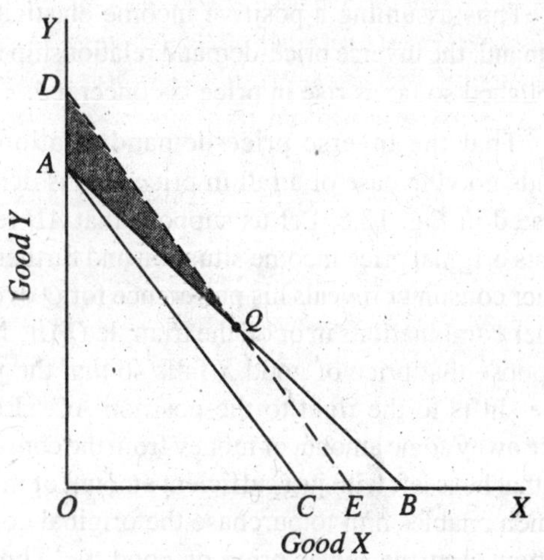

Fig. 12.5. *Proving Fundamental Demand Theorem in Case of Rise in Price*

Now, suppose that price of good X rises, price of Y remaining unchanged. With the rise in price of X the budget line shifts to the new position AC. The budget line AC represents new price-income situation. We now want to know what is the effect of this rise in price of good X on its quantity demanded, assuming that demand varies directly with income (*i.e.*, income elasticity of demand is positive). It is evident from Fig.12.5 that combination Q is not available to the consumer in price-income situation AC. Let us compensate the consumer for the higher price of X by granting him extra money so that he can buy the same combination Q even at the higher price of X. The amount of money which is required to be granted to the consumer so that he could buy the original combination Q at the higher price of X has been called *Cost-difference* by Prof. J. R. Hicks. In Fig. 12.5, a line DE parallel to AC has been drawn so that it passes through Q. DE represents the higher price of X and the money income after it has been increased by cost difference.

Now, the question is which combination will be chosen by the consumer in price-income situation DE. The original combination Q is available in price-income situation DE. It is evident from Figure 12.5 that he will not choose any combination lying below Q on the line DE. This is because if he chooses any combination below Q on the line DE, his choice would be inconsistent. All combinations below Q on DE, that is, all combinations on QE could have been bought by the consumer but had been rejected by him in price-income situation AB in favour of Q. (All points on QE were contained in the original choice triangle OAB.). Since we are assuming consistency of choice behaviour on the part of the consumer he will not choose in price-income situation DE, any combination below Q on QE in preference to Q when Q is available in the new situation. It follows, therefore, that in the price-income situation DE the consumer will either choose the original combination Q or any other combination on QD segment of DE or within shaded area QAD. It should be noted that choice of any other combination on QD or within the shaded area QAD in preference to Q by the consumer will not be inconsistent since combinations lying above Q on QD or within shaded region QAD were not available in price-income situation AB. In price-income situation DE if the consumer chooses the original combination Q, it means he will be buying the same amount of goods X and Y as before, and if he chooses any combination above Q on QD or within the shaded area QAD, it means that he will be buying less amount of commodity X and greater amount of Y than before.

Thus, even after sufficient extra income has been granted to the consumer to compensate him for the rise in price of good X, he purchases either the *same* or the *smaller* quantity of X at the higher price. Now, if the extra money granted to him is *withdrawn*, he will definitely buy the smaller amount of X at the higher price, if the demand for good X is known always to fall with the decrease in income (that is, if income elasticity of demand fox X is positive). In other words, when the price of good X rises and no extra money is granted to the consumer so that he faces price-income situation AC, he will purchase less amount of good X than at Q. Thus assuming a positive income-elasticity of demand, the inverse price-demand relationship is established so far as rise in price is concerned.

That the inverse price-demand relationship holds good in case of a fall in price also is demonstrated in Fig. 12.6. Let us suppose that AB represents original price income situation and further that other consumer reveals his preference for Q over all other combinations in or on the triangle OAB. Now, suppose that price of good X falls so that the price line shifts to the right to the position AC. Let us take away some amount of money from the consumer so that he is left with just sufficient amount of money which enables him to purchase the original combination Q at the lower price of good X. Thus, in Figure. 12.6, a line DE is drawn parallel to AC so that it passes through Q. Price line DE represents lower price of X as given by AC and the money income after it has been reduced by the cost difference.

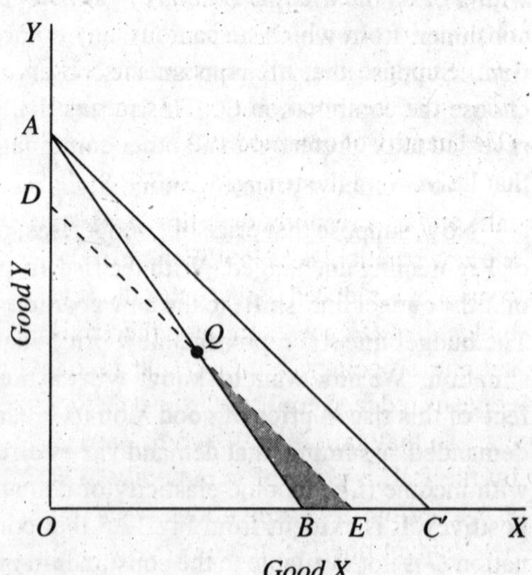

Fig. 12.6. *Proving Fundamental Demand Theorem in Case of Fall in Price*

It is obvious that in price-income situation DE, the consumer cannot choose any combination above Q on QD, since all such combinations were available to him in the original price-income situation AB and were rejected by him in favour of Q. The consumer will, therefore, choose either Q or any other combination on QE or from within the shaded region QEB. In price-income situation DE, his choice of Q means that he buys the same quantity of goods X and Y as in original price-income situation AB, and his choice of any other combination on QE or from *within the shaded region QEB* means that he buys a larger amount of good X and a smaller amount of good Y than in the original price-income situation AB. Thus, even after consumer's income has been reduced, he buys either the same quantity of X or more at the lower price. And if we give him back the amount of money taken away from him so that he confronts again price-income situation AC he will definitely buy more of X at the lower price, provided that his demand for X rises with the rise in income (*i.e.*, his income elasticity of demand for good X is positive).

The two demonstrations given above together prove the fundamental theorem of consumption theory, according to which any good whose demand varies directly with income must definitely shrink in demand when its price rises and expands in demand when its price falls. It may be noted that Samuelson's theory involves two implicit assumptions which have not been explicitly stated. In the first place the consumer is always shown to choose a combination *on* the price line. In other words, he is never shown to choose a combination from within the triangle. This is based upon the assumption that a consumer always prefers a larger collection of goods to a smaller one. Secondly, another implicit assumption involved in Samuelson's theory is that the consumer is shown to choose only one combination of goods in every price-income situation. With these two implicit assumptions the inverse price-demand relationship is deduced by Samuelson by making explicit assumptions of consistency of choice and a positive income elasticity of demand.

Breaking up of Price Effect into Substitution Effect and Income Effect

Having now explained the derivation of law of demand from revealed preference approach we are now in a position to show how in the revealed preference approach price effect can be broken up into substitution and income effects. We will explain this by considering the case of fall in price of a commodity. Now consider Figure 12.7 where, to begin with, price-income situtation faced by a consumer is given by the budget the *AB*. With price-income situation represented by the budget line, *AB* suppose the consumer chooses combination *Q* and buys *OM* quantity of commodity *X*.

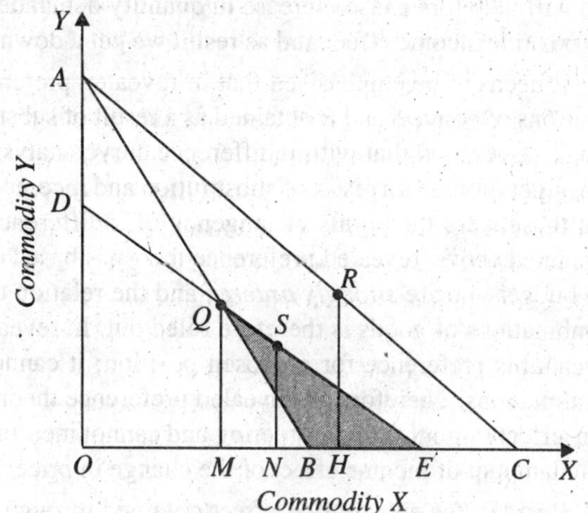

Fig. 12.7. *Breaking up Price Effect into Substitution and Income Effects.*

Now, suppose price of commodity *X* falls and as a result budget line shifts to the new position *AC*. Now, income of the consumer is reduced so much that the new budget line *DE* passes through the original chosen combination *Q*. That is, income is reduced equal to the cost difference so that gain in real income caused by the fall in price of commodity *X* is cancelled out . As seen above, with the new budget line *DE*, to be consistent in his behaviour the consumer can either choose the original combination *Q* or any combination lying on the segment *QE* of the budget line *DE*. If he chooses again the original combination *Q*, the Slutsky substitution effect well be zero. However, suppose that the consumer actually chooses combination *S* on the segment *QE* of the new budget line *DE*. Now, choice of the combination *S* shows that there will be substitution effect due to which the consumer will buy *MN* more of good *X*.

Note that subsitution effect is negative in the sense that the relative *fall* in price has led to the *increase in quantity demanded* of *X*, that is, change in quantity demanded *is in opposite direction* to the change in price. It should be noted that choice of combination *S* on segment *QE* in preference to combination *Q* of the budget line *DE* is not inconsistent because combinations on *QE* segment and within the shaded area were not available before when combination *Q* was earlier chosen in price-income situation *AB*. Thus, with the new budget line *DE* after consumer's income has been adjusted to cancel out the gain in real income resulting from a relative fall in price of *X*, the consumer chooses either *Q* (when substitution effect is, zero or a combination such as *S* on segment *QE* when substitution effect leads to the increase in quantity demanded of good *X* by *MN*. This is generally known as **Slutsky theorem** *which states that if income effect is ignored substitution effect will lead to the increase in quantity demanded of the good whose price has fallen and therefore the Marshallian law of demand describing inverse relationship between quantity demanded and price of a good will hold good,* that is, due to substitution effect alone demand curve slopes downward.

Now, if the consumer choose the combination *S* on the line segment *QE* of budget line *DE* it means that he buys *MN* more due to the substitution effect. Thus he prefers combination *S* to combination *Q*. In other words, his choice of *S* instead of *Q* reveals that he will be *better off* at *S* as compared to *Q*. Now, if money income withdrawn from him is restored to him so that he is faced with the budget line *AC′*. If income effect is positive, he will choose a combination, say *R*) on the budget line *AC′* to the right of point *S* indicating that as a result of income effect he buys *NH* more of the commodity *X*.

Thus quantity demanded of commodity *X* increases by *MN* as a result of substitution effect and by *NH* as a result of income effect. This proves the law of demand stating inverse relationship between price and quantity demanded.

On budget line *DE*, if the consumer chooses combination *Q* and consequently substitution effect is zero, the whole increase in quantity demanded *MH* as a result of decline in price of good *X* will be due to positive income effect. However, which is more likely the substitution effect will lead to the choice by a consumer a combination such as *S* that lies to the right of *Q* on the line segment *QE* and will therefore cause increase in quantity demanded.[3] This substitution effect, is reinforced by the positive income effect and as result we get a downward sloping demand curve.

It needs to be emphasised that in revealed preference theory it is not possible to locate exact positions of points *S* and *R* obtained as a result of substitution effect and income effect respectively. It will be recalled that with indifference curve analysis we could obtain precise points to which a consumer moves as a result of substitution and income effects and as we saw in the previous chapter that these were the points of tangency of indifference curves with the relevant budget lines. As explained above, revealed preference theory is based on the assumption that all points on or below the budget line are *strongly ordered* and the relation of indifference of a consumer between some combinations of goods is therefore ruled out. In revealed preference theory, choice of a consumer reveals his preference for a chosen position; it cannot reveal indifference of consumer between combinations. Therefore, in revealed preference theory we can say about the *direction* of substitution effect through logical ordering and cannot measure the exact size of it, nor we can measure the exact amount of income effect of the change in price.

Besides, the substitution effect obtained through variation in income through cost difference method, does not represent *pure* substitution effect in the Hicksian sense in which the consumer's satisfaction remains constant. In substitution effect obtained by the revealed preference theory through Slutskian method of cost difference, the consumer moves from point *Q* to point *S* on budget line *DE*. His choice of *S* on budget line *DE* instead of *Q* under the influence of substitution effect shows that he prefers *S* to *Q*. That is, he is *better off* in position *S* as compared to the position *Q*. Therefore, it is maintained by some economists that the substitution effect obtained in revealed preference theory is not a pure one and contains also some income effect.[4]

However, the present author is of the view that the two types of substitution effect (Hicksian and the one obtained in revealed preference theory) differ with regard to the *concept of real income* used by them. In indifference curve analysis the term real income is used in the sense of level of satisfaction obtained by the consumer, whereas in revealed preference theory real income is used in the sense of purchasing power. Thus, Hicksian substitution effect involves the change in the quantity demanded of a good when its *relative price alone changes, level of his satisfaction remaining the same*. On the other hand, *revealed preference* theory considers substitution effect as the result of change in relative price of a good on its quantity demanded, ***purchasing power remaining the same***. In Fig. 12.7 we obtain budget line *DE* after variation in income by cost difference so that it passes through the original combination *Q* chosen by the consumer before the fall in price. This implies that with budget line *DE*, he can buy, if he so desires the original combination *Q*, that is, the gain in purchasing power or real income caused by fall in price of *X* has been cancelled out by the reduction in his money income.

CRITICAL APPRAISAL OF REVEALED PREFERENCE THEORY

Samuelson's revealed preference theory has gained some advantages over the Marshallian

---

3. However, it may be noted that substitution effect, if not equal to zero, is *always negative*. A bit confusion has been created by Professors Stonier and Hague in their well-known book "*A Textbook of Economic Theory*" wherein they write substitution effect is *always positive* (see, op. cit. second edition pp.96-97). What Professors Stonier and Hague want to convey is that "Change in quantity demanded of good *X* whose price has fallen is *more that zero*" (that is, $\Delta X > 0$). This is of course correct. However, when examining substitution effect we refer to the '*relation* between ***change in quantity demanded and a change in relative price of a good*** and it is this relationship which is always negative and not positive. This is because change in quantity demanded (ΔX) is ***in opposite direction*** to the relative change in price (ΔP).

4. See Stonier and Hague, *op. cit.*, p. 96.

cardinal utility theory and Hicks-Allen indifference curve theory of demand. It is the first to apply behaviouristic method to derive demand theorem from observed consumer's behaviour. In contrast, both the earlier theories, namely, Marshallian utility analysis and Hicks-Allen indifference curve theory were psychological or introspective explanations of consumer's behaviour.

Now, the question is whether it is the behaviouristic approach or the psychological approach which is more correct to explain consumer's demand. We are of the opinion that no prior ground for choosing between behaviourist and introspective methods can be offered which would be acceptable irrespective of personal inclinations. Commenting on the behaviourist-ordinalist controversy, Professor Tapas Majumdar says, "*Behaviourism certainly has great advantages of treading only on observed ground; it cannot go wrong.*" But whether it goes far enough is the question. It may also be claimed for the method of introspection that operationally it can get all the results which are obtained by the alternative method, and it presumes to go further, it not only states, but also expalins its theorems"[5]. We may conclude that which of the two methods is better and more satisfactory depends upon one's personal philosophical inclinations. However, behaviourist method has recently gained wide support from the economists and has become very popular.

The concept of reveal preference is a powerful tool which can provide a significance information about consumer's preferences from which we can derive law of demand or downward sloping demand curve. Revealed preference theory does this without assuming that a consumer possesses complete information about his preferences and indifferences. In indifference curve analysis it was supposed that consumers had complete and consistent scale of preferences reflected in a set of indifference curves. His purchases of goods were in accordance with the scale of preferences. It is as if consumers were carrying complete indifference maps in their mind and purchasing goods accordingly. Therefore, it was considered better to derive demand theorem by observing consumer's behaviour in making actual choices. Most economists now-a-days believe that it is unrealistic to assume that a consumers have complete knowledge of their scale of preferences depicted in a set of indifference curves. The merit of revealed preference theory is that it has made possible to derive law of demand (*i.e.* downward sloping demand curve) on the basis of revealed preference without using indifference curves and associated restrictive assumptions. Further, it has enabled us to divide the price effect into its two component parts, namely, substitution and income effects through cost difference method and axiom of revealed preference. Cost difference method requires only market data regarding purchases of goods in different market situations. Cost difference (ΔC) can be simply measured by change in price (ΔP) multiplied by the quantity initially purchased by him. Thus,

$$\Delta C = \Delta P_x . Q_x$$

where ΔC stands for the cost difference, ΔP_x stands for the change in price of good X. Q_x is the quantity purchased by the consumer before the change in price of the good X.

Further, with revealed preference theory we can even establish the *existence* of indifference curves and their important property of *convexity*. However, it is notworthy that indifference curves are not required for deriving law of demand or downward sloping demand curve. Indifference curve analysis requires less information than Marshall's cardinal utility theory. But it still requires a lot of information on the part of a consumer since indifference curve analysis requires him to be able to rank consistently all possible combinations of goods. On the other hand, in Samuelson's revealed preference theory of demand the consumer does not require to rank his preferences on the basis of his introspection. It is based on the preferences revealed by his purchases or choices in the different market situations and on the axiom of revealed preference. If consumer's preferences and tastes do not change, revealed preference theory enables us to derive demand theorem just from observation of his market behaviour, that is, what purchases or choices he makes in different market situations. It

5. *Op. cit.*

is however assumed that his preference pattern or tastes do not change. As said above, we can even construct indifference curves from consumers' revealed preferences even though they are not required for establishing law of demand.

A Critique of Revealed Preference Theory

Although Samuelson's revealed preference approach has made some important improvements upon the earlier theories of demand but it is not free from all flaws. Various criticisms have been levelled against it.

First, Samuelson does not admit the possibility of indifference in consumer's behaviour. As has been explained above, the rejection of indifference by Samuelson follows from his strong ordering preference hypothesis. Prof. J.R. Hicks in his later work "*A Revision of Demand Theory*" does not consider the assumtion of strong ordering as satisfactory and instead employs weak ordering from of preference hypothesis. Whereas under strong ordering, the chosen combination is shown to be preferred to all other combinations *in* and *on* the triangle, under weak ordering the chosen combination is preferred to all positions *within* the triangle but *may be either preferred to or indifferent to other combinations on* the same triangle (*i.e. on* the budget line).

Further, in Samuelson's theory, preference is considered to be revealed for a single act of choice. It has been pointed out that if preference is to be judged from a large number of observations, then the possibility of indifference also emerges. Thus, an individual reveals preference for *A* over *B* if he chooses *A* rather than *B more frequently* than he chooses *B* rather than *A* over a given number of observations. Now, we can say that an individual is indifferent between the two situations *A* and *B* if a definite preference for either does not emerge from a sufficiently large number of observation. Thus only because Samuelson regards preference to be revealed from a single act of choice that indifference relation is methodologically inadmissible to his theory. The possibility of indifference relation clearly emerges if the existence of preference or otherwise is to be judged from a sufficiently large number of observations.

Furthermore, if we assume that an *individual is able to compare his ends*, which is a very valid assumption to be made about the individual's behaviour. Then the possibility of indifference or in other words, remaining at the same level of satisfaction by sacrificing some amount of one good for a certain amount of another good will emerge clearly. Thus, commenting on the Samuelson's revealed preference theory from 'welfare' point of view Prof. Tapas Majumdar remarks : "It may be remembered that in all forms of welfare theory, indeed in any integral view of human activity, we have to assume that the individual can always compare his ends. If this axiom is not granted, the whole of welfare economics falls to the ground. And if this axiom is granted, then the idea of remaining on the same level of welfare while sacrificing something of one commodity for something else of another will emerge automatically."[6]

Since Samuelson proves his demand theorem on the basis of positive income elasticity of demand, it cannot derive the demand theorem when income effect or income elasticity is negative. Thus, Samuelson is able to establish the demand theorem in case in which, in terms of Hicksain indifference curve theory, substitution effect has been reinforced by positive income effect of the price change. When the income elasticity is negative, Samuelson's revealed preference theory is unable to establish the demand theorem. In other words, given negative income elasticity of demand, we cannot know on the basis of revealed preference theory as to what will be the direction of change in demand as a result of change in price. Thus Samuelson's revealed preference theory cannot derive the demand theorem when (*i*) the income elasticity is negative and the negative income effect is smaller than the substitution effect; and (*ii*) the income elasticity is negative and the negative income effect is greater than the substitution effect.

---

6. Tapas Majumdar, *Measurement of Utility,* p. 90.

From above it follows that Samuelson's theory cannot account for Giffen's Paradox. The case of Giffen goods occurs when the income effect is negative and this negative income effect is so powerful that it outweighs the substitution effect. In case of Giffen goods, demand varies directly with price. Since he assumes income elasticity to be positive in his establishment of demand theorem, his theory cannot explain Giffen good. We thus conclude that though Samuelson makes improvement over Hicks-Allen indifference curves theory of demand in respect of methodoology adopted (that is, its behaviourist method is superior to Hicks-Allen's introspective method) but in respect of the content of the demand theorem established by it , it is a few steps backward as compared to Hicks-Allen indifference curve theory of demand.

Lastly, Samuelson's fundamental axiom 'choice reveals preference' has been criticised. Under conditions of perfect competition choice of a collection by a consumer may well reveal his preference for it but "this axiom is invalid for situations where the individual choosers are known to be capable of employing strategies of a game theory type" [7] It should, however, be noted that even indifference curve theory does not apply to the situation where strategies of a game theory type are to be employed.

In the end, we may emphasise the point that superiority of Samuelson's theory lies in his applying scientific or behaviouristic method to the consumer's demand and his description of preference hypothesis.

QUESTIONS FOR REVIEW

1. What is meant by 'revealed preference hypothesis'? Explain Samuelson revealed preference theory of demand based on it.
2. Carefully state the assumptions of the revealed preference theory of demand. Explain how law of demand is derived from these assumptions. *(D.U.B. A.(Hons.)1998*
3. Define substitution effect. *Substitution effect is alwasy negative*. How can you prove it with revealed preference approach to demand theory. *(D.U. 1990)*
4. Distinguish between strong ordering and weak ordering forms of preference hypothesis.
5. What is Slutsky equation ? How will you establish it with the help of revealed preference approach to demand analysis ?
6. Explain how price effect is broken up into income effect and substitution effect with the aid of revealed preference theory of demand. *(B.A. (Hons.) D.U. 1996)*
7. The price of a good increases. We know that the substitution effect is always negative. Does it follow that the income and substitution effects of the price rise always work in the same direction if the income elasticity of demand for the good is negative ? Will the demand curve be downward sloping ? Explain. *(D.U. B.A.(Hons.)1998)*
8. Show with the help of a diagram that the substitution effect of a fall in price of a commodity will make a consumer either consume the same quantity or more but not less of it. *(D.U. B.A. (Hons.) 1987)*
9. (*a*) State Samuelson's "*Weak Axiom of Revealed Preference*" (WARP).

   (*b*) Consider two commodities, apples and oranges initially when both apples and oranges cost Re. 1 per unit each, a consumer buys 4 apples and 6 oranges. When the price of apples rises to Rs. 2 per unit and that of oranges falls to Rs. 0.50 per unit, she buys 8 apples and 3 oranges. Does she violate WARP. *(D.U. B.A.(Hons.) 1998)*
10. Revealed preference theory makes a major advancement in the theory of demand. Discuss.

---

6. Tapas Majumdar, *op. cit.*

CHAPTER 13
ELASTICITY OF DEMAND

Various Concepts of Demand Elasticity

We have discussed in the preceding chapter that when the price of a good falls, its quantity demanded rises and when the price of it rises, its quantity demanded falls. This is generally known as *law of demand*. This law of demand indicates only the *direction* of change in quantity demanded in response to a change in price. This does not tell us by *how much* or to what extent the quantity demanded of a good will change in response to a change in its price. This information as to how much or to what extent the quantity demanded of a good will change as a result of a change in its price is provided by the concept of elasticity of demand.

It is price elasticity of demand which is usually referred to as elasticity of demand. But, besides price elasticity of demand, there are various other concepts of demand elasticity. As we have seen in the previous chapter, demand for a good is determined by its price, incomes of the people, prices of related goods, etc. Quantity demanded of a good will change as a result of change in any of these determinants of demand. The concept of elasticity of demand therefore refers to the degree of responsiveness of quantity demanded of a good to a change in its price, consumers' income and prices of related goods. Accordingly, there are three concepts of demand elasticity : price elasticity, income elasticity, and cross elasticity. Price elasticity of demand relates to the degree of responsiveness of quantity demanded of a good to the change in its price. Income elasticity of demand refers to the sensitiveness of quantity demanded to a change in income. Cross elasticity of demand means the degree of responsiveness of demand of a good to a change in the price of a related good, which may be either a substitute for it or a complementary with it.

The concept of elasticity of demand forms the subject-matter of the present chapter. The concept of elasticity has a very great importance in economic theory as well as for formulation of suitable economic policies.

PRICE ELASTICITY OF DEMAND

As mentioned above, price elasticity of demand indicates the degree of responsiveness of quantity demanded of a good to the change in its price, other factors such as income, prices of related commodities that determine demand are held constant. Precisely, *price elasticity of demand is defined as the ratio of the percentage change in quantity demanded of a commodity to a percentage change in price. Thus*

$$e_p = \frac{\text{Percentage change in quantity demanded}}{\text{Percentage change in price}}$$

It follows from the above definition of price elasticity of demand that when the percentage change in quantity demanded a commodity is greater than the percentage change in price that brought it about, price elasticity of demand (e_p) will be greater than one and in this case demand is said to be *elastic*. On the other hand, when a given percentage change in price of a commodity leads to a smaller percentage change in quantity demanded, elasticity will be less than one and demand in this case is said to be *inelastic*. Further, when the percentage change in quantity demanded of a commodity is equal to the percentage change in price that caused it, price elasticity is equal to one. Thus in case of elastic demand, a given change in price causes quite a large change in quantity demanded. And in case of inelastic demand, a given change in price brings about a very small change in quantity demanded of a commodity.

It is a matter of common knowledge and observation that there is a considerable difference between different goods in regard to the magnitude of response of demand to the changes in price. The demand for some goods is more responsive to the changes in price than those for others. In terminology of economics, we would say that demand for some goods is *more elastic* than those for the others or *the price elasticity of demand of some* goods is greater than those of the others. Marshall who introduced the concept of elasticity into economic theory remarks that the *elasticity or responsiveness of demand in a market is great or small according as the amount demanded increases much or little for a given fall in price, and diminishes much or little for a given rise in price.*[1] This will be clear from Figures 13.1 and 13.2 which respresent two demand curves. For a *given fall* in

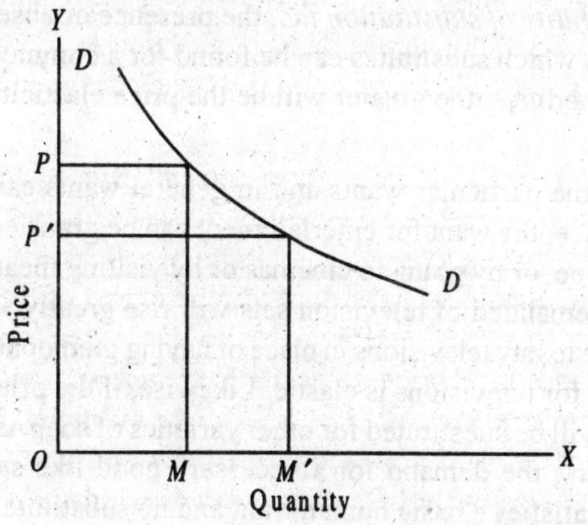

Fig. 13.1. *Elastic Demand*

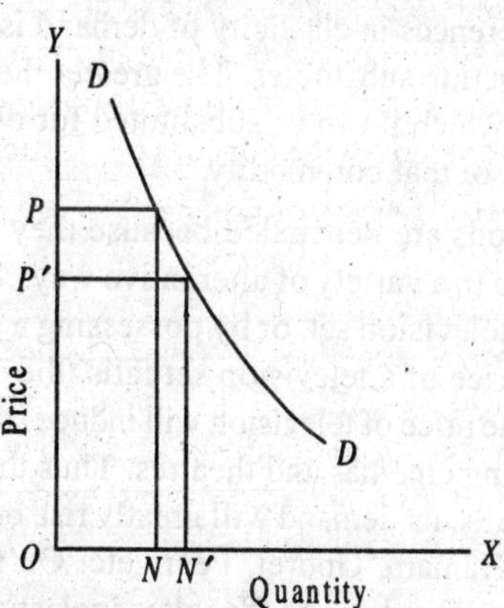

Fig. 13.2. *Inelastic Demand*

price, from *OP* to *OP′*, increase in quantity demanded is much greater in Figure 13.1 than in Figure 13.2. Therefore, demand in Figure 13.1 is more elastic than the demand in Figure in 13.2 for a given fall in price for the portion of demand curves considered. Demand for the good represented in Fig. 13.1 is generally said to be elastic and the demand for the good in Fig. 13.2 to be inelastic.

It should, however, be noted that *terms elastic and inelastic demand are used in the relative sense*. In other words, elasticity is a matter of degree only. Demand for some goods is only more or less elastic than others. Thus, when we say that demand for a good is elastic, we mean only that the demand for it is relatively more elastic. Likewise, when we say that demand for a good is inelastic, we do not mean that its demand is absolutely inelastic but only that it is relatively less leastic. In economic theory elastic and inelastic demands have come to acquire precise meanings. Demand for a good is said to be *elastic* if price elasticity of demand for it is *greater than one*. Similarly, the demand for a good is called *inelastic* if price elasticity of demand for it is *less than one*. Price elasticity of demand equal to one, or in other words, *unit elasticity* of demand therefore represents the dividing line between elastic and inelastic demand. It will now be clear that by inelastic demand we do not mean perfectly inelastic but only that price elasticity of demand is less than unity, and by elastic demand we do not mean absolutely elastic but that price elasticity of demand is greater than one.

1. Alfred Marshall, *Principles of Economics* (8th Edition), Vol. 2.

Thus,

Elastic demand	:	$e_p > 1$
Inelastic demand	:	$e_p < 1$
Unitary elastic demand	:	$e_p = 1$

Price Elasticity of Demand for Different Goods Varies a Good Deal

As said above, goods show great variation in respect of elasticity of demand *i.e.*, their responsiveness to changes in price. Some goods like common salt, wheat and rice are very unresponsive to changes in their prices. The demand for salt remains practically the same for a small rise or fall in its price. Therefore, demand for common salt is said to be 'inelastic'. Demand for goods like televisions, refrigerators etc., is elastic, since changes in their prices bring about large changes in their quantity demanded. We shall explain later at length those factors which are responsible for the differences in elasticity of demand of various goods. It will suffice here to say that the main reason for differences in elasticity of demand is the *possibility of substitution i.e.*, the presence or absence of competing substitutes. The greater the ease with which substitutes can be found for a commodity or with which it can be substituted for other commodities, the greater will be the price elasticity of demand of that commodity.

Goods are demanded because they satisfy some particular wants and in general wants can be satisfied in a variety of alternative ways. For instance, the want for entertainment can be gratified by having television set, or by possessing a gramophone, or by going to cinemas or by visiting theatres. If the price of a television set falls, the quantity demanded of television sets will rise greatly since fall in the price of television will induce some people to buy televisions in place of having gramophones or visiting cinemas and theatres. Thus the demand for televisions is elastic. Likewise, if the price of `Lux' falls, its demand will greatly rise because it will be substituted for other varieties of soapÅsuch as Jai. Hamam, Godrej, Pears etc. On the contrary, the demand for a necessary good like salt is inelastic. The demand for salt is inelastic since it satisfies a basic human want and no substitutes for it are available. People would consume almost the same quantity of salt whether it becomes slightly cheaper or dearer than before.

Perfectly Inelastic and Perfectly Elastic Demand

We will now explain the two extreme cases of price elasticity of demand. First extreme situation is of perfectly inelastic demand which is depicted in Fig. 13.3. In this case changes in price of a

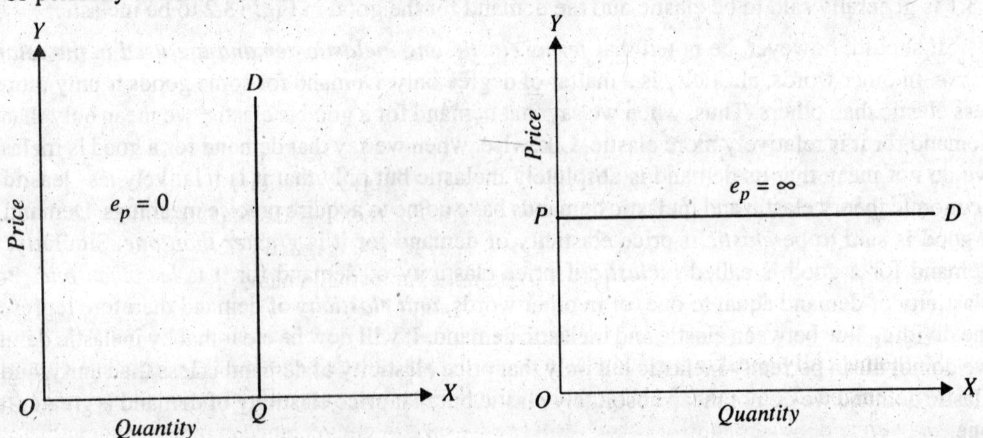

Fig. 13.3. *Perfectly Inelastic Demand ($e_p = 0$)* **Fig. 13.4.** *Perfectly Elastic Demand $e_p = \infty$*

commodity does not affect the quantity demand of the commodity at all. In this perfectly inelastic demand, demand curve is a vertical straight line as shown in Fig. 13.3. As will be seen from this figure, whatever the price quantity demanded of the commodity remains unchanged at *OQ*. An approximate example of perfectly inelastic demand is the demand of acute diabetic patient for insulin. He has to get the prescribed doze of insulin per week whatever its price.

The second extreme situation is of perfectly elastic demand in which case demand curve is a horizontal straight line as shown in Fig. 13.4. This horizontal demand curve for a product implies that a small reduction in price would cause the buyers to increase the quantity demanded from zero to all they could obtain. On the other hand, a small rise in price of the product will cause the buyers to switch completely away from the product so that its quantity demanded falls to zero. We will see in later chapters that perfectly elastic demand curve is found for the product of an individual firm working under perfect competition. Products of different firms working under perfect competition are completely identical. If any perfectly competitive firm raises the price of its product, it would lose all its customers who would switch over to other firms and if it reduces its price somewhat it would get all the customers to buy the product from it.

MEASUREMENT OF PRICE ELASTICITY

As said above, price elasticity of demand expresses the response of quantity demanded of a good to changes in its price, given the consumer's income, his tastes and prices of all other goods. Thus price elasticity means the degree of responsiveness or sensitiveness of quantity demanded of a good to a change in its price. An important method to measure price elasticity of demand is the percentage method which we explain below.

Percentage Method. Price elasticity can be precisely measured by dividing the the percentage change in quantity demanded in response to a small change in price, divided by the percentage change in price. Thus we can measure price elasticity by using the following formula:

$$\text{Price Elasticity} = \frac{\text{Percentage change in quantity demanded}}{\text{Percentage change in price}}$$

$$e_p = \frac{\dfrac{\Delta q \times 100}{q}}{\dfrac{\Delta p}{p}} = \frac{\Delta q}{q} \div \frac{\Delta p}{p}$$

$$= \frac{\Delta q}{q} \times \frac{p}{\Delta p}$$

$$= \frac{\Delta q}{q} \times \frac{p}{q}$$

where e_p stands for price elasticity
q stands for the original quantity
p stands for the original price
Δ stands for a small change

Mathematically speaking, price elasticity of demand has a *negative sign* since the change in quantity demanded of a good is in opposite direction to the change in its price. When price falls, quantity demanded rises and vice versa. But for the sake of convenience in understanding the *magnitude of response* of quantity demanded of a good to a change in its price we ignore the negative sign and take into account only the numerical value of the elasticity. Thus, if 2% change in price leads to a 4% change in quantity demanded of good *A* and 8% change in that of *B*, then the above formula of elasticity will give the value of price elasticity of good *A* equal to 2 and that of good *B* equal to 4. It indicates that the quantity demanded of good B changes relatively much more than that of good A in response to a given change in price. But if we had written minus signs before the numerical values of elasticities of the two goods, that is, if we had written the elasticity as – 2 and 4 respectively as strict mathematics would require us to do, then since – 4 is smaller than – 2, we would have been misled in concluding that price elasticity of demand of B is less than that of good A. But, as we have noted above, response of demand for good B to the change in its price is greater than that of A, it is better to ignore minus sign and draw conclusion from the absolute values of elasticities. Hence, *by convention minus sign before the value of price elasticity of demand is generally ignored in economics* unless otherwise mentioned.

Midpoint Method : Calculating Percentage Changes

When we calculate the price elasticity of demand we face a problem whether to use the *initial price* as the base for calculating percent change in price and *initial quantity* as the base for calculating the percent change in quantity demanded in response to a given percent change in price. For example, suppose price of a commodity rises from Rs. 4 to Rs. 6 per unit and as a result, the quantity demanded falls from 120 units to 80 units. If we take initial price Rs. 4 as the base for change in price, then change in price by Rs. 2 amounts to 50 percent change in price $\left(\frac{6-4}{4}\times 100=\frac{1}{2}\times 100=50\right)$ And taking initial quantity 120 units as the base for calculating percent change in quantity demanded, then there is 33.3 percent change in quantity demanded $\left(\frac{120-80}{120}\times 100=\frac{1}{3}\times 100=33.3\right)$. Thus we get price elasticity of demand as

$$e_p=\frac{33}{50}=0.66$$

Let us now reverse the direction. Suppose the price of the commodity falls from Rs. 6 to Rs. 4 per unit, and as a result quantity demanded increases from 80 units 120 units, then now taking initial Rs. 6 as the base for calculating percentage change in price, then there is 33 per cent change in price $\left(\frac{6-4}{6}\times 100=\frac{2}{6}\times 100=33\right)$ and taking 80 units as the base for calculating percentage change in quantity, then the quantity demanded rises by 50 percent $\left(\frac{120-80}{80}\times 100=\frac{40}{80}\times 100=50\right)$. Thus, we will now get $\frac{50}{33}=1.5$ as the price elasticity of demand. It therefore follows that for the same absolute change in price and absolute change in quantity demanded we get different values of price elasticity of demand if we use Rs. 4 or Rs. 6 as the base for calculating percentage change in price and 120 units or 80 units as the base for calculating percentage change in quantity demanded. To avoid this problem we use *midpoint method* for calculating the percentage changes in price and quantity demand. In mid-point method we calculate the percentage change in price or quantity demanded by *taking midpoint of the initial and final values of price and quantity demanded* respectively as the base. Thus, in our above example, midpoint (or, in other words, average) of prices of Rs. 4 and Rs. 6 is $\frac{4+6}{2}=5$ and midpoint (or average) of quantities demanded is $\frac{80+120}{2}=100$. Using this midpoint method the percentage change in price is $\frac{6-4}{5}\times 100=40$ and percentage change in quantity demanded is $\frac{120-80}{100} \times 100 = 40$. With these percentage changes in price and quantity demanded price of elasticity of demand will be

$$e_p = \frac{40}{40} = 1$$

It should be carefully noted that for *large changes in price, we must use midpoint method of calculating rice elasticity of demand.* If change in price is *very small*, then we can use initial price and initial quantity demanded.

If p_1 stands for initial price and p_2 for the new price and q_1 for the initial quantity and q_2 for the new quantity, then midpoint formula for calculating price elasticity of demand (e_p) can be written as

$$e_p = \frac{(q_2 - q_1)}{\frac{q_1 + q_2}{2}} \div \frac{p_2 - p_1}{\frac{p_1 + p_2}{2}}$$

$$= \frac{\Delta q}{\frac{q_1 + q_2}{2}} \times \frac{\frac{p_1 + p_2}{2}}{\Delta p}$$

$$= \frac{\Delta q}{\Delta p} \times \frac{p_1 + p_2}{q_1 + q_2}$$

Arc Elasticity of Demand

The concept of arc elasticity of demand should be distinguished from the *point elasticity of demand.* Point elasticity of demand refers to the price elasticity at a point on the demand curve or, in other words, it refers to the price elasticity when the changes in the price and the resultant changes in quantity demanded are infinitesimally small. In this case if we take the initial or the original price and original quantity or the subsequent price and quantity after the change in price as the basis of measurement, there will not be any significant difference in the coefficient of elasticity. However, as explained above, when the price change is quite large or we have to measure elasticity over an *arc of the demand curve* rather than at a *specific point* on it, the measure of point elasticity, namely, $\frac{\Delta q}{\Delta p} . \frac{p}{q}$ does not provide us the true and correct measure of price elasticity of demand and therefore we use the midpoint method of measuring price elasticity of demand. Therefore, in cases when large changes in price and quantity demanded are involved or in other words when we have to find the price elasticity of the arc of a demand curve as between points *A* and *B* on demand curve *DD* in Figure 13.4(a). We use *midpoint formula* (or what is also known as arc elasticity formula) for correctly calculating price elasticity of demand. As explained above, in such cases, the coefficient of price elasticity would be different depending upon whether we choose original price and quan-

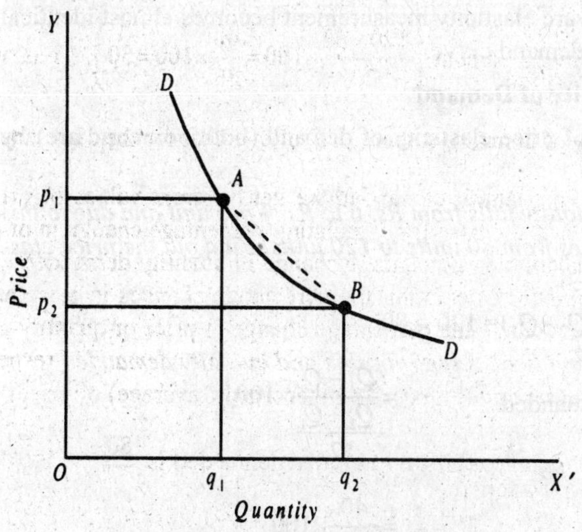

Fig. 13.4(a). *Arc Elasticity of Demand*

tity demanded or the subsequent price and quantity demanded as the base for measurement of price elasticity and therefore there will be significant difference in the two coefficients of elasticity obtained from using the two bases.

Therefore, when the change in price is quite large, say more than 5 percent, then accurate measure of price elasticity of demand can be obtained by taking the *average of original price and subsequent price as well as average of the original quantity and subsequent quantity* as the basis of measurement of percentage changes in price and quantity. Thus, in Figure 13.4(a) if price of a good falls from p_1 to p_2 and as a result its quantity demanded increases from q_1 to q_2, the average of the two prices is given by $\frac{p_1+p_2}{2}$ and average of the two quantities (original and subsequent) is given by $\frac{q_1+q_2}{2}$. Thus, in Figure 13.4(a) the formula for measuring arc elasticity, we use midpoint method of measuring price elasticity which is given by :

$$e_q = \frac{\Delta q}{\frac{q_1+q_2}{2}} \div \frac{\Delta p}{\frac{p_1+p_2}{2}}$$

$$= \frac{\Delta q}{q_1+q_2} \cdot \frac{p_1+p_2}{\Delta p} = \frac{\Delta q}{\Delta p} \cdot \frac{p_1+p_2}{q_1+q_2}$$

It should be carefully ntoed that, the greater the convexity of the demand curve between *A* and *B*, the greater the divergence between the dashed line *AB* and the true demand curve and therefore the poorer the approximation of arc elasticity measure (of the dashed line *AB*) for the true curve between *A* and *B*. Moreover, the larger the distance between *A* and *B* on the demand curve, the greater will be the divergence between the dashed straight line *AB* and the true curve from *A* to *B* and consequently the greater will be the discrepancy between the elasticity on the true curve from *A* to *B* and consequently the greater will be the discrepancy between the elasticity on the true curve and the elasticity on the dashed line *AB* measured by the arc elasticity formula given above. That is why even the concept of arc elasticity is relevant in case when the arc involved in small, that is, two points *A* and *B* lie close together. Therefore, the arc elasticity formula or midpoint method of measuring price elasticity should be used when the change in price is quite *large*. On the other hand, when the two points on the demand curve are *very close* together, arc (dashed straight line) becomes almost indentical with the true curve and the arc elasticity measurement becomes almost identical with the point elasticity measurement on the demand curve.

Some Numerical Problems of Price Elasticity of Demand

Let us solve some numerical problems of price elasticity of demand (both point and arc) by percentage method.

Problem 1. *Suppose the price of a commodity falls from Rs. 6 to Rs. 4 per unit and due to this quantity demanded of the commodity increases from 80 units to 120 units. Find out the price elasticity of demand.*

Solution: Change in quantity demand ($Q_2 - Q_1$)= 120 – 80

Percentage chagne in quantity demanded $= \frac{Q_2 - Q_1}{\frac{Q_2+Q_1}{2}} \times 100$

$$= \frac{40}{\frac{200}{2}} \times 100$$

$= 40$

Change in price $= P_2 - P_1 = 4 - 6 = -2$

% Change in price $= \dfrac{P_2 - P_1}{\dfrac{P_2 + P_1}{2}} \times 100 = \dfrac{-2}{\dfrac{10}{2}} \times 100$

$= -40$

Price elasticity of demand $= \dfrac{\text{\% change in quantity demanded}}{\text{\% Change in price}}$

$-\dfrac{40}{-40} = -1$

We ignore the minus sign. Therefore, price elasticity of demand is equal to one.

Problem 2. *A consumer purchases 80 units of a commodity when its price is Re. 1 per unit and purchases 48 units when its price rises to Rs. 2 per unit. What is the price elasticity of demand for the commodity ?*

Solution: It should be noted that the change in price from Re. 1 to Rs.2 in this case is very large (*i.e.*, 100%). Therefore, to calculate the elasticity coefficient in this case midpoint elasticity formula should be used.

Change is price (Δp) = Rs. 2 – 1 = 1

Average of the original and subsequent prices $= \dfrac{p_1 + p_2}{2}$

$= \dfrac{1+2}{2} = \dfrac{3}{2} = 1.5$

Change in quantity demanded (Δq) $= 80 - 48 = 32$

Average of the original and subsequent quantities $= \dfrac{q_1 + q_2}{2}$

$$e_p = \frac{\Delta q}{\dfrac{q_1 + q_2}{2}} \div \frac{\Delta p}{\dfrac{p_1 + p_2}{2}} \quad = \frac{80+48}{2} = \frac{128}{2} = 64$$

$$= \frac{32}{64} \div \frac{1}{1.5}$$

$$= \frac{32}{64} \times \frac{1.5}{1} = \frac{1}{2} \times \frac{15}{10} = \frac{3}{4} = 0.75$$

Thus, the price elasticity of demand obtained is equal to 0.75.

Problem 3. *Suppose a seller of a textile cloth wants to lower the price of its cloth from Rs. 150 per metre to Rs. 142.5 per metre. If its present sales are 2000 metres per month and further it is estimated that its elasticity of demand for the product equals – 0.7. Show*

(a) Whether or not his total revenue will increase as a result of his decision to lower the price; and

(b) Calculate the exact magnitude of its new total revenue.

Solution. (*a*) Price elasticity $= \dfrac{\Delta q}{\Delta p} \cdot \dfrac{p}{q}$

p = Rs. 150

$$q = 2000 \text{ metres}$$
$$\Delta p = 150 - 142.5 = 7.5$$
$$e_p = 0.7$$
$$\Delta q = ?$$

Substituting the values of p, q, Δp and e_p in the price elasticity formula we have

$$0.7 = \frac{\Delta q}{7.5} \times \frac{150}{2000}$$

$$\Delta q = \frac{0.7 \times 7.5 \times 2000}{150} = 70$$

Since the price has fallen the quantity demanded will increase by 70 metres. So the new quantity demanded will be 2000 + 70 = 2070.

(*b*) Total Revenue before reduction in price = 2000 × 150 = Rs. 3,00,000

Total revenue after price reduction = 2070 × 142.5 = Rs. 2,94,975

Thus with reduction in price his total revenue has decreased.

TOTAL REVENUE, TOTAL EXPENDITURE AND PRICE ELASTICITY OF DEMAND

Total revenue is the amount received by the seller from the sale of the quantity of the good sold in the market. It is worthnoting noting that total revenue received by the seller from sale of the quantity of a good is the expenditure made by the buyers. Total revenue (or total expenditure) from the sale of a good is intimately related to the price elasticity of demand. Total revenue is the product of price (*P*) and the quantity (*Q*) of the commodity sold (*i.e.*, Total revenue or total expenditure = *P* × *Q*) .. Consider Fig. 13.4(b) where *DD* is the demand curve. At price *OP* or Rs. 5, the quantity demanded and sold of the commodity is *OQ* (or 100 units). Thus the area of the rectangle *OPAQ* (or 5× 100 = 500) represents the total revenue made by the sellers or the expenditure made by the buyers on the commodity :

Change in total revenue following a change in price of the good depends on price elasticity of demand. We can classify the commodities into the following three categories.

1. When demand is elastic (e_p>1). When demand for a commodity is elastic ($e_p > 1$), the percentage increase in quantity demanded of the commodity will be greater than the percentage fall in price that caused the former. As a result, total revenue will increase following the reduction in price of the commodity. Conversely, this also implies that when demand is elastic (e_p>1), rise in price will cause the total revenue to decrease.

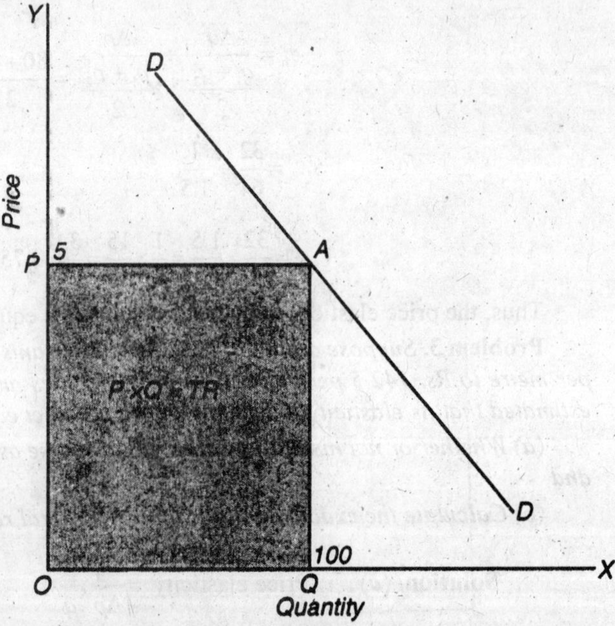

Fig. 13.4(b). *Total Revenue* = *P* × *Q*

2. When Demand is Inelastic (e_p <1). When demand for a commodity is inelastic, with a fall in price the quantity demanded of a good increases proportionately less then the fall in price. Therefore, in this case of inelastic demand, with a fall in price, total revenue (or expenditure) decreases. This also implies that when demand is inelastic, the rise in price will lead to a *percentage decline in quantity demanded that is proportionately less than the rise in price*. As a result, if demand is inelastic, rise in price will cause total revenue to increase.

3. **When demand is unit-elastic (e_p = 1).** When the demand for a commodity is unit-elastic, with the fall or rise in price, the quantity demanded rises or falls in the same proportion as the change in price . As a result, in case of unit-elastic demand, total revenue ($P \times Q$) remains the same when price changes.

Thus we arrive at the following conclusions about the relationship between changes in price of a good and total revenue.

1. *When demand for good is elastic ($e_p > 1$), a fall in price raises total revenue and a rise in price reduces total revenue.*

2. *When demand for a good is inelastic ($e_p < 1$), a fall in price reduces total revenue and a rise in price raises total revenue.*

3. *When demand for a commodity is unit-elastic ($e_p = 1$), changes in its price do not affect total revenue.*

Estimating Price Elasticity of Demand from Changes in total Revenue (or Total Expenditure)

We can now use the relationship between changes in price and total revenue explained above for estimating price elasticity of demand. It may be noted that total revenue received by sellers is the expenditure made by the buyers on a commodity. Therefore, estimating price elasticity from changes in total revenue is also called *expenditure method* of measuring price elasticity of demand. Moreover, from changes in total revenue or expenditure caused by changes in price we can only estimate whether price elasticity is greater than one, equal to one or less than one, we cannot measure exact coefficient of price elasticity of demand. Thus, for estimating price elasticity from changes in total expenditure or revenue, we use the following lists.

1. *If fall in price of a commodity causes total expenditure (or total revenue) to increase, demand for the good is elastic ($e_p > 1$).*

2. *If fall in price of a commodity causes total expenditure (or total revenue) on a commodity to decrease, demand for the commodity is inelastic ($e_p < 1$).*

3. *If changes in price of a good does not bring about any change in total expenditure, (i.e. total revenue) demand for it is unitary-elastic.*

Illustration of Expenditure Method

Let us illustrate how we judge the elasticity of demand as to whether it is greater than one, equal to one or less than one. Consider Table 13.1, which gives quantity demanded of pens at various prices. It will be seen from Table 13.1 that quantity demanded increases from 30 pens at price Rs. 5 per pen to 87 pens at price Rs. 3.25. We have calculated the total outlay by multiplying the quantity demanded with the corresponding price of the pen. It will be observed from the table that when price of the pen falls from Rs. 5 to Rs. 4.75, from Rs. 4.75 to Rs. 4.50, from Rs. 4.50 to Rs. 4.25 and from Rs. 4.25 to Rs. 4 the quantity demanded increases so much that the total outlay on pens increases indicating thereby that elasticity of demand is greater than one at these prices.

When price falls from Rs. 4.00 to Rs. 3.75, the quantity demanded increases from 75 pens to 80 pens so that total outlay remains the same at Rs. 300. This shows that price elasticity of demand is unity. When price of the pen further falls from Rs. 3.75 to Rs. 3.50 and then to Rs. 3.25 the total outlay spent on pens decreases. Thus, the price elasticity of demand for pens at these prices is less than unity.

TAble 13.1. Price Elasticity of Demand and Total Expenditure

Price of Pen (Rs.) P	*Quantity Demand Q*	*Total Expenditure or Revenue (Rs.) P × Q*	*Price Elasticity of Demand (e_p)*
5.00	30	150	
4.75	40	190	e > 1
4.50	50	225	e > 1
4.25	60	255	e > 1
4.00	75	300	e > 1
3.75	80	300	e = 1
3.50	84	294	e < 1
3.25	87	282.75	e < 1

Graphic Illustration of Expenditure Method

This relationship between price elasticity of demand and total outlay can also be graphically illustrated with the aid of the demand curve. This relationship between price elasticity of demand and total expenditure made on a good is illustrated with the aid of Fig. 13.5 where demand curve *DD* is given. In the Fig. 13.5 when the price is *OP*, the total expenditure made on the good is equal to *OP* × *OQ i.e.*, area *OPRQ* and when the price falls to *OP′*, the total expenditure is equal to *OP′R′Q′*. It will be seen from he Figure 13.5 that the area *OP′ HQ* is common in both the rectangles *OPRQ* and *OP′R′Q′*. Now, by comparing the remaining areas *PRHP′* and *QHR′Q′* we find that two are equal to each other. That is, the total outlay *OP′R′Q′* is equal to the original outlay *OPRQ*. This means that with the fall in price the total outlay (expenditure) made on the good has remained the same. Hence the price elasticity of demand is here equal to unity.

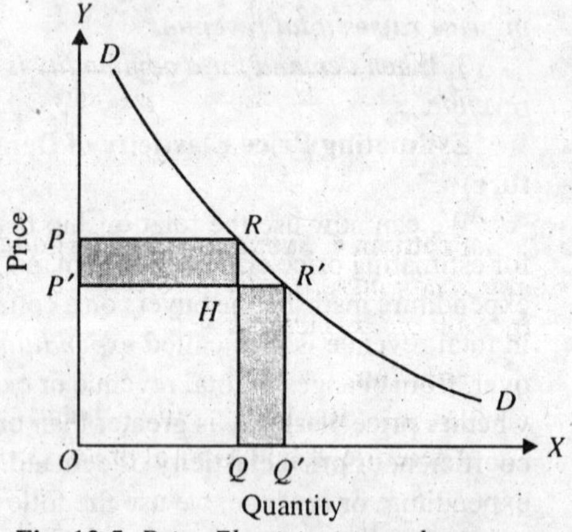

Fig. 13.5. *Price Elasticity is equal to one*

That when the price elasticity of demand is greater than one, the total expenditure made on the good increases with the fall in price of the good is illustrated in Fig. 13.6 in which a demand curve *DD* is given. When price of the good is *OP*, *OQ* quantity of the good is demanded. At the price of *OP*, the total expenditure made on the good is equal to the area *OPRQ*. Now, if price of the good falls to *OP′*, the quantity demanded of the good rises to *OQ′*. Therefore, now at price *OP′* total expenditure on the good is equal to the area *OP′R′Q*. It will be seen in Fig. 13.6 that the area *OP′HQ* is present in both the rectangles *OPRQ* and *OP′R′Q′*. The remaining areas in the two rectangles are *PRHP′* and *QHR′Q′*. Now, a galance at Fig. 13.6 will show that the area *QHR′Q* is greater than the area *PRHP′*. It is thus clear that the expenditure (*OP′R′Q*) on the good at price *OP′* is greater than the expenditure (*OPRQ*) at price *OP*. That is, with the fall in price the total expenditure on the commodity has increased. Hence, the price elasticity of demand is here greater than unity.

Now, consider Fig. 13.7. In this figure demand for the good is such that with the fall in price the total expenditure made on the good declines. At price *OP* the total expenditure is *OPRQ* and when the price falls to *OP′* the total expenditure made on it is equal to *OP′R′Q′*. Now, by comparing the two total expenditure it is evident that the expenditure *OP′R′Q′* is less than the expenditure *OPRQ* in Figure 13.7. Therefore, the price elasticity of demand is here less than unity.

From the above analysis it is clear that from the changes in the total expenditure as a result of the changes in price we can know the price elasticity of demand for a good. We repeat once again that with the total expenditure method we cannot know the exact and precise measure of the price elasticity; with this we can only know whether price elasticity is equal to one, greater than one or less than one.

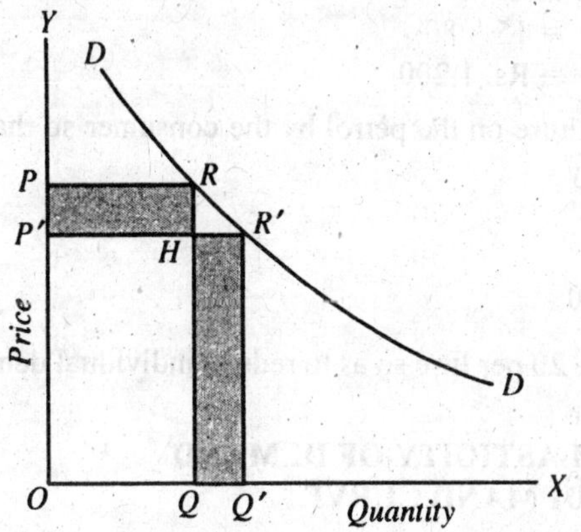

Fig. 13.6. *Price Elasticity is greater than one*

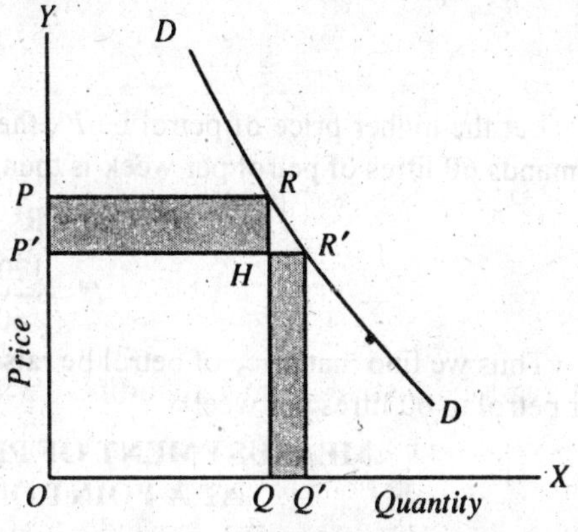

Fig. 13.7. *Price Elasticity is less than*

Problem 4. *Suppose price of a good falls from Rs. 10 to Rs. 8 per unit. As a result, its quantity demanded increases from 80 units to 100 units. What can we say about price elasticity of demand by total outlay method.*

Solution.

At price Rs. 10, quantity demand is 100 units

Therefore, total outlay at price Rs. 10 = $P \times Q$

$= 10 \times 80$

= Rs. 800

At the lower price Rs. 8, quantity demand increases to 100 units

Therefore, total expenditure at price Rs. 8 = $P \times Q$

$= 8 \times 100$

= Rs. 800

We thus find that with the change in price of the good, total outlay on the commodity remains constant. Hence price elasticity of demand is equal to one.

Problem 5. *Suppose price of a commodity rises from Rs. 15 to Rs. 16 per unit. As a result, its quantity demanded falls from Rs. 100 units to 80 units. Find out the price elasticity of demand by expenditure method.*

Solution.

Expenditure on the commodity at price Rs.15 = P × Q

= 15 × 100

= Rs. 1500

Expenditure on the commodity at price Rs. 16 = 16 × 80

= Rs. 1,280

Thus we find with the rise in price, expenditure on the commodity decreases. This means the price elasticity of demand is greater than one (*ep* > 1).

Problem 6. *Suppose that price elasticity of demand for petrol is equal to unity and at Rs. 15 per litre an individual consumes (i.e., demands) 80 litres of petrol in a week. How much price of petrol should be fixed so that he demands 60 litres of petrol ?*

Solution.

Since the given price elasticity of demand for petrol is equal to unity, the expenditure on the petrol by the individual will remain constant at different prices.

$$\text{Expenditure on petrol at price of Rs. 15 per litre} = P \times Q$$
$$= 15 \times 80$$
$$= \text{Rs. } 1{,}200$$

Let the higher price of petrol be P', the expenditure on the petrol by the consumer so that he demands 60 litres of petrol per week is then given by

$$P' \times 60 = \text{Rs. } 1200$$

$$P' = \frac{1200}{60} = Rs.20$$

Thus we find that price of petrol be raised to Rs. 20 per litre so as to reduce individual demand for petrol to 60 litres per week.

MEASUREMENT OF PRICE ELASTICITY OF DEMAND AT A POINT ON THE DEMAND CURVE

Let a straight line demand curve DD' is given and it is required to measure price elasticity at a point R on this demand curve. It will be seen from Fig. 13.8 that corresponding to point R on the demand curve DD', price is OP and quantity demand at it is OQ.

The measure of price elasticity of demand is given by :

$$e_p = \frac{\Delta q}{\Delta p} \cdot \frac{p}{q}$$

The first term in this formula, namely, $\frac{\Delta q}{\Delta p}$ is the reciprocal of the slope of the demand curve DD' (Note that the slope of the demand curve DD' is equal to $\frac{\Delta p}{\Delta q}$ which remains constant all along the straight line demand curve). The second term in the above point elasticity formula is the original price (p) divided by the original quantity (q). Thus

$$e_p = \frac{1}{slope} \cdot \frac{p}{q}$$

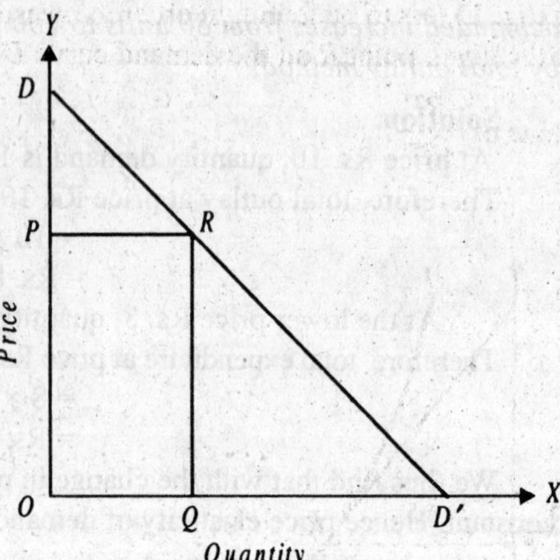

Fig. 13.8. *Measuring Price Elasticity at a a Point on a Straight-Line Demand Curve*

It will be seen from Fig. 13.8 that at point R, original price $p = OP$ and original quantity $q = OQ$. Further, slope of the demand curve DD' is $\frac{\Delta P}{\Delta Q} = \frac{PD}{PR}$

Substituting these values in the above formula we have

$$e_p = \frac{1}{\frac{PD}{PR}} \times \frac{OP}{OQ}$$

$$= \frac{PR}{PD} \times \frac{OP}{OQ}$$

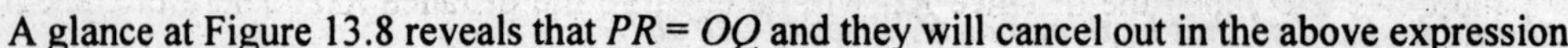

A glance at Figure 13.8 reveals that $PR = OQ$ and they will cancel out in the above expression.

Therefore, $$e_p = \frac{OP}{PD} \qquad ...(1)$$

Measuring price elasticity by taking the ratio of these distances on the vertical axis, that is, $\frac{OP}{PD}$ is called *vertical axis formula.*

In a right-angled triangle *ODD'*, *PR* is paralled to *OD'*. Therefore,

$$e_p = \frac{OP}{PD} = \frac{RD'}{RD}$$

RD' is the lower segment of the demand curve *DD'* at point *R* and *RD* is its upper segment. Therefore,

$$e_p = \frac{RD'}{RD} = \frac{\text{lower segement}}{\text{upper segment}} \qquad ...(2)$$

Measuring price elasticity at a point on the demand curve by measuring the ratio of the distances of lower segment and upper segment is another popular method of measuring point price elasticity on a demand curve.

Measuring price elasticity on a non-linear demand curve. If the demand curve is not a straight line like *DD'* in Fig. 13.8 but is, as usual, a non-linear curve, then how to measure price elasticity at a given point on it. For instance, how price elasticity at point *R* on the demand curve *DD* in Fig. 13.9 is to be found. In order to measure elasticity in this case, we have to draw a tangent *TT'* at the given point *R* on the demand curve *DD'* and then measure price elasticity by finding out the value of $\frac{RT'}{RT}$.

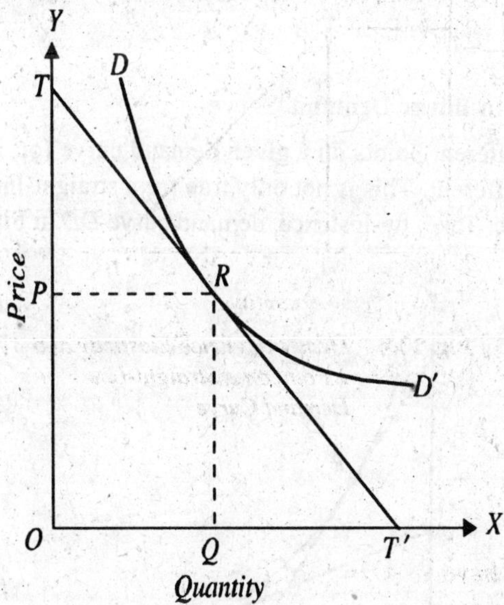

Fig. 13.9. *Measuring Price Elasticity at a Point on a Non-Linear Demand Curve*

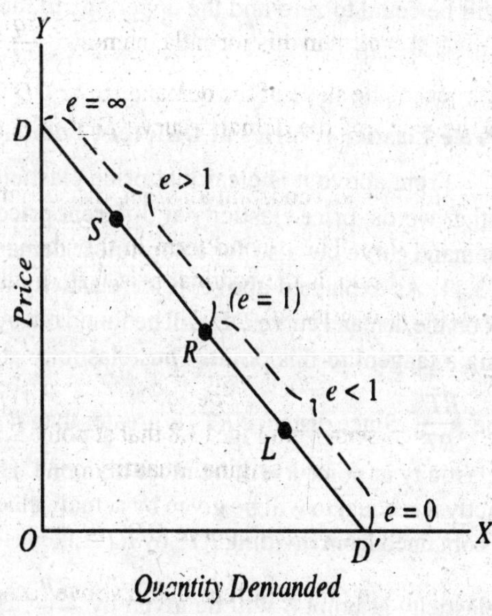

Fig. 13.10. *On a linear demand curve price elasticity varies from infinity to zero.*

On a linear demand curve price elasticity varies from zero to infinity. Now again, take the straight-line demand curve *DD'* (Fig. 13.10). If point *R* lies exactly at the middle of this straight-line demand curve *DD'*, then the distance *RD* will be equal to the distance *RD'*. Therefore, elasticity which is equal to $\frac{RD'}{RD}$ will be equal to one at the middle point of the straight-line demand curve. Suppose a point *S* lies above the middle point on the straight-line demand curve *DD'*. It is obvious that the distance *SD'* is greater than the distance *SD* and price elasticity which is equal to $\frac{SD'}{SD}$ at point *S* will be more than one. Similarly, at any other point which lies above the middle point on the straight-line demand curve, price elasticity will be greater than unity. Moreover, price elasticity will go on increasing as we move further towards point *D* and at point *D* price elasticity will be equal to infinity. This is because price elasticity is equal $\frac{RD'}{RD}$ *i.e.*, $\frac{\text{lower segment}}{\text{upper segment}}$ and as we move towards *D* the lower segment will go on increasing while the upper segment will become smaller. Therefore, as we move towards *D* on the demand curve, the price elasticity will be increasing. At point *D*, the lower segment will be equal to the whole *DD'*, and the upper segment will be zero. Therefore,

$$\text{Price elasticity at point } D \text{ on the demand curve } DD' = \frac{DD'}{0} = \text{infinity.}$$

Now, suppose a point *L* lies below the middle point on the linear demand curve *DD'*. In this case, the lower segment *LD'* will be smaller than the upper segment *LD* and therefore price elasticity at *L* which is equal to $\frac{LD'}{LD}$ will be less than one.

Moreover, price elasticity will go on decreasing as we move towards point *D'*. This is because whereas lower segment will become smaller and smaller, the upper one will be increasing as we move towards point *D'*. At point D′ the price elasticity will be zero, since at *D'* the lower segment will be equal to zero and the upper one to the whole *DD'*. At point *D'*,

$$e_p = \frac{0}{DD'} = 0$$

Price Elasticity Varies at Different Points on a Non-linear Demand Curve

From above it is clear that price elasticity at different points on a given demand curve (or, in other words, price elasticity at different prices) is different. This is not only true for a straight-line demand curve but also for a non-linear demand curve. Take, for instance, demand curve *DD* in Fig. 13.11. As explained above, price elasticity at point *R* on the demand curve *DD* will be found out by drawing a tangent to this point. Thus elasticity at *R* will be $\frac{RT'}{RT}$. Since distance *RT'* is greater than *RT*, price elasticity at point *R* will be more than one. How exactly it is equal to will be given by actual value which is obtained from dividing *RT'* by *RT*. Likewise, price elasticity at point *S* will be given by $\frac{SJ'}{SJ}$. Because *SJ'* is smaller than *SJ*, elasticity point at *S* will be less than one. Again, how exactly it is, will be found from actually dividing *SJ'* by *SJ*. It is thus evident that elasticity at point *S* is less than that at point *R* on he demand curve *DD*. Similarly, price elasticity at other points of the demand curve *DD* will be found

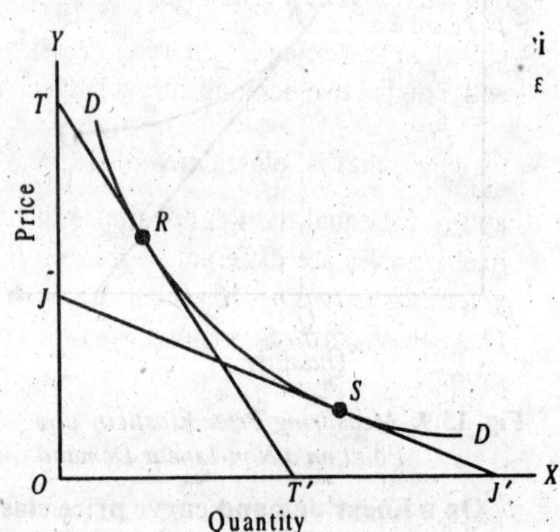

Fig. 13.11. *Price elasticity declines as we move down on a demand curve.*

to be different.

Comparing Price Elasticity of Two Demand Curves With Different Slopes

Having explained the concept of price elasticity of demand we will now explain how to compare price elasticity on two demand curves. First, we take up the case of two *demand curves with different slopes* starting from a given point on the *Y*-axis. This case is illustrated in Fig. 13.12 where two demand curves *DA* and *DB* which have different slopes but are starting from the same point *D* on the *Y*-axis. Slope of demand curve *DB* is less than that of *DA*. Now, it can be proved that at any given price the price elasticity on these two demand curves would be the same. If price is *OP*, then according to demand curve *DA*, *OL* quantity of the good is demanded and according to demand curve *DB*, *OH* quantity of the good is demanded. Thus, at price *OP* the corresponding points on the two demand curves are *E* and *F* respectively. We know that price elasticity at a point on the demand curve is equal to $\frac{\text{lower segment}}{\text{upper segment}}$. Therefore, the price elasticity of demand at point *E* on the demand curve *DA* is equal to $\frac{EA}{ED}$ and the price elasticity of demand at point *F* on the demand curve *DB* is equal to $\frac{FB}{FD}$.

Now, take triangle *ODA* which is a right-angled triangle in which *PE* is parallel to *OA*. It follows that in it, $\frac{EA}{ED}$ is equal to $\frac{OP}{PD}$. Thus, the price elasticity at point *E* on the demand curve *DA* is equal to $\frac{OP}{PD}$.

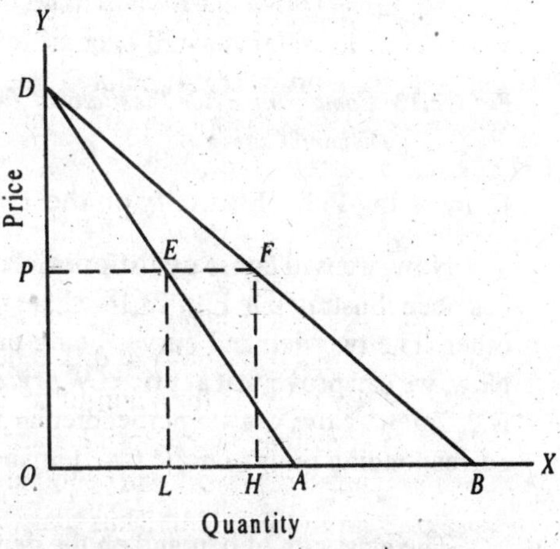

Fig. 13.12. *Comparing Price Elasticity on the Two Demand Curves with Different Slopes*

Now, in the right-angled triangle *ODB*, *PF* is parallel to *OB*. Therefore, in it $\frac{FB}{FD}$ is equal to $\frac{OP}{PD}$. Thus, price elasticity of demand at point *F* on the demand curve *DB* is also equal to $\frac{OP}{PD}$. From above it is clear that price elasticity of demand on points *E* and *F* on the two demand curves respectively is equal to $\frac{OP}{PD}$, that is, elasticities of demand at points *E* and *F* are equal though the slopes of these two demand curves are different. *It follows therefore that price elasticity is not the same thing as slope. Therefore, price elasticity on two demand curves should not be compared by considering their slopes alone.*

Comparing Price Elasticity on Two Intersecting Demand Curves

We now take up the case of *comparing price elasticity at a given price where the two demand curves intersect*. In Fig. 13.13 we have drawn two *demand curves AB* and *CD* which intersect at point *E*. It will be noticed from the figure that demand curve *CD* is flatter than the demand curve *AB*. Now, it can be easily proved that at every price on the flatter demand curve *CD*, price elasticity will be greater than that on the relatively steeper demand curve *AB*. For example at price *OP*, corresponding to the intersecting point E, using the vertical axis formula, elasticity at point E on demand curve $CD = \frac{OP}{PC}$. Similarly, elasticity at point E on the demand curve $AB = \frac{OP}{PA}$. It will be seen from Fig. 13.13 that $\frac{OP}{PC} > \frac{OP}{PA}$ because distance PC is less than the distance PA. Hence at the price OP, elasticity is greater on the flatter demand curve CD, as compared to the steeper demand curve AB. Likewise, it can be shown at any other given price, price elasticity of demand will be greater on the flatter demand curve CD as compared to the steeper demand curve AB.

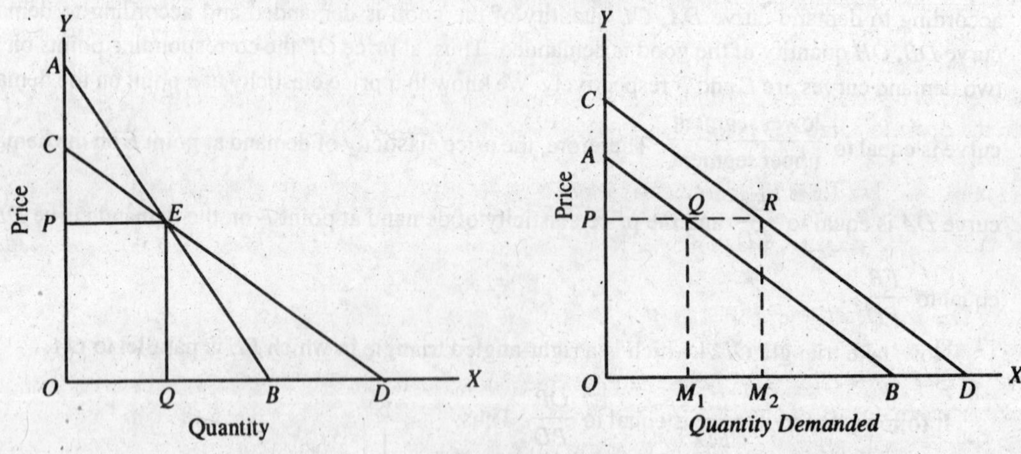

Fig. 13.13. *Comparing Price Elasticity of Two Intersecting Demand Curves*

Fig. 13.14. *Comparing Price Elasticity of Two Parallel Demand Curves*

Comparing Price Elasticity on the Two Parallel Demand Curves

Now, we will compare the price elasticity at two parallel demand curves at a given price. This has been illustrated in Fig. 13.14 where the given two demand curves AB and CD are parallel to each other. The two demand curver being parallel to each other imlies that they have the same slope. Now, we can prove that at price OP price elasticity of demand on the two demand curves AB and CD is different. Now, draw a perpendicular from point R to the point P on Y-axis. Thus, at price OP the corresponding points on the two demand curves are Q and R respectively.

The elasticity of demand on the demand curve AB at point Q will be equal to $\frac{QB}{QA}$ and at point R on the demand curve CD it is equal to $\frac{RD}{RC}$.

Because in a right-angled triangle OAB, PQ is parallel to OB :

Therefore, $$\frac{QB}{QA} = \frac{OP}{PA}$$

Hence, price elasticity at point Q on the demand curve $AB = \frac{OP}{PA}$

At point R on the demand curve CD, price elasticity is equal to $\frac{RD}{RC}$. Because in the right-angled triangle OCD, PR is parallel to OD.

Therefore, $\frac{RD}{RC} = \frac{OP}{PC}$. Hence, on point *R* on the demand curve *CD*, price elasticity = $\frac{OP}{PC}$

On seeing Figure 13.14 it will be clear that at point *Q* on the demand curve *AB*, the price elasticity = $\frac{OP}{PA}$ and at point *R* on the demand curve *CD*, price elasticity = $\frac{OP}{PA}$ which are not equal to each other. Because *PC* is greater than *PA*,

Therefore $$\frac{OP}{PC} < \frac{OP}{PA}$$

It is, therefore, clear that at point *R* on the demand curve *CD* the price elasticity is less than that at point *Q* on the demand curve *AB*, when the two demand curves being parallel to each other have the same slope. It also follows that *as the demand curve shifts to the right the price elasticity of demand at a given price goes on declining*. Thus, as has been just seen, price elasticity at price *OP* on the demand curve *CD* is less than that on the demand curve *AB*.

DETERMINANTS OF PRICE ELASTICITY OF DEMAND

The following are the main factors which determine price elasticity of demand for a commodity.

The Availability of Substitutes. Of all the factors determining price elasticity of demand the availability of the number and kinds of substitutes for a commodity is the most important factor. If for a commodity close substitutes are available, its demand tends to be elastic. If price of such a commodity goes up, the people will shift to its close substitutes and as a result the demand for that commodity will greatly decline. The greater the possibility of substitution, the greater the price elasticity of demand for it. If for a commodity good substitutes are not available, people will have to buy it even when its price rises, and therefore its demand would tend to be inelastic.

For instance, if the price of Coca Cola were to increase sharply, many consumers would turn to other kinds of cold drinks, and as a result, the quantity demanded of Coca Cola will decline very much. On the other hand, if the price of Coca Cola falls, many consumers will change from other cold drinks to Coca Cola. Thus, the demand for Coca Cola is elastic. It is the availability of close substitutes that makes the consumers sensitive to the changes in the price of Coca Cola and this makes the demand for Coca Cola elastic. Likewise, demand for common salt is inelastic because good substitutes for common salt are not available. If the price of common salt rises slightly, the people would consume almost the same quantity of salt as before since good substitutes are not available. The demand for common salt is inelastic also because people spend a very little part of their income on it and even if its price rises it makes only negligible difference in their budget allocation for the salt.

The Proportion of Consumer's Income Spent On a commodity. Another important determinant of the elasticity of demand is how much it accounts for in consumer's budget. In other words, the proportion of consumer's income spent on a particular commodity also influences the price elasticity of demand for it. The greater the proportion of income spent on a commodity, the greater will be generally its elasticity of demand, and vice versa. The demand for common salt, soap, matches and such other goods tends to be highly inelastic because the households spend only a fraction of their income on each of them. When price of such a commodity rises, it will not make much difference in consumers' budget and therefore they will continue to buy almost the same quantity of that commodity and, therefore, the demand for them will be inelastic. On the other hand, demand for cloth in a country like India tends to be elastic since households spend a good part of their income on clothing. If price of cloth falls, it will mean great saving in the budget of many households and therefore they will tend to increase the quantity demanded of the cloth. On the other hand, if price of cloth rises many households will not afford to buy as much quantity of cloth as before, and therefore, the quantity demanded of cloth will fall.

The Number of Uses of a Commodity. The greater the number of uses to which a commodity can be put, the greater will be its price elasticity of demand. If price of a commodity having several uses is very high, its demand will be small and it will be put to the most important uses and if price of such a commodity falls it will be put to less important uses also and consequently its quantity demanded will rise significantly. To illustrate, milk has several uses. If its price rises to a very high level, it will be used only for essential purposes such as feeding the children and sick persons. If price of milk falls, it would be devoted to other uses such as preparation of curd, cream, ghee and sweets. Therefore, the demand for milk tends to be elastic.

Complementarity Between Goods. Complementarity between goods or joint demand for goods also affects the price elasticity of demand. Households are generally less sensitive to the changes in prices of goods that are complementary with each other or which are jointly used as compared to those goods which have independent demand or used alone. For example, for the running of automobiles, besides petrol, lubricating oil is also used. Now, if the price of lubricating oil goes up, it will mean a very small increase in the total cost of running the automobile, since the use of oil is much less as compared to other things such as petrol. Thus, the demand for lubricating oil tends to be inelastic. Similarly, the demand for common salt is inelastic, partly because consumers do not use it alone but along with other things.

It is worth mentioning here that for assessing the elasticity of demand for a commodity all the above three factors must be taken into account. The three factors mentioned above may reinforce each other in determining the elasticity of demand for a commodity or they may operate against each other. The elasticity of demand for a commodity will be the net result of all the forces working on it.

Time and Elasticity. The element of time also influences the elasticity of demand for a commodity. Demand tends to be more elastic if the time involved is long. This is because consumers can substitute goods in the long run. In the short run, substitution of one commodity by another is not so easy. The longer the period of time, the greater is the ease with which both consumers and businessmen can substitute one commodity for another. For instance, if the price of fuel oil rises, it may be difficult to substitute fuel oil by other types of fuels such as coal or cooking gas. But, given sufficient time, people will make adjustments and use coal or cooking gas instead of the fuel oil whose price has risen. Likewise, when the business firms find that the price of a certain material has risen, then it may not be possible for them to substitute that material by some other relatively cheaper one. But with the passage of time they can undertake research to find substitute material and can redesign the product or modify the machinery employed in the production of a commodity so as to economise in the use of the dearer material. Therefore, given the time, they can substitute the material whose price has risen. We thus see that demand is generally more elastic in the long run than in the short run.

IMPORTANCE OF PRICE ELASTICITY OF DEMAND

The concept of elasticity of demand plays a crucial role in the pricing decisions of the business firms and the Government when it regulates prices. The concept of price elasticity is also important in judging the effect of devaluation or depreciation of a currency on its export earnings. It has also a great use in fiscal policy because the Finance Minister has to keep in view the price elasticity of demand when it considers to impose taxes on various commodities. We shall explain below the various uses, applications and importance of the elasticity of demand.

Pricing Decisions by Business Firms. *The business firms take into account the price elasticity of demand when they take decisions regarding pricing of the goods.* This is because change in the price of a product will bring about a change in the quantity demanded depending upon the coefficient of price elasticity. This change in quantity demanded as a result of, say a rise in price by a firm, will affect the total consumer's expenditure and will therefore, affect the revenue of the firm. If the demand for a product of the firm happens to be elastic, then any attempt on the part of the firm to raise the price of its product will bring about a fall in its total revenue. Thus, instead of gaining from the increase in price, it will lose if the demand for its product happens to be elastic. On the other hand, if the demand for the product of a firm happens to be inelastic, then the increase in price by it will raise its total revenue. Therefore, for fixing a profit-maximising price, the firm cannot ignore the price elasticity of demand for its product.

Price elasticity of demand can be used to answer the following types of questions:

1. What will be the effect on sales if a firm decides to raise the price of its product, say by 5 per cent.

2. How large a reduction in price of a product is required to increase sales, say by 25 percent.

It has been found by some empirical studies that business firms often fail to take elasticity into account while taking decisions regarding prices, or they give insufficient attention to the coefficient of price elasticity. No doubt, the main reason for this is that they don't have the means to calculate price elasticity for their product, since sufficient data regarding past prices and quantity demanded at those prices are not available. Even if such data are available, there are difficulties of interpretation of it because it is not clear whether the changes in quantity demanded were the result of changes in price alone or changes in some other factors determining the demand. However, recently big corporate business firms have established their research departments which estimate the coefficient of price elasticity from the data concerning past prices and quantities demanded. Further, they are also using statistical techniques to isolate the price effect on the quantity demanded from the effects of other factors.

Uses in Economic Policy Regarding Price Regulation, Especially of Farm Products. Governments of many countries, especially the United States of America, regulate the prices of farm products. This price regulation involves the increase in the prices of farm products and this is done with the expectation that the demand for the farm products is inelastic. That the demand for farm products is inelastic in countries like USA has been found by empirical studies. By restricting supply in the market, Government succeeds in raising the price for the farm products. The demand for farm products being inelastic, the quantity demanded does not fall very much and as a result the expenditure of the consumers on farm products increases, which raises the incomes of the agricultural class. If the demands for farm products were elastic, any rise in their price brought about by Government's restricted supply of them, would have caused the decrease in the incomes of the agricultural class. Therefore, *the crop restriction programme and keeping part of the crop off the market by the Government would never have been considered, had the demand for farm products been elastic rather than inelastic.*

Explanation of the 'Paradox' of Plenty. The concept of price elasticity of demand also helps us to explain the so-called 'paradox of plenty' in agriculture, namely, that a bumper crop reaped by the farmers brings a smaller total income to them. The fall in the income or revenue of the farmers as a result of the bumper crop is due to the fact that with greater supply the prices of the crops decline drastically and in the context of inelastic demand for them, the total expenditure on the crop output declines, bringing about fall in the incomes of the farmers. Thus, bumper crop instead of raising their incomes, reduces them. Therefore, in order to ensure that the farmers do not lose incentive to raise their production, they need to be assured certain minimum price by the Government. At that minimum price the Government should be prepared to buy the crop from the farmers.

Use in International Trade. The concept of price elasticity of demand is also crucially important in the field of international economics. The Governments of the various countries have to decide about whether to devalue their currencies or not when their exports are stagnant and imports are mounting and as a result their balance of payments position is worsening. The effect of the devaluation is to raise the price of the imported goods and to lower the prices of the exports. *If the demand for a country's exports is inelastic, the fall in the prices of exports as a result of devaluation will lower their foreign exchange earnings rather than increasing them.* This is because, demand being inelastic, as a result of the fall in prices quantity demanded of the exported products will increase very little and the country would suffer because of the lower prices. On the other hand, if the demand for a country's exports is elastic, then the fall in the prices of these exports due to devaluation will bring about a large increase in their quantity demanded which will increase the foreign exchange earnings of the country and will thus help in solving the balance of payments problem. Thus, the decision to devalue or not, depends upon the coefficient of the demand elasticity of exports.

Likewise, if the objective of devaluation is to reduce the imports of a country, then this will be realised only when the demand for the imports is elastic. With elastic demand for imports, the imports will decline very much as a result of rise in their prices brought about by devaluation and the country will save a good amount of foreign exchange. On the other hand, if the demand for imports is inelastic, the increase in prices as a result of devaluation will adversely affect the balance of payments, because at higher prices of the imports and almost the same quantity of imports, the country would have to spend more on the imports than before.

Importance in Fiscal Policy. The elasticity of demand is also of great significance in the field of fiscal policy. The Finance Minister has to take into account price elasticity of damand of the product on which he proposes to impose the tax if the revenue for the Government is to be increased. The imposition of an indirect tax, such as excise duty or sales tax, raises the price of a commodity. Now, if the demand for the commodity is elastic, the rise in price caused by the tax, will bring about a large decline in the quantity demanded and as a result the Government revenue will decline rather than increase. *The Government can succeed in increasing its revenue by the imposition a of commodity tax only if the demand for the commodity is inelastic.*

The elasticity of demand also determines to what extent a tax on a commodity can be shifted to the consumer. Thus, the incidence of a commodity tax on the consumers depends on their price elasticity of demand for the commodity. *If the demand for a commodity is perfectly inelastic, the whole of the burden of the commodity tax will fall on the consumers.* When a tax is imposed on a commodity, its price will rise. As in the case of perfectly inelastic demand, the quantity demanded for the commodity remains the same, whatever the price, the price will rise to the extent of the tax per unit. Therefore, the consumers will bear the whole burden of the tax in the form of a higher price they pay for the same quantity demanded.

On the contrary, *if the demand for a commodity is perfectly elastic, the imposition of the tax on it will not cause any rise in price and, therefore, the whole burden of the tax will be borne by the manufacturers or sellers.* When demand is neither perfectly inelastic, nor perfectly elastic, then respective burdens borne by the consumers and the producers will depend upon the elasticity of demand as well as on the elasticity of supply. We thus see that a Finance Minister cannot ignore price elasticity of demand for products while levying taxes.

CROSS ELASTICITY OF DEMAND

Very often demands for two goods are so related to each other that when the price of any of them changes, the demand for the other good also changes, its own price remaining the same. Therefore, *degree of responsiveness of demand for one good in response to the change in price of another good represents the cross elasticity of demand of one good for the other.*

The concept of cross elasticity of demand is illustrated by Fig. 13.15 and 13.16 where demand curves of two goods X and Y respectively are given. Initially, the price of good Y is OP_1, at which OQ_1 quantity of it is demanded and the price of good X is OP at which OM_1 quantity of it is demanded.

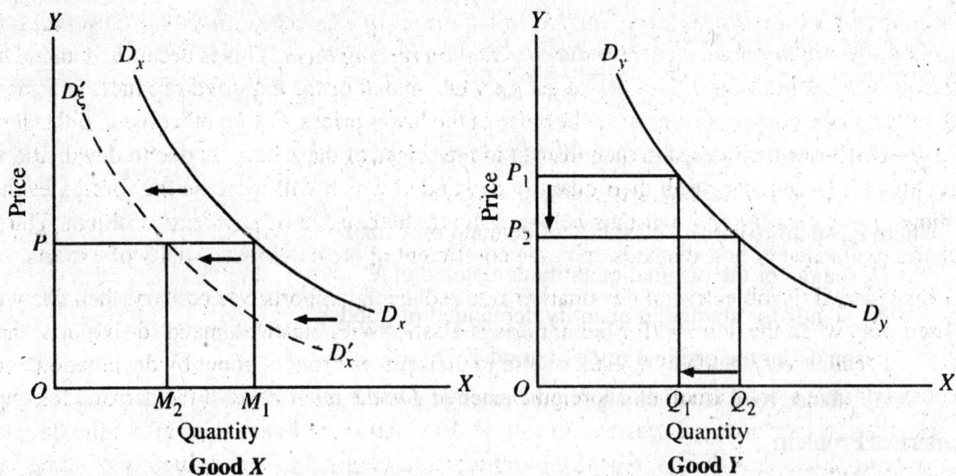

Fig. 13.15 & 13.16. *The Effect of Change in Price of Good Y on the Demand for Good X*

Now suppose and 13.16 the price of good Y falls from OP_1 to OP_2, while price of good X remains constant at OP. As a consequence of the fall in price of good Y from OP_1 to OP_2, its quantity demanded rises from OQ_1 to OQ_2. In drawing the demand curve, D_xD_x for good X, it is assumed that the prices of other goods (including good Y) remain the same. Now that the price of good Y has fallen and as a result its quantity demanded has increased, it will have an effect on the demand for good X. *If good Y is a substitute for good X, then as a result of the fall in price of good Y from OP_1 to OP_2, in Fig. 13.16 the demand curve of good X in Fig. 13.15 will shift to the left, that is, the demand for good X will decrease.* This is because *as the quantity of a good increases, the marginal utility of its substitute good declines and therefore the entire marginal utility curve of the substitute good shifts to the left.* As shall be seen from the Fig. 13.16 that with the fall in price of good Y, its quantity demanded increases for Q_1 to Q_2, and as a result the demand curve of good X in 13.15 shifts from D_xD_x to the dotted position $D'_xD'_x$ so that at price OP now less quantity OM_2 of X is demanded. M_1M_2 of good X has been substituted by Q_1Q_2 of good Y.

It should be noted that if good X instead of being substitute is complement of good Y, the resultant increase in its quantity demand of good Y due to fall in its price would have caused the increase in demand for good X and a result the entire demand curve of good X, instead of shifting to the left, would have shifted to the right. This is because *when the price of a good falls and consequently its quantity demanded increases, the marginal utility of its complement would increase and therefore its entire demand curve would shift to the right.* With a rightward shift of the demand curve of good X, the greater quantity of it will be demanded at the given price OP. It should be noted again that in the concept of cross elasticity of demand, while the price of *one good* changes, there is a change in the quantity demanded of *another good.*

When the quantity demanded of good X falls as a result of the fall in the price of good Y, the coefficient of cross elasticity of demand of X for Y will be equal to the percentage change in the quantity demanded of good X in response to a given percentage change in the price of good Y. Therefore,

$$\text{Coefficient of cross elasticity} = \frac{\text{Percentage change in the quantity demanded of } X}{\text{Percentage change in the price of good } Y}$$

$$e_c = \frac{\frac{\Delta q_x}{q_x}\times 100}{\frac{\Delta p_y}{p_y}\times 100} = \frac{\Delta q_x}{q_x} \div \frac{\Delta p_y}{P_y}$$

$$= \frac{\Delta q_x}{q_x} \times \frac{P_y}{\Delta p_y}$$

$$= \frac{\Delta q_x}{\Delta p_y} \cdot \frac{P_y}{q_s}$$

where e_c, stands for cross elasticity of demand of *X* for *Y*

Q_q stands for the original quantity demanded of *X*

Δ_q, stands for change in quantity demanded of good *X*

p_y stands for the original price of good *Y*

Δp_y stands for a small change in the price of good *Y*

Numerical Problem

Let us take an example. If the *price of coffee* rises from Rs. 4.50 per hundred grams to Rs. 5 per hundred grams and as a result the consumer's *demand for tea* increases from 60 hundred grams to 70 hundred grams, then the cross elasticity of demand of tea for coffee can be found out as follows:

In the above example:

$$\Delta q_x = 70 - 60 = 10 \text{ hundred grams}$$
$$q_x = 60 \text{ hundred grams}$$
$$\Delta p_y = \text{Rs. } 5 - 4.50 = 50 \text{ paise}$$
$$p_y' = \text{Rs. } 4.50 = 450 \text{ paise}$$

Cross elasticity of demand $= \frac{\Delta q_x}{\Delta p_y} \times \frac{P_y}{q_s}$

$$= \frac{10}{50} \times \frac{450}{60}$$

$$= \frac{3}{2} = 1.5$$

Substitute and Complementary Goods

As we have seen in the example of tea and coffee above, when two goods are substitutes of each other, then as *a result of the rise in price of one good, the quantity demanded of the other good increases*. Therefore, the *cross elasticity of demand between the two substitute goods is positive*, that is, in response to the *rise in price of one good, the demand for the other good rises*. Substitute goods are also known as *competing goods*. On the other hand, when the two goods are complementary with each other just as bread and butter, tea and milk etc., the rise in price of one good brings about the *decrease in demand* for the other. Therefore, the *cross elasticity of demand between* the two complementary goods is negative. Therefore *according to the classification based on the concept of cross elasticity of demand, goods X and Y are substitutes or complements according as the cross elasticity of demand is positive or negative.*

The concept of cross elasticity of demand is very important in economic theory. The substitute and complementary goods, as we have seen above, are defined is terms of cross elasticity of demand. *The goods between which cross elasticity of demand is positive are known as substitute goods and the goods between which cross elasticity of demand is negative are complementary goods.*

Besides, classification of various types of market structures is made on the basis of cross elasticity of demand. Thus, Professor Triffen has employed the concept of cross elasticity of demand in distinguishing the various forms of markets. Perfect competition is defined as that in which the cross elasticity of demand between the products produced by many firms in it is infinite. Monoploy is said to exist when a producer produces a product the cross elasticity of demand for which with any other product is very low. In fact, the pure or absolute monopoly is sometimes defined as the production by a single producer of a product whose cross elasticity of demand with any other product is zero. Monopolistic competition is said to prevail in the market when a large number of firms produces those products between which cross elasticity of demand is large and positive, that is, they are close substitutes of each other.

Importance of Cross Elasticity of Demand for Business Decision Making

The concept of cross elasticity of demand is of great importance in managerial decision making for formulating proper price strategy. Multi-product firms often use this concept to measure the effect of change in price of one product on the demand for other products. For example, Maruti Udyog Ltd. produces Maruti Vans, Maruti 800 and Maruti Esteem. These products are good substitutes of each other and therefore cross elasticity of demand between them is very high. If Maruti Udyog decides to lower the price of Maruti 800, it will significantly affect the demand for Maruti Vans and Maruti Esteem. So it will formulate a proper price strategy fixing appropriate price for its various products. Further, Gillete Company produces both razors and razor blades which are complements with high cross elasticity of demand. If it decides to lower the price of razors, it will greatly increase the demand for razor blades. Thus there is need for adopting a proper price strategy when a firm produces products with high positive or negative cross price-elasticity of demand.

Second, the concept of cross elasticity of demand is frequently used in defining the boundaries of an industry and in measuring interrelationship between industries. An industry is defined as a group of firms producing similar products (that is, products with a high positive cross elasticity of demand. For example cross elasticity of demand between Maruti Esteem, *I-Kon Ford*, Opel Astra is positive and quite high. They therefore belong to the same industry (*i.e.*, automobiles). It should be noted that because of interrelationship of firms and industries between which cross price-elasticity of demand is positive and high, any one cannot raise the price of its product without losing sales to other firms.

Further, the concept of cross elasticity of demand is extremly used in the United States in deciding cases relating to Antitrust laws and monopolistic practices used by firms. It so happens that in order to reduce competition that one dominant firm producing a product with high cross elasticity of demand with the products of other firms tries to take over them and thereby establish a monopoly, or various firms producing close substitutes with high cross elasticity of demand try to merge with each other to form a cartel to enjoy monopolistic profits. These actions are held illegal by Antitrust or anti-monopoly laws. An interesting attempt was made in India by Caca-Cola in 1995 when it returned to India following the adoption of policy of liberalisation. In order to reduce competition, Coca-Cola company purchased the firm producing Thums Up, Gold Spot, Limca which have high positive cross elasticity of demand with Coca-Cola. Thus, it succceeded in significantly reducing competition. With this its competition has been mainly with other multinational rival firm Pepsi-Cola.

INCOME ELASTICITY OF DEMAND

Another important concept of elasticity of demand is income elasticity of demand. *Income elasticity of demand shows the degree of responsiveness of quantity demanded of a good to a small change in the income of consumers*. The degree of response of quantity demanded to a change in income is measured by dividing the proportionate change in quantity demanded by the proportionate change in income. Thus, more precisely, the income elasticity of demand may be defined as the ratio of the percentage change in purchases of a good to a percentage change in income which induces the former.

$$\text{Income elasticity} = \frac{\text{Percentage change in purchases of a good}}{\text{Percentage change income}}$$

Let Y stand for an initial income, ΔY for a small change in income, q for the initial quantity purchased, Δq for a change in quantity purchased as a result of a change in income and e_i for income elasticity of demand. Then,

$$e_i = \frac{\frac{\Delta q}{q} \times 100}{\frac{\Delta y}{y} \times 100} = \frac{\Delta q}{q} \div \frac{\Delta Y}{Y} = \frac{\Delta q}{\Delta Y} \times \frac{Y}{q}$$

If, for instance, consumer's daily income rises from Rs. 300 to Rs. 320, his purchase of the good X increases from 25 units per week to 30 units, then his income elasticity of demand for X is :

$$e_i = \frac{\frac{5}{25} \times 100}{\frac{20}{300} \times 100}$$

$$= \frac{\frac{1}{5}}{\frac{1}{15}} = \frac{1}{5} \times 15 = 3$$

Income elasticity of demand being zero is of great significance. Zero income elasticity of demand for a good implies that a given increase in income does not at all lead to any increase in quantity demanded of a good or expenditure on it. In other words, zero income elasticity signifies that quantity demanded of the good is quite unresponsive to changes in income.

Income Elasticity, Normal Good and Inferior Goods

Besides, zero income elasticity is significant because it represents dividing line between positive income elasticity on the one side and negative income elasticity on the other. On the one side, when income elasticity is more than zero (that is, positive), then an increase in income leads to the increase in quantity demanded of the good. This happens in case of normal goods. On the other side of zero income elasticity are all those goods whose income elasticity is less than zero (that is, negative) and in such cases increases in income will lead to the fall in quantity demanded of the goods. *Goods having negative income elasticity are known as inferior goods*. Goods with positive income elasticity are called *normal goods*. We thus see that zero income elasticity is a significant value, for it helps us to distinguish normal goods from inferior goods.

Income Elasticity, Luxuries and Necessities

Another significant value of income elasticity is unity. This is because when income elasticity of demand for a good is equal to one, then proportion of income spent on the good remains the same as consumer's income increases. Income elasticity of unity also represents a useful dividing line. If the income elasticity for a good is greater than one, the proportion of consumer's income spent on the good rises as consumer's income increases, that is, that good bulks larger in consumer's expenditure as he becomes richer. On the other hand, if income elasticity for a good is less than one, the proportion of consumer's income spent on it falls as his income rises, that is, the good becomes relatively less important in consumer's expenditure as his income rises. *A good having income elasticity more than one and which therefore bulks larger in consumer's budget as he becomes richer is called a luxury. A good with an income elasticity less than one and which claims declining proportion of consumer's income as he becomes richer is called a necessity.* It should, however, be noted that the definitions of luxuries and necessities on the basis of income elasticity may not conform to their definitions in Engligh dictionary because the dictionary's luxuries may be necessities and its necessities may be luxuries according to the above definition. But in economic theory it is useful to call the goods with income elasticity greater than one as luxuries and goods with income elasticity less than one as necessities.

Importance of Income Elasticity for Business Firms

The concept of income elasticity is important for decision making both by business firms and industries. First, the firms producing products which have a high income elasticity have great potential for growth in an expending economy. For example, if for a firm's product income elasticity of demand is greater than one, it means that it will gain more than proportionately to the increase in national income. Thus firms which are producing products having high income elasticity are more interested in forecasting the level of aggregate economic activity (*i.e.*, level of national income) because the demand for their products will greatly depend on the level of overall econmic activity. Further, as seen above, the demand for luxuries is highly income elastic. Therefore, the demand for luxuries fluctuate very much during different phases of business cycles. During boom periods, demand for luxuries increase very much, and decline sharply during recessionary periods.

On the other hand, the demand for products with low income elasticity will not be greatly affected by the fluctuations in aggregate economic activity. During booms the demand for their products will not increase much and during recessions it will not decrease sharply. Therefore, the firms with low income elasticity for their products would not be much interested in forecasting future business activity. Remember it is generally necessities for which demand is not much income elastic. However, there is one good thing for the firms which face low income elasticity. They are to a good extent recession-proof. In the periods of recession, their incomes do not fall to the extent of decline in aggregate income. Of course, to share the benefits of increasing national income firms currently producing products with low income elasticity would try to enter the industries demand for whose products is highly income elastic as this would ensure better growth opportunities.

The knowledge of income elasticity of demand also plays a significant role in designing marketing strategies of the firms. If income of people is an important determinant of demand for a product, the firms producing product with high income elasticity of demand will be located in those areas or set up their sales outlets in those cities or regions where incomes are increasing rapidly. Besides, the firms will direct their advertising campaigns and other sales production activities to those segments of people whose income is high and also increasing rapidly. This is to ensure higher growth of sales of their products.

The concept of income elasticity of demand shows clearly why farmers income do not rise equal to that of urban people engaged in manufacturing industries. Income elasticity of demand for agricultured products such as foodgrains is less than one. This implies that it is defficult for the farmers' income from agriculture to increase in proportion to the expanding national income. Thus farmers cannot keep up with the urban people who derive their incomes from industries producing goods with high income elasticity of demand.

THE ELASTICITY OF SUBSTITUTION

The elasticity of substitution is another important concept of demand elasticity. The elasticity of substitution between the two goods is a relative measure of the degree of substitution possibility between the two goods for consumption by the consumers. As we move along an indifference curve, we substitute one commodity for another in our combination. Thus elasticity of substitution is measured as the proportionate change in the ratio of the quantities of the two goods consumed divided by the proportionate change in the marginal rate of substitution (MRS_{xy}) between the two goods along a given indifference curve.

$$\sigma = \frac{\text{Proportionate change in the ratio of the two goods consumed}}{\text{Proportionate change in } MRS_{xy}}$$

$$\sigma = \frac{\Delta\left(\frac{q_x}{q_y}\right) \Big/ \frac{q_x}{q_y}}{\Delta MRS_{xy} \,/\, MRS_{xy}}$$

where σ stands for elasticity of substitution q_x are q_y are the quantities of the two goods X and Y consumed.

As a consumer moves along an indifference curve downward to the right, he substitutes the commodity X for commodity Y in consumption and as a result the ratio of consumption of the two

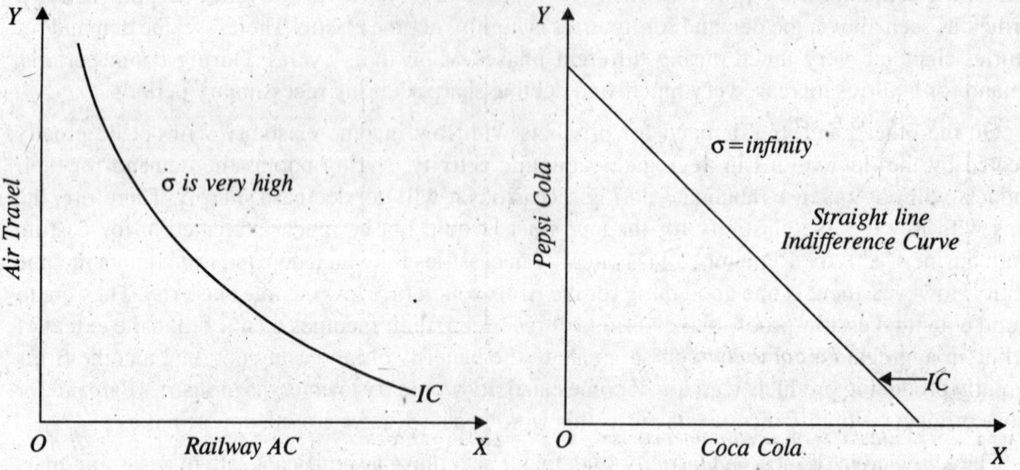

Fig. 13.17(a) *Elasticity of substitution (σ) is very high.*

Fig. 13.17(b) *Elasticity of substitution ($\sigma = \infty$).*

commodities changes, his level of statisfaction remaining the same. Besides, with the movement along an indifference curve marginal rate of substitution (MRS_{xy}) between the two commodities changes. It may be noted that change in the marginal rate of substitution between the two goods is measured by the change in absolute value of the slope of the indifference curve at relevant points on it. Further, as a consumer moves downward along an indifference curve he consumes more and more of X and less and less of Y, marginal rate of substitution of good X for good Y diminishes. Changes in the marginal rate of substitution indicate the extent to which one good can be substituted for another, his level of satisfaction remaining the same. When the substitution between the two goods is easy, then as a consumer moves along an indifference curve a proportionate change in the ratio of the two goods consumed (q_x/q_y) is large compared with the relative change in the marginal rate of substitution (MRS_{xy}) between the two goods. In such cases, elasticity substitution between the two goods is large. Therefore, the goods which are close substitutes of each other as, for example, railway AC coach and air travel, tea and coffee, the elasticity of substitution between them is high and the indifference curve is close to the straight line as shown in Fig. 13.17(a).

In the limiting case when the two goods are perfect substitutes, as perhaps Coca Cola and Pepsi

Cola, the indifference curve between the two goods is a straight line as shown in Fig. 13.17(b) where there are infinitely large possibilities of substitution between the two goods as compared with the relative change in marginal rate of substitution which is zero (Note that the slope of a straight line is constant). Thus, in case of perfect substitutes.

$$\sigma = \frac{\Delta\left(\frac{q_x}{q_y}\right) \bigg/ \frac{q_x}{q_y}}{\Delta MRS_{xy} / MRS_{xy}} = \frac{\Delta\left(\frac{q_x}{q_s}\right) \bigg/ \frac{q_x}{q_y}}{0} = \infty$$

It may be noted that in real life it is very difficult to find the examples of perfect substitutes and if such goods do exist then from economic point of view they should be considered as the same goods.

On the other hand, when the two goods are bad substitutes and therefore it is difficult to substitute one good for another, as for instance, between shirts and trousers, the indifference curves between them are highly convex, and in their case the ratio of the two goods consumed by an

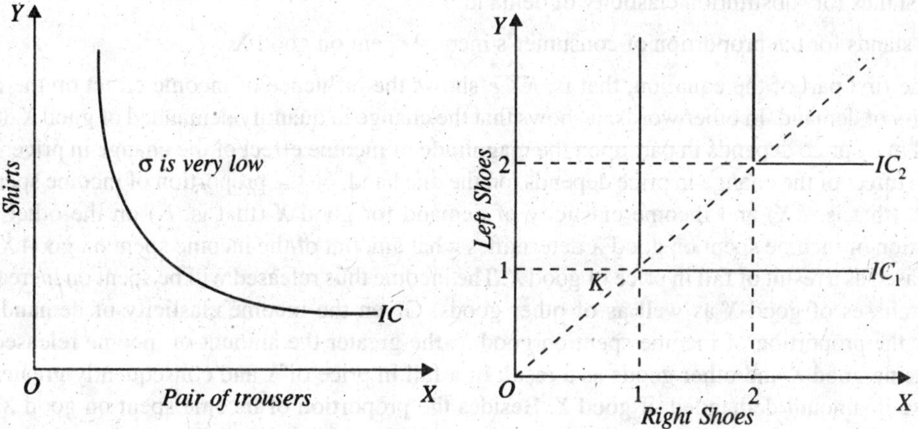

Fig. 13.18(a) *Elasticity of substitution between complementary goods is very low*

Fig. 13.18(b) *Elasticity of substitution between perfect complements is zero ($\sigma = 0$)*

individual changes very little. For example, one would not like to have more or less than two or three shirts to each pair of trousers. The convexity of indifference curve between complementary goods is very high and elasticity of substitution between them is very small. In the extreme case when the goods are perfect complements to each other they cannot be substituted for each other and must be used in a fixed proportion as, for example, right shoes and left shoes. The elasticity of substitution between them is zero as depicted in Fig. 13.18(b). Therefore, indifference curves of perfect complements are L-shaped (i.e. right angled) and elasticity of substitution between them is zero. In case of perfect complements since $\Delta\left(\frac{q_x}{q_y}\right)$ is zero, we have

$$\sigma = \frac{0}{\text{Proportionate change in } MRS_{xy}} = 0$$

Since the cases of perfect substitutes and perfect complements are remote possibilities, the absolute value of elasticity of substitution between the two goods in the real world is greater than zero but less than infinity ($0 < \sigma < \infty$).

RELATIONSHIP BETWEEN PRICE ELASTICITY, INCOME ELASTICITY AND SUBSTITUTION ELASTICITY

As already explained, price effect, that is, the effect on the quantity demanded of a good due to a change in price, depends upon income effect on the one hand and substitution effect on the other. Similarly, price elasticity of demand which is the relative measure of the price effect depends upon the income elasticity on the one hand and substitution elasticity on the other. Thus, *price elasticity, in a way, is a compromise between income elasticity and substitution elasticity of demand.* The relationship between these three elasticities can be expressed in the form of *Slutsky equation*. Thus, the price elasticity of demand for good X is given by the following Slutsky equation :

$$e_p = KX.e_i + (1 - KX)e_s$$

where

e_p stands for price elasticity of demand.

e_i stands for income elasticity of demand.

e_s stands for substitution elasticity of demand.

K_t stands for the proportion of consumer's income spent on good X.

The first part of the equation, that is, $KX.e_i$ shows the influence of income effect on the price elasticity of demand. In other words, it shows that the change in quantity demanded of good *X* due to the fall in its price depends in part upon the magnitude of income effect of the change in price. This income effect of the change in price depends, on the one hand, on the proportion of income spent on good *X* (that is, *KX*) and income elasticity of demand for good *X* (that is, e_i) on the other. The proportion of income spent on good *X* determines what amount of the income spent on good *X* will be released as a result of fall in price of good *X*. The income thus released will be spent on increasing the purchases of good *X* as well as of other goods. Given the income elasticity of demand, the greater the proportion of income spent on good *X*, the greater the amount of income released for purchasing good *X* and other goods as a result of a fall in price of *X* and consequently greater the increase in amount demanded of good *X*. Besides the proportion of income spent on good *X*, the increase in amount demanded of good *X* due to income effect of the price fall depends on the income elasticity of demand for good *X*. This is because income elasticity of demand for good *X* determines how much of the income released by the fall in price of good *X* will be spent on good *X* whose price has fallen and how much will be spent on other goods. Proportion of income spent on good *X* being given, the greater the income elasticity of demand for good *X*, greater the part of income released will be spent on good *X* and consequently there will be a greater increase in quantity demanded of good *X*. We thus see that first part of the equation, that is *KX. e.i.*, shows the impact of income effect on the price elasticity of demand.

The quantity demanded of the good does not increase only because of the income effect of the fall in price, it also increases because of substitution effect. As the price of good *X* falls, more of it is purchased at the expense of others because *X* has now become relatively cheaper than others. The second part of the equation, that is, $(1 - KX)\ e_s$ shows the influence of the substitution effect on the price elasticity of demand for good *X*. The magnitude of substitution effect in turn depends in part on the elasticity of substitution (e_s), that is, the extent to which good *X* can be substituted for other goods now that it is relatively cheaper. The substitution effect also depends on the amount of other goods which were being purchased before the fall in price of good *X*. This is because only to the extent one is already purchasing other goods, the substitution of *X* for other goods is possible. Elasticity of substitution being given, the greater the amount of other goods being purchased by the consumer, the greater is the possibility of substitution of good *X* for other goods when *X* becomes cheaper. Since KX stands for the proportion of income spent on good *X*, (1–*KX*) will give the proportion of income not being spent on good *X*. In other words, (1–*KX*) stands for the proportion of income spent on goods other than *X*. Therefore, (1–*KX*) indicates the proportion of consumer's income within which substitution of *X* for other goods is possible.

From the above analysis it follows that the price elasticity of demand for a good is determined by the following four factors :

1. *Proportion of income spend on a good*
2. *Income elasticity of demand*
3. *Elasticity of substitution*
4. *Proportion of income spent of other goods*

Price elasticity can be known if the first three factors are known. Let us consider the following examples.

Suppose that a consumer is spending 1/5th of his income on any good *X* and the income elasticity of demand for the good *X* is 2 and elasticity of substitution between good *X* and all other good is 3. What will be the price elasticity of demand in this case ?

$$e_p = KX.e_t + (1 - KX)e_s$$
$$= 1/5 \times 2 + (1 - 1/5) \times 3$$
$$= 2/5 + 4/5 \times 3$$
$$= 2/5 + 12/5$$
$$= 14/5 = 2.8$$

Thus, price elasticity of demand for good *X* is equal to 2.8.

From the above formula of price elasticity of demand, it follows that whatever the proportion of income spent on a good, if income elasticity and substitution elasticity are equal to one, then price elasticity will also be equal to one. For instance, if a proportion of income spent on a good is 1/5 and income and substitution elasticities are equal to one, then price elasticity will be:

$$e_p = KX.e_i + (1 - KX)e_x$$
$$= 1/5 \times 1 + 4/5 \times 1$$
$$= 1/5 + 4/5 = 1$$

Likewise, if proportion of income spent on a good is 1/3, and given that both the income and substitution elasticities are equal to one, price elasticity will be found to be equal to one.

PRICE CONSUMPTION CURVE AND PRICE ELASTICITY OF DEMAND

It is also possible to know with indifference curve analysis whether price elasticity is more than one, equal to one or less than one. It is from the slope of *price consumption curve* that we are able to judge the price elasticity of demand. Let us take Fig. 13.19 where on the *Y*-axis money income is measured and on *X*-axis the quantity of a commodity *X*. It is assumed that the consumer has *OA* amount of money to spend. Each of the indifference curves drawn between the two axes will show the various combinations of money and good *X* among which consumer is indifferent. To begin with, *AB* is the price line. The slope of the price line *AB*, *i.e.*, $\frac{OA}{OB}$ will give the price of good *X*. At this price (*i.e.*, with price line *AB*) the consumer is in equilibrium at point Q_1 on indifference curve IC_1 and is buying OX_1 of good *X*. Thus, in this equilibrium position, he is having combination of OX_1 of good *X* and OY_1 of money. It means that he has spent AY_1 of money on the good *X* and has obtained OX_1 of its quantity. Let price of good *X* falls, money income of the consumer remaining the same, so that we get a new price line AC. The new price of good X will be given by the slope of the new price line AC, *i.e.*, $\frac{OA}{OC}$. With this lower price or with price line AC, the consumer is in equilibrium at Q_2 on indifference curve IC_2. At this new equilibrium position Q_2 the consumer is getting OX_2 of good X and amount OY_2 of money is let with him. It means that at the lower price of good X he has spent AY_2 amount of money on it which is greater than the amount AY_1 of money which he spent at the original price. Thus, with the fall in price, his expenditure on the good X has increased. Similarly, when the price of good X falls further so that AD is now the relevant price line, consumer is in equilibrium at Q_3 where he is spending AY_3 amount of money and is having OX_3 quantity of the good X. Money expenditure AY_3 is greater than AY_2. It is thus clear that in the present case when the price *consumption curve is sloping downward* (*i.e*, *PCC* has a negative slope), with the reduction in price of the good X the consumer's money outlay on the good X increases. In Fig. 13.19 indifference map depicting preferences of the consumer is such that we get a downward sloping consumption curve which means, as explained above, that with the fall in the price of good X, consumer's expenditure on it rises. We know that when consumer's money expenditure on a good rises with the fall in price of the good, the demand for the good is elastic, i.e., elasticity of demand is more than one. We thus conclude that *when price consumption curve for a good slopes downward, price elasticity of demand is more than one, that is, demand is elastic.*

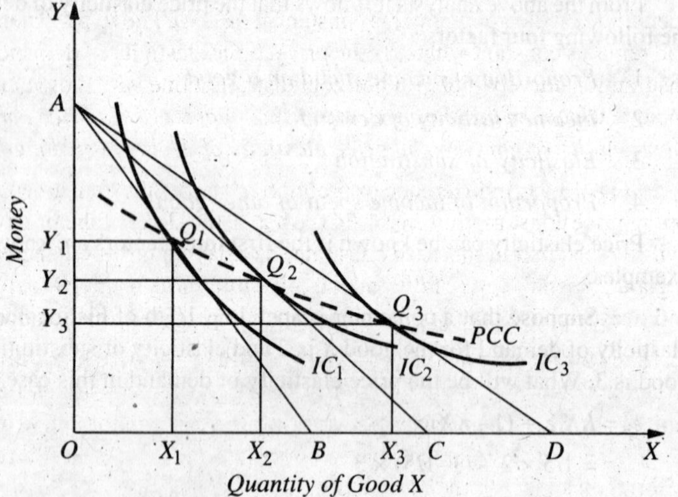

Fig. 13.19. *Elastic Demand*

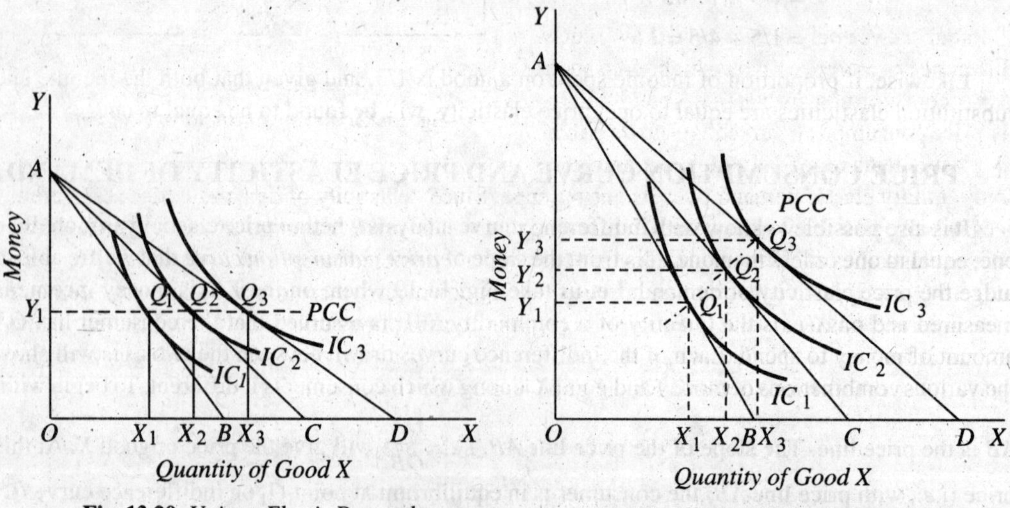

Fig. 13.20. *Unitary Elastic Demand*

Fig. 13.21. *Inelastic Demand*

In Fig. 13.20, we have depicted such an indifference-preference map of the consumer that gives us a price consumption curve *PCC* which is a horizontal straight line, parallel to the *X*-axis (that is, price consumption curve has a zero slope). In this case, with the fall in the price of the good, though quantity purchased of good *X* rises first from OX_1 to OX_2 and then from OX_2 to OX_3, but consumer's expenditure on the good remains constant at AY_1. We know that when consumer's expenditure on the good remains constant whatever the price, price elasticity of demand is equal to one. Thus, the price consumption curve which is a horizontal straight line will show unit elasticity of demand. We thus conclude that *when indifference map is such that it gives a price consumption curve of the shape of a horizontal straight line, the price elasticity of demand for the good X is equal to unity.*

In Fig. 13.21, indifference or preference map of the consumer is such that it yields an upward-sloping price consumption curve *PCC* (that is, the slope of the price consumption curve is positive). It will be seen that in this case consumer's outlay on the good decreases with the fall in the price of the good. When the price falls and the price line shifts from *AB* to *AC*, the quantity demanded of the good rises from OX_1 to OX_2 but consumer's expenditure on the good *X* falls from AY_1 to AY_3.

Likewise, when price falls further and as a result price line shifts from *AC* to *AD*, though quantity demanded of the good *X* rises from OX_2, to OX_3, consumer's expenditure on the good *X* falls from AY_2 to AY_3. Thus upward sloping price consumption curve means a decline in consumer's expenditure as the price of the good *X* falls. Since a fall in consumer's expenditure as a result of the fall in price means that demand for the good is inelastic, *upward-sloping price consumption curve will therefore show inelastic demand, i.e., elasticity will be less than one.*

To sum up, downward-sloping price consumption curve for a good means that demand for the good is elastic, upward-sloping price consumption curve means that demand for the good is inelastic and horizontal straight-line price consumption curve means that demand for the good is unit elastic.

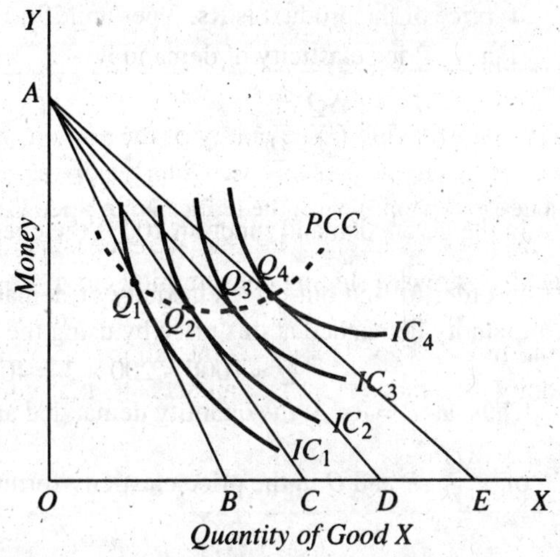

Fig. 13.22. *Varying Elasticity of Demand*

In our above analysis, we have drawn such indifference-preference maps which yield such a price consumption curve that shows either only price consumption curve that shows either only elastic demand, or only inelastic demand, or only unitary elastic demand over its entire range. Since elasticity of demand varies at different prices, we can also draw such an indifferent map that yields price consumption curve which shows different elasticities at different price levels. This we have depicted in fig. 13.22 where it will be seen that from Q_1 to Q_2 price consumption curve is sloping downward, therefore over this range demand for the good is elastic (*i.e.*, $e_p > 1$). From Q_2 to Q_3 price consumption curve is horizontal, therefore, the elasticity is here equal to unit (*i.e.* $e_p = 1$). From Q_3 to Q_4 and onward price consumption curve slopes upward, so over this range demand for the good is inelastic (*i.e.* $e_p < 1$).

QUESTIONS AND PROBLEMS FOR REVIEW

1. Explain the following concepts of elasticity of demand :

(*a*) Price elasticity of demand (*b*) Income elasticity of demand

(*c*) Cross elasticity of demand (*d*) Point price elasticity of demand (*e*) Arc price elasticity of demand

2. (*a*) How would you measure point price elasticity of demand at a point on the demand curve?
(*b*) What happens to point price elasticity at a given price when the demand curve shifts to the right in a parallel manner ?

3. What are the factors which determine price elasticity of demand ? What role does price elasticity of demand play in decision-making by business firms ?

4. What would you say about the price elasticity of demand for a good when
(*a*) price consumption curve slopes downward
(*b*) price consumption curve slopes upward
(*c*) price consumption curve slopes backward

5. Suppose that in a year the excise duty on cigarettes is doubled and as a result the total revenue from the excise duty decreases. What conclusions about price elasticity of demand for cigarettes would you draw ?

6. Do you think that price elasticity of demand would be greater for car industry as a whole or for Maruti 800 of the Maruti firm.

7. Demand for a firm's product has been estimated to be

$$Q_d = 1000 - 200P$$

If price of the product is Rs. 3 per unit, find out the price elasticity of demand at this price.
[Hints : Price elasticity of demand is

$$e_p = \frac{\Delta Q}{\Delta P} \cdot \frac{P}{Q}$$

In the given demand function 200 is the coefficient of price which measures $\frac{\Delta Q}{\Delta P}$.

In order to find out price elasticity of demand at price Rs. 3, we have first to find out the quantity demanded at this price by using the given demand equation. Thus,

$$Q = 1000 - 200 \times 3 = 400$$

Thus, at P = Rs. 3, the quantity demanded at this price is 400 units. Substituting the values of $\frac{\Delta Q}{\Delta P}$, P and Q in the price elasticity formula, we have

$$e_p = \frac{\Delta Q}{\Delta P} \times \frac{P}{Q} = 200 \times \frac{3}{400} = 1.5$$

8. Given : $P.Q = 500$, what happens to price elasticity of demand as price falls (P = price, and Q = quantity purchased) ?

D.U. B.A. (H) Economics 2001

[**Hints :** $P.Q$ represents expenditure on a commodity which remains constant at 500 even when price changes. When expenditure on a commodity remains constant as price changes, its price elasticity of demand is equal to one]

9. An individual spends all his income on two goods, X and Y. if with the rise in price of good X, the quantity purchased of good Y remains unchanged, what is the price elasticity of demand for X? *D.U. B.A. (Hons.) 1996, 2001*

[**Hints :** Given individual's income if quantity purchased of good Y remaining the same even when price of good X rises, means that expenditure on good X (*i.e.*, $P_x \cdot Q_x$) remains constant. This implies that price elasticity of demand for good X equals one.]

10. *The price elasticity of demand for colour TVs is estimated to be –2.5. If the price of colour TVs is reduced by 20 per cent, how much percentage increase in the quantity of colour TVs sold do you expect ?*

[**Hints :** Price elasticity of demand being equal to –2.5 means that one per cent change in price causes 2.5 per cent change in quantity demanded or sold. Besides, minus sign only indicates there is *inverse* relationship between price and quantity sold. Thus, 20 per cent *reduction in price* of colour TVs will cause *increase in quantity sold* by 2.5 × 20 = 50 per cent.]

11. In an attempt to increase sales and profits, a firm is considering 5 per cent increase in price and 15 per cent increase in advertising expenditure. If the price elasticity of demand is –1.5 and advertising elasticity of demand is +0.7, would there be increase or decrease in total revenue ?

[**Hints :** 5 per cent increase in price will cause 5 × 1.5 = 7.5 *per cent decrease* in quantity sold. However, 15 per cent increase in advertising will cause 0.7 × 15 = 10.5 per cent *increase* in quantity sold. Thus, there is net *increase in quantity sold* by 3 per cent. Since there is also 5 per cent *increase in price*, the total revenue (which is equal to *P.Q.*) will increase.]

12. Explain the relationship between the total revenue of a firm and the price elasticity of demand for price reduction.

(**Hints :** Note that expenditure on a product by the consumers is revenue for the firm. Therefore, the relationship between price elasticity and total expenditure on it applies to relation between total revenue and price elasticity of demand.

13. *(a) Explain why a firm facing a downward sloping demand curve would never produce at the inelastic ($e_p < 1$) portion of the demand curve.* *D.U.BA. (Hons) 2002*

14. Show that on a linear demand curve, price elasticity of demand decreases continuously from infinity at the price axis to zero at the quantity axis.

15. From the demand schedule given below calculate price elasticity of demand and total revenue.

Price (Rs.	*Quantity demanded*	*Price elasticity*	*Total revenue*
10	*20*	–	–
8	*30*	–	–
6	*35*	–	–
4	*40*	–	–

16. Explain the concept of income elasticity of demand. How would you define necessities and luxuries on the basis of income elasticity of demand ?

17. Explain the importance of income elasticity of demand for business firms especially in designing marketing strategies.

18. Explain the concept of cross elasticity of demand. Using the concept of cross elasticity of demand, define substitutes and complements.

19. Explain the importance of the concept of cross elasticity of demand in (*a*) formulating proper price strategy by a firm (*b*) in analysing the degree of competition prevailing in an industry.

20. *Colgate sells its standard size toothpaste for Rs. 25. Its sales have been on an average 8000 units per month over the past year. Recently, its close competitor Binaca reduced the price of its same standard size toothpaste from Rs. 35 to Rs. 30. As a result, colgate sales declined by 1500 units per month.*

(i) Calculate the cross elasticity between the two products.

(ii) What does your estimate indicate about the relationship between the two ?

21. For the demand curve $Q(P) = a + bP$, find the equation for point elasticity of demand.

DU, B.A(Hons.) Ist year 2008

Hint:

In demand function, $Q = a + bP$

$$\frac{dQ}{dP} = b$$

Price elasticity of demand $(e_p) = \dfrac{dQ}{dP} \cdot \dfrac{P}{Q}$

Substituting b for $\dfrac{dQ}{dP}$ in the above elasticity expression we have

$$e_p = b.\frac{P}{Q}$$

Since $Q = a + bP$ in the given demand function we have

$$e_p = b.\frac{P}{a+bP}$$

Numerical Problems on Cross Elasticity of Demand

22. *Suppose the following demand function for coffee in terms of price of tea is given. Find out the cross elasticity of demand when price of tea rises from Rs. 50 per 250 grams pack to Rs. 55 per 250 grams pack.*

$Q_C = 100 + 2.5P_t$

where Q_C is the quantity demanded of coffee in terms of packs of 250 grams and P_t is the price of tea.

Solution. The positive sign of the derivative of P_t shows that rise in price of tea will cause an increase in quantity demanded of coffee. This implies that tea and coffee are substitutes.

In order to determine cross elasticity of demand between tea and coffee, we first find out quantity demanded of coffee when price of tea is Rs. 50 per 250 grams. Thus,

$Q = 100 + 2.5 \times 50 = 225$

$$\text{Cross elasticity, } e_c = \frac{dQ_c}{dP_t} \times \frac{P_t}{Q_c}$$

$$\frac{dQ_c}{dP_t} = 2.5$$

$$e_c = 2.5 \times \frac{50}{225} = \frac{125}{225} = 0.51$$

23. *Two goods have a cross-price elasticity of demand of +1.2 (a) Would you describe the goods as substitutes or complements ? (b) If the price of one of the goods rises by 5 per cent, what will happen to the demand for the other good, holding other factors constant ?*

Solution. (*a*) The goods with positive cross-price elasticity of demand are substitute goods. (*b*) If the price of one of the two goods increases by 5 per cent, it will be substituted by the other good so that the quantity demanded of this other good will rise. With positive cross-price elasticity being equal to 1.2, the quantity demanded of the other good will increase by 1.2 × 5 = 6 per cent.

APPENDIX TO CHAPTER 13

APPLICATIONS OF ELASTICITY OF DEMAND

Elasticity of demand has important applications for formulation of proper economic policies to be adopted by the government and also to explain several economic events. In this chapter we will explain the following with the help of elasticities of demand and supply.

1. The paradox of poverty amongst plenty in agriculture or what is also described as *good news for agriculture is bad news for farmers* ?
2. How crop restriction programmes in the United States raise incomes of the farmers ?
3. Why did OPEC fail to keep the price of oil high ?
4. How the burden of a tax on a commodity borne by buyers and sellers depends on elasticities of demand and supply ?
5. How does campaign against use of illegal drugs help to reduce the problem of drug addiction ?
6. How can Government stabilise agricultural prices and incomes through proper policies ?

PARADOX OF POVERTY AMIDST PLENTY

How a good news that a good weather or good monsoon which will substantially increase agricultural production may possibly be bad news for the farmers. The bumper crop as a result of good weather may cause such a large fall in prices of agricultural products that the sales revenue or income of the farmers falls. Similarly, if due to research there is improvement in agricultural technology which leads to the substantial increase in agricultural output instead of raising farmers' income may actually brings about reduction in it. This strange phenomenon is due to the *inelastic nature of demand for agricultural products*. Consider Fig. 13A.1. Suppose initially the demand curve *DD* and supply curve S_1 determine price of an agricultural crop, say wheat, equal to P_1 (or Rs. 5 hundred per quintal) at which the quantity Q_1 (or 100 quintals, are bought and sold. Suppose due to good weather (or in case of India due to good monsoon), there is bumper crop of wheat and as result supply curve of wheat shifts from S_1 to S_2. The new supply curve S_2 intersects the inelastic demand curve *DD* at point *B* and determines price P_2 (or Rs. 4 hundred per quintal) and quantity bought and sold increases to Q_2 or 110 quintals. Thus, there is a large fall (Rs. 100 per quintal) in price of wheat but due to inelastic demand of the agricultural product there is only a small increase in quantity bought and sold.

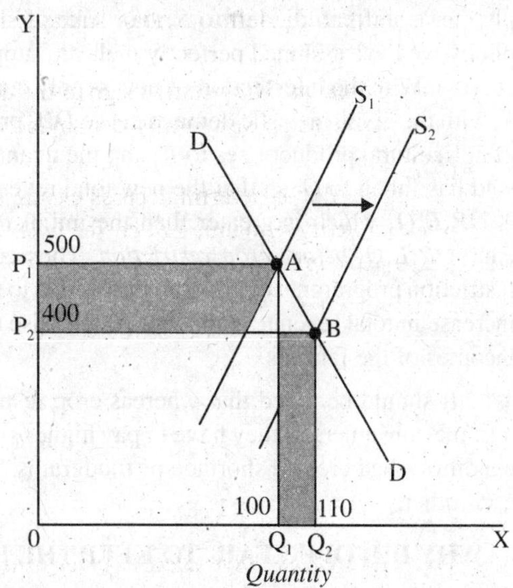

Fig. 13A.1. *Bumper crop leads to lower income of the farmers*

Now, as explained above, in an earlier chapter, total sales revenue made by the farmers is equal to the product of price and the quantity sold ($TR = P \times Q$). In view of the fact that demand for agricultural product is inelastic, small expansion in output (Q) causes a relatively large fall in price resulting in decrease in total revenue of the farmers. It will be seen from Fig. 13A.1 that increase in supply from S_1 to S_2 causes price to fall from P_1 (= Rs. 5 hundred per quintal to P_2 (= Rs. 400 per quintal). As a result, total revenue which was equal to the area OP_1AQ_1 (or 500 × 100 = 50,000) falls and is now equal to the area OP_2BQ_2 (or 400 × 110 = 44,000). Thus, good news leading to bumper crop has led to the fall in total revenue or income of the farmers. This is usually described as farmers face a 'pardox of poverty amongst plenty' or a good news (in the form of good weather or good monsoon) turns out to be actually a bad news for the farmers as it leads to the decline in their incomes and they have become worse off. [1]

Crop Restriction Programme and Farmers' Income

In the previous chapter we explained through demand and supply analysis that government often helps the farmers by giving them subsidy for every bushel of wheat or any other crop such as rice produced by the farmers. However, during the last over three decades, government in the United States helps farmers by requiring them to restrict production. To induce them to restrict output government provides subsidy to them for not planting crops on all their land (that is, for keeping some land uncultivated). The purpose of restricting production in this way is to reduce their supply in the market so that price of the agricultural product in the market rises. *In view of the fact that demand for agricultural product is inelastic a fall in production will cause their revenue or income to rise and will thus make them better off.* Consider Fig. 13A.2 where without intervention by government demand curve *DD* and supply curve S_1 determine equilibrium price P_1 and the farmer's sales revenue is equal to the area $OP_1E_1Q_1$. As a result of crop restriction programme of government supply curve shifts to the left to S_2 (For sake of simplicity we have assumed perfectly inelastic supply curves). With the intersection of new supply curve S_2 with the given inelastic demand curve *DD*, price of agricultural product rises to P_2 and the quantity sold has fallen to Q_2 so that the new total revenue is $OP_2E_2Q_2$ which is greater than the initial revenue $OP_1E_1Q_1$ *before crop restriction.* Thus crop restriction programme of government has led to the increase in total revenue and hence it will raise the incomes of the farmers.

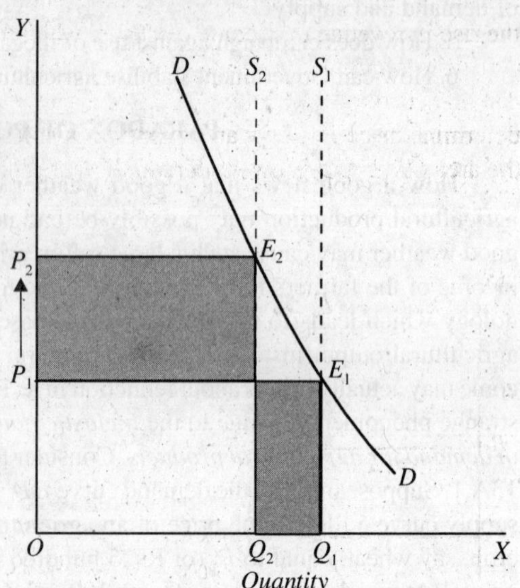

Fig. 13A.2. *Crop restriction programme raises both price and income of the farmers.*

It should be noted that whereas crop restriction has raised the incomes of the farmers, it has hurt the consumers as they have to pay higher prices for foodgrains as they would if flood or drought conditions had created shortage of foodgrains. Thus, interests of farmers and consumers clash with each other.

WHY DID OPEC FAIL TO KEEP THE PRICE OF OIL HIGH IN THE LONG RUN ?

Petroleum exporting countries have formed a cartel to promote interests and raise their incomes. This certel is known as OPEC (Organisation of Petroleum Exporting Countries). In the early 1970s OPEC gave a shock to the world when it decided to raise the price of oil by jointly deciding

1. Strictly speaking, our analysis indicates decline in sales revenue. From decline in sales revenue we are concluding fall in farmers' income. However, income is equal to total revenue minus cost. In our conclusion however we have assumed that cost does not change much.

to reduce the supply of oil they supply. In 1973 and 1974, OPEC raised the price of oil by more than 50 per cent that created energy crisis in the world. Again price of oil was raised by 14 per cent in 1979, 34 per cent in 1980 and further 34 per cent 1981. However, after 1981, OPEC failed to maintain high price of oil and from 1982 to 1985, oil prices fell by about 50 per cent. In 1986 cooperation among OPEC countries completely failed that caused a further decline in price of oil by 45 per cent. In 1990, price of oil (adjusted for overall inflation) came down to the level of 1970. Price of oil remained at the low level throughout the decade of 1990s.

Now, the important question is why OPEC failed to maintain high price ? Why was it not able to raise oil prices in 1990s by reducing the supply of oil. The model of elasticities of demand and supply answers this question. As explained earlier both demand and supply of oil are inelastic in the short run. The rise in oil price by reducing supply brought about a substantial rise in price and due to inelastic demand in the short run, the quantity demanded and sold fell only by a small amount. This brought about increase in sales revenue and incomes of members of OPEC in the short run. Supply of oil is inelastic in the short run because the amount of oil in reserves and capacity for extracting oil cannot be adjusted quickly. Demand for oil in the short run is also inelastic because buying habits of consumers of oil also could not be adjusted quickly to changes in price of oil. This helps to explain the rise in revenue or income of OPEC when they succeeded in raising price of oil by cutting down production and supply of oil in the market. This is illustrated in Figure 13A.3 where *DD* is the demand curve of oil which is quite steep (i.e. inelastic) and S_1 is the initial supply curve and the two determine price P_1 of oil and quantity Q_1 sold. The total revenue of members of OPEC is given by the area $OP_1E_1Q_1$. Now, with reduction in production by members of OPEC, supply curve shifts to

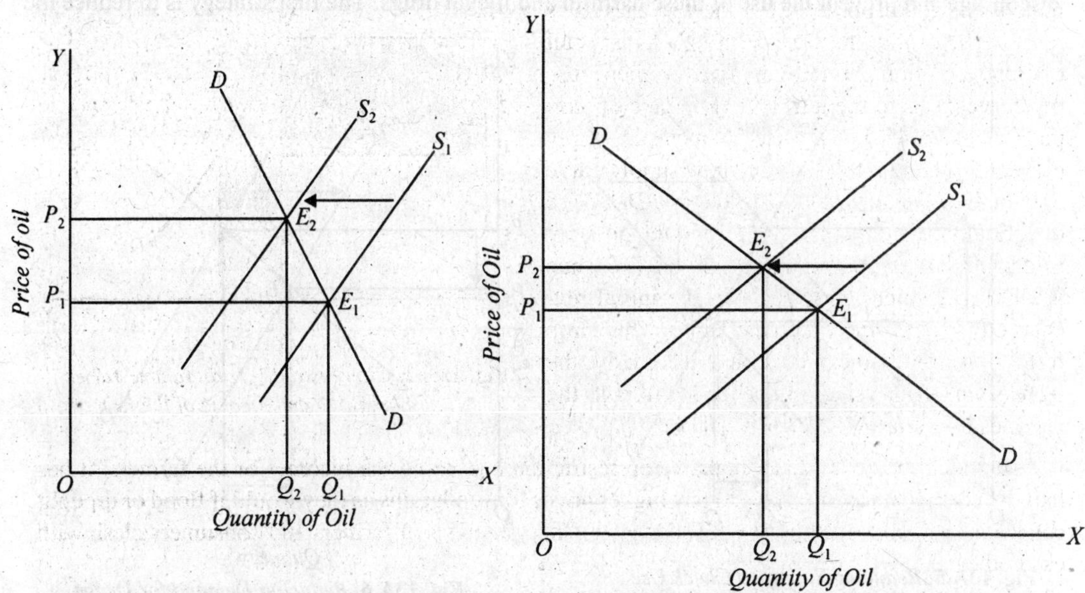

Fig. 13A.3. *Restricting Output to Raise Oil Price : Short-run Effect*

Fig. 13A.4. *Due to elastic demand and supply curves in the long run, output restriction does not lead to rise in income.*

the the left to S_2 and given the inelastic demand curve *DD* causes a substantial rise in oil price to P_2 and the quantity sold falls by only a small amount from Q_1 to Q_2. As result, the new total revenue earned $OP_2E_2Q_2$ is greater than the revenue $OP_1E_1Q_1$ earned before the reduction in production. Thus joint action by OPEC resulted in rise in incomes of members of OPEC in the short run.

However, the situation in the long run is different. In the long run, the producers who were not members of OPEC tried to raise their production by increasing oil exploration and also by expanding their extraction capacity. This response of producers made supply curve quite elastic in the long run as is shown in Fig. 13A.4. Similarly, in the long run consumers responded to high oil prices by making attempts to conserve oil. For example, they replaced old fuel-inefficient cars with more fuel-efficient ones. As a result, demand for oil is also elastic in the long run as shown in Figure 13A.4. Now, in Fig. 13A.4, with elastic supply and demand curves in the long run the same reduction in production by OPEC bringing about leftward shift in the supply curve by the same amount as in Fig. 13A.3 causes only a small rise in price. As will be seen from Fig. 13A.4 the reduction in output by OPEC and shift in supply curve from S_1 to S_2 by the same horizontal distance as in Fig. 13A.3 price rises only a little from P_1 to P_2 and quantity sold declines from Q_1 to Q_2. It will be seen that in the long run reduction in production has resulted in fall in revenue and therefore it is not profitable to make a cut in oil production in the long run. That is why OPEC could not succeed to maintain high oil prices in the long run.

FIGHT AGAINST DRUGS

An important problem faced by a modern society is the extensive use of illegal drugs such as cocaine, heroine, etc. The use of these harmful drugs not only impairs the health of individuals who consume them but they also ruin the families as the drug addicts often spend a lot of incomes of their families. Besides, drug-addicts often commit burglaries and robberies to make quick money to spend on drugs. There are other drug-related crimes. Therefore, governments of different countreis including India often adopt measures to discourage the use of drugs. There are two main strategies to discourage and prevent the use of these harmful and illegal drugs. The first strategy is to reduce the

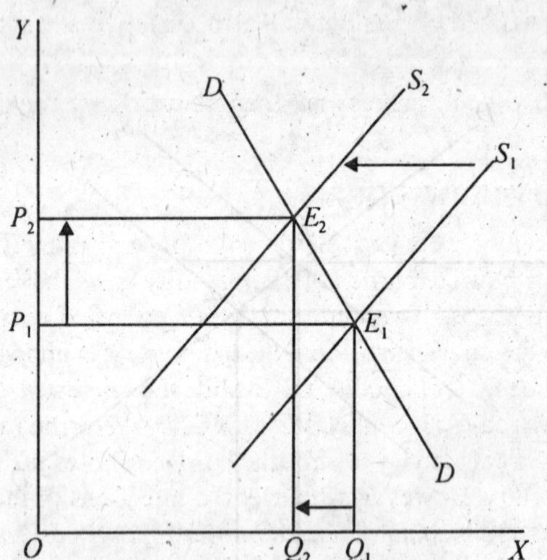

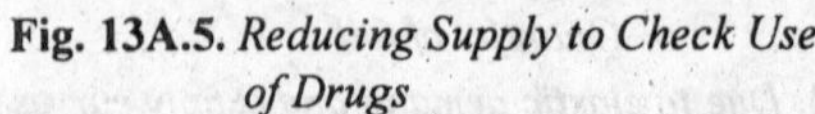
Fig. 13A.5. *Reducing Supply to Check Use of Drugs*

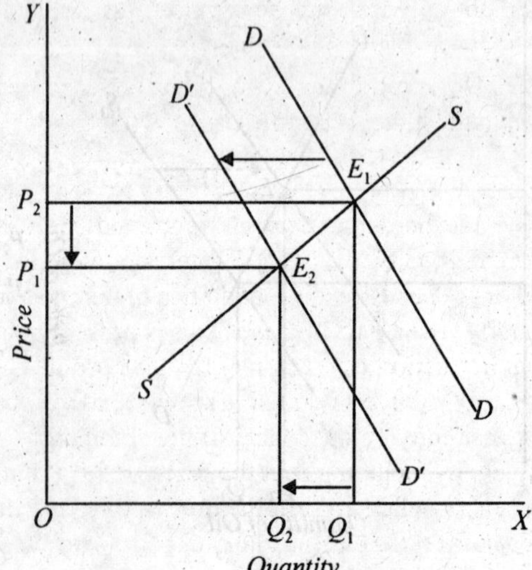

Fig. 13A.6. *Reducing Demand for Drugs throught Education*

supply of drugs and thereby raising prices of drugs. The second strategy is to reduce the demand for drugs by giving education to the people, especially the young ones about the harmful effects of these drugs. To reduce the use of these illegal drugs governments of various countries (including India) prohibit the flow of drugs into their countries and arrest and put heavy penalties on smugglers of these drugs. As a result, cost of selling these drugs rises which reduces the supply of these drugs in a country. This policy of discouraging the use of these harmful drugs by reduction in their supply is depicted in Fig. 13A.5. It will be seen from this figure that initially with the given demand curve *DD* and supply curve S_1, the equilibrium price is P_1 at which quantity Q_1 is bought and sold. Now, as a result of various measures adopted by government to reduce the supply of these drugs, supply curve shifts to the left to S_2. It will be seen that with the leftward shift in with supply curve to S_2, price of drug rises to P_2 and quantity demanded and sold falls to Q_2. Thus, drug interdiction has led to reduce the drug use.

However, some economists have criticized this strategy of reducing drug use by reducing supply. According to them, this will not prevent the drug-related crimes. This is because demand for drugs is likely to be inelastic as has been drawn in Fig. 13A.5. It has been pointed out that drug users are unlikely to forego their habits of using drugs in response to higher price of these drugs. In fact, given the inelastic demand, at a higher price P_2 of these drugs the users of these drugs will be spending more money than before. In Fig. 13A.5, the total expenditure as measured by the area $OP_2E_2Q_2$ is greater than the area $OP_1E_1Q_1$ before the reduction in supply. Thus, the need for money to fulfil their desire for these drugs they will commit more crimes to make sufficient money. Besides, high price of drugs make them very profitable to produce or sell these drugs. The persons engaged in this business will make efforts to procure these drugs from whatever sources they can do so.

Due to the above drawbacks of the strategy of reducing supply, the alternative strategy proposed is to reduce the demand for these drugs by educating people about their harmful effects on health. If education about harmful effects of drugs is successful, it will reduce the demand for these drugs and cause a leftward shift in their demand curve as shown in Fig. 13A.6. As a result of education about harmful effects, demand curve shifts to the left from *DD* to *D'D'*. The equilibrium price falls from P_2 to P_1 and as will be seen from Fig. 13A.6 the total revenue which is equal to price times the quantity ($P \times Q$) also declines. Thus, by bringing down the price, alternative strategy of drug education makes it less profitable to produce, sell or smuggle these illegal drugs. Thus drug education not only reduces the use of drugs and drug related crimes but will also make it unattractive to produce and sell these drugs.

However, in our view, both the supply-reducing measures and drug education are required if war against these harmful drugs is to be won.

ELASTICITY AND BURDEN OF A TAX

The burden of a tax on a commodity is shared between the sellers (or producers) and buyers of the commodity. We are now interested in showing how the burden of a commodity tax on buyers and sellers depends on the elasticities of demand and supply. Two important taxes are levied on a commodity and a part of these taxes is passed on to the consumers. First, the excise duty is imposed on the production of a commodity. The producers of the commodity try to shift the burden of excise duty to the buyers by raising the price of the commodity. Secondly, sales tax is levied on the sales of a commodity on the sellers of the commodity. Sellers also try to shift the burden of sales tax to the buyers by including it in the price of the commodity. However, whatever the intentions of the producers or sellers to shift the burden of a commodity tax, *actual burden borne by buyers and sellers depends on the elasticities of demand and supply.* The money burden of a tax on buyers and sellers is called *incidence of a tax.*

A commodity tax, excise duty or sales tax drives a wedge between the price paid by the buyers and the price received by the sellers. Consider Figure 13A.7 where the demand curve *DD* is inelastic and supply curve *SS* is elastic. Suppose now sales tax equal to *CB* per unit is imposed. The producers or sellers will be willing to sell a *given quantity of a commodity*, if they receive the same *net price* as before. That is, the producers or sellers will treat the sales tax *CB* per unit as an extra cost of production and therefore, they would add it to the cost per unit. As a result of the imposition of a sales tax per unit of the commodity, supply curve will shift upward to S_2 and will be parallel to the supply curve S_1 without a tax. Demand curve *DD* will remain unaffected as a result of the imposition of sales tax. It will be seen from Fig. 13A.7 that the new supply curve S_2 intersects the demand curve

DD at point *B* and determines higher equilibrium price OP_2 and the quantity sold falls to OQ_2. It will be seen from Fig. 13A.7 that in this present case when demand is inelastic and supply elastic, the burden of the tax falls more on the buyers and less on the sellers. The buyers have to pay *EB* more price than before. Therefore, *EB* is the burden or incidence of the tax on buyers. Sellers receive *EC* less price than before and therefore *EC* is the burden of tax on the sellers. And $EB > EC$.

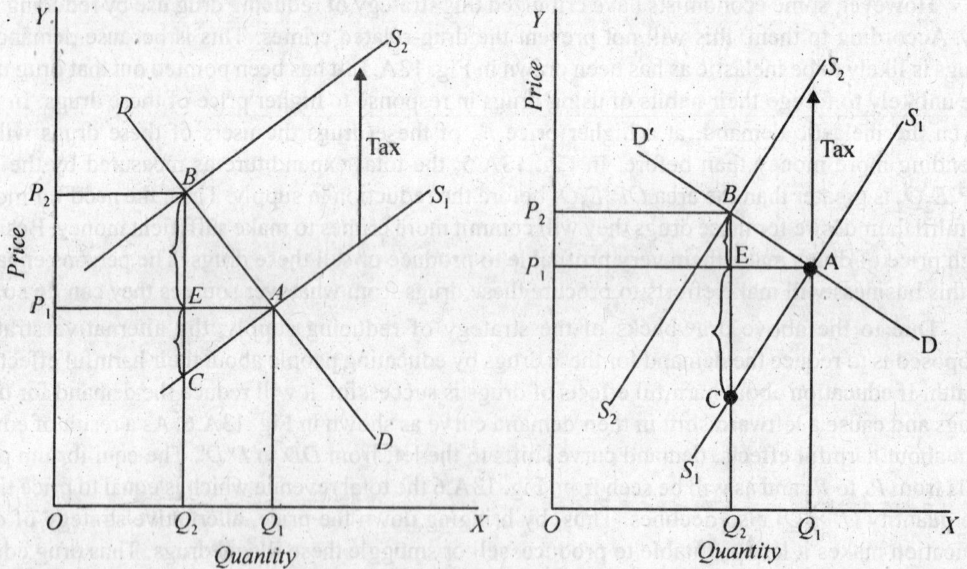

Fig. 13A.7. *In case of inelastic demand the burden of a commodity tax falls more on buyers.*

Fig. 13A.8. *In case of elastic demand the burden of a commodity tax falls more on the sellers.*

Now consider Fig. 13A.8 where demand curve *DD* is elastic and supply curve S_1S_1 is relatively inelatic. Before the imposition of tax P_1 is the price at which quantity Q_1 is being bought and sold consequent to imposition of tax equal to *CB*, supply curve shifts to S_2S_2. Price rises from P_1 to P_2 and equilibrium quantity sold and bought falls to Q_2. In this case when demand is elastic and supply relatively inelastic, burden of tax *EB* per unit borne by the buyers is much less than the burden *CE* borne by the sellers.

It follows from above that *the burden or the incidence of taxes borne by the producers and the consumers will depend upon the elasticity of demand as well as elasticity of supply. The lower the elasticity of demand, the greater will be the incidence of tax borne by the consumers.*

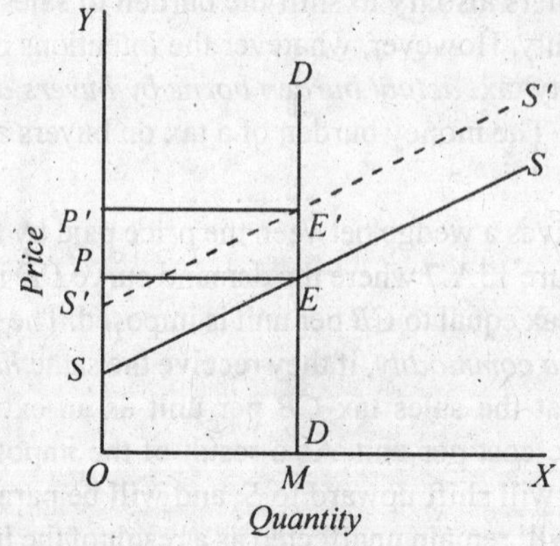

Fig. 13A.9. *Incidence of Tax in Case of Perfectly Inelastic Demand*

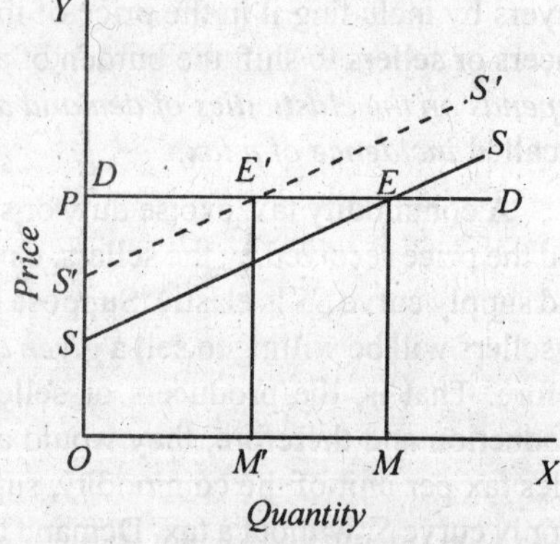

Fig. 13A.10. *Incidence of Tax in Case of Perfectly Elastic Demand*

If the demand for a commodity is perfectly inelastic the whole of the burden of the commodity tax will fall on consumer. This is shown in figure 13A.9. In this figure demand curve *DD* is a vertical straight line showing that demand for the commodity is completely inelastic. As a result of the intersection of the demand and supply curves, price *OP* is determined. If now the tax equal to *SS′* is imposed on the commodity, the supply curve will shift vertically upward to the dotted position *S′S′*. It will be seen that the new supply curve *S′ S′* intersects the demand curve *DD* at point *E′* and the new equilibrium price *OP′* is determined. It will be noticed from Fig. 13A.9 that in this case the price of the commodity has risen by *PP′* or *EE′* which is equal to the full amount of the tax *SS′*. It means that producers have succeeded to pass on the full tax to the consumers and they themselves do not bear any incidence. It, therefore, follows that *in case of perfectly inealstic demand, the whole incidence of the indirect tax falls on the consumers.*

On the contrary, if the consumer's demand for a quantity is perfectly elastic, as is shown by *DD* curve in Figure 13A.10 the imposition of the tax on it will not cause any rise in price. In this case, the whole burden of commodity tax will be borne by the manufacturers or sellers. It will be seen from Fig. 13A.10 that as a result of the indirect tax by the amount *SS′* and the resultant upward shift in supply curve to *S′ S′* the equilibrium price remains unchanged at the leve *OP*. Since the price has not risen, the consumers would not bear any burden of the tax in this case. Therefore, the whole incidence of the tax will fall on the producers or sellers in case of perfectly elastic demand.

It should be noted that the more inelastic the demand for a commodity, the greater the rise in the price paid by the consumers and the vice versa.

The predictions about the incidence of taxes borne by the consumers and the producers have been generally found to be true in the real world situation when the commodities on which taxes are imposed are sold under competitive conditions.

QUESTIONS FOR REVIEW

1. Explain with reference to agriculture 'Paradox of poverty amongst plenty, Illustrate diagrammatically.
2. How a good news for agriculture can be a bad news for farmers ?
3. How does a crop-restriction programe by government of the Untied States help farmers ?
4. Show that what is good for farmers is not necessarily good for the society as a whole ?
5. How might a drought that destroys half of all farm crops be good for farmers ? If such a drought is good for farmers, why don't farmers destroy their own crops in the absence of a drought ?

   (**Hint.** No single farmer will benefit from destroying his crops *as he takes the market price as given.* But if all farmers destroy their crops together, it will result in rise in prices of crops, and given the inelastic nature of demand for agricultural products, price will rise substantially whereas there will be a little fall in quantity demanded of them. But there is no guarantee that all farmers in a country willingly act together, whereas drought is a natural phenomenon which reduces supply or production of all).
6. In the 1970s, OPEC caused a dramatic increase in the price of oil. What prevented it from maintaining the high price through 1980s ?
7. What strategies can be adopted to reduce the use of drugs ? Comment on the efficiency of each strategy.

Incidence of Taxes

8. Analyse the incidence of a per unit tax imposed on a commodity with perfectly inelastic demand. Assume that the conditions in the market are perfectly competitive.

   (D.U. B.A.(Hons) 1980)

9. A unit excise duty is imposed on a firm in a competitive market. Examine its short-run and long-run effects on industry and firm. *(D.U.B.A.(Hons.) 1996)*
10. Analyse the incidence of a per unit tax imposed on a commodity with (*i*) perfectly elastic demand and (*ii*) perfectly inelastic demand. *(D.U.B.A.(Hons.) 1987)*
11. Explain the circumstances under which rise in price of a commodity as a result of the imposition of a per unit tax on it is more than the tax. *(D.U.B.A.(Hons.) 1997)*

    [**Hints.** This happens in case of a decreasing-cost industry where supply curve slopes downward].
12. How is a specific duty imposed on a commodity is shared by the consumers and producers? Show that the lower the price elasticity of demand, the higher is the incidence of a specific commodity tax on the consumers.

CHAPTER 14
CONSUMER SURPLUS

Meaning of Consumer Surplus

The concept of consumer surplus was first formulated by Dupuit in 1844 to measure social benefits of public goods such as canals, bridges, national highways. Marshall further refined and popularised this in his '*Principles of Economics*' published in 1890. The concept of consumer surplus became the basis of old welfare economics. Marshall's concept of consumer's surplus was based on the cardinal measurability and interpersonal comparisons of utility. According to him, every increase in consumer's surplus is an indicator of the increase in social welfare. As we shall see below, *consumer's surplus is simply the difference between the price that 'one is willing to pay' and 'the price one actually pays' for a particular product.*

Concept of consumer's surplus is a very important concept in economic theory, especially in theory of demand and welfare economics. This concept is important not only in economic theory but also in formulation of economic policies such as taxation by the Government and price policy pursued by the monopolistic seller of a product. The essence of the concept of consumer's surplus is that a consumer derives extra satisfaction from the purchases he daily makes over the price he actually pays for them. In other words, people generally get more utility from the consumption of goods than the price they actually pay for them. It has been found that people are prepared to pay more price for the goods than they actually pay for them. This extra satisfaction which the consumers obtain from buying a good has been called consumer surplus. Thus, Marshall defines the consumer's sruplus in the following words: "*excess of the price which a consumer would be willing to pay rather than go without a thing over that which he actually does pay is the economic measure of this surplus satisfaction.... it may be called consumer's surplus.*"[1]

The amount of money which a person is willing to pay for a good indicates the amount of utility he derives from that good; the greater the amount of money he is willing to pay, the greater the utility he obtains from it. Therefore, the marginal utility of a unit of a good determines the price a consumer will be prepared to pay for that unit. The total utility which a person gets from a good is given by the sum of marginal utilities (ΣMU) of the units of a good purchased and the total price which he actually pays is equal to the price per unit of the good multiplied by the number of units of it purchased. Thus:

Consumer's surplus = What a consumer is willing to pay minus what he actually pays.

= Σ Marginal utility – (Price × Number of units of a commodity purchased)

The concept of consumer surplus is derived from the law of diminishing marginal utility. As we purchase more units of a good, its marginal utility goes on diminishing. It is because of the diminishing marginal utility that consumer's willingness to pay for additional units of a commodity declines as he has more units of the commodity. The consumer is in equilibrium when marginal utility from a commodity becomes equal to its given price. In other words, consumer purchases the number of

1. Alfred Marshall, *Principles of Economics*, 8th edition, p. 103.

units of a commodity at which marginal utility is equal to price. This means that at the margin what a consumer will be willing to pay (*i.e.*, marginal utility) is equal to the price he actually pays. *But for the previous units which he purchases, his willingness to pay (or the marginal utility he derives from the commodity) is greater than the price he actually pays for them. This is because the price of the commodity is given and constant for him and therefore price of all the units is the same.*

Marshall's Measure of Consumer Surplus

Consumer surplus measures extra utility or satisfaction which a consumer obtains from the consumption of a certain amount of a commodity over and above the utility of its market value. Thus the total utility obtained from consuming water is immense while its market value is negligible. It is due to the occurrence of diminishing marginal utility that a consumer gets total utility from the consumption of a commodity greater than its market value. Marshall tried to obtain the monetary measure of this surplus, that is, how many rupees this surplus of utility is worth to the consumer. It is the monetary value of this surplus that Marshall called consumer surplus. To determine this monetary measure of consumer surplus we are required to measure two things. First, the total utility in terms of money that a consumer expects to get from the consumption of a certain amount of a commodity. Second, the total market value of the amount of commodity consumed by him. It is quite easy to measure the total market value as it is equal to market price of a commodity multiplied by its quantity purchased (*i.e.*, *P.Q.*). An important contribution of Marshall has been the way he devised to determine the monetary measure of the total utility a consumer obtained from the commodity. Consider Table 14.1 which has been graphically shown in Fig. 14.1.

Table 14.1. Marginal Utility and Consumer Surplus

No. of Units	*Marginal Utility*	*Price*	*Net Marginal Benefit*
1	₹ 20	₹ 12	₹ 8
2	₹ 18	₹ 12	₹ 6
3	₹ 16	₹ 12	₹ 4
4	₹ 14	₹ 12	₹ 2
5	₹ 12	₹ 12	₹ 0
6	₹ 10	₹ 12	₹ (– 2)
	Total Consumer Surplus (from 5 units)		= 20

Suppose for the first unit of the commodity the consumer is prepared to pay ₹ 20. This means that the first unit of the commodity is at least worth ₹ 20 to him. In other words, he derives marginal utility equal to ₹ 20 from the first unit. For the second unit of the commodity, he is willing to pay ₹ 18, that is, the second unit is at least worth ₹ 18 to him. This is in accordance with the law of diminishing marginal utility. Similarly, the marginal utility of the third, fourth, fifth and sixth units of the commodity falls to ₹ 16, 14, 12 and 10 respectively. However, actually the consumer has not to pay the sum of money equal to the marginal utility or marginal valuation he places on them. For all the units of the commodity he has to pay the current market price of the commodity. Suppose the current market price of the commodity is ₹ 12. It will be seen from the Table 14.1 and Fig. 14.1 that the consumer will buy 5 units of the commodity at this price because his marginal utility of the fifth unit just equals the market price of ₹ 12. This shows that his marginal utility of the first four units is greater than the market price which he actually pays for them. He will therefore obtain surplus or net marginal benefit of ₹ 8 (₹ 20 – 12) from the first unit, ₹ 6 (= ₹ 18 – 12) from the second unit, ₹ 4 from the third unit and ₹ 2 from the fourth unit and zero from the fifth unit. He thus obtains total consumer surplus or *total net benefit* equal to ₹ 20.

Measurement of Consumer Surplus as an Area Under the Demand Curve

The analysis of consumer surplus made above is based on discrete units of the commodity. If we assume that the commodity is perfectly divisible, which is usually made in economic theory, the

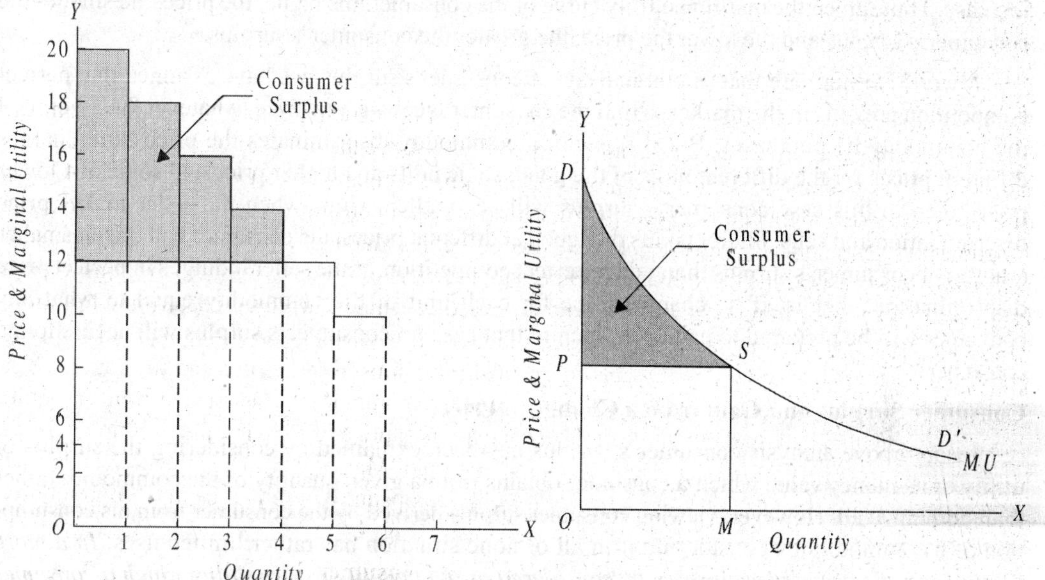

Fig. 14.1. *Consumer Surplus* **Fig. 14.2.** *Marshall's Measure of Consumer's Surplus*

consumer surplus can be represented by an area under the demand curve. The measurement of consumer surplus from a commodity from the demand or marginal utility curve is illustrated in Fig. 14.2 in which along the *X*-axis the amount of the commodity has been measured and on the *Y*-axis the marginal utility (or willingness to pay for the commodity) and the price of the commodity are measured. *DD'* is the demand or marginal utility curve which is sloping downward, indicating that as the consumer buys more units of the commodity falls, marginal utility of the additional units of the commodity. As said above, marginal utility shows the price which a person is willing to pay for the different units rather than go without them. If *OP* is the price that prevails in the market, then the consumer will be in equilibrium when he buys *OM* units of the commodity, since at *OM* units, marginal utility from a unit of the commodity is equal to the given price *OP*. The *M*th unit of the commodity does not yield any consumer's surplus to the consumer since this is the last unit purchased and for this price paid is equal to the marginal utility which indicates the price that he is prepared to pay rather than go without it. But for the intra-marginal units *i.e.*, units before *M*th unit, marginal utility is greater than the price and, therefore, these units yield consumer's surplus to the consumer. The total utility of a certain quantity of a commodity to a consumer can be known by summing up the marginal utilities of the various units purchased.

In Fig. 14.2, the total utility derived by the consumer from *OM* units of the commodity will be equal to the area under the demand or marginal utility curve up to point *M*. That is, the total utility of *OM* units in Fig. 14.2 is equal to *ODSM*. In other words, for *OM* units of the good the consumer will be prepared to pay the sum equal to Rs. *ODSM*. But given the price equal to *OP*, the consumer will actually pay the sum equal to Rs. *OPSM* for *OM* units of the good. It is thus clear that the consumer derives extra utility equal to *ODSM* minus *OPSM* = *DPS*, which has been shaded in Fig. 14.2. To conclude when we draw a demand curve, the monetary measure of consumer surplus can be obtained by the area under the demand curve over and above the rectangular area representing the total market value (*i.e.*, *P.Q.* or the area *OPSM*) of the amount of the commodity purchased.

If market price of the commodity rises above *OP*, the consumer will buy fewer units of the commodity than OM. As a result, consumer's surplus obtained by him from his purchase will decline. On the other hand, if price falls below OP, the consumer will be in equilibrium when he is purchasing more units of the commodity than OM. As a result of this, the consumer's surplus will increase. Thus, given the marginal utility curve of the consumer, the higher the price, the smaller the consumer's surplus and the lower the price, the greater the consumer's surplus.

It worth noting here that in our analysis of consumer's surplus, we have assumed that perfect competition prevails in the market so that the consumer faces a given price, whatever the amount of the commodity he purchases. But if seller of a commodity discriminates the prices and charges different prices for the different units of the good, some units at a higher price and some at a lower price, then in this case consumer's surplus will be smaller. Thus, when the seller makes price discrimination and sells different units of a good at different prices, the consumer will obtain smaller amount of consumer's surplus than under perfect competition. If the seller indulges in perfect price discrimination, that is, if he charges price for each unit of the commodity equal to what any consumer will be prepared to pay for it, then in that case no consumer's surplus will accure to the consumer.

Consumer Surplus and Gain from a Change in Price

In our above analysis consumer's surplus has been explained by considering the surplus of utility or its money value which a consumer obtains from a given quantity of the commodity rather than nothing at all. However, viewing consumer surplus derived by the consumer from his consumption of a commodity by considering it in all or none situation has rather limited uses. *In a more useful way, consumer's surplus can be considered as net benefit or extra utility which a consumer obtains from the changes in price of a good or in the levels of its consumption.*

Consider Fig. 14.3 where DD shows the demand curve for food. At a market price OP of the food, the consumer buys OQ quantity of the food. The total market value which he pays for OQ food is equal to the area $OPEQ$, that is, price OP multiplied by quantity OQ. The total benefit, utility or use-value of OQ quantity of food is the area $ODEQ$. Thus, consumer's surplus obtained by the consumer would be equal to the area PED. Now, if price of food falls to OP', the consumer will buy OQ' quantity of food and the consumer surplus will increase to $P'TD$. The net increase in the consumer's surplus as a result of fall in price is the shaded area $PETP'$, ($P'TD - PED = PETP'$). This measures the net benefit or extra utility obtained by the consumer from the fall in price of food. This net benefit can be decomposed into two parts. First, the increase in consumer surplus arising on consuming previous OQ quantity of food due to fall in price.

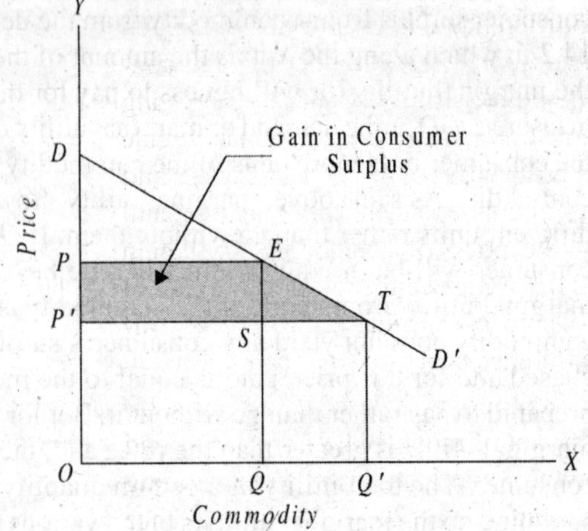

Fig. 14.3. *Gain in Consumer Surplus with a Fall in Price*

Second, the increase in consumer surplus equal to the small triangle EST arising due to the increase in consumption of the food following the lowering of its price ($PETP' = PESP' + EST$).

Measurement of Consumer's Surplus through Indifference Curve Analysis

We have explained above the Marshallian method of measuring consumer's surplus. Marshallian method has been criticised by the advocates of ordinal utility analysis. Two basic assumptions made by Marshall in his measurement of consumer's surplus are: (1) utility can be quantitatively or cardinally measured, and (2) when a person spends more money on a commodity, the marginal utility of money does not change or when the price of a commodity falls and as a result consumer becomes better off and his real income increases, the marginal utility of money remains constant. Economists like Hicks and Allen have expressed the view that utility is a subjective and psychic entity and, therefore, it cannot be cardinally measured. They further point out that marginal utility of money does not remain constant with the rise and fall in real income of the consumer following the changes in price of a commodity. The implication of Marshallian assumption of constant marginal utility of money is that he neglects the income effect of the price change. But in some cases income effect of the price change is very significant and cannot be ignored. Marshall defended his assumption of constancy of marginal utility of money on the ground that an individual spends a negligible part of his income on an individual commodity and, therefore, a change in its price does not make any significant change in the marginal utility of money. But this need not be so in case of all commodities.

Prof. J.R. Hicks rehabilitated the concept of consumer's surplus by measuring it with indifference curve technique of his ordinal utility analysis. Indifference curve technique does not make the assumption of cardinal measurability of utility, nor does it assume that marginal utility of money remains constant. However, without these invalid assumptions, Hicks was able to measure the consumer's surplus with his indifference curve technique. The concept of consumer's surplus was criticised mainly on the ground that it was difficult to measure it in cardinal utility terms. Therefore, Hicksian measurement of consumer's surplus in terms of ordinal utility went a long way in establishing the validity of the concept of consumer's surplus.

How consumer's surplus is measured with the aid of Hicksian indifference curve technique is illustrated in Fig. 14.4. In Fig. 14.4, we have measured the quantity of commodity X along the X-axis, and money along the Y-axis. It is worth noting that money represents *other goods* except the commodity X. We have also shown some indifference curves between the given commodity X and money for the consumer, the scale of his preference being given. We know that consumer's scale of preferences depends on his tastes and is quite independent of his income and market prices of the good. This will help us in understanding the concept of consumer's surplus with the aid of indifference curves.

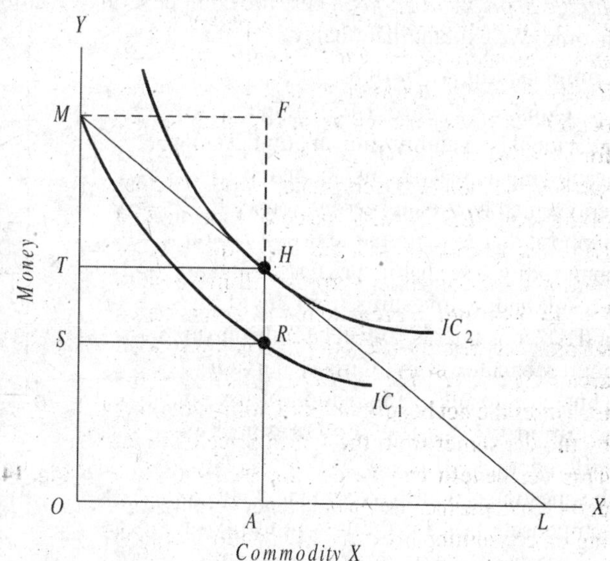

Fig. 14.4. *Measurement of Consumer Surplus with Indifference Curves*

Suppose, a consumer has OM amount of money which he can spend on the commodity X and the remaining amount on other goods. The indifference curve IC_1 touches the point M indicating thereby that all combinations of money and commodity X represented on the indifference curve IC_1 give the same satisfaction to the consumer as OM amount of money. For example, take combination R on an indifference curve IC_1. It follows that OA amount of commodity X and OS amount of money will give the same satisfaction to the consumer as OM amount of money because both M and R combinations lie on the same indifference curve IC_1. In other words, it means that the consumer is willing to pay MS amount of money for OA amount of the commodity X. It is thus clear that, given the scale of preferences of the consumer, he derives the same satisfaction from *OA* amount of the commodity *X* as from *MS* amount of money. In other words, he is prepared to give up *MS* (or *FR*) for *OA* amount of commodity *X*.

Now, suppose that the price of commodity *X* in the market is such that we get the budget line *ML* (price of *X* is equal to $\frac{OM}{OL}$). We know from out analysis of consumer's equilibrium that consumer is in equilibrium where the given budget line is tangent to an indifference curve. It will be seen from Fig. 14.4 that the budget line *ML* is tangent to the indifference curve IC_2 at point *H*, where the consumer is having *OA* amount of commodity *X* and *OT* amount of money. Thus, given the market price of the commodity *X*, the consumer has actually spent *MT* amount of money for acquiring *OA* amount of commodity *X*. But, as mentioned above, he was prepared to forego *MS* (or *FR*) amount of money for having *OA* amount of *X*. Therefore, the consumer actually pays *TS* or *HR* less amount of money than he is prepared to pay for *OA* amount of the commodity *X* rather than go without it. Thus, *TS* or *HR* is the amount of consumer's surplus which the consumer derives from purchasing *OA* amount of the commodity. In this way, Hicks explained consumer's surplus with his indifference curves technique without assuming cardinal measurability of utility and without assuming constancy of the marginal utility of money. Since Marshall made these dubious assumptions for measuring consumer surplus, his method of measurement is regarded as invalid and Hicksian method of measurement with the technique of indifference curves is regarded as superior to the Marshallian method.

Welfare Gains from Price Change Terms of Compensating Variation and Equivalent Variation in Income

As explained above, J.R. Hicks explained consumer surplus with his indifference curve analysis, that is, in ordinal utility terms. Two of his four concepts of consumer surplus are particularly useful in *measuring in money terms the gain in utility or welfare of the individuals caused by change in prices of goods*. These are compensating variation in income and equivalent variation in income. We explain them below.

Compensating Variation

Consider Figure 14.5 Suppose an individual is in equilibrium at point *Q* and is enjoying a level of satisfaction or utility represented by the indifference curve IC_1. Suppose the government levies a tax on commodity *X* so that its price rises and as a result budget line shifts from BL_1 to BL_0 and the consumer is now in equilibrium at point *R* on a lower indifference curve IC_0. Thus as a result of imposition of tax on commodity *X*, the consumer has suffered a loss of utility or welfare. Now the question is if the government wants to compensate him for the loss in utility or welfare due to the rise in price of commodity *X* following the imposition of tax on it, *how much income he should be given to compensate him for the loss in utility due to rise in price so that he comes back to his original indifference curve IC_1 (i.e. his original level of welfare)*.

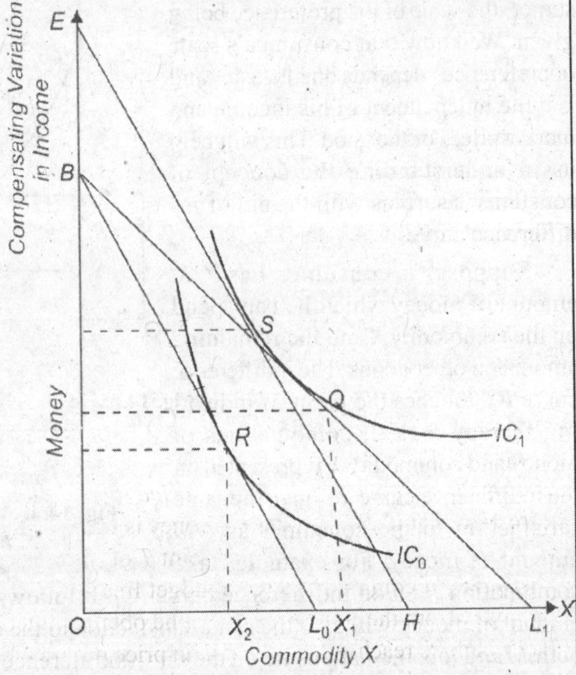

Fig. 14.5. *Compensating Variation in Income*

From Figure 14.6 it will be seen that if with new equilibrium at point *R* on lower indifference curve IC_0, he is given the amount of money *BE* the consumer comes back to his original indifference curve IC_1 (that is, his original level of utility or welfare). With getting *BE* as money compensation, the budget line shifts from BL_0 to the budget line *EH* which is tanget to the original indifference cruve IC_1 at point *S*. Thus the amount of money *BE* which should be given to the consumer so as to bring him back to the original indifference curve IC_1 is called compensation variation in income and provides us with a *money measure of loss welfare* sufferred by the consumer as a result of rise in price of the commodity following the imposition of tax on it by the government. Thus, the *change in income necessary to restore the consumer to his original indifference curve when price of a commodity rises is called the* ***compensating variation*** *in income since it is the change in income that will just compensate the consumer for the price change. The compensating variation measures how much money the government would have to give to the consumer if it wanted to exactly compensate the consumer for the price change.*

Equivalent Variation in Income

An alternative measure of the change in welfare or utility in money terms resulting from a change in price is called equivalent variation in income by J.R. Hicks, *Equivalent variation in income refers to the amount of money that has to be taken away from the consumer when the price of a commodity falls so that he is as better off as he would be after the price change.* This is called equivalent variation in income because its impact on welfare is equivalent to that of price change. This is illustrated in Figure 14.6 where initially the consumer is in equilibrium at point *Q* at which the given budget line BL_1 is tangent to indifference curve IC_1. Now suppose the price of commodity *X* rises which shifts the budget line from BL_1, to BL_0. With this new budget line BL_0, the consumer is in equilibrium at point *R* on lower indifference curve IC_0. Now, with initial equilibrium position *at Q* on indifference curve IC_1 at the higher prior price representing by the budget line BL_1, *how much money income has to be taken away from the consumer so that he reaches the subsequent indifference curve IC_0 at which he reached with higher price represented by the budget line BL_0*. It will be seen from Figure 14.6 that if *BG* amount of money is taken away from the consumer budget line shifts from BL_1 to *GH* which just touches the point *T* of indifference curve IC_0 at which he reaches with the higher price of commodity *X* and budget line BL_0. Thus, the *BG* amount of money would have to taken away from the consumer so that he obtains the level of utility represented by the indifference IC_0 to which he reaches with the rise in price of commodity *X*. Thus *BG is the equivalent variation in income which measures the maximum amount of money income that the consumer would be willing to pay to prevent the rise in price.* Thus the equivalent variation in income is equal to the

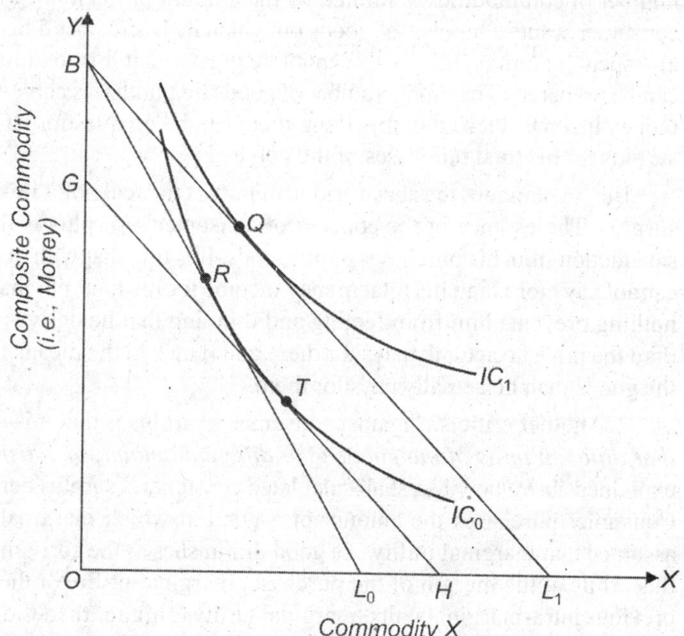

Fig. 14.6. *Equivalent Variation is Incomes as a measure of welfare gain from Price Change*

impact of change in price on consumer welfare or utility. Besides, the *equivalent variation in income measures the change in welfare in terms of money as a result of change in price.*

It may be noted that in general equivalent variation in income will be different from compensating variation in income because "the amount of money that the consumer would be willing to pay to avoid a price change would be different than the amount of money that the consumer would have to be paid to compensate him for the price change"[3].

Critical Evaluation of the Concept of Consumer's Surplus

The concept of consumer's surplus has been severely criticised ever since Marshall propounded and developed it in his *Principles of Economics*. Critics have described it as quite imaginary, unreal and useless. Most of the criticisms of the concept has been levelled against the Marshallian method of measuring it as an area under the demand curve. However, some critics have challenged the validity of the concept itself. Marshallian concept of consumer's surplus has also been criticised on the ground of its being based upon unrealistic and questionable assumptions. We explain below the various criticisms levelled against this concept and will critically appraise them.

1. It has been pointed out by several economists that the concept of *consumer's surplus is quite hypothetical, imaginary and illusory*. They say that a consumer cannot afford to pay for a commodity more than his income. The maximum amount which a person can pay for a commodity or for a number of commodities is limited by the amount of his money income. And, as is well-known, a consumer wants a number of goods on which he has to spend his money. Total sum of money actually spent by him on the goods cannot be greater than his total money income. Thus what a person can be prepared to pay for a number of goods he purchases cannot be greater than the amount of his money income. Viewed in this light, there can be no question of consumer getting any consumer's surplus for his total purchases of the goods.

But, in our view, the above criticism misses the real point involved in the concept of consumer's surplus. The essence of the concept of consumer's surplus is that consumer gets excess psychic satisfaction from his purchases of the goods. It is true that with his limited money income, consumer cannot pay more than his total money income for his total purchases than that he actually pays. But nothing prevents him from feeling and thinking that he derives more satisfaction from the goods than the price he actually pays for them and if he had the means he would have paid much more for the goods than he actually pays for them.

2. Another criticism against consumer's surplus is that it is *based upon the invalid assumption that different units of the goods give different amount of satisfaction to the consumer*. We have explained above how Marshall calculated consumer's surplus derived by the consumer from a good. Consumer purchases the amount of a good at which marginal utility is equal to its price. It is assumed that marginal utility of a good diminishes as the consumer has more units of it. This means that while at the margin of the purchase, marginal utility of the good is equal to its price, for the previous intra-marginal units, marginal utility is higher than the price and, on these intra-marginal units, a consumer obtains consumer's surplus. Now, the critics point out that when a consumer takes more units of a commodity it is not only the utility of the marginal unit that declines but also all previous units of the commodity he has taken. Thus, as all units of a commodity are assumed alike, all would have the same utility. And when, at the margin, price is equal to the marginal utility of the last unit purchased, the price will also be equal to the utility of the previous units and consumer would, therefore, not get any consumer's surplus.

But this criticism is also not acceptable because even though all units of a commodity may be alike, they do not give same satisfaction to the consumer; as the consumer takes the first unit, he

3. Hal R. *Varian, Intermediate Microeconomics (New York, W.W. Norton & Company)* Second edition, 1990, p. 248
4. Hal R. Varian, *op. cit.*, p.249

derives more satisfaction from it and when he takes up the second unit, it does not give him as much satisfaction as the first one, because while taking the second unit, a part of his want has already been satisfied. Similarly, when he takes the third unit, it will not give him as much satisfaction as the previous two units, because now a part of his want has been satisfied. Similarly, when he takes the third unit, it will not give him as much satisfaction as the previous two units. If we accept the above criticism, we then deny the law of diminishing marginal utility. But diminishing marginal utility from a good describes the fundamental human tendency and has also been confirmed by observation of actual consumer's behaviour. The concept of consumer's surplus is derived from the law of diminishing marginal utility. If law of diminishing marginal utility is valid, the validity of the Marshallian concept of consumer's surplus cannot be challenged.

3. The concept of consumer's surplus has also been criticised on the ground that it *ignores the interdependence between the goods*, that is, the relations of substitute and complementary goods. Thus, it is pointed out that if only tea were available and no other substitute drinks such as milk, coffee, etc., were there, then the consumer would have been prepared to pay much more price for tea than that in the presence of substitute drinks. Thus, the magnitude of consumer's surplus derived from a commodity depends upon the availability of substitutes. This is because if only tea were available, consumer will have no choice and would be afraid that if he does not get tea, he cannot satisfy his given want by consuming any other commodity. Therefore, he will be willing to pay more for a cup of tea rather than go without it. But if substitutes of tea are available, he would not be prepared to pay as much price since he will think that if he is deprived of tea, he will take other substitute drinks like milk and coffee. Thus, it is said that consumer's surplus is not a definite, precise and unambiguous concept; it depends upon the availability of substitutes. The degree of substitutability between different goods is different for different consumers, and this makes the concept of consumer's surplus a little vague and ambiguous. Marshall was aware of this difficulty and, to overcome this, he suggested that for the purpose of measuring consumer's surplus, substitute products like tea and coffee be clubbed together and considered as one single commodity.

4. *Prof. Nicholson described the concept of consumer's surplus as hypothetical and imaginary.* He writes, "of what avail is it to say that the utility of an income of (say) £100 a year is worth (say) £1000 a year". According to Prof. Nicholson and other critics, it is difficult to say how much price a consumer would be willing to pay for a good rather than go without it. This is because consumer does not face this question in the market when he buys goods; he has to pay and accept the price that prevails in the market. It is very difficult for him to say how much he would be prepared to pay rather than go without it. However, in our view, this criticism only indicates that it is difficult to measure consumer's surplus precisely. That a consumer gets extra satisfaction from a good than the price he pays for it is undeniable.

Moreover, as J.R. Hicks has pointed out "*the best way of looking at consumer's surplus is to regard it as a means of expressing it in terms of money income gain which accrues to the consumer as a result of a fall in price.*"[2] When the price of a commodity falls, the money income of the consumer being given, the budget line will switch to the right and the consumer will be in equilibrium at a higher indifference curve and as a result his satisfaction will increase. Thus, consumer derives more satisfaction at a lower price than that at the higher original price of the good. This implies that fall in the price of a commodity, and, therefore, the availability of the commodity at a cheaper price adds to the satisfaction of the consumer and this is in fact the change in consumer's surplus brought about by change in the price of the good. Prof. J.R. Hicks has further extended the concept of consumer's surplus considering it from the viewpoint of gain which a consumer gets from a fall in price of a good.[3] Moreover, the concept of consumer's surplus is useful and meaningful and not unreal because it indicates that he gets certain extra satisfaction and advantages from the use of amenities available in modern towns and cities.

5. The concept of consumer's surplus has also been criticised on the ground that *it is based upon questionable assumptions of cardinal measurability of utility and constancy of the marginal*

utility of money. Critics point out that utility is a psychic entity and cannot be measured in quantitative cardinal terms. In view of this, they point out that consumer's surplus cannot be measured by the area under the demand curve, as Marshall did it. This is because Marshallian demand curve is based on the marginal utility curve in drawing which it is assumed that utility is cardinally measurable.

Further, as has been explained in earlier chapters, by assuming constant marginal utility of money, Marshall ignored income effect of the price change. Of course, income effect of the price change in case of most of the commodities is negligible and can be validly ignored. But in case of some important commodities such as foodgrains, income effect of the price change is quite significant and cannot be validly ignored. Therefore, the Marshallian method of measurement of consumer surplus as area under the demand curve, ignoring the income effect, is not perfectly correct. However, this does not invalidate the concept of consumer's surplus. As has been explained above, J.R. Hicks has been able to provide *a money measure of consumer's surplus* with his indifference curve technique of ordinal utility analysis which does not assume cardinal measurement of utility and constant marginal utility of money. Hicks has not only rehabilitated the concept of consumer's surplus but has also extended and developed it further.

Despite some of the shortcomings of the concept of consumer surplus, some of which are based on wrong interpretation of the concept of consumer surplus, it is of great significance not only in economic theory but also in the formulation of economic policies by the Government. The concept of consumer's surplus has a great practical importance in the formulation of economic policies by the Government. We explain below some important uses and applications of consumer surplus.

USES AND APPLICATIONS OF CONSUMER SURPLUS

The concept of consumer surplus has several applications both in economic theory and economic policy. This concept has been used to resolve water-diamond paradox of value theory, to explain the effects of taxes and subsidies on people's welfare, to make cost-benefit analysis of public projects, to show gains from trade etc. We will explain below some of the applications of the concept of consumer surplus.

Explaining Water-Diamond Paradox

One of the most famous puzzles in economic theory is why diamonds are more expensive than water. Water is essential for life; it is so useful that without its consumption one cannot live or survive. On the other hand, diamonds, though attractive and beautiful, satisfy less important human needs than water. Then, how it can be that in the market a less useful commodity like diamond is so expensive and a highly useful commodity as water is very cheap. Some thinkers in the past therefore complained that something was wrong with the market system which determines high price of commodities such as diamond, gold etc. which are least useful and low price of a commodity such as water which is necessary and highly useful. Therefore, this came to be known as water-diamond paradox. However, for modern economists there is no paradox about it as they are able to explain the large price differential between water and diamond.

The notion of marginal utility or marginal benefit of a commodity and the concepts of consumer surplus based on it, can be used to resolve the water-diamond paradox. The marginal benefit or marginal valuation per litre of water for the consumer is very low as the actual supply of water per period is very large. On the other hand, the marginal utility or marginal benefit of diamonds is very high because the amount of diamond actually available is very small. If, in fact, only a few litres of water were available marginal valuation of water would have been much greater than that of dia-

2. J.R. Hicks, *Value and Capital*, Oxford University Press, 2nd edition 1946, p. 40.
3. In the chapter on Indifference curve analysis we have explained the concept of Compensating Variation in Income and Equivalent Variation in Income. They are in fact measures of consumer surplus obtained by the consumer from a fall in price of a good.

monds. Note that *marginal valuation of a commodity reflects how much amount of money consumer is prepared to pay for a commodity*. This indicates marginal utility or use-value of the commodity for the consumer. It is worth noting that downward-sloping demand curve for a commodity can be interpreted as showing the marginal valuation or marginal utility in terms of money to the consumer of various units of a commodity. If the quantity actually available of a commodity in the market is very large, its marginal valuation or marginal utility will be very small, though its total use-value or total benefit may be very large. On the other hand, as the actually available quantity of a commodity such as diamonds, gold etc. is very small, its marginal valuation or marginal utility is very high, though its total value-in-use or total utility is small.

Market price of a commodity is determined not by its total use-value but by its marginal valuation or marginal utility which in turn depends on the actually available quantity. The total use-value or total utility which a consumer gets from a quantity of a commodity equals the amount actually paid and the consumer surplus he obtains from it. In case of water market price as determined by its marginal utility is very low but consumer surplus from it is very large. On the other hand, in case of diamond due to their greater scarcity, marginal utility and hence its price is very high but consumer surplus from it is very small. Thus, the concept of consumer's surplus shows that price should not be confused with total use-value of a commodity and this helps us to resolve the water-diamond paradox.

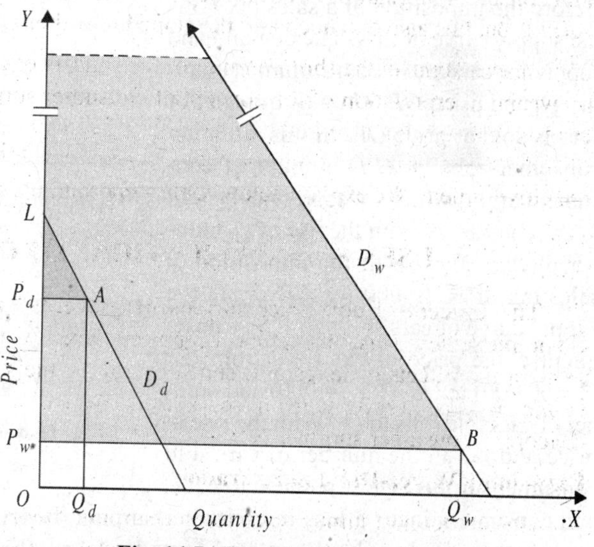

Fig. 14.7. *Water-Diamond Paradox*

This is illustrated in Fig. 14.7 where consumer's demand curve D_d depicts the marginal valuation curve for diamonds. On the X-axis quantity of diamonds in grams per time period and along the Y-axis marginal utility or valuation and price of diamonds are measured. Since the total use-value (*i.e.*, total utility) of diamonds is small, the demand curve is at a low level. Suppose the quantity of diamonds actually available is OQ_d and, as will be seen from the figure, price of diamond determined by demand and supply is P_d which is quite high, whereas the consumer surplus equal to LAP_d (shaded area) obtained by the consumers over and above what they actually pay is small.

Figure 14.7 also illustrates the price determination of water. Demand curve D_w representing marginal valuation or marginal utility of different quantities of water is at a higher level. If the quantity of water available is a very large quantity OQ_w, its marginal utility equals Q_wB and therefore price determined is OP_w. Though the market price of water is very low, consumer surplus obtained by the consumers will be the whole shaded area (not fully shown) above the price line P_wB which is very large compared with those of diamonds.

To sum up, the total utility or satisfaction derived from water consumed is much greater compared with diamonds but its marginal utility is low due to its abundant supply. The difference is large consumer surplus. On the other hand, whereas total utility (value in use) of diamonds is very small, due to its scarcity its marginal utility and therefore its price is relatively very high as compared with water. The difference is very small consumer surplus.

Evaluating Loss of Benefit from Tax

The notion of consumer surplus is applied for evaluating benefits and losses from certain economic policies. The losses and gains from taxes and subsidies to the consumers can be analysed using market demand curve and the concept of consumer's surplus. First, we explain the loss in consumer's surplus or welfare caused by the imposition of an indirect tax (say, sales tax) on cars. We assume that supply curve of cars is perfectly elastic, indicating constant-cost conditions under which the car industry is working. Under these conditions, imposition of a sales tax, say ₹ 10,000 per car sold would raise the price of car by exactly this amount, say from ₹ 2,60,000 to ₹ 2,70,000. The rise in price of car will result in fall in its quantity demanded and sold.

The loss in benefits incurred by the consumers as a result of the sales tax is illustrated in Fig. 14.8. The *DD* represents the demand curve for cars. This demand curve for cars can also be interpreted as marginal utility or marginal valuation curve of the cars for the consumers. Before the imposition of a sales tax *PS* is the supply curve of cars. The demand and supply for cars are in equilibrium at quantity Q_1 and price *OP*. Thus Q_1 quantity of cars is sold at price *OP*. In this situation consumers obtain *APD* amount of consumer surplus which measures net benefit to the consumers from the use of Q_1 number of cars. Now, with the imposition of sales tax of ₹ 10,000 (or $PP' = T$) the supply curve of cars shifts to *P'S'*. Consequently, the price of car rises from *OP* (₹ 2,60,000) to *OP'* (₹ 2,70,000) and number of cars sold falls to Q_2. With the rise in price and fall in the number of cars sold consumer surplus is now reduced to *BP'D*

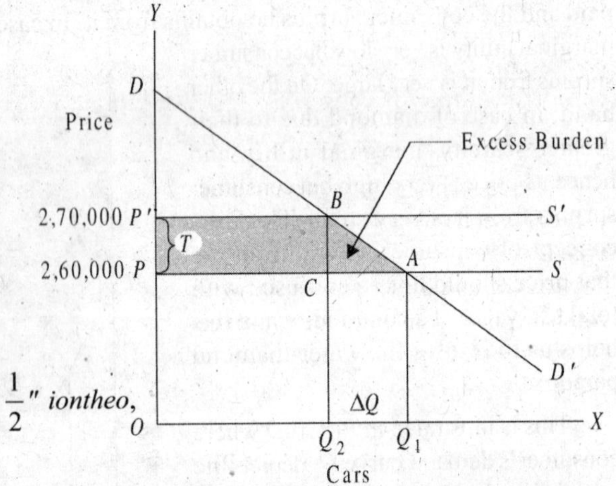

Fig. 14.8. *Evaluating Loss of Consumer Surplus from Sales Tax*

and consumers incur a loss in consumer surplus (benefit) equal to the area *APP'B*. This loss in consumer surplus can be decomposed into two parts. The first part is the rectangular area, *PP'BC* which is equal to the tax (*T*) multiplied by the reduced number of cars Q_2, ($PP'BC = T.Q_2$) and arises due to the increased expenditure on Q_2 number of cars consequent to the imposition of the sales tax. The area *PP'BC* or $Q_2 \cdot T$ also represents the revenue collected by the Government from levying sales tax. The second component of loss in consumer's surplus is the triangular area *ABC* which measures the loss in consumer surplus on account of the decrease in number of cars sold, that is, ΔQ or Q_1Q_2 as a result of levying of sales tax. In this way, the total loss in consumer surplus is $PP'BA = PP'BC + ABC$. Where *PP'BC* is also equal to tax per car (*i.e.*, *T*) multiplied by the reduced numbers of cars sold (*i.e.*, Q_2), that is, $T.Q_2$ and the triangular area *ABC* which equals $1/2\ T.\Delta Q$. Thus, loss in consumer surplus $(PP'BA) = T.Q_2 + 1/2\ T.\Delta Q$.

It is worth noting that the loss in consumer surplus *PP'BA* is greater than the revenue collected by the Government which is equal to the area *PP'BC* and this extra loss in consumer surplus is equal to the triangular area *ABC*. This area *ABC* represents the *excess burden of sales taxation*. The net loss in welfare or consumer surplus in excess of tax revenue received by the Government *is also called dead weight loss*. If instead of sales tax, a lump-sum tax of an equal amount were levied, there would have been no excess burden. Thus, sales tax distorts the price of cars, reduces the number of cars sold and thereby results in loss in consumer welfare in excess of the amount of tax collected. Therefore, ***economists dub indirect taxes such as sales tax or excise duty as economically inefficient.***

Thus, it follows that the burden of indirect tax (such as sales tax or excise duty) is greater than the direct tax such as lump-sum tax or income tax. Therefore, many economists hold that from the viewpoint of social welfare or optimum allocation of resources, the direct taxes such as a lump-sum tax or income tax is superior to an indirect tax such as sales tax or excise duty. Let us show and illustrate it with the help of Fig. 14.8 *which represents the case of constant cost industry*. With the given demand and supply curves *DD'* and *PS* respectively price *OP* and equilibrium quantity OQ_1 are determined. This is the position before the imposition of any tax and represents the maximum satisfaction or welfare of the people. Now, if the sales tax equal to *PP'* per unit of the commodity is imposed, the supply curve will shift upward to the position *P'S'* . As a result, the price will rise to *OP'* and the quantity demanded and sold will fall to Q_2. As explained above, tax collected by the Government in this case will be equal to *PP'BC*, but the loss in consumer's surplus suffered by the consumer will be equal to *PP'BA*. Now, if the Government takes away the sum equal to *PP'BC* through a direct tax, say lump sum tax or income tax, then the people would not have to suffer the loss equal to the area *ABC*. This is so because whereas ***an indirect tax distorts the price of a commodity* (*i.e.* it raises the price), *a lump-sum or income does not affect the price.*** Thus, it is clear that a direct tax causes less loss of welfare than a price-distorting indirect tax.

Evaluating Gain from a Subsidy

The concept of consumer surplus can be used to evaluate the gain from subsidies. The Government these days provide subsidies on many commodities such as foodgrains, fertilizers, power. Let us take the example of subsidy on foodgrains production being given by the Government. Suppose the subsidy reduces the price of foodgrains from ₹ 400 to ₹ 300 per quintal. As a result of the fall in price of foodgrains due to subsidy being provided for its production, the quantity demanded of foodgrains increases from 10 thousand quintals (Q_1) to 12 thousand quintals (Q_2). Now, the question to be answered is what will be net social benefit or gain from this subsidy. Consider Fig. 14.9 where *DD* is the demand curve for foodgrains which, as explained above, can also be interpreted as *marginal utility (or marginal valuation)* curve. To begin with, *PS* is the supply curve, assuming constant cost conditions. Price determined is *OP* or ₹ 400 per quintal. With the grant of subsidy equal to ₹ 100 per quintal, supply curve shifts below to P_1S_1 and as a result price falls to OP_1 or ₹ 300 per quintal. With the reduction in price to OP_1 (*i.e.*, ₹ 300 per quintal) quantity demanded increases to from OQ_1 to OQ_2. It will be seen from Fig. 14.9 that the total gain in consumer surplus is equal to the area $PACP_1$ which can be divided into two parts, namely, the area $PABP_1$ ($= R.Q_1$) where *R* is the subsidy per quintal of foodgrains plus triangle *ABC*, which equals 1/2 $R.\Delta Q$. Thus, the gain in consumer surplus $= R.Q_1 + \frac{1}{2} R.\Delta Q$. where $R.Q_1$ represents the reduction in expenditure on the quantity Q_1 that would have cost ₹ *R* (= ₹ 100) per quintal more without subsidy. Thus $R.Q_1$ represents the benefit or gain in consumer surplus to those who were purchasing foodgrains before the grant of subsidy but would now do so at a lower price. The amount 1/2 $R.\Delta Q$ represents the gain in consumer surplus due to the increase in quantity demanded at a lower price made possible by the grant of subsidy. Thus, the total gain in consumer surplus is the area $PACP_1$ which equals $R.Q_1 + 1/2\ R.\Delta Q$.

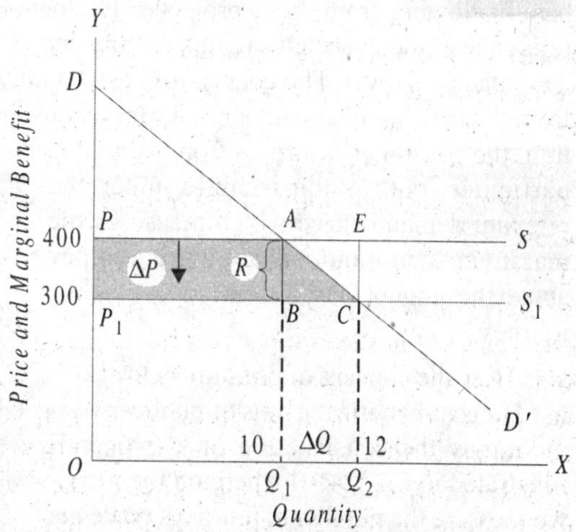

Fig. 14.9. *Gain from a Price Subsidy*

But the cost of subsidy to the Government is $R.Q_2$ or the area P_1PEC which is greater than the gain in consumer surplus by the area of the triangle ACE. Thus, if the buyers would have been given the lump-sum grant equal to the area $PACP_1$ they would have been as well off as in case of subsidy which costs more to the Government. Thus, *subsidy causes excess burden equal to the area of triangle ACE as compared to the lump sum grant.*

Use of Consumer Surplus in Cost-Benefit Analysis

An important application of consumer surplus is its use in cost-benefit analysis, especially of public investment projects. In fact, Dupuit, the originator of the idea of consumer surplus in his paper. "*On the Measurement of Public Works*" in 1844 used the concept of consumer surplus for describing the impact of public investment projects on social welfare. In recent years Prof. E.J. Mishan has based his cost-benefit analysis on consumer surplus approach. Consumer's surplus has been treated as benefits in various cost-benefits analysis of investment projects. The cost-benefit analysis has become very popular these days to judge the desirability of public investment in particular projects. It should be noted that *costs and benefits in cost-benefit analysis do not merely mean money costs and money benefits but real costs and real benefits in terms of satisfaction and resources.* Further, cost-benefit analysis looks at costs and benefits from social point of view; it is concerned with social benefits and social costs. The amount of consumer's surplus expected to be derived from certain projects such as a bridge, road, park, dam etc. are considered as an important benefit flowing from these projects.[4] The benefit of a new motor way or flyover is estimated by reference to the expected savings of time and cost of fuel by all motorists who will make use of the new road or flyover. The concept of cost-saving however, as we shall see below, is derived directly from the concept of consumer's surplus. Thus, prior to the introduction of the new flyover in question, the consumer's surplus from using this particular route is the triangle under the relevant demand curve which measures the maximum sum motorists are willing to pay above the amount they currently spend on the journey.[5]

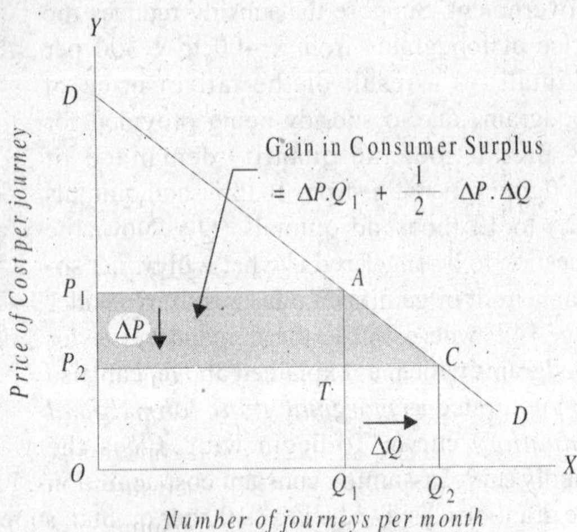

Fig. 14.10. *Use of Consumer Surplus in Cost-Benefit Analysis of the Construction of a Flyover*

How the concept of consumer surplus is used in cost-benefit analysis of public investment, say the construction of a flyover is illustrated in Fig. 14.10 where on the X-axis we measure the number of journeys made per month on a particular route where flyover is proposed to be undertaken and on the Y-axis we measure the price or cost per journey. DD is the demand curve for the journey on that route which, as explained above, shows the maximum price the motorists are willing to pay for making journeys on that route. If the current price or cost per journey, that is, prior to the construction of flyover is OP_1, the motorists make OQ_1 number of journeys on that route and pay $OP_1 . OQ_1$ as the total cost for the OQ_1 journeys made. It will be seen from the demand curve that the *total amount of money that the motorists will be willing to pay for OQ_1 journeys equals the area $ODAQ_1$* and thus the triangle P_1DA represents the consumer surplus they derive from making OQ_1 journeys. Now suppose the flyover is constructed which by reducing their fuel consumption reduces the cost per journey to OP_2. At the lower price or

4. See E.J. Mishan, *Cost-Benefit Analysis: An Informal Introduction*, George Allen & Unwin Ltd.
5. E.J. Mishan, *op. cit.*, p. 33.

cost per journey, they will make OQ_2 number of journeys and their consumer surplus will increase by the shaded area P_1ACP_2. This is the benefit the motorists receive from the construction of flyover.

This increase in consumer surplus can be divided into two parts. First, we have the cost-saving component equal to the rectangular area P_1P_2TA which is calculated as the saving per journey multiplied by the original number of journeys OQ_1. The other part of the increase in consumer surplus is represented by the area of the triangle ATC which is the gain in consumer's surplus obtained from the additional journeys made by the same motorists or the new ones. It is worth noting that it is the cost-saving segment of the increment in consumer surplus that often enters into the cost-benefit calculations of the investment projects. But, as we have just seen, this cost-saving is the main component of the addition to the consumer surplus due to fall in the cost per journey brought about by the construction of the flyover.

We have seen above that the concept of consumer's surplus in the context of an individual and in the context of a particular good is a meaningful and useful concept. However, it is worth noting here that the use of the concept of consumer's surplus as a tool for formulation of policies such as choice of investment projects based on cost-benefit calculation, requires the summation of con-sumer's surpluses derived from a good or project by various consumers belonging to different income groups. Such summation and comparison of consumer's surplus of different individuals can be validly made if one rupee worth of consumer's surplus means the same thing to different individuals. However, this is based on the assumption that marginal utility of money is the same for all individuals regardless of the size of their income. This lands us into interpersonal comparison of the utility which is not regarded as scientific and justified by many economists.

QUESTIONS FOR REVIEW

1. Define consumer surplus show *h* one would you measure it on a consumer demand curve for a commodity.
2. What is value paradox ? Using demand curves for water and diamonds and their associated price explain how you will resolve the paradox using the concept of consumer's surplus. *D.U. B.A. (Hons) 1999.*
3. Explain the concept of consumer surplus. How did Marshall measure it ?
4. How is consumer's surplus measured with the help of indifference curves ? Under what conditions consumer surplus as measured by the area under the demand curve is exactly equal to that measured by indifference curves. *I.A.S. (Main Examination 1996)*
5. Using the concept of consumer surplus show that indirect tax, that is, excise duty or sales tax, causes excess burden on the consumer as compared to a direct tax.
6. Using the concept of consumer surplus show that a consumer will prefer the subsidy in cash rather than a price subsidy on a commodity.
7. Explain the use of consumer surplus in cost-benefit analysis of projects.
8. With the help of consumer surplus show that social welfare will be increased by imposing a tax on the product of an increasing cost industry and revenue so collected be used for subsidising the product of a decreasing cost industry.
9. Consumer's surplus is hypothetical having no practical importance. Examine critically.
10. Explain compensating variation in income and Equivalent Variation in income. How change in welfare in money terms as a result of a price change is measured through them.

PART - III

THE THEORY OF PRODUCTION AND COST

- Factors of Production
- The Theory of Production : Returns to a Factor
- Production Function with Two Variable Factors
- Optimum Factor Combination
- Cost of Production and Cost Curves

CHAPTER 15
FACTORS OF PRODUCTION

Factors of Production: Meaning

Production of goods and services requires the use of factors of production which are also called agents of production. Volume of production and therefore national income depends upon the supply of various factors of production and their productivity. Since economic growth consists in expansion in total production or national income, the supply and productivity of the factors are vital to the process of economic growth.

But, what do we exactly mean by a factor of production. Fraser defines "factor of production as a group or class of productive sources".[1] More explicitly, the term 'factor' of production is used for a class of productive elements, the individual members of which are known as '*units*' of the factor and all units of a factor are homogeneous and interchangeable. Technically speaking, all units of a factor are perfect substitutes of one another. This also implies that two different factors of production cannot be perfect substitutes of each other.

It may also be noted that modern economists prefer to talk in terms of *productive services* or more recently of merely *inputs* rather than the conventional factors of production such as land, labour, capital and entreprepreneur. Thus, the goods or services which are used for the production of goods are called inputs and what they produce are called outputs. This *input-output analysis* has become an important tool of modern economic analysis.

Classification of Factors of Production

As mentioned above, factors of production have been classified as *land, labour, capital and organisation* (*or entrepreneurship*). Land in economics does not mean mere soil. Land in economics is synonymous with all natural resources available from air, water, from above the land surface and below it which can be used for production. Likewise, labour does not mean merely physical exertion, but all types of work, physical or mental, done by man for a monetary reward. By capital is meant the whole of the stock of wealth consisting of machines, tools, implements, raw materials etc. which is used for the production of further goods. Organisation or entrepreneurship consists in bringing the above three factors together, assigning work to each and bearing the risk and uncertainty of production. The entrepreneur who supplies this factor, initiates and directs production and bears risk and uncertainty.

Some economists have classified factors into two categories, land and labour (or nature and man) on the ground that they are the only *original or primary factors*. It is said that capital has no independent origin and is merely the outcome of combined efforts of land and labour, while organisation or enterprise is merely a special form of labour. But, whatever the origin, being man - made instrument of production, capital is capable of being expanded while the supply of land as a whole is fixed. This has made capital an important factor of production as a separate and distinct factor from land. Similarly, the entrepreneur's work is of a distinct type from that of labour and he is remunerated on a different basis. Thus, the four-fold classification of factors into land, labour, capital and enterprise is being followed even today.

1. L. M. Fraser, *Economic Thought and Language,* 1947, Ch.12.

LAND

Meaning and Significance

The term 'land' has been given a special meaning in economics. It does not mean soil, as in the ordinary speech, but it is used in a much wider sense. In the words of Marshall, land means "the materials and the forces which nature gives freely for man's aid, in land and water, in air and light and heat."[2] Land stands for all natural resources which yield an income or which have exchange value. "It represents those natural resources which are useful and scarce, actually or potentially."[3]

In every stage of economic evolution, nature has been man's most useful ally. In the hunting and the fishing stage, nature supplied food freely and sustained human life. In the pastoral stage, but for land surface and the pastures and meadows, herds of cattle and sheep could not have been reared and kept. The utility of land is obvious in the agricultural stage for how else could man grow his crops without soil, air and sunshine? When the agricultural stage has given place to the industrial stage, land still remains essential. Land is the chief agent in the production of wage goods, such as foodgrains, cloth and sugar. Every commodity that we use can, directly or indirectly, be traced ultimately to land. Look in whatever direction we may, our debt to nature is deep and obvious. Our very existence would be impossible without it. In Marshall's worlds. "Earth's surface is a primary condition of anything that a man can do, it gives him room for his action.[4]

The quantity and quality of natural resources (including agricultural land) plays a vital role in the economic development of a country. Important natural resources are those of agricultural land, minerals and oil resources, water, forests, climate, etc. The quantity of natural resources available in a country puts a limit on the level of output of goods which can be attained. Without a minimum of natural resources there is not much hope for economic development. It should, however, be noted that resource availability is not a sufficient condition for economic growth. For instance, India, though sufficiently rich in natural resources, has remained poor and under-developed. This is because resources have not been fully utilised for productive purposes. Thus, it is not only the availability of natural resources but also the ability to use them for production, which determines growth of an economy.

Supplies of natural resources can be increased as a result of new discoveries of resources in a country and technological changes which facilitate new discovery or transform certain previously useless materials into highly useful ones. It should also be noted that the scarcity of certain natural resources can be overcome by synthetic substitutes. For example, the synthetic rubber is being increasingly used in place of natural rubber in advanced countries. Further, nylon which is a synthetic commodity is being largely used in place of silk which is a natural commodity.

The use of natural resources and the role they play in the process of economic growth depends, among other things, on the type of technology. One does not have to go back very far in history to find that an item currently as valuable as petroleum was of little or no significance. In many developing economies there are deposits of many minerals which are not being used because of technological deficiencies, Thus, natural resources are in themselves passive in their influence on economic growth. They remain dormant and largely unknown till such time as the change in technology reveals their use-value. They acquire a dynamic character largely through changes in technology introduced by man.

Land as a Renewable and Non-Renewable Resource

Natural resources are often divided into two categories – (*a*) the exhaustible resources or nonrenewable resources, (*b*) the renewable resources. *The exhaustible resources are those natural*

2. Marshall,
3. L. M. Fraser, *Ibid* p. 222.
4. Alfred Marshall, *Principles of Economics,* Eighth Edition, p.138.

resources which when used once cannot be renewed. Natural resources such as mineral deposits of iron ore, copper, deposits of coal and petroleum get depleted as they are used by the economy. Their stocks are limited and cannot be renewed, that is, their stocks cannot be increased. According to the data available with the Planning Commission if we assume roughly an annual average growth rate in exploitation of say about 6% to 7%, cooking-coal reserves will be exhausted by about 2150 A.D., iron ore by' about 2050 A.D., manganese ore and chromite by about 2000 A.D. and bauxite by about 2033 A.D.[5] It may, however, be noted that all potential stock of these non-renewable resources may not be known at a given time and therefore their supply may increase through new discoveries as has happened in India where deposits of mineral oil and gas have been discovered at several places in the last few years.

On the other hand, *renewable resources are those which go on being used again and again and year after year for production.* Thus, agricultural land which is a very important natural resource can be cultivated again and again for production of foodgrains and other crops without much loss of productivity. Moreover, not only the productivity of land can be maintained but it can be significantly improved by human efforts. Thus, land in the sense of agricultural soil is renewable resource. Water resources, fisheries and forest resources are other examples of renewable resources: If some part of the forest resources are used, they can be replanted and their stock can be increased in the long run.

It is clear from above that land in its wider meaning which includes all natural resources is in part renewable and in part non-renewable. Agricultural land, water resources, forest resources, etc. are renewable but mineral and power resources such as deposits of iron ore, coal, petroleum, etc., are non-renewable resources.

Inelastic Supply of Land

An important characteristic of land is that it is fixed in supply. Land is a free gift from nature and its quantity is fixed by nature. Therefore, more land cannot be produced in response to greater demand for it. Whatever the rent, high or low, for the use of land its supply to the economy as a whole remains unchanged. In other words, the supply of land to the entire economy is not dependent on the price *i.e.*, rent for its use. Hence, from the standpoint of the whole economy, the supply of land (which includes natural resources) is *perfectly inelastic.* Since supply of land is a free gift from nature and not a produced factor, cost of production has no relevance for supply. For the society as a whole, land has got no cost of production, since society did not produce it; it got it free from nature.

But the supply of land to a *single use or a particular* industry is not perfectly inelastic. The supply of land to a particular use or industry can be increased by the shifting of land from other uses or industries. By offering attractive rents, the supply of land for a particular use can be taken away from other competitive uses. Therefore, *the supply curve of land to a particular use or industry is elastic and slopes upward from left to right.*

CAPITAL : PHYSICAL AND HUMAN

Meaning of Capital

The term capital is used in economics in various senses. In ordinary language and sometimes in economics also capital is used in the sense of money. But when we talk of capital as a factor of production, to confuse capital with money is quite wrong. Of course, money is used to purchase various factors such as raw materials, machinery, labour which help to produce goods, but money *itself* does not directly help in the production of goods. The money which is available for investment and productive purposes has been called *money capital or financial capital* by some economists. But money capital is not the real capital. The real capital consists of machinery, tools, tubewell,

---

5. See Planning Commission, *Revised Fifth Plan*, Chapter 2, pp. 11-12.

factories; tractors, etc., which *directly* assist in the production of goods. Similarly, government securities and bonds, shares and debentures of public limited companies do not represent real capital. Securities, bonds, stocks, etc., possessed by individuals yield income to them but they cannot be called real capital because they represent only titles of ownership rather than factors of production.

Capital has been rightly defined as "*produced means of production*". This definition distinguishes capital from both land and labour because both land and labour are not produced factors. Land and labour are often considered as *primary or original factors of production*. But capital is not a primary or original factor; it is a produced factor of production. Capital has been produced by man by working with nature. Therefore, capital may well be defined as *man-made instrument of production*. Capital thus consists of those physical goods which are produced for use in future production. Machines, tools and instruments, factories, canals, dams, transport equipment, stocks of raw materials are some of the examples of capital. All of them are produced by man to help in the production of further goods. According to Prof. Richard T. Gill, "*A country's capital is its stock of produced or man-made means of production, consisting of such items as buildings, factories, machinery, tools, equipment and inventories of goods in stock.*"[6]

Fixed Capital and Working Capital

Capital may be classified into fixed capital and working capital. *Fixed Capital* are durable-use producer goods which are used in production again and again till they wear out. Machinery, tools, railways tractors, factories *etc*., are all fixed capital. Fixed capital does not mean fixed in location. Capital like plant, tractors, and factories are called fixed because money spent upon these durable goods, remains fixed or unrealised for a long period in contrast with the money spent on purchasing raw materials which is recovered as soon as goods made with them are sold. *Working Capital*, on the other hand, are the single-use producers' goods like raw materials, fertilizers, goods in process and fuel. They are used up in a single act of production. Moreover, money spent on them is fully recovered when goods made with them are sold in th› market.

Human Capital

We have explained above the concept of *physical capital*. For a long time in economics, it was thought that it was the physical capital which played a crucial role in expanding production. In recent years, a new concept of '*human capital*' has been evolved and emphasised. *By human capital is meant the stock of people equipped with education, skills, health*, etc. It has now been found that the rate of growth achieved in the developed countries cannot be wholly explained by the increases in physical capital and advances in technology. A good part of economic growth has occurred due to the accumulation of human capital. It has now been realised that human capital formation is as important in increasing production and productivity as the physical capital formation. An educated, trained and skilled man is much more productive than an uneducated, untrained, and unskilled. Likewise, a person with good health contributes to production to a greater degree than the person with frail and poor health. Since investment in education, skill and health adds greatly to the productivity of men, investment in human capital has also been called *investment in men*, or *investment in human beings*. One of the major tasks confronting the developing countries is the building of human capital. There is a growing realisation that a rapid rate of 'human capital formation' is as important a pre-condition of economic growth as the rapid rate of 'physical capital formation'.

ROLE OF CAPITAL

Capital plays a vital role in the modern productive system. Production without capital is hard for us even to imagine. Nature cannot furnish goods and materials to man unless he has the tools and

6. Richard Gill "*Economic Development: Past and Present*," Third Edition; 1975, Prentice-Hall of India Private Limited, p. 14.

machinery for mining, farming, forestry, fishing, etc. If man has to work with his hands on barren soil, productivity would be very low indeed. Even in the primitive stage, man used some tools and implements to assist him in the work of production. Primitive man made use of elementary tools like bow and arrow for hunting and fishing net for catching fishes. With the growth of technology and specialisation, capital has become more complex and is of superior and advanced type. More goods can be produced with the aid of capital. In fact, greater productivity of the modern economy like that of U.S.A. is mainly due to the extensive use of capital, *i.e.* machinery, tools or implements in the production process. Capital adds greatly to the productivity of workers and hence of the economy as a whole. Because of its strategic role in raising productivity, capital occupies a central position in the process of economic development. In fact, capital accumulation is the very core of economic development.

Capital goods are man-made instruments of production and increase the *productive capacity* of the economy. Therefore, accumulation of capital goods every year greatly increases the national product or income. Capital accumulation is necessary to provide people with tools and implements of production. If the population goes on increasing and no net capital accumulation takes place, then the growing population would not be able to get necessary tools, instruments, machines and other means of production with the result that their capacity to produce would be seriously affected.

Thus, capital accumulation makes possible the use of *indirect or roundabout methods of production* which greatly increase the productivity of the workers. Under these indirect or roundabout methods of production, workers instead of working with bare hands, work with the aid of more productive tools, instruments and machinery. Under these indirect or roundabout methods some labourers and other productive resources are first employed in producing capital goods and then with the help of these capital goods workers produce consumer goods. The greater the extent to which the methods, of production would be indirect or roundabout, the greater their productivity and efficiency. But, as we have seen above, for the use of indirect or roundabout methods of production capital has to be accumulated. Therefore, we see that capital accumulation makes the use of indirect or roundabout methods of production possible and thereby greatly increases the national product and is helpful in bringing about rapid economic growth. Moreover, productivity of the workers depends upon the amount of capital per worker. The greater the quantity of capital per worker, the greater the productivity and efficiency of the worker.

From the viewpoint of economic growth capital formation is important also because it make large scale production and greater degree of specialisation possible. Thus, with capital accumulation the *advantages of large-scale production and specialisation* are obtained. The advantage of large-scale production and specialisation is that they greatly increase output and productivity and thereby bring down the *cost of production per unit.* Without adequate capital accumulation neither the scale of production can be increased nor greater specialisation and division of labour in the production process is possible. Hence, capital accumulation by increasing the scale of production and specialisation increases the production and productivity in the economy and thereby promotes economic growth.

Another contribution of capital accumulation is that it makes the *technological progress of the economy* possible. Different technologies need different types of capital goods. Therefore, when new, superior and better technology is discovered, its use can be made for production only if that technology is embodied in new capital goods, that is, if capital goods according to that technology are made. Therefore, without capital accumulation, not much technical progress can be made. If there is no capital accumulation, then the various new inventions or discoveries will remain unused for production. It is therefore, clear that capital accumulation promotes technical progress and thereby accelerates the economic growth of the country.

Another important economic role of capital formation is the *creation of employment opportuni-*

ties in the country. Capital formation creates employment at two stages. First, when the capital is produced, some workers have to be employed to make capital like machinery, factories, dams, irrigation works, etc. Secondly, more men have to be employed when capital has to be used for producing further goods. In other words, many workers have to be engaged to produce goods with the help of machines, factories etc. Thus, one sees that employment will increase as capital formation is stepped up in the economy. Now. if the population grows faster than the increase in the stock of capital the entire addition to the labour force cannot be absorbed in productive employment because not enough instruments of production will be there to employ them. This results in unemployment. The rate of capital formation must be kept sufficiently high so that employment opportunities are enlarged to absorb the additions to the working force of the country as a result of population growth. In India the stock of capital has not been growing at a fast enough rate so as to keep pace with the growth of population. That is why there is huge unemployment and underemployment in both the urban and rural areas. The fundamental solution to this problem of unemployment and under-employment is to speed up the rate of capital formation so as to enlarge employment opportunities.

HUMAN CAPITAL, EDUCATION AND ECONOMIC GROWTH

Gross domestic product of a country depends on not only the amount of labour (i.e. work-hours) used for producing goods and services but also on its productivity. One of the important factors that determines productivity of worker is human capital, that is, education. As seen above, in the modern economics the concept of capital is not confined to physical capital such as machines, tractors, capital equipment etc. that raises productivity of labour but also includes what is called human capital. *By human capital we mean the skills and knowledge that workers acquire through education and training*. This human capital, that is, knowledge and skills, are accumulated by human beings through education during the time they spend in primary and secondary schools and upto graduation and post graduation in college or universities. Besides, specialised professional education such as engineering, computer training, management education and others raises greatly the productivity of workers. Therefore, accumulation of human capital is generally called *investment in people*.

Human capital though less tangible than physical capital, is similar to it in many ways. First, like physical capital, accumulation of human capital increases the ability of a country to produce more goods and services. Second, like physical capital, human capital is a produced factor of production. Producing human capital requires investment in inputs such as student time, teachers, books and libraries, college buildings. Thirdly, like the physical capital, the accumulation of human capital increases the productivity of workers and therefore causes their wages to rise. Fourthly, like the accumulation of physical capital, the accumulation of human capital requires the sacrifice of some present consumption so as to have more consumption in future.

Cost of Human Capital : Human capital is built through acquiring more education by spending more time in school, college or university. Thus, in spending more time in acquiring more education, one not only delays one's entry into labour force but also sacrifices income or wages which he could have earned by working during the time he spends for acquiring education. This is the *opportunity cost* of acquiring more education, skills and grades (*i.e.* accumulating more human capital). But they spend time in acquiring more human capital with the expectation that they would be able to earn higher income, or wages in the future as more education and higher skills raises the productivity of the workers and therefore their wages. Thus, the students, like the people who save, face a trade-off between less consumption today for more consumption in the future.

Thus, "spending more on education today (reducing consumption) raises future income but each additional investment in education provides a smaller and smaller return"[7]. It follows from

7. Joseph, E. Stiglitz, *and C.E. Walsh Principles of Economics*, W.W. Norton & Co. New York 1997, p.170

above that, like physical capital, expenditure on education also represents investment in capital which raises productivity in the future. Besides, investment in education is tied to specific human being and therefore it is called human capital. Thus, according to Mankiw, "*Like all forms of capital, education represents an expenditure of resources at one point in time to raise productivity in the future. But unlike an investment in other forms of capital investment in education is tied to a specific person and this linkage is what makes it human capital*"[8]. It is important to note that workers endowed with higher education (*i.e.* more human capital) earns more income or wages than those having less education. The differences in wages between those with more education and those with less education are quite large and has been increasing. For example "College graduates in the United States earn about twice as much as those workers who end their education with a high school diploma"[9] It may be noted that this difference in earnings between workers with more human capital and those with less human capital on an average tends to be even larger in developing countries where educated workers are in scarce supply.[10]

Human Capital and Sources of Economic Growth

The supply of human capital plays a crucial role in promoting economic growth. In an important study Edward F. Denison[11] has measured the relative importance of various sources of economic growth in the United States for the 50 years period, 1929-69.

Table 1 : Sources of US Economic Growth

Percent of Growth Rate

Source	*1929-1969*	*1948-1969*
Advances in knowledge	31.1	34.1
More work done	28.7	23.9
Capital accumulation	15.8	21.6
Increased education	14.1	11.9
Others	10.3	8.5
Total	100	100

Rate of economic growth in the US economy was on an average 3.3 percent during the 50 years period (1929-69) of the study. It will be seen from Table-I that the most important source of economic growth (31.1 to 34 per cent) was *advances in knowledge* (which includes improvement in technological knowledge) that takes place as a result of increase in education and in research and development activity. The next important source of economic growth was increase in labour force (*i.e.* more work done) as measured by increase in hours worked by labour which contributed about 28 per cent during the 50 years period of study. Contrary to expectations of economists, accumulation of physical capital contributed only 15.8 per cent during the entire period (1929-69) and 21.6 per cent during 1948-69 to the growth in GDP. For the entire 50 years period of study (1929-69) increase in eduction (*i.e. number of years spent in* schools, colleges and universities) contributed almost the same as accumulation of physical capital (14.1 percent as against 15.8 per cent of physical capital. However, if we club the contribution of increased education and advances in knowledge their contribution is as high as about 45 percent to growth.

8. N. Gregory Mankiw, *Principles of Economics*, Thomson, 2nd edition, 2001, p. 419
9. Mankiw op. cit., p.419
10. See, Stiglitz, op. cit. p. 171. and Mankiw, op. cit. pp. 419-420.
11. Edward, E. Denison, *Accounting for US Economic Growth, 1929-1965* (Wshington D.C. Brookings Institution, 1974.

Other sources include the *efficient use of available resources, economies of scale,* a shift of labour force from low-productivity agricultural sector to higher productivity industrial sector which contributed about 10 per cent to growth in GDP. It may however be noted that Denison could not measure directly the contribution of advances in knowledge. He measured the contributions of other four sources of growth, namely, more labour work, accumulation of physical capital accumulation, increased education, and others (as mentioned above) and assumed that all economic growth that could not be explained by other sources was the contribution of advances in knowledge.

LABOUR

The contribution of labour to the national product and income depends not only on the size of labour force but also on its quality. By quality of labour we mean how much productive it is, that is, what is its level of productivity. A given labour force with higher productivity will yield a larger national product and income. Therefore, in this chapter we shall discuss the factors on which productivity or efficiency of labour depends. An important factor determining efficiency of labour force is the division of labour.

Whereas land and capital are material factors of production, labour is a human factor. Because of this, labour should not be treated as a saleable commodity like land and capital. Labour exhibits the following characteristics :

1. *Labour cannot be separated from the labourer himself*, whereas land and capital are distinct from their owners *i.e.,* landlords and capitalists.
2. *The labourer does not sell himself; he sells only his labour.* It was only when the slavery system prevailed that labourers were sold and purchased. But in modern times workers sell only their labour in return for wages but not their persons as such.
3. *Labour is a perishable factor* and it is not possible to store it for future use. If a worker does not get employment for some days, then the time so lost cannot be recovered. The labour time lost once is lost for ever.
4. *Labour lacks mobility.* It is less mobile than even capital. This is because labourer is a human being with all his feelings of affection and attachment with the place he is presently residing and with the friends and relatives who live there. It is difficult for him to leave them and shift from one place to another. However, despite this, some workers do migrate from one part of a country to another or even from one country to another in search of their livelihood.
5. *Supply of labour is elastic* but it takes time to increase its overall supply by expanding population and providing them suitable training and skills required.
6. *Efficiency of labour varies a good deal.* Some workers are more efficient than others. The differences in efficiency are caused by their physical and mental capabilities as well as by training and skill imparted to them. Their productivity differs also because of different quantity and quality of capital equipment used by them and different technologies with which they work.

The contribution of labour to the national product and income depends not only on the size of labour force but also on its quality. By quality of labour we mean how much productive it is, that is, what is its level of productivity. A given labour force with higher productivity will yield a larger national product and income. Therefore, an important factor determining efficiency of labour force is the division of labour. We, therefore, start our study of the qualitative aspect of labour force with the discussion of division of labour.

Division of labour

Division of labour is an important feature of modern industrial organisation. Division of labour occupies so important a place in the modern production process and adds so greatly to the total output and wealth of a country that Adam Smith, the father of economics, selected it as the first topic for discussion in his book. "*An Enquiry into the Nature and Causes of Wealth of Nations*."

Division of labour may be simple or complex. Simple division of labour refers to the *production of a single commodity by a person*. In a society where simple division of labour prevails every worker would be producing only one commodity. Some would be producing cloth, some will be making shoes, some others will be producing farm products but every body would be producing either farm products or cloth or shoes. In the old village societies there prevailed this simple division of labour and, therefore, the old village society composed of farmers who produced agricultural goods, weavers who made cloth, cobblers who made and repaired shoes, etc.

But, in the modern days, division of labour is of complex type. In fact, it is the complex division of labour which has increased so greatly the productivity of the modern productive system. *Complex division of labour means that the making of an article is split up into several processes and each process is carried out by a separate worker or a separate group of workers*. Thus, complex division of labour refers to the specialisation in one operation or process. Every group of workers specialises only in one process in the production of a commodity. The process may be split up into sub-processes and thus division of labour may become more complex. In the modern tailoring shops, making of a shirt is broken up into different processes. Some workers only do the job of "cutting", some others only do the work of "sewing", and still a separate group of workers puts buttons on it, etc. This is complex division of labour in the making of shirts.

Several advantages are claimed for the system of division of labour. The system of division of labour has proved to be of immense benefit to society.

Advantages of Division of Labour

1. Increase in Productivity. The greatest advantage of division of labour is that it increases immensely the productivity per worker. This point can be illustrated by the famous example of pin making given by Adam Smith. The process of pin making is divided into 18 distinct operations. Ten men make 48,000 pins in a day. One worker may, therefore, be considered to have made 4,800 pins in a day. In the absence of division of labour one man could have made only one pin in a day or at the most only 20 pins. Thus, with the division of labour the productive capacity of the individual and of the community has greatly increased.

2. The Right Man in the Right Place. Another great advantage is that the work under division of labour is allotted according to the ability and capacity of the individual worker. This ensures a high degree of efficiency as the right man is put in the right job. Thus, it eliminates the possibility of fitting a square peg in a round hole.

3. Dexterity and Skill. The worker becomes highly skilled and acquires high degree of dexterity because of the repeated performance of the same operation. As the age-old dictum goes, *practice makes a man perfect*. The worker acquires perfection in his skill because he has to carry out the same operation over and over again. This adds to his productivity.

4. Inventions are Facilitated. Another significant advantage is that it promotes the development of new ideas and better techniques of doing the work. It is due to the fact that when a worker is performing the same operation over and over again, he can think of doing that process in a better and improved manner. Even some mechanical device may occur to him to do that task easily and more efficiently. Thus, division of labour results in inventions of new machinery and better tools.

5. Saving in Time. Under division of labour, a worker performs a part of the whole process and therefore he needs to learn only that much. Long periods of training are, therefore, rendered unnecessary. This saves great time and money.

Further as the worker remains employed on the same process, he does not waste his time in moving from one process to another. He, therefore, goes on working without loss of time. This further results in saving in time.

6. Economy in the Use of Tools. A worker is not provided with a complete set of tools required for the whole process. He is provided with only those tools which are required by him for the performance of that part of the process which is allotted to him. Thus, one set of tools can be made use of by many workers. This is a great economic gain.

7. Use of Machinery Encouraged. By breaking up the production of a commodity into small and simple operations, division of labour encourages the use of machinery and its introduction. These simple operations easily can be carried out by suitable machines. Machines can be economically used only when they are fully used, that is, when their productive capacity is fully utilised. Division of labour involves production on a large scale and therefore permits the economical use of machinery.

8. Cheaper Goods. Another distinct advantage of division of labour is that the economies of large scale are reaped. The cost per unit tends to fall down when the commodity is produced on a large scale which ensures the production of cheaper goods. Even poor people can buy them. As a result of this, the standards of living of the people rise.

9. Rise of Entrepreneurs. Since the work is divided into various processes, someone is required to coordinate the work. This has resulted in the rise of entrepreneurs whose job is to specialise in the art of organisation. The rise of entrepreneurs has greatly contributed to the increase in efficiency and productivity of the modern economy.

ENTREPRENEUR

Having explained three factors–land, labour and capital–we now turn to the explanation of the fourth important factor, namely, the entrepreneur. It is not enough to say that production is a function of land, capital and labour. There must be some factor which combine these factors in the right proportion and initiates the process of production and also bear the risk involved in it. This factor is known as the entrepreneur. He has also been called the organiser, the manager and the risk taker. But in these days of specialisation, the task of manager and organiser has become different from that of the entrepreneur. While the organisation and management include decision-making of routine type, *the real task of the entrepreneur is to initiate the production work* and not to manage the business affairs. Indeed, the entrepreneur may employ on wage basis managers who manage day-to-day affairs of the organisation. Further, whereas the hired managers get fixed wages, *the entrepreneurs bear risk and uncertainty of the production work.*

Functions of the Entrepreneur

There is a controversy about the proper and true functions of the entrepreneur. Various economists have laid stress on the different functions of the entrepreneur. According to Schumpeter, the function of the entrepreneur is to introduce innovations. By innovations, he means new combinations of factors or new processes or the discovery of new products or the discovery of new markets or any change in production methods which reduce cost of production. In other words, anything which reduces cost of production or raises the demand for the product is called innovation by Schumpeter. F.H. Knight emphasised the uncertainty bearing function of the entrepreneur. Alfred Marshall assigns to the entrepreneur the function of risk bearing, provision of finance, introduction of innovations and management of a business enterprise. We shall explain below these various functions of the entrepreneur, but it should be carefully noted that different economists have emphasised different functions. Further, with the passage of time and change in the organisational structure of the business enterprises, there has been division of labour and specialisation in the various tasks which were previously assigned to entrepreneur. Thus, in a corporate form of business organisation co-ordination between the various factors, day-to-day management of the organisation and decisions regarding price, output, selling costs, investment are taken by specialised or professional managers. The important functions of entrepreneure are explained below :

(1) **Initiating a business enterprise and bringing about resource co-ordination.** The first and foremost function of an entrepreneur is to initiate a business enterprise. For this he has to collect different factors of production, such as labour, capital, land or factory building and bring about co-ordination among them. In other words, he does all what is required to set up a new firm or a productive enterprise. These various other factors of production are paid fixed contractual remunerations; the labourers are paid at the fixed rate of wages, the land or factory building gets fixed rate of rent for its use and on capital the fixed rate of interest is paid. But the reward for the entrepreneur, that is, profits is not fixed. If his planning and anticipation go very much wrong, he may get even negative profit, that is, losses. Thus, to start a business, the entrepreneur has to confront the possibility of earning profits or making losses. On the other hand, the other factors get their fixed contractual payments irrespective of whether the entrepreneur makes profits or losses.

(2) **Risk taking or uncertainty bearing.** Ultimate responsibility of the business lies with the entrepreneur. As pointed out above, what is planned and anticipated by the entrepreneur may not come true and the actual course of events may differ from what was anticipated and planned. The economy is dynamic and changes in it are occurring every day: the demand for commodities may change, the cost structure may change, fashions and tastes of the people may change. Changes in Government's policy regarding taxation, interest may also change. All these changes bring about changes in the cost or demand conditions of the business firms. It may happen that as a result of certain particular changes, which were not anticipated by the entrepreneur, the firm has to incur a heavy loss. To bear the financial losses arising out of the uncertainty is the task of the entrepreneur. Therefore, many economists have emphasised that true function of the enterprise is to bear risk and uncertainty. F. H. Knight distinguished between risk taking and uncertainty bearing. He divided the risk into two kinds. The first kind of risks are those which can be insured against and the entrepreneur can avoid them by getting them insured and pay premium for such insurance. This premium is included in cost of production. Therefore, such risks are not borne by the entrepreneur, Risks of fire, theft, burglary, etc. are this type of risks which can be insured. The second type of risks are those which cannot be insured. The risk of incurring losses as a result of changes in the demand or cost conditions cannot be insured. The bearing of this non-insurable risk has been called uncertainty bearing by Knight. According to Knight, the entrepreneur earns profits because he bears uncertainty in the economy where dynamic changes are occurring every day.

(3) **Innovations.** As said above, according to Schumpeter, the true function of the entrepreneur is to introduce innovations. Schumpeter uses innovations in a very broad sense which include introduction of new production methods, utilisation of new source of raw materials, adoption of new forms organisation, introduction of a new product including quality improvements, discovering new markets. The first three types of innovations are primariy cost reducing and the last two are primarily of a demand creating nature. There is always uncertainty attached to the introduction of new innovations. They may succeed in the sense that they may bring profits to the entrepreneur or they may fail in the sense that entrepreneur has to suffer losses for introducing them. The tasks of the entrepreneur is to continuously introduce new innovations. When, a new innovation is introduced for the first time by the entrepreneur and it proves successful, it will be imitated by others and all will be adopting that innovation after some time lag. Therefore, the innovations may yield profits for the entrepreneur for some time but when it is widely adopted by others, the profits would disappear. But the entrepreneur may introduce further new innovations to make profits.

It is through innovations that technological progress occurs in an economy. If the science and technology is confined merely to new inventions or discoveries, it will be fruitless if they are not practically used in the productive processes or for commercial purposes. By introducing new innovations and thereby contributing to technological progress in the economy the entrepreneurs promote economic growth of the country. But innovations also involve risks. Therefore, only a few individuals in the society are capable of introducing new innovations. The greater the innovating ability, the greater the supply of entrepreneurs in the economy and the greater will be the rate of technological progress.

CHAPTER 16

THE THEORY OF PRODUCTION : RETURNS TO A FACTOR

So far we have been discussing the demand side of the pricing problem. In this chapter and the next few ones we shall be discussing the supply side of the pricing of products. The supply of a product, as we shall see in a later chapter, depends upon its cost of production, which in turn depends upon (a) the physical relationship between inputs and output, and (b) the prices of inputs. The physical relationship between inputs and output plays an important part in determining the cost of production. It is the general description of this physical relation between inputs and output which forms the subject-matter of the theory of production. In other words, the theory of production relates to the physical laws governing production of goods.

The act of production involves the transformation of inputs into outputs. The word production in economics is not merely confined to bringing about physical transformation in the matter, *it is creation or addition of value*. Therefore, production in economics also covers rendering of services such as transporting, financing, marketing. Laws of production, or in other words, the generalisations regarding relations between inputs and outputs developed in this chapter will apply to all these types of production.

The relation between inputs and output of a firm has been called the 'Production Function'. Thus, the theory of production is the study of production functions. The production function of a firm can be studied by holding the quantities of some factors fixed, while varying the amount of other factors. This is done when the *law of variable proportions* is derived. The production function of a firm can also be studied by varying the amounts of all factors. The behaviour of production when all factors are varied is the subject-matter of the laws of *returns to scale*. Thus, in the theory of production, the study of (a) the law of variable proportions and (b) the laws of returns to scale is included. Besides this, the theory of production is also concerned with explaining *which combination of inputs (or factors of production) a firm will choose* so as to minimise its costs of production for producing a given level of output or to maximise output for a given level of cost.

IMPORTANCE OF THE THEORY OF PRODUCTION

The theory of production plays a double role in the price theory. First, it provides a basis for the analysis of relation between costs and amount of output. Costs govern supply of a product which, together with demand, determines the price of a product. The prices of inputs (factors) of production influence the cost of production and hence play a part in determining the prices of product. Secondly, the theory of production provides a basis for the theory of firm's demand for factors (inputs) of production. Demand for factors of production or inputs, together with the supply of them, determines their prices.

The theory of production has great relevance for the theory of firm. The theory of firm is concerned with what level of output it will produce so as to maximise its profits. In order to fix this profit-maximizing output, besides the demand conditions (average and marginal revenues), the firm will be guided by the marginal and average costs of production. In addition to the prices of the factors of production, the changes in marginal and average costs of production as a result of increase in output are determined by the physical relationship between inputs and output.

Demand for factors of production depends upon the marginal revenue productivity of the factors and therefore demand curves for factors of production are derived, given the price for output, from their marginal productivity curves. And the theory of production explains the forces which determine the marginal productivity of the factors. As we shall study in a later part concerning the theory of distribution, the *relative prices of factors*, that is, wages of labour, rent of land, interest on capital etc. depend a good deal on the demand for them and hence on their marginal productivity. Thus, the theory of production has a great relevance to the theory of relative prices of factors, that is, to the microtheory of distribution.

The theory of production is also relevant to the macrotheory of distribution. The aggregate distributive shares of the various factors, for instance, aggregative shares of wages and profits in national income, depend upon the elasticity of substitution between factors which is an important concept of the theory of production. In fact, in the neo-classical macro-theory of distribution, elasticity of substitution is the crucial factor which determines the aggregative shares of the various factors.

PRODUCTION FUNCTION: TRANSFORMING INPUTS INTO OUTPUT

The act of production involves the transformation of inputs into output. Production is a transformation of physical inputs into physical output. The output is thus a function of factors which are also called *inputs*. The functional relationship between physical inputs and physical output of a firm is known as production function. Algebraically, production function can be written as

$$Q = f(L, K, M)$$

where Q stands for the quantity of output, L, K and M stand for the quantities of factors labour, capital and raw materials respectively.

The above equation shows that the quantity (Q) of output produced depends upon the quantities of the factors used. The production function expresses the relationship between the quantity of output and the quantities of the various inputs used for the production. More precisely, *the production function states the maximum quantity of output that can be produced with any given quantities of various inputs*. If a small firm produces wooden tables in a day, its production function will consist of the *maximum* number of tables that can be produced from a given quantities of various inputs such as wood, varnish, labour time, machine time, floor space.

Two things must be noted in respect of production function. First, production function, like the demand function, must be considered with reference to a *particular period of time*. Production function expresses *a flow of inputs* resulting in *a flow of output* in a specific period of time. Secondly, production function of a firm is determined by the state of technology. When the technology advances, the production function changes with the result that greater flow of output can be obtained from the given inputs, or smaller quantities of inputs can be used for producing a given quantity of output.

In economic theory we are interested in two types of production functions. First, we study the production function when the quantities of some inputs such as capital and land are kept constant and the quantity of one input such as labour (or quantities of few inputs) is varied. This kind of production function [$Q = f(L, \bar{K})$] is called *short-run production function*. The study of short-run production is the subject-matter of the law of diminishing returns which is also called the *law of variable proportions*. Secondly, we study production function (input-output relation) by varying all inputs and this is called *long-run production* function and can be expressed as $Q = f(L, K, M)$. This forms the subject-matter of the *law of returns to scale*. Generally, the terms constant and increasing returns are used with reference to constant and increasing returns to scale.

CONCEPTS OF PRODUCT

Regarding physical production by factors there are three concepts (1) *Total Product,* (2) *Average Product,* and (3) *Marginal Product.*

Total Product. Total product of a factor is the amount of total output produced by a given amount of the factor, other factors held constant. As the amount of a factor increases, the total output increases. It will be seen from Table 16.1 (on Page 191) that when with a fixed quantity of capital (*K*), more units of labour are employed total product is increasing in the beginning. Thus, when one unit of labour is used with a given quantity of capital 80 units of output are produced. With two units of labour 170 units of output are produced, and with three units of labour total product of labour increases to 270 units and so on. After 8 units of employment of labour total output declines with

Table 16.1: Returns to Labour

Units of Labour	*Total Product (Quintals)*	*Marginal Product (Quintals)*	*Average Product (Quintals)*
L	Q	$\frac{\Delta Q}{\Delta L}$	$\frac{Q}{L}$
1	80	80	60
2	170	90	85
3	270	100	90
4	368	98	92
5	430	62	86
6	480	50	80
7	504	24	72
8	504	0	63
9	495	–9	55
10	480	–15	48

further increase in labour input. But the *rate* of increase in total product varies at different levels of employment of a factor. Graphically the total product curve is shown by *TP* curve in Fig. 16.1. It will be seen that in the beginning total product curve rises at an increasing rate, that is, the slope of the *TP* curve is rising in the beginning. After a point total product curve starts rising at a diminishing rate as the employment of the variable factor is increased. The fact that ultimately total product increasses at a diminishing rate has been proved by empirical evidence, as shall be seen later in our discussion of the law of diminishing returns.

Average Product. Average product of a factor is the total output produced per unit of the factor employed. Thus,

$$\text{Average Product} = \frac{\text{Total Product}}{\text{Number of units of a factor employed}}$$

If Q stands for total product, L for the number of a variable factor employed, then average product (AP) is given by:

$$AP = \frac{Q}{L}$$

We can measure the average product from the total product data given in Table 16.1. Thus when two units of labour are employed, the average product is $\frac{Q}{L} = \frac{170}{2} = 85$. Similarly, when three units of labour are employed, average product is $\frac{270}{3} = 90$ and so on. From a total product curve *TP* in

Fig. 16.1, we can measure the average product of labour. Thus, when OL_1 units of labour are employed, total product is equal to L_1A and therefore average product of labour equals $\frac{L_1A}{OL_1}$ which would be equal to the slope of the ray OA. Similarly, when OL_2 units of labour are employed, total product (TP) is L_2B which would give us average product to be equal to $\frac{L_2B}{OL_2}$ or the slope of the ray OB. Further, with the employment of labour equal to OL_3, the average product will be measured by the slope of the ray OC.

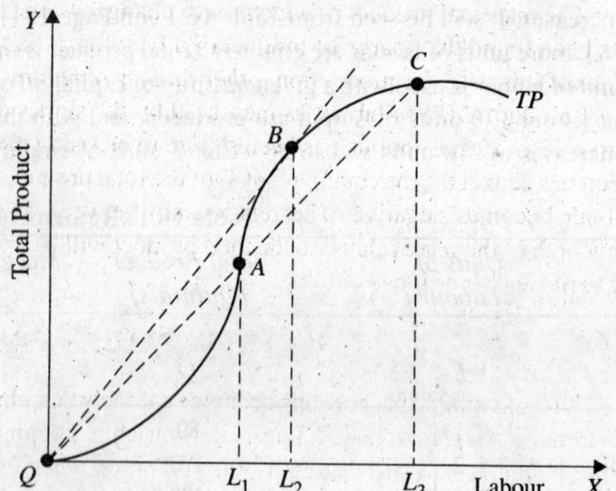

Fig. 16.1. *Measuring Average Product on a Total Production Function Curve*

It has been generally found that as more units of a factor are employed for producing a commodity, the average product first rises and then falls. As shall be seen from Table 16.1 and the Fig. 16.1, the average product curve of a variable factor first rises and then it declines. That is, the average product curve has an inverted U-shape.

Marginal Product. *Marginal product of a factor is the addition to the total production by the employment of an extra unit of a factor.* Suppose when two workers are employed to produce wheat in an agricultural farm and they produce 170 quintals of wheat per year. Now, if instead of two workers, three workers are employed and as a result total product increases to 270 quintals, then the third worker has added 100 quintals of wheat to the total production. Thus 100 quintals is the marginal product of the third worker.

It will be seen from Table 16.1 that marginal product of labour increases in the beginning and then diminishes. Marginal product of 8th unit of labour is zero and beyond that it becomes negative.

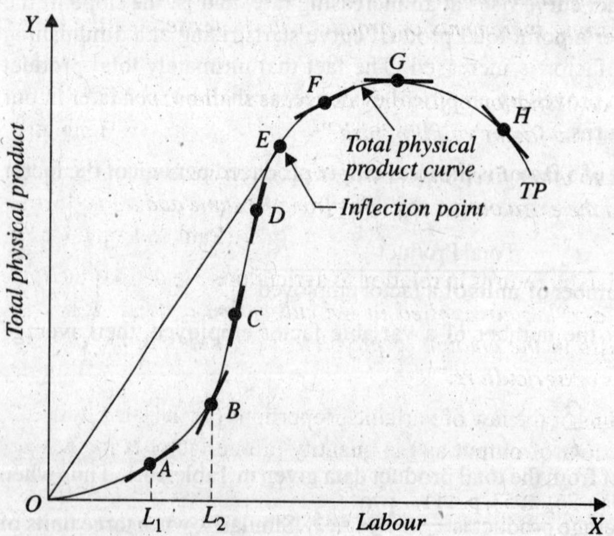

Fig. 16.2. *Measuring Marginal Physical Product of Labour*

Mathematically, if employment of labour increases by ΔL units which yield an increase in total output by ΔQ units, the marginal physical product of labour is given by $\frac{\Delta Q}{\Delta L}$. That is,

$$MP_L = \frac{\Delta Q}{\Delta L}$$

The marginal physical product curve of a variable factor can also be derived from the total physical product curve of labour. At any given level of employment of labour, the marginal product of labour can be obtained by measuring the slope of the total product curve at a given level of labour employment. For example, in Fig. 16.2

when OL_1 units of labour are employed, the marginal physical product of labour is given by the slope of the tangent drawn at point A to the total product curve *TP*. Again, when OL_2 units of labour are employed, the marginal physical product of labour is obtained by measuring the slope of the tangent drawn to the total product curve *TP* at point *B* which corresponds to OL_2 level of labour employment and so on for further units of labour employed.

The marginal product of a factor will change at different levels of employment of the factor. It has been found that marginal product of a factor rises in the beginning and then ultimately falls as more of it is used for production, *other factors remaining the same*. That is why in Fig. 16.2 marginal product (*MP*) of labour as measured by the slopes of the tangents drawn to the total product curve TP at various points has been shown to be rising in the beginning and then diminishing till it becomes zero at the maximum point *G* of the total product curve. Thereafter, the marginal product of labour becomes negative. The relationship between average product and marginal product and how both of them are related to the total product will be explained in detail in our analysis of the law of variable proportions.

LAW OF VARIABLE PROPORTIONS

Law of variable proportions occupies an important place in economic theory. This law examines the production function with one factor variable, keeping the quantities of other factors fixed. In other words, it refers to the input-output relation when output is increased by varying the quantity of one input. When the quantity of one factor is varied, keeping the quantity of other factors constant, the proportion between the variable factor and the fixed factor is altered; the ratio of employment of the variable factor to that of the fixed factor goes on increasing as the quantity of the variable factor is increased. *Since under this law we study the effects on output of variation in factor proportions, this is also known as the law of variable proportions.* Thus law of variable proportions is the new name for the famous "*Law of Diminishing Returns*" of classical economics. This law has played a vital role in the history of economic thought and occupies an equally important place in modern economic theory. This law has been supported by the empirical evidence about the real world. The law of variable proportions or diminishing returns has been stated by various economists in the following manner:

As equal increments of one input are added; the inputs of other productive services being held constant, beyond a certain point the resulting increments of product will decrease, i.e., the marginal products will diminish."[1] (G. Stigler)

"As the proportion of one factor in a combination of factors is increased, after a point, first the marginal and then the average product of that factor will diminish."[2] (F. Benham)

"An increase in some inputs relative to other fixed inputs will, in a given state of technology, cause output to increase; but after a point the extra output resulting from the same addition of extra inputs will become less."[3] (Paul A. Samuelson)

Marshall discussed the law of diminishing returns in relation to agriculture. He defines the law as follows: *"An increase in the capital and labour applied in the cultivation of land causes in general a less than proportionate increase in the amount of product raised unless it happens to coincide with an improvement in the arts of agriculture."*[4]

It is obvious from the above definitions of the law of variable proportions (or the law of diminishing returns) that it refers to the behaviour of output as the quantity of one factor is increased,

---

1. G.J. Stigler, *Theory of Price*, The MacMillan Co., 1953, p. 111.
2. F.Benham, *Economics*, 2nd edition, 1950 p. 110.
3. Paul A. Samuelson, *Economics*, 8th edition, p. 25.
4. Alfred Marshall, *Principles of Economics*, 6th edition, p. 150.

keeping the quantity of other factors fixed and further it states that the marginal product and average product will eventually decline.

Assumptions of the Law. The law of variable proportions or diminishing returns, as stated above, holds good under the following conditions:

1. First, the state of technology is assumed to be given and unchanged. If there is improvement in the technology, then marginal and average products may rise instead of diminishing.

2. Secondly, there must be some inputs whose quantity is kept fixed. This is one of the ways by which we can alter the factor proportions and know its effect on output. This law does not apply in case all factors are proportionately varied. Behaviour of output as a result of the variation in all inputs is discussed under "*returns to scale*".

3. Thirdly, the law is based upon the possibility of varying the proportions in which the various factors can be combined to produce a product. The law does not apply to those cases where the factors must be used in fixed proportions to yield a product. When the various factors are required to be used in rigidly fixed proportions, then the increase in one factor would not lead to any increase in output, that is, the marginal product of the factor will then be zero and not diminishing. It may, however, be pointed out that products requiring fixed proportions of factors are quiet uncommon. Thus, the law of variable proportion applies to most of the cases of production in the real world.

The law of variable proportions is illustrated in Table 16.1. and Fig. 16.3. We shall first explain it by considering Table 16.1. Assume that there is a given fixed amount of land, with which more units of the variable factor, labour, is used to produce agricultural output. With a given fixed quantity of land, as a farmer raises employment of labour from one unit to 7 units, the total product increases from 80 quintals to 504 quintals of wheat. Beyond the employment of 8 units of labour, total product diminishes. It is worth noting that upto the use of 3 units of labour, total product increases at an increasing rate. This fact is clearly revealed from column 3 which shows successive marginal products of labour as extra units of labour are used. *Marginal product of labour, it may be recalled, is the increment in total output due to the use of an extra unit of labour.*

It will be seen from Col. 3 of Table 16.1, that the marginal product of labour initially rises and beyond the use of three units of labour, it starts diminishing. Thus when 3 units of labour are employed, marginal product of labour is 100 and with the use of 4th and 5th units of labour marginal product of labour falls to 98 and 62 respectively. Beyond the use of eight units of labour, total product diminishes and therefore marginal product of labour becomes negative. As regards average product of labour, it rises upto the use of fourth unit of labour and beyond that it is falling throughout.

Three Stages of the Law of Variable Proportions

The behaviour of output when the varying quantity of one factor is combined with a fixed quantity of the other can be divided into three distinct stages. In order to understand these three stages it is better to graphically illustrate the production function with one factor variable. This has been done in Fig. 16.3. In this figure, on the *X*-axis the quantity of the variable factor is measured and on the *Y*-axis the total product, average product and marginal product are measured. How the total product, average product and marginal product a variable factor change as a result of the increase in its quantity, that is, by increasing the quantity of one factor to a fixed quantity of the others will be seen from Fig. 16.3. In the top panel of this figure, the total product curve *TP* of a variable factor goes on increasing to a point and after that it starts declining. In the bottom panel, average and marginal product curves of labour also rise and then decline; marginal product curve starts declining earlier than the average product curve. The behaviour of these total, average and marginal products of the variable factor as a result of the increase in its amount is generally divided into three stages which are explained below.

Stage 1. In this stage, total product curve *TP* increases at an increasing rate up to a point. In Fig. 16.3. from the origin to the point *F*, slope of the total product curve *TP* is increasing, that is, up to the point *F*, *the total product increases at an increasing rate* (the total product curve *TP* is concave upward upto the point *F*), which means that the marginal product *MP* of the variable factor is rising. From the point *F* onwards during the stage 1, the total product curve goes on rising but its slope is declining which means that from point *F* onwards *the total product increases at a diminishing rate* (total product curve *TP* is concave down-ward), *i.e.*, marginal product falls but is positive. The point *F* where the total product stops increasing at an increasing rate and starts increasing at the diminishing rate is called the *pont of inflection. Vertically corresponding to this point of inflection marginal product is maximum,after which it starts diminishing.* Thus, marginal product of the variable factor starts diminishing beyond *OL* amount of the variable factor. That is, law of diminishing returns starts operating in stage 1 from point *D* on the *MP* curve or from *OL* amount of the variable factor used.

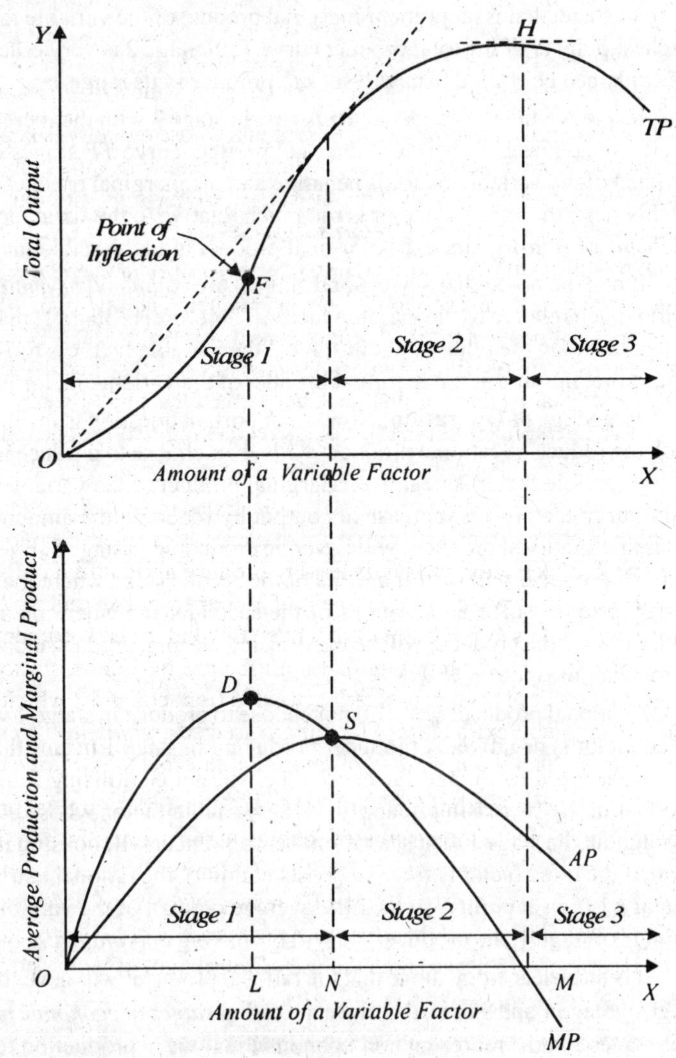

Fig. 16.3. *Three Stages of the Law of Variable Proportions*

This first stage ends where the average product curve *AP* reaches its highest point, that is, point *S* on *AP* curve or *ON* amount of the variable factor used. During stage 1, when marginal product of the variable factor is falling it still exceeds its average product and so continues to cause the average product curve to rise. Thus, during stage 1, whereas marginal product curve of a variable factor rises in a part and then falls, the average product curve rises throughout. In the first stage, the quantity of the fixed factor is too much relative to the quantity of the variable factor so that if some of the fixed factor is withdrawn, the total product will increase. Thus, in the first stage *marginal product of the fixed factor is negative.*

Stage 2. In stage 2, the total product continues to increase at a diminishing rate until it reaches its maximum point H where the second stage ends. In *this stage both the marginal product and the average product of the variable factor are diminishing but remain positive*. At the end of the second stage, that is, at point M marginal product of the variable factor is zero (corresponding to the highest point H of the total product curve TP). Stage 2 is very crucial and important because as will be explained below the firm will seek to produce in its range.

Stage 3. Stage of Negative Returns. In stage 3 with the increase in the variable factor the total product declines and therefore the total product curve TP slopes downward. As a result, marginal product of the variable factor is negative and the marginal product curve MP goes below the X-axis. In this stage the variable factor is too much relative to the fixed factor. This stage is called the *stage of negative returns*, since the marginal product of the variable factor is negative during this stage.

It may be noted that stage 1 and stage 3 are *completely symmetrical*. In stage 1 the fixed factor is too much relative to the variable factor. Therefore, in stage 1, marginal product of the fixed factor is negative. On the other hand, in stage 3 the variable factor is too much relative to the fixed factor. Therefore, in stage 3, the marginal product of the variable factor is negative.

The Stage of Operation. Now, an important question is in which stage a rational producer will seek to produce. A rational producer will never choose to produce in stage 3 where marginal product of the variable factor is negative. Marginal product of the variable factor being negative in stage 3, a producer can always increase his output by reducing the amount of the variable factor. It is thus clear that a rational producer will never be producing in stage 3. Even if the variable factor is free, the rational producer will stop at the end of the second stage where the marginal product of the variable factor is zero. At the end point M of the second stage where the marginal product of the variable factor is zero, the producer will be maximising the total product and will thus be making maximum use of the variable factor.

A rational producer will also not choose to produce in statge 1 where the marginal product of the fixed factor is negative. A producer producing in stage 1 means that he will not be making the best use of the fixed factor and further that he will not be utilising fully the opportunities of increasing production by increasing quantity of the variable factor whose average product continues to rise throughout the stage 1. Thus, a rational entrepreneur will not stop in stage 1 but will expand further. Even if the fixed factor is free (*i.e.*, costs nothing), the rational entrepreneur will stop only at the end of stage 1 (*i.e.*, at point N) where the average product of the variable factor is maximum. At the end point N of stage 1, the producer the will be making maximum use of the fixed factor.[5]

It is thus clear from above that the rational producer will never be found producing in stage 1 and stage 3. Stage 1 and 3 may, therefore, be called *stages of economic absurdity or economic non-sense*. The stages 1 and 3 represent non-economic regions in production function. A rational producer will always seek to produce in stage 2 where both the marginal product and average product of the variable factor are diminishing. At which particular point in this stage, the producer will decide to produce depends upon the prices of factors. The stage 2 represents the range of rational production decisions.

We have seen above *how output varies as the factor proportions are altered* at any given moment. We have also noticed that this input-output relation can be divided into three stages. Now, the question arises as to what causes increasing marginal returns to the variable factor in the beginning, diminishing marginal returns later and negative marginal returns to the variable factor ultimately.

---

5. The statement in respect of the non-operation by a rational producer in stage 1 applies to the producer who is working under *perfect competition* in both the product and factor markets where the price of the product sold by him and the prices of factors bought by him remain fixed. In monopoly and imperfect competition in product and factor markets where the prices of product and factors do not remain fixed with the changes in the level of output and employment, the producer might find his most profitable level of output in stage 1.

Causes of Initial Increasing marginal Returns to a Factor

In the beginning, the quantity of the fixed factor is abundant relative to the quantity of the variable factor. Therefore, when more and more units of a variable factor are added to the constant quantity of the fixed factor, the *fixed factor is more intensively and effectively utilised*. This causes the production to increase at a rapid rate. When, in the beginning the variable factor is relatively smaller in quantity, some amount of the fixed factor may remain unutilised and therefore when the variable factor is increased *fuller utilisation of the fixed factor* becomes possible with the result that increasing returns are obtained. The question arises as to why the fixed factor is not initially taken in an appropriate quantity which suits the available quantity of the variable factor. Answer to this question is provided by the fact that generally those factors are taken as fixed which are *individisble*. Indivisibility of a factor means that due to technological requirements a minimum amount of that factor must be employed whatever the level of output. Thus, as more units of variable factor are employed to work with an indivisible fixed factor, output greatly increases in the beginning due to fuller and more effective utilisation of the latter. Thus, we see that *it is the indivisibility of some factors which causes increasing returns* to the variable factor in the beginning.

The second reason why we get increasing returns to the variable factor in the initial stage is that as more units of the variable factor are employed the efficiency of the variable factor itself increases. This is because *when there is a sufficient quantity of the variable factor, it becomes possible to introduce specialisation or division of labour which results in higher productivity*. The greater the quantity of the variable factor, the greater the scope of specialisation and hence the greater will be the level of its productivity or efficiency.

Causes of Diminishing marginal Returns to a Factor

The stage of diminishing marginal returns in the production function with one factor variable is the most important. The question arises as to why we get diminishing marginal returns after a certain amount of the variable factor has been added to a fixed quantity of the other factor. As explained above, increasing returns to a variable factor occur initially primarily because of the more effective and fuller use of the fixed factor becomes possible as more units of the variable factor are employed to work with it. Once the point is reached at which the amount of the variable factor is sufficient to ensure the efficient utilisation of the fixed factor, then further increases in the variable factor will cause marginal and average products of a variable factor to decline because the fixed factor then becomes inadequate relative to the quantity of the variable factor. In other words, *the contributions to the production made by the variable factor after a point become less and less because the additional units of the variable factor have less and less of the fixed factor to work with*. The production is the result of the co-operation of various factors aiding each other. Now, how much aid one factor provides to the others depends upon how much there is of it. Eventally, the fixed factor is abundant relative to the number of the variable factor and the former provides much aid to the later. Evantally, the fixed factor becomes more and more scarce in relation to the variable factor so that as the units of the variable factor are increased they receive less and less aid from the fixed factor. As a result, the marginal and average products of the variable factor decline ultimately.

The phenomenon of diminishing marginal returns, like that of increasing marginal returns, rests upon the indivisibility of the fixed factor. As explained above, the important reason for increasing returns to a factor in the beginning is the fact that the fixed factor is indivisible which has to be employed whether the output to be produced is small or large. When the indivisible fixed factor is not being fully used, successive increases in a variable factor add more to output since fuller and more efficient use is made of the indivisible fixed factor. But there is generally a limit to the range of employment of the variable factor over which its marginal and average products will increase. There will usually be a level of employment of the variable factor at which indivisible fixed factor is being as fully and efficiently used as possible. It will happen when the variable factor has increased to such an amount that the fixed indivisible factor is being used in the '*best or optimum proportion*' with the variable factor.

Once the optimum proportion is disturbed by further increases in the variable factor, returns to a variable factor (*i.e., marginal product and average product*) will diminish primarily because the indivisible factor is being used too intensively, or in other words, the fixed factor is being used in non-optimal proportion with the variable factor. Just as the marginal product of the variable factor increases in the first stage when better and fuller use of the fixed indivisible factor is being made, so the marginal product of the variable factor diminishes when the fixed indivisible factor is being worked too hard. *If the fixed factor was perfectly divisible, neither the increasing nor the diminishing returns to a variable factor would have occurred.* If the factors were perfectly divisible, then there would not have been the necessity of taking a large quantity of the fixed factor in the beginning to combine with the varying quantities of the other factor. In the presence of pefect divisibility, the optimum proportion between the factors could have always been achieved. Perfect divisibility of the factors implies that a small firm with a small machine and one worker would be as efficient as a large firm with a large machine and many workers. The productivity of the factors would be the same in the two cases. Thus, we see that if the factors were perfectly divisible, then the question of varying factor proportions would not have arisen and hence the phenomena of increasing and diminishing marginal returns to a variable factor would not have occurred. Prof. Bober rightly remarks: "Let divisibility enter through the door, law of variable proportions rushes out through the window."[6]

Joan Robinson goes deeper into the causes of diminishing returns. She holds that *the diminishing marginal returns occur because the factors of production are imperfect substitutes for one another.* As seen above, diminishing returns occur during the second stage since the fixed factor is now inadequate relatively to the variable factor. Now, a factor which is scarce in supply is taken as fixed. When there is a scarce factor, quantity of that factor cannot be increased in accordance with the varying quantities of the other factors, which, after the optimum proportion of factors is achieved, results in diminishing returns. If now some factors were available which was perfect substitute of the scarce fixed factor, then the paucity of the scarce fixed factor during the second stage would have been made up by the increase in supply of its perfect substitute with the result that output could be expanded without diminishing returns. Thus, even if one of the variable factors which we add to the fixed factor were perfect substitute of the fixed factor, then when, in the second stage, the fixed factor becomes relatively deficient, its deficiency would have been made up the increase in the variable factor which is its perfect substitute.

Thus, Joan Robinson says, "*What the Law of Diminishing Returns really states is that there is a limit to the extent to which one factor of production can be substituted for another, or, in other words, that the elasticity of substitution between factor is not infinite.* If this were not true, it would be possible, when one factor of production is fixed in amount and the rest are in perfectly elastic supply, to produce part of the output with the aid of the fixed factor, and then, when the optimum propertion between this and other factors was attained, to substitute some other factor for it and to increase output at constant cost."[7] *We, therefore, see that diminishing returns operate because the elasticity of substitution between factors is not infinite.*

Explanation of Negative Marginal Returns to a Factor

As the amount of a variable factor continues to be increased to a fixed quantity of the other factor, a stage is reached when the total product declines and the marginal product of the variable factor becomes negative. *This phenomenon of negative marginal returns to the variable factor in stage 3 is due to the fact that the number of the variable factor becomes too excessive relative to the fixed factor* so that they obstruct each other with the result that the total output falls instead of

6. M.M. Bober, *Intermediate Price and Income Theory.*
7. Joan Robinson, *The Economics of Imperfect Competition*

rising. Besides, too large a number of the variable factor also impairs the efficiency of the fixed factor. The proverb "*too many cooks spoil the broth*" aptly applies to this situation. In such a situation, a reduction in the units of the variable factor will increase the total output.

APPLICABILITY OF THE LAW OF DIMINISHING RETURNS

We have discussed above the law of variable proportions which states marginal physical product of a variable factor eventually diminishes, even if it increases in the beginning. Uptill Marshall, it was thought that there were three laws of production–diminishing, constant and increasing returns – which were quiet distinct and separate. Now, modern economists have veered round to the view that diminishing, constant and increasing returns to a factor are not three separate laws but they are three phases of one general law of variable proportions. Moreover, uptill Marshall it was thought that law of diminishing returns applied to agriculture while the manufacturing industries were characterised by increasing or constant returns. But this is no longer believed to be correct, Law of diminishing returns has a vast general applicability. This law applies as much to industries as to agriculture. Whenever some factors are fixed and the amount of an other increases, then the technology remaining the same, diminishing returns to factor are bound to occur eventually both in agriculture and industries. We have given above the various definitions of the law of variable proportions which lay stress on its general and universal applicability.

We have given the theoretical reasons for the occurrence of diminishing returns. The occurrence of diminishing marginal physical returns after a point has been confirmed by the overwhelming empirical evidence. Indeed, *if the diminishing returns did not occur we could grow sufficient amount of foodgrains even in a flower pot by using more doses of labour and capital.* If the constant returns could be obtained by applying more labour on a given piece of land, then as the population increased we could use more labour on that land to get proportionate increase in agricultural output. In that case the world, especially the developing countries like India, would not have to face the problems of food shortage and over-population. Professor R.G. Lipsey is right when he says, "Indeed, were the hypothesis of diminishing returns incorrect, there would need to be no fear that the present population explosion will bring with it a food crises. If the marginal product of additional workers applied to a fixed quantity of land were constant, then world food production could be expanded in proportion to the increase in population merely by keeping the same proportion of the population on farms. As it is, diminishing returns means an inevitable decline in the marginal product of each additional labourer as an expanding population is applied with static techniques, to a fixed world supply of aggricultural land."[8]

But from above it should not be understood that because of diminishing returns there can be no hopes for raising the living standards of mankind, especially of the people in developing countries. To predict such a gloomy prospects for the future of mankind on the basis of the law of diminishing returns is wholly unwarranted.

Technological Progress and Diminishing Returns

Some people misunderstood the law and asserted that as the population increased, the quantity of land remaining unchanged, the productivity per person would necessarily decline. But this is quite wrong. The law of diminishing returns, as stated above, has a great proviso that technical knowledge, equipment, etc., remain the same. In the present-day developed countries, though population has increased, agricultural productivity has greatly gone up instead of diminishing. This is so because present-day developed countries have made an impressive progress in technical knowledge, resulting in new and superior machinery and other equipments and the use of fertilisers. Capital equipment per worker engaged in agriculture has greatly increased. As a result, agricultural productivity has registered a tremendous increase in the present-day advanced countries. On the other hand, developing countries have not made much progress in technical knowledge and in

8. Richard G.Lipsey, *Introduction to Positive Economics*, 3rd edition, p. 216.

accumulating and using sufficient capital equipment like machinery, tools, fertilisers, etc. It is no wonder, therefore, that agricultural productivity has not risen. In fact, marginal productivity of labour has gone down. The phenomenon of disguised unemplyment found in agriculture of developing countries reveals that marginal productivity of a worker is zero or nearly zero. It is thus clear that actual experience regarding the behaviour of agricultural productivity in both developed and developing countries is in no way a contradiction to the law of diminishing returns, the operation of which is subject to the condition that technical knowledge, capital equipment and other aids of production remain the same.

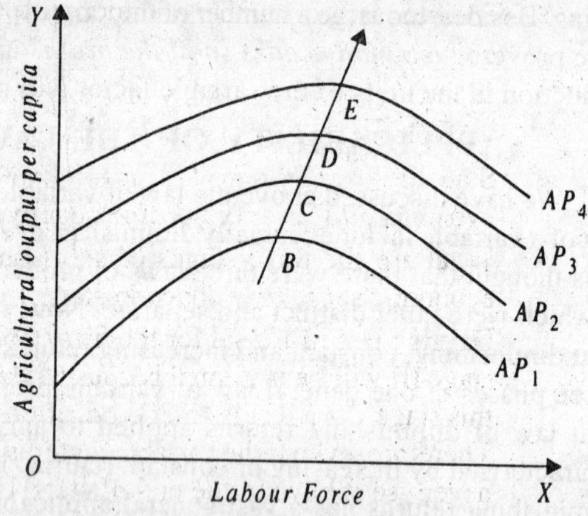

Fig. 16.4. *Rising Agricultural Productivity due to Technological Progress*

That the increase in agriculture productivity or output per capita in agriculture on account of the advances in technology is in no way contradiction to the principle of diminishing returns can be illustrated with the help of Figure 16.4. It will be seen from Fig. 16.4 that the curves of agricultural output per capita rise up to a certain point and then begin to fall due to the diminishing returns. However, in the developed countries agrigultural productivity curve has been shifting upward because of the progress in technology in agriculture over time. It is this progress in agricultural technology that has brought about shift in the productivity curve AP_1 to AP_2, from AP_2 to AP_3, and from AP_3 to AP_4. If there had been no progress in technology and increase in capital equipment, the agricultural productivity curve would have remained unchanged at AP_1 and therefore with increase in population and hence in labour force, the agricultural productivity would have diminished as is indicated by the falling part of AP_1 curve. But in actual practice along with the increase in the labour force, the average productivity of labour in agriculture has been rising due to the progress in technology, that is, due to the upward shift of *AP* curve. As a result of progress in technology, the economies of developed countries have been moving along the arrow mark line *BE* which indicates the rising average productivity despite the increase in the labour force. Thus, we see that diminishing returns with a proviso that 'other things remaining unchanged' is in no way contradiction to the actual experience of rise in average agricultural productivity over time in developed countries. It is the proviso 'other things remaining unchanged' that has not been fulfilled.

We thus see that despite the validity of the diminishing returns developing countries like India can rapidly increase their agricultural production by making advancement in agricultural technology. As demonstrated above, we can suspend the operation of diminishing returns by continually improving the techniques of production through progress in science and technology. Of course, if we fail to improve our technology sufficiently, diminishing returns would assert themselves and create the problems of food shortage and starvation. We, therefore, conclude "unless there is continual and rapidly accelerating improvements in the techniques of production, the population explosion must bring with it declining living standards over much of the world and eventual widespread famine."[9]

QUESTIONS FOR REVIEW

1. What is production function ? Distinguish between fixed inputs and variable inputs. Is the distinction between the two relevant in the long run ?

---

9. R.G. Lipsey, op. cit., p. 216

2. Explain the concept of production function ? Why is it useful in the analysis of firm's behaviour ?
3. What is the relationship between marginal product and average product of labour (or a variable input) ?
4. State the law of diminsihing returns. Why does diminsihing returns to a variable input occur eventually ? Can they become negative? If so, why ?
5. What are the three stages of short-run production function? Why does it not make any economic sense to produce in stage 1 or 3?

   [**Hints :** It is irrational for the firm to produce in either stage I or stage III. The operating in stage III will be irrational because the marginal product of the variable factor is negative in this stage. As a result, total production can be increased by using less of the variable factor. Therefore, even if the variable factor is absolutely free (that is, its price is zero), the firm will never use it beyond the end of stage II.

   The production in stage I is also irrational. In stage 1, the fixed factor, capital or land whichever be the fixed factor, is so abundant in relation to the variable factor that its marginal product is negative. Since a firm operating in stage I where the marginal product of the fixed factor is negative, can increase the level of output by reducing the amount of the fixed factor, it does not make any economic sense to produce in stage 1.]
6. How is the law of diminishing returns reflected in the shape of the total produce curve ? If the total product curve increases at a decreasing rate from the very beginning what would be the shapes of corresponding marginal and average product curves ?
7. Explain the law of diminishing returns. Mention on what assumptions it is based. How Malthus used the law to predict gloomy forecast for future mankind ? What mistake did he commit in making this gloomy forceast ?
8. Fill in the blanks in the following table :

Number of variable input	Total output (number of of units)	Marginal product of the variable input	Average product of the variable input
3	—	18	30
4	—	20	—
5	130	—	—
6	—	5	—
7	—	—	19.5

9. As the quantity of a variable input increases, explain why the point where marginal product begins to decline is reached before the point where average product begins to decline. Also explain why the point where average product begins to decline is reached before the point where total output begins to decline.

   [**Hints.** This is due to the usual average-marginal relationship in the production process. Due to the operation of diminishing marginal returns, marginal returns begin to decline at some point but for some range though diminishing it remains greater than average product. Therefore, average product continues to increase. Only when in its diminishing phase marginal product becomes less than average product, average product starts declining. That is, why marginal product curve cuts the average product curve at the latter's highest point. Marginal product continues diminishing after it is equal to the maximum average product but remains positive for some range which causes the total output to continue increasing. When marginal product becomes zero, the total product reaches its maximum level. As a result, total output continues increasing even after the maximum average product and begins to decline only when marginal product becomes negative]

CHAPTER 17
PRODUCTION FUNCTIONS WITH TWO VARIABLE FACTORS

In the last chapter we explained the production function with a single variable factor, holding other factors constant. In the present chapter we are concerned with the analysis of production function when two factors are taken as variables in the production process. For the analysis of production function with two variable factors we make use of the concept called isoquants or iso-*product curves* which are similar to indifference curves of the theory of demand. Therefore, before we explain the production function with two variable factors and returns to scale, we shall explain the concept of isoquants (that is, equal product curves) and their properties.

ISOQUANTS

Isoquants, which are also called equal product curves, are similar to the indifference curves of the theory of consumer's behaviour. An isoquant represents all those factor combinations which are capable of producing the same level of output. The *isoquants are thus contour lines which trace the loci of equal outputs.* Since an isoquant represents those combinations of inputs which will be capable of producing an equal quantity of output, the producer would be indifferent between them. Therefore, another name which is often given to the equal product curves is *production-indifference curves.*

Table 17.1

Factor Combinations to Produce a Given Level of Output

Factor Combinations	*Labour*	*Capital*
A	1	12
B	2	8
C	3	5
D	4	3
E	5	2

The concept of isoquant can be easily understood from Table 17.1. It is presumed that two factors labour and captial are being employed to produce a product. Each of the factor combinations *A, B, C, D* and *E* produces the same level of output, say 100 units. To start with, factor combination *A* consisting of 1 unit of labour and 12 units of capital produces the given 100 units of output. Similarly, combination *B* consisting of 2 units of labour and 8 units of capital, combination *C* consisting of 3 units of labour and 5 units of capital, combination *D* consisting of 4 units of labour and and 3 units of capital, combination *E* consisting of 5 units of labour and 2 units of capital are capable of producing the same amount of output, *i.e.*, 100 units. In Fig. 17.1 we have plotted all these combinations and by joining them we obtain an isoquant showing that every combination represented on it can produce 100 units of output.

Though isoquants are similar to be indifference curves of the theory of consumer's behaviour, there is one important difference between the two. An indifference curve represents all those combinations of two goods which provide the same satisfaction or utility to a consumer but no attempt is made to specify the level of utility in exact quantitative terms it stands for. This is so because the car-

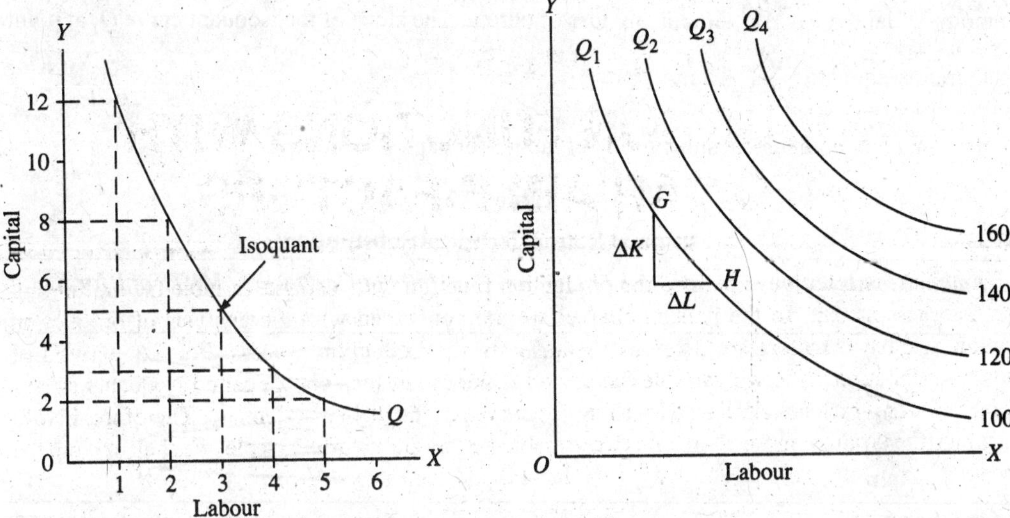

Fig. 17.1. *Isoquant* **Fig. 17.2.** *Isoquant map*

dinal measurement of satisfaction or utility in unambiguos therms is not possible. That is why we usually label indifference curves by ordinal numbers as I, II, III etc. indicating that a higher indifference curve represents a higher level of satisfaction than a lower one, but the information as to how much one level of satisfaction is greater than another is not provided. On the other hand, we can label isoquants in the physical units of output without any difficulty. Production of a good being a physical phenomenon lends itself easily to absolute measurement in physical units. Since each isoquant represents a specified level of production, it is possible to say by how much one isoquant indicates greater or less production than another. In Fig. 17.2 we have drawn an *isoquant-map or equal-product map* with a set of four isoquants which represent 100 units, 120 units,140 units and 160 units of output respectively. Then, from this set of isoquants it is very easy to judge by how much production level on one isoquant curve is greater or less than on another.

MARGINAL RATE OF TECHNICAL SUBSTITUTION

Marginal rate of technical substitution in the theory of production is similar to the concept of marginal rate of substitution in the indifference curve analysis of consumer's demand. Marginal rate of technical substitution indicates the rate at which factors can be substituted at the margin without altering the level of output. More precisely, *marginal rate of technical substitution of labour for capital may be defined as the number of units of capital which can be replaced by one unit of labour, the level of output remaining unchanged.* The concept of marginal rate of technical substitution can be easily understood from Table 17.2.

Each of the factor combinations *A*, *B*, *C*, *D*, and *E* yields the same level of output. Moving down from combination *A* to combination *B*, 4 units of capital are substituted by 1 unit of labour in the production process without any change in the level of output. Therefore, marginal rate of technical substitution of labour for capital is 4 at this stage. Switching from input combination *B* to input combination *C* involves the replacement of 3 units of capital by an additional unit of labour, output remaining the same. Thus, the marginal rate of technical substitution is now 3. Likewise, marginal rate of technical substitution of labour for capital between factor combinations *C* and *D* is 2, and between factor combinations *D* and *E* it is 1.

The marginal rate of technical substitution at a point on an isoquant (an equal product curve) can be known from the slope of the isoquant at that point. Consider a small movement down the equal product curve from G to H in Fig. 17.2 where a small amount of capital, say ΔK is substituted by an amount of labour say ΔL without any loss of output. The slope of the isoquant curve Q_1 at point G is therefore equal to $\frac{\Delta K}{\Delta L}$. Thus,

$$\text{marginal rate of tehcnical substitution of labour for capital} = \text{slope} = \frac{\Delta K}{\Delta L}.$$

Table 17.2.

Marginal Rate of Technical Substitution

Factor Combinations	*Units of Labour (L)*	*Units of Capital (K)*	*MRTS of L for K*
A	1	12	
B	2	8	4
C	3	5	3
D	4	3	2
E	5	2	1

Slope of the isoquant at a point and therefore the marginal rate of technical substitution (*MRTS*) between factors can also be known by the slope of the tangent drawn on the isoquant at that point. In Fig. 17.3 the tangent TT' is drawn at point K on the given isoquant Q. The slope of the tangent TT' is equal to $\frac{OT}{OT'}$. Therefore, the marginal rate of substitution at point K on the isoquant Q is equal to $\frac{OT}{OT'}$. JJ' is the tangent at point L drawn to the isoquant Q. Therefore, the marginal rate of technical substitution of labour for capital at point L is equal to OJ/OJ'.

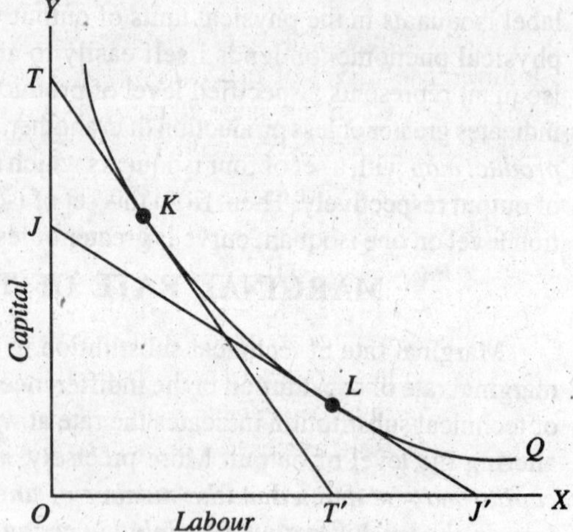

Fig. 17.3. *MRTS is given by the slope of an isoquant at a point.*

An important point to be noted about the marginal rate of technical substitution is that it is equal to the ratio of the marginal physical products of the two factors. Since, by definition, output remains constant on an isoquant the loss in physical output from a small reduction in capital will be equal to the gain in physical output from a small increment in labour. The loss in output is equal to the marginal physical product of capital (*MP*) multiplied by the amount of reduction in capital. The gain in output is equal to the marginal physical product of labour (*MP*) multiplied by the increment in labour.

Accordingly, along an isoquant

$$\Delta K.MP_K + \Delta L.MP_L = 0$$

$$\Delta K \times MP_K = \Delta L \times MP_L$$

$$\frac{\Delta K}{\Delta L} = \frac{MP_L}{MP_K}$$

But $\frac{\Delta K}{\Delta L}$, by definition, is the marginal rate of technical substitution of labour for capital

Therefore, $MRTS_{LK} = \frac{MP_L}{MP_K}$

We thus see that marginal rate of technical substitution of labour for capital is the ratio of marginal physical product of the two factors.

Diminishing Marginal Rate of Technical Substitution. An improtant characteristic of marginal rate of technical substitution is that it diminishes as more and more of labour is substituted for capital. In other words, as the quantity of labour used is increased and the quantity of capital employed reduced, the amount of capital that is required to be replaced by an additional unit of labour so as to keep the output constant will diminish. This is known as the principle of diminishing marginal rate of technical substitution. This principle of diminishing marginal rate of technical substitution is merely an extension of the law of diminishing returns to the relation between the marginal physical products of the two factors. Along an isoquant as the quantity of labour is increased and the quantity of capital is reduced, the marginal physical product of labour diminishes and the marginal physical product of capital increases. Therefore, less and less of capital is required to be substituted by an additional unit of labour so as to maintain the same level of output.

It may also be noted that the rate at which marginal rate of technical substitution diminishes is a measure of the extent to which the two factors can be substituted for each other. The smaller the rate at which the marginal rate of technical substitution diminishes, the greater the degree of substitutability between the two factors. If marginal rate of substitution between any two factors does not diminish and remains constant, the two factors are *perfect substitutes of each other*.

GENERAL PROPERTIES OF ISOQUANTS

The isoquants normally possess properties which are similar to those generally assumed for indifference curves of the theory of consumer's behaviour. Moreover, the properties of isoquants can be proved in the same manner as in the case of indifference curves. The following are the improtant properties of isoquants.

1. **Isouants, like indifference curves, slope downward from left to right (i.e., they have a negative slope).** This is so because when the quantity of a factor, say labour, is increased, the qunatity of other capital *i.e.*, capital must be reduced so as to keep output constant on a given isoquant. This downward-sloping property of isoquants follows from a valid assumption that the marginal physical products of factors are positive, that is, the use of additional units of factors yield positive incre*ments* in output. In view of this when one factor is increased yielding positive marginal products, the other factor must be *reduced* to hold the level of output constant otherwise the output will increase and we will switch over to a higher isoquant.

The assumption that the marginal physical product of a factor is positive is quite reasonable. In the discussion of the law of variable proportions we saw that in the stage III, when the units of the variable factor, say labour, become excessive, it causes such an overcrowding on a fixed capital equipment (or on a given piece of land if land is the fixed factor) that they obstruct each other resulting in negative marginal products of labour, that is, the use of additional units of labour reduce total output. This could happen but no rational producer who aims to minimise cost or maximise profits will employ units of a factor to the point where its marginal product has become negative because positive prices have to be paid for them. Thus, in view of the positive prices that have to be paid for the units of a factor, we rule out the use of the units of a factor that have negative or zero marginal products.

Thus, with labour measured on the *X*-axis and capital on the *Y*-axis if the isoquant is a horizontal straight line, this would indicate that the marginal products of labour (MP_L) are zero. Likewise, vertical isoquant would indicate marginal products of capital (MP_K) are zero. Further, an upward sloping isoquant implies that either the marginal products of the two factors are zero or one of the two factors has negative marginal products and the other has positive marginal products. It is also worth noting that the *upward-sloping isoquant implies that the same output can be produced with the use of less of both the factors*, that is, marginal products of at least one factor is negative. In this situation when every reduction in both the factors used does not affect output, the producer will not reach an equilibrium position. It follows from above that over the economically relevant stage of production when the marginal products of the factors are positive we have *downward sloping isoquants*.

2. **No two isoquants can intersect each other.** If the two isoquants, one corresponding to 20 units of output and the other to 30 units of output intersect each other, there will then be a common factor combination corresponding to the point of intersection. It means that the same factor combination which can produce 20 units of output according to one isoquant can also produce 30 units of output according to the other isoquant. But this is quite absurd. How can the same factor combination produce two different levels of output, technique of production remaining unchanged.

3. **Isoquants, like indifference curves, are convex to the origin.** The convexity of isoquant curves means that as we move down the curve successively smaller units of capital are required to be substituted by a given increment of labour so as to keep the level of output unchanged. Thus, the convexity of equal product curves is due to the diminishing marginal rate of technical substitution of one factor for the other.

If the isoquants were concave to the origin, it would mean that the marginal rate of technical substitution increased as more and more units of labour were substituted for capital. This could be valid if the law of increasing returns applied. Since it is the law of diminishing returns which is more true of the real world, the principle of diminishing marginal rate of technical substitution generally holds good and it makes the isoquants convex to the origin. We have seen above that marginal rate of technical substitution diminishes because of diminishing marginal returns to a factor as we increase its quantity used. Therefore, the *convexity of isoquants implies the diminishing returns to a variable factor*. We have seen that there are diminishing returns to a factor because of the fact that different factors are imperfect substitutes of each other in the production of a good.

In general, convexity of isoquants implies that *it becomes progressively more difficult or harder to substitute one factor for another* as we move along an isoquant and increase the use of one factor substituting the other factor. Thus, if it is difficult to substitute a factor, say labour for capital, it will then require a relatively larger amount of labour to replace a unit of capital, the level of output being held constant. Thus, *the curvature or convexity of the isoquants indicates the ease with which one factor can be substituted for another. The more convex an isoquant, the harder it is to substitute one factor for another*.

Isoquants of Perfect Substitutes and Complements

There are two exceptions to this general property of the convexity of isoquants. One is the case of factors which are perfect substitutes of each other. When the two factors are perfect substitutes of each other, then each of them can be used equally well in place of the other. For all intents and purposes they can be regarded as the same factor. Therefore, the *marginal rate of technical substitution between two perfect substitute factors remains* constant. Since marginal rate of technical substitution remains the same throughout, the isoquants of perfect substitutes are straight lines, as shown in Fig. 17.4 instead of being convex to the origin.

Another exceptional case is of factors which are perfect complements and for which the isoquants are right-angled as shown in Fig. 17.5. The *perfect complementary factors are those which are jointly used for production in a fixed proportion*. Thus, in Fig. 17.5, *OA* of factor *X* and *OB* of factor Y are used to yield a level of output represented by isoquant Q_1. An increase in one factor without the required proportionate increase in the other factor will yield no additional output whatsoever.

That is why the isoquant is right-angled (with two arms, one is a vertical straight line and the other is a horizontal straight line) at the combination consisting of a given proportion of the two factors.

Consider isoquant or equal product curve Q_1 in Fig. 17.5 where output Q_1 can be produced by the combination *H* consisting of *OA* amount of factor *X* and *OB* amount of factor *Y*. If now the amount

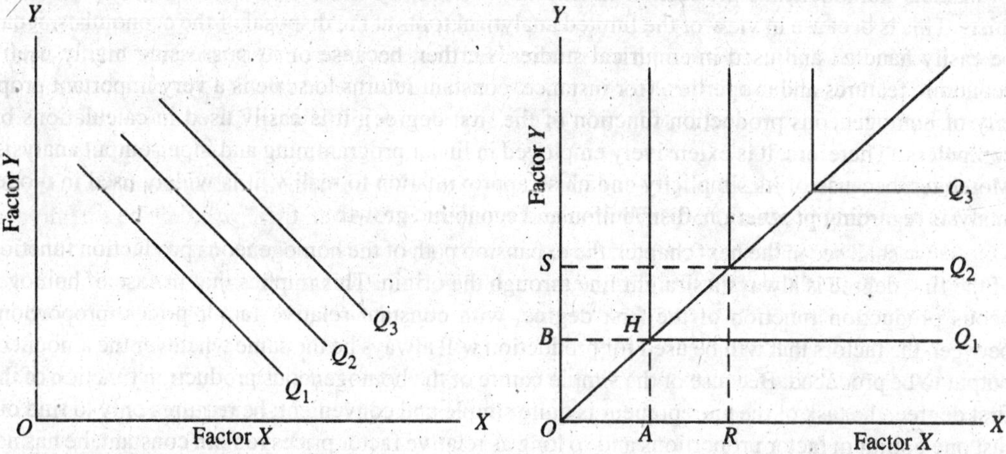

Fig. 17.4. *Perfect Substitutes* **Fig. 17.5.** *Perfect Complementary Factors*

of factor *X* is increased beyond *OA* without the increase in the factor *Y*, output will not rise and hence the lower portion of isoquant is a horizontal straight line. Likewise, if the amount of factor *Y* is increased beyond *OB* without the increase in factor *X*, the output will remain the same and hence the upper portion of the equal product curve is a vertical straight line. In case of perfect complementary factors, output can be increased only by increasing the amount of both the factors by the required given proportion. Thus, in Fig. 17.5, if the amount of factor *X* is increased to *OR* (which is twice *OA*), then the amount of factor *Y* will have to increase by *OS* (which is twice *OB*) so that we have the same factor proportion, output increases by the same proportion as the increase in factors and we have a new isoquant Q_2. It should be noted that no substitution of factors is possible in case of perfect complements.

LINEAR HOMOGENEOUS PRODUCTION FUNCTION

Production function can take several forms but a particular form of production function enjoys wide popularity among the economists. This is a linear homogeneous production function, that is, production function which is homogeneous of the first degree. *Homogeneous production function of the first degree implies that if all factors of production are increased in a given proportion, output also increases in the same proportion.* Hence linear homogeneous production function represents the case of constant returns to scale. If there are two factors *X* and *Y*, then homogeneous production function of the first degree can be mathematically expressed as:

$$mQ = f(mX, mY)$$

where *Q* stands for the total production and *m* is any real number.

The above function means that if factors *X* and *Y* are increased by *m*-times, total production *Q* also increases by *m*-times. It is because of this that homogeneous function of the first degree yields constant returns to scale.

More generally, a homogeneous production function can be expressed as

$$Qm^k = (mX, mY)$$

where *m* is any real number and *k* is constant. This function is homogeneous of the kth degree. If *k* is equal to one, then the above homogeneous function becomes homogeneous of the first degree. If k is equal to two, the function becomes homogeneous of the 2nd degree. If k is greater than one, the production function will yield increasing returns to scale. If, on the other hand, k is less than 1, it will yield decreasing returns to scale.

Linear homogeneous production function is extensively used in empirical studies by economists. This is because in view of the limited analytical tools at the disposal of the economists, it can be easily handled and used in empirical studies. Further, because of its possessing highly useful economic features and properties, (for instance, constant returns to scale is a very important property of homogeneous production function of the first degree), it is easily used in calculations by computers. Therefore, it is extensively employed in linear programming and input-output analysis. Moreover, because of its simplicity and close approximation to reality, it is widely used in model analysis regarding production, distribution and economic growth.

As we shall see in the next chapter, the expansion path of the homogeneous production function of the first degree is always a straight line through the origin. This implies that in case of homogeneous production function of the first degree, with constant relative factor prices, proportions between the factors that will be used for production will always be the same whatever the amount of output to be produced. Because of the simple nature of the homogeneous production function of the first degree, the task of the entrepreneur is quite simple and convenient; he requires only to find out just one optimum factor proportions and so long as relative factor prices remain constant, he has not to make any fresh decision regarding factor proportions to be used as he expands his level of production. Moreover, the use of the same optimum factor proportions (with constant relative factor prices) at different levels of output in homogeneous production function of the first degree is also very useful in input-output analysis. Homogeneous production function of the first degree, which, as said above, implies constant returns to scale, has been actually found in agriculture as well as in many manufacturing industries. In India, farm management studies have been made for various states and data have been collected for agricultural inputs and outputs. Analysing the data collected in these farm management studies, Dr. A.M. Khusro has reached the conclusion that constant returns to scale prevail in Indian agriculture.[1] Likewise, empirical studies conducted in the United States and Britain have found that many manufacturing industries are characterised by a long phase of constant long-run average cost (*LAC*) curve which again implies constant returns to scale and homogeneous production function of the first degree.

Cobb-Douglas Production Function

Many economists have studied actual production functions and have used statistical methods to find out relations between changes in physical inputs and physical outputs. A most familiar empirical production function found out by statistical methods is the Cobb-Douglas production function. Originally Cobb-Douglas production function was applied not to the production process of an individual firm but to the whole of the manufacturing industry. Output in this function was thus manufacturing production. Two factor Cobb-Douglas production function takes the following mathematical form:

$$Q = AL^a K^b$$

where Q is the manufacturing output, L is the quantity of employed, K is the quantity of capital employed and A, a and b are parameters of the function.

Roughly speaking, Cobb-Douglas production function found that about 75% of the increase in manufacturing production was due to the labour input and the remaining 25% was due to the capital

1. See his article "Returns to Scale in Indian Agriculture, *The Indian Journal of Agricultural Economics*, Vol. XIX-Dec. 1964, reprinted in "*Readings in Agricultural Development*", edited by A.M. Khusro, Allied Publishers, 1968.

input. Cobb-Douglas production can be estimated by regression analysis by first converting it into the following log form.

$$\log Q = \log A + a \log L + b \log K$$

Cobb-Douglas production function in log form is a linear function.

Cobb-Douglas production function is used in empirical studies to estimate returns to scale in various industries as to whether they are increasing, constant or decreasing. Further, Cobb-Douglas production function is also frequently used to estimate output elasticities of labour and capital. *Output elasticity of a factor shows the percentage change in output as result of a given percentage change in the quantity of a factor.*

Cobb-Douglas production has the following useful properties :

1. The sum of the exponents of factors in *Cobb-Douglas production function, that is, a+b measures returns to scale.*

   If $a + b = 1$, returns to scale are constant

   If $a + b > 1$, returns to scale are increasing

   If $a + b < 1$, returns to scale are decreasing

2. In a linear homogeneous Cobb-Douglas production function, $Q = AL^aK^{1-a}$, *average and marginal products of a factor depend on ratio of factors used in production* and is independent of the absolute quantities of the factors used. In the linear homogeneous Cobb-Douglas production function :

$$Q = A\,L^aK^{1-a} \qquad \text{where} \qquad a + 1 - a = 1$$

Average product of labour can be obtained from dividing the production function by the amount of labour L

$$\text{Average product of labour} = \frac{AL^a K^{1-a}}{L} = \frac{AK^{1-a}}{L^{1-a}} = A\left(\frac{K}{L}\right)^{1-a}$$

Since A and a are *constants, average product of labour will depend on the ratio of factors* $\left(\frac{K}{L}\right)$ of the factors used *and will not depend upon their absolute quantities.*

Like the average product of a factor, the marginal product of a factor of a *linear homogeneous* Cobb-Douglas production function also depends upon the *ratio* of the factors used and is independent of *the absolute quantities of the factors used.* Note that marginal product of a factor, say labour, is first derivative of the production function with respect to labour. The marginal product of labour of Cobb-Douglas production can be obtained as under:

$$Q = AL^a K^{1-a}$$

$$\text{Marginal Product of labour,} \quad \frac{dQ}{dL} = AaL^{a-1} K^{1-a}$$

$$= \frac{AaL^a k^{1-a}}{L}$$

$$= \frac{AaL^{a-a} K^{1-a}}{L^{1-a}} = \frac{AaK^{1-a}}{L^{1-a}}$$

$$= Aa\left(\frac{K}{L}\right)^{1-a}$$

Since A and a are constants, marginal product of labour will depend on capital-labour ratio $\left(\frac{K}{L}\right)$, that is, capital per worker and is independent of the *absolute quantities* of the factors employed.

3. **Thirdly, the exponents of labour and capital in *Cobb-Douglas production function measure output elasticities of labour and capital respectively*. Remember that output elasticity of a factor shows the percentage change in output resulting from a given percentage change in the quantity of a factor, other factors remaining constant. Thus,**

Output elasticity of labour $= \frac{\partial Q}{\partial L} \cdot \frac{L}{Q}$

$\frac{\partial Q}{\partial L}$ **= marginal productivity of labour (MP_L). Substituting the value of marginal productivity of labour in Cobb-Douglas production function as obtained above (*i.e.*, $MP_L = a\frac{Q}{L}$) in the output-elasticity expression we have**

$$\text{Output elasticity of labour} = \frac{\partial Q}{\partial L} \cdot \frac{L}{Q}$$

$$= a\frac{Q}{L} \cdot \frac{L}{Q} = a$$

Thus exponent '*a*' of labour in the Cobb-Douglas production function is equal to the output elasticity of labour.

$$\text{Output elasticity of capital} = \frac{\partial Q}{\partial K} \cdot \frac{K}{Q}$$

$$\text{Marginal productivity of capital, } \frac{\partial Q}{\partial K} = b \cdot \frac{Q}{K}$$

$$\text{Therefore, output elasticity of capital} = b \cdot \frac{Q}{K} \cdot \frac{K}{Q} = b$$

4. ***Linear homogenous Cobb-Douglas Production Function exhibits diminishing returns to a variable factor.***

To prove that the linear cobb-Douglas production function exhibits diminishing marginal product of a variable factor we have to show that the second derivative of the function with respect to a variable factor (say labour) is negative. Linear Cobb-Douglas production function can be written as

$Q = AL^{0.75}K^{0.25}$ **where** $0.75 + 0.25 = 1$

$$MP \text{ of labour } \left(\frac{\partial Q}{\partial L}\right) = 0.75\, AL^{0.75-1}\, K^{0.25}$$

$$= 0.75AL^{-0.25}\, K^{0.25}$$

$$\text{Second derivative } \left(\frac{\partial^2 Q}{\partial L^2}\right) = -\,0.25 \times 0.75\, AL^{-1.25}\, K^{0.25}$$

Thus second derivative of Cobb-Douglas production function is negative and therefore it shows diminishing marginal returns to the variable factor i.e., labour.

5. ***Linear Homogenous Cobb-Douglas production function shows constant returns to scale.*** **That is, when in Cobb-Douglas production function, $Q = AL^aK^b$, the sum of exponents $a + b = 1$ returns to scale are constant. We can easily prove this. When the sum of exponents $a + b = 1$, we can write b as $1 - a$. Writing Cobb-Douglas production function in this way we have**

$$Q = AL^a K^{1-a}$$

If the inputs of labour (L) and capital (K) are increased by a constant g, then the quantity of output will be increased to

$A(gL)^a (gK)^{1-a} = g^a g^{1-a} AL^aK^{1-a}$

Since $g^a g^{1-a} = g$,

Therefore, $A(gL)^a (gK)^{1-a} = g\, AL^a K^{1-a}$

$= gQ$

Thus, when the inputs of capital and labour are increased by a constant g, the output Q also increases by g. That is, returns to scale are constant.

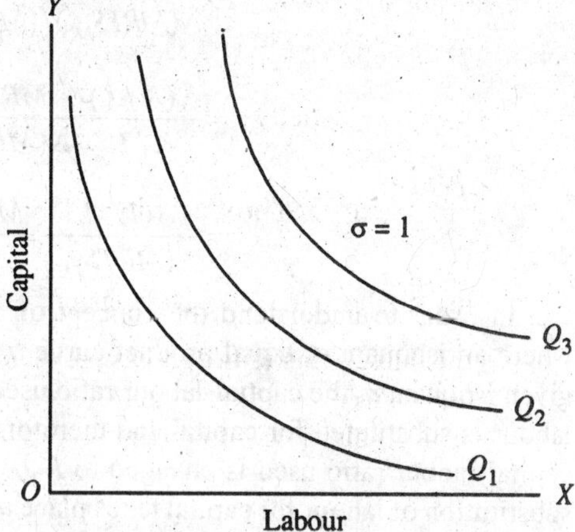

Fig.17.6. *Isoquants of Cobb Douglas Production Function*

6. *The elasticity of substitution between two factors, labour and capital, in Cobb-Douglas production function is equal to unity.* This unit elasticity of factor substitution in Cobb-Douglas production lies in between infinite substitution elasticity in case of perfect substitute factors and zero substitution elasticity between two perfect complementary factors. Due to this unit elasticity of substitution between two factors in this production function, isoquants curves are convex to the origin as shown in Fig 17.6.

ELASTICITY OF TECHNICAL SUBSTITUTION (BETWEEN FACTORS)

In part 2 concerning the theory of demand, we explained the concept of elasticity of substitution between goods (products) in consumption. In the theory of production we are concerned with the elasticity of substitution between factors (or inputs) in the production of goods. Thus, in the theory of production we are concerned with what may be called *elasticity of technical substitution.*

As seen above, marginal rate of technical substitution (*MRTS*) or factor X for factor Y declines as more of factor X is substituted for factor Y along an isoquant. In other words, marginal rate of technical substitution is different at different factor-proportions (*i.e.*, input ratios) used in the production of a good. This responsiveness of the proportions or ratios in which factors (or inputs) are used as there is a movement along an isoquant may be compared with the change in substitution possibilities in production as measured by the change in the marginal rate of technical substitution. *The proportionate change in the factor-proportions (or input ratios) divided by change in the marginal rate of technical substitution is known as elasticity of technical substitution between factors.* If the elasticity of substitution between the two factors is high, one factor can easily be substituted by another.

The concept of elasticity of technical substitution has been widely discussed in economic literature in connection witht the substitution between labour and capital. Therefore, we too shall explain the concept of elasticity of substitution with reference to capital and labour as factors of production. If K stands for the quantity of capital, L for the quantity of labour and σ for the elasticity of substitution, then in accordance with the above definition, elasticity of substitution between labour and capital can be expressed as follows :

$$\sigma = \frac{\text{proportionate change in the ratio of } (K/L) \text{ used}}{\text{proportionate change in the marginal rate of technical substitution of } L \text{ for } K}$$

$$= \frac{\text{proportionate change in } K/L}{\text{proportionate change in } MRTS_{LK}}$$

$$= \frac{\frac{\Delta(K/L)}{K/L}}{\Delta(MRTS_{LK})/(MRTS)_{LK}}$$

$$= \frac{\Delta(K/L)}{K/L} \cdot \frac{MRTS_{LK}}{\Delta(MRTS_{LK})}$$

$$= \frac{\Delta(K/L)}{\Delta(MRTS_{LK})} \cdot \frac{MRTS_{LK}}{K/L}$$

In order to understand the concept of elasticity factor of substitution, consider Figure 17.9 where an isoquant or equal product curve q has been drawn. It will be seen that at point A on the given isoquant q, the captial-labour ratio used is K_1/L_1 which is equal to the slope of the ray OA. As labour is substituted for capital and therefore we move down on the isoquant q from point A to B, capital-labour ratio used is changed to K_2/L_2 which is equal to the slope of the ray OB. If further substitution of labour for capital takes place and we come down to point C on the isoquant q, capital-labour ratio further falls to K_3/L_3 which is equal to the slope of the ray OC. It is, therefore, clear that as we substitute more labour for capital along the isoquant, while labour-capital ratio is rising, capital-labour ratio is falling.

Now, as we have already seen, marginal rate of technical substitution at point A is given by the absolute value of the slope of the isoquant at that point (which is equal to the slope of the tangent t_1t_1 drawn to that point). At point B, the $MRTS_{LK}$ is equal to the absolute value of the slope of tangent t_2t_2 and at point C, the $MRTS_{LK}$ is equal to the absolute of value of the slope of tangent t_3t_3. It will be seen that the slope of tangent t_2t_2 is less than that of t_1t_1; slope of t_3t_3 is less than that of t_2t_2, that is, $MRTS_{LK}$ diminishes as more labour is substituted for capital.

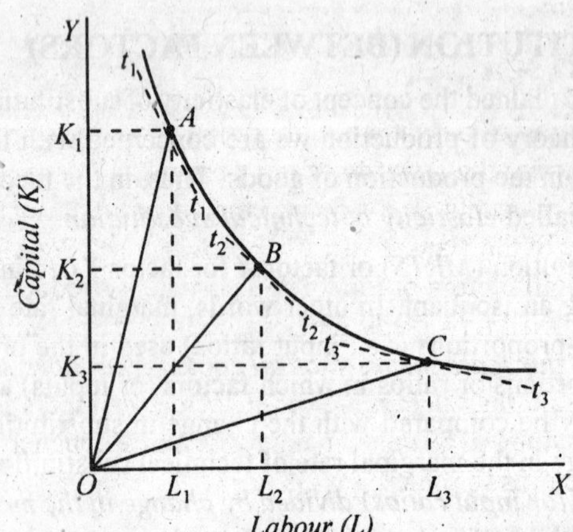

Fig. 17.7. *$MRTS_{LK}$ and Capital-Labour Ratios*

The greater the ease with which one factor can be substituted for another to produce a given level of output, the higher will be the elasticity of technical substitution between them. Thus, in case of good substitutable factors, since the proportionate change in the rate of the quantities of the two factors used as one moves along an isoquant is relatively large as compared with the change in marginal rate of technical substitution (*MRTS*) between them, elasticity of technical substitution between them is very high. In the extreme case of factors which are perfect substitutes, there is infinite possibilities of substituting one factor for another to produce a given level of output without causing any change in *MRTS*, the elasticity of factor substitution is equal to infinity and the isoquants between them are straight lines as shown in Fig. 17.4. Thus, in case of perfect substitutes :

$$\sigma = \frac{\Delta\left(\frac{K}{L}\right) \Big/ \frac{K}{L}}{\Delta MRTS_{LK} / MRTS_{LK}} = \frac{\infty}{0} = \infty$$

On the other extreme case when the two factors are perfect complements which are used in a fixed ratio in the production of a commodity and hence there is no possibility of substitution between them at all (*i.e.*, $\Delta\left(\frac{K}{L}\right)\Big/\frac{K}{L}=0$), the substitution elasticity between them is zero. Therefore, in case of perfectly complementary factors, isoquants are L = shaped as depicted in Fig. 17.5.

Elasticity of Substitution and Factor Price Ratio

Since, in equilibrium position, the marginal rate of technical substitution is equal to the ratio of factor prices, the marginal rate of substitution in the formula for elasticity of substitution may therefore be replaced by the ratio of factor-prices. Thus,

$$\sigma = \frac{\text{proportionate change in the factor ratio}}{\text{proportionate change in the ratio of factor prices}}$$

$$= \frac{\Delta(K/L)}{K/L} \times \frac{P_L/P_K}{\Delta(P_L/P_K)} = \frac{\Delta(K/L)}{\Delta(P_L/P_K)} \times \frac{P_L/P_K}{K/L}$$

The replacement of factor-price ratio for marginal rate of technical substitution in the formula of elasticity of substitution is greatly helpful in practical applications of the concept of elasticity of substitution. This is because information regarding prices is more easily available than the information regarding marginal rate of technical substitution. Further, changes in factor-proportions in which factors are used are generally induced by the relative factor prices.

Elasticity of factor substitution occupies an important place in the theory of distribution. According to neo-classical theory of distribution, distributive shares of labour and capital in national income depends on the elasticity of factor substitution.

RETURNS TO SCALE

In the previous chapter we explained the behaviour of output when alteration in factor proportions is made. Factor proportions are altered by keeping the quantity of one or some factors fixed and varying the quantity of the other. The changes in output as a result of the variation in factor proportions, as seen before, forms the subject-matter of the "law of variable proportions." We shall now undertake the study of changes in output when all factors or inputs in a particular production function are increased together. In other words, we shall now study the behaviour of output in response to the changes in the scale. *An increase in the scale means that all inputs or factors are increased in a given proportion.* Increase in the scale thus occurs when all factors or inputs are increased keeping factor proportions unaltered. The study of changes in output as a consequence of changes in the scale forms the subject-matter of "returns to scale".

Changes in Scale and Factor Proportions Distinguished

Before explaining returns to scale it will be instructive to make clear the distinction between changes in the scale and changes in factor proportions. The difference between the changes in scale and changes in factor proportions will become clear from the study of Fig. 17.8 where the two factors, labour and capital, have been measured on the *X*-axis and *Y*-axis respectively. We suppose that only labour and capital are required to produce a particular product. An isoquant map has been drawn. A point *S* has been taken on the *Y*-axis and the horizontal line *ST* parallel to *X*-axis has been drawn. *OS* represents the amount of capital which remains fixed along the line *ST*. As we move towards right on the line *ST*, the amount of labour varies while the amount of capital remains fixed at *OS*. In other words, proportion between the two factors undergoes a change along the line *ST*; the ratio of the variable factor 'labour' to the fixed factor 'capital' rises as we move towards right on the line *ST*. Thus, the movement along the line *ST* represents variation in factor proportions. Likewise, a vertical line *GH* parallel to the *Y*-axis has been drawn which also indicates changes in factor proportions. But in this case the quantity of labour remains fixed while the quantity of capital varies.

Now, draw a straight line *OP* passing through the origin. It will be seen that along the line *OP* the inputs of both the factors, labour and capital, vary. Moreover, because the line *OP* is a straight line through the origin, the ratio between the two factors along *OP* remains the same throughout. Thus, the upward movement along the line *OP* indicates the increase in the absolute amounts of two factors employed with the proportion between two factors remaining unchanged. Assuming that only labour and capital are needed to produce a product, then the increase in the two factors along the line *OP* represents the *increase in the scale* since along the line *OP* both the factors increase in the same proportion and therefore proportion between the two factors remains unaltered. If any other straight line through the origin such as *OQ* or *OR* is drawn, it will show, like the line *OP*, the changes in the scale but it will represent a different given proportion of factors which remains the same along the line. That is, the various straight lines through the origin will indicate different proportions between the two factors but on each line the proportion between the two factors remains the same throughout.

Validity of the Concept of Returns to Scale

We now proceed to discuss how the returns vary with the changes in scale, that is, when all *factors* are increased in the same proportion. But some economists have challenged the concept of returns to scale on the ground that all factors cannot be increased and therefore the proportions between factors cannot be kept constant. For instance, it has been pointed out that entrepreneurship is a factor of production which cannot be varied (in the single firm), though all other factors can be increased. The entrepreneur and his decision-making are indivisible and incapable of being increased. Thus, the entrepreneur is a fixed factor in all production functions. If labour and capital could produce a product with no one to supervise and take decisions, then the returns to scale in the sense of returns to all factors could be validly visualised. But the idea that labour and capital can produce goods without an entrepreneur is quite unrealistic. Thus, the concept of returns to scale involves a puzzle for economists which still remains unresolved. However, this puzzle can be resolved by assuming entrepreneurship to be variable in the sense that the greater the other inputs or factors, the greater the entrepreneurial work to be performed. This will be valid even if an entrepreneur is a single person because as he employs more units of other factors he uses his entrepreneurial ability to that extent greater. Thus, when labour and capital are increased in a proportion, the entrepreneurship can be assumed to be increased automatically in the same proportion. In this sense, returns to scale, that is, returns when *all factors* are varied, can be conceived.

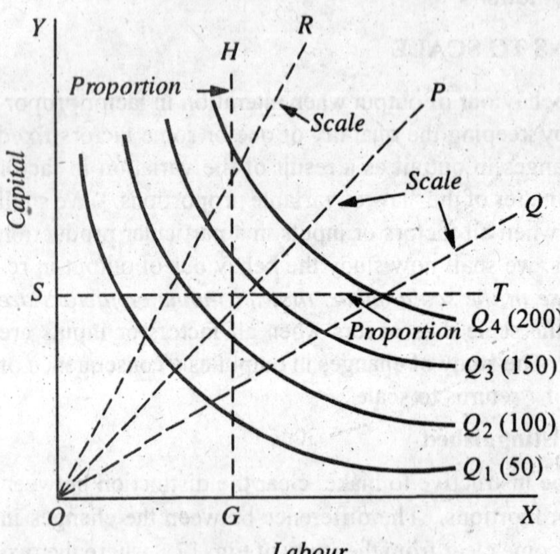

Fig. 17.8. *Changes in Scale and Factor Proportions Distinguished*

But we shall explain below the concept of returns to scale by assuming that only two factors, labour and capital, are needed for production. This makes our analysis simple and also enables us to proceed our analysis in terms of isoquants or equal-product curves.

CONSTANT RETURNS TO SCALE

Returns to scale may be constant, increasing or decreasing. *If we increase all factors (i.e., scale) in a given proportion and the output increases in the same proportion, returns to scale are said to be constant.* Thus, if a doubling or trebling of all factors causes a doubling or trebling of outputs, returns to scale are constant. But, if a given percentage increase in all factors leads to a more than proportionate increase in output, returns to scale are said to be increasing. Thus, if all factors are doubled and output increases by more than a double, then the returns to scale are increasing. On the other hand, if the increase in all factors leads to a less than proportionate increase in output, returns to scale are decreasing. We shall explain below these various types of returns to scale.

As said above, the constant returns to scale means that with a given percentage increase in the scale or the amounts of all factors leads to the same percentage increase in output, that is, doubling of all inputs doubles the output. In mathematics the case of constant returns to scale is called *linear homogeneous production function or homogeneous production function of the first degree.* Production function exhibiting constant returns to scale possesses very important mathematical properties which make it very useful for theoretical analysis. There are a number of special theorems which apply when production function exhibits constant returns to scale. Empirical evidence suggests that production function for the economy as a whole is not too far from being homogeneous of the first degree. Empirical evidence also suggests that in the production function for an individual firm there is a long phase of constant returns to scale.

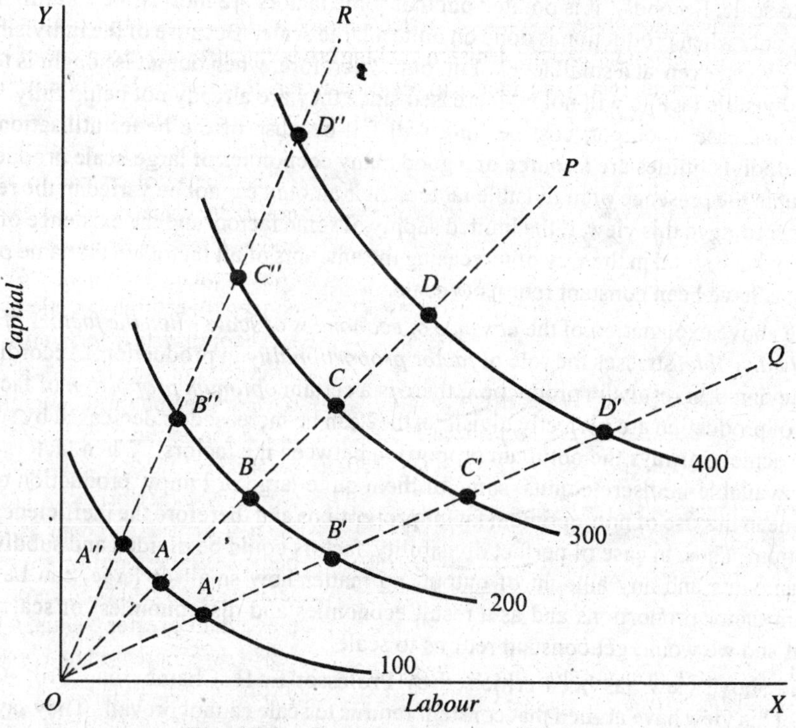

Fig. 17.9. *Constant Returns to Scale*

Let us illustrate diagrammatically the constant returns to scale with the help of equal product curves *i.e.* isoquants. Fig. 17.9 depicts an isoquant map. It is assumed that, in the production of the good, only two factors, labour and capital, are used. In order to judge whether or not returns to scale are constant, we draw some straight lines through the origin. As shown above, these straight lines passing through the origin indicate the increase in scale as we move upward. It will be seen from the figure, that successive isoquants are equidistant from each other along each straight line drawn from the origin. Thus along the line *OP*, $AB = BC = CD$, and along the line *OQ*, $A'B' = B'C' = C'D'$ and along the line *OR*, $A''B'' = B''C'' = C''D''$. The distance between the successive equal product curves being the same along any straight line through the origin, means that if both labour and capital are increased in a given proportion, output expands by the same proportion. Therefore, Fig. 17.9 displays constant returns to scale.

Divisibility, Proportionality and Constant Returns to Scale

Some economists are of the view that if the factors of production are perfectly divisible production function must necessarily exhibit constant returns to scale. It is thus argued by them that if, for instance, all factors or inputs are doubled, then what is there to prevent the output from being doubled. Suppose we build three exactly same type of factories by using exactly same type of workers, capital equipment and raw materials, will we not produce three times the output of a single factory ? Economists such as Joan Robinson, Nicholas Kaldor, A. P. Lerner, F. H. Knight who hold this view argue that if it is possible to increase or diminish all factors or inputs in the same proportion, then the constant returns to scale must occur. They say that if constant returns to scale does not prevail in some industries it is because it is not possible to increase or diminish factors used in them in exactly the same proportion. They advanced two reasons for our inability to vary the factors in the same proportion. First, there are some factors whose amount cannot be increased in a given proportion because their supplies are scarce and limited. The scarcities of these factors cause diminishing returns to scale. Secondly, it is pointed out that some factors are indivisible and full use of them can be made only when production is done on quite a large scale. Because of the indivisibility they have to be employed even at a small level of output. Therefore, when output is sought is to be expanded, these indivisible factors will not be increased since they are already not being fully utilised. Thus, with the increase in output, cost per unit will fall because of the better utilisation of indivisible factors. Indivisibilities are a source of a good many economies of large-scale production. It is thus clear that in the presence of indivisible factors their amount cannot be varied in the required proportion. According to this view, if the limited supply of some factors and the existence of indivisibilities would not have stood in the way of increasing the amounts of all factors in the same proportion, then there must have been constant returns to scale.

The above explanation of the *absence of economies of scale when the factors of production are perfectly divisible*, stresses the role of *factor proportionality* in production. According to this view, for achieving best results in production, there is a certain *optimum proportion* of factors. When the factors of production are perfectly divisible, they can be increased or decreased by suitable amounts so as to achieve always the optimum proportion between the factors. When factors are indivisible, that is, available in discrete units, some of them quite large or lumpy, production on a small scale would mean the use of non-optimum factor proportions and therefore the inefficiency of small-scale production. Thus, in case of perfect divisibility, factors could be divided and subdivided by appropriate amounts and any amount of output, no matter how small or large, can be produced with optimum factor proportions and as a result economies and diseconomies of scale would be non-existent and we would get constant returns to scale.

The above view has been criticised by Professor E. H. Chamberlin. Prof. Chamberlin and others of his view have argued that constant returns to scale cannot prevail. They say that even if all factors could be varied in required quantities and even if all factors were perfectly divisible there could be increasing returns to scale. In their view even in case of perfect divisibility and variation of the factors, increasing returns to scale can occur with the increase in the scale or size (*i.e.*, increase in all factors, because at a larger scale, (1) greater specialization of labour becomes possible and (2) introduction of specialized machinery or other inputs of a superior technology is made possible by a wise selection from among the greater range of technical possibilities opened up by greater resources. Thus, Professor Chamberlin lays stress on *size* (or *scale*), in causing economies of scale. According to him, when the size or scale of operations, or in other words when the *absolute amounts* of all factors increase, the efficiency of the factors is increased by the use of greater specialisation of labour and by the introduction of specialised and superior machinery. Thus, according to Chamberlin, the above view which stresses divisibility and proportionality neglects the effect of *scale* on the efficiency of factors.[2]

It has been further pointed out that one cannot meaningfully speak of doubling all the factors in a given situation. For instance, two factories existing nearby is simply not the same thing as doubling of one factory in isolation. The existence of another factory at a close distance affects labour discipline, air pollution, cost of labour training etc. It is thus argued that in practice it is not possible to vary all the factors in a given proportion and obtain increases in output in the same proportion.

More significantly, it is pointed out that if a large single factory is more efficient than two small factories (the two having total capacity equal to the large one), then there would be no incentive on the part of an entrepreneur to double or duplicate his factors in the sense of setting up another small factory, near to his previous one. In other words, when the entrepreneur sees the opportunity of getting increasing returns to scale by setting up a large factory, then he would not set up a duplicate factory of his previous size and obtain constant returns to scale. In this connection, it is pointed out that there are many types of economies of scale due to which there is a great possibility of getting, at least in the beginning, increasing returns to scale.

Cobb-Douglas Production Function and Constant Returns to Scale. As seen above, though some economists look at constant returns to scale with suspicion, empirical evidence shows that in the expansion of a single firm, after a phase of increasing returns to scale, there is a long phase of constant returns to scale covering a wide range of output. Cobb-Douglas production function found out empirically and which applies to the manufacturing industry as a whole and to several individual industries also exhibits constant returns to scale. As noted in the previous chapter, Cobb-Doughlas production function takes the following form : $Q = AL^aK^{1-a}$ where Q stands for quantity of output, L for the quantity of labour and K for the quantity of capital employed. A and a are positive constants and where $a < 1$. As shown above, according to the Cobb-Douglas production function returns to scale are constant. The production function of the type of constant returns to scale plays an important role in the theory of distribution, input-output analysis and linear programming analysis of production.

INCREASING RETURNS TO SCALE

As stated above, increasing returns to scale means that output increases in a greater proportion than the increase in inputs. If, for instance, all inputs are increased by 25%, and output increases by 40% then the increasing returns to scale will be prevailing. When a firm expands, the increasing returns to scale are generally obtained in the beginning. Several factors account for increasing returns to scale, at least in the initial stages.

Indivisibility of the Factors. Many economists, such as Joan Robinson, Kaldor, Lerner and Knight ascribe increasing returns to scale to the indivisibility of factors. Some factors are available in large and lumpy units and can therefore be utilised with utmost efficiency at a large scale of output. Therefore, in the case of some indivisible and lumpy factors, when output is increased from a small level to a large one, indivisible factors are better utilised and therefore increasing returns are obtained. According to this view, as stated above, if all factors are perfectly divisible, increasing returns to scale would not occur.

Greater Possibilities of Specialisation of Labour and Machinery. As stated above, Chamberlin is of the view that returns to scale increase because of greater possibilities of specialisation

2. For the views of Professor Chamberlin regarding the controversial question of Divisibility, Proportionality and Economies of Scale, see his article in *Quarterly Journal of Economics*. Vol. LXII, Feb. 1948.

of labour and machinery. According to him, even if the factors were perfectly divisible, with the increase in the scale, returns to scale can increase because the firm can introduce greater degree of specialization of labour and machinery (because now greater resources or amounts of factors become available) and also because it can install technologically more efficient machinery.

Integration of Processes. Integration of successive processes in the production of a commodity is another factor which gives rise to some economies of large-scale production. For example, a book publishing company may set up its own printing press, opens up a binding section with suitable binding machinery, and also starts varnishing the book covers itself. Likewise, a steel firm may start doing various processes such as melting of iron, making of steel and converting steel into different shapes and sizes. This integration of successive stages in a single firm increases the productivity and efficiency of the firm and proves to be highly economical.

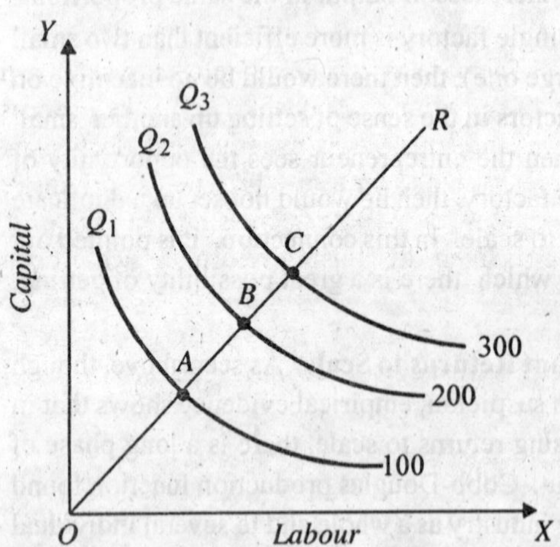

Fig. 17.10. *Increasing Returns to Scale*

Dimensional Economies. Another important cause of increasing returns to scale lies in dimensional relations, which have been emphasised by Professor Baumol.[3] A wooden box of 3 foot-cube contains 9 times greater wood than the wooden box of 1 foot-cube, that is, 3 foot-cube wooden box contains 9 times greater input. But the capacity of the 3 foot-cube wooden box is 27 times greater than that of 1 foot-cube. Another example is the construction of a warehouse. Suppose a rectangular whorehouse is proposed to be constructed. Most important input used in this construction-work is the number of bricks and other inputs which almost vary in proportion to the number of bricks used. The number of bricks used depends upon the wall area of the building. The elementary mathematics tells us that the wall area will increase equal to the square of the perimeter of the warehouse, while its volume, that is, its storage area will increase equal to the cube of the perimeter. In other words, double the number of bricks and other inputs that go with them, the storage capacity of the warehouse will be more than doubled. This is thus a case of increasing returns to scale. Similarly, if the diameter of a pipe is doubled, the flow through it is more than doubled.

Increasing returns to scale can be shown through isoquants. When increasing returns to scale occur, the successive isoquants will lie at decreasingly smaller distances along a straight line ray *OR* through the origin. In Fig. 17.10 the various isoquants Q_1, Q_2, Q_3 are drawn which successively represent 100, 200 and 300 units of output. It will be seen that distances between the successive isoquants decrease as we expand output by increasing the scale. Thus, increasing returns to scale occur since $AB < OA$ *and* $BC < AB$ which-means that *equal increases in output are obtained by smaller and smaller increments in inputs.*

DECREASING RETURNS TO SCALE

As stated above, when output increases in a smaller proportion than the increase in all inputs, decreasing returns to scale are said to prevail. When a firm goes on expanding by increasing all his inputs, *eventually* diminishing returns to scale will occur. But among economists there is no agreement on a cause or causes of diminishing returns to scale. Some economists are of the view that the entrepreneur is a fixed factor of production ; while all other inputs may be increased, he cannot be. According to this view, decreasing returns to scale is therefore actually a special case of the law of variable proportions. Thus, they point out that we get diminishing returns to scale beyond a point

3. W.J. Baumol, *Economic Theory and Operations Analysis;* Prentice Hall, 3rd edition, p. 382

because varying quantities of all other inputs are combined with a fixed entrepreneur. Thus, according to this view, decreasing returns to scale is a special case of the law of variable proportions with entrepreneur as the fixed factor. Other economists do not treat decreasing returns to scale as the special case of the law of variable proportions and argue that decreasing returns to scale eventually occur because of the *increasing difficulties of management, co-ordination and control with the expansion in scale and output.* When the firm has expanded to a too gigantic size, it is difficult to manage it with the same efficiency as previously.

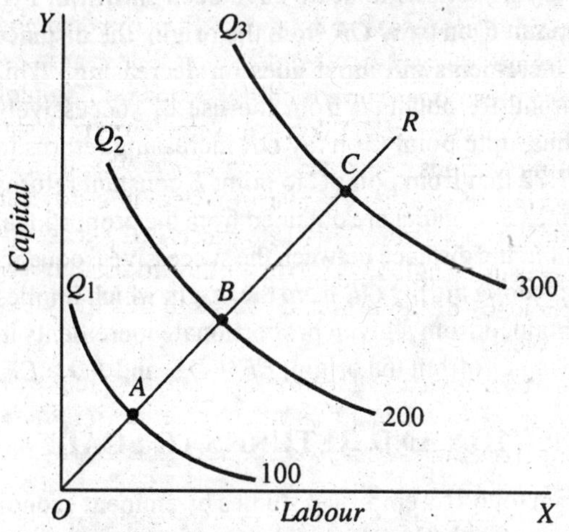

Fig. 17.11. *Decreasing Returns to Scale*

The case of decreasing returns to scale can-be shown with an isoquant map. When successive isoquants lie at progressively larger and larger distance on a ray through the origin, returns to scale will be decreasing. In Fig. 17.11 successively decreasing returns to scale occur since *AB* > *OA*, and *BC* > *AB*. It means that successively more and more of inputs (labour and capital) are required to obtain equal increments in output.

Varying Returns to Scale in a Single Production Process

It should be noted that it is not always the case that different production functions should exhibit different types of returns to scale. It generally happens that there are three phases of increasing constant and diminishing returns to scale in a single production function. In the beginning when the scale increases, increasing returns to scale are obtained because of greater possibilities of specialization of labour and machinery. After a point, there is a phase of constant returns to scale

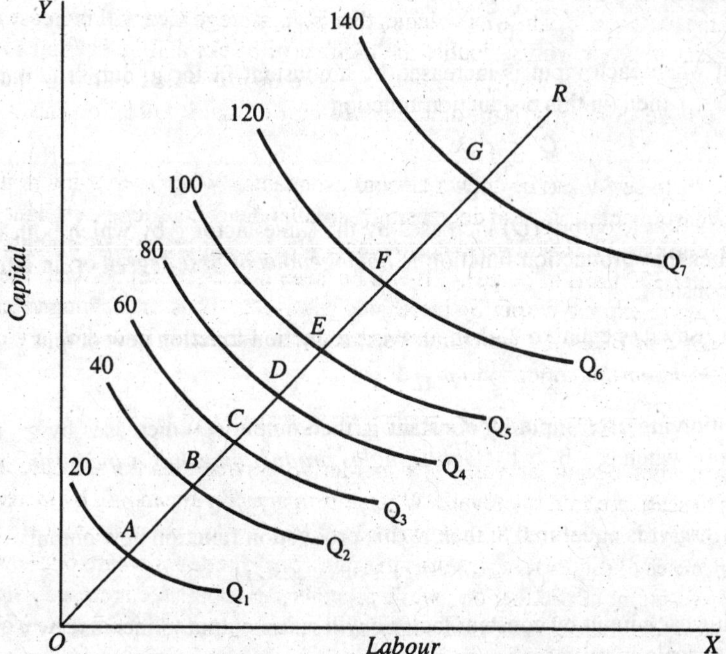

Fig. 17.12. *Varying Returns to Scale*

where output increases in the same proportions as inputs. Empirical evidence suggests that the phase of constant returns to scale is quite long. If the firm continues to expand, then eventually a point will be reached beyond which decreasing returns to scale will occur due to the mounting difficulties of co-ordination and control. These varying returns to scale have been shown in Fig. 17.12. It will be seen from Figure 17.12 that upto point C on a ray OR from the origin, the distance between the successive isoquants showing equal increments in output goes on decreasing. This implies that upto point C equal increments in output are obtained from the use of successively smaller increases in inputs (labour and capital). Thus, upto point C on ray OR increasing returns to scale occur. Further, it will be seen from Figure 17.12 that from point C to point E constant returns to scale are obtained as the same proportionate increments in output are obtained from the proportional increase in inputs of labour and capital. Beyond point E, the distance between the successive isoquants representing equal increments in output is decreasing along the ray OR from the origin which implies that less than proportionate increase in output is obtained from a given proportionate increments in the use of the two factors, labour and capital on the ray OR from the origin, $EF > DE$ and $FG > EF$.

COBB-DOUGLAS PRODUCTION FUNCTION AND RETURNS TO SCALE

An important production function which has been found by empirical studies by eminent economists Cobb and Douglas and known after their name as Cobb-Douglas production function is given below :

$$Q = AL^{\alpha}K^{\beta}$$

In this production function the sum of exponents $(\alpha + \beta)$ measures returns to scale. Multiplying each input, labour (L) and capital (K), by a constant factor g, we have

$$Q' = A\,(gL)^{\alpha}\,(gK)^{\beta}$$
$$= g^{\alpha+\beta}\,(AL^{\alpha}K^{\beta})$$

Expression in bracket $AL^{\alpha}K^{\beta} = Q$. Therefore,

$$Q' = g^{\alpha+\beta}Q$$

This means that when each input is increased by a constant factor g, output Q increases by $g^{\alpha+\beta}$. Now, If $\alpha + \beta = 1$ then, in this production function

$$Q' = g^{1}Q$$

or

$$Q' = gQ$$

That is, when $\alpha + \beta = 1$, output (Q) increases by the same factor g by which both inputs are increased. This implies that production function is *homogenous of first degree* or, in other words, returns to scale are constant.

When $\alpha + \beta > 1$, say it is equal to 2, then, in this production function new output

$$Q' = g^{\alpha+\beta}AL^{\alpha}K^{\beta} = g^{2}Q$$

In this case multiplying each input by constant g, then output (Q) increases by g^2, that is by more than g. Therefore, when $\alpha + \beta > 1$. *Cobb Douglas production exhibits increasing returns to scale.*

When $\alpha + \beta < 1$, say it is equal to 0.8, then in this production function new output

$$Q' = g^{\alpha+\beta}AL^{\alpha}K^{\beta} = g^{0.8}Q$$

That is, increasing each input by constant factor g will cause output to increase by $g^{0.8}$, that is, less than g. Returns to scale in this case are decreasing.

RETURNS TO SCALE AND MARGINAL RETURNS TO A VARIABLE FACTOR

Constant Returns to Scale and Returns to a Variable Factor

We now turn to study the relationship between returns to scale and marginal returns to a variable factor. In other words, we want to study whether marginal productivity of a factor diminishes or rises when the returns to scale are constant, diminishing and increasing. We first take the case of constant returns to scale. As seen above, in case of constant returns to scale, or what is called in mathematics, homogeneous production function of the first degree, the distance between the successive equal product curves along a straight line through the origin is always the same. Consider Fig. 17.13 in which here equal product curves showing 100, 200 and 300 units of output respectively are drawn. A straight line *OL* through the origin and cutting the equal product curves is drawn. Line *OL* displays returns to scale. Since returns to scale are constant, *PQ* is equal to *QR*. A horizontal line *ST* is also drawn, which shows the behaviour of output when the amount of the variable factor labour is increased to a fixed quantity *OS* of capital. Now, it is to be proved that when the returns to scale are constant, the marginal physical product of the variable factor diminishes. In terms of Fig. 17.13 where returns to scale are constant, we can prove that more units of the variable factor labour will be required to be added to a fixed quantity of capital to obtain equal increments in output, that is, *QN* is greater than *MQ*. Thus, given that *PQ* = *QR* (*i.e.*, returns to scale are constant), we have to prove that *QN* is greater than *MQ*. *QN* being greater than *MQ* means that marginal physical product of labour diminishes as varying amounts of it are added to the fixed quantity of *capital*. This can be proved in the following way :

In triangles *QRF* and *QPE* in Fig. 17.13

$$QR = PQ \text{ (given, because of constant returns to scale)}$$

$$\angle QRF = \angle QPE \text{ (alternate angles)}$$

$$\angle RQF = \angle PQE \text{ (vertically opposite angles)}$$

Therefore, triangles *QRF* and *QPE* are congruent, *i.e.*, equal in every respect.

Hence, $QF = EQ$

It will be seen from Fig. 17.13 that *MQ* is less than *EQ* and *QN* is greater than *QF*. Therefore, *QN* is greater than *MQ*.

It is thus proved that *when returns to scale are constant, (or when production function is homogeneous of the first degree) marginal physical product (i.e., marginal returns) of a variable factor diminishes. In other words, constant returns to scale imply diminishing marginal returns to a varaible factor.*

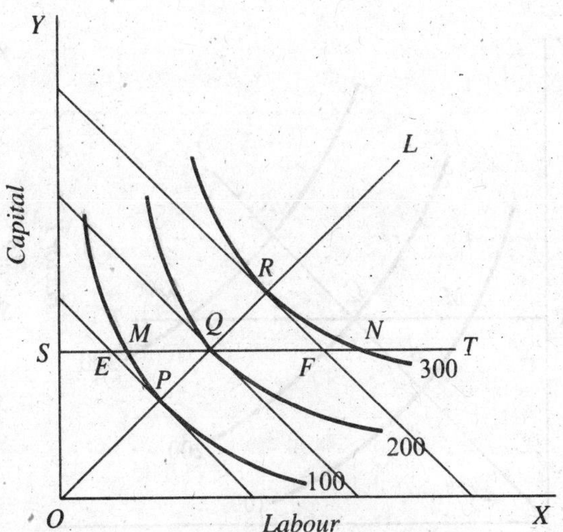

Fig. 17.13. *When returns to scale are constant, returns to a variable factor diminish*

Mathematical Proof*. That when returns to scale are constant, marginal product of a variable factor diminishes can be proved mathematically. Let us take Cobb-Douglas production function with sum of

* Those who are not interested in mathematical proof, they may omit this section

exponents equal to one which implies constant returns to scale. Such a Cobb-Douglas production function can be written as

$$Q = AL^{\frac{3}{4}} K^{\frac{1}{4}} \qquad ...(i)$$

Since in the above Cobb-Douglas production function sum of exponents $\left(\frac{3}{4}+\frac{1}{4}\right)$ equals one, this represents constant returns to scale.

Marginal product of labour $(MP_L) = \frac{\partial Q}{\partial L}$

Now, in order to obtain marginal product of labour we differentiate the given production function (*i*) with respect to labour. Thus

$$MP_L = \frac{\partial Q}{\partial L} = \frac{3}{4} A L^{\frac{3}{4}-1} K^{\frac{1}{4}}$$

$$= \frac{3}{4} AL^{-\frac{1}{4}} K^{\frac{1}{4}} \qquad ...(ii)$$

For marginal product of labour to diminish as more labour is used, its second derivative must be negative. To obtain the second derivative we differentiate (*ii*) with respect to labour

Thus $$\frac{\partial^2 Q}{\partial L^2} = -\frac{1}{4} \cdot \frac{3}{4} AL^{-\frac{1}{4}-1} K^{\frac{1}{4}}$$

Likewise, it can be shown that with a given quantity of labour, if capital increases, marginal product of capital would diminish.

Decreasing Returns to Scale and the Marginal Physical Product of the Variable Factor

It also follows from above that when returns to scale are decreasing, the marginal physical product of the variable factor will diminish more than in the case of constant returns to scale. In

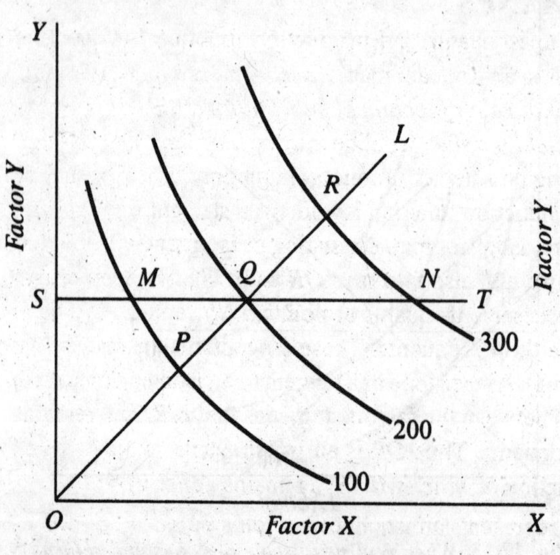

Fig. 17.14. *When returns to scale are decreasing returns to a variable factor diminish rapidly*

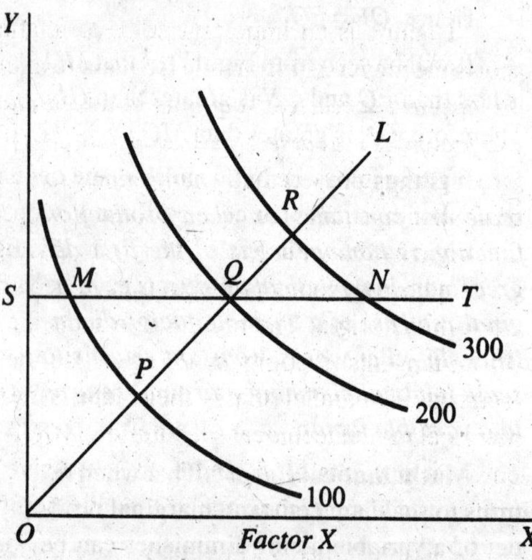

Fig.17.15. *Marginal physical product can diminish even when returns to scale are increasing.*

product of the variable factor will diminish more than in the case of constant returns to scale. In Fig. 17.14 returns to scale are diminishing, since *QR* is greater than *PQ*. It is quite obvious from Fig. 17.14 that along the horizontal line *ST* which represents the varying quantities of factor *X* with a fixed quantity of factor *Y*, the intercept *QN* is much greater than the intercept *MQ*. It follows *therefore that when returns to scale are diminishing, marginal physical product of the variable factor falls rapidly.*

Increasing Returns to Scale and Marginal Physical Product of the Variable Factor

Finally, how the marginal physical product of the variable factor behaves when returns to scale are increasing. This case is illustrated in Fig. 17.15 where returns to scale are increasing *strongly*. *QR* is much less than *PQ*. It will be seen from Fig. 17.15 that along the horizontal line *ST*, *QN* is less than *MQ*. It means that as the varying quantities of factor *X* are successively added to the given quantity of the fixed factor *Y*, smaller quantity of factor *X* than before is required to be increased to get an equal increment in output. Thus, *QN* being less than *MQ* means that marginal physical product of the variable factor *X* increases. It is therefore concluded that when returns to scale are *strongly* increasing, the marginal returns to a variable factor (used with a fixed quantity of the other factor) increases. However, when the returns to scale are *slightly increasing*, then the marginal returns of the variable factor will diminish.

Thus, the law of diminishing marginal returns to a factor is even consistent with increasing returns to scale. As just seen above, increasing returns to scale can yield increasing returns as well as diminishing returns to a variable factor depending upon whether returns to scale are strongly increasing or slightly increasing.

From the foregoing analysis we conclude that if returns to scale are constant the marginal physical product of a variable factor used in combination with a fixed factor will always diminish as more of the variable factor is used. Similarly, when returns to scale are decreasing, marginal physical product of a variable factor always diminish, and when returns to scale are increasing marginal physical product of a factor will still diminish unless the returns to scale are increasing sufficiently strongly.

ISOCLINES

Isocline is an important concept relating to isoquants and production function. An isocline shows the movement from one isoquant to another in an isoquant map. *An isocline is a locus of points on various successive isoquants at which marginal rate of technical substitution (MRTS) between two factors is the same, that is, constant at a particular value.* Isocline may be a straight line through the origin or it may be of irregular shape depending on whether production function is homogeneous or nonhomogeneous. In case of homogeneous production function isocline is a straight line through the origin as shown in Fig 17.16 (*a*). In this figure, isoquant map consisting of isoquants Q_1, Q_2 and Q_3 of a homogeneous production have been drawn and also two rays *OR* and *OS* have been drawn through the origin. The ray *OR* intersects the successive isoquants at points a_1, b_1 and c_1. We have drawn tangents at points a_1, b_1 and c_1 to the the three isoquants. These tangents to the successive isoquants are parallel (that is, their slope is the same). As the slope of a tangent to an isoquant measures marginal rate of technical substitution ($MRTS_{LK}$) between the factors, it means that $MRTS_{LK}$ remains constant at points a_1, b_1 and c_1 at successive isoquants. Thus *OR* is an isocline as it is the locus of points of different isoquants of a production function at which $MRTS_{LK}$ remains constant.

Similarly, ray *OS* in Figure 17.16 (*b*) also represents an isocline as it joins points a_2, b_2 and c_2 on different isoquants at which $MRTS_{LK}$ (as measured by the slopes of tangents drawn to those points) is constant, though with a different value as compared to that of isocline *OR*. Note that tangents at points a_2, b_2 and c_2 to isoquants Q_1, Q_2 and Q_3 are relatively flatter as compared to those at a_1, b_2 and c_2.

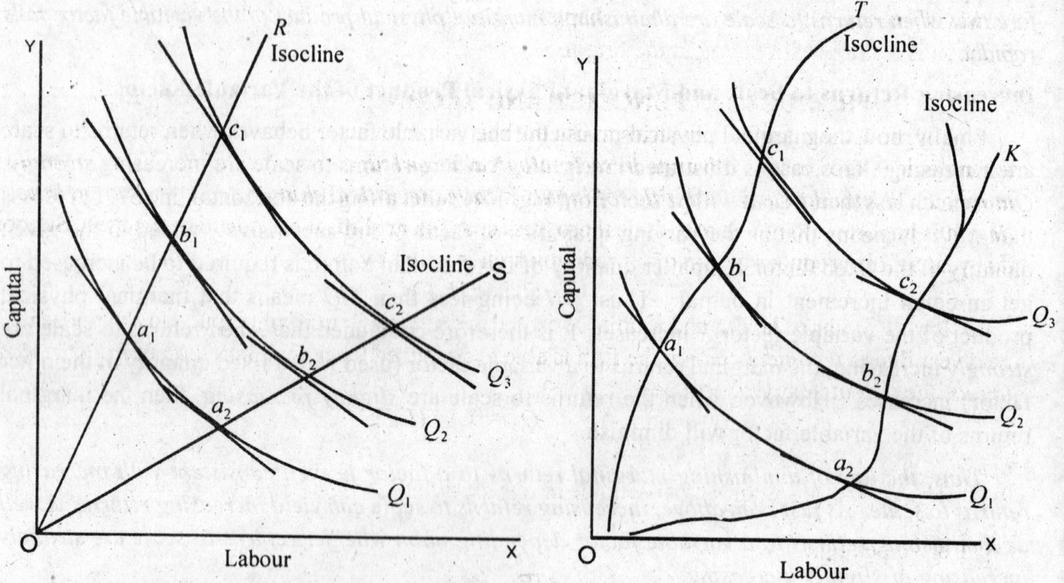

Fig. 17.16. (*a*) *Isocline of an Homogeneous Production Function*

Fig. 17.16. (*b*) *Isoclines of a Non-homogeneous Production Function*

Two things must be noted in respect of isoclines of a homogeneous production function. First, in case of homogeneous production function, isoclines are straight lines through the origin as are isoclines *OR* and and *OS* in Fig. 17.16(a). Secondly, isoclines of homogeneous production functions being straight lines through the origin, capital - labour ratio (that is, $\frac{K}{L}$ ratio) remains the same. The slope of isocline mesures capital-labour $\left(\frac{K}{L}\right)$ ratio. However, $\frac{K}{L}$ ratio along different isoclines such as *OR* and *OS* is different. It will be seen from Fig. 17.16 (a) that $\frac{K}{L}$ ratio along isocline line *OR* is greater than that of *OS*.

Isoclines of Non-homogeneous Production Function. If production function is non-homogeneous, then the isoclines will not be straight lines through the origin but would be of an irregular shape as shown in Figure 17.16 (*b*) by the curves *OT* and *OK*. Moreover, capital labour ratio $\left(\frac{K}{L}\right)$ along isoclines of a non-homogeneous production will be different at various points on each isocline.

Isoclines and Production Path. It is important to note that an isocline which is the locus of points on successive isoquants at which $MRTS_{LK}$ is the same is *drawn independently of the prices of factors of production.* The shape of isoclines depends on the physical characteristics of the production function. Therefore, the concept of isocline is different from the concept of expansion path along which also $MRTS_{LK}$ remains the same, but with the *given prices of factors*. But expansion path represents the optimum or least-cost combination of factors, given the prices of factors of production. Hence, unlike an isocline, the expansion path shows the actual choice of factor combinations by a rational producer and this choice of factor combination depends on the prices of factors of production. However, as we will study in the next chapter, expansion path of a linear homogeneous production function is a straight line through the origin.

PRODUCTION FUNCTION AND TECHNOLOGICAL CHANGE

For producing goods a firm tries to use the best available production process, given the state of technological knowledge. ***Advance in technological knowledge that enables the firms to produce more output with the same quantities of inputs is called technical change or technological innovation.*** It is important to note that technical progress changes or shifts the production function. Suppose this year a firm produces output of a product which is given by

$$Q_1 = f(L,K)$$

It uses L units of labour and K units of capital to produce Q_1 units of output. Now suppose in the next year due to *technical change* the firm is able to produce 10 per cent more output from the *given inputs,* the output next year will be

$$Q_2 = 1.1\, f(L,K)$$

The firm's rate of growth of output in our example is 10 per cent as $\dfrac{1.1f(L,K)-f(L,K)}{f(L,K)}$ = 0.1 or 10 per cent.

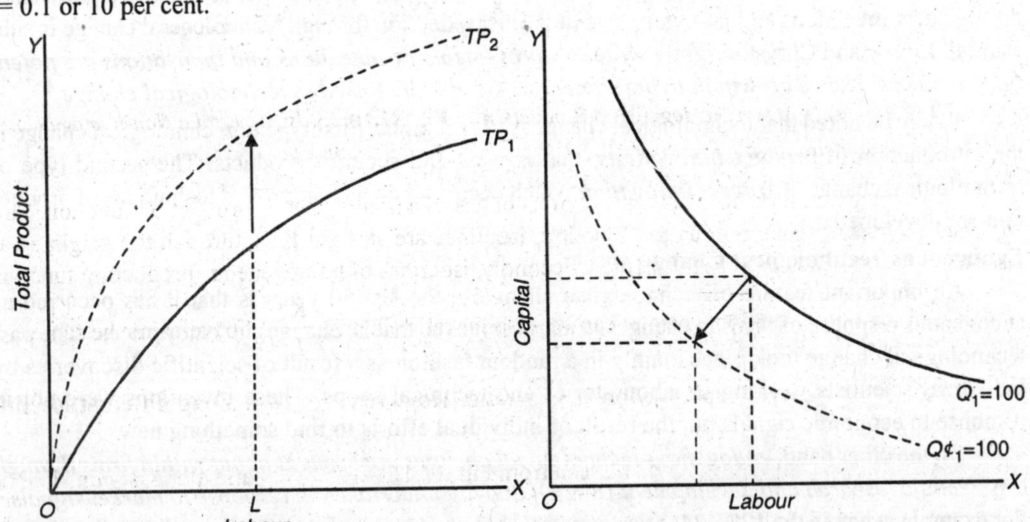

Fig. 17.17. *Upward Shift in the Total Product Curve of Labour due to Technological Change*

Fig. 17.18. *Downward Shift in the Isoquant due to Technological Change*

This increase in productivity in a year is due to technical change. As noted above, the technical change brings about a shift in the production function and will therefore cause a shift in the productivity curve of factors and isoquant as shown in Fig. 17.17 and 17.18. It will be seen from Fig. 17.17 that total product curve of labour shifts upward to a higher level indicating that from a given quantity of labour such OL, the firm can produce more, that is, productivity of labour has risen. In Fig. 17.18 the isoquant Q_1 representing output of 100 units has shifted downward Q'_1 due to technological advancement that shows use of lower amounts of labour and capital can now yield 100 units of output. That is, productivity of both labour and capital or what is often called *total factor productivity* has gone up. In recent years, various empical studies have been made to measure technical change or growth in productivity. In Table 17.3 we have given the estimates of growth ın productivity during 1949-1983 in the USA. The growth in productivity varies in different industries.

It will be seen from Table 17.3 that in the manufacturing sector as a whole in the United States, productivity increased at the rate of 1.1 per cent annum during 1949-1983.

Table 17.3. Annual Rate of Productivity Growth in United States, 1949-83

Industry	*Growth rate (%)*
Food and Kindred products	0.7
Tobacco manufactures	0.2
Lumber and Wood Products	1.3
Paper and Allied Products	1.5
Total Manufacturing	1.1

Source: Gullickson and Harper, "*Multi-Factor Productivity in US Manufacturing,* 1949-83"

Growth in productivity or technical change over years is an important factor in determining rate of economic growth of a country. The lower growth of productivity causes slowdown in economic growth. If developing countries such as India have to catch up with the presently developed countries the key factor to achieve this is to bring about adequate technical change.

Since technological change raises productivity of inputs, it reduces average cost of producing output. Empirical evidence shows that possibilities of reducing cost of production through choice among available techniques of production are limited, while cost per unit can be reduced significantly through new inventions and innovations, that is, cost reduction through technological change is substantial. Lipsey and Chrystal rightly write, "*improvements by inventions and innovations are potentially limitless. Hence growth in living standards is critically linked to technological change.*[4]

It may be noted that technological change is of two kinds. First type of technological change is the introduction of ***product innovations,*** that is, new and superior products. The second type of technological change is ***process innovation*** which occurs when new improved techniques of production are developed.

Endogenous Technological Change

An important feature of technological change in the last 50 years is that it has occurred as endogenous response of firms to changes in market signals, that is, changes in factor prices. The past technological change took place mainly in a random fashion as a result of scientific discoveries by individual scientists working in labouratories and technical shops. These inventions were not in response to economic signals but the result of individual efforts to find something new.

On the other hand, *endogenous technological changes are brought about within firms through a systematic research and development (R & D) activity undertaken in response to market signals.*[5] For example, when in the 1973-74, price of petrol shot up, car manufacturing firms directed their R & D activity to develop more fuel efficient cars. Similarly,when prices of natural rubber rose, firms through their research and development activity developed synthetic rubber and plastic to substitute natural rubber. Thus, Lipsey and Chrystal write, "Changes in technology are often *endogeneous responses to changing economic signals,* that is, they result from *responses by firms* to the same things that induce substitution of one input for another."[6] That is, as firms substitute one input for another within the confines of a given technology in response to change in relative prices of these inputs, similarly in the very long-run, firms develop new technologies in response to changes in market prices of inputs.

---

4. Richard G. Lipsey, K. Alex Chrystal, *Economics,* 10th edition, 2004, p. 152.

5. Lipsey and Chrystal, *op. cit.* p. 152.

6. *Ibid,* p. 153

NUMERICAL PROBLEMS

Problem 1. *You are given the following production function :* $Q = L^{0.75}K^{0.25}$

(*i*) *Find the marginal product of labour*

(*ii*) *If the fixed quantity of capital in the short run equals 10,000 units, what is the short-run production function?*

(*iii*) *Show that marginal product of labour (MP_L) is less than average product of labor in the short-run production function in (ii) above*

Solution :

(*i*) To get marginal product of labour, we differentiate the given production function with respect to labour. Thus

$$MP_L = \frac{\partial Q}{\partial L} = 0.75L^{-0.25} \cdot K^{0.25} = 0.75\left(\frac{K}{L}\right)^{0.25}$$

(*ii*) $Q = L^{0.75} \cdot K^{0.25}$

$Q = L^{0.75} \cdot (10{,}000)^{0.25}$

Since the fourth root of 10,000 is 10

Thus short-run production function is

$Q = L^{0.75} \cdot 10 = 10L^{0.75}$

(*iii*) $MP_L = \frac{\partial Q}{\partial L} = 10 \times 0.75L^{-0.25} = \frac{7.5}{L^{0.25}}$

(*ii*) $AP_L = \frac{Q}{L} = \frac{10L^{0.75}}{L} = 10L^{0.75-1} = \frac{10}{L^{0.25}}$

Comparing the values of MP_L and AP_L we find that $MP_L < AP_L$

Problem 2. *You are given the following production functions. What types of production function they are? Draw isoquants for these production functions.*

(*i*) $Q = 2L + K$ (*ii*) $Q = \text{Min}(2L, K)$

Solution:

(*i*) Production function,. $Q = 2L + K$ is a linear production function. This is proved as follows.

Let L and K are increased by a given number λ, thus

$$Q' = 2\lambda L + \lambda K$$

λ can be factored out. Thus

$$Q' = \lambda(2L + K) = \lambda Q$$

Thus increasing each inputs by λ, output also increases by λ. This shows this production function is linear homogeneous.

(*ii*) *Production function,* $Q = \text{Min}(2L, K)$ is a Leontief production function. This is so called because a noted American economist Wassely Leontief used this production function to describe the American economy. This is a fixed proportion production function in which labour and capital are combined in the ratio $2L$ and $1K$.

(*iii*) **Drawing isoquants of the above two functions** :

To draw the isoquants for the production function $Q = 2L + K$, let $K = 0$, then $L = \frac{Q}{2}$ and let $L = 0$, then $K = Q$. This implies that isoquant for $Q = 2L + K$ is a straight line that intersects the horizontal axis along which labour is measured at $L = \frac{Q}{2}$ and intersects

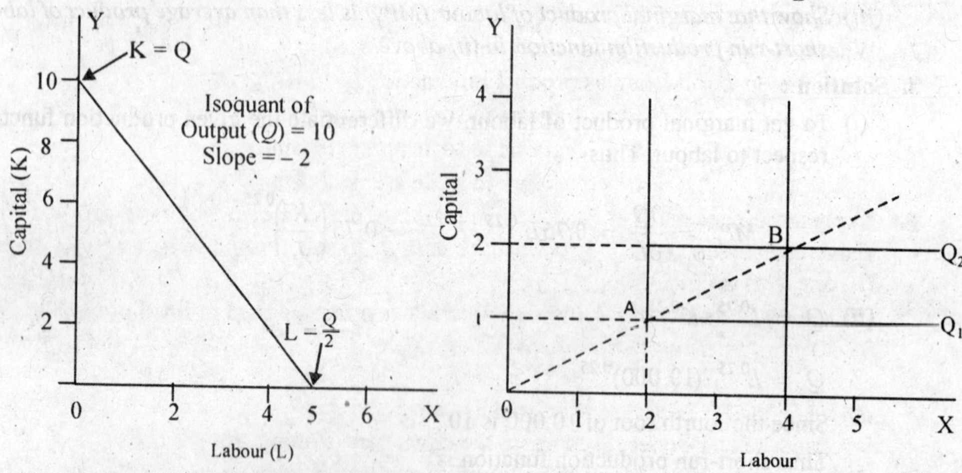

Fig. 17.19. *Straight line isoquant of* $Q = 2L + K$ **Fig. 17.20.** Isoquants of $Q = \text{Min}(2L, K)$

the y-axis along which capital is measured so that $K = Q$. In Figure 17.19 we have drawn the isoquants representing the production function $Q = 2L + K$, assuming output level (Q) equal to 10 units. It will be seen from Figure 17.18 that isoquant for $Q = 2L + K$ is a downward-sloping straight.

Drawing Isoquants of production function, Q = Min(2L, K). This production function indicates that capital and labour are used in fixed production so that $\frac{K}{L} = \frac{1}{2}$, that is, for each unit of capital (K), minimum 2 units of labour (L) are employed to produce an output. Isoquants of such a fixed factor proportions production function are right angles at the points A and B as shown in Figure 17.20.

QUESTIONS FOR REVIEW

1. What are isoquants ? Why does an isoquant slope downward ? Why cannot isoquants cut each other ? Why are they convex to the origin ?
2. What is meant by marginal rate of technical substitution between factors ($MRTS_{LK}$) ? How is it related to marginal products of factors ? Why does marginal rate of technical substitution of labour for capital diminish as more labour is used by substituting capital ?
3. "The slope of an isoquant is a measure of the relative marginal productivities of the factors." Explain.

[**Hints** : Slope of an isoquant is equal to *MRTS* between factors. Since

$$MRTS_{LK} = \frac{MP_L}{MP_K}$$

Therefore, the slope of an isoquant measures the ratio of marginal products of the two factors. For the proof that $MRTS_{LK} = \frac{MP_L}{MP_K}$, see the text in the book.

4. Distinguish between fixed proportions and variable proportions production function. Draw the isoquants of fixed proportions production function.

5. (*a*) In case of perfect substitutes, what can you say about the equilibrium of the producer ?

6. What is meant by linear homogeneous production function. What are its important properties ?

[**Hint.** Cobb-Douglas production function is the chief example of linear homogeneous production function. Therefore, you can explain the properties of linear homogneous production by taking the example of Cobb-Douglas production function)

7. What is Cobb-Douglas production function ? What are its important properties ? Explain.

8. Show that in Cobb-Douglas production function $Q = AL^aK^b$ when

a + b > 1, returns to scale are constant

a + b > 1, returns to scale are increasing

a + b < 1, returns to scale are decreasing

9. Explain the concept of elasticity of substitution between two factors of production. What shope does the isoquant take when the elasticity of substitution between factors is (i) zero, (*ii*) one, (*iii*) infinity. *D.U. B.A. (Hons) 1988*

[**Hints.** (*i*) Elasticity of substitution between two factors used in fixed proportions is zero. The isoquants are right-angled. (*iii*) Elasticity of substitution between two factors in Cobb-Douglas production function ($Q = AL^aK^b$) is equal to one. Their isoquants are convex to the origin; (*iii*) The elasticity of substitution between two perfect substitutes is infinity. The isoquants of two perfect substitutes are downward-sloping straight lines]

10. Distinguish between returns to scale and returns to a variable factor with the help of isoquants.

11. What is meant by constant returns to scale ? Represent it by an isoquant map. Show that empirically discovered Cobb-Douglas production function represents constant returns to scale.

12. If all factors were perfectly divisible, constant returns to scale would have occurred". Examine critically. On what grounds E.H. Chamberlin challenged this viewpoint.

13. What is meant by *increasing returns to scale* ? Explain the factors that cause increasing returns to scale.

14. A production function is subject to constant returns to scale. What can you say about the returns to a variable factor. Explain diagrammatically.

D.U. B.A. (Hons) 1986; D.U., B.A. (H) 2009

15. If a production function reveals increasing returns to scale, what can you say about the returns to a variable factor ? Explain diagrammatically. *D.U. B.A (Hons) 1998*

16. What are increasing returns to scale ? Show them on an isoquant map. Explain the causes of increasing returns to scale.

17. Show the increasing cost and and decreasing returns to scale with the help of isoquants. What causes decreasing returns to scale beyond a point ?

18. Is decreasing returns to a variable factor compatible with constant returns to scale ? Explain *D.U. B.A. (Hons) 2001*

19. Show that when returns to scale are constant, marginal returns to a variable factor diminish (*a*) Prove geometrically (*b*) Give an algebraic proof of it using a linear homogeneous production function.

20. A firm's production function is given by $Q = K.L$, where K and L are the inputs used by the firm and Q represents output.

(*i*) Check the returns to scale for this production function.

(*ii*) Draw the isoquant map.

(*iii*) Calculate the marginal rate of technical substitution between L and K. What will the expansion path look like ?

[**Hints.** This production function ($Q = K.L$) is a Cobb-Douglas type production function ($Q = K^a L^b$) with each of the two exponents, a and b, are equal to one (implied). Thus, the given production function can be written as

$$Q = K^1.L^1$$

(*i*) Returns to scale are measured by the sum of exponents, they are increasing in this production function as a + b is here greater then one (1 + 1 = 2)

(*ii*) As in Figure 17.10 in this chapter.

(*iii*) $MRTS_{LK} = \dfrac{MP_L}{MP_K}$ Now, in the production function, $Q = K.L$

$$MP_L = \frac{\partial Q}{\partial L} = K$$

$$MP_K = \frac{\partial Q}{\partial K} = L$$

Therefore, $MRTS_{LK} = \dfrac{K}{L}$

Since along an expansion path $MRTS_{LK}$ remains constant, the ratio of two factors, $\dfrac{K}{L}$ which is equal to $MRTS_{LK}$ in the given production function will also remain constant. Hence expansion path will be straight line through the origin.

21. Show that linear homogenous Cobb-Douglas production function shows constant returns to scale. *D.U. B.Com (Hons.) 2009*

22. What is meant by constant returns to scale ? Show them with an iso-product map. Is it correct to say that returns to scale would have been constant if the factors of production had been perfectly divisible ?

23. Consider the following data on output and inputs. What type of returns to scale does it represent and why ?

K	*L*	*Q*
5	8	3
10	16	6
20	32	12
40	64	24

Where K denotes units of capital, L denotes units of labour used and Q denotes output produced.

24. Explain the laws of returns to scale. Show the three kinds of returns to scale with the help of isoquants. Why do we get decreasing returns to scale ? *D.U. B.Com (H) 2000*

25. You are given the following production functions. Which ones represent constant returns to scale, which one increasing returns to scale and which one decreasing returns to scale and why ?

(*a*) $Q = AK^{0.5} L^{0.7}$ (*b*) $Q = AK^{0.25} L^{0.75}$

(*c*) $Q = AK^{0.3} L^{0.6}$ (*d*) $Q = 10\sqrt{L}\sqrt{K}$

(**Hints** : Sum of the exponents in Cobb-Douglas production function indicates returns to scale. In (*b*) and (*d*) sum of exponents is equal to one. Hence these show constant returns to scale. In (*a*) sum of exponents (0.5 + 0.7 = 1.2) exceeds one, it is therefore the case of increasing returns to scale type of production function. (*c*) depicts decreasing returns to scale as in it the sum of exponents is less than 1 (0.3 + 0.6 = 0.9)

26. A firm has the following production function :

$$Q = K^{\frac{1}{2}} L^{\frac{1}{2}}$$

Calculate marginal product function for labour and capital. Also calculate $MRTS_{LK}$.

What type of returns to scale does it represent ?

27. You are given the following production function :

$Q = L^a K^b$

(*i*) Does this production function represent increasing, decreasing or constant returns to scale.

(*ii*) If $(a + b) > 1$, what would the isoquant map look like ? *D.U. B.A. (Hons.) 2001*

28. *Consider the production function represented by $Y = AL^{\alpha} K^{\beta}$ where Y is output and α and β are positive constants.*

(a) Show that this production function exhibits constant returns to scale when $\alpha + \beta = 1$.

(b) Show that marginal product of labour depends on the input ratio $\frac{K}{L}$ only.

(c) When is the expansion path linear ?

(d) Define the range of values of α for which this function depicts diminishing MP of labour.

[**Hints** : (*c*) Expansion path is linear when the sum of α + β = 1 and production function becomes linear homogenous. For proof, see next chapter of this book]

(*d*)
$$MP_L = \frac{\partial Y}{\partial L} = AaL^{a-1} K^{\beta} \quad ...(i)$$

$$\text{Slope of } MP_L = \frac{\partial^2 Y}{\partial L^2} = Aa(a-1)L^{\alpha-2} K^{\beta} \quad ...(ii)$$

For diminishing marginal product of labour to occur, $\frac{\partial^2 Y}{\partial L^2}$ must be negative.

From (*ii*) it follows that MP_L will be diminishing if $0 < a < 1$.

29. Show in linear homogeneous Cobb-Douglas production function $X = Ak^a L^{1-a}$, average product of labour and marginal product of labour depends on ratio of factors and it shows constant returns to scale. *D.U., B.Com. (Hons.) 1st Year 2009*

CHAPTER 18
OPTIMUM FACTOR COMBINATION

In the last three chapters we explained the law of variable proportions and returns to scale which underlie the process of production. An important problem facing an entrepreneur is to decide about a particular combination of factors which should be employed for producing a product. There are various technical possibilities open to a firm from which it has to choose, that is, there are various combinations of factors which can yield a given level of output and from among which a producer has to select one for production. As explained in an earlier chapter, various combinations of factors which produce equal level of output are represented by an equal product curve or what is also called insoquant. An isoquant or iso-product map represents various technical possibilities of producing different levels of output.

It is assumed that the entrepreneur aims at maximising his profits. A profit maximising entrepreneur will seek to minimise his cost for producing a given output, or to put it in another way, he will maximise his output for a given level of outlay. The choice of a particular combination of factors by an entrepreneur depends upon (*a*) technical possibilities of production, and (*b*) the prices of factors used for the production of a particular product. Technical possibilities of production are represented by the isoquant map. Before explaining how a producer will arrive at the optimum or least-cost combination of factors, we shall first explain how the prices of factors can be introduced into the study.

The Economic Region of Production and Ridge Lines

Before explaining which factor combination a firm will use for production, it will be useful to demonstraste the region in which the optimal factor combination will lie. The traditional economic theory focuses on only those combinations of factors which are technically efficient and the marginal products of factors are diminishing but positive. According to this isoquants are sloping downward (*i.e.* their slope is negative) and convex to the origin. however, there are regions in a production function, where isoquants may have positively sloped segments that is, bend backwards. In fig. 18.1 we represent a production function through isoquants and measure labour along the *X*-axis and capital along the Y-axis. It will be seen from this figure that above the line *OA* and below the line *OB* slope of the isoquants is *positive* which means that increases in both capital and labour are *required to produce a given fixed quantity of output*. Obviously, the production techniques (that is, factor combinations) lying on these positively sloping segments of the isoquants are technically inefficient. It may be recalled that a *technique or factor combination is technically inefficient if it requires more quantity of both the factors for producing a given level of output*. The positively sloping segments of isoquants implies that marginal product of one of the factors has become negative. Thus, above the line *OA*, marginal product of capital has become negative, which means output can be increased by using less capital, while the amount of labour is held constant. On the other hand, below the line *OB*, marginal product of labour becomes negative, which means output can be increased by using less labour, keeping capital constant. The lines *OA* and *OB* are called the **ridge lines** which bound a region in which marginal products of the two factors are positive. The ridge line OA connects those points of the isoquants where marginal product of capital is zero ($MP_k = 0$). On the other hand, the ridge line OB connects those points of the isoquants where marginal product of labour is zero ($MP_L = 0$). Thus, the ridge lines are the locus of points of isoquants where marginal product of one of the factors is zero.

No rational enterpreneur will operate at a point outside the ridge lines since marginal product of one of the factors is negative and production is technically inefficient. In other words, production outside the ridge lines is inefficient, because *same output can be produced with less quantity of the factors which must be cheaper*. This can be better understood from fig. 18.1. Consider point R on isoquant Q_2, R is the point where the isoquant is positively sloping and therefore lies outside the ridge line. It will be seen from fig. 18.1 that production at point R to produce output Q_2 requires more of both capital and labour than some other points, such as point H, on the same isoquant. Since, both capital and labour have to paid positive prices, it will be cheaper to produce a given quantity of output at point H than at point R. Thus, since production outside the ridge lines are technically inefficient and marginal product of one or the other factor is negative, no rational entrepreneur will like to operate outside the ridge lines if he aims at minimising cost to produce a given output. Thus, *regions outside the ridge lines are called regions of economic nonsense*. A rational producer will produce in the region bounded by the two ridge lines OA and OB where the isoquants are negatively sloping, marginal products of factors are diminishing but positive. Therefore, the region bounded by the two ridge lines, OA and OB is called the *region of economic production* which has been shaded by us. Exactly at what point in the economic region, a firm will operate depends on the outlay it has to make on purchasing the factors and also on prices of the factors. In what follows we now turn to explain this choice by a firm. We will first explain the concept of iso-cost line which is used in the study of optimum factor combination.

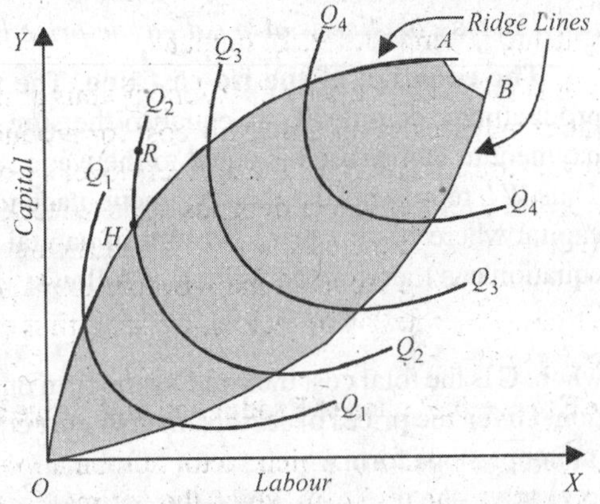

Fig. 18.1. *Economic Region of Production*

The above analysis also shows that there is a limit to which one factor can be substituted for another. As the substitution of one factor for another is carried out mor and more, it becomes progressively more difficult unti a point is reached beyond which substitution between factors becomes impossibe. As a result, the marginal product of the increasing factor first becomes zero and then it becomes negative so that isoquant becomes positively sloping.

ISO-COST LINE

The prices of factors are represented by the iso-cost line. The iso-cost line plays an important part in determining what combination of factors the firm will choose for production. An iso-cost line shows various combinations of two factors that the firm can buy with a given outlay. How the iso-cost line is drawn is shown in Fig. 18.2 where on the X-axis we measure units of labour and on the Y-axis we measure units of capital. We assume that prices of factors are given and constant for the factor. In other words, we are considering a firm which is working under perfect competition in the factor markets. Further suppose that a firm has ₹ 300 to spend on the factors, labour and capital and price of labour is ₹ 4 per labour hour and the price of capital is ₹ 5 per machine hour. With outlay of Rs. 300, he can buy 75 units of labour or 60 units of machine hours (*i.e.*, capital). Let *OB* in Fig. 18.2 represent 75 units of labour and *OA* represent 60 units of capital. In other words, if the firm spends its entire outlay of Rs. 300 on factor *X*, it buys 75 units or *OB* of labour hours and if it spends its entire outlay of Rs. 300 on capital it buys 60 units or *OA* of machine hours. The straight line *AB* which joins points *A* and *B* will pass through all combinations of labour and capital which the firm can buy with outlay of Rs. 300, if it spends the entire sum on them at the given prices. This line *AB* is called *iso-cost* line, for whichever combination lying on it the firm buys it has to incur the same cost or outlay at the given prices. *An iso-cost line is defined as the locus of various combinations of factors which a firm can buy with a constant outlay. The iso-cost line is also called the price line or outlay line.*

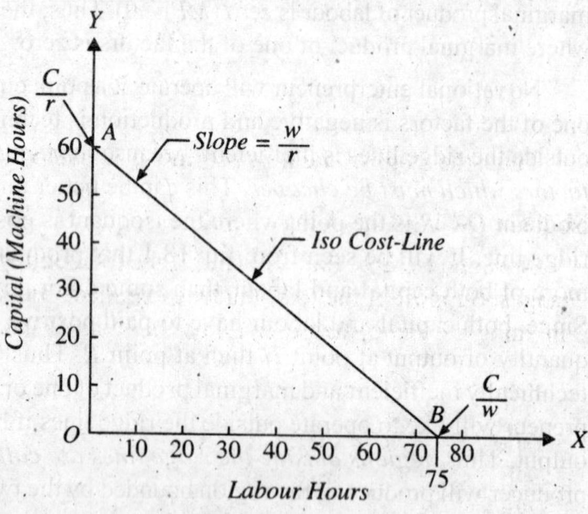

Fig. 18.2. *Iso-Cost Line*

The equation of the iso-cost line. The total cost incurred on the factors of production for producting a commodity is equal to the sum of the payments made to labour and capital. Now, payment to labour used is equal to the wage rate (*w*) multiplied by the amount of labour used (*L*). Thus *W.L* represents the total payment made to labour. Similarly, *rK* is the total payment made for capital where *r* is the price per unit of capital and *K* is the quantity of capital used. The total cost equation can therefore be written as follows:

$$C = w.L + rK$$

where C is the total cost incurred by the firm on purchasing the quantities of factors used for production. Given the prices of factors, the iso-cost equation can be rearranged as under to express it in the intercept-slope form:

$$C = wL + rK$$

$$rK = C - w.L$$

$$K = \frac{C}{r} - \frac{w}{r}.L \quad \text{...(i)}$$

where $\frac{C}{r}$ represents the intercept of the iso-cost line on the *Y*-axis and $\frac{w}{r}$ represents the factor price ratio and is equal to the slope of the iso-cost line.

Slope of the iso-cost line. The slope of the iso-cost line can be proved to be equal to the ratio of price of labour (*w*) and price of capital (*r*). Let, according to the iso-cost line *AB*, which given the factor prices, represents the total outlay or cost incurred on the two factors, labour and capital, the total cost equals *C*.

As explained above, the vertical intercept *OA* that represents the quantity of capital if entire cost-outlay is spent on it is equal to $\frac{C}{r}$. Similarly, the horizontal intercept *OB* representing the quantity of labour purchased if entire cost is incurred on purchasing it is equal to .

Now, the slope of the iso-cost line is:

$$\frac{OA}{OB} = \frac{C}{r} \div \frac{C}{w} = \frac{C}{r} \cdot \frac{w}{C} = \frac{w}{r}$$

Thus, the slope of the iso-cost line is equal to the ratio of factor-prices $\left(\frac{w}{r}\right)$.

Shifts in the Iso-Cost Line

Now, the iso-cost line will shift if the total outlay which the firm wants to spend on the factors changes. Suppose if the total outlay to be made by the firm increases to Rs. 400, prices of factors remaining the same, then it can buy 100 units of labour hours (*i.e.*, *OB′* of labour) or 80 units of

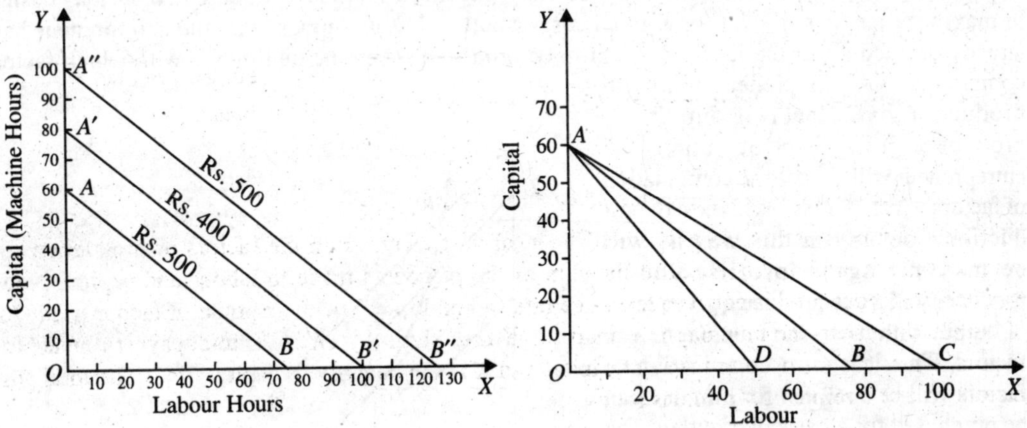

Fig. 18.3. *Iso-cost Line Resulting from increase in outlay or total cost.*

Fig. 18.4. *Changes in Iso-Cost Line as a Result of Changes in the Price of Labour X*

machine hours (*i.e.*, *OA′* of capital) if it spends the entire sum on either of them. Thus, the new iso-cost line will be *A″ B″* which will be parallel to the original iso-cost line *AB* (see Fig. 18.3). If the outlay which the firm intends to make further increases to Rs. 500, then iso-cost line will shift to the position *A′ B′*. Thus any number of iso-cost lines can be drawn, all parallel to one another, and each representing the various combinations of two factors that can be purchased for a particular outlay. The higher the outlay, the higher the corresponding iso-cost line.

The iso-cost line will also change if the prices of factors change, outlay remaining the same. Suppose the firm's outlay is Rs. 300 and the prices of labour and capital are Rs. 4 and Rs. 5 respectively. Then the iso-cost line will be *AB* as shown in Fig. 18.4. If now the price of labour falls to Rs. 3, then with the outlay of Rs. 300 and Rs. 3 as the price of labour the firm can buy 100 units of labour if it spends the entire outlay on it. *OC* represents 100 units of labour. Therefore, as a result of the fall in price of labour from Rs. 4 to Rs. 3, the price line changes from *AB* to *AC*. If the price of labour rises from Rs. 4 to Rs. 6 per hour the iso-cost line will shift to *AD*. Likewise, if the price of capital changes, the outlay and the price of labour remaining the same, the iso-cost line will shift.

It is clear from above that the iso-cost line depends upon two things : (*i*) prices of the factors of production, and (*ii*) the total outlay which the firm has to make on the factors. Given these two things, an iso-cost line can be drawn. It should also be noted that the slope of the iso-cost line, like that of the price line in indifference curve analysis of demand, is equal to the ratio of the price of two factors. Thus, slope of the iso-cost line *AB*

$$= \frac{\text{Price of Labour}}{\text{Price of Capital}} = \frac{w}{r}$$

OPTIMUM OR LEAST-COST COMBINATION OF FACTORS

An equal product map or isoquant map represents the various factor combinations which can yield various levels of output, every equal product curve or isoquant showing those factor combinations each of which can produce a specified level of output. Thus, *an equal product map represents the production function of a product with two variable factors*. Therefore, an equal product map represents the technical conditions of production for a product. On the other hand, a family of iso-cost line represents the various levels of total cost or outlay, given the prices of two factors. The entrepreneur may desire to minimize his cost for producing a given level of output, or he may desire to maximize his output level for a given cost or outlay. Let us suppose that the entrepreneur has already decided about the level of output to be produced. Then the question is with which factor combination the entrepreneur will try to produce a given level of output. To produce a given level of output, the entrepreneur will choose the combination of factors which minimizes his cost of production, for only in this way he will be maximizing his profits. Thus, a producer will try to produce a given level of output with *least-cost combination* of factors. This least-cost combination of factors will be *optimum* for him that can be purchased for a particular outlay. The higher the outlay, the higher the corresponding iso-cost line.

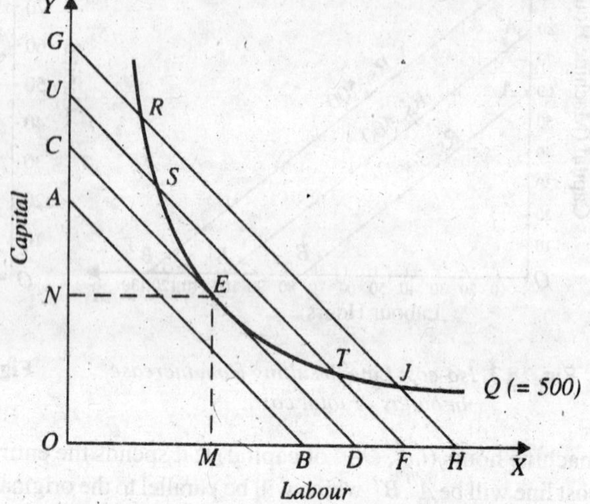

Fig. 18.5. *Minimising Cost for a Given Level of Output*

Which will be the least-cost combination of factors can be understood from considering Fig. 18.5. Suppose the entrepreneur has decided to produce 500 units of output which is represented by isoquant *Q*. The 500 units of output can be produced by any combination of labour and capital such as *R*, *S*, *E*, *T* and *J* lying on the isoquant. Now, a glance at the Fig. 18.5 will reveal that for producing the given level of output (500 units) the cost will be minimum at point *E* at which the iso-cost line *CD* is tangent to the given isoquant. At no other point such as *R*, *S*, *T* and *J*, lying on the isoquant *Q* the cost is minimum. It will be seen from Fig. 18.5 that all other points on isoquant *Q*, such as *R*, *S*, *T*, *J* lie on higher iso-cost lines than *CD* and which will therefore mean greater total cost or outlay for producing the given ouput. Therefore, the entrepreneur will not choose any of the combinations *R*, *S*, *T* and J. We thus see that factor combination *E* is the least-cost combination of labour and capital for producing a given output. Factor combination *E* is therefore an *optimum combination* for him under the given circumstances. Hence we conclude that the entrepreneur will choose factor combination *E* (that is, *OM* units of labour and *ON* units of capital) to produce 500 units of output. It is thus clear that the tangency point of the given isoquant with an iso-cost line represents the least-cost combination of factors for producing a given output.

How an entrepreneur arrives at the least-cost factor combination can also be explained with the help of the concept of marginal rate of technical substitution (*MRTS*) and the price ratio of the two factors. As has been shown earlier, the marginal rate of technical substitution (*MRTS*) is given by the slope of the isoquant at its various points. On the other hand, the price ratio of the factors is given by the slope of the iso-cost line. The entrepreneur will not choose to produce a given output at point *R* because at point *R* marginal rate of technical substitution of labour for capital is greater than the price ratio of the factors (at point *R* the slope of the isoquant *Q* is greater than the slope of the iso-cost line *GH*). Therefore, if he is at point *R* he will use more of labour in place of capital and go down on the isoquant. Likewise, he will not stop at point *S*, since the marginal rate of technical substitution of labour for capital is still greater than the price ratio of the factors; slope of the isoquant at point *S* being greater than the slope of the iso-cost line *UF*. Therefore, the entrepreneur will further substitute labour for capital and will go down further on the isoquant *Q*.

When the entrepreneur reaches point *E*, marginal rate of technical substitution of labour for capital is here equal to the price ratio of the factors, since the slopes of the isoquant and the iso-cost; line *CD* are equal to each other. The entrepreneur will have no incentive to go further down, for he will not be lowering his cost in this way, but in fact he will be reaching higher iso-cost lines. At points *J* and *T* on the isoquant *Q* marginal rate of technical substitution of labour for capital is smaller than the price ratio of the factors and the entrepreneur will try to substitute capital for labour and move upward on the isoquant *Q* until he reaches the point of tangency *E*, where marginal rate of technical substitution is equal to the price ratio of the factors. It is thus clear that the entrepreneur will be minimising his cost when the factor combination for which marginal rate of technical substitution is equal to the price ratio of the factors. Thus at his equilibrium point *E*.

$$MRTS_{LK} = \frac{w}{r} \begin{cases} \text{where } w \text{ stands for the wages rate} \\ \text{of labour and } r \text{ for the price of capital} \end{cases}$$

But, as we saw in the last chapter, the marginal rate of technical substitution of labour for capital is equal to the ratio of the marginal physical products of the two factors.

Therefore,

$$MRTS_{LK} = \frac{MP_L}{MP_K} = \frac{w}{r}$$

$$\frac{MP_L}{MP_K} = \frac{w}{r}$$

We can rearrange the above equation to have

$$\frac{MP_L}{w} = \frac{MP_K}{r}$$

We therefore reach an important conclusion about the entrepreneur's choice of the quantities of the two factors. The entrepreneur will be in equilibrium in regard to his use and purchases of the two factors when he is using such quantities of the two factors that the marginal physical products of the two factors are proportional to the factor prices. If, for instance, the price of labour is twice as much as that of capital, then the entrepreneur will purchase and use such quantities of the two factors that the marginal physical product of labour is twice the marginal physical product of capital.

Output Maximisation for a Given Level of Outlay (I.E. cost)

We have explained earlier in this chapter the condition for minimisation of cost to produce a given level of output, namely, marginal rate of technical substitution between factors should be equal to the ratio of factor prices $\left(MRTS_{LK} = \frac{w}{r}\right)$. The dual of cost-minimization problem for a given level of output is of output maximization for a given level of cost or outlay. Suppose the firm has decided upon an outlay which it has to incur for the production of a commodity. With a given level of outlay, there will be a single iso-cost line that represents the outlay that firm has decided to spend. The firm will have to choose a factor combination lying on the given iso-cost line. Obviously, with a given cost or outlay, a rational producer will be interested in maximising output of the commodity. Consider Fig. 18.6. Suppose the firm has decided to incur an outlay of Rs. 200 on labour and capital which is represented by the iso-cost line *AB*. The firm has a choice to use any factor combination of labour and capital such as *R, S, E, T, J* etc. lying on the given iso-cost line *AB* to produce the product. An isoquant map showing a set of isoquants that represents various levels of output (200, 300, 400, 500 units) has been superimposed on the given iso-cost line *AB*. A glance at the Fig. 18.6 reveals that the firm will choose the factor combination *E* consisting of *ON* of labour and *OH* of capital. This is because of all the factor combinations that lie on the given iso-cost line *AB*, only the factor combination *E* enables the firm to reach the highest possible isoquant Q_3 and thus produce 400 units of output. All other combinations of labour and capital that lie on the given iso-cost line *AB* such as *R, S, T, J* etc., lie on lower isoquants showing lower levels of output than 400 units.

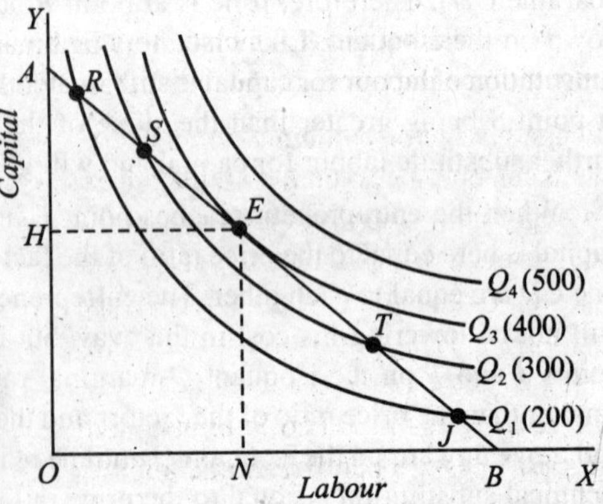

Fig. 18.6. *Output-maximisation for a given cost.*

At point *E*, $MRTS_{LK} = \frac{w}{r}$

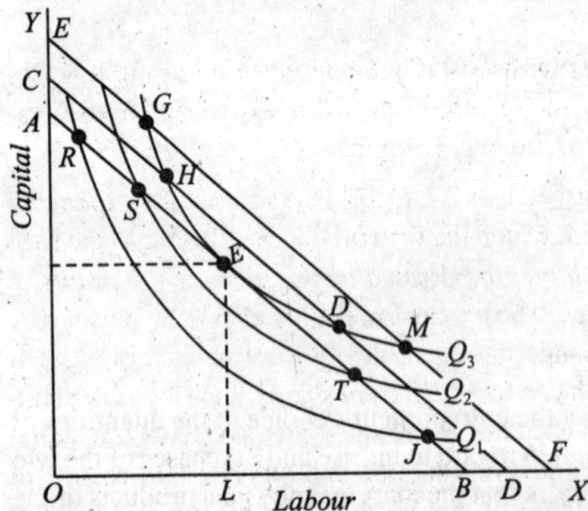

Fig. 18.7. *Cost Minimisation for a Given Output and Output Maximisation for a Given Cost.*

Cost-Minimisation for a Given Output and Output-Maximization for a Given Cost-Outlay yield same results.

This can be easily shown with the help of Fig. 18.7. Suppose *AB* is the given iso-cost line depicting the given cost constraint. Maximisation of output subject to this cost-constraint is achieved at point *E* which lies on the highest possible isoquant Q_3, while other points on the iso-cost line *AB* such as *R, S, T* or *J* lie on lower isoquants. Hence *E* represents maximum-output factor combination. Now, *given the output level* Q_3, point *E* also represents the least-cost factor combination as other points on isoquant Q_3 such as *G,H,D, M* lie on higher iso-cost curves.

It is quite clear from above that the entrepreneur's behaviour in choosing the quantities of factors is exactly symmetrical with the behaviour of the consumer. Both the entrepreneur and the consumer purchase things in such quantities as to equate marginal rate of substitution with their price ratio. The consumer, to be in equilibrium, equates marginal rate of substitution (or the ratio of the marginal utilities of two goods) with the price-ratio of the goods. The entrepreneur equates marginal rate of technical substitution (or, the ratio of the marginal physical products of the two factors) with the price-ratio of the twofactors.

EXPANSION PATH

We explained above which factor combination a firm will choose to produce a specified level of output, given the prices of the two factors. We are now interested to study how the entrepreneur will change his factor combination as he expands his output, given the factor prices. To begin with, suppose the prices of the two factors *X* and *Y*, are such that are represented by the slope of the iso-cost line *AB*. In Fig. 18.8, four iso-cost lines, *AB*, *CD*, *UF*, and *GH* are drawn which show different levels of total cost or outlay. All iso-cost lines are parallel to one another indicating that prices of the two factors remain the same. If the firm wants to produce the output level denoted by Q_1 (= 100 units of output), it will choose the factor combination E_1 which minimisses cost of production; E_1 is the point of tangency between theequal product curve Q_1 and the iso-cost line *AB*. Now, if a firm wants to produce a higher level of output as denoted by the equal product curve Q_2, then it will choose the factor combination E_2 which is the least-cost combination for new output. Likewise, for still higher output levels as denoted by Q_3 and Q_4, the firm will respectively choose tangency combination E_3 and E_4 which minimise cost for the given outputs.

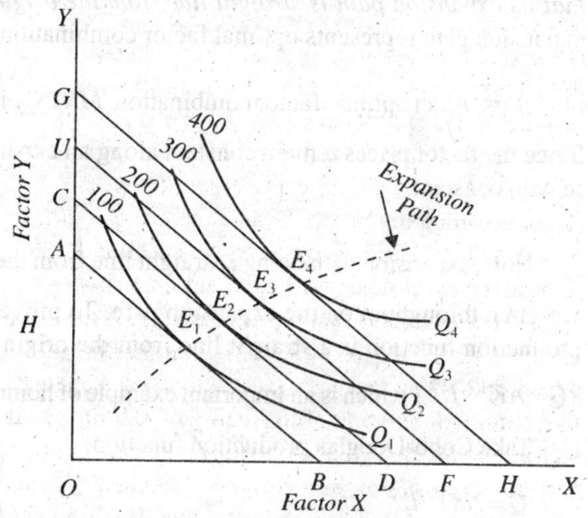

Fig. 18.8. *Expansion Path*

The line joining the minimum cost combinations such as E_1, E_2, E_3, E_4 is called the *expansion path* because it shows how the factor combination with which the firm produces will alter as the firm expands its level of output. *Thus the expansion path may be defined as the locus of the points of tangency between the isoquants and the iso-cost lines.* The expansion path is also known as *scale-line* because it shows how the entrepreneur will change the quantities of the two factors when it increases the scale of production. The expansion path can have different shapes and slopes depending upon the relative prices of the productive factors used and the shape of the isoquants (*i.e.* equal product curves). As we shall prove below, when production function exhibits constant returns to scale, the expansion path will be a straight line through the origin. Further, for a given equal product map there will be different expansion paths for different relative prices of the factors.

Since expansion path represents the minimum-cost combinations for various levels of output, it shows the cheapest way of producing each level of output, given the relative prices of the factors. When two factors are variable, the entrepreneur will choose to produce at some point on the expansion path. One cannot say exactly at which particular point on the expansion path the entrepreneur will in fact be producing unless one knows either the output which he wants to produce or the size of the cost or outlay it wants to incur. But this is certain that where both factors are variable and the prices of factors are given, a rational entrepreneur will seek to produce at one point or the other on the expansion path.

Expansion Path of a Linear Homogenhous Production Function

Whether expansion path is linear or non-linear depends on the nature of technology involved in the production function. An *important property of a linear homogeneous production function is that its expansion path is straight line from the origin* as shown in figure 18.9. As we saw above expansion path represents optimal factor combinations as firm expands its output, given the prices of factors. At an optimal factor combination, $MRTS_{LK}$ is equal to factor price ratio $\left(MRTS_{LK} = \frac{w}{r}\right)$. Since the factor prices remain constant along an expansion path, this implies that $MRTS_{LK}$ will also remain constant.

Now, expansion path being a straight line from the origin implies that factor ratio $\left(\frac{K}{L}\right)$ remains the same throughout on the expansion path. To prove that expansion path of a linear homogenous production function is a straight line from the origin we take Cobb–Douglas production function $\left(Q = AK^{1/2} L^{1/2}\right)$ which is an important example of homogenous production function of the first degree.

Take Cobb-Douglas production function,

$$Q = AK^{1/2} L^{1/2}$$

Differentiating it with respect to labour

$$\frac{\partial Q}{\partial L} = \frac{1}{2} AK^{1/2} L^{-1/2} \quad ...(1)$$

Differentiating it with respect to capital,

$$\frac{\partial Q}{\partial K} = \frac{1}{2} AK^{-1/2} L^{1/2} \quad ...(2)$$

Dividing (1) by (2) we have

$$\frac{MP_L}{MP_K} = \frac{\partial Q}{\partial L} \Big/ \frac{\partial Q}{\partial K} = \frac{\frac{1}{2} AK^{\frac{1}{2}} L^{\frac{-1}{2}}}{\frac{1}{2} AK^{\frac{-1}{2}} L^{\frac{1}{2}}} = \frac{K}{L}$$

or $$MRTS_{LK} = \frac{MP_L}{MP_K} = \frac{K}{L}$$

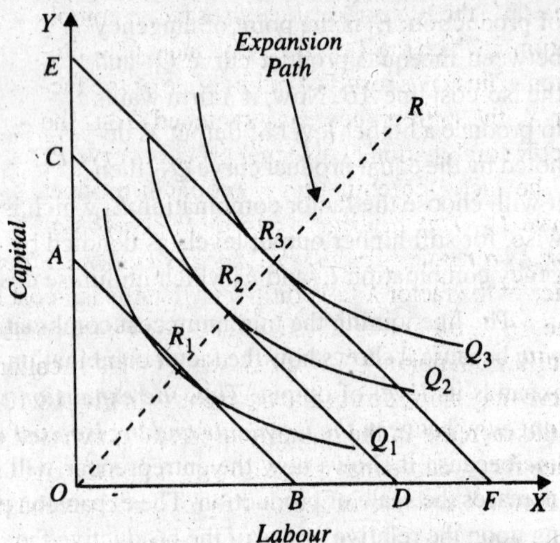

Fig. 18.9. *Expansion path of a linear homogeneous production function is a straight line from the origin.*

Thus, $MRTS_{LK}$ in the given linear homogenous Cobb-Douglas production function is equal to

$\frac{K}{L}$. As explained above, at optimal factor combinations on the expansion path, $MRTS_{LK}$ equals $\frac{w}{r}$ and, therefore, given the factor prices, $MRTS_{LK}$ remains constant along an expansion path. Thus $\frac{K}{L}$ which is equal $MRTS_{LK}$ in a linear homogenous Cobb-Douglas production will remain constant. Constant factor ratio $\frac{K}{L}$ along the expansion path implies that it is a straight line from the origin.

PRICE EFFECT : EFFECT OF CHANGE IN FACTOR PRICE ON FACTOR USAGE

Now we proceed to study what happens to the quantities of factors used and purchased when the prices of the factors undergo a change. Consider Fig. 18.10. To begin with, a firm is in equilibrium at point Q on equal product curve P_1, given the total outlay and factor prices as denoted by the iso-cost line AB. He is, in this situation, buying the quantities of two factors as denoted by the combination Q. Now, suppose the price of factor X falls, price of factor Y and the total outlay or cost remaining unaltered, so that the iso-cost line assumes the position AB'. The entrepreneur will now seek to produce at the point where the iso-cost line AB' is tangent to an equal product curve. It is evident from Fig. 18.10 that with iso-cost line AB', the entrepreneur chooses factor combination R which maximises output under new situation. Thus, as a result of fall in price of the factor X, the entrepreneur has switched from the factor combination Q on equal product curve P_1 to the factor combination R on equal product curve P_2. *This alternation in factor combination as a result of change in price is known as factor-price effect or simply price effect.* Suppose price of the factor X falls further so that the iso-cost line shifts to the position AB''. With the iso-cost line AB'', the entrepreneur will choose factor combination S on equal-product curve P_3. By joining equilibrium points Q, R, and S, we get what is called the *price-factor curve* (*PFC*). The price factor curve may slope upward to the right as in Fig. 18.10 indicating that fall in price of the factor X leads to the increase in the quantity used and purchased of both factors X and Y. On the other hand, the price factor curve may slope downward to the right showing that as price of the factor X falls, more of factor X and less of factor Y is used and purchased.

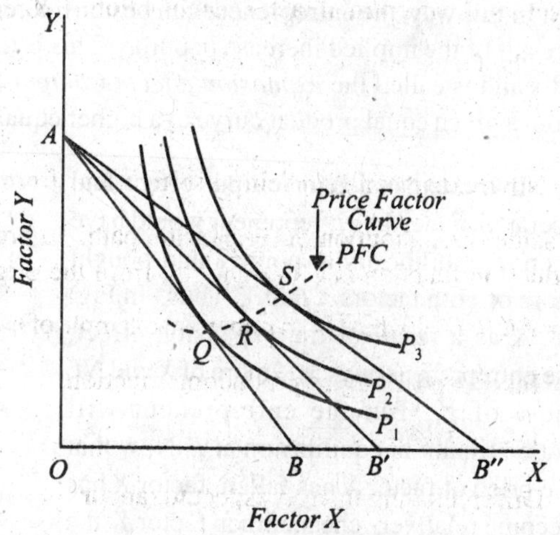

Fig. 18.10. *Factor Price Effect*

Price Effect: Separation of Output Effect and Technical Substitution Effect

In the indifference curve theory of consumer's behaviour we studied that effect of the change in price of a good on its purchases is the resultant of two forces—the income effect and the substitution effect. Likewise, the effect of the change in price on its quantity used and purchased is the resultant of similar two forces. Thus, the factor-price effect can be broken up into output effect and technical substitution effect. Consider Fig. 18.11 to begin with, the iso-cost line is *AB*, given the prices of factors and a total outlay. Now if the price of factor *X* falls, the total outlay and the price of factor *Y*, remaining the same, the iso-cost line shifts to *AB′*, with iso-cost line *AB′* the entrepreneur will be in equilibrium by choosing factor combination *R* on the equal product curve P_2. This change from combination *Q* to combination *R* as a result of the fall in price of factor *X* is the price effect. This price effect can be viewed as the resultant of two forces. First, now when the price of factor *X* has fallen, the entrepreneur can obtain larger output from the same given outlay because with lower price of *X*, he will be able to buy more quantities of the productive factors *X* and *Y* with the given outlay. It is as if the total outlay had increased, relative prices of factors remaining unaltered. The increase in total outlay, factor prices remaining unchanged, is shown by a parallel shift in the iso-cost line. Thus an iso-cost line *CD* is drawn parallel to *AB* so as to be tangent to the equal product curve P_2. With iso-cost line *CD*, the entrepreneur will choose factor combination *T*. Thus, the entrepreneur can be visualised to move from combination *Q* to *T* as a result of the increase in the outlay due to the fall in price of factor *X*. Actually, it is purchasing power of the given outlay which increases due to the fall in the factor price. But the increase in the purchasing power of a given outlay is equivalent to an increase in outlay. In this way, the entrepreneur can be considered to move along the expansion path from *Q* to *T* as a result of the implied increase in outlay. This is the first force that operates when price of the factor falls and is called the *expnasion effect* or *output effect* because due to this the entrepreneur moves from a given equal product curve to a higher equal product curve and thus expands his output.

If the expansion or output effect had operated alone, the entrepreneur would have been in equilibrium at point *T* and bought more of both factors *X* and *Y*. Thus, in Fig. 18.11 as a result of the expansion effect, the entrepreneur buys *MK* more of *X* and *NL* more of *Y*. But the entrepreneur will not be finally in equilibrium at *T*. Now that the price of factor *X* has fallen, factor *X* has become relatively cheaper than factor *Y*, the entrepreneur will, therefore, not stay at point *T* on the equal product curve P_2 but will substitute factor *X* for factor *Y*, that is, he will move down along the equal product curve *P*, by using more of *X* in place of *Y*. This second force is called the *technical substitution effect* and involves the movement on the same equal product curve from one point to another. It will be seen from Fig. 18.11 that as a result of the technical substitution effect (*i.e.* moving from *T* to *R*) the entrepreneur buys *KG* more of factor *X* and *LH* less of factor *Y*. The substitution effect always induces the entrepreneur to buy more of the factor whose price has relatively fallen.

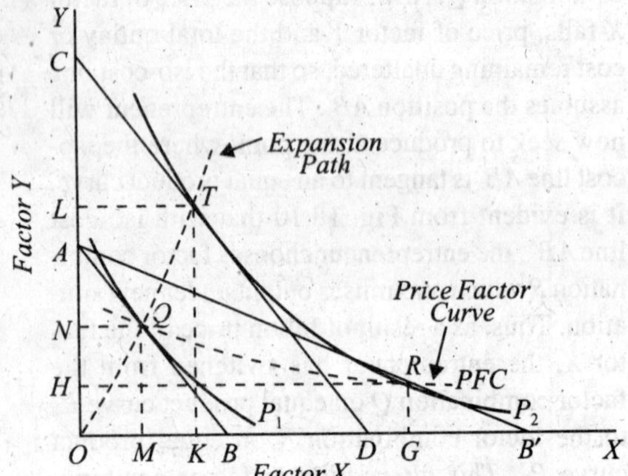

Fig. 18.11. *Output and Substitution Effects of the Price Change*

It is thus clear that the movement from *Q* to *R* as a result of the price effect can be separated into two distinct movements, first from *Q* to *T* along the expansion path due to expansion or output effect, and second, from *T* to *R* along the equal product curve P_2 due to technical substitution effect. In Fig. 18.11 price effect effect of the fall in price of *X* on the purchase of factor *X* is the increase in its quantity purchased by *MG* which is equal to *MK* (output effect) plus *KG* (technical substitution effect). On the other hand, the price effect of the fall in price of *X* on the purchases of factor *Y* is the decrease in its quantity purchased by *NH* which is equal to *NL* (expansion effect) minus *LH* (substitution effect).

SUBSTITUTE AND COMPLEMENTARY FACTORS

It is clear from Fig. 18.11 that fall in the price of factor *X* leads to the fall in the quantity purchased of factor *Y*. *When a fall in the price of one of the two variable factors leads to the decline in the quantity purchased of the other factor, the two factors are said to be substitutes of each other in production*. Thus Fig. 18.11 illustrates the case of two factors which are substitutes of each other. It should be noted that the fall in price of the factor *X* has led to the decline in quantity purchased or used of *Y*, because the substitution effect which works negatively for factor *Y* is greater than the positive expansion (output)effect. We may therefore say *two factors X and Y are substitutes if the substitution effect on Y of the change in price of X is greater than the output effect on it.* In figure 18.11, the substitution effect of the fall in the price of factor *X* on factor *Y* is *LH* which is greater than the output effect *NL*. The two effects work in opposite direction on the quantity used of factor *Y*; the substitution effect tends to reduce it and output effect tends to increase it. Since the substitution effect is greater than the output effect, the net result is the fall in the quantity used of the factor *Y* by *NH* amount. Thus, Fig. 18.11 represents the case of the two factors which are substitutes of each other.

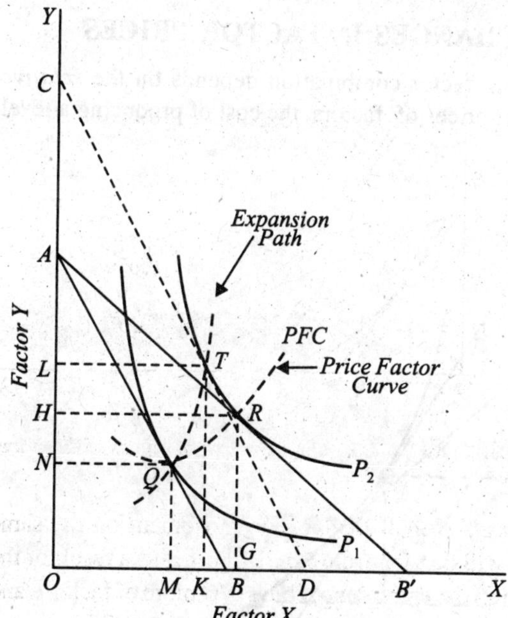

Fig. 18.12. *Complementary Factors*

In Fig. 18.12 the marginal rate of technical substitution diminishes rapidly along the equal product curves, that is, the equal product curves are highly convex when looked from origin. In this case therefore the substitution effect will be very small. Thus, in Fig. 18.12 the output effect of the fall in price of *X* on the quantity used or purchased of *Y* is greater than the substitution effect and therefore the net effect of the fall in price of *X* on *Y* is the increase in the quantity purchased of *Y*. In Fig. 18.12, the substitution effect on *Y* as a result of the fall in the price of factor *X* is *LH*, whereas the output effect on *Y* is *NL* which is greater than *LH*. In this case, therefore, the fall in price of *X* leads to the increase in the quantity purchased and used of both the factors. *When a fall in the price of one of the two factors causes the increase in quantity purchased of both the factors, the two factors are said to be complementary*. Thus fig. 18.12 illustrates the cases of two complementary factors. In terms of output and technical substitution effects, the *complementary factors may be defined as those factors in which case the output effect of the relative fall in the price of one factor on the purchases of the other is greater than the substitution effect.*

Perfect Complements

It should be noted that the factors represented in Fig. 18.12 are complements but not perfect complements. The two perfect complementary factors are used in a given fixed proportion and, as explained in the previous chapter, the equal product curves of the two perfect complementary factors are right-angled. The technical substitution effect in case of two perfect complements is therefore zero. The case of perfect complements is illustrated in Fig. 18.13 where substitution effect being nil, price effect consists of only the output effect and the quantities of both factors increases in a given proportion as a result of the fall in price of a factor and the resultant change in the iso-cost line from AB to AB'. It will be seen from Fig. 18.13 that when iso-cost line CD is drawn parallel to AB so as to be tangent to the equal-product curve P_2, it touches the same point R where the new iso-cost line AB' is tangent to the equal product curve P_2. This shows that substitution effect is zero and price effect contains only the output effect.

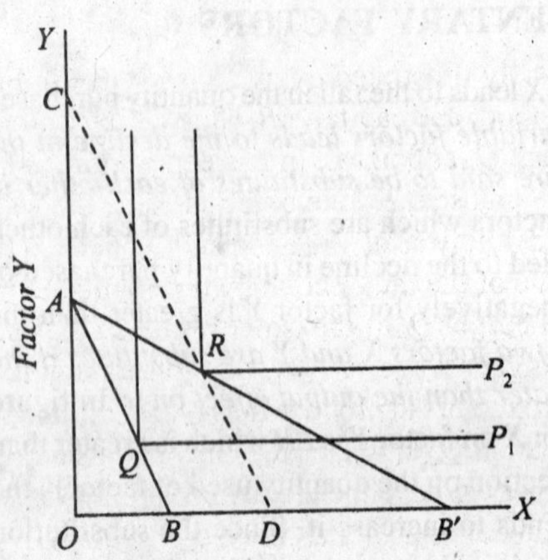

Fig. 18.13. *Perfect Complementary Factors*

FACTOR SUBSTITUTION AND CHANGES IN FACTOR PRICES

We have seen above that the cost-minimising factor combination depends on the *relative prices* of factors used. As shown above, given the prices of factors, the cost of producing a level of output is minimised by using a factor combination at which

$$MRTS_{LK} = \frac{w_0}{r_0}$$

or

$$\frac{MP_L}{w_0} = \frac{MP_k}{r_0}$$

where w_0 is the price of labour *i.e.* wage rate and r_0 is the price of capital.

Now, if either the price of labour (w) or the price of capital (r) changes, the producer will respond to this change in factor prices as their cost-minimisation state will be disturbed. For example, if the wage rate *rises* from w_0 to w_1, then at the initial equilibrium position,

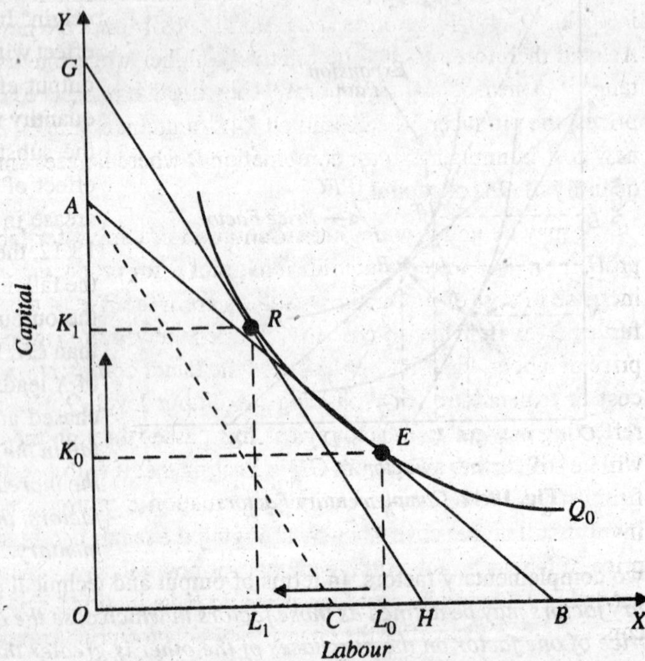

Fig. 18.14. *Rise in wage rate (price) of labour causes substitution of capital for labour.*

$$\frac{MP_L}{w_1} < \frac{MP_k}{r_0} \text{ or, } \frac{MP_K}{r_0} > \frac{MP_L}{w_1}$$

This will induce a rational producer to substitute capital for relatively more expensive labour. That is, he will try to use more capital and less labour and continue substituting capital for labour until $MRTS_{LK} = \frac{w_1}{r}$ or $\frac{MP_L}{w_1} = \frac{MP_K}{r}$.

The substitution of one factor for another is graphically illustrated by using isoquants in Fig. 18.14, where with factor prices w_0 and r_0 respectively of labour and capital, *AB*, which is the iso-cost line for a given amount of outlay, is tangent to the isoquant Q_0 at point *E*. In this equilibrium situation, he is using OL_0 of labour and OK_0 of capital. Now suppose the price of labour (*i.e.*, the wage rate) rises so that the iso-cost line, price of capital (*r*) and outlay remaining constant, rotates to the new position *AC*. It will be seen from Fig. 18.14 that none of the factor combinations lying on the iso-cost line *AC* will be sufficient to produce the level of output Q_0 as the iso-cost line *AC* lies at a lower level than the isoquant Q_0. In other words, with higher wage rate w_1, the given amount of outlay is not enough to buy the required amounts of the two factors to produce the level of output Q_0. Thus, if the producer wants to produce the same level of output Q_0, it will have to increase its outlay. The increase in outlay on factors implies moving to a higher iso-cost line that will be parallel to the new iso-cost line *AC*. Now, with new relative prices of labour and capital, the iso-cost line *GH* is drawn parallel to *AC* so that it is tangent to the isoquant Q_0.

It will be observed from the Fig. 18.14 that the new iso-cost line *GH* will not be tangent at the initial equilibrium point *E* since its slope reflecting the new relative factor prices differs from the slope of the initial iso-cost line *AB*. Thus, *the initial point E no longer minimises cost in the context of new relative factor prices.*

Now that the wage rate is higher, that is, the labour is relatively more expensive, to produce the initial level of output, a producer will substitute capital for labour by moving upward along the isoquant Q_0. It will be observed from Fig. 18.14 that the new iso-cost line *GH* which is parallel to *AC* and therefore reflects the relatively higher wage rate as compared to the iso-cost line *AB*, is tangent to the isoquant Q_0 at point *R* showing that in order to minimise cost at the new relative factor prices, the producer has substituted K_0K_1 amount of capital for L_0L_1 amount of labour to reach the new cost-minimising factor combination *R* where he uses smaller amount OL_1 of labour and larger quantity of OK_1 of capital.

It may be noted again that substitution of capital for labour and thereby changing the factor-proportion used to reach equilibrium point *R* for producing a given level of output Q_0 involves the increase in cost of production resulting from the rise in the price of labour (iso-cost line *GH* lies further away from the iso-cost line *AC* when viewed from the origin). However, if with the new higher price of labour, the producer had used the factor combination *E*, he would have incurred still higher cost or expenditure for producing the output level Q_0. If iso-cost line is drawn parallel to *AC* reflecting new relative factor prices that passes through the original factor combination point *E* it will lie still further away from *GH* indicating that if with new relative prices of labour and capital the firm uses the same labour-capital combination *E* to produce that initial level of output Q_0, it will involve still higher cost. Thus by changing the factor combination from *E* to *R* following the rise in price of labour by substituting capital for now relatively more expensive labour, the firm has succeeded in lowering its cost than it would have incurred if it had continued to use the same factor combination *E* even after the change in the factor-price situation.

From the foregoing analysis we arrive at the conclusion that change in relative factor prices causes a substitution of a factor that has become relatively more expensive by a factor that has become relatively . In the real world there are several examples of factor substitution in response to changes in relative factor prices. When price of petroleum increased many countries tried to substitute other types of energy resources using inputs such as coal, electricity to reduce costs of production. Again, in the United States the firms use more machines (*i.e.* capital) and relatively less labour as labour there is very costly than is the case in some developing countries where wages are comparatively low. Further, recently when prices of computers have fallen, there has been substitution of manual labour for doing such work as book-keeping, making architectural maps, composing books and journals by computers (*i.e.* capital).

QUESTIONS AND PROBLEMS FOR REVIEW

1. Explain the concept of production function. The information about production function facing a firm is inadequate for making decision regarding economically efficient use of factors or resources. Explain.

   [**Hints:** Production function describes the technological aspect of production, that is, maximum possible output that can be produced by various combinations of factors. On the other hand, *economic efficiency in resource use implies least-cost combination of factors to produce a given output or alternatively it implies maximisation of output for a given cost outlay*. Thus, for deciding about optimal or economically efficient resource use we require not only the data about the production function but also about prices of factors.]

2. What is meant by efficient or optimum factor combination in production ? Explain with the help of isoquants (*i.e.*, equal product curves) and iso-cost lines how a producer achieves this combination of factors.

3. Show with the help of isoquants that a firm will be in equilibrium regarding use of a factor combination when marginal rate of technical substitution (MRTS) between factors is equal to the ratio of factor prices.

4. Given the prices of the two factors for the individual firm, explain the conditions for producing a given output at least cost. [*C.U., B.Con ., (Hons.),* 1998]

5. Show with the isoquant-iso-cost apparatus, a firm is in equilibrium with regard to the use of factors when the ratios of marginal products of factors to their respective prices are equal.
   D.U. B.Com (Hons.)

6. Show that maximisation of output subject to a given cost constraint and minimisation of cost subject to a given output will yield identical results. [*C.U. B.Com., 1993*]

(*a*) Suppose a firm is using a combination of labour and capital to produce a certain level of output. Now suppose that wage rate of labour rises, price of capital remaining the same. Explain using diagram what will be its effect on the use of labour and capital, while output of the firm remains constant.

(*b*) (*i*) What are ridge lines? Explain the economic region of product using isoquant map .

(*ii*) Suppose labour is free, show with the help of an isoquant map how much labour will be employed, given a certain fixed quantity of capital. *D.U. B.Com (Hons.) and B.A. (Hons.)*

7. Define substitute and complementary factors. Show that in case of perfectly complementary factors substitution effect is zero.

8. What is an expansion path? Show that expansion path of a linear homogeneous production function is a straight line through the origin. [*D.U. B.A. (Hons.) 1996*]

[**Hint:** For the later part see mathematical portion in the text of the book.]

9. Explain using isoquants (*i.e.*, equal product curves) (*a*) the effect of rise in wage rate of labout, price of capital remaining, constant on the use of labour and capital, (*b*) the effect of fall in price of capital, wage rate of labour remaining the same.

10. Explain using isoquants-iso-cost apparatus how a change in price of a factor is split up into output effect and substitution effect.

11. A firm is producing output using labour and capital in such quantities that marginal product of labour is 15, and marginal product of capital is 8. The wage of labour is Rs. 3 and price of capital is Rs. 2. Is the firm using efficient factor combination for production ? If not, what it should do to achieve economic efficiency?

[**Hints:** Efficiency condition for factor use (that is, optimal factor combination) requires that the following condition should be fulfilled:

$$\frac{MP_L}{w} = \frac{MP_K}{r}$$

Now, $$\frac{MP_L}{w} = \frac{15}{3} \text{ and } \frac{MP_K}{r} = \frac{8}{2}$$

Thus, $$\frac{15}{3} > \frac{8}{2}$$

The given factor combination cannot therefore be efficient or optimal factor combination *because the firm is getting more output per unit of rupee spent on labour than on capital.* To achieve efficiency or maximum profits the firm should substitute labour for capital so that $\frac{MP_L}{w}$ becomes equal to $\frac{MP_K}{r}$.]

12. The wage rate of labour is Rs. 6 and price of raw materials is Rs. 2. The marginal product of labour is 16 and that of raw materials is 4. Can a firm operating under these conditions be maximising profits ?

[**Hints:** Profit maximisation requires the following conditions:

$$\frac{MP_L}{w} = \frac{MP_{RM}}{P_{RM}}$$

$$\frac{MP_L}{w} = \frac{16}{6}, \quad \frac{MP_{RM}}{P_{RM}} = \frac{4}{2}$$

$$\frac{16}{6} > \frac{4}{2} \text{ or } \frac{MP_L}{w} > \frac{MP_{RM}}{P_{RM}}$$

Thus, use of inputs is inefficient and the firm will not be maximising profits.]

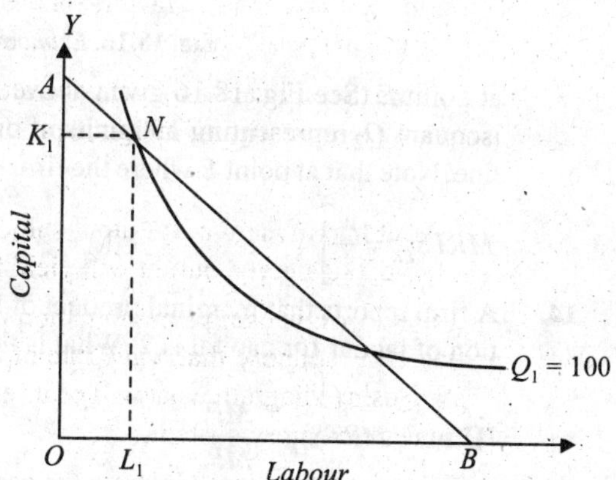

Fig. 18.15. *Economicin efficiency in Resource Use.*

13. What is meant by economic efficiency in the use of resources in production? In the diagram given in Fig. 18.15, AB is the given iso-cost line and Q_1 is the isoquant representing 100 units of output. Does the factor combination depicted by point N in the diagram represent economically efficient use of resources ?

[Hints: Economic efficiency in the use of resources means either minimisation of cost for a given output or maximisation of output for a given cost-outlay. In the diagram point N does not represent economically efficient use of resources, because this does not ensure maximum output for a given iso-cost line. It will be rational behaviour on the part of the firm to move down along the given iso-cost line AB by substituting labour for capital as in doing so it will be reaching higher isoquants showing higher levels of output. The firm will reach the efficient factor combination

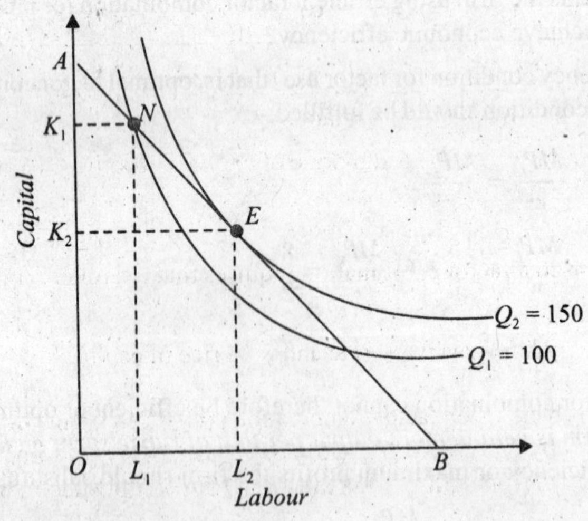

Fig. 18.16. *Economic Efficiency in Resource Use*

at point E (See Fig. 18.16 given above) at which the given iso-cost line is tangent to the isoquant Q_2 representing 150 units of output and maximises output with a given iso-cost line. Note that at point E where the firm uses L_2 amount of labour and K_2 amount of capital,

$$MRTS_{LK} = \frac{w}{r} \Big]$$

14. A firm reports that marginal product of labour is 5 and marginal rate of technical substitution of labour for capital is 2. What is the marginal product of capital ?

[Hints : $MRTS_{LK} = \dfrac{MP_L}{MP_K}$

$$2 = \frac{5}{MP_K}, \quad MP_K = \frac{5}{2} = 2.5 \Big]$$

15. A firm employs labour as the only variable factor along with a fixed quantity of capital. Wage rate of labour is Rs. 100 per day and its marginal product is 20 units of output. What is *marginal cost* of the product.

[**Hints:** Marginal cost is the additional cost incurred on producing an extra unit of output. Marginal cost can be obtained from dividing the wage that has to be paid to the additional unit of labour by the number of units of output produced by it (that is, its marginal product). Thus,

$$MC = \frac{W}{MP_L} = \frac{100}{20} = 5.$$

16. A biscuit producing company reports the following data about its production and factors used :

Q	K	L	Q	K	L
490	15	99	470	14	100
500	15	100	500	15	100

where Q = output, K = capital, L = labour.

If wage rate of labour is Rs. 5 and price of capital is Rs. 10. Does the input combination of 15K and 100L represent the least-cost factor combination. If not, should it use more labour and less capital or less labour and more capital?

[**Hints** : Least-cost factor combination requires that the following condition must be met:

$\frac{MP_L}{w} = \frac{MP_K}{r}$, where w is wage rate and r is price of capital.

Now, in the problem when factor combination is changed from $15K + 100L$ to $15K + 99L$, the output declines by 10 units ($500 - 490 = 10$). Thus, $MP_L = 10$. Similarly, when factor combination is changed from $15K + 100L$ to $14K + 100L$, output declines by 30 ($500 - 470 = 30$). Thus,

$MP_K = 30$. Substituting these values of marginal products of labour and capital and the factor prices in the condition for least-cost factor combination, we have

$$\frac{MP_L}{w} = \frac{MP_K}{r}$$

$$\frac{10}{5} \neq \frac{30}{10} \text{ or } \frac{10}{5} < \frac{30}{10}$$

The company will use more capital and less labour as output per unit of a rupee (3) spent on capital is greater than the output per unit of rupee $\left(\frac{10}{5} \text{ or } 2\right)$ spent on labour.

17. Suppose that a product requires two inputs for its production, then is it correct to say that if the prices of inputs are equal, optimal behaviour on the part of producers will dictate that these inputs be used in equal amounts.

[**Hints:** The answer is 'NO'. This is because optimal use of factors depends not only on the prices of factors, but also on their marginal products which are governed by the nature of production function (that is, technology of production)]

CHAPTER 19
COST OF PRODUCTION AND COST CURVES

In the last chapter we studied the laws of returns underlying the production conditions of goods. These production conditions determine to an appreciable degree the supply of goods. In this chapter we carry further the analysis of the forces determining supply of goods. We shall examine here how the cost of production of a firm changes with the change in its output. In other words, cost-output relations form the subject matter of the present chapter. The relation between cost and output is called "*cost function*". The cost function of the firm depends upon the production conditions and the prices of the factors used for production. How much costs a firm will incur on production depends on the level of output. Moreover, the quantity of a product that will be offered by the firm for supply in the market depends to a great degree upon the cost of production incurred on the various possible levels of output. Costs of production is the most important force governing the supply of a product. It should be pointed out here that it is assumed that a firm chooses a combination of factors which minimises its cost of production for a given level of output. It is thus assumed that whatever the level of output a firm produces, it is produced at the minimum cost possible.

In microeconomic theory, economists are generally interested in two types of cost function : the short-run cost function and the long run cost function. Accordingly, they derive the short-run and long-run cost curves. We first explain below the various concepts of costs which are used in modern economic theory and then turn to study the derivation of the short-run and the long-run cost curves.

THE CONCEPTS OF COST

Accounting Costs and Economic Costs

It is necessary for the proper understanding of the price theory to know the various concepts of cost that are often employed. When an entrepreneur undertakes production of a commodity he has to pay prices for the factors which he employs for production. He thus pays wages to the labourers employed, prices for the raw materials, fuel and power used, rent for the building he hires for the production work, and the rate of interest on the money borrowed for doing business. All these are included in his cost of production. An accountant will take into account only the payments and charges made by the entrepreneur to the suppliers of various productive factors.

But an economist's view of cost is somewhat different from this. It generally happens that the entrepreneur invests a certain amount of his own money capital in his productive business. If the money invested by the entrepreneur in his own business had been invested elsewhere, it would have earned a certain amount of interest or dividends. Moreover, an entrepreneur devotes time to his own work of production and contributes his entrepreneurial and managerial ability to it. If the entrepreneur had not set up his own business, he would have sold his services to others for some positive amount of money. Therefore, economists would also include in the cost of production (*i*) the *normal return on money capital* invested by the entrepreneur himself in his own business, which he could have earned if invested outside and (*ii*) *the wages or salary* he could have earned if he had sold his services to others. The accountant would not include these two items in a firm's cost of production but the economists consider them as *bona-fide* costs and will accordingly include them in cost. Likewise, the money rewards for other factors owned by the entrepreneur himself and employed by him in his own business are also considered by the economists as parts of the cost of production.

It follows from above that the accountant considers those costs which involve cash payments to *others* by the entrepreneur of the firm. The economist takes into account all of *these accounting costs*, but in addition, he also takes into account the *amount of money the entrepreneur could have earned if he had invested his money and sold his own services and other factors in next best alternative uses*. The accounting costs are contractual cash payments which the firm makes to other factor owners for purchasing or hiring the various factors are also known as *explicit costs*. The normal return on money-capital invested by the entrepreneur and the wages or salary for his services and the money rewards for other factors which the entrepreneur *himself owns and employs* them in his own firm are known as *implicit costs or imputed costs*. The econimists take into consideration both the explicit and implicit costs. Therefore,

Economic Costs = Accounting Costs + Implicit Costs

It may be pointed out that the firm will earn *economic profits* only if it is making revenue *in excess of the total of accounting and implicit costs*. Thus, when the firm is in no profit and no loss position, it means that the firm is making revenue equal to the total of accounting and implicit costs and no more. Therefore,

Economic Profits = Total Revenue – Total Economic Costs

Opportunity Cost

The concept of opportunity cost occupies a very important place in modern economic analysis. *The opportunity cost of any good is the next best alternative good that is sacrificed*. The factors which are used for the manufacture of a car may also be used for the production of an equipment for the army. Therefore, the opportunity cost of production of a car is the output of the army equipment foregone or sacrificed, which could have been produced with the same amount of factors that have gone into the making of a car. To take another example, a farmer who is producing wheat can also produce prtatoes with the same factors. Therefore, the opportunity cost of a quintal of wheat is the amount of output of potatoes given up. Professor Benham defines the opportunity costs thus : "*the opportunity cost of anything is the next best alternative that could be produced instead by the same factors or by a equivalent group of factors, costing the same amount of money*."[1]

Two points be noted in the above definition of opportunity cost. First, the opportunity cost of anything is only the *next-best alternative* foregone. That is say, the opportunity cost of producing a good is not any other alternative good that could be produced with the same factors; it is only the *most valuable other good* which the same factors could produce. Second point worth noting in the above definition is the addition of the qualification "or by an equivalent group of factors costing the same amount of money". The need for the addition of this qualification arises because all the factors used in the production of one good may not be the same as are required for the production of the next best alternative good. For instance, the farmer who is employing land, workers, water, fertilisers, wheat seed, *etc.*, for the production of wheat may use the same land, the same workers, the same water, the same fertilisers for the production of potatoes, but a different type of seed will be needed. Likewise, a manufacturing firm may shift from the production of one product to another without any changes in plant and equipment or its workers but it will require different types of raw materials. In such cases therefore the opportunity cost of a good should be viewed as the next best alternative good that could be produced with the *same value* of the factors which are more or less the same.

1. Frederic Benham, *Economics*, 6th edition, p. 195.

The concept of opportunity cost is very fundamental to economics. Robbins' famous definition of economics goes in terms of the scarcity of resources and their ability to be put into various uses. If the production of one good is increased, then the resources have to be withdrawn from the production of other goods. Thus, when the resources are fully employed, then more of one good could be produced at the cost of producing less of the others. If 100 units more of good *X* are produced by withdrawing resources from the industry producing good *Y*, then the opportunity costs of producing additional hundred units of *X* is the amount of good *Y* sacrificed.

The alternative or opportunity cost of a good can be given a money value. In order to produce a good the producer has to employ various factors of production and have to pay them sufficient prices to get their services. These factors have alternative uses. *The factors must be paid at least the price they are able to obtain in the next best alternative uses.* The total alternative earnings of the various factors employed in the production of a good will constitute the opportunity cost of the good.

A significant fact worth mentioning is that *relative prices of goods tend to reflect their opportunity costs*. The resources will remain employed in the production of a particular good when they are being paid at least the money rewards that are sufficient to induce them to stay in the industry, *i.e.*, equal to the value they are able to obtain and create elsewhere. In other words, a collection of factors employed in the production of a good must be paid equal to their opportunity cost. The greater the opportunity cost of a collection of factors used in the production of a good, the greater must be the price of the good. Thus, if the same collection of factors can produce either one tractor or 2 scooters, then the price of one tractor will be twice that of one scooter.

Private Cost Versus Social Cost

It is important to note the distinction made by the economists between the private cost and social cost. The sum of the explicit and implicit costs incurred by a firm to produce a product constitutes his private cost. It is these private costs that it takes into account while making decisions regarding price and output of the commodity it produces. However, in addition to the private costs, the *production of a commidity by a firm bestows some benefits or causes some damage or loss to others which he does not take into account while taking decisions regarding price and output of the commodity.* These external damages or benefits, if any caused by the production of a firm to other firms or consumers also constitute a part of the social cost which are ignored by a firm but may be of great significance from the social point of view. For example, a firm producing pesticides pay prices for the purchase of raw materials, labour and capital used by it. These are the private costs of the firm. But in the production process of pesticides some by products such as foul smell, polluted air and effluents that are emitted along the production of pesticides cause economic damage or costs to those people who live in the adjoining areas. These harmful external effects are also called *negative externalities*. The beneficial external effects created by firm are called positive externalities. *The social costs are the sum of the private costs and the net of negative externalities over positive externalities.* If there are no any negative externalities, social cost will be greater than private costs. If social welfare is to be maximised, it is the total social cost and not the private cost alone that has to be minimised. We shall discuss in detail the concept of social cost in the part relating to the welfare economics where we will explain when there occur market failures due to the presence of external damages and benefits of the production by firms, the intervention by the government becomes necessary to promote social welfare.

Short Run and Long Run Defined

There are some inputs or factors which can be readily adjusted in the short run with the changes in the output level. Thus, a firm can readily employ more workers, if it has to increase output. Likewise, it can secure and use more raw materials, more chemicals without much delay if it has to expand production in the short run. Thus, factors such as *labour, raw materials, chemicals etc.*, *which can be readily varied with the change in output are called variable factors.* On the other hand, there are factors such as capital equipment, building, top management personnel which cannot be so readily varied. It requires a comparatively long time to make variations in them. It takes time to expand a factory building or to build a new factory building with a large area or capacity. Similarly, it also takes time to order and install new machinery. The *factors such as capital equipment, factory building which cannot be readily varied and require comparatively a long time to make adjustment in them are called fixed factors.*

Corresponding to the distinction between variable factors and fixed factors, economists distinguish between the short run and the long run. *The short run is a period of time in which output can be increased or decreased by changing only the amount of variable factors such as labour, raw materials, chemicals, etc.* On the other hand, in the long run, quantities of the fixed factors such as capital equipment, factory building, etc., can also be varied for making changes in output.

Thus, in the long run, the output can be increased not only by using more quantities of labour and raw materials but also by expanding the size of the existing plant or by building a new plant with a larger productive capacity.

Short Run Costs : Total Fixed and Variable Costs

Fixed costs are those which are independent of output, that is, they do not change with changes in output. These costs are a fixed amount which must be incurred by a firm in the short run, whether output is small or large. Even if the firm closes down for some time in the short run but remains in business, these costs have to be borne by it. Fixed costs are also known as *overhead costs* and include charges such as contractual rent, insurance fee, maintenance costs, property taxes, interest on the capital invested, minimum administrative expenses such as manager's salary, watchman's wages etc. Thus *fixed costs are those which are incurred in hiring the fixed factors of production whose amount cannot be altered in the short run.*

Variable costs, on the other hand, are those costs which are incurred on the employment of variable factors of production whose amount can be altered in the short run. Thus the total variable costs change with changes in output in the short run, *i.e.*, they increase or decrease when the output rises or falls. These costs include payments such as wages of labour employed, prices of the raw materials, fuel and power used, the expenses incurred on transporting and the like. If a firm shuts down for some time in the short run, then it will not use the variable factors of production and will not therefore incur any variable costs. Variable costs are made only when some amount of output is produced and the total variable costs increase with the increase in the level of production. Variable costs are also called *prime costs* or *direct costs*. Total costs of a business is the sum of its total variable costs and total fixed costs. Thus:

$$TC = TFC + TVC$$

where TC stands for total cost, TFC for total fixed cost and TVC for total variable cost.

Because one component, *i.e.*, the total variable cost (TVC) varies with the change in output, the total cost of production (TC) will also change with the changes in the level of output. The total cost increases as the level of output rises. The concepts of total cost, total variable cost and total fixed cost in the short run can be easily understood with the help of the following Table 19.1.

It will be seen from the below table that the total fixed costs are equal to Rs. 50 and remain constant when the output is increased from 1 to 8 units of output. Even if no output is produced, the firm has to bear the fixed costs of production. This is because, as said above, the firm cannot dispense with the fixed factors of production in the short run. It has therefore to keep the fixed factors idle in the short run and bear costs incurred on them If demand conditions are not favourable for production.

Table 19.1 Total Cost, Total Fixed Cost, and Total Variable Cost

No. of Units of Output	*Total Fixed Cost (TFC)*	*Total Variable Cost (TVC)*	*TotalCost (TC)*
0	50	0	50
1	50	20	70
2	50	35	85
3	50	60	110
4	50	100	150
5	50	145	195
6	50	190	240
7	50	237	287
8	50	284	334

As regards the variable costs, it will be seen from Table 19.1, that variable costs are equal to Rs. 20 when only one unit of output is produced and they rise to Rs. 284 when eight units are produced. Since variable costs are incurred on factors such as labour, raw materials, fuel etc., which vary with the change in the level of output, the total variable costs increase wih the increases in output throughout.

As the total cost is the sum of fixed cost and the variable cost, it can be obtained by adding the figures of column 2 (fixed cost) and column 3 (variable cost). For example, when two units of output are produced, the total cost works out to be Rs. 70 (Rs. 50 + Rs. 20 = 70). The total cost also varies directly with output because a significant part of it (*i.e.*, variable cost) increases as output is increased.

Total fixed cost and total variable costs are portrayed in Fig. 19.1 where output is measured on the *X*-axis and cost on the *Y*-axis. Since the total fixed cost remains constant whatever the level of output, the total fixed cost curve (*TFC*) is a horizontal straight line. It will be seen from Fig. 19.1 that total fixed cost curve (*TFC*) starts from a point *B* on the *Y*-axis meaning thereby that the total fixed cost equal to *OB* will be incurred even if the output is zero. On the other hand, the total variable cost curve (*TVC*) rises upward showing thereby that as output is increased, the total variable cost also increases. The total variable cost curve *TVC* starts from the origin which shows that when output is zero the variable costs are nil.

It should be noted that total cost (*TC*) is a function of total output (*Q*); the greater the output, the greater will be the total cost. In symbols, we can write:

$$TC = f(Q)$$

where *Q* stands for output

We can prove this as follows :

$$TC = TFC + TVC.$$

Suppose *TFC* is equal to *K* whihc is a constant amount whatever the level of output. *TVC* is equal to the amount used of the variable factor, say, *L*, multiplied by the given price of the variable, say, *w*

$$TVC = L.w \quad \ldots \text{(i)}$$

$$TC = \overline{K} + L.w \quad \ldots \text{(ii)}$$

Now, *L.w*, that is, *TVC* must rise with the increase in output, because only by increase in the amount of variable factor, that is, by increase in

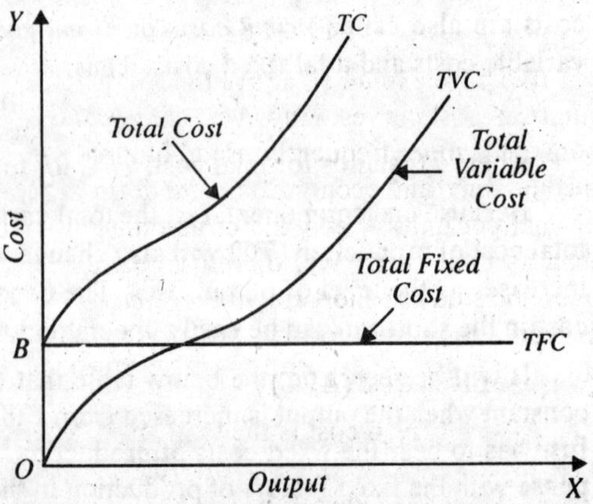

Fig. 19.1. *Total Fixed Cost, Total Variable Cost and Total Cost*

L, the output can be increased. From equation (*ii*) it follows that with the increase in $L.w$ as output rises, *TC* must also rise. In other words, total cost (*TC*) is a function of total output (*Q*) and varies directly with it.

Total cost curve (*TC*) is obtained by adding up vertically total fixed cost and total variable cost curves because the total cost is sum of total fixed cost and total variable cost. It will be seen from Fig. 19.1 that the vertical distance between the *TVC* curve and *TC* curve is constant throughout. This is because the vertical distance between the *TVC* and *TC* curves represents the amount of total fixed cost which remains unchanged as output is increased in the short run. It should also be noted that the vertical distance between the total cost curve (*TC*) and the total fixed curve (*TFC*) represents the amount of total variable costs which increase with the increase in output. The shape of the total cost curve (*TC*) is exactly the same as that total variable cost curve (*TVC*) because the same vertical distance always separates the two curves.

Sunk Costs

There is an important difference between the approach of economists from accountants regarding the treatment of fixed costs incurred on durable capital goods such as machines, buildings. The accountants take *historical costs* of these capital goods, that is, the price at which they were originally purchased and a given percentage of the original price is taken as *depreciation* which is charged to current costs of production per year. However, economists consider the historical costs of these capital goods as *sunk cost* which is irrelevant to the current costs of production and therefore cannot be the basis of decision-making with regard to production and pricing of commodities. **Sunk costs are those expenditures incurred by a firm that cannot be recovered.** The economists adopt the principle that "bygones are bygones" and consider the *current* opportunity costs of these capital goods that is relevant for decision making in the current period. If the capital goods can be put to an alternative use or can be let out to others, the earnings in the next best alternative or the rental value of the machines if they are hired by others would constitute the opportunity costs of these capital goods and could be counted by the economists as part of the current cost of production. However, if the durable capital goods, especially specialized equipment such as machines, have no alternative use, their opportunity cost will be zero and economists would not include them in current costs of production, despite their depreciation during a year. It may, however, be noted that conventional accounting method of including depreciation charge in current cost of production may be useful for other purposes, for instance, for determining income tax liability. But economists look at things from the point of view of opportunity costs which affect the decision-making process. Thus, when determining the rental value of specialized capital equipment, economists consider its opportunity cost and ignore its historical price.

THE SHORT-RUN AVERAGE COST CURVES

We have explained above the short-run total cost curves. However, the cost concept is more frequently used both by businessmen and economists in the form of cost per unit, or average costs rather than as total costs. We, therefore, pass on to the study of short-run *average cost curves*.

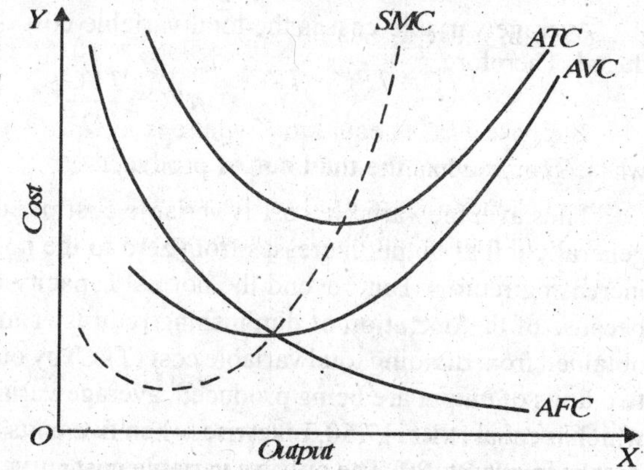

Fig. 19.2. *Short-Run Average and Marginal Cost Curves*

Average Fixed Cost (AFC)

Average fixed cost is the total fixed cost divided by the number of units of output produced. Therefore,

$$AFC = \frac{TFC}{Q}$$

where Q represents the number of units of output produced.

Thus average fixed cost is the fixed cost per unit of output. Suppose for a firm the total fixed cost is Rs. 2,000 when output is 100 units, average fixed cost (*AFC*) will be Rs. 2,000/100 = Rs. 20 and when output is expanded to 200 units, average fixed cost will be Rs. 2,000/200 = Rs. 10. Since total fixed cost is a constant quantity, average fixed cost will steadily fall as output increases. Therefore,

Table 19.2. Average Fixed Cost, Average Variable Cost and Average Total Cost

Units of output (Q)	*Total Fixed Cost (TFC)*	*Total Variable Cost (TVC)*	*Total Cost (TC)*	*Average Fixed Cost (AFC)*	*Average Variable Cost (AVC) TVC/Q*	*Average Total Cost (ATC) TC/Q*
0	50	0	50	0	0	0
1	50	20	70	50.00	20.00	70.00
2	50	35	85	25.00	17.50	42.50
3	50	60	110	16.67	20.00	36.67
4	50	100	150	12.50	25.00	37.50
5	50	145	195	10.00	29.00	39.00
6	50	190	240	8.33	31.67	40.00
7	50	237	287	7.14	33.86	41.00
8	50	284	334	6.25	35.50	41.75

average fixed cost curve slopes downward throughout its length. As output increases, the total fixed cost spreads over more and more units and therefore average fixed cost becomes less and less. When output becomes very large, average fixed cost approaches zero. Consider Table 19.2 where total cost is Rs. 50 when one unit of output is produced, the average fixed cost is obviously Rs. 50(50/1=50). On raising output to 2 units, average fixed cost will be Rs. 25. (i.e. 50/2 = 25). Further, if output is increased to 8 units, average fixed cost falls to Rs. 6.25 (i.e. 50/8 = 6.25). Average fixed cost curve (AFC) is shown in Fig. 19.2. It will be seen that average fixed cost curve continuously falls throughout. Mathematically speaking, average fixed cost curve approaches both axes asympotically. In other words, *AFC* curve gets very nearer to but never touches either axis.

The average fixed cost curve, *AFC*, possesses another important property. If we pick up any point on the average fixed cost curve and multiply the average fixed cost at that point with the corresponding quantity of output produced, then the product is always the same. This is because the product of the average fixed cost and the corresponding quantity of output will yield total fixed cost which remains constant throughout. A curve with such a property is called *rectangular hyperbola*.

Average Variable Cost (AVC)

Average variable cost is the total variable cost divided by the number of units of output produced. Therefore,

$$AVC = \frac{TVC}{Q}$$

where Q represents the total output produced.

Thus average variable cost is variable cost per unit of output. The average variable cost will generally fall as output increases from zero to the normal capacity output due to the occurrence of increasing returns. But beyond the normal capacity output average variable cost will rise steeply because of the operation of diminishing returns. Thus, in Table 19.2 average variable cost can be obtained from dividing total variable cost (*TVC*) by output. It will be seen from Table 19.2 that when two units of output are being produced, average variable cost can be found by dividing Rs. 35 by 2 which is equal to Rs. 17.50. Likewise, when five units of output are being produced, average variable cost becomes Rs. 29. The average variable cost curve is shown in Fig. 19.2 by the curve *AVC* which first falls, reaches a minimum and then rises.

Average total cost (*ATC*) is the sum of the average variable cost and average fixed cost. Therefore, as output increases and average fixed cost becomes smaller and smaller, the vertical distance between the average total cost curve (*ATC*) and average variable cost curve (*AVC*) goes on declining. When average fixed cost curve (*AFC*) approaches the *X*-axis, the average variable cost curve approaches the average total cost curve (*ATC*).

Relationship between AVC and Average Product

Average variable cost bears an important relationship with the average product per unit of the variable factor. Let *Q* stand for quantity of total product produced; *L* for the amount of the variable factor, say labour, used and *w* for the price per unit of the variable factor and *AP* for the average product of the variable factor. We assume that the price of the variable factor remains unaltered as more or fewer units of the variable factor are employed.

Total product (or output *Q*) $= AP \times L$

where *AP* stands for average product of labour, the variable factor and *L* for the amount of labour used.

$$\text{Average variable cost } (AVC) = \frac{TVC}{Q}$$

Since the total variable cost (*TVC*) is equal to the amount of the variable factor (*L*) employed multiplied by the price per unit (*w*) of the variable factor, ($TVC = L.w.$). Therefore

$$AVC = \frac{L.w}{Q}$$

Since $$Q = AP \times L$$

$$\therefore \quad AVC = \frac{L.w}{AP \times L} = \frac{w}{AP} = w\left(\frac{1}{AP}\right)$$

Thus, given the price of the variable factor *w*, the average variable cost is equal to the reciprocal of the average product $\left(\frac{1}{AP} \text{ is the reciprocal of } AP\right)$ multiplied by a constant *w*. It follows that average variable cost and average product of the variable factor vary inversely with each other. Therefore, when average product of the variable factor rises in the beginning as more units of the variable factor are employed, the average variable cost must be falling. And when the average product of the variable factor falls, the average variable cost must be rising. At the level of output at which the average product of the variable factor is maximum, the average variable cost is minimum. Thus the average variable cost (*AVC*) curve looks like the average product (*AP*) curve turned upside down with minimum point of the *AVC* curve corresponding to the maximum point of the *AP* curve.

Average Total Cost (ATC)

The average total cost or what is simply called average cost is the total cost divided by the number of units of output produced.

$$\text{Average total cost} = \frac{\text{Total Cost}}{\text{Output}}$$

or $$ATC = \frac{TC}{Q}$$

Since the total cost is the sum of total variable cost and the total fixed cost, the average total cost is also the sum of average variable cost and average fixed cost. This can be proved as follows :

$$ATC = \frac{TC}{Q}$$

Since $$TC = TVC + TFC$$

Therefore, $$ATC = \frac{TVC + TFC}{Q}$$

$$= \frac{TVC}{Q} + \frac{TFC}{Q}$$

$$= AVC + AFC$$

Average total cost is also known as *unit cost*, since it is cost per unit of output produced. As the average total cost is the sum of average variable cost and average fixed cost, in Table 19.2 it can be obtained by summing up the figures of columns 5 and 6 corresponding to different levels of output. Thus, for example, with two units of output, average total cost is Rs. 25 + Rs. 17.50 = Rs. 42.50 and with three units of output it is equal to Rs. 16.67 + Rs. 20 = Rs. 36.67 and so on for other levels of output. Alternatively, the average total cost can be obtained directly from dividing the total cost by the number of units of output produced. Thus average total cost of 2 units of output is equal to Rs. 85/2 or Rs. 42.50. Likewise, when output is raised to 6 units, total cost rises to 240 and average total cost works out to be Rs. 240/6 = Rs. 40.

It follows from above that the behaviour of the average total cost curve will depend upon the behaviour of the average variable cost curve and average fixed cost curve. In the beginning, both *AVC* and *AFC* curves fall, the *ATC* curve therefore falls sharply in the beginning. When *AVC* curve begins rising, but *AFC* curve is falling steeply, the *ATC* curve continues to fall. This is because during this stage the fall in *AFC* curve weighs more than the rise in the *AVC* curve. But as output increases further, there is a sharp rise in *AVC* which more than offsets the fall in *AFC*. Therefore the *ATC* curve rises after a point. Thus, the average total cost curve (*ATC*) like the *AVC* curve first falls, reaches its minimum value and then rises. The average total cost curve (*ATC*) is therefore almost of a 'U' shape.

MARGINAL COST (MC)

The concept of marginal cost occupies an important place in economic theory. Marginal cost is *addition* to the total cost caused by producing one more unit of output. In other words, marginal cost is the addition to the total cost of producing *n* units instead of *n* – 1 units (*i.e.*, one less) where *n* is any given number. In symbols:

$$MC_n = TC_n - TC_{n-1}$$

Suppose the production of 5 units of a product involves the total cost of Rs. 206. If the increase in production to 6 units raises the total cost to Rs. 236, then marginal cost of the sixth unit of output is Rs. 30 (236 – 206 = 30). Let us illustrate the computation of marginal cost from a table of total cost and output. In the table 19.3 when output is zero in the short run, the producer is incurring total cost of Rs. 100 which represents the total fixed cost of the production. When one unit of output is produced, the total fixed cost rises to Rs. 125. The marginal cost of the first unit of output is therefore Rs. 25 (*i.e.*125 – 100 = 25). When output is increased to 2 units, the total cost goes up to Rs. 145. Therefore, the marginal cost is now Rs. 20 (*i.e.*, 145 – 125 = 20). In this way marginal cost can be found for further units of output.

$$MC = \frac{\Delta TC}{\Delta Q}$$

where ΔTC represents a change in total cost and ΔQ represents a unit change in output or total product. Since in the short run its is only the total variable cost (*TVC*) that varies with change in output, $MC = \frac{\Delta TVC}{\Delta Q}$

If we consider the total cost curve, $\frac{\Delta TC}{\Delta Q}$ represents the slope of it. Therefore, if we want to measure the marginal cost at a certain output level, we can do so by measuring the slope of the total cost curve corresponding to that output by drawing a tangent at it.

Table 19.3 : Computation of Marginal Cost

Output	*Total Cost*	*Marginal Cost*
Q	*TC*	$MC = \frac{\Delta TC}{\Delta Q}$
0	100	—
1	125	25
2	145	20
3	160	15
4	180	20
5	206	26
6	236	30
7	273	37

It is worth pointing out *that marginal cost is independent of the fixed cost and depends on the changes in the variable factors*. Since fixed costs do not change with output, there are no marginal fixed costs when output is increased in the short run. It is only the variable costs that vary with output in the short run. Therefore, the marginal costs are in fact due to the changes in variable costs, and whatever the amount of fixed cost, the marginal cost in unaffected by it.

The Relationship between Marginal Cost and Marginal Product of a Variable Factor

It should be noted that *marginal cost of production is intimately related to the marginal product of the variable factor*. Thus, if *MC* stands for marginal cost of output, *MP* for marginal product of the variable factor, *w* for the price of the variable factor, then

$$MC = \frac{\Delta TVC}{\Delta Q} \qquad ...(i)$$

Since, given the price of the variable factor, change in total variable cost can occur by increasing the quantity of the variable factor (*e.g.*, labour), we have

$$\Delta TVC = w.\Delta L$$

$$MC = \frac{\Delta TVC}{\Delta Q} = \frac{w.\Delta L}{\Delta Q} \qquad ...(ii)$$

where *w* is the given price of the variable factor 'labour', $\frac{\Delta L}{\Delta Q}$ is the reciprocal of marginal product of labour which we simply write as *MP*.

Thus, from (*ii*) we have,

$$MC = w.\frac{1}{MP} = \frac{w}{MP} \qquad ...(iii)$$

Thus, marginal cost of production is equal to the reciprocal of the marginal product of the variable factor multiplied by the price of the variable factor. In other words, *marginal cost* is *the price of the variable factor divided by its marginal product*. Therefore, marginal cost varies inversely with the marginal product of the variable factor. Now, if the price of the variable factor, *i.e.*, *w* is assumed to be constant, then from the relation between *MC* and *MP* represented in the above equation, we can ascertain the shape of the marginal cost curve. We know from the study of the law of variable proportions that as output increases in the beginning, marginal product of the variable factor rises. This means that constant *w* in the equation (*iii*) is being divided by increasingly larger *MP*. This will cause the marginal cost (*MC*) to decline as output increases in the beginning. Further, according to the law of variable proportions, marginal product of a variable factor falls after a certain level of output, which means that now constant *w* in the above equation (*iii*) is being divided by increasingly smaller *MP*. This causes the marginal cost (*MC*) to rise after a certain level of output. Thus, the fact that marginal product first rises, reaches a maximum and then declines ensures that the marginal cost curve of a firm declines first, reaches a minimum and then rises. In other words, marginal cost curve of a firm has a U-shape. The relation between marginal product of labour and marginal cost curve is shown in Fig. 19.3, where marginal product curve (*MP*) of the variable factor labour is shown at the top pannel, the marginal cost curve is shown in the panel at the bottom of the figure is labelled as *MC*.

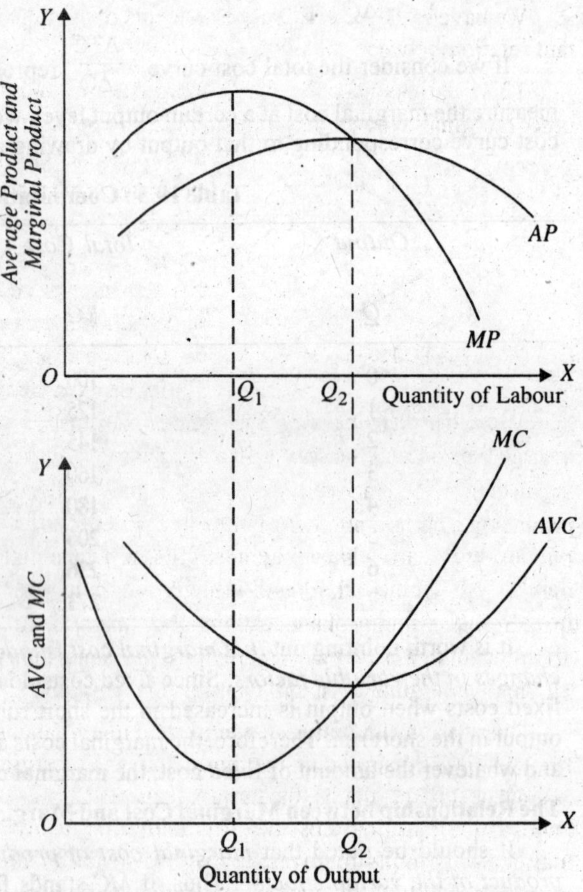

Fig. 19.3. *The Relationship between Product Curves and Cost Curve*

It is clear from above that the law of variable proportions, or in other words, the behaviour of marginal product (*MP*) curve determines the shape of marginal cost (*MC*) curve. Indeed, marginal cost (*MC*) curve is an inverse of the marginal product (*MP*) curve, with maximum of marginal product curve corresponding to the minimum of marginal cost curve. Marginal cost is simply the transformation of marginal product from physical terms into money terms. The relation between marginal product and marginal cost is quite similar to the relationship between average product and average cost. Three points are worth noting in regard to our above analysis of marginal cost. First, marginal cost is due to the changes in variable cost and is therefore independent of the fixed cost. Secondly, the shape of the marginal cost curve is determined by the law of variable proportions, that is, by the behaviour of the marginal product of the variable factor. Thirdly, the assumption that the price of the variable factor remains constant as the firm expands its output is greatly significant, since a change in the factor price may disturb our conclusion.

THE RELATION BETWEEN THE AVERAGE AND MARGINAL COST CURVES

We have explained above the concepts of average and marginal cost curves. There is an important relation between the two.

This relationship between the marginal cost and average cost is the same as that between any other marginal-average quantities. *When marginal cost is less than average cost, average cost falls and when marginal cost is greater than average cost, average cost rises.* This marginal-average relationship is a matter of mathematical truism and can be easily understood by a simple example. Suppose that a cricket player's batting average is 50. If in his next innings he scores less than 50, say 45, then his average score will fall because his marginal (additional) score is less than his average score. If instead of 45, he scores more than 50, say 55, in his next innings, then his average score will increase because now the marginal score is greater than his previous average score. Again, with his present average runs of 50, if he scores 50 also in his next innings, then his average score will remain the same because now the marginal score is just equal to the average score. Likewise, suppose a producer is producing a certain number of units of a product and his average cost is Rs. 20. Now, if he produces one unit more and his average cost falls, it means that the additional unit must have cost him less than Rs. 20. On the other hand, if the production of the additional unit *raises* his average cast, then the marginal unit must have cost him more than Rs. 20. And finally, if as a result of production of an additional unit, the average cost remains the same, then marginal unit must have cost him exactly Rs. 20, that is, marginal cost and average cost would be equal in this case.

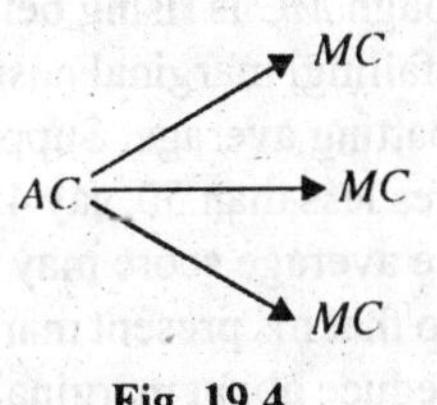

Fig. 19.4

The relationship between average and marginal cost can be easily remembered with the help of Fig. 19.4. It is illustrated in this figure that when marginal cost (*MC*) is above average cost (*AC*), the average cost rises, that is, the marginal cost (*MC*) pulls the average cost (*AC*) upwards. On the other hand, if the marginal cost (*MC*) is below the average cost (*AC*), average cost falls, that is, the marginal cost pulls the average cost downwards. When marginal cost (*MC*) stands equal to the average cost (*AC*), the average cost remains the same, that is, the marginal cost pulls the average cost horizontally.

Now, take Fig. 19.5. where short-run average cost curve *AC* and marginal cost curve *MC* are drawn. As long as short-run marginal cost curve *MC lies below* short-run average cost curve, the average cost curve *AC* is falling. When marginal cost curve *MC lies above* the average cost curve *AC*, the latter is *rising*. At the point of intersection *L* where *MC* is equal to *AC*, *AC* is neither falling nor rising, that is, at point *L*, *AC* has just ceased to fall but has not yet begun to rise. It follows that point *L*, at which the *MC* curve crosses the *AC* curve to lie above the *AC* curve is the minimum point of the *AC* curve. Thus, *marginal cost curve cuts the average cost curve at the latter's minimum point.*

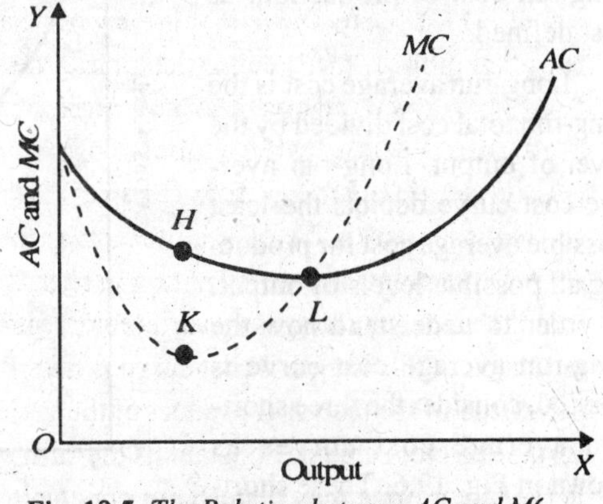

Fig. 19.5. *The Relation between AC and MC Curves*

It is important to note that *we cannot generalise about the direction in which marginal cost is moving from the way average cost is changing*, that is, when average cost is falling we cannot say that marginal cost will be falling too. When average cost is falling, what we can say definitely is only that the marginal cost will be below it but the marginal cost itself may be either rising or falling. Likewise, when average cost is rising, we cannot deduce that marginal cost will be rising too. When average cost is rising, the marginal cost must be above it but the marginal cost itself may be either rising or falling. Consider Fig. 19.5 where up to the point *K*, marginal cost is falling as well as below the average cost. As a result, the average cost is falling. But beyond point *K* and up to point *L* marginal cost curve lies below the average cost curve with the result that the average cost curve is falling. But it will seen that between *K* and *L* where *the marginal cost is rising, the average cost is falling.* This is because though *MC* is rising between *K* and *L*, it is below *AC*. It is therefore clear that when the average cost is falling, marginal cost may be falling or rising. This can also be easily illustrated by the example of batting average. Suppose a cricket player's present batting average is 50. If in his next innings he scores less than 50, say 45, his batting average will fall. But his marginal score of 45, though less than the average score may itself have risen. For instance, he might have scored 40 in his previous innings so that his present marginal score of 45 is greater than his previous marginal score. Thus one cannot deduce about marginal cost as to whether it will be falling or rising when average cost is falling or rising.

DERIVATION OF LONG-RUN AVERAGE COST CURVE

We now turn to explain the cost curves in the long-run. The long-run, as noted above, is a period of time during which the firm can vary all its inputs. In the short run, some inputs are fixed and others are varied to increase the level of output. In the long-run, none of the factors is fixed and all can be varied to expand output. The long-run production function has therefore no fixed factors and the firm has no fixed costs in the long run. It is conventional to regard the size or scale of plant as a typical fixed input. The term 'plant' is here to be understood as consisting of capital equipment, machinery, land etc. In the short run, the size of the plant is fixed and it cannot be increased or reduced. That is to say, one cannot change the amount of capital equipment in the short run, if one has to increase or decrease output. On the other hand, long-run is a period of time sufficiently long to permit the changes in plant, that is, in capital equipment, machinery, land etc. in order to expand or contract output. Thus whereas in the short run the firm is tied with a given plant, in the long run the firm moves from one plant to another; the firm can make a larger plant if it has to increase its output and a smaller plant if it has to reduce its output. *The long-run average cost of production is the least possible average cost of production of producing any given level of output when all inputs are variable, including of course the size of the plant.* A long-run cost curve depicts the functional relationship between output and the long-run cost of production, as just defined.

Long-run average cost is the long-run total cost divided by the level of output. Long-run average cost curve depicts the least possible average cost for producing all possible levels of output. In order to understand how the long-run average cost curve is derived, consider the three short-run average cost curves as shown in Fig. 19.6. These short-run average cost curves are also called *plant curves*, since in the

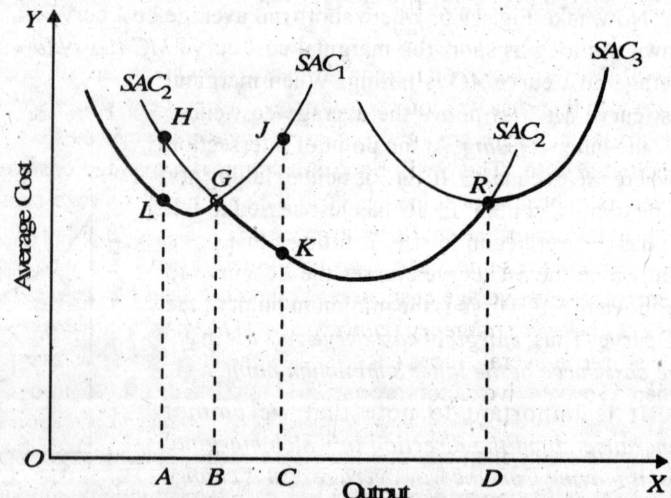

Fig. 19.6. *The Relation between AC and MC Curves*

short run plant is fixed and each of the short-run average cost curves corresponds to a particular plant. In the short run, the firm can be operating on any short-run average cost curve, given he size of the plant. Suppose that there are only these three technically possible sizes of plant, and that no other size of the plant can be built. Given a size of the plant or a short-run average cost curve, the firm will increase or decrease its output by varying the amount of the variable inputs. But, in the long run, the firm can choose among the three possible sizes of plant as depicted by short-run average cost curves SAC_1, SAC_2 and SAC_3. In the long-run the firm will decide about with which size of plant or on which short-run average cost curve it should operate to produce a given level of output at the minimum possible cost.

It will seen from Fig. 19.6. that up to *OB* amount of output, the firm will operate on the short-run average cost curve SAC_1, though it could also produce with short-run average cost curve SAC_2, because up to *OB* amount of ouput, production on SAC_1 curve entails lower cost than on SAC_2. For instance, if the level of output *OA* is produced with SAC_1, it will cost *AL* per unit and if it is produced with SAC_2 it will cost *AH* per unit. It will be seen from the Fig. 19.6 that *AL* is smaller than *AH*. Similarly, all other output levels up to *OB* can be produced more economically with the smaller plant SAC_1 than with the larger plant SAC_2. It is thus clear that in the long run the firm will produce any output up to *OB* on SAC_1. If the firm plans to produce an output which is larger than *OB* (but less than *OD*), then it will not be economical to produce on SAC_1. It will be seen from Fig. 19.6 that the output larger than *OB* but less then *OD*, can be produced at a lower cost per unit on SAC_2 than on SAC_1. Thus, the output *OC* if produced on SAC_2 costs *CK* per unit which is lower than *CJ* which is the cost incurred when produced on SAC_1. Therefore, if the firm plans to produce between output *OB* and *OD*, it will employ the plant corresponding to short-run average cost curve SAC_2. If the firm has to produce an output which exceeds *OD*, then the cost per unit will be lower on SAC_3 than on SAC_2. Therefore, for output larger than *OD*, the firm will employ plant corresponding to the short-run average cost curve SAC_3.

It is thus clear that in the long-run the firm has a choice in the use of a plant, and it will employ that plant which yields possible minimum unit cost for producing a given output. *The long-run average cost curve depicts the least possible average cost for producing various levels of output when all factors including the size of the plant have been adjusted.* Given that only three sizes of plants, as shown in Fig. 19.6, are technically possible, then the long-run average cost curve is the curve which has scallops in it. This heavily scalloped long-run average cost curve consists of some segments of all the short-run average cost curves as explained above.

Suppose now that the *size of the plant can be varied by infinitely small gradations* so that there are infinite number of plants corresponding to which there will be numerous short-run average cost curves. In that case, the long-run average cost curve will be a smooth and continuous curve without any scallops. Such a smooth long-run average cost curve has been shown in Fig. 19.7 and has been labelled as *LAC*. There will be infinite short-run average cost curves in such a case, though only seven have been shown in Fig. 19.7. This long-run average cost curve *LAC* is drawn so as to be tangent to each of the short-run average cost curves. Since an infinite number of short-run average cost curves is assumed, every point on the long-run average cost curve is a tengency point with some short-run average cost curve. In fact, *the long-run, average cost curve is nothing else but the locus of all these tangency points with short-run average cost curves.* It is again worth noting that the long-run average cost curve shows the least possible average cost of producing any output when all productive factors are variable. If a firm desires to produce particular output in the long-run, it will pick a point on the long-run average cost curve corresponding to that output and it will then build a relevant plant and operate on the corresponding short-run average cost curve.

In the situation as depicted in Fig. 19.7, for producing output *OM*, the corresponding point on the long-run average cost curve *LAC* is *G* at which the short-run average cost curve SAC_2 is tangent to the long-run average cost curve *LAC*. Thus, if a firm desires to produce output *OM*, the firm will construct a plant corresponding to SAC_2 and will operate on this curve at point *G*. Similar would be the case for all other outputs in the long-run. Further, consider that the firm plans to produce output

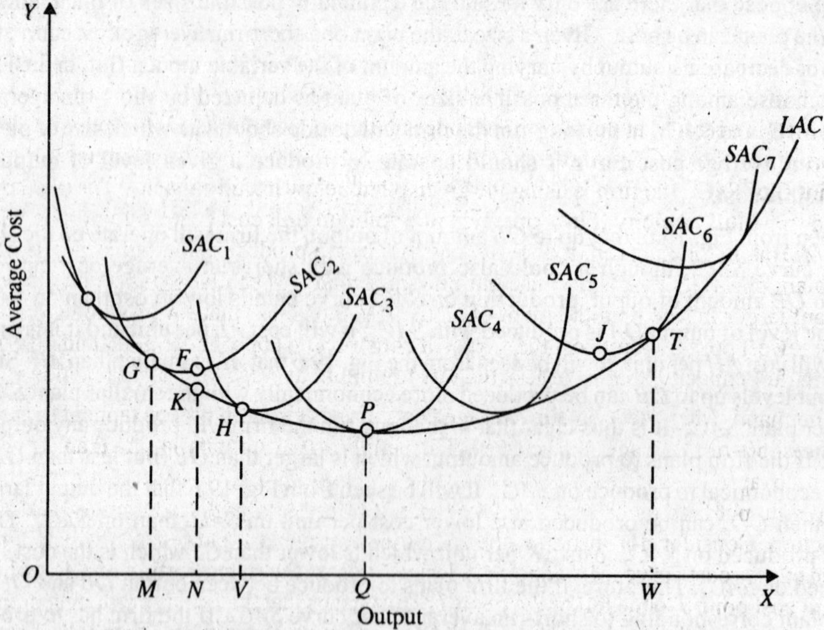

Fig. 19.7. *Deriving Long-Run Average Cost Curve from Short-Run Average Cost Curves*

ON, which corresponds to point *K* on the long-run average cost curve *LAC*. As already noted, every point on the long-run average cost curve is a tangency point with some short-run average cost curve and that there are infinite number of short-run average cost curves, so there will be some short-run average cost curve (not shown in Fig. 19.7) which will be tangent to the long-run average cost curve *LAC* at point *K* corresponding to *ON* output. Thus, for producing output *ON*, the firm will build a plant which will correspond to that short-run average cost curve which is tangent to the long-run average cost curve *LAC* at point *K* corresponding to *ON* output. The long-run average cost curve *LAC* is also called '*envelope*' since it envelops or supports a family of short-run average cost curves from below.

It is evident from Fig. 19.7 that larger outputs can be produced at the lowest cost with the larger plants, whereas smaller outputs can be produced at the lowest cost with smaller plants. Thus, output *OV* can be produced with the lowest possible cost with the plant represented by the SAC_3. To produce *OM* output with a larger plant corresponding to SAC_3, will entail higher unit cost than that on SAC_2. But a larger output *OV* can be produced most economically with a larger plant represented by SAC_3 while to produce *OV* with the smaller plant of SAC_2 will mean higher unit cost. This is as it should be expected. A larger plant which is more expensive when employed to produce a small output will not be fully utilised and its underutilisation will cause higher unit cost. In other words, using a larger plant and to operate it much below its capacity in order to produce a small output will naturally mean higher average cost. On the other hand, a large output with a small plant will also involve higher cost per unit because of its limited capacity.

It will be seen in Fig. 19.7 that the long-run average cost curve first falls and then beyond a certain point it rises, that is, the long-run average cost curve is U-shaped, though the U-shape of the long-run average curve is less pronounced than that of the short-run average cost curve. In Fig. 19.7 long-run average cost is minimum at output *OQ*. The long-run average cost falls up to the output *OQ* and it rises beyond output *OQ*. Why does the long-run average cost first decline and then after some point rises will be explained a little later.

An important fact about the long-run average cost curve is worth mentioning. It is that the *long-run average curve LAC is not tangent to the minimum points of the short-run average cost curves.* When the long-run average cost curve is declining, that is, for output less than *OQ*, it is tangent to the *falling protions* of the short-run average cost curves. This means that for any output smaller than *OQ*, it will not pay to operate a plant, that is, work at a short-run average cost (*SAC*) at its minimum unit cost. Consider, for instance, the plant corresponding to the short-run average cost curve SAC_2, which is operated at point *G* in the long run to produce output *OM*. The point *G* lies on the falling portion of the short-run average cost curve SAC_2 which has a minimum point *F*. By working at point *G* of SAC_2, the firm is using the given plant below its full capacity. The plant of SAC_2 will be utilised to its full capacity if it is operated at minimum unit cost point *F* to produce a larger output than *OM*. But, in the long run, it does not pay the firm to produce an output larger in size than *OM* with the plant of SAC_2. This is because output larger than *OM* can be produced at a lower unit cost with a plant larger in size than the plant of SAC_2. It is thus clear that for producing output less than *OQ* at the lowest possible unit cost the firm will construct an appropriate plant and will operate it at less than its full capacity, that is, at less than its minimum average cost of production.

On the other hand, when the long-run average cost curve is rising, it will be tangent to the *rising portions* of the short-run average cost curves. This implies that outputs larger than *OQ* will be produced most cheaply by constructing a plant with a given optimal capacity and operating it to produce a larger output than its capacity, that is, using it to produce at more than its minimum unit cost of production. Consider, for instance, the short-run average cost curve SAC_6 which is tangent to the long-run curves cost curve *LAC* at point *T*. Point *T* lies on the rising portion of SAC_6 which has a minimum unit cost point *J* to the left of the point *T*. This means that the firm is producing output *OW* by operating at point *T* on the plant of SAC_6 which has a optimum capacity less than *OW*. That is, the firm for producing output *OW* at lowest possible cost has built a plant corresponding to SAC_6 and works it at more than its capacity.

Long-run average cost curve is often called the '**planning curve**' of the firm by some economists, because a firm plans to produce any output in the long run by choosing a plant on the long-run average cost curve corresponding to the given output. The long-run average cost curve reveals to the firm that how large should be the plant for producing a certain output at the least possible cost. Thus while making decisions regarding the choice of a plant, the firm has to look at its long-run average cost curve enveloping a family of plant or short-run overage cost curves. What different sizes of plants are available at a time and what short-run average cost curves they will have for being used for production are known to the firm either from experience or from engineering studies.

WHY LONG-RUN AVERAGE COST CURVE IS OF U-SHAPE?

In Fig. 19.7, we have drawn the long-run average cost curve as having an approximately U-shape. It is generally believed by economists that the long-run average cost curve is normally U-shaped, that is, the long-run average cost curve first declines as output is increased and then beyond a certain point it rises. Now, what is the proper explanation of such a behaviour of the long-run average cost curve.

We saw above that the U-shape of the short-run average cost curve is explained with the law of variable proportions. *But the shape of the long-run average cost curve depends upon the returns to scale.* Since in the long run all inputs including the capital equipment can be altered, the relevant concept governing the shape of this long-run average cost curve is that of returns to scale. In a previous chapter we have explained that returns to scale increase with the initial increases in output and after remaining constant for a while, the returns to scale decrease. *It is because of the increasing returns to scale in the beginning that the long-run average cost of production falls as output is increased and, likewise, it is because of the decreasing returns to scale that the long-run average cost of production rises beyond a certain point.*

Why does LAC fall in the beginning : Economies of Scale

But the question is why we first get increasing returns to scale due to which long-run average cost falls and why after a certain point we get decreasing returns to scale due to which long-run average cost rises. In other words, what are the reasons that the firm first enjoys *internal economies of scale* and then beyond a certain point it has to suffer *internal diseconomies of scale*. Three main reasons have been given for the economies of scale which accrue to the firm and due to which cost per unit falls in the beginning.

First, as the firm increases its scale of operations, *it becomes possible to use more specialized and efficient form of all factors, especially capital equipment and machinery*. For producing higher levels of output, there is generally available a more efficient machinery which when employed to produce a large output yields a lower cost per unit of output.

Secondly, when the scale of operations is increased and the amount of labour and other factors becomes larger, *introduction of a great degree of division of labour or specialisation* becomes possible and as a result the long-run cost per unit declines. Thus, whereas the short-run decreases in cost (the downward sloping segment of the short-run average cost curve) occur due to the fact that the ratio of the variable input comes nearer to the optimum proportion, decreases in the long-run average cost (downward segment of the long-run average cost curve) take place due to the use of more efficient forms of machinery and other factors and to the introduction of a greater degree of division of labour in the productive process.

Indivisibility of Factors. Some economists explain economies of scale as arising from the *imperfect divisibility of factors*. In other words, they think that the economies of scale occur and therefore the long-run average cost falls because of the 'indivisibility' of factors. They argue that most of the factors are 'lumpy', that is, they are available in *large indivisible units* and can therefore yield lower cost of production when they are used to produce a larger output. If a small output is produced with these costly indivisible units of the factors, the average cost of production will naturally be high. If the factors of production were perfectly divisible, then, according to them, suitable adjustment in the factors could be made so that the optimum proportions between the factors were maintained even for producing small amounts of output and hence the average cost of production would not have been higher. Thus, according to them, if the factors were perfectly divisible, the small-scale production would be as good and efficient as the large-scale production and the economies of scale would be non-existent. Thus, Joan Robinson remarks, "If all the factors were finely divisible, like sand, it would be possible to produce the smallest output of any commodity with all the advantages of large-scale industry."[2]

Why does LAC Rise Eventually : Diseconomies of Scale

So much for the downward sloping segment of the long-run average cost curve. As noted above, beyond a certain point the long-run average cost curve rises which means that the long-run average cost increases as output exceeds beyond a certain point. In other words, beyond a certain point a firm experiences net *diseconomies of scale*. There is also divergence of views about the proper explanation for this upward sloping of the long-run average cost curve. The first view as held by Chamberlin and his followers is that when the firm has reached a size large enough to allow the utilisation of almost all the possibilities of division of labour and the employment of more efficient machinery, further increases in the size of the plant will entail higher long-run unit cost because of the *difficulties of management*. When the scale of operations exceeds a certain limit, the management may not be as efficient as when the scale of operations is relatively small.

After a certain sufficiently large size these inefficiencies of management more than offset the economies of scale and thereby bring about an increase in the long-run average cost and make the

2. Joan Robinson, *The Economics of Imperfect Competition*, p. 334.

LAC curve upward-sloping after a point. It should be noted that this view regards the entrepreneurial or managerial functions to be divisible and variable and explains the diseconomies of scale or the rising part of the long-run average cost curve as arising from the mounting difficulties of management (*i.e.* of supervision and coordination) beyond a certain sufficiently large-scale of operations.

The second view considers *the entrepreneur to be a fixed indivisible factor*. In this view, though all other factors can be increasesd, the entrepreneur cannot be. The entrepreneur and his functions of decision-making and ultimate control are indivisible and cannot be increased. Therefore, when a point is reached where the abilities of the fixed and indivisible entrepreneur are best utilised, further increases in the scale of operations by increasing other inputs cause the cost per unit of output to rise. In other words, *there is a certain optimum proportion between an entrepreneur and other inputs* and when that optimum proportion is reached, further increases in the other inputs to the fixed entrepreneur means the proportion between the inputs is moved away from the optimum and, therefore, this results in the rise in the long-run average cost. Thus,in this view, increases in the long-run average cost is explained by the law of variable proportions. Economists who hold this view think that the decreasing returns to scale or rising long-run average cost is actually a special case of variable proportions with entrepreneur as the fixed factor.

Long-Run Average Cost Curve in Case of Constant Returns to Scale

If the production function is linear and homogeneous (that is, homogeneous of the first degree) and also the prices of inputs remain constant, then the long-run average cost will remain constant at all levels of output. As explained in the previous chapter, linear homogeneous production function implies constant returns to scale which means that when all inputs are increased in a certain proportion, output increases in the same proportion. Therefore, with the given prices of inputs, when returns to scale are constant, the cost per unit of output remains the same. In this case, the long-run average cost curve will be a horizontal straight line as depicted in Fig. 19.8. Though there will be infinite number of short-run average cost curves as we continue to assume that the size of the plant can be varied by infinitely small gradations, only *SAC* curves of three plants have been shown in Fig. 19.8.

It will be noticed from Fig. 19.8 that all short-run average cost curves such as SAC_1, SAC_2, SAC_3 have the same minimum average cost of production. This means whatever the size of the plant, the minimum average cost of production is the same. This implies that all factors can be adjusted in the long-run in such a way that the proportions between them always remain optimum. In such a case, the optimum size of the firm is indeterminate, since all levels of output can be produced at the same long-run average cost which represents the same minimum short-run average cost throughout. It is useful to note that though all levels of output will be produced at the same minimum cost of production the different sizes of plants will be used for producing different levels of output. Thus, for producing output *OA*, the plant of SAC_1 will be employed; for output *OB*, the plant of SAC_2 will be employed; and for output *OC* the plant of SAC_3 will be employed and so on. This is because the production at the lowest possible cost for output *OA* is possible with plant SAC_1, for output *OB* with plant SAC_2 and for output *OC* with plant SAC_3.

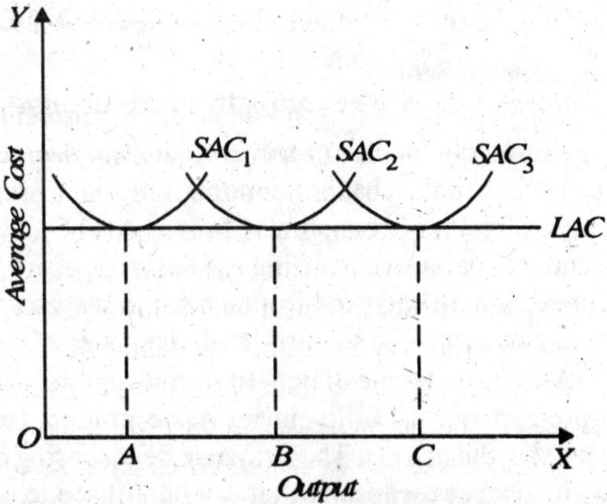

Fig. 19.8. *When returns to scale are constant, long-run average cost curve is a horizontal straight line.*

Some economists like Kaldor, Joan Robinson, Stigler are of the view that when all factors of production are "*perfectly divisible*" then there would be no internal economies of scale (and no internal diseconomies). Therefore, according to them, in case of 'perfect divisibility' of all factors, the long-run average cost curve will be a horizontal straight line showing that the long-run average cost is constant whatever the level of output. In their view, all internal economies of scale are due to the indivisibility of some factors. Therefore, they argue that if perfect divisibility of factors is assumed, then it implies the absence of internal economies of scale and therefore in such a case the long-run average cost curve will still be a horizontal straight line. But Prof. Chamberlin has challenged this viewpoint. According to him, perfect divisibility has nothing to do with efficiency, that is to say, perfect divisibility does not mean the absence of internal economies of scale. Thus, according to him, even if all factors were perfectly divisible, the economies of scale will still be reaped due to the use of more specialised machinery and a greater degree of division of labour at higher levels of output. Therefore, according to Prof. Chamberlin, constant returns to scale cannot exist and long-run average cost cannot remain constant.

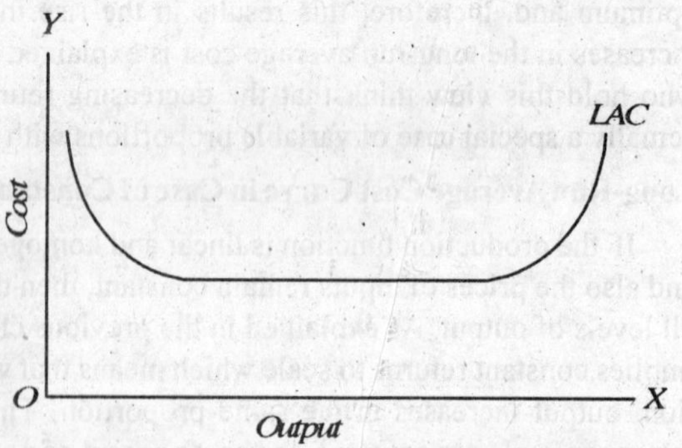

Fig. 19.9. *Saucer-Shaped Long-Run Average Cost Curve*

Saucer-Shaped Long-run Average Cost Curve

However, many empirical studies have shown that U-shape of the long-run average cost curve is not smooth and regular as it is shown in Fig. 19.7, but a wavy and irregular one. Further, a very important feature of long-run average cost curve revealed by empirical studies is that there is *a relatively very large flat portion* or in other words, a large horizontal region in the centre of long-run average cost curve, as is depicted in Fig. 19.9. In such a real case, long-run average cost curve has a saucer-shaped appearance. Such a long-run average cost curve with a very large flat portion in the centre can arise if the economies of scale are exhausted at a very modest scale of operation and then for a relatively large further expansion in output, diseconomies of scale do not occur. Only after a very large increase in output, diseconomies of scale exert themselves and bring about a rise in the long-run average cost. A long horizontal or flat section in the long-run average cost curve can also occur because economies of scale which are mostly of technological type may be offset by the diseconomies over a wide range of output.

Economies of Scope

Economies of scope should be distinguished from economies of scale. Economies of scope refer to the *reduction in cost that occurs when a firm produces two or more commodities together rather than a single one*. That is, economies of scope are the economies that accrue to a multi-product firm. Many examples of economies of scope can be given. For example, a passenger air line can profitably extend its operations by using the same air plane for providing cargo services which lowers its cost of operation. In such an airoplane some seats have to be removed and packets and bags containing goods can be placed to carry to their places of destination.

Another example of benefit from economies of scope which is often cited is when a firm extends its product line by utilising its waste product to produce a useful commodity for which there is demand in the market. The firm may be disposing of its waste product earlier at a cost. Besides, a firm may have excess capacity that can be utilised to produce other products with little or no increase in capital cost. This results in lowering overall cost per unit of output of a firm.

In the real world the firms greatly benefit from their comparative advantage in the production of related products. For example, Hindustan Unilever does not produce only bathing soap 'Lux' but a whole range of detergents and cleansing products. This is quite cost effective and lowers the overall unit cost of products.

THE CONCEPT OF OPTIMUM FIRM

It is important to explain the concept of optimum firm. The optimum firm refers to the best or ideal size of the firm. More specifically optimum or best firm is considered as one that has set up a plant with lowest possible cost and is also operating it at its lowest average cost point. E.A.G. Robinson who has done a good deal of research on the issue of optimum firm writes, "*an optimum firm is the one which operates at the scale at which, in the existing conditions of technique and organising ability, has the lowest average cost of production when all those costs which must be covered in the long run are included*". This means that optimum firm is one which operates at the lowest point of long-run average cost curve of production. Production at the minimum point of the long-run average cost curve is called optimum because at it resources of the society are most efficiently used. When a firm expands its size to the lowest point of the long.run average cost (*LAC*), it sets up a plant which, given the state of technology, has the lowest unit cost of production when operated at its full capacity. As has been explained above that long-run average cost of a firm is influenced by the various economies and diseconomies of scale. These economies and diseconomies are determined by various technical, managerial, financial and marketing factors. The optimum size is achieved when all the internal economies of scale such as division of labour, use of specialised machinery, managerial advantage of large scale production etc. are being fully enjoyed by the firm and the internal diseconomies of scale have not yet started accruing to it.

It is worth noting that in the determination of optimum size, the state of technology and methods of organising business remain unchanged. In Fig. 19.7 optimum firm is one that has set up a plant represented by short-run average cost curve SAC_4 and operating at the minimum point *P* on it and producing output *OQ*.

It is clear from Fig. 19.7 that in the continuous long-run average cost curve both for outputs less than *OQ* and more than *OQ* no plant is used at its point of minimum averge cost. It is only the plant, the minimum point of whose short-run average cost curve coincides with the minimum point of the long-run average cost curve, which is operated at the point of minimum point of its short-run average cost curve. In Fig. 19.7 for producing output *OQ*, the plant of SAC_4 is being utilized to produce its optimum output *OQ*, that is to say, it is being used at its full capacity.

It should be noted that in Fig. 19.7 the plant of SAC_4 is optimum plant, since its minimum cost of production is the lowest of the minimum costs of all other plants. If the size of the plant is increased beyond SAC_4, it results in higher average cost of production. Similarly, if the size of the plant is smaller than SAC_4, average cost of production is higher. Further, the least-cost output, or in other words, the optimum output of the plant SAC_4 is *OQ*. Now, if the firm produces output *OQ* with the optimum plant SAC_4, it is said to have achieved the optimum size. Thus, *an optimum firm is that firm which is producing optimum output (i.e., least-cost output) with the optimum plant*. In our Fig. 19.7 the firm is of optimum size if it employs plant SAC_4 and uses it to produce *OQ*. Since the point of minimum cost of the optimum plant SAC_4 coincides with the minimum point of the long-run average cost curve, *the optimum firm can also be defined as one which produces at the minimum point of the long-run average cost curve* (*LAC*).

The optimum size of the firm varies a great deal in different industries. In agriculture, extractive industries, wholesale and retail trade, optimum size is relatively small, that is, the minimum point of the long-run average cost curve is reached at a comparatively small output. Fig. 19.10 shows a firm whose optimum size is relatively small. On the other hand, the optimum size of the firm in steel industry, automobile industry, other heavy industries and public utilities is relatively very large, that is, the minimum point of their long-run average cost curve is reached at a relatively very large

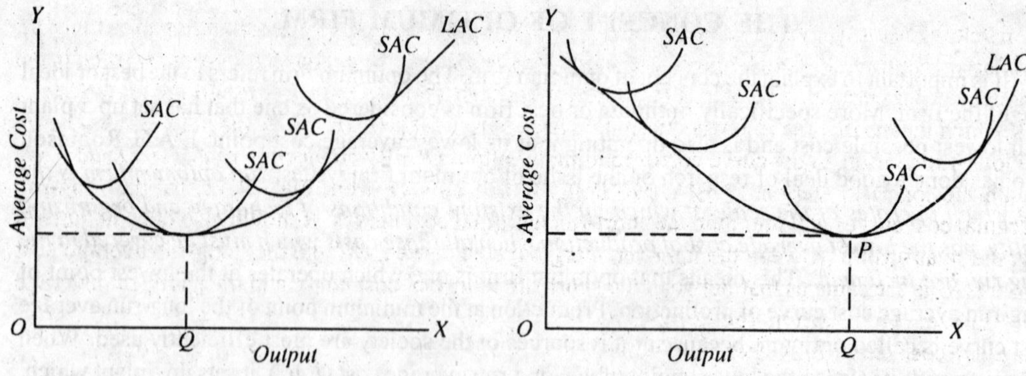

Fig. 19.10. *Small Optimum size* **Fig. 19.11.** *Large Optimum Size*

output. Fig. 19.11 depicts a firm whose optimum size is very large. In the industry in which the optimum size of the firm is very large, there are generally a few number of firms, each with a large size.

DERIVATION OF LONG-RUN MARGINAL COST CURVE

In a previous section we explained what is the marginal cost and how the short-run marginal cost curve is obtained and what relation it bears to the short-run average cost curve. Since marginal cost curve is important both from the viewpoint of the short run and the long run, it will be useful to know how the long-run marginal cost curve is derived. The long-run marginal cost curve can be directly derived from the long-run total cost curve, since the long-run marginal cost at a level of output is given by the slope of the total cost curve at the point corresponding to that level of output. Besides, the long-run marginal cost curve can be derived from the long-run average cost curve, because the long-run marginal cost curve is related to the long-run average cost curve in the same way as the short-run marginal cost curve is related to short-run average cost curve. In Fig. 19.12, it is depicted that how the long-run marginal cost curve *LMC* is derived from a long-run average cost curve *LAC* enveloping a family of short-run average and marginal cost curves.

If the output *OA* is to produced in the long run, then it must be produced on the long-run average cost curve *LAC* at point *H* which is a tangency point with the short-run average cost curve SAC_1. Thus, when output *OA* is to be produced in the long run, it will be produced with the plant corresponding to the short-run average cost curve SAC_1 and the short-run marginal cost curve SMC_1. Corresponding to the tangency point *H* between the short-run average cost curve SAC_1 and the long-run average cost curve *LAC*, there is a point *N* on the short run marginal cost curve *SMC*. This means that the production of output *OA* in the long run involves the marginal cost *AN*. Therefore, point *N* must lie on the long-run marginal cost curve corresponding to output *OA*. If output *OB* is to be produced in the long run, it will be produced at point *Q* which is the tangency point between *LAC* and SAC_2. *Q* is also

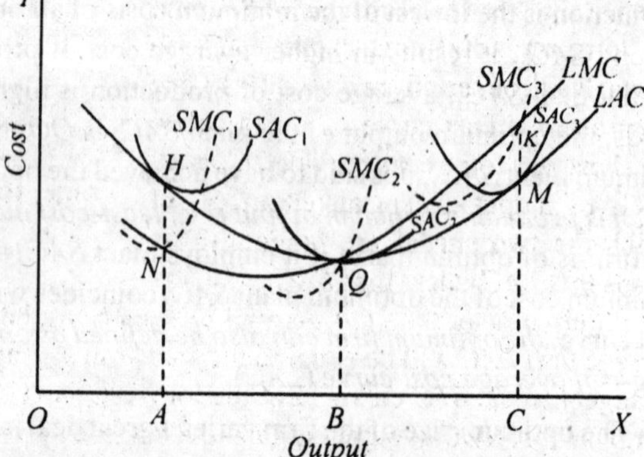

Fig.19.12. *Derivation of Long-Run Marginal Cost Curve*

the point on the short-run marginal cost curve SMC_2, corresponding to output *OB*. (*Q* is the common point between SAC_2 and SMC_2 because *Q* is the minimum point of SAC_2 at which the SMC_2 cuts it from below). Thus Q must also lie on the *long-run* marginal cost curve corresponding to output *OB*. Similarly, if output *OC* is to be produced in the long run, it will be produced at point *M* which is the tangency point between *LAC* and SAC_3. Corresponding to point *M*, the relevant point on the SMC_3 is *K* which means that the long-run marginal cost of producing *OC* is *CK*. Thus point *K* must lie on the long-run marginal cost curve corresponding to output *OC*. By connecting points *N*, *Q* and *K* we obtain the long-run marginal cost curve *LMC*. It will be seen from Fig. 19.12 that the long-run marginal cost curves is flatter than the short-run marginal cost curves. It should also be remembered that the relationship between the long-run marginal cost curve *LMC* and the long-run average cost curve *LAC* is the same as that between the short-run marginal cost curve and the short -run average cost curve. Thus, when the long-run marginal cost curve *LMC* lies below the long-run average cost curve, the latter will be falling, and when the long-run marginal cost curve lies above the long-run average cost, the latter will be rising. When the the long-run marginal cost is equal to the long-run averäge cost, the latter will be neither rising nor falling.

Relationship of LAC and LMC with SAC and SMC

It is important to note that *LAC* and *SAC* curves are related in an important way with *SMC* and *LMC* curves. This relationship shows, as will be seen from Fig. 19.13, that at the level of output at which a particular *SAC* curve is tangent to the *LAC* curve, the corresponding *SMC* curve interesects the *LMC* curve. This relationship can be proved using a short-run total cost curve and the long run total cost curve and this has been done in Figure 19.13 where a short-run total cost curve *STC* and the long-run total cost curve *LTC* are drawn. It will be seen from Figure 19.13 that long-run total cost curve *LTC* lies below the short-run total cost curve *STC* at all levels of output except at output *OA* at which the two curves are tangent. This means that *LAC* is less than *SAC* at all levels of output other than *OA*. As will be seen from the bottom of pannel Figure 19.13 that long-run average cost *LAC* will be equal to the short-run average cost *SAC* at output *OA* at which *LTC* curve is tangent to the *STC* curve. But the long-run marginal cost *LMC* must also be equal to short-run marginal cost *SMC* at output *OA i.e.* the tangency point *P*. This is because marginal cost is given by the slope of the total cost curve at any point, and the *LTC* curve and *STC* curve have the same slope at the tangency point *P*. It will be seen from the bottom pannel of Fig. 19.13 that at output level *OA*, where the *SAC* is equal to the *LAC*, *SMC* is also equal to the *LMC*.

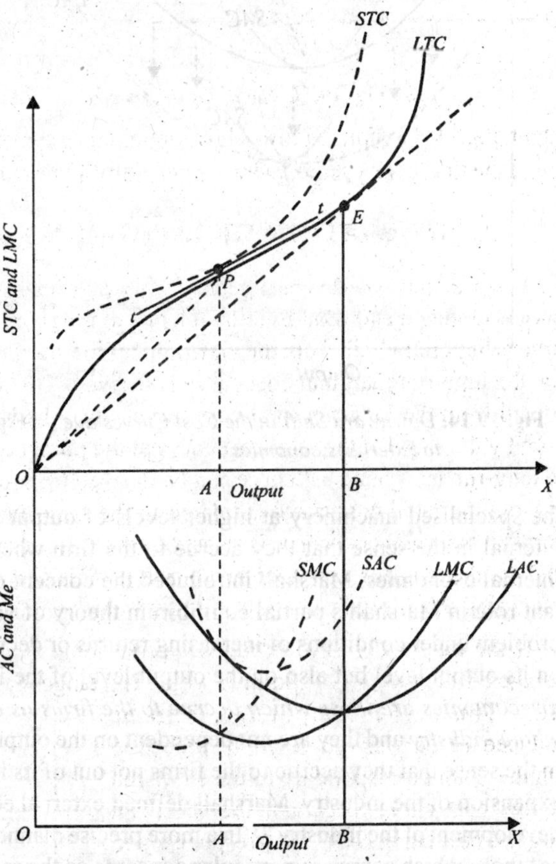

Fig. 19.13. *Relationship between SAC & LAC with SMC and LMC*

EXTERNAL ECONOMIES AND DISECONOMIES AND COST CURVES

We have explained above that the long-run average cost curve falls downward in the beginning because of economies of scale, namely, the use of greater degree of division of labour and the specialised machinery at higher levels of output. The use of greater degree of division of labour and

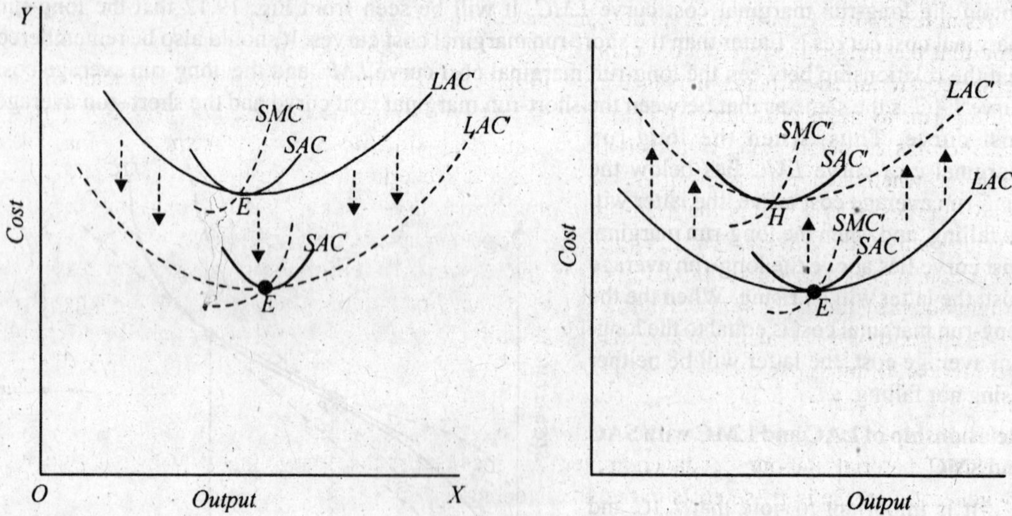

Fig. 19.14. *Downward Shift in the Cost Curves due to External Economies*

Fig. 19.15. *Downward Shift in the Cost Curves due to External diseconomies*

the specialised machinery at higher levels of output are called the *internal economies*. They are internal in the sense that they accrue to the firm when *its own output or scale* increases. Besides internal economies, Marshall introduced the concept of *external economies* which plays an important role in Marshall's partial equilibirum theory of value especially in his analysis of equilibrium problem under conditions of increasing returns or decreasing costs. Costs of a firm depend not only on its output level but also on the output level of the industry as a whole. *External economies and diseconomies are those which accrue to the firms as a result of the expansion in the output of the whole industry* and they are not dependent on the output level of individual firms. They are external in the sense that they accrue to the firms not out of its internal situation but from otuside it *i.e.*, from expansion of the industry. Marshall defined external economies as "those dependent on the general development of the industry."[3] In a more precise manner Jacob Viner has defined external economies as "those which accrue to particular concerns as the result of expansion of output by the industry as a whole and which are independent of their own individual output."[4]

External economies accrue to the individual firms, if the increase in the output of industry *lowers* the cost curves of each firm in the industry. On the other hand, external diseconomies accrue to the firms, when the expansion of the output of the industry *raises* the cost curves of each firm. Thus, when the industry expands and as a result of it certain external economies accrue to the firms, the cost curves of a firm will shift down as is shown in Figure 19.14. It should be noted that external economies will cause all types of firm's cost curves—long-run average and marginal cost curves, short-run average and marginal cost curves—to shift down. In Figure 19.14, initially the long-run average cost curve is *LAC* (thick curve) and as a result of the expansion of the whole industry and the creation of external economies it shifts down to a new position *LAC'* (dotted).

3. A. Marshall, *Principle of Economics*, 8th edition, p. 266.
4. Jacob Viner, Cost Curves and Supply Curves, *Readings in Price Theory*, A.E.A., p. 217.

On the other hand, when the external diseconomies accrue to the firms as a result of the expansion of the industry, cost curves of the firms will shift upward as is depicted in Figure 19.15. In the beginning, the long-run average cost curve is *LAC* and with the expansion of the industry output and consequent emergence of external diseconomies causes the long-run average cost curve (along with its short-run average and marginal cost curves) to shift upward to a new position *LAC'* (dotted).

As noted above in a previous section, internal economies and diseconomies of scale affect the shape that the long-run average cost curve takes; internal economies of scale cause the long-run average cost to fall as output is increased in the initial stage and internal diseconomies of scale cause the long-run average cost curve to rise. On the other hand, external economies and external diseconomies cause the long-run average cost curve to shift down or up, as the case may be. Moreover, when we are considering the effect of external economies and external diseconomies on the cost curves, it is not only the long-run average cost curve but all short-run and long-run cost curves, whether total, average or marginal, shift together up or down as the case may be. In this connection, it is also worth noting that shifts in cost curves of a firm are not always, nor necessarily brought about by the exapsnion or contraction of an industry's output alone. For instance, a *general increase* in cost of materials, such as cement, steel, oil, electricity, a *general increase* in the prices of machinery and equipment, an *all-round* increase in wages and interest rates in the economy will also shift up the cost curves of a firm. Therefore, in economics when we speak of increasing-cost industries and decreasing cost industries, we consider only the effect of expansion of industry's output on costs of materials, labour, capital equipment *etc.* incurred by the firms in that industry and rule out any general increase in these costs in the whole economy.

Types of External Economies

Now, the question arises when an industry grows or expands its output, what types of external economies it generates which reduce the costs of the firms in it. The chief examples of external economies provided by Marshall are: (*i*) "improved methods of machinery which are accessible to the whole industry"[5] when it expands, (*ii*) economies which result from the growth of correlated branches of industry which mutually assist one another and "being concentrated in the same localities"[6] encourage the development of "*hereditary skill*", 'the growth of subsidiary trades supplying it with implements and machinery' (*iii*) economies which are "connected with the growth of knowledge and the progress of arts,[7] especially in matters of trade knolwedge: newspapers, trades, trade and technical publications.[8]

Like Marshall, Joan Robinson who analysed the phenomenon of increasing returns (*i.e.* decreasing costs) in the context of partial equilibrium analysis, provided the following main examples of external economies: (*i*) the cases "where the machinery can be bought more cheaply when the industry presents a large market to the machine-making industry"[9] and (*ii*) the cases "where a large labour force is accustomed to work in a certain trade" and develops "traditional skill"[10].

From the above examples mentioned by Marshall and Joan Robinson we explain below some of important external economies which accrue to the firms and reduce their costs of production when the industry as a whole expands.

1. Cheaper Materials and Capital Equipment. First, the expansion of an industry may lead to new and cheaper raw materials, machinery and other types of capital equipment. The expansion of an industry means that demand for the various kinds of materials and capital equipment required by it

5. A. Marshall, *Principle of Economics*, 8th edition, p. 615.
6. *Ibid*, p. 317.
7. *Ibid*, p. 267.
8. *Ibid*, p. 284
9. Joan Robinson, *The Economics of Imperfect Competition*,. p. 340.
10. *Ibid*, p. 341.

increases. This makes it possible to produce them on a large scale by other industries. This large-scale production of materials and capital equipment lowers their costs of production and hence their prices. Thus the firms in the industry which use these materials and capital equipment will be able to get them at lower prices. This will favourably affect their costs of production. This, of course, will happen in cases where there are increasing returns (*i.e.* decreasing costs) in the industries supplying the materials and capital equipment.

2. **Technological External Economies.** Secondly, with the growth of an industry some external economies of technological type may accrue to the firms of that industry. In our discussion of returns to scale we mentioned that as an individual firm expands its scale it may become possible for it to use more specialised and productive machinery and to introduce greater degree of division of labour. These are *internal* technological economies, which change the technical coefficients of production and improve the firm's productivity. Similarly, when the whole industry expands, it may lead to the discovery of new technical knowledge and in accordance with that the use of improved and better machinery than before. This will change the technical coefficients of production and will enhance the productivity of the firms in the industry and will reduce their costs of production.

3. **Development of Skilled Labour.** Another example of external economies that has been suggested is the development of hereditary or traditional skills among labour. When an industry expands in an area, the labour in that area is well accustomed to do the various productive processes and learns a good deal from the experience. As a result, with the growth of an industry in an area a pool of trained labour equipped with the traditional skills is developed which has a favourable effect on the level of productivity and costs of the firms in the industry.

4. **The Growth of Subsidiary and Correlated Industries.** Another external economy accuring to the frims from the growth of an industry is the growth of subsidiary and correlated industries. These subsidiary and correloted industries may specialise in the production of raw materials, tools and machinery and therefore can provide them at lower prices to the main industry. Likewise, some specialised firms may come into existence, which process the '*waste product*' of the industry into some useful product, when the expansion of the industry makes the waste product large enough to make it worthwhile to set up separate plants for transforming the waste products into useful ones. When this happens, then the firms of the industry can sell their waste products at a good price. This will tend to reduce their cost of production.

5. **Improved Transportation and Marketing Facilities**. These external economies are greatly relevant when an infant industry grows up in a new territory. In the beginning, transportation and marketing facilities both for the purchase of materials and for the sale of its product may not be well-developed. However, the expansion of the industry by the entry of new firms in it may make possible the development of transportation and marketing facilities which will greatly reduce the costs of the firms.

6. **Development of Industry Information Servives.** As an industry expands, the firms may form a trade association that distributes information regarding technical knowledge and market possibilities about the industry through publication of trade and technical hournals with the expansion of the industry the firms may jointly set up a central research institute which will be engaged in discovering new improved techniques for the firms in the industry. Thus, besides providing market information, the growth of the industry may help in discovering and spreading improved technical knowledge.

External Diseconomies

We have explained above the external economies which accrue to the firms as a result of the growth of the industry. But, as said above, the expansion of an industry is also likely to generate external diseconomies which raise the cost curves of the firms. The main example of external

11. K.J. Arrow, "The Economic Implications of Learning by Doing" *Revenue of Economic Studies*. Vol. 29 (June 1962) pp. 154-179.

diseconomies is *the rise in some factor prices* when the industry expands and its demand for various factors needed by it increases. The expansion of an industry will definitely raise the prices of those raw materials and capital goods which are in short supply. Likewise, the expansion of the industry is likely to raise the wages of skilled labour, at least in the short run, since it always takes time for the labour to get training and acquire specialised skill needed in a particular industry.

Since the productive factors such as various types of raw materials, cement, steel, various kinds of machinery and tools and skilled labour are scarce, the increase in demand for them resulting from the expansion in the industry is likely to push up their industry will expand by snatching away the scarce resources from other industries, it will bid up their prices. Thus, in the real world of scarcity, an expanding industry will create more external diseconomies than external economies. Therefore, most industries in the real world encounter rising costs when they expand.

LEARNING CURVE

The learning curve is an important modern concept according to which cumulative experience in the production of a product over time increases efficiency in the use of inputs such as labour and raw materials and thereby lowers cost per unit of output. K.J. Arrow, one of the pioneers in putting forward this concept calls it "*Learning by doing*"[11]. According to Arrow, as a firm or its manager produces successive lots of output over various periods of time, it learns to produce more with a given quantity of resources or it is capable of producing a given output by using lesser quantities of inputs or resources than before. Thus, either with the increase in efficiency of resources or with saving in resources such as labour and raw materials, cost per unit of output declines. This learning curve effect mostly occurs in the reduction of labour requirements per unit of output.

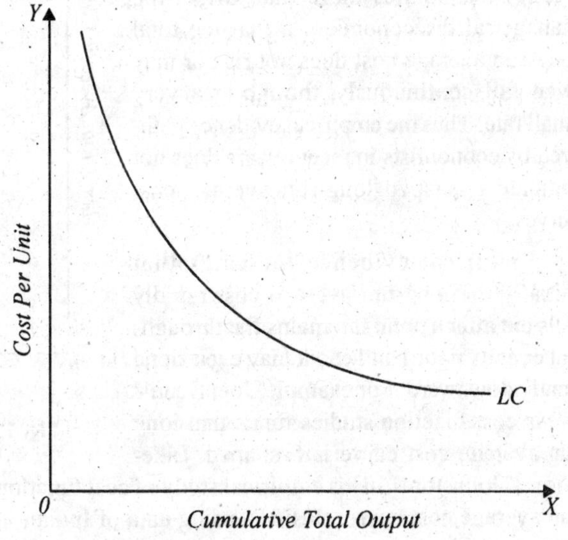

Fig. 19.16. *The Learning Curve*

A number of factors bring this learning curve effect. As cumulative volume of output over successive periods of time increases, labour and supervisors become more familiar with the work methods or the production process, which leads to the reduction in the amount of scrap and other types of wastes. Besides, raw materials cost per unit of output may also decline as cumulative volume of output in successive periods over time increases and as a result a firm gains more experience in doing a production process repeatedly over successive time periods. The learning curve is graphically shown in Fig. 19.16 where on the *X*-axis cumulative total output over successive periods of time and on the *Y*-axis cost per unit of output are measured. It will be seen from Fig. 19.16 that the learning curve shopes downward which shows declining cost per unit of output as cumulative output increases over time and the firm learns from its work experience.

The learning curve effect is usually expressed as a constant percentage. This percentage represents the proportion by which cost per unit of output declines with the increase in cumulative output in each successive time period. For example, if in a production process labour-input cost experiences 80 per cent learning curve effect, this means that if in the first period production of a unit of output requires labour cost of Rs. 1000, in the next period labour cost per unit will decline to Rs. 800 and so forth. This learning-curve relationship between cost output is expressed algebraically as follows:

$$C = aA^b.$$

Where C is the input cost of Qth unit of output, Q is successive unit of output produced, a is the input cost per unit of output in the first period and b is the rate of decline in cost per unit of output in the successive period. Since the learning curve is downward sloping, the value of b is negative.

It is important to note that reduction in cost per unit due to the learning curve effect is different from economies of scale. Whereas economies of scale refer to the decline in cost per unit of output as a *firm's output per time period increases, the learning curve describes the reduction in cost per unit of output as a firm's ccumulative output over successive time periods increases, while output per period may remain the same.*

L-SHAPED LONG RUN AVERAGE COST CURVE : MODERN COST THEORY

A significant recent development in cost theory is that the long-run average cost curve is L-shaped rather than *U*-shaped. The L-shape of the long-run average cost curve implies that in the beginning when output is expanded through increase in plant size and associated variable factors, cost per unit falls rapidly due to economies of scale. Even after a sufficiently large scale of output, the long-run average cost does not rise; it may either remain constant or it may even go on falling slightly. At a very large scale of production, the managerial cost per unit of output may rise, but the technical or production economies more than offset the managerial diseconomies so that the total long-run average cost does not rise or may even fall continuously, though at a very small rate. Thus the empirical evidence gathered by economists in recent years does not indicate U-shaped long-run average cost curve.

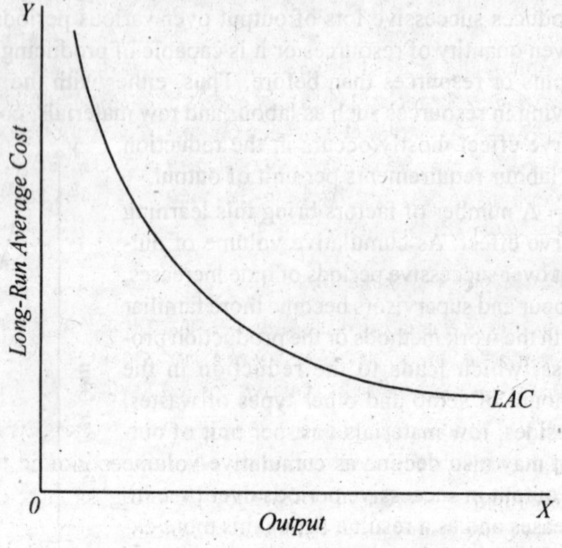

Fig. 19.17. L-*Shaped Long-Rum Average Cost Curve*

Empirical evidence indicates that initially the long-run average cost rapidly falls but after a point it remains flat throughout or at its right-hand end it may even slope gently downward. For example, Joel Dean[12] in his cost function studies funds that long run average cost curve is L-shaped. Likewise, J. Johnston[13] in his empirical study of cost functions found strong evidence for L-shaped long-run average cost curve. Besides, using data of Indian industries Vinod Gupta[14] who studied long-run average cost functions for 29 manufacturing Indian industries found that in 18 of them long-run cost was L-shaped. *L*-shaped long-run average cost curve is illustrated in Fig. 19.17. The difference between L-shaped *LAC* of Fig. 19.17 and the *U*-shaped *LAC* is that there is no rising portion in the former. Indeed, as stated just above, the empirical evidence shows that *LAC* may even slope gently downward at its right hand end. Thus, there is an apparent contradiction between traditional economic theory according to which *LAC* is U-shaped and the results of empirical cost-function studies which find *LAC* to be L-shaped. Two reasons have been given for the continuous occurrence

12. See Joel Dean, *Managerial Economics,* Prentice Hall, 1951, pp. 292-31.
13. J.Johnston, *Statistical Cost Analysis*, McGraw Hill, New York.
14. Vinod K. Gupta, Cost Function, Concentration and Barriers to entry in Twenty Nine Manufacturing Industries in India, *Journal of Industrial Economics*, Vol. 17, Nov. 1948.

of economies of scale which cause falling cost per unit of output.

Production or Technical Economies. First, it is pointed out that there are substantial technical economies of scale enjoyed by a firm when it expands its scale of output in the beginning. This causes the long-run average cost to fall steeply with the initial increases in scale of production. However, it has been asserted that even after most of the economies of scale have been achieved and the firm reaches a minimum *optimal scale*, given the technology of the industry, the *unit cost of production may fall due to some technical economies which it can continue to enjoy even after the minimum optimal scale.* First, the *new techniques* of production are adopted at a large scale of production due to which cost per unit falls. Besides, even with the existing known techniques some economies can always be obtained due to (1) decentralisation and improved skills and prodctivity of labour, (2) lower repair costs after a certain scale is achieved and (3) producing by a firm itself some of the materials and equipment it needs at a lower cost for its production process instead of buying them from other firms.

Development of Appropriate Managerial Techniques. In the traditional cost theory, the rising part of the *LAC* is explained by the difficulties in management, supervision, coordination and control which pushes up the unit cost of production after a certain scale of production is attained. In this regard, it has been pointed out that modern management science has developed for each plant size appropriate organizational and managerial set-up for efficient working of the firm. For different scales of plant and sizes of firms different appropriate management techniques have been evolved and each management technique is applicable to a range of output. Only at a very large scale, managerial costs may rise. However, it has been claimed that any rise in managerial costs even after a very large scale of output may be offset by production economies that continue to accrue. However, there is controversy as to whether the long-run average cost is really L-shaped when usual assumptions made in economic theory hold.

A Critical Evaluation

Now, the question is how L-shaped long-run average cost curve can be explained and apparent contradiction between theory and empirical evidence be removed. The following two explanations have been provided to remove this contradiction.

1. Technical Progress. One reason why modern empirical studies do not find U-shaped long-run average cost curve is that whereas economic theory assumes that technology remains unchanged or there is no technological progress, in the real world, technological progress does take place over time. As a result of technological progress in the real world, long-run average cost curve will shift downward over time. The empirical investigations which are based on times series data would not find the rising average cost in view of the existence of technological progress. Thus while in the case of unchanged technology, as is assumed in traditional cost theory, long-run average cost curve (*LAC*) is *U*-shaped, empirical studies conducted on the basis of data belonging to different points of time between which technological progress had taken place or inter cross section studies where both small and large firms using different technologies are included would find the average cost falling. In view of the technological improvement we cannot therefore find the average cost rising in emprical cost function studies. This is illustrated in Fig. 19.18.

Suppose initially the firm is producing OQ_1 output at cost OK_1 by operating on LAC_1. If the demand for the firm's product increases to OQ_2, then in the context of unchanged technology the firm will expand production along LAC_1 and will produce OQ_2 at cost *OH*. Now, if the technological progress has taken place and in accordance with new technology the firm instals a new plant whose long-run average cost is LAC_2, the firm will produce on the new curve LAC_2 the output OQ_2 at cost per unit which is less than both OK_1 and *OH*. Likewise, when the firm at some later date has expanded output to OQ_3 in response to the increase in demand for its product, the technology might have advanced in the mean time so that the firm produces OQ_3 at OK_3 cost per unit which is less than OK_2. By joining the minimum points of long-run average cost curves we get a curve *LAC* which gently slopes downward due to technological improvement that has taken place over time, whereas with unchanged technology long-run average cost curves LAC_1, LAC_2, and LAC_3 each with a different but unchanged technology is *U*-shaped. Empirical cost-function studies made by economists at different points of time would estimate OK_1, OK_2 and OK_3 unit costs at output OQ_1, OQ_2 and OQ_3 respectively and would therefore suggest that long-run average cost curve was like the thick curve *LAC*.

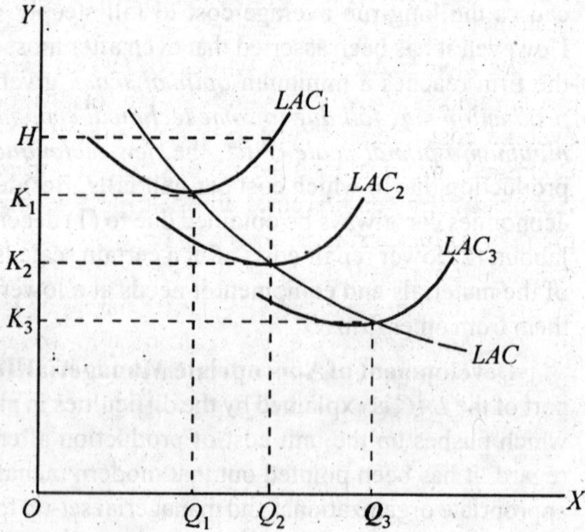

Fig. 19.18. *Shifting down of LAC due to Technology Progress*

We therefore conclude that while with a given and unchanged technology long-run average cost curves are *U*-shaped, the empirical evidence would find *L*-shaped long-run average cost curve due to technological progress that takes place over time. The fact that technology changes does not in itself contradict our convention that, if only because it is harder to manage a larger firm than a smaller one, long-run average cost curves will be U-shaped in a given state of technology. What the empirical evidence does suggest is that technological progress may often be rapid enough to reduce unit cost even in a situation where, with given technology, the problem of managing a bigger firm would increase unit costs.[15]

2. **Learning Curve Effect.** Learning curve effect or learning by doing is another factor which causes the long-run average cost to slope downward throughout. It is now common knowledge that a person learns while doing some productive work. The greater the amount of work he has done since the time he started doing a particular work, the greater the experience he attains and with the experience he learns to do things in a better way than before. This tends to reduce cost per unit. A firm learns to produce a commodity more efficiently as the aggregate amount of output produced by it increases over time. A good deal of empirical evidence is available which goes to prove that firm's cost of production depends not only on the amount of output of a commodity it produces each month or year but also on the aggregate amount of that commodity produced since the time it started its production. This is because the aggregate output by a firm to date determines the degree of learning it has acquired and the efficiency gained by it.

Therefore, we can draw a learning curve (as we did in Fig. 19.17) which relates the average cost of production of a commodity to the aggregate amount of output produced so far of that commodity. This learning curve slopes downward indicating thereby that as the aggregate amount of output produced of a commodity by a firm increases over time, cost per unit goes on declining. This is because, as said above, with greater production, a firm learns to produce a commodity more efficiently and therefore cost per unit declines. It should be noted that with the increase in aggregate production of a commodity over time, learning gained by a firm is not only in respect of improving efficiency in physical operations in the production of a commodity but also in respect of improving the organisation of the plant. Thus, besides the factor of technological progress, learning provides us another reason why long-run average cost curves are L-shaped rather than U-shaped. To quote

15. Stonier and Hague, *A Textbook of Economic Theory*, 4th edition, 1972, p.140.

Professors Stonier and Hague, "Even, with a given technology, a firm can 'learn' to produce at a lower unit cost the longer the period of time that has elapsed since a previous observation and the greater the aggregate amount of that product that has consequently been made. It may be, therefore, that technological change is not the only reason why long-run cost curves are L-shaped rather than U-shaped.[16]

We have stated above that according to empirical evidence long-run average cost after the initial rapid fall, either remains constant or declines throughout; it does not rise. That is, long-run average cost does not turn up as is required if it is *U*-shaped. Professor G.A. Smith[17] who has examined empirical evidence in this connection has concluded that with a very large size of firm, labour costs, assembly costs and distribution costs increase very much and therefore large-sized plants *with increasing average cost are not set up in actual practice* and therefore empirical evidence cannot assess the cost situation in them. Therefore, according to Professor Smith, empirical evidence does not refute the U-shaped nature of long-run average cost curve. Walters[18] after examining the empirical studies by Dean and Johnston reached the conclusion that, there is no large body of data which convincingly contradicts the hypothesis of a *U*-shaped long-run average cost curve and the fruitful results which depend on it".

NUMERICAL EXERCISES

Exercise 1. *Suppose a firm faces a cost function of* $C = 8+4q+q^2$

(i) What is the firm's fixed cost?

(ii) Derive an expression for the firm's variable cost and marginal cost.

DU. BA (Hons.) 2003

Solution :

(*i*) As fixed cost of the firm does not vary with output, the term in the given cost function which has no output (q) variable will be the fixed cost. From the given cost function it is evident that fixed cost is 8.

(*ii*) Total variable cost (TVC) = $TC - TFC$

$$= (8+4q+q^2)-8 = 4q+q^2$$

and,
$$AVC = \frac{TVC}{Q} = \frac{4q+q^2}{q} = 4+q$$

Marginal cost is the first derivative of total cost function or total variable cost function. Thus, taking the first derivative of the total variable cost function we have

$$MC = \frac{d(TVC)}{dq} = 4+2q$$

Exercise 2. *Given the total cost function* $TC = 1000 + 4Q + 0.5Q^2$
Determine the functions for TFC, TVC, MC, AVC and AC

Solution :

$$TC = 1000 + 4Q + 0.5Q^2$$

Total fixed cost is independent of level of output to be produced.

Therefore, $TFC = 1000$

$$TVC = TC - TFC$$

Therefore, $TVC = 4Q + 0.5Q^2$

16. Stonier and Hague, *op. cit.*, p. 141.
17. C.A. Smith, Empirical Evidence of Economies of Scale, printed in *Theory of Firm* (Penguin)
18. A. Walters, Production and Cost Fucntions, An Econometric Survey, *Econometrica* Vol. 31, 1963, p. 52.

$$AVC = \frac{TVC}{Q}$$

$$\therefore \quad AVC = \frac{4Q+0.5Q^2}{Q} = 4+0.5Q$$

$$MC = \frac{\Delta TVC}{\Delta Q} = 4+1.0Q$$

or

$$MC = 4+Q$$

$$AC = AFC + AVC$$

$$AFC = \frac{TFC}{Q} = \frac{1000}{Q}$$

Therefore

$$AC = \frac{1000}{Q} + 4 + 0.5Q$$

Exercise 3. *We give below short-run total cost function :*

$$TC = 100 + 50Q - 12Q^2 + Q^3$$

where TC is total cost and Q is level of output.

(*i*) *Determine* : (*a*) *total fixed cost function* (b) *total variable cost function*, (c) *average variable cost function*, (*d*) *marginal cost function.*

(*ii*) *Calculate total cost, ATC, AVC and MC when the firm produces 10 units of output.*

(*iii*) *Calculate the level of output at which AVC is minimum.*

Solution. (*a*) From the total cost function it is evident that when level of output is zero, the firm's cost will be Rs. 100. Thus, $TFC = 100$

(*b*) If we deduct Rs. 100 from the total cost function we obtain the total variable cost function.

Thus, $TVC = TC - TFC$

$$\therefore \quad TVC = 50Q - 12Q^2 + Q^3$$

(*c*) If we divide the *TVC* function by output (*Q*) we get *AVC* function. Thus,

$$AVC = \frac{50Q - 12Q^2 + Q^3}{Q}$$

$$= 50 - 12Q + Q^2$$

(*d*) Marginal cost is the first derivative of total variable cost function. Thus,

$$MC = \frac{dTVC}{dQ} = 50 - 24Q + 3Q^2$$

(*ii*) Given total output (*Q*) equal to 10, we have

$$TC = 100 + 50(10) - 12(10)^2 + (10)^3$$
$$= 100 + 500 - 1200 + 1000$$
$$= 400$$

$$ATC = \frac{100}{Q} + 50 - 12Q + Q^2 = \frac{100}{10} + 50 - 12\times10 + (10)^2$$
$$= 10 + 50 - 120 + 100$$
$$= 40$$

$$AVC = 50 - 12Q + Q^2$$
$$= 50 - 12 \times 10 + 100$$
$$= 30$$

$$MC = 50 - 24Q + 3Q^2$$
$$= 50 - 240 + 300$$
$$= 110$$

(*iii*) The level of *AVC* is minimum at the level of output at which first derivative of *AVC* function is zero. Thus,

$$AVC = 50 - 12Q + Q^2$$
$$\frac{d(AVC)}{dQ} = -12 + 2Q = 0$$
$$2Q = 12$$
$$Q = 6$$

Thus at 6 units of output, *AVC* is minimum.

Exercise 4. *Given the following total cost function* $TC = 1500 + 15Q - 6Q^2 + Q^3$

(i) Determine the total fixed cost for producing 1000 units of output and 500 units of output.

(ii) What is AFC at (a) 1000 units of output, and (b) 500 units of output

(iii) Determine TVC, AVC, MC and AC at 50 units of output.

Solution :

(*i*) *TFC* = 1500 irrespective the level of output

(*ii*) *AFC* at 1000 units of output :

$$AFC = \frac{TFC}{Q} = \frac{1500}{1000} = 1.5$$

AFC at 500 units of output

$$AFC = \frac{TFC}{Q} = \frac{1500}{500} = 3$$

(*iii*)
$$TVC = TC - TFC$$

$$\therefore \quad TVC = 15Q - 6Q^2 + Q^3$$

If output is 50 units

$$TVC = 15 \times 50 - 6 \times (50)^2 + (50)^3$$
$$= 750 - 15000 + 125000$$
$$= 1,10,750$$

$$AVC = \frac{TVC}{Q} = \frac{1,10,750}{50} = 2215$$

$$MC = \frac{dTVC}{dQ} = 15 - 12Q + 3Q^2$$

$$MC \text{ with } Q = 50, = 15 - 600 + 7500 = 6915$$
$$AC = AFC + AVC$$

$$AC \text{ with } Q = 50, = \frac{1500}{50} + 2215 = 30 + 2215 = 2245$$

Exercise 5. *A firm producing hocky sticks has a production function given by* $Q = 2\sqrt{KL}$. *In the short run, the firm's amount of capital equipment is fixed at K = 100. The rental rate for K is Re. 1 and the wage rate is Rs. 4.*

(i) Calculate the firm's short-run total and average costs.

(ii) What are STC, SAC and SMC for producing 25 sticks. *D.U. BA (Hons.) 2003*

Solution.

The given production function of firm is

$$Q = 2\sqrt{KL}$$

With $K = 100$ in the short run, the short-run production function is

$$Q = 2\sqrt{100L} = 2 \times 10\sqrt{L} = 20\sqrt{L}$$

Cost, $C = wL + rK$

Given that $w = 4$ and $r = 1$

$$C = 4L + 1K$$

With the given $K = 100$

$$C = 4L + 100 \quad \text{...(1)}$$

The short-run production function is

$$Q = 20\sqrt{L}$$

Taking square of both sides we have

$$Q^2 = 400L$$

or $$\frac{Q^2}{400} = L \quad \text{...(2)}$$

Substituting (2) in (1) we have

$$C = 100 + 4 \cdot \frac{Q^2}{400}$$

or $$C = 100 + \frac{Q^2}{100} \quad \text{...(3)}$$

The above equation (3) represents the short-run total cost function. To get the short-run average cost function we divide the short-run total cost function in (3) by output (Q). Thus

$$SAC = \frac{100 + \frac{Q^2}{100}}{Q} = \frac{100}{Q} + \frac{Q}{100}$$

Short-run Marginal Cost Function :

Short-run marginal cost function can be obtained by taking the first derivative of short-run total cost function.

Short-run total cost function is

$$C = 100 + \frac{Q^2}{100}$$

$$SMC = \frac{dC}{dQ} = 2\frac{Q}{100} = \frac{Q}{50}$$

If output of hocky sticks = 25, then

$$STC = 100 + \frac{(25)^2}{100} = 100 + \frac{625}{100}$$

$$= 106.25$$

$$SAC = \frac{STC}{Q} = \frac{106.25}{25} = 4.25$$

$$SMC = \frac{Q}{50} = \frac{25}{50} = 0.5$$

Exercsie 6. *If $Q = A(KL)^{0.5}$, what is the short-run cost function when K = 100? What is MC function?*

Solution. With $K = 100$, short-run production function can be written as

$$Q = A(100L)^{0.5} = 10A(L)^{0.5}$$

Squaring both sides we have

$$Q^2 = 100\,A^2 L \qquad \text{...}(i)$$

Now, the short-run cost function is

$$C = TFC + TVC$$

$$= 100r + wL \qquad \text{...}(ii)$$

where r is the rental price of capital and w is the wage rate of labour and given $K = 100$

From equation (i) we have

$$L = \frac{Q^2}{100A^2}$$

Substituting this value of L in (ii) we get the following shrot-run cost function

$$C = 100r + w.\frac{Q^2}{100A^2}$$

$$MC = \frac{TVC}{dQ} = \frac{2wQ}{100A^2}$$

Exercise 7. *Given the production function, $Q = A(LK)^{0.5}$, derive the cost function.*

Solution. A firm minimises its cost production for a given level of output when

$$MRTS_{LK} = \frac{w}{r} \qquad \text{...}(i)$$

where w = wage rate of labour

r = rental price of use of capital

In the given Cobbe-Douglas production function,

$$Q = A(LK)^{0.5}, \qquad MRTS_{LK} = \frac{K}{L}$$

Therefore, at cost-minimisation

$$\frac{K}{L} = \frac{w}{r}$$

or

$$wL = r.K$$

$$K = \frac{wL}{r} \qquad \text{...}(ii)$$

Iso-cost curve equation can be written as

$$C = wL + rK \qquad \text{...}(iii)$$

Substituting the optimum value of K as obtained in (*ii*) in the iso-cost equation (*iii*) we have

$$C = wL + r\cdot\frac{wL}{r}$$

$$C = 2wL$$

or
$$L = \frac{C}{2w} \qquad ...(iv)$$

Similarly, the optimum value of K can be obtained by eliminating L. Thus

$$K = \frac{C}{2r} \qquad ...(v)$$

Substituting the optimum values of L and K in the given production function we have

$$Q = A\left(\frac{C}{2w}\right)^{0.5}\left(\frac{C}{2r}\right)^{0.5}$$

Solving for C we have $C = \dfrac{2Q(w.r)^{0.5}}{A}$

QUESTIONS AND PROBLEMS FOR REVIEW

1. Distinguish between economic costs and accounting costs. Which should be taken into account for calculating the economic profits of the firm? *D.U., B.Com. (Hons.) Ist Year 2009*
2. What is the difference between explicit costs and implicit costs? Should both be considered for optimal business decision-making by the firm?
3. Explain the concepts of total fixed cost, total variable costs and total costs. How are they related to each other ? Illustrate them through curves. Is the distinction between the fixed costs and variable costs relevant in the long run ?
4. Explain the following concepts of cost :
   (*a*) Average fixed cost (*AFC*)
   (*b*) Average variable cost (*AVC*)
   (*c*) Average total cost (*ATC*)
   (*d*) Marginal cost (*MC*)
   Draw these curves with usual shapes.
   Why does *ATC* curve reaches its lowest point after the *AVC* curve? Why does the *MC* curve intersects both the *AVC* and *ATC* curves at their lowest points?
5. Fill in the blanks in the table below:

Output	*Total Cost (Rs)*	*Total Fixed Costs (Rs)*	*Total Variable Costs (Rs)*	*AFC (Rs)*	*AVC (Rs)*
0	50	—	—	—	—
1	70	—	—	—	—
2	100	—	—	—	—
3	120	—	—	—	—
4	135	—	—	—	—
5	150	—	—	—	—
6	160	—	—	—	—
7	165	—	—	—	—

[**Hint:** Since at zero output level variable costs are zero, the whole total cost of Rs. 50 at zero output level represents total fixed cost. Thus, Rs. 50 is the total fixed cost at all levels of output.]

6. From your knolwedge of the relationships between various concepts of cost of production, fill in the blanks in the following table :

Q	*TC*	*TFC*	*TVC*	*ATC*	*AFC*	*AVC*	*MC*
0	125	—	—	—		—	—
10	—	—	—	—	—	—	5
20	—	—	—	10.5	—	—	—
30	—	—	110	—	—	—	—
40	255		—	—	—	—	—
50	—	—	—	—	—	3	—
60	—	—	—	—	—	—	3
70	—	—	—	5	—	—	—
80	—	—	295	—	—	—	—

7. *What is the relationship between average cost and marginal cost? If the marginal cost is rising, does it mean that average cost must also be rising?*
8. Derive long-run average cost curve from short-run average cost curves. How are they related to each other ? Does the curve joining the minimum points of the short-run average cost curves constitutes long-run average cost curve?
9. Give reasons for the U-shape of long-run average cost curve. Why is long-run average cost curve usually called 'planning curve'?
10. Explain the various economies of scale and diseconomies of scale that accrue to the firm when it expands its scale of production.
11. Empirical studies have found that long-run average cost curve (*LAC*) is L-shaped. How would you explain it ? Does it not contradict the U-shaped long-run average cost curve?
12. What would be the shape of long-run average cost (*LAC*) curve when constant returns to scale occur?
13. What is Learning Curve? What are the factors that bring about learning curve effect? How does reduction in cost per unit due to the learning curve effect different from economies of scale?'
D.U., B.Com (Hons.) Ist Year 2009
14. (*a*) Describe relationship between *AVC* and average product (*AP*), between marginal cost (*MC*) and marginal product (*MP*).
(*b*) How is U-shape of the average variable cost explained by the law of variable proportions ?
15. The production function for a firm exhibits constant returns to scale. Input prices paid by the firm are constant, regardless of the quantity purchased. Draw the LRAC curve for the firm. Draw a SRAC for the same firm at some plant size. *D.U.B.A. (Hons.) 1987*
15. Briefly discuss the factors affecting the shape of the long-run average cost curve.
17. Explain how the long-run envelope cost curve is derived from short-run average cost curves. Illustrate with (*i*) the case of a few plant sizes, and (*ii*) the case of many and continuously varied plant sizes. *D.U.B.A. (Hons.)*
18. Given U-shaped long-run average cost curve and the relevant short run cost curves, derive long-run marginal cost curve. *D.U.B.A.(Hons.)*
19. *Distinguish between a firm's short-run cost of production from its long-run cost of production. Why is it that at the output where SAC = LAC short run marginal cost also equals long-run marginal cost ?* *D.U.B.A. (Hons)* 1989

[Hints. Proof of the later part

$SAC = LAC$

Since $SAC \cdot Q$ = short run total cost and $LAC.Q$ is long-run total cost, we have $STC = LTC$

Differentiating both with respect to output (Q) we have

$$\frac{d(STC)}{dQ} = \frac{d(LTC)}{dQ}$$

Therefore, $SMC = LMC$]

20. Of the increasing segment of a firm's long-run marginal cost curve and short-run marginal cost curve which is steeper ? Why ?
[Hints. *SMC* is steeper. This is because in the short run size of the plant is fixed and output is varied by increasing the amount of the variable factors. In the long-run fixed factors represented by plant size can also be varied to minimise cost of production].

21. When the law of diminishing returns operates, the *TVC* rises at decreasing rate. True or false? Give reasons.

22. (*a*) A typical production function has three stages. Explain and illustrate. Relate these stages of production function with the shape of the total cost of production curve. Also explain why it implies a U-shaped marginal cost curve. *D.U.BA(Hons.) 1991*

23. What can you infer about the average cost curve from the information that marginal costs are less than average costs ? Give reasons.
(Hint: When *MC* is less than *AC*, average cost curve slopes downward)

24. The long-run average cost curve is the locus of the minimum points of the short run average cost curves. True of false? Explain. *D.U. B.A.(Hons.), 1999*
[Hint. False; the long-run average cost curve is the locus of the *tangency points* of the short-run average cost curves with the long-run average cost curve.]

25. "If wage rate falls, marginal production cost must fall" True or False? Explain. *D.U.B.A.(Hons.)*

[Hint: $MC = \frac{W}{MP_L}$. Therefore, given marginal product of labour (MP_L) when, wage rate (w) falls, marginal cost (MC) must fall].

26. (*a*) What is the relationship between average cost and marginal cost as the average cost is falling, rising and at its minimum point.

(*b*) Why does the minimum of the average variable cost curve occur before the minimum of the average cost curve ? *D.U. BA(Hons.) 1999*

CHAPTER 20

ELASTICITY OF SUPPLY

The Concept of Elasticity of Supply

We have the explained the concept of supply and the factors that determine it a previous chapter. In the present chapter we will explain the concept of elasticity of supply. When a small fall in price leads to a large contraction in supply, the supply is comparatively elastic. But when a big fall in price leads to a very small contraction in supply, the supply is said to be comparatively inelastic. Conversely, a small rise in price leading to a big increase in supply shows more elastic supply, and a big rise in price leading to a small increase in supply indicates inelastic supply. The elasticity of supply is really the measure of the increase to which the supply of output by an industry can be expanded and changes in. the marginal costs of production.

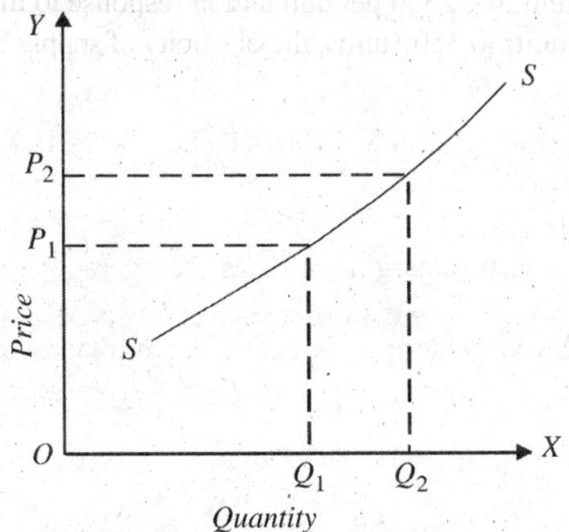

Fig. 20.1. *Elastic Supply*

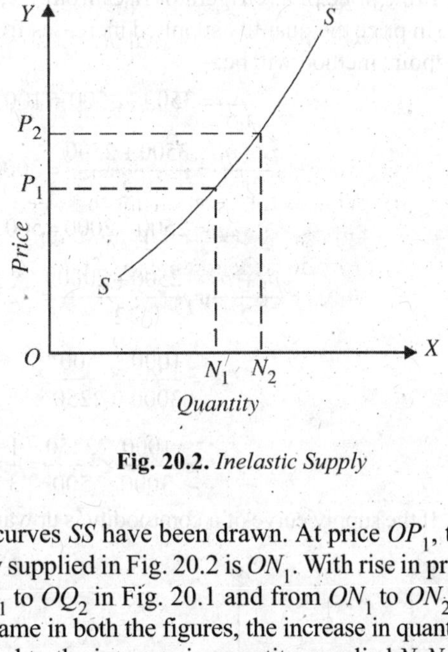

Fig. 20.2. *Inelastic Supply*

Consider Figs. 20.1 and 20.2 where two supply curves *SS* have been drawn. At price OP_1, the quantity supplied in Fig. 20.1 is OQ_1, and the quantity supplied in Fig. 20.2 is ON_1. With rise in price of the product, quantity supplied increases from OQ_1 to OQ_2 in Fig. 20.1 and from ON_1 to ON_2 in Fig. 20.5. Whereas the relative change in price is the same in both the figures, the increase in quantity supplied Q_1Q_2 in Fig. 20.1 is much larger as compared to the increase in quantity supplied N_1N_2 in Fig. 20.1. Therefore, supply in Fig. 20.1 is said to be elastic, whereas that in Fig. 20.2 is inelastic. The elasticities of supply of various products differ very much from each other. What are the factors which determine elasticity of supply of products will be explained in some detail later.

The concept of elasticity of supply, like the elasticity of demand, is a relative measure of the responsiveness of quantity supplied of a commodity to the changes in its price. The greater the responsiveness of quantity supplied of a commodity to the changes in its price, the greater its elasticity of supply. In precise terms, the elasticity of supply can be defined as under :–

$$\text{Elasticity of supply} = \frac{\text{Proportionate change in quantity supplied}}{\text{Proportionate change in price}}$$

$$e_s = \frac{\Delta q}{q} \div \frac{\Delta p}{p} = \frac{\Delta q}{q} \times \frac{p}{\Delta p} = \frac{\Delta q}{\Delta p} \times \frac{p}{q}$$

For an accurate measure of elasticity of supply ***mid-point method***, as explained in case of elasticity of demand, should be used. Using midpoint formula, elasticity of supply can be measured as

$$e_s = \frac{q_2 - q_1}{\frac{q_1 + q_2}{2}} \div \frac{p_2 - p_1}{\frac{p_1 + p_2}{2}}$$

$$q_2 - q_1 = \Delta q \text{ and } p_2 - p_1 = \Delta p$$

Therefore, $$e_s = \frac{\Delta q}{q_1 + q_2} \times \frac{p_1 + p_2}{\Delta P}$$

$$e_s = \frac{\Delta q}{\Delta p} \times \frac{p_1 + p_2}{q_1 + q_2}$$

If the price of a refrigerator rises from ₹ 2,000 per unit to ₹ 2500 per unit and in response to this rise in price the quantity supplied increases from 2500 units to 3500 units, the elasticity of supply by midpoint method will be:–

$$\Delta q = 3500 - 2500 = 1000$$

$$\frac{q_2 + q_1}{2} = \frac{3500 + 2500}{2} = 3000$$

$$\Delta p = 2500 - 2000 = 500$$

$$\frac{p_1 + p_2}{2} = \frac{2500 + 2000}{2} = 2250$$

$$e_s = \frac{1000}{3000} \div \frac{500}{2250}$$

$$= \frac{1000}{3000} \times \frac{2250}{500} = \frac{1}{3} \times \frac{4.5}{1} = \frac{4.5}{3} = 1.5$$

If the supply curve of a commodity is upward sloping as is generally the case (See Figure 20.1) the

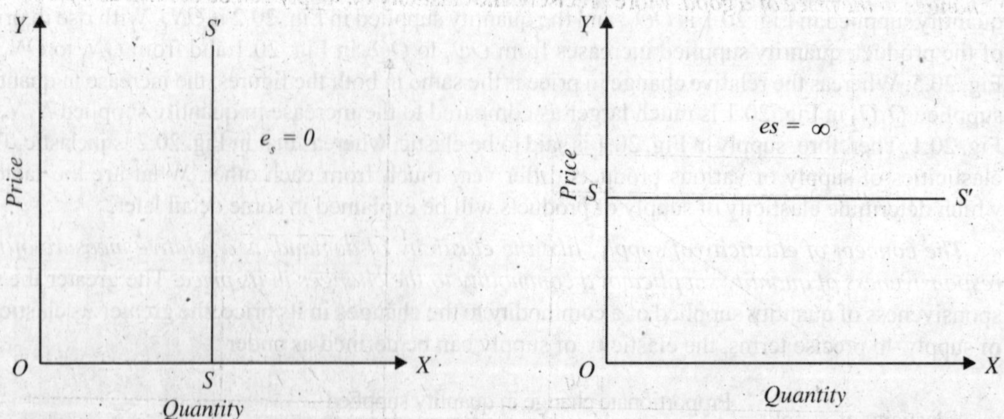

Fig. 20.3. *Perfectly Inelastic Supply* ($e_s = 0$) **Fig. 20.4.** *Perfecly Elastic Supply* ($es = \infty$)

coefficient of elasticity of supply will have a positive sign. When the supply curve is upward sloping, the elasticity of supply will be anything between zero and infinity.

When the quantity supplied of a commodity does not change at all in response to the changes in response to the changes in its place, the elasticity of supply is zero. In the case of zero elasticity of supply, the supply curve will be vertical straight line parallel to the Y-axis and is said to be *perfectly inelastic* in which case elasticity of supply is zero ($C_s = 0$) (see Fig. 20.3). On the other hand, if at a price, any quantity of the good is supplied, its elasticity will be equal to infinity and its supply curve will be a horizontal straight line parallel to the quantity axis and is said to be *perfectly elastic* in which case elasticity of supply is infinite ($e_s = \infty$). Perfectly elastic supply curve is shown in Figure 20.4.

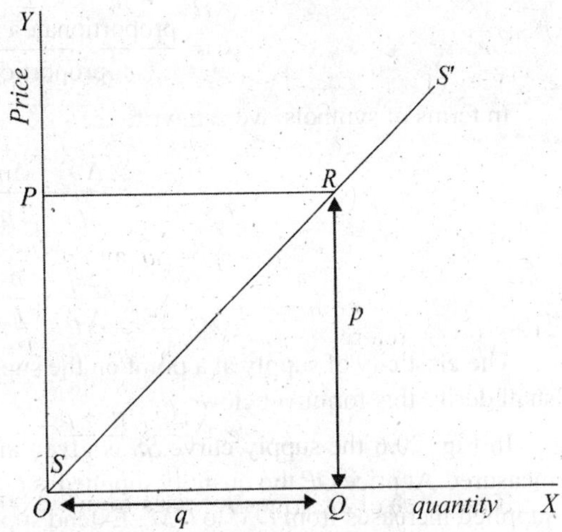

Fig. 20.5. *Unitary Elastic Supply Curve*

A third special case of supply curve is found when a straight-line supply curve passes through the origin such as the one shown in Figure 20.5. In this case elasticity of supply at any point such as R is *unity*. This follows from the elasticity formula; $\frac{\Delta q}{\Delta q} \cdot \frac{p}{q} \cdot$ It will be seen from Fig. 20.5 that in case of supply curve passing through the origin, the ratio $\frac{p}{q}$ is equal to the slope *i.e.* $\frac{\Delta p}{\Delta q}$ of the supply curve SS'. Thus substituting $\frac{\Delta p}{\Delta q}$ for $\frac{p}{q}$ in the elasticity formula we have $e_s = \frac{\Delta q}{\Delta p} \times \frac{\Delta p}{\Delta q} = 1$.

MEASUREMENT OF POINT ELASTICITY OF SUPPLY

The concept of elasticity of supply, like the elasticity of demand, occupies an important place in price theory. As explained above, *the elasticity of supply is the degree of responsiveness of supply to changes in the price of a good*. More precisely, the elasticity of supply can be defined as a proportion-

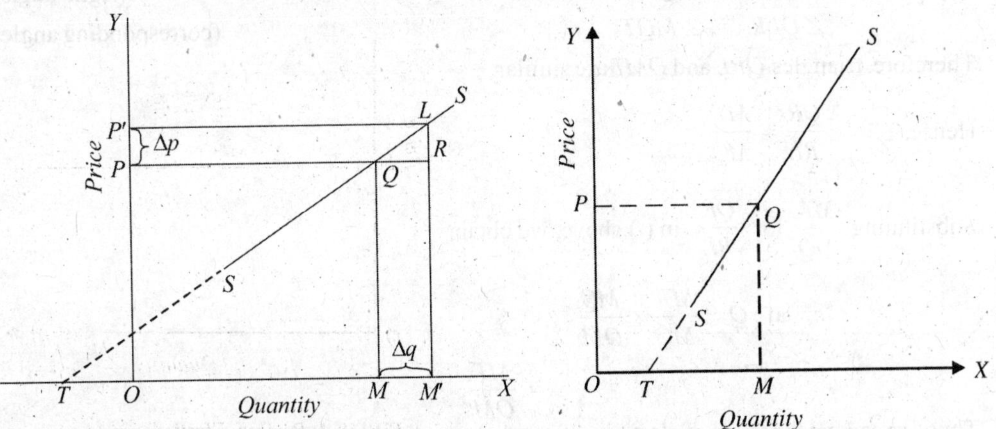

Fig. 20.6. *Measurement of Point Elasticity of Supply ($e_s > 1$)*

Fig. 20.7. *Measurement of Point Elasticity of Supply, $e_s < 1$*

ate change in quantity supplied of a good in response to a given proportionate change in price of the good. Therefore,

$$e_s = \frac{\text{proportionate change in quantity supplied}}{\text{proportionate change in price}}$$

In terms of symbols, we can write :

$$e_s = \frac{\Delta q}{q} \div \frac{\Delta p}{p} = \frac{\Delta q}{q} \times \frac{p}{\Delta p}$$

$$= \frac{\Delta q}{\Delta p} \times \frac{p}{q}$$

The elasticity of supply at a point on the supply curve can be easily measured by a formula. We shall derive this formula below.

In Fig. 20.6 the supply curve *SS* is given and elasticity of supply at point *Q* is required to be measured. At price *OP* the quantity supplied is *OM*. With the rise in price from *OP* to *OP′* the quantity supplied increases from *OM* to *OM′*. Extend supply curve *SS* downward so that it meets the *X*-axis at *T*.

The elasticity of supply at point $Q = \frac{\Delta q}{q} \div \frac{\Delta p}{p}$

or, $$e_s = \frac{MM'}{OM} \div \frac{PP'}{OP} = \frac{MM'}{OM} \times \frac{OP}{PP'}$$

$$= \frac{MM'}{PP'} \times \frac{OP}{OM}$$

Substituting *QR* for *MM′*, *RL* for *PP′* and *MQ* for *OP*, we get

$$e_s \text{ at point } Q = \frac{QR}{RL} \times \frac{MQ}{OM} \qquad ...(i)$$

Now, in triangles *QRL* and *QMT*

$\angle LQR = \angle QTM$ (corresponding angles)

$\angle QRL = \angle QMT$ (right. angles)

$\angle QLR = \angle MQT$ (corresponding angles)

Therefore, triangles *QRL* and *QMT* are similar

Hence, $\frac{QR}{RL} = \frac{MT}{MQ}$

Substituting $\frac{MT}{MQ}$ for $\frac{QR}{RL}$ in (*i*) above, we obtain

$$e_s \text{ at } Q = \frac{MT}{MQ} \times \frac{MQ}{OM}$$

$$= \frac{MT}{OM}$$

Thus, we can get the value of elasticity of supply from dividing *MT* by *OM*. Since in Fig. 20.6, *MT* is greater than *OM*, supply elasticity, $\frac{MT}{OM}$, will be greater than one.

In Fig. 20.7 supply curve when extended meets the *X*-axis to the right of the point of origin so that *MT* is smaller than *OM*. Therefore, in Fig. 20.7 the elasticity of supply $\frac{MT}{OM}$ is less than unity.

In Fig. 20.8 supply curve *SS* when extended meets the *X*-axis exactly at the point of origin so that the *MT* is equal to *OM*. Therefore, in Fig. 20.8 elasticity of supply will be equal to one.

In Fig. 20.6 elasticity of supply will be greater than one at every point of the curve, but it will differ from point to point. Similarly, in Fig. 20.7 supply elasticity is less than one at every point of the curve, but will differ from point to point. However, in Fig. 20.8 elasticity of supply will be equal to one at every point of the supply curve.

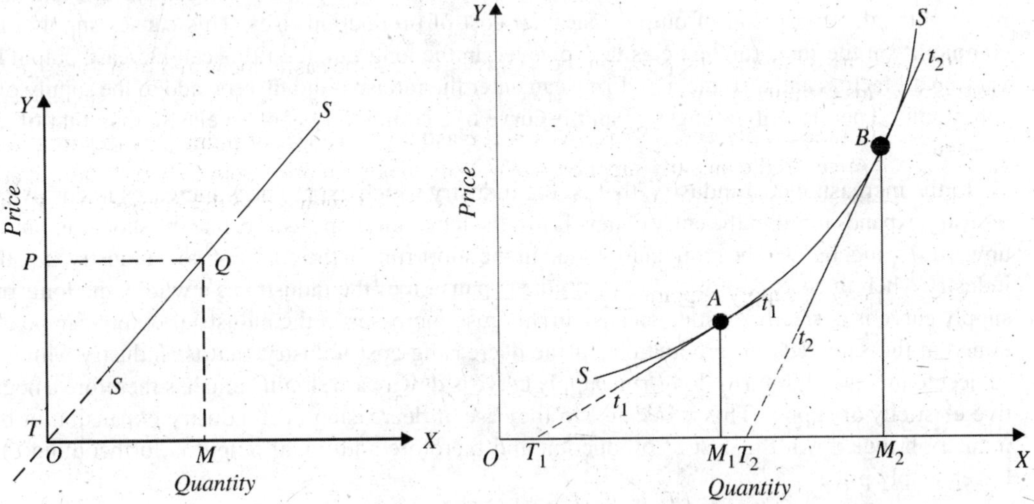

Fig. 20.8. $e_s = 1$

Fig. 20.9. *Varying Elasticity at Different Points on the Supply Curve*

We have studied above how the elasticity of supply is measured at a point on the straight-line supply curve. But now the question is how the point elasticity of supply can be measured on the real curve-type supply curve. Consider Fig. 20.9 where a supply curve of true curve type has been drawn and it is required to measure elasticity at point *A* on it. The general principle involved is the same as described above. In order to apply the above principle for estimating the point elasticity at point *A* on the supply curve *SS*, we have to draw a tangent at it.

Now, a tangent $t_1 t_1$ has been drawn at point *A*. On being extended, tangent t_1t_1 meets the *X*-axis at point T_1. Therefore, elasticity of supply at point *A* on the supply curve is $\frac{M_1T_1}{OM_1}$.

Likewise, we can find out the elasticity of supply at point *B* on the supply curve. For this, tangent t_2t_2 has been drawn at point *B* and has been extended to meet the *X*-axis at point T_2. Thus, the elasticity at point *B* on the supply curve *SS* is equal to $\frac{M_2T_2}{OM_2}$. It is also evident from Figure 20.9 that elasticity of supply at point *A* and *B* is different. Since $\frac{M_2T_2}{OM_2}$ is less than $\frac{M_1T_1}{OM_1}$, the elasticity of supply at point *B* is less than that at *A*.

FACTORS DETERMINING ELASTICITY OF SUPPLY

Elasticity of supply plays an important role in determining prices of products. To what extent price of a product will rise following the increase in demand for it depends on the elasticity of supply. The greater the elasticity of supply of a product, the less the rise in its price when demand for it increases. We explain below the factors which determine elasticity of supply of a product.

Changes in Marginal Cost of Production. Elasticity of supply of a commodity depends upon the ease with which increases in output can be obtained without bringing about rise in cost of production. If with the increase in production, the marginal cost of production goes up the elasticity of supply to that extent would be less. In the short run, with some factors of production being fixed, the increase in the amount of a variable factor eventually causes diminishing marginal returns and as a result with the expansion of output marginal cost of production rises. This causes supply of a commodity in the short run less elastic. However, in the long run, the firms can increase output by varying all factors and also the new firms can enter the industry and thereby add to the supply of a commodity. Therefore, the long-run supply curve of a commodity is more elastic than that of the short run.

In the increasing cost industry, that is, the industry which experiences increases in cost when industry expands through the entry of new firms, the long-run supply curve, like the short-run one, is upward sloping, but will be more elastic than in the short run. In the constant-cost industry, *i.e.*, the industry wherein costs do not change with the expansion of the industry as a whole, the long-run supply curve is perfectly elastic, because in this case increases in the industrial output can be obtained at the same cost of production. In the decreasing-cost industry, that is, industry which is subject to increasing returns, long-run supply curve is downward sloping and has therefore a negative elasticity of supply. This is because in the case of decreasing-cost industry expansion in the industry brings down the cost of production and therefore additional output is forthcoming at a lower supply price.

Response of the Producers. Besides the change in cost of production, the elasticity of supply for a product depends on the responsiveness of producers to changes in its price. If the producers do not respond positively to the increase in prices, the quantity supplied of a product would not increase as a result of rise in its price. A profit-maximising producer will increase the quantity supplied of a product following the rise in its price. However, producers who not always exhibit profit-maximising behaviour may not raise supply in response to the rise in price. For example, it has been argued by some with some empirical evidence that farmers in developing countries respond negatively to the rise in price of their agricultural products. They point out that with the higher agricultural prices, their need for fixed money income is met by selling smaller quantities of foodgrains and therefore at higher prices they may produce and sell smaller quantities rather than more.

Availability of infrastructure facilities and other inputs for expanding output. The extent to which the producers would raise supply of their products also depends on the availability of infrastructure facilities and inputs required for the production of goods. For example, when there is lack of fertilisers, irrigation facilities, the farmers would not be able to raise the supplies of agricultural products in response to the rise in their prices even if they want to do so. Likewise, in the industrial field if there is shortage of power, fuel, essential raw materials, the expansion in supply would not be forthcoming in response to the rise in prices of industrial products.

Possibilities of Substitution of one Product for the others. The change in quantity supplied of a product following the change in its price depends on the possibilities of substitution of one product for others. For example, if market price of wheat rises, the farmers will try to shift resources such as land, fertilisers away from other products such as pulses to devote them to the production of wheat. The greater the extent of possibilities of shifting of resources from the other products to wheat production, the greater the elasticity of supply of wheat.

The Length of Time. The elasticity of supply of a product also depends on the length of time during which producers have to respond to a given change in price of a product. Generally, the longer the time producers get to make adjustments for changing the level of output in response to the change in price, the greater the response of output, that is, the greater the elasticity of supply. From the viewpoint of the influence of the length of time on the elasticity of supply we distinguish between three time periods : (1) market period or very short run, (2) short run and (3) long run. The market period is a very short period and during this no more production is possible. Therefore, market-period supply curve is a vertical straight line (*i.e.*, perfectly inelastic). In the short run, firms can change output by changing the amounts of only variable factors, short-run supply curve is somewhat elastic. In the long run since firms can adjust all factors of production and also new firms can enter or leave the industry, long-run supply curve is more elastic.

QUESTIONS AND PROBLEMS FOR REVIEW

1. Distinguish between supply and stock. Explain the factors that determine the elasticity of supply.
2. Distinguish between supply and quantity supplied. Illustrate graphically.
3. Distinguish, between '*movement along a Supply Curve*' and '*Shift in Supply Curve*'. What factors cause such changes ?
4. What is the law of supply? How would you explain it ? Are there any exceptions to this law?
5. What are the assumption of low of supply ? Explain them.
6. Explain why the concept of supply curve relevant only in case of perfect or pure competition.
7. Why does the supply curve generally slope upward to the right?
8. Distinguish between extension and increase of supply on the one hand, and contraction and decrease in supply on the other. Illustrate the difference with a diagram.
9. Explain the factors which determine supply of a commodity.
10. What is meant by Elasticity of Supply? How is it measured ?
11. What are the factors which determine the elasticity of supply of a commodity. Give some examples of elastic supply.
12. The coefficient of elasticity of supply of a commodity X is 2, what quantity of the commodity will the seller supply at a price of ₹ 5 per unit, if he supplies 80 units of it at ₹ 4 per unit.

    [**Hints:** $e_s = \frac{\Delta q}{\Delta p} \cdot \frac{p}{q}$. Where given are $e_s = 2$, $\Delta P = 5 - 4 = 1$, $p = 4$ and $q = 80$. Substituting in the elasticity formula we have

    $$2 = \frac{\Delta q}{1} \cdot \frac{4}{80}$$

    $$\Delta q = 40$$

    Thus with rise in price to Rs. 5 the quantity supplied will increase from 80 to 80 + 40 =120]
13. Draw a supply curve with unitary elasticity.
14. A vertical supply curve means that elasticity of supply
    (*a*) infinity, (*b*) zero,
    (*c*) equal to one, (*d*) greater than one but less than infinity.
15. A horizontal supply curve means that elasticity of supply is
    (*a*) zero, (*b*) infinity,
    (*c*) equal to one, (*d*) greater than one but less than infinity.

16. A linear supply curve cuts the *Y*-axis (*i.e.*, price axis). What can you say about its elasticity? *D.U. B.A. (Hons.)*

17. Show that an upward sloping supply curve curve with its intercept on the X-axis has a price elasticity of supply less than one. *D.U. B.A. (Hons.)*

18. What shape will a supply curve have if it is unitary elastic? Is the *slope* of the supply curve indicative of its elasticity.

(**Hint.** $e_s = \dfrac{\Delta q}{\Delta p} \dfrac{p}{q}$. Where $\dfrac{\Delta q}{\Delta p}$ is the *inverse of the slope* of supply curve. Thus elasticity of supply depends not only on the slope of the supply curve but also on price-output ratio $\left(\dfrac{p}{q}\right)$. Thus, slope is not the correct indicative of elasticity of supply curve.

19. Explain the concept of *supply function*. How do changes in technology and factor prices influence it ?

PART – IV

THEORY OF FIRM AND PRICING IN DIFFERENT MARKET STRUCTURES

- Main Market Forms and Concepts of Revenue
- Equilibrium of the Firm : A General Analysis
- Equilibrium of the Firm and Industry Under Perfect Competition
- Price Determination Under Perfect Competition
- Applications of Demand and Supply Analysis
- Price and Output under Monopoly
- Price Discrimination
- Price and Output Under Oligopoly
- Sales Maximisation Model of Oligopoly
- Theory of Games and Competitive Strategy

CHAPTER 21

MAIN MARKET FORMS AND CONCEPTS OF REVENUE

The determination of prices and outputs of various products depends upon the type of market structure in which they are produced, sold and purchased. In this connection economists have classified the various markets prevailing in a capitalist economy into (*a*) perfect competition or pure competition, (*b*) monopolistic competition, (*c*) oligopoly and (*d*) monopoly. Three market forms, monopolistic competition, oligopoly and monopoly, are generally grouped under the general heading of imperfect competition, since these three forms of market differ with respect to the degree of imperfection in the market. Monopolistic competition is highly imperfect and monopoly is the most imperfect form of market structure.

But before explaining the salient features of various market forms, it will be useful to explain what is meant by market in economics.

Meaning of Market

Market is generally understood to mean a particular place or locality where goods are sold and purchased. However, in economics, by the term market we do not mean any particular place or locality in which goods are bought and sold. The idea of a particular locality or geographical place is not necessary to the concept of the market. What is required for the market to exist is the contact between the sellers and buyers so that transaction (*i.e.*, sale and purchase of a commodity) at an agreed price can take place between them. The buyers and sellers may be spread over a whole town, region or a country but if they are in close communication with each other either through personal contact, exchange of letters, telegrams, telephones, *etc.* so that they can sell and buy a good on agreed price, the market would be said to exist. Further, it is notworthy that because in a market, there is close and free communication between various buyers and sellers price of a homogeneous commodity settled between different sellers and buyers tends to be the same. Thus, in the words of Cournot, a French economist, "*Economists understand by the term market not any particular market place in which things are bought and sold but the whole of any region in which buyers and sellers are in such free intercourse with one another that the price of the same good tends to equality easily and quickly*".

Thus, the essentials of a market are: (*a*) commodity which is dealt with; (*b*) the existence of buyers and sellers; (*c*) a place, be it a certain region, a country or the entire world; and (*d*) such communication between buyers and sellers that only one price should prevail for the same commodity at the same time.

CLASSIFICATION OF MARKET FORMS

The popular basis of classifying market structures rests on three crucial elements, (1) the number of firms producing a product, (2) the nature of product produced by the firms, that is, whether it is homogenous or differentiated, and (3) the ease with which new firms can enter the industry. The price elasticity of demand for a firm's product depends upon the number of competitive firms producing the same or similar product as well as on the degree of substitution which is possible between the product of a firm and other products produced by rival firms. Therefore, a distinguishing feature of different market categories is the degree of price elasticity of demand faced by an individual firm.

We present in the table given below the classification of market forms based on the number of firms, the nature of product produced by them and price elasticity of demand.

1. **Perfect Competition.** As is evident from Table 21.1 perfect competition is said to prevail where there is a large number of producers (firms) producing a homogeneous product. The maximum output which an individual firm can produce is very small relatively to the total demand of the industry product so that a firm cannot affect the price by varying its supply of output.

There are following four important features of perfect competition :

1. There is a large number of firms (producers and sellers) and buyers of a product,
2. Products of all firms are homogeneous,
3. There is freedom of new firms to enter the industry and old ones to to leave it,
4. All firms and buyers have perfect information about the prevailing market price of the product.

With many firms and homogenous product under perfect competition, no individual firm in it is in

TABLE 21.1

The Classification of Market Forms

Form of Market Structure	*Number of Firms*	*Nature of Product*	*Price Elasticity of Demand for an Individual Firm*	*Degree of Control over Price*
(*a*) Perfect Competition	A large number of firms	Homogeneous product	Infinite	None
(*b*) **Imperfect Competition**				
(*i*) Monopolistic Competition	A large number of firms	Differentiated Products (but they are close substitues of each other)	Large	Some
(*ii*) Pure Oligopoly, (*i.e.*, Oligopoly without Product Differentiation)	Few firms	Homogeneous Product	Small	Some
(*iii*) Differentiated Oligopoly (*i.e.*, Oligopoly with Product Differentiation)	Few firms	Differentiated Products (which are close substitutes of each other)	Small	Large
(*c*) Monoply	One	Unique Product without Close Substitutes	Very small	Very large

a position to influence the price of the product and therefore the demand curve facing it will be horizontal straight line at the level of the prevailing price of the product in the market, that is, price elasticity of demand for a single firm will be infinite. Mrs. Joan Robinson writes: "Perfect competition prevails when the demand for the output of each producer is perfectly elastic. This entails, first, that the number of sellers is large so that the output of any one seller is negligibly small proportion of the total output of the commodity and the second that the products of various sellers are homogeneous from the viewpoint of consumers[1]. Many economists use perfect competition and pure competition interchangeably. But some such as E.H. Chamberlin, F.H. Knight draw a distinction between 'perfect' competition and 'pure' competition which we shall explain in a later chapter.

2. **Imperfect Competition**. Imperfect competition is an important market category wherein individual firms exercise control over the price to a smaller or larger degree depending upon the degree of imperfection present in a case. Control over price of a product by a firm and therefore the existence of imperfect competition can be caused either by the 'fewness' of the firms or by the product differentiation. Therefore, imperfect competition is divided into the following sub-categories.

(*a*) **Monopolistic Competition** : The first important sub-category of imperfect competition is monopolistic competition, on which Professor E.H. Chamberlin laid a great stress in his original thought-provoking work "*The Theory of Monopolistic Competition*". Monopolistic Competition, as is now understood, is characterised **by a large number of firms and product differentiation.**[2] That is, in *monopolistic competition* a large number of firms produce somewhat different products which are close substitutes of each other. As a result, demand curve facing a firm under monopolistic competition is highly elastic and this indicates that a firm working in it enjoys some control over the price. Besides, there is freedom of entry and exit under monopolistic competition.

(*b*) **Pure Oligopoly** : The second sub-category of imperfect competition is **oligopoly without product differentiation** which is also known as *pure oligopoly*. Under it there is competition among the few firms producing homogeneous or identical product. The fewness of the firms ensures that each of them will have some control over the price of the product and the demand curve facing each firm will be downward sloping which indicates that the price elasticity of demand for each firm will not be infinite.

(*c*) **Defferentiated Oligopoly** : The third sub-category of imperfect competition is **oligopoly with product differentiation** which is also called *differentiated oligopoly*. As its name shows, it is characterised by competition among the few firms producing differentiated products which are close substitutes of each other. The demand curve facing individual firms under oligopoly with product differentiation is downward sloping[3] and the firms would have fairly large control over the price of their individual products.

---

1. Joan Robinson, *The Economics of Imperfect Competition*. Macmillan and Co., London, 1954, p. 18.
2. It should be carefully noted that Prof. E.H. Chamberlin called any market structure, which was a blend of monopoly and competition, as monopolistic competition. A blend of monopoly and competition could be there if there was either a few firms producing a identical or differentiated product or there was a large number of firms producing differentiated products. The former is the case of oligopoly with and without product differentiation and the latter is the monopolistic competition with many firms. Thus, in Chamberlin's terminology, the concept of monopolistic competition covers both oligopoly (with as well as without product differentiation) and monopolistic competition with a large number of firms producing differentiated products. However, in standard modern economic theory, the term monopolistic competition is used only for the latter.
3. The nature of demand curve under oligopoly is, however, a controversial matter. In some models of oligopoly without product differentiation, it is assumed that the demand curve for an oligopolist is perfectly elastic (*i.e.*, horizontal straight line). Further, another important model of oligopoly assumes a kinked demand curve (with a kink at the prevailing price) for an oligopoly firm.

3. Monopoly.[4] Monopoly, as is now generally understood, means the existence of *a single producer or seller which is producing or selling a product which has no close substitutes*. Since a monopoly firm has a sole control over the supply of a product, which can have only remote substitutes, it has a very large control over the price of its product. The expansion and contraction in output of the product by a monopolist will considerably affect the price of the product, contraction in output will raise its price and expansion in output will lower it. Therefore, the demand curve facing a monopolist is downward sloping and has a steep slope. Thus, according to Prof. F. Machlup, "Monopolistic Competition would then comprise the cases of closer substitutes and more elastic demand curves, while monopoly would comprise those of remote substitutes and steeper demand curves."[5] Besides, in monopoly there are strong barriers to the entry of new firms in the industry.

Market Classification and Cross Elasticity of Demand

The concept of cross elasticity of demand has been used by Robert Triffin[6] to measure the amount and kind of competition among firms and therefore for classifying the market structure. In perfect competition the cross elasticity of demand for the product of a single firm with respect to a change in the price of the rest of the industry is infinite. That is to say, the proportionate fall in the demand for the product of a single firm is infinitely large in response to any given proportionate fall in the price of the product of the whole industry. Similarly, in monopolistic competition the cross elasticity of demand for the product of a single firm with respect to a change in the price of other products made in the monopolistic 'group' is very high. The cross elasticity of demand for the product of a monopolist with respect to a fall in the price of the other products in the economy is very low. We present below the different market categories and the cross elasticity of demand (e_c) found in them in a tabular form.

TABLE 21.2
Market Classification on the Basis of Cross Elasticity of Demand

Market Form	*Cross Elasticity of Demand*
1. Perfect Competition	Cross elasticity is infinite ($e_c = \infty$)
2. Monopolistic Competition	Cross elasticity (e_c) is very high
3. Monopoly	Cross elasticity (e_c) is very low or zero

The concept of cross elasticity of demand as a measure of classifying market forms is very much inadequate and sometimes leads to wrong conclusions. "The basic objection to the concept of cross elasticity is that it causes neglect of the two basic determinants of market structure: the degree of closeness or remoteness of substitution among products and the number of firms in the relevant group or industry. The concept of cross elasticity leads to the neglect of the two elements which are fundamental to an understanding or market structure."[7]

It has been pointed out by several economists[8] such as E.H. Chamberlin, W. Fellner, E.F. Beach

4. For monopoly, sometimes the terms *absolute* monopoly, *pure* monopoly, *complete* monopoly are used. All these terms have the same meaning since all visualise a single producer or seller producing a product which has no close substitutes. However, Sraffa used the term 'Pure Monopoly' in a different sense. *By pure monopoly Sraffa means that a single seller of a product is so powerful that he is in a position to take the whole income of all the consumers whatever the level of his output. Obviously, such a pure or absolute monopoly cannot exist in the real world.*
5. Fritz Machlup, Monopoly and Competition: A classification of Market Positions, *American Economic Review*, September 1937, p.448.
6. *See* his book *"Monopolistic Competition and General Equilibrium Theory"*.
7. M. Olson and D. Mcfarland "The Restoration of Pure Monopoly and the Concept of Industry", *Quarterly Journal of Economics*. Vol. 76 (November 1962), pp. 613-31.

and A.G. Papandreou that cross elasticity of demand of any perfectly competitive firm, instead of being infinity, is zero. Now, as said above, under pure monopoly, cross elasticity of demand is also zero. Thus, in two market situtaions of pure competition and pure monopoly which are two opposite extreme cases, cross elasticity is found to be the same. Therefore, cross elasticity of demand is a very unsatisfactory measure of a market structure. The cross elasticity of demand of a perfectly or purely competitive firm is zero because it produces a product which has so many homogeneous substitutes produced by other firms in the competitive industry. The number of firms producing homogeneous products, that is, perfect substitutes, is so great that *no one of them* will be noticeably affected when a single firm changes its price or output. If a purely competitive firm tries to reduce its price unilaterally, it will not be able to fully meet the demand for its product as the consumers of the homogeneous products of other firms will be attracted to it. But the crucial point is that no other single firm will perceive any noticeable change because the number of firms involved is very large.

We, therefore, conclude that cross elasticity of demand as a means of market classification is unsatisfactory. The classification of market forms made on the basis of (*i*) number of firms in the industry, (*ii*) the nature of product (*i.e.* the closeness or remoteness of substitution among products and the ease with which new firms can enter the industry or the old ones can leane it, which we have explained above, is quite adequate and satisfactory.

CONCEPTS OF AVERAGE REVENUE AND MARGINAL REVENUE

In the previous few chapters we discussed the nature of demand from the viewpoint of the consumer. But a producer or seller of good is also very much concerned with the demand for a good, because revenue obtained by him from selling the good depends mainly upon the demand for the good. He is, therefore, interested in knowing what sort of demand curve faces him. The demand curve of the consumers for a product is the average revenue curve from the standpoint of the sellers, since the price paid by the consumers is revenue of the sellers.

Average Revenue

Price paid by the consumer for the product forms the revenue or income of the seller. The whole income received by the seller from selling a given amount of the product is called *total revenue*. If a seller sells 15 units of a product at price Rs. 10 per unit and obtains Rs. 150 from this sale, then his total revenue is Rs. 150. Thus total revenue can be obtained from multiplying the quantity of output sold by the market price of the product (*P.Q*). On the other hand, average revenue is revenue earned *per unit of output*. Average revenue can be obtained by dividing the total revenue by the number of units sold. Thus,

$$\text{Average revenue} = \frac{\text{total revenue}}{\text{total output sold}}$$

$$AR = \frac{TR}{Q}$$

where *AR* stands for average revenue, *TR* for total revenue and *Q* for total output produced and sold.

In our above example, when total revenue *Q* equal to Rs. 150 is received from selling 15 units of the product, the average revenue will be equal to Rs. 150/15 = Rs. 10. Rs. 10 is here the revenue

8. E.H. Chamberlin, *Toward a More General Theory of Value*, pp. 79–81 : William Fellner. *Competition among the Few*, pp. 50–54; E.F. Beach, Triffin's Classification of Market Positions, *Canadian Journal of Economics and Politics*, Feb. 1943, pp. 69–74; A.G. Papandreou, Market Structure and Monopoly Power, *American Economic Review*, September 1949, pp. 883–97.

earned per unit of output. Now the question is whether average revenue is different from price or these two concepts mean the same thing. If a seller sells various units of a product at the same price, then average revenue would be the same thing as price. But when he sells different units of a given product at different prices, then the average revenue will not be equal to price. An example will clarify this point. Suppose a seller sells two units of a product, both at a price of Rs. 10 per unit. Total revenue of the seller will be Rs. 20 and the average revenue will be 20/2 = Rs. 10. Thus average revenue is here equal to the price of the product. Now suppose that the seller sells the two units of his product, one unit to the consumer *A* at price Rs. 12 and one unit to the consumer *B* at price Rs. 10. His total revenue from the sale of two units of the product will be Rs. 22. Average will be here equal to 22/2 = Rs. 11. Thus in this case when two units of the product are sold at different prices, average revenue is not equal to the prices charged for the product.

But in the actual life we find that different units of a product are sold by the seller at the same price in the market (except when he discriminates and charges different prices for different units of the good), average revenue equals price. Thus in economics we use average revenue and price as synonyms except when we are discussing price discrimination by the seller. Since the buyer's demand curve represents graphically the quantities demanded or purchased by the buyers at various prices of the good, it also, therefore, shows the average revenue at which the various amounts of the good are sold by the seller. This is because the price paid by the buyer is revenue from seller's point of view. Hence, average revenue curve of the firm is really the same thing as the demand curve of the consumers.

Marginal Revenue

On the other hand, marginal revenue is the *net revenue* earned by selling an additional unit of the product. In other words, *marginal revenue is the addition made to the total revenue by selling one more unit of a commodity.* Putting it in algebraic expression, marginal revenue is the addition made to total revenue by selling *n* units of a product instead of *n* – 1 where *n* is any given number. If a producer sells 10 units of a product at price Rs. 15 per unit, he will get Rs. 150 as the total revenue. If he now increases his sales of the product by one unit and sells 11 units, suppose the price falls to Rs. 14 per unit. He will, therefore, obtain total revenue of Rs. 154 from the sale of 11 units of the good. This means that 11th unit of output has added Rs. 4 to the total revenue. Hence Rs. 4 is here the marginal revenue.

Total revenue when 10 units are sold at price of Rs. 15 $= 10 \times 15 = \text{Rs. } 150$

Total revenue when 11 units are sold at price of Rs. 14 $= 11 \times 14 = \text{Rs. } 154$

Marginal revenue $= 154 - 150 = \text{Rs. } 4$

The word *net* in the first definition of marginal revenue given above is worth noting. The full understanding of the word 'net' in the definition will reveal why the marginal revenue is not equal to the price. The question is, taking our above numerical example, why the marginal revenue due to the 11th unit is not equal to the price of Rs. 14 at which the 11th unit is sold. The answer is that the 10 units which were sold at the price of Rs. 15 before will now all have to be sold at the reduced price of Rs. 14 per unit. This will mean the loss of one rupee on *each* of the previous 10 units and total loss on the previous 10 units due to price fall will be equal to Rs. 10. The loss in revenue incurred on the previous units occurs because the sale of additional 11th unit reduces the price to Rs. 14 *for all*. Thus in order to find out the net addition made to the total revenue by the 11th unit, the loss in revenue (Rs. 10) on previous units should be deducted from the price of Rs. 14 at which the 11th unit is sold along with others. The marginal revenue in this case will, therefore, be equal to Rs. 14 – 10 = 4. Marginal revenue is thus less than the price at which the additional unit is sold.

It is clear from above that marginal revenue can either be found directly by taking out the difference between total revenue before and after selling the additional unit, or it can be obtained by subtracting the loss in revenue on previous units due to the fall in price from the price at which the additional unit is sold.

Therefore, marginal revenue = difference in total revenue in increasing sales from $n - 1$ units to n units.

= price of the additional unit minus loss in revenue on previous units resulting from price reduction.

It follows from above that when the price falls as additional unit is sold, marginal revenue is less than the price. But when the price remains the same as additional unit is sold, as under perfect competition, the marginal revenue will be equal to average revenue, since in this case there is no loss incurred on the previous units due to the fall in price. The relationship between average revenue and marginal revenue is the same as between any other average and marginal values. When average revenue falls marginal revenue is less than the average revenue. When average revenue remains the same, marginal revenue is equal to average revenue.

If TR stands for total revenue and Q stands for output, then marginal revenue (MR) can also be expressed as follows :

$$MR = \frac{\Delta TR}{\Delta Q}$$

$\frac{\Delta TR}{\Delta Q}$ indicates the slope of the total revenue curve.

Thus, if the total revenue curve is given to us, we can find out marginal revenue at various levels of output by measuring the slopes at the corresponding points on the total revenue curve.

Average and Marginal Revenue Under Imperfect Competition

The meaning of the concepts of total, average and marginal revenues under conditions of imperfect competition will become clear from Table 21.3. As has been stated above, when imperfect competition prevails in the market for a product, an individual firm producing that product faces a downward sloping demand curve. In other words, as a firm working under conditions of imperfect competition increases production and sale of its product its price falls. Now, when all units of a product are sold at the same price, the average revenue equals price. How marginal revenue can be obtained from the changes in total revenue and what relation it bears to average revenue will be easily grasped from looking at Table 21.3.

Table 21.3
Total, Average and Marginal Revenues

No. of Units Sold	*Total Revenue (Rupees)*	*Average Revenue or Price (Rs.)*	*Marginal Revenue (Addition made to Total Revenue) (Rupees)*
I	II	III	IV
1	16	16	16
2	30	15	14
3	42	14	12
4	52	13	10
5	60	12	8
6	66	11	6
7	70	10	4
8	72	9	2
9	72	8	0
10	70	7	–2

It will be seen from the Col. III of the table that price (or average revenue) is falling as additional units of the product are sold. Marginal revenue can be found out by taking out the difference between the two successive total revenues. Thus, when 1 unit is sold, total revenue is Rs. 16. When 2 units are sold, price (or *AR*) falls to Rs. 15 and total revenue increases to Rs. 30. Marginal revenue is therefore here equal to 30–16 = 14, which is recorded in Col. IV. When 3 units of the product are sold, price falls to Rs. 14 and total revenue increases to Rs. 42. Hence marginal revenue is now equal to Rs. 42–30 = Rs. 12 which is again recorded in Col. IV. Likewise, marginal revenue of further units can be obtained by taking out the difference between two successive total revenues. Marginal revenue is positive as long as total revenue is increasing. Marginal revenue becomes negative when total revenue declines. Thus when in our table 22.3 quantity sold is increased from 9 units to 10 units the total revenue declines from Rs. 72 to 70 and therefore the marginal revenue is negative and is equal to –2.

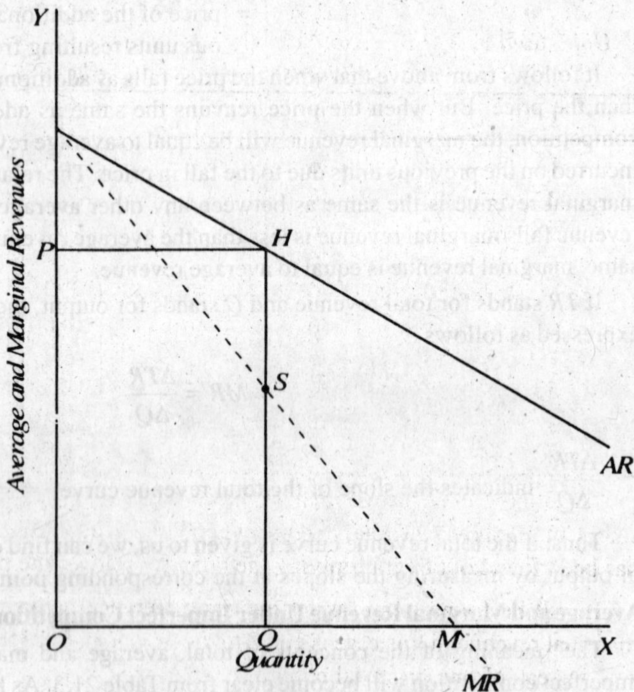

Fig. 21.1. *Average and Marginal Revenue Curves under Imperfect Competition*

It may be noted that in all forms of imperfect competition, that is, monopolistic competition, oligopoly and monopoly, average revenue curve facing an individual firm slopes downward as in all these market forms when a firm lowers the price of its product, its quantity demanded and sales would increase and vice versa.

The case, when average revenue (or price) falls when additional units of the product are sold in the market is graphically represented in Fig. 21.1. In Fig. 21.1 it will be observed that average revenue curve (*AR*) is falling downward and marginal revenue curve (*MR*) lies below it. The fact that *MR* curve is lying below *AR* curve indicates that marginal revenue declines more rapidly than average revenue. When *OQ* units of output are sold, *AR* is equal to *QH* or *OP* and *MR* is equal to *QS*. When *OM* units of the product are sold, marginal revenue is zero. If the quantity sold is increased beyond *OM*, marginal revenue becomes negative.

Average and Marginal Revenue uder Perfect Competition

When there prevails perfect competition in the market for a product, demand curve facing an individual firm is perfectly elastic and the price is beyond the control of a firm, average revenue remains constant. If the price or average revenue remains the same when more units of a product are sold, the marginal revenue will be equal to average revenue. This is so because if one more unit is sold and the price does not fall, the addition made to the total revenue by that unit will be equal to the price at which it is sold, since no loss in revenue is incurred on the previous units in this case. Consider the following table:

TABLE 21.4
Average and Marginal Revenues Under Perfect Competition

No. of Units Sold	*Price (or AR) (Rupees)*	*Total Revenue (Price × Output) (Rupees)*	*Marginal Revenue (MR) (Rupees)*
I	II	III	IV
1	16	16	16
2	16	32	16
3	16	48	16
4	16	64	16
5	16	80	16
6	16	96	16
7	16	112	16
8	16	128	16
9	16	144	16
10	16	160	16

In the above table, price remains constant at the level of Rs. 16 when more units of the product are sold. Col. III shows the total revenue when various quantities of the product are sold. Total revenue has been found out by multiplying the quantity sold by the price.

It will be found from taking out the difference between two successive total revenues that marginal revenue in this case is equal to the price *i.e.*, Rs. 16. Thus, when two units of the good are sold instead of one, the total revenue rises from Rs. 16 to Rs. 32, the addition made to the total revenue *i.e.* marginal revenue will be equal to Rs. 32 – 16 = Rs. 16. Similarly, when three units of the product are sold, the total revenue increases to Rs. 48, and the marginal revenue will be equal to Rs. 48 – 32 = Rs. 16 Likewise, it will be found for further units of the product sold that marginal revenue is equal to price. The case of perfect competition when for an individual firm average revenue (or price) remains constant and marginal revenue is equal to average revenue is graphically shown in Fig. 21.2 Average revenue curve in this case is a horizontal straight line (*i.e.*, parallel to the *X*-axis). Horizontal-straight-line average revenue curve (*AR*) indicates that price or average remains the same at *OP* level when quantity sold is increased. Marginal revenue (*MR*) curve coincides with average revenue (*AR*) curve since marginal revenue is equal to average revenue.

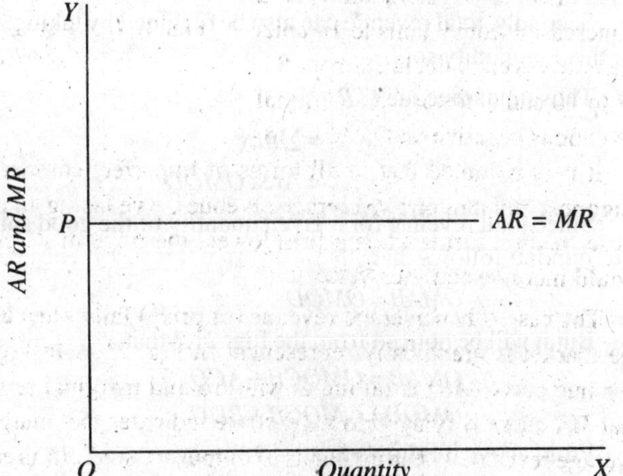

Fig. 21.2. *Average and Marginal Revenue Curves under Perfect Competition*

RELATIONSHIP BETWEEN AR AND MR CURVES

Given that both average revenue (*AR*) and Marginal revenue (*MR*) curves are of straight-line shape, it can be shown that (*MR*) curve will cut the distance between *AR* curve and the *Y*-axis in the middle. In other words, when both *AR* and *MR* curves are straight lines, then if a perpendicular is drawn from a point on the *AR* curve to the *Y*-axis, *MR* curve will cut this perpendicular at its middle point. Consider Fig. 21.3, where both *AR* and *MR* curves are straight lines. Point *A* is taken on the average revenue curve and a perpendicular *AB* is drawn to the *Y*-axis. *MR* curve cuts the perpendicular *AB* at point *C*. Now, if *MR* curve cuts halfway the distance between *AR* curve and the *Y*-axis, then *AC* must be equal to *BC*. So in order to show that *MR* cuts halfway the distance between *AR* and the *Y*-axis, we have to prove in Fig. 21.3 that *AC* = *BC*.

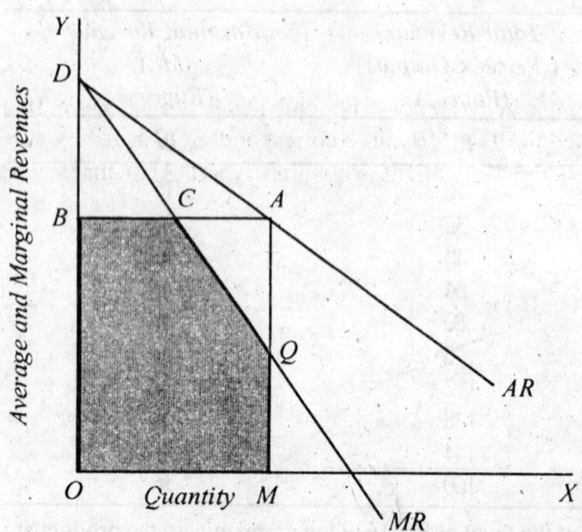

Fig. 21.3. *Relationship between AR and MR Curves*

Draw a vertical straight line from *A* so as to meet the *X*-axis at *M*. It means that when *OM* quantity of the commodity is sold, average revenue is equal to *AM*. Now, there are two ways in which we can find out the total revenue earned by the sale of *OM* units of the commodity.

First, total revenue (*TR*) = *AR* × quantity sold

$= AM \times OM$

= area *OMAB* ...(*i*)

Secondly, total revenue can also be obtained by taking a sum of marginal revenues of all the units of the commodity sold.

Thus, total revenue (*TR*)

$= \Sigma MR$

= Area *OMQD* ...(*ii*)

Since total revenue for a given quantity of the good sold is to be the same whichever way it may be found, it follows that

$OMAB = OMQD$

But it will be noticed from the Fig. 21.3 that

$OMAB = OMQCB + ACQ$

$OMQD = OMQCB + BDC$

From above it follows that :

$OMQCB + ACQ = OMQCB + BDC$

$ACQ = BDC$

or

Thus triangles *ACQ and BDC are equal in area*

Now, in Δs *ACQ* and *BDC*

$QAC = \angle DBC$ (right angles)

$\angle ACO = \angle BCD$ (vertically opposite angles)

$\angle AQC = \angle BDC$ (alternate angles)

Therefore, ΔACQ and ΔBDC are similar.

We have proved above that triangles *ACQ* and *BDC* are equal in area as well as similar. Now, when the two triangles are both equal and similar, then they are congruent (*i.e.* equal in all respects).

Therefore Δs ACQ and BDC are congruent

Hence, $AC = BC$

It is thus proved that given the straight-line average and marginal revenue curves, the marginal revenue curve will lie half-way from the average revenue curve.

From above, we also learn the way of drawing *MR* curve corresponding to a given *AR* curve. If any *AR* curve is given to you, and you are asked to draw *MR* curve corresponding to it, then you should first extend the *AR* curve so that it meets the *Y*-axis (if it is not already so). After that you should draw *MR* curve starting from the *Y*-axis so that it *bisects* any perpendicular line drawn from a point on the *AR* curve to the *Y*-axis.

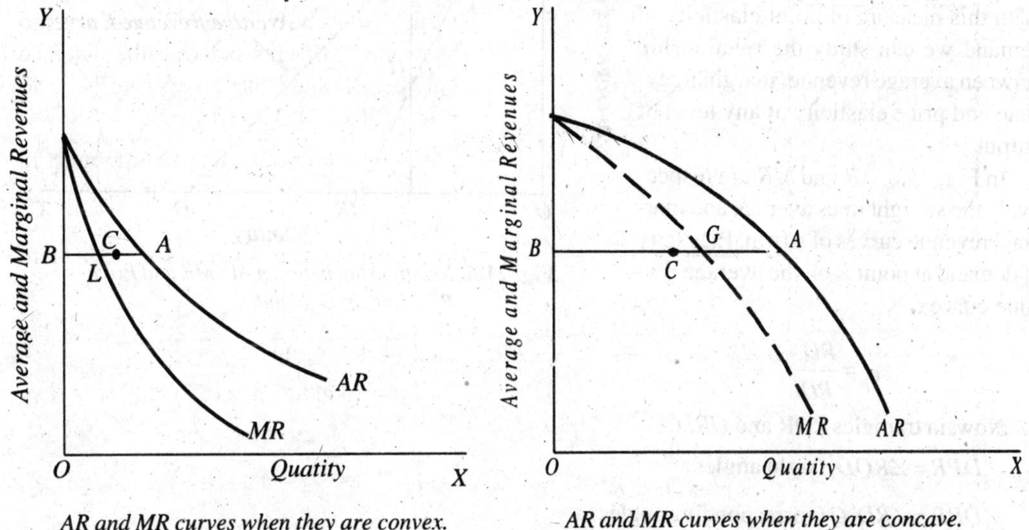

AR and MR curves when they are convex.

Fig. 21.4.

AR and MR curves when they are concave.

Fig. 21.5.

Marginal revenue curve corresponding to a convex or concave average revenue curve is not of straight-line shape but is either convex or concave to the origin. What relationship *MR* curve will bear to *AR* curve when average and marginal revenue curves are either convex or concave ? In either of these cases the marginal revenue curve will not lie halfway from the average revenue curve. If the average revenue curve is convex to the origin as in Fig. 21.4 the marginal revenue curve *MR* will also be convex to the origin and will cut any perpendicular drawn from *AR* curve to the *Y*-axis *more than halfway a*s measured from the average revenue curve. On the other hand, if the average revenue curve is *concave* to the origin as in Fig. 21.5, the marginal revenue curve will also be concave and will cut any perpendicular line from the average revenue curve to the *Y*-axis *less than halfway* as measured from the average revenue curve.

In Figs. 21.4 and 21.5, *C* is the middle point on the perpendicular line *AB*.

AVERAGE REVENUE MARGINAL REVENUE AND PRICE ELASTICITY OF DEMAND

There is a very useful relationship between elasticity of demand, average revenue and marginal revenue at any level of output. We will make use of this relation extensively when we come to the study of price determination under different market conditions. Let us study what this relation is.

We have stressed above that the average revenue curve of a firm is really the same thing as the

demand curve of consumers for the firm's product. Therefore, elasticity of demand at any point on a consumer's demand curve is the same thing as the elasticity of demand on the given point on the firm's average revenue curve. We know that elasticity of demand at point R on the average revenue curve DD' in Fig. $21.6 = \frac{RD'}{RD}$.

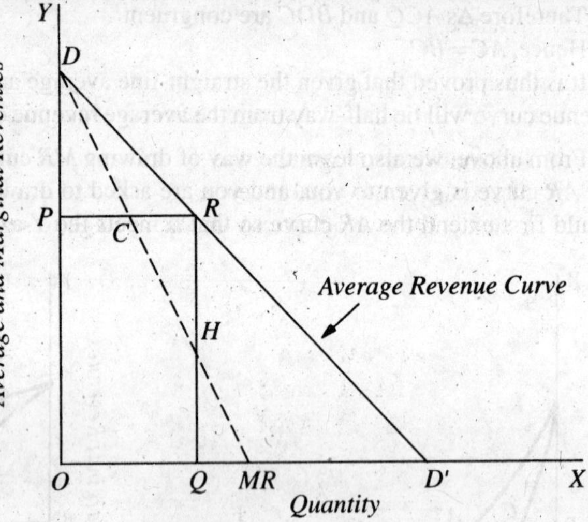

Fig. 21.6. *Relationship between AR, MR and Price Elasticity of Demand*

With this measure of point elasticity of demand we can study the relationship between average revenue, marginal revenue and price elasticity at any level of output.

In Fig. 21.6, AR and MR are respectively the straight lines average and marginal revenue curves of a firm. Elasticity of demand at point R on the average revenue curve :

$$e_p = \frac{RD'}{RD}$$

Now, in traingles PDR and QRD'

$\angle DPR = \angle RQD'$ (right angles)

$\angle DRP = \angle RD'Q$ (corresponding angles)

Third $\angle PDR = \angle QRD'$

Therefore, triangles PDR and QRD' are equiangular

Hence $$\frac{RD'}{RD} = \frac{RQ}{PD} \quad \ldots\text{(i)}$$

In the triangles PDC *and* CRH

$PC = RC$

$\angle PCD = \angle RCH$ (vertically opposite angles)

$\angle DPC = \angle CRH$ (right angles)

Therefore, triangles PDC and CRH are congruent (*i.e.*, equal in all respects).

Hence $PD = RH$ ... *(ii)*

From (i) and (ii), we get

Price elasticity at $R = \frac{RD'}{RD} = \frac{RQ}{PD} = \frac{RQ}{RH}$

Now, it is seen from Fig. 21.6 that

$$\frac{RQ}{RH} = \frac{RQ}{RQ - HQ}$$

Hence, price elasticity at point $R = \frac{RQ}{RQ - HQ}$

It will be seen from Fig. 21.6 that RQ is the average revenue (AR) and HQ is the marginal revenue

(MR) at the level of output OQ corresponding to point R on the demand or average revenue curve DD'. Therefore,

$$\text{Price Elasticity at } R = \frac{\text{Average Revenue}}{\text{Average Revenue} - \text{Marginal Revenue}}$$

If A stands for average revenue
M stands for marginal revenue
e stands for point elasticity on the average revenue curve,

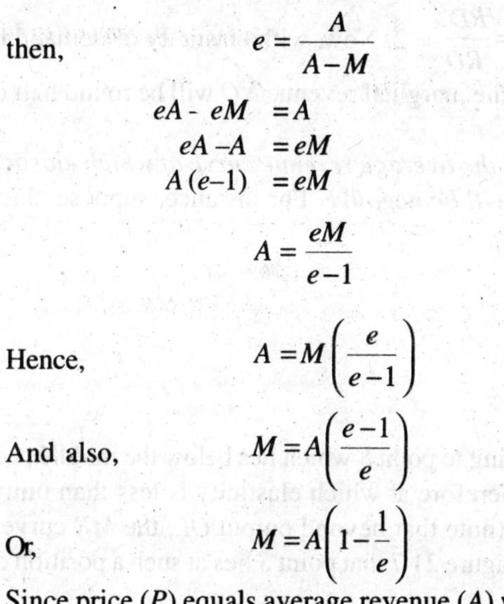

then, $$e = \frac{A}{A-M}$$

$$eA - eM = A$$

$$eA - A = eM$$

$$A(e-1) = eM$$

$$A = \frac{eM}{e-1}$$

Hence, $$A = M\left(\frac{e}{e-1}\right)$$

And also, $$M = A\left(\frac{e-1}{e}\right)$$

Or, $$M = A\left(1 - \frac{1}{e}\right)$$

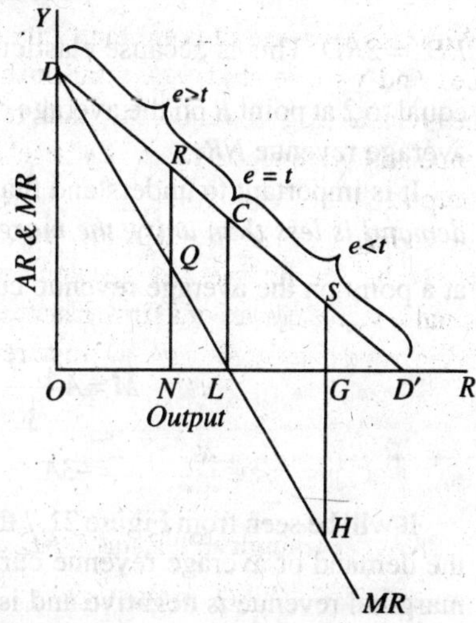

Fig. 21.7. *Average Revenue, Marginal Revenue and Price Elasticity of Demand*

Since price (P) equals average revenue (A) we have

$$M = P\left(1 - \frac{1}{e}\right)$$

where e stands for price elasticity of demand at a given point on the average revenue curve.

With the help of the above formulae we can find out marginal revenue at any level of output from average revenue at the same output provided we know the point price elasticity of demand on the average revenue curve. *If the price elasticity of a firm's average revenue curve at a given level of output is equal to one, marginal revenue equals zero.* This can be proved as under :

$$M = A\left(1 - \frac{1}{e}\right)$$

$$= A\left(1 - \frac{1}{1}\right)$$

$$= A \times 0$$

$$= 0$$

It will be seen from Figure 21.7 that corresponding to the middle point C on the average revenue curve DD' where elasticity of demand equals unity, the marginal revenue is zero.

By applying the above formula it can be shown that at a point on the average revenue curve where elasticity of demand is greater than one, marginal revenue will be positive though less than the average revenue. *Thus when demand elasticity on a firm's average revenue curve is 2, the marginal revenue will be positive and will equal half the average revenue.* This is because

$$M = A\left(1 - \frac{1}{e}\right)$$

$$= A\left(1 - \frac{1}{2}\right)$$

$$= \frac{1}{2}A$$

If price elasticity of demand at a point on the average revenue curve equals 2, then the relevant point on the average revenue curve *DD′* in Figure 21.7 is *R* corresponding to output *ON* such that *RD′= 2RD*. This is because elasticity at point $R = \frac{RD'}{RD} = 2$. Now, with elasticity of demand being equal to 2 at point *R* on the average revenue curve the marginal revenue *NQ* will be found half of the average revenue *NR*.

It is important to understand that *at a point on the average revenue curve at which elasticity of demand is less than unity, the marginal revenue will be negative.* For instance, suppose elasticity at a point on the average revenue curve is $\frac{1}{4}$. Then,

$$M = A\frac{\frac{1}{4} - 1}{\frac{1}{4}} = A\left(-\frac{3}{4}\right) \times 4$$

$$= -3A$$

It will be seen from Figure 21.7 that corresponding to point *S* which lies below the middle point on the demand or average revenue curve *DD′* and therefore at which elasticity is less than unity, the marginal revenue is negative and is equal to *GH* (note that beyond output *OL*, the *MR* curve goes below the *X*-axis). Further, it will be noticed from Figure 21.7 that point *S* lies at such a position on the average revenue curve *DD′* so that $SD' = \frac{1}{4}SD$ and, therefore, $e_p = \frac{SD'}{SD} = \frac{1}{4}$.

Thus on measurement it will be found that corresponding to point *S* at which elasticity is equal to $\frac{1}{4}$ the marginal revenue *GH* is three times the average revenue *GS*.

To sum up, *marginal revenue is always positive at any point or output where the elasticity of the average revenue curve is greater than one and marginal revenue is always negative where the elasticity of average revenue curve is less than one and marginal revenue is zero corresponding to unit elasticity at the average revenue curve.*

THREE TYPES OF REVENUE (*AR, MR, TR*) AND PRICE ELASTICITY (E)

We are now in a position to describe the relationship between three types of revenue, namely, *AR*, *MR*, and *TR* on the one side and price elasticity of demand on the other. From the formula $MR = AR\left(\frac{e-1}{e}\right)$ we can know what would be the marginal revenue, if elasticity and *AR* are given to us. When *the elasticity is equal to one, it follows from the above formula that marginal revenue will be equal* to zero.

Thus $$MR = AR\left(\frac{e-1}{e}\right)$$

$$MR = AR\left(\frac{1-1}{1}\right)$$

$$MR = AR \times 0 = 0$$

Likewise, it can be proved that,

If $e > 1$, MR is positive, and

if $e < 1$, MR is negative.

In a straight-line demand curve we know that the elasticity at the middle point is equal to one. It follows that marginal revenue corresponding to the middle point of the demand curve (or *AR* curve) will be equal to zero.

Consider Fig. 21.8. *C* is the middle point of the average revenue or demand curve *DD′*. At point *C* price elasticity is equal to one. Corresponding to *C* on the *AR* curve, marginal revenue will be zero. Thus *MR* curve is shown cutting the *X*-axis at point *N* which corresponds to point *C* on the *AR* curve. At a quantity greater than *ON* price elasticity on the demand curve, curve is less than one and the marginal revenue is negative. Marginal revenue being negative beyond *ON* means that total revenue will diminish if a quantity greater than *ON* is sold. Total revenue will be increasing upto *ON* output, since upto this marginal revenue remains positive. It follows therefore that total revenue will be maximum where elasticity is equal to one. Thus *TR* curve drawn in the bottom panel of Fig. 21.8 is shown to be at its highest level corresponding to the point *C* on *AR* curve or *ON* output where marginal revenue is zero and elasticity is equal to one.[9]

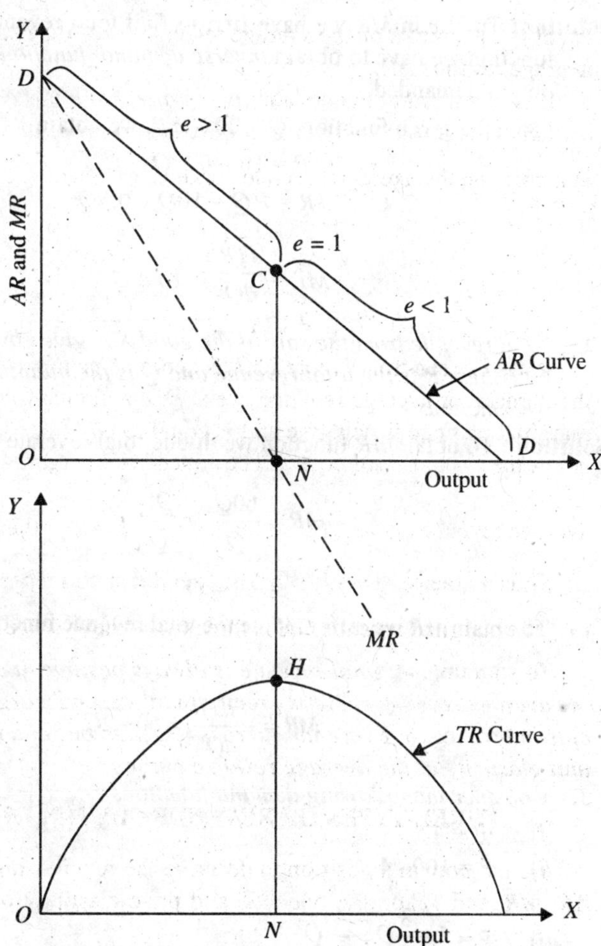

Fig. 21.8. *Relationship between AR, MR, TR and Price Elasticity*

We can also prove that total revenue is maximum corresponding to the unit elasticity point on the *AR* curve even without bringing in the marginal revenue. We know from the relationship between elasticity and total outlay (or total revenue) that the total revenue increases when elasticity is greater than one and total revenue diminishes when elasticity is less than one. Thus, in Fig. 21.8 beginning from point *D* on the average revenue or the demand curve *DD′* and coming down to the middle point *C*, elasticity remains greater than one and therefore the total revenue will go on increasing as we descend from point *D* to point *C* on the demand curve. Below point *C* on the demand or *AR* curve, elasticity is less than one, therefore the total revenue will start diminishing as we descend from point *C* downward. It, therefore, follows that corresponding to the

9. It should be noted that the *scale* on the *Y*-axis for *TR* curve is different from the scale used for *AR* and *MR* curves at the top panel.

middle point C on the demand curve where elasticity is equal to one, the total revenue will be maximum.

It will be seen from Fig. 21.8 that total revenue curve starts from O and goes on rising till it reaches its peak at point H. Then it starts declining till it meets point D' on the X-axis. It means that at output OD' total revenue is zero. This is because at output OD' average revenue or price is zero.

NUMERICAL PROBLEMS

1. *Suppose demand function facing a firm is $Q = 20 - 2P$ where Q is output demanded and P is price. Find the marginal revenue function.*

Solution: To obtain MR we have first to find total revenue function. For obtaining total revenue function we have to obtain *inverse demand function*, that is, price expressed as a function of output demanded.

From the given function, $Q = 20 - 2P$, we obtain

$$P = 10 - 0.5Q$$

$$TR = P.Q = 10Q - 0.5Q^2$$

$$MR = \frac{dTR}{dQ} = 10 - Q$$

2. *Total revenue from the sale of the good X is given by the equation $R = 60Q - Q^2$ for $0 \leq Q \leq 60$ (where R is the total revenue and Q is the quantity bought at price P). Calculate MR and AR functions.*

Solution : To obtain AR function we divide total revenue function by output. Thus

$$AR = \frac{60Q}{Q} - \frac{Q^2}{Q}$$

$$= 60 - Q$$

To obtain MR we differentiate the total revenue function ($R = 60Q - Q^2$) with respect to output. Thus,

$$MR = \frac{dTR}{dQ} = 60 - 2Q$$

3. *Consider the following demand functions :*

(*i*) $P = 4$

(*ii*) $P = 100 - 4Q$

(*iii*) $P = 1 + \frac{3}{2}Q - \frac{4}{3}Q^2$

Calculate total, average and marginal revenue functions for each one. At what point is total revenue maximised in each case. *(D.U.B.A (Hons.) 1997)*

Solution :

(*i*) $P = 4$

$$TR = P.Q = 4Q$$

$$AR = \frac{PQ}{Q} = P = 4$$

$$MR = \frac{dTR}{dQ} = \frac{d(4Q)}{dQ} = 4$$

Note that in this case MR equals AR.

(ii) $P = 100 - 4Q$

$TR = P.Q = 100Q - 4Q^2$

$$AR = \frac{P.Q}{Q} = 100 - 4Q$$

$$MR = \frac{dTR}{dQ} = 100 - 8Q$$

TR is maximum at output level where $MR = 0$

Thus, setting MR function equal to zero we have

$100 - 8Q = 0$

$8Q = 100$

$$Q = \frac{100}{8} = 12.5$$

Thus, at output level 12.5, TR will be maximum.

(iii) $P = 1 + \frac{3}{2}Q - \frac{4}{3}Q^2$

$$TR = P.Q = Q + \frac{3}{2}Q^2 - \frac{4}{3}Q^3$$

$$AR = \frac{PQ}{Q} = 1 + \frac{3}{2}Q - \frac{4}{3}Q^2$$

$$MR = \frac{dTR}{dQ} = 1 + 3Q - 4Q^2$$

TR will be maximised at output level where $MR = \frac{dTR}{dQ} = 0$

Setting MR equal to zero we have

$1 + 3Q - 4Q^2 = 0$

(Find the value of Q)

Problem 4. *The demand function equation faced by HP for its personal computers is given by*

$$P = 50,000 - 4Q$$

1. *Write the total revenue function and marginal revenue equation.*
2. *At what price and quantity marginal revenue will be zero?*
3. *At what price and quantity total revenue will be maximized?*

Solution. (1) To obtain total revenue function, we multiply the given *inverse* demand equation by Q.

$$TR = PQ = 50,000Q - 4Q^2 \quad \text{..(1)}$$

Taking the first derivative of the total revenue function would give us marginal revenue equation. Thus, seting MR function equal to zero we have :

$$MR = \frac{d(TR)}{dQ} = \frac{d(PQ)}{dQ} = 50,000 - 8Q \quad \text{..... (2)}$$

(2) Setting *MR* equation equal to zero would give us the quantity at which *MR* is zero. Thus, setting *MR* function equal to zero we have :

$$50,000 - 8Q = 0$$
$$8Q = 50,000$$
$$Q = 6250$$

Now, to obtain price associated with the quantity (6250), we substitute the value of Q in the given inverse demand equation ($P = 50,000 - 4Q$). Thus.

$$P = 50,000 - (4 \times 6250)$$
$$= 50,000 - 25,000 = 25,000$$

It follows from above that at the quantity of 6250 units and price of ₹ 25,000 per computer, marginal revenue is zero.

(3) To obtain quantity at which *TR* is maximum, we set the *first derivative of TR function* (*i*), that is, *MR* equal to zero.

$$TR = 50.000Q - 4Q^2$$

$$\frac{d(TR)}{dQ} = MR = 50,000 - 8Q$$

Setting *MR* equal to zero we have :

$$50,000 - 8Q = 0$$
$$8Q = 50,000$$
$$Q = 6250$$

Thus, at the quantity of 6250 units the total revenue is maximum.

Important Conclusion. It is clear from the answers to the questions (2) and (3) of this problem that the *quantity at which MR is equal to zero, total revenue is maximum*. This is because, as stated above, it follows from the very definition of marginal revenue. Marginal revenue is the increase in total revenue resulting from the sale of an additional unit of output. As long as marginal revenue is positive, total revenue is increasing and beyond the output level where total revenue is maximum, marginal revenue becomes negative and, therefore, total revenue declines. Thus, at the output level where marginal revenue is zero, total revenue is maximum.

Problem 5. *Outside an airport, a shopkeeper is running a coffee shop. The demand function for coffee cups is*

$$Q = 150 - 10P$$

where Q is the quantity demanded of coffee cups and P is price per coffee cup.

1. Write total revenue function and determine at what quantity of coffee cups sold and price fixed, total revenue is maximised.

2. Show that at the quantity sold where total revenue is maximised, price elasticity of demand is equal to unity.

Solution: 1. The given demand function is

$$Q = 150 - 10P \quad \text{...(i)}$$

In order to determine the total revenue, we have to first obtain *inverse demand function*, that is, demand expressed in terms of *price as a function of quantity demanded*. Rearranging the demand equation (*i*) above we have

$$10P = 150 - Q$$

$$P = 15 - \frac{Q}{10} \qquad \text{......}(ii)$$

Now, $$TR = PQ$$

$$= Q\left(15 - \frac{Q}{10}\right)$$

Thus total revenue function is : $TR = 15Q - \dfrac{Q^2}{10}$ ......(*iii*)

Taking the first derivative of the *TR* function (Note that the first derivation of *TR* function measures *MR*). We have :

$$\frac{d(TR)}{dQ} = MR = 15 - \frac{2}{10}Q = 15 - \frac{1}{5}Q$$

In order to find out quantity sold at which *TR* is maximised, we set first derivative of *TR* i.e., *MR* function, equal to zero. Thus

$$\text{Thus } \frac{d(TR)}{dQ} = 15 - \frac{1}{5}Q = 0$$

$$\frac{1}{5}Q = 15$$

$$Q = 75$$

Thus at quantity of output 75 total revenue is maximised.
Substituting the value of *Q* into the given demand equation (*ii*)

$$P = 15 - \frac{1}{10}.75 = 15 - 7.5$$

$$= ₹ 7.5$$

Thus, the quantity at which total revenue is maximized is 75 and associated price is ₹ 7.5 per coffee cup.

2. Price elasticity of demand $(e_p) = \dfrac{dQ}{dP} \cdot \dfrac{P}{Q}$

From the demand function equation (*i*), we find that the coefficient of *P* is 10 which means.

$\dfrac{dQ}{dP} = 10.$

We have found above that *TR*–maximizing quantity is 75 and associated price is 7.5, Substituting these values into the price elasticity formula

$$e_p = \frac{dQ}{dP} \cdot \frac{P}{Q} = 10 \times \frac{7.5}{75} = 1$$

Thus, price elasticity of demand at the *TR*–maximising quantity is equal to one.

QUESTIONS AND PROBLEMS FOR REVIEW

1. Define Market. Does it necessarily mean a particular price where goods and services are bought and sold ?
2. Into what main categories market structures are classified? Explain the basis of such classification.
3. Differentiate between perfect competition, monopoly and monopolistic competition. Briefly explain their features with regard to

(1) the number of firms
(2) the nature of product being produced
(3) freedom to enter the industry
(4) control over the price of the product.

4. What is meant by cross elasticity of demand? Explain how it is used as a basis for classifying various market structures.

5. Explain the concepts of average revenue, marginal revenue and total revenue. Show how they are related to each other.

6. Show that in case of linear demand curve marginal revenue curve cuts *half-way the distance* between the average revenue curve and the *Y*-axis. Prove geometrically.

7. Explain how average revenue and marginal revenue are related to each other through price elasticity of demand. Give a geometric and mathematical proofs of this relation.

(Hint. *For mathematic proof see Appendix to this chapter*)

8. Show how marginal revenue and total revenue depend on the price elasticity of demand on a demand curve. Represent this relationship graphically.

9. Explain and illustrate with diagrams the nature of average and marginal revenue curves of a firm working under :

(*a*) Perfect competition
(*b*) Monopoly
(*c*) Monopolistic Competition

10. Define marginal revenue. How is it related to (*a*) average revenue, and (*b*) total revenue?

11. Complete the following table.

Price (₹)	*Output* (*Units*)	*Total Revenue* ₹	*Marginal Revenue* ₹	*Price Elasticity Demand*
6	0			
5	1			
4	2			
2	4			
1	5			
0	6			

12. Why is marginal revenue curve of a firm under perfect competition identical with average revenue curve? Explain.

13. When average revenue curve of a firm is falling, marginal revenue curve lies below it. Why?

14. When marginal revenue is zero, total revenue is maximum. Why ? Explain.

15. Demand for a firm's product is given by the following demand function

$$Q_d = 1000 - 200P$$

(1) Find the inverse demand function
(2) Find the quantity of output at which total revenue is maximum
(3) What is the price of the product corresponding to revenue-maximising output.

16. Given the following demand function for a firm's product

$$P = 50{,}000 - 4Q$$

Show that price elasticity of demand is equal to one at the output level at which *TR* is maximum

APPENDIX TO CHAPTER 21

Mathematical Treatment of AR and MR Curves

In this appendix we mathematically prove the two types of relationship: (1) Relationship between linear *AR* and *MR* curves, (2) Relationship between *AR*, *MR* and price elasticity of demand

Relationship between Linear *AR* and *MR* Curves

When demand or average revenue curve is linear, marginal revenue curve is also linear. An important relationship exists between the linear average revenue curve and linear marginal revenue curve. This relationship is described in the following theorem.

Theorem. *Marginal revenue curve cuts the linear demand or average revenue curve halfway the horizontal distance between the vertical axis and the linear average revenue curve. Alternatively,* the theorem states that *marginal revenue curve bisects the distance between the vertical axis and the linear demand curve.*

We can mathematically prove the above theorem. The equation for the linear average or demand curve is

$$P = a - bQ \qquad \text{....(1)}$$

where P = price, Q = quantity, $-b$ is the slope of the linear demand curve.

Now, total revenue, $TR = P \cdot Q$

Substituting $a - bQ$ for P, we have

$$TR = (a-bQ)\,Q$$

or

$$TR = aQ - bQ^2 \qquad \text{...(2)}$$

Differentiating (2) with respect to Q, we have

$$\frac{dTR}{dQ} = a - 2bQ$$

$\frac{dTR}{dQ}$ is the expression for marginal revenue

Therefore, $\quad MR = a - 2bQ \qquad$ ...(3)

Equation (3) implies that *marginal revenue curve of a linear demand curve is also linear.* Further, according to equation(3), the *slope of the marginal revenue curve is twice that of linear demand or average revenue curve.* This also implies that marginal revenue curve will cut halfway the horizontal distance between the vertical axis and the linear demand or average curve. However, this can be explicitly shown as under:

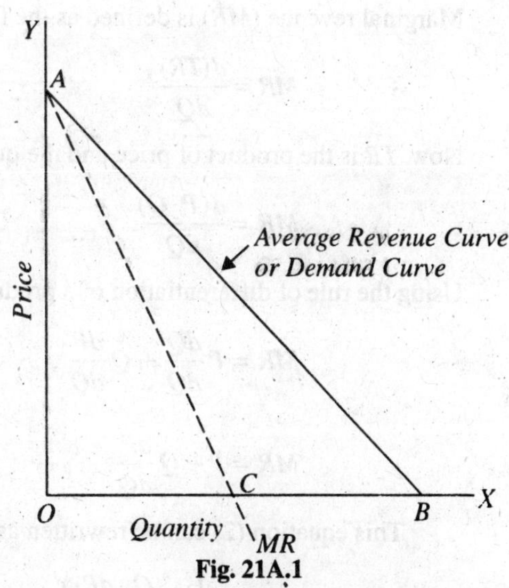

Fig. 21A.1

It may be noted that setting demand equation $P = a - bQ$ equal to zero will give us the *intercept on the horizontal axis of the demand or average curve* (that is, *OB* in the adjoining figure) and setting marginal revenue function, $MR = a - 2bQ$ equal to zero will give us the *intercept on the horizontal axis of the marginal revenue curve* (that is, *OC* in the adjoining figure). Thus,

$$P = a - bQ = 0$$

$$Q = \frac{a}{b}$$

That is, Q or intercept OB of the AR curve on the horizontal axis is equal to $\frac{a}{b}$.

Now, $$MR = a - 2bQ = 0$$

$$Q = \frac{1a}{2b} = \frac{1}{2}\frac{a}{b}$$

That is, Q or intercept OC of the marginal revenue curve on the horizontal axis $= \frac{1a}{2b}$. This explicitly shows that intercept OC of MR curve is half of the intercept OB of the linear average revenue curve. Therefore, in the adjoining figure $OC = \frac{1}{2}OB$ shows that marginal revenue curve *bisects* the linear AR or demand curve.

Relationship between Price (i.e. Average Revenue), Marginal Revenue and Price Elasticity of Demand : Mathematical Derivation

There exists an important relationship between price, marginal revenue and price elasticity or demand which is extensively used in making price decisions by firms. This relationship can be written algebraically as

$$MR = P\left(1 - \frac{1}{e}\right)$$

where P = price and e = point price elasticity of demand.

The above relation can be mathematically derived as follows:

Marginal revenue (MR) is defined as the first derivative of total revenue (TR) function. Thus,

$$MR = \frac{d(TR)}{dQ} \quad ...(1)$$

Now, TR is the product of price and the quantity of the product sold ($TR = P \cdot Q$). Thus,

$$MR = \frac{d(P \cdot Q)}{dQ}$$

Using the rule of differentiation of a product, we have

$$MR = P\frac{dQ}{dQ} + Q\frac{dP}{dQ}$$

$$MR = P + Q\frac{dP}{dQ} \quad ...(2)$$

This equation (2) can be rewritten as

$$MR = P\left(1 + \frac{Q}{P} \cdot \frac{dP}{dQ}\right) \quad ...(3)$$

Now, recall that point price elasticity of demand

$$= \frac{P}{Q} \cdot \frac{dQ}{dP}.$$

It will thus be noticed that the expression $\frac{Q}{P} \cdot \frac{dP}{dQ}$ in equation (3) above is the reciprocal of point price elasticity of demand $\left(\frac{P}{Q} \cdot \frac{dQ}{dP} \right)$. Thus,

$$\frac{Q}{P} \cdot \frac{dP}{dQ} = \frac{1}{e} \qquad \text{....(4)}$$

Substituting equation (4) into equation (3), we obtain

$$MR = P\left(1 + \frac{1}{e}\right)$$

Remember that price elasticity of demand has a negative sign which is generally ignored. However recognizing it, we have

$$MR = P\left(1 + \frac{1}{-e}\right)$$

or $$MR = P\left(1 - \frac{1}{e}\right)$$

This relationship can be easily used to show that

When $e = 1$, $MR = 0$

When $e > 1$, $MR > 0$, *i.e*, MR is positive.

When $e < 1$, $MR < 0$, *i.e.*, MR is negative.

Exercise. *If AR curve is rectangular hyperbola, draw the corresponding MR curve. Comment on the nature of elasticity of demand.* *D.U.B.Com. (H), 2000*

[**Hints:** *AR* curve being rectangular hyperbola shows that total area which represents total revenue or total expenditure (*P.Q*) remains constant as price of the commodity changes. Total revenue remaining constant with changes in price implies that price elasticity of demand is equal to one. Now,

$$MR = P\left(1 - \frac{1}{e}\right) = P\left(1 - \frac{1}{1}\right)$$

$$= P(0) = 0$$

Thus, *MR* curve will overlap the *X*-axis throughout].

CHAPTER 22

OBJECTIVES OF THE FIRM AND ITS EQUILIBRIUM : A GENERAL ANALYSIS

In last chapter we have discussed the various forms of market in which a producer or firm may sell his product. Analysis of equilibrium of the firm and the industry under various market forms occupies an important place in economic theory. The theory of price with which we are concerned in this book is primarily an analysis of equilibrium of the firm and the industry under various market forms. When different firms are producing differentiated products, it is difficult to define an industry and the analysis of equilibrium of the industry under such conditions is full of conceptual difficulties. When different firms are producing differentiated products, each would have its separate demand and supply of its particular product. Therefore, in this case we cannot sum up the demand and supply of the various firms producing differentiated products to obtain the supply and the demand for the industry. *It was in connection with the industry composed of various firms producing homogeneous, undifferentiated products that the concepts of supply and demand were forged by Marshall.*

When various firms are producing same or homogeneous products, it is possible to identify an industry and the supply and the demand for the product of that industry can be ascertained. But when different firms are producing differentiated (but similar) products, it is not easy to identify an industry having its own supply and demand. Prof. Chamberlin in his concept of monopolistic competition where various firms produce differentiated but similar products has called the collection of these firms as *'group'* rather than industry. Moreover, it is because of this difficulty of viewing supply and demand for 'group' of firms producing differentiated products and also because of greater importance of behaviour of individual firms having control over their own products that in recent years emphasis has been shifted from the equilibrium of the industry to the equilibrium of the firm. However, equilibrium of the industry under conditions of perfect competition, where various firms produce homogeneous products, retains its importance and usefulness.

Meaning of Firm's Equilibrium

Word 'equilibrium' means a state of balance. When two opposing forces working on an object are in balance so that the object has no tendency to change, it is said to be in equilibrium. In other words, when the object under the pressure of forces working in opposite directions has no tendency to move in either direction, the object is in equilibrium. Thus, by consumer's equilibrium we mean that in regard to the allocation of money expenditure among various goods the consumer has reached the state where he has no tendency to reallocate his money expenditure. Similarly, *a firm is said to be* in *equilibrium when it has no tendency to change its level of output, that is, when it has no tendency either to increase or to contract its level of output.* The firm will produce the equilibrium level of output and will charge the price at which the equilibrium output can be sold in the market. In fact, in a previous chapter, we discussed the equilibrium of the firm in respect of the combination of factors it has to employ for producing a given level of output. But the problem for a producer is not simply what combination of factors it has to choose for producing a given level of output but it has to go further to decide what level of output it should produce. Thus, the equilibrium of the firm is generally conceived in respect of output it has to produce. In this regard, to repeat what has been just said above, the firm is in equilibrium, when, given certain demand and cost conditions, it has struck upon the level of output at which it will stick on and will have no tendency to change it.

OBJECTIVES OF THE FIRM

Before analysing conditions of equilibrium of the firm, we shall first explain the objectives of the firm because only when the firm is achieving its objective it will have no tendency to change the level of its output, that is, it will be in equilibrium position. Like that of a consumer the entrepreneur or firm is assumed to behave in a rational manner. The rationality on the part of a firm is generally understood to imply that a firm attempts to maximise its profits. Until a few years back, maximisation of profits was considered to be the valid objective of a firm. However, in recent years apart from profit maximisation, several other objectives of the firm have been pointed out by several economists. The various alternative objectives of the firm that have been stressed by different economists are:—

1. Profit Maximisation
2. Achieving Steady flow of Secure Profits
3. Satisficing Objective
4. Maximisation of Sales
5. Maximisation of Utility
6. Maximisation of Growth

We explain below the above objectives of the firm.

Profit Maximization Objective

Profit maximisation assumption about the behaviour of the firm is one of the most fundamental assumptions of economic theory. The attempt of the entrepreneur to maximise his profits is regarded as a rational behaviour. It has been said that as the rationality on the part of the consumer means that he tries to maximize his satisfaction, the rationality on the part of the entrepreneur implies that he tries to maximise his profits.

It should be carefully noted as to what the entrepreneur is supposed to maximise under profit maximisation objective. An entrepreneur's income consists of two elements. Firstly, he gets wages for his work of routine management and supervision which he is supposed to pay to himself and include in his regular cost calculations. Thus, the total costs of output comprise not only the costs incurred on the hired factors by the entrepreneur but also the entrepreneur's own wages of routine management and supervision. When we say that the entrepreneur tries to maximise the difference between total revenue and total costs, these total costs include entrepreneur's wages of management and supervision. Thus the entrepreneur's wages of management do not form part of that income which the entrepreneur has to maximise. Secondly, the entrepreneur gets what is left after meeting all costs (including his own wages of routine management). This surplus of total revenue over total cost which is called his residual income. This residual income is the profits which is his true or net profits that the entrepreneur is assumed to maximise. Thus, we see that the entrepreneur's income comprises his own wages of routine management and the residual income which accrues to him.

Marshall called entrepreneur's wages of management and supervision as normal profits, and the residual income as super-normal profits.This dichotomy of entrepreneur's income is very fundamental to the theory of firm. *The normal profits are the minimum income which the entrepreneur must get in order to stay in a business or industry*. As has been just said above, the normal profits are included in costs and do not come under the maximising problem. It is the super-normal profits, *i.e*, true economic profits which is the residual income which the entrepreneur aims at maximising. These *susper-normal or pure eonomic profits are of the nature of economic rent since they are over and above the normal profits which must be paid to the entrepreneur to make him to remain in the industry or business.*

Another important thing to note is that in the traditional theory of the firm maximisation of pure profits is considered to be *maximisation of short-run profits*. This short run is generally considered to be a year.

A Critique of Profit-Maximisation Objective

The profit maximization objective has been subjected to severe criticisms in recent years. It has been pointed out that all firms do not maximise profits. Further, some economists have asserted that apart from making profits, firms in the real world also try to achieve other objectives. Some other alternative objectives have been suggested by prominent economists. First, Prof. Rothschild[1] has asserted that entrepreneurs try to secure a steady flow of profits over a long period of time. Prof. Baumol[2] is of the view that firms attempt to maximise sales (i.e. total revenue) subject to a minimum profit constraint. Williamson[3] argues that in case of corporate business firms, managers maximise their own utility function rather than maximising profits for shareholders who are the owners of the firm. On the other hand, H.A. Simon and Cyert and March express the view that rather than maximise any thing the firms just *satisfice*, that is, want satisfactory performance regarding profits made, market share and sales revenue.

With the growth of managerial capitalism, the two developments have taken place which have been the basis of criticism of profit maximisation objective. The traditional assumption of profit a maximisation implies that a firm was owned by an entrepreneur himself and therefore it was perfectly rational for him to maximise profits. Now, in large corporate firms it is managers who make business decisions while the corporate firm is owned by shareholders. In other words, there is separation between **control and ownership of corporate a firm.** It has been asserted that managers who make business decisions may not be interested in maximising profits, instead they may try to achieve their own goals or objectives which may not be in the interests of owners *i.e.* shareholders. This situation has been described as **managerial capitalism**. Profs. Nellis and Parker rightly write "With managers in control it is easy to question the validity of the profit maximisation assumption of traditional theory. Some managers may seek to keep shareholders happy by reporting a certain level of profit while leaving themselves the flexibility to achieve, perhaps personal objectives (such as business growth, diversification, salary, etc)".[4]

The second development on the basis of which the validity of profit maximisation has been questioned is the emergence of oligopoly as the most common form of market structure. In the traditional theory the firms which were assumed to work under condition of either perfect competition or monopoly, they were considered to work *independently* and *possess full and accurate information* about demand and cost conditions. They could therefore easily determine profit maximisation by equating marginal cost with marginal revenue. However, the assumption of perfect maximisation fails to provide a satisfactory explanation decision making under oligopoly because in this type of market structure (1) the firms are quite **interdependent** and (2) there exists a **lot of uncertainly** about demand and cost conditions. Mutual interdependence arises in oligopoly because there are a few firms in this market structure and each of them produces a sufficiently large proportion of the industry's output so that its price-output decisions affect the market share of its rival firms which are expected to retaliate. Uncertainty exists because under oligopoly form of market structure a firm's decision is influenced not just by what its competitors are doing but also by what it thinks its rivals might do in reponse to its initiative regarding change in price, quantity of output, product variation and advertising.

---

1. R.W. Rothschild, Price Theory and Oligopoly, *The Eonomic Journal*, 1947, pp. 299-320.
2. W.J. Baumol, *Business Behavaiour, Value and Growth*, p.49
3. O.E. Williamson, *The Economics of Discretionary Behaviour: Managerial Objectives in a Theory of the Firm*, Marsham Publishing Co. Chicago, 1967.
4. Joseph G. Nellis and David Parker, "*The Essence of Business Economics*" Prentice-Hall of India, New Delhi, 2002

In the context of development of managerial capitalism and the emergence of oligopoly as the chief form of market structure, Baumol put forward the view that managers of firms maximise sales value (*i.e.* total revenue) rather than profits, O.E. Williamson laid stress on the view that managers or business executives of large corporate firms are motivated by self-interest and therefore they **maximise their own utility function** rather than profits for the shareholders. Still another view has been presented by Marris[5] according to whom the managers try to **maximise growth of their companies** which raise their own status, power and prestige rather than maximising profits which are mostly bagged by shareholders.

In addition to the above altrenative maximising objectives in place of profit maximisation, there are two other theories of the firm which emphasize that managers or firms **do not maximise any thing but pursue non-maximising goals.** There are mainly two non-maximising approaches to firm's behaviour. Firstly, on the basis of empirical study two Oxford economists professors Hall and Hitch expressed the view that businessmen do not maximise profits but charge price according to what is called **mark-up principle** to achieve normal profit. According to this principle, firms calculate average cost on the basis of expected output or sales of the product and add to it, (*i.e.* mark up) a normal profit margin. In this way they prevent the entry of new firms in the industry which enable them to earn a steady flow of profits over time.

The second approach to non-maximising behaviour is the behaviourist theory initially put forward by Professor H.A. Simon[6] but was further developed by R.M Cyert and J.G. March.[7] According to this behaviourist approach managers of the firms **do not try to maximise any thing,** whether it is profits, sales value, utility or growth. They just pursue the goal of **satisficing.** According to this, they try to achieve only a **satisfactory performance** with regard to profits, sales, market share. We shall explain these approaches in detail later in this chapter. We explain below alternative objectives of firm which have been proposed by some economists.

Case for the Objective of Maximising Profits

We have explained above the various alternatives to profit maximization objective. However, the various alternatives to profit maximisation are not free from drawbacks and no comprehensive theory of the firm has been developed on the basis of non-profit maximising assumption so that till now the theory of the firm based on profits-maximizing behaviour dominates the economic theory. Several reasons can be given in favour of the assumption of profit-maximizing behaviour of the firms.

In the first place there is a question of survivorship. The firm which is working in a very competitive environment if it does not maximise profits it will run the risk of not being able to survive in the long run. Thus, profit maximising is quite a rational behaviour in the fields where intense competition prevails. It may appear under certain circumstances that the firms are not maximising profits, but they may be doing so only for the short run. For instance, the firms working in oligopolistic or monopolistic market structures do not maximise profits in the short run in order to prevent the potential competitors to enter the industry. Under these circumstances, the firms try to maximise profits in the long run. Similarly, some other goals such as maximising the growth of output, sales maximisation, increasing the market share are only the means to achieve maximum profits in the long-run and therefore from the long-run point of view, they are not inconsistent with the goal of profit maximisation.

In defence of profit maximisation hypothesis, it may also be noted that the managers are not permanent in a firm and are likely to be changed by the owners (shareholders in the corporate firms) if they feel that managers are not providing them adequate return or profits on their investment. Thus,

---

5. R. Marris, A Model of Managerial Enterprise, *Quarterly Journal of Economics*, 1963.
6. W.J. Baumol, *Business Behaviour, Value and Growth*, p.49.
7. R.M. Cyert and J.C. March, *A Behavioural Theory of the Firm*, Prentice Hall, 1963.

given the fact that managers are liable to be changed, if they deviate much from profit maximisation, they will not be allowed to continue for long in the firm. Of course, if control over management is absent, the managers may continue to behave in a non-profit maximising manner. However, if the managers of corporate firms are not maximising profits in the long-run, the prices of its shares will fall greatly and it may be taken over by others who will change the current management and install a new team of managers who are efficient and try to maximise profits in the long run.

Finally, it may be said that no model, nor its assumptions can be completely realistic. Models are built and assumptions are made so as to bring out the crucial aspects and relations of the economic phenomena. For this purpose we need not fully take into account the massive and confusing details of the real world. We must abstract from reality to draw purposeful conclusions which can adequately explain the economic phenomenon. This is also true of the profit maximisation assumption. The profit maximisation may not truly and exactly reflects the behaviour of the managers in the real world, but on the basis of the profit maximisation assumption, correct predictions regarding determination of prices and outputs of commodities have been made. In this regard we may refer again to the viewpoint of Friedman[8] who has argued that the *ultimate test of the validity of an assumption is its capability to predict correctly*; the assumption itself may be unrealistic. Defending the assumption of profit maximisation on these grounds he writes, "unless the behaviour of businessmen in some way or other is approximated behaviour consistent with the maximisation of returns, it seems unlikely that they would remain in business for long."[9] He points out that profit maximisation assumption is valid because predictions regarding changes in prices and output based on it have been shown to be correct.

ALNERNATIVES TO PROFIT MAXIMISATION OBJECTIVES

Maximisation of Long-run Profits : Achieving a Steady Flow of Secure Profits

Prof. Rothschild[10] maintains that maximization of short-run profits may be the valid objective to be pursued by the firms working under conditions of perfect competition and monopolistic competition when a large number of firms are competing with each other to sell a product and under monopoly when a firm controls the supply of a product which has no close substitutes. Under these market conditions, firms do not feel insecure in making profits over a long period as they do not have to face effective competition and do not expect their profits will be competed away by the actions of their *existing* rivals. But under conditions of oligopoly where the firms are quite interdependent and face a lot of uncertainty regarding the activities of their few rivals, the firms desire to obtain secure profits. This is because in deciding about his price and output policies the entrepreneur does not maximise his profits at a particular time or for a particular short period of time but tries to have a *steady flow of profits* over a long period of time. Therefore, this has been also called the security or survival objective.

It is generally conceded that under conditions of oligopoly the firms strive for secure profits over a long period of time rather than maximising short-run profits at a particular point of time.

Satisficing Objective

According to the satisficing hypothesis, corporate managers aim at achieving satisfactory rate of profits rather than maximising profits. The advocates of this hypothesis say that a corporate manager sets for himself a minimum standard for performance or what is called the *aspiration level*. Once the satisfactory rate of profit according to this aspiration level is achieved, the firm will slack off. This approach is based on behavioural theory of the firm and explain how firms actually behave.

---

8. Milton Friedman, "The Methodology of Positive Economics", in *Essays in Positive Economics,* University of Chicago Press, Chicago, 1953.
9. *Ibid.*
10. R.W. Rothschild, Price Theory and Oligopoly, *The Economic Journal*, 1947, pp. 299-320

H.A. Simon[11], one of the pioneers of the behavioural approach to the theory of the firm, points out that most psychological theories assume that instead of maximising, rational men normally satisfice. Applying this to the business decisions of the firm, he suggests that instead of maximising profits, firms aim at satisficing, that is, want to achieve satisfactory level or rate of profit. Simon has further postulated that a firm has normally an 'aspiration level'. An aspiration level of a firm is based on its goal as well as its past experience, and in fixing it future uncertainties are duly taken into account. If the actual performance of the firm reveals that a given aspiration level can be easily achieved, it will be revised upward. On the other hand, if it is found that a given aspiration level is difficult to be achieved, it will be lowered. Simon points out that when the actual performance of a firm falls short of an aspiration level, 'search' activity is started to find out the ways of better performance in the future and therefore achieving the aspiration level. But, according to Simon, there is limit to 'searching activities' which a firm will undertake because for searching activities such as obtaining of information firms have to incur cost. And therefore the gain from search activity must be balanced against its cost. That is why if searching activities relatively cost more, aspiration level is adjusted downward to a level which is more likely to be achieved. Since the firm limits its searching activity on account of its cost, it does not maximise profits. Therefore, the firms behave rationally when they aim at 'satisficing' rather than 'maximising'.

According to an other prominent satisficing theory put forward by Cyert and March[12], in these days of large-scale corporate type of business firms, we can no longer consider them as single major decision makers (*i.e.*, the entrepreneur), but instead we should look at them as complex group or complex organisation composed of various individuals whose interests may conflict with each other. Cyert and March call this complex organisation or group as organisational coalition which may include managers, stockholders, workers, customers and so on. They assert that all these different individuals participate in setting the goals of the organisation. Another argument for satisficing behaviour on the part of the corporate managers advanced is that top management serves as trustee of the organisation which has a responsibility not only to shareholders but also to employees, customers, creditors, suppliers etc. Thus, corporate managers pursuing a satisficing goal strike a statesman like balance among the claims of shareholders for dividends and higher share price for the shareholders, the demands of employees for higher wages, the pressures from consumers for lower prices and better quality products.

Thus, the hypothesis of satisficing behaviour implies that instead of maximising profits for owners, corporate managers strive for attaining satisfactory rate of profit. The satisficing model of behaviour of the corporate managers rightly stresses that the problem of decision-making in large firms, especially in oligopoly environment, is quite complex as they have to reconcile the interests of various pressure groups in the organisation. But the major problem with the satisficing hypothesis is that it does not provide a clear definition of satisfactory rate of profits. A number of standards of profits which may be considered as satisfactory may be mentioned. Thus, on the one hand, a satisfactory rate of profit may be that which is high enough to attract outside capital on a sustained basis. On the other hand, the firms may fix their satisfactory rate of profits at a low level so as to prevent the entry of new firms which may offer a strong competition and erode their profits. The satisfactory rate of profits may also be fixed at a low level in order to prevent the government control and regulation. Thus the standard of satisfactory profit may vary a good deal depending on the nature of competition and environment in which a particular firm may find itself. The satisficing model, therefore, does not provide us any general guideline for determination of satisfactory rate of profits for the fixation of output and price.

11. Important works by H.A. Simon, in which he has developed his behavioural theory of the firm are : (1) A Behavioural Model of Rational Choice, *Quarterly Journal of Economics*. Feb. 1955. (2) Theories of Decision Making in Economics and Behavioural Sciences, *American Eonomic Review*. June 1959. (3) *Models of Men*, Wiley, New York, 1957.
12. R.M. Cyert and J.C. March, *A Behavioural Theory of the Firm*, Prentice-Hall, 1963.

Sales Maximization : Baumol's Approach

Prof. Baumol has also challenged the assumption of profit maximization. He has argued that maximisation of sales rather than of profits is the ultimate objective of the firm. He says that the firm tries to promote sales not merely as a means to further its other objectives, namely, operational efficiency and profits, but for businessman "sales have become an end of themselves." He, therefore, thinks that sales maximization is the most valid assumption about the behaviour of the firm. It may be noted that by sales Baumol does not mean the **total quantity of a good sold but the total revenue earned** by producing and selling the product.

Thus sales = total revenue = $P \times Q$ where P stands for price and Q for quantity produced and sold. It is worth noting that Baumol is concerned with managerial behaviour of a corporate firm where there is separation of management from ownership.

Prof. Baumol thinks that empirical evidence for his hypothesis that sales rank ahead of profits as the main object of the oligopolist's concern is quite strong. He says, "Surely it is common experience that when one asks an executive,. "How's business?' he will answer that his sales have been increasing (or decreasing), and talk about profits only as an after-thought, if at all."[13] Thus Prof. Baumol very strongly believes that sales maximisation has become the ultimate objective of the firms and therefore they direct their energies in promoting and maximising sales instead of profits.

Prof. Baumol gives several reasons for maximisation of sales value :

1. Manager's salaries generally depend on fast growth of sales. The managers who show better results in terms of sales growth are rewarded with higher salries revenue.

2. High and rising sales revenue help in raising more capital resources from external sources such as financial institutions.

3. High sales help in distributing and marketing large quantitities of products resulting in economies of scale.

But Prof. Baumol softens his sales maximisation hypothesis by pointing out that in their attempt to promote sales businessmen do not completely disregard cost incurred on output, and profits to be made. He also concedes that there is some conflict between the firm's sales goal and its profit objective. He points out that in the actual word, businessmen usually promote sales subject to the limitation that costs incurred are covered plus a usual rate of return on investment is earned. According to him, "*management is not concerned to obtain profits higher than this. Once this minimum profit level is achieved, sales rather than profits become the overriding goal.*"[14] Thus Prof. Baumol asserts that "the typical oligopolist's objective can usefully be characterized approximately as sales maximization subject to minimum profit constraint. Doubtless this premise overspecifies a rather vague set of attitude but I believe it is not too far from truth. So long as profits are high enough to keep stockholders satisfied and contribute adequately to the financing of company growth, management will bend its efforts to the augmentation of sales revenue rather than to further increase its profits".[15]

It may be objected that maximisation of sales instead of profits means irrational behaviour of the entrepreneur. But Prof. Baumol rightly points out that his hypothesis in no way conflicts with the assumption of rationality. He presents a different conception of rationality which is more scientific. According to him, rationality does not consist in choosing the ends, it only means *pursuing the ends efficiently and consistently*. He says, "People's objectives are whatever they are. Irrationality surely must be defined to consist in decision patterns which make it more difficult to attain one's own ends that are for some reason considered to be right. Unless we are prepared to determine other people's

13. W.J. Baumol, *Business Behaviour, Value and Growth*, pp. 47-48.
14. *Ibid.*, p.49
15. *Ibid.*, p.49

values, or unless they pursue incompatible objectives, *we must class behaviour as rational if it efficiently pursues whatever goals happen to have been chosen*", Thus he thinks that given the sales-maximisation as objective, the entrepreneur will be rational if he works most efficiently and consistently towards maximising his sales.

We shall explain in detail sales maximisation *regarding fixation of price and output and level of advertising expenditure* in a later chapter 30 and graphically represent it. However, it may be noted that given the downward sloping demand curve with a total revenue (*TR*) curve bulging outward, sales maximisation point will be to the right of profit maximisation point (see Fig. 30.1 of Chapter 30). From this we draw the following conclusions :

1. The higher level of output will be produced under sales maximisation than under profit maximisation objective.
2. Given the downward sloping demand curve, the *lower price* will be set under sales maximisation objective than under profit maximisation objective.
3. More advertising expenditure will be incurred under sales maximisation objective so as to boost demand for the project which will increase the sales revenue.

Utility Maximization

Since satisfaction or utility is the ultimate end which an individual aspires to get, some economists have pointed out that entrepreneur-owners and managers of joint stock companies try to maximise their utility rather than money profits. The objective of utility maximisation has been discussed in the context of two types of firms: First, in case of firms owned and managed by the entrepreneur himself, the utility maximization implies that in choosing an output level, *the entrepreneur-owner not only considers the money profits which he will make but also the sacrifice of leisure which he would have to make in doing the necessary activity for producing that level of output.* Second, in case of large firms owned and organised in the form of corporate firms where there exists separation of management from ownership. The utility function of managers or business executives of these corporate companies includes not only the profits which they earn for shareholders but also the promotion of sales, maintaining lavish offices, seeking to have a larger member of staff under their supervision *etc.* In this case manager will maximise his utility by attaining a best combination of profits and other objectives. We discuss below utility maximisation in both these cases.

Utility Maximization by Entrepreneur-Owner. It has been pointed out by some economists as Higgins, Reder and Scitovsky that profit maximisation does not necessarily mean utility or satisfaction maximization. If the entrepreneur is supposed to maximise his utility, then not only the satisfaction which he gets from material goods which are obtained with the money profits earned from putting in entrepreneurial activity or work, but also the satisfaction which he obtains from the leisure at his disposal. The leisure or what Hicks calls 'quiet life' is an essential ingredient of an individual's welfare. But more activity or work put in by the entrepreneur, the less leisure he will be able to enjoy. The preference for leisure must, therefore, be incorporated into the analysis of an entrepreneur who is supposed to maximise his satisfaction or utility.

We now proceed to show that as long as we do not make a special assumption about the entrepreneur's attitude or behaviour regarding work and leisure, maximisation of profits will not ensure maximum utility or satisfaction. Let us draw the entrepreneur's indifference curves between money profits and leisure. In Fig. 22.1 money profits are measured on *Y*-axis and leisure (from left to right) is measured on the *X*-axis. An indifference curve in such a diagram will represent the various combinations of money profits and leisure which will give the entrepreneur equal amount of satisfaction. The higher the level of such an indifference curve, the greater the level of entrepreneur's satisfaction or utility.

We further assume that *entrepreneurial activity (i.e., work) is a variable factor, that is, we assume entrepreneurship to be divisible* but whose quantity per unit of output is fixed. In this way, we can measure entrepreneurial activity in terms of output. The greater the amount of output produced, the greater the amount of entrepreneurial activity done to earn net money profits. More entrepreneurial activity and therefore more output means less leisure. Point *W* in Fig. 22.1 represents zero output which means that entrepreneur does not put in any activity and spends his whole time in enjoying leisure. In other words, *OW* represents total leisure or entrepreneurial inactivity. At *W* he does not work at all and therefore produces zero output with the result that he spends whole of his time in leisure. When he puts in some entrepreneurial activity, he will produce some output and will earn some net profits. These net profits are the difference between his total revenue and total costs and in these total costs are also included his own wages of routine management *(i.e.,* normal profits). In Fig. 22.1 net profit curve *PC* starting from *W* is drawn which shows the net profits made by the entrepreneur by producing various levels of output or, in other words, by putting in various amounts of entrepreneurial activity which is measured from left to right from point *W*.

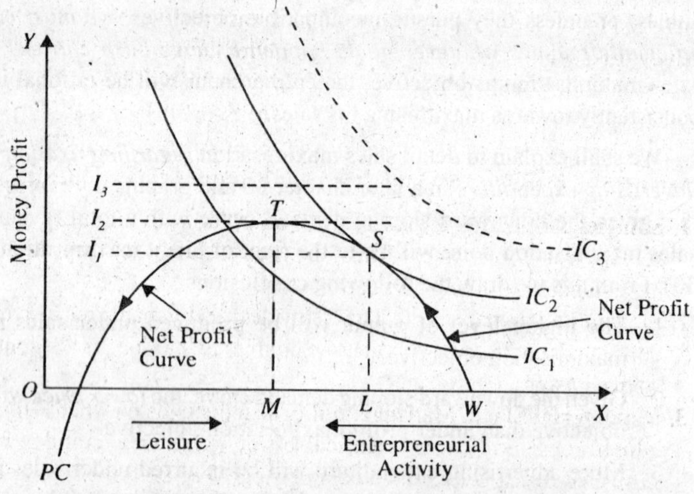

Fig. 22.1. *Utility Maximisation vs. Profit Maximisation*

Now, the entrepreneur who wants to maximize his satisfaction or utility would try to reach the highest possible indifference curve. He would get maximum possible satisfaction where his net profit curve is tangent to an indifference curve. It will be seen from the Fig. 22.1 that net profit curve *PC* is tangent to indifference curve IC_2 at point *S*. Therefore, at point *S* he is getting maximum possible utility or satisfaction by putting in *WL* amount of entrepreneurial activity. In this maximum utility position, he is getting total net money profits equal to *LS* and *OL* is the amount of leisure which he will be enjoying. It should be noted that at point *S* where his utility is maximum, his net profits are not maximum. Net profits are maximum when he is producing *WM* output or putting in entreprenurial activity equal to *WM* and *MT* is the greatest difference between net profit curve and the *X*-axis, *T* being the highest point of the net profit curve *PC*. It is, therefore, clear that utility-maximizing output which is equal to *WL* is less than profit-maximizing output which is equal to *WM*. We thus see that *when leisure enters into preference function of the entrepreneur he will fix the level of output below the profit-maximizing output level.*

A little reflection will show that maximization of utility or satisfaction can be achieved at point *T*, the profit-maximizing point, only if we assume that instead of convex indifference curves as IC_1, IC_2 in Fig. 22.1, the **entrepreneur has horizontal indifference curves** (*between money profits and leisure*). But horizontal indifference curves between money profits and leisure will mean that it does not make any difference to the entrepreneur's satisfaction whether he has more or less leisure, that is, leisure does not enter into his preference function.

Utility Maximisation by Managers of Corporate Business Firms. According to O.E. Williamson, managers or business executives of large firms are motivated by self-interest and they maximise their own utility function. Willianson argued that managers of large firms have enough discretion to pursue those polices which increase their personal utility.[16] Utility function of managers include their salaries, the number of staff under their control, lavishly furnished offices, *discretional* non-essential investment expenditure. However, the objective of utility maximisation by managers is subject to the constraint that after-tax profits are large enough to pay acceptable dividends to shareholders and also to pay for necessary investment expenditure. According to Willianson,[16] utility maximisation by self-seeking managers of corporate firms depend on the following factors.

1. **Salaries.** The higher the salaries and other forms of monetary compensation which the managers receive from the business firms, the greater the utility they have. The high salaries ensure them high standard of living and high status.
2. **Staff under their control.** The utility desired by managers also depend upon the number of staff under their control. The greater the number of staff under the control of a manager, the higher his status, power and prestige.
3. **Managerial Slack.** Mananger utility also depends on what Williamson calls '*managerial slack*' which consists of non-essentical eapenditure and includes such benefits such as lavishly furnished office, a luxurious company car, free air travel.
4. **The Discretionary Investment Expenditure-** This includes expenditure which manager can spend according to his discrection. This discretionary expenditure is over and above the essential investment expenditure which is necessary for the growth of the firm.

The utility function of the managers of corporate firms and the factors on which it depends can be written as under:

$U = f(S, N, M, I_d)$

U = utility of a manager

S = the salary and other forms of monetary compensation which the managers obtain from the business firms.

N = the number of staff under the control of a manager

M = *management slack* which means the amount of non-essential management perquisites such as lavishly furnished offices, luxurious company cars, large expenses accounts, etc.

I_d = the amount of discretionary investment expenditure by the manager.

Thus the managers maximise the above utility function, that is, the composite utility derived from the above mentioned four factors. However, the objective of utility maximisation by the managers is subject to the constraint that after-tax profits are large enough to pay acceptable dividends to the shareholders and also to pay for economically necessary investments.

Hall and Hitch's Mark-up Pricing Approach : Seeking Normal Profits

Further, reference may also be made to the empirical study made by Oxford economists, Hall and Hitch, who interviewed some thirty-eight entrepreneurs on price policy. From their empirical study Professors Hall and Hitch concluded that the businessmen did not try to maximise profits. They also concluded from their study that businessmen charged prices that cover their average cost of production and they add profit mark-up to this average cost to fix the price of their products. According to this principle, businessmen do not seek abnormal profits, that is, more than conventional profits which are considered as reasonable. Thus the mark-up pricing which Hall and Hitch found in their enquiry, is claimed to be opposed to the principle of profit maximisation. It may however be pointed out that the market situation in which businessmen of Hall and Hitch enquiry were placed was one of monopolistic competition with an admixture of oligopoly elements. In such a market situation, the desire to obtain secure profits in the long run greatly governs the businessmen in charging prices of their products. If they try to earn large economic profits by charging high prices, new firms will

16. Oliver E. Williamson, *The Economics of Discretionary Behaviour: Managerial Objectives in a Theory of the Firm,* Prentice-Hall, 1964.

invade their field. Thus in a market situation where the obstacles for newcomers to enter the field are verv small and as a result the businessmen already in the field fear that new comers will enter the industry they will not seek to maximise economic profits.

It is thus asserted that the practice of mark-up pricing contradicts the hypothesis of profit maximisation. However, it may be noted that a relevant question in this regard is what will determine the profit mark-up on the basis of which price will be fixed. On the face of it, it appears that since in this mark-up pricing principle demand is not taken into account in determining the profit mark-up it cannot possibly lead to the maximisation of profits. However, in our view this profit mark-up is not a fixed magnitude but varies depending on the price elasticity of demand or the intensity of competition in the market. In actual practice, businessmen determine this profit mark-up keeping in view the price elasticity of demand for their product or the intensity of competition from rival products. Empirical studies made in the USA confirm this varying profit mark-up in case of different products. For example, in an empirical study made for pricing by the U.S. Steel Corporation, it was found that profit mark-up or margins fixed in case of steel rails was relatively high because this was the product in which US steel faced little competition. On the other and, profit mark-up fixed in case of stainless steel and tin plates was low because for them competition from aluminium and lumber products were quite strong. We thus see that mark-up principle of price fixation can be consistent with the objective of profit maximisation.

Growth Maximisation

According to another important theory the managers of corporate firms try to **maximise the growth rate of their firms** rather than maximisation of profits. This theory was put forward by the Cambridge economist Robert Marris[17] in 1960s, Prof. Marris also considers the case of market structure in which competition is limited. Besides, he is concerned with the behaviour of the corporate firm where management is separated from ownership so that there is ample scope for managerial discretionary behaviour. Prof. Marris regards the corporate firm as a typically bureaucratic organisation where corporate growth and the security associated with it is a desirable goal. According to him, the goal of the corporate manager is to achieve balanced rate of growth of the firm which requires maximising rate of growth of demand for the products on the one hand and rate of growth of capital supply for increase in investment on the other.

Rationale for Maximising Growth of the Firm. Now, an important question is why managers seek to maximise the balanced growth rate of the firm, that is, why do they jointly maximise the rate of growth of demand for firm's products and the growth rate of capital supply. This is because by doing so they maximise their own utility function and the utility function of their owners. Before Marris, it was generally argued by the management theorists that the goals of the manager and the owner often clash because the utility functions which they try to maximise greatly differ. The utility function which managers seek to maximise include variables such as salaries, status, job security. On the other hand, utility function which owners seek to maximise include variables such as profits, capital supply, size of output, market share and image or reputation in the public.

According to Marris, despite the difference in the variables in the utility functions of managers and owners, the most of the variables included in both of them are positively correlated with a single variable, namely, the growth rate of the firm. Further, according to him, the growth of the firm may be measured by the increase in the level of output, capital supply, sales revenue or market share. However, Marris regards steady balanced growth rate over time as the objective of the managers because most of the variables such as sales, output, capital supply, included in their utility function increase simultaneously so that maximising long-run growth of any variable amounts to maximising long-run growth of others.

---

17. R. Marris, A. Model of Managerial Enterprise, *Quarterly Journal of Economics (1963). Aslo R. Marris, Theory of Managerial Capitalism*, Macmillan, 1964

It is evident from above that Marris thinks that corporate managers would recognise the relationship between the growth of the company with profits being ploughed back into investment for expansion of production capacity on the hand and their own personal goals (such as increased status, power and salary) on the other. Besides, according to Marris, managers try to balance growth against the impact of their decision on profits and dividends. They are expected to be aware of the risk of low dividends lowering share prices which put the firms vulnerable to being taken over by the rival companies. Thus, according to Marris, minimisation of risk requires Prudent approach in deciding about investment and raising of capital. Profs. Nellis and Parker rightly state that there may be trade off between securing profits to pay dividends and taking risk when investing to increase the growth of the firm. At the same time while profits provide the retained earnings to help finance new investment which leads to growth of the firm, excessive company liquidity may attract predators. Cash rich companies attract takeover bids. In Marris's model. This conflict is summarised as management seeking **"optimal dividend-to-profit retention ratio"**.

EQUILIBRIUM OF THE FIRM : MAXIMISING PROFITS

As stated above, *a firm is said to be in equilibrium when it has no tendency either to increase or to contract its output*. Since we are assuming that the firm aims at maximizing its profits, it will, therefore, be in equilibrium when it is making maximum money profits. In order to simplify our analysis we also assume that our firm produces a single product. It is true that a firm in the real world may produce more than one product and our assumption of single product firm may, therefore, be unrealistic. But the assumption of multi-product firm which seems to be more realistic will not, given the assumption of profit maximization, involve any significant modification in the method or results of our analysis. It is to make our analysis simple that we are making the assumption of a single product firm.

It should be noted that in the present chapter we are concerned with the analysis of equilibrium of the firm in general terms. We shall explain the equilibrium of the firm with reference to specific market forms, namely, perfect competition, monopoly, monopolistic competition when we take up their separate detailed study. Here we shall derive general conditions of equilibrium which are valid under all types of market.

There are two ways of explaining how a firm reaches its equilibrium position by maximising profits. In the first method we use the concepts of total cost and total revenue. In the second method, which is generally used in modern economic theory, we use the concepts of marginal revenue and marginal cost to explain firm's maximising behaviour. We explain below the equilibrium of the firm in both these ways.

Firm's Equilibrium: Total Revenue and Total Cost Approach

A firm will go on increasing its output if its profits are thereby increasing. It will fix its output at the level where it is making maximum money profits. The profits is the difference between total revenue (*TR*) and total cost (*TC*). Therefore, a firm will maximise its profits at a level of output where the difference between total revenue and total cost is the largest. Consider Table 22.1 which shows the changes in total revenue and total cost when it raises its output from one to 10 units.

It will be seen from the table that when firm is producing 2 units of output, its total revenue is ₹ 90 and total cost is ₹ 80. This yields profits of ₹ 10. Now when the firm raises its output level to 7 units, its profits go up to ₹ 108. Increase in output beyond 7 units will lower profits, and further if it raises output beyond 8 the losses will accrue to the firm. It is therefore clear that profits are maximum when the firm produces 7 units of output. Thus the firm will be in equilibrium by producing 7 units of output.

TABLE 22.1. Firm's Equilibrium: Maximising Profits

Output *Q*	*Total Revenue* *TR*	*Total Cost* *TC*	*Total Profits* *TR–TC*
1	45	50	–5
2	90	80	+10
3	135	90	+45
4	180	105	+75
5	225	130	+95
6	270	165	+105
7	315	207	+108
8	350	270	+80
9	375	385	–10
10	395	505	–110

Fig. 22.2 portrays what is called break-even chart by businessmen. In this are shown total revenue curve *TR* and total cost curve *TC*. Total revenue curve *TR* starts from the origin which means that when no output is produced the revenue is zero. Total revenue goes on increasing as more output is produced. However, it will be noticed that total cost curve *TC* starts from a point *F* which lies above the origin. In other words, it is assumed that even when there is no production the firm has to incur some costs equal to *OF*. For instance, when the firm has to stop production in the short run, it has to bear the fixed costs. Thus our Fig. 22.2 depicts short-run total revenue and total cost curves of the firm. As a firm starts from zero output and increases its production of the good, in the very initial stages total cost is greater than total revenue and the firm is not making any profits at all. When it is producing *OL* level of output, total revenue just equals total cost and the firm is therefore, making neither profits nor losses, that is, the firm is only breaking even. Thus the point *S* corresponding to *OL* output is called *Brak-Even Point*.

When the firm increases its output beyond *OL*, total revenue becomes larger than total cost and profits begin to accrue to the firm. It will be seen from the figure that profits are rising as the firm increases production to output *OM*, since the distance between the total revenue curve (*TR*) and total cost curve (*TC*) is widening. At *OM* level of output the distance between the *TR* curve and *TC* curve is the greatest and, therefore, the profits will be maximum. Thus the firm will be in equilibrium at the *OM* level of output. The firm will not produce any output larger than *OM* since after it the gap between *TR* and *TC* curves goes on narrowing down and therefore the total profits will be declining. At *OH* level of output *TR* and *TC* curves again intersect each other, which means that total revenue is equal to total cost at output *OH*. Thus point *K* (corresponding to *OH* output) is again a break-even point. Beyond output *OH*, total revenue is less than

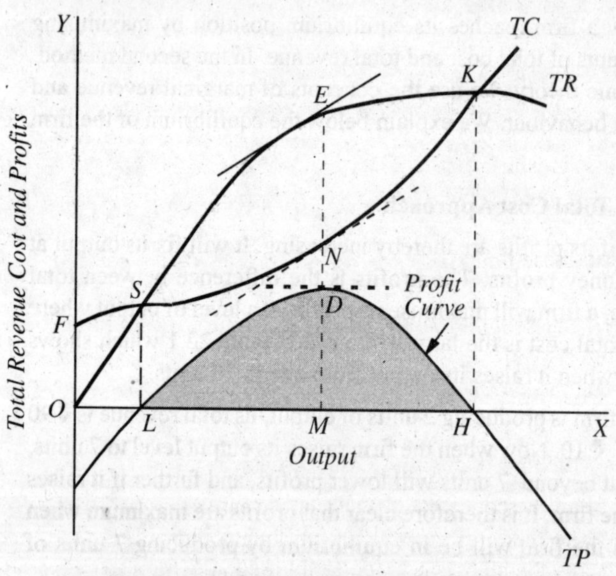

Fig. 22.2. *Profit Maximisation by a Firm*

total cost and the firm will make losses if it produces any output larger than *OH*.

From above it is clear that the firm will be in equilibrium at *OM* level of output where the total revenue exceeds total cost by the largest amount and hence profits are maximum. Now the question is how to locate this profit-maximising output level. By vision it is not easy to locate where exactly is the largest distance between *TR* and *TC* curves. In order to do so we have to draw tangents at the various points on the *TR* and *TC* curves. Where the tangents at the corresponding points on the *TR* and *TC* curves are parallel to each other, as is shown in Fig. 22.2 by tangents at points *E* and *N* on *TR* and *TC* curves respectively, the distance between *TR* and *TC* curves will be the largest and hence profits the maximum.

Another way to find out the profit-maximizing output is to draw directly total profit curve showing the difference between total revenue and total cost at various levels of output. In Fig. 22.2, *TP* is such a total profit curve which indicates the distance between revenue and total total cost at various levels of output. The level of output at which this profit curve stands highest from the *X*-axis will be the profit maximising level of output.

It will be noticed from Fig. 22.2 that total profit curve *TP* lies below the *X*-axis upto point *L* which shows that the firm is making negative profits (*i.e.*, losses) upto *OL* level of output. At *L*, the profit curve cuts the *X*-axis indicating that at output *OL*, the profits are equal to zero. As the firm increases its output beyond *OL*, profits curve is rising which indicates that total revenue and total profits are increasing. At output *OM*, profit curve stands highest from the *X*-axis and beyond *OM* the profit curve slopes downward indicating that total profit are declining when output is raised beyond *OM*. It may also be pointed out that tangent drawn to point *D* on the profit curve (corresponding to output *OM*) will be parallel to the *X*-axis which indicates the greatest distance between the profit curve and the *X*-axis at output *OM*. It follows that at output *OM* the firm will be making maximum profits and hence will be in equilibrium position. The profits earned at *OM* level of output are equal to *NE* or *MD*.

This method of finding out the profit-maximizing level of output by curves of total revenue and total cost seems to be quite reasonable and is also often employed by businessmen too, but it has some limitations. In the first place, the longest vertical distance between total revenue and total cost curves is difficult to find out at a glance. Many tangents have to be drawn before one finds the corresponding tangents to two curves to be parallel to each other indicating the level of output which yields maximum money profits. Of course, when profit curve is also drawn, it is relatively less difficult to locate the maximum profit point, because output corresponding to the highest point of profit curve is profit-maximising output. Secondly in this method, price per unit of output cannot be known at first sight from the diagram since price is not directly shown in the diagram. In order to know the price we have to divide the total revenue at the profit-maximising point by the total output. Thus in Fig. 22.2 at maximum profit output *OM* the total revenue is *ME*. The price charged by the firm will be equal to $\frac{\text{total revenue}}{\text{total output}} = \frac{ME}{OM}$ in Figure 22.2. With these limitations, complicated problems of the equilibrium analysis of the firm cannot be easily discussed with this method of showing equilibrium of the firm. In modern economic theory, marginal analysis involving marginal cost and marginal revenue curves are therefore employed for explaining the equilibrium of the firm. We now turn to explain this alternative method.

Equilibrium of the Firm: Marginal Revenue and Marginal Cost Approach

In an earlier chapter we explained in detail the concepts of marginal revenue and marginal cost. Marginal revenue means the addition made to the total revenue by producing and selling an additional unit of output and marginal cost means the addition made to the total cost by producing an additional unit of output. Now, a firm will go on expanding its level of output so long as an extra unit of output adds more to revenue than to cost, since it will be profitable to do so. The firm will not produce an additional unit of the product which adds more to cost than to revenue because to produce that unit will mean losses. In other words, it will pay the firm to go on producing additional units of output so long as the marginal revenue exceeds marginal cost. The firm will be increasing its total profits by increasing its output to the level at which marginal revenue just equals marginal cost. It will not be profitable for the firm to produce a unit of output for which marginal cost is greater than marginal revenue.

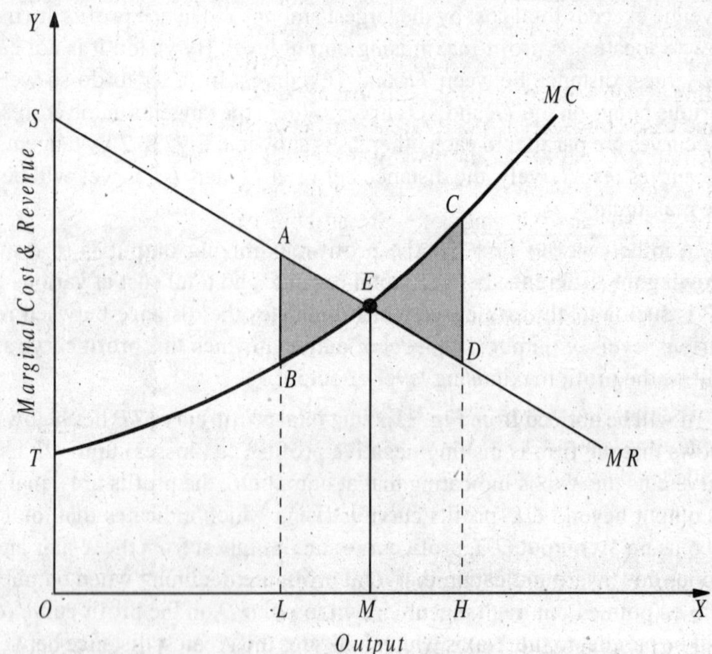

Fig. 22.3. *Equilibrium of the Firm: Profit-Maximising Output*

The firm will be making maximum profits by expanding output to the level where marginal revenue is equal to marginal cost. If it goes beyond the point of equality between marginal revenue and marginal cost, it will be incurring losses on the extra units of output and therefore will be reducing its total profits. Thus, *the firm will be in equilibrium position when it is producing the amount of output at which marginal revenue equals marginal cost.* It will be earning maximum profits at the point of equality between marginal revenue and marginal cost. Therefore, the condition for the equilibrium of the firm is that marginal revenue should be equal to marginal cost or $MR = MC$.

The whole argument can be better understood with the aid of Fig. 22.3 which depicts hypothetical marginal revenue and marginal cost curves of the firm. In this Fig. 22.3 firm's marginal revenue curve *MR* is sloping downward and firm's marginal cost curve *MC* is sloping upward and they intersect each other at point *E* which corresponds to output *OM*. Up to *OM* level of output, marginal revenue exceeds marginal cost and at *OM* the two are just equal to each other. The firm will be maximising its profits by producing *OM* output. The total profits will be less if it produces less than or more than *OM*. For instance, if the firm produces *OL* level of output (which is less than *OM*), its total profits will be less than at *OM*, because by producing *OL* it will be forgoing the opportunity to earn more profits which it can if it raises output to *OM*. This is so because additional units between *L* and *M* add more to revenue than to cost (*i.e.*, their *MR* is greater than *MC*) and it will therefore be profitable for the firm to produce them. The extra units between *L* and *M* can give to the firm extra profits equal to the area *ABE* which it would be forgoing if it produces *OL* output.

It is now clear that at any output level which is smaller than *OM*, the profits will be smaller than at *OM*. Likewise, profits will be smaller if the firm produces more than *OM*. Thus, at the greater output *OH*, profits will be less than at *OM*. This is so because extra units beyond *OM* add more to cost than to revenue (*i.e.*, their marginal cost is greater than their marginal revenue) and therefore the firm will be incurring a loss on these extra units with the result that its total profits will be reduced to that extent. On the units from *M*th to *H*th, the firm will be incurring a loss equal to the area *CDE* and total profits made by producing *OH* output will be equal to area *STE* minus area *CDE*. It is thus clear that total profits at *OH* output will be less than at *OM* output.

To conclude, the firm will be making maximum profits and will therefore be in equilibrium at the level of output at which marginal revenue is equal to marginal cost, or where the marginal revenue and marginal cost curves intersect each other. The amount of total profits earned by the firm in its equilibrium position at *OM* output will be equal to the area *STE*. A point about profits is worth noting. It will be seen from Fig. 22.3 that as output is increased from zero to point *M*, the gap between *MR* and *MC* curves is narrowing down till it disappears to *OM* output. Since gap or distance between *MR* and *MC* indicates the amount of profit earned on the additional unit of output, it means therefore the marginal profit earned on successive units of output goes on declining and is equal to zero at *OM*. Thus at *OM* output, marginal profit on the *M*th unit is zero but total proits will be maximum. It means that by expanding output to *OM* level, the firm has availed of the whole opportunity of making profits and therefore its total profits are maximum at *OM*.

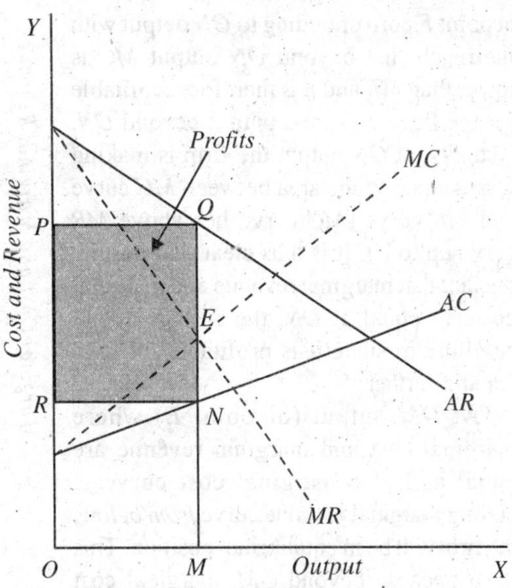

Fig. 22.4. *Equilibrium of the Firm: Equilibrium Ouput, Price and Profits*

In Fig. 22.3 only marginal revenue and marginal cost curves are shown and price cannot be directly read or known from this figure. In order to read price directly from the figure, it is customary to draw corresponding average revenue and average cost curves along with the marginal curves. This is exhibited in Fig. 22.4. The firm is in equilibrium at output *OM* at which marginal revenue and marginal cost curves cut each other. It will be seen from *AR* curve that *OM* output yields *MQ* (=*OP*) as average revenue or, in other words *OM* output can be sold at price *MQ*(=*OP*). Thus, we can directly read the price at which the firm sells its output from this figure. In Fig. 22.4 the total profits made by the firm can also be represented and known in a different way from that of Fig. 22.3.

Total profits = Total Revenue – Total Cost
= *AR* (or Price) × Output – *AC* × Output

In Fig. 22.4 *AR* or price = *MQ*, output = *OM*, average cost or *AC* = *MN*

Total profits = *MQ* × *OM* – *MN* × *OM*
= area *OMQP* – area *OMNR*
= area *RNQP*

Second Order Condition for Equilibrium of the Firm

The first order condition for the equilibrium output of the firm is that its marginal revenue should equal marginal cost. There is a second order condition which must also be fulfilled if the firm is to be in a stable equilibrium position. Thus, *equality between marginal revenue and marginal cost is a necessary but not a sufficient condition of firm's equilibrium. The second order condition requires that for a firm to be in equilibrium marginal cost curve must cut marginal revenue curve from below at the point of equilibrium.* If at point of equality between *MR* and *MC*, the *MC* curve is cutting *MR* curve from above, then beyond this equality point, *MC* would be lower than *MR* and it will be profitable for the firm to expand output beyond this equality point. It is thus clear that the output at which marginal revenue is equal to marginal cost but marginal cost curve is cutting marginal revenue curve from above cannot be a position of equilibrium because the firm will have a tendency to increase its output further in spite of the equality between marginal revenue and marginal cost. For instance, consider Fig. 22.5. Here *MR* curve is a horizontal straight line and *MC* curve is U-shaped and is cutting *MR* curve at two points, *F* and *E*. The firm cannot be in equilibrium at point *F* (or output *ON*) at which *MC* is equal to *MR*. This is because *MC* curve is cutting *MR* curve from above at point *F* corresponding to *ON* output with the result that beyond *ON* output *MC* is lower than *MR* and it is therefore profitable for the firm to expand output beyond *ON*. Actually, at *ON* output the firm is making losses equal to the area between *MC* curve and *MR* curve (*MC* curve lies above *MR* curve up to *F*). It is thus clear that despite the fact that marginal revenue and marginal cost are equal at *ON*, the firm is not in equilibrium since it is profitable for it to expand further.

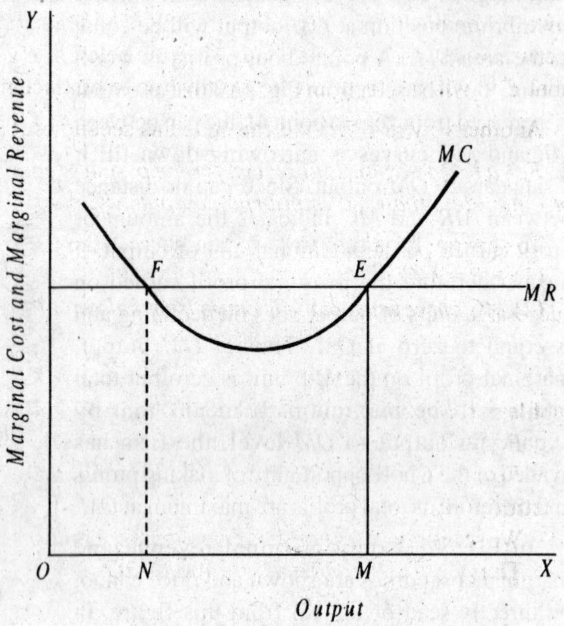

Fig. 22.5. *MC curve mus cut MR curve from below at the point of equilibrium*

At *OM* output (or point *E*) where marginal cost and marginal revenue are equal and also marginal cost curve is cutting marginal revenue curve *from below*, the firm will be in equilibrium position. This is so because beyond *OM*, marginal cost curve lies above marginal revenue curve and therefore it will not be worthwhile to produce more than *OM*. The firm will not stop short of *OM* output, for it can increase its profits by expanding output up to *OM*. To conclude, in Fig. 22.5 the firm is in equilibrium at *OM* output (point *E*) and not at output *ON* (point *F*).

Similarly, point *F* in Fig. 22.6(*a*) cannot be the position of equilibrium though *MC* equals *MR*. This is because at *F*, *MC* curve is cutting *MR* curve from above with the result that *MC* is lower than *MR* after point *F*. The firm will go on expanding output beyond *F* since the additional units will add

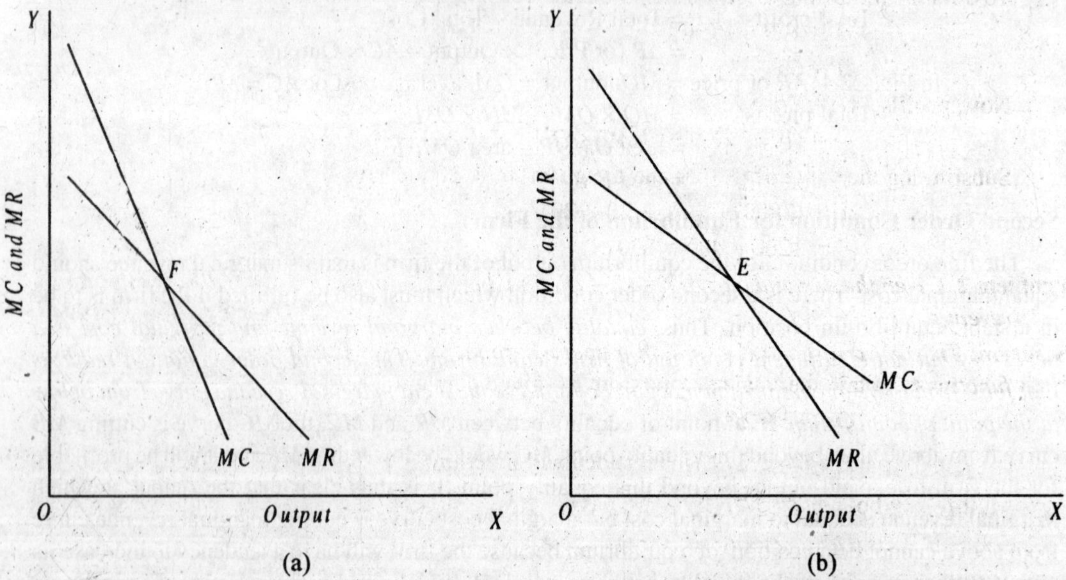

Fig. 22.6 (a) *Firm is not in equilibrium at F*   **Fig. 22.6** *(b) Firm is in equilibrium at E*

more the revenue than to cost. In the situation depicted in Fig. 22.6(a) there is no determinate posit.on of firm's equilibrium. In this figure determinate position of equilibrium can only be established if marginal cost curve begins to rise so that it then cuts MR curve from below at some point. It shoulc, however, be noted that point E in Fig. 22.6(b) denotes position of equilibrium of the firm. This is because MC curve is cutting MR curve from below at E with the result that MC is higher than MR after point E. It will not therefore be worthwhile to produce more output than that indicated by point E.

Another way in which we can state this second order condition of firm's equilibrium is:

For a firm to be in equilibrium, for the output greater than the equilibrium output, $MC > MR$, and for output less than the equilibrium output, $MC < MR$.

To sum up, for a firm to be in equilibrium, the following two conditions must be satisfied.

(1) $MR = MC$;

(2) *MC curve must cut MR curve from below at the point of equilibrium.*

NUMERICAL PROBLEMS

Problem 1. *Suppose a firm is facing the following demand function:*

$P = 100 - 2Q$

Firm's $AC = MC = 20$. Determine the equilibrium levels of firm's output, price and profits.

Solution :

We multiply the given inverse demand function by output (Q) to obtain total revenue (TR). Thus

$$TR = P.Q = 100\,Q - 2Q^2$$

$$MR = \frac{d(TR)}{dQ} = 100 - 4Q$$

Equating MR with MC we have

$$100 - 4Q = 20$$

$$4Q = 100 - 20 = 80$$

$$Q = {}^{80}\!/_{4} = 20 \qquad \text{.... }(i)$$

To obtain equilibrium price we substitute the value of $Q = 20$ in the demand function. Thus

$$P = 100 - 2\,(20)$$

$$P = 60 \qquad \text{...}(ii)$$

Now, profits, $\pi = TR - TC$

$$= (100Q - 2Q^2) - AC \times Q$$

Substituting the value of $Q = 20$ and the given $AC = 20$ we have

$$\pi = (2000 - 800) - (20 \times 20)$$

$$= 1200 - 400 = 800$$

Problem 2. *Given the demand curve $Q = 12 - 2P$, find the output and price that will maximise total revenue.* *D.U. B.A. (Hons.) 1994*

Solution: *TR is maximised at the level of output where $MR = 0$.* We first find the *inverse demand function* to obtain the total revenue from the given demand function.

$$Q = 12 - 2P$$

$$P = 6 - 0.5\,Q \text{ (inverse demand function)} \qquad \text{...}(i)$$

Multiplying both sides of (i) by Q we have

$$TR = P.Q = 6Q - 0.5\,Q^2$$

$$MR = \frac{dTR}{dQ} = 6 - Q$$

Setting *MR* function (*i.e.* the first derivative of total revenue function) equal to zero we have

$$6 - Q = 0$$
$$Q = 6$$

At output level of 6 units, total revenue will be maximum

Substituting the value of $Q = 6$ in (*i*) we have

$$P = 6 - 0.5 \times 6$$
$$= 6 - 3 = 3$$

Thus, Rs. 3 per unit is the revenue-maximising price of the product.

Problem 3. *A firm faces demand curve given by q = 100 – 2P. Marginal and average costs for the firm are constant at ₹ 10 per unit. What output levels should the firm produce to (i) maximise profits and (ii) maximise slaes revenue? What are the respective profits at each output level.*

Solution. The given demand function is $q = 100 - 2P$

We first convert this demand function into inverse demand function. Thus

$$2P = 100 - q$$

$$P = 50 - \frac{1}{2}q \quad \text{... (i)}$$

Total revenue is $P.q = 50q - \frac{1}{2}q^2$ ... (*ii*)

$$MR = \frac{d(P.q)}{dq} = 50 - q \quad \text{... (iii)}$$

$$MC = AC = ₹\ 10$$

Equating *MR* with *MC* to find out profit-maximising output level we have

$$50 - q = 10$$
$$q = 50 - 10 = 40$$

With $q = 40$, price (P) is

$$P = 50 - \frac{1}{2} \cdot 40 = 30$$

(*ii*) **Maximisation of Sales revenue**

Sales revenue is maximised at the output level whose total revenue (*TR*) is maximum. *TR* is maximum at the output level at which $MR = 0$.

Thus, setting *MR* function obtained in (*iii*) equal to zero we have

$$50 - q = 0$$
$$q = 50$$

(*iii*) Profits at profit - maximising output level 40 are :

$$\text{Profits} = TR - TC$$
$$= p.q - AC.q$$
$$= (30 \times 40) - 10(40)$$
$$= 1200 - 400$$
$$= ₹\ 800$$

To obtain profits at sales revenue maximising output level 50 we substitute $q = 50$ in the inverse demand function we have is

$$\text{Profits} = \left(50q - \frac{1}{2}q^2\right) - (AC \times q)$$

$$= \left(50 \times 50 - \frac{1}{2} \times 2500\right) - (10 \times 50)$$

$$= (2500 - 1250) - 500$$

$$= 1250 - 500 = 750$$

QUESTIONS AND PROBLEMS FOR REVIEW

1. Critically examine important objectives of a business firm. Are they consistent with each other?

2. What is meant by profit maximisation? On what grounds it has been criticised by some economists.

3. Critically evaluate profit-maximisation objective of business firms. What arguments would you give in defence of profit maximisation?

4. What is meant by economic profits? Is profit maximisation an appropriate goal for owners of a firm? For managers? What tends to happen if owners are not themselves managers ?

D.U. B.A.(Hons.) 1990

5. Two Oxford economists, Hall and Hitch contended that businessmen do not maximise profits but follow "*mark-up pricing principle*" to obtain only normal profit. Is mark-up pricing principle consistent with profit-maximisation principle? Examine.

6. Given the separation of ownership from control in the modern corporate form of business organisation managers often strive to maximise their utility rather than maximising profits for the owners. Evaluate critically. Also mention the factors that enter into the utility functions of managers.

7. According to Prof. Baumol sales maximisation rather than profit maximisation is the valid objective of business executive today. Examine critically. Is it not irrational on the part of business managers to seek sales maximisation rather than profit maximisation?

8. H.A. Simon, one of the pioneers of the behavioural approach to the theory of the firm, suggests that instead of maximising profits, managers of business firms aim at '*satisficing*'. Discuss and explain what is meant by satisficing.

9. Write short critical notes on the following objectives of firm,

1. Sales maximisation
2. Maximisation of Growth
3. Utility maximisation

10. What is meant by equilibrium of the firm ? Using total revenue-total cost approach explain how firm maximises profits to attain equilibrium.

11. Define firm's equilibrium. Show that equality of marginal revenue with marginal cost is the necessary condition for firm's equilibrium regarding price and output. Illustrate with a diagram.

12. Equality of marginal cost with marginal revenue is necessary but not a sufficient condition of firm's equilibrium.

13. "Profit maximising output is smaller than the sales maximising output". Explain.

14. An author is to receive 10% of the sales revenue of a book as royalty. Would he favour a price which is lower than the one suggested by profit maximising publishers ? Why?

D.U.B.A. (Hons.) 1994

[**Hints:** Author's royalty will be maximum when sales revenue is maximum. The price is lower at the output level where total sales revenue is maximum as compared to that at profit-maximising level of output. Therefore, the author will prefer a lower price].

CHAPTER 23

EQUILIBRIUM OF THE FIRM AND INDUSTRY UNDER PERFECT COMPETITION

MEANING AND CONDITIONS OF PERFECT COMPETITION

In an earlier chapter we made a general analysis of the equilibrium of the firm and its conditions. In this chapter we will study the equilibrium of the firm and industry under conditions of perfect competition. It would be in the fitness of things if we first describe what we mean by perfect competition. Perfect competition, as is generally understood, is said to prevail when the following conditions are found in the market :

1. There are a large number of firms producing and selling a product.
2. The product of all firms is homogeneous.
3. Both the sellers and buyers have perfect information about the prevailing price in the market.
4. Entry into and exit from the industry is free for the firms.

We shall discuss below in detail the above four conditions of perfect competition.

Large Number of Firms

The first condition of perfect competition is that there are a large number of firms in the industry. The position of a single firm in the industry containing numerous firms is just like a drop in the ocean. The existence of a large number of firms producing and selling the product ensures that an individual firm exercises no influence over the price of the product. The output of an individual firm constitutes a very small fraction of the total output of the whole industry so that any increase or decrease in output by an individual firm has a negligible effect on the total supply of product of the industry. As a result, a single firm is not in a position to influence the price of the product by the increasing or reducing its output. The individual firm under perfect competition therefore takes the price of the product as a given datum and adjusts its output to earn maximum profits. In other words, *a firm under perfect competition is price-taker and output-adjuster.*

Homogeneous Products

The second condition of perfect competition is that the products produced by all firms in the industry are fully homogeneous and identical. It means that the products of various firms are indistinguishable from each other; they are perfect substitutes for one another. In other words, cross elasticity between the products of the firms is infinite. In case of homogeneous products, trade marks, patents, special brand labels etc. do not exist since these things make the products differentiated. It should be noted that if there are many firms, but they are producing differentiated products, each one of them will have influence over the price of his own variety of the product. The control over price is completely eliminated only when all *firms are producing homogeneous products.*

But whether or not products are homogeneous should be judged from the viewpoint of the buyers. Products would be homogeneous only when the buyers consider them to be so. Even if the buyers find some imagined differences between the products, the products would not be homogeneous, howsoever physically alike they may be. Anything which makes buyers prefer one seller to another, be it personality, reputation, convenient location, or the tone of his shop, differentiates the product to that degree, since what is bought is really a bundle of utilities of which these things are a part. Therefore, for the products to be homogeneous utilities offered by all sellers to buyers must be identical. If the bundle of utilities offered by all sellers is not the same, then the buyers would have a preference for some sellers who will have a degree of control over their individual prices. Thus the existence of homogeneous products signifies that the products of all sellers are completely identical in the eyes of consumers who therefore do not have any preference for one seller over another. Under such conditions it is evident that "buyers and sellers will be paired in random fashion in a large number of transactions. It will be entirely a matter of chance from which seller a particular buyer makes his purchases, and purchases over a period of time will be distributed among all sellers according to the law of probability. After all this is only another way of saying that the product is homogeneous."[1]

Perfect Information about the Prevailing Price

Another condition for perfect competition to prevail is that both the buyers and sellers are fully aware of the ruling price in the market. Because only when all buyers know fully the current price of the product in the market, sellers cannot charge more than the prevailing price. If any seller tries to charge a higher price than that ruling in the market, then the buyers will shift to some other sellers and buy the good at the ruling price since they know what the ruling price in the market is. Similarly, all sellers are also aware of the prevailing price in the market and no one will charge less price than this.

Free Entry and Exit

Lastly, perfect competition requires that there must be complete freedom for the entry of new firms or the exit of the existing firms from the industry in the long run. There must be no barriers to the entry of firms. Since, in the short run, firms can neither change the size of their plants, nor new firms can enter or old ones can leave the industry, the condition of free entry and free exit therefore applies only to the long-run equilibrium under perfect competition. If the existing firms are making super-normal profits in the short run, then this condition requires that in the long run new firms will enter the industry to compete away the profits. If, on the other hand, firms are making losses in the short run, some of the existing firms will leavc the industry in the long run with the result that the price of the product will go up and the firms left in the industry will be earning at least normal profits.

The Demand Curve of a Product Facing a Perfectly Competitive Firm

The first three conditions ensure that a single price must prevail under perfect competition and the demand curve or average revenue curve faced by an individual firm under perfect competition is perfectly elastic at the ruling price in the market. Perfectly elastic demand curve signifies that the firm does not exercise any control over the price of the product but can sell any amount of the product as it likes at the ruling price. If the firm raises its price slightly above the ruling price, it will lose all its customers to its rivals. Because it can sell as much as it likes at the prevailing price it has no incentive to lower it. Without being able to raise the price and having no incentive to lower it, the firm is content it to accept the ruling price in the market. Once the price in the market is established, a firm accepts as a given datum and adjusts its output at the level which gives it maximum profits. Consider Fig. 23.1. To begin with, demand curve *DD* and supply curve *SS* intersect at point *E* and determine price *OP*. Now, the firm, having no influence over the price, will take the price *OP* as given and therefore average-marginal revenue curve facing it will be a horizontal straight line at the level of *OP*. When the demand increases and as a result the price rises to *OP′*, the firm will now

1. E. H. Chamberlin, *Theory of Monopolistic Competition*, 7th ed., p.8.

confront average-marginal revenue curve at the level of OP'. And if the demand decreases and price falls to OP'' the firm's average-marginal revenue curve will shift below to the level of OP''.

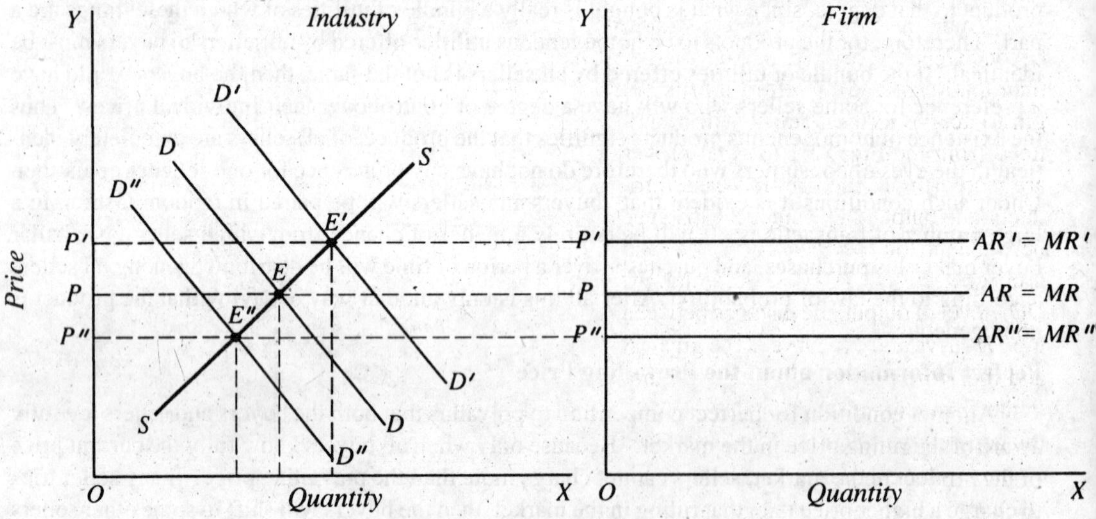

Fig. 23.1 *Demand Curve facing an Individual Firm*

The fourth condition, namely, free entry and free exit, ensures that the firm will make only normal profits in the long run. On the one hand, super-normal profits will disappear by the entry of new firms in the industry and, on the other, losses will disappear as a result of some firms leaving the industry.

PROFIT MAXIMIZATION BY A COMPETITIVE FIRM : TR-TC APPROACH

As seen in the previous chapter there are twc aproaches to explain the equilibrium or profit maximisation by the firm; (*a*) Total-revenue and total cost approach, and (*b*) *MR* and *MC* approach. Though in modern economic analysis, the equilibrium of a firm is usually explained through *MR* & *MC* approach, for some purposes total revenue and total cost approach is highly useful (for example, to show break even level of output). Therefore, we first explain how a perfectly competitive firm maximises its economic profits using total revenue and total cost curves. Since under perfect competition marginal revenue is constant, total revenue curve is an upward-sloping straight line. On the other hand, due to varying returns to the factors used, total cost (*TC*) curve first increases at a decreasing rate and then after a point it increases at an increasing rate.

Equilibrium of a firm working under perfect competititon which aims at profit maximisation is graphically illustrated in Figure 23.1 (*a*) where *TR* represents total revenue curve and *TC* represents total cost curve. Total revenue curve starts from the origin which means that when no output is produced, total revenue is zero. As output is increased total revenue goes on increasing at a constant rate. This is because price for a firm working under perfect competition remains constant whatever its level of output. Consequently, total revenue curve *TR* is a straight line from the origin. However, it will be noticed that the total cost curve *TC* starts from a point *F* which lies above the origin. It means that *OF* is the fixed cost which the firm has to incur even if it stops production in the short run. It will be seen that the short-run total cost curve *TC* initially increases at a decreasing rate and then after a point it increases at an increasing rate. This implies that average total cost curve is roughly of U-shape. Total profits can be measured as the vertical distance between the *TR* and *TC* curves. It will be observed from Fig. 23.1 (*a*) that upto the level of output OQ_B, *TC* curve lies above *TR* curve showing that as the firm raises its output in the initial stages total cost is greater than total revenue and the firm is incurring losses. When the firm produces OQ_B level of output, total revenue just equals total cost and the firm is therefore neither making profits, nor losses. That is, the firm is only breaking even at output level OQ_B. Thus the point B or output level OQ_B is called ***Break-Even Point***.

When the firm increases its output beyond OQ_B total revenue becomes larger than total cost and therefore profits begin to accrue to the firm. It will be noticed from the Fig. 23.1 (*a*) that profits are increasing as the firm increases production to output OQ_M, since the distance between the total revenue curve (*TR*) and total cost curve (*TC*) is widening. At OQ_M level of output, the distance between the *TR* curve and *TC* curve is the greatest and therefore profits will be maximum. If the firm expands output beyond Q_M, the gap between *TR* and *TC* curves goes on narrowing down and therefore the total profits will be declining. It is therefore clear that the firm will be in equilibrium at O_M level of output where total revenue exceeds total cost by the largest amount and hence its profits are maximum.

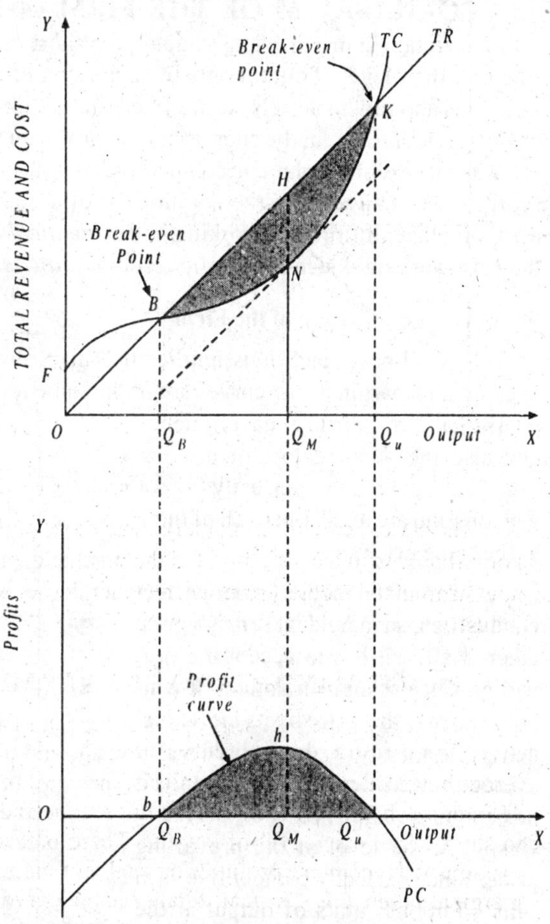

Fig. 23.1(a). *Profit Maximisation under Perfect Competition : TC - TR Approach*

It will be observed from Figure 23.1 (*a*) that at output level Q_U, total revenue is again equal to total cost (*TR* curve cuts *TC* curve at point *K* corresponding to output Q_U). Thus, point *K* is again a break-even point, usually called *upper break-even point*. It may however be noted that this upper break-even point *K* or output level Q_U is not of much relevance as it lies beyond firm's profit maximising level and may actually lie beyond firm's capacity to produce. It is the first break-even point *B* or output level Q_B which is highly significant as a firm will not plan to produce if it cannot sell output equal to at least Q_B at which total revenue just covers total cost of production so that its economic profits are zero.

For a more vivid representation of profit-maximising level of output we have drawn in the lower panel of Figure 23.1 (*a*) the profit curve *PC* which measures the distance between *TR* and *TC* curves. It will be seen from this lower panel of Fig. 23.1 (*a*) that up to output level Q_B profit curve lies below the *X*-axis showing that the firm is making losses if it produces less than Q_B . At output level Q_B the firm's economic profits are zero because at this output level total revenue just covers total cost of production. Therefore, output Q_B *is break-even level of output*. As the firm expands its level of output beyond Q_B, profit curve is rising until it reaches its maximum point corresponding to level of output Q_M. Beyond level of output Q_M, profit curve slopes downward indicating that profits decline beyond output Q_M. Thus, *at output level Q_M, the firm maximises economic profits*. At a higher output level Q_U, profits are gain zero indicating the upper break-even point.

There is a major shortcoming of the *TC* and *TR* approach of analysing firm's equilbrium. It is that in this approach what price will be charged by the firm in its equilibrium position is not directly known. Therefore, in what follows we explain the modern *MC* = *MR* approach to firm's equilibrium.

EQUILIBRIUM OF THE FIRM UNDER PERFECT COMPETITION

As explained in a previous chapter, the short run means a period of time within which the firms can alter their level of output only by increasing or decreasing the amounts of variable factors such as labour and raw materials, while fixed factors like capital equipment, machinery etc. remain unchanged. Moreover, in the short run, new firms can neither enter the industry, nor the existing firms can leave it. Before explaining competitive equilibrium we assume that a firm tries to maximize money profits. We shall explain the equilibrium of a perfectly competitive firm in two stages : first, by assuming that all firms are working under *identical cost conditions* and, secondly, by assuming that they are working under *differential cost conditions*.

Short-run Equilibrium of the Firm

Identical cost conditions implies that all firms are facing same cost-conditions, that is. their average and marginal cost curves are of the same level and shapes. This would be so if the entrepreneurs of all firms are of equal efficiency and also the other factors of production used by them are perfectly homogeneous and are available to all of them at the same prices.

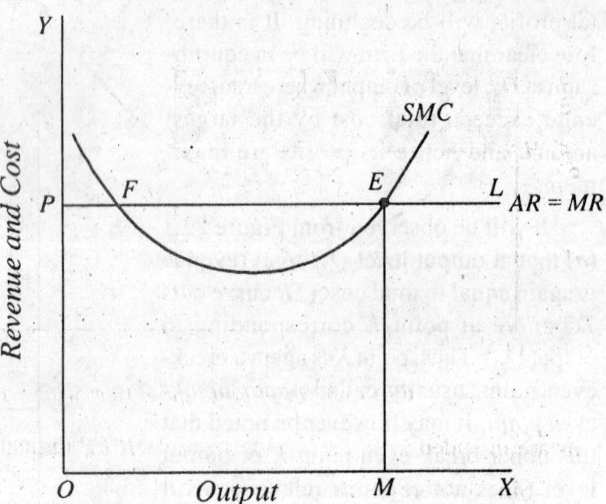

Fig. 23.2. *Firm's Equilibrium under Perfect Competition*

As explained earlier, under perfect competition, an individual firm is a price taker, that is, it has to accept the prevailing price as a given datum. It cannot influence the price by its individual action. As a result, demand curve or average revenue curve of the firm is a horizontal straight line (*i.e.*, perfectly elastic) at the level of the prevailing price. Since perfectly competitive firm sells additional units of output at the same price, marginal revenue curve coincides with average revenue curve. Marginal cost curve, as usual, is U-shaped. Now, in order to decide about its equilibrium output, the firm will compare marginal cost with marginal revenue. It will be in equilibrium at the level of output at which marginal cost equals marginal revenue and marginal cost curve is cutting marginal revenue curve from below. At this level it will be maximising its profits. Since marginal revenue is the same as price (or average revenue) *under perfect competition, the firm will equalise marginal cost with price to attain equilibrium output.*

Consider Fig. 23.2 in which price *OP* is prevailing in the market. *PL* would then be the demand curve or the average and marginal revenue curve of the firm. It will be seen from Fig. 23.2 that marginal cost curve cuts average and marginal revenue curve at two different points, *F* and *E*. *F* cannot be the position of equilibrium, since at *F* second order condition of firm's equilibrium, namely, that marginal cost curve must cut marginal revenue curve from below at the point of equilibrium, is not satisfied. The firm will be increasing its profits by increasing production beyond *F* because marginal revenue is greater than marginal cost. The firm will be in equilibrium at point *E* or output

OM since at *E* marginal cost equals marginal revenue (or price) as well as marginal cost curve is cutting marginal revenue curve from below. As under perfect competition marginal revenue curve is a horizontal straight line, the marginal cost curve must be rising so as to cut the marginal revenue curve from below. Therefore, in case of perfect competition the second order condition of firm's equilibrium requires that marginal cost curve must be rising at the point of equilibrium. Hence the twin conditions of firm's equilibrium under perfect competition are :

(1) *MC* = *MR* = Price

(2) *MC curve must be rising at the point of equilibrium.*

But the fulfillment of the above two conditions does not guarantee that the profits will be earned by the firm. In order to know whether the firm is making profits or losses and how much of them, average cost curve must be introduced in the figure. This has been done in Fig. 23.3 where *SAC* and *SMC* curves are short-run average cost and short-run marginal cost curves respectively. Profit per unit of output is the difference between average revenue (price) and average cost. In Fig. 23.3, at the equilibrium output *OM*, average revenue is equal to *ME*, and average cost is equal to *MF*. Therefore, the profit per unit of output is *EF*, the difference between *ME* and *MF*. The total profits earned by the firm will be equal to *EF* (profit per unit) multiplied by *OM* or *HF* (total output). Thus, the total profits will be equal to the area *HFEP*. Because normal profits are included in average cost, the area *HFEP* indicates super-normal profits.

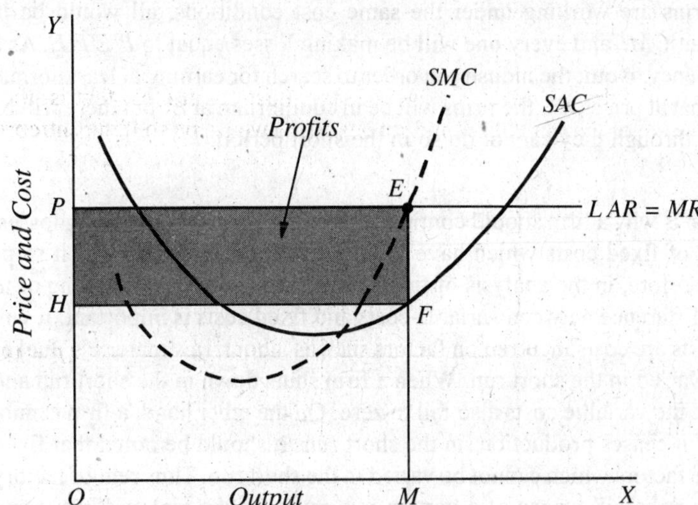

Fig. 23.3. *Short-Run Equilibrium with Profits*

Since we are assuming that all firms in the industry are working under same cost conditions and also for all of them price is *OP*, all will be earning super-normal profits equal to the area *HFEP*. Thus, while all firms in the industry will be in short-run equilibrium, but the industry will not be in equilibrium since there will be a tendency for the new firms to enter the industry to complete away the super-normal profits. But the short run is not a period long enough for the new firms to enter the industry. The existing firms will therefore continue

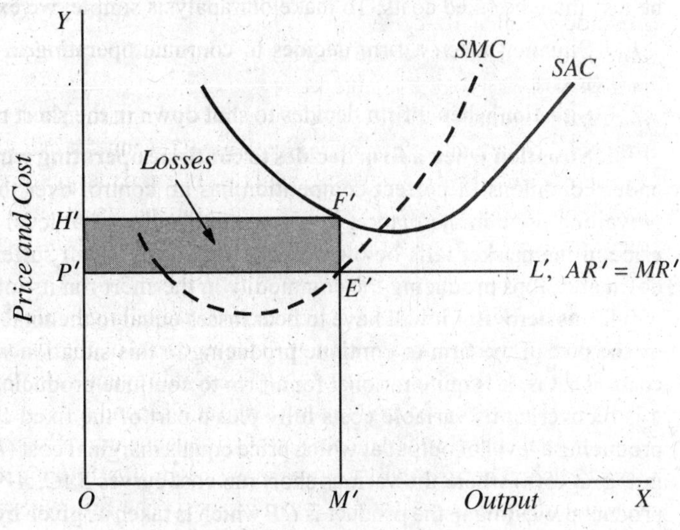

Fig. 23.4. *Short-Run Equilibrium with Losses*

earning super-normal profits equal to *HEFP* in the short period. It is evident that in the situation depicted in Fig. 23.3 all firms will be in equilibrium at *E* and each will be producing *OM* output, but the tendency for the new firms to enter the industry will be present, though they cannot enter during the short period.

Now suppose that the prevailing market price of the product is such that the price line or average and marginal revenue curve lies below average cost curve throughout. This case is illustrated in Fig. 23.4 where the ruling price is *OP'* which is taken as given by the firm. *P' L'* is the price line which lies below *AC* curve at all levels of output. The firm will be in equilibrium at point *E'* at which marginal cost is equal to price (or marginal revenue) and marginal cost curve is rising. Firm would be producing *OM'* output but would be making losses, since average revenue (or price) which is equal to *M'E'* is less than average cost which is equal to *M'F'*. The loss per unit of output is equal to *E'F'* and total loss will be equal to *P'E'F'H'* which is the minimum loss that a firm can make under the given price-cost situation. Since all the firms are working under the same cost conditions, all would be in equilibrium at point *E'* or output *OM'* and every one will be making losses equal to *P'E'F'H*. As a result, the firms will have a tendency to quit the industry in order to search for earning at least normal profits elsewhere. We thus see that at price *OP'* the firms will be in equilibrium at *E'* but there will be a tendency for firms to leave it through they cannot do so in the short period.

Deciding to Shut Down

Now, an important question is why a firm should continue operating when it is incurring losses. The answer lies in the concept of fixed costs which have to be borne by the firm even if it stops production in the short run. Therefore, in the analysis of firm's decision to continue operating or to shut down in the short run, the difference between variable costs and fixed costs is important. It will be remembered that variable costs are costs incurred on factors such as labour, raw materials, fuel or electricity which can be easily varied in the short run. When a firm shuts down in the short run and stops producing the commodity, the variable costs also fall to zero. On the other hand, a firm cannot escape from fixed costs even if it ceases production in the short run. It should be noted that fixed costs are costs incurred on those factors which cannot be varied in the short run. Thus rent of factory building, costs on machinery purchased, wages of a certain minimum managerial staff are some examples of fixed costs. *When a firm stops production, that is, shuts down in the short run, it will have to bear losses equal to the fixed costs.* Therefore, it will be wise to continue operating in the short run when firm's total revenue exceeds total fixed costs because in that case firm's losses will be less than the fixed costs. To make our analysis simple, we examine the question in two parts.

1. Situation when a firm decides to continue operating in the short run even when incurring losses.
2. Situation when a firm decides to shut down in the short run.

1. Situation when a firm decides to continue operating when incurring losses. A firm working under conditions of perfect competition has no control over the price of the product. It takes the prevailing price in the market as given and decides what level of output it should produce. When price in the market falls below average total cost, it will suffer losses. To avoid losses if it shuts down and stops producing the commodity in the short run its total revenue as well as variable costs will fall to zero. But it will have to bear losses equal to the total fixed costs. Therefore, it is prudent on the part of the firm to continue producing in this situation when losses are less than total fixed costs. That is, it is quite rational for a firm to continue producing the commodity in the short run, if it is recovering its variable costs fully plus a part of the fixed costs. But it will minimise losses by producing a level of output at which price equals marginal cost ($P = MC$). This situation is illustrated in Fig. 23.5(a) where the various short run cost curves *SAC*, *AVC* and *SMC* are shown. Price of the product prevailing in the product is *OP* which is taken as given by the firm. The firm is in equilibrium at point *E* where it produces *OQ* output at which the given price *OP* is equal to marginal cost of production (*SMC*). It will be seen from Fig. 23.5(a) that at the equilibrium output *OQ*, average variable cost is *QL*, which is less than the price *OP* (=*QE*) or Price > *AVC*. This means the firm is recovering variable costs plus a part of the fixed cost. Total revenue (*TR*) earned by producing output *OQ* is equal to the area *OPEQ*, while the total costs are equal to the area *ORTQ*.

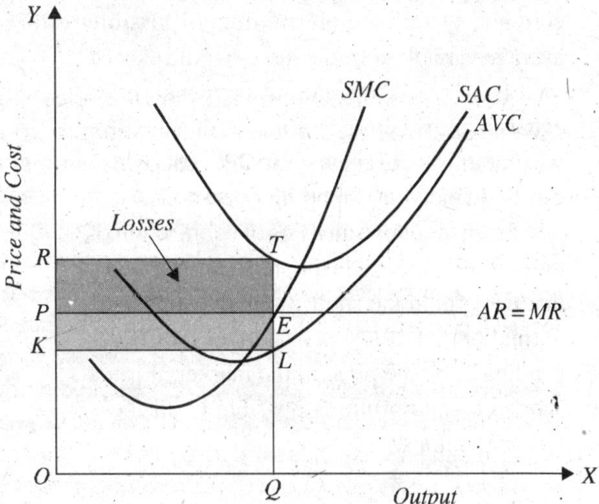

Fig. 23.5(a). *It is rational to operate when losses < TFC*

It is evident from Fig. 23.5(a) that when price is *OP* total revenue is less than the total costs and the firm is making losses equal to the area *RTEP*. It should be noted that average fixed cost at output level *OQ* is given by the vertical distance *TL* between short-run average total cost (*SAC*) and the average variable cost (*AVC*). Multiplying this average fixed cost by output *OQ* (= *KL*) we get the total fixed costs being equal to the area *RTLK*. It is thus clear by working at point *E* and producing output *OQ*, the firm is recovering the entire variable costs equal to the area *OQLK* and a part of the fixed cost equal to the area *KLEP*. Thus losses made equal to the area *RTEP* are less than the total fixed cost equal to the shaded area *RTLK*. If a firm shuts down in the short run and ceases to produce the product, its losses will be equal to the total fixed cost *RTLK*. It will therefore be a rational decision on the part of the firm to continue operating as shutting down in this situation will mean greater losses equal to the entire total fixed cost.

To conclude, *the firm will continue operating in the short run at a loss when total revenue exceeds total variable costs. This enables the firm to earn revenue to recover a part of the fixed costs*. We state below the condition when it is rational for the firm to continue production in the short run even when it is incurring losses:

$$TR > TVC$$

Since $\quad TR = P.Q, \text{ and } \quad TVC = AVC.Q$

Therefore, $\quad P.Q > AVC.Q$

$$P > AVC$$

2. Situation when a firm decides to shut down in the short run. This situation is depicted in Fig. 23.5(b) where it will be seen that price has fallen to the level OP_1. With price OP_1, equilibrium is attained at point *D* corresponding to output OQ_1 at which price is equal to both marginal cost (*MC*) and minimum average variable cost. By producing OQ_1 output and selling it at price OP_1, the firm earns total revenue equal to the area OQ_1DP_1. The total cost of producing OQ_1 output is equal to the area OQ_1HB. Thus with price OP_1 the firm is incurring losses equal to the area P_1DHB. It should be noted that average fixed cost is *DH* at OQ_1 output, that is, the vertical distance between *SAC* and *AVC*. The total fixed cost is then given by the area P_1DHB. Thus when price falls to OP_1, firm's losses are equal to the total fixed cost. Even when the firm closes down, its losses will be equal to the total fixed cost. Therefore, if price falls below OP_1 which is equal to the minimum possible average variable cost (*AVC*), the losses will become greater than the fixed costs and the firm will shut down. Point *D* which indicates the minimum possible average variable cost represents the *shut-down point*. The situation when firm actually shuts down when price falls below average variable cost is explained below.

3. Situation when firm actually shut down and does not operate. When price of the commodity falls below minimum possible average variable cost, the losses would exceed total fixed cost at the output for which price equals marginal cost. This means that the firm will not fully recover even variable costs which can be avoided by stopping operations.

From the above analysis of equilibrium of the competitive firm in the short run, it follows that the firm in the short run may earn super-normal profits or losses or normal profits depending upon the price in the market. Firm's short-run equilibrium is possible in all these three situations.

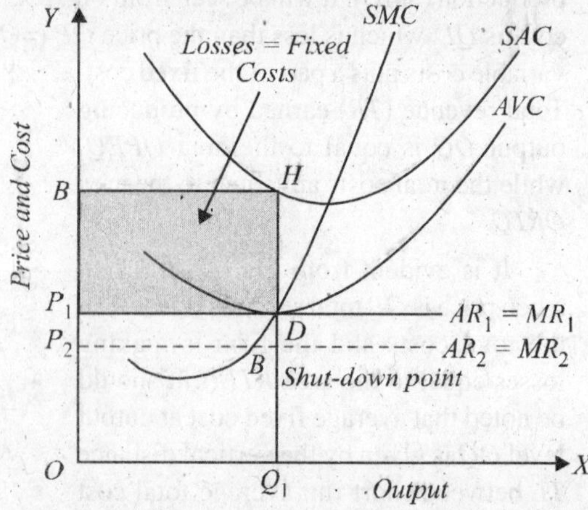

Fig. 23.5(b). *When Price (P) = minimum AVC, losses are equal to total fixed costs. If price falls below it, the firm will shut down.*

Long-run Equilibrium of the Firm under Perfect Competition

The long-run is a period of time which is sufficiently long to allow the firms to make changes in all factors of production. In the long-run, all factors are variable and none fixed. The firms, in the long run, can increase their output by changing their capital equipment; they may expand their old plants or replace the old lower-capacity plants by the new higher-capacity plants or add new plants. Besides, in the long-run, new firms can enter the industry to compete the existing firms. On the contrary, in the long run, the firms can contract their output level by reducing their capital equipment; they may allow a part of the existing capital equipment to wear out without replacement or sell out a part of the capital equipment. Moreover, the firms can leave the industry in the long run. The long-run equilibrium then refers to the situation when free and full adjustment in the capital equipment as well as in the number of firms has been allowed to take place. It is therefore long-run average and marginal cost curve which are relevant for deciding about equilibrium output in the long-run. Moreover, in the long run, it is the average total cost which is of determining importance, since all costs are variable and none fixed.

As explained above, a firm is in equilibrium under perfect competition when marginal cost is equal to price. But for the firm to be in long-run equilibrium, besides marginal cost being equal to price, the price must also be equal to average cost. For, if the price is greater or less than the average cost, there will be tendency for the firms to enter or leave the industry. If the price is greater than the average cost, the firms will earn more than normal profits. These supernormal profits will attract other firms into the industry. With the entry of new firms in the industry, the price of the product will go down as a result of the increase in supply of output and also the cost will go up as a result of more intensive competition for factors of production. The firms will continue entering the industry until the price is equal to average cost so that all firms are earning only normal profits.

On the contrary, if the price is lower than the average cost, the firms would make losses. These losses will induce some of the firms to quit the industry. As a result, the output of the industry will fall which will raise the price. On the other hand, with some firms going out of the industry, cost may go down as a result of fall in the demand for certain specialised factors of production. The firms will continue leaving the industry until the price is equal to average cost so that the firms remaining in the field are making only normal profits. It, therefore, follows that for a perfectly competitive firm to be in long-run equilibrium, the following two conditions must be fulfilled.

1. *Price = Marginal Cost*
2. *Price = Average Cost*

If price is equal to both marginal cost and average cost, then we have a double condition of long-run perfectly competitive equilibrium :

Price = Marginal Cost = Average Cost

But from the relationship between marginal cost and average cost we know that marginal cost is equal to average cost only at the minimum point of the average cost curve. Therefore, the condition for long-run equilibrium of the firm can be written as :

Price = Marginal Cost = Minimum Average Cost

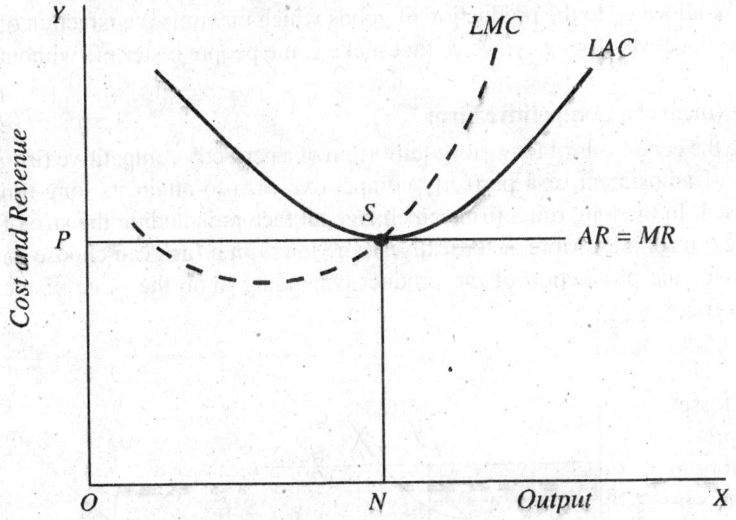

Fig. 23.6. *Long-Run Equilibrium of the Firm*

Fig. 23.6 represents long-run equilibrium of firm under perfect competition. The firm cannot be in the long-run equilibrium at a price greater than *OP* in Fig. 23.6. This is because if price is greater than *OP*, then the price line (demand curve) would lie somewhere above the minimum point of the average cost curve so that marginal cost and price will be equal where the firm is earning abnormal profits. Since there will be tendency for new firms to enter and compete away these abnormal profits, the firm cannot be in long-run equilibrium at any price higher than *OP*. Likewise, the firm cannot be in long-run equilibrium at a price lower than *OP* in Fig. 23.6 under perfect competition. If price is lower than *OP*, the average and marginal revenue curve will lie below the average cost curve so that the marginal cost and price will be equal at the point where the firm is making losses. Therefore, there will be tendency for some of the firms in the industry to go out with the result that price will rise and the firms left in the industry make normal profits. We therefore conclude that the firm can be in long-run equilibrium under perfect competition only when price is at such a level that the horizontal demand curve (that is, *AR* curve) is tangent to the average cost curve so that price equals average cost and firm makes only normal profits.

It should be noted that a horizontal demand curve can be tangent to a U-shaped average cost curve only at the latter's minimum point. Since at the minimum point of the average cost curve the marginal cost and average cost are equal, price in long-run equilibrium is equal to both marginal cost and average cost. In other words, double condition of long-run equilibrium is fulfilled at the minimum point of the average cost curve.

It is clear from above that *long-run equilibrium of the firm under perfect competition is established at the minimum point of the long-run average cost curve.* Working at the minimum point of the long-run average cost curve signifies that the firm is producing with the plant of optimum scale, that is, with lowest possible level of short-run average cost curve. Besides, the perfectly competitive firm will be producing at the minimum point of the long-run average curve *LAC*. In doing so *it is enjoying all possible economies of scale,* or in other words, it has exhausted the economies of scale and has no incentive to move to any other point on the long-run average cost curve *LAC*. Working at the minimum point of long-run average cost curve implies that, it is working *at the minimum efficient scale*. The fact that the firm, working under conditions of perfect competition, tends to be working with optimum scale plant and at the minimum point of *LAC* in the long run is beneficial from the social point of view in two ways.

First, by working at the minimum point of long run average cost curve by a perfectly competitive firm means that it works with utmost technical efficiency and thus resources are being used most efficiently. Secondly, since at the minimum point of long-run average cost curve marginal cost equals average cost this ensures price is also equal to marginal cost (Price = *MC*). We will explain later that producing output at which price equals marginal cost ensures *allocative efficiency*. Allocative efficiency means the resources are allocated to the production of goods which maximise satisfaction of the people. Having achieved allocative efficiency, we cannot make some people better off without making some others worse off.

Long-Run Equilibrium Adjustment of a Competitive Firm

We have explained above the conditions of long-run equilibrium of a perfectly competitive firm. In what follows the process of adjustment of a perfectly competitive firm to attain its long-run equilibrium position is analysed. In the long run a firm can change all factors including the size of plant by installing more or new machines. More specifically, in the long run a firm can choose an appropriate size of the plant for the production of the product depending upon the price of the product and the long-run average and marginal cost of production. In the long run, a firm can even decide to leave the industry to avoid losses or if it thinks it can earn more profits elsewhere. The long-run equilibrium adjustment of competitive firm is illustrated in Fig. 23.7.

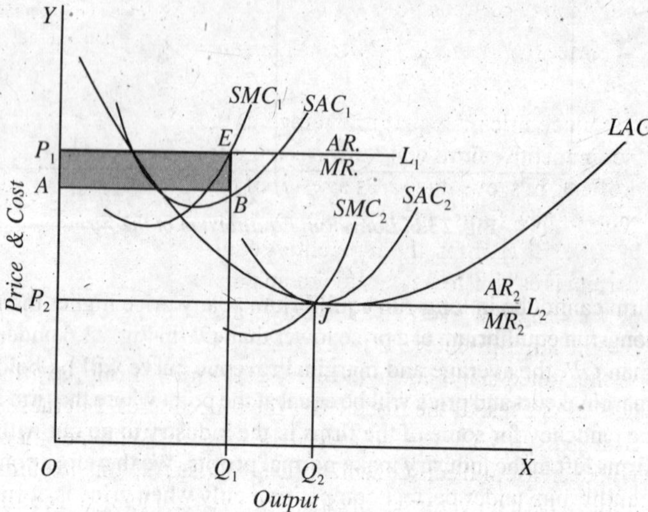

Fig. 23.7. *Long-run Adjustment of a Competitive Firm*

As in the short run, in the long run also a competitive firm faces a perfectly elastic (horizontal) demand curve as being incapable of influencing the price, it takes the market price as given. In Fig. 23.7, the price of the product in the market, to begin with, is equal to OP_1 and therefore the demand curve facing the firm is P_1L_1. Suppose the firm is working with a plant of the size having short-run average cost curve, SAC_1 with its short run marginal cost curve SMC_1. With P_1L as the demand curve, the firm will maximise its profits in the short run by producing level of output equal to OQ_1 where its *SMC* = Price OP_1. With this short-run equilibrium output OQ_1, the firm is making positive economic profits equal to the area of the rectangle $ABEP_1$. (Note that *EB* is the difference between *AR* and *AC* and therefore represents profit per unit). Though the firm is making positive economic profits in the short run by producing output OQ_1, this does not represent its long-run equilibrium position. This is because the firm can increase its profits by expanding the size of plant and other associated factors. The decision regarding which plant size to employ and what level of output to produce with it is governed by the long-run average and marginal cost curves. The long-run average cost curve is also U-shaped which shows that as the firm expands the size of its plant and output there are economies of scale up to an output level OQ_2 and beyond this the diseconomies of scale occur. As long as the firm is earning economic profits and economies of scale exist, the firm will expand its scale.

It will be seen from Figure 23.7 that if firm can reduce reduce its average cost of production by expanding output to the the level OQ_2 and and installing a plant of scale whose short-run average cost curve is SAC_2. Thus, the firm will tend to shift to SAC_2 and produce output OQ_2. However, at the same time lured by the economic profits made by the existing firms, new firms having same costs as the existing firm will enter the industry which will cause the supply of output to increase. Thus supply of output of the product increases in two ways: First, the existing firms expand their size to take advantage of the economies of scale and secondly new firms enter the industry to take advantage of the profit opportunities in the industry.

As a consequence of the expansion of output by all the existing firms and the entry of new firms in the industry, the supply of the product of the industry will increase which will cause a reduction in its price. The entry of new firms will continue and price go on falling under the pressure of more supply until the price falls to OP_2 equal to the level of minimum long-run average cost curve. It will be seen from Fig. 23. 7 that with price OP_2, the competitive firm will be in equilibrium by producing output equal to OQ_2 where the following conditions hold good:

Price $(OP_2) = LMC = SMC =$ Minimum LAC

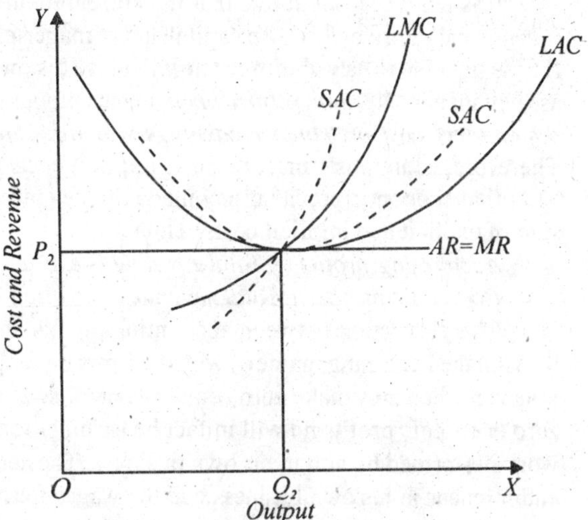

Fig. 23.8. *Long-Run Equilibrium of the Competitive Firm with Zero Economic Profits*

Since price is equal to average cost, the competitive firms will earn no economic profits. Thus, eventually, as a result of the entry of new firms and expansion of scale by the existing firms, the competitive equilibrium is established at the minimum point of the long-run average cost curve and firms charge price equal to it. It may be further noted that if due to the entry of too many firms the price falls below the long-run average cost curve. As a result, the firms will experience losses. But these losses will be only temporary as some firms will go out of the industry in the long run. With the exit of some firms, the supply of the product will decrease and consequently price will rise resulting in elimination of profits or, in other words, can hope to earn only normal profits. The eventual long-run equilibrium of the competitive firm when it makes zero economic profits or in other words, earns only normal profits has been shown in Fig. 23.8.

Zero Economic Profits in the Long Run under Perfect Competition : Economic Profits and Accounting Profits.

We have seen above that firms working under perfect competition earn zero economic profits in the long run. This gives rise to an important question why firms operate under perfect competition in the long run at all when they do not make any economic profits. To solve this puzzle it should be remembered that economic profits have different meaning from the accounting profits as commonly understood. As explained in a previous chapter, while calculating cost and profits accountants generally consider only the *explicit costs* incurred by the firm and ignores its *implicit costs*. Explicit costs refer to the payments made to the other factors hired by a firm such as wages paid to workers employed, rent on the factory building leased in, interest paid on capital borrowed from others and prices paid for raw materials purchased from others. Then the accounting profits is obtained as follows :

Accounting profits = Total revenue – Explicit costs

But while calculating economic profits or what are called pure profits the economists take into account not only explicit costs but also implicit costs. As seen in a previous chapter, implicit costs refer to the money rewards to the factors owned by the entrepreneur which he employs in his own business firm. There are two important examples of implicit costs. First, *the normal return on owned money–capital* which the entrepreneur has invested in his own business. If he invests this money capital in shares and debentures of companies or deposit them in the banks in fixed account he would get some return. Therefore, the normal return on his money-capital elsewhere must be counted as costs for the business firm owned by an entrepreneur. Second, the wages or salary for managerial work of coordination, hiring manpower, supervision and control which an entrepreneur does for his own firm must also be counted as cost. This is because instead of doing his own business he can get employment as a manager in others' firm and gets wages or salary from them.

It is evident from above that the entrepreneur must earn income equal to these implicit costs (*i.e.* normal return on his own capital and managerial services performed by him in his own business. If he is not able to earn this much he will close his own business firm and seek employment elsewhere as a manager. *Normal return on his own money capital and managerial work are in fact his opportunity cost or transfer earnings which he must earn if he has to stay in his own business.* Therefore, economists include these implicit costs as a part of his economic costs of his business. Note that economic profits if any made by the entrepreneur are the excess of total revenue over the sum of explicit and implicit costs. Thus

Accounting profits = Total revenue – explicit costs

Economic profits = Total revenue – (explicit costs + implicit costs)

The distinction between accounting profits and economic profits answers the question raised by us in the beginning, namely, why the firms under perfect competition operate in the industry in the long run when they make zero economic profits. As a matter of fact when the entrepreneur is making zero economic profits he will in fact be earning normal return on his money capital and managerial work performed by him in his own business. The normal rewards for self-owned capital invested by the entrepreneur in his own business and the wages for his management work are generally referred to as *normal profits*. And since these normal profits are implicit costs representing the opportunity costs of the factors, they are included in the cost of production. Therefore, when in the long run under perfect completion price equals average cost of production and therefore the entrepreneur is said to be making zero economic profits, he is in fact earning normal profits, that is, getting normal returns (equal to his transfer earnings) on their owned capital invested by him in his own business and wages for the management tasks done by him in his own firm. It is these normal profits that motivate him to continue operating under perfect competition in the long run.

NUMERICAL PROBLEMS

Q.1. *The following table shows the total cost schedule of a competitive firm. What is total fixed cost of the firm. Using marginal analysis find the profit-maximising level of output if price of the product for the firm is Rs. 8. Calculate the profits at this output level.*

Quantity sold (units)	*TC* (Rs)
0	5
1	7
2	10
3	12
4	15
5	23
6	33
7	40

Solution. Since the firm incurs a cost of Rs. 5 even at zero level of output, the firm's total fixed cost is Rs. 5. In order to determine the profit-maximising level of output (i.e. equilibrium output) we have to first calculate marginal costs at different levels of output. We do so in the following table.

Quantity sold (units)	*TC* (Rs.)	*MC* (Rs.)
0	5	–
1	7	2
2	10	3
3	12	2
4	15	3
5	23	8
6	33	10
7	45	12
8	58	13

To maximise profits the competitive firm will equate price with the marginal cost. It will be seen from the table that at output level of 5 units, price equals marginal cost (Rs. 8). Thus the firm's maximising-profit level of output is 5 units.

$$\text{Profits} = TR - TC = (P.Q) - TC$$
$$= 8 \times 5 - 23 = \text{Rs. } 17$$

Q.2. A competitive firm has the following data

Output, (Q)	*TFC (Rs.)*	*TVC (Rs.)*
0	100	0
1	100	50
2	100	90
3	100	140
4	100	200
5	100	280
6	100	380

(*i*) *If price = Rs. 60, how many units will the firm produce ?*
(*ii*) *What will be level of profits/losses at this level of production ?*
(*iii*) *Will the firm operate in the short run ?* (*iv*) *What happens in the long run ?*

Solution. (*i*) In order to obtain how many units of output, the competitive firm will produce given the price, depends on the marginal cost of production. Note that $MC = \frac{\Delta TVC}{\Delta Q}$ where $\Delta Q = 1$ or, in other words, $MC = TVC_n - TVC_{n-1}$. We calculate below *MC* at different levels of output.

Output (Q)	*TVC (Rs.)*	*ΔMC* $TVC_n - TVC_{n-1}$
0	0	–
1	50	50
2	90	40
3	140	50
4	200	60
5	280	80
6	380	100

In order to be in equilibrium a perfectly competitive firm will produce the number of units of output at which price = *MC*. It will be seen from the above table that price of Rs. 60 equals marginal cost when it is producing 4 units of output.

(*ii*) With 4 units of output total cost = *TVC* + *TFC* = 200 + 100 = 300. Total revenue (*TR*) earned by producing 4 units of output will be $P \times Q = 60 \times 4 = 240$. Since total cost (Rs. 300) exceeds total revenue (Rs. 240), the firm will be incurring losses equal to $300 - 240 = 60$ rupees through it will be minimising losses.

(*iii*) Since at 4 units of output total revenue of Rs. 240 exceeds the total variable cost (200), the firm will continue to operate in the short run.

(*iv*) In the long run, some firm will leave the industry causing price of the product to rise. The firms that remain in the industry must earn zero economic profits, that is, for them price must be equal to the long-run average cost.

EQUILIBRIUM OF THE INDUSTRY

Since the price of a product under perfect competition is determined by the intersection of the demand and supply curves of the product of an industry, we need to know the nature and shape of the supply curve of a product under perfect competition. In our chapters on demand theory we have already explained how the market demand curve for a product is derived and what shape it normally takes. We shall now explain how the supply curve of a product under condition of perfect competition is derived and the shape it takes both in the short run and the long run. Before explaining the derivation of the supply curve, we shall discuss the concept of the equilibrium of the industry under perfect competition. It should be noted that the concept of industry is only relevant in case of perfect competition since only under perfect competition, a large number of firms produce identical or homogeneous product.

An industry is in equilibrium when there is no tendency on the part of the industry to vary its output, that is, neither to expand output and nor to contract it. Now, the essential condition for the absence of any tendency for expansion or contraction of industry output is that the demand for the product of the industry and the supply of it by the industry are in balance that is, in equilibrium. Unless the quantity demanded of the industry's product and the quantity supplied of it are equal, there will always be a tendency for the industry output to vary. If at the given price the quantity demanded of the product exceeds the quantity supplied of it by the industry, price of the product will tend to rise and also the output of the industry will tend to be increased. On the other hand, if at a price the quantity demanded of the product falls short of the quantity supplied of it, the price and output of the industry will tend to fall. Thus, only when the quantity demanded and quantity supplied of the product of the industry demanded and quantity supplied of the product of the industry are equal, there will be no tendency for the industry either to expand its output or to contract it. We therefore conclude that *industry is in equilibrium at the level of output at which the quantity demanded and quantity supplied of its product are equal*, or in other words, at which the demand curve for the product of the industry and the supply curve of it by the industry intersect each other.

Now, the output of the product of an industry can vary in two ways. Firstly, the output of an industry can vary if the existing firms in it vary their output levels. And the firms will have no tendency to vary their output when they are individually in equilibrium by equating market price with marginal cost and are thus maximising their profits. Secondly, the output and therefore the supply of the product of an industry can vary by a change in the number of firms in it; the industry output will increase if new firms enter the industry and the industry output will decline if some of the existing firms leave it.

Thus, given the external conditions regarding demand for the product an industry would be in equilibrium when neither the individual firms have incentive to change their output nor there is any tendency for the new firms to enter the industry or for the existing firms to leave it. Therefore, in addition to the equality of demand and supply of the industry's product, two conditions which must be satisfied if there is to be equilibrium of the industry. First, each and every firm should be in equilibrium. It should be noted here that, according to Marshall, for the equilibrium of the industry each firm in it may not be in equilibrium. To Marshall, equilibrium of the industry meant the equality of demand and supply of the industry's product, nothing more. According to Marshall, given the equilibrium of the industry some firms in it may be growing *i.e.*, expanding their output), some may be declining (*i.e.*, contracting their output), and some others may be holding their outputs constant. It is in this connection that Marshall evolved the concept of representative firm, the firm which was in equilibrium (*i.e.*, holding its output steady) when the industry was in equilibrium. There was a serious shortcoming in Marshall's concept of the equilibrium of the industry in that he did not demonstrate that for the industry to be in equilibrium, the outputs of growing firms are equal to the outputs of the declining firms. In the modern economic theory, Marshall's concept of representative firm has not been adopted and therefore in modern microeconomics, for the industry to be in equilibrium, all firms must also be in equilibrium. This will happen at the output of a firm where marginal cost is equal to marginal revenue and marginal cost curve cuts the marginal revenue curve from below. Second, the number of firms should be in equilibrium, *i.e.*, there should be no tendency for the firms either to move into or out of the industry. This will happen when all the entrepreneurs, *i.e.*, owners of the firms of the industry, are making zero economic profits which means they earn only '*normal profits*', *that is, profits which are just sufficient to induce them to stay in the industry, and when no entrepreneur outside the industry thinks that he could earn at least normal profits if he were to enter it.*

Normal Profits and Equilibrium of the Industry

Thus, the concept of normal profits is important in defining and describing equilibrium of the industry. If we assume that all entrepreneurs in a certain industry have the same opportunity costs, that is, the same transfer earnings if they leave the industry, then there would be a given fixed amount of normal profits for the whole industry. Every entrepreneur must earn at least this fixed amount of normal profits if he is to stay in the industry. If all the firms in the industry are earning profits above normal, there will be incentive for the firms outside the industry to enter it since there is every reason for the entrepreneurs outside the industry to expect that they would be able to earn at least normal profits if they enter. Thus, there will be a tendency for the firms in that industry to increase. If, on the other hand, the firms in the industry are earning profits below normal (*i.e.*, when they are incurring losses), it implies that the firms cannot cover their opportunity costs. Therefore, some of them will leave the industry and search for profits elsewhere. Thus, the number of firms in that industry will tend to diminish. In conclusion, we can say that *equilibrium of the industry or full equilibrium, as it is sometimes called, would be attained when the number of firms in the industry is in equilibrium, (i.e., no movement into or out of the industry) and also all the individual firms in it are in equilibrium, that is, they are equating marginal cost with marginal revenue, and MC curve cuts MR curve* from below.

It should be noted that normal profits of entrepreneur are included in the average cost of production. Therefore, if the price is equal to the average cost of production, it means that the entrepreneur is earning only normal profits.

Short-Run Equilibrium of the Industry

We must distinguish between the *short-run and the long-run equilibrium of the industry.* In the short run only existing firms can make adjustment in their output while the number of firms remains the same, that is, no new firms can enter the industry, nor any existing firms can leave it. Since, in the short run, by definition, the entry or exit of the firms is not permitted, for the short-run equilibrium of the industry, the condition of making only normal profits by the existing firms (or, in other words, the equality of average cost with average revenue) is not required. Thus, the industry is in short-run equilibrium when the short-run demand for and supply of the industry's product are equal and all the firms in it are in equilibrium. In the short-run equilibrium of the industry, though all firms must be in equilibrium, they all may be making supernormal profits or all may be having losses depending upon the demand conditions of the industry's product.

Short-run equilibrium of the industry is illustrated in Fig. 23.9 where in the right hand panel, industry's demand curve *DD* and short-run supply curve *SRS* respectively are shown. These curves

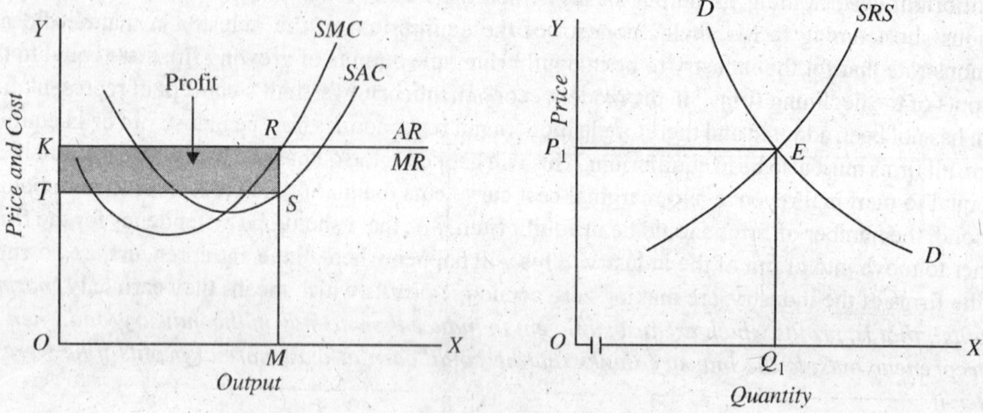

Fig. 23.9. *Short-run Equilibrium of the Industry*

intersect at point *E* and thereby determine the equilibrium price OP_1 and the equilibrium output OQ_1 of the industry. Firms will take price OP_1 as given and will adjust their output at the profit-maximising level. The left hand panel of Figure 23.9 shows that a firm in the industry will be in equilibrium at *OM* output. (It should be noted that the scale on the *X*-axis of the diagrams in the right-hand and left-hand panels are different). With *OM* output, the firm is making super normal profits equal to the area *KRST*. If it is assumed, as is being done here, that all firms in the industry are alike in respect of cost conditions, then all firms like the one shown in Fig. 23.9 (left-hand panel) will be making profits. Thus, while the industry is in short-run equilibrium, that is, the demand and supply of its product are equal and also all the firms in it are in equilibrium; the firms are making supernormal profits.

If the demand conditions for the product of the industry are not so favourable, for instance, if the demand curve of the industry's product is at a much lower position than shown in Figure 23.9, then the intersection of demand and supply curves may take place at the price at which the firms will be having losses in their equilibrium positions. In this case too the industry will be in short-run equilibrium. We, therefore, reach the following two conditions for the short-run equilibrium of the industry under perfect competition.

1. *The short-run demand for and supply of the product of the industry must be equal.*
2. *All the firms in the industry should be in equilibrium whether they are making profits or having losses.*

Long-run Equilibrium of the Industry

If in the short run the firms are making super normal profits, as shown in Panel (a) of Fig. 23.10 at price OP_1, they are in equilibrium by producing output OQ_1 at which they equate the given price OP_1 with their short-run marginal cost curve. The price OP_1 is determined by intersection of demand curve *DD* and short-run supply curve SRS_1 of the industry. In the long run, the existing firms will expand their scale in order to make more profits and lured by profits the new firms will enter the industry. With these two adjustments the short-run supply curve *SRS* of the industry will shift to the right. The short-run supply curve will go on shifting to the right and price of the product will go on falling until all the firms will be in long-run equilibrium at the minimum points of their long-run average cost curves and will therefore be making only normal profits. In the short run, if the existing firms make losses, some of the firms will leave the industry so that the short-run supply curve of the industry will shift to the left and as a result the price of the industry will rise to the level of average cost. Thus, as a consequence of the exit of some firms, the remaining firms come to be in long-run equilibrium where they are earning only normal profits.

The industry is in long-run equilibrium when in addition to the equality of supply of and demand for the industry's product, all firms are in equilibrium and also there is neither a tendency for the new firms to enter the industry, nor for the existing firms to leave it. The long-run equilibrium of the industry is depicted in Fig. 23.10 in which, in the right hand panel, demand and short-run supply curve of the industry are shown which intersect at point R and thereby determine the price OP_1. It

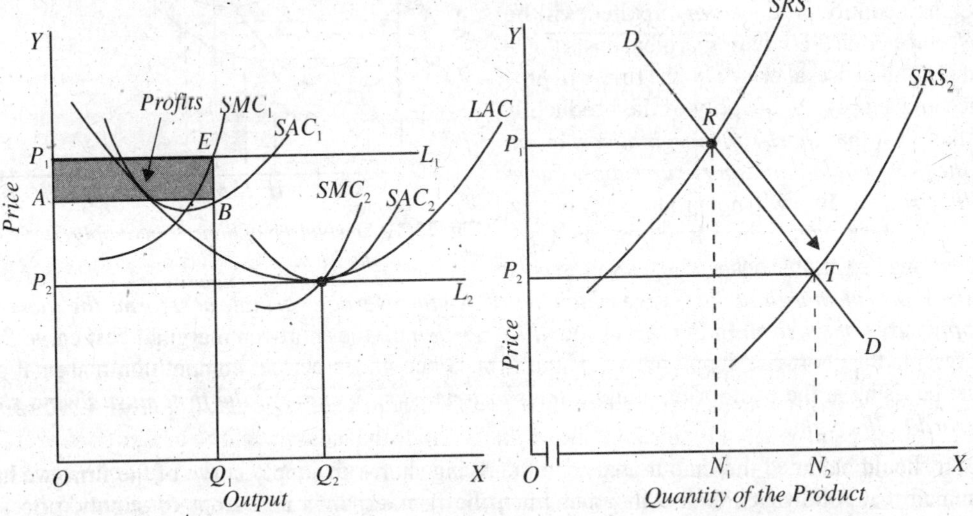

Fig. 23.10. *Long-run Adjustment and Equilibrium of the Perfectly Competitive Industry*

will be seen from left-side panel of Fig. 23.10 that with price OP_1, the firm is in equilibrium at point E and producing OQ_1 output and making supernormal profits. As explained above, with the expansion of scale of production by the existing firms and the entry of new firms in the long run, the short-run supply curve of the industry will continue shifting to the right until it intersects the demand curve DD at point T at which price OP_2 is determined. It will be seen from the left-hand panel of Figure 23.10 that price OP_2 is equal to the minimum long-run average cost curve LAC and the firm is making only normal profits. Since all firms have identical cost conditions, all firms in the industry will be making only normal profits. Under these circumstances, there will be no tendency for the firms to enter or leave the industry. We therefore arrive at the following three conditions for the long-run equilibrium of the industry.

1. *The supply of the product has been fully adjusted to the given demand for the product of the industry and the two are in balance.*

2. *All firms in the industry should be in equilibrium.*

3. *There should be no tendency for the new firms to enter the industry or for the existing firms to leave it. In other words, number of firms should be in equilibrium.* This implies that all firms in the industry will be earning only normal profits in the long run.

SHORT-RUN SUPPLY CURVE OF THE PERFECTLY COMPETITIVE FIRM

As is known, the short-run is a period in which more quantity of the good is produced by working the given capital equipment or plant more intensively by employing more amounts of the variable factors. We have seen above that the firm under perfect competition produces that amount of the good at which marginal cost equals price. Since the price for a perfectly competitive firm is given and constant for it, price line will be a horizontal straight line. The horizontal coordinate of a point on the rising marginal cost curve measures the quantity of the good that the firm will produce at that price. The short-run marginal cost curve of the firm therefore indicates the quantities which the firm will produce in the short run at different prices.

Consider Figure 23.11 at price OP, the firm will produce and offer for sale OM quantity of the good, because at OM quantity of the good, price OP equals marginal cost. Similarly, at price OU the quantity produced or supplied will be ON, since price OU equals marginal cost at output ON. Likewise, at price OS, the firm will produce and supply OL quantity of the product. It is thus clear that *short-run marginal cost curve of the firm is in fact the short-run supply curve of the firm*. The firm will not produce any output at a price below OD, since it will not be fully recovering its variable costs. Thus, *only the part of the short run marginal cost curve which lies above the average variable cost forms the short-run supply curve of the firm*. In Fig. 23.11 the *thick portion* of the short-run marginal cost curve SMC represents the short-run supply curve of the firm. Since under perfect competition marginal cost must be rising at the equilibrium output, *the short-run supply curve of the firm must always slope upward to the right.*

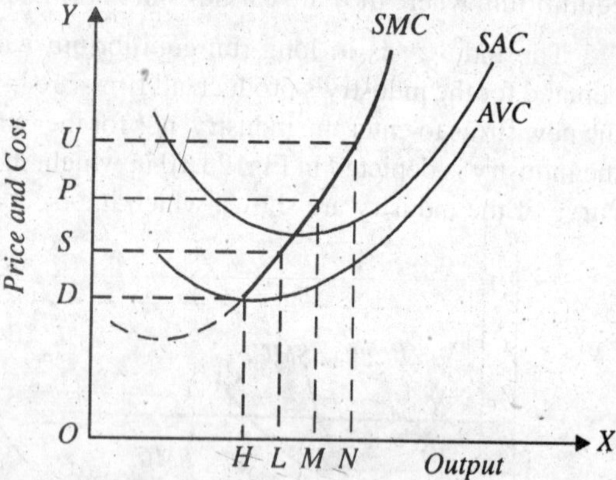

Fig. 23.11. *Derivation of Short-run Supply Curve of the Firm*

It should be noted that in our analysis of deriving short-run supply curve of the firm, we have assumed that following the rise in price when the firm expands its output or supply, prices of resources or inputs it uses for production do not go up. It is a valid assumption because an individual firm under perfect competition is only one among many and its demand for inputs or resources is insignificant part of the total market demand for them and therefore the increase in demand for these resources by the firm as it expands will have no effect on their prices.

SHORT-RUN SUPPLY CURVE OF THE COMPETITIVE INDUSTRY

We now proceed to derive the short-run supply curve of the competitive industry. As the market demand curve is found by the horizontal summation of demand curves of all individual consumers of a product, similarly *the supply curve of the industry is obtained by lateral summation (horizontal addition) of short-run supply curves of all individual firms in the industry*. How the short-run supply curves (short-run marginal cost curves) of the firms are added to obtain the short-run supply curve of the competitive industry is illustrated in Fig. 23.12. Suppose there are 200 firms in the competitive industry. We further assume that all firms are alike in respect of cost of production. In Fig. 23.12(*a*). SMC represents short-run supply curve of an individual firm. At price OP_1, an individual firm will produce and supply OM_1 quantity of the product. Since there are 200 such firms in the industry, the whole industry will produce and supply $200 \times OM_1$ quantity of the product. Therefore, in Fig. 23.12(*b*), $200 \times OM_1$, quantity is plotted against the price OP_1.

ON_1 is equal to $200 \times OM_1$. It should be carefully noted that in Fig. 23.12(*a*) and (*b*) whill the scale on Y-axis is the same, the scale on X-axis differs very much. The scale on X-axis in Fig. 23.12(*b*), has been compressed very much to accommodate large quantities. At price OP_2 the individual firm will produce and supply OM_2 amount of the good, while the whole industry will supply ON_2 which is equal to $200 \times OM_2$ amount of the product. In the same way, industry will produce and supply $(200 \times OM_3) = ON_3$ output at price OP_3, and $(200 \times OM_4)$ or ON_4 at price OP_4. Likewise, the industry's supply can be determined for all other prices. *The short-run supply curve of the industry will always slope upward*. This is because the short-run marginal cost curves of the firms (*i.e.*, their short-run supply curves) always slope upward above the minimum point of the average variable cost curves. The slope and the elasticity of short-run supply curve of the industry will obviously depend upon the slope and elasticity of the marginal cost curves of individual firms in the industry.

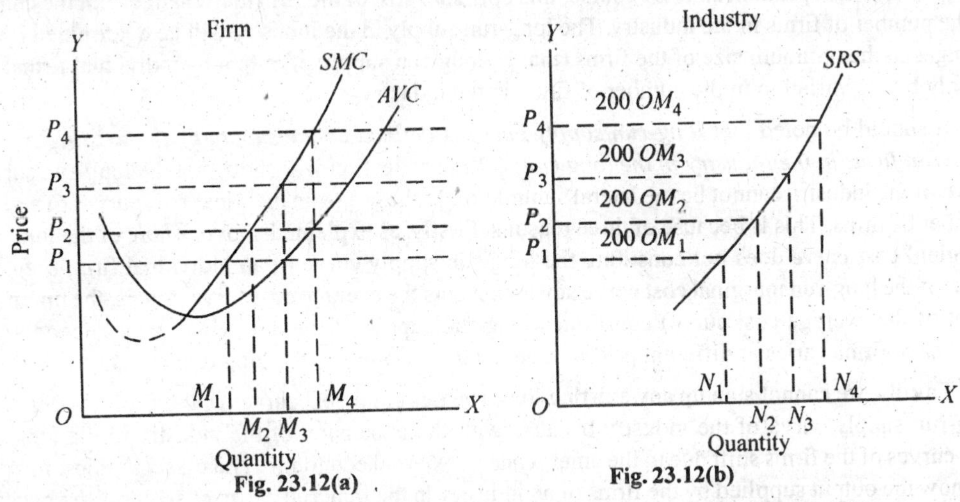

Fig. 23.12(a) **Fig. 23.12(b)**

Derivation of the Short-Run Supply Curve of the Perfectly Competitive Industry

That the short-run supply curve of the industry under perfect competition is a lateral or horizontal summation of the short-run supply curves (*i.e.*, *SMC*) of the firms in it is subject to an important qualification. This is that the simultaneous expansion of output by all the firms in it (*i.e*, the expansion of output by the industry) and therefore the increase in demand for the resources or inputs to be used for production will have no effect on the prices of these resources, that is, for the whole industry these resources or inputs are perfectly elastic. But whereas the expansion or contraction of output of the individual firm and therefore the changes in its demand for resources is not likely to affect their prices, the simultaneous expansion or contraction of all firms in the industry may mean a significant change in the demand for these resources and will therefore affect their prices. If expansion of industry output and therefore the increase in demand for resources raises the prices of these resources, then the cost curves of the individual firms will shift upward. On the other hand, if the expansion of the industry brings about a fall in the prices of resources, the cost curves of individual firms will shift downward. It may be that prices of some resources may rise and some others may fall with the expansion of the industry. In that case, the shift in the cost curves of the firms will depend upon whether the increase or decrease in resource prices is predominant.

When the cost curves of individual firms shift due to the change in resource prices, then the supply curve of industry cannot be obtained by summing up laterally the short-run supply curves of the firms, because then with every increase in the industry output, cost curves of firms change. In this case, therefore, when external effects are present, that is, when resource prices change with the expansion of industry, the short-run supply curve of the industry can be obtained by summing up the *equilibrium outputs* with different cost curves of all firms at each possible market price of the product.

LONG-RUN SUPPLY CURVE OF THE INDUSTRY UNDER PERFECT COMPETITION

In the long run the firms can change their capital equipment and the other fixed factors and also the number of firms can vary in response to changes in the demand for a commodity. In the long run, when new firms can enter and old ones can leave the industry the firm is in equilibrium at the minimum point of the long-run average cost curve, where the long-run marginal cost curve intersects it. Thus a firm under perfect competition in the long-run equilibrium is forced to produce only at one point of the long-run marginal cost curve at which it cuts the average cost curve. Price in the long run is equal to both long-run marginal cost and minimum average cost. Therefore, the firm in the long run will produce and supply an output indicated by the minimum point of its long-run average cost curve, that is, its optimum size. Of course, this optimum size of the firm may change with the change in the number of firms in the industry. The long-run supply in the industry will be determined by the changes in the optimum size of the firms (that is, long-run supply of output by individual firms) but mainly by the variation in the number of firms in the industry.

It should be noted that *long-run supply curve is defined as the supply by the existing as well potential firms in the industry in the long run.* A little reflection will show that the long-run supply curve of the industry cannot be the lateral summation of the long-run marginal cost curves of a given number of firms. This is because of three reasons. Firstly, as explained above, *whole* of the long-run marginal cost *curve* does not constitute the long-run supply curve of an individual firm, *only one point* of the long-run marginal cost curve at which it cuts the average cost curve (that is, the minimum point of the average cost curve) constitutes long-run supply of the individual firm. Secondly, the number of firms varies at different prices or demand conditions in the long run.

Thirdly, we cannot sum up any existing long-run marginal cost curves of the firms to obtain the long-run supply curve of the industry because with the expansion of the industry in the long run cost curves of the firms shift due to the emergence of external economics and diseconomies. In order to know the output supplied by the firms of an industry in the long run, we need to know the position or level of the cost curves of the firms as well as number of firms in the industry at a given demand and price of the product.

External Economies and Diseconomies and Long-run Supply Curve of an Industry

As we explained in a previous chapter, *external economies and diseconomies are those which are realised by all firms in an industry as a result of the expansion of the industry as a whole.* The creation of external economies by an expanding industry will shift the cost curves of the firms downward. On the other hand, the creation of external diseconomies will shift the cost curves of the firms downward. Whether a given industry will experience upward or downward shift in the cost curves depends upon the *net or combined effect* of the external economies and diseconomies. When with the expansion of an industry the external economies outweight the external diseconomies, so that there are *net external economies* cost curves of the firms will shift downward. On the other hand, if with the expansion of an industry external diseconomies are stronger than the external economies so that there are **net external diseconomies**, cost curves of the firms will shift upward.

In a previous chapter, we mentioned the important examples of external economies which may accrue to the firms of an expanding industry. To repeat in brief, main examples of external economies which an expanding industry may reap are : (*i*) the availability of tools machinery, raw materials *etc*., at lower prices, (*ii*) discovery and diffusion of a superior technical knowledge, and (*iii*) economic use of the waste-products. We explain these below.

With the growth of an industry some raw materials, tools, capital equipment *etc.* may become available because some specialised subsidiary and correlated firms may be set up which produce them on a large scale at lower cost per unit and are therefore in a position to supply them at lower prices. Thus, while explaining the reasons for falling costs in an industry due to external economies. Professor Robert Heilbroner writes: "The source of these changes in cost does not lie within the firm, in the relative efficiency of various factors mixed. Rather they are changes thrust upon the firm–for better or worse—by the interaction of the growing industry of which it is a part and the economy as a whole. A new industry, for example by its very expansion may bring into being satellite firms that provide some of its necessary inputs; and as the main new industry grows, the *satellites also expand and thereby realise economies of scale* that will benefit the main industry itself. The automobile industry was surely an instance of such long-run falling costs (for a long period, at least) resulting from the economies of scale enjoyed by makers of tires, makers of batteries, and other equipment"[3].

Further, as the industry expands, trade journals may appear which help in discovering and spreading technical knowledge. Again, with the growth of an industry some specialised firms may come into existence which work up its waste products. The industry can then sell them at good price. There is every possibility of external economies to be reaped when a young industry grows in a new territory.

On the country, when a well-established and good-sized industry expans further, it may experience **external diseconomies.** *As more firms enter the industry, competition among them may push up the prices of scarce raw materials, skilled labour and other specialised inputs.* Moreover, the additional units of productive inputs being obtained by the industry may be less efficient than the previous ones. All these external diseconomies will raise the average and marginal cost curves of the firms. To quote Professor Heilbrone again, "Industries may also experience long-run rising costs if their expansion pushes them up against factor scarcity of a stubbornly inelastic kind. Extractive industries, for example, may be forced to use progressively less accessible mineral deposits; or agricultural industries may be forced to use progressively less fertile or less-conveniently located land. Such industries would experience a gradual rise in unit costs as their output is increased".[4]

We thus see that external economies and diseconomies play a vital role in shaping the long-run supply of an industry. *Whether a particular industry on expansion will experience the phenomenon of rising costs or falling costs or constant costs will depend upon the net result of external economies and diseconomies.* The long-run supply curve of perfectly competitive industry will therefore have different shapes depending upon whether the industry in question is a (*i*) constant cost industry, (*ii*) increasing cost industry; (*iii*) decreasing cost industry.

It follows from above that at a given price the quantity supplied by an industry in the long run will be determined by the optimum output of a firm in the long run (*i.e.*, output corresponding to minimum long-run average cost) multiplied by the number of firms in the industry at that price. With the change in the price of the product following a change in demand conditions, the number of firms in the industry will change and also the cost curves of the firms will shift on account of the creation of external economies and diseconomies. As a result, the quantity supplied by the industry will change at a new price. *The long-run supply curve of the industry may either be sloping upward or be a horizontal straight line, or be sloping downward depending upon whether the industry in question is increasing cost, constant cost, or decreasing cost.* How the long-run supply curve of a perfectly competitive industry under these three types of cost conditions is obtained is explained in the next chapter.

NUMERICAL PROBLEMS

Problems 1. *Suppose a firm is operating under perfectly competitive conditions in the market in the short run. It faces the following revenue and cost conditions :*

$$TR = 12Q$$

$$TC = 2 + 4Q + Q^2$$

Determine the equilibrium level of output and total profits made.

Solution. Profits are maximised when the firm equates marginal cost (MC) with MR and marginal cost is rising. Thus, in order to obtain the equilibrium output we equate $MC = MR$.

$$TR = 12Q$$

3. Robert L. Heilbrone, *The Economic Problem*, Prentice Hall, 1970, P.512 (italics added)
4. Ibid, p. 512

$$MR = \frac{dTR}{dQ} = 12$$

$$MC = \frac{dTC}{dQ} = 4 + 2Q$$

In equilibrium,

$$MC = MR$$
$$4 + 2Q = 12$$
$$Q = 4$$

Total profits $(\pi) = TR - TC = 12Q - (2 + 4Q + Q^2)$

Substituting $Q = 4$, we have

$$\pi = (12 \times 4) - 2 - (4 \times 4) - 16$$
$$= 48 - 34 = 14$$

Note that in order to ensure the fulfillment of second order condition, we have to test whether *MC* is rising. For this, we take the derivative of *MC*, that is, the second derivative of *TR* function.

$$MC = \frac{dTC}{dQ} = 4 + 2Q$$

Therefore $\frac{d^2TC}{dQ^2} = +2$

The positive sign of the second derivative of *TC* function implies that *MC* is rising.

Problem 2. *Suppose that revenue and total cost of a firm are given by the equations $R = 60Q$ and $C = 10 + 5Q^2$, (Q = output).*

What will be the profit-maximising output and total profit of the firm ?

[*C.U.,B.Com., (H), 1998*]

Solution. We have solved he above example through $MC = MR$ approach. Let us solve this example through *TC* and *TR* approach.

$$\pi = TR - TC$$
$$= 60Q - 10 - 5Q^2 \quad \ldots(i)$$

Profits will be maximum at the level of output at which first derivative of total profit function = 0. Thus,

$$\frac{d\pi}{dQ} = 60 - 10Q = 0$$

$$10Q = 60$$
$$Q = 6$$

For the second order condition to be fulfilled, the second derivative of profit function should be negative. Taking the second derivative of the profit function, we have

$$\frac{d^2\pi}{dQ^2} = -10$$

Thus, the second order condition is satisfied. Substituting $Q = 6$ in the profit function (*i*), we have

$$\pi = 60 \times 6 - 10 - 5(6)^2$$
$$= 360 - 10 - 5 \times 36$$
$$= 360 - 10 - 180 = \text{Rs. } 170$$

Problem 3. *A firm's total variable cost is given by the following :*

$$TVC = 75Q - 10Q^2 + Q^3$$

Will the firm produce the product if price of the product is Rs. 40.

Solution. A firm produces a product if price of the product exceeds its minimum average variable cost,

$$AVC = \frac{TVC}{Q} = \frac{75Q - 10Q^2 + Q^3}{Q}$$

$$= 75 - 10Q + Q^2 \qquad ...(1)$$

AVC is minimised at the output level when

$$\frac{d(AVC)}{dQ} = 0$$

Taking a derivative of AVC we have :

$$\frac{d(AVC)}{dQ} = -10 + 2Q$$

Therefore, AVC will be minimum when

$$-10 + 2Q = 0$$
$$2Q = 10$$
$$Q = \frac{10}{2} = 5$$

Now substituting the value of Q in equation for AVC we have

$$\text{Minimum } AVC = 75 - 10 \times 5 + 25$$
$$= 100 - 50 = 50$$

Thus price of the product is less than the minimum average cost, the firm will therefore not produce the product at price equal to Rs. 40

Problem 4. *Given the following short-run cost function of a firm*

$$TC = 1000 + 10Q^2$$

What is the firm's shut-down point ? Derive the expression for firm's short-run supply curve.

Solution. A firm's short-run supply curve is firm's short-run marginal cost curve. To obtain marginal cost function we have to obtain the derivative of total cost function. Thus

$$MC = \frac{dTC}{dQ} = 2 \times 10Q = 20Q.$$

To get the short-run supply curve of a firm we set price equal to marginal cost. Thus

$$P = 20Q$$

or

$$Q = \frac{P}{20} \qquad ...(1)$$

The supply curve of a firm is that portion of marginal cost curve that lies above the minimum point of of the average variable cost (AVC) curve. AVC is minimised at the output level where its first derivative equals zero.

$$AVC = \frac{TVC}{Q} = \frac{10Q^2}{Q} = 10Q$$

Setting the first derivative of AVC equal to zero we have

$$\frac{d(10Q)}{dQ} = 0$$

or $$Q = 0$$

Thus, *AVC* is minimised when output (Q) is equal to zero. Thus, the firm's shut-down point is $Q = 0$. It therefore follows that the entire marginal cost function found in (1) above, namely,

$Q = \frac{P}{20}$ or $P = 20Q$ represents the short-run supply curve of the firm.

QUESTIONS AND PROBLEMS FOR REVIEW

1. Explain the various features of a perfectly competitive market. How is price of a commodity determined under it ?
2. What is meant by firm's equilibrium ? Explain the conditions of short-run equilibrium of a firm under perfect competition. Is equality of marginal revenue with marginal cost sufficient condition for equilibrium of the firm ?
3. Can a firm under perfect competition operate in the short run when it is making losses ? If so, under what conditions ?
4. When does a firm working under perfect competition decide to (*a*) shut down in the short-run, (*b*) leave the industry in the long-run.
5. Explain the conditions of long-run equilibrium of a firm operating under conditions of perfect competition. A firm operating under perfect competition tends to be of optimum size. Explain. What is significance of this for the consumer and the community as a whole?
6. "If there is free entry of new firms in the competitive industry, price must fall to the level of minimum long-run average cost." Explain.
7. "In the long-run equilibrium, every firm in a competitive industry earns zero profits. Thus, if the price falls, all of these firms will be unable to stay in business." Examine this statement.
8. A perfectly competitive firm has the following total cost function :

Total output (Units)	*Total cost (Rs)*
0	20
1	30
2	42
3	55
4	69
5	84
6	100
7	117

How much the firm will produce if the price of the product in the market is Rs. 14 per unit? How will it change its output if price rises to Rs. 16 per unit ?

[**Hints** : Under perfect competition *MR* = Price which is given to be equal to Rs. 14 or Rs. 16. For equating this *MR* or Price with *MC*, make the third column in the above table calculating *MC* at various level of output and see at what output level *MC* = *MR*.]

9. (*a*) Explain the concept of supply curve. How is this relevant only under perfect competition ?

(*b*) Derive a short-run supply curve of the firm operating under perfect competition. Explain that short-run supply curve of a firm *always* slopes upward.

10. What is the short-rule supply curve of a competitive firm ? What is its likely shape and why ? *D.U. B.A (Hons) 1988*

11. What is meant by equilibrium of the industry ? How would you derive short-run supply curve of the competitive industry ? Does it always slope upward ?

12. What are external economies and external diseconomies ? Give some examples. What role do they play in determining the long-run supply curve of a competitive industry ?

13. Explain why a firm working under perfect competition is in equilibrium at the level of output at which marginal cost is equal to price and also at which marginal cost is rising.

14. Show for a perfectly competitive firm to be in long-run equilibrium price should not only be equal to marginal cost but must also be equal to long-run average cost of production.

15. Explain under perfect competition how the conditions of firm's long-run equilibrium differ from those of short-run equilibrium.

16. What are external economies and external diseconomies ? Give some examples. What role do they play in determining the long-run supply curve of a competitive industry ?

17. Firms working under perfect competition earn *zero economic profits* in their long-run equilibrium. Why then firms do not quit the industry in the long run ?

18. Tick the right answer. The demand curve for a perfectly competitive firm :
(*a*) is a horizontal straight line (*b*) is downward sloping
(*c*) is perfectly inelastic (*d*) is positively sloping

19. Tick the right answer. Price in equilibrium of a perfectly competitive firm
(a) equals marginal cost (*MC*) of production.
(b) is greater than *MC* (c) is less than *MC*

20. Which ones of the following are correect ? Perfectly competitive firms :
(*a*) are price makers (*b*) are price takers
(*c*) are quantity adjusters, but not price makers
(*d*) do not earn even normal profits in the long run.
[**Hint.** Both (*b*) and (*c*) are correct answers.]

21. Which of the following is *not correct* in case of long-run equilibrium of a firm under perfect competition.
(*a*) occurs where average revenue curve of a firm is tangent to its long-run average total cost curve (*LAC*).
(*b*) occurs when a firm earns zero economic profits.
(*c*) occurs when a firm makes only normal profits in the long run.
(*d*) some firms may suffer losses.
[**Hint.** (*D*) is incorrect because firms leave the industry in the long run if they suffer losses.]

22. Short-run supply curve of a perfectly competitive firm :
(*a*) It is a horizontal straight line (*b*) It always slopes upward
(*c*) It can slope downward
Give reasons for the correct answer.

23. Which is correct in case of long-run supply curve of a perfectly competitive industry :
(*a*) is a lateral summation of the long-run marginal cost curves of the firms
(*b*) always slopes upward
(*c*) is always perfectly elastic (*d*) none of the above

24. Explain whey a perfectly competitive firm has a *horizontal demand curve* ? Does it imply that a firm can sell as much as it likes at the given price ? If so then why does not a perfectly competitive firm expand its output and sales without limit at the current given price ?

25. Show that a competitive firm will continue expanding in the long run when increasing returns to scale are present *D.U., B.A (Hons.) Ist Year 2009*

Appendix to Chapter 23
FIRMS' EQUILIBRIUM OF UNDER PERFECT COMPETITION : DIFFERENTIAL COST CONDITIONS

Short-run Equilibrium of the Competitive Firms : Differential Cost Conditions

We now pass on to explain the short-run equilibrium of perfectively competitive firms when they are working under different cost conditions. Differences in the quality of raw materials used by the various firms, differences in production techniques, differences in efficiency of managers employed by them, differences in the size of plants built by them and differences in the ability of the entrepreneurs themselves account for the differences in costs of the various firms. Some firms may enjoy the advantage of more convenient location, purer raw materials and more skilled managers that are not available to other firms. Under any of these differential conditions, cost curves of various firms will not be identical. We thus see that *most of the cost-differences arise because various factors of production employed by different firms are heterogeneous* and most important and relevant case is the case when different *entrepreneurs themseleves are heterogeneous*, that is, when entrepreneurs of various firms are of different efficiency and ability. More efficient firms employing better resources will have lower cost curves than others. For the sake of convenience we divide the firms having differential cost conditions into three categories *A*, *B* and *C* whose cost curves are shown in Fig. 23.A1 which represents short-run equilibrium of the firms under differential cost conditions.

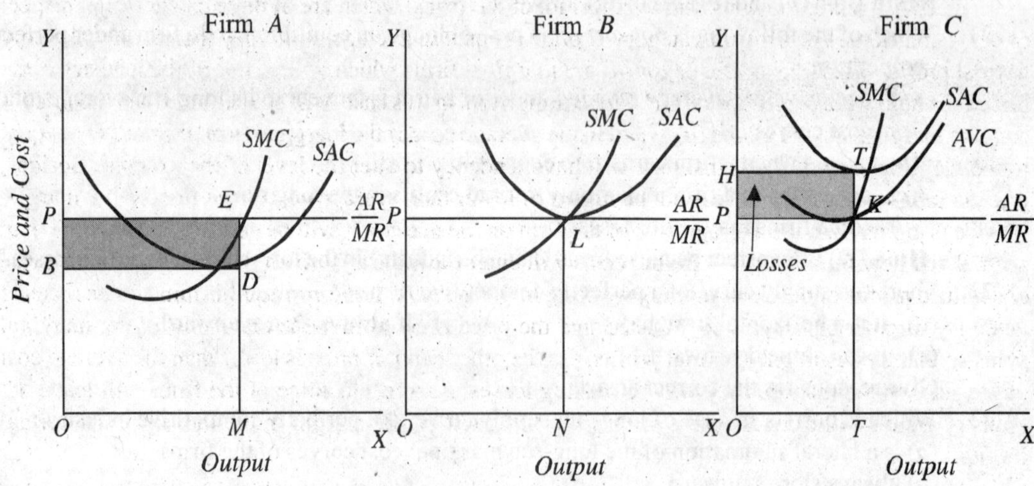

Fig. 23A.1. *Short-run Equilibrium of the Competitive Firms : Differential Cost Conditions*

If price in the market is *OP*, then the firm of every category will adjust output where price *OP* equals its marginal cost. Firm *A* will be in equilibrium at *E* and will be producing *OM* output, firm *B* will be in equilibrium at *L* and will be producing *ON*, firm *C* will be in equilibrium at *K* and will be producing *OT*. While for all the firms, price equals their marginal cost at equilibrium output, but firm *A* is making super-normal profits, *B* is earning only normal profits and *C* is making losses. This is so because cost conditions are different for the three firms. Thus under conditions of different costs and in short-run equilibrium, some firms in the industry may be earning super-normal profits, some may be making only normal profits, and some others may be incurring losses.

Long-run Equilibrium of Firms : Differential Cost Conditions

What would be the long-run equilibrium position of the firms when they are operating under differential cost conditions ? In this connection the concept of marginal firm is relevant. *A marginal firm is one which will be the first to leave the industry if price falls. The marginal firm is the highest-cost firm which earns only normal profits.* Since the marginal firm is the highest-cost firm making only normal profits, it will be the first to quit the industry if the price falls as with the fall in price its profits will sink below normal.

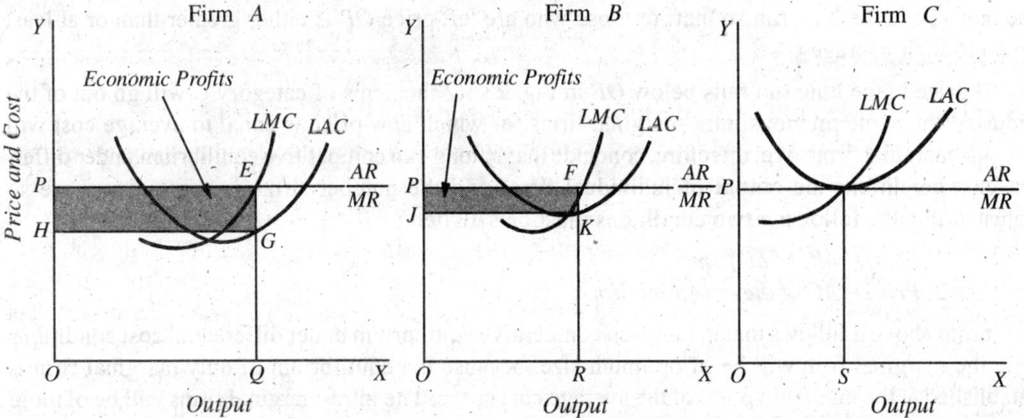

Fig. 23A.2. *Long-Run Equilibrium of the Competitive Firms Under Differential*

Fig. 23A.2 represents long-run equilibrium of the firms, which are of three categories in respect of cost conditions. For firms of category *C* price is equal to average cost, they therefore, make only normal profits. Thus, firms of category *C* are marginal firms which will go out of the industry if the price falls below the present price *OP*. Full equilibrium, in this case, will be realised when the price is equal to marginal cost of all the firms and to the average cost of the marginal firm. If price is not equal to the marginal cost of the firms, they will have tendency to alter the level of their output. Besides, price in long-run equilibrium cannot be higher or lower than average cost of the firm on the margin. If price is higher than the average cost of the firm on the margin, it will be earning profits more than normal and new firms with still higher costs will enter the industry, which will bring down the price and reduce profits of the firms already working in the industry. Long-run equilibrium will be reached when the number of firms is so adjusted that the price is equal to the average cost of the marginal firms so that they earn only normal profits. On the other hand, if price is lower than the average cost of the firm on the margin, they will be making losses. As a result, some of the firms will leave the industry which will raise the price so that the firms left on the margin in the industry earn normal profits.

Fig. 23A.2 represents long-run equilibrium of competitive firms under differential cost conditions. Three categories of firms in respect of the cost are assumed and from each category one firm is shown. The price prevailing in the long run is *OP* which equals marginal cost of firm *A* at output *OQ*, marginal cost of firm *B* at output *OR*, and marginal cost of firm *C* at output *OS*. Besides, price *OP* is equal to average cost of the marginal firm C and therefore it makes only normal profits. But price *OP* is greater than average cost at equilibrium outputs of intra-marginal firms *A* and *B* and therefore they make super-normal profits. Price being equal to the marginal cost of all firms ensures equilibrium of all individual firms including the marginal one. The price being equal to average cost of the marginal firm guarantees that the marginal firm will be making only normal profits and therefore there will be no tendency for new firms to enter or for some of the existing firms to leave the industry. The question now arises: Can the new firms having lower costs than the marginal firm *C* enter the industry at price *OP* and earn profits more than normal ? Our answer is in the negative because firms having lower costs than firms *C* would have already entered and would be working as intra-marginal firms. New firms having higher costs than category *C* will not enter since they will not be able to earn even normal profits. Besides, all firms in the industry incurring losses at price *OP* would have gone out of the industry in the long run so that for those who are left price *OP* is either greater than or at least equal to their average cost.

If price in the long run falls below *OP* in Fig. 23A.2 the firms of category *C* will go out of the industry and some previous intra-marginal firms for which new price is equal to average cost will become marginal firms. We, therefore, conclude that in long-run competitive equilibrium under different cost conditions the output of individual firms and the number firms in the industry are so adjusted that the following two conditions must be satisfied :

1. *Price = MC of all firms* ;
2. *Price = AC of the marginal firm.*

From above it follows that in long-run competitive equilibrium under differential cost conditions only the marginal firm will be of optimum size, because the equilibrium of only marginal firm is established at the minimum point of the average cost curve. The intra-marginal firms will be of more than optimum size as will be seen from Fig. 23A.2.

Differential Cost Conditions and Economic Rent

We have explained above that in long-run competitive equilibrium under differential cost conditions, the marginal firm makes only normal profits, while the intra-marginal firms which have lower costs than the marginal firm will earn profits more than normal. The lower costs of the intra-marginal firms and hence their abnormal profits are due to the fact that the intra-marginal firms employ better or more productive resources than those employed by the marginal firms.

Now, the question arises whether the prices of better or more efficient resources employed by the intra-marginal firms will not be bid up sufficiently high so as to wipe out the differences in costs between the marginal and intra-marginal firms. In fact, this would be so and the prices of the better or more efficient resources will be higher than those of the resources of the marginal firm to the extent of their higher efficiency. Competition among the firms in the long run ensures that differences in costs of the various firms due to differences in the efficiency of the various resources employed will dispapear as a result of bidding up of prices of more efficient resources. For instance, if manager *A* employed by a firm runs the firm at Rs. 12,000 more cheaply per year than can the manager *B* employed by another firm, then manager *A*'s salary will tend to be bid up until it is Rs. 12,000 higher per annum than the salary of manager *B*. If the firm employing manager *A* pays him only Rs. 10,000 more than the manager *B*, it will then be in the interest of the other firms to try to get *A* by offering him to pay Rs. 11,000 more than the manager *B* and it will pay firm employing *A* to try to keep him by offering him Rs. 11,500 more than the manager *B* and so forth until the manager *A* is offered Rs. 12,000 more than the manager *B*. We thus see that the lower costs or super-normal profits of intra-marginal firms made possible by the employment of more efficient resources tend to be paid out to the owners of those resources.

It follows from above that no differential profit advantage can be derived from employing better or more efficient resources, since extra payment equal to the reduction in costs made by them will have to be paid to the owners of those resources. In other words, *entire profits in excess of the normal profits will be extracted by the owners of more efficient resources. The extra payments made to the more efficient resources are over and above their transfer earnings, since their transfer earnings are already included in firms' costs of production. These extra payments made to the more efficient resources over and above their transfer earnings are called rent in economics.* This 'rent' is as much a part of cost of production as any other payment. We, therefore, conclude that differential profit advantage enjoyed by the intra-marginal firms using more efficient resources is wiped out by the extra 'rent' they must pay. If an entrepreneur happens to own the more efficient resources himself, then no actual payment of rent by the entrepreneur would take place. But the rent to more efficient resources will no doubt accrue, though it will be bagged by the entrepreneur himself, since he happens to own them. *Economic rent is defined to be the part of the earnings of a factor which is over and above the minimum amount necessary to retain it in the given industry or occupation.* These excess earnings will accrue to the more efficient units of a factor and will be received by him who happens to own them.

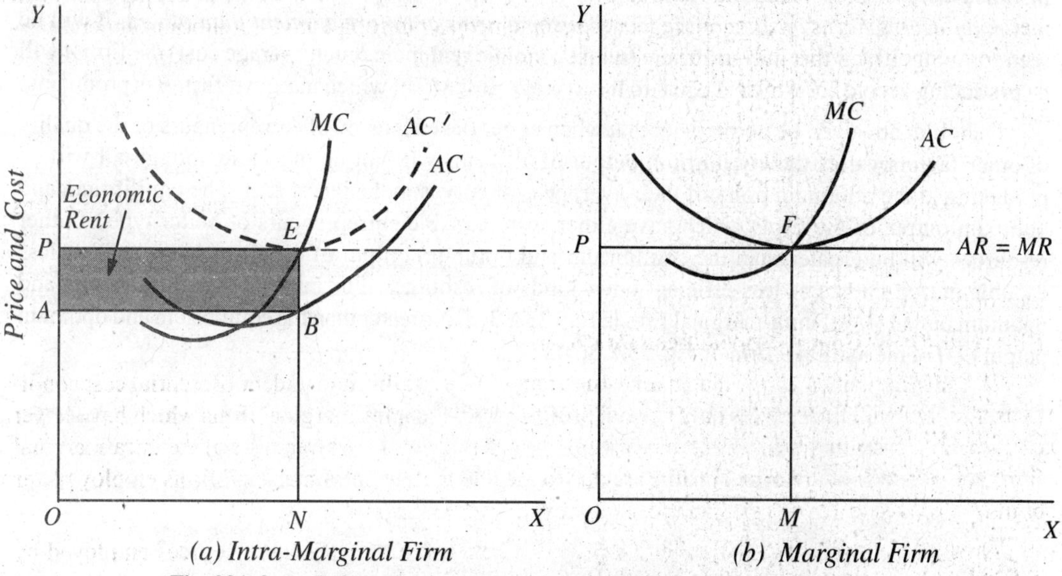

Fig. 23A.3. *Including Economic Rent of More Efficient Factors in Cost*

If the rent earned by the more efficient resources is, therefore, included in costs, then the long-run equilibrium of *all* firms under so called differential cost conditions will be established at the point of minimum average cost. This is illustrated in Fig. 23A.3, Fig. 23.A(*b*) represents the marginal firm and Fig. 23A.3 (*a*) represents an intra-marginal firm. *OP* is the price of the product. The price *OP* is equal to both marginal cost and average cost of the marginal firm. With price *OP*, the intra-marginal firm is in equilibrium at point *E* of the marginal cost. The average cost *AC* in Fig. 23A.3 (*a*) represents the cost of production exclusive of extra rent which has to be paid to the more efficient resources employed by it. The economic rent earned by the more efficient resources is equal to *ABEP*. Now, if this economic rent is included in the average cost, then average cost curve inclusive of rent is represented by *AC*′. By including rent into total cost, we add a fixed amount which is independent of the firm's output (given the price of the product), the marginal cost curve *MC* will therefore cut *AC* as well as *AC*′ at their minimum points. It is therefore clear that the long-run equilibrium of the intra-marginal firms will be fixed at the minimum point of the average cost curve inclusive of rent. Price equals both marginal cost and minimum average cost for all the firms, marginal as well as intra-marginal. In fact, when average cost is understood to be inclusive of rent that has to be paid to the more efficient units of the factors, there is no sense in calling some firms as marginal and some intra-marginal; the level of the average cost curve inclusive of rent will be the same for all firms and all will be making only normal profits.

Now suppose that the differences in the average cost are due to the differences in efficiency of entrepreneurs themselves while all other resources or factors used by the various firms are perfectly homogeneous. Then economic rent of entrepreneurship will accrue to the more efficient entrepreneurs and they will therefore make more than normal profits, while the marginal entrepreneur will make only normal profits. Should then the economic rent of entrepreneurship be included in average cost just as the economic rent earned by the more efficient units of other factors of production are included in average cost. Similarly of the treatment demands that the economic rent of entrepreneurship be also included in average cost. If this is done, then price would be equal to marginal cost and average cost of all firms in long-run competitive equilibrium, even though some entrepreneurs would be more efficient than others. Further, our analysis that when *economic* rent *earned by factors is included in* cost of production, then *every firm in equilibrium must be producing at the same minimum average csot in spite of the fact that some firms are more efficient than others.* It will be seen from Fig. 23A.3 that in equilibrium (with economic rent included in average cost) the firm *A* will be producing at cost *NE* which is equal to the average cost *MF* at which marginal firm *B* is producing.

It should, however, be pointed out that when either the efficiency of entrepreneurs or the quality of other factors varies the equilibrium output of all firms will not be the same, though all will be producing at the minimum point of their average cost curves inclusive of rent. The equilibrium and optimum output of the firms which have either more capable entrepreneurs or better type of other resources will be greater than the equilibrium and optimum output of the firms having either less capable entrepreneurs or less efficient other kinds of resources. For instance, the equilibrium and optimum output *ON* of intra-marginal firm in Fig. 23A.3(*a*) is greater than the equilibrium and optimum output *OM* of the marginal firm of Fig. 23A.3(*b*).

Chapter 24
PRICE DETERMINATION UNDER PERFECT COMPETITION

We are now in a position to explain how price is determind under perfect competition . In the preceding chapters we have explained in detail the forces of demand and supply which by their interaction determine the price of the product. In the discussion of the theory of demand we assumed that an individual buyer is unable to influence the price of the product and therefore takes the prevailing price of the product as a given for him and spends so much money on various goods as to obtain maximum satisfaction from his total outlay. On this assumption we derived the demand curve for a product with the aid of Marshallian cardinal utility analysis as well as with indifference curve technique. Likewise, we discussed the theory of supply by assuming that an individual entrepreneur or a firm cannot individually affect the price of the product and accepts the ruling price in the market as given and constant for him. With this assumption we have explained how much quantity of a product the firm and indsutry will supply at various prices.

Now, the intersection of demand and supply curves determines the price of the product. It is not the demand of a single buyer and the supply of a single seller that go to determine the price of the product, but the demand of all buyers of a product taken together (*i.e.*, market or industry's demand curve) and the supply of all firms selling the product taken together (*i.e.*, the supply curve of the industry) that determine the price of the product. The industry's demand curve shows the various quantities of the good which will be demanded by the consumers at different prices. On the other hand, the industry's supply curve shows the various quantities of the good that the industry will be ready to supply at different prices. That particular price at which quantity demanded is equal to quantity supplied will finally settle down in the market.

TWO APPROACHES IN PRICE THEORY

In regard to pricing under perfect competition, two main approaches have been adopted. One approach has been followed by famous English economist Alfred Marshall who adopted the *partial equilibrium approach* and the second approach has been adopted up by Walras and is called *general equilibrium approach*. We shall explain below both these approaches in price theory.

Partial Equilibrium Analysis : Marshall's Approach

In partial equilibrium approach to the pricing, we seek to explain the price determination of commodity, keeping the prices of other commodities constant and also assuming that the various commodities are not interdependent. In explaining partial equilibrium approach, Marshall writes: "The forces to be dealt with are, however, so numerous that it is best to analyse a few at a time and to work out a number of partial solutions as auxiliaries to our main study. Thus we begin by isolating the primary relations of supply, demand and price in regard to a particular commodity. We reduce to inaction all other forces by the phrase '*other things being equal*'. We do not suppose that they are inert, but for the time we ignore their activity. This scienctific device is a great deal older than science; it is the method by which consciously or unconsciously sensible men dealt from time immemorial with every difficult problem of everyday life."[1]

1. Alfred Marshall, *Principles of Economics*, 8th ed. Macmillan.

Thus in Marshallian explanation of pricing under perfect competition, demand function for a commodity is drawn with the assumption that prices of other commodites, tastes and incomes of the consumers remain constant. Similarly, supply curve of commodity is constructed by assuming that prices of other commodities, prices of resources or factors and production function remain the same. Then Marshall's partial equilbrium analysis seeks to explain the price determination of a single commodity through the intersection of demand and supply curves, with prices of other goods, resource prices etc., remaining the same. Prices of other goods, resource prices, incomes, *etc*., are the *data* of the system which are taken as given to explain the determination of price-output equilibrium of a single commodity. Given the assumption of *ceteris paribus* it explinas the determination of a price of a goods, say *X*, *independently of the prices of all other goods*. With the change in the data, new demand and supply curves will be formed and, corresponding to these, new price of the commodity will be determined. Thus partial equilibrium analysis of price determination also studies how the equilibrium price changes as a result of change in the data. But given the independent data the partial equilibrium analysis explains only the price determination of a commodity in isolation and does not analyse how the prices of various goods are interdependent and inter-related and how they are *simultaneously* determined.

It should be noted that *partial equilibrium analysis is based on the assumption that the changes in a single sector do not significantly affect the rest of the sectors*. Thus, in partial equilibrium analysis, if the price of a good changes, it will not affect the demand for other goods. Prof. Lipsey rightly writes: "All partial equilibrium analyses are based on the assumption of *ceteris paribus*. Strictly interpreted, the assumption is that all other things in the economy are unaffected by any changes in the sector under consideration (say sector *A*). This assumption is always violated to some extent, for anything that happens in one sector must cause changes in some other sectors. What matters is that the changes induced throughout the rest of the economy are sufficiently small and diffiuse so that the effect they in turn have on the sector A can be safely ignored".[2]

General Equilibrium Analysis : Walras Approach

In general equilibrium analysis, the price of a good is not explained to be determined independently of the prices of other goods. Since the changes in price of good *X* affect the prices and quantities demanded of other goods and in turn the changes in prices and quantities of other goods will affect the quantity demanded of the good *X*, *the general equilibrium approach explains the simultaneous determination of prices of all goods and factors*.

As stated above, partial equilibrium approach assumes that the effect of the change in price of a good *X* will be so diffused in the rest of the economy (*i.e.*, over all other goods) so as to have negligible effect on the prices and quantities of other individual goods. Therefore, where the effect of a change in the price of a good, on the prices and quantities of some other goods is significant, as is there in the case of inter-related goods, that is, substitutes and complementary goods, the partial equilibrium approach cannot be validly applied in such cases and therefore the need for applying general equilibrium analysis which should explain the mutual and simultaneous determination of their prices and quantities.

General equilibrium analysis deals with inter-relationship and inter-dependence between equilibrium ajustment with each other. General equilibrium exists when at the going prices, the quantities demanded of each product and each factor are equal to their respective quantities supplied. A change in the demand or supply of any good, or factor would cause changes in prices and quantities of all other goods and factors and there will begin the process of adjustment and readjustment in demand, supply and prices of other goods and factors till the new general equilibrium is established. Indeed, the general equilibrium analysis is solving a system of simultaneous equations. In a general

2. R.G. Lipsey, *An Introduction to Postive Economics*, 3rd edition 1971. p. 404

equilibrium system, the quantity demanded of *each good* is described by an equation in which its quantity demanded is a function of *prices of all goods*. Likewise, in general equilibrium analysis, quantity supplied of each good is considered to be the function of price of all factors of production.

In a general equilibrium system the prices of all *goods* affect the quantity demanded of *each* good. Further, the prices of the all factors affect the quantity supplied of each good. Besides these crucial equations, there will be equations determining *the price of each of the factors of production*. As noted above, a change in any of the demand or supply equations would cause changes in *all prices and quantities* and as a result the system will tend to move to the new general equilibrium.

To explain the inter-relationship and interdependence among the prices and quantities of goods and and factors and ultimately to explain the determination of the relative prices of all goods and factors, the proportion in which different goods are being produced and different factors are being used for the production of different goods is the essence of general equilibrium analysis. However, in this book we shall mainly confine ourselves to the partial equilibrium approach to the determination of relative prices. In a separate part of this book we shall explain the general equilibrium analysis using Edgeworth Box diagram.

DEMAND – SUPPLY MODEL OF PRICING

We have explained in detail in a previous chapter how in a perfectly competitive market demand for and supply of a commodity determine price and quantity bought and supplied of a commodity. Consider Fig. 24.1 where *DD* is the demand curve and *SS* is the supply curve of a commodity. It will be seen from the figure that the two curves intersect at point *E* and determine price P_0 and equilibrium quantity *ON* demanded and sold. It will seen from the Figure 24.1 that a price higher than P_0, (for example at price P_1, the quantity supplied exceeds quantity demanded. Under the pressure of excess supply, price will fall to P_0. On the other hand, if price is lower than P_0, say it is P_2, then as will be seen from Fig. 24.1 the quantity demanded exceeds quantity supplied. As a result of this excess demand there will be pressure on price to go up to P_0 at which quantity demanded is equal to the quantity supplied of it.

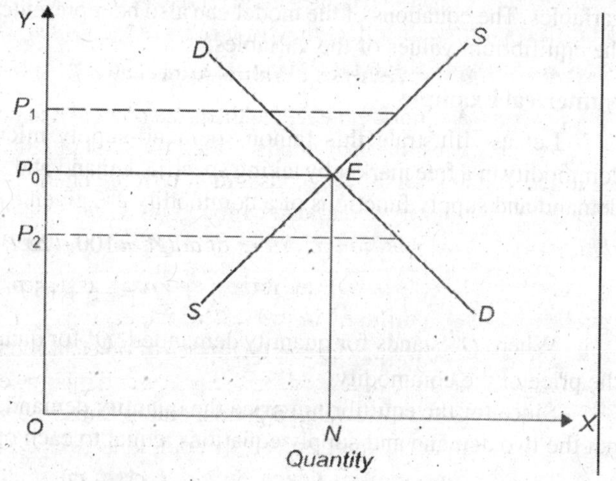

Fig. 24.1. *Determination of Price in a Perfectly Competitive Market*

It is quite often more useful and illuminating to study economic problems through mathematical equations. Demand-supply model of pricing can be presented in mathematical equations and solved for equilibrium price and quantity. In this model it is assumed that both demand and supply functions are of linear type. Further, in this demand-supply model of pricing it is assumed that perfect competition forevails in the market for the product. This implies that there are a large number of sellers and buyers of a homogeneous product so that no single seller or buyer has any influence over the price of the product. This demand-supply model consists of the following three equations:

$$Q^d = a - bP \quad \ldots (i)$$

$$Q^s = c + dP \quad \ldots (ii)$$

$$Q^d = Q^s \quad \ldots (iii)$$

Where,

Q^d stands for quantity demanded

Q^s stands for quantity supplied

P stands for price of a commodity

a, b, c and d are constants

The above set of three equations constitutes a model. Here, in this model, the variables considered are price, quantity demanded, quantity supplied. The objective is to obtain the price and quantities demanded and sold when the system attains the equilibrium position. To find the equilibrium values of these variables, the above three equations are required to be solved simultaneously. The equation (*i*) describes that the quantity demanded is a decreasing function of price, that is, as price falls quantity demanded increases and *vice versa.* Equation (*ii*) describes that quantity supplied is increasing function of price, that is, as price rises quantity supplied increases and *vice versa.* Equation (*iii*) describes the equilibrium condition meaning thereby that the price that equates quantity demanded and quantity supplied will clear the market. Equilibrium price implies that both the buyers and sellers are satisfied with their purchases and sales and hence there is no tendency on their part to raise or lower the price. It is in this way that Marshall explained the determination of price of a commodity.

Equations of the model can be solved mathematically to obtain the equilibrium values of the variables. The equations of the model can also be represented by graphs to determine geometrically the equilibrium values of the variables.

Numerical Example

Let us illustrate this famous demand-supply micro-model of price determination of a commodity in a free market by taking specific demand and supply functions. Suppose the following demand and supply functions of a commodity are given :

$$Q^d = 100 - 20\,P$$

$$Q^s = -5 + 15\,P$$

Where Q^d stands for quantity demanded, Q^s for quantity supplied of a commodity and P for the price of the commodity.

Since for the equilibrium price the quantity demanded is equal to the quantity supplied, we put the two demand and supply equations equal to each other. Thus, we have

$$Q^d = Q^s$$

$$100 - 20\,P = -5 + 15\,P$$

$$15\,P + 20\,P = 100 + 5$$

$$35\,P = 105$$

$$P = \frac{105}{35} = 3$$

Thus we get Rs. 3 as price per unit of the commodity. Putting the value of P in either the demand or supply equation we can obtain the equilibrium quantities Q^d and Q^s. Thus

$$Q^d = 100 - 20 \times 3 = 40$$

$$\text{Or, } Q^s = -5 + 15 \times 3 = 40$$

Thus equilibrium price of the commodity equals Rs. 3 and the equilibrium quantity sold and purchased equals 40 units in a period.

Are Demand and Supply Final Answers to the Pricing Problem ?

From above it follows that price is determined by equilibrium between demand and supply. But it is worth mentioning that demand and supply do not provide final answer to the princing problem. Demand and supply which by their intersection determine price are themselves governed by several factors. There are many forces or factors which work behind demand and supply to determine price. 'Demand and supply' is only a superficial formula. Real factors that determine the prices of goods are those upon which demand and supply depend. But demand and supply are very useful concepts serving outer cover for two distinct categories of factors. Prof. Samuelson rightly remarks: "*Supply and demand are not ultimate explanations of price. They are simply useful catch-all categories of analysing and describing multitude of forces, causes and factors impinging on price.* Rather than final answers, supply and demand simply represent initial questions. Our work is not over but just begun."[5] For instance, market demand for a good depends upon the incomes of the people, their perferences for the goods, the total population, availability and prices of substitute goods. Any change in them will cause a change in demand for the good and hence in its equilibrium price. Similarly, supply depends upon the availability and price of labour, raw materials, machines, chemicals etc., and techniques of production, all of which govern cost of production. Any change in them will bring about change in cost of production and supply and will therefore alter the equilibrium price. It is thus clear that factors like availability of raw materials, cost of production, incomes of the people, the size of population, consumers' preferences for goods, etc., are ultimate determinants of the prices of various goods but all of them work through either demand or supply. For explaining any price behaviour of a good we have to go behind demand and supply and search for those factors which are responsible for the price behaviour for a commodity.

IMPORTANCE OF TIME ELEMENT IN THE THEORY OF PRICE

Marshall, who propounded the theory that price is determined by both demand and supply, also gave a great importance to the time element in the determination of price. Time element is of great relevance in the theory of value, since one of the two determinants of price, namely supply, depends on the time allowed to it for adjustment. It is worth mentioning that *Marshall divided time into different periods from the viewpoint of supply and not from the viewpoint of demand*. Time is short or long according to the extent to which supply can adjust itself. Marshall felt it necessary to divide time into different periods on the basis of response of supply because it always takes time for the supply to adjust fully to the changed conditions of demand. The reason why supply takes time to adjust itself to a change in the demand conditions is that nature of technical conditions of production is such as to prohibit instantaneous adjustment of supply to changed demand conditions. A period of time is required for changes to be made in the size, scale and organisation of firms as well as of the industry.

Another point is worth noting. When Marshall distinguished short and long periods he was not using clock or calendar time as his criterion, but '*operational*' time in terms of economic forces at work. In this regard, as said above, supply forces were given the major attention and a time was short or long according to the extent of adjustment in the forces of supply. The greater the adjustability of the supply forces, the greater the length of the time irrespective of the length in clock-time.

Marshall divided time into following three periods on the basis of response of supply to a given and permanent change in demand.

(1) **Market Period.** The market period is a very short period in which the supply is fixed, that is, no adjustment can take place in supply conditions. In other words, supply in the market period is

limited by the existing stock of the good. The maximum that can be supplied in the market period is the stock of the good which has already been produced. In this period more good cannot be produced in response to an increase in demand. This market period may be a day or a few days or even a few weeks depending upon the nature of the good. For instance, in case of perishable goods, like fish, the market period may be a day and for a cotton cloth, it may be a few weeks.

(2) **Short Run.** Short run is a period in which supply can be adjusted to a limited extent. During the short period the firms can expand output with given equipment by changing the amounts of variable factors employed. Short periods is not long enough to allow the firm to change the plant or given capital equipment. The plant or a capital equipment remains fixed or unaltered in the short run. Output can be expanded by making intensive use of the given plant or capital equipment by varying the amounts of variable factors.

(3) **Long Run.** The long run is a period long enough to permit the firms to build new plants or abandon old ones. Further, in the long run, new firms can enter the industry and old ones can leave it. Since in the long run all factors are subject to variation, none is a fixed factor. During the long period forces of supply fully adjust themselves to a given change in demand; the size of individual firms as well as the size of the whole industry expands or contracts according to the requirements of demand.

From above, it is clear that because of the varying response of supply over a period of time to a sudden and once-for-all increase in demand Marshall found, it necessary and useful to study the pricing process in (*a*) the market period, (*b*) the short-run and (*c*) the long-run depending respectively upon whether the supply conditions have time to make (*i*) *no adjustment*, (*ii*) *some adjustment of labour and other variable factors, and* (*iii*) *full adjustment of all factors and all costs*. Therefore, Marshall explained how the equilibrium between demand and supply was established in three time periods and determined market price, short-run price and long-run price.

We thus see that the price that will prevail depends upon the period under consideration. If a sudden and a once-and-for all increase in demand takes place, the market price will register a sharp increase, since supply cannot increase in the market period In this market period, firms can sell only the output that has already been produced. However, in the short run some limited adjustment in supply will take place as a result of the firms moving along their short run marginal cost curves by expanding output with the increase in the amount of variable factors. Consequently, the short run price will come down from the new high level of the market price. But this short-run price will stand above the level of original market price which prevailed before the increase in demand occurred. In the long run the firms would expand by building new plants, that is, by increasing the size of their capital equipment. In other words, firms would expand along the long-run marginal cost curves. Besides, the new firms will enter the industry in the long run and will add to the supply of output. As a result of this long-run adjustments in supply, the price will decline. Thus the long run price will be lower than the short-run price. But this long-run price will be higher than the original price which ruled before the increase in demand took place, if the industry happens to be increasing-cost industry.

The adjustment of supply over a period of time and consequent changes in price is illustrated in Fig. 24.2 where long-run supply curve *LRS* of an increasing-cost industry along with the market-period supply curve *MPS* and the short-run supply curve *SRS* have been drawn. Originally, demand curve *DD* and market-period supply curve *MPS* intersect at point *E* and price *OP* is determined. Suppose that there is a once-for-all increase in demand from *DD* to *D′ D′*. Supply cannot increase in the market period and remains the same at *OM*. Market-period supply curve *MPS* intersects the new demand curve *D′D′* at point *Q*. Thus, the market price sharply rises to *OP′* . Short-run supply curve *SRS* intersects the new demand curve *D′D′* at point *R*. The short-run price will therefore be *OP″* which is lower than the new market price *OP′*. As a result of the long-run adjustment the price will fall to *OP'''* at which the long-run supply curve *LRS* intersects the demand curve *D' D'*. The new long-run price *OP'''* is lower than the new market price *OP'* and the short-run price *OP''*, but will be higher than the original price *OP* which prevailed before the increase in demand took place. This is so because we are assuming an increasing-cost industry. If the industry is subject to constant costs, the long-run price will be equal to the original price. Further, if the industry is subject to decreasing costs, the long-run price will be lower than the original price.

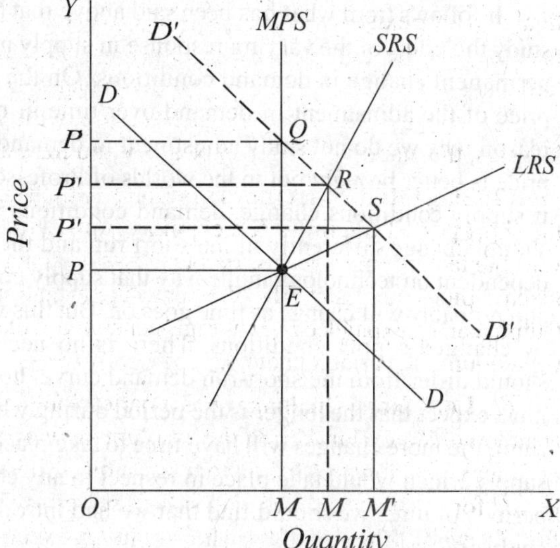

Fig. 24.2. *The Role of Time Element in the Determination of Price*

It follows from above that the price which prevails in the market depends upon the period under consideration. It is thus clear that the time plays an important role in the determination of price. Another significance of the time-period analysis of pricing is that it enabled Marshall to resolve the controversy current among economists whether it is demand or supply which determines price. Marshall propounded the view that both demand and supply took part in the determiantion of price. But, "as a general rule", said Marshall, "*the shorter the period which one considers the greater must be the share of our attention which is given to the influence of demand on value, and the longer the period more important will be the influence of cost of production on value.* Actual value at any time—the market value as it is often called—is often influenced by passing events and causes whose action is fitful and shortlived than by those which work peristently. But in the long run these fitful and irregular causes in a larger measure efface one another's influence so that in the long run persistent causes dominate value completely".[6]

From the abvoe quotation from Marshall it follows that in the market period, demand exercises a predominant influence over price but in the long run it is the supply which is of overwhelming importance as a determinant of price. Roughly speaking, we can say that in the market period it is the force of demand which determines price and in the long period it is the force of supply which governs price. Thus those economists who held that value was governed by demand were in a way right and so were those who contended that cost of production (*i.e.*, force working on the supply side) determines price. The difference in the two views was due to the fact that one gorup of economists was emphasising the determination of the *marekt price* over which demand has determining influence and over which cost of production does not exercise much influence, while the other group was stressing on the determination of *long-run price* over which cost of production has got paramount influence. It is thus clear that Marshall by putting forth the view that both demand and supply determine price by their interaction brought about synthesis between the views of earlier economists.

Both the two opposite views of earlier economists were in a way right but each was one-sided. Each view provided us with a force which governed price. The two forces of supply and demand furnished by the two opposing views were sufficient determining factors. Therefore, Marshall gave equal importance to both demand and supply as determinants of price, though the influence of the two varied in different time periods. Marshall introduced time period analysis into pricing process to bring out the varying influence of each of two forces over price of the product in different time periods.

6. Alfred Marshall, *Principles of Economics,* 8th edition,p.350.

It follows from what has been said above that Marshall and modern economists following him study the effect of the varying response in supply in different time periods on price to a sudden and permanent change in demand conditions. On the contrary, economists do not study the effect on price of the adjustment in demand over time in response to a change in supply conditions. The reason why we do not study adjustment in demand to a change in supply and consequent effect on price is better brought out in the worlds of Professors Stonier and Hague. "There is no reason why, if supply conditions change, demand conditions should change as well, or if they do, why they should change differently in the short run and the long run. Change in consumer's tastes are not dependent on technology in the way that supply conditions are. Admittedly, consumers' tastes may and probably will change as time goes on. But this will be a change of data and not a change induced by changed supply conditions. There is no necessary reason why the long-run demnad curve should differ from the short-run demand curve, however odd the behaviour of supply has been–we must expect that the longer is the period during which demand and supply are coming into equilibrium, the more changes will have time to take place. If we were to study the changes in demand and supply which would take place in respect to any change of data during many successive very short periods of time, we should find that we had introduced unnecessary and intolerable detail into the analysis."[7]

We shall explain below in detail the market-period equilibrium, short-run equilibrium, long-run equilibrium between demand and supply and thus the determination of market price, short-run price and long-run price under conditions of perfect competition.

DETERMINATION OF MARKET PRICE

Market price is the price of a good which prevails at any given time. Market price is determined by the momentary equilibrium between demand and supply at a time. In the market period, as has been already mentioned, the supply of the good is limited by the available stock of the good. But the quantity that may be supplied in the market period may not be equal to the given stock of the good. Whether the whole stock of the good is offered for sale or not depends upon whether the good in question is perishable or durable. The perishable goods like fish and milk cannot be stored or kept back; they will go waste if stored. Therefore, the whole of the given stock of a perishable good has to be supplied in the market whatever the price of the good. As a result, the market-period supply curve of a perishable commodity is perfectly inelastic, or a vertical straight line. On the other hand, the sellers can hold back a durable good and wait for the time when the price of the good rises. Out of a given stock of the good, they will be prepared to sell a lesser amount at lower price, and a greater amount at a higher price. At some price, they will be willing to supply the whole stock of the good and beyond that price the supply of the good will be completely inelastic. Consequently, the supply curve of a durable commodity slopes upward to a point but becomes a vertical straight line after that.

Fig. 24.3illustrates the determination of market price of a perishable commodity. *OM* is the given stock of the good and *MPS* is the market-period supply curve. Suppose, to begin with, *DD* is the demand curve of the commodity. Demand and supply are in equilibrium at price *OP*. Therefore, *OP* is the equilibrium market price. Now if the demand incereases from *DD* to *D′D′*, the market price will sharply rise from *OP* to *OP′*, the supply of the good remaining fixed at *OM*. On the contrary, if the demand decreases from *DD* to *D″D″*, the market price falls from *OP* to *OP″* the supply of the good again remaining constant at *OM*. We thus see that changes in demand produce sharp changes in price in the market period, supply being constant during this period.

Fig. 24.4illustrates the determination of market price of a durable, non-perishable commodity. As pointed out above, the market-period supply curve of a durable good is not a vertical straight line throughout its length. In this connection, it is essential to note two important price levels. First, there is a price level which is sufficiently high so that the sellers will be prepared to supply the whole stock

7. Stonier and Hague: *A Textbook of Economic Theory*, 4th edition, 1972, p. 155

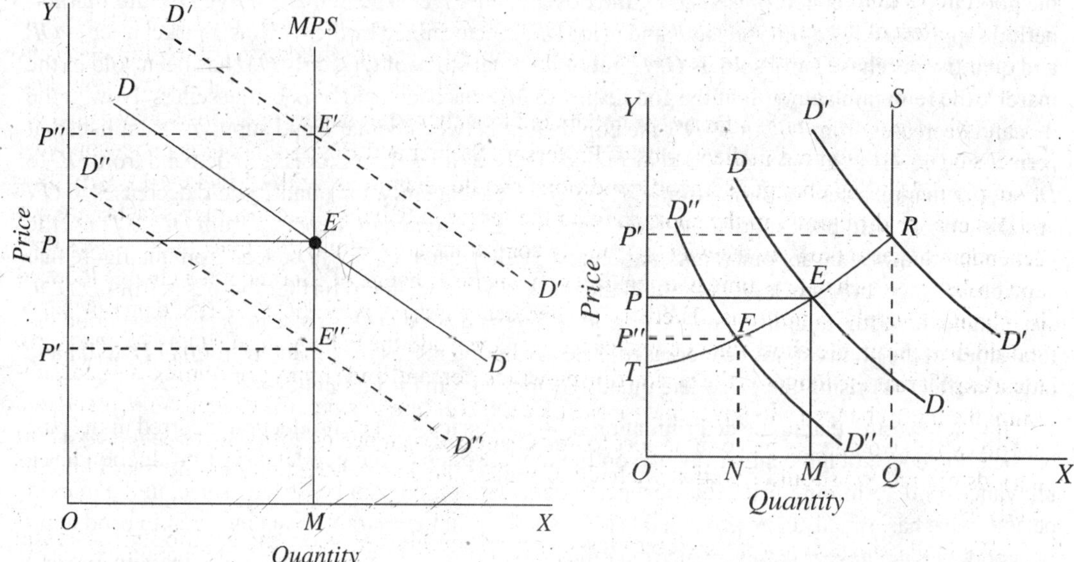

Fig. 24.3. *Determination of Market Price of a Perishable Commodity*

Fig. 24.4. *Determination of Market Price of a Durable commodity*

of the good. Secondly, there is a minimum price at which the sellers will not be prepared to sell at all, instead they will hold back the whole stock of the good. This minimum price at which the sellers refuse to supply the good at all and store it with themselves is known as *reserve price*. The reserve price is determined by several factors which are as follows :

(*a*) First, the reserve price of a good depends upon the *expectations of sellers regarding the future movements in price* of the good. If they expect the price of the good to go up in the near future, their reserve price will be higher and *vice versa*. (*b*) Another factor which governs the reserve price is the *sellers preference for liquidity*. If their need for cash money is great, they will be more anxious to sell the good and consequently their reserve price will be low. The opposite will be the case if their need for liquidity is small. (*c*) The reserve price also depends upon the *costs of stroage* which have to be incurred for holding back the stock of the good for a period. The length of the period for which the stock or a part of it has to be stored is therefore important. The longer the period and the higher the storage cost, the lower will be the reserve price and *vice versa*. (*d*) Still another factor determining reserve price is the *durability of the good*. The greater is the durability; the higher will be the reserve price. (*e*) *Production cost* to be incurred in the future on a good also governs the reserve price to some extent. In view of the higher costs of producing a good, the sellers will fix a higher reserve price.

Given the two price levels, one at which the sellers will be willing to suply the whole stock of the good, and the other at which the sellers will hold back the whole stock, the amount of the good which will be supplied in the market will vary with price. The sellers will supply more quantity of the good at a higher price than at a lower one within the above two price limits. Thus, at a reserve price the quantity supplied of the good will be zero, and as the price rises the quantity supplied will increase until a price is reached at which the whole stock of the good will be offered for sale. Therefore, the supply curve of a durable commodity slopes upward to a point and then it becomes a vertical straight line.

Determination of market price of a durable commmodity is illustrated in Figure 24.4 where *TRS* is the market-period supply curve, *OQ* being the total stock of the good. To begin with, the demand for

5. Paul A. Samuelson, *Economics*, 8th edition, 1970, pp. 369-70

the good in the market is represented by the demand cure *DD*. The demand curve *DD* and market-period supply curve *TRS* intersect at *E* and price *OP* is determined by them. Thus, market price is *OP* and quantity purchased and sold is *OM*. Out of the total stock of *OQ*, only *OM* has been sold in the marekt, the remaining amount of the good equal to *MQ* has been held back by the sellers. Now, if the demand decreases from *DD* to *D''D''*, the equlibrium between demand and supply is established at point *F* and new marekt price *OP''* is determined. Thus, as a result of decrease in demand from *DD* to *D''D''*, the market price has fallen from *OP* to *OP''*. Consequently, the quantity sold decreases to *ON* and the amount held back increases to *NQ*. Suppose, if the demand increases from *DD* to *D'D'*, the new equilibrium will be at point *R* and market price will rise to *OP'*. It will be seen from the figure that at price *OP'* the whole stock *OQ* is sold in the market. If the demand further increases from *D'D'* to some higher level, the quantity supplied or sold will remain fixed at *OQ*, since in the market period the total stock of the good cannot be increased. The further increases in demand beyond *D'D'* will have only the effect of raising the price, the quantity supplied remaining unchanged.

It is noteworthy that in the determination of market price, cost of production incurred in the past on the good does not have any influence on the market price of the good. Cost of production has a relevance for determining price during a period in which output can be varied. Since, in the marekt period, what has already been produced is to be supplied in the market, costs incurred in producing the good does not have much influence over the market price. However, cost of production exercises a determining influence over the short-run price and long-run price of the good. This is because in the short run and the long-run output can be increased or decreased and what amount of the good will be supplied in the marekt depends to a great extent upon the cost of producing it.

Since a product under perfect competition is homogeneous, it will have a single uniform price in the market. Moreover, because there are a very large number of firms producing and selling homogeneous product, no one can influence the price by its own individual acton. Therefore, once the market price is established an individual firm will take this price as given and constant for it and will so adjust its level of output as to get maximum profits.

DETERMINATION OF SHORT-RUN PRICE

Short-run price is determined by short-run equilibrium between demand and supply. Supply curve in the short run under perfect competition is a lateral summation of the short-run marginal cost curves of the firm. Also, the short-run supply curve of the industry always slopes upward, since the short-run marginal cost curves of individual firms slope upward. It was explained in a previous chapter that in the short run fixed costs are not taken into account while deciding about whether to produce or not.If the price does not cover fixed cost, the firms will continue producing provided the price stands above the average variable cost. It is, therefore, the average variable cost and not the average total cost (which includes average fixed cost) which determines whether to produce or not. If the price falls below average variable cost, the firms will close down (suspend production in order to avoid unnecessary losses). Thus, the average variable cost sets a minimum limit to the price in the short run, since at prices below it no amount of output will be produced and offered for sale.

Figure 24.5 illustrates the process of the price determination in the short run. In Fig. 24.5 (*b*) *DD* represents the demand curve for the product of the industry, and *SRS* is the short-run supply curve of the industry. To begin with, *OP* is the short-run price since the given demand curve *DD* intersects the short-run supply curve *SRS* at point *E*. The individual firm will take the price *OP* as a given datum for it and will adjust its output at *OM* at which the price *OP* is equal to it short-run marginal cost

In order to further clarify the process of determination of short-run price, we suppose that in Fig. 24.5 (*b*) the demand increases from *DD* to *D'D'*. In the market period since the supply cannot be increased in response to this increase in demand and consequently with the increase in the the demand from *DD* to *D'D'* the market period price will sharply rise. But, in the short period, the supply of output will be increased by increasing the employment of variable factors to the given fixed capital equipment and therefore the short-run supply curve *SRS* slopes upward to the right. The

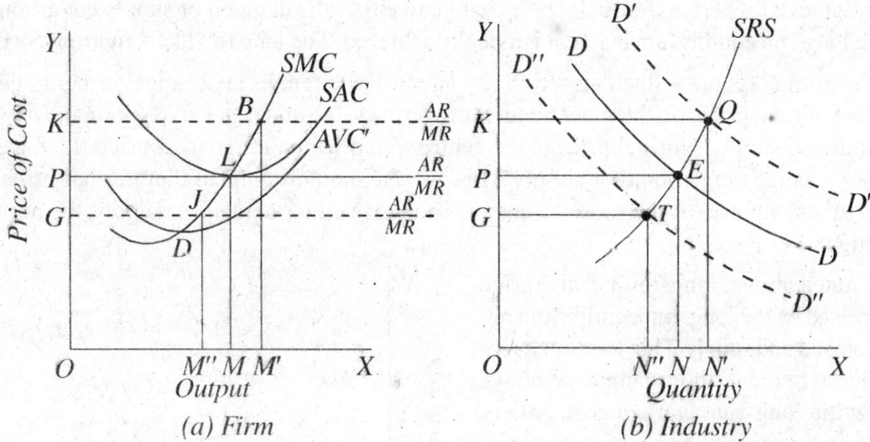

Fig. 24.5. *Determination of Short-Run Price under Perfect Competition*

new demand curve *D'D'* intersects the short-run supply curve *SRS* at point *Q* and therefore new short-run price *OK* is determined, which is higher than the original price *OP*. This is because the marginal cost rises as more is produced by the firms in the short run, short-run marginal cost curve being upward sloping. The individual firms will take this new short-run price *OK* as given and will produce *OM'* output at which price *OK* equals the marignal cost. It is clear from Fig. 24.5 (*a*) that at price *OK* the firm will be making supernormal profits, since price *OK* is greater than the average cost at equilibrium output *OM'*.

Now, suppose that instead of increase in demand, there is a decrease in demand for the product of the industry from *DD* to *D''D''*. In the market period, supply will remain fixed at *ON* and the new marekt price will fall sharply. But in the short period the firms will reduce output by reducing the employment of labour and other variable factors in response to the decrease in demand. New demand curve *D''D''* cuts the short-run supply curve *SRS* at point *T* and short-run price *OG* is determined, which is lower than the original short-run price *OP*. At price *OG*, the firm is producing *OM''* output and will be making losses, since the price *OG* is smaller than the average total cost at output *OM''*. But because the price *OG* is greater than the average variable cost, the firm will continue producing the product. A firm will not produce at a price which is lower than the average variable cost, since it will not be recovering variable costs fully and will be incurring losses more than the fixed costs. A firm will rather close down than to produce at a price lower than average variable cost. Thus we see that the short-run price cannot fall below the average variabel cost. Average variable cost sets a minimum limit to the price in the short run.

DETERMINATION OF NORMAL PRICE AND DERIVATION OF LONG-RUN SUPPLY CURVE OF THE INDUSTRY

Long-run price is also known as long-run normal price or simply normal price. Long-run price or normal price is determined by long-run equilibrium between demand and supply when the supply conditions have fully adjusted themselves to the given demand conditions. Marshall says, "Normal or natural value of a commodity is that which economic forces, would tend to bring about in the long run". Given the demand, a price will tend to prevail in the long run when supply has fully adjusted and that price is known as long run price or normal price. It is worth noting that normal price of a good is not the same thing as the average price of the good. Normal price is the price to which actual prices tend to reach in the long run, while the average price is the arithmetical average of all actual prices over a period of time. Moreover, it should be borne in mind that long-run normal price may never be actually achieved. There will usually be a change in either the demand or supply conditions underlying the long-run equilibrium before it is actually achieved. The long run like tomorrow never comes.

Whereas market price fluctuates from day to day due to temporary changes either in demand or supply, the normal price, on the other hand, remains the same under the given permanent conditions of demand and supply. Normal price is the centre round which the market price fluctuates due to temporary changes in demand or supply. However, it should be noted that normal price is not a permanently fixed level. If there is a permanent change in either demand or supply, the normal price will change.

As stated above, long-run normal price is determined by the long-run equilibrium between demand and supply. This long-run price under perfect competition cannot be above or below the long-run average cost. A firm under perfect competition is in long-run equilibrium at the output where price is equal to both marginal cost and average cost. If the price is greater than average cost, the firms will earn more than normal profits. Attracted by the supernormal profits new firms will enter the industry in the long run and will add to the supply of the product. As a result of this process, the price will fall to the level of minimum long-run average cost. On the other hand, if the price is below the average cost, the firms will be making losses and as a result some of the existing firms will quit the industry in the long run. With some of the firms going out of the industry, the supply of the product will fall and price will rise to the level of long-run average cost so that the remaining firms make only normal profits.

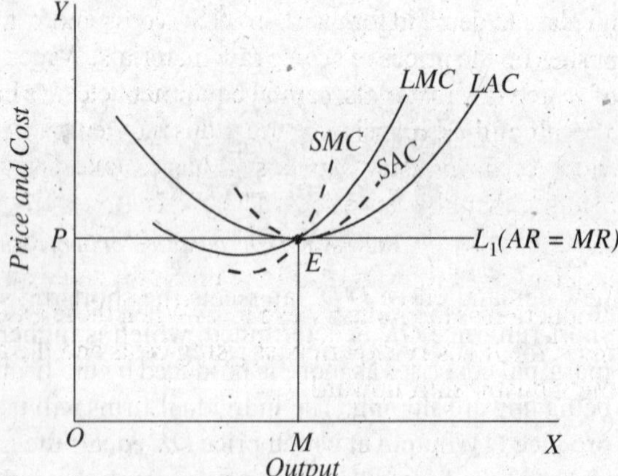

Fig. 24.6. *Long-run price is equal to minimum long-run average cost.*

It follows from above that when price is either above or below the long-run average cost certain forces in the system so operate as to bring the long-run normal price to the level of minimum long-run average cost. It will be seen from Fig. 24.6 that long-run equilibrium of a firm is established at the minimum point of the long-run average cost and the long-run price *OP* is established which is equal to the minimum long-run average cost. It will be noticed from Figure 24.6 that long-run normal price is equal to both the minimum short-run as well as long-run average cost. Thus

$$Long\text{-}Run\ Price = SMC = SAC = LAC = LMC$$

But to say that, in the long run, price will be equal to the minimum long-run average cost is not enough since what would be the level of minimum long-run average cost and hence of price depends upon what happens to the cost curves when industry expands or contracts in response to a given increase or decrease in demand. The long-run average cost shifts upward or downward or remains at the same level when the industry expands depending upon whether the industry in question is increasing-cost industry, decreasing-cost industry or constant-cost industry. We shall explain below what causes the industry to be increasing-cost, decreasing-cost or constant-cost and how long-run normal price is determined in each case. Besides, we shall also explain how long-run supply curve of the perfectly competitive industry is derived in these three types of industry.

Determination of Normal Price and Derivation of Long-Run Supply Curve in Increasing Cost Industry

When an industry expands in response to an increase in demand it experiences some *external economies* as well as some *external diseconomies*. Whereas external economies tend to reduce the cost and thereby tend to shift the long-run average cost downward, the external diseconomies tend to raise the costs and thereby shift the long-run average cost curve upward. So we have an increasing-cost industry when external diseconomies outweigh the external economies, that is, when there are *net external diseconomies*.

The external diseconomies which accrue to an expanding industry are generally the rise in prices of raw materials or factors used for production in the industry. As more firms enter the industry in response to the increase in demand for the product, the prices of scarce factors rise due to the increase in demand for them. In other words, more intensive bidding by the increased number of firms pushes up the prices of scarce raw materials. Wages of specialised labour, rent of land and the prices of scarce raw materials, capital equipment etc. are bound to rise as the demand for them increases as a result of the expansion of the industry. Generally, the same resources are used in different industries. As an industry expands, it has to take away the scarce resources from other industries by offering them higher prices. The rise in prices of the scarce factors raises the costs of production. Furthermore, the additional factors of production coming into the industry are generally less efficient or of inferior quality than the previous ones and this also brings about increase in cost of production as the industry expands. When these external diseconomies outweigh the external economies, the industry experiences rising costs and the average and marginal cost curves of the firms in the industry shift upward.

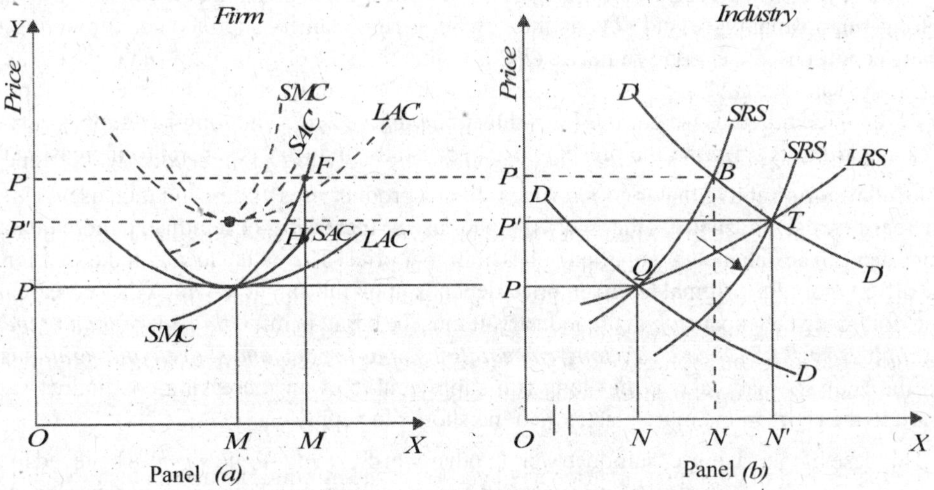

Fig. 24.7. *Long-Run Normal Price and Derivation of Long-Run Supply Curve of the Increasing-Cost Industry*

Figure 24.7 illustrates the determination of long-run normal price in an increasing-cost industry. The left-hand side of the diagram in Fig. 24.7 shows long-run equilibrium of the firm at two different long-run normal prices, while the right-hand side of diagram shows the demand and supply curves of the industry with the horizontal scale compressed. To begin with, a given demand curve intersects

7. Stonier and Hague, *A Textbook of Economic Theory*. 4th edition, 1972. p.178

the short-run supply curve at *Q* therefore, the short-run price *OP* is determined. It will be seen from the left side of the diagram that price *OP* is equal to minimum long-run average cost of firms. It means that the sizes of firms as well as the number of firms have already been fully adjusted to the given demand conditions as represented by the curve *DD*. Therefore, price *OP* is also a long-run normal price corresponding to the demand curve *DD*.

Now, let us see what happens to the long-run normal price when a once-for-all increase in demand from *DD* to *D′D′* occurs. In the short-run price will rise to *OP′* and quantity exchanged to *ON′* as a result of the given increase in demand. From the left-hand diagram it will be seen that in the short run the individual firm will expand its output along the short-run marginal cost curve and will be in equilibrium at point *F* on *SMC*. The firms will therefore expand output from *OM* to *OM′* in response to the increase in demand from *DD* to *D′D′* and the rise in short-run price from *OP* to *OP′*. It will be further seen from the panel (*a*) side of Fig. 24.7 that the individual firm will be making supermormal profits equal to *FH* per unit of output in the short run at price *OP′*. Lured by these supernormal profits new firms will enter the industry to produce the homogeneous product and will add to the supply of the product. As a result, the short-run supply curve will shift to the right. The new firms will continue entering the industry as long as supernormal profits are made and short-run supply curve will continue shifting rightward until its intersection with the new demand curve *D′D′* determines a price at which supernormal profits are reduced to zero.

It is evident from Fig. 24.7 (*b*) above that when short-run supply curve has shifted to the position *SRS′* due to the entry of a certain number of firms, it intersects the new demand curve *D′D′* at point *T* and determines a price *OP″* at which firms make only normal profits (*i.e.*, supernormal profits are reduced to zero). Price *OP″* is equal to the minimum average cost of the new long-run average cost curve *LAC″*(dotted). The long-run average cost curve has shifted upward from *LAC* to *LAC″* due to increasing costs which have come about with the expansion of the industry. Thus *OP″* is a long-run normal price and *ON″* is the new long-run quantity supplied corresponding to the demand conditions *D′D′*. Long-run price *OP″* is higher than the original long-run price *OP* and also the quantity supplied *ON″* at price *OP″* is greater than the quantity supplied at price *OP*. If points *Q* and *T* are joined together we get the long-run supply curve *LRS*. The long-run supply curve *LRS* slopes upward to the right in the present case because the industry is subject to increasing costs.

It follows from above that the long-run price of a product rises as demand increases in the case of increasing-cost industry. In other words, in the case of increasing-cost industry, more quantity of the product can be obtained or supplied only at a higher price. The extent to which the new long-run price differs from the original long-run price depends upon the extent to which the increase in cost occurs following the expansion of the industry. It must be borne in mind *that every point of the long-run supply curve LRS represents a long-run equilibrium as the demand shifts to the right*. It is clear from the analysis made above that long-run supply curve of an increasing-cost industry slopes upward to the right and is more elastic than the short-run supply curve.

This case of increasing-cost industry or, in other words, *rising supply price* is believed to be the most typical of the competitive industries in the actual world. This is so because productive resources are scarce and are currently being used in various industries. Therefore, when an industry expands and requires more resources, it has to take away resources from others by paying higher prices for them. Thus, Professor Samuelson writes : "*The case of increasing cost is "the normal one to be met in most sizeable competitive industries. Why normal? Because when a large industry (which has already achieved the economies of large-scale production) expands, it must coax men and other productive factors away from the other industries by bidding up their prices and thus its own cost. So the long-run supply curve will usually be sloping gently upward.*"[9]

---

8. Paul A. Samuelson, *Economics, 8th edition*, p.366

Normal Price and Derivation of Long-run Supply Curve in the Constant Cost Industry

If an industry on its expansion gives rise to some external economies and external diseconomies which cancel each other so that the constituent firms do not experience any shift in the cost curves, then that industry is a constant-cost industry. *In case of constant-cost industry, we have neither net external economies, nor net external diseconomies*. An industry can also be a constant-cost industry if its expansion breeds neither external economies, nor external diseconomies. As more firms enter an industry the demand for productive factors like raw materials, labour, chemicals and machinery will increase and if prices of these productive resources go up as a result of the increase in demand, then the cost is bound to rise. It is, therefore, evident that an industry can be constant-cost industry if it makes little impact on the market for these productive resources, that is, if its demand for productive resources is a negligible part of the total demand for them so that the increase in demand for them by the industry does not push up their prices. To quote Prof. Samuelson, "*only if the industry is small compared with the total of all other uses will Marshall's long-run supply curve be horizontal—which is called the case of constant-cost.*"[10] If the industry on its expansion does not create external diseconomies, it will be a constant-cost industry only when its expansion also does not give rise to any external economies.

Thus an industry can be constant-cost in two ways. First, when the expansion of an industry creates both external economies and diseconomies but they cancel each other in their effect on costs, and, secondly, when the expansion of an industry creates neither external economies nor external diseconomies. Figure 24.8 depicts the determination of long-run normal price in the constant-cost industry. To begin with, a given demand curve *DD* intersects the short-run supply curve *SRS* at point *Q* and short-run price *OP* is determined. The price *OP* is equal to the minimum long-run average cost of the firm. This means that the number of firms has already been fully adjusted to the given demand conditions. Therefore, price *OP* is also the long-run price corresponding to the demand conditions represented by the curve *DD*. Now, suppose that the demand increases from *DD* to *D′D′*. As a result, price will rise to *OP′* in the short run at which the short-run supply curve *SRS* intersects the new demand curve *D′D′* . The quantity supplied by the industry will increase to *ON′* in the short run. At price *OP* a firm will be in equilibrium at *F* and will be producing *OM′* amount of the product. It will be seen from the figure that at price *OP′* the firm is making abnormal proits equal to *FH* per unit of output. This will attract other firms to the industry in question. As more firms enter the industry, the short-run supply curve will shift to the right. The new firms will go on entering the industry and short-run supply curve will go on shifting righward until its intersection with the demand curve *D′D′* determines a price at which super-normal profits of the firms disappear completely.

It will be seen from Fig. 24.8 that when the short-run supply curve has shifted to *SRS′* it intersects the new demand curve *D′D′* at point *T* and once again determines price *OP* at which firms will make only normal profits. Thus, price *OP* is also a long-run price corresponding to the new demand curve *D′D′*. The cost curves of the firms have not shifted because external economies and diseconomies have offset each other's effect. As a result of the increase in demand, the price went up in the short run but has returned to the original level of *OP* in the long run. *In a constant-cost industry, long-run normal price remains the same whatever the level of demand.* If points like *Q* and *T* are joined together we get a long-run supply curve *LRS* which is a horizontal straight line in the present case. It is thus clear that in the constant-cost industry new firms enter the industry without raising or lowering cost curves of firms and make available additional supplies of output at the same price which is equal to the minimum long-run average cost of the firms. *Since long-run supply curve of the constant-cost industry is a horizontal straight line, any increase or decrease in demand will not produce any effect on the long-run price*. In this case, increase or decrease in demand will in the long run only change the supply of output by causing a change in the number of firms without producing any effect on the long-run normal price.

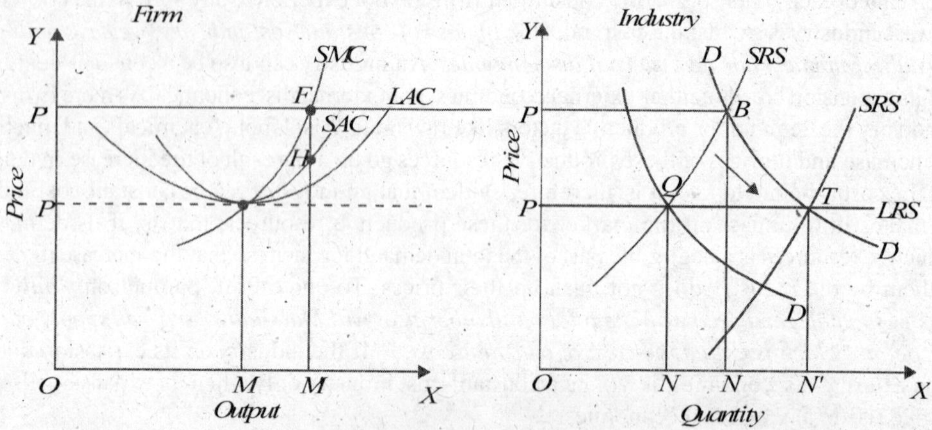

Fig. 24.8. *Long-Run Pricing in a Constant Cost Inustry*

Here, a point is worth noting. *While the long-run marginal cost curve of the firm will be sloping upward in its relevant part, the long-run supply curve of the industry in this case is a horizontal straight line.* It is manifest from this that the long-run supply curve of an industry cannot be the lateral summation of the long-run marginal cost curves of the firms.

Determination of Normal Price and Derivation of Long-run Supply Curve in the Decreasing Cost Industry

When an industry grows in size by the increase in the number of firms, it may be that the external economies outweigh the external diseconomies so that there is a decline in the production costs of the firms. In other words, when an industry reaps *net external economies* as it expands, it is a decreasing-costs industry. There is every possibility of external economies to outstrip the external diseconomies when an industry grows in a new territory. In earlier stages of the growth of an industry in a new territory, not much diseconomies are created, while external economies are likely to accrue in greater amount. Costs may decline with the expansion of the industry due to the following external economies.

1. Some raw materials, tools and capital equipment may be made available to the industry at reduced prices since as the industry grows subsidiary and correlated firms may spring up in the vicinity of the industry which produce them on a large scale and therefore can provide the expanding industry with raw materials, tools and capital equipment at the reduced rates.

2. Cheaper and better trained labour may become available with the expansion of the industry.

3. With the growth of industry, certain specialised firms may come into existence which work up its waste products. The industry can then sell its waste products at good prices, while previously it may be throwing them away.

4. As the industry expands it may become worthwhile to publish trade journals which may help in discovering and spreading technical knowledge concerning the industry.

5. When there is enlargement of the industry, better information centres, research institutions etc. may emerge which greatly benefit the firms in the industry.

In case the above-mentioned external economies are more powerful than the external diseconomies that may arise, the cost curves of all firms in the industry will shift to a lower position as the industry expands.

Long-run pricing in a decreasing cost industry is illustrated in Fig. 24.9. To start with, demand curve *DD* and short-run supply curves *SRS* intersect at *Q* and determine short-run price *OP*. Price *OP* is also the initial long-run price since price *OP* is equal to the miminum long-run average cost of the firms which are therefore making only normal profits. With the increase in demand from *DD* to *D′ D′* short-run price rises to *OP′* and the quantity exchanged to *ON′*. As a result of the rise in price from *OP* to *OP′*, each firm of the industry will expand output to *OM′* in the short run. Price *OP′* yields supernormal profits to the firms. These supernormal profits will attract other firms into the industry and as a result the industry will expand.

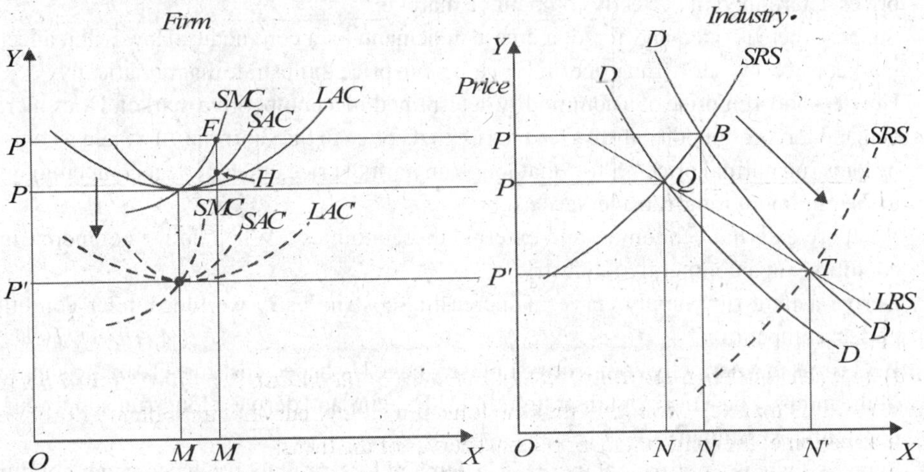

Fig. 24.9. *Long-Run Pricing in the Decreasing Cost Industry*

As the industry expands, its short-run supply curve will shift to the right and the industry being a decreasing cost industry, cost curves of the firms will shift downward. The short-run supply curve will continue to shift to the right and cost curves of the firms continue to shift downward until the price *OP″* is reached at which firms make only normal profits. Price *OP″* is therefore long-run price corresponding to the demand curve *D′D′* . As is evident from Fig. 24.9, new long-run price *OP′* is lower than the original long-run price *OP*. Connecting points *Q* and *T*, we get the downward sloping long-run supply curve *LRS*. We thus see that the *long-run supply curve of a decreasing-cost industry slopes downward from left to right*. In this case the greater supplies of the product will be forthcoming at reduced prices in the long run. Every increase in demand in this case will bring about a fall in the long-run price of the good. This is in sharp contrast to the increasing-cost industry in which case long-run price rises as the demand increases.

It follows from the analysis of long-run pricing made above that with the increases in demand, long-run price rises, remain constant, or falls depending upon whether the industry is subject to increasing cost, constant cost or decreasing cost.

QUESTIONS FOR REVIEW

1. Distinguish between partial equilibrium analysis and general equilibrium analysis of pricing. When are they used in explaining prices of commodities ?
2. What is meant by partial equilibrium analysis of pricing ? On what basic assumption is it based ? Explain how Marshall defended the use of partial equilibrium analysis of pricing of commodities.
3. "General equilibrium analysis explaines simultaneous determination of prices of all goods and factors". Explain when it is more useful to adopt general equilibrium approach to explain the determination of prices of goods.

4. The credit of finding the true answer to the pricing problem goes to Marshall who held that both demand and supply were equally important in determining prices of commodities". Discuss.
5. "Supply and demand are not ultimate explanations of price. They are simply useful catch-all concepts of deseribing many factors and forces that go to determine price" Discuss
6. Explain the importance of time element in the determination of prices in perfectly competitive markets.
7. Distinguish between a perishable commodity and durable commodity. How are their market prices determined in perfectly competitive marekts.
8. Suppose there is once-and-for all increase in demand for a commodity. How will it affect its (*a*) market price, (*b*) short-run price and (*c*) long-run price ? Illustrate diagramatically.
9. How is short-run price of a commodity determined in a competitive market. Does increase in demand for a commodity always lead to rise in its price in the short run ? Explain what is meant by long-run normal price ? Show that long-run normal price under perfect competition is equal to the minimum long-run average cost.
10. What are external economies and external diseconomies ? When do we get increasing cost conditions in a competitive industry ?
11. Derive a long-run supply curve of increasing-cost industry working under conditions of perfect competition. *D.U. B.A.(Hons), 1997, 1999.*
12. If all firms in a perfectly competitive industry have U-shaped cost curve, can the supply curve of the industry be a horizontal straight line ? Explain and derive a long-run supply curve of a constant-cost industry.
13. Suppose there is a permanent increase in demand for a product produced under conditions of perfect competition by an increasing-cost industry. What would be its effect on price and output in the shrot run and long run.
14. A perfectly competitive industry is in long-run equilibrium. What are the long-run effects of an increase in demand for its product given that it is an increasing-cost industry. *D.U.B.A. (Hons) 2002*
15. Under what conditions long-run supply curve of a competitive industry can slope downward ? If in such an industry demand for the product increases, how will its price change in (*a*) the shrot run, (*b*) the long run.
16. If all the firms in a perfectly competitive industry have U-shaped cost curve, can the supply curve of the industry be downward sloping ? Give reasons. *D.U. B.A. (Hons) 1998.*
17. Is it possible for an industry to be constant-cost industry though each firm in the industry has increasing marginal costs. Explain.
18. Can the supply curve of an industry under perfect competition be downward sloping in (i) Short run, (ii) Long run *D.U., Eco. (Hons.) Year 2006*

    [**Hint.** Supply curve of a perfectly competitive industry *cannot be downward sloping in the short run*. (see text).]

    Long-run supply curve of an industry under perfect competition can be downward sloping when there are *net* external economies, when the industry expands following the entry of new firms.

CHAPTER 25

STABILITY OF EQUILIBRIUM AND COBWEB MODEL

Stable and Unstable Equilibrium : Walras Price Adjustment Approach

We now turn to the problem of stability of market equilibrium. The equilibrium between demand and supply is attained at a price-quantity combination at which both buyers and sellers are satisfied about what they are buying and selling respectively and therefore they do not have any incentive to change their behaviour. Furthermore, changes in demand due to changes in preferences of the consumers and changes in supply due to technological changes or variation in factor prices often occur which disturb the equilibrium. These changes either in demand or supply will determine new equilibrium price but there is no guarantee that the new equilibrium price will be restored. Thus, when actual price differs from the equilibrium price due to certain disturbances, it is very relevant to ask whether some forces will come into operation which would cause the system to return to the equilibrium level. *The equilibrium is stable, if following a disturbance in it, the equilibrium is established again, and unstable if the system tends to move away from the equilibrium situation.* Whether or not equilibrium is restored when it is disturbed depends on the behaviour of agents, that is, buyers and sellers. Further when there is disequilibrium whether it is changes in price or changes in quantity through which adjustment takes place to restore equilibrium. *Walras thought it is through changes in price that adjustment takes place.* According to him, behaviour of buyers is such that they tend to bid up the price when quantity demanded exceeds the quantity supplied at a given price and the behaviour of sellers is such that they tend to lower it when the quantity supplied of the commodity is greater than the quantity demanded of it. With such changes in price equilibrium will be stable.

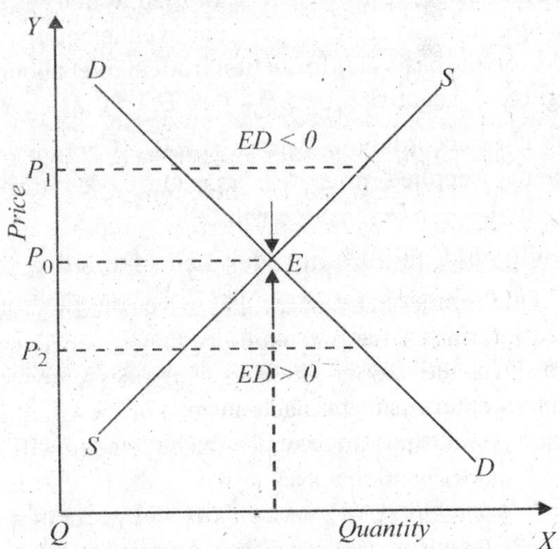

Fig. 25.1. *Stable Equilibrium Walras Approach*

If demand curve is downward sloping (*i.e.*, has a negative slope) and supply curve is upward sloping (*i.e.*, has a positive slope), as is normally the case, the equilibrium between demand and supply; if it exists, will be stable. This is illustrated in Fig. 25.1. At price, P_1, the quantity supplied exceeds quantity demanded (that is, *at price P_1, excess demand is negative* ($ED < 0$). This means at price P_1, the sellers would not be able to sell the quantity they would like, that is, disequilibrium exists. According to the profit-maximising behaviour, in these circumstances the sellers would bid down price until price P_0 is reached at which demand and supply are again in equilibrium. On the other land, if price is P_2, in Fig. 25.1, the quantity demanded exceeds quantity supplied (that is, excess demand ED is positive), buyers would push up the price until P_0, is reached. Thus, *with negatively sloping demand curve and positively sloping supply curve equilibrium when exists is stable as market price when disturbed moves toward equilibrium due to the assumed behaviour of buyers and sellers.*

In Fig. 25.2 both demand and supply curves are negatively sloping but the supply curve is less steep as compared to the demand curve. In this situation quantity demanded equals quantity supplied at price P_0. If the market price is initially at this equilibrium level P_0, it will stay there unless there is some external disturbance. However, if due to some disturbance, price happens to be P_1 which is above the equilibrium price P_0, quantity demanded exceeds quantity supplied (that is, $ED > 0$ where ED stands for excess demand), Now, given the behaviour pattern of buyers, they would tend to bid up the price and therefore the market price instead of returning to the equilibrium level P_0, will tend to move away from it. This shows *the equilibrium at price P_0 in Fig. 25.2 is unstable*. On the other hand, in Fig. 24.2 if due to some disturbance, price happens to be P_2, which is below the equilibrium price, the quantity supplied exceeds the quantity demanded (that is, $ED < 0$), the sellers will tend to lower the price and price will not go up to the equilibrium level but will move away from it. This again shows the *equilibrium at P_0 in Fig. 25.2 represents unstable equilibrium in Walrasian approach.*

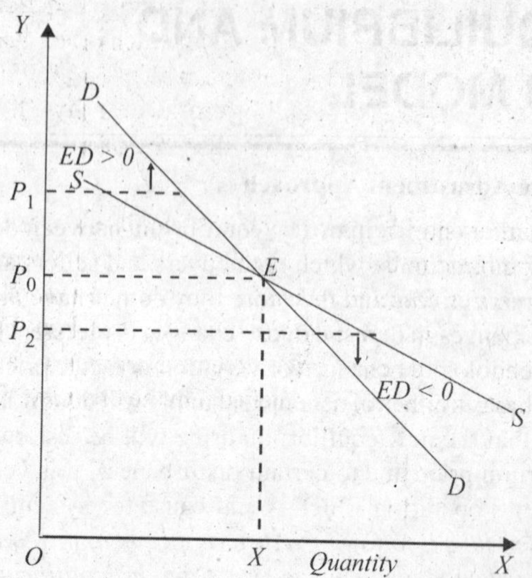

Fig. 25.2. *Unstable Equilibrium under Walrasian Price Adjustment Approach*

Walrasian Stability of Equilibrium and Excess Demand. We have seen above that due to a certain external disturbance market may go out of equilibrium. This creates an adjustment in the market. But whether adjustment is made in price or quantity has been a controversial issue. Walras thought that it is price which is adjusted. When current price is below the equilibrium price, price is bid up and when current price is above the equilibrium, it is bid down. These changes in price are made on the basis of information from market about the nature of excess demand as to whether it is positive or negative (*i.e.*, $ED > 0$ or $ED < 0$).

Thus according to Walras, if $ED > 0$, price goes up, that is, if quantity demanded exceeds quantity supplied, price will rise. On the contrary, if quantity demanded is less than quantity supplied, *i.e.*, $ED < 0$, price will fall.

Stability of Equilibrium : Marshall's Quantity Adjustment Approach

On the other hand, according to Marshall it was quantity which was adjusted in case of market disequilibrium. To restore equilibrium between demand and supply, buyers and sellers make adjustments in quantity, whereas changes in prices follow from the adjustments in quantity. In Marshallian quantity adjustment approach, instead of viewing the situation as quantity demanded and quantity supplied *at a price*, price which the buyers are willing to pay for a *given quantity* (which is *called demand price*) and the price at which the producers are willing to supply that quantity (which is called the *supply price*) are considered. In case of negatively sloping demand curve and positively sloping supply curve, there is a *stable equilibrium* at the quantity where demand and supply curves intersect. This is illustrated in Fig. 25.3. At the quantity Q_0 at which demand and supply curves intersect (that is, demand price equals supply price at the quantity Q_0), market equilibrium is reached and this equilibrium is stable even according to Marshallian approach, as was the case in Walrasian price adjustment approach. For example, suppose the quantity Q_1 is being produced and sold. It will be observed from Fig. 25.3 that for quantity Q_1, demand price which is equal to Q_1H exceeds the supply price which is equal to Q_1G (the price at which producers are willing to sell quantity Q_1 and which depends upon the marginal cost of production). Therefore, it is profitable for the producers to increase the quantity produced, and this adjustment in quantity will continue until the quantity Q_0 is reached where demand price becomes equal to supply price. Further, it will be observed from Fig. 25.3 that if quantity will happens to be Q_2, demand price at it is equal to Q_2L which is less than the supply price Q_2K at it. As a result, quantity will be reduced to the equilibrium quantity Q_0. This shows, according to Marshallian quantity adjustment approach, equilibrium at quantity Q_0 in Fig. 25.3 is *stable*, as was so under Walrasian price adjustment approach in this case of negatively sloping demand curve and positively sloping supply curve.

However, in case of both demand and supply curves sloping downward with supply curve being less steep, as shown in Fig. 25.4, the two approaches lead to different results. In this case whereas according to *Walrasian price adjustment, equilibrium is found to be unstable, under Marshallian quantity adjustment approach*, the equilibrium at Q_0 in Fig. 25.4 is *stable*. It will be seen from Fig. 25.4 that if current quantity of commodity produced is Q_1 demand price exceeds supply price at it with the result that this would tend to increase the quantity until Q_0 is reached. On the contrary, if at

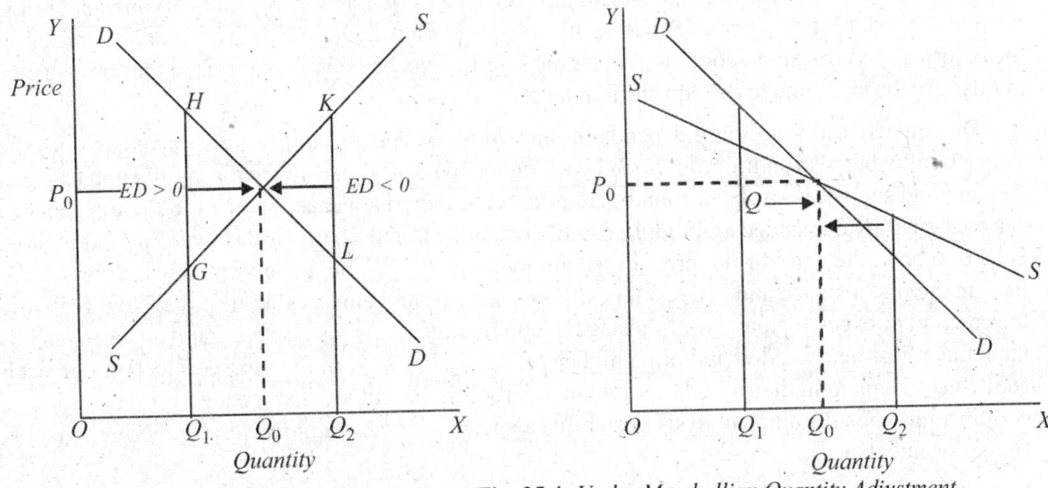

Fig. 25.3. *Stability of Equilibrium : Marshallian Quantity Adjustment*

Fig. 25.4. *Under Marshallian Quantity Adjustment Approach, Equilibrium at Q_0 is Stable.*

any time output happens to be Q_2, demand price is less than the supply price. Consequently, producers would be induced to reduce the quantity to Q_0 where demand price equals supply price and therefore quantity adjustment ceases.

STATIC STABILITY VS DYNAMIC STABILITY

Two types of stability of equilibrium may be distinguished. As mentioned above, when an equilibrium is disturbed, it creates an adjustment process in the market. For example, if price is below the equilibrium level, some buyers bid up the price leading to the restoration of equilibrium. *Static analysis of stability does not consider how price and quantity change or adjust through time when there is disequilibrium between demand and supply*; it merely considers the nature of changes or tendencies that exist as to whether the market will move towards or away from equilibrium. It is important to note that stability conditions are derived from assuming a certain behaviour pattern on the part of buyers and sellers. In the foregoing analysis we have made static analysis of stability of equilibrium and distinguished between Walrasian and Marshallian conditions of static stability. We now turn to explain dynamic stability of equilibrium.

Dynamic stability considers how price and quantity change through time when the system is thrown into disequilibrium state. In other words, starting from a disequilibrium state, the dynamic analysis of stability investigates *the time path of the adjustment process* of the movement of price and quantity towards the equilibrium levels. It always takes time for the adjustment to be made in price and quantity and therefore instantaneous adjustment to the new equilibrium is not feasible. The process of dynamic adjustment is often explained through what is called *recontracting model*. According to this, buyers and sellers enter into series of provisional contracts about price and quantity until they reach a final equilibrium situation when recontracting ceases. Let us explain this recontracting in some greater detail.

Suppose that at an initial price, the quantity demanded by buyers is not equal to the quantity supplied, that is, there is, disequilibrium. Adjustment process starts and recontracting takes place. If at the new price there is still a discrepancy between demand and supply, the price will be further changed by what is called an auctioneer — a middle man through whom contracts are being made. This process of recontracting continues and price bids go on changing from period to period over the course of time until equilibrium price is reached at which quantity demanded equals quantity supplied. Thus, "*equilibrium is stable in the dynamic sense if the price converages to or approximates the equilibrium over time ; it is unstable if the price change is away from equilibrium*".[1] Note that dynamic stability has been defined in this quotation according to Walrasian condition of stability. In terms of Marshallian condition, dynamic stability can be defined in terms of the convergence of quantity through time to the equilibrium level.

Dynamic stability not only depends on the *slopes* of demand and supply curves as does the static stability but also on the *magnitude* by which the market adjusts to the disequilibrium between demand and supply. It has been found that quite often there is over-adjustment to the discrepancy between quantity demanded and supplied until right adjustment finally occurs over a period of time. For instance, if the equilibrium price of a commodity is Rs. 20/- but buyers actually bid for Rs. 15/ for it in the first instance and as a result positive excess demand emerges at this price. Now, realising the creation of excess demand (*i.e.* shortage of commodity at this lower price), and buyers overestimate the adjustment needed and bid a higher price, say Rs. 22/-, in the next period. Though each adjustment is made in the right direction but is larger in magnitude than needed for restoration of equilibrium. Thus dynamic analysis of stability also considers the *magnitude of reactions* to disturbances or imbalances.

Dynamic Stability with Lagged Adjustment : Cobweb Model

We shall now explain the notion of dynamic stability with a well known theorem often referred to as cobweb model. Cobweb theorem is the simplest model of economic dynamics when equilibrium reached over time between demand, supply and price is investigated. Producers' supply function (curve) shows how producers adjust their output to changes in price. At a higher price, they respond to produce more and at a lower price they cut down their production. But this adjustment in production in response to changes in price does not occur instantaneously but takes a good deal of time. Thus, there is a *time lag* between a change in price and appropriate adjustment in supply in response to it. The time gap between the decision to change the quantity supplied in response to a given price and its actually being supplied is known as *supply lag*. The supply lag is often found in case of agricultural commodities, animal rearing etc. For instance, it takes four-five months for wheat crop to be grown and raised.

It should be noted that supply lag often results in *cyclical movements or oscillations* in price and quantity over time. The dynamic analysis of stability investigates whether these oscillations coverage to the equilibrium values or move away from them.

Cobweb Model. Let us explain the dynamics of cobweb model. We consider the market for wheat as an example of a market where the supply of wheat is lagged function of price. In order to

1. J.M. Henderson, R.E. Quandt, *Microeconomic Theory*, 2nd ed. 1971. p. 136 (Italics added).

keep our analysis simple we assume that there is a one-year lag in the response of quantity supplied of wheat to a given market price of it. Thus

$$S_t = f(P_{t-1})$$

which means that the quantity of wheat supplied in a year t depends on the price prevailing in the previous period (P_{t-1}). Further, in accordance with this the present year price (i.e. P_t) will determine the quantity supplied in the next period (*i.e.* S_{t+1}).

On the side of demand function there is no lag, that is, the quantity demanded of this year depends on price of this year. The equilibrium price in any year is determined at the level at which the quantity demanded of any year t equals the quantity supplied in that year t. This means the price in a period adjusts to bring about equality in the quantity demanded in the year (D_t) and the quantity supplied in that year (S_t) which of course in this model is determined by the price prevailing in the previous year, *i.e.* $t - 1$. It should be noted that there is perfectly inelastic supply in any year as in case of agricultural commodities like wheat no more quantity can be grown until next year to augment supply. Thus in any year t

$$D_t = S_t \quad or \quad D_t - S_t = 0$$

This is the equilibrium situation brought about by adjustment in price in a year. In any year there is clearing of the market, that is, no producer is left with unsold stocks and no consumer with unsatisfied demand. Possible time paths of change in price and consequently the nature of oscillations depends upon the particular demand and supply functions. The demand and supply functions according to cobweb model can be written as :

$$D_t = bP_t + a \qquad \ldots (i)$$

$$S_t = gP_t + C \qquad \ldots (ii)$$

where b and a in the demand function are constants ; whereas b is a slope coefficient showing relation between price of a commodity and demand for it, a is the constant intercept term. Similarly, g and C in the supply functions are constants; whereas g denotes the slope coefficient showing the relation between price of a commodity and the quantity supplied which is forthcoming at it and C is the intercept term of this supply function.

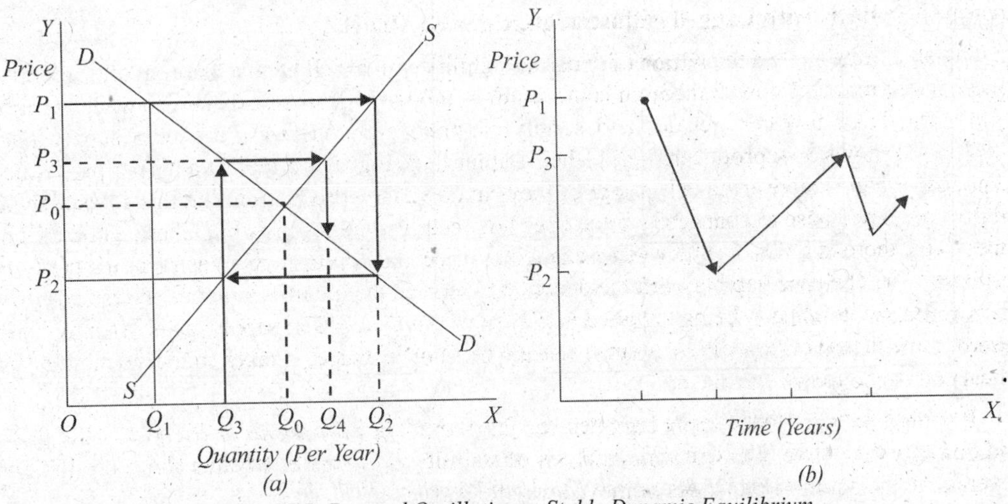

Fig. 25.5. *Damped Oscillations : Stable Dynamic Equilibrium*

Now, the path of price as a function of time depends on the absolute values of the slope coefficient of the demand function [*i.e.* b in (*i*) above] and the slope coefficient of supply function [*i.e.* g in (*ii*) above]. If the slope of the supply curve i.e. $\frac{1}{|g|}$ is greater (in absolute value) than the slope of the demand curve i.e. $\frac{1}{|g|}$ (that is, supply curve is *steeper* or less elastic than the demand curve), we get the case of *damped oscillations*, which as will be seen from panel (a) of Fig. 25.5 appears like a cobweb. Fig. 25.5 describes the time path of price and quantity as we start from price-quantity combination (P_1, Q_1). Let us explain this path of price in greater detail. It will be seen from panel (a) of Fig. 25. 5 that demand and supply curves intersect at price P_0 and Q_0 which are therefore equilibrium price and quantity.

Suppose there is a disturbance such as occurrence of a drought which causes the output (quantity) of wheat to fall to Q_1. Now, with Q_1 as the quantity supplied and given the demand curve *DD*, the price P_1 is determined. From the supply curve *S* in panel (a) of Fig. 25.5 it will be observed that at the price P_1, the quantity supplied Q_2 will be forthcoming in the next year t_2. With Q_2 as the supply and the demand curve *DD*, price P_2 is determined. Thus price falls from P_1 in year 1 to price P_2 in year 2. Now, as will be observed form Fig. 25.5 [panel (a)] price P_2 will induce the quantity supplied Q_3 in the next year 3. With Q_3 as the quantity supplied and demand curve *DD*, the price P_3 is the equilibrium price in period 3. This will further cause a change in supply in the next period and bring about further change in price. But, as will be seen from Fig. 25.5 price is oscillating but it is damping, that is, tending towards the equilibrium price P_0. It is thus clear that in the present case *when the absolute slope of the supply curve exceeds that of the demand curve we have damped oscillations in price*, that is, price fluctuates but over a time it tends to move towards the equilibrium level. Therefore, the cobweb model of damped oscillations represents the case *of stable dynamic equilibrium.* It will be seen from panel (*b*) of Fig. 25.5 which directly depicts the time path of price over the years and shows that over time the price tends to converge to the equilibrium level.

Perpetual Oscillations. If the absolute slopes of the supply and demand curves are equal, we will get a cobweb model of perpetual oscillations as shown in Fig. 25.6. The equal slopes of supply and demand curves in economic sense imply that the response of quantity demanded and supplied to the changes in price is the same. Consider panel (a) of Fig. 25.6. To start with, in year 1 the quantity

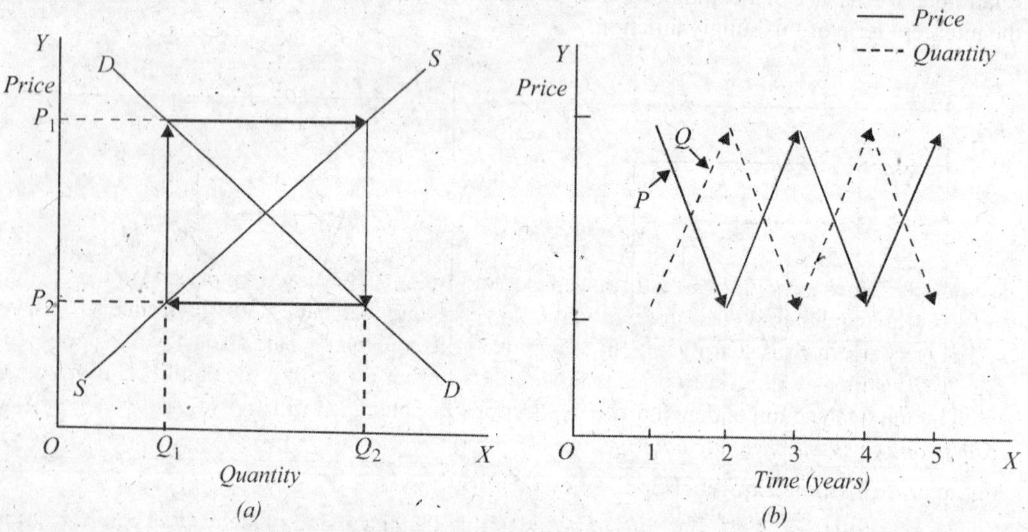

Fig. 25.6. *Cobweb Theorem : Perpetual Oscillations.*

of the good produced is Q_1 and, given the demand curve *DD*, the price P_1 is determined in year 1. Price P_1 in year 1 calls forth quantity produced and supplied Q_2 in year 2. With Q_2 as the quantity supplied and the demand curve *DD*, a lower price P_2 is determined in year 2. It will be seen from supply curve *SS* that at the lower price P_2, the producers reduce the quantity produced and supplied again to Q_1. With Q_1 as the quantity supplied and the demand curve *DD*, price again rises to P_1 in year 3 and so on. The price goes on fluctuating between P_1 and P_2 perpetually and quantity goes on oscillating ceaselessly between Q_1 and Q_2. It should be noted that these perpetual oscillations remain constant in amplitude. As will be seen from Fig. 25.6 (*b*) that *in this case of perpetual oscillations, price and quantity do not move towards equilibrium price and quantity*. Therefore, equilibrium once disturbed is never restored. In fact equilibrium is never attained in this case. It should be noted that when quantity is low, price is high, and when quantity is high, price is low.

Explosive Oscillations. Finally, we have cobweb model in which prices and quantities move further away from equilibrium instead of moving towards equilibrium as indicated by the intersection of demand and supply curves. This occurs when the *absolute value* of the slope of the supply curve is less relative to that of the demand curve. In economic terms this implies that when the supply responds to changes in prices to a greater degree than the demand, (that is, supply is more elastic than the demand) the amplitude of oscillations of price and quantity go on increasing over time and become too much excessive. Therefore, these ever-widening oscillations of price and quantity

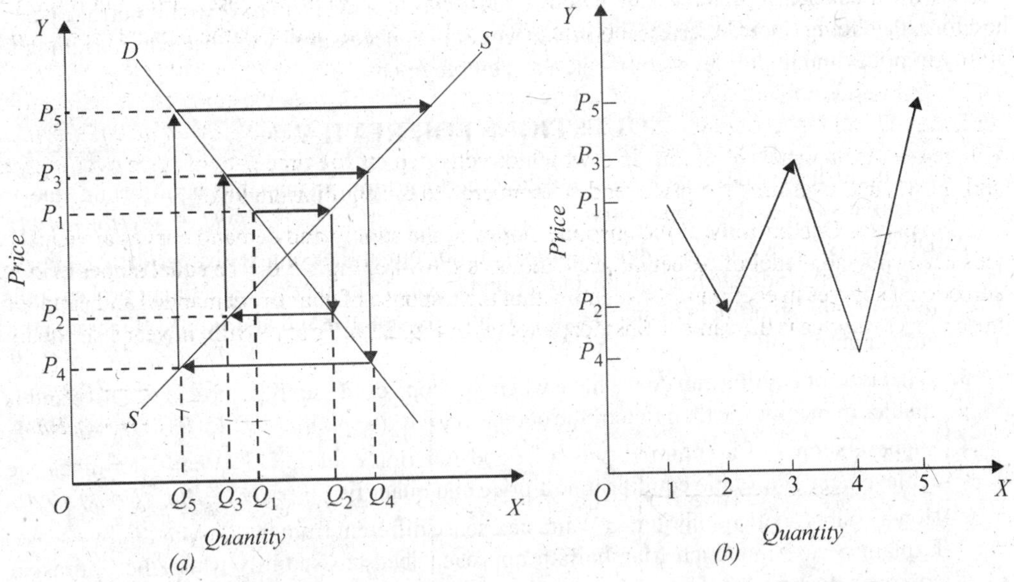

Fig. 25.7. *Cobweb Model : Explosive Oscillations.*

are called *explosive oscillations* and are depicted in Fig. 25.7. Starting from price P_1 in year 1 it falls to P_2 in year 2 and then it goes up sharply to P_3 in year 3 and then have a drastic decline to P_4 in year 4. The price again rises sharply to P_5 in year 5. The price movements are also shown in panel (*b*) of Fig. 25.7 where as will be seen price tends to move further away from the equilibrium price indicated by the intersection of demand and supply curves. Thus, *the explosive oscillations model represents and unstable dynamic equilibrium.*

Stable and Unstable Equilibrium : Policy Implications

The students are likely to gather impression that the discussion of stability of equilibrium is a futile theoretical exercise without any economic significance. But this is far from truth. The stability of equilibrium of a market has important implications for economic policy. If a competitive market is in stable equilibrium, it implies that it can survive any external disturbances, however large and drastic they may be. That is, if any disturbance causes disequilibrium, the stable nature of market equilibrium ensures that certain forces will automatically come into play to bring it back into equilibrium. For instance, if due to certain factors, given the demand and suppıy curves, if price rises above the equilibrium level, that is, there is inflation in the economy, then if market equilibrium is stable, rise in price will be self-corrected without any interference from the Government. Similarly, if due to some reasons equilibrium is disturbed and consequently there prevail deflation and unemployment, the stability of equilibrium, if it is stable, ensures that the adjustment in wages, prices and labour employment would occur which will bring the market back into equilibrium without unemployment. This is a very important conclusion because if market equilibrium is stable and automatic correction of disequilibrium is possible, theoretically there is no need for Government interference in a free market economy in times of inflation, recession or unemployment. On the contrary if market equilibrium is unstable the Government has to play an important role by intervening in the economy to restore equilibrium. The economists who are in favour of market-friendly approach tend to argue that less the interference by the Government in the working of a free market private enterprise system, the better it is. However, this argument in favour of free market and private sector is theoretically justified only if the market equilibrium is stable. In case of unstable market disequilibrium free competitive market could collapse under the pressure of either high inflation or recession. In fact, in the real world we witness unstable eqilibrium in some commodity markets, labour markets, foreign exchange markets and therefore self-correction by the market would not take place. Therefore, the Government interference in the economy is necessary to achieve equilibrium with stability in prices and higher levels of income and employment.

QUESTIONS FOR REVIEW

1. Distinguish between stable and unstable equilibrium. Is unstable equilibrium due to negative slope of the supply curve ? *D.U. B.A. (Hons) 1987*
2. Distinguish between stable and unstable equilibrium in the context of a perfectly competitive industry. Indicate the circumstances under which the market adjustment process fails to ensure the attainment of stable equilibrium between demand and supply. Illustrate your answer graphically. *D.U. B.A. (Hons) 1989*
3. What type of equilibrium do we have when the slope of the supply curve is negative and is smaller in magnitude than that of the demand curve ? Explain *D.U. B.A.(Hons) 1986.*
4. Suppose supply of a commodity is a lagged function of its price. What determines the achievement of a stable equilibrium of price and quantity *D.U. B.A. (Hons) 1990.*
5. How is stability of equilibrium in Walrasian sense different from that in Marshallian sense. Explain a case in which Marshallian approach leads to stability white the Walrasian approach does not. *D.U. B.A. (Hons) 1996*
6. Explain Cobweb model. Show how it explains cyclical movements or oscillations in price and quantity of agricultural products.
7. When there is lagged response of supply to changes in price of a commodity. under what conditions we get
   1. Damped oscillations
   2. Perpetual oscillations
   3. Explosive oscillations.

CHAPTER 26

PRICE AND OUTPUT UNDER MONOPOLY

In the last two chapters, we discussed the equilibrium of the firm and the industry under perfect competition and as a consequence the determination of price and output under it. Monopoly is another important market from which merits detailed study in respect of output equilibrium of the firm as well as how price is determined under it. About seventy years ago it was thought that the existence of monopoly was an exceptional case. But now monopoly form of market structure extensively prevails in capitalist economies of the world, including that of India. Monopolistic market structure prevails in many large-scale manufacturing industries and public utility services. Therefore, the analysis of price and output determination under monopoly has assumed vital importance. As has been pointed out in chapter 22, monopoly, as it is now generally understood, is an extreme form of imperfect competition. Pure or perfect competition and pure or absolute monopoly are the two extreme opposite cases and between them the various intermediate market situations lie, which differ from each other in respect of the degree of monopoly. In this chapter we shall explain the principles which underlie the price and output equilibrium under monopoly and will compare them with those of perfectly competitive equilibrium.

MONOPOLY : ITS MEANING AND CONDITIONS

What is monopoly ? *Monopoly is said to exist when one firm is the sole producer or seller of a product which has no close substitutes.* Three points are worth noting in this definition. First, there must be a single producer or seller of a product if their is to be monopoly. This single producer may be in the form of an individual owner or a single partnership or a joint stock company. If there are many producers producing a product, either perfect competition or monopolistic competition will prevail depending upon whether the product is homogeneous or differential. On the other hand, when there are few producers or sellers of a product, oligopoly is said to exist. If then there is to be monopoly, there must be one firm in the industry. Even literally monopoly means one seller. 'Mono' means one and 'poly' means seller. Thus monopoly means one seller or one producer.

But to say that monopoly means one seller or producer is not enough. A second condition which is essential for a firm to be called monopolistic is that *no close substitutes for the product of that monopolistic firm should be available in the market.* If there are some other firms which are producing close substitutes for the product in question there will be competition between them. In the presence of this competition a firm cannot be said to have monopoly. Monopoly implies absence of all competition. For instance, there is one firm in India which produces 'Binaca' toothpaste but this firm cannot be called monopolist since there are many other firms which produce close substitutes of Binaca toothpaste such as Colgate, Promise, Forhans, Meclean etc. These various brands of toothpaste compete with each other in the market and the producer of any one of them cannot be said to have a monopoly. Prof. Bober[1] rightly remarks, "The privilege of being the only seller of a product does not by itself make one a monopolist in the sense of possessing the power to set the price. As

1. M.M. Bober, *Intermediate Price and Income Theory*, revised edition (1962), p. 237

the one seller, he many be a king without a corwn."

We can express the second condition of monopoly in terms of cross elasticity of demand also. Cross elasticity of demand shows a change in the demand for a good as a result of change in the price of another good. Therefore, if there is to be monopoly *the cross elasticity of demand between the product of the monopolist and the product of any other producer must be very small.*

The fact that there is one firm under monopoly means that other firms for one reason or other are prohibited to enter the monopolistic industry. In other words, strong barriers to the entry of firms exist wherever there is one firm having a sole control over the production of a commodity. The barriers which prevent the firms to enter the industry may be economic in nature or else of institutional and artificial nature. In case of monopoly, barriers are so strong that prevent entry of all firms except the one which is already in the field.

From above it follows that for the monopoly to exist, three conditions are necessary:

1. There is a single producer or seller of a product.
2. There are no close substitutes for the product.
3. Strong barriers to the entry into the industry exist.

THE NATURE OF DEMAND AND MARGINAL REVENUE CURVES UNDER MONOPOLY

It is important to understand the nature of the demand curve facing a monopolist. The demand curve facing *an industrial firm* under perfect competition, as explained in a previous chapter, is a horizontal straight line, but the demand curve facing the *whole industry* under perfect competition is sloping downward. This is so because the demand is by the consumers and the demand curve of consumers for a product usually slopes downward. The downward-sloping demand curve of the consumers faces the whole competitive industry. But an individual firm under perfect competition does not face a downward-sloping demand curve. This is because an individual firm under perfect competition is one among numerous firms constituting the industry so that it cannot affect the price by varying its individual level of output. A perfect competitive firm has to accept the ruling price as given and constant for it. It can sell as much as it likes at the ruling price of the product. Therefore, the demand curve facing an individual firm under perfect competition is a horizontal straight line at the level of prevailing price of the product. A perfectly competitive firm is a mere quantity adjuster; it has no influence over price.

But in the case of monopoly one firm constitutes the whole industry. Therefore, the entire demand of the consumers for a product faces the monopolist. Since the demand curve of the consumers for a product slopes downward, the monopolist faces a downward sloping demand curve. If he wants to increase the sale of his good, he must lower the price. He can raise the price if he is prepared to sacrifice some sales. To put it in another way, a monopolist can lower the price by increasing his level of sales and output, and he can raise the price by reducing his level of sales or output. A perfectly competitive firm merely adjusts the quantity of output it has to produce, price being a given and constant datum for him. But the monopolist encounters a more complicated problem. He cannot merely adjust quantity at a given price because each quantity change by him will bring about a change in the price at which the product can be sold. Consider Fig. 26.1. *DD* is the demand curve facing a monopolist. At price *OP* the quantity demanded is *OM*, therefore he would be able to sell *OM* quantity at price *OP*. If he wants to sell a greater quantity *ON*, then price the to *OL*. If would he restricts his quantity to *OG*, fall price will rise to *OH*. Thus every quantity change by him entails a change in price at which the product can be sold. Thus the problem faced by a monopolist is to choose a price-quantity combination which is optimum for him, that is, which yields him maximum possible profits.

Demand curve facing the monopolist will be his average revenue curve. Thus, the average revenue curve of the monopolist slopes downward throughout its length. Since average revenue curve slopes downward, marginal revenue curve will lie below it. This follows from usual average-

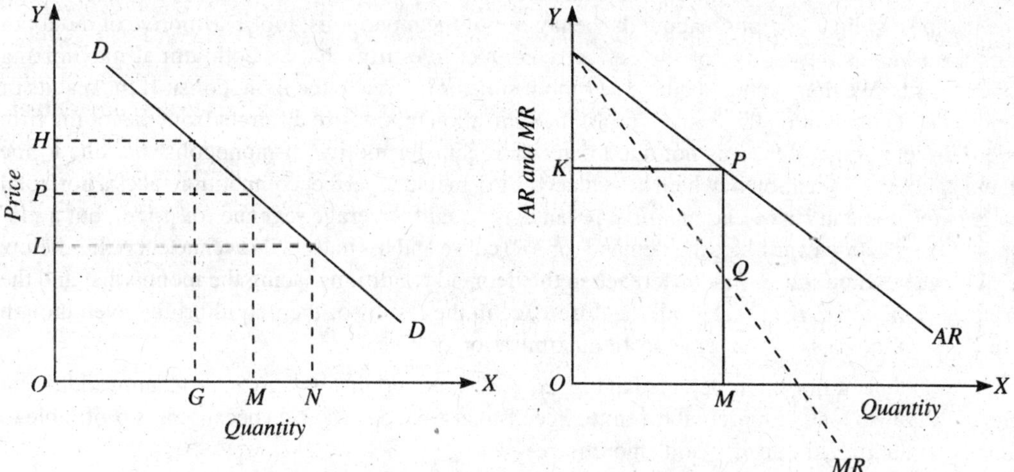

Fig. 26.1. *Demand curve of the monopolist slopes downward.*

Fig. 26.2. *Average and Marginal Revenue Curves under Monopoly*

marginal relationship. The implication of marginal revenue curve lying below average revenue curve is that the marginal revenue will be less than the price or average revenue. When monopolist sells more, the price of his product falls; marginal revenue therefore must be less than the price. In Fig. 26.2 *AR* is the average revenue curve of the monopolist and slopes downward. *MR* is the marginal revenue curve and lies below *AR* curve. At quantity *OM*, average revenue (or price) is *MP* and marginal revenue is *MQ* which is less than *MP*. In an earlier chapter we have explained that average and marginal revenue at a quantity are related to each other through price elasticity of demand and in this connection we derived the following formula :

$$MR = AR\frac{(e-1)}{e}$$, where *e* stands for price elasticity.

Since AR is the same thing as price

Therefore, $$MR = \text{price}\frac{(e-1)}{e}$$

or $$\text{price} = MR\frac{e}{e-1}$$

Since the expression $\frac{e-1}{e}$ will be less than unity, *MR* will be less than price, or price will be greater than *MR*. The extent to which *MR* curve lies below *AR* curve depends upon the value of the fraction $\frac{e-1}{e}$.

The monopolist has a clearly distinguished demand curve for his product, which is identical with the consumers' demand curve for the product in question. It is also worth mentioning that, unlike oligopolist or a firm under monopolistic competition, monopolist does not consider the repercussions of the price change by him upon those of other firms. Monopoly, as defined here, requires that the gap between the monopoly product and those of other firms is so sharp that changes in the price policies of the monopolist will not affect other firms and will therefore not evoke any readjustments of the policies by these firms.

PRICE–OUTPUT EQUILIBRIUM UNDER MONOPOLY

Monopolist, like a perfectly competitive firm, tries to maximize his profits. Profit maximization assumption on which is based the equilibrium analysis of the perfectly competitive firm is also taken to be the most valid assumption about the behaviour of the monopolist too. The motive of monopolist is the same as the motive of the perfectly competitive firm, that is, both aim at maximizing money profits. We thus do not attribute any more sinister motive to the monopolist. If the results of monopolist' behaviour on the basis of profit maximisation motive are different from that of the firm under perfect competition, it is not due to any more sinister motive of monopolist but due to the circumstances and situation in which he is placed. A firm under perfect competition faces a horizotal straight-line demand curve and marginal revenue is equal to average revenue (or price), but a monopolist faces a downward-sloping demand (or *AR*) curve and his marginal revenue curve lies below the average revenue curve. The difference in the demand conditions facing the monopolist and the perfectly competitive firm makes all the difference in the results of their equilibrium, even though both work on the basis of the same profit maximisation motive.

Monopoly equilibrium is depicted in Fig. 26.3. The monopolist will go on producing additional units of output so long as marginal revenue exceeds marginal cost. This is because it is profitable to produce an additional unit if it adds more to revenue than to cost. His profits will be maximum and he will attain equilibrium at the level of output at which marginal revenue equals marginal cost. If he stops short of the level of output at which *MR* equals *MC*, he will be unnecessarily forgoing some profits which otherwise he could make. In Fig. 26.3, marginal revenue is equal to marginal cost at *OM* level of output. The firm will be earning maximum profits and will therefore be in equilibrium when it is producing and selling *OM* quantity of the product. If he increases his output beyond *OM*, marginal revenue will be less than marginal cost, that is, additional units beyond *OM* will add more to cost than to revenue. Therefore, the monopolist will be incurring loss on the additional units beyond *OM* and will thus be reducing his total profits by producing more than *OM*. Thus he is in equilibrium at *OM* level of output at which marginal cost equals marginal revenue (*MC* = *MR*).

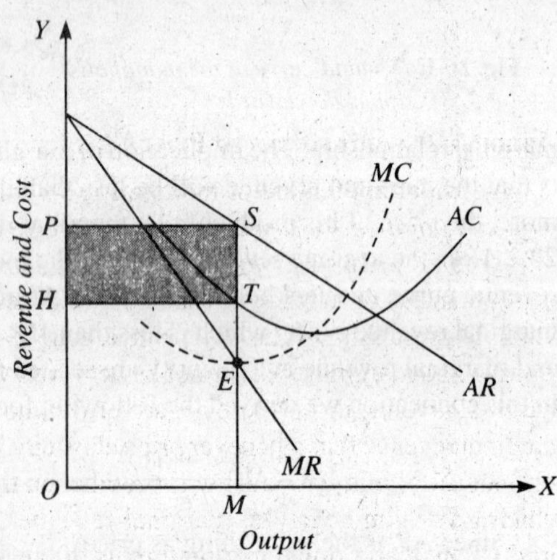

Fig. 26.3. *Firm's Equilibrium under Monopoly: Maximisation of Profits*

It will be seen from the *AR* curve in Fig. 26.3 that he will be getting the price *MS* or *OP* by selling *OM* quantity of output. The total profits earned by him are equal to the area *HTSP*. There is here a significant difference between monopoly and perfect competition. *The price under perfect competition is equal to marginal cost, but under monopoly price is greater than marginal cost.* The monopolist, unlike perfectly competitive firm, faces a downward-sloping average revenue curve and his marginal revenue lies below average revenue curve. Therefore, in monopoly equilibrium when marginal cost is equal to marginal revenue, it is less than price (or average revenue). From Fig. 26.3 it will be noticed that at equilibrium output *OM*, marginal cost and marginal revenue are equal and both are here equal to *ME*, while price fixed by monopolist is *MS* or *OP*. It thus follows that price under monopoly is greater than marginal cost.

$$MR = P\left(\frac{e-1}{e}\right)$$

where *MR* stands for marginal revenue, *P* for price and *e* for price elasticity of demand at the equilibrium output.

Since in equilibrium, $MR = MC$, therefore

$$P\left(\frac{e-1}{e}\right)=MC$$

or $$P=MC\frac{e}{e-1} \qquad \ldots (2)$$

Equation (2)* provides us with *rule of thumb for pricing* by the monopolist. If the knows marginal cost for his product and value of price elasticity of demand at or near the equilibrium output, he can easily calculate what price he should fix to maximise profits. In Equation (2) since $\frac{e}{e-1}$ is greater than one, $P > MC$. Further, it shows that *price is inversely* related to elasticity of demand. The greater the price elasticity of demand, the smaller the price fixed by the monopolist and vice-versa. Thus, if price elasticity of demand for the firm's product is equal to – 4 marginal cost of production is 12, the profits-maximising price of the monopolist will be

$$P=MC\frac{e}{e-1}=12\frac{4}{4-1}=16$$

Monopoly Equilibrium and Price Elasticity of Demand

An important feature of monopoly equilibrium is that the *monopolist will never be in equilibrium at a point on the demand curve or average revenue curve at which price elasticity of demand is less than one*. In other words, the monopolist will never fix his level of output at which elasticity of the demand or average revenue curve is less than one, provided the marginal cost is positive which is most usually the case. Since marginal cost can never be negative, equality of marginal revenue and marginal cost cannot be achieved where price elasticity of demand is less than one and marginal revenue is therefore negative. We know from the relationship between price elasticity and marginal revenue that whenever price elasticity is less than one, marginal revenue is negative. Therefore, no sensible monopolist will produce on that portion of the demand or average revenue curve which gives him negative marginal revenue, that is, which reduces his total revenue, while the production of additional marginal units of output adds to his total cost.

That the equilibrium of the monopolist will never be at the level of output at which the elasticity of demand curve or average revenue curve is less than one is illustrated in Fig. 26.5. It will be seen from Fig. 26.5 (upper panel) that upto *ON* level of output, *MR* is positive and total revenue is increasing because upto this output level, price elasticity of demand on the demand or average revenue curve is greater than one. *Monopoly equilibrium will always lie where price elasticity is greater than one if marginal cost is positive.* We know that at the middle point *R* of the straight-line demand or *AR* curve, elasticity is equal to one and corresponding to this unit elasticity point, marginal revenue is equal to zero. Below the middle point *R* on the average revenue curve, elasticity is less than one and marginal revenue is negative. The equilibrium of the monopolist, will never lie below the middle point of the average revenue curve *AR* as over this range, marginal revenue becomes negative and total revenue (*TR*) decreases as is evident from the falling the *TR* curve beyond *ON* output in the bottom part of Fig. 26.4. Thus, given that *MC* is positive, the equilibrium cannot lie below the middle point of the average revenue curve where elasticity is less than one. It will always lie above the middle point of the average revenue curve where elasticity is greater than one. The precise point on which equilibrium point lies depends, as already explained, upon the position of marginal cost curve and its intersection point with the marginal revenue curve.

Monopoly Equilibrium in Case of Zero Marginal Cost

There are, however, some cases where marginal cost is zero, that is, it costs nothing to produce additional units of output. For instance, in case of mineral spring, cost of production of mineral water is zero. Furthermore, in the very short period when a product is already on hand in excessive amount, it is not relevant to consider cost of production while determining the quantity of output to sell. *In these cases where cost of production is either zero or is irrelevant to consider the monopoly equilibrium will lie at a unit elasticity point on the demand curve.* This is because in such cases monopolist has only to decide at which output the total revenue will be maximum. And total revenue is maximum at the output level at which marginal revenue is zero. When marginal cost is zero, the condition of profit maximisation, that is, the equality between marginal cost and marginal revenue is achieved only at the output where the latter is zero. In Fig. 26.4 if marginal cost is zero, monopoly equilibrium will be achieved at *ON* level of output at which *MR* is zero. The price set by him in this situation will be *NR* or *OP*. *ON* quantity of output will yield maximum total revenue since beyond this marginal revenue becomes negative and total revenue will, therefore, start declining. Since cost of production is zero, the whole revenue will represent profits and because total revenue is maximum at *ON* output, the total profits will be maximum at this output. As at *ON* level of output, *MR* is zero and, as already seen, corresponding to zero marginal revenue, elasticity of the demand on the average revenue curve is equal to one or unity. We therefore conclude that *when cost of production is zero, monopoly equilibrium will be established at a level where price elasticity of demand is one*. If the marginal cost is positive, then, as explained above, monopolist will be in equilibrium at a point where elasticity on average revenue curve is greater than one.

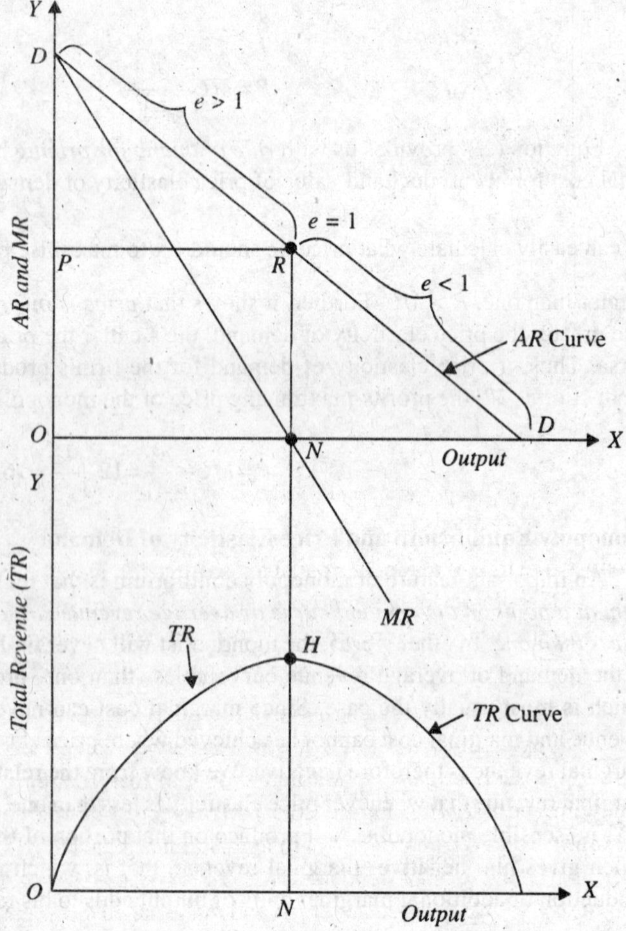

Fig. 26.4. *Monopolist cannot be in equilibrium at a level of output where elasticity of demand is less than one.*

LONG-RUN EQUILIBRIUM UNDER MONOPOLY

In the long run monopolist would make adjustment in the size of his plant. The long-run average cost curve and its corresponding long-run marginal cost curve portray the alternative plants, i.e., various plant sizes from which the firm has to choose for operation in the long-run. The monopolist would choose that plant size which is most appropriate for a particular level of demand. In the short run the monopolist adjusts the level of output while working with a given existing plant. His profit-maximising output in the short run will be where only the short-run marginal cost curve (*i.e.*, marginal cost curve with the existing plant) is equal to marginal revenue. But in the long run he can further increase his profits by adjusting the size of the plant. *So in the long run he will be in equilibrium at the level of output where given marginal revenue curve cuts the long run marginal cost curve.* Fixing output level at which marginal revenue is equal to long-run marginal cost shows that the size of the plant has also been adjusted. That is, a plant size has been chosen which is most optimal for a given demand for the product. It should be carefully noted that, in the long run, marginal revenue is also equal to short-run marginal cost. But this short-run marginal cost is of the plant which has been selected in the long run keeping in view the given demand for the product. Thus while, in the short run, marginal revenue is equal only to the short-run marginal cost of the given existing plant, in the long run marginal revenue is equal to the long-run marginal cost as well as to the short-run marginal cost of that plant which is appropriate for a given demand for the product in the long run. In the long-run equilibrium, therefore, both the long-run marginal cost curve and short-run marginal cost curve of the relevant plant intersect the marginal revenue curve at the same point.

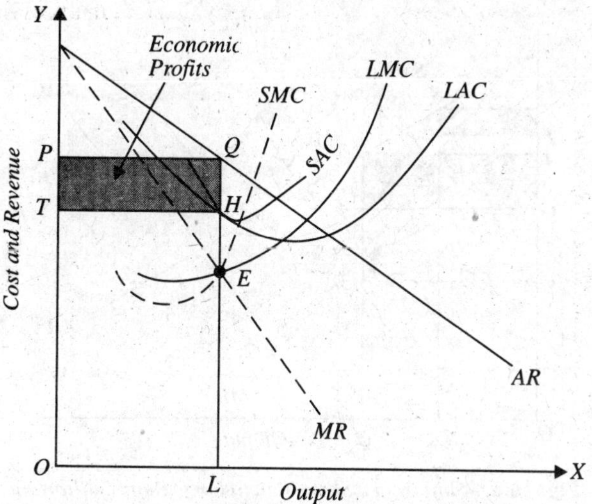

Fig. 26.5. *Long-Run Equilibrium under Monopoly*

Further, it is important to note that, in the long run, the *firm will operate at a point on the long-run average cost curve (LAC) at which the short-run average cost is tangent to it*. This is because it is only at such tangency point that short-run marginal cost (*SMC*) of a plant equals the long-run marginal cost (*LMC*). Figure 26.5 portrays the long-run equilibrium of the monopolist. He is in equilibrium at *OL* output at which long-run marginal curve *LMC* intersects marginal revenue curve *MR*. Given the level of demand as indicated by positions of *AR* and *MR* curves he would choose the plant size whose short-run average and marginal cost curves are *SAC* and *SMC*. He will be charging price equal to *LQ* or *OP* and will be making profits equal to the area of rectangle *THQP*.

It therefore follows that for the monopolist to maximise profits in the long run, the following conditions must be fulfilled

$$MR = LMC = SMC$$

$$SAC = LAC$$

$$P \geq LAC$$

The last condition implies that in *long-run monopoly equilibrium* price of the product should be either greater than long-run average cost or at least equal to it. The price cannot fall below long-run average cost because in the long run the monopolist will quit the industry if it is not even able to make normal profits.

Long-run Equilibrium Adjustment under Monopoly

In order to understand fully the difference between the short-run equilibrium and long-run adjustment under monopoly, it is necessary to show short-run equilibrium and long-run equilibrium in one figure. This has been done in Fig. 26.6 which shows that for a given level of demand, the monopolist will be in short-run equilibrium at point E or at output OQ_1 if he has plant size SAC_1 at that time. But in the long run he would not be in equilibrium at E since in the long run he can also change the plant and will employ that plant which is most appropriate for a given level of demand. In the long run he will be in equilibrium at point F where marginal revenue curve cuts his long-run marginal cost curve (*LMC*). But every point of the long-run marginal cost curve corresponds to a point of some short-run marginal cost curve. Long-run equilibrium point F at which marginal revenue curve cuts long-run marginal cost curve is also the point on short-run marginal cost curve SMC_2 which corresponds to the short-run average cost curve SAC_2. It means that, in long-run equilibrium position, monopolist has chosen the plant with short-run average and marginal cost curves SAC_2 and SMC_2. The plant having short-run cost curves SAC_2 and SMC_2 is optimal for him in the long run, given the level of demand as given by *AR* and *MR* curves. It is now clear that the monopolist who was in equilibrium at E in the short run with the given plant having cost curves SAC_1 and SMC_1 has shifted to the plant having cost curves SAC_2 and SMC_2 in his long run adjustment, level of demand being given. It will be noticed that, in the long run, the output has increased from OQ_1 to OQ_2 and price has fallen from *OP* to *OJ*. Profits have also increased in the long run; area *GHKJ* is larger than the area *TRSP*

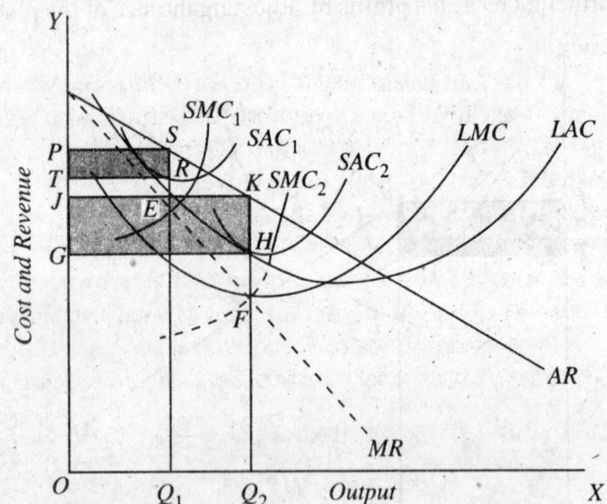

Fig. 26.6. *Shift from a Short-Run to Long-Run Equilibrium Position under Monopoly*

SOURCES OR REASONS OF MONOPOLY POWER

There are five major reasons or sources of monopoly. It is because of these reasons that monopolist enjoys a high degree of monopoly power. These sources relate to the factors which prevent the entry of new firms into an industry. Thus, these factors serve as barriers to the entry of new firms. We have explained earlier that strong barriers to the entry of new firms is an essential condition for the existence of monopoly. We explain below some of the important factors that serve as barriers to the entry of new firms and therefore constitute sources of monopoly.

1. Patent or Copyright. First important source of monopoly is that a firm may possess a patent or copyright which prevents others to produce the same product or use a particular production process. Generally, when the firms introduce *new products*, they get patent rights from the Governments so that others cannot produce them. These patent rights is granted for a certain period of time. For example, when copying machine was invented, its inventor '*Xerox*' Company had monopoly in its production based on a patent granted to it by the Government. Likewise, when a new medicine is invented by a medical company, it gets patent right from the Government so that it retains monopoly power over its production. Patents and copyrights constitute strong barrier to the entry of potential competitors.

2. Control over an Essential Raw-Material. Another source of monopoly is a control by a particular firm over an essential raw material or input used in the production of a commodity. For example, before World War II, Aluminium Company of America exercised exclusive control over almost every source of bauxite, which is an essential input for the manufacture of aluminium, had the monopoly power over the production of aluminium in the USA. Likewise OPEC (Organisation of Petroleum Exporting Countries) exercises monopoly power in the world over the supply of petroleum products from the Middle East countries as it has control over the supply of Crude Oil of these countries.

3. Grant of Franchise by the Government. Another important reason for monopoly is the grant of franchise by the Government to a firm. A firm is granted the exclusive legal right to produce a given product or service in a particular area or region. For example in Delhi the Government has granted the exclusive right to the Government owned Company DVB to provide or distribute electricity in Delhi. Likewise, Mahanagar Telephone Nigam Ltd. (MTNL) enjoys exclusive legal rights to provide landline telephone service in Delhi. It may be noted that when a company is given a franchise to produce a particular product or provide a particular service by the Government, the Government keeps with itself the right to regulate its price and quality.

4. Economies of Scale: Natural Monopoly. Another important source of monopoly is significant economies of scale over a wide range of initial output. When significant economies of scale are present, *average cost of production goes on falling over a wide range of output and reaches a minimum at an output rate that is large enough for a single firm to meet the entire market demand at a price that is profitable.* In such a situation if more than one firm operate to produce the product each firm must be producing the product at a higher than minimum cost per unit. In such a situation each firm is inclined to cut price to increase its output and reduce average cost of the product. This leads to price warfare and one who survives in this economic warfare emerges as monopolist.

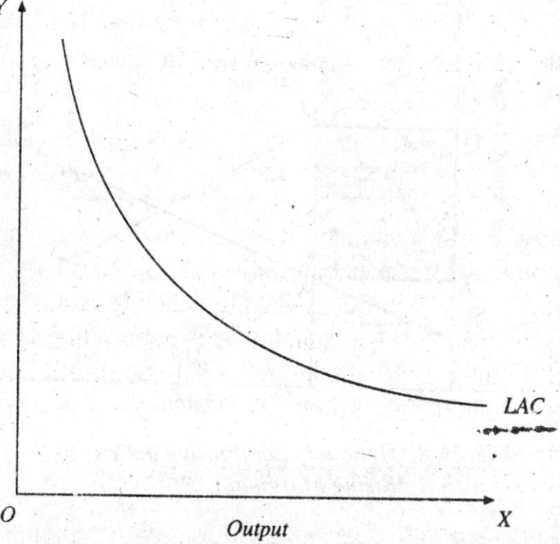

Fig. 26.7. *Significant Economies of Scale of a Natural Monopoly*

When there are significant economies of scale and as a result average cost decreases over a wide range of output, *natural monopoly is said to exist.* Natural monopolies are regulated by the Government so that they should not charge high prices and exploit the consumers.

5. Advertising and Brand Loyalties of the Established Firm. Another important reason that prevents the entry of new competitors in the industry is strong loyalties to the brands of the established firms and their heavy advertising campaigns to promote their brand. For example, strong loyalty of the consumers for 'Britannia Bread' makes it difficult for the potential competitors to enter. Further, for a long time in the USA the firm producing Coca Cola was a well-established firm to produce a famous cold drink and no one dared to enter this field till Pepsi Cola, another giant, came and broke its monopoly. Huge advertising campaigns and customer service programmes are often undertaken to enhance the market power of the producer and prevent the entry of potential competitors. Besides, if well-established firms are expecting new potential competitors, they cut prices of their products so that potential competitors find it unprofitable to enter the industry.

MONOPOLY EQUILIBRIUM AND PERFECTLY COMPETITIVE EQUILIBRIUM COMPARED

We have explained, in the preceding chapters, equilibrium of a perfectly competitive firm and industry and also how price was determined under. In the present chapter we have explained above the equilibrium under monopoly. It is now in the fitness of things to make a comparative study of the two. Only similarity between the two is that a firm under both perfect competition and monopoly is in equilibrium at the level of output at which marginal revenue equals marginal cost. But there are many important points of difference which we spell out below.

A significant difference between the two is that while *under perfect competition price equals marginal cost at the equilibrium output, under monopoly equilibrium price is greater than marginal cost*. Why? Under perfect competition average revenue curve is a horizontal straight line and therefore marginal revenue curve coincides with average revenue curve and as a result marginal revenue and average revenue are equal to each other at all levels of output. Therefore, at the equilibrium output marginal cost not only equals marginal revenue but also equals average revenue, that is, price. On the other hand, average revenue curve contronting a monopolistic firm slopes downward and marginal revenue curve therefore lies below it. Consequently, under monopoly, average revenue (or price) is greater than marginal revenue at all levels of output. Hence, at the equilibrium output of the monopolist where marginal cost equals marginal revenue, price stands higher than marginal cost. Thus, under perfectly competitive equilibrium, price = $MR = MC$. In monopoly equilibrium, price > MC.

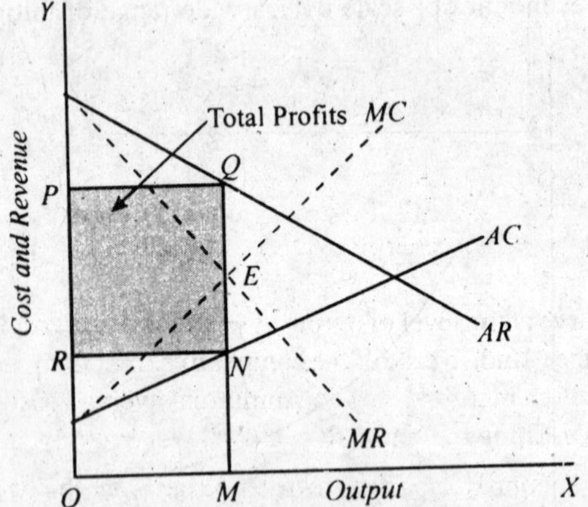

Fig. 26.8. *Monopoly Equilibrium in Case of Rising Marginal Cost*

A second important difference between the two is that while *under perfect competition, equilibrium is possible only when marginal cost is rising at the point of equilibrium, but monopoly equilibrium can be reached whether marginal cost is rising, remaining constant or falling at the equilibrium output*. This is so because the second order condition of equilibrium, namely, *MC* curve should cut *MR* curve from below at the equilibrium point, can be satisfied in monopoly in all the three cases, whether *MC* curve is rising, remaining constant or falling, whereas in perfect competition the second order condition is fulfilled only when *MC* curve is rising. Since in perfect competition the marginal revenue curve is a horizontal straight line, marginal cost curve can cut the marginal revenue curve from below only when it (*MC* curve) is rising. But, under monopoly, marginal revenue curve is falling downward and, therefore, marginal cost curve can cut the marginal revenue curve from below whether it (*MC* curve) is rising, remaining at constant level, or falling.

The equilibrium of the monopolist in these three cases is shown in Figs. 26.8, 26.9 and 26.10. Fig. 26.8 illustrates the equilibrium of the monopolist when marginal cost curve is rising at the equilibrium output. Fig. 26.9 shows monopoly equilibrium when marginal cost is constant at and near the equilibrium output. In Fig. 26.10 monopolist is in equilibrium when marginal cost is falling at and near the point of equilibrium. In all these three cases, *OP* represents the price determined, *OM* represents the equilibrium output, and *RNQP* represents total positive profits made, though their amount differs in different cases.

Another significant difference between the two is that *whereas a perfectly competitive firm is in long-run equilibrium at the minimum point of the long-run average cost curve, monopolistic firm is generally in equilibrium at the level of output where average cost is still declining* and has not yet reached its minimum point. In other words, whereas a perfectly competitive firm tends to be of optimum size in the long run, a monopolist firm stops short of the optimum size. This is so because it pays a competitive firm to expand production so long as average cost is falling since average revenue and marginal revenue remain constant but it does not pay a monopolist firm to expand production to the minimum point of the average cost curve because it is often not worthwhile for it to do so. More frequently, the marginal revenue curve of the monopolist intersects the marginal cost

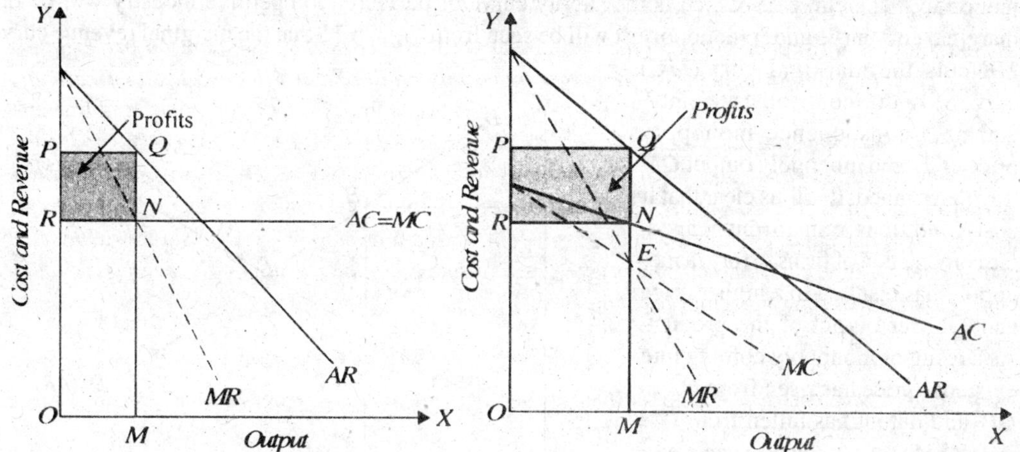

Fig. 26.9. *Monopolist Equilibrium in Case of Constant Costs*

Fig. 26.10. *Monopoly Equilibrium in Case of Falling Cost*

curve at the level of output at which average cost is still falling, as will be seen from Fig. 26.6. On the other hand, in case of the competitive firm, marginal revenue or price, in long-run equilibrium, is equal to both marginal cost and minimum average cost. In other words, profits of the competitive firm are, in the long run, maximum at the level of output at which long-run average cost is minimum.

Fourth important difference between the two is that *while the perfectly competitive firm is, in the long run, able to make only normal profits, a monopolist can make supernormal profits even in the long run.* Under perfect competition, if firms in the short run are making profits above normal, the new firms will enter the industry to compete away the profits. But under monopoly the firm continues earning supernormal profits even in the long run since there are strong barriers to the entry of new firms in the monopolistic industry. It should not however be understood from this that monopoly always guarantees super-normal profits. As already explained above, *the monopoly can even make losses, though only in the short run.* These short-run losses are not due to competition from any new firms but due to low demand and high costs. The point is, if a monopolist in the short run is making profits above normal, they cannot he eliminated by the entry of new firms in the long run with the result that these supernormal profits will persist in the long run provided that the demand and cost situations are nor changed unfavourably.

Another important difference between monopoly equilibrium and perfectly competitive equilibrium is that *under monopoly price is higher and output smaller than under perfect competition,* assuming cost conditions in the two cases to be the same. Suppose a number of firms are producing homogeneous products and pure or perfect competition in the sense so that no one can individually affect the price exists among them . Price and output will be determined at the level where demand and supply curves intersect each other. Suppose that all the firms constituting the competitive industry combine together so as to form a monopoly. We assume that no economies, internal or external, accrue when the firms combine together so that the cost or supply conditions remain unchanged. Note that the price and output under monopoly are determined by equality between marginal cost and marginal revenue and not by the intersection of demand and supply curves.

Price-output equilibrium under perfect competition and monopoly are graphically shown in a single diagram (Fig. 26.11). Curves *DD* and *SS* are respectively demand and supply curves of the perfectly competitive industry. The two curves intersect each other at point E and as a result price OP and output OM are determined under perfect competition. The marginal revenue curve MR is drawn corresponding to the demand curve DD. Now, what is the marginal cost curve of the monopoly? The curve SS which is the supply curve of perfectly competitive industry will be the marginal cost curve under monopoly. It will be seen from Fig. 26.11 that the marginal revenue curve MR cuts the marginal cost (MC) curve SS of the monopolist at point F and as a consequence monopoly price $O'P'$ and monopoly output OM' are determined. It is thus clear that if cost conditions remain unchanged, the combination of firms to form a monopoly has resulted in a higher price and a lower output of the product. As a result of monopoly coming into existence price has risen from OP to OP' and output has fallen from OM to OM' *Monopoly thus restricts output to raise price.*

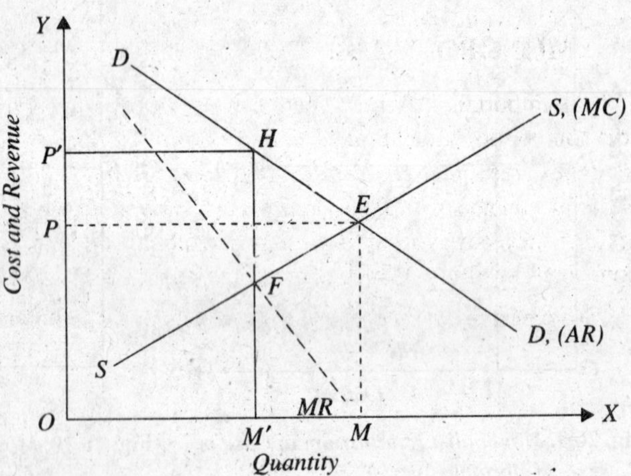

Fig. 26.11. *Under monopoly price is higher and output smaller than under perfect competition.*

Now, a pertinent question is whether cost conditions are likely to remain the same when a number of firms combine to become a monopoly? In other words, whether some extra economies will not accrue when the monopoly comes into existence and works on a large scale than that of a large number of small firms under perfect competition. There are two opinions on this issue. One view is that monopolist can introduce various economies such as greater specialisation in the work by bringing about suitable lateral and vertical integration, organization of sales on a large scale, buying raw materials and machinery on a big order, getting cheap credit, discovering and introducing new methods of production, and undertaking various measures which are generally associated with modernisation. These economies, it is held, will lower the cost of production of the monopolist with the result that the marginal cost curve (SS) in Fig. 26.11 will shift to a downward position when monopoly comes into existence. If these economies are large enough so that there is substantial fall in the cost curve, the monopoly price may be lower than the competitive price MP and monopoly output will be larger than the competitive output.

But in view of Mrs. Joan Robinson, "*perfect competition would bring about all the economies which monopoly could introduce.*"[2] She holds therefore that the cost curve will not shift downward significantly as a result of the establishment of monopoly in place of a large number of firms working under perfect competition. Thus, according to her, monopoly price is always higher and monopoly output always smaller than that under perfect competition.

Last significant difference between monopoly and perfect competition is that while a *monopolist can discriminate prices for his product, a perfect competition cannot.* The monopolist will be increasing his total profits by discriminating prices if he finds that elasticities of demand at the single monopoly price are different in different markets. But it is not possible for a firm under perfect competition to charge different prices from different buyers. This is because a seller under perfect competition confronts a perfectly elastic demand curve at the level of going market price. Therefore, if he tries to charge a bit higher price than the going market price from some buyers, they will turn to

2. Joan Robinson, *Economics of Imperfect Competition*, p. 168

other sellers and purchase the same product at the going market price. But the monopolist has the sole control over the supply of a product which has no close substitutes and therefore the demand curve of his product is very much less elastic. If the monopolist is able to break up his market into different parts on one basis or the other, it will be possible for him to discriminate prices in different parts of the market. But it will be profitable for him to charge prices in the different parts only if the elasticity of demand at the single monopoly price is different in different parts.

MONOPOLY AND INEFFICIENCY : SOCIAL COST OF MONOPOLY

An important difference between monopoly and perfect competition is that whereas under perfect competition allocation of resources is optimum and therefore social welfare is maximum, under monopoly resources are misallocated causing loss of social welfare. As seen above, when a product is produced and sold under conditions of monopoly, the monopolist gains at the expense of consumers, for they have to pay a price higher than marginal cost of production. This results in loss of consumers' welfare. Which is greater ? monopolist's gain or consumers' loss.

To measure welfare gain or loss some economists have used the concept of consumer's surplus. Consumer's surplus, it will be recalled, is the surplus of price which consumers are prepared to pay for a commodity over and above what they actually pay for it. The dead-weight loss in consumer's welfare due to monopoly can be shown through Figure 26.12 where *TD* is the demand curve for the monopolsist product, *MR* is the corresponding marginal revenue curve. It is assumed that the industry is a constant cost industry so that average cost (*AC*) remains the same as output is increased and marginal cost is equal to it.

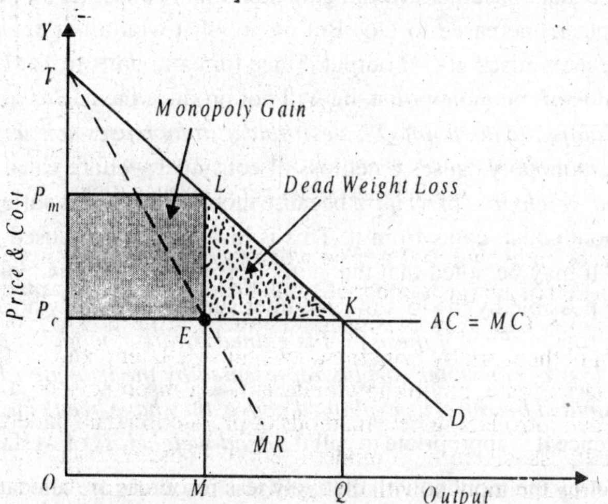

Fig. 26.12. *Dead-weight Loss or Social Cost of Monopoly*

Under perfect competition firms equate price with marginal cost and industry's output is determined by demand for and supply of the product. Since we are considering a constant cost industry, a horizontal line (*AC* = *MC*) is the supply curve of the industry. It will be seen from Figure 26.12 that under perfect competition price determined is equal to *QK* (or OP_C) and output *OQ* is being produced. Firms will be equating price OP_C with their marginal cost. The consumer surplus enjoyed by the consumers is equal to the area TKP_C. It may be noted that consumer surplus reflects social welfare as it is excess of what consumers are willing to pay (that is, the utility that they obtain) over and above what they actually pay.

Now, the monopolist would not produce OP_C output as he equates marginal revenue (*MR*) with marginal cost (*MC*) to maximise his profits. It will be seen from Fig. 26.12 that marginal revenue and marginal cost are equal at output level *OM*. Therefore the monopolist will produce *OM* output and charge *ML* or OP_m price. Thus, monopolist has restricted output to *OM* and raised price to OP_m. As a result monpolist makes profits equal to the area P_mLEP_c. On the other hand, as a result of rise in price to P_m, the consumers' surplus has been reduced to the area TLP_m and they suffer a loss of consumer surplus equal tot he area P_cKLP_m. Thus there is a redistribution of income from consumers to the monopolist, but it is important to note that loss of consumer surplus P_cKLP_m which is greater than the profits made by the monopolist by the area of triangle *LKE*.

The loss in consumer surplus can be divided into two components. First part is the profits equal to the area P_mLEP_c made by the monopolist at the expense of the consumers. This component of loss in consumer surplus is suffered by those who are still purchasing the product. The second component of the loss of consumer surplus is equal to the area of triangle *LKE* which is due to allocative inefficiency caused by the monopolist by reducing output of the product and raising its price. This second component of loss in consumer surplus as measured by the area of triangle *LKE* is called *dead-weight loss* of welfare caused by the monopolist. This represents **social cost of monopoly**. It will be seen from Figure 26.12 that price which the last existing consumer is willing to pay for *M*th unit is M_L while the marginal cost which has to be incurred by the society is *ME* and therefore from *M*th unit, consumer enjoys consumer surplus equal to *EL*. In other words, consumer values the product more than the opportunity cost of production as measured by the marginal cost (*MC*). Likewise, the price which the consumers are willing to pay for additional *MQ* units exceeds the marginal cost (*MC*) to the society and therefore generates additional consumer surplus.

Thus, the social welfare or consumer surplus would be increased if output is extended to the point *Q*. It will be seen from Figure 26.12 that consumers would gain additional consumer surplus equal to the area of triangle *LKE* if output is increased to *OQ*. But monopolist would not extend output to point *Q* because his profits are maximised at *OM* output. Since for extra units from *M* to *Q*, marginal cost exceeds marginal revenue of the monopolist, he will not produce them. *But from the social point of view, the extension of output to the point Q is desirable as it increases consumer surplus gained by the consumers.* Thus, monopoly causes a net loss of consumer welfare equal to area of triangle *LKE*. This is called *a dead weight loss of welfare* because though consumers suffer a loss of welfare, no one else, not even monopolist, gains from it. This is loss of welfare caused by allocative inefficiency of the monopoly. It may be noted that the gain of profits by the monopolist equal to the area P_mLEP_c has been made possible by the loss of consumer surplus of those who are still purchasing the *OM* quantity of the product. *Even if these profits gained by the monopolist are redistributed among the consumers, the loss of consumer surplus represented by the triangle LKE would still remain and would not be eliminated because, as explained above, they have been caused by allocative inefficiency of monopoly.* Hence it is appropriate to call it a *dead-weight loss* of welfare.

With lower production of the product by the monopolist, relatively less resources are allocated to its production. For optimum allocation of resources *OQ* amount of the product, at which marginal cost equals price should have been produced and resources allocated accordingly. To conclude, *monopoly causes misallocation of resources and dead-weight loss of welfare.* This is also called social cost of monopoly.

Dead - Weight Loss (Social Cost) under Monopoly in Case of Increasing Marginal Cost

In our above analysis of dead-weight welfare loss (or, in other words, social cost of monopoly) due to reduction in output and hike in the price by a monopolist as compared to the perfectly competitive equilibrium, it has been assumed that marginal cost curve is a horizontal straight line. When marginal cost curve is a horizontal straight line, the loss in welfare occurs only in consumer surplus. But when marginal cost curve is rising, the loss in welfare due to reduction in output by the monopolist will occur not only in reduction in consumer surplus but also in producer surplus. Producer surplus, it will be recalled, is the total revenue earned over and over all the opportunity costs (explicit and implicit) represented by the marginal cost curve. It may be noted that *maximum social welfare or economic efficiency is achieved when the sum of consumer surplus and producer surplus is the maximum.* In a perfectly competitive equilibrium where quantity demanded equals quantity supplied or price equals marginal cost, the sum of consumer surplus and producer surplus is maximum and therefore perfect competition ensures maximum social welfare or economic efficiency. But to maximize profits monopolist does not equate price with marginal cost. Instead, he equates marginal revenue with marginal cost and therefore reduces output and raises price and thereby causes loss of welfare. Loss in welfare as measured by the reduction in the sum of consumer surplus and producer surplus is illustrated in Figure 26.12(a).

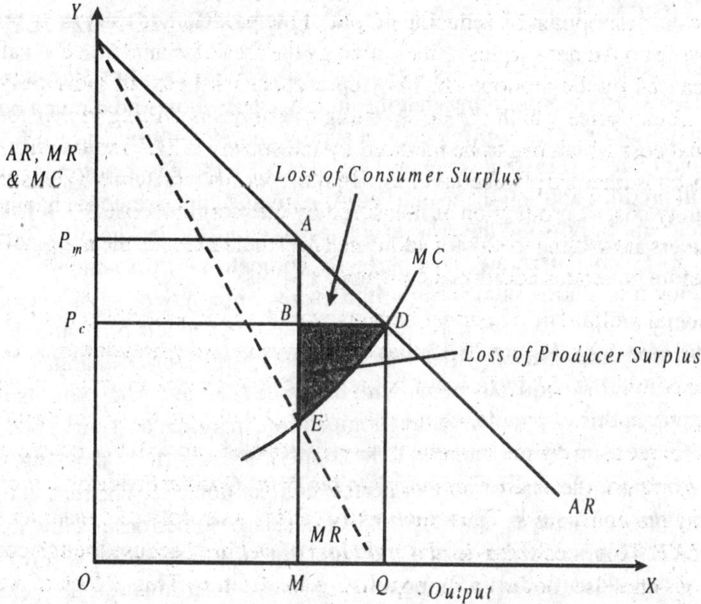

Fig. 26.12(a). *Dead-Weight Loss in Welfare in Case of Increasing Marginal Cost.*

It will be seen that, under perfect competition, equilibrium will be at point *D* where price is equal to marginal cost (*MC*) and *OQ* output is being produced and P_C price lis being charged. Now, if monopoly comes into existence, the monopolist-producer will maximize profits by producing lower output *OM* and will charge higher price P_m. It will be observed that the loss in consumer surplus suffered suffered by the buyers is equal to area P_cDAP_m. Due to the higher price charged by the monopolist, his gain in profits or producer surplus equals the rectangel P_cBAP_m. (It may be noted that this gain in producer surplus by the monopolist occurs at the expense of consumers who suffer a loss in consumer surplus and is equal to the price differential $P_m - P_c$ or *AB* multiplied by the monopoly output *OM*). Thus the gain in producer surplus represented by the area P_cBAP_m is just a transfer of income from the consumers to the monopolist. Net loss of consumer surplus or welfare is therefore the area of the triangle *ABD*.

However, in the situation depicted in Figure 26.12(a) where marginal cost is rising, apart from the net loss of consumer surplus, there is also a loss of producer surplus due to reduction in output by *OM* amount under monopoly. It will be seen from Figure 26.12(a) that under perfect competition with price equal to OP_c or *QD*, the extra profits or producer surplus earned over and above the marginal costs in the region of *MQ* output equals the area *BDE* which is lost due to the reduction in output equal to *QM* by the monopolist. This loss in producer surplus *BDE* is also a *dead weight loss* caused by the inefficiency or lower production due to monopoly because this has not benefited any other. Thus, the total dead weight loss of welfare caused by the monopoly is equal to the whole area *AED* which is the sum of net loss of consumer surplus (*ABD*) and the loss of producer surplus equal to *BDE* represents *social cost of monopoly*.

It follows from the partial equilibrium approach to the measurement of loss of welfare that monopoly is economically inefficient and causes misallocation of resources as it does not extend production of a product to the level at which the sum of consumer surplus and producer surplus is the maximum.

ABSENCE OF SUPPLY CURVE UNDER MONOPOLY

An important feature of the monopoly is that, unlike a competitive firm, *the monopolist does not have the supply curve.* It is worth noting that the supply curve shows how much output a firm will produce at various *given prices* of a product. The supply curve of a product by a firm traces out the *unique price-output relationship,* that is, against a given price there is a particular amount of output which the firm will produce and sell in the market. As explained in a previous chapter, the concept of supply curve is relevant only when the firm exercises no control over the price of the product and therefore takes it as given. Therefore, it is perfectly competitive firm which is a price taker and demand curve facing it is a horizontal straight line that a unique price-output relationship is established. For a perfectly competitive firm, marginal revenue *(MR)* equals price and therefore to maximize profits, the firm equates price (= *MR)* with marginal cost. As price changes due to the shift in demand, the competitive firm equates the new higher price *(i.e.* new *MR)* with its marginal cost at higher level of output. In this way under perfect competition, marginal cost curve becomes the supply curve of the firm. To quote professor Baumol, "The supply curve is strictly speaking, a concept which is usually relevant only for the case of pure or perfect competition .... The reason for this lies in its definition ... the supply curve is designed to answer question of the form, "How much will firm A supply if it encounters a price which is at *P* dollars. But such a question is most relevant to the behaviour of firms that actually deal with price over whose determination they exercise no influence."[3]

But a monopolist does not take the price as given and exercises control over the price of the

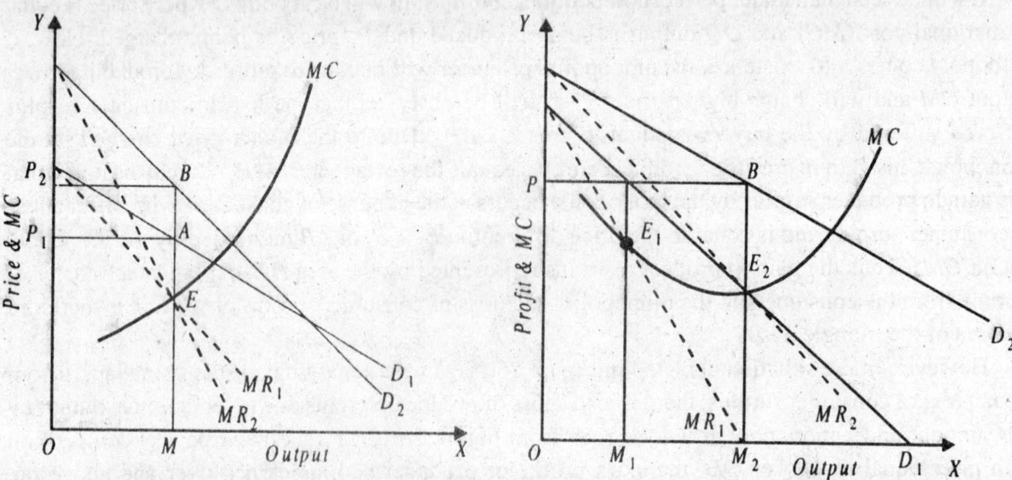

Fig. 26.13. *Under monopoly a shift in demand leading to the same output being supplied at two different prices.*

Fig. 26.14. *Under monopoly a shift in demand may lead to a change in output being supplied at the same price.*

product as he is the sole producer of the product. Further, for a monopoly firm demand curve slopes downward and marginal revenue *(MR)* curve lies below it. Therefore, a monopolist in order to maximise profits does not equate price with marginal cost; instead he equates marginal revenue with marginal cost. As a result, shifts in demand causing changes in price do not trace out a unique price-output series as happens in case of a perfectly competitive firm. In fact, under monopoly shifts in demand can lead to a change in price with no change in output or a change in output with no change in price or they can lead to changes in both price and output. This renders the concept of supply curve inapplicable and irrelevant under conditions of monopoly. Thus, there is no unique price-quantity relationship, since quantity supplied by a firm under monopoly is not determined by price but instead by marginal revenue, given the marginal cost curve. Thus, Joan Robinson writes, "When competition is not perfect, the demand curve for the output of each individual producer is not perfectly elastic and each producer will sell that output at which his marginal cost is equal to his marginal receipts Marginal revenue will not be equal to price, it is marginal revenue and not price that determines output of the individual producer."[4]

That, under monopoly, we do not get a series of unique price-output relationship or supply curve of a product is illustrated in Figure 26.13. Suppose the demand curve is initially D_1, corresponding to which MR_1 is the marginal revenue curve. Given the marginal cost curve MC, monopolist is in equilibrium at OM level of output and charging price OP_1. Now, suppose that demand curve shifts to the position D_2 corresponding to *which* MR_2 is the marginal revenue curve. It will be seen from Fig. 26.13 that the new marginal revenue curve MR_2 also intersects the given marginal cost curve MC at the same level of output OM as before the shift in the demand curve but price has risen to OP_2. Thus we see that under monopoly, a shift in demand may lead to the production and *supply of the same output at two different prices.* This clearly shows that there is no unique price-output relationship which is essential for the concept of supply curve to be applicable.

Figure 28.14 illustrates another special case where shift in demand leads to the *different levels of output being supplied at the same* price. Initially, with D_1 and MR_1 as the demand and marginal revenue curves respectively, the monopolist maximises his profits by producing output OM_1 and charging price OP. With the shift in demand curve to D_2 and the marginal revenue curve to MR_2, the marginal cost curve MC cuts the new MR_2 curve at E_2 and it will be observed from Figure 28.14 that in the new equilibrium, the monopolist produces higher quantity OM_2 at the same price OP. This again shows that under monopoly there is no any *specific* quantity of the product supplied at a price.

To sum up, under monopoly, there is no supply curve associating a unique output with a price. Shift in demand may lead to either change in price with the same output being produced and supplied or it may lead to the change in output with same price. However, usually the shift in demand would lead to the changes in both output and price. *How price and output will change as a result of shift in demand depends not only on the marginal cost curve but also on the price elasticity of demand.* The important thing to remember is that in sharp contrast to the case of a perfectly competitive firm, under monopoly marginal cost curve does not serve as the supply curve of the firm and further that there is no supply curve under monopoly depicting unique price-output relationship.

MEASUREMENT OF MONOPOLY POWER

Professor A.P. Lerner has put forward a measure of monopoly power which has gained great popularity and is most widely cited. Lerner takes perfect competition as the basis of departure for measuring monopoly power. He regards pure or perfect competition as the state of social optimum or maximum welfare and any departure from it would indicate the presence of some monopoly power leading to misallocation of resources or state of less than social optimum. As we know, in perfect competiton price is equal to marginal cost of the product in the equilibrium position. And it is this equality of price with marginal cost under perfect competition that ensures maximum social welfare or optimum allocation of resources.

Now, when competition is less than pure or perfect the demand curve facing a firm will be sloping downward and marginal revenue curve will lie below it. Consequently, when competition is

3. W.J. Baumol, *Economic Theory and Operations Analysis*, 2nd edition, p.342
4. Joan Robinson, *The Economics of Imperfect Competition*, p. 66

less than pure (perfect), that is, when it is imperfect, in a seller's equilibrium position, marginal cost will be equal to marginal revenue but price will stand higher than marginal cost or marginal revenue. *This divergence between price and marginal cost, according to Professor Lerner, is the indicator of the existence of monopoly power.* The greater this divergence between price and marginal cost, the greater the degree of monopoly power possessed by the seller. Based on this, Lerner has given the following precise index of the degree of monopoly power:

$$\text{Degree of monopoly power } = \frac{P-MC}{P}$$

where P denotes price and MC denotes marginal cost at the equilibrium level of output.

When competition is pure or perfect, price *(P)* is equal to marginal cost and therefore Lerner's index of monopoly power is equal to zero indicating no monopoly power at all, for when price is equal to marginal cost, $P - MC$ will be equal to zero and the above formula will yield the value of index as zero.

Thus, under perfect competition, Lerner's index of monopoly power $\left(\frac{P-MC}{P}\right) = \frac{0}{P} = 0$. On the other hand, when the monpolised product entails no cost of production, that is, when the product is a free good whose supply is controlled by one person, the marginal cost will be equal to zero and Lerner's index of monopoly power $\left(\frac{P-MC}{P}\right)$ would be equal to one or unity. Thus when MC is equal to zero $\frac{P-MC}{P} = \frac{P-0}{P} = \frac{P}{P} = 1$.

It is thus clear that Lerner's index of monopoly power can vary from zero to unity. Within this range, the greater the value of the index $\left(\frac{P-MC}{P}\right)$, *the greater the degree of monopoly power possessed by the seller.* For instance, if the price of a product is equal to Rs. 15 per unit and its marginal cost is Rs. 10, then the value of index of monopoly power will be $\frac{15-10}{15} = \frac{5}{15} = 1/3$ and when the price is equal to Rs. 20 and marginal cost is equal to 10, the index of monopoly power will be equal to $\frac{20-10}{20} = \frac{10}{20} = 1/2$.

Monopoly Power and Price Elasticity of Demand

Now, it has been shown that Lerner's index of monopoly power is equal to the inverse of the price elasticity of demand. We can prove this as follows:

Since at the equilibrium level, marginal cost is equal to marginal revenue, we can substitute in the above formula marginal revenue for marginal cost.

Thus

$$\text{Lerner's index of monopoly power } = \frac{P-MC}{P}$$

Since in equilibrium, $MC = MR$

$$\text{Lerner's index of monopoly power } = \frac{P-MR}{P} \quad \ldots \text{(i)}$$

We know that $MR = P\left(1 - \frac{1}{|e|}\right)$ where e is absolute value of the price elasticity of demand at the equilibrium output. Thus, putting $P\left(1-\frac{1}{|e|}\right)$ in place of MR in (i) above we get,

$$\text{Lerner's index of monopoly power} = \frac{P-MC}{P} = \frac{P-P\left(1-\frac{1}{|e|}\right)}{P} = 1-1+\frac{1}{|e|} = \frac{1}{|e|}.$$

It therefore follows that Lerner's index of monopoly power is equal to the inverse of price elasticity of demand. Thus degree of monopoly power can be judged by merely knowing the price elasticity of demand at the equilibrium output. *The degree of monopoly power varies inversely with the absolute value of price elasticity of demand for the good.* It is worth noting that the price elasticity of demand in Lerner's index refers only to the price elasticity at the equilibrium output.

Critique of Lerner's Measure of Monopoly Power

Lerner's measure has many shortcomings. First, the chief shortcoming of Lerner's measure is its inability to measure the strength of monopoly and competitive elements in the *non-price competition* and in cases of product differentiation as found in monopolistic competition and differentiated oligopoly. Lerner's index at the best measures the strengths of monopoly and competitive elements when the competition between the sellers is on the basis of price. When instead of competing on the basis of price the sellers in monopolistic competition and oligopoly compete on the basis of product variation, advertising and other of selling costs, Lerner's index fails to indicate truly the degree of monopoly and competition involved in such market structures. Suppose Lerner's monopoly index for a firm selling a differentiated product yields a high figure. But this does not necessarily mean that the seller will be possessing a high degree of monopoly power and facing less competition. It may be that the sellers of the various varieties of the product may not be competing on the basis of price and instead may be engaged in highly intense competition in product variation and advertising and other forms of selling costs to promote the sales of their products.

On the basis of the above non-price factors some firms may enjoy greater monopoly control over their products than others. Thus Professor Chamberlin rightly says that elasticity and Lerner's index measures "*pass over completely the important problems of competition and monopoly in the non price area; quality and other aspects of the product including location and advertising and other forms of selling costs.*"[5]

Secondly Lerner's measure is based upon only one aspect of monopoly, namely, its control over price which depends upon the *availability and effectiveness of existing substitutes*. It ignores the restraints on monopoly power put by the *potential substitutes* which would come to exist with the entry of new firms into the industry as a powerful factor limiting be monopoly power of the existing sellers. To quote Chamberlin again, "Neither elasticity nor the Lerner's index measures anything the effectiveness of existing substitutes; it gives no indication as to potential substitutes (the important problem of entry)."[6]

Thirdly, Lerner's index is criticised on the ground that monopoly power does not express itself only in the divergence of price from marginal cost, it also expresses itself in the restriction of output.

THE RULE OF THUMB FOR PRICING

We have explained above Lerner's index of monopoly power according to which degree of

5. E.H. Chamberlin, Measuring the Degree of Monopoly and Competition, printed in his "*Towards a General Theory of Value.*"
6. E.H. Chamberlin, *op. cit.*

monopoly is given by

$$\frac{P-MC}{P} = \frac{1}{e}$$

where $\frac{P-MC}{P}$ is the *mark-up* over marginal cost as a proportion of price. According to the above equation, this mark-up over price is equal to inverse of the absolute value of the price elasticity of demand for the product. It follows from above that there are following relations of mark-up over marginal cost with price elasticity of demand :

(*a*) The lower the price elasticity of demand, the greater the mark-up as a proportion of price and greater the monopoly power.

(*b*) The greater the price elasticity of demand, the smaller the mark-up as a proportion of price and less the monopoly power.

For example, if marginal cost of production at the equilibrium output is 9 and price elasticity of demand is 4. What will be the price ? Note that absolute value of price elasticity of demand is 4. Therefore,

$$\text{Mark up} = \frac{P-MC}{P} = \frac{P-9}{P} = \frac{1}{4}$$

$$P = 4P - 36$$

$$3P = 36$$

$$\text{Thus price or } P = \frac{36}{3} = 12$$

Now if at the equilibrium output with $MC = 9$, price elasticity of demand is 2, then

$$\frac{P-MC}{P} = \frac{P-9}{P} = \frac{1}{2}$$

$$P = 2P - 18$$

$$2P - P = 18$$

$$P = 18$$

It follows from above that given the marginal cost, the lower absolute value of price elasticity of demand, the greater the mark-up over marginal cost and, therefore, higher the level of price fixed by the producer.

Diagrammatic Illustration

The relation of price mark-up over marginal cost with monopoly power and price elasticity of demand is illustrated in Figure 26.14(A). In panel (*a*) of Fig. 26.14(A) price elasticity of demand at the equilibrium output *OQ* is relatively more, and therefore the power of the producer to raise price above marginal cost is less and as a result the mark-up (*P–MC*) is small. On the other hand, in panel (*b*) of Figure 26.14(A) price elasticity of demand at equilibrium output is less and therefore the greater the power of the producer to set price above marginal cost. As a result, price mark up $\left(\frac{P-MC}{P}\right)$ is much higher in panel (b) Fig. 26.14(A).

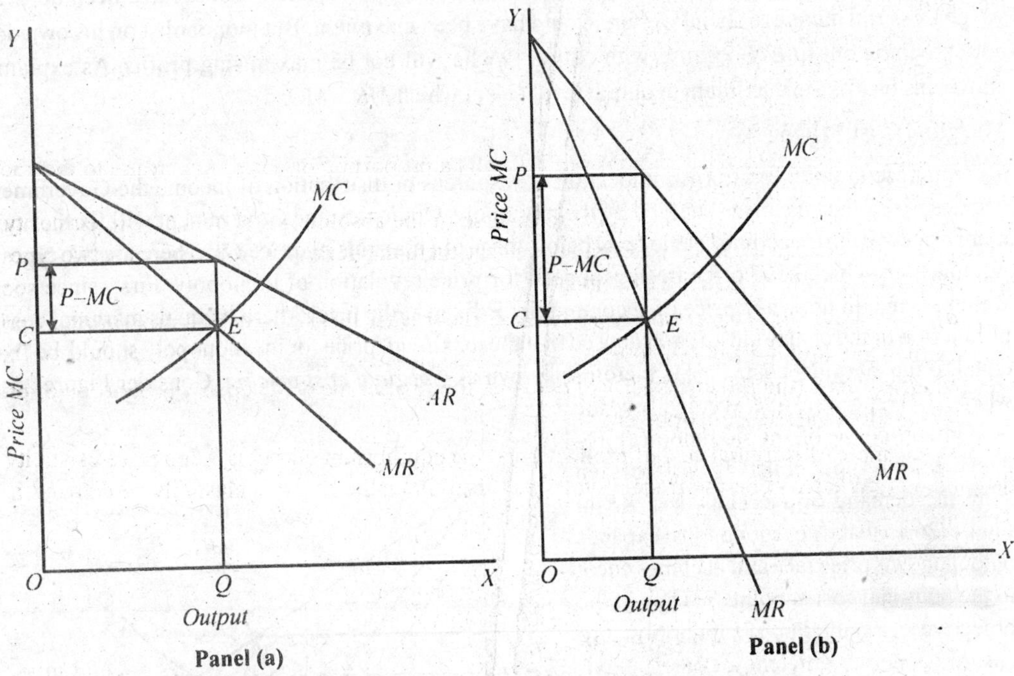

Figure 26.14(A). *Price Elasticity of Demand and Price Mark-up*

Thus, the relationship $\frac{P-MC}{P} = \frac{1}{e}$ provides us a rule of thumb for price fixation by a firm enjoying monopoly power. It has to fix price as a mark-up over marginal cost which is determined by the absolute value of the price elasticity of demand.

REGULATION OF MONOPOLY

It has been seen above that monopolists restrict output and raise price of their products, In this way they are not only generally able to make supernormal profits and increase inequalities in income distribution but also cause inefficiency in the allocation of resources of the society. It has therefore been felt to regulate monopoly with a view to achieving two objectives. First, it is regulated to improve income distribution and prevent exploitation of consumers by the monopolists. Secondly, monopoly is regulated so as to ensure economically efficient allocation of resources. Further, monopoly can be regulated either through suitable taxation or through fixation of the maximum price it can charge for its product. It is the *price regulation* of monopoly that we will discuss below.

Consider Figure 26.15 which gives cost and demand conditions faced by a monopolist. Without regulation of price charged by him, he is in equilibrium by producing the level of output *OQ* and setting price equal to *OP* at which his profits are maximum, and are equal to the area *PKLT*. He has been able to make these supernormal profits by producing a level of output less than what is socially desirable and also charging a price higher than what would be prevailing under perfect competition. It should be noted that by setting price equal to *OP* and producing output equal to *OQ* to maximise his profits the monopolist causes a *dead-weight loss* equal to the area *EKS* which represents loss of social welfare. This is because in the range of output *QN* the consumers are willing to pay more than the marginal cost (*MC*) of the monopolist (Note that the segment *KS* of the consumers' demand curve *DA* lies above the segment *ES* of the marginal cost curve of the monopolist. If the monopolist had extended his output level *ON* (i.e., point *S*) at which price = *MC*, there would have been no dead-weight loss and therefore social welfare would have been maximum. But monopolist on his own does not extend output to *ON* because with output *ON* he will not be maximising profits. As explained above, his profits are maximum at output level *OQ* at which *MR* = *MC*.

Marginal Cost Pricing

Suppose in order to improve allocation of resources or distribution of income the Government: decides to regulate the price charged by the monopoly. Obviously, the Government will fix the maximum price *(i.e.,* price ceiling) at the level below the profit maximising price *OP*. There are two types of pricing rules which have often been proposed for price regulation of monopoly. First, since social welfare is maximum when price of a commodity is fixed at the level where it equals marginal cost of production of the commodity, it is proposed that the maximum price for the monopoly should be fixed equal to the marginal cost. This is therefore known as *marginal cost pricing.* Consider Figure 26.15 where *AR* represents the average revenue or demand curve of the commodity produced by the monopolist. It will be seen from the demand or average curve *AR* in Figure 26.15 that when monopolist expands output on *ON*, price falls and becomes equal to the marginal cost at point *S*. Thus, if the objective of regulation of monopoly is to ensure economic efficiency, that is, maximum social welfare, the maximum price to be charged by the monopolist should be fixed at the level of marginal cost *OH* corresponding to the level of output *ON*. With this, the dead-weight loss will be eliminated and maximum social welfare will be attained.

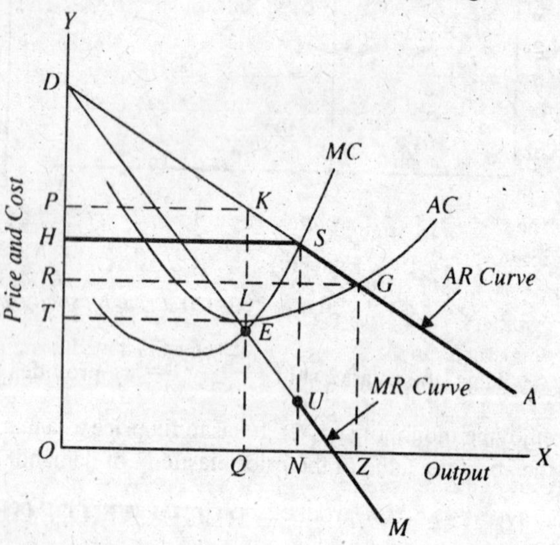

Fig. 26.15. *Regulation of Price Charged by a Monopoly: Marginal Cost Pricing*

It is important to note that with the maximum price *OH* fixed by the Government the monopolist will sell all units of output upto *N* at the same price *OH*. Therefore, with *OH* as the maximum regulated price for the monopolist, the part of the average revenue curve *DS* now becomes irrelevant. This is because he can sell any amount upto point *N* at the given regulated price *OH*. Therefore, his new average revenue curve upto the level of output *ON* becomes the horizontal straight line *HS*. Since average revenue curve remains constant over the range of output *ON*, marginal revenue curve would now coincide with the average revenue curve *HS* which has been thickened. Therefore, with regulation of price at *OH*, part *DU* of the marginal revenue curve also becomes irrelèvant. With regulated price at *OH*, the portion of demand or average revenue curve *SA* lying below the price *OH* would remain intact and unaffected and marginal revenue curve corresponding to this part of the average revenue curve is the thickened portion *UM*. Thus, with maximum regulated price *OH*, the average revenue curve for the monopolist becomes *HSA* and the marginal revenue curve is *HSUM* with the broken or discontinues portion *SU*.

It should be noted that with the given marginal cost curve *MC* and the new marginal revenue curve *HSUM* formed after the fixation of regulated price *OH*, the monopolist will be maximising his profits by producing *ON*. This is because if with the regulated price *OH* the monopolist produces more than *ON*, its marginal revenue will fall below the marginal cost showing losses on the extra units produced. And if with the regulated price *OH*, he produces less than *ON* level of output, marginal revenue exceeds marginal cost indicating the possibility of increasing profits by expanding output to the level *ON*. Thus, with the regulated price *OH* fixed on the basis of marginal cost principle, the monopolist is in equilibrium and maximising profits by producing *ON* level of output.

It is interesting to observe that in case of monopoly, when maximum regulated price *OH* is fixed below its free market profit-maximizing price *OP*, the monopolist expands his output from *OQ* to *ON* and buyers demand this much output at price *OH* and therefore no shortage of output is created as a result of the fixation of regulated price below its free-market profit maximising price *OP* of the monopolist. This is in sharp contrast to the price regulation of an industry working under perfect competition in which case when maximum price is fixed below the free-market equilibrium price at which the quantity demanded equals the quantity supplied, at the lower regulated price the quantity demanded exceeds the quantity supplied which results in shortage of the commodity. However, in monopoly, fixation of a lower price can lead to a greater output up to the point of equality of price with marginal cost. This is because if left free a monopolist restricts output to raise the price of the commodity. Now, with the fixation of the maximum price which he can charge, the reason for restricting output no longer exists. Indeed, at the maximum regulated price below his free-market price *OP*, if he continues to produce the same level of output *OQ*, his profits will decline. And further with regulated maximum price *OH*, he can increase his profits by raising output to the *ON* level.

Average Cost Pricing

Now, it will be seen from the Figure 26.15 that even with the imposition of maximum price equal to the marginal cost and his producing *ON* level of output, he is making supernormal profits, as his average revenue exceeds average cost of production. Those who want to regulate monopoly to improve the distribution of income or to ensure that lowest possible price be charged from the consumers, they propose that monopolist should not be allowed to make more than *fair return* on his capital investment, especially when he is producing an essential commodity. Their proposal is to adopt the average cost pricing for regulating the product-price of monopolist. Consider Figure 26.15. According to the average-cost pricing principle, the maximum price should be fixed at the level *OR* corresponding to which at point *G* average revenue or demand curve *DA* cuts the average cost curve *AC* at output level *OZ*. Thus with price equal to *OR* and output *OZ*, the monopolist is just covering his average cost of production. However, it may be noted that his *average cost includes normal profits or fair return on his capital investment*. This normal profits or fair return on capital is the opportunity cost of his capital, that is, the earnings which he can make elsewhere if he invests his capital in some other industry. Of course, what exactly is the fair return on capital has been a subject of severe controversy and Governments which regulate monopoly often appoint committees to decide about the fair return on capital investment which then become a part of the cost of production. To conclude, when average cost pricing principle is followed, it actually ensures fair return on capital.

Price Regulation of Natural Monopoly

Price regulation in case of a natural monopoly presents some problems. *A natural monopoly is said to exist when there occur economies of scale over a large expansion of output due to which average cost of production steadily declines and the extent of market demand for a commodity is such that it can support only one big optimum-size firm.* Under these circumstances a large-sized firm enjoying economies of scale and therefore having lower average cost of production can compete away the small-sized firms having higher average cost through setting a lower price. Thus, in case of occurrence of economies of scale upto quite a large output, one firm tends to dominate and succeed in establishing its monopoly.

Now, for a regulation of natural monopoly through marginal cost pricing a difficult problem is to faced. Figure 26.16 illustrates the case of marginal cost pricing in case of natural monopoly. Owing to economies of scale average cost is steadily declining throughout and marginal cost curve lies below it. *AR* and *MR* are the average and marginal revenue curves representing the demand conditions. It will be seen that marginal cost curve intersects the average revenue curve at point E, that is, if marginal cost pricing is followed, then price will be fixed at the level OP_m at which OQ_m quantity of the commodity will be sold. A glance at the Figure 26.16 will reveal that price OP_m is less than the average cost of production equal to OL at OQ_m level of output. This means that if marginal cost pricing is imposed on the monopolist he will have to incur losses equal to $LCEP_m$ and therefore will go out of business. In order that he continues to produce with price regulated at the marginal cost level, *he will have to be provided subsidies equal to the area $LCEP_m$*. This amount of subsidy will ensure him fair return on his capital investment, while producing OQ_m level of output.

However, if the Government does not want to give subsidies because of its financial constraint, average cost pricing policy may be adopted. It will be seen from Figure 26.16 average cost curve cuts the demand or average revenue curve AR at point S and therefore according to the rule of average cost pricing, price should be fixed at the level of OP_a at which the monopolist will produce OQ_a. With price equal to the average cost, the monopolist will make fair return on capital (included in average cost). It is worth noting that unregulated monopoly price will be equal to OP and if left free and unregulated, the monopolist will produce output equal to OQ and will therefore make profits equal to $PTKJ$. Thus, *even regulation of monopoly through average cost pricing leads to the expansion in output by the monopolist to OQ_a level and thereby cause expansion of output towards economically more efficient output* (the consumer's surplus or welfare will increase by expanding output from OQ to OQ_a). In other words, loss in welfare or economic efficiency suffered in case of unregulated monopoly will be reduced under average cost pricing due to the expansion in output and lowering of price. It should be further noted that with average cost pricing, the producer would not be making any monopoly profits; he will be earning only normal profits and fair return on his capital investment. Of course, as mentioned above, full economic efficiency or maximum social welfare is reached if marginal cost pricing is adopted. But, as seen above, in a case of natural monopoly, marginal cost pricing requires provision of subsidy by the Government if he is to be induced to stay in business.

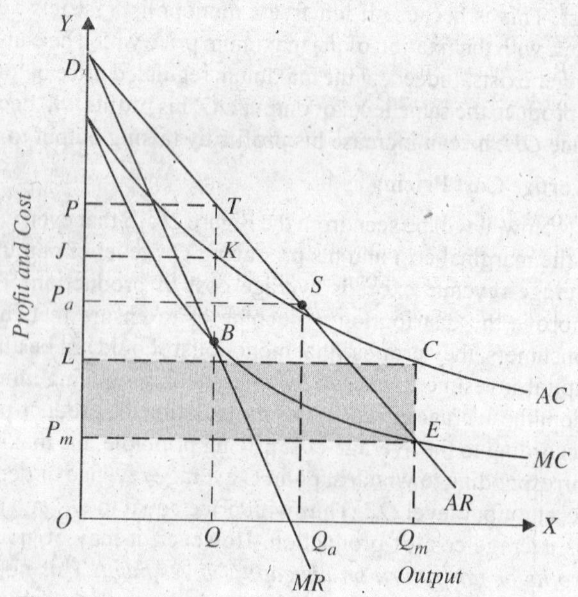

Fig. 26.16. *Regulating the Price of a Natural Monopoly*

MULTIPLANT MONOPOLY

In our analysis of determination of price and output under monopoly we considered the case of single plant monopoly. That is, a monopolist was producing a product by operating a single plant. We will now analyse determination of price and output of a monopolist who is producing an identical product in different plants. For the sake of simplicity we assume the monopolist operates two plants. It is further assumed that the cost structure of the two plants is different. In order to achieve his goal of profit maximisation, he has to take the following two decisions :

1. How much total output he should produce and what price he should fix for his product.

2. How to allocate the total profit-maximising output between the two plants for producing the product. That is, of the total output how much he should produce with plant *A* and how much with plant *B*.

Price-Output Equilibrium

As before we assume that monopolist is aware of demand for his product. Demand curve for his product is downward sloping and marginal revenue curve lies below it. In order to determine price and output that maximises his profits, the monopolist has to find out the total or combined marginal cost of production in the two plants. To obtain the total or combined marginal cost of production of the two plants, he will sum up horizontally the marginal cost (*MC*) curves of the two plants. In panel (*c*) of Fig. 26.17 combined marginal cost curve *CMC* has been obtained by adding up horizontally MC_a and MC_b of the two plants *A* and *B*. In order to maximise profits, the monopolist equates this combined marginal cost *CMC* with marginal revenue. It will be seen from panel (c) of Fig. 26.17 that combined marginal cost is equal to marginal revenue at *OQ* level of output, which can be sold at price *OP*. Therefore, the multiplant monopolist will produce *OQ* output and charge price *OP* of his product which will yield him maximum profits.

Allocation of Production between the Plants

To maximise profits for producing a given level of output cost needs to be minimised. Cost of producing a given level of output will be minimised if a given level of production is allocated between the two plants so that marginal costs in each plant are equal to each other and to the marginal revenue at the equilibrium level of total output. This is because if marginal cost of production in plant *A* is lower than *MC* in plant *B*, then cost of producing a given output can be reduced by increasing

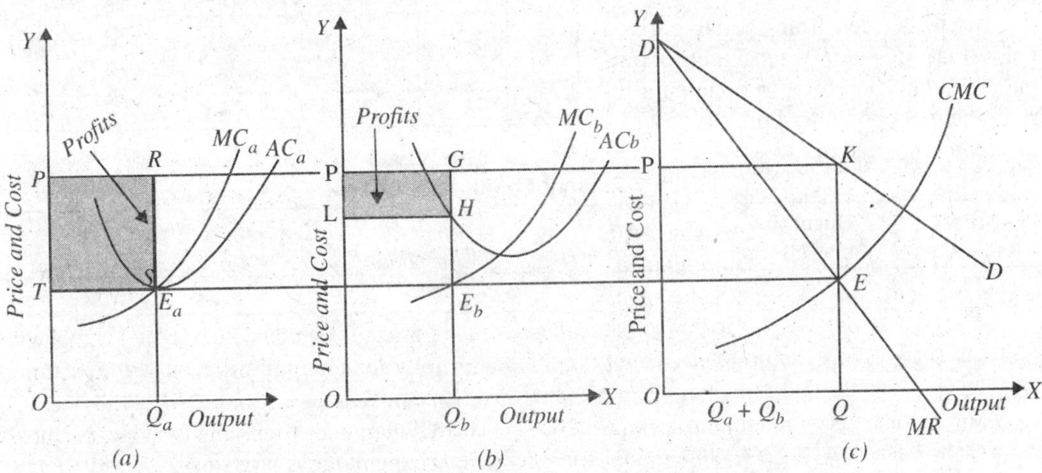

Fig. 26.17. *Multiplant Monopoly : Allocation of Production Between the Plants*

production in plant *A* and reducing production in plant *B* until the *MC* in the two plants becomes equal. Thus the total cost will be minimised and profits maximised by allocating production between the two plants when the following rule is satisfied :–

$$MC_a = MC_b = CMC = MR$$

In graphic terms the above rule is fulfilled when from the equilibrium point *E* in panel (*c*) we draw a horizontal straight line which intersects the marginal cost curve MC_a of plant *A* at point E_a and marginal cost curve MC_b of plant *B* at point E_b. At these points equilibrium condition ($MC_a = MC_b = MR = CMC$) is satisfied if output OQ_a (corresponding to point E_a) in plant A and output OQ_b

(corresponding to point E_b) in plant B are produced. It may be noted that sum of outputs OQ_a and OQ_b of the two plants will be equal to the total equilibrium output OQ because by summing up horizontally such outputs we have obtained the combined marginal cost curve CMC.

Since cost structure in the two plants is different, (in plant A, cost of production is lower than in plant B). profits earned in the two plants will also differ as the price charged for the product is the same. It will be seen from Fig. 26.17 that with output OQ_a and price OP, the profits earned by plant A are equal to the area $PRST$, and with output OQ_b in plant B, the profits made by the producer in plant B are equal to the area $PGHL$. Thus profits in plant A are much larger than that in plant B. This is as was expected because cost of production is lower in plant A as compared to plant B.

NUMERICAL PROBLEMS

Q.1. *The following demand function and total cost function of a monopolist are given. Calculate his marginal revenue and marginal cost. At what level of output, the monopolist will be in equilibrium. What price will be set at the equilibrium output and calculate total profits made by him.*

Price (Rs.)	Quantity sold	Total cost (Rs.)
15	1	12
14	2	22
13	3	31
12	4	39
11	5	46
10	6	54
9	7	64
8	8	75

Solution. In order to find marginal revenue (MR) we have first to calculate total revenue (TR). $MR = TR_n - TR_{n-1}$ and marginal cost which is $TC_n - TC_{n-1}$ The monopolist will be in equilibrium at the level of output at which $MR = MC$. Calculating TR, MR and MC we have the following table.

It will be seen from the table given below that $MC = MR$ when 5 units of output are sold. Therefore, to be in equilibrium the monopolist will produce 5 units to maximise his profits.

Table : Finding Equilibrium Output

Price (P) Rs.	Quantity sold (Q)	TR ($P \times Q$)	MR $TR_n - TR_{n-1}$	TC Rs.	MC $TC_n - TC_{n-1}$
15	1	15	15	12	12
14	2	28	13	22	10
13	3	39	11	31	9
12	4	48	9	39	8
11	5	55	7	46	7
10	6	60	5	54	8
9	7	63	3	64	10
8	8	64	1	75	11

Table : Finding Equilibrium Output Price $= AR = \frac{TR}{Q} = \frac{55}{5} = 11$

Total profits $= TR - TC = 55 - 46 = 9$

Numerical Problem 2

Suppose a monopolist faces the following demand schedule

(*i*) *Calculate the marginal revenue. If marginal cost is Rs. 50 what is the profit-maximising level of output and price.*

(*ii*) *If price is set equal to marginal cost, what will be the output that the monopoly will produce ?*

DU B.A. (Honours) Economics 2008

Solution. Note that in this problem quantity demanded (or sold) increases by blocks of 5 units and price changes by blocks of Rs. 10. This should be kept in mind while calculating marginal revenue.

To obtain marginal revenue we have first to calculate total revenue (TR) which is equal to $P \times Q$. Then marginal revenue $(MR) = \frac{\Delta TR}{\Delta Q}$. We calculate MR below.

Demand Schedule

Price, P	Quantity, Q
100	0
90	5
80	10
70	15
60	20
50	25
40	30
30	35

Price (P) Rs.	Quantity demanded or sold (Q)	Total Revenue (TR) ($P \times Q$)	$MR\left(=\frac{\Delta TR}{\Delta Q}\right)$
100	0	0	0
90	5	450	$\frac{450}{5}=90$
80	10	800	$\frac{350}{5}=70$
70	15	1050	$\frac{250}{5}=50$
60	20	1200	$\frac{150}{5}=30$
50	25	1250	$\frac{50}{5}=10$
40	30	1200	$\frac{-50}{5}=-10$
30	35	1050	$\frac{-150}{5}=-30$

Given marginal cost equal to Rs.50, the profit-maximising condition of $MC = M_1R$ is satisfied when 15 units of the product are sold. It will be seen from the above table that with 15 units of output sale price of the product is Rs. 70 per unit.

(*ii*) If price is set equal to marginal cost, that is, Rs. 50, then as will be seen from the above table, 25 units of output will be produced and sold by the monopolist.

NUMERICAL PROBLEMS

Problem 1. *A monopolist faces a demand curve, $P = 100 - 2Q$. If marginal cost is constant and is equal to 20. What is the amount of profits made by the monopolist ? What is dead weight welfare loss on account of monopoly?*

Solution. For monopoly equilibrium, $MR = MC$. The given demand curve is $P = 100 - 2Q$

$$TR = PQ = 100Q - 2Q^2$$

$$MR = \frac{d(TR)}{dQ} = \frac{d(PQ)}{dQ}$$

$$= 100 - 4Q$$

Equating MR with $MC(= 20)$ we have

$$100 - 4Q = 20$$
$$4Q = 100 - 20 = 80$$
$$Q = \frac{80}{4} = 20$$

To obtain equilibrium price we substitute $Q = 20$ in the given demand function. Thus

$$P = 100 - 2 \times 20$$
$$= 100 - 40 = \text{Rs. } 60$$

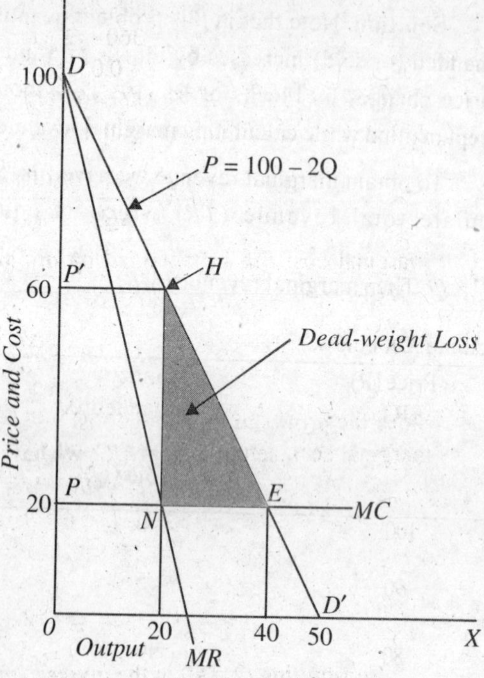

Fig. 26.18. *Monopoly Equilibrium and Dead-Weight Loss*

Calculating Dead-Weight Loss

Welfare is maximised. when at the output produced price equals marginal cost as under conditions of perfect competition. Thus, equating price with marginal cost we have

$$P = MC$$
$$100 - 2Q = 20$$
$$2Q = 100 - 20 = 80$$
$$Q = 40$$

In Fig. 26.18 consumer's surplus with output equal to 40 and price equal to 20 is equal to the area *DPE*. Monopoly restricts output to 20 and raises price to 60 or *OP′*. Therefore, under monopoly, consumer surplus is reduced to the area *DP′H*. Thus, consumers suffer a loss of welfare (*i.e.* consumer's surplus) equal to the area *PP′HE*. The monopolist's profits as a result of restriction of output from 40 units to 20 units and rasing of price of the product from 20 to Rs. 60, is equal to the area *PNHP′* (*i.e.* 40 × 20 = Rs. 800). But consumers suffer a greater loss of consumer surplus equal to the area *PP′HE*, that is, *NHE* more than the gain in profits by the monopolist. The welfare loss of consumers equal to the area *NHE* represents the **dead weight loss** of welfare and is equl to

$$= \frac{1}{2}(40 \times 20) = \frac{1}{2}(800)$$
$$= 400$$

This dead-weight loss represents social cost of monopoly.

Problem 2. *Suppose the following demand and total cost functions of a monopolist are given (demand function)*

$$Q = 360 - 20P$$
$$TC = 6Q + 0.05Q^2 \quad \textit{(cost function)}$$

Determine equilibrium output of the monopolist. What price will be charged in this equilibrium solution ?

Solution. In order to find the profit-maximising solution we have to derive the marginal revenue and marginal cost from the demand and cost equations given above. In order to find out the marginal revenue we have to first obtain the total revenue function.

Rearranging to obtain the *inverse* demand function

$$Q = 360 - 20P$$
$$20P = 360 - Q$$
$$P = 18 - 0.05Q \quad \text{(inverse demand function)} \quad \ldots \text{(i)}$$

Total revenue $(TR) = P.Q = 18Q - 0.05Q^2$

Differentiating TR function with respect to output Q, we can get MR. Thus,

$$MR = \frac{\Delta TR}{\Delta Q} = \frac{\Delta(P.Q)}{\Delta Q} = 18 - 0.1Q \quad \ldots \text{(ii)}$$

Marginal cost can be obtained by differentiating the given total cost function ($TC = 6Q + 0.05Q^2$)

$$MC = \frac{\Delta TC}{\Delta Q} = 6 + 0.1Q \quad \ldots (iii)$$

Since the profits of the monopolist will be maximised when he equates marginal revenue with marginal cost, setting $MR = MC$, we have

$$MR = MC$$
$$18 - 0.1Q = 6 + 0.1Q$$
$$0.2Q = 18 - 6 = 12$$
$$Q = 12.\frac{10}{2} = 60$$

Substituting $Q = 60$ in the inverse demand function (*i*) we have

$$P = 18 - 0.05 \times 60 = 15$$
$$TR = P.Q = 15 \times 60 = 900$$
$$TC = 6Q + 0.05Q^2 = 6 \times 60 + 0.05\,(60)^2$$
$$= 360 + \frac{5}{100} \times 3600 = 540$$

Profits $= TR - TC = 900 - 540 = 360$

Thus, output $(Q) = 60$; price $(P) = 15$ and profits = Rs. 360

Problem 3. *A monopolist has the following total cost function $TC = 10 + 5Q$*

(1) *If the price elasticity of demand for his products is – 2, find out pirce he will fix for his product.*

(2) *If the price elasticity of demand for his product changes to –4, how will he change his price ?*

Solution.

$$TC = 10 + 5Q$$
$$MC = \frac{\Delta TC}{\Delta Q} = 5 \quad \ldots (1)$$

The relationship between MR, price and price elasticity of demand (e) is

$$MR = P\left(1 + \frac{1}{e}\right)$$

Given that price elasticity of demand is – 2,

$$MR = P\left(1 + \frac{1}{-2}\right) = P\left(1 - \frac{1}{2}\right)$$

$$MR = \frac{1}{2}P \qquad \ldots (2)$$

In equilibrium $MR = MC$

$$\frac{1}{2}P = 5$$

$$P = 5 \times 2 = \text{Rs. } 10$$

Given that price elasticity of demand, $e = -4$

$$MR = P\left(1 + \frac{1}{-4}\right) = P\left(1 - \frac{1}{4}\right) = \frac{3}{4}P$$

In equilibrium $MR = MC$

$$\frac{3}{4}P = 5; \quad P = 5 \times \frac{4}{3} = 6.67$$

Thus, with the increase in absolute value of price elasticity of demand, monopolist will reduce the price of his product.

Problem 4. *Suppose the price elasticity of demand for the product of a monopolist is –2.0. Show that price fixed by him will be twice the marginal cost of pröduction.*

Solution. In price-output equilibrium of the monopolist

$$MR = MC$$

Since $MR = P\left(1 - \frac{1}{|e|}\right)$

In equilibrium, $MC = P\left(1 - \frac{1}{|e|}\right)$

If $e = 2.0$

$$MC = P\left(1 - \frac{1}{2}\right) = \frac{1}{2}P, \quad \text{or} \quad P = 2MC$$

Problem 5. *Given the following linear demand and cost functions, show that monopolist will produce half the output under perfect competition*

$Q = 300 - 2P$ (Linear demand function)

$TC = 150 + 10Q$

Solution.

$$TC = 150 + 10Q$$

$$MC = \frac{\Delta TC}{\Delta Q} = 10 \qquad \ldots (i)$$

Now, the given linear demand function is

$$Q = 300 - 2P$$

$$2P = 300 - Q$$

$$P = 150 - 0.5Q \qquad \ldots (ii)$$

$$TR = PQ = 150Q - 0.5Q^2$$

$$MR = \frac{\Delta(PQ)}{\Delta Q} = 150 - Q \qquad \ldots (iii)$$

Ouput under perfect competition is determined where $MC = P$

Thus, in equilibrium under perfect competition

$$10 = 150 - 0.5Q$$

$$0.5Q = 150 - 10 = 140$$

Hence, $Q_{PC} = 280$ ... (*iv*)

In equilibrium under monopoly,

$$MR = MC$$

From (*iii*) we know $MR = 150 - Q$ and from (*i*) we know that $MC = 10$

Thus, in equilibrium under monopoly

$$150 - Q = 10$$

$$Q = 150 - 10 = 140$$

Thus, $Q_m = 140$ ... (*v*)

Comparing (*iv*) nad (*v*) we find that output under monopoly is half of that under perfect competition.

QUESTIONS AND PROBLEMS FOR REVIEW

1. What is monopoly? Explain the three conditions necessary for the existence of monopoly.
2. Explain the relationship between average revenue, marginal revenue and price elasticity of demand under the conditions of monopoly.
3. Explain the equilibrium of a monopoly firm ? Show that price fixed by the monopolist is less than marginal cost of production.
4. How are price and output determined under monopoly. Show that under monopoly price is higher and output smaller than under perfect competition.
5. *Show that a monopolist will always operate on the elastic part of the demand curve.* *D.U. B.A. (Hons.) 2002*
6. A monopolist will never be in equilibrium on the *inelastic* ($e_p < 1$) portion of the demand curve. Explain. *D.U.B.A.(H) 2001*
7. A monopolistic firm has the following total cost function and demand function.

Price (Rupees)	*Quantity demand (Units)*	*Total cost (Rs)*
8	5	20
7	6	21
6	7	22
5	8	23
4	9	24
3	10	25

Explain what price will be charged and what output will be produced.

[**Hint**: From the given data of price and quantity demanded, first find out total revenue ($TR = P.Q$). From *TR*, marginal revenue can be obtained at different levels of quantity demanded or sold. From total cost data, *MC* can be obtained. Then the output level at which $MC = MR$, will be the equilibrium output and price at that will be equilibrium price. In the above table, *MC* is constant at Re. 1. When 6 units of sold, MR =2 and when 7, units are sold, $MR = 0$, therefore the firm should produce 6 units of output to maximise profits].

8. *How is monopoly power measured ? State Lerner's measure of degree of monopoly power. Show that degree of monopoly power* is *inverse of the price elasticity of demand.*
9. A simple monopolist is in equilibrium. At the point of equilibrium the coefficient of price elasticity is - 2.0 and the marginal cost is Rs. 4.0. Calculate his equilibrium price. How will this price be effected by an increase in the fixed cost of the monopolist. *D.U. B.A. (Hons). 1996.*

[**Hints** : In equilibrium, $MC = MR$

Since $MR = P\left(1 - \frac{1}{|e|}\right)$

Given $MC = 4$ and $e = -2$

$$i.e.\quad 4 = P\left(1-\frac{1}{2}\right)$$

$$P = 4\times\frac{2}{1}=8]$$

10. When a monopolist is maximising profits price is greater than marginal cost. Thus consumers will be paying more for additional units of output than it costs to produce. So why does not the monopolist produce more ? *D.U. B.A (Hons) 1988*

11. A monopolist plans to produce 100 units of a commodity and observes that the price elasticity of demand at this output is 0.5. What advice would you give to the monopolist ?

D.U. B.A. (Hons) 1993

[**Hints.** Since *MR* is negative at an output level where price elasticity is less than one, the monopolist will not be making maximum profits. In fact, he may be making losses if he pursues his plan. Therefore, the monopolist should restrict output of the commodity to the level where price elasticity of demand is greater than one and where his *MC* = *MR*]

12. A monopolist will never sell its product at a price less than its average total cost. Is it true or false ? Give reasons. *D.U. B.A. (Hons) 1993*

13. Explain why marginal revenue of a monopolist is less than the price charged.

D.U. B.A. (Hons) 1993

14. Explain why a perfectly competitive firm will never operate when marginal cost is declining but a monopoly firm can do so. *D.U. B.A. (Hons) 1993*

15. If a price making monopolistic firm wants to maximise its sales revenue, it should :

(*a*) set the highest price it can get.

(*b*) set the lowest price it can get.

(*c*) choose a selling price at which the elasticity of demand for its product is unity.

(d) choose a selling price where the extra revenue received from the last unit sold exceeds the extra cost of making that unit.

Tick the right answer.

16. Suppose that at the profit maximising output, a monopolist price is twice as high as his marginal cost. What is the price elasticity of demand. *D.U. B.A. (Hons) 1991*

17. Does a monopolist always set his price above marginal cost ? Will he ever produce at the minimum point of long-run average curve.

[**Hints.** As explained in the text a monopolist always sets his price above marginal cost of production. Further, in the long run he usually produces less than the minimum point of LAC, that is, he produces with excess capacity in the long run. *However, this is not necessary* as it depends on the demand conditions facing him. If demand for his product is sufficiently large he may produce at or near the minimum point of long-run average curve, that is, produces with a optimal scale of plant and uses it at its full capacity (see Fig. 26.19). However, there is no certainty that monopolist will produce at this optimal level, as is the case under perfect competition. This is because unlike in competitive market conditions, no market forces operate under monopoly that compel the monopolist to work wtih optimum plant size and uses it at its full capacity.

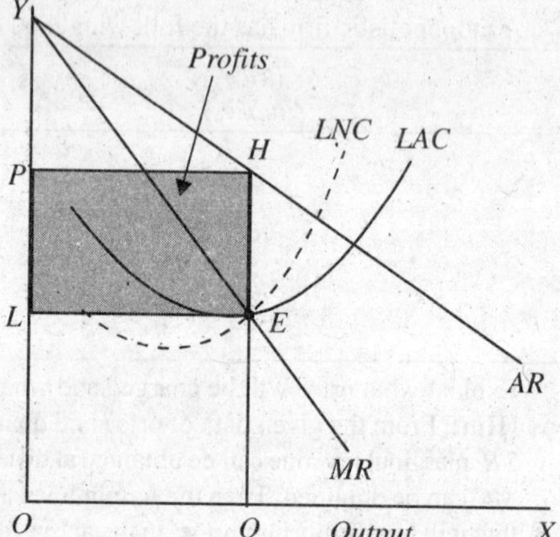

Fig. 26.19. *Monopolist working at the minimum point of LAC*

18. A monopolist has attained equilibrium on a point on the demand curve where the coefficient of price elasticity is – 2.5 and the equilibrium price is Rs. 20.00. Calculate his marginal revenue.

19. What do you understand by 'dead-weight loss' of monopoly ? If the gains to producers be redistributed to consumers, would the "dead-weight loss" be eliminated ? *D.U. B.A (Hons) 2000*

20. What is a social cost of monopoly ? If the gains to the monopolist could be redistributed to consumers, would the social cost of monopoly be eliminated. Explain briefly. *D.U. B.A. (Hons) 1995*

21. Let the demand function for an industry's output be $Q = 50 - 5P$, where P is price and Q is the output. Assume constant costs at Rs. 6 per unit of output.

(*i*) How much would a profit-maximising monopolist produce ? What would be the equilibrium price ?

(*ii*) Now assume the commodity is produced by a public sector undertaking which follows the *marginal* cost *pricing principle*. What would be the optimal quantity produced ?

[**Hints** (*ii*) A public sector undertaking following marginal cost-pricing principle would set the price equal to marginal cost of production. Thus

$$Q = 50 - 5P \quad \ldots (1)$$

$$5P = 50 - Q$$

$$P = 10 - 1/5\,Q \quad \ldots (2)$$

Setting price (*P*) equal to marginal cost we have

$$6 = 10 - 1/5\,Q$$

$$1/5Q \quad \text{or} \quad = 10 - 6 = 4, \quad Q = 20]$$

22. Consider a shift in demand under monopoly. In two separate diagrams, show that this can result in:

(*i*) Different quantities being supplied at the same price.

(*ii*) Different prices supporting the same quantity. Hence show that a monopolist does not have a unique supply curve. *D.U. B.A. (Hons) 1999*

23. We write the percentage make-up of price over marginal cost as $(P - MC)/P$. For a profit maximising monopolist, how does this mark-up depend on the elasticity of demand ? Why can this marke-up be viewd as a measure of monopoly power ? *D.U. B.A. (Hons) 1995*

24. Show why supply curve does not exist under monopoly. Explain with diagrams. *[D.U.B. Com. (H), 2006, 2007, C.U., B.Com., (H), 1998, 95]*

25. Explain how average revenue curve, marginal revenue curve and elasticity of demand are related to one another. Why should a monopoly firm not sell below the price where elasticity of demand is less than one? *D.U., B. Com (Hons) 2000*

26. Explain the long-run equilibrium under monopoly. Explain the adjustment process how a monopoly firm with shift from the short-run equilibrium to the long-run equilibrium position. Why is monopoly profits not likely to be eliminated ?

27. Show how monopoly causes misallocation of resources and thereby causes loss of social welfare

OR

Monopoly is said to be economically inefficient. Explain and show how it causes dead weight loss. *[D.U., B.Com. (H), 1996]*

28. If natural monopoly is regulated to produce the perfectly competitive output, it would have losses. Do you agree ? Explain. *DU., B.A. (Hons.) Ist Year 2006*

29. Regulators require a natural monopoly to charge a price equal to marginal cost, the monopoly will incur losses. State whether true or false. *DU., B.A (Hons.) Ist Year 2007*

30. How will a multi-plant monopolist maximise profits and how will he decide how much of that output each plant should produce? *DU., B.Com (Hons) 2006,2007*

31. Explain price regulation of a monpoly. How price regulation can eliminate deadweight loss that results from monopoly power ? *DU., B.Com (Hons.) 2006*

32. What do you mean by degree of monopoly power? (*i*) How can Lerner's index be used to measure monopoly power. (*ii*) what are the social cost of such a power ? *DU., B.Com (Hons.) 2007, 2008, 2009*

33. Derive the *Rule of Thumb* for pricing under monopoly. Using this concept show how a zero cost firm will determine its profit-maximising output and price. Show it diagrammatically also. *DU., B.Com (Hons.) 2008*

Chapter 26A
GOVERNMENT POLICIES TOWARDS MONOPOLY AND COMPETITION

Introduction

People look at monopolies with suspicion and they are considered as undesirable form of market structure. The existence of monopolies in an economy is an important cause of glaring income inequalities and monopolists wield a lot of economic power which they use to exploit both consumers and workers. Economists generally criticise monopolies as they restrict output and raise prices of their products. Thus monopolies and oligopolies not only increase income inequalities but also cause inefficiency in the allocation of resources of a society. In this chapter we analyse the economic effects of monopolies and imperfect competition represented by oligopolies and what policies government can adopt to reduce their bad effects and to achieve economic efficiency.

THE DRAWBACKS OF MONOPOLIES AND LIMITED COMPETITION

The effect of monopolies and limited competition as in oligopolies is that they lead to economic inefficiency which reduce social welfare. There are four major sources of emergence of economic inefficiency under monopolies and oligopolies. First, *monopolies restrict output* and produce levels of output which are less than what are economically efficient. Second, there exists *managerial slack* under monopoly due to which cost per unit of output is higher. Thirdly, monopolies *spend less on research and development* and therefore hampers technological progress. Fourth, monopolies and oligopolies often indulge in *rent-seeking activities* to raise or sustain their monopoly profits. We briefly explain below these drawbacks of monopolies and oligopolies.

1. Restriction of Output to Charge Higher Price

Monopolists, like firms working under perfect competitions, aim at maximising profits. But as seen in the earlier chapters, to maximise profits a monopolist is able to charge higher price by restricting output of product or service he produces. Given the same demand and cost conditions as prevailing in a competitive industry, the monopolist who maximises his profits at output level at which his marginal cost equals marginal revenue, produces less than the competitive industry. Thus, by producing less and charging higher price, the monopolist works in an economically inefficient way and causes a loss of consumer welfare. Consider Figure 26A.1 where *DD* is the demand curve for a competitive industry consisting of a large number of firms. *SS* is the short-run supply curve of the competitive industry which is obtained by summing up the marginal cost curves of the firms. The competitive industry is in equilibrium at point *E* at which demand curve and supply curve intersect and produces Q_C quantity of the product and price set equals P_C. Note that under competitive equilibrium price P_C is equal to marginal cost of production at output level Q_C.

Now, with monopolist equating marginal revenue (*MR*) with marginal cost (*MC*) to maximise profits restricts output to Q_m and sets price equal to P_m. Note that when all competitive firms are merged to form a monopoly supply curve *SS* of the competitive industry will become marginal cost (*MC*) curve of the monopolist. Thus, output under monopoly is lower and price higher than in a competitive industry and this leads to loss of consumer welfare.

How monopoly causes loss of consumer welfare can be explained by reinterpreting the demand curve. On this interpretation, demand curve for a product shows *how much money a consumer is willing to pay for an extra unit of the product* as he consumers more quantity of the product. In other words, demand curve which depicts various prices at different quantities of goods purchased measures *marginal benefit* to a consumer of extra units of a product as he purchases more units of it. Since under perfect competition the output level is determined at which demand curve (which reflects marginal benefit) intersects the supply curve (which represents marginal cost curve), under it consumer welfare is maximised. Price paid by the consumers depicting marginal benefit is equal

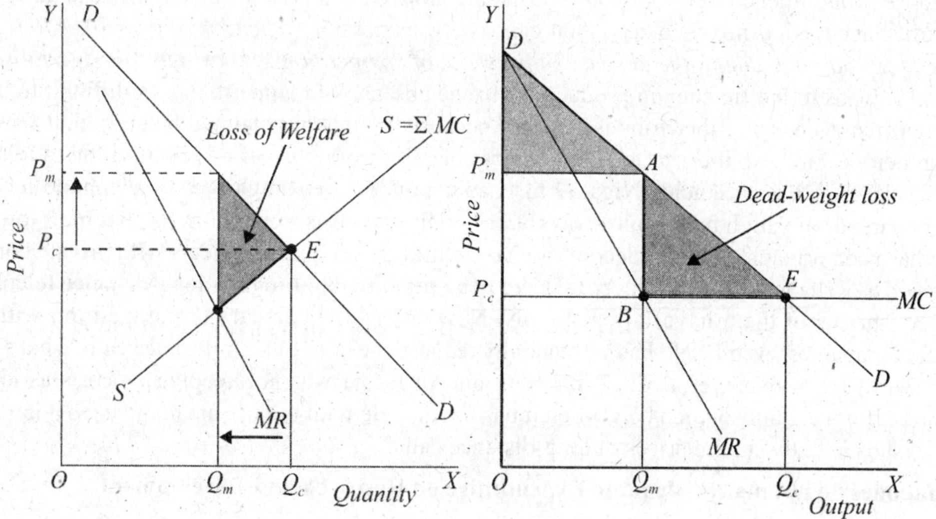

Fig. 26A.1. *Monopolist restricts output to to raise price.*

Fig. 26A.2. *Dead-Weight Loss under Monopoly and Reduction in Consumer Surplus*

to marginal cost under perfect competition and this ensures maximum welfare. Alternatively, as explained in earlier chapters, allocative economic efficiency is achieved when total surplus (i.e. sum of consumer surplus and producer surplus is maximised. Under perfect competition the sum of consumer surplus and producer surplus is maximised at output level Q_C in Fig. 26A.1 at which demand curve *DD* intersects the supply curve *SS*.

On the other hand, by producing level of output at which price exceeds marginal cost, monopolist reduces social welfare and causes allocative inefficiency. This is explicitly illustrated in Figure 26A.2. To keep the analysis simple we assume that marginal cost curve (which is the supply curve under perfect competition) is a horizontal straight line which shows that marginal cost remains constant as output is increased. Under perfect competition as price is equated with marginal cost, output Qc will be produced. With output Q_C and price P_C, consumer surplus enjoyed by consumers will be *EPCD*. On the other hand, monopolist will equate marginal cost with marginal revenue and will produce lower amount of output Q_m and charge higher price P_m. As a result, consumer surplus is reduced to AP_CD which represents the loss of consumer welfare equal to the area $AE\ P_CP_m$. But this loss of consumer welfare can be broken into two losses. (1) the rectangle ABP_CP_m which represents the profits made by the monopolist by restricting output to Q_m and raising price to P_m. But this loss of consumer surplus is not a loss to the society as a whole. It is a transfer of income from the consumers to the monopolist – as price of the product is raised and output reduced by the latter. But there is additional loss of consumer surplus equal to the area *ABE* because of restriction of output from Q_C to Q_m by the monopolist. As will be seen from the segment of demand curve *AE* in Fig. 26A.2 for the units of output from Q_m to Q_C, the consumers are prepared to pay higher price than marginal cost (*MC*) of these units of output. Thus, this second type of loss of consumer surplus is a complete loss to society as no one in the society has gained as result of this loss suffered by the consumers. Therefore, the loss of consumer surplus equal to the area of triangle *ABE* is called *dead-weight loss* and represents inefficiency caused by the monopolist.

Managerial Slack

It is generally pointed out that a firm which aims at maximising profits will try to minimise cost as far as possible for producing a given level of output. However, in actual practice it has been found that those firms either enjoying monopoly or facing limited competition which are able to make a lot of profits lack the incentives to keep their cost as low as possible. *The lack of incentives to reduce costs as far possible due to the absence of pressure of competition is known as managerial slack.* This also leads to inefficiency in production. In the absence of competition it is difficult to know whether management of the firms is efficient because it is always claimed by them that they are doing their best to keep their costs as low as possible. For example, before privatisation of telecom services BSNL (Bharat Sanchar Nigam Ltd.) had a monopoly of long distance telephone services and it charged very high prices but always claiming that its costs were as low as possible. Now that there has been privatisation of Telecom services in India in the past few years with private companies such as Reliance, Tata, Hutch, Airtel have been permitted to provide long-distance telephone services, prices of them have fallen sharply. Now, under the pressure of competition with the private companies, even BSNL has substantially reduced the rates of long-distance calls. That shows there was a lot of managerial slack in BSNL and in fact it was not keeping its costs as low as possible. If it were not so, then how when it has to compete with the private companies it has been able to substantially cut the prices of long-distance calls.

Monopolies do not make Adequate Expenditure on Research and Development

It has often been found that because they do not have to face competition in selling their products, monopolies do not make enough expenditure to develop new products and new and better techniques of production. Since monopolists are able to make a large amount of profits without any effort to make progress in technology, there is lack of incentives on their part to make adequate effort and spend enough expenditure on research and development to develop new technologies which improve productivity and lower costs of production. Of course, there may be some exceptions to this general tendency on the part of monopolies. For example, it has been pointed out that the US telephone company AT & T made important innovations throughout the period when it held almost a monopoly position in providing telephone services in the United States. The invention of laser technology and transistor were two of its important contributions. However, Professor Stiglitz point out that *greater expenditure on research and development by AT & T was due to the regulation by government*. He writes, AT & T was in a unique position. The prices it charged were set by government regulators and those prices were set to encourage the expenditure of money on research. From this perspective AT & T's research contribution was as much a consequence of government regulatory policy as of anything else."[1]

Rent-Seeking Activities

The last important source of economic inefficiency under monopoly is *their attempt to spend a lot of money in maintaining their monopoly position in the market rather than using their resources or profits for productive purposes*. By maintaining their monopoly position, the monopolists continue making large monopoly profits. It may be noted that since these monopoly profits are over and above the opportunity costs of the capital invested by them and wages for the managerial

1. Joseph. E. Stiglitz, op. cit., p.290.

services performed by the monopolists, they are often referred to as *monopoly rents*. Therefore, *the attempts by the monopolists to maintain or acquire monopoly positions in some industries or in sale of some products or services is referred to as rent-seeking behaviour.*

Sometimes, monopoly position of a firm is the result of protection granted by government. Many developing countries grant a license to a firm or few firms within their country to produce a product and thus providing a large market power or monopoly power to them which they use to make large profits. In addition, they ban the imports of some goods from abroad so as to prevent any competition from foreign manufacturers. To get these licences and protection from imports from abroad, these firms spend a lot of money for lobbing for them to maintain regulations that restrict competition and yield large profits to them. They contribute to the election expenses of members of parliament and political parties. They even bribe bureaucrats to enforce regulations that favour them. Commenting on these rent-seeking activities, Prof. Stiglitz write "*such activities are socially wasteful. Real resources (including labour times) are used to win favourable rules, not to produce goods and services. There is thus legitimate concern that the willingness of government to restrict competition will encourage firms to spend money on rent-seeking activities rather than on making a better product.*"[4]

Further Disadvantages of Limited Competition

We have seen in the earlier chapters that oligopolies dominate the economy. In these oligopolies, there is limited competition among the few firms that operate to produce either the same or similar product. In oligopolies the output produced is lower than in perfect competition but is more than in monopoly. Though the expenditure on research and development to introduce new products and to discover superior techniques of production to reduce costs is quite intense under oligopoly, but other inefficiences are worse in oligopolies with limited competition. Oligopolistic firms spend more resources on practices to prevent entry of new firms in the industry so as to continue making large profits. An important way to deter entry of potential firms is to issue threat that if they dare to enter, they will reduce price to such a low level that the new entrants will suffer a great monetary loss. To make the threat credible, the existing oligopolistic firms *build excess capacity*. With excess capacity the existing firms can easily expand output to lower price of the product. This convince the potential entrants, if they enter the industry, the existing firms will lower price to compete them out. To deter entry the existing oligopolistic firms even resort to *predatory pricing*. **Predatory pricing means the existing firms set price below even cost of production so as to inflict heavy losses on the new entrants**. Unable to bear losses when the new entrants leave the industry, **the existing firms** raise prices so as not only to recover the earlier losses but to ensure high sustained profits in future.

Besides, the oligopolists incur a lot of expenditure on competitive advertising to keep their market share in the product. Further, a large advertising expenditure is incurred to deter entry of potential entrants by influencing the consumers that their products are far better than others. However, the expenditure to detry entry may increase the profits of the existing oligopolistic firms facing limited competition but from the social point of view it involves wasteful expenditure and make consumers worse off. Thus, under oligopoly, firms facing limited competition operate with economic inefficiency.

PUBLIC POLICY TOWARDS MONOPOLY AND COMPETITION

Having discussed the drawbacks of monopolies and oligopolies, we will now explain how government intervenes to influence price charged and quantity produced by the firms working in monopolistic and oligopolistic markets. There are three ways in which government can influence these markets to achieve economic efficiency and to protect the interests of consumers.

4. Op. cit., p. 290

1. *Nationalisation or Public Ownership* of the monopolistic and oligopolistic firms.

2. *Regulation of monopolies* so that they should charge such price and produce such quantities of goods which ensure economic efficiency and work in the best interests of public.

3. To create competitive conditions and discourage monopolistc practices.

It may be noted that the first two measures have been adopted to deal with monopolies, especially natural monopolies. In case of oligopolies, there is limited competition among the few firms and they often adopt certain business practices to prevent the entry of new firms or they join hand with each other to enter into agreements to promote collusion, formal or tacit. In this respect, the general public policy is to *encourage competition.* When encouraging competition does not work, government *passes legislation to enforce competition.*

We will discuss all the above three types of public policies to deal with monopolies and oligopolies.

Public Policy Towards Natural Monopoly : Nationalisation or Public Ownership

The first public policy approach towards natural monopoly is that government should take it under its ownership and run it as a nationalised enterprise. Before explaining the merits and demerits of public ownership of natural monopoly, it is necessary to clarify the meaning of natural monopoly. *Natural monopoly in an industry is said to exist when there occur economies of scale over a large range of output due to which average cost of production steadly declines and the extent of market demand for a commodity is such that it can support only one big optimum-size firm.* Under these circumstances a large-sized firm enjoying economies of scale and operating with a lower average cost of production can compete away the small-sized firms having higher average costs and can therefore succeed in establishing its monopoly. The examples of industries in which natural monopoly exists is distribution of electricity, water and gas in a city, rail transportation, air transportation, telephone services etc.

Let us first see analyse how the working of a natural monopoly leads to economic inefficiency and causes loss of consumer's welfare. This is illustrated in Figure 26A.3 where DD' is the demand curve facing the natural monopolist. ATC is the average cost curve of the natural monopoly which, as will be seen from Fig. 26A.3, is sloping downward throughout due to economies of scale. Marginal cost curve MC which shows changes in variable costs as extra units of output are produced is a horizontal straight line. Note that average total cost curve ATC is falling throughout due to the fall in average fixed costs as more units of output are produced. Under perfect competition output Q_C will be produced at which marginal cost equals price of product P_C. But the natural monopoly maximises its profits by producing output Q_m at

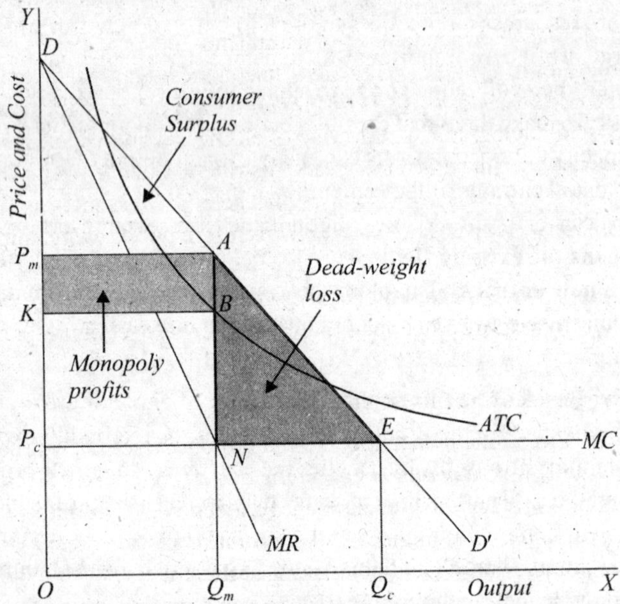

Fig. 26A.3. *Profit Maximisation by a Natural Monopoly and its Economic Inefficiency*

which its marginal revenue equals marginal cost and will set price equal to P_m and will make profits equal to $ABKP_m$. Natural monopoly is causing dead-weight loss equal to ANE and is therefore operating with economic inefficiency.

But, as explained above, in the case of natural monopoly because of falling average cost throughout due to economies of scale, competition is ruled out. Under natural monopoly, average cost curve is declining throughout and marginal cost is less than it. Hence if a firm having a natural monopoly is asked to equate marginal cost with price, it will suffer losses as shown by the shaded area $EBSP_C$ in Fig. 26A.4. If government wants the natural-monopoly firm to adopt this marginal cost pricing policy it would have to grant subsidies to the firm equal to the shaded area. To finance subsidies, taxes would have to be imposed on the public. Thus grant of subsidies to the natural monopoly to make it work efficiently will impose costs on the society. Besides, it is very difficult to ascertain the amount of subsidies since the firm may inflate its costs. As a result, instead of subsidising, government may decide to takeover the ownership of the firm having natural monopoly and operate it as nationalised enterprise. In the UK this policy of nationalisation of natural monopolies in the field of railways, telephones, supply of electricity, gas and water was adopted during the period 1945 to 1951. In India too until recently the natural monopolies belonging to railways, post and telegraph, distribution of electricity and water, gas, telephone services have been in public ownership. In the last few years, distribution of electricity in cities like Delhi, Mumbai and Kolkata has been privatised. Also there has been privatisation of Telecom services and air transportation. But railways, post and telegraph are still in public ownership and are operated as nationalised enterprises.

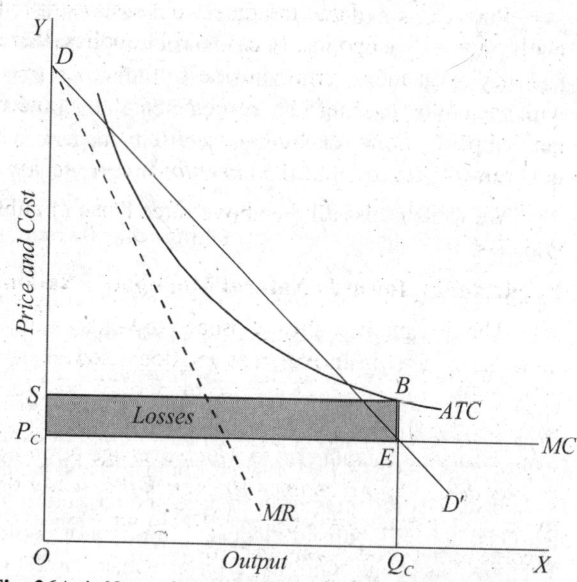

Fig. 26A.4. *Natural Monopoly Making Losses on Equating MC with Price.*

It was expected that, under government ownership, the natural monopolies would not abuse their monopoly power and would neither restrict output, nor charge high prices and thus work in public interest and achieve economic efficiency.

Problems of Nationalised Industries

But public ownership of natural monopolies has not been without problems. First, it has been pointed out that *managers of public owned enterprises lack the incentives to minimise cost.* Managers of a privately owned firms have incentives to minimise costs to make sufficient profits for the owners-shareholders in case of corporations to keep them satisfied. If the managers of a private firm are doing a bad job and not making sufficient profits, they will be fired by the owners of the firm. On the other hand, if bureaucrats who run a government-owned natural monopoly do a bad job, it is consumers and taxpayers who suffer because it is by taxing them that the losses of public-owned enterprises have to be met. The ability of managers of government-owned enterprises to obtain subsidies to cover the losses weaken their incentives to minimise cost. For the same reasons, bureaucrats who manage government-owned companies do not have any incentives to introduce any innovations to cut costs and improve the technology of production.

Besides, it has been found that in running public-sector enterprises governments often yield to temptation to interfere with the working of public sector undertakings to seek goals other than efficient operation. For example, in India it has been observed that *public sector undetakings have been overstaffed* for sake of generating more employment. In Britain and some other European countries such as Sweden also the experience has been to provide public sector jobs to keep unemployment low, no matter whether extra employees are really required or not.

Further, as a result of incurring losses year after year public sector enterprises in the field of public utilities such as railways, electricity, telephone services etc. their investment plans have been severely constrained. For example, in India losses of state electricity boards have been enormous which have adversely affected investment in the power sector. Government enterprises running the public utilities such as railways, electricity have been pressurised to provide some services at below their marginal cost, with the losses so incurred are made up by the profits made in other parts of business. This is often called *cross-subsidisation*. For example, Indian Railways are required to maintain services on the loss-making routes which are financed by revenue obtained from more profitable routes. Another example of cross-subsidisation is the practice of Post and Telegraph Department of charging the same fee for delivering a piece of mail (e.g. registered letter or a parcel) between any two places within India as a whole or within any two points in a large city like Delhi.

Due to heavy losses made by nationalised or public sector enterprises and their inefficient working, there has been a tendency all over the world (including India) to sell these enterprises to the private sector. This is called *privatisation*. For example, in Delhi electricity distribution has been handed over to BSES (a Reliance Company) and NDPL (a Tata Company) . In Mumbai and Kolkata also, private companies are in charge of distribution of electricity. In Britain, British Telecom, British Gas and nationalised electricity and water companies were sold to the private sector in the 1980s. It has been found that after privatisation, these companies have made large profits and the prices of their shares rose sharply. However, in order to cut costs, after privatisation these companies have made large cuts in employment and have contributed to growing unemployment in Britain and other European countries.

Regulation of Natural Monopolies

Another important way in which government can deal with natural monopolies is to regulate their price and output. Privatisation can lead to more operational efficiency and enormous profits earned by the private owners but it cannot solve the basic problem and drawback of natural monopoly that it leads to a large market power enjoyed by private firms which exploits consumers by making enormous profits and causes loss of economic inefficiency. It is therefore necessary to regulate them and put restrictions on their behaviour so that they work in public interest and in economically efficient way. Therefore, even in Britain where previously nationalised industries in the field of public utilities have been privatised, regulatory commissions or committees have been appointed to regulate their behaviour.

Marginal-Cost Pricing. One important theory of regulation is the *public interest theory*. According to public interest theory, the regulation of the firm having natural monopoly should be such as to ensure that it works with economic efficiency, that is, it should fix such price and output of the product or service that maximise the total surplus (sum of consumer surplus and producer surplus). Therefore, according to public interest theory, the regulation requires the firm to adopt *marginal cost pricing*, as illustrated in Figure 26A.4. It will be seen from this figure that natural monopoly should be so regulated that it should charge price P_C and produce output Q_C at which marginal cost curve *MC* cuts the demand curve *DD′* . However, as explained above with marginal-cost pricing the natural monopoly makes losses. This is because in a natural monopoly average total cost is falling throughout and marginal cost curve lies below it. Therefore, at output level at which marginal cost (*MC*) curve cuts demand curve and becomes equal to price, the average total cost will exceed price. As a result, with marginal cost equal to price the firm will make losses as shown by the shaded area in Figure 26A.4. Therefore, instead of charging such a low price that equals marginal cost and causes losses to the firm, the monopoly firm will just leave the industry. One response of public policy to this problem is to provide subsidy to the monopolist to compensate him for the losses. But, as pointed out above, to pay subsidy to the monopolist government will levy taxes on the people. Taxation as seen in an earlier chapter involves dead-weight loss and reduce economic efficiency.

The second problem with marginal cost pricing as a regulatory policy is that it does not provide any incentive to reduce costs. Every firm working in a competitive market tries to minimise costs because lower costs mean more profits for it. But in case a of a regulated monopoly the firm knows whenever costs are reduced, the regulator will reduce prices and it will therefore not gain from making efforts to reduce costs. That is why to furnish incentives to reduce costs in actual practice regulators often allow the monopolists to retain some of the profits obtained through reduction in costs. However, this practice represents deviation from marginal cost pricing.

Average Cost Pricing. Due to the problems faced in marginal cost-pricing policy, especially when government does not want to give subsidies to the natural monopoly because of its financial costraint, average-cost pricing policy may be adopted. But if it is worthwhile to make investment in a public utility the monopolist must be assured of *fair return on capital*. The fair return on capital represents normal profits which are included in average cost of production. Thus, in average-cost pricing policy regualtor fixes prices equal to average cost of production which includes fair rate of return on capital invested by the firm. Consider Figure 26A.5 *DD′* is demand curve facing the firm owning a natural monopoly. *ATC* is the average total cost curve which includes fair return on capital invested. *MC* is the marginal cost curve. The regulator following average-cost pricing will set price P_a corresponding to which average total cost curve *ATC* intersects the given demand curve *DD′*. At this regulated price P_a, the firm will produce Q_a quantity of the product. It will be seen from Figure 26A.5 that output Q_a is less than the output Q_c at which marginal cost (*MC*) equals price. Therefore, *average-cost pricing leads to the level of output produced being less than the economically efficient output.* As a result, average cost pricing causes *dead-weight loss of welfare* as shown by the shaded area.

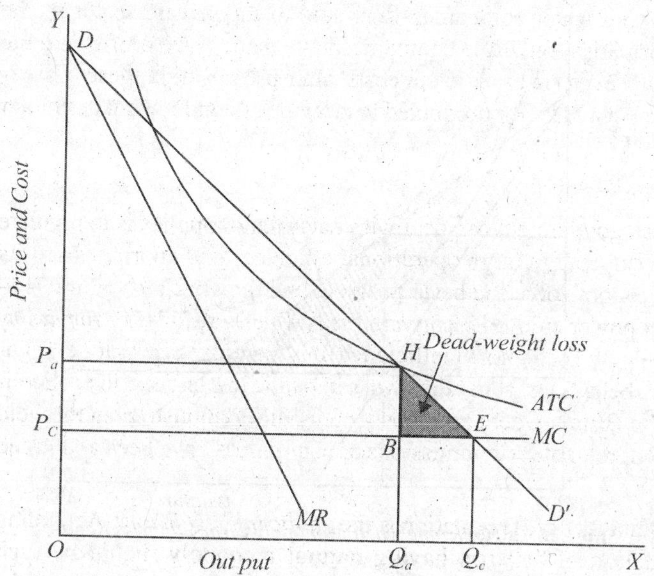

Fig. 26A.5. *Average Cost Pricing to Regulate Natural Monopoly*

The second problem facing average cost pricing policy is that under it monopoly firm has no incentive to reduce cost as it knows that if it cuts its costs, the regulatory authority will reduce the price and it will not therefore benefit from making efforts to reduce costs.

The third problem facing average-cost pricing is that since the firms are assured of a fair return on capital, they have a tendency to increase investment in capital as much as possible so as to obtain higher return on capital. This leads to too much investment. Besides, another problem of regulation through average cost pricing is that firms have no incentives to innovate. This is because technological innovations reduce costs and as a result regualtors reduce price of the product, and therefore firms do not benefit from innovations introduced by them. In recent years, regulatory commissions in both the USA and the UK have realised that unless they reward the firms for introducing innovations, these will not be forthcoming. Therefore, in recent years business firm who by introducing technological innovations succeed in making profits, the regulators have allowed them to retain much of increased profits, at least for few years.

But, the most serious problem of average-cost pricing is that *regulators are often captured by the firms whom they are supposed to regulate*. In contrast to public interest theory, according to capture theory such regulations are framed that enable the monopolistic firms to maximise their producer surplus. So as a result of regulatory capture, regulatory authorities instead of trying to promote public interest, promote the interests of the monopoly firm. The monopoly firm often bribes the regulators to win over them. The fair return on capital is crucial for calculating average cost and fixing price on that basis. The monopoly firms often through bribe or otherwise succeed in misleading the regulators about true costs and fair return on capital. The managers of a monopoly firm often succeed in inflating their costs by spending a part of firm's revenues on inputs that are not really required. Keeping luxury cars, expensive office suits, lavish international travel, keeping company jets or helicopters, lavish entertainment expenditure are some of the ways in which monopoly firm inflates costs. Explaining the reasons for capturing regulators based on experience of the UK and the US, Prof. Stiglitz writes, "regulators are pulled frequently into the cramps of those they regulate. This could happen through bribery and corruption but the much likelier way is just that over time employees of a regulated industry develop personal friendship with the regulators who in turn come to rely on their expertise and judgement. Worse, regulatory agencies (of necessity) tend to hire persons from the firms in the regulated industry. By the same token, regulators who demonstrate an "understanding " of the industry may be rewarded with good jobs in that industry after they leave government service"[5]. The above reasons apply equally well to India.

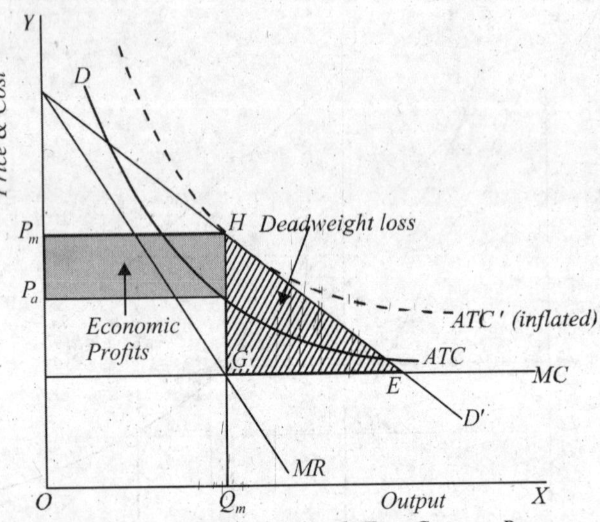

Fig. 26A.6. *Outcome when Monopoly Firm Captures Regulator or Inflates Cost.*

When the monopoly firm captures the regulator or succeeds in inflating the cost by misleading the regulator, the outcome is shown in Figure 26A.6. It will be seen from Fig. 26A.6 that the firm of natural monopoly is maximising its profits by equating marginal cost (*MC*) with marginal revenue when it produces Q_m and charges P_m price. When the firm captures the regulator it makes the latter to fix price P_m which maximises its economic profits. The economic profits made by the monopoly firm in this situation when it captures regulator are shown by the shaded area in Figure 26A.6.

The same outcome of profit maximising situation for the monopoly firm prevails if it succeeds in inflating its costs by misleading the regulator. If with inflated costs, average total cost curve (*ATC*) shifts to the dotted position *ATC* (inflated) which is tangent to the demand curve exactly vertically above the point *G* at which marginal cost equals marginal revenue and monopoly firm maximises its profits by producing output O_m. It will be further observed that with capturing the regulator or succeeding in inflating costs, dead-weight loss has increased to the stripped area *HGE*.

Encouraging Competition

The last way in which government can deal with natural monopoly is to encourage competition between firms, however imperfect competition it may be. This raises question as to how competition can be promoted in the field of natural monopoly when it is generally believed that competition in natural monopoly when average cost is falling over a large relevant range of output, is not viable. Suppose the two firms divide the market for a product of natural monopoly. Thus, we have duoplolists competing in this natural monopoly industry. Why is competition not viable between the two ? This is illustrated in Figure 26A.7 where *ATC* is average total cost curve and *DD'* is the market demand curve for the product of natural monopoly which the two firms are sharing. Suppose if there was one monopolistic firm operating to meet the market demand, its profits were maximised by producing output Q_m and charging price P_m. Now, when the two firms are sharing the market, suppose each is producing Q_d (half of Q_m) and its cost is AC_d. Now, any one firm can capture the entire market by cutting price below that of its rival firm. By expanding output beyond Q_d, it will be reducing its average cost. Having established its monopoly, it can set its price above AC_d and earn profits without worrying about the entry of any potential rivals trying to capture some of the profits. Potential rivals knows that on the entry by them existing firm can afford to lower the price since it can enjoy economies of scale by expanding output. This deters the entry of new firms.

However, in the last three decades, in many countries efforts have been to introduce more competition in the industries of natural monopoly. In Britain bus services were deregulated and competition was promoted by allowing more firms to operate bus services. Competition has been introduced in telephone services in Britain by allowing more firms to use the cables already laid. In

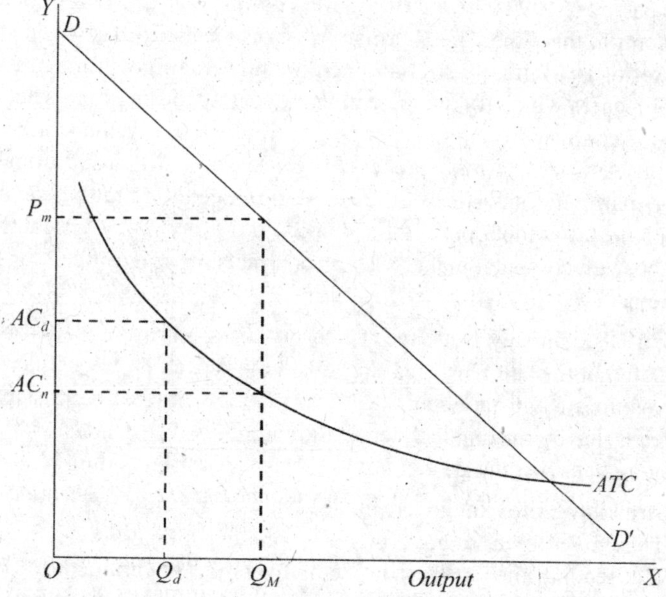

Fig. 26A.7. *Natural Monopoly and Need for Competition*

India too with the advances in telecom technology and advent of cellular telephones, more firms such as Airtel, Tata Indicom, Reliance have been allowed to provide telephone services. In Britain and India electricity generation has been separated from electricity distribution and more firms have been permitted to compete in generating electricity. Even electricity distribution has been privatised, different private firms have been given licenses to distribute electricity in specific areas.

In the USA and various countries of Europe and India too, airlines have been substantially deregulated and more than one air company has been allowed to compete. Thus, in India, Air Sahara, Jet Air ways, Air Decean have been allowed to operate both within India and outside to compete with public sector companies. Increased competition has lowered fares and improved air services. Even there is now competition in the postal services with private courier companies providing the same service.

But *an important way monopoly firm can be subjected to competition is to allow imports of goods*. When domestic monopolistic companies have to compete with the imported products, they will tend to charge lower prices to remain in business. However, competition from imports is more valid in case of other monopolistic and oligopolistic industries than natural monopolies.

Increasing Competition through Antitrust Law

In our above analysis, we have explained how public policy has tried to deal with natural monopolies. Government has also intervened to prevent *mergers* of the companies so as to prevent the creation of monopolies and to promote competition between them. When there is oligopoly, that is, there are a few firms in the industry, there is often a tendency among them to merge and form a cartel. A cartel is a collusive agreement among a number of firms aimed at restricting output and achieving a larger profits for the member firms. In many countries *formation of cartel is illegal as it leads to monopoly and exploitation of the consumers*..However, international cartels such as famous OPEC (The Organisation of Petroleum Producing Countries) legally operate.

The oligopolies are regulated through enacting legislation such as *Anti Trust Law* which forbids the mergers of the firms which leads to the creation of monopolies. In the USA Sherman Anti Trust Law was passed in 1890 to reduce the market power of 'trusts' (oligopolies) that dominated the American economy at that time. The Sherman Act was amended in 1914 by the enactment of Clayton Act. Clayton Act of 1914 greatly strengthened the powers of government to proceed against any company or companies which try to create monopolies. According to this act, private law suits can also be filed in the courts if any company or companies try to create monopoly or adopt monopolistic practices. It is this Anti-trust law that prevented Software giant Microsoft from buying Intuit in 1994. Similarly, the department of Justice of the US started to enquire into the complaints of Microsoft competitors that the latter monopolised the market for PC operating system (DOS and Windows by making contracts with computer makers. These contracts made it difficult for firms producing other operating systems.

Recently, a US company Netscape which produces a browser called Navigator complained against Microsoft that the latter was making available its web browser 'Internet Explorer' at a zero price which was unfair and monopolistic trade practice and not permissible under the US law. Microsoft's plea is that by making its Internet Explorer free of cost along with its Windows operating system it is giving consumers a greater value. The case is still pending in the court.

The Antitrust laws provide government various ways in which it can intervene to promote competition. They give power to government to prevent mergers so as to prevent the creation of monopolies. The second, the antitrust law empowers the government to break up companies to encourage competition. Thus, in the US a famous telecommunication company AT & T was split up into eight small companies to encourage competition. Thirdly, antitrust laws prevent companies from coordinating their activities in ways that make markets less competitive.

It may be noted that all mergers of companies are not undersirable. Sometimes different firms merge not to reduce competition but to increase efficiency by joint operation and thus lower costs. The recent Indian Competition Act allows mergers of companies if they result in higher efficiency and lower costs but not in restricting competition. Some banks in India have merged in recent years to strengthen their financial position and to improve efficiency.

Thus crucial question is to examine whether formation of mergers of firms is to reduce competition or to improve efficiency and strengthen financial position. If merger is designed to reduce competition it is bad and undesirable, but if it is to improve efficiency and strengthen financial position of the firms without reducing competition it is desirable.

QUESTIONS FOR REVIEW

1. What is meant by managerial slack ? What does it mean when economists say that monopoly output is 'too little' or a monopoly price is "too high". What benchmark do they use to claim this ?
2. Give reasons for the lack of incentives for the monopoly firm to lower costs as far as possible.
3. Why does a monopolistic firm lack incentives to make adequate expenditure on research and development (R & D) to make advances in technology ?
4. What is a natural monopoly ? Explain why average cost curve of a natural monopoly falls throughout ? What are the consequences of this ?
5. If regulatory authority of a natural monopoly sets price equal to marginal cost, what problem will arise ? How does nationalisation or regulation solve this problem?
6. What is public interest theory of regulation ? What price policy for a natural monopoly does it suggest ?
7. What is regulatory capture hypothesis? What are it consequence ?
8. How oligopolies are regulated so as to prevent them from merging and reducing competition ?
9. Explain how competition is not viable in case of natural monopoly. How has government sought to promote competition in this case ?
10. What are the drawbacks of monopolies and limited competition ? Explain why there is need for regulation of monopolies and oligopolies with limited competition.
11. If natural monopoly is regulated to produce the perfectly competitive output, it would have losses. Do you agree ? Explain. *DU B.A (Hons.) Ist Year 2006*
12. Regulators require a natural monopoly to charge a price equal to marginal cost, the monopoly will incur losses. State whether true or false. *DU B.A (Hons.) Ist Year 2007*

CHAPTER 27
PRICE DISCRIMINATION

MEANING OF PRICE DISCRIMINATION

Price discrimination refers to the practice of a seller of selling the same product at different prices to different buyers. A seller makes price discrimination between different buyers when it is both possible and profitable for him to do so. If the manufacturer of a refrigerator of a given variety sells it at Rs. 5000 to one buyer and at Rs. 5,500 to another buyer (all conditions of sale and delivery being the same in two cases), he is practising price discrimination.

Price discrimination, as defined above, is not a very common phenomenon. It is very difficult to charge different prices for the identical product from the different buyers. More often, the product is slightly differentiated to practise successfully price discrimination. Thus, the concept of price discrimination can be broadened to include the sale of the various varieties of the same good at prices which are not proportional to their marginal costs. Thus, Prof. Stigler defines price discrimination as *"the sales of technically similar products at prices which are not proportional to marginal costs."*[1] On this definition, a seller is doing price discrimination when he is charging different prices from different buyers for the different varieties of the same good if the differences in prices are not the same as or proportional to the differences in the costs of producing them. For example, if a book costs the publisher Rs. 58 per unit and its deluxe edition Rs. 65 per unit, then he will be practising price discrimination if he sells the ordinary edition at Rs. 70 per unit and the deluxe edition at Rs. 130 per unit. In this case, he is said to be practising price discrimination because the price difference between the two editions (Rs. 130 – 70 = 60) is greater than the cost difference between them (Rs. 65 – 58 = 7).

Though this second case of price discrimination is very relevant, but is more complicated. Therefore, for the purpose of analysis given below, we shall restrict ourselves to the simple case of price discrimination—the sale of the same product at different prices to different buyers. But the conclusions arrived at in this simple case will be generally valid in case of the more complicated case mentioned above.

Three types of price discrimination may be noted. Price discrimination may be (*a*) *personal*, (*b*) *local*, or (*c*) *according to use or trade*. Price discrimination is personal when a seller charges different prices from different persons. Price discrimination is local when the seller charges different prices from people of different localities or places. For instance, producer may sell a commodity at one price at home and at another price abroad. Discrimination is according to use when different prices of a commodity are charged according to the uses to which the commodity is put. For example, the electricity is usually sold at a cheaper rate for domestic uses than for commercial purposes.

Degrees of Price Discrimination

Prof. A.C. Pigou has distinguished between the following three types of price discrimination on another ground : (*i*) price discrimination of the first degree; (*ii*) price discrimination of the second degree; and (*iii*) price discrimination of the third degree.

1. G.J. Sitgler, *The Theory of Price*, revised edition 1952, p. 215.

Price discrimination of the first degree involves maximum possible exploitation of each buyer in the interest of a seller's profits. *Price discrimination of the first degree is also called perfect price discrimination. Price discrimination of the first degree or perfect price discrimination is said to occur when the monopolist is able to sell each separate unit of the output at a different price.* Thus under discrimination of the 'first degree' every buyer is forced to pay the price which is equal to the maximum amount he would be willing to pay rather than do without the good altogether. In other words, under perfect price discrimination, the seller leaves no consumer's surplus to any buyer.

Price discrimination of the *second degree* would occur when a monopolist is able to charge *separate prices for different blocks or quantities of a commodity from buyers* and in this way he takes away a part, but not all of consumer surplus from them . Thus, under the second degree price discrimination a monopolist may charge a high price for first block of say 10 units, the medium price for the additional block of 10 units, and a lower price for additional units of a commodity. For example, a monopolist may charge from a buyer a price of Rs. 50 per unit for the first 10 units, Rs. 40 per unit for the next 10 units and Rs. 30 per unit for the additional units of the commodity.

Price discrimination of the *third degree* is said to occur *when the seller divides his buyers into two or more than two sub-markets or groups depending on the price elasticity of demand and charges a different price in each sub-market.* The price charged in each sub-market depends upon the output sold in that sub-market and the demand conditions of that sub-market. Price discrimination of the third degree is most common. A common example of such discrimination is found in the practice of a manufacturer who sells his product at a higher price at home and at a lower price abroad. Again, the third degree price discrimination is found when an electric company sells electric power at a lower price to the households and at a higher price to the manufacturers who use it for industrial purposes. In our analysis of price discrimination made below, we will assume only third degree price discrimination since this is usually more practicable as well as most commonly found in case of the real world.

WHEN IS PRICE DISCRIMINATION POSSIBLE?

Two fundamental conditions are necessary for the price discrimination to become possible. First, price discrimination can occur only *if it is not possible to transfer any unit of the product from one market to another.* In other words, a seller can practise price discrimination only when he is selling in different markets which are divided in such a way that product sold by him in the cheaper market cannot be resold in the dearer market. Price discrimination by the original seller will break down if his buyers in the cheaper market purchase the product from him and resell it to the buyers of the dearer market. Buyers in the dearer market of the original seller will instead of buying from him will buy the product from the buyers of his cheaper market. Thus, a seller can charge different prices in the two markets when there is no possibility of the product being transferred from the cheaper market to the dearer market.

Second essential condition for price discrimination to occur is that *it should not be possible for the buyers in the dearer market to transfer themselves into the cheaper market to buy the product* or *service at the lower price.* For instance, if a doctor is charging a smaller fee from the poor than from the rich, then his price discrimination will break down if a rich man can pretend to be poor and pay a poor man's charges to the doctor.

It is clear from above that for the price discrimination to become practicable, neither the unit of the good, nor the unit of demand (*i.e.*, buyer) can be transferred from one market to the other. In other words, there should not be any seepage or communication between the two markets. Thus price discrimination depends upon the ability of the seller to keep his two markets quite separate. If he is not able to keep the different markets separate, the price discrimination by him will break down. Price discrimination is possible in the following cases.

1. **The Nature of the Commodity.** The nature of the commodity or service may be such that there is no possibility of transference from one market to the other. The most usual case is the sale of direct personal services like that of a surgeon or lawyer. The surgeons usually charge different fees from the rich and the poor for the same kind of operation. This is possible for them since the service has to be delivered personally by the surgeon and therefore it cannot be transferred. Neither is it possible for the rich men to assume to be poor so easily in order to pay the smaller fee.

2. **Long Distances or Tariff Barriers.** Discrimination often occurs *when the markets are separated by long distance or tariff barriers* so that it is very expensive to transfer goods from a cheaper market to be resold in the dearer market. A monopolist manufacturer at Chennai may sell his product in one town, say Kolkata, at Rs. 20 and in another town, say Delhi, at Rs. 15. If the transport cost between Delhi and Kolkata is greater than Rs. 5 per unit it will not be worthwhile for the buyers in Delhi to transfer the goods to Kolkata on their own. Similarly, if a seller is selling his good in two different markets, say, in a home market which is protected by a traiff and in a foreign market without a tariff, he can take advantage of the tariff barrier and can raise the price of his product in the home market (which is protected by the tariff). As a result, he will be selling the product in the foreign market at a lower price than at home. *This practice of selling the product at cheaper rates abroad than at home is known as dumping.*

3. **Legal Sanction.** In some cases there may be *legal sanction for price discrimination*. For example, an electricity company sells electricity at a lower price if it is used for domestic purposes and at a higher price if it is used for commercial purposes. In this case customers are liable to be fined if they use electricity for commercial purposes if the sanction has been granted for domestic purposes only. The same is the case with railways which charge different fares for travelling in First Class, and Second Class compartments. Though the service of carrying rendered in two classes of compartments slightly differs in each case but the differences in fares are out of porportion to the differences in comforts provided. So this is a clear case of price discrimination by legal sanction. It is unlawful and a criminal offence to travel in the first class with a ticket for the second class.

4. **Preferences or Prejudices of the Buyers.** Price discrimination may become possible due to *preferences or prejudices of the buyers*. The same good is generally converted into different varieties by providing different packings, different names or labels in order to convince the buyer that certain varieties are superior to others. Different prices are charged for different varieties, although they differ only in name or label. In this way the producers are usually able to break up their market and sell the so-called superior varieties to the rich people at higher prices and the so-called inferior varieties to the poor people. Sometimes there is some actual difference in the various varieties of the good, for instance, generally there is a difference in the paper used and quality of the binding between the deluxe edition and ordinary edition of a book, but the difference in prices of the two kinds of editions is more than proportional to the extra costs incurred on the de luxe edition. So, this is a clear case of price discrimination based on the preferences or prejudices of the various buyers of the product. It is worth quoting Joan Robinson in this connection. "Various brands of a certain article which in fact are almost exactly alike may be sold as different qualities under names and labels which induce rich and snobbish buyers to divide themselves from poor buyers, and in this way the market is split up and the monopolist can sell what is substantially the same thing at several prices.[2]"

Another case of price discrimination falling in this category is that when some people prefer to buy goods in a particular locality at a higher price. For example, if a seller has two shops, one in Cannaught Place which is the most fashionable shopping centure in Delhi and another at Sadar Bazar which is very congested and ugly locality in Delhi, he may be selling the same product at a higher price in Connaught Place and at a lower price in Sadar Bazar. It is the fashionable and rich people who usually buy goods in Connaught Place and they will be prepared to pay a higher price rather than go for shopping in the congested and ugly locality of Sadar Bazar.

2. Joan Robinson, *Economics of Imperfect Competition*, pp. 180-81.

5. **Ignorance and Laziness of Buyers.** Price discrimination may become possible due to *ignorance and laziness of buyers*. If a seller is discriminating between two markets but the buyers of the dearer market are quite ignorant of that fact that the seller is selling the product at a lower price in another market, then price discrimination by the seller will persist. Price discrimination will also persist if the buyers of the dearer market are aware of the seller's act of selling the same product at a lower price in another market but due to laziness may not go for shopping in the cheaper market. In these cases if the ignorance is removed or laziness is given up, the price discrimination will break down.

6. Price discrimination may become possible *when several groups of buyers require the same service for clearly differentiated commodities*. For example, railways charge different rates of fare for the transport of cotton and coal. In this case price discrimination is possible since bales of cotton cannot be turned into loads of coal in order to take advantage of the cheaper rate of transport for coal.

Under Which Market Structure Price Discrimination is Possible ? We have seen above those conditions under which price discrimination is possible. Now, the question arises under what market form a seller can practise price discrimination. It is obvious that *under perfect or pure competition no seller can charge different prices from different buyers for the same product*. Under perfect or pure competition, there are many sellers selling the homogeneous product. If any seller tries to charge from some buyers a higher price than the prevailing market price, they will refuse to buy from him and will buy the same product at the prevailing price from other sellers. It is worth noting that under conditions of perfect or pure competition price discrimination cannot prevail even if the market can be easily divided into separate parts. This is so because if conditions of perfect or pure competition prevails in each part of the whole market, then will confront a perfectly elastic demand curve in each part and will like to sell the whole of his output in that part of the market in which the highest price prevails. But the attempt by all sellers to do so would force down the price to the competitive level so that a single price will prevail throughout the whole market. But if all sellers under perfect competition, combine or arrive at some understanding, then they can discriminate prices. "*So long as market is perfect it is only if all sellers are combined or are acting in agreement that they can take advantage of the barriers between one part of a market and another to charge different prices for the same thing*."[3] However, it may be pointed out that if all sellers combine or enter into an agreement regarding price discrimination, perfect competition ceases to exist. We thus see that price discrimination is not possible under perfect competition.

Under imperfect or monopolistic competition, price discrimination can occur. The degree of price discrimination practised depends upon the degree of imperfection in the market. The imperfect or monopolistic competition prevails when the product is differentiated and every seller has some attached customers who will not move so readily from one seller to another. Therefore, if imperfect or monopolistic competition exists and also the market can be divided into different parts by a seller, then price discrimination becomes possible. It should be noted that in this case an individual seller may not produce a single variety of the product but may produce various varieties of his product and thus may break up his market into different parts and charge different prices for different varieties of his good. Price discrimination will occur only if extra prices charged for the so-called superior varieties are not proportional to the extra costs incurred on them.

But *price discrimination is more likely to occur when there is monopoly of the product by a single seller or when there is agreement among the various sellers selling the same product or service*. Monopoly exists when there are no other sellers selling the same good or its close substitutes. Therefore, monopolist is in a position to charge different prices from different buyers for the same good. Price discrimination also usually occurs when there are various sellers selling the same product or same service but there is agreement among them for charging different prices from differ-

3. Joan Robinson. *Economics of Imperfect Competition*, p. 179.

ent groups of buyers. For instance, doctors have generally some understanding with each other to charge higher fees from the rich and lower fees from the poor.

WHEN IS PRICE DISCRIMINATION PROFITABLE ?

We have seen above under what conditions price discrimination is possible. Price discrimination may be possible yet it may not pay the monopolist to discriminate prices in the separate markets. In other words, the monopolist may be able to discriminate prices but it may not be profitable for him to do so. We have to see now under what conditions it is profitable for the monopolist to discriminate prices between the two markets. *Price discrimination is profitable only if elasticity of demand in one market is different from elasticity of demand in the other.* Therefore, the monopolist will discriminate prices between two markets only when he finds that the price elasticity of demand of his product is different in the different sub-markets. We shall analyse below this condition for the profitability of price discrimination.

(*a*) *When Demand Curves in the Separate Markets are Iso-elastic.* If the demand curves in the two markets are iso-elastic so that at every price the elasticity of demand in the two markets is the same, then it will not pay the monopolist to charge different prices in the two markets. Why? When elasticity of demand is the same in the two markets, it follows from the formula, $MR = AR\,\dfrac{e-1}{e}$ that marginal revenues in the two markets *at every price* (i.e. every *AR*) of the good will also be the same. Now, if marginal revenue at every price of the product is the same in the two markets, it will not be profitable for the monopolist to transfer any amount of the good from one market to the other and thus to charge different prices of the good in the two markets.

(*b*) *When Elasticity of Demand is Different in Various Markets at the Single Monopoly Price.* It will be to the advantage of the monopolist to set different prices if price elasticities of demand in the two markets at the single monopoly price are not the same. In fact, if he wants to maximise profits he must discriminate prices if the price elasticities of demand in the two markets *at the single monopoly price* are different. If the producer regards the two markets as one and charges a single monopoly price on the basis of aggregate marginal revenue and marginal cost of the output, he would not be maximising profits if elasticities of demand in the two markets at the single monopoly price are different. If price elasticity of demand is the same in the two markets at the single monopoly price, it will not pay the monopolist to discriminate between the two markets, even if the elasticities are different at other prices.

Suppose on the basis of aggregate marginal revenue and marginal cost, a monopolist fixes a single price (which is called the single monopoly price) and charges the same price in both the markets. If he now finds that price elasticity of demand at this single monopoly price is different he can increase his total profits by discriminating prices between the two markets. How is it profitable for the monopolist to charge different prices in the two markets when price elasticities of demand in them at the single monopoly price are different? This follows from the formula, $MR = AR\,\dfrac{e-1}{e}$

When average revenue in both the markets is the same, that is, when the monopolist charges a single monopoly price in both the markets, but price elasticities are different in the two markets, then marginal revenues in the two markets will be different. Suppose the single monopoly price is Rs. 15 and price elasticity of demand in markets *A* and *B* is 2 and 5 respectively. Then,

$$MR \text{ in market } A = AR_a\,\frac{e_a - 1}{e_a}$$

$$=15\frac{2-1}{2}=15\times\frac{1}{2}=7.5$$

$$MR \text{ in market } B = AR_b \frac{e_b - 1}{e_b}$$

$$=15\times\frac{5-1}{5}$$

$$=15\times\frac{4}{5}=12$$

It is thus clear that marginal revenues in the two markets are different when elasticities of demand at the single monopoly price are different. Further, from the above numerical example, it is evident that the marginal revenue in the market in which price elasticity is higher is greater than the marginal revenue in the market where price elastiticy is lower. Now, it is profitable for the monopolist to transfer some amount of the product from the market *A* where elasticity is less and therefore marginal revenue is low to the market *B* where elasticity is higher and, therefore, marginal revenue is larger. In this way, the loss of revenue by reducing sales in market *A* by some marginal units will be smaller than the gain in revenue from increasing sales in market *B* by those units. Thus, in the above example, if one unit of the product is withdrawn from market *A*, the loss in revenue will be Rs. 7.5, while with the addition to sales by one more unit of the product in market B, the gain in revenue will be about Rs. 12. It is thus clear that the transference of some units of the product will be profitable, when there is difference in price elasticities of demand and hence in marginal revenues.

It is worth mentioning that when some units of the product are transferred from market A to market *B*, price in market *A* will rise and price in the market *B* will fall. This means that the monopolist will now be discriminating prices between the two markets.

But here a relevant question arises: how long will it be profitable for the monopolist to continue shifting his product from the market with lower elasticity of demand to the market with higher elasticity of demand? It is worthwhile for the monopolist to go on transferring units from market *A* (with lower elasticity of demand) to market *B* (with higher elasticity of demand) until the marginal revenues in the two markets become equal. This is because as long as marginal revenue in market *B* is greater than that in market *A*, he will be making addition to revenue in market *B* by selling an additional unit of the product more than the loss he will be incurring in market *A* from reducing sales by one unit. When the marginal revenues in the two markets become equal as a result of transference of some units of output, it will no longer be profitable to shift more units of output from market *A* to market *B*. When the position of equality of the marginal revenues in the two markets is reached, he will be charging different prices in the two markets—a higher price in market A with lower elasticity of demand and a lower price in market *B* with a higher elasticity of demand.

EQUILIBRIUM UNDER PRICE DISCRIMINATION

We have explained above the conditions under which price discrimination is possible and profitable. We now turn to analyse the equilibrium of a discriminating monopolist. Under simple monopoly, a single price is charged for the whole output; but under price discrimination the monopolist will charge different prices in different sub-markets. First of all, therefore, the monopolist has to divide his total market into various sub-markets on the basis of differences in price elasticity of demand in them. The monopolist can divide his total market into *several sub-markets* according to the differences in demand elasticity, but for the sake of making our analysis simple we shall explain the case when the total market is divided into *two sub-markets*.

In order to reach the equilibrium position, the discriminating monopolist has to take two decisions: (1) how much total output should be produced; and (2) how the total output should be distributed between the two sub-markets and what prices he should charge in the two sub-markets.

The same marginal principle will guide the decision of the discriminating monopolist to produce a total output as that which guides a perfect competitior or a simple monopolist. In other words, the discriminating monopolist will compare the marginal revenue with the marginal cost of the output. But he has to find out first the aggregate marginal revenue (*AMR*) of the two sub-markets taken together and then compare this aggregate marginal revenue with the marginal cost of the total output. Aggregate marginal revenue curve is obtained by summing up laterally the marginal revenue curves of the sub-markets. Consider Fig. 27.1. MR_a is the marginal revenue curve in sub-market *A* corresponding to the demand curve D_a. Similarly, MR_b is the marginal revenue curve in sub-market *B* corresponding to the demand curve D_a. Now, the aggregate marginal revenue curve *AMR*, which has been shown in diagram (*iii*) of Fig. 27.1, has been derived by adding up laterally MR_a and MR_b. This aggregate marginal revenue curve depicts the total amount of output that can be sold in the two sub-markets taken together corresponding to each value of the marginal revenue. Marginal cost curve of the monopolist is shown by the curve *MC* in Fig. 27.1 (*iii*).

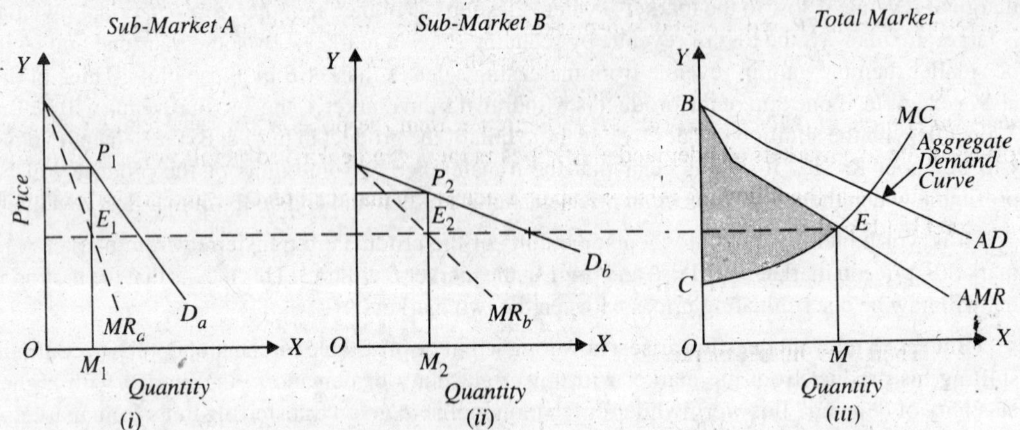

Fig. 27.1. *Determination of total output and different prices in the two markets*

The discriminating monopolist will maximise his profits by producing the level of output at which marginal cost curve *MC* intersects the aggregate marginal revenue curve *AMR*. It will be seen from Fig. 27.1 (*iii*) that profit-maximising output is *OM*, for only at *OM* aggregate marginal revenue (*AMR*) is equal to the marginal cost (*MC*) of the total output. Thus the discriminating monopolist will decide to produce *OM* level of output.

Once the total output to be produced has been determined the next task for the discriminating monopolist is to distribute the total output between the two sub-markets. He will distribute the total output *OM* in such a way that marginal revenues in the two sub-markets are equal. Marginal revenues in the two sub-markets must be equal if the profits are to be maximised. If he is so allocating the output in the two markets that the marginal revenues in the two are not equal, then it will pay him to transfer some amount of output from the sub-market in which the marginal revenue is less to the sub-market in which the marginal revenue is greater. Only when the marginal revenues in the two markets are equal, it will be unprofitable for him to shift any amount from one market to the other.

But for the discriminating monopolist to be in equilibrium it is essential not only that the marginal revenues in the two markets should be the same but that they should also be equal to the marginal cost of the whole output. Equality of marginal revenues in the two markets with marginal cost of the whole output ensures that the amount sold in the two markets will together be equal to the whole output *OM* which has been fixed by equalising aggregate marginal revenue with marginal cost. It will be seen from Fig. 27.1 [diagram (*iii*)] that at equilibrium output *OM*, marginal cost is *ME*. Now, the output *OM* has to be distributed in the two markets in such a way that marginal revenue in them should be equal to the marginal cost *ME* of the whole output. It is clear from the diagram (*i*) that OM_1 should be sold in sub-market *A*, because marginal revenue M_1E_1 at amount OM_1 is equal to marginal cost *ME*. Similarly, OM_2 should be sold in sub-market *B*, since marginal revenue M_2E_2 at amount OM_2 is equal to the marginal cost *ME* of the whole output. To conclude, demand and cost conditions being given, the discriminating monopolist will produce total output *OM* and will sell amount OM_1 in sub-market *A* and amount OM_2 in sub-market *B*. It should be carefully noted that the total output *OM* will be equal to $OM_1 + OM_2$.

Thus, for the discriminating monopolist to be in equilibrium, the following conditions must be fulfilled:

1. $AMR = MC$
2. $MR_1 = MR_2 = MC$

Another important thing to know is what prices will be charged in the two markets. It is clear from the demand curve that amount OM_1 of the good can be sold at price M_1P_1 in sub-market *A*. Therefore, price M_1P_1 will be set in sub-market *A*. Likewise, amount OM_2 can be sold at price M_2P_2 in sub-market *B*. Therefore, price M_2P_2 will be set in sub-market *B*. Further, *it should be noted that price will be higher in market A where the demand is less elastic than in market B where the demand is more elastic*. Thus, price M_1P_1 is greater than the price M_2P_2. The relation between prices in the two markets and demand elasticities in them can be derived as follows.

We know that the following relationship between price, marginal revenue and price elasticity in a market holds good.

$$MR = \text{Price}\left(\frac{e-1}{e}\right)$$

Therefore, in sub-market *A*,

$$MR_a = P_a\left(\frac{e_a-1}{e_a}\right) \quad ...(i)$$

where P_a stands for price, MR_a for marginal revenue and e_a for price elasticity in market *A*.

Likewise, in sub-market *B*,

$$MR_b = P_b\left(\frac{e_b-1}{e_b}\right) \quad ...(ii)$$

where P_b stands for price, MR_b for marginal revenue and e_b for price elasticity in market *B*.

Since in equilibrium under price discrimination, $MR_a = MR_b$, from (*i*) and (*ii*) we get

$$P_a\left(\frac{e_a-1}{e_a}\right) = P_b\left(\frac{e_b-1}{e_b}\right)$$

$$\frac{P_a}{P_b} = \frac{\dfrac{e_b-1}{e_b}}{\dfrac{e_a-1}{e_a}} = \frac{\left(1-\dfrac{1}{e_b}\right)}{\left(1-\dfrac{1}{e_a}\right)}$$

Suppose absolute value of price elasticity in market *A* is equal to 2 and in market *B* it is equal to 3, then

$$\frac{P_a}{P_b} = \frac{\frac{3-1}{3}}{\frac{2-1}{2}} = \frac{\frac{2}{3}}{\frac{1}{2}}$$

$$= \frac{2}{3} \times \frac{2}{1} = \frac{4}{3}$$

Thus, when elasticities in markets *A* and *B* are 2 and 3 respectively, the prices in the two markets will be in the ratio of 4 : 3.

From the forgoing analysis it follows that the following two conditions are required to be satisfied for the equilibrium of a discriminating monopolist :

(1) Aggregate Marginal Revenue (*AMR*) = Marginal Cost (*MC*) of the total output.

(2) $MR_a = MR_b = MC$.

Equilibrium under Price Discrimination in the Dumping Case

A special case of price discrimination occurs when a producer is selling in two markets, one in which he faces perfect competititon, while in the other he has a monopoly. The demand curve for the product will be perfectly elastic for him in the market in which he faces perfect competition, while the demand curve will be sloping downward in the market in which he enjoys monopoly position. Such situation might occur when a producer sells his product in his home country in which he has a monopoly and in the world market which is perfectly competitive. Equilibrium in this situation is depicted in Fig. 27.2. In the home market in which the producer has a monopoly, demand curve or the average revenue curve AR^H is sloping downward. So does the marginal revenue curve MR^H. In the international or world market in which he faces perfect competition, the demand for his product is perfectly elastic. The average revenue curve AR^W of the producer in the world market is therefore a horizontal straight line and marginal revenue curve MR^W coincides with it. *MC* is the marginal cost curve of output. Aggregate marginal revenue (*AMR*) curve in this case is the composite curve *BFED* which is the lateral summation of MR^H and MR^W. The marginal cost curve *MC* intersects the aggregate marginal revenue curve *BFED* at point *E* and equilibrium output *OM* is determined. The total output *OM* is to be distributed between the home market and the world market in such a way that marginal revenue in each market is equal to each other and to the marginal cost *ME*. It is clear from Fig. 27.2 that when amount *OR* is sold in the home market, the marginal revenue is *RF* which is equal to marginal cost *ME*. Thus, out of total output *OM*, amount *OR* will be sold in the home market. From the curve AR^H, it is clear that price OP^H will be charged in the home market. Rest of

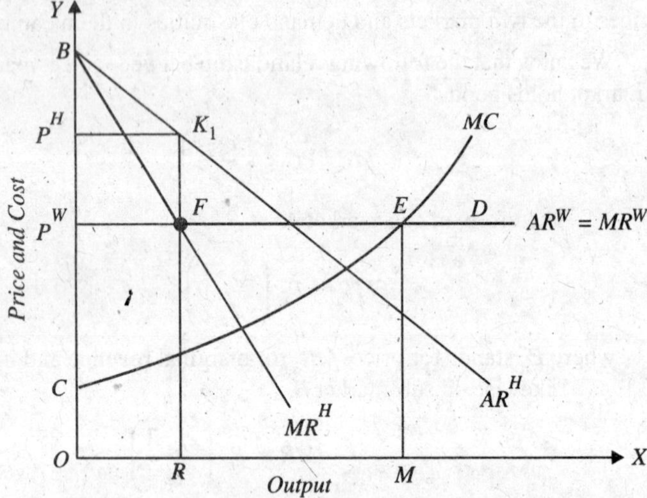

Fig. 27.2. *Equilibrium of the discriminating monopolist when he has a monopoly in the home market and faces perfect competition in the world market.*

the amount *RM* will be sold in the world market at price OP^W. Area *CEFB* represents the total profits earned by the producer from both the markets. Price in the world market OP^W is lower than the price OP^H in the home market. *When a producer charges a lower price in the world market than in the home market, he is said to be dumping in the world market.*

PERFECT PRICE DETERMINATION : OUTPUT DETERMINATION

We have studied above that under perfect price discrimination, the monopolist is able to charge different prices for different units and leaves no consumer surplus with the buyers of his product. For each unit perfect price discriminator charges maximum price which consumers are willing to pay for them and thus consumers are left with no consumer surplus. In this way with perfect price discrimination he is able to increase his revenue and profits more than what he gets under third degree and second degree price discrimination.

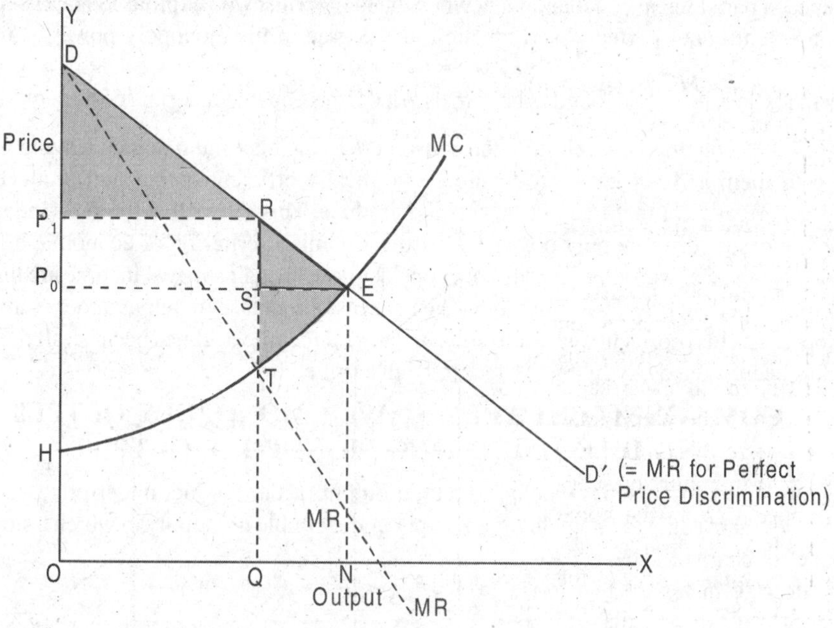

Fig. 27.3. *Output Determination under Perfect Price Discrimination*

Now, what output a monopolist practising perfect price discrimination will produce. For this it is important to understand what is marginal revenue (*MR*) curve of the perfect price discriminator. Since the perfect price discriminator charges the maximum price that the consumers are willing to pay for each unit, his marginal revenue from sale of different units of the product will be equal to the price of the units. As result his, marginal revenue curve will coincide with the market demand curve *DD′*. Consider Figure 27.3 where *DD′* is market demand curve for the product which has been obtained by horizontal summation of all individual consumers' demand curves for the product. If the monopolist does not practice price discrimination and charges a single price (*i.e.* he is simple monopolist), his marginal revenue curve *MR* lies below the market demand curve *DD′*. The simple monopolist will equate his marginal revenue with marginal cost ($MR = MC$) to maximize profits. It will be seen from Figure 27.3 that the simple monopolist will produce *OQ* output corresponding to point *T* at which his $MR = MC$ and charge price equal to OP_1 (= *QR*) and will leave consumer surplus equal to the area DP_1R with the buyers. However, since he produces less than the economically efficient output *ON* (at which Price = *MC*), there is dead-weight loss of welfare equal to area *TRE*.

Now, as explained above, a monopolist practising perfect price discrimination, marginal revenue (MR) curve will coincide with the market demand curve DD'. Therefore, perfect price discriminator will produce output ON at which his marginal cost (MC) curve intersects the market demand curve (DD') which is also his marginal revenue curve. Thus in equilibrium at output ON, for monopolist practicing perfect price discrimination marginal cost equals price as is the case price of a firm working under perfect competition.

Since at equilibrium output ON of perfect price discriminator price equals marginal cost, there is no dead weight loss and he is achieving economic efficiency. In other words, dead-weight loss has been eliminated under perfect price discrimination. In fact, perfect price discriminator grabs the dead-weight loss for increasing his profits and consumers are left with no consumer surplus at all. Total profits of perfect price discriminating monopolist equal to the area HDE, that is, the area within demand curve and MC curve upto the point E.

We reach paradoxical conclusion that when the monopolist who exploits his market power to the maximum extent under perfect discrimination, the degree of his monopoly power as measured by Lerner's Index $\left(\frac{P-MC}{P}\right)$ is found to be zero as price (P) is equal to marginal cost at equilibrium point E in Fig. 27.3. Though he is exploiting the consumers to the maximum degree leaving no consumer surplus with them and yet he is producing economically efficient output and produces the same output as a perfectly competitive industry would produce. This shows that Lerner's index is quite an inadequate measure of monopoly power and also economists' criterion of economic efficiency is a poor measure of social welfare as its does not consider how the gains in real income are distributed. In our example of perfect price discrimination, the benefits of increase in output under it are grabbed by the monopolist as his profits increase and consumer's real income declines because all their consumer surplus has been taken away by the perfect price discriminator.

COMPARING BETWEEN SIMPLE MONOPOLY OUTPUT AND DISCRIMINATING MONOPOLY OUTPUT

It is now proper to discuss whether the total output of the product under price discrimination will be greater than, equal to or smaller than output under simple monopoly in which a single price for the product is charged. There is no single rule in regard to the effect of price discrimination on output. Whether the price discrimination will increase output or reduce output or leave output unchanged depends upon the various conditions.

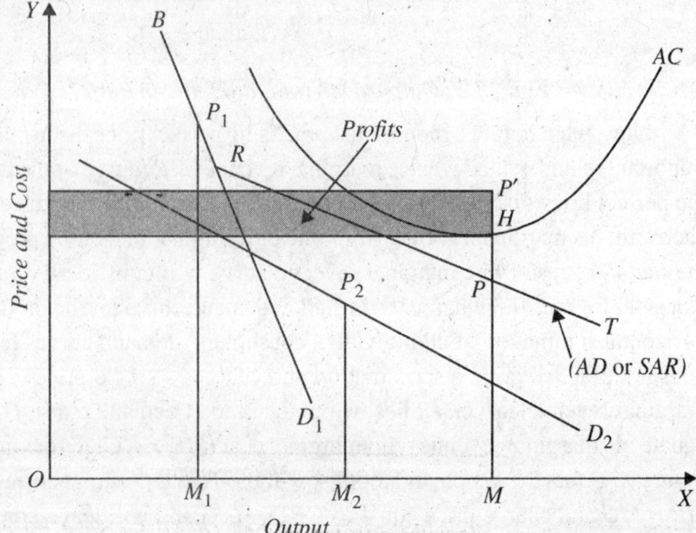

Fig. 27.4. *The case where production is possible only under price discrimination.*

First of all, there are cases in which no output will be produced at all under simple monopoly. In such cases, output of the product is possible only under price discrimination. The fact that the average revenue under price discrimination is greater than the average revenue under simple monopoly has an important bearing over this question. If the average cost curve of a product lies above the demand curve for it throughout its length, then it will not be profitable for the simple monopolist to produce any output at all. He may find that if he breaks up the market and charges different prices in the various separate markets, it may be profitable for him to produce some output of the product. This is so because the average revenue obtained by discriminating prices in the two separate markets is greater than the average revenue under simple monopoly. The average revenue under price discrimination (*DAR*) may therefore be greater than the average cost, when average revenue under simple monopoly (*SAR*) is less than the average cost. This situation is depicted in Fig. 27.4 in which average cost of output is shown by the curve *AC*. D_1 is the demand curve facing the monopolist in one market and D_2 is the demand curve facing him in the other market. The composite curve *BRT* is the aggregate demand curve (*AD*) or the average revenue curve under simple monopoly (*SAR*).

PRICE DISCRIMINATION AND SOCIAL WELFARE

It is evident from Fig. 27.4 that aggregate demand curve (*AD*) lies below the average cost curve *AC* throughout its length. In other words, average cost is greater than average revenue at all levels of output when a single price is charged for the product. For instance, suppose a simple monopolist decides to produce *OM* level of output, the single price which he will be able to charge from both markets is *MP* which is less than the average cost *MH*. So it will not pay the simple monopolist to produce *OM* output and charge the single price. But it will be profitable for him to produce *OM* output if he discriminates prices in the two markets. Under discrimination he may sell output OM_1 in one market at price M_1P_1 and output OM_2 in the other market at price M_2P_2, ($OM_1 + OM_2 = OM$). By discriminating prices in this way, suppose the average revenue obtained by him is equal to MP'. It will be seen from Fig. 27.4. That MP' is greater than the average cost *MH* of output *OM*. Thus, wereas it is not profitable for the simple monopolist to produce any output under single price system, it pays him to produce output by discriminating prices in the two markets.

We have discussed above the extreme case when there will be no output without price discrimination. In less extreme cases, output under price discrimination can be larger than the output without price discrimination.

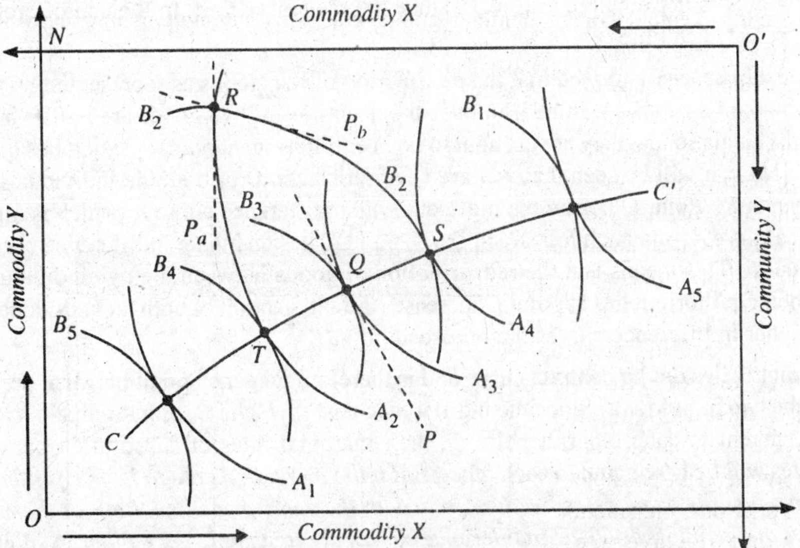

Fig. 27.5. *Price discrimination reduces social welfare by causing maldistribution of goods between the individuals.*

Whether price discrimination promotes social welfare or not is difficult to say, Judgement as to whether price discrimination promotes social welfare partly depends upon whether with the adoption of price discrimination, total output of the product increases or not. If we put aside the output effect of price discrimination and consider the *distribution of a given output* in case when price discrimination is being practised, then economist's verdict would be that this price discrimination will adversely affect the social welfare since it will be misallocating the output between the various individuals. Acccording to the economists, ideal market situation from the point of view of social welfare is perfect competition in which there is no price discrimination. *One of the marginal condition for maximum social welfare is that the marginal rate of substitution (MRS) of different consumers between any two goods should be the same.* And it is this condition of maximum social welfare that is violated by price discrimination.

That the price discrimination violates the optimum condition of distribution (or exchange) and therefore leads to maldistribution of goods between individuals and misallocation of resources between the goods is illustrated in Figure 27.5. We have assumed that there are two individuals A and B. Individual A's indifference curves between two goods are shown in this figure as A_1, A_2, A_3 etc. with O as the origin and indifference curves of individual B are B_1, B_2, B_3 etc. with O' as the origin. Individual B's Indifference map has been turned upside down by rotating it 180°. Further, suppose the output of commodity X is OM and output of commodity Y is ON.

Now, on account of price discrimination between two individuals, different prices of commodities X and Y are charged from the two individuals. Therefore, price lines facing the two individuals would not be the same. Suppose the price line faced by an individual A is P_a and price line faced by an individual B is P_b. These two price lines are shown to be intersecting at point R. At point R, individual A, given the prices of two goods, is maximizing his satisfaction by equating the price ratio for him to his marginal rate of substitution. (Price line P_a is tangent to his indifference curve A_2 at point R). Likewise, at point R individual B is maximizing his satisfaction, by equating the given price ratio for him with his marginal rate of substitution(price line P_b is tangent to his indifference curve B_2 at point R). Thus, in the presence of price discrimination, the distribution of two goods between the individuals A and B is depicted by the point R. It should be noted that at point R marginal rate of substitution of A is not equal to that of B, since the tangents drawn to their indifference curves at point R intersect each other.

Now, it can be easily proved that the distribution of two goods as represented by the point R is not one of maximum social welfare. Suppose the quantities of two goods are redistributed between the two individuals so that they are brought to be in equilibrium at point Q which lies on the contract curve CC'. Now, it will be seen that welfare (*i.e.*, satisfaction) of both the individuals is greater at point Q than at R. Point Q lies on the individual A's indifference curve A_3 which is higher than the indifference curve A_2 on which R lies. Similarly, point Q lies on higher indifference curve B_3 than B_2 of individual B. This means that the redistribution of goods between the two individuals in such a way that their equilibrium lies at point Q increases the satisfaction of both the individuals by putting them on higher indifference curves than those at point R.

But point Q lies on the contract curve and is therefore tangency point between the indifference curves of the two individuals. Since the indifference curves A_3 and B_3 of individuals A and B respectively are tangent to each other at point Q, their marginal rates of substitution between the two commodities will be here equal to each other. *But if the individuals are to be in equilibrium at point Q, they must pay the same price because only with the same price line, both of them would be in equilibrium at a point where their indifference curves are tangent to each other.* At point R, the two individuals are not paying the same price for the two goods on account of price discrimination. If price discrimination is removed, and the same price is charged, they will move to the equilibrium position on the contract curve CC'. Thus we see that by removing price discrimination and charging the same price from both the individuals, they would come to be in equilibrium at a point on the contract curve such as point Q and in this way their welfare will increase. Hence, *price discrimination is not conducive to optimum distribution of goods.*

It may be noted that between indifference curves A_2 and B_2 there are also other points lying on the contract curve CC', where the indifference curves of the two individuals are tangent to each other, that is, between points T and S on the contract curve besides point Q there are other points at which the indifference curves of the individuals will be tangential to each other. All the points between T and S on the contract curve will be on higher indifference curves than A_2 and B_2 on which the point R lies. The equilibrium at different points between T and S on the contract curve will be there with the different levels of the uniform prices of the two goods charged from the two individuals. If the uniform prices of the goods charged from the individuals are given by the price line P, the equilibrium of both the individuals will be at point Q. But, as shown above, with price discrimination (*i.e.*, when different prices are charged from the two individuals), the distribution of the goods between two individuals does not lie at a point on the contract curve, but away from it. In other words, with price discrimination the distribution of goods between the individuals is such that they are at a lower level of welfare than at a point on the contract curve. G.J. Stigler rightly writes : "*given the quantities of the commodities and the buyers' money incomes, all buyers can gain by the elimination of price discrimination, for price discrimination prevents them from reaching the contract curve*".[4]

SOCIAL JUSTIFICATION OF PRICE DISCRIMINATION

But the above argument against price discrimination is based on the assumption that the quantity of commodities produced of two goods is given. The question of their optimum distribution is analysed, by taking the given outputs of the goods. But a relevant question is *when the price discrimination leads to the increase in output, this extra output made possible by price discrimination has socially beneficial effect flowing from it and which should be put against the possible loss of social welfare due to misallocation of goods between the two individuals.* As we explained above, following Joan Robinson, price discrimination in many cases leads to the increase in output. That is, output of a commodity in many cases is greater under price discrimination than under simple monopoly. Thus, from the point of view of output, especially when a society prefers a greater output to a smaller output, *price discrimination in all those cases where it leads to the increase in output can be held to be promoting social welfare and is therefore justified.* We agree with Mrs Joan Robinson when she writes:

"From the point of view of society as a whole, it is impossible to say whether price discrimination is desirable or not. From one point of view, therefore, *price discrimination must be held to be superior to simple monopoly in all those cases in which it leads to an increase of output*, and these cases are likely to be more common. But against this advantage must be set the fact that *price discrimination leads to maldistribution of resources as between different uses...* Before it is possible to say whether discrimination is desirable or not it is necessary to weigh up the benefit from the increase in output against this disadvantage. In those cases in which discrimination will decrease output, it is undersirable on both counts."[5]

There is another important reason for which in some cases price discrimination is socially justified. This is the case when under a single uniform price, no output of a commodity is produced and only under price discrimination production of a commodity becomes profitable. Rail transportation is a case in point. It has been observed by many that if railway authorities are not permitted to charge higher fare from the rich people who travel in first or AC class, then it may not be profitable for the authorities to run the railways on a single uniform fare from all, rich and poor.

---

4. G.J. Stigler, *The Theory of Price*, revised edition, p.93, 1952.
5. John Robinson, *The Economics of Imperfect Competition, p.206.(italics added)*

We have already graphically explained above with the aid of Fig. 27.4 that when aggregate demand curve (*AD*) for a commodity lies below the average cost curve throughout and therefore at no level of output average revenue (when single price is charged) is greater than the average cost, the commodity would not be produced at all with a single uniform price, because it is not profitable to do so. When in such cases, price discrimination is practised the average revenue under price discrimination (*DAR*) may become higher than the average cost of production, it becomes worthwhile or profitable to produce a commodity (for full explanation of this point, see above the explanation given in connection with Figure 27.4). In those cases, where under single uniform price no production is done and under price discrimination, production becomes possible (to be more exact, becomes profitable), then price discrimination is socially desirable and justified, if the production of that commodity is considered essential and important for the society.

Price Discrimination and Equity. Finally, price discrimination may be socially justified on grounds of equity. We have discussed above the desirability of price discrimination from the point of view of *efficiency criterion*. As regards *optimum distribution of goods*, (that is, distributive efficiency), we have found that price discrimination leads to the maldistribution of the commodities between the individuals and thus violates the criterion of distributive efficiency. But this whole analysis of distributive efficiency is based on the given present distribution of income. If the present distribution of income is not considered equitable, then the mere distributive efficiency is not enough. *Under price discrimination when price is raised for the rich and is lowered for the poor, it has a redistributive effect; the poor are benefited at the expense of the rich.* Therefore, in order to reduce inequalities of personal real incomes, Government often itself practises price discrimination or when it controls prices in the private sector, it may permit or even encourage price discrimination. We thus see that equity criterion may outweigh the efficiency criterion and may make the price discrimination socially justified.

We, therefore, conclude that from the point of view of distributive efficiency and optimum allocation of resources, given the present distribution of income, price discrimination is not socially desirable. But from the point of view of expansion in output as well as for making the distribution of real incomes more equitable, price discrimination is socially justified. Thus, to pass judgement on the social desirability of a particular case of price discrimination, all these various considerations have to be weighed against each other.

NUMERICAL PROBLEM ON PRICE DISCRIMINATION

Problem. *Suppose a discriminating monopolist is selling a product in two separate markets in whcih demand functions are*

$$P_1 = 12 - Q_1$$
$$P_2 = 20 - Q_2$$

The monopolist's total cost fucntion is

$$TC = 3 + 2Q$$

As the economic adviser you are asked to determine the prices to be charged in the two markets and amount of output to be sold in each market so that profits are maximised. You are also asked to calculate the total profits to be made from the strategy of price discrimination. What advise will you give?

Solution. As profits in case of price discrimination are maximised when $MR_1 = MR_2 = MC$. Therefore, we have to calculate the marginal revenue in the two markets from the given demand functions of the two markets.

Total revenue in market $1 = P_1Q_1 = 12Q_1 - Q_1^2$ ...(1)

MR_1 in market $1 = \dfrac{\Delta(P_1Q_1)}{\Delta Q_1} = 12 - 2Q_1$

Total revenue in market $2 = P_2Q_2 = 20Q_2 - Q_2^2$ ... (2)

MR_2 in market $2 = \dfrac{\Delta(P_2Q_2)}{\Delta Q_2} = 20 - 2Q_2$

We can derive the marginal cost from the total cost function

$$TC = 3 + 2Q$$

$$MC = \frac{\Delta TC}{\Delta Q} = 2$$

Profit-maximising amounts of output to be sold in the two markets are determined by applying the equilibrium condition $MR_1 = MR_2 = MC$ and solving the following equations:

$$MR_1 = MC$$
$$12 - 2Q_1 = 2$$
$$2Q_1 = 12 - 2 = 10$$
$$Q_1 = 5$$
$$MR_2 = MC$$
$$20 - 2Q_2 = 2$$
$$2Q_2 = 20 - 2$$
$$Q_2 = 18/2 = 9$$

Substituting these equilibrium outputs, Q_1 and Q_2 in the demand functions, we obtain the profit-maximising prices:

$$P_1 = 12 - Q_1 = 12 - 5 = 7$$
$$P_2 = 20 - Q_2 = 20 - 9 = 11$$

Total profits can be obtained in the usual way

Total profits $\pi = (TR_1 + TR_2) - TC$

$$= (P_1Q_1 + P_2Q_2) - (3 + 2Q)$$
$$= 7(5) + 11(9) - [3 + 2(5 + 9)]$$
$$= (35 + 99) - 31 = 103$$

Numerical Example 2: *An Indian monopoly firm sells its product in the Indian and the US markets. The Indian demand function for the product is $P_i = 100 - Q_i$ and the US demand function for the product is $P_0 = 80 - 2Q_u$ where both prices are measured in rupees. The firm's marginal cost of product is Rs. 20 in both countries. If the Indian monopoly firm can prevent any resale what price will it charge in both markets ?*

Solution. Note that in both the markets *inverse demand functions* are given, namely, $P_i = 100 - Q_i$ and $P_u = 80 - 2Q_{2u}$. In order to find the equilibrium output prices in the two markets we have to first find the marginal revenue functions corresponding to the given linear demand functions. Further note that a marginal revenue function is *twice as steep as the slope of the linear demand function*. Therefore,

Marginal revenue in the Indian market is $MR_i = 100 - 2Q_i$

Marginal revenue in the US market is $MR_u = 80 - 4Q_u$

Since resale of the product between one market to another is not possible, the monopolist firm will equate the marginal revenue in each market with the given marginal cost which is equal to 20.

Thus, in India

$$MR_i = 100 - 2Q_i = 20$$
$$2Q_i = 100 - 20 = 80$$
$$Q_i = 80/2 = 40 \text{ units}$$

Similarly in the US

$$MR_u = 80 - 4Q_u = 20$$
$$4Q_u = 80 - 20 = 60$$
$$Q_4 = \frac{60}{4} = 15$$

Now, in order to find the prices charged in the two markets we substitute the equilibrium quantities sold in the two markets in their demand functions. Thus,

Substituting $Q_i = 40$ in the demand function of India we have

$$P_i = 100 - Q_i$$
$$= 100 - 40 = 60$$

Substituting $Q_u = 80 - 2Q_u$

in the demand function of the US we have

$$P_u = 80 - 2 \times 15$$
$$= 80 - 30 = 50$$

Thus, price discriminating monopolist charges price of Rs. 60 in India, while he sells it at Rs. 50 in the US.

QUESTIONS AND PROBLEMS FOR REVIEW

1. A monopolist is able to spearate two markets. In one market, the demand can be expressed as $Q_1 = 14 - P_1$. In the second market the demand is $Q_2 = 20 - 2P_2$.
   The monopolist's *MC* (marginal cost) equals 4. Find the profit maximising output, its allocation between the two markets and the prices charged. What happens to profit ?
2. Define price discrimination. Under what conditions can a monopolist discriminate between different buyers in fixing the price of his product? How does a discriminating monopolist allocate his output and charge different prices in different markets.
   (D.U., B.Com. (H), 2007)
3. Explain the conditions under which monopolistic price discrimination is both possible and profitable. *(D.U.B.A.(Hons)1990, C.U., B.Com., (H), 1994)*
4. Discuss the equilibrium of a monopolist, if one of the markets in which he operates is perfectly competitive.
   [Hint. This is the situation just like the dumping case discussed in the text]
5. A distinguish between simple and discriminating monopoly. Show graphically how a monopolist practicing third degree price discrimination maximise his profits.
6. Suppose a monopolist sells his product in the home market and also exports a part of it. The foreign elasticity of demand for its product is below that of the domestic market. If consumer arbitrage betwen the two markets is impossible, how do the domestic and foreign prices compare ?
7. A firm supplies its product in two markets, demand being more elastic in one than in the other. Assuming that the firm aims to maxmise its profits, show how the price and output in each market are determined.

8. A discriminating monopolist finds price elasticity of demand of his product –2.0 in one market and –1.5 in the other. What would be the ratio of prices charged by him in the two markets ?

[**Hint :** In equilibrium, $MR_1 = MR_2$

$MR_1 = P_1\left(1-\frac{1}{e_1}\right)$ and $MR_2 = P_2\left(1-\frac{1}{e_2}\right)$. Therefore, in equilibrium

$$\therefore \quad P_1\left(1-\frac{1}{e_1}\right) = P_1\left(1-\frac{1}{e_2}\right)$$

$$\frac{P_1}{P2} = \frac{1-\frac{1}{e_2}}{1-\frac{1}{e_1}} = \frac{1-\frac{1}{1.5}}{1-\frac{1}{2}} = \frac{\frac{1}{3}}{\frac{1}{2}}$$

$$\frac{P_1}{P_2} = \frac{2}{3}$$

Prices in two markets will be in the ratio of 2 :3. In market price where elasticity is higher price will be lower.

9. Explain and distinguish between 1st degree and 2nd degree price discrimination. What additional profit will the firm get while practising perfect 1st degree price discrimination.
D.U., B.Com (Hons.) 2009

10. What is Pareto optimality in the distribution of goods between individuals ? Show that price discrimination is not conducive to optimum distribution of goods.

11. When will a monopolist discriminate prices between buyers of his product ? Is price discriminations socially justified ? *D.U. B.Com. (Hons.)*

APPENDIX TO CHAPTER 27

PEAK - LOAD PRICING AND TWO-PART TARIFF PRICING

Similar to price discrimination the monopolist often adopts two other pricing practices, namely, peak-load pricing and two part tariff pricing. Under the peak-load pricing the monopolist charges higher price for a commodity during the peak period and the lower price during off-peak period. Two-part tariff pricing is also an important practice adopted by the monopolist to increase his profits by extracting more consumer surplus from the buyers. Under the two-part tariff pricing the monopolist charges *initial price* for the right to buy a commodity or service and the *usage* fee per unit of the number of units purchased by the buyers. We will explain below in detail both these pricing practices of the monopolist.

PEAK-LOAD PRICING

Now, we shall shed light on an important policy issue. When demand for a commodity or service varies at different periods of time, it has been generally suggested that higher price of a commodity or service be charged for the peak period when demand is greater and lower price be charged for off-peak period when demand is lower. This *dual pricing, that is, higher price for peak period and lower price for off-peak period is known as peak-load pricing*. It may be noted that peak-load pricing is suggested when not only the demand varies between peak and off-peak periods but also cost of production is different in the two time periods. In the peak period when capacity is strained marginal cost is higher as compared to the off-peak period. Thus, different prices of a commodity for two periods reflects the different costs of production of the commodity in the two periods.

Various examples of peak load pricing can be given. In India charges for trunk or STD calls during day time which is the peak period is higher and charges for the off-peak period from 9 P.M. to 6 A.M. are lower. In many countries electric companies are permitted to charge higher rates during the day time which is the peak period for the use of electricity and lower rates for the night which is off-peak period for the use of electricity. Similarly, air-lines often follow peak-load pricing; in off season they often lower their rates as compared to the peak periods of travel.

It may be noted that peak-load pricing is generally recommended for regulated monopolies such as electric companies telephone companies. As explained in a previous chapter, economic efficiency requires that *marginal cost pricing principle* should be followed. *According to marginal cost principle, price of a commodity or service is set equal to the marginal cost of production.* We will therefore explain peak-load pricing in the context of a regulated monopoly. We will analyse it by taking the example of electricity company. The Government generally appoints a commission to regulate electric company by fixing price for the use of electricity. Use of electricity varies a good deal over 24 hours in a day. During the day time when most commercial firms and industries are operating, the use or demand for electricity is the highest, that is, day time is the peak period. On the other hand, during late evening and night, the demand for electricity is lower. Thus there are different demand curves for electricity in the peak and off-peak periods.

Cost of producing electricity also varies over the day. Since production of electricity must be greater during the peak period, the electric company must have sufficient generating capacity to meet the higher demand for it in this period. As a result, much of the generating capacity required during the peak period remains unutilised during off-peak period. Thus, marginal cost of producing and supplying electricity during peak hours is higher when capacity is strained and lower during off-peak period when only the most efficient generators are used for producing electricity.

Average Cost Pricing : Is it Feasible ?

The case for adoption of peak-load pricing in case of an electric company which is regulated by the Government is illustrated in Fig. 27A.1 where $D_1 D_1$ is the demand curve of the electricity in off-peak period and $D_2 D_2$ is the demand curve of the electricity in the peak period. *The regulatory commissions generally follow average cost pricing under which a single, uniform price or rate is charged in both the peak and off-peak periods.* This average cost is calculated to cover its labour, capital, fuel and other costs plus a fair return on investment. Suppose a uniform price based on this average cost of producing electricity in the two period is fixed at *OP*. It will be seen from Fig. 27A.1 that at the single uniform price *OP*, the demand for electricity in the off-peak period is *OA*, while it is *OB* in the peak period. However, during the peak period the company would like to produce *OQ* electricity. This is because at this output, the uniform price *OP* is equal to marginal cost (*MC* = Price) and thus with the *given price OP* it will be maximising its profits by producing *OQ* rate of output. Thus company's rate of production equal to *OQ* during the peak period and quantity demanded of electricity equal to *OB* in this period, *shortage of electricity supply would emerge during the peak period.* To meet this shortage regulatory commission of the electric supply company makes it mandatory for it to produce and supply *OB* quantity of electricity during the peak period. But, as will be observed from Fig. 27A.1, it is not profitable for the electric company to generate electricity more than *OQ* during the peak period because beyond output *OQ* price (or *MR*) is less than marginal cost. Thus, the interests of the electric company which produces electricity and of the public which uses it clash with each other. It has been observed that *regulated electric companies deliberately resort to black-outs or load shedding quite often during the peak periods*. This shows the reluctance of the companies to generate sufficient electricity at the regulated price to meet the peak-period demand for it. It is because of these pitfalls of uniform-price policy of Public Utility Companies which produce commodities or services such as electricity, telecommunication that in recent years the commissions appointed to regulate these monopolies have recommended peak-load pricing. Which, as explained above, requires different prices to be charged in peak and off-peak periods.

Peak-Load Pricing : Marginal Cost Pricing

It is important to note that to achieve economic efficiency in the use of resources, peak-load pricing policy for regulated public utility companies (which are generally monopolies) follows marginal cost pricing principle. That is, under peak-load pricing price in each period is set equal to marginal cost of production in that period. Thus, in the cost situation depicted in Fig. 27A.1 price in each period will be fixed where marginal cost curve *MC* intersects the demand curves of the peak and off-peak periods. It will be seen from fig. 27A.1 that marginal cost curve *MC* intersects the demand curve $D_1 D_1$ of the off-peak period at point *R* and therefore price set in the off-peak period will be OP_1. At price OP_1, consumers will use or purchase OQ_1 quantity of electricity. Figure 27A.1 further reveals that marginal cost curve *MC* intersects the demand curve $D_2 D_2$ of the peak period at point *T* and therefore in the peak period price will be set equal to OP_2. At price OP_2, the consumers will use or buy OQ_2 quantity in the peak period. With this dual price structure, consumers have incentive to be economical in the use of electricity during the peak period

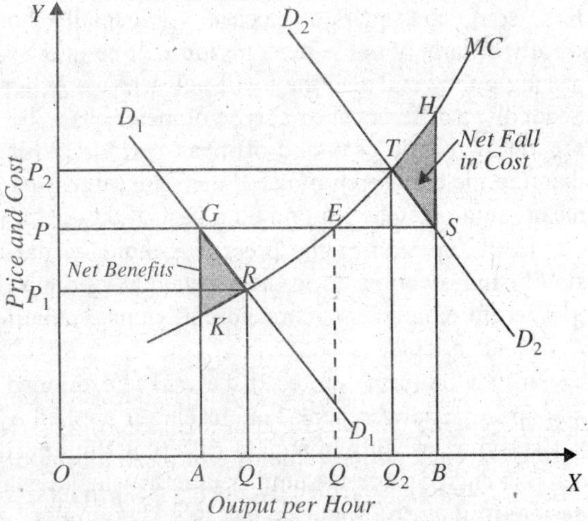

Fig. 27A.1. *Peak Load Pricing and Its Effect*

when its price is higher. Secondly, consumers have incentive to reduce peak-period consumption of electricity by shifting it as far as possible to the off-peak period when its price is low.

Advantages of Peak-Load Pricing

There are two distinct benefits of peak-load pricing as compared to uniform pricing. First, peak-load pricing ensures more efficient distribution of the use of electricity between the peak and non-peak periods. As has been explained above, as a result of peak-load pricing consumers reduce the consumption of electricity in the peak-period when its price is higher and increase its consumption in the off peak-period when its price is lower. Consequently, a given amount of electric power is produced with lower cost than before. This implies more efficient production. It will be seen from Fig. 27A.1 that with the adoption of peak-load pricing when consumption of electricity falls from OB to OQ_2, costs are reduced by the area under the marginal cost curve, that is, area $BHTQ_2$ over this range of output while benefits, as indicated by the area under the demand curve, fall by the amount equal to the area $BSTQ_2$. It is evident from Fig. 27A.1 that there is *net fall in costs* equal to the shaded are HST. Similarly, with the increase in consumption of electric power in the off-peak period from OA to OQ_1, there is gain in benefits equal to the area $AGRQ_1$ while there is increase in costs equal to the area $AKRQ_1$ which is less than the gain in benefits. Consequntly, there is net *gain in benefits* equal to the shaded area KGR. Note that since we are explaining peak-load pricing in the context of regulated monopoly in which firm makes zero economic profits, the efficiency gain of peak-lead pricing will go to the consumers of electricity. This is quite evident from the fact that the peak-load pricing leads to the reduction in total cost of production and given that the total output of electricity remains the same, peak-load pricing will cause the average price of electricity for the consumers to fall.

A second benefit that accrues from peak-load pricing refers to cost saving on account of planning a productive capacity in the long run. In planning for setting up a scale of operations, an electric company must have sufficient generating capacity to meet demand in the peak period. It will be observed from Fig. 27A.1 that with peak load pricing quantity demanded of electricity in the peak period falls to OQ_2 under peak-load pricing from OB in case of uniform pricing. In view of lower demand in the peak period, the firm has to design a smaller scale of operations under peak-load pricing. Thus, with *peak-load pricing a firm has to install, maintain and house fewer generators to meet the demand in the peak period.* This means a good deal of cost savings which shows another efficiency gain from the peak-load pricing.

Disadvantages

Peak-load pricing is not without disadvantages. Its two disadvantages are worth mentioning. First, some consumers of electricity, especially those businesses whose demand for electricity is wholly or largely in the peak period will be hurt by the higher peak-period price under peak-load pricing policy and also they will not derive any benefits from lower price in the off-peak period. Secondly, a different special type of meter has to be installed to register consumption of electricity separately for the peak and off-peak periods. While these special meters do not cost much more than the meters currently used; the replacement of the existing meters by the new ones however means some increase in one time cost of the firms.

In the opinion of the present author, the disadvantages of peak-load pricing are not very significant as compared to the substantial gain in efficiency and reduction in cost that result from it. Therefore, in recent years, commissions regulating monopolies are increasingly recommending peak-load pricing.

It may be further noted that we have examined peak-load pricing in the context of regulated monopoly. However, peak-load pricing is applied by the firms working under other forms of market structure when demand in different time periods is different. For instance, hotels in hill stations charge more in summer months when demand is high and charge lower rate during other periods. Similarly, some restaurants charge more at dinner time when demand is high than at lunch. Further, some cinema halls in Delhi charge more in the evening shows than in the afternoon and morning shows. It should be noted that these and other similar case of peak-load pricing do net reflect price discrimination. Instead, these are the adjustments in the rate structure according to market conditions when demand varies systematically over time.

TWO-PART TARIFF PRICING

Similar to the price discriminating practice, another price practice that is sometimes adopted by the monopolist is two-part tariff policy. Two-part tariff policy by the monopolist is an important way to extract consumer surplus from the buyers of a product or service. Under the two-part tariff, the monopolist charges *initial fee* for the right to buy a product or service and the *specified price* or *usage fee for each unit* purchased by the consumer or buyer of a product or service. The initial fee which is a lump sum payment for right to buy is the first tariff and the specified price or the usage fee to be paid for each unit of the product purchased by the consumer is the second tariff.

Many examples of two-part tariff pricing practice can be given. First, a telephone company requires its user to pay *a monthly connection fee or rent* and a fee per minute of its use. Golf and tennis clubs often charge an *annual membership fee* as the initial fee as well as the fee for *each round or game* played. Pricing by an amusing park provides another example of two-part tariffs. Management of an amusement park requires its visitors to pay an admission fee and also a fee or price for each ride they take.

It is worth noting again that the purpose of the two-part tariff pricing by the *monopolist, like* price discrimination, is *to extract as much consumer surplus as possible from the consumers of the product and therefore to maximise his profits.*

To pursue two-part tariff policy successfully a firm must have a large market power, that is, he must have a sufficient monopoly power to fix price and should know the demand curves of the consumers and further how demands of consumers differ for a product. Besides, for two-part tariff policy it is necessary that the monopolist must successfully prevent *resales by the buyers*. In what follows we first explain how with two parts tariff, the monopolist is able to extract consumer

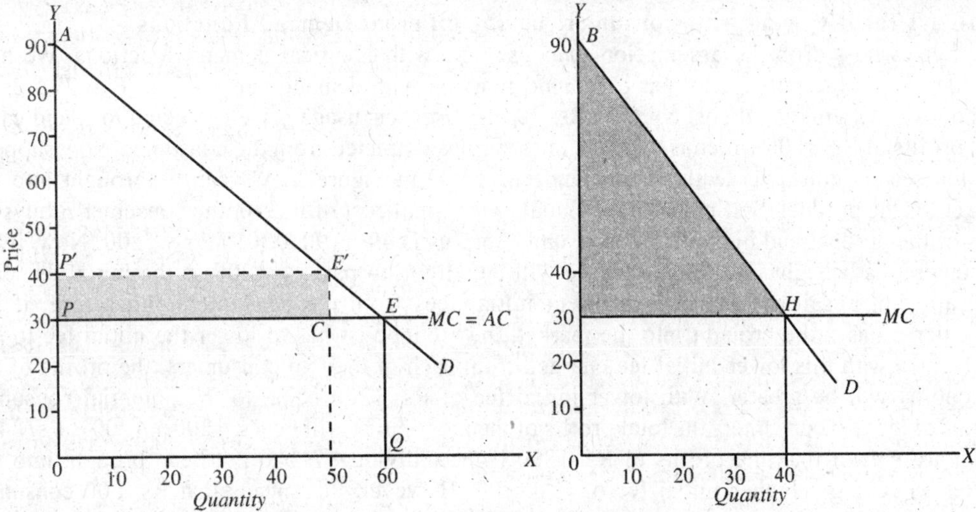

Fig. 27A.2. *Two-part Tariff Pricing with one Consumer in the Market*

Fig. 27A.3. *Two-part Tariff Pricing with Second Consumer with Different Demand Function*

surplus from the buyers. The monopolist is able to maximise his profits *by charging usage fee or per unit price equal to marginal cost* and the *initial fee* equal to the entire potential consumer surplus of the buyers. To explain this we assume that demand functions of all consumers are identical as given by demand curve *AD* in Figure 27A.2. Now suppose that marginal cost of the monopolist is Rs. 30 and remains constant. Under the two-part tariff pricing strategy the monopolist will set price or usage fee of its product equal to Rs. 30 at which a consumer buys 60 units. As price is equal to marginal cost (which is equal to average cost as *MC* remains constant), the monopolist will just cover its costs by charging this usage fee equal to marginal cost. However, under the two -part tariff policy, the monopolist will also charge *initial membership* or *admission fee* to earn profits. By setting usage price equal to marginal cost it maximises the potential consumer surplus of the buyers of the product or service. Now, the monopolist will set the *initial fee* so as to extract the entire consumer surplus of the buyers. It will be seen from Figure 27A.2 that by buying *OQ* (= 60 units) quantity at price *OP* = (Rs. 30 per unit), consumer's surplus is equal to the area *AEP*. To extract this entire consumer surplus *AEP* which is equal to 60 × (90 – 30) × ½ = 1800, the monopolist will charge a lump sum of Rs. 1800 as the initial fee in addition to usage price per unit for the number of units of the product purchased by a buyer. The total profits made by him is equal to the consumer surplus of Rs. 1800 extracted from the consumer for the sale of 60 units of the product.

It may be noted that the profits of the monopolist will be lower at any other price. Suppose he sets price of the product equal to *OP′* (Rs. 40 per unit) which results in lower quantity (50 units) bought by the consumer. With price equal to Rs. 40 or *OP′*, the monopolist will get profits of Rs. 10 more per unit and the gain in profits by charging a higher usage price will increase by 10 × 50 = Rs. 500. But his total profits will fall because of the decline in consumer surplus at the higher price (Rs. 40) . At this higher price of Rs. 40 or *OP′*, the consumer surplus to be extracted from the buyer by charging an initial lump sum will fall. With Rs. 40 (or *OP′*) as the price charged and 50 units of sale, the consumer surplus falls to 50 × (90 – 40) × ½ = Rs. 1250. With this the total profits will be 1250 + 500 = Rs. 1750. Thus at a higher price of Rs. 40 or *OP′*, the total profits fall. In fact, the decline in total profits will be equal to the area of the small triangle *ECE′*. Further, at any price lower than Rs. 30 (or *OP*), the monopolist will incur a loss on each unit of the product sold and this total loss will be greater than the gain in consumer surplus extracted from the buyer by lowering price so that total profits will be less at any price lower than *OP* or Rs. 30 which is equal to marginal cost.

Two-Part Tariff Pricing with Consumers having different Demand Functions

Let us now drop the assumption of consumers with identical demand functions. We now consider one consumer A who has a demand function with demand curve *AD* in Fig. 27A.2. As seen above, with marginal cost equal to Rs. 30, the firm sets usage price *OP* equal to it and earns total profits of Rs. 1800 which is the consumer surplus extracted from the consumer. Now suppose that the second consumer with the demand curve *BD* in Figure 27A.3 can be brought into the market for the product. Setting price *OP* equal to marginal cost of Rs. 30, the consumer *B* buys 40 units of the product and his potential consumer surplus is 40 × (90 – 30) × ½ = 1200. Now, if the consumer *B* is brought into the market he will be willing to pay Rs. 1200 as the initial fee. It is generally not possible to charge different initial fees from the consumers. Therefore, if the consumer *B* has to be brought into the market, the monopolist has to lower the initial fee to Rs. 1200. Even with this lower initial fee charged from each of the two consumers, the profits of the monopolist will be greater. With lower initial fee of Rs. 1200 equal to the potential consumer surplus of the two consumers the total profits of the monopolist will be Rs. 1200 + 1200 = Rs. 2400 which are greater than the profits of Rs. 1800 if the individual *B* had not been brought into the market by setting a higher initial fee of Rs. 1800. However, this means that Rs. 600 consumer surplus will be left with the consumer *A*. The monopolist could extract this consumer surplus from consumer *A* if he somehow goes on charging initial fee of Rs. 1800 from consumer *A* and gives a special discount membership to consumer *B* with initial fee of Rs. 1200.

QUESTIONS FOR REVIEW

1. What do you mean by peak-load pricing ? Show how peak-load pricing can be a better policy than uniform pricing in case of a public utility company producing electricity.
D.U., B.Com (Hons.) 2006, 2009
2. Explain peak-load pricing by a monopolistc public utility company. Explain why under a regulated public utility company peak-load pricing follows marginal cost pricing.
3. What is two-part tariff pricing ? Show how under it a monopolist firm extracts consumer surplus to maximise his profits.

CHAPTER 28

PRICE UNDER MONOPOLISTIC COMPETITION

IMPERFECT COMPETITION : MONOPOLISTIC COMPETITION AND OLIGOPOLY

Perfect competition and monopoly are rarely tound in the real world and thus they do not represent, for the most part, the acutal market situations. Therefore, the conclusions which follow from the theories of pure competition were found to be inapplicable to the behaviour of business firms in the actual world. For instance, in the real world, firms were found to be enjoying 'internal economies of scale' which were incompatible with the theory of perfect competition. The urgent need was therefore felt to reformulate the theory of price so as to bring it nearer to the actual world. This was accomplished by E.H. Chamberlin and Joan Robinson who worked quite independently and brought out simultaneously "*The Theory of Monopolistic Competition*" and "*The Economics of Imperfect Competition*" respectively. Joan Robinson got the clues for her theory of imperfect competition from who in his article "The Laws of Returns under Competitive Conditions" in *Economic Journal* asserted, "*It is necessary, therefore, to abandon the path of free competition and turn in the opposite direction, namely, towards monopoly.*"

Monopolistic competition theory of Prof. Chamberlin and imperfect competition theory of Joan Robinson, though similar in various ways differ in some important respects. The nutshell of these theories, especially of the theory of monopilstic competition, is that the pure competition and pure monopoly are the two opposite limiting cases, lying between which is a series of intermediate cases, which differ from each other in relative strengths of monopoly and competitive elements, or in other words, in *degrees of imperfection*. It may be noted that the extreme limit of monopoly is reached when a seller does not face competition from any substitute product. Since every good has to complete with others for buyer's money income, every good is a substitute of others to some extent. It follows that the extreme limit of monopoly, which Sraffa denotes as *pure monopoly*, will be reached only when a single person or agency comes to have a "control over the supply of all economic goods". At the other extreme is pure or perfect competition in which case an individual seller has to compete with the products (of rival sellers) which are perfect substitutes of his own product, since products of all sellers are completely identical or homogeneous. Between these two extremes of pure monopoly and pure competition, there are all gradations in which both the monopolistic and competitive elements are present. In the terminology of Robinson and Chamberlin, pure monopoly in the sense of a single seller of a product which has got no close substitutes is an extreme form of imperfect competition. *The two important forms of imperfect competition are : (a) monopolistic competition, (b) oligopoly.*

The fundamental distinguishishing feature of imperfect competition is that unlike that under perfect or pure competition, the demand curve confronting an individual firm under it slopes downward. As a result, the marginal revenue curve lies below it. Marginal revenue curve plays such a crucial role because of its definite relation with price and elasticity ($MR = \text{Price}\ \frac{e-1}{e}$). It is the nature of this relation which distinguishes a state of competititon that is pure from one that is impure or imperfect. The difference between mrginal revenue and price at an output level depends upon the size of price elasticity of demand at it. Under perfect competition, price is equal to marginal revenue since price elasticity of demand is infinite, while under imperfect competition, price is greater than marginal revenue since price elasticity of demand is less than infinite. Therefore, the difference between the price and marginal revenue (or marginal cost) at equilibrium output is regarded as the *degree of imperfection or degree of monopoly*. Thus, the relative magnitudes of price and marginal revenue at equilibrium output help us to distinguish between different degrees of imperfection or monopoly power in various market structures. The greater the difference between the price and the marginal revenue, the greater the degree of imperfection or monopoly element and *vice versa*.

PRODUCT DIFFERENTIATION AND MONOPOLISTIC COMPETITION

The concept of monopolistic competition put forth by Chamberlin is a true revolutionary as well as more realistic than either perfect competition or pure monopoly. Before Chamberlin, monopoly and competition were regarded as two mutually exclusive alternatives; one would be absent when the other exists. On the other hand, according to Chamberlin, in most of the real world economic situations, both monopoly and competitive elements are present. Chamberlin's concept of monopolistic competition is thus a blending of competition and monopoly.

The distinguishing feature of monopolistic competition which makes it as a blending of competition and monopoly is the *differentiation of the product*. This means that the products of various firms are not homogeneous but differentiated though they are closely related to each other. Product differentiation does not mean that the products of various firms are altogether different. They are only slightly different so that they are quite similar and serve as close substitutes of each other. When there is any degree of differentiation of products, monopoly element enters the situation. And, the greater the differentiation, the greater the element of monopoly involved in the market situation. When there is a large number of firms producing differentiated products, each one has a monopoly of its own product but is subject to the competition of close substitutes. Since each is a monopolist and yet has competitors, we have a market situation which can be aptly described as "monopolistic competition." It is thus clear that monopolistic competititon involves both the monopoly and competitive elements. Here, it is worth quoting Chamberlin himself "With differentiation appears monopoly and as it proceeds further, the element of monopoly becomes greater. Where there is any degree of differentiation whatever, each seller has an absolute monopoly of his own product, but is subject to the competition of more or less imperfect substitutes. Since each is a monopolist and yet has competitors we may speak of them as 'competing monopolists' and with peculiar appropriateness, of the forces at work as those of monopolistic competition."[1]

It is thus clear from above that in monopolistic competition, products are not identical as in perfect competition, but neither are they remote substitutes as in monopoly. The products of various sellers are fairly similar (but not the same) and serve as close substitutes of each other. Every seller has a monopoly of his own differentiated product but he has to face a stiff competition from his rival sellers which are selling close substitutes of his product.

Many examples of product differentiation can be given from the Indian scene. For instance, in India there are various manufacturers of toothpaste which produce different brands such as Colgate, Binaca, Forhans , Pepsodent , Signals, Neem etc. Thus, the manufacturer of 'Colgate' has a monopoly of producing it (nobody else can produce and sell the toothpaste with the name 'Colgate') but he faces competition from the manufacturers of Forhans, Binaca, Pepsodent etc. which are close substitutes of Colgate. The manufacturer of Colgate cannot therefore decide about its price-output policies without considering the possible reactions of rival firms producing close substitutes. Other examples of monopolistic competition are the producers of bathing soaps (Lux, Godrej, Breeze, Hamam,

---

1. E.H. Chamberlin, *The Theory of Monopolistic Competition*, 7th ed., 1956, p. 904,

Palmolive, Jai etc.); the manufacturers of tooth brushes (Colgate, Dr. West's, Wisdom, Binaca, etc.); retailers' shops in the towns; barbers' shops in the towns, etc. We thus see that monopolistic competititon corresponds more to the real world economic situation than perfect competition or monopoly.

A general class of product is differentiated if a basis exists for preferring goods of one seller to those of others. Such a basis for preference may be real or fancied, it will cause differentiation of the product. When such differentiation of the product exists, even if it is slight, buyers will be paired with sellers not in a random fashion (as in perfect competition) but according to their preferences, There are, broadly speaking, two bases of product differentiation. Firstly, differentiation may be based upon certain *characteristic of the product itself* such as exclusive patented features, trade marks and trade names, peculiarities of packages or wrappers if any, or difference in quality, design, colour or style. Real qualitative differences like those of materials used, design and workmanship are no doubt important means of differentiating products. But imaginary differences created through advertising, the use of attractive packets, the use of trade marks and brand names are more usual methods by which products are differentiated, even if physically they are identical or almost so. Secondly, Differentiation may be based upon the *conditions surrounding the sale of the product.* This means that product is differentiated if the services rendered in the process of selling the product by one seller or firm are not identical with those rendered by any other seller or firm. Thus, in retail trade to take only one instance, the conditions surrounding the sale of the product include "the convenience of the seller's location, the general tone or character of his establishment, his way of doing business, his reputation for fail dealing, courtesy, efficiency, and all others which attach his customers either to himself or to those employed by him".[2] If these and other intangible factors surrounding the sale of the product are different in case of different sellers, the product in each case will be different since the buyers take these intangible factors into consideration while making purchases. These factors like the patents, trade marks etc. serve as a basis for preference.

If the above two aspects of differentiation are borne in mind, then it will be quite manifest that virtually all products in the real world are more or less differentiated. It should be carefully noted that even when product differentiation is caused by the circumstances surrounding the sale of the products, both monopolistic and competitive elements are present. In retail trade, to take the above example, every product is rendered differentiated by the individuality of the establishment in which it is sold including the location factor, the general tone, reputation, goodwill of the establishment, way of dealing with customers etc. Each retail trader has complete and absolute control over the supply of his 'product' when this is taken to include location factor, general tone and reputation, way of dealing with the customers etc; this is the monopolistic aspect. Again, every retail trade is subject to the competition of other 'products' sold under different conditions and at different locations; this is the competitive aspect. Thus, as in the case of patents and trade marks, both monopoly and competition are present in the case of 'products' differentiated by the conditions surrounding their sale.

Under monopoly, the demand curve for the product of the monopolist is given. But the demand curve for the product of an individual producer or seller under monopolistic competition cannot be taken as given since there exist, in monopolistic competition, close competitive interrelationships among various producers selling close substitutes. The demand curve for the product of an individual depends upon the nature and prices of its closely competing substitues. Thus, according to Chamberlin, "Monopolistic competition concerns itself not only with the problem of an *individual equilibrium* (the ordinary theory of monopoly), but also with that of a *group equilibrium* (the adjustment of economic forces within a group of competing monopolists, ordinarily regarded as merely a group of competitors). In this, it differes both from the theory of competition and from the theory of monopoly".[3]

3. *Ibid.*, p. 69,
2. E.H. Chamberlin, *op. cit.*, p. 68

This leads us to Chamberlin's concepts of group and group equilibrium. Chamberlin has used the word group instead of industry in order to draw distinction between pure competition and monopolistic competition. The word industry is generally used in economics in the context of pure or perfect competition and *refers to a collection of firms that produce homogeneous products.* But, as explained above, under monopolistic competition we have product hetrogeneity. Therefore, the word 'industry' loses its significance under monopolistic competition. Therefore, Prof. Chamberlin has used the word 'group'. *By group he means "a number of producers whose goods are fairly close substitutes"*. We thus see that the Chamberlin's 'group' refers to a collection of firms that produce closely related but not identical products. It became necessary for Prof. Chamberlin to evolve the concept of 'group' as distinct from industry because in the case of group where products are differentiated there are special problems which are absent in the case of industry where products are homogeneous. The various firms in a given group produce products which are close substitutes of each other and therefore compete with each other in the market. The demand for the product of one producer depends upon the price and the nature of the products of his close rivals. These competitive interrelationships among firms are absent in the case of an industry under pure or perfect competition since all of them produce homogeneous products and each of them can sell his entire supply of the product at the going market price.

An individual producer in the 'group' under monopolistic competition cannot therefore be treated in complete isolation from his rivals producing close substitutes, since the demand for his product depends upon the nature and price of the close substitutes. To quote Prof. Chamberlin: "From our point of view, each producer within the group is a monopolist, yet his market is interwoven with those of his competitors, and he is no longer to be isolated from them"[4].

Lastly, it may be noted that the sense in which the word 'competition' is generally used in the business world is in conformity more with the monopolistic competition than with the pure competition. The phrases such as price cutting, under-selling, unfair competition, meeting competition, cut-throat competition, securing market etc. often used in the business world are irrelevant in the context of pure competition. This is because each seller under so-called 'pure competition' accepts the going market price and can dispose of his entire supply of the product without affecting price. For a pure competitor there is no problem of choosing a price policy, problem of advertising in order to attact customers. Thus, the competition in the ordinary sense of the competitive phrases, just noted above, has meaning only in the context of monopolistic competition (and also of oligopoly) where products of various sellers are differentiated but closely related. Sellers really compete in the ordinary sense of the word only under the monopolistic competition and oligopoly.

IMPORTANT FEATURES OF MONOPOLISTIC COMPETITION

It is important to understand the important characteristics of monopolistic competition. The knowledge of these features will enable the students to know how this form of market structure is different from perfect competition and oligopoly. We explain below its important features.

1. A large number of firms. The first important feature of monopolistic competition is that under it there are a relatively large number of firms each satisfying a small share of the market demand for the product. Because there is a large number of firms under monopolistic competition, there exists stiff competition between them. Unlike perfect competition these large number of firms do not produce identical products. Instead, they produce and sell differentiated products which are close substitutes of each other. This makes the competition among firms real and tough.

Further, the fact that there is a large number of firms under monopolistic competition, size of each firm will be relatively small. This is unlike oligopoly where there are a few firms of big size.

4. E.H. Chamberlin, *op. cit.* p.8.

2. Product differentiation. The second important feature of monopolistic competition is that the products produced by various firms are not identical but are slightly different from each other. Though different firms make their products slightly different from others, they remain close substitutes of each other. In other words, the products of various firms working under monopolistic competition are not the same but are similar. Therefore, their prices cannot be very much different from each other. It is because of the fact that their products are similar and close substitutes of each other that the various firms under monopolistic competition compete with each other.

3. Some influence over the price. Each firm under monopolistic competition produces a product variety which is close substitute of others. Therefore, if a firm lowers the price of its product variety, some customers of other product varieties will switch over to it. This means as it lowers the price of its product variety, quantity demanded of it will increase. On the other hand, if it raises the price of its product, some of its customers will leave it and buy the similar products from its competing firms. This implies that demand curve facing a firm working under monopolistic competition slopes downward and marginal revenue curve lies below it. This means that under monopolistic competition an individual firm is not a price taker but will have some influence over the price of its product. If it fixes a higher price, it will be able to sell a relatively smaller quantity of output. And if it fixes a lower price, it will be able to sell more. *Thus under monopolistic competition, a firm has to choose a price-output combination which will maximise its profits.*

4. Non-price competition: Expenditure on advertisement and other selling costs. An important feature of monopolistic competition is that firms incur a considerable expenditure on advertisements and other selling costs to promote the sales of their products. Promoting sales of their products through advertisement is an important example of non-price competition. The expenditure incurred on advertisement is prominent among the various types of selling costs. The advertisement and other selling outlays by a firm change the demand for its product as well as its costs. Like the adjustments of price and product, a seller under monopolistic competition will also adjust the amount of his advertisement expenditure so as to maximise his profits. This problem of adjusting one's selling outlay is unique to monopolistic competition, because the firm under perfect competition has not to incur any expenditure on advertisement. The advertisement expenditure by a purely competitive firm will be without purpose since it can sell as much amount as it pleases at the going market price without any advertisement expenditure. The rival firms under monopolistic competition keenly compete with each other through advertisement by which they change the consumers' wants for their products and attract more customers. Thus, a full explanation of the equilibrium under monopolistic competition must also involve equilibrium in regard to the amount of expenditure on advertisement and other sales promotion activities.

5. Product variation. Another form of non-price competition which a firm under monopolistic competition has to face is the variation in products by various firms. A firm, under perfect competition, does not confront this problem, for the product is homogeneous under perfect competition. The problem of product variation under monopolistic competition exists because there is differentiation of products of various firms. The firm will try to adjust its product so as to conform more to the wishes of the buyers. The variation of the product may refer to a change in the quality of the product itself, technical changes, a new design, better materials, and it may mean only a new package or container. It may also mean more prompt or courteous service, and a different way of doing business. The amount of the product which a firm will be able to sell in the market depends in part upon the manner in which its product differs from others. Where the possibility of product differentiation exists, sales depends upon the skill with which a product is distinguished from others and made to appeal to a particular group of buyers. The profit maximisation principle applies to the choice of the nature of the product as to its price. In other words, a firm will choose that nature of the product, given its price, which gives it maximum profits. Therefore, in a full explanation of the firm's equilibrium under monopolistic competition we have also to explain product equilibrium in addition to price equilibrium and selling-costs equilibrium.

6. Freedom of entry and exit. This is another important feature of monopolistic competition. In a monopolistically competitive industry it is easy for the new firms to enter and the existing firms to leave it. Free entry means that when in the industry existing firms are making super-normal profits, the new firms enter the industry which leads to the expansion of output. As a result, price of product tends to fall in the long run. However, it may be noted that under monopolistic competition entry may not be as easy or free as under perfect competition. Whereas under perfect competition the new firms which enter the industry can produce identical products, but under monopolistic competition, the new firms can produce only new brands or product varieties which may initially find it difficult to compete with the already well-established brands and product varieties.

The Nature of Demand and Marginal Revenue Curves under Monopolistic Competition

It is important to understand the nature of the demand curve facing an individual firm under monopolistic competition. As has been explained in previous chapters, demand curve facing a firm working under perfect competition is perfectly elastic at the ruling market price since it has absolutely no control over the price of the product. On the contrary, a firm working under monopolistic competition enjoys some control over the price of its product since its product is somewhat differentiated from others. If a firm under monopolistic competition raises the price of its product, it will find some of its customers going away to buy other products. As a result, the quantity demanded of its product will fall. On the contrary, if it lowers the price, it will find that buyers of other varieties of the product will start purchasing its product and as a result the quantity demanded of its product will increase. It therefore follows that the demand curve facing an individual firm under monopolistic competition slopes downward.

If a firm working under monopolistic competition wants to increase the sales of its product, it must lower the price. It can raise the price if it is prepared to sacrifice some sales. To put it in another way, a firm working under monopolistic competition can lower the price by increasing its level of sales and output. A purely competitive firm merely adjusts the quantity of output it has to produce, price being a given and constant datum for it. But a firm working under monopolistic competition faces a more complicated problem. It cannot merely adjust quantity at a given price because each quantity change by it will bring about a change in the price at which the product can be sold. Consider Fig. 28.1. *DD* is the demand curve facing an individual firm under monopolistic competition. At price *OP* the quantity demanded is *OM*. Therefore, the firm would be able to sell *OM* quantity at price *OP*. If it wants to sell greater quantity *ON*, then it will have to reduce price to *OL*. If it restricts its quantity to *OG*, price will rise to *OH*. Thus, every quantity change by it entails a change in price at which the product can be sold. Thus *the problem faced by a firm working under monopolistic competition is to choose the price-quantity combination which is optimum for it, that is, which yields it maximum possible profits.*

Demand curve facing a firm will be his average revenue curve. Thus the average revenue curve of the monopolistically competitive firm slopes downward throughout its length. Since average revenue curve slopes downward, marginal revenue curve lies below it. This follows from usual average-marginal relationship. The implication of marginal revenue curve lying below average revenue curve is that the marginal revenue will be less than the price or average revenue. When a firm working under monopolistic competition sells more, the price of its product falls; marginal revenue therefore must be less than price. In Fig. 28.2 *AR* is the average revenue curve of the firm under monopolistic competition and slopes downward. *MR* is the marginal revenue curve and lies below *AR* curve. At quantity *OM*, average revenue (or price) is *OP* and marginal revenue is *MQ* which is less than *OP*. In an earlier chapter we have explained that average and marginal revenues at a level of output are related to each other through price elasticity of demand and in this connection we derived the following formula:

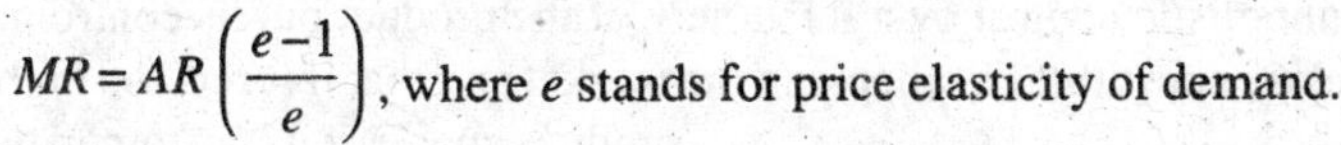

$$MR = AR\left(\frac{e-1}{e}\right)$$, where e stands for price elasticity of demand.

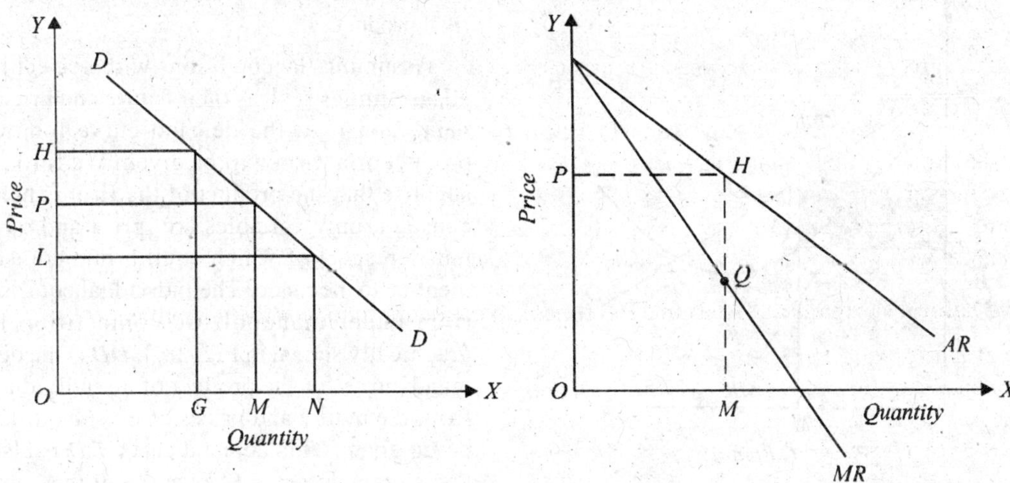

Fig. 28.1. *Demand Curve Facing a Monopolistically Competitive Firm*

Fig. 28.2. *Average and Marginal Revenue Curves under Monopolistic Competition*

PRICE-OUTPUT EQUILIBRIUM UNDER MONOPOLISTIC COMPETITION

A firm under monopolistic competition has to face various problems which are absent under perfect competition. Since the market of an individual firm under perfect competition is completely merged with the general one, it can sell any amount of the good at the ruling market price. But, under monopolistic competition, individual firm's market is isolated to a certain degree from those of its rivals with the result that its sales are limited and depend upon (1) its price, (2) the nature of its product, and (3) the advertising outlay it makes. Thus, the firm under monopolistic competition has to confront a more complicated problem than the perfectly competitive firm. Equilibrium of an individual firm under monopolistic competition involves equilibrium in three respects, that is, in regard to the price, the nature of the product, and the amount of advertising outlay it should make.

Equilibrium of the firm in respect of three variables simultaneously—price, nature of product, selling outlay—is difficult to discuss. Therefore, the method of explaining equilibrium in respect of each of them separately is adopted, keeping the other two variables given and constant. Moreover, as noted above, the equilibrium under monopolistic competition involves "individual equilibrium" of the firms as well as "group equilibrium". We shall discuss these two types of equilibrium first in respect of price and output and then in respects of product and advertising expenditure adjustments.

Individual Firm's Equilibrium under Monopolistic Competition

The demand curve for the product of an individual firm, as noted above, is downward sloping. Since the various firms under monopolistic competition produce products which are close substitutes of each other, the position and elasticity of the demand curve for the product of any of them depend upon the availability of the competiting substitutes and their prices. Therefore, the equilibrium adjustment of an individual firm cannot be defined in isolation from the general field of which it is a part. However, for the sake of simplicity in analysis, conditions regarding the availability of substitute products produced by the rival firms and prices charged for them are held constant while the equilibrium adjustment of an individual firm is considered in isolation. Since close substitutes for its product are available in the market, the demand curve for the product of an individual firm working under conditions of monopolistic competition is fairly elastic. Thus, although a firm under monopolistic competition has a monopolistic control over its variety of the product but its control is tempered by the fact that there are close substitutes available in the market and that if it sets too high a price for its product, many of its customers will shift to the rival products.

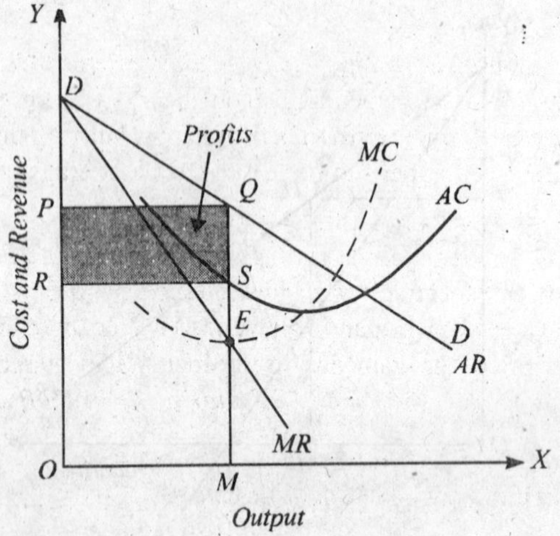

Fig. 28.3. *Individual Firm's Equilibrium under Monopolistic Competition (with Profits)*

Assuming the conditions with respect to all substitutes such as their nature and prices being constant, the demand curve for the product of a firm will be given. We further suppose that the product of the firm is held constant, only variables are price and output in respect of which equilibrium adjustment is to be made. The individual equilibrium under monopolistic competition is graphically shown in Fig. 28.3. *DD* is the demand curve for the product of an individual firm, the nature and prices of all substitutes being given. This demand curve *DD* is also the average revenue (*AR*) curve of the firm. *AC* represents the average cost curve of the firm, while *MC* is the marginal cost curve corresponding to it. It may be recalled that average cost curve first falls due to internal economies and then rises due to internal diseconomies.

Given these demand and cost conditions a firm will adjust his price and output at the level which gives it maximum total profits. Theory of value under monopolistic competition is also based upon the profit maximisation principle, as is the theory of value under perfect competition. Thus a firm in order to maximise profits will equate marginal cost with marginal revenue. In Fig. 28.3, the firm will fix its level of output at *OM*, for at *OM* output marginal cost is equal to marginal revenue. The demand curve *DD* facing the firm in question indicates that output *OM* can be sold at price *MQ* = *OP*. Therefore, the determined price will evidently be *MQ* or *OP*. In this equilibrium position, by fixing its price at *OP* and output at *OM*, the firm is making profits equal to the area *RSQP* which is maximum. It may be recalled that profits *RSQP* are in excess of normal profits because the normal profits which represent the minimum profits necessary to secure the entrepreneur's services are included in average cost curve *AC*. Thus, the area *RSQP* indicates the amount of supernormal or economic profits made by the firm.

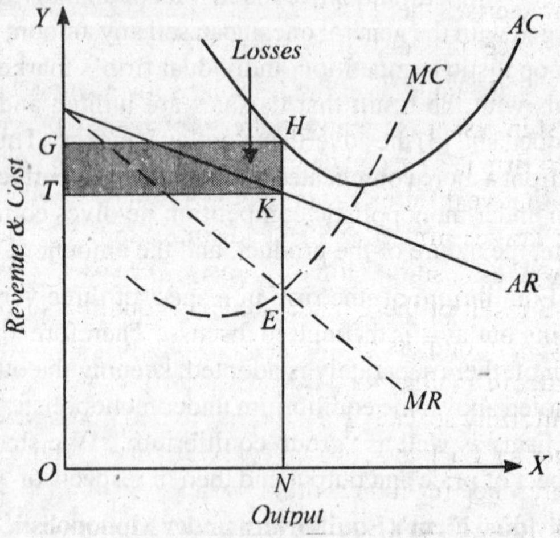

Fig. 28.4. *Individual Firm's Equilibrium under Monopolistic Competition (with Losses)*

In the short-run, the firm, in equilibrium, may make supernormal profits, as shown in Fig. 28.3 above, but it may make losses too if the demand conditions for its product are not so favourable relative to cost conditions. Fig. 28.4 depicts the case of a firm whose demand or average revenue curve *DD* for the product lies below the average cost curve throughout indicating thereby that no output of the product can be produced at positive profits. However, the firm is in equilibrium at output *ON* and setting price *NK* or *OT*, for by adjusting price at *OT* and output at *ON*, it is rendering the losses to the minimum. In such an unfavourable situation there is no alternative for the firm except to make the best of the bad bargain.

We thus see that a firm in equilibrium under monopolistic competition, as under pure or perfect competition, may be making supernormal profits or losses depending upon the position of the demand curve relative to the position of the average cost curve. Further, a firm may be making only normal profits even in the short run if the demand curve happens to be tangent to the average cost curve.

It should be carefully noted that in individual equilibrium of the firm both in Fig. 28.3 and Fig. 28.4, the firm having once adjusted price at *OP* and *OT* respectively will have no tendency to vary the price any more. If it varies its price upward, the loss due to fall in quantity demanded will be more than made up by the higher price. If it cuts down its price, the gain due to the increase in quantity demanded will be less than the loss due to the lower price. Hence, price will remain stable at *OP* and *OT* in the two cases respectively.

Long-Run Firm's Equilibrium and Group Equilibrium under Monopolistic Competition

We may now turn to see how the 'group' comes to be in equilibrium. In other words, We have now to explain how the equilibrium adjustment of prices and outputs of a number of firms whose products are close substitues comes about. As explained above, each firm within a group has monopoly of its own particular product, yet its market is interwoven with those of his competitors who produce closely related products. The price and output decisions of a firm will affect his rival firms who may in turn revise their price and output policies. This dependence of the various producers upon one another is aprominent feature of monopolistic competition. The question now is: what characterises the system of relationship into which the group tends to fall as a result of producers's influence on each other ?

A difficulty faced in describing the group equilibrium is the vast diversity of conditions which exist in respect of many matters between the various firms constituting the group. The product of each firm has special characteristics and adapted to the tastes and preferenes of its customers. The qualitative differences among the products lead to the large variations in cost and demand curves of the various firms. The demand curves of the products of various firms differ in respect of elasticity as well as position. Similary, cost curves of the various firms differ in respect of shape and position. As a result of these heterogeneous conditions surrounding each firm, there will be differences in prices, in outputs (scales of production) and profits of the various firms in the group. Putting this matter in another way, E.H. Chamberlin says: "The differentiation of the product is not, so to speak, 'uniformly spaced'; it is not distributed homogeneously among all the products which are grouped together. Each has its own individuality, and the size of its market depends on the strength of the preference for it over other varieties".[5]

In order to simplify the analysis of equilibrium, Chamberlin ignores these diverse conditions surrounding each firm and takes an assumption what has been called "*uniformity assumption*". Thus Chamberlin says: "We, therefore, proceed under the heroic assumption that both demand and cost curves for all the 'products' are uniform throughout the group."[6] Chamberlin points out that by taking this assumption we do not reduce the differentiation of products. Under the uniformity assumption, "It is required only that *consumer's preferences be evenly distributed among the different varieties*, and that differences between them be not such as to give rise to differences in cost."[7]

5. *Op. cit.* p.82
6. *Ibid.*, p. 82
7. *Ibid*, p. 83 (*italics added*)

Further, to facilitate exposition of his theory, Chamberlin introduces a further assumption which has been called '*symmetry assumption*' by Prof. Stigler. It is that the number of firms being large under monopolistic competition, an individual's actions regarding price and output adjustment will have a negligible effect upon its numerous competitors so that they will not think of retaliation for readjusting their prices and outputs. He thus says, specifically, we assume for the present that any adjustment of price of a "product" by a single producer spreads its influence over so many of his competitors that the impact felt by any one is negligible and does not lead him to any readjustment of his own situation. A price cut, for instance, which increases the sales of him who made it draws inappreciable amounts from the markets of each of his many competitors, achieving a considerable result for the one who cut, but without making incursions upon the market of any single competitor sufficient to cause him to do anything he would not have done any way."[8]

Given the above assumptions, we proceed to explain how under monopolistic competition an individual firm and a group of firms producing close substitutes come to be in equilibrium position. To begin with, suppose that the demand and cost curves of each of the firms in the group are *DD* and *AC* as depicted in Fig. 28.3. Each firm will set price *OP* at which marginal cost is equal to marginal revenue and hence profits are maximum. Although all firms are making supernormal profits, there is no reason for any one to cut down price below *OP* because the sales gained thereby will be insufficient to make up the loss due to the lower price. These supernormal profits will, however, attract new firms into the field in the long run.

Here it may be pointed out that full freedom of entry cannot prevail under monopolistic competition. Entry can be fully free only if the new firms who propose to enter the field can produce exactly identical products as those of the existing firms. But under monopolistic competition, this is not possible. Therefore, entry in the full and strict sense cannot exist under monopolistic competition. However new entrants are free to produce closely related products which are very similar to the products of the existing firms. Thus, *under monopolistic competition there can be freedom of entry only in the sense of a freedom to produce close substitutes.*

Turning to the above argument, when the new firms lured by the abnormal profits enjoyed by the existing firms enter the field, the market would be shared between more firms and a result the demand curve (or average revenue curve) for the product of each firm will shift downward *i.e.*, to the left. This process of entry of new firms and the resultant shift in the demand (average revenue) curve to the left will continue until the average revenue curve becomes tangent to the average cost curve and the abnormal profits are completely wiped out. This is shown in Fig. 28.5 where average revenue curve is tangent to average cost curve at point *T*. Marginal cost and marginal revenue curves intersect each other exactly vertically below *T*. Therefore, *the firm is in long-run equilibrium by setting price QT or OP and producing OQ quantity of its product.* Because average revenue is equal to average cost, the firm will be making only normal profits. Since all firms are alike in respect of demand and cost curves (by assumption), the average revenue of all will be tangent to their average cost curves and all firms will, therefore, be earning only normal profits. Because only normal profits are accruing to the firms there will be no more tendency for the new competitors to enter the field and the group as a whole will, therefore, be in equilibrium.

An important point is worth nothing here. It is that a *firm in long-run equilibrium under monopolistic competition makes only normal profits, as in perfect competition, but its price is higher and output smaller than under perfect competition.* Under perfect competition, long-run equilibrium of the firm is established at the minimum point of the average cost curve. In other words, a firm under perfect competition tends to be of the optimum size. But a firm under

8. *Ibid., p.* 83

monopolistic competition, as is evident from Fig. 28.5, stops short of the optimum point and operates at the point at which average cost is still falling. In Fig. 28.5 the firm produces output *OQ*, while a firm under perfect competition would have produced outut *OR* at which average cost is minimum. The firm under monopolistic competition can reduce its cost of production by expanding output to the point *R* but it will not do so because by expanding output beyond *OQ* it will be reducing price more than the average cost. It is, therefore, clear that by producing *OQ* instead of *OR*, the firm under monopolistic competition does not use its capacity fully. (The firm would be using its capacity fully, if it produces optimum or full capacity output *OR*). Thus capacity equal to *QR* is lying unused in the firm's long-run equilibrium under monopolistic competition. This *unused capacity is called excess capacity which is a prominent feature of long-run equilibrium under monopolistic competition.*

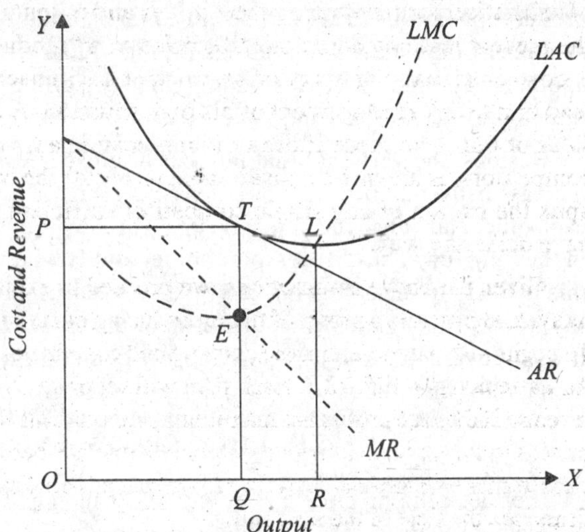

Fig. 28.5 *The Group is in equilibrium when average revenue curves of the firms are tangent to their long-run average cost curves.*

Further, it may be noted that in the long-run equilibrium, firms under monopolistic competition make only normal profits as under pure competition, but the price set under monopolistic competition is higher than competitive price. In Fig. 28.5, price set in long-run equilibrium under monopolistic competition is *QT* while competitive price would have been equal to *RL*. This higher price under monopolistic competition is due to monopoly element contained in it. The monopoly element involved in monopolistic competition makes the demand or average revenue curve facing an individual firm downward sloping and a downward-sloping average revenue curve can be tangent to the average cost curve only to the left of its minimum point.

Thus price under monopolistic competition will be higher than the competitive price due to the monopoly element in monopolistic competition. But, in spite of the higher price, a firm under monopolistic competition will not be making profits above normal in the long run. We may, therefore, say that a *firm under monopolistic competition, in the long-run equilibrium, charges higher price without enjoying monopoly profits*. A significant result follows from this. It is that the non-existence of abnormal profits is no indicator of the absence of monopoly element. In long-run equilibrium under monopolistic competition, as seen above, the firm has monopoly power (it has a sole control over its own differentiated product with the result that demand curve for it slopes downward) but does not make any supernormal profits. Further, the existence of abnormal or excessive profits does not necessarily mean the presence of monopoly power. Under perfect competition, a firm in the short run may enjoy excessive supernormal profits due to the increase in demand for the product. Thus "*he skates on thin ice who identifies profits with monopoly and monopoly with profits.*"[9]

Another noteworthy point about long-run equilibrium under monopolistic competition is that with the increase in the number of firms in the long run *demand curves facing individual firms will become more elastic in the sense that they will flatten out*. Although Chamberlin denies it, it is now commonly believed that as the number of firms gets larger in the long run, the cross elasticities of demand between the products of various firms will increase and as a result

9. M.M. Bober, *Intermediate Price and Income Theory.*

the demand curves of the firms will become more elastic (or graphically less steep). When, in the short run, abnormal profits are accuring to the firms due to the large demand for their brands or varieties of the product, lured by these abnormal profits the new firms will enter and try to produce brands or varieties as similar to the existing brands as possible. Thus, in the long run, products of various firms will become more similar or in other worlds, come closer together and as a result the demand curves facing individual firms will become more elastic. To put it in another way, the new firms which enter the group will come "in between" the old ones and thereby result in increasing the elasticities of demand curves (that is, make them flatten out).

Besides, the very fact that number of close substitutes in the long run increases due to the increase in the number of firms means that each brand will become more closely competitive with each other and hence the demand curve for the product of any one firm will become more elastic in the long run. Thus Professors Stonier and Hague write: "If new producers enter the industry this is likely to mean that instead of, say, twenty similar cars being produced there will now be, say, forty. This again means that each of the cars is likely to be more similar to each other than it was previously. And the more closely competitive substitutes there are, the more elastic the demand for the product of any one firm in the group will be."[10]

SELLING COSTS AND ADVERTISING

For determining price and output under monopolistic competition and oligopoly, firms often compete through incurring selling costs or advertisement expenditure. For firms working under conditions of monopolistic competition and oilgopoly, besides adjustments of price, output and product, an important decision that has to be taken is that of how much selling costs or advertisement expenditure it should undertake so as to achieve its aim of profit maximisation. The first problem that is encountered in connection with selling costs is how do they differ from production costs. The other important question which arises is why firms under monopolistic competition and oligopoly incur selling costs and not the firms working udner conditions of perfect competition and monopoly. Further, how the firm will decide about the optimum level of selling costs or advertisement expenditure. And, lastly, what is the influence of selling costs on price and output of the product. We shall discuss all these questions concerning selling costs below.

Selling Costs Distinguished from Production Costs

The term "selling costs" is broader than advertisement expenditure. Whereas advertisement expenditure includes costs incurred only on getting product advertised in newspapers and magazines, on radio and television, selling costs include the salaries and wages of salesmen, allowances to retailers for the purpose of getting their product *displayed* by them and so many other types of promotional activities besides advertisement. Chamberlin who introduced the analysis of selling costs in price theory distinguished selling costs from production costs. According to Chamberlin, cost of production includes all those expenses which are incurred to manufacture and provide a product to the consumer to meet his *given demand or want*, while the selling costs are those which are incurred to *change, alter or create the demand for a product*. Costs of production therefore include manufacturing costs, transportation costs, and cost of handling, storing and delivering a product to the consumers, since all of these activities add utilities to a commodity. And the addition or creation of utilities to satisfy the given wants is called production in economics. To quote Chamberlin, "Cost of production includes all expenses which must be met in order to provide the commodity or service, transport it to the buyer, and put it into his hands ready to satisfy his wants. *Cost of selling includes all outlays made in order to secure a demand or market* for the product. The former costs create utilities in order that given demands may be satisfied; the *latter create and*

10. Stonier and Hague, *A Textbook of Economic Theory*, 4th edition, 1972, p.209

snift *the demands themselves*. A simple criterion is this: of all the costs incurred in the manufacture and sale of a given product, *those which alter the demand curve for it are selling costs*, and those which do not are costs of production."[11] The selling costs, according to Chamberlin, include "advertising in its many forms, salaries of salesmen and the expenses of sales departments and sales agencies (except where these agencies actually handle the goods), window displays, and displays and demonstration of all kinds,"[12]

It should be noted that transportation snould not be construed as *increasing the demand*, as it apparently appears. This is because the transportation does not really increase the demand; it merely enables the producer to meet the demand of the consumer which is already there whether the transport cost is incurred by the producer or by the consumer himself. Likewise, a high site rent for a shop in a well-located area will increase the sales of the firm but cannot be considered as a part of selling costs, since in this the firm is meeting the given or existing demand for the product more accurately or exactly and not *altering* the demand for the product. By paying a high rent for a shop or a factory building in the well-located area, the producer is merely adapting the product or himself more exactly to the given demand and not altering the demand or adapting his customers. Therefore, Chamberlin while drawing the distinction between production costs and selling costs writes that those costs which are "*made to adapt the product to the demand are costs of production; those made to adapt the demand to the product are costs of selling*".[13]

It should, however, be noted that the distinction between production costs and selling costs cannot always be sharply made and there are cases where it cannot be said whether product is being adapted to meet the given demand, or the demand is being adapted to sell the product. For instance, it is difficult to say whether the extra cost on attractive packaging is production cost or selling cost. However, as far as advertisement expenditure is concerned, there is little doubt about its being a selling cost, since purpose of advertisement is to increase or create the demand for the product. Thus Chamberlin's distinction is quite applicable so far as advertisement expenditure is concerned. Because advertising expenditure is the most important and dominant form of selling costs, we in our analysis below shall use them interchangeably and discuss the various questions concerning selling costs by taking the case of advertisement expenditure.

Role of Selling Costs under Perfect Competition, Monopoly and Imperfect Competition

As has been explained in previous chapters, there is no need for a firm working under perfect competition to undertake advertisement expenditure or to incur other types of selling costs, since by assumption, the product produced by all firms in the perfectly competitive industry is homogeneous, and an individual firm can sell as much quantity of the product as it likes at the given price. If a perfectly competitive firm advertises for the product, the consumers who are influenced by it may purchase the product from other firms in the industry, since all are selling homogeneous products. Of course, the whole perfectly competitive industry, that is, all firms together or their association may advertise to promote the sales of their product at the expense of the *products of other industries*. Such advertising is known as *promotional advertising*, as compared to competitive advertising with which we are here concerned. In India, there has been advertising by *Terene* industry producing terylene fabrics for increasing the demand for its product at the cost of other kinds of fabrics. We, therefore, conclude that under perfect competition, there can be promotional advertising by the whole industry but not competitive advertising by individual firms to snatch away the customers from each other.

Under monopoly also, there is no competitive advertising since, by definition, a monopolist

---

11. Edward, H. Chamberlin, *The Theory of Monopolistic Competition*, 6th edition, p. 123 (italics added).
12. *Op. cit.*, p. 124
13. *Ibid.*, p. 125

produces a product which has no close substitutes. The monopolist only needs to inform or remind the buyers that his product exists and he need not emphasise the competitive nature of its product. Of course, the monopolist may advertise to promote his sales or demand but it will not be at the expense of its rivals, since no rivals producing close substitutes are there under monopoly. Hence the advertisement by the monopolist is informative and promotional and not competitive.

It is under conditions of imperfect competition, that is, monopolistic competition and oligopoly with product differentiation that advertisement and other selling costs become important as a competitive weapon at the disposal of one firm to increase its sales at the expense of others. This is because differentiated products produced by different firms under monopolistic competition and differentiated oligopoly are close substitutes of each other. Therefore, each firm under monopolistic competition tries to convince the buyers that its product is better than those of others in the industry. A firm under monopolistic competition and differentiated oligopoly may keep its price and product design constant and seek to increase the demand for its product by increasing the amount of advertisement expenditure and through it persuading the buyers that its brand of the product is of superior quality than others. Thus, this is competitive advertising which is aimed at attracting the customers to their product and weaning them away from the closely related products of the rivals. Thus, "*the fundamental aim of all 'competitive' advertising is to attract the customers' attention and to imprint the name of a particular product on his mind; the aim is to persuade the consumer to put his hand in his pocket and buy the product in question........... the main aim is to increase the sales of one firm at the expense of others and not to increase the sales of the 'group' as a whole.*"[14] For instance, we all know that all tooth pastes are based upon the same chemical formula recommended by the medical science. But the firm producing Colgate through its radio and television commerical programmes has been propagating that the tooth paste of 'Colgate' variety is very much better than others and has special and superior qualities which are absent in other brands of toothpaste. The fundamental aim of Colgate advertisment is not to increase the aggregate demand for toothpaste in the country but to increase the demand for 'Colgate toothpaste' by competing away the buyers from other brands of toothpaste. Similarly, the manufactures of other brands of toothpaste such as Binaca, Pepsodent, Oral–B, Signal, Forhans etc. are also incurring expenditure on advertisement through various means and trying to convince the buyers that their particular brand of tooth paste is better than others. Such competitive advertisement by a firm often proves to be successful in its objective of increasing the demand for a particular brand of the product. Thus, as a result of advertisement, demand curve facing an individual firm shifts to the right which indicates that at a given price, a greater quantity of the product can be sold.

It follows from above that in the presence of selling costs or advertisement, demand curve for a product cannot be taken as an objective fact given by the tastes or wants of the consumers. A firm can alter or shift the demand curve for its product through its own efforts by incurring advertisement expenditure and other forms of selling costs.

Effect of Selling Costs (Advertising Expenditure) on Demand

The purpose and effect of successful advertising is to increase the demand, that is, to shift the demand curve for the product to the right. However, these selling costs or advertising outlays are subject to the varying returns. That is, equal increments in advertising outlay first yield increasing returns and then eventually diminishing returns in terms of its effect on demand for the product. In the beginning, increases in advertising outlay will bring about increasing returns in raising demand for the product for two reasons. Firstly, increase in advertising outlay (or selling costs) permits a firm to *repeat many times* the advertisement for the product. And this repetition of advertisement produces favourable effects on demand. "It is well established that repetition is essential if advertising

14. Stonier and Hague, *op. cit.*, p. 222. (italics added)

for the product for two reasons. Firstly, increase in advertising outlay (or selling costs) permits a firm to *repeat many times* the advertisement for the product. And this repetition of advertisement produces favourable effects on demand. "It is well established that repetition is essential if advertising is to make an impact on the consumer's mind. A single advertisement seen once will have at the most a negligible, and probably no effect on the consumer. The outlay for it is wasted. But continued advertising over a period of time and in different media is far more likely to impinge on the consumers' thoughts and consequent consumption choices."[15]

Second reason for occurrence of increasing returns as the advertisement outlay is increased in the beginning is the *economies of large scale selling operations or advertising.* The main economy or adventage is the specialisation which is made possible by large-scale selling or advertising activity. To quote Prof. Hibdon again, "Large-scale activities permit the *use of specialised personnel with greater expertise and effectiveness.* There may also be *economies in the use of advertising media.* Greater total spending permits a shift in the technique and media that are used in the selling effort as well as the use of combinations of media."[16] As a result of the increasing returns from advertising outlay in the beginning, the demand increases more than proportionately to the equal increases in advertising outlay.

But as the advertising outlay is stepped up, diminishing returns are likely to set in eventually. Firstly, this is because potential buyers differ in tastes, income and wealth. These differences among the potential buyers of the product mean that they will vary in their responses to selling operations or advertising by a firm. Initial advertisements will cause large increases in demand as the more susceptible buyers respond to advertisement. But further increase in advertisements is likely to bring about relatively less increases in demand as they fail to influence other buyers who do not prefer the good so much.

Second reason for the ultimate occurrence of diminishing returns from the increases in advertisement is that the existing buyers may not further increase the demand for the product as a result of more advertising by the firm. This is because as the consumer buys more of a product, its marginal utility to him falls. Further, in order to purchase one good more, he has to give up more of some other goods, his income being limited. As a result, marginal utility of 'other goods' increases. Thus, on the one hand, marginal utility of a good declines as it is purchased more under the influence of advertisement, and, on the other hand, the opportunity cost of buying this good increases on account of the rise in the marginal utility of 'other goods'. This makes the existing buyers of a product reluctant to buy more units of it when advertising effort by a firm is greatly increased. Thus this also causes diminishing returns to advertising outlay.

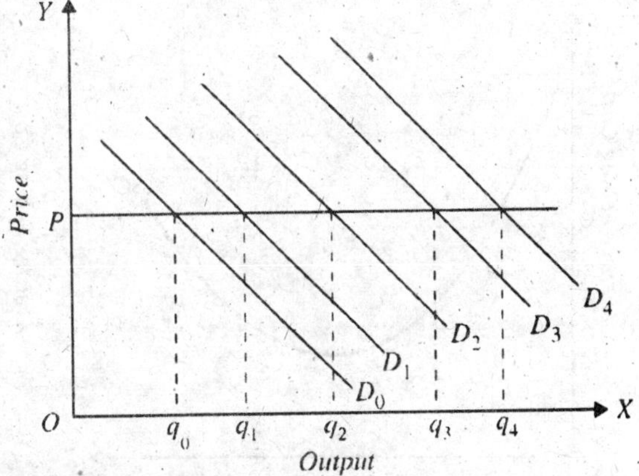

Fig. 28.6. *Effect of Selling Cost on Demand*

The effect of selling costs on the demand for a product and the varying returns in this connection are illustrated in Fig. 28.6. Demand curve before any advertisement expenditure is undertaken is D_0. Now, equal increments in advertisement expenditure successively bring about rightward shift in the demand curve to D_1, D_2, D_3 and D_4 respectively. We have assumed that the shift in the demand curve is parallel, while in the real world it may not be so. Because in the beginning there are increasing returns and then after a point dimin-

15. James E. Hibdon, *Price and Welfare Theory,* McGrawHill, 1969, p. 302
16. *Op., cit.*, p. 302.

q_3 to q_4. It will be seen from the Fig. 28.6 that after D_3, diminishing returns to extra advertising outlay occur.

The Curve of Average Selling Costs

The concept of the curve of average selling cost should be fully understood. There are two concepts regarding average selling cost, and average selling cost curves drawn according to these two concepts are different. Since the shape of the average selling cost curve is different in these two concepts, for analysing selling cost and its effect on equilibrium price and output, it must, therefore, be known according to which concept the curve of average selling cost is drawn. A firm can choose among various amounts of advertising outlay (*i.e.*, selling costs). Therefore, the firm may at the outset treat the selling costs as variable amounts. Thus, with varing amounts of selling costs (advertising outlay) incurred in a period, the average selling cost per unit will depend upon the output sold as a result of the rightward shift in the demand curve brought about by a particular amount of selling costs. This average selling cost is obtained by dividing the amount of selling costs incurred by the quantity of output sold. And as a firm plans to increase the amount of selling costs incurred in a period, the average selling cost will change depending, on the one hand, upon the increase in selling costs and, on the other, upon the resultant increase in output demanded (or sold) at a *given price*. As explained above, it is generally believed that *selling costs (advertisement outlay) is subject to varying returns*. In the beginning, increasing returns to selling costs are obtained, that is, equal increases in advertisement outlay cause more than proportionate increase in the amount demanded of the product at the *given price*. In other words, selling costs per unit will fall in the beginning. After a point diminishing returns to selling costs set in and increases in advertisement outlay cause less than proportionate increases in the amount demanded of the product. In other words, after a point, average selling cost will rise. Hence, with varying amounts of selling cost average selling cost in the beginning falls due to increasing returns; reaches the minimum level and then rises due to diminishing returns. Thus with varying amounts of selling cost, a curve of average selling cost, like the ordinary average production-cost curve, is U-shaped, which is shown in Fig. 28.7 by the curve *ASC*.

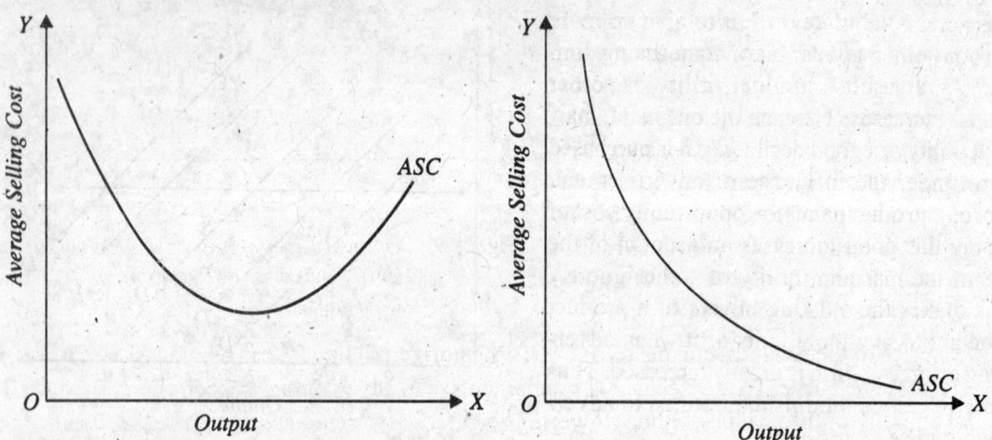

Fig. 28.7. *Average Selling Cost Required to Sell Various Amounts of Output*

Fig. 28.8. *Curve of Average Selling Cost with a Fixed Amount of Total Selling Costs*

However, the average selling cost curve *ASC* drawn in Fig. 24.7 should be carefully interpreted. It does not mean how the average selling cost per unit changes as output is increased. But *it means the average selling cost per unit which is required to be undertaken to sell various amounts of output.* Ultimately the average selling cost curve *ASC* will become vertical. This is because quite often saturation point regarding the effect of extra selling costs on raising the demand for the product is reached, beyond which no further increases in selling costs can cause any expansion in amount demanded of the product.

We have discussed above the nature of the average selling cost curve when the total selling costs are treated as variable magnitudes and, in fact, the firm treats them as such when it has to plan for an amount of selling or advertisement cost it should incur in a period so as to maximise profits. However, *once a firm commits itself to a particular amount of selling costs or advertisement outlay to be incurred in a period, it may regard that cost as a fixed cost during that period.* In other words, when a *given fixed amount* of total selling costs is decided or considered to be incurred, then greater the level of output sold, the selling cost per unit would continue to decline. In other words, when a firm commits itself to a given amount of selling costs, it will be then treat them as a fixed cost. Given a fixed amount of selling costs, average selling cost will change in the same manner as does the average fixed cost. Like the average fixed cost curve, this type of average selling cost curve will have a shape of rectangular hyperbola, as shown in Fig. 28.8.

Optimum Level of Advertising Outlay (Selling Costs): With Price and Product Design as Constants

An important question is how much selling costs (advertisement outlay), a firm will undertake so as to maximise profits. In other words, what is the *optimum amount* of advertisement expenditure for a firm. The determination of optimal advertising outlay (selling costs) for the firm can be explained by the average and marginal cost curves. For explaining the optimal amount of advertising expenditure with average and marginal costs, we have to use the concept of average selling cost when advertisement outlay is taken to be variable. Consider Fig. 28.9 where *ASC* and *APC* are average selling cost and average production cost curves respectively. Average selling cost curve *ASC* has been superimposed over the average production cost curve *APC* to obtain average total curve *AC* (*AC* = *APC* + *ASC*). It should, therefore, be noted that the vertical distance between the *AC* and *APC* curves measures the average selling cost. *MC* is the marginal cost curve to the average total cost curve *AC*. We assume that price *OP* has already been fixed by the firm which is kept constant. Further, the nature of the product is also held unchanged and it is only the advertising expenditure which is varied and consequently demand shifts to the right and output sold increases.

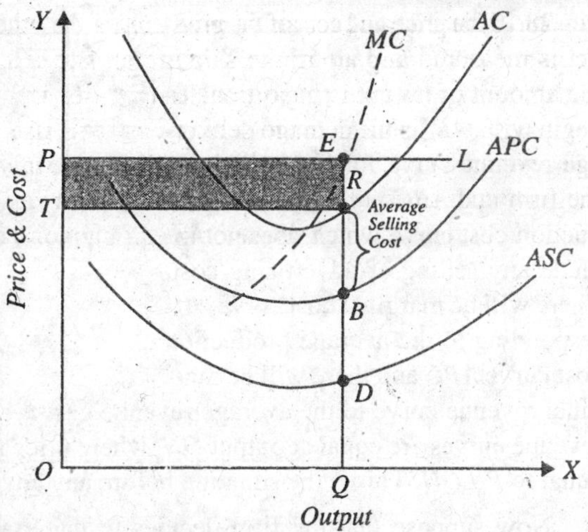

Fig. 28.9. *Optimal Level of Advertising Expenditure (with price and Product Design as Constants)*

Since price of the product remains fixed at *OP*, the horizontal line *PL* can be viewed as if it were a marginal revenue curve. This is because through increase in advertisement expenditure, a firm can sell more quantity of the product without lowering price. *If the firm aims to maximise profits, then it will be in equilibrium regarding advertising outlay where the marginal cost (which is inclusive of both production cost and selling cost) is equal to the marginal revenue, i.e., given price OP.* It will be seen from the Fig. 28.9 that marginal cost is equal to marginal revenue (or price) at *OQ* level of output at which profits will be maximised. With *OQ* as the output produced and sold, total profits made by the firm are equal *PERT* and, as is evident from the figure, average selling cost incurred by the firm in its equilibrium position is equal to *QD* or *BR*. Therefore, the optimal amount of advertisement outlay, incurred by the firm will be equal to (*QD* or *BR*) multiplied by the output *OQ*.

Optimal Level of Advertising Expenditure with both Price and Output Variable

We have discussed above how much advertising expenditure a firm will undertake so as to maximise its profits when the price as well as nature of the product remain constant. We shall now explain the case of optimal level of advertising expenditure when price also varies. In other words, we have to explain optimal combination of advertising expenditure, price and output, only the physical make-up of the product will not be varied. We shall illustrate our analysis with two dimensional diagram. Here we shall be taking *a given sum of advertising expenditure and then analyse its effect on demand, output, price and profits*. With a given sum of advertising expenditure, average selling cost per unit will go on declining as more output is produced. It is because of this that the distance between the two successive average cost curves will become smaller and smaller as output is expanded. However, it should be noted that we will be increasing this given sum of advertising expenditure and assess its effect on demand and profits to obtain the optimal levels of advertising expenditure and output.

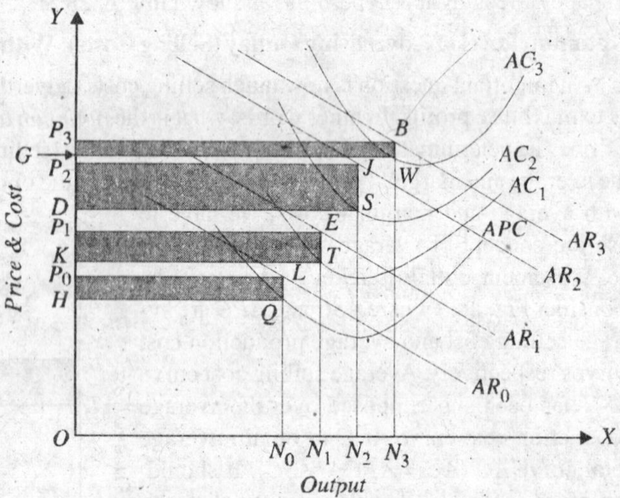

Fig. 28.10. *Optimal Advertising Expenditure*

The optimal amount of advertising outlay and the choice of price-output combination by a firm is illustrated in Fig. 28.10. It should be noted that we continue to assume that the firm aims to maximise profits. Along the *Y*-axis in Fig. 28.10 the price and cost of the product is measured and along the *X*-axis the amount of output is measured. To begin with, AR_0 is the demand or average revenue curve for the product of the firm and *APC* is the average production cost curve which does not include any selling or advertising cost. There will be marginal cost curve corresponding to the average production cost curve *APC* and there will be marginal revenue curve to the average revenue curve AR_0. Suppose these marginal cost and marginal revenue curves are equal at output ON_0 where price P_0 is determined and the firm is making profits equal to P_0LQH. This is the situation before any advertisement expenditure is undertaken.

Now suppose that the firm decides to undertake advertisement expenditure equal to 1,000 rupees. This advertisement expenditure will not only increase demand by shifting the average revenue curve to the right, but will also add to costs. Assume that with advertisement expenditure of Rs. 1,000, the demand curve shifts to the curve AR_1 and the new average cost (inclusive of advertising cost) is AC_1. Suppose with AR_1, as the new demand curve and AC_1 as the average cost curve, equilibrium is at output ON_1 and price P_1 (this price-output equilibrium is determined by the equality of new marginal revenue and marginal cost curves which are not drawn in the figure for sake of avoiding confusion). It will be seen from the figure that profit has now risen to the area P_1ETK. It should be noted that profits will increase only when the addition to *net* revenue earned from advertising outlay is greater than the advertising outlay incurred. It should be further noted that as a result of advertising outlay, output increases and therefore total production cost also increases. And the addition *to net* revenue attributable to advertising outlay is obtained by subtracing the addition to production cost from the addition to gross revenue.

Since as a result of advertisement expenditure, profits have increased, firm will be tempted to

17. Stonier and Hague, *op. cit.*, p. 224.

undertake further advertisement expenditure. Suppose the firm incurs additional advertising expenditure of Rs. 1,000 (i.e., now total Rs. 2,000) and with this the demand (or average revenue curve) shifts to the position AR_2 and average cost curve to AC_2. Now, the new equilibrium position is reached at output ON_2 and price P_2, and profits are further increased to P_2JSD. It may again be mentioned that profits increase only when additional revenue generated (net of production cost) is greater than the additional advertising cost. "*Indeed it will pay the firm to go on increasing selling costs in this way so long as each increment of advertising expenditure adds more to revenue than to costs. Only when the additional revenue generated (net of production costs) equals the extra (marginal) amount spent in order to generate that net revenue, will profit be at the highest possible level.*"[17]

In Fig. 28.10 now assume that lured by the increase in profits to P_2JSD, firm undertakes additional advertising expenditure of Rs. 1,000 (that is, now total advertising expenditure is raised to Rs. 3,000). With this, the average revenue curve shifts to AR_3 and average cost curve to AC_3. It will be seen from the figure that now profits earned by the firms are equal to the area P_3BWG. It will be observed that profits P_3BWG are less than the previous profits P_2JSD. The decline in profits must be due to the additional net revenue (*i.e.*, additional revenue net of increase in production costs) made possible by the additional advertising expenditure being smaller than the extra cost of one thousand rupees on advertisement.

It is thus clear that the firm will not undertake the third additional outlay of one thousand rupees and will be in equilibrium by incurring advertising expenditure of two thousands rupees at which its profits are largest (that is, equal to P_2JSD) and additional net revenue made possible by the advertising is equal to the additional advertising outlay. Thus in the situation depicted in Fig. 28.10 two thousand rupees per period is the optimal advertising expenditure for the firm.

It should be noted for each level of advertising expenditure, that is, for one thousand, two thousand and three thousand rupees there is profit-maximising price and output. Various levels of profits P_0LQH, P_1ETK, P_2JSD, and P_3BWG are all maximum with different levels of advertising expenditure. The task for the firm is to choose the combination of advertising expenditure, price and output which yields maximum out of the various maxima of profits. That is, the firm has to determine the combination of advertising expenditure, price and output which yields him *maximum-maximorum* level of profits. And we have seen above that in the situation depicted in Fig. 28.10 this *maximum-maximorum* equilibrium is reached when advertising expenditure is two thousand rupees, price is P_2 and output is ON_2.

Effect of Advertising (Selling Costs) on Elasticity of Demand

We have seen above that as a result of advertising expenditure demand for the product increases, that is, demand curve shifts to the right. For the sake of convenience, we have assumed that the new demand curves after advertising is undertaken are parallel to the old one, though in actual practice it need not be so. However, in this connection it is useful to consider whether when the demand increases and demand curve shifts to the right, elasticity of demand at each price remains the same, declines or rises. The purpose of competitive advertising or other forms of selling costs is to influence the consumers to buy a particular brand of the product rather than other substitute brands of it. The intention of the producer who advertises for his brand of the product is to differentiate his brand more from the viewpoint of the consumers and try to prove his brand to be superior to others. Thus if the purpose and intention of advertisement is achieved, then the consumers would begin to consider a particular brand of the product much superior to others. That is, they will now regard the other competitive brands as less closely substitutes than they were thinking before. This greater degree of differentiation and consequently fall in the elasticity of substitution will cause a decline in the price elasticity of demand for the product at each price as the demand curve shifts to the right under the influence of the advertisement. It is, therefore likely that price elasticity of demand should decline under the influence of advertising or other forms of selling costs. The extent to which price elasticity will decline is of course very uncertain. As we shall see below, changes in price elasticity of demand as a result of advertisement expenditure have significant implications for price-output equilibrium.

Effect of Advertising (Selling Costs) on Price and Output

The effect of advertising and other forms of selling costs on price and output are quite uncertain. This effect depends, on the one hand, upon the change in price elasticity of demand as a result of advertising expenditure and, on the other, upon the behaviour of average cost of production. If when the demand curve shifts to the right under the influence of advertising, price elasticity of demand at the current price remains the same and average cost of production is falling sharply with the expansion in output, then it may be profitable for the firm to set a lower price after advertisement. In this case profit-maximising price will be lower and output larger than those before advertisement. On the other hand, if price elasticity of demand declines very much as demand curve shifts to the right as a result of advertisement, and the average cost of production is rising sharply with the increase in production, then in order to maximise profits in the new situation after advertisement, the firm may raise the price and reduce its level of output. In this case, the advantage of the increase in demand due to advertisement expenditure will be enjoyed in the form of higher price of the product rather than of increased sales of the product. But the most likely case to occur is that price elasticity of demand declines after advertisement and the average cost of product is not rising very sharply, and as a result of these the firm may find it profitable to raise price of the product somewhat and also increase output after advertising expenditure is undertaken. Thus, according to Stonier and Hague, "The most probable result for a profit-maximising firm will be that the elasticity of demand will fall somewhat at each price, that the volume of demand will increase at each price and that price and output will both increase to some extent as a result of advertising campaign."[18] And this is the case which we have considered in our analysis of advertising expenditure as depicted in Fig. 28.10. It will be seen from Fig. 28.10 that with successive increments in advertising expenditure price has risen from P_0 to P_1, P_1 to P_2 and P_2 to P_3 and also output has increased from N_0 to N_1, N_1 to N_2 and N_2 to N_3. Thus in our analysis of Fig. 28.10 both price and output have increased as a result of advertisement outlay.

EXCESS CAPACITY UNDER MONOPOLISTIC OR IMPERFECT COMPETITION

Theories of Chamberlin's monopolistic competition and Joan Robinson's imperfect competition have revealed that a firm under monopolistic competition or imperfect competition in long-run equilibrium produces an output which is less than socially optimum or ideal output. This means that firms operate at the point on the falling portion of long-run average cost curve, that is, they do not produce the level of output at which long-run average cost is minimum. Long-run equilibrium of a firm under monopolistic competition is achieved when the demand curve (or average revenue curve) facing a firm becomes tangential to the long-run average cost curve so that it earns only normal profits. Under such circumstances a firm can reduce average cost (and hence price) by expanding output to the minimum level of long-run average cost, but it will not do so because its profits are maximised (equality of marginal revenue with marginal cost is attained) at the level of output smaller than that at which its long-run average cost is minimum.

Society's productive resources are fully utilised when they are used to produce the level of output which renders long-run average cost minimum. Thus a monopolistically competitive firm produces less than the socially optimum or ideal output, that is, the output corresponding to the lowest point of long-run average cost curve. This is in sharp contrast to the position of the firm in long-run equilibrium under perfect competition, which operates at the minimum point of the long-run average cost curve.

---

18. Stonier and Hague, *op. cit.*, p. 226.

The amount by which the actual long-run output of the firm under monopolistic competition falls short of the socially ideal output is a measure of *excess capacity* which means unutilised capacity.

The existence of excess-capacity under imperfect or monopolistic competition can be understood from Figures 28.11 and 28.12. Figure 28.12 depicts the long-run position of a perfectly competitive firm which is in long-run equilibrium at the level of output *ON* corresponding to which long-run average

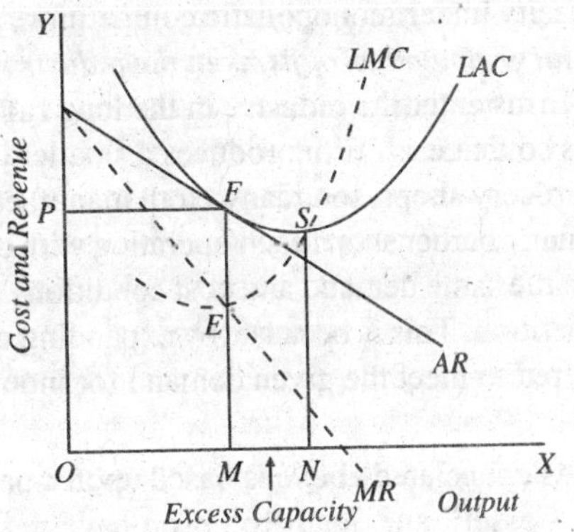

Fig. 28.11. *Excess Capacity under Monopolistic Competition*

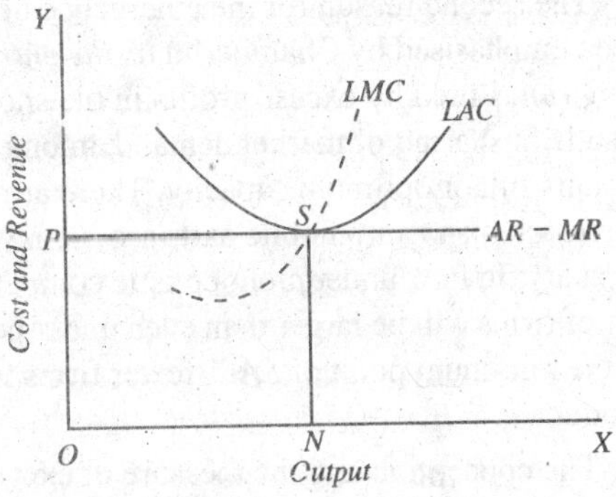

Fig. 28.12. *Ideal or Socially Optimum Output under Perfect Competition*

cost is minimum. It is at output *ON* that the double condition of long-run equilibrium, namely Price = *MC* = *AC* is fulfilled. It is thus clear that firms under perfect competition produce socially ideal output. On the other hand, a firm under monopolistic competition depicted in Fig. 28.11 is in long-run equilibrium at output *OM* at which its marginal revenue is equal to marginal cost and price is equal to average cost (Average revenue curve *AR* is tangential to average cost curve *LAC* at point *F* corresponding to output *OM*). It will be noticed that at output *OM* long-run average cost is still falling and goes on falling up to output *ON*. This means that the firm can expand its production up to *ON* and reduce his long-run average cost to the minimum. Ideal output is the output at an which long-run average cost is minimum. Therefore, the firm is *producing MN less than the ideal output. Thus MN output represents the excess capacity which emerges under monopolistic competition.* It is worth nothing that the concept of excess capacity refers only to the long run. This is because in the short run under any type of market structure (including perfect competition) there can be all sorts of departures from the ideal reflecting incomplete adjustment to the existing market conditions.

Causes of Excess Capacity

What factors are responsible for the existence of excess capacity under monopolistic competition? It is due to the existence of excess capacity that average cost of production and price of product are higher and output smaller monopolistic competition than under perfect competition. There are three main causes of the emergence of excess capacity under monopolistic competition. First, the most important cause of the eixstence of excess capacity under monopolistic competition is *downward-sloping demand curve (or average revenue curve) of the firm.* A downward-sloping curve can be tangent to a U-shaped average cost curve only at the latter's falling portion. It is only the horizontal demand curve or average revenue curve (as is actually found under perfect competition) which can be tangent to a U-shaped average cost curve at the latter's minimum point. From this, it also follows that the greater the elasticity of average revenue (or demand) curve confronting a monopolistically competitive firm, the less the excess capacity and *vice versa.* When the demand curve facing a firm is perfectly elastic, there is no ecess capacity, as is the case under perfect competition.

Now, demand curve facing individual firms under monopolistic competition slopes downward due to *product differentiation* found in it. Various firms produce different varieties and brands of product and each has a certain degree of monopoly power over the variety or brand it produces for fixing price and output. If products were homogeneous the demand curve would not have been downward sloping and equilibrium would have been established at the minimum point of *LAC* without there being any excess capacity.

The second reason for the emergence of excess capacity under monopolistic competition, as has been emphasised by Chamberlin, *is the entry of a very large a number of firms in the industry in the long run*. Lured by excess profits in the short run new firms enter the industry in the long run. This results in sharing of market demand among many firms so that each firm produces a smaller output than its full or optimum capacity. There are too many grocery shops, too many cloth manufacturing firms, too many automobile parts producing firms, too many barber shops each operating with excess capacity. In fact, under monopolistic competition, given the same demand and cost conditions, number of firms will be larger than even under perfect competition. This is because by expanding output to the minimum point of *LAC*, fewer firms will be required to meet the given demand for industry's product.

The conception and the measure of excess capacity as enunciated above is based upon a particular notion of ideal output. Marshall, Kahn[19], Harrod[20], Cassel[21] and Joan Robinson have regarded *ideal output or optimum size of the firm as that output at which its long-run average cost is minimum*. To quote Joan Robinson, "In a perfectly competitive industrv each firm in full equilibrium will produce that output at which its average costs are minımum. Each firm will then be ot the optımum size... If competition is imperfect, the demand curve for the output of the individual firm will be falling and the double condition of equilibrium can only be fulfilled for some output at which average cost if falling. The firms will, therefore, be of less than optimum size when profits are normal... It is only if conditions of perfect competition prevail that firms will be of the optimum size and there is no reason to expect that they will be of optimum size in the real world since in the real world competition is not perfect."[22]

Benefits of Excess Capacity. However, many modern economists are of the view that excess capacity under monopolistic competition is *desirable in some respects*. According to them, excess capacity under monopolistic competition provides some benefits which increase consumer welfare. As mentioned above, the excess capacity comes into existence mainly due to product differentiation under monopolistic competition. Now, this *product differentiation leads to product variety* which is highly beneficial to the consumers. The ability to choose among a wide variety of clothes, furniture, restaurant meals and other types of styles of product designs add greatly to the satisfaction or welfare of the consumers. Therefore, according to this view, social benefits of excess capacity should be weighed against the cost to the society of excess capacity.

EQUILIBRIUM UNDER MONOPOLISTIC COMPETITION: CHAMBERLIN'S ALTERNATIVE APPROACH

Concepts of Proportional and Perceived Demand Curves

The process of equilibrium adjustment under monopolistic competition has also been explained by an alternative approach put forward by Chamberlin. This alternative approach makes use of two types of demand curves, namely, *perceived demand curve and proportional demand curve*. The

19. R.F. Khan, "Some Notes on Ideal Output", *Economic Journal*, XIV (1935), pp. 1-35.
20. R.F. Harrod, Doctrines of Imperfect Competition, *Quarterly Journal of Economics*, XLIX (1934-35), pp. 442-70.
21. J.M. Cassels, Excess Capacity and Monopolistic Competition, *Quarterly Journal of Economics*, LI (1936-37), pp. 426-43.
22. Joan Robinson, *Economics of Imperfect Competition*, pp. 96-97.

demand curve facing an individual firm, as perceived by it, describes the demand for the product of one firm on the assumption that all other firms in the industry or group keep the *prices of their products constant*. The perceived demand curve shows the increase in quantity demanded of a product of a firm when a firm cuts down its price provided others keep their prices at the present level. On the contrary, it shows the fall in quantity demanded of the product of a firm which will occur if it raises its price on the assumption that others would not raise their prices. This type of demand curve in the present alternative approach, is known as *perceived demand curve* and is based upon the above important assumption. This type of demand curve is also known as *subjective or imagined or expected demand* curve because this is based on the individual firm deciding subjectively what it perceives or imagines its demand curve looks like. The number of firms being large in a product group under monopolistic competition, it is assumed that each firm is so small relative to the whole group that it thinks that the price change by it will have negligible impact upon its competitive firms with the result that they would not think of reacting to the change in price by it in retaliation.

The other type of the demand curve used in this approach is *proportional demand curve* facing an individual firm. This shows the demand or sales of the product of a firm when the prices of all firms in a product-group or industry *change, all of them simultaneously in the same direction and by the same amount* so that they charge same or uniform price. Obviously, the proportional demand curve of a firm will be less elastic than its perceived demand curve, since equal change in price by all firms of the industry (*i.e.*, group) will prevent the movement of customers from one seller to another. The proportional demand curve of each firm slopes downward because the market demand for the general class of the product increases as a result of the fall in price. In fact, the proportional demand curve facing an individual firm is a proportinate part of the total market demand curve for the general class of the product and will be of the same elasticity. Thus, since each firm gets some proportional share of the total market demand for the general class of the product, the proportional demand for each firm varies with the number of firms in the product group. The greater the number of firms in a product-group, the smaller the share of an individual firm at a given price. Therefore, the proportional demand curve facing an individual firm shifts to the left as more and more firms enter the product-group or industry. We designate the proportional demand curve as *DD′* curve and, the perceived demand curve as *dd′* curve. The two types of demand curves are graphically shown in Fig. 28. 13. The two demand curves have been shown to be intersecting at point *A* corresponding to price *OP* and quantity demanded *OQ*. This means that at price *OP* of the product, the proportional share of each firm of the market demand for the industry product is equal to *OQ*. Since it is assumed that all firms charge the same price, all firms in the industry will be producing and selling *OQ* quantity and each charging *OP* price. Therefore, point *A* lies on the proportional demand curve. From the initial situtation at *A* on the proportional demand curve *DD′* (with price equal to *OP* and quantity demanded of each equal to *OQ*) we can draw the perceived demand curve of a firm. An individual firm believes that if it makes small alternation in price, it will have negligible effect on each of its many competitors so that they will not think of readjusting their prices. Prices of other firms remaining unchanged at *OP*, an individual firm thinks that if it reduces its price, the sales or quantity demanded of its product will greatly increase as it will attract customers of other firms. Thus, an individual firm perceives that its demand is more elastic than the proportinal demand curve and it can increase its profits by cutting down its price. Therefore, we construct the

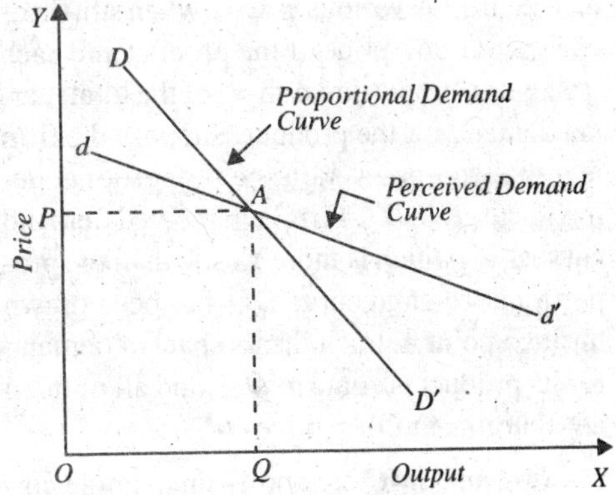

Fig. 28.13. *Chamberlin's Concepts of Perceived and Proportional Demand Curves*

perceived demand curve dd' passing through point A as being more elastic than the proportinal demand curve DD'. However, it may be pointed out that since *each* firm in the product group will think independently that its price reduction will have a negligible effect upon each of his rivals and therefore assumes that others would keep their prices constant, each firm will cut its price and therefore the actual movement would not be along the perceived demand curve dd' but along the proportional demand curve DD' which shows actual sales by each firm when the prices of all change equally and are identical.

Short-Run Firm's Equilibrium under Monopolistic Competition

Price-output equilibrium of an individual firm in the short run in terms of two demand curves (proportional demand curve and perceived demand curve) is illustrated in Figure 28.14. The proportional demand curve $D_0D'_0$ shows the quantity demanded of the product of the firm at various prices when all firms charge uniform price of the product and each firm gets a proportional share of the total market demand for the product. Suppose the firm is initially at point A on the proportional demand curve $D_0D'_0$. Firm's perceived demand curve $d_0d'_0$ which is more elastic than the proportional demand curve DD' has been drawn through point A. Each firm's share of demand for its product is equal to OQ_0 and all of them are charging uniform price OP_0.

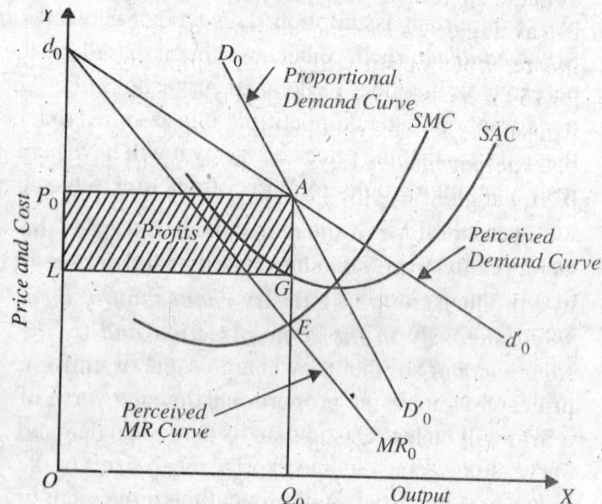

Fig. 28.14. *Short-run Equilibrium of the Firm under Monopolistic Competition: Proportional and Perceived Demand Curves Approach*

SAC and *SMC* are short-run average cost curve and short-run marginal cost curve respectively. Marginal revenue curve MR_0 corresponding the perceived demand curve dd'_0 has been drawn. *SMC* and MR_0 curves intersect at point E and accordingly output OQ_0 is equilibrium output of the firm and OP_0 is the equilibrium price charged with proportional and perceived demand curves cutting each other at point A in the present price-quantity equilibrium. It will be seen from Fig. 28.14. that price OP_0 exceeds average cost of production at OQ_0 output level and therefore the firm is making supernormal profits equal to the shaded area P_0AGL. Thus, according to Chamberlin's altenative approach short-run equilibrium under monopolistic competition is reached when the following two conditions are satisfied:

(1) The price-output combination is such at which *perceived marginal revenue curve intersects the marginal cost curve* so that $MR = MC$

(2) The price-output combination where $MR = MC$ is such that corresponds to the point at which *perceived demand curve dd' intersects the proportional demand curve D_0D_0'*.

Only when the above two conditions are fulfilled, the firm will be maximising its profits and will have no incentive to change its price. Thus firm's equilibrium in the short run occurs at the point on proportional demand curve and perceived demand curve which also corresponds to the output level where marginal revenue is equal to marginal cost.

Long-Run Adjustment

Chamberlin explains adjustment to long-run equilibrium at two stages. In the first stage he explains adjustment in the number of firms alone without price competition. In the second stage he discusses price competition among firms to reach long-run equilibrium position with zero economic profits. We have shown this adjustment to reach long-run equilibrium in Fig. 28.15. It has been assumed that firms face same demand and cost conditions. Lured by the supernormal profits made by the firms in the short run new firms enter the industry and as a result proportional market demand curve D_0D_0' starts shifting to the left as a given market demand is shared by more firms. Entry of the new firms will stop when the proportional market demand curve becomes tangent to the long-run average curve so that supernormal profits are wiped out. It will be seen from Fig. 28.15 that proportional demand curve facing firms in the absence of price competition has become tangent to the long-run average curve (*LAC*) at point *H*. However, this will not be long-run equilibrium situation if each of the existing firms working independently thinks that it can secure larger market share and thereby can increase its profits. From Figure 28.15 it is evident that *in its position at point H, a firm has more elastic perceived demand curve $d_0d'_0$ than its proportinate market demand curve $D_1D'_1$.*

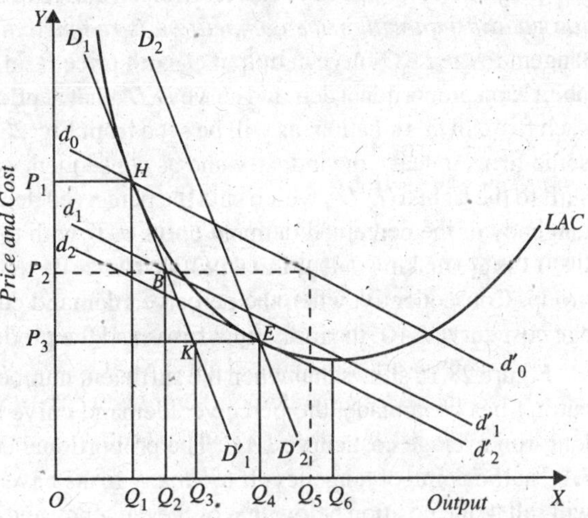

Fig. 28.15. *Long-run Equilibrium under Monopolistic Competition with Free Entry and Price Competition: Chamberlin's Alternative Approach*

Thus, with its position at point *H*, the firm perceives that it can increase its profits by cutting down price to P_2 ($AR > LAC$) by securing more than proporionate increase in demand for its product assuming that other firms will not react and would maintain their prices at the current level P_1. However each firm in monopolistically competitive industry will perceive, through independently of each other, that if it lowers its price below the current one, it can lure away customers from others assuming that others would keep their prices constant. Though this is a naive and myopic behaviour on the part of the firms, Chamberlin assumes it and thinks that in the real world firms do behave in this manner when they indulge in price competition.

But as a matter of fact since all firms working in this myopic manner cut down their prices, each firm *will not be in equilibrium* at point *H* producing Q_1 quantity of the product. Instead, the firms will find themselves at point *B* on the proportinoal demand curve $D_1D'_1$ getting a proportinale share of the increase in market demand at the lower price OP_2. Thus each firm will be working at point *B* on the proportinal demand curve $D_1D'_1$, and producing OQ_2 output. Thus, as a result of price cutting the perceived demand curve of each firm will slide down the proportinate demand curve to point *B*. In other words, from a new point *B* on the proportional demand curve $D_1D'_1$ at which the firms land themselves as a result of price reduction, the new perceived demand curve d_1d_1' has to be drawn. It will be seen from Figure 28.15 that with point *B* on the new perceived demand curve d_1d_1', a firm still thinks that it can increase its demand if it lowers its price below OP_2 provided other rival firms keep their prices constant. Thus, though its earlier attempt to increase profits by lowering price was frustrated by others also cutting down their prices by an equal amount, each firm again believes, though still suffering from illusion, that if it lowers the price, it can bring about increase in quantity demanded of its product and make profits.

However, since each firm perceives in the same way and cuts down its prices, though acting independently, it would not succeed in snatching away customers from its rival firms and its attempt to increase profits would again be frustrated. As a result, each firm instead of moving to a point on the perceived demand curve for increasing its profits it will land itself on the proportional demand curve $D_1D'_1$ getting the same proportionate share from the increase in quantity demanded of the product at the lower price. In this way the process of price-cutting competition and sliding down of perceived demand curve on the proportional demand curve would continue until a firm has reached a situation where it cannot perceive to increase its profits by reducing its price. In fact, In this situation it will be in equilibrium and will have therefore no incentive to lower further the price of the product. This long-run *equilibrium with price competition is reached at point E where the perceived demand curve* is tangent to the *LAC* curve at output Q_4 with price P_3 in Fig. 28.15. It will however be noticed from the point *K* on proportional demand curve $D_1D'_1$ that at price P_3 actually amount Q_3 will be demanded from each firm. In this siuation, as will be seen from Fig. 28.15 firms will be making losses. This will force some firms to leave the industry and as consequence the proportional demand curve amount Q_3 will shift to the right to $D_2D'_2$ which cuts the perceived demand curve $d_2d'_2$ at the point of tangency *E*. The tangency of the perceived demand curve $d_2d'_2$ with the long-run average cost curve *LAC* shows that the fi.ms are making only normal profits. Hence there will be no tendency for the firms to enter into the group. Consequently, when the perceived demand curve *dd′* becomes tangent to the long-run average cost curve *LAC*, the individual firms and the product group as a whole will be in equilibrium.

Figure 28.15 shows that when the sufficient number of new firms have entered the group and price cutting has been made, the perceived demand curve has fallen to the position of tangency with the long-run average cost curve *LAC*. The proportional demand curve $D_2D'_2$ will intersect the d_2d_2' and *LAC* at the point of tangency. If too many firms have entered the group the perceived demand curve will fall to the position below that of the tangency and the firms will be making losses. The result will be that some firms will leave the group and the proportional demand curve along with perceived demand curve curve will shift to the right. For the achievement of long-run equilibrium of the firms and the group equilibrium, the two conditions are necessary.

(*i*) The perceived demand curve *dd′* must be tangent to the long-run average cost curve *LAC*.

(*ii*) The proportional demand curve *DD′* facing individual firm must intersect both the *dd′* and *LAC* curves at the point of tangency.

In the above discussion, the two competitive forces, namely, the entry of firms and the price cutting have been shown to be operating separately with the net result that the perceived demand curve *dd′* curve falls to the position of tangency with the *LAC* curve and the proportional demand curve *DD′* cuts both of them at the point of tangency. In actual world, the two competitive forces operate simultaneously but for analytical purposes, it is better to describe separately the working of these two forces.

It may be noted that, according to Chamberlin, with the entry of new firms, and *before the price competition taking place, that is, when firms operate* at point *H*, there exists excess capacity equal to Q_1Q_4 as according to him, OQ_4 is socially ideal output in the presence of product differentiation and price competition having been fully worked out. It may be further noted that Chamberlin does not regard Q_4Q_6 as excess capacity as according to him this much lower output is inevitable under monopolistic competition due to the existence of product differentiation and product variety.

Chamberlin's Concepts of Ideal Output and Excess Capacity

The view of ideal output described earlier rests upon the perfect competition and its associated product homogeneity which gives rise to the horizontal demand curve confronting an individual firm under it and consequently the establishment of the long-run equilibrium of the firm under perfect competition at the minimum point of the long-run average cost curve. The output at this minimum long-run average cost under perfect competition with product homogeneity is regarded as "ideal" from the viewpoint of social welfare. But Prof. Chamberlin argues that this "*Competitive Ideal*" cannot be considered as "ideal" under monopolistic competition.

Under monopolistic competition there is product differentiation which inevitably gives rise to the downward-sloping demand curve. Downward sloping demand curve along with free entry into the product group and active price competition necessarily involves long-run equilibrium to the left of minimum point of the long-run average cost curve. According to Chamberlin, product differentiation is desired *per se* and therefore the long-run equilibrium output of the monopolistically competitive firm under free entry and *active price competition* represents the "ideal output". The departure from the long-run equilibrium output under free entry and active price competition from the long-run minimum average cost does not prevent the output to be ideal because this departure is only due to product differentiation which is desired by the consumers for its own sake.

Chamberlin regards product differentiation a quality of the product which carries a cost just as any other quality. The cost of product differentiation is represented by production in the long run to the left of the minimum long-run average cost. This means that "the difference between the actual long-run equilibrium output and output at minimum cost is then a measure of the cost of producing differentiation rather than a measure of excess capacity"[23]. But according to Chamberlin, this is true only when effective price competition in the market is present, because it is only when effective price competition among the sellers is present that the buyers would have the degree of product differentiation they wish to purchase.

The ideal output as conceived by Chamberlin is illustrated in Figure 28.15. According to Chamberlin, the long-run equilibrium under monopolistic competition is established at the point where the subjective or perceived demand curve $d_2d'_2$ is tangent to the long-run average cost curve and also proportional demand curve $D_2D'_2$ curve cuts this point of tangency. This is achieved at point E where $d_2d'_2$ is tangent to LAC and the proportional demand curve $D_2D'_2$ is cutting LAC at this point. This long-run equilibrium point has been achieved after adjustment in the number of firms in the 'group' has taken place and also price competition has fully worked itself out. Corresponding to this long-run equilibrium point E, the firm is producing output OQ_4. But point E lies on the falling portion of the long-run average cost curve. Chamberlin regards long-run equilibrium output OQ_4 corresponding to point E as the ideal output under monopolistic competition in which there is product differentiation. According to Chamberlin, output which corresponds to the minimum point of the long-run average cost curve LAC cannot represent ideal output under monopolistic competition involving product differentiation.

Thus with active price competition when long-run equilibrium is at pont E where perceived demand curve $d_2d'_2$ is tangent to the long-run average cost curve and the firm is producing OQ_4 output which represents ideal one under product differentiation, There is no excess capacity. Therefore, *according to Chamberlin, so long as there is active price competition in the market, monopolistic competition does not create excess capacity. In his view, excess capacity arises when there is free entry of firms but no price competition.* Thus it is the entry of firms in the long run in the monopolistically competitive group which, *in the absence of price competition*, gives rise to the excess capacity.

Chamberlin[24] has given various reasons for the lack of price competition between the firms in monopolistic competition. First, the business firms may follow the policy of "*to live and let live*" and therefore they may not indulge in price cutting. They may set prices with reference to cost (including normal profits) rather than demand and accordingly seek only normal profits rather than maximum profits; more or less taking it granted that they will enjoy usual share of the total market demand. Secondly, the business firms in monopolistic competition may have entered into formal or tacit agreements. They might have formed 'price association' which builds up the spirit of 'maintaining price' among the competitors and preventing them from price cutting. Thirdly, *business or professonal ethics*, also prevents them from disturbing the market by price cutting. It is generally considered unethical in the professions to compete on the basis of price. The fourth factor preventing price cutting is the fear of business firms that the lower price may lead the consumers to regard the particular product as of inferior quality. It is generally seen in the real world that many consumers blindly link quality with price.

23. C.F. Ferguson, *Microeconomic Theory* (1966), p. 262.
24. *Op. Cit.*, pp. 105-107.

In the fifth place, the business firm may make disguised or hidden price cuts while maintaining the price openly. Since open price cuts generally bring about retaliation from the rivals, it is considered desirable to give certain non-price concessions, offer facilities free of charge, such as free coupons, premiums, etc., while displaying and charging the same price as competitors. All these extra non-price concessions or facilities are regarded as hidden price cuts. Finally, the prices may not be free to move at all, for they are often set by custom or tradition.

As pointed out above, if price competition is in fact absent individual firms will have no regard for the existence of perceived demand curve *dd´*. They will be concerned only with market demand curve *DD´* which represents the effects of price rise or price decline when all firms in the group simultaneously raise or reduce price. According to Chamberlin, the result of the absence of price competition among the firms in monopolistic competition "is excess productive capacity for which there is no automatic corrective. Such excess capacity may develop, of course, under pure competition owing to miscalculation on the part of producers or to sudden fluctuations in demand or cost conditions. *But it is the peculiarity of monopolistic competition* that it may develop over long periods *with impunity*, prices always covering costs, and may, in fact, become permanent and normal through the failure of price competition to function. The surplus capacity is never case off, the result is high prices and waste" [25]. He further says that his theory of monopolistic competition "affords an explanation of such wastes in the economic system—wastes which are usually referred to as "wastes of competition". In fact they could never occur under pure competition. They are wastes of monopoly—of the monopoly elements in monopolistic competition".[25]

PRICE-OUTPUT EQUILIBRIUM UNDER MONOPOLISTIC COMPETITION COMPARED WITH THAT UNDER PERFECT COMPETITION

It is useful to explain how price-output equilibrium under monopolistic competition differs from that under perfect competition.

1. Price is greater than MC under monopolistic competition. A significant difference between the two relates to the relation between price and marginal cost. Whereas in equilibrium under perfect competition, price is equal to marginal cost, in equilibrium under monopolistic competition price is greater than marginal cost. Since under perfect competition, an individual firm cannot influence the price of its product and takes price as given and constant, the demand or average revenue curve is a horizontal straight line and marginal revenue (*MR*) is equal to average revenue (*AR*) or price. Therefore, under perfect competition when a firm equates marginal cost with marginal revenue so as to maximise its profits, the former also becomes equal to price.

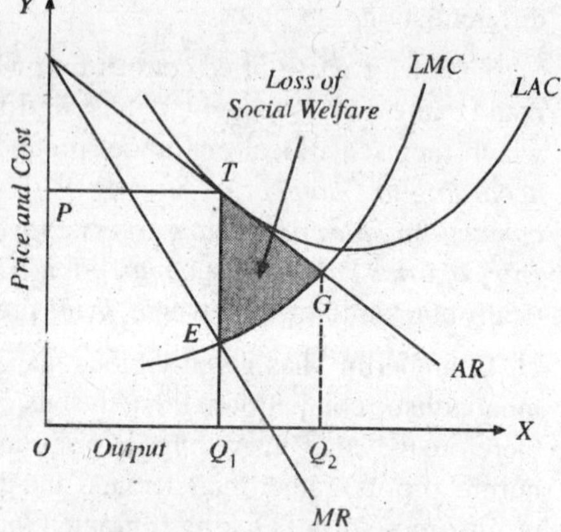

Fig. 28.16. *Loss of Social Welfare.*

On the other hand, under monopolistic competition, a firm exercises some control over the price of its product and the demand curve for it, representing prices at various quantities, slopes downward. As a result, marginal revenue (*MR*) curve lies below average revenue (*AR*) curve. Therefore, in order to maximise profits when a firm under monopolistic competition equates marginal cost with marginal revenue, price stands at a higher level than marginal cost. This is clear from Fig. 28.3 where, in equilibrium, price determined is equal to *MQ* or *OP*, which is greater than marginal cost (*ME*).

It should be noted that *producing level of output much less than at which marginal cost equals price implies a loss of social welfare.* It should be noted that social welfare is maximum when output

25. E.H. Chamberlin, *op. cit.*, p. 109.

is extended to the point where price is equal to long-run marginal cost. It will be seen from Fig. 28.16 that such point is *G* where price or *AR* = *LMC*. But as will be seen from Fig. 28.16 the firm working under conditions of monopolistic competition produces OQ_1 in the long-run equilibrium. Thus, the area *TEG* represents loss of social welfare which is also called *dead weight loss*. This indicates inefficiency of monopolistic competition.

2. Long-run equilibrium under monopolistic competition is established at less than optimum size. Another important difference between the equilibrium under monopolistic competition and perfect competition is that whereas a firm in long-run equilibrium under monopolistic competition produces less than its optimum size of output, under perfect competition long-run equilibrium of the firm is established at the minimum point of the long-run average cost curve. In other words, a firm under perfect competition tends to be of the optimum size. But a firm under monopolistic competition, as is evident from Fig. 28.5 stops short of the optimum point and operates in the long run at the point at which long-run average cost is still falling. In Fig. 28.5 the firm produces output *OQ*, while a firm under pure or perfect competition would have produced output *OR* at which long-run average cost is minimum. The firm under monopolistic competition can reduce its cost of production by expanding output to the point *R* but it will not do so because by expanding output beyond *OQ* it will be reducing price more than the average cost. It is, therefore, clear that by producing *OQ* instead of *OR* in the long run, the firm under monopolistic competition does not use its capacity fully. (The firm would be using its capacity fully if it produces optimum output *OR*). Thus, capacity equal to *QR* lies unused in the firm under monopolistic competition. This unused capacity is called excess capacity which is a prominent feature of long-run equilibrium under monopolistic competition.

3. Price under monopolistic competition is greater than competitive price. Further, it may be noted that in the long-run equilibrium, firms under monopolistic competition make only normal profits as under perfect competition, but the price set under monopolistic competition is higher than competitive price. In Fig. 28.5, price set in long-run equilibrium under monopolistic competition is *QT* while competitive price in the long run would have been equal to *RL*. This higher price under monopolistic competition is due to monopoly element contained in it. The monopoly element involved in monopolistic competition makes the demand or average revenue curve facing an individual firm downward sloping and a downward-sloping average revenue curve can be tangent to the average cost curve only to the left of its minimum point.

Thus price under monopolistic competition will be higher than the competitive price due to the monopoly element in monopolistic competition. But, in spite of the higher price, a firm under monopolistic competition will not be making profits above normal in the long run. We may, therefore, say that a firm under monopolistic competition, in the long-run equilibrium, charges higher price without enjoying monopoly profits. A significant result follows from this. It is that the ***non-existence of abnormal profits is no indicator of the absence of monopoly element***. In long-run equilibrium under monopolistic competition, as seen above, the firm has monopoly power (it has a sole control over its own differentiated product with the result that demand curve for it slopes downward) but it does not make any super-normal profits in the long-run.

4. Excess capacity and other wastes of competition under monopolistic competition. Further, it is evident from the long-run equilibrium situation of a firm under monopolistic competition (see Fig. 28.5) that it occurs at the output level which falls short of the output *OR* at which the long-run average cost is minimum. This implies, that maximum economic efficiency is not achieved under monopolistic competition because the resources are not being used to produce the good at the minimum possible average cost. That is why economists such as Harrod, Cassel have called the output difference *QR* as *the excess capacity that tends to prevail under monopolistic competition which represents waste of resources*. However, it is worth noting that some economists do not consider *QR* as the excess capacity. According to them, this small loss of output and consequently higher average cost is price which people are paying for the product variety which they get under monopolistic competition due to product differentiation as compared to perfect competition. Further, *firms under monopolistic competition spend a lot of money on advertisement and other sales promotion activities which also represents* wastes of competition.

According to Chamberlin, *a lot of excess capacity is created under monopolistic as a result of entry of a large number of firms only if price competition does not prevail.* If price competition prevails then there is not much excess capacity under monopolistic competition. In the long-run too mainy firm enter the industry so that market is shared among many and in the absence of price competition each produces much less than its full capacity.

MONOPOLISTIC COMPETITION AND ECONOMIC EFFICIENCY

Perfect competition is said to be the ideal market form as it ensures maximum possible social welfare. In partial equilibrium analysis welfare is measuerd by the consumer surplus gained by the consumers and producer surplus earned by the producers. Under perfect competition, given the demand and cost conditions the maximum possible sum of consumer surplus and producer surplus is achieved so that social welfare is maximised. Besides, under perfect competition in the long run firms operate at the minimum point of the long-run average cost curve which ensures maximum efficiency in the use of resources. According to this, not only *optimum scale of plant* (*i.e*, plant with minimum *LAC*) is set up but also that plant is operated at its *optimum* or full *capacity*, that is, at the minimum point of short-run average cost curve of the plant.

On the other hand, firms operating in monoplistic competitive environment earn zero economic profits in their long-run equilibrium but they operate with *two types of inefficiencies*. First, as discussed above in detail, firms opeate in the long run with *excess capacity* which implies inefficiency or waste in the use of resources and impedes the achievement of maximum social welfare. In long-run equilibrium under monopolistic competition, firms operate at less than the scale of output at which long-run average cost is minimum. In this long-run equilibrium situation, neither the optimum scale of plant is set up, nor the plant actually set up is operated at its optimum capacity (*i.e.*, at minimum point of short-run average cost). This implies higher cost and price as well as lower output than if production had been done at minimum point of *LAC*. Thus, the existence of excess capacity under monopolistic competition causes inefficiency in the use of resources and loss of consumer welfare.

The second type of inefficiency that prevails under monopolistic competition is called *allocative inefficiency* which refers to the misallocation of resources among products which also causes loss of welfare. *Allocative efficiency is achieved if price of a product is fixed equal to the marginal cost of production.* However, under monopolistic competition firms are in long-run equilibrium at the level of output at which price exceeds marginal cost of production. Consider Fig. 28.16, firm is in long-run equilibrium at output OQ_1 at which *MR* equals *MC* but price fixed is Q_1T or *OP* which exceeds marginal cost Q_1E at the equilibrium output. The ideal output from the viewpoint of allocative efficiency is OQ_2 at which price equals *MC*. It will be observed from the *AR* curve in the figure that the price which consumers are willing to pay for additional units from Q_1 to Q_2 exceeds the marginal cost of production to be incurred by the society. If output were extended to Q_2 at which demand (*AR*) curve cuts the long-run marginal cost curve *LMC*, the total surplus (sum of consumer surplus and producer surplus) could be increased by an amount equal to the shaded area *ETG*. This shaded area *ETG* represents *dead weight loss* of welfare. This dead-weight loss accrues due to the monopoly element involved in monopolistic competition. It may be recalled that monopoly element is present in monopolistic competition because products of different firms are differentiated and each of them has some control over the price of its product. Expansion of output to Q_2 requires allocation of more resources to the production of the product. By restricting output to Q_1 and thereby raising price of the product, firms operating under monopolistic competition do not allocate resources efficiently which cause dead weight loss in welfare. This is called dead weight loss because there is no compensating gain by any one else.

Comments. Due to the existence of above two types of inefficiencies monopolistic competition is considered socially undesirable form of market structure by traditional economists. However, modern economists do not think so. This is for two reasons. First, the excess capacity that exists under monopolistic competition is very small because in the long run under monopolistic competition demand curve facing each firm becomes highly elastic as a result of the entry of new firms in the industry making available more close substitutes in the market.

Second, due to the demand (*AR*) curve becoming highly elastic in the long run monopolistic competition ensures that the difference between the price and marginal cost will also be very small which means whatever dead weight loss in welfare occurs is not very significant.

Above all there is gain or benefits to consumers because of *product variety* found in this market structure. Most consumers derive great satisfaction from the ability to choose among a wide variety of products and brands that exist under monopolistic competition. The gain in consumer welfare or benefits due to product diversity may be weighed against the cost of little inefficiency that prevails under monopolistic competition.

QUESTIONS AND PROBLEMS FOR REVIEW

1. What is monopolistic competition? Explain the important features of monopolistic competition.
2. What is product differentiation? What role does it play in the determination of price and output under monopolistic competition?
3. Analyse the short-run and long-run equilibrium of a firm working under monopolistic competition. *[D.U., B.Com (Hons.) 2007, C.U., B.Com., (H), 1999]*
4. What is group equilibrium? Explain how group equilibrium is achieved under monopolistic competition.
5. (*a*) What is meant by excess capacity? Show that how a firm working under monopolistic competition works with excess capacity in the long run. Is this outcome necessarily undesirable ? *[D.U.B.Com. (H) 2001]*
   (*b*) What causes excess capacity under monopolistic competition? Why is it undesirable? *[D.U., B. Com (H) 2006, 2008]*
6. *Are there any benefits of excess capacity associated with monopolistc competition*?
7. What are wastes of competition? How are they found under monopolistic competition?
8. Compare price-output equilibrium under monopolistic competition with that under (*a*) perfect competition, (*b*) monopoly.
9. Distinguish between selling costs and production cost? Explain the optimal level of advertising expenditure.
10. Explain Chamberlin's concepts of *proportional* and *perceived* demand curves of firms operating under monopolistic competition. Explain with their help short-run and long-run firm's equilibrium under monopolistic competition.
11. Explain Chamberlin's concept of excess capacity. What, according to him, is responsible for the emergence of excess capacity under monopolistic competition?
12. Explain the concept of economic efficiency. Evaluate econmic inefficiency of firms operating under monopolistic competition.
13. Distinguish between production cost and selling costs. How does monopolistically competitive firm determine the optimal amount of selling costs. *[D.U. B.A.(Hons.) 1997]*
14. "Monopolistically Competitive industries are characterised by too many firms each of which produces too little" *[D.U. B.A.(Hons.) 1987]*
15. Assuming that a firm operating under monopolistic competition does not engage in price competition and that it has already decided what kind and quality of product it will produce, how will the firm decide how much selling costs to incur in order to maximise its profits? *[D.U. B.A.(Hons.)]*
16. Under monopolistic competition, which demand curve (perceived demand or proportionate demand curve) determines the firm's choice of output and price? Why is the firm's perceived demand curve flatter than the total market demand curve? Why must the two demand curves intersect at the equilibrium point? *[D.U. (B. Com Hons.) 2004]*
17. Explain the short-run equilibrium under monopolistic competition with the help of perceived and proportionate demand curves. *D.U., B. Com (H) 2008*

CHAPTER 29

PRICE AND OUTPUT UNDER OLIGOPOLY

We have studied price and output determination under three market forms, namely, perfect competition, monopoly, and monopolistic competition. However, in the real world economies we find that many of the markets or industries are oligopolistic. Oligopoly is an important form of imperfect competition. Oligopoly is said to prevail when there are few firms or sellers in the market producing or selling a product. In other words, when there are two or more than two, but not many, producers or sellers of a product, oligopoly is said to exist. Oligopoly is also often referred to as "*Competition among the Few*". *The simplest case of oligopoly is duopoly which prevails when there are only two producers or sellers of a product.* Analysis of duopoly raises all those basic problems which are confronted while explaining oligopoly with more than two firms.

Although there is no borderline between few and many but when the number of sellers of a product are two to ten, oligopoly situation is said to exist. When products of a few sellers are homogeneous, we talk of *Obligopoly without Product Differentiation or Pure Oligopoly.* On the other hand, when products of the few sellers or firms, instead of being homogeneous, are differentiated but close substitutes for each other, *Oligopoly with Product Differentiation or Differentiated Oligopoly* is said to prevail.

CHARACTERISTICS OF OLIGOPOLY

In oligopoly some special characteristics are found which are not present in other market structures. We discuss some of these characteristics below:

Interdependence. The most important feature of oligopoly is the interdependence in decision-making of the few firms which comprise the industry. This is because when the number of competitors is few, any change in price, output, product etc. by a firm will have a direct effect on the fortune of its rivals, which will then retaliate in changing their own prices, output or products as the case may be. It is, therefore, clear that the oligopolistic firm must consider not only the market demand for the industry's product but also the reactions of the other firms in the industry to any action or decision it may take. Since more than one reaction-pattern is possible from the other firms, we have to make some assumptions about the reaction of the others before we can provide a definite and determinate solution of price-output fixation under oligopoly.

Importance of advertising and selling costs. A direct effect of interdependence of oligopolists is that the various firms have to employ various aggressive and defensive marketing weapons to gain a greater share in the market or to prevent a fall in their market share. For this various firms have to incur a good deal of costs on advertising and on other measures of sales promotion. Therefore, there is a great importance of advertising and selling costs under conditions of market situation characterised by oligopoly. Prof. Baumol rightly says that "it is only under oligopoly that advertising comes fully into its own."[1] Under perfect competition, advertising by an individual firm is unnecessary in view of the fact that it can sell any amount of its product at the going price. A monopolist has

1. William J. Baumol, *Economic Theory and Operations Analysis*, 3rd ed., p. 352.

also not to make any competitive advertisement since he is the only seller of a product. A monopolist may perhaps advertise when he has to inform the public about his introduction of a new model of his product or he may advertise in order to attract potential consumers who have not yet tried his product. Under monopolistic competition advertising plays an important role because of the product differentiation that exists under it, but not as much important as under oligopoly. "Under oligopoly, advertising can become a life-and-death matter where a firm which fails to keep up with the advertising budget of its competitors may find its customers drifting off to rival products".[2]

In view of the fact that a firm in an oligopolistic industry competes by changing the advertisement costs, quality of the product, prices, output etc., *the presence of competitive conditions in it can hardly be denied*. To an oligopolist "Competition can consist not in the quiescent stalemate of perfect competition where there is no battle because there is never anyone strong enough to disturb the peace. Rather to him, true competition consists of the life of constant struggle, rival against rival, which one can only find under oligopoly (or, on a smaller scale, under conditions of monopolistic competition)."[3]

Group behaviour. Further, another important feature of oligopoly is that for the proper solution to the problem of determination of price and output under, it analysis of group behaviour is important. Theories of perfect competition, monopoly and monopolistic competition present no difficult problem of making suitable assumption about human behaviour. In cases of perfect competition and monopolistic competition (with a large number of firms), the economists assume that the business firms behave in such a way as to maximise their profits. Assumption of profit maximisation gives overall good results in these situations where mass of people are involved and there is no interdependence of firms. On the other end, the theory of monopoly deals with a sole individual and it is also appropriate to assume profit-maximising behaviour on his part.

But the theory of oligopoly is a theory of *group behaviour* not of mass or individual behaviour and to assume profit-maximising behaviour on the part of a producer of a group may not be very valid. There are few firms in a group which are very much interdependent. Given the present state of our economic and social science, there is no generally accepted theory of group behaviour. Do the members of a group agree to pull together in promotion of common interests or will they fight to promote their individual interests? Does the group possess any leader? If so, how does he get the others to follow him? These are some of the questions that need to be answered by the theory of group behaviour.

Indeterminateness of demand curve facing an oligopolist. Another important feature is the indeterminateness of the demand curve facing an oligopolist. The demand curve shows what amounts of its product a firm will be able to sell at various prices. Now, under perfect competition, an individual firm's demand curve is given and definite. Since a perfectly competitive firm is one among a large number of firms producing an identical product, it is incapable of influencing the price of its product by its own individual action. Therefore, a firm under perfect competition faces a perfectly elastic demand curve at the level of the going price in the market. On the other hand, a monopolist produces a product which has only remote substitutes. Therefore, a monopolist can safely ignore the effects of its own price changes on his distant rivals and therefore the monopolist faces a given and definite demand curve depending upon the consumer's demand for his product. Under monopolistic competition, where there is a large number of firms producing products which are close substitutes for each other, changes in price by an individual firm will have a negligible effect on each of its many rivals. Therefore, a firm under monopolistic competition can validly assume the prices of its rivals to remain unchanged when it makes changes in the price of its product. Thus, the demand curve for a firm under monopolistic competition can be taken as definite and is given by the buyers' preferences for its product.

2. *Ibid*, p. 352.
3. *Ibid*, p. 352

But the situation under oligopoly is quite different because of interdependence of the firms in it. Under oligopoly, a firm cannot assume that its rivals will keep their prices unchanged when it makes changes in its own price. As a result of this, the demand curve facing an oligopolistic firm loses its definiteness and determinateness because it goes on constantly shifting as the rivals change their prices in reaction to price changes by a firm.

ARE PRICE AND OUTPUT UNDER OLIGOPOLY INDETERMINATE ?

We have explained above the various characteristics and problems of oligopoly. The readers will now like to know how the economists analyse the determination of price and output under oligopoly. Because of the interdependence of firms in oligopoly and the uncertainty about the reaction patterns of the rivals, the easy and determinate solution to the oligopoly problem is not possible. In other words, interdependence of firms in an oligopoly and consequently firm's reactions to each other's behaviour poses serious difficulties in establishing the theory of the determination of price and output in an oligopolistic market.

Interdependence of Firms in Oligopoly

A significant consequence of interdependence of firms in an oligopolistic market situation is that under it a *wide variety of behaviour patterns becomes possible*. "Rivals may decide to get together and co-operate in the pursuit of their objectives, at least so far as the law allows or, at the other extreme, they may try to fight each other to the death. Even if they enter into an agreement it may last or it may break down. And the agreements may follow a wide variety of patterns."[4] Therefore, a large variety of models analysing price-output determination under oligopoly have been evolved by the economists depending upon the different assumptions about the behaviour of the oligopolistic group and the reaction patterns of rivals to a change in price or output by a firm.

Another difficulty that arises from interdependence of oligopolistic firms is the *indeterminateness of the demand curves facing individual firms*. As has been stated earlier, because of the interdependence an oligopolistic firm cannot assume that its rival firms will keep their price and quantities constant when it makes changes in its price. When an oligopolistic firm changes its price, its rival firms will retaliate or react and change their prices which in turn would affect the demand for the product of the former firm. Therefore, an oligopolistic firm cannot have sure and definite demand curve, since it keeps shifting as the rivals change their prices in reaction to the price changes made by it. Moreover, there is quite uncertainty about the rivals' reactions to a price change by one firm. That is, when an oligopoly firm cuts its price, whether its rivals will also cut their prices similarly, or whether they will keep their prices unchanged. If they cut their prices, whether they will cut their prices by the same amount, or by a smaller or greater amount. A definite and determinate demand curve for a firm can be drawn if its rivals' prices remain unchanged or if it is known before hand that they will change their prices in a *certain particular way* in response to price changes by one firm. But under oligopoly there is no certainty about the reactions of the rivals to the price changes made by a firm. Hence the demand curve of an oligopolistic firm cannot be easily determined.

Now, when an oligopolist does not know the demand curve confronting him, what price and output he will fix cannot be ascertained by economic analysis. In other words, in view of the indeterminateness of demand curve for a firm under oligopoly, the solution for the determination of price and output under oligopoly cannot be provided by the economic theory. Under conditions of perfect competition, monopoly and monopolistic competition, an individual firm faces a determinate demand curve which has a corresponding definite marginal revenue curve. Then, on the basis of profit maximisation principle, the determinate solution for the price and output fixation under perfect competition, monopoly and monopolistic competition is found by the equality of marginal revenue with marginal cost. This solution cannot be applied to price and output determination under oligopoly

4. William J Baumol, *op. cit*, pp. 223–24.

without qualification or making some additional as assumptions because the individual firm's demand curve and therefore the marginal revenue curve is indeterminate or unknown. Thus even if profit maximisation assumption is considered as valid under conditions of oligopoly, no determinate solution for price-output fixation can be provided because of the indeterminateness of demand curve.

Even when the firms of an oligopoly do not enter into collusion, tacit or formal, or choose a leader from among themselves and instead try to compete with each other no single and simple solution is possible as to how a firm will fix its price and output. This is because of the uncertainty about the reaction patterns of the rivals to a move by one firm. This uncertainty about the reaction patterns of competitors poses a serious analytical difficulty in the way of providing a determinate solution for the oligopoly problem. Quoting Prof. Baumol again. "When a businessman wonders about his competitors' likely response to some move which he is considering, he must recognize that his competitors, too, are likely to take this interdependence phenomenon into account. The firms' attempts to outguess one another are then likely to lead to an *interplay of anticipated strategies and counterstrategies which is tangled beyond hope of direct analysis*."[5] Thus under oligopoly a firm is likely to imagine an infinite sequence of compounded hypotheses such as "If I make move A, he may consider making countermove B, but he may realise that I might then respond by making move C, in which case..., and so an *ad infinitum*."

Profit-Maximising Assumption Challenged in Case of Oligopoly

Again, a determinate solution to the price-output problem in other market forms (perfect competition, monopoly and monopolistic competition) is arrived at by assuming profit-maximising motive on the part of the firms. But some economists have challenged the validity of the profit-maximising hypothesis in oligopolistic situations. According to Prof. Rothschild, *oligopolists aim at maximising their security or achieving reasonable amount of stable profits* over a long period of time rather than maximising profits at a time.[6] On the other hand, Prof. Baumol thinks that in oligopolistic circumstances it is legitimate to assume *sales maximising objective* on the part of the firms.[7] Some other economists think that managers of oligopolistic firms maximise their own *utility function*. Still others like R.L. Morris think that firms try to maximise their *growth rate*. Finally, some economists assert that oligopolists do not maximise anything, they merely *satisfice*. In other words, they aim to obtain satisfactory profits rather than maximum profits. All this controversy about the real objective of the firms relates especially to the oligopolistic firms. This controversy about the most probable objective of the oligopolists further introduces indeterminacy in the analysis of price and output under oligopoly.

In view of above, there is no single determinate solution of the oligopoly problem but a wide variety of possible solutions, each depending upon different assumptions. It is worth noting as to what exactly economists mean by *indeterminacy*. When no single solution of a problem is possible, economists generally say that the problem has no determinate solution. Thus economists usually speak of indeterminacy where mathematicians would speak of a multiplicity of solutions. Prof. Fritz Machlup explains the meaning of indeterminancy as follows:

"In a general way, economists speak of indeterminacy if not enough information is available to give a safe and unambiguous answer to a question before them. If they wish to solve a problem—for example, how the price of a certain commodity will change under certain conditions—but find that the data which are assumed to be "given" *would permit of two or more (perhaps of an infinite number of)* answers, they will say that the problem has no determinate solution."[8]

5. *Op. cit.*, p. 224 (italics added)
6. See for Rothschild's view about security motive in chapter 22.
7. See for Baumol's view about sales maximization objective, chapter 30.
8. Fritz Machlup, The *Economics of Sellers' Competition,* p. 415 (italics added).

Various Approaches to Determination of Price and Output under Oligopoly

It may, however, be pointed out that in spite of what has been said above, economists have tried to provide a determinate solution to the oligopoly problem. But there is no any *single determinate solution, but a number of determinate solutions* depending upon different assumptions. The determinate solution to the oligopoly problem has been provided in the following ways.

Ignoring interdependence. First, for providing a determinate solution to the price-output determination, some economists have assumed that oligopolistic firms *ignore interdependence.* Now, when interdependence disappears from decision-making of the oligopolistic firms, the demand curve facing them becomes determinate and can be ascertained. With this, the standard analysis of the theory of the firm can be applied to provide a determinate solution for price and output problem of oligopoly. Classical models of duopoly put forward by Cournot and Bertrand fall in this category. In both those models, oligopolistic interdependence has been ignored. Cournot[9] in his famous model assumed that each oligopolistic firm would set its output in the belief that its rival firms output would remain constant. On the other hand, Bertrand[10] assumed that an oligopolistic firm would set its price in the belief that its rival firm would keep its price unchanged. But for providing a solution for price and output determination under oligopoly by ignoring the interdependence is a fundamentally mistaken approach. Rothschild rightly writes, "The determinate solution can be reached.... if it is assumed that the oligopolists do not take into account the éffect of their action on the policy of their rivals as in the famous Cournot and Bertrand's solutions; ...But this type of approach is absolutely valueless, because it only solves the oligopoly problem by removing from the analysis its most essential differentiating aspect: the oligopolists' consciousness of their interdependence."[11]

Predicting reaction pattern and counter-moves of rivals. The second approach to provide a determinate solution to the price and output problem of oligopoly is to assume that oligopolistic firm is able to *predict the reaction patterns and counter moves of his rivals*. In this approach various oligopoly models based on different assumptions regarding the particular reaction patterns have been propounded. Chamberlin[12] while recognizing that oligopolistic firms are conscious of their interdependence took some assumptions regarding the reaction pattern and provided a determinate solution according to which under duopoly or oligopoly, monopoly output and price are determined so that *profits of duopolists (oligopolists) are jointly maximised.* P.M. Sweezy and Oxford economists, Hall and Hitch, assumed that an oligopolist firm considers that while the price increase by it will not be followed by its rival firms, the price reduction will be matched by them. With such an assumption about the reaction pattern, demand curve facing an individual oligopolistic firm is of a kinked type with a kink at the current price. We shall discuss the kinked demand curve approach to oligopoly problem in detail later in this chapter. Many other economists assuming other reaction patterns have propounded various other oligopoly models.

Forming a collusion to maximise joint profits. The third approach to oligopoly problem assumes that oligopolistic firms, realising their interdependence, will pursue their common interest and will form a collusion, formal or tacit, that is, will enter into agreement and work in the pursuit of their common interest. They will maximise joint profits and share profits, market or output as agreed to between them. A variant of this approach is that firms in an oligopoly would accept one firm as a leader, which may be a dominant or low-cost firm, and they will follow their leader in the fixation of price of the product. Both the collusive and price leadership oligopoly models will be critically examined later in this chapter. In case of collusion and price leadership, the problem of indeterminateness of demand curve is not encountered.

---

9. A. Cournot, "*Researches into the Mathematical Principles of the Theory of Wealth*", translated by Nathaniel T. Bacon, the Macmillan Co., New York, 1897.
10. J. Bertrand, "Theorie Mathematique de la Richesse Sociale", *Journal des Savants*, Paris, September 1893.
11. K.W. Rothschild, "Price Theory and Oligopoly, *Economic Journal*," Vol. 57, 1947, reprinted in *Reading in Price Theory* (AEA).
12. E.H. Chamberlin, *The Theory of Monopolistic Competition*, chapter 3 and Appendix A.

Game theory approach to oligopoly. Another significant approach to the oligopoly is that of the *theory of games*, put forward by Neuman and Morgenstern. In the theory of games, an oligopolistic firm does not guess at its rivals' reaction pattern, but *calculates the optimal moves by rival firms*, that is, their best possible strategies and in view of that adopts its own policies and counter moves. The explanation of the application of the theory of games to the oligopoly problem is an advanced-level study and will not be discussed in this book.

From our above analysis it follows that there is no single determinate solution to the price-output fixation under oligopoly. As said above, economists have developed a large number of models by taking different assumptions regarding the behaviour of the oligopolistic group (that is, whether they will cooperate together or fight with each other), regarding the objective they seek to achieve (that is, whether they are assumed to maximise individual or joint profits or they are assumed to maximise security or sales), and regarding the *different reaction patterns* of rival firms to price and output changes by one firm.

COLLUSIVE OLIGOPOLY : CARTELS

In order to avoid uncertainty arising out of interdependence and to avoid price wars and cut throat competition, firms working under oligopolistic conditions often enter into agreement regarding a uniform price-output policy to be pursued by them. The agreement may be either formal (open) or tacit (secret). But since formal or open agreements to form monopolies are illegal in most countries, agreements reached between oligopolists are generally tacit or secret. When the firms enter into such collusive agreements formally or secretly, collusive oligopoly prevails. But collusions are of two main types: (*a*) cartels and (*b*) price leadership. In a cartel type of collusive oligopoly, firms jointly fix a price and output policy through agreements. But under price leadership one firm sets the price and others follow it. The one which sets the price is a price leader and the others who follow it are its followers. The follower firms adopt the price of the leader, even though they have to depart from their profit-maximising position, as they think that it is to their advantage not to compete with their leader and between themselves. In this present section we confine ourselves to explain the determination of price and output under the cartel type of collusive oligopoly and in the next section we will explain price and output determination under price-leadership form of collusive oligopoly.

Originally, the term 'cartel' was used for the agreement in which there existed a common sales agency which alone undertook the selling operations of all the firms that were party to the agreement. But now-a-days all types of formal or informal and tacit agreements reached among the oligopolistic firms of an industry are known as cartels. Since these cartels restrain competition among the member firms, their formations have been made illegal in some countries by the Governments passing laws against them. For instance, the formation of a cartel is illegal in U.S.A. under the Anti-Trust Laws passed there. However, in spite of the illegality of cartels they are still formed in U.S.A. through secret devices and by adopting some means or the other shrewd businessmen are able to evade the anti-monopoly laws.

Formal collusion or agreement among the oligopolists may itself take various forms. An extreme form of collusion is found when the member firms agree to surrender completely their rights of price and output determination to a 'Central Administrative Agency' so to secure maximum joint profits for them. Formation of such a formal collusion is generally designated as *perfect cartel*. Thus under perfect cartel type of collusive oligopoly, the price and output determination of the whole industry as well as of each member firm is determined by the common administrative authority so as to *achieve maximum joint profits for the member firms*.

The total profits are distributed among the member firms in a way already agreed between them. The share from total profits of each member firm is not necessarily in proportion to the output quota it has to supply and the cost it incurs on it. The output quota to be produced by each firm is decided by the central administrative authority in such a way that the total costs of the total output produced is minimum. In fact, under perfect cartel, the central authority determines the separate outputs to be produced by the various members and the price they have to charge in the same way as a monopolist operating multiple plants would do. Now, the question arises as to what outputs different firms in a cartel will be asked to produce so that the total cost is made minimum. Total cost will be minimised when the various firms in the cartel produce such separate outputs so that their marginal costs are equal. This is because if the marginal costs of the member firms are not equal, then the marginal units of output could be produced at a smaller cost by the firms with a lower marginal cost than by those with a higher marginal cost.

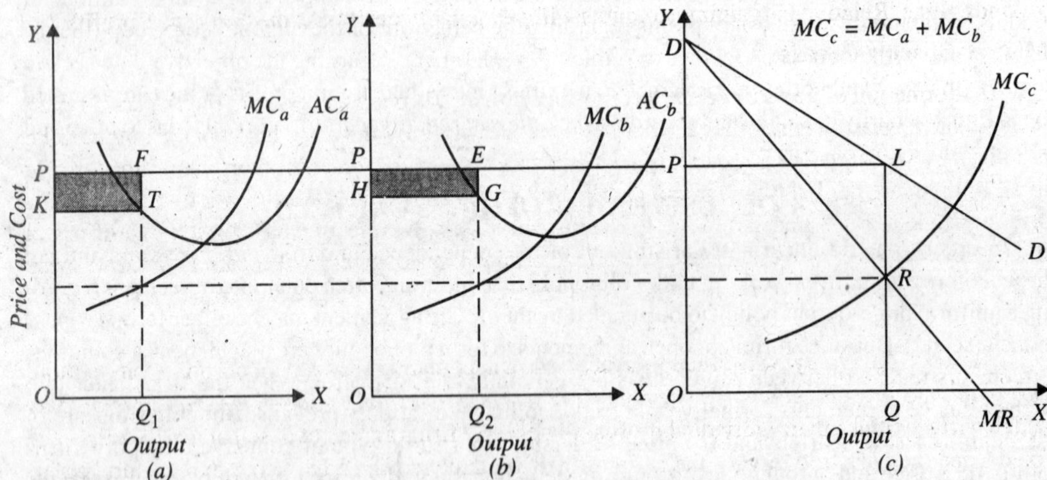

Fig. 29.1. *Price and Output Determiantion under Cartel : Joint Profit Maximization*

Let us now see how the cartel works and determines its price and output. Let us assume that two firms have formed a cartel by entering into an agreement. We assume that the *cartel will aim at maximising joint profits for the member firms*. First of all, the cartel will estimate the demand curve of the industry's product. As the demand curve facing a cartel will be the aggregate demand curve of the consumers of the product, it will be sloping downward as is shown by the curve *DD* in Fig. 29.1(*c*) Marginal revenue curve *MR* showing the addition to cartel's revenue for successive additions to its output and sales will lie below the demand curve *DD*. Cartel's marginal cost curve (MC_C) will be given by the horizontal addition of the marginal cost curves of the two firms. This has been done in Fig. 29.1(*c*) where MC_C curve has been obtained by adding horizontally marginal cost curves MC_a and MC_b of firms *A* and *B* respectively. It should be noted that cartel's marginal cost curve MC_c, obtained as it is by horizontal addition of marginal cost curves of the two firms, will indicate the minimum possible total cost of producing each industry output on it; each industry output being distributed among the two firms in such a way that their marginal costs are equal.

Now, the cartel will maximise its profits by fixing the industry's output at the level at which *MR* and *MC* curves of the cartel intersect each other. It will be seen in Fig. 29.1(*c*) that *MR* and *MC* curves cut each other at point *R* or output *OQ*. It will also be seen from the demand curve *DD* that the output *OQ* willdetermine price equal to *QL* or *OP*. Having decided the total output *OQ* to be produced, the cartel will allot output quota to be produced by each firm so that the marginal cost of each firm is the same. This can be known by drawing a horizontal straight line from point *R* towards the Y-axis. It will be seen from the figure that when firm *A* produces OQ_1 and firm *B* produces OQ_2, the marginal costs of the two firms are equal. The output quota of firm *A* will be OQ_1, and of firm *B* will be OQ_2. It is worth noting that the total output *OQ* will be equal to the sum of OQ_1 and OQ_2.

Thus, the determination of output *OQ* and price *OP* and the outputs OQ_1 and OQ_2 by the two firms *A* and *B* will ensure the maximum joint profits for the member firms constituting the cartel. It will be seen from Fig. 29.1(*a*) that with output *OQ* and cartel price *OP*, the profits made in firm *A* are equal to *PFTK* and with output OQ_2 and cartel price *OP* the profits made in firm *B* are equal to *PEGH*. The sum of the profits, that is, the joint profits made by the cartel will be maximum under the given demand and cost conditions as they have been arrived at as a result of equating combined marginal cost (MC_c) with the combined marginal revenue (*MR*). *The allocation of output quota to each of them is made on the grounds of minimissing cost and not as a basis for determining profit distribution.* Prof. J.S. Bain rightly says, "There is no particular reason for believing that the operating firms will retain just the profits resulting from the sale of their quotas, which are determined on cost grounds alone. Relative bargaining strengths will presumably determine the division of profits."[13]

Market -Sharing Cartels

The formation of perfect cartels, as described above, has been quite rare in the real world even where their formation is not illegal. In a perfect cartel not only the price but also the output to be produced by each member of a cartel is decided by a central management authority and profits made in all of them are pooled together and distributed among the members according to the terms of a prior agreement. But when cartels are loose, instead of being perfect, the distribution of profits and fixation of outputs of individual firms are not determined in a manner perfect cartel does. In a loose type of cartel the market-sharing by the firms occurs. Further, there are two methods of market sharing: non-price competition and quotas.

Market-Sharing by Non-Price Competition. Under market sharing by non-price competition, *only a uniform price is set and, the member firms are free to produce and sell the amount of outputs* which will maximise their individual profits. Though the firms agree not to sell at a price below the fixed price they are free to vary the style of their product and the advertising expenditure and to promote sales in other ways. That is, the price being a fixed datum, the firms compete on non-price basis. If the different member firms have identical costs, then the agreed uniform price will be the monopoly price which will ensure maximisation of joint profits. But when there are cost differences between the firms as is generally the case, the cartel price will be fixed by bargaining between the firms. The level of this price will be such as will ensure some profits to high-cost firms.

But with cost differences such loose cartels are quite unstable. This is because the low cost firms will have an incentive to cut price to increase their profits and therefore they will tend to break away from the cartel. However, they may not openly charge lower price than the fixed one and instead cheat the other firms by giving secret price concessions to the buyers. However, as the rivals gradually loose their customers, the cheating by the low-cost firms will be ultimately discovered and consequently open price war may commence and cartel breaks down.

Market-Sharing by Output Quota. The second type of market-sharing cartel is the agreement reached between the oligopolistic firms regarding quota of output to be produced and sold by each of them at the agreed price. If all firms are producing homogeneous product and have same costs, the monopoly solution (that is, the maximisation of joint profits) will emerge with the market being equally shared by them. However, when costs of member-firms are different, the different quotas for various firms will be fixed and therefore their market shares will differ. The quotas and market shares in case of cost differences are decided through bargaining between the firms. During the bargaining process, two criteria are usually adopted to fix the quotas of the firms. One is the past level of sales of the various firms and the second is the productive capacity of the firms. However, the 'past-period sales' and 'productive capacity' of various firms are not very firm criteria as they can be easily manipulated. Ultimately the quotas fixed for various firms depend upon their bargaining power and skill.

13. J.S. Bain, "*Pricing, Distribution and Employment*," 1953, p. 286.

The second common basis for the quota system and market sharing is the division of market regionwise, that is, the geographical division of the market between the cartel firms. In this arrangement, price and also style of the product of cartel firms may vary.

It is worth noting that all types of cartels are unstable when there exists cost differences between firms. The low cost firms always have a tendency to reduce price of the product to maximise their profits which ultimately results in the collapse of the collusive agreement. Further, if the entry of firms in the oligopolistic industry is free, the instability of the cartel is intensified. The new entrants may not join the cartel and may fix a lower price of the product to sell a large quantity. This may start a price war between the cartel firms and the new entrants. We thus see that the stability of the cartel arrangement is always in danger.

PRICE LEADERSHIP

As mentioned above, price leadership is an important form of collusive oligopoly. Under it, one firm sets the price, others follow it. Price leadership also comes into existence either through tacit or formal agreement. But as the formal or open agreement to establish price leadership are generally illegal, price leadership is generally established as a result of informal and tacit understanding between the oligopolists. The competing oligopolists in an informal meeting choose a leader and agree to follow him in setting price.

Types of Price Leadership

Price leadership is of various types. Firstly, there is a *price leadership by a low-cost firm.* In order to maximise profits the low-cost firm sets a lower price than the profit-maximizing price of the high-cost firms. Since the high-cost firms will not be able to sell their product at the higher price, they are forced to agree to the low price set by the low-cost firm. Of course, the low-cost price leader has to ensure that the price which he sets must yields some profits to the high-cost firms—their followers.

Secondly, there is a *price leadership of the dominant firm.* Under this one of the few firms in the industry may be producing a vary large proportion of the total production of the industry and may therefore dominate the market for the product. This dominant firm wields a great influence over the market for the product, while other firms are small and are incapable of making any impact on the market. As a result, the dominant firm estimates its own demand curve and fixes a price which maximises its own profits. The other firms which are small having no individual effects on the price, of the product, follow the dominant firm and accepting the price set by it and adjust their output accordingly.

Thirdly, there is a *barometric price leadership* under which an old, experienced, largest or most respected firm assumes the role of a custodian who protects the interests of all. He assesses the change in the market conditions with regard to the demand for the product, cost of production, competition from the related products etc. and makes changes in price which are best from the viewpoint of all the firms in the industry. Naturally, other firms follow him willingly.

Fourthly, there is *exploitative or aggressive price leadership* under which a very large or dominant firm establishes its leadership by following aggressive price policies and thus compel the other firms in the industry to follow him in respect of price. Such a firm will often initiate a move threatening to compete the others out of market if they do not follow him in setting their prices.

Price-Output Determination under Low-Cost Price Leadership

Economists have developed various models concerning price-output determination under price leadership making different assumptions about the behaviour of price leader and his followers. We shall first explain price-output determination under price leadership by a low-cost firm. In order to simplify our analysis we make the following assumptions:

(1) There a.e two firms, *A* and *B*. The firm *A* has a lower cost of production than firm *B*.

(2) The product produced by the two firms is homogeneous so that the consumers have no preference between them.

(3) Each of the two firms has equal share in the market. In other words, demand curve facing each firm will be the same and will be half of the total market demand curve of product.

Given the above assumptions, price and output determination under price leadership is illustrated in Fig. 29.2. Each firm is facing demand curve *Dd* which is half of the total market demand curve *DD* for the product. *MR* is the marginal revenue curve of each firm. AC_a and MC_a are the average and marginal cost curves of firm *A* and AC_b and MC_b are the average and marginal cost curves of firm *B*. Cost curves of firm *A* lie below the cost curves of firm *B* because we are assuming that firm *A* has a lower cost of production than firm *B*.

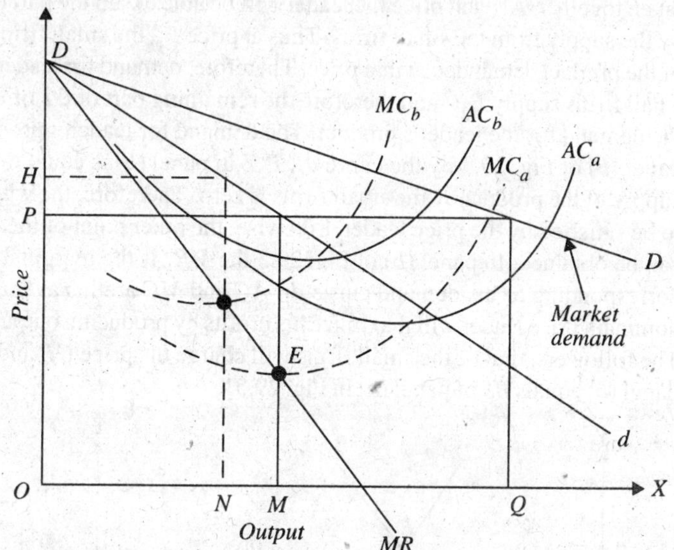

Fig. 29.2. *Price-Output Determination under Low-Cost Price Leadership*

The firm *A* will be maximising its profits by selling output *OM* and setting price *OP*, since at output *OM*, its marginal cost is equal to the marginal revenue. Firm *B*'s profits will be maximum when it fixes price *OH* and sells output *ON*. It will be seen from the figure that profit-maximising price *OP* of firm *A* is lower than the profit-maximising price *OH* of firm *B*. Since the two firms are producing a homogeneous product, they cannot charge two different prices. Because the profit-maximising price *OP* of firm *A* is lower than the profit-maximising price *OH* of firm *B*, firm *A* will dictate the price to the firm *B* or, in other words, firm *A* will win if there is price war between the two and will emerge as a price leader and firm *B* will be compelled to follow. Given these facts, the agreement reached between them, even though tacit it may be, will require that the firm *A* will act as the price leader and firm *B* as the price follower.

It should be noted that firm *B* after having accepted firm *A* as the price leader will actually charge price *OP* and produce and sell *OM*. This is because at price *OP*, it can sell *OM* output like firm *A* because the demand curve facing each firm is the same. Thus both the firms will charge the same price *OP* and sell the same amount (*OM*). Note that the total output of the two firms will be *OM* + *OM* = *OQ* which will be equal to the market demand for the good at price *OP*. But there is an important difference between the two. While firm *A*, the price leader, will be maximising its profits by selling output *OM* and charging price *OP*, the firm *B* will not be making maximum profits with this price-output combination because its profits are maximum at output *ON* and price *OH*. Profits earned by firm *B* by producing and selling output *OM* and charging price *OP* will be smaller than those of firm *A* because its costs are greater.

When the products of the price leader and his price-followers are differentiated, then the price charged by them will be different but the prices charged by the followers will be only slightly different either way from that of the price leader and they will conform to a definite pattern of differentials.

Price-Output Determination Under Price Leadership by the Dominant Firm

We now proceed to explain the determination of price and output when there exists price leadership by a dominant firm which is having a large share of the market with a number of small firms as followers each of which has a small share of the market. To explain this we assume that the dominant firm knows the total market demand curve for the product. Further, the dominant firm also knows the marginal cost curves of the smaller firms whose lateral summation yields the total supply of the product by the small firms at various prices. This implies that from his past experience the dominant firm can estimate fairly well the likely supply of the product by the small firms at various prices. With this information, the leader can obtain his demand curve. Consider panel (*a*) of Fig. 29.3 where *DD* is the market demand curve for the product S_m is the supply curve the product of all the small firms taken together. At each price the leader will be able to sell the part of the market demand not fulfilled by the supply from the small firms. Thus at price P_1, the small firms supply the whole of the quantity of the product demanded at that price. Therefore, demand for leader's product is zero. At price P_2, the small firms supply P_2C and therefore the remaining part of *CT* of the market demand will constitute the demand for the leader's product. The demand for leader's product has been separately shown in panel (*b*) of Fig. 29.3 by the curve d_L. P_2Z in panel (*b*) is equal to *C T* in panel (*a*). At price P_3, the supply of the product by the small firms is zero. Therefore, the whole market demand P_3U will have to be satisfied by the price leader. Likewise, the other point of the demand curve for the price leader can be obtained. In panel (*b*) of Fig. 29.3 the MR_L is the marginal revenue curve of the price leader corresponding to his demand curve d_L. *AC* and *MC* are his average and marginal cost curves. The dominant price leader will maximize his profits by producing output *OQ* (or *PH*) and setting price *OP*. The followers, that is, the small firms will charge the price *OP* and will together produce *PB*. [*PH* in panel (*b*) equals *BS* of panel (*a*) in Fig. 29.3].

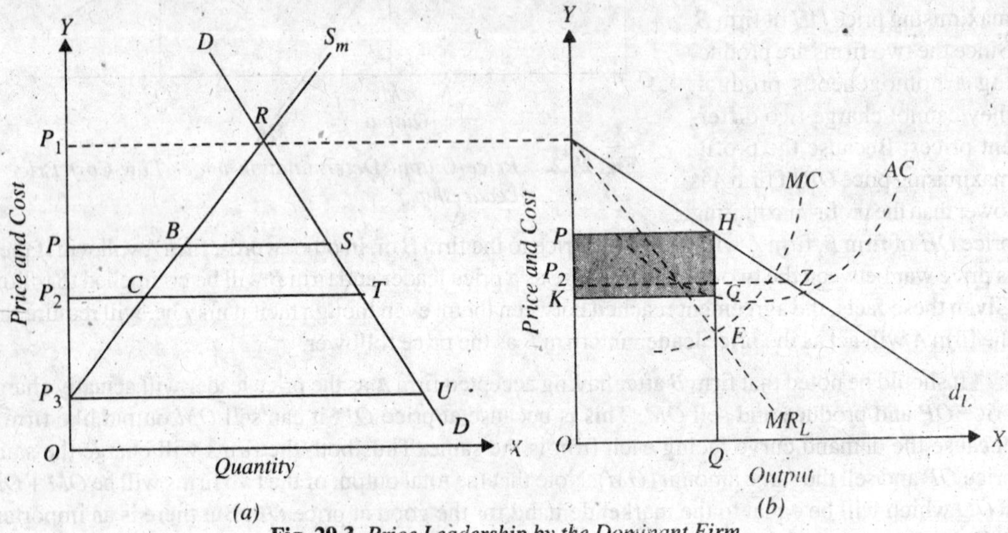

Fig. 29.3. *Price Leadership by the Dominant Firm*

It is worth noting that in order that profits of the leader are maximised it is not enough that followers should charge profit-maximizing price *OP* set by him, he will also have to ensure that they produce output *PB*. If the followers produce more or less than this, given the market demand *DD*, the leader will be pushed to a non-profit maximising position. This implies that if price-leadership is to remain, there must be some definite market-sharing agreement tacit though it may be.

Difficulties of Price Leadership

Price leadership involves many difficulties in the real world. First, the success of price leadership of a firm depends upon the correctness of his estimates about the reactions of his followers. If his estimates about the reactions of his rivals to price changes by it prove to be incorrect, then not only the success of his price policy but also his leadership in the market will be jeopardised. Secondly, when a price leader fixes a higher price than the followers would prefer, there is a strong tendency for the followers to make hidden price cuts in order to increase their shares of the market without openly challenging the price leader. A good number of devices which amount to secret price cutting are used by business firms. Some of these secret price-cutting devices are the offer of rebates, favourable credit terms, 'money back' guarantees, after-delivery free services, sale on the payment of price in easy installments with low rates of interest etc., and liberal entertainment of the buyers. Price leaders are generally fed up with the increasing number of concessions granted by their rivals and they make an open price cut to prevent further fall in their share of the market. In such circumstances price leadership becomes infructuous.

Another important difficulty of maintaining price leadership is the tendency on the part of the rivals to indulge in *non-price competition* to increase sales while go on charging the price set by the price leader. The devices used under 'non-price competition' include advertising and other methods of the sales promotion, like improvement of the quality of the product, in addition to the hidden price-product concessions mentioned above. While charging the same price, the rivals try to increase their share of the market by increasing the advertisement expenditure. As a result of this non-price competition, the price leader has also to adopt similar devices to prevent the fall in its sales or has to make outright cut in price in order to achieve his objective. In view of these facts, the price leader may not be able to maintain his leadership for a long time.

Further, there is a great limitation on the price leader to fix a high price of his product. This is because the high price will induce the rivals to make secret price cuts which will adversely affect the sales of the price leader. Moreover, a high price fixed by the price leader will attract new competitiors into the industry which may not accept his leadership. Lastly, differences in costs also pose a problem. If the price leader has higher costs, then the high price fixed by him will, as mentioned above, induce the rivals to undercut price or will attract the entry of new firms into the industry. If the price leader has lower costs than his rivals, he will set a low price which will antagonise his rivals who will disturb him quite frequently.

THE KINKED DEMAND CURVE THEORY OF OLIGOPOLY

It has been observed that many oligopolistic industries exhibit an appreciable degree of price rigidity or stability. In other words, in many oligopolistic industries prices remain sticky or inflexible, that is, there is no tendency on the part of the oligopolists to change the price even if the economic conditions undergo a change. Many explanations have been given of this price rigidity under oligopoly and most popular explanation is the so-called kinked demand curve hypothesis. The kinked demand curve hypothesis was put forward independently by Paul M. Sweezy[14], an American economist, and by Hall and Hitch[15], Oxford economists.

It is for explaining price and output *under oligopoly with product differentiation*, that economists often use the kinked demand curve hypothesis. This is because when under oligopoly products are differentiated, it is unlikely that when a firm raises its price, all customers would leave it because some customers are intimately attached to it due to product differentiation. As a result, demand curve facing a firm under differentiated oligopoly is not perfectly elastic. On the other hand, under oligopoly without product differentiation, when a firm raises its price, all its customers would leave it so that demand curve facing an oligopolist producing homogeneous product may be perfectly elastic. Further, under oligopoly without product differentiation, there is a greater tendency on

14. Paul M. Sweezy, "Demand under Conditions of Oligopoly", *Journal of Political Economy*, Vol. XLVIII, August 1939, reprinted in American Economics Association, *Readings in Price Theory*.
15. R.L. Hall and C.J. Hitch, "Price Theory and Business Behaviour" *Oxford Economic Papers*, No. 2, May, 1939.

the part of the firms to join together and form a collusion, formal or tacit, and, alternatively, to accept one of them as their leader in setting their price. No doubt, kinked demand curve has a special relevance for differentiated oligopoly, but it has also been applied for explaining price and output under oligopoly without product differentiation.

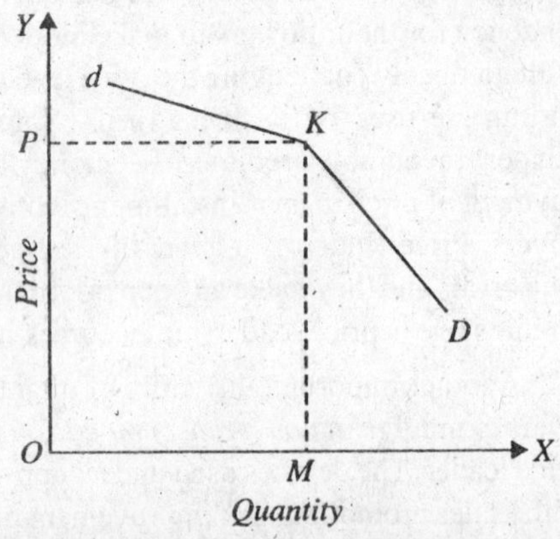

Fig. 29.4. *Kinked Demand Curve under Oligopoly*

The demand curve facing an oligopolist, according to the kinked demand curve hypothesis, has a 'kink' at the level of the prevailing price. The kink is formed at the prevailing price level because the segment of the demand curve above the prevailing price level is highly elastic and the segment of the demand curve below the prevailing price level is inelastic. A kinked demand curve *dD* with a kink at point *K* has been shown in Fig. 29.4. The prevailing price level is *OP* and the firm is producing and selling the output *OM*. Now, the upper segment *dK* of the demand curve *dD* is relatively elastic and the lower segment *KD* is relatively inelastic. This difference in elasticities is due to the particular competitive reaction pattern assumed by the kinked demand curve hypothesis.

The competitive reaction pattern assumed by the kinked demand curve oligopoly theory is as follows:

Each oligopolist believes that if he lowers the price below the prevailing level, his competitors will follow him and will accordingly lower their prices, whereas if he raises the price above the prevailing level, his competitors will not follow his increase in price.

In other words, each oligopolistic firm believes that though its rival firms will not match his increase in price above the prevailing level, they will indeed match its price cut. These two different types of reaction of the competitors to the increase in price on the one hand and to the reduction in price on the other make the portion of the demand curve above the prevailing price level relatively elastic and the lower portion of the demand curve relatively inelastic. This is explained below:

(*a*) **Price reduction.** If the oligopolist reduces its price below the prevailing price level *OP* in order to increase his sales, the competitors will fear that their customers would go away from them to buy the product from the former oligopolist which has made a price cut. Therefore, in order to retain their customers they will be forced quickly to match the price cut. Because of the competitors quickly following the reduction in price by an oligopolist, he will gain in sales only very little. (His sales will increase not at the expense of his competitors but because of the rise in total quantity demanded due to the reduction in price of the good. In fact each will gain in sales to the extent of a proportionate share in the increase in total demand). Very small increase in sales of an oligopolist following his reduction in price below the prevailing level means that the demand for him is inelastic below the prevailing price. Thus the segment *KD* of the demand curve in Fig. 29.4 which lies below the prevailing price *OP* is inelastic showing that very little increase in sales can be obtained by a reduction in price by an oligopolist.

(*b*) **Price increase.** If an oligopolist raises his price above the prevailing level, there will be a substantial reduction in his sales. This is because as a result of the rise in his price, his customers will withdraw from him and will go to his competitors who will welcome the new customers and will gain in sales. These happy competitors will have therefore no motivation to match the price rise. The oligopolist who raises his price will be able to retain only those customers who either have a strong preference for his product (if the products are differentiated) or who cannot obtain the desired quantity of the product from the competitors because of their limited productive capacity. Large reduction in sales following an increase in price above the prevailing level by an oligopolist means that demand with respect to increases in price above the existing one is highly elastic. Thus, in Fig. 29.4 the segment *dK* of the demand curve which lies above the current price level *OP* is elastic showing a large fall in sales if a producter raises his price.

It is now evident from above that each oligopolist finds himself placed in such a position that while, on the one hand, he expects his rivals to match his price cuts very quickly, he does not expect his rivals to match his price increases on the other. Given this expected competitive reaction pattern, each oligopolist will have a kinked demand curve *dKD* with the upper segment *dK* being relatively elastic and the lower segment *KD* being relatively inelastic.

Why Price Rigidity Under Oligopoly?

From what has been said above, it is easy to see why an oligopolist confronting a kinked demand curve will have no incentive to raise its price or to lower it. *Since the oligopolist will not gain a large share of the market by reducing his price below the prevailing level, and will have substantial reduction in sales by increasing his price above the prevailing level, he will be extremely reluctant to change the prevailing price*. In other words, each oligopolist will adhere to the prevailing price seeing no gain in changing it. Thus, rigid prices are explained in this way by the kinked demand curve theory. In Fig. 29.4, the prevailing price is *OP* at which kink is found in the demand curve *dKD*. The price *P* will tend to remain stable or rigid as every member of the oligopoly will not see any gain in lowering it or in increasing it. It should be noted that if the prevailing price *OP* is greater than average cost, more than normal profits will be made.

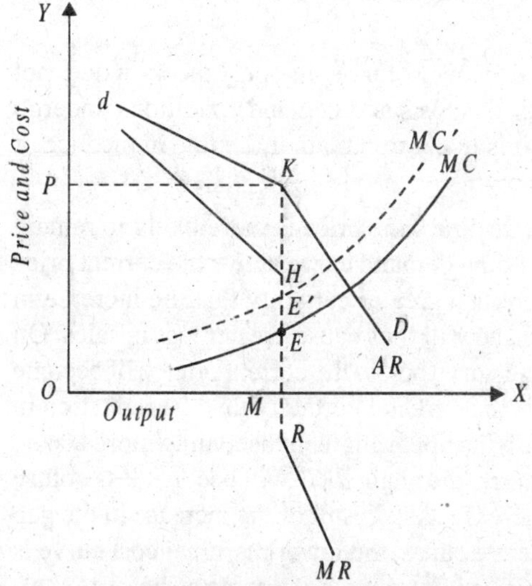

Fig. 29.5. *Changes in costs within limits do not affect the oligopoly price.*

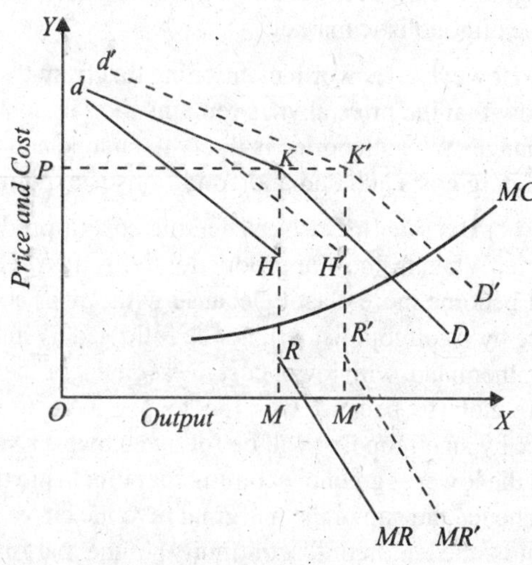

Fig. 29.6. *Changes in demand do not affect the oligopoly price.*

Further, it is worth mentioning that the oligopolist confronting a kinked demand curve will be maximising his profits at the current price level. For finding the profit-maximizing price-output combination, marginal revenue curve *MR* corresponding to the kinked demand curve *dKD* has been drawn. It is worth mentioning that the marginal revenue curve associated with a kinked demand curve is discontinuous, or in other words, it has a broken vertical portion. The length of the discontinuity depends upon the relative elasticities of two segments *dK* and *KD* of the demand curve at point *K*. The greater the difference in the two elasticities, the greater the length of the discontinuity. In Fig. 29.5 marginal revenue curve *MR* corresponding to the kinked demand curve *dKD* has been drawn which has a discontinuous portion or gap *HR*. Now, if the marginal cost curve of the oligopolist is such that it passes anywhere, say from point *E*, through the discontinuous portion *HR* of the marginal revenue curve *MR*, as shown in Fig. 29.5, the oligopolist will be maximizsing his profits at the prevailing price level *OP*, that is, he will be in equilibrium at point *E* or at the prevailing price *OP*. *Since the oligopolist is in equilibrium, or in other words, maximising his profits at the prevailing price level, he will have no incentive to change the price.*

Furthermore, even if there are changes in costs, the price will remain stable so long as the marginal cost curve passes through the gap *HR* in the marginal revenue curve. In Fig. 29.5 when the marginal cost curve shifts upward from *MC* to *MC′* (dotted) due to the rise in cost, the equilibrium price and output remain unchanged since the new marginal cost *MC′* also passes from point *E′* through the gap *HR*.

Likewise, the kinked demand curve theory explains that even when the demand conditions change, the price may remain stable. This is illustrated in Fig. 29.6 in which when the demand for the oligopolist increases from *dKD* to *d′K′D′*, the given marginal cost curve *MC* also cuts the new marginal revenue curve *MR′* within the gap. This means that the same price *OP* continues to prevail in the oligopolistic market.

However, it is worth mentioning that from the kinked demand curve oligopoly theory it does not follow that the price always remains the same whenever the costs and demand conditions undergo a change. When the price is likely to change and when it is likely to remain inflexible in the face of changing costs and demand conditions is explained below:

(1) **Decline in Costs.** When the cost of production declines, the price is more likely to remain stable. When the cost of production falls, then segment of the demand curve above the current price will become more elastic because with lower costs there is a greater certainty that the increase in price by an oligopolist will not be followed by his rivals and will thus cause greater loss in sales. On the other hand, with lower cost the segment of the demand curve below the current price will become more inelastic because with the decline in costs, there is then greater certainty that the reduction in price by an oligopolist will be followed by his rivals. With the upper segment becoming more elastic and the lower segment becoming more inelastic than before, the angle *dKD* will become less obtuse and hence the gap in the marginal revenue curve will increase. As a result of the increase in the gap (that is, the length of discontinuity) in the marginal revenue curve, the lower marginal cost curve is likely to pass through this gap showing that the price and output remain the same as before.

(2) **Rise in Cost.** *If there is a rise in the cost of the oligopolistic industry, the price is not likely to stay rigid.* When there is a rise in cost of industry an oligopolist can reasonably expect that his increase in price will be followed by the others in the industry. Consequently, the segment of the demand curve above the prevailing price will become less elastic and thereby make the angle *dKD* more obtuse and this will narrow down the gap in the marginal revenue curve. With the smaller gap in the marginal revenue curve, the *higher marginal cost curve is likely to cut it above the upper point H* indicating that the equilibrium price will rise and the equilibrium output will fall. Thus it follows from the kinked demand curve theory that price is not likely to remain stable in the event of rise in cost.

(3) **Decrease in Demand.** In case of decrease in demand, the price is very likely to remain inflexible and will not fall. When the demand decreases, it becomes more certain that if one oligopolist initiates the reduction in price, others will follow with the result that the lower segment of the demand curve will become more inelastic. On the other hand, in the face of a decline in demand it is very certain that the increase in price by one oligopolist will never be followed by others. As a result, the upper segment of the demand curve becomes more elastic, that is, it becomes more nearly horizontal. With the increase in the elasticity of the upper segment and the decrease in the elasticity of the lower segment, the gap in the marginal revenue curve becomes wider and there it is most likely

that the given marginal cost curve will cross the marginal revenue curve inside the gap when the demand curve *dKD* shifts downward. This indicates that the price will remain unchanged in the case of decrease in demand.

(4) **Increase in Demand.** *When the demand increases, the price is unlikely to remain stable, instead the price is likely to rise*. In the event of increase in demand, an oligopolist can expect that if he initiates the increase in price, his competitors will most probably follow him. Therefore, the upper segment *dK* of the demand curve will become less elastic and the angle *dKD* will become more obtuse. As a result, the gap *HR* in the marginal revenue curve will decrease and if this gap decreases much, it is very likely that the marginal cost curve crosses the marginal revenue curve above the upper point *H*, that is, above the gap, indicating that the price will rise above *OP*.

From above, it is clear that the kinked demand curve analysis of oligopoly explains stability in price in the face of falling costs or declining demand, whereas, price are likely to rise when either the costs rise or demand increases. M.M. Bober, thus rightly writes:

"The kinky demand curve analysis points to the likelihood of price rigidity in oligopoly when a price reduction is in order and of price flexibility when conditions warrant a rise in price. There is hardly any disposition to lower the price when there is decline in demand or in costs, but the price may be raised in response to increased demand or to rising cost."[16]

Critical Apprisal of Kinked Demand Curve Theory

1. We saw above how the kinked demand curve theory of oligopoly provides an explanation of price rigidity under oligopoly. But there is a major drawback in the theory. It only explains why once an oligopoly price has been determined it would remain rigid or stable, *it does not explain how the price has been determined.* There is nothing in the kinked demand theory which explains how the price which is prevailing is determined. In other words, whereas this theory shows why price tends to stay where it is, it tells us nothing about why the price is where it is. In Fig. 29.4 the kink occurs at the price *OP* because *OP* happens to be the prevailing or established price. The theory does not explain how the price got to be equal to *OP*. Commenting upon kinked demand curve theory Prof. Silberston rightly writes, "The most interesting question is not 'why are prices sticky in the short run?' (if they are), but who decides what the price is to be and on what principles."[17]

However, it may be mentioned that the above criticism applies especially to P.M. Sweezy's version of the kinked demand curve analysis. Hall and Hitch's version of kinked demand curve analysis also explains the determination of oligopoly price. According to Hall and Hitch, equilibrium price is determined by average cost (including normal profits), that is, by the tangency between average cost curve and the demand curve, as shown in Fig. 29.7. However, Hall and Htch version runs into difficulty when the average cost curve of the various firms in an oligopolistic industry are different.

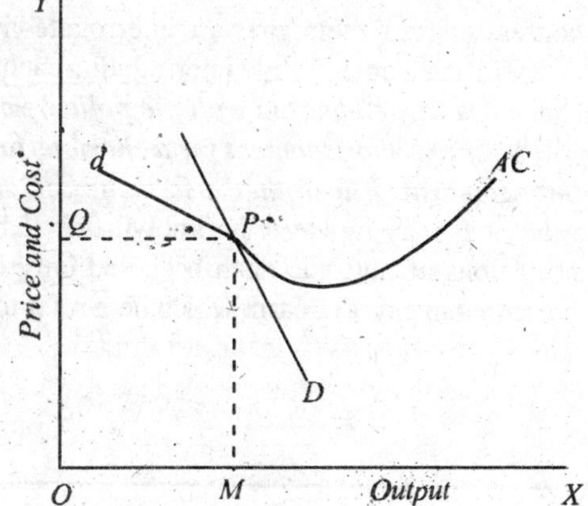

Fig. 29.7. *Full-Cost Pricing and Kinked Demand Curve.*

2. Another shortcoming of the kinked-demand oligopoly theory is that it does not apply to the oligopoly cases of prices leadership and price cartels which account for quite a large part of the oligopolistic markets. When price leadership and price cartels exist in oligopolistic markets there is concerted behaviour in regard to the price changes and

16. M.M. Bober, *Intermediate Price and Income Theory.*
17. Aubrey Silberston, Price Behaviour of Firms, *Economic Journal*, September 1970.

hence there is no kink in the demand curve in these cases.

3. Finally, even in the case of pure oligopoly (*i.e.* oligopoly with homogenous products), the kinked demand curve theory does not furnish a complete explanation for price rigidity observed in oligopolistic markets. As explained earlier, from the kinked demand curve analsysis it follows that prices are likely to remain stable when demand or cost conditions decrease, whereas under pure oligopoly prices are likely to rise in the case of increase in cost or demand.

4. Finally, it has been rightly asserted that explanation of price stability by Sweezy's kinked demand curve theory applies only to depression periods. In periods of depression, demand for the products decreases. As has been explained above, in the context of decreased demand, price in kinked demand curve theory is likely to remain sticky. But in periods of boom and inflation when the demand for the product is high and increasing, the price is likely to rise rather than remaining stable.

We, therefore, conclude that from Sweezy as well as Hall and Hitch's versions of kinked demand curve, it follows that prices are likely to remain stable during depression periods but not during boom and inflationary periods. Our analysis shows that whether we use kinked demand curve of the type postulated by Sweezy, or Hall and Hitch prices are unlikely to be stable during the boom periods.

PRISONERS' DILEMMA AND OLIGOPOLY THEORY

The Prisoners' Dilemma

The firms working in oligopolistic markets make decisions in face of uncertainty about how their rivals will react to their moves. The game theory is a mathematical technique of analaysing the behaviour of rival firms with regard to changes in price, output and advertisement expenditure in the situations of conflicts of interest among individuals or firms. An important game model that has significant implications for the behaviour of the oligopolists is popularly known as prisoner's dilemma. Model of prisoner's dilemma explains how rivals behaving selfishly act contrary to their mutual or common interests. We first explain prisoner's dilemma with the examples which was originally given while propounding this model.

Suppose two persons, Billa and Ranga, have been caught for committing a bank robbery. Suppose the prosecution has no enough evidence for their committing the crime. In order to procure confession from them, they are interrogated in two separate rooms so that they could not communicate with each other. While interrogating each accused, the police offers to Billa *"If you confess to the crime (that is, cooperate with the police) while the other keeps silent (i.e., does not confess) you will be given imprisonment for a short period, say, 1 year only but punish the other with 10 years imprisonment. If the other also confesses, then both of the you would be sentenced to jail for 5 years."* It may however be known that if both prisoners do not confess, then according to the provisions of law, each can be jailed only for two years. The choices open to each accused are presented in payoff matrix which here refer to years of imprisonment.

TABLE 29.1

Prisoners' Dilemma

		Ranga's Choice	
		Confesses	Doesn't confess
Billa's Choice :	Confesses	Ranga : 5 years Billa : 5 years	Ranga : 10 years Billa : 1 year
	Doesn't confess	Ranga : 1 year Billa : 10 years	Ranga : 2 years Billa : 2 years

It will be seen from the payoff matrix that the outcome (*i.e.*, length of sentences to each) is determined by the specific strategy, (that is, choice) adopted by each prisoner. The two strategies (choices) refer to (*i*) confesses and (*ii*) does not confess. If both Ranga and Billa confess, each gets 5 years imprisonment. If one confesses, but the other does not, the one who confesses (*i.e.*, cooperate with the police) gets a very light punishment, namely, imprisonment for 1 years only, and the one who does confess is sentenced for 10 years imprisonment. It will be further seen from the table that if both don't confess (that is, they remain loyal and faithful to each other and do not cooperate with the police), both are sentenced to 2 years imprisonment.

Now, each prisoner faces an uncertain situation regarding how the other person will behave, that is, whether or not he will confess. Though each person has to make an independent choice whether to confess or not but the outcome, *i.e.*, payoff depends on what the other does.

Now, under these circumstances what choice will be made by the prisoners when they cannot communicate with each other and have to choose between the two alternatives independently. *The model of prisoners' dilemma suggest that both behaving selfishly and working in self-interest will confess to the crime and cheat each other.* Since both confess, each will get imprisonment for 5 years. Why do they make this choice and confess can be shown as under. Take Ranga first. Most probably, he would confess when he does not know how his co-accused will act. Ranga would reason like this. If I do not confess it is very likely that I will be imprisoned for 10 years as the other prisoner will most probably confess. If I confess, I will get 5 years imprisonment if the other one also confesses and only one year imprisonment even if he does not confess. So in the presence of uncertainty about the other prisoner's choice, and behaving in self-interest, Ranga is likely to confess. Billa too reasoning similarly would confess. As a result, both prisoners confess and therefore would be sentenced for 5 years, though they would have received a light sentence of only two years if they had not confessed and remained loyal to each other. However, it is self-interest which leads each prisoner to confess and prevents them from attaining the best solution for themselves (2 years imprisonment) if both do not confess to the crime and remain loyal to each other. *But the decision of each prisoner in favour of confession is quite rational because each person works in self-interest and tries to make the "best" of the "worse outcomes" in an uncertain situation.*

Prisoners' Dilemma and Oligopolistic Behaviour : Instability of a Carter

The game of prisoner's dilemma is of important relevance to the oligopoly theory. The incentive to cheat by a member of a cartel (*i.e.*, in the model of collusive oligopoly) and eventual collapse of cartel agreement is better explained with the model of prisoner's dilemma. Instead of two prisoners we take the two firms *A* and *B* which have entered into a cartel agreement and have fixed the price of the product each has to charge and output each has to produce and sell (*i.e.*, share of the market). The choice problem facing each member firm of the cartel is whether to cooperate and abide by the

TABLE 29.2

Payoff Matrix for Cartel Members

		Firm *A*	
		Cheat	Cooperate
Firm *B*	Cheat (lower the price)	*A* : 5 lakhs *B* : 5 lakhs	*A* : 2 lakhs *B* : 25 lakhs
	Cooperate	*A* : 25 lakhs *B* : 2 lakhs	*A* : 15 lakhs *B* : 15 lakhs

agreement and thus sharing the joint monopoly profits or to cheat the other and try to make higher individual profits. But if both cheat and violate the agreement, the cartel would break down and profits would fall to the competitive level. We will show that though both would lose by cheating others but as seen in case of prisoner's dilemma their selfish behavior would lead them to cheat others. The payoff matrix for two member firms of a cartel from the various combination of choices to be made by them is presented in Table 29.2.

It will be seen from the above payoff matrix, that if both firms cooperate and abide by cartel agreement, they share monopoly profits; 15 lakhs to each of them (right hand bottom). If both firms cheat and thus violate the agreement, profits to each firm fall to the competitive level, Rs. 5 lakh to each firm (left hand top). If firm *A* cheats, while firm *B* cooperates, *B*'s profits drop to low level of Rs. 2 lakh and *A*'s profits rise to Rs. 25 lakhs (left hand bottom). On the other hand, if firm *B* cheats and firm *A* adheres to the agreement, profits of *A* declines to Rs. 2 lakh and *B*'s profits shoot up to Rs. 25 lakhs (left hand top).

It is evident from the payoff from the different choices that each firm has a strong incentive to cheat. Under the prevailing circumstances. *A*'s best strategy is to cheat, rather than cooperate. The same is true for firm *B* whose best strategy is also to cheat. Again, *it is the pursuit of self-interest rather than common interest that prompts the firms to cheat each other.* Thus, both firms will cheat and this will bring about the break down of the cartel.

Graphical illustration. The strong incentive to cheat on the part of cartel members and consequently causing a break-down of a cartel is graphically illustrated in Fig. 29.8, where *DD* is market demand curve facing the cartel consisting of two firms *A* and *B*. MC_a in panel (*i*) is the marginal cost curve of the firm *A*. Summing up horizontally marginal cost curves of the two firms forming a cartel we get the combined marginal cost curve MC_{a+b}. The cartel maximises its profits by equating *MR* with MC_{a+b} and accordingly output *OQ* and price *OP* are fixed. The output share of each firm will be fixed where marginal cost of each firm equals the combined marginal cost of the cartel members. Accordingly, the output share of firm *A* shown in panel (*i*) is Oq_a at which marginal cost of firm *A* equals the combined marginal cost *OT* or *QE* in the equilibrium situation. Oq_a will be the agreed share of output of firm *A*. To simplify our analysis we have not shown the cost situation of firm *B*, the other member of the cartel.

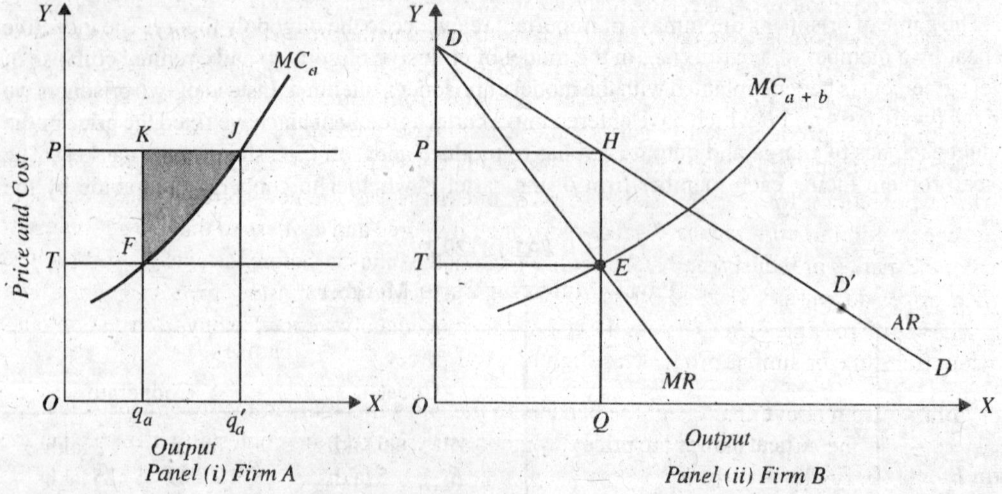

Fig. 29.8. *Instability of a Cartel Due to Cheating by a Member*

Thus, under the cartel agreement, firm *A* will be producing Oq_a, and charging price *OP*. Now, a glance at panel (*i*) in Fig. 29.8, reveals that given the price *OP*, fixed by the cartel, if the firm *A* increases its output from agreed share Oq_a to Oq'_a, it can increase its profits by the shaded area *FKJ* This means that in order to increase its profits the firm *A* will have incentive to cheat by trying to produce and sell more at the agreed price *OP*. Similarly, the firm *B*, other member of the cartel (not shown in Fig. 29.8) will also find that it can increase its profits by violating the cartel agreement by producing and selling more than its agreed output share. To sum up, *it is due to the promotion of self-interest by cartel members that accounts for the instability of cartel arrangements and frequent price wars.*

THE THEORY OF CONTESTABLE MARKETS

Baumol, Panzor and Willing have developed a new theory of markets known as the theory of contestable markets. According to this theory, even when there prevail monopoly and oligopoly in the product markets, the firms may find it most profitable to behave in setting price of its product as if they were working in a perfectly competitive market. This is because a firm thinks that if it sets a price higher than competitive market, other firms will enter the market and compete for the customers and thereby push down the price. Hence, the threat of new entrants in the markets forces the existing firm or firms to charge no more than the competitive price and therefore make only normal profits.

Important conditions for contestable markets to prevail are :

1. The new firms can enter the market with the same cost conditions as the existing firm or firms. If the existing firm enjoys some cost advantage as compared to the potential entrants in the market, then the new firms that enter the market cannot succeed in competing with the existing one which can afford to lower the price and inflict losses on the new entrants.
2. The second condition for the contestable markets is that firms should be able to leave or exit the market (*i.e.* industry) without incurring any capital loss. If the production in an industry involves much capital investment which is specific to that industry and therefore of no use elsewhere, leaving the industry will entail losses equal to the sunk costs. Recall that *sunk costs are the costs incurred on capital assets which are specific to an industry and cannot be recovered by selling them or which cannot be deployed or used elsewhere for commercial or production purposes.* Sunk costs act as an important barrier to the entry of new firms and are therefore deterrant to the existence of contestable markets.
3. The third condition for contestable markets to exist is that the potential entrants must be at no disadvantage as compared to the existing firms with regard to the *production technology or product quality as perceived by the consumers.* Any lack of access to the same production technology as used by the existing firms prevents the new entrants from competing the existing firms on the basis of cost or product quality. This would work to reduce the threat by potential entrants and enable the existing firms to charge higher than competitive price and earn supernormal profits.
4. The last condition for the contestable markets to exist is that the new entrants must be able to engage in **'hit and run'** tactics. That is, entry should be free and costless so that the new entrants enter the market or industry and make profits and exit the industry before the existing firms adjust their prices downward. Hit and run tactics can succeed when the existing firms can adjust their prices with some time - lags whereas the consumers immediately respond to buy from new entrants who offer same or similar products at slightly lower prices.

It follows from above that fewer the barriers to the entry in a market, the more contestable the market is. So to the extent monopolistic and oligopolistic markets are contestable depends on the barriers to the entry of new firms into a market or industry.

---

1. See William J. Baumol, John C. Panzar and Robert D. Willing, *Contestable Markets and the Theory of Industrial Structure,* (New York : Harcourt, Brace, Jovanorich, 1982)

When there are absolutely no barriers to the entry of new firms, the perfectly contestable markets would exist even though the existing firms may be working in monopolistic or oligopolistic market structures. In perfectly contestable markets, the existing firms are forced to keep their prices equal to average cost and therefore make only normal profits.

Price setting in a contestable market is illustrated in Figure 29.9 Suppose there are two firms in an industry, that is, there is duopoly in the product market. *DD* is the demand curve for the industry's product. The average and marginal cost curves of each firm are shown. The threat of entry of new firms leads each duopolist to charge a price *OP* (which is equal to their minimum average cost) and produces output equal to *Oq*. The total output *OQ* will be equal to two times *Oq*. (That is $OQ = 2Oq$). Each firm earns zero economic profits.

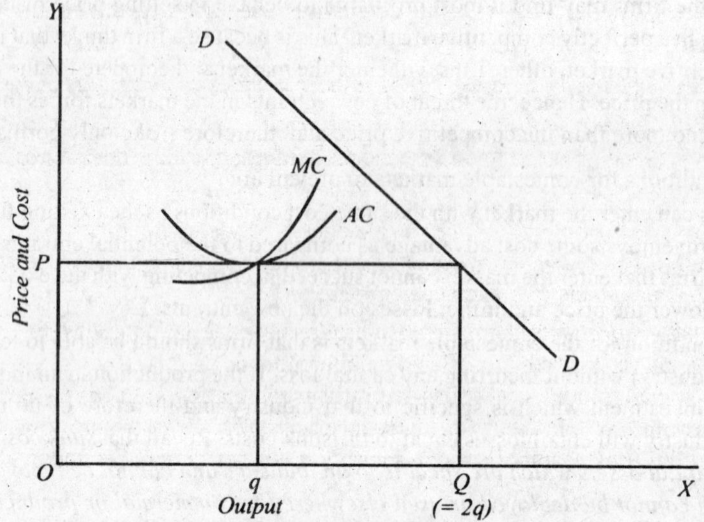

Fig. 29.9 *A Constestable Market : The threat of potential entrants leads the duopolists to behave like competitors.*

Though the two firms can enter into tacit collusion and push up the price and earn supernormal profits, they do not do so because they think new entrants will enter industry quickly and undercut price and in this way inflict losses on them. To prevent entry of new firms and avoid competiting with them each duopolist produces *OQ* output and charges *OP* price. By producing at the lowest minimum average cost they are able to enjoy all the economies of scale. Thus, in producing the level of output at the minimum average cost and charging a price equal to it, the two firms behave like a perfectly competitive firm.

The theory of contestable markets has been criticised, among others by Shepherd who points out that it is based on extremely unrealistic assumptions regarding entry and exit of new firms. According to him, in the real world entry is not free and exit is not costless. He contends that most monopolistic and oligopolistic markets are not contestable because there exist a good amount of sunk costs in most of the industries. These sunk costs act a barrier to the entry of potential entrants as they cannot exit the market without much loss. Because some of the investment involves sunk cost, the new competitors would have to set a price high enough to cover all their costs, whereas the existing firm could set a slightly lower price and make more than normal profits.

To conclude, the threat of new entrants can lead to the the existing monopolists and oligopolists to behave like a competitive firm in some situations but when there exist substantial sunk investment

2. William G. Shepherd, Contestability vs Competition, *American Economic Review*, Sep. 1984, pp. 572–587.

costs, the existing firms have an edge over the new entrants and charge higher than competitive price and make large supernormal profits. We thus see that contestable market theory does not apply to all monopolistic and oligopolistic market situations.

QUESTIONS AND PROBLEMS FOR REVIEW

1. What is oligopoly ? Explain the important features of oligopoly. Do you think price and output under oligopoly is indeterminate?
2. There is no unique solution to the problem of determination of price and output under oligopoly. Discuss.
3. What is Collusive Oligopoly ? How are price and output determined under it?
4. What is Cartel ? Explain how a cartel determines price and output of a product to maximise joint profits. *D.U., B. Com (Hons.) 2006*
5. Why are cartels generally unstable ? Why is there a tendency on the part of members of cartels to cheat ?
6. Explain Sweezy's kinked demand curve model of oligopoly. How does it explain price rigidity under oligopoly ?
7. What is non-price competition ? What role does it play in oligopolistic market situation ? [**Hints** : Selling costs (*e.g.*, advertisement expenditure etc.) and product variation by the firms are two important forms of non-price competition.]
8. What alternative objectives to profit maximisation have been proposed which the firms working under oligopoly seek to achieve? Briefly explain them.
   [**Hints** : Three alternative objectives to profit maximization are : (*a*) to seek normal profits which is assumed in the theory of mark-up pricing (*b*) sales maximisation which has been emphasised by Prof. Baumol and (*c*) security motive or to achieve maximum profits in the long run.]
9. What are the different types of price leadership that may be established in oligopolistic market situation ? Assuming that there are two firms producing homogeneous products explain how price and output are determined where there is price leadership by the lower cost firm.
10. Explain determination of price and output under price leadership of the dominant firm *D.U., B. Com (Hons.) 2006*
11. Explain determination of price and output under price leadership when the two firms have :
    (*a*) equal market share
    (*b*) unequal market share.
12. *What is kinked demand curve ? How does it help in explaining price rigidity under oligopoly?* *D.U. B.A(Hons.)*
13. What is kinked demand curve ? How does the kinked demand curve hypothesis explain price stability under oligopoly. *D.U. B. Com. (Hons.), 2006*
14. Using the kinked demand curve model explain how the increase and reduction in marginal cost need not lead to any change in price or output. *D.U. B.A. (Hons.), 1993, 1997*
15. What is meant by price rigidity ? Why are prices rigid under oligopoly ? Explain with the help of a model. *D.U. B.Com. (Hons.)* 1998, 1999
16. Can a kinked demand curve arise in a duopoly market with homogeneous products ? If so what would be the equilibrium price and output ? *D.U. B.A (Hons.)*, 1991

17. What is prisoner's dilemma ? How does it help.to explain the likelihood of firms opting for sub-optimal solution in oligopoly ? *B.Com. (Hons.) D.U.* 2002

18. What are the chief difficulties of maintaining price leadership in oligopolistic market situation? Examine the view that price leadership is likely to break down as there is generally a tendency on the part of the rival firms to indulge in *non-price competition* to promote their sales.

19. What is meant by interdependence of firms in oligopoly ? How does it affect price-output equilibrium of a firm ?

20. Explain briefly the various approaches that have been offered to explain the determination of price and output under oligopoly.

21. Which of the following statements are true and which false?
    (*a*) Interdependence of firms is an important feature of an oligopolistic market.
    (*b*) Advertisement expenditure does not play any role in an oligopolistic market.
    (*c*) Firms working in oligopolistic market have kinked demand curve.
    (*d*) Demand curve facing a firm working in an oligopolistic market is indeterminate.
    (*e*) There is no unique solution to the determination of price and output under oligopoly.
    (*f*) Price rigidity is one of the features of oligopoly.
    (*g*) It is the pursuit of self-interest by members that is often responsible for break-down of a cartel.

    [**Hint.** (*a*) Correct. (*b*) Incorrect. (*c*) Correct (according to the kinked demand curve theory) (*d*) Correct. (*e*) Correct. (*f*) Correct. (*g*) Correct.]0

22. An oligopolistic firm suspects that if it cuts price, its rivals will follow suit. How will this action on the part of the rivals affect the elasticity of demand curve facing the firm?
    (*a*) It will make the firm's demand curve more elastic.
    (*b*) It will make the firms demand curve less elastic.
    (*c*) It will not affect the elasticity of firm's demand curve.
    (*Which is correct answer and Why*?) *D.U. B.A. (Hons.)* 1989

23. Explain Prisoner's dilemma. How does it help to explain that cartels are quite unstable ?

24. (*a*) Use the prisoner's dilemma to show why firms attempt to form cartels and yet cheat.
    (*b*) How does a cartel determine the joint profit maximising quantity and allocate it among the firms. *D.U. B.Com (Hons.) 2004*

25. Why has OPEC oil cartel succeeded in raising price substantially ? What conditions are essential for successful cartelization. *D.U., B. Com (Hons.) 2006, 2008, 2009*

APPENDIX TO CHAPTER 29

Cournot's, Chamberlin Stachelberg and Models of Oligopoly

In this appendix we will discuss two important models of oligopoly. A model of oligopoly was first of all put forward by Cournot a French economist, in 1838. Cournot's model of oligopoly is one of the oldest theories of the behaviour of the individual firm and relates to non-collusive oligopoly. In Cournot model it is assumed that an oligopolist thinks that his rival will keep their output fixed regardless of what he might do. That is, each oligopolist does not take into account the possible reactions of his rivals in response to his actions.

Another important model of non-collusive oligopoly which we will discuss below was put forward by E.H. Chamberlin in his famous work *"The Theory of Monopolistic Competition"*. Chamberlin made an important improvement over the classical models of oligopoly, including that of Cournot. In sharp contrast to Cournot and other classical models Chamberlin assumes in his model that oligopoly firms recognise their inter-dependence while fixing their output and price. Through his model Chamberlin arrives at a monopoly solution of pricing and output under oligopoly wherein oligopolistic firms in an industry *jointly maximise their profits.*

COURNOT'S DUOPOLY MODEL

As said above, Augustin Cournot, a French economist, published his theory of duopoly in 1838. But it remained almost unnoticed until 1880's when Walras called the attention of the economists to Cournot's work. Cournot dealt with the case of duopoly. Let us first state the assumptions which are made by Cournot in his analysis of price and output under duopoly. First, Cournot takes the case of two identical mineral springs operated by two owners who are selling the mineral water in the same market. Their waters are identical. Therefore, *his model relates to the duopoly with homogeneous products.* Secondly, it is assumed by Cournot, for the sake of simplicity, that the owners operate mineral springs and sell water without incurring any cost of production. Thus, in Cournot's model, cost of production is taken as zero; only the demand side of the market is analysed. It may be noted that the assumption of zero cost of production is made only to simplify the analysis. His model can be presented when cost of production is positive. Thirdly, the duopolists fully know the market demand for the mineral water; they can see every point on the demand curve. Moreover, the market demand for the product is assumed to be linear, that is, market demand curve facing the two producers is a straight line.

Lastly, Cournot assumes that *each duopolist believes that regardless of his actions and their effect upon market price of the product, the rival firm will keep its output constant,* that is, it will go on producing the same amount of output which it is presently producing. In other words, the duopolist will decide about the amount of output which is most profitable for him to produce in the light of his rival's *present* output and assumes that it will remain constant. In other words, for determining the output to be produced, he will not take into account reactions of his rival in response to his variation in output and thus decides its level of output *independently.*

Cournot's Approach to Equilibrium of the Duopolists

Suppose the demand curve confronting the two producers of the mineral water is the straight line *MD* as shown in Fig. 29A.1. Further suppose that *ON* = *ND* is the maximum daily output of each mineral spring. Thus, the total output of both the springs is $OD = ON + ND$. It will be seen from the figure that when the total output OD of both the springs is offered for sale in the market, the price will be zero. It may be noted here that if there was a perfect competition, the long-run equilibrium price would have been zero and actual output produced equal to OD. This is because cost of production being assumed to be zero, price must also be zero so as to provide a zero profit long-run equilibrium under perfect competition.

Assume for the moment that one producer A of the mineral water starts the business first. Thus, to begin with he will be the monopolist. He will then produce daily ON output because his profits will be maximum at output ON' and will be equal to $ONKP$ (since the costs are zero, the whole of total revenue $ONKP$ will represent profits). The price which that producer will charge will be OP. Suppose now that the owner of the other spring enters into the business and starts operating his spring. This new producer B sees that the former producer A is producing ON amount of output. According to the assumption made by Cournot, the producer B believes that the former producer A will continue producing $ON (= \frac{1}{2} OD)$ amount of output, regardless of what output he himself decides to produce. Given this belief, the best that the new producer B can do is to regard segment KD as the demand curve confronting him. With his demand curve KD, and corresponding marginal revenue curve MR_B, the producer B will produce $NH (= \frac{1}{2} ND)$ amount of output. The total output will now be $ON + NH = OH$, and as a result the price will fall to OP' or HL per unit. The total profits made by the two producers will be $OHLP'$ which are less than $ONKP$. Out of total profits $OHLP'$, profits of producer A will be $ONGP'$ and profits of producer B will be $NHLG$. Thus entry into the market by producer B and producing output NH by him, the producer A 's profits has been reduced. A will therefore reconsider the situation. But he will assume that producer B will continue to produce output NH. With producer B producing output NH, the best that the producer A can do is to produce $\frac{1}{2}$ $(OD - NH)$. He, will, therefore, reduce his output.

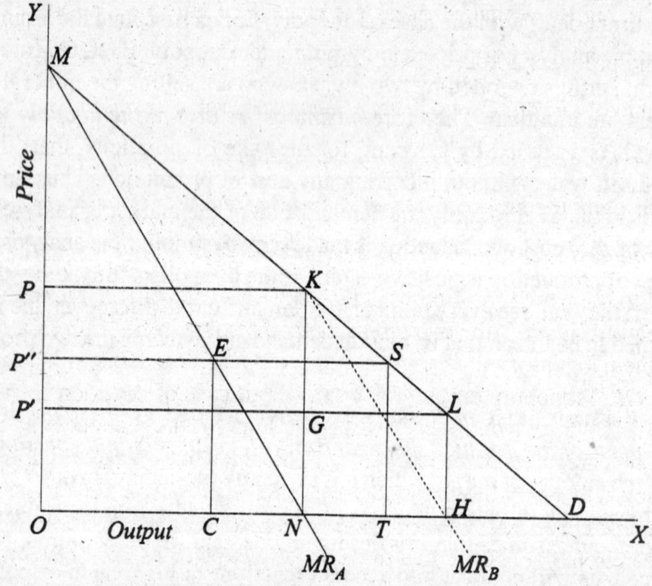

Fig. 29A.1 *Output Cournot's Duopoly Solution*

1. When cost of production is zero, the marginal cost will also be zero. With demand curve MD is a straight line, the marginal revenue curve will pass through the middle of OD, that is, through N so that $ON = ND$.Thus, at ON output MR will zero. Therefore, a monopolist with zero marginal cost will be in equilibrium at output ON where marginal revenue and marginal cost will be equal (both being zero at output ON). In such a situation, the monopolist will make maximum profits by producing output ON, given the linear demand curve MD.

Now that the producer *B* has been surprised by the reduction of output by producer *A* and will also find that his share of total profits is less than that of producer *A*, he will reconsider his situation. Learning nothing from his earlier experience and believing that producer *A* will continue producing its new current level of output, the producer *B* will find that he will now be making maximum profits by producing output equal to $\frac{1}{2}$ (*OD* – New output of *A*). Producer *B*, accordingly, will increase his output. With this move of producer *B*, producer *A* will find his profits reduced. The producer *A* will therefore again reconsider his position and will find that he can increase his profits by producing output equal to $\frac{1}{2}$ (*OD* – Current output of producer *B*). This process of adjustment and readjustment will continue and producer *A* being forced gradually to reduce his output and producer *B* being able to increase his output gradually until the total output *OT* is produced ($OT = \frac{2}{3}$ *OD*) and each is *producing the same amount of output* equal to $\frac{1}{3}$ *OD*. In this final position, producer *A* produces *OC* amount of output and producer *B* produces *CT* amount of output, and *OC* = *CT*. Throughout this process of adjustment and readjustment, each producer assumes that the other will keep his output constant at the present level and then always finds his maximum profits by producing output equal to $\frac{1}{2}$ (*OD* – the present output of the other).

As seen above, producer *A* starts by producing *ON* = ($\frac{1}{2}$ *OD*) and continuously reduces his output until he produces *OC*. The final output *OC* of producer *A* will be equal to $\frac{1}{3}$ *OD* (= $\frac{1}{2}$ *OT*). On the other hand, producer *B* begins by producing $\frac{1}{4}$th of *OD* and continuously increases his output until he produces *CT*. His final output *CT* will be equal to $\frac{1}{3}$ *OD* (= $\frac{1}{2}$ *OT*). Thus, the two producers together will produce total output equal to $\frac{1}{3}$ *OD* + $\frac{1}{3}$ *OD* = $\frac{2}{3}$ *OD* (= *OT*).

Cournot's Duopoly Equilibrium

It will be seen from Fig. 29A.1 that when each producer is producing $\frac{1}{3}$ *OD* (that is, when producer *A* is producing *OC* and producer *B* equal to *CT*), the best that his rival can do is to produce $\frac{1}{2}$ (*OD* – $\frac{1}{3}$ *OD*) which is equal to $\frac{1}{3}$ *OD* = *OC* = *CT*. Thus, *when each producer is producing* $\frac{1}{3}$ *OD so that the total output of the two together is* $\frac{2}{3}$ *OD, no one will expect to increase his profits by making any further adjustment in output. Thus, in Cournot's model of duopoly, stable equilibrium is reached when total output produced is* $\frac{2}{3}$ *rd of OD and each producer is producing* $\frac{1}{3}$ *rd of OD.*

It will be useful to compare the Cournot' s duopoly equilibrium with the monopolistic and the purely competitive equilibriums. If the two producers had combined and formed a coalition, then the output produced by them together will be the monopoly output *ON* and, therefore, the price set will be the monopoly price *OP*. Monopoly output *ON* produced in case of coalition is much less than the output *OT* produced in Cournot's duopoly equilibrium. Further, the monopoly price *OP* charged in case of coalition is much greater than the price *OP''* determined in Cournot's duopoly equilibrium. In case of coalition, they will enjoy the monopoly profits *ONKP* which are *maximum possible joint profits*, given the demand curve *MD*. These monopoly or maximum joint profits can be shared equally by them. It will be seen from Fig. 29A.1, that these monopoly profits *ONKP* made in case of coalition are much greater than the total profits *OTSP"* made by them in Cournot's duopoly equilibrium. It is thus clear that in case of the duopolists competing with each other as conceived by Cournot's duopoly solution, the price and the profits are lower and output is greater than if they had combined together and formed a monopoly.

On the other hand, if the market were perfectly competitive, the output would have been *OD* and price would have been zero. This is because with assumed marginal cost being equal to zero, perfectly competitive equilibrium will be reached at the output level where price is equal to zero. That is, perfectly competitive solution would have resulted in greater output and lower price than under Cournot's duopoly equilibrium.

To sum up, under Cournot's duopoly equilibrium, output is two thirds of the maximum possible output (*i.e.*, perfectly competitive output) and price is two-thirds of the most profitable price (*i.e.*, monopoly price).

Following Cournot, the cost of production in the above discussion of Cournot's oligopoly solution has been taken to be zero. However, it should be noted that above conclusions will not change if the cost curves with positive cost of production are introduced into the discussion.

Reaction Functions and Cournot Duopoly Solution

Cournot solution of duopoly problem can also be obtained with *reaction functions* of the two firms. A*n output reaction function depicts the profit-maximising output of a firm, on the assumption that the other firm's output remains constant.* We have seen above that the profit-maximising output of a Cournot's duopolist is one-half of the difference between the other firm's output and the market demand for output at which price equals marginal cost. This is called reaction function of a firm. This output at which price equals marginal cost (MC) is the maximum output which can be produced because any output beyond this will cause the price to go below marginal cost (which is equal to AC under constant cost conditions) and will therefore not be worthwhile to produce.

The following example will make clear the concept of reaction functions. Let the market demand function is: $Q = 100 - P$ and marginal cost is Rs. *10. In order to determine reaction functions of two duopolist firms, we set price equal to the given marginal cost to determine market demand at price (P)* = *MC*. Thus, from the given demand function

$$P = 100 - Q \quad \text{....}(i)$$

Setting it equal to MC we have

$$100 - Q = 10$$

Or

$$Q = 100 - 10 = 90$$

Thus, the reaction function of firm A is :

$$Q_a = \frac{90 - Q_b}{2} \quad \text{....}(ii)$$

Where Q_a and Q_b are the outputs of firm A and B respectively.

Similarly, reaction function of firm B is :

$$Q_b = \frac{90 - Q_a}{2} \quad \text{....}(iii)$$

The above two equations (*ii*) and (*iii*) can be solved simultaneously to determine Q_a and Q_b. To do so we substitute the value of $Q_b = \frac{90 - Q_a}{2}$ in equation (*ii*) and have :

$$Q_a = \frac{90 - \left(\frac{90 - Q_a}{2}\right)}{2}$$

$$Q_a = \frac{90 - 45 + \frac{Q_a}{2}}{2} = 45 - 22.5 + \frac{1}{4}Q_a$$

$$Q_a - \frac{1}{4}Q_a = \frac{3}{4}Q_a = 22.5$$

$$Q_a = 22.5 \times \frac{4}{3} = \frac{90}{3} = 30$$

With $Q_a = 30$,

$$Q_b = \frac{90 - Q_a}{2} = \frac{90-30}{2} = 30$$

$$Q = Q_a + Q_b = 60$$

Solving equation (*i*) for P we get

$$P = 100 - Q = 100 - 60 = 40$$

Cournot Equilibrium as Nash Equilibrium

John F. Nash, a noted American Mathematician and a Nobel Prize winner in economics, has put forward the concept of equilibrium known as *Nash Equilibrium*. Cournot duopoly equilibrium is an example of Nash equilibrium. *According to Nash equilibrium, competing firms reach their equilibrium state when each of them thinks that it is doing its best, that is, maximising its profits in response to the given strategy adopted by others which think they are also maximising their profits with the given strategies.* As a result, no one has a tendency to change its strategy. Therefore, we have a stable equilibrium. Since in Cournot duopoly equilibrium each firm choses to produce an output level that maximises its profits, given the profit-maximising level of output of the other firm, Cournot duopoly is generally called *Cournot-Nash duopoly equilibrium.*

Cournot's Duopoly Equilibrium Explained with the Aid of Reaction Curves

Some economists have employed the reaction curves to explain Cournot's duopoly equilibrium. The reaction curves may be output reaction curves or price reaction curves depending upon whether it is the output or the price which is the adjustment viable. Since, in Cournot's model, it is the output which is subject to the adjusting variation, output reaction curves are relevant. It should be carefully noted that these *reaction curves refer not to the reactions which a seller expects will be forthcoming from his rivals but to the sellers' own reactions to the moves of his rival.*

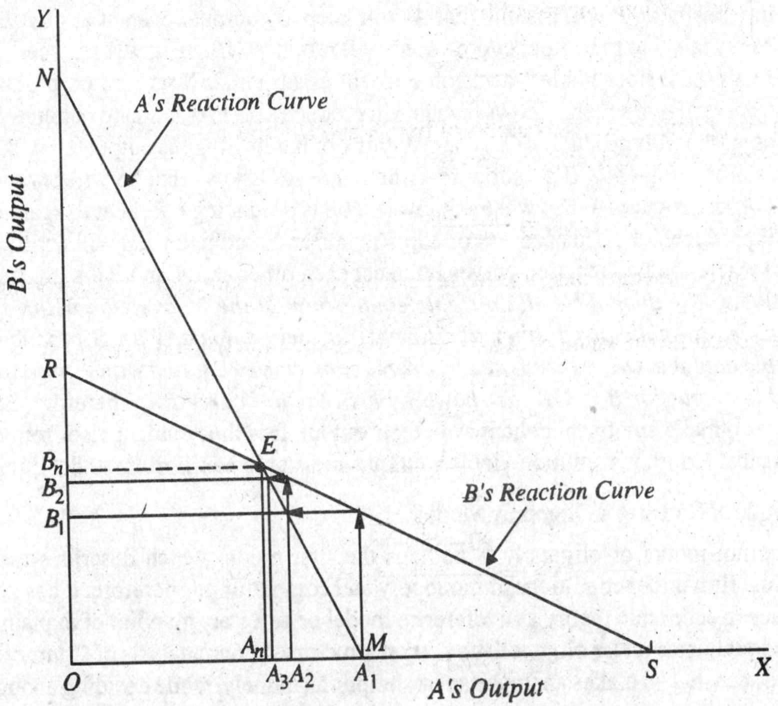

Fig. 29A.2. *Output Reaction Curves According to Cournot's Model*

In Fig. 29A.2 output reaction curves of two producers (sellers) *A* and *B* are shown, *MN* is the output reaction curve of *A* and *RS* is the output reaction curve of *B*. The output reaction curve *MN* of seller *A* shows how *A* will react to any change in output by *B*, that is, *A's* output reaction curve shows how much output *A* will decide to produce for each given output of producer *B*. In other words, *A's* output reaction curve *MN* indicates the most profitable output for *A* for each given output of *B*. Likewise, *B's* output reaction curve *RS* shows how much output *B* will decide to produce (that is, what will be *B'* s most profitable output) for each given output of *A*. For example, if *B* produces output OB_1, *A's* output reaction curve *MN* shows that *A* will produce output OA_2 in response to *B's* output OB_1. Similarly, for all other outputs. On the other hand, if *A* produces OA_2, *B's* output reaction curve shows that *B* will produce OB_2 and so forth for all other outputs.

It will be seen from Fig. 29 A.2, that output reaction curves have been drawn to be straight lines. This is because we are assuming that market demand curve for the product of duopolist is a straight line and that the marginal costs of production of both producers *A* and *B* are constant (at zero). It should be noted that output *OM* is the monopoly output since producer *A* will produce output *OM* if producer *B's* output is zero. In other words, producer *A* will produce and sell output *OM* if he were the monopolist. On the other hand, *A* will produce zero output if *B'S* output is *ON*. Given the marginal cost equal to zero, a producer will be forced to produce zero output when the price has fallen to zero and, therefore, production is no longer profitable. Output *ON* will be produced under conditions of perfect competition since at output *ON* the price will be zero and therefore equal to marginal cost which is assumed to be zero in the present case. Thus, *while OM is the monopoly output, ON is the perfectly competitive output*. We assume the two producers *A* and *B* to be completely identical, *OR* will, therefore, be equal to *OM*, and *OS* will be equal to *ON*.

Output reaction curves, as interpreted above, can be used to explain Cournot's duopoly equilibrium. Each producer, as before, assumes that his rival will continue producing the same amount of output regardless of what he might himself decide to produce. To begin with, suppose producer *A* goes into business first and is therefore initially a monopolist. Therefore, in the beginning *A* will produce output *OM* which is a monopoly output as output by the firm *B* is zero. Suppose now *B* also enters into business, *B* will assume that *A*, will keep his output constant at *OM*. *B*'s output reaction curve *RS* reveals that for output *OM* of *A*, he will produce OB_1. But when *A* sees that *B* is producing OB_1 he will reconsider his last decision but will assume that *B* will go on producing OB_1. Output reaction curve *NM* of seller *A* shows that he will produce OA_2 in reaction to output OB_1, of firm *B*. Now when *B* sees that *A* is producing OA_2, he will think of readjusting his output but will assume that *A* will continue producing OA_2. *B*'s ,output reaction curve *RS*, shows that he will produce output OB_2 for output OA_2 of producer *A*, But when *A* knows that *B* is producing OB_2 he will again readjust his output and will produce OA_3, This process of adjustments and readjustments will continue until point *E* is reached where the two reaction curves intersect each other and *A* and *B* are producing OA_n and OB_n respectively. *The duopolists attain stable equilibrium at the intersection point, since they will not feel induced to make any further adjustments in their outputs. With B producing* OB_n, *A's most profitable output is* OA_n *as indicated by his reaction curve NM, and with A producing* OA_n, *the most profitable output for B is* OB_n *as shown by his reaction curve RS,* Therefore, no one will have a tendency to make any further changes in their output. It is thus evident also from the reaction curve analysis that Cournot's solution yields a unique and stable equilibrium under duopoly.

A Critique of Cournot's Oligopoly Model

Cournot model of oligopoly is perhaps the first model which describes the behaviour of an individual firm under conditions of monopoly and competition. Therefore, it has occupied an important place in economic theory as a reference model or as a starting point of explaining the behaviour of individual firms under oligopolistic market structure. In our analysis of Cournot's duopoly model, we have seen that he makes an important assumption,, namely, while deciding about his output policy, each duopolist believes that his rival will hold output constant at the present level whatever output he himself might produce. Further, a producer remains unshaken in this erroneous belief even when he constantly finds himself to be proved incorrect since after his action the rival does react and changes his output. This is a chief logical error in Cournot's model.

Furthermore, by assuming that duopolist (oligopolist), will think that his rival will continue producing the current level of output *Cournot model ignores the mutual interdependence* **between the** duopolist which is the chief characteristic of oligopoly, Thus, Cournot model provides solution for oligopoly problem by removing from it its most important feature.

PROBLEMS ON COURNOT'S MODEL

Problem 1. *Let the market for telecommunications equipment be represented by a duopoly, where the two firms produce outputs q_1 and q_2 respectively. The inverse market demand function is represented by $P = 100 - 2Q$ (Where $Q = q_1 + q_2$). The marginal cost that each firm faces is 4* :

(i) What are the reaction functions of the Cournot duopolists?

(ii) Calculate each firm's output and the market price at Cournot equilibrium.

D.U. B.A. (*Hons.*)

Solution :

We first find out market demand for output (Q) when $P = MC$. For this, setting the given inverese demand function equal to MC, we have

$$100 - 2Q = 4$$
$$Q = 48$$

Reaction function of firm B :

$$Q_a = \frac{48 - Q_b}{2} \quad ...(i)$$

Reaction function of firm A :

$$Q_b = \frac{48 - Q_a}{2} \quad ...(ii)$$

To determine Q_a we substitute the value of Q_b in (*i*) and have

$$Q_a = \frac{48 - \left(\frac{48 - Q_a}{2}\right)}{2}$$

$$= \frac{48 - 24 + \frac{1}{2}Q_a}{2}$$

$$Q_a = 24 - 12 + \frac{1}{4}Q_a$$

$$\frac{3}{4}Q_a = 12$$

$$Q_a = 12 \times \frac{4}{3} = 16$$

To obtain Q_b we substitute the value of Q_a in (*ii*).

$$Q_b = \frac{48 - Q_a}{2} = \frac{48 - 16}{2} = 16$$

Total output (Q) under Cournot duopoly equilibrium = 16 + 16 = 32

Substituting the value of Q in the inverse demand function we have

$$P = 100 - 2Q = 100 - 2 \times 32$$
$$= 36$$

Problem 2. *Suppose the market demand curve for a commodity is $P = 70 - Q$. Suppose that there are two firms each with constant MC of Rs. 10/-. Assuming they behave as Cournot duopolists what will be the price and total industry output ? Compare with the outcome under pure monopoly and perfect competition.* D.U. B.A. (Hons.) 1989

Solution :

Market demand for output at which $P = MC$:

$$70 - Q = 10$$
$$Q = 60$$

Let the output of the two firms A and B are Q_a and Q_b respectively

$$Q_a = \frac{60 - Q_b}{2} \quad ...(i)$$

$$Q_b = \frac{60 - Q_a}{2} \quad ...(ii)$$

Substituting the value of Q_b in (i) we have

$$Q_a = \frac{60 - \left(\frac{60 - Q_a}{2}\right)}{2} = \frac{60 - 30 + \frac{1}{2}Q_a}{2}$$

$$= 30 - 15 + \frac{1}{4}Q_a$$

$$\frac{3}{4}Q_a = 15$$

$$Q_a = 15 \times \frac{4}{3} = 20$$

$$Q_b = \frac{60 - Q_a}{2}$$

$$= \frac{60 - 20}{2} = 20$$

Total output (Q) under Cournot duopoly equilibrium = $Q_a + Q_b = 40$

Price under Cournot duopoly equilibrium :

$$P = 70 - Q$$
$$= 70 - 40 = 30$$

MR under Pure Monopoly

$$MR = \frac{dTR}{dQ} = \frac{d(PQ)}{dQ} = \frac{d(70Q - Q^2)}{dQ}$$
$$= 70 - 2Q$$

Now, in equilibrium output under monopoly : $MR = MC$

$$70 - 2Q = 10$$
$$2Q = 60$$
$$Q = 30$$

Price under Pure Monopoly

$$P = 70 - Q = 70 - 30 = 40$$

Output and Price under Pefect Competition

For equilibrium output under perfect competition :

$$\text{Price} = MC$$

$$70 - Q = 10$$

$$Q = 70 - 10 = 60$$

Price under perfect competition :

$$P = 70 - Q$$

$$= 70 - 60 = 10$$

It is evident from above that output (40) under Cournot duopoly is $\frac{2}{3}$rd of output (60) under perfect compeitition and monopoly output (30) is half of the output under perfect competition. Price under perfect competition (Rs. 10) is lower than those under Cournot duopoly and pure monopoly.

Problem 3. *In a constant cost industry having zero costs, the inverse demand function is given by $P = 12 - Q$. Estimate the equilibrium value of the price and output for monopoly, Cournot Duopoly and perfect competition.* D.U. B.A. (Hons.) 1999

Solution:

Monopoly :

For price and output under monopoly :

$$MR = MC$$

$$MR = \frac{d(TR)}{dQ} = \frac{d(PQ)}{dQ} = \frac{12(12Q - Q^2)}{dQ}$$

$$= 12 - 2Q$$

Since $MC = 0$ (given)

$$12 - 2Q = 0$$

$$Q = 6$$

Price under monopoly

$$P = 12 - Q = 12 - 6 = 6$$

Cournot Duopoly :

Setting price equal to marginal cost (which is zero) we have $12 - Q = 0$ or $Q = 12$

$$\text{Output of Firm 1 } (Q_1) = \frac{12 - Q_2}{2} \qquad ...(i)$$

$$\text{Output of Firm 2 } (Q_2) = \frac{12 - Q_1}{2} \qquad ...(ii)$$

Substituting the value of Q_2 in (*i*) we have

$$Q_1 = \frac{12 - \left(\frac{12 - Q_1}{2}\right)}{2}$$

$$Q_1 = \frac{12 - 6 + \frac{1}{2}Q_1}{2}$$

$$Q_1 = 6 - 3 + \frac{1}{4} Q_1$$

$$\frac{3}{4} Q_1 = 3$$

$$Q_1 = 3 \times \frac{4}{3} = 4$$

Similarly $$Q_2 = \frac{12 - Q_1}{2} = \frac{12 - 4}{2} = 4$$

Cournot Duopoly output, $Q_1 + Q_2 = 4 + 4 = 8$

Price under Cournot duopoly :

$$P = 12 - Q$$
$$= 12 - 8 = 4$$

Under Perfect Competition :

Perfectly competitive output : Price = MC

$$12 - Q = 0$$
$$Q = 12$$

Perfectly competitive price :

$$P = 12 - Q = 12 - 12 = 0$$

CHAMBERLIN'S OLIGOPOLY MODEL

In his now famous work *"The Theory of Monopolistic Competition"* Chamberlin made an important contribution to the explanation of pricing and output under oligopoly. His oligopoly model makes an advance over the classical models of Cournot, Edgeworth and Bertrand in that in sharp contrast to these classical models *his model is based on the assumption that the oligopolists recognise their interdependence and act accordingly*. Chamberlin criticises the behavioural assumption of Cournot, Bertrand and Edgeworth that the oligopolists behave independently in the sense that they ignore their mutual dependence and while 'deciding about their output or price assume that their rivals will keep their output or price constant at the present level. According to him, oligopolists behave quite intelligently as they recognise their interdependence and learn from the experience when they find that their action in fact cause the rivals to react and adjust their output level. This *realisation of mutual dependence on the part of the oligopolists leads to the monopoly output being produced jointly and thus charging of the monopoly price*. In this way, *according to Chamberlin, maximisation of joint profits and stable equilibrium are achieved by the oligopolists even though they act in a non-collusive manner*. Given identical costs, they will also equally share these monopoly profits.

Chamberlin's Approach to Stable Equilibrium under Oligopoly

The process by which stable equilibrium under oligopoly is reached in Chamberlin's oligopoly model is illustrated in Figure 29A.3. Chamberlin, considers the case of a duopoly with zero cost of production of the two producers, *A* and *B*. Like Cournot he also assumes that the market demand curve for the product is linear. In Figure 29A.3, *MD* represents this linear demand curve for the homogeneous product of the duopolists. As in Cournot's model, suppose producer *A* is the first to start production. He will view the whole market demand curve *MD* facing him and corresponding to it MR_a is the marginal revenue curve. In order to maximise his profits he will equate marginal revenue with marginal cost (which is here taken to be equal to zero). It will be seen from Fig. 29A.3 that he will be in equilibrium ($MR = MC$) when he produces *OQ* output (*i.e.* half of *OD*), which is in fact the monopoly output, and will fix price equal to *OP*.

Now, suppose producer B enters the market. He thinks, as in Cournot' s model, that producer A would continue to produce OQ output and therefore views ED portion of the demand curve as the

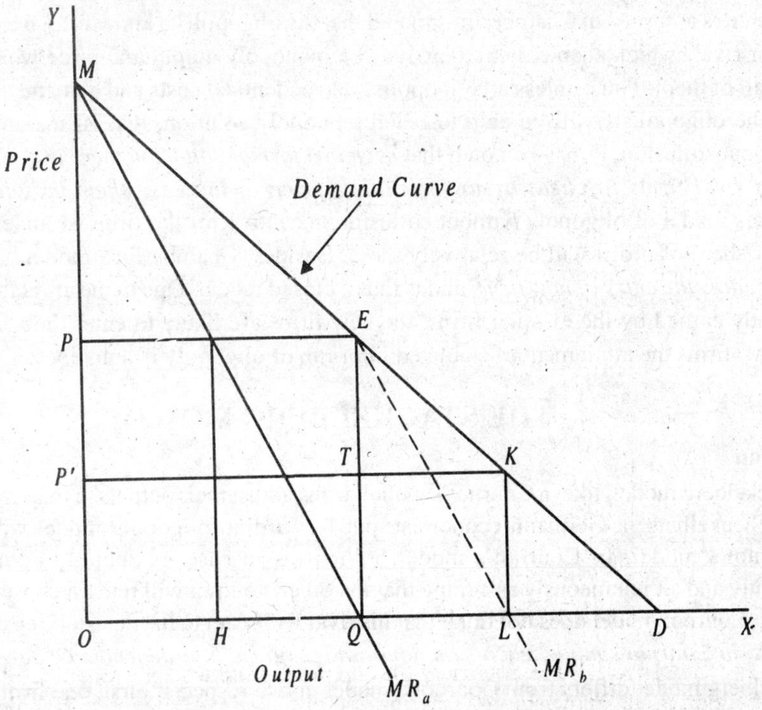

Fig. 29A.3 *Chamberlin's Stable Model of Duopoly with Mutual Dependence Recognised*

relevant demand curve facing him and corresponding to him MR_b is the marginal revenue curve. With marginal cost being equal to zero, for maximing profits he will produce half of QD, that is, QL or at point L at which his marginal revenue curve intersects the X-axis along which output is measured. With aggregate output OL ($OL = OQ$ of $A + QL$ of B), price will fall to the level LK or OP' with the result that profits earned by producer B will be equal to the area of rectangle $QLKT$, and due to the fall in price the profit of producer A will decrease from $OPEQ$ to $OP'\ TQ$.

However, from this point onward Chamberlin's analysis deviates from Cournot's model. Whereas in Cournot's model, the firm A will readjust his output and will continue to assume that his rival will keep his output constant at QL level, but in Chamberlin's model producer A learns from his experience that they are interdependent. With the realisation of mutual dependence, producer A decides to produce output OH equal to output QL of producer B and half of monopoly output OQ so that the aggregate output of both of them is the monopoly output ($OQ = OH$ of $A + QL$ of B). With OQ as the aggregate output level, price will rise to QE or OP. Firm B also realises that in view of interdependence it is in the best interest for both of them to produce half of monopoly output and will therefore maintain output at the QL or OH level which is half of the monopoly output. Thus, *each producer producing half of monopoly output, will result in maximisation of joint profits though they do not enter into any formal collusion*. In this way Chamberlin explains that duopolists behaving intelligently and realising their interdependence reach a stable equilibrium and together produce monopoly output and charge monopoly price each sharing profits equally.

Comments. Chamberlin's model is an advance over the classical models in that the firms behave intelligently and recognise their interdependence. Their behaviour leads them to the *monopoly solution of output and pricing which ensures maximisation of joint profits though they do not formally collude*. This implies that firms have full information about the market demand curve and quickly learn from the experience and realise that the ultimate consequence of alternative chain of adjustments to rival's moves will be less profitable than sharing the monopoly profits equally with him.

Further, it is assumed in Chamberlin's model that the oligopolists know fully the costs of production of their rivals which enable them to arrive at a monopoly output and price which is in the best interest of all of them. Thus, unless all oligopolists have identical costs and demands, it seems impossible that the oligopolists will be able to reach monopoly solution, that is, maximisation of joint profits without collusion. It may be noted that *even in a formal collusion there is always incentive on the part of rival firms to cheat by under-cutting price to increase their individual profits.* In Chamberlin's model of oligopoly without collusion, incentive for the firms to undercut price to increase their share of profit will be relatively more. Besides, Chamberlin's model has another great flaw as *it ignores the entry of new firms* and is thus a closed model. Due to the attraction of monopoly profits jointly earned by the existing firms, the new firms are likely to enter the industry. With the entry of new firms the attainment of stable equilibrium of oligopoly is unlikely to occur.

THE STACKELBERG MODEL

Introduction

In Stackelberg model, like in Cournot's model, firms adjust their outputs to maximise their profits. However, Stackelberg, a Germann economist, put forward an oligopoly model which is different from Cournot's model. In Cournot's model both firms in case of duopoly adjust their output independently and simultaneously assuming that the other's output will remain constant, that is, each duopolist in Cournot model does not think that his rival will react to his decision regarding output. *In other words, in Cournot's model each firm does not recognise interdependence between them.*

Stackelberg model differs from Cournot's model in two respects. First, one firm recognises that his rival firm will take into account the quantity of output it decides to produce. Thus, firms recognise their interdependence and thus behave in a sophisticated manner. Secondly, in Stackelberg duopoly model the two firms do not take their decisions simultaneously; one firm fixes its output first, that is, it moves first to produce a quantity of a commodity. The other firm follows and produces its profit-maximising output by taking the output of the first mover as given and constant. That is, the follower behaves like a Cournot's duopolist. Stackelberg model shows that it is a advantageous for a firm to go first, that is, to become a leader so that others follow him.

The Follower's Problem

Let us start with the firm 2 which follows firm 1 which sets its output first. We assume that market demand for the product is of the following form :

$$P = a - bQ$$

where a is constant intercept of the demand curve and b is the slope of the demand curve. Marginal cost of the production of both the firm is zero. P is price of the product and Q is output. Let output of firm 1 is denoted by Q_1 and output of firm 2 is denoted by Q_2. With this, the given demand function can be written as

$$P = a - b(Q_1 + Q_2) \quad \text{... } (i)$$

The follower firm 2 will decide about its profit-maximising output after firm 1 has taken its output decision, and further that firm 2 will fix its profit-maximising output taking the first mover firm 1's output as given and constant. That is, the follower firm 2's output is given by Cournot's reaction curve which is obtained by a profit-maximising firm taking the output of the other firm as given and constant. Recall that to derive Cournot's reaction curve, a firm equates marginal revenue with marginal cost, given the output of the rival firm. Thus, to determine the follower firm's profit-making output, given the output of the other firm, we obtain its marginal revenue function and then equate it with the given marginal cost.

To obtain total revenue of the follower firm 2, we multiply the inverse demand function equation (*i*) by its output which is denoted by Q_2. Thus

$$TR = PQ_2 = aQ_2 - bQ_1Q_2 - bQ_2^2$$

$$MR_2 = \frac{d(PQ_2)}{dQ_2} = a - bQ_1 - 2bQ_2$$

Setting MR_2 equal to marginal cost which is here given to be equal to zero we have

$$a - bQ_1 - 2bQ_2 = 0$$

$$2bQ_2 = a - bQ_1$$

$$Q_2 = \frac{a - bQ_1}{2b} \qquad \text{... (ii)}$$

The equation (*ii*) describes the reaction function curve of the follower firm 2.

The Leader's Profit-Maximising Problem

Having explained how the follower firm will decide about its output, given the output of the leader, we now turn to explain how the leader firm will determine its profit - maximising output. According to Stackelberg model, the leader is a sophisticated firm which recognises that its output decision will influence the choice of output by the follower firm. The choice of profit-maximising output by the follower (firm 2), given an output of the other firm (in this case the output of the leader firm 1), is given by its reaction function curve as derived above. Hence making its output choice, the leader firm 1 will take into account the reaction func ion curve of the follower. Accordingly, in order to know the profit-maximising output of the leader, given the reaction function curve of the follower firm 1, we obtain the total revenue function of the leader firm 1. Thus, multiplying the given inverse demand function equation (*i*) by output Q_1 of the leader we have

$$TR_1 = PQ_1 = aQ_1 - bQ_1^2 - bQ_1Q_2 \qquad \text{... (iii)}$$

Substituting the reaction function equation (*ii*) of the follower firm for Q_2 in the total revenue function of the leader firm 1 we have

$$PQ_1 = aQ_1 - bQ_1^2 - bQ_1\left(\frac{a - bQ_1}{2b}\right)$$

Simplifying it we get

$$PQ_1 = aQ_1 - bQ_1^2 - \frac{aQ_1}{2} + \frac{bQ_1^2}{2}$$

$$PQ_1 = \frac{1}{2}aQ_1 - \frac{1}{2}bQ_1^2$$

MR of the above total revenue function is

$$MR_1 = \frac{d(PQ_1)}{dQ_1} = \frac{a}{2} - bQ_1 \qquad \text{... (iv)}$$

To obtain profit - maximising output of the leader firm we equate marginal revenue obtained in equation (*iv*) above with marginal cost (*MC*) which given to be equal to zero we get

$$\frac{a}{2} - bQ_1 = 0$$

$$bQ_1 = \frac{a}{2}$$

or leader's profit maximising output, $$Q_1^* = \frac{a}{2b} \qquad \text{... (v)}$$

(Note that * mark over Q_1 indicates equalibrium or profit maximising output)

Now in order to find out the follower firm 2's output we substitute the value of Q_1^* into the reaction function obtained in (*ii*) of the follower firm 2. Thus

$$Q_2 = \frac{a - bQ_1^*}{2b} = \frac{a - b\left(\frac{a}{2b}\right)}{2b}$$

$$Q_2 = \frac{a - \frac{a}{2}}{2b} = \frac{a\left(1 - \frac{1}{2}\right)}{2b} = \frac{\frac{a}{2}}{2b}$$

$$Q_2^* = \frac{a}{4b} \qquad \text{... (vi)}$$

Thus, the output of leader firm 1 is $\frac{a}{2b}$ and the follower firm 2 is $\frac{a}{4b}$. We can obtain the price (*P*) of the product by substituting total output ($Q^* = Q_1^* + Q_2^*$) produced in the given demand function, $P = a - bQ^*$

Exercise 1. *Given the demand function, P = 30 – Q, and the two firms 1 and 2 in an industry producing a product. Marginal cost of production of each firm is zero. Suppose firm 1 behaves as a Stackelberg's leader and firm 2 as its follower :*

What output will be produced by them and what price will be determined ?

Solution. Follower firm 2 makes its decision after leader firm 1 assuming leader firm's output as given and constant. Here the constant term of the demand function, $a = 30$ and slope of the demand function $b = 1$.

Reaction function the follower firm is : $$Q_2 = \frac{a - bQ_1}{2b}$$

or $$Q_2 = \frac{30 - Q_1}{2} = 15 - \frac{1}{2}Q_1 \qquad \text{... (i)}$$

Total revenue of the leader firm 1 is

$$TR_1 = PQ_1 = 30Q_1 - Q_1(Q_1 + Q_2)$$

$$= 30Q_1 - Q_1^2 - Q_1Q_2 \qquad \text{... (ii)}$$

Substituting $Q_2 = 15 - \frac{1}{2}Q_1$ in total revenue function equation (*ii*) of the leader firm we have

$$TR_1 = 30Q_1 - Q_1^2 - Q_1\left(15 - \frac{1}{2}Q_1\right)$$

$$= 30Q_1 - Q_1^2 - 15Q_1 + \frac{1}{2}Q_1^2$$

$$= 15Q_1 - \frac{1}{2}Q_1^2 \qquad \text{... (iii)}$$

Marginal Reveue (MR_1) of the leader firml is

$$\frac{d(TR_1)}{dQ_1} = 15 - Q_1 \qquad \text{... (iv)}$$

Setting MR_1 equal to marginal cost which is zero we have

$$15 - Q_1 = 0$$

$$Q_1^* = 15$$

Substituting the value of leader output Q_1 in the reaction function equation (i) of the follower firm 2 we have

$$Q_2^* = 15 - \frac{1}{2}Q_1$$

$$= 15 - \frac{1}{2} \times 15 = 7.5$$

Thus the leader firm's production is 15 and follower firm's output is 7.5. Hence total output (Q^*) is 15 + 7.5 = 22.5

To obtain price we substitute the total output of 22.5 in the given demand function. Thus

$$P = 30 - Q$$

$$= 30 - 22.5 = 7.5$$

Exercise 2. *The Market demand curve for a Stackelberg leader and follower is given by* $P = 10 - Q$. *If each has a marginal cost of 2 what will be the equilibrium quantity and price for each producer.*

Solution. In this exercise we are given a positive marginal cost instead of zero marginal cost.

Follower's reaction function : Let us first derive follower's reaction function. The producer 2 is the follower

$$P = 10 - Q$$

or, $$P = 10 - (Q_1 + Q_2) \qquad \text{... (i)}$$

Multiplying the demand function equation (i) by the output Q_2 of producer 2 to obtain total revenue function we have

$$TR_2 = PQ_2 = 10Q_2 - Q_1Q_2 - Q_2^2$$

$$MR_2 = 10 - Q_1 - 2Q_2$$

Setting MR_2 equal to marginal cost we get the reaction function for the follower. Thus

$$10 - Q_1 - 2Q_2 = 2$$

$$2Q_2 = 10 - 2 - Q_1 = 8 - Q_1$$

$$Q_2 = 4 - \frac{1}{2}Q_1 \qquad \text{... (ii)}$$

Equation (ii) describes the reaction function equation for the follower.

Leader's Equilibrium :

Demand function for the leader is

$$P = 10 - (Q_1 + Q_2)$$

Multiplying both sides by output Q_1 of leader we have

$$TR_1 = PQ_1 = 10Q_1 - Q_1^2 - Q_1Q_2 \qquad \text{... (iii)}$$

Substituting the value of $Q_2 = 4 - \frac{1}{2}Q_1$ in TR_1 equation (iii) we have

$$TR_1 = 10Q_1 - Q_1^2 - Q_1\left(4 - \frac{1}{2}Q_1\right)$$

$$= 10Q_1 - Q_1^2 - 4Q_1 + \frac{1}{2}Q_1^2$$

$$TR_1 = 6Q_1 - \frac{1}{2}Q_1^2$$

$$MR_1 = \frac{d(TR_1)}{dQ} = 6 - Q_1 \quad \text{... (iv)}$$

Setting MR_1 equal to marginal cost (MC) we have

$$6 - Q_1 = 2$$
$$Q_1 = 6 - 2 = 4$$

Thus, the leader produces 4 units of the product.

Substuting $Q_1 = 4$ in the follower's reaction function equation (*ii*) we have

$$Q_2 = 4 - \frac{1}{2}Q_1 = 4 - \frac{1}{2} \times 4$$
$$= 2$$

Thus, the follower will produce 2 units of the product.

Total output = 4 + 2 = 6

Substituting the total output produced in the given demand function we get price at which the product will be sold. Thus

$$P = 10 - Q = 10 - 6$$
$$= 4$$

Thus price equals Rs. 4.

QUESTIONS FOR REVIEW

1. Explain how equilibirum output and price are determined in Cournot's duopoly model. State the underlying assumptions.
2. How is Cournot–Nash equilibrium determined ? Why is it stable ? Why don't the duopolists set the output at joint-profit maximizing level by tacit collusion. *D.U. B.A. (Hons.)* 2001
   [**Hint:** Cournot equilibrium is also called Cournot–Nash equilibrium.]
3. Explain Cournot's model of duopoly. Why is equilibrium under it called a Nash equilibrium ? *D.U., B.Com (Hons.) 2007*
4. (*a*) Explain Cournot's duopoly model. What should the firms do to maximise their profits. *D.U. B.Com. (Hons.)* 1996
   (*b*) Bring out precisely the difference between Cournot equilibrium and profit maximising behaviour. *D.U. B.A. (Hons.)* 1988
5. What are the reaction function curves of duopolists ? How are they used to explain Cournot's equilibrium under duopoly ? *D.U., B.Com (Hons.) 2008.*
6. Duopolists face the following market demand curve : P = 30 – Q. Q is total production of both firms, $Q = Q_1 + Q_2$. Both firms have zero marginal cost $MC_1 = MC_2 = 0$. Calculate Cournot equilibrium with the help of reaction curves and compare it with competitive equilibrium and also compare it if the firms collude. *D.B., B. Com (Hons.) 2009.*
7. Explain Chamberlin's model of duopoly. How does it differ from Cournot's solution of duopoly problem. *D.U. B.Com. (Hons.)* 2001
8. Let the market for telecommunications equipment be represented by a duopoly where the two firms produce outputs q_1 and q_2 respectively. The inverse demand function is represented by $P = 100 - 2Q$ (where $Q = q_1 + q_2$). The marginal cost that each firm faces is 4 :
   (*i*) What are the reaction functions of the Cournot's duopolists ?
   (*ii*) Calculate each firm's output and the market price at Cournot's equilibrium. *D.U. B.A. (Hons.) 2003*
9. In the Stackelberg model, the firm that sets output first has an advantage. Explain. Give reasons. *D.U. B.Com (Hons.) II Year 2009*

CHAPTER 30

SALES MAXIMISATION MODEL OF OLIGOPOLY

Sales maximisation model of obligopoly is another important alternative to profit maximization model. This has been propounded by W.J. Baumol, an American economist. In an earlier chapter we have explained sales maximisation objective and saw how Baumol challenged the profit maximisation assumption regarding business behaviour in these days of manager-dominated corporate form of business organisation and showed how sales maximisation was more valid and realistic assumption of business behaviour. Further, we pointed out there that sales maximisation was quite consistent with *rationality* assumption about business behaviour. It may also be noted that sales maximisation model represents one of the managerial theories of the firm because in it, the great importance has been given to the manager's role and to his pursuing self-interest in making price, output and advertising policies. Prof. Baumol thinks that *managers are more interested in maximizing sales than profits*.

Sales Maximisation vs Profit Maximisation

It should be noted that by sales maximisation Baumol does not mean the maximisation of the *physical volume* of sales but the maximisation of *total revenue from sales*, that is, the rupee value of the sales made. Therefore, his theory is also known as revenue maximisation model. Further, as has been mentioned in a previous chapter, Prof. Baumol does not ignore profit motive altogether. He argues that there is a *minimum acceptable level of profits* which must be earned by the management so as to finance future growth of the firm through retained profits and also to induce the potential shareholders for subscribing to the share capital of the company. Thus, according to him, management of oligopolistic firms *seeks to maximise sales or, in other words, total revenue subject to this minimum profit constraint*.

He thus writes: "My hypothesis then is that oligopolists typically seek to maximize their sales subject to a minimum profit constraint. The determination of the minimum just acceptable profit level is a major analytical problem and I shall only suggest here that it is determined by long-run considerations. Profits must be high enough to provide the retained earnings needed to finance current expansion plans and dividends sufficient to make future issues of stocks attractive to potential purchasers"[1]

Sales Maximisation: Price-output Determination

It is better to explain graphically price-output determination in Prof. Baumol's sales or total revenue maximization model. Consider Fig. 30.1 where on the *Y*-axis we measure total revenue, total cost and total profits in terms of rupees and on the *X*-axis we measure the total output. *TR* and *TC* are respectively total revenue and total cost curves. Since total cost curve *TC* starts from the origin, it means the diagram refers to the long-run cost-revenue situation. *TP* is the total profit curve

1. W.J. Baumol, On the Theory of Oligopoly, *Economica*, new series, Vol. 25, 1958.

which first rises and then after a point falls downward. Since total profits are the difference between total revenue and total costs at various levels of output, the total profit curve measures the vertical difference between the *TR* and *TC* curves at various levels of output.

If the firm aims at maximising profits, it will produce *OA* output. This is because corresponding to *OA* output, the highest point of *TP* curve lies. But, as we have seen above, according to Prof. Baumol, the firm does not seek maximisation of profits. On the other hand, if the firm wants to maximise sales (or total revenue) it will fix output at *OC* level which is greater than *OA*. At output *OC* total revenue is CR_2, which is maximum in the diagram. At this total revenue (sales) maximising output level *OC*, the firm is making total profits equal to *CG* which are less than the maximum attainable profits *AH*. It will be clear from the figure that sales (or total revenue) maximisation output *OC* is larger than profit-maximising output *OA*. Prof. Baumol contends that the business firms aim at total revenue (sales) maximisation subject to a minimum profit constraint. Now, if *OM* is the minimum total profits which a firm wants to obtain, then *ML* is the minimum profit line. Now, this minimum profit line *ML* cuts the total profit curve *TP* at point *E*. Therefore, if the firm wants total revenue (sales) maximisation subject to the minimum profits of *OM*, as has been contended by Prof. Baumol, then it will produce and sell output *OB*. At output *OB*, the firm will be having total revenue equal to BR_1 which is less than the maximum possible total revenue of CR_2. But the total revenue BR_1 is the maximum obtainable revenue to earn the minimum desirable profits *OM*.

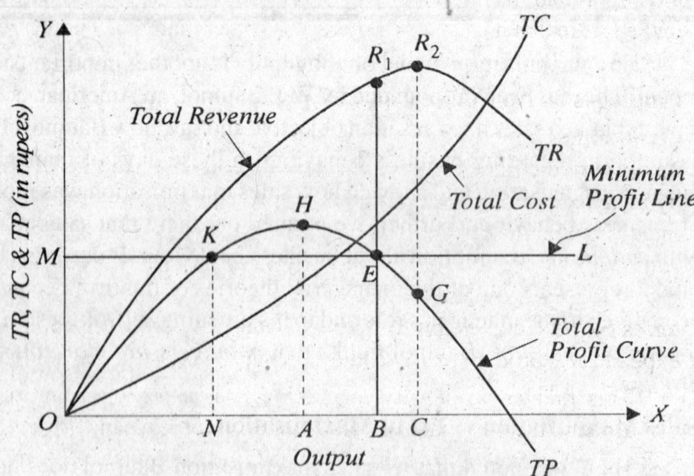

Fig. 30.1. *Prof. Baumol' Sales Maximisation Hypothesis.*

It should be noted that the firm can earn the minimum profit *OM* even by producing *ON* output. (Minimum profit line *ML* also cuts the total profits curve *TP* at point *K*). But the total revenue at output *ON* is much less than at output *OB*. Therefore, given the firm's objective of maximising the total revenue subject to the minimum profit constraint, the firm will not produce *ON* output or at point *K*. It will be noticed from the figure that the output *OB* lies in between *OA* and *OC*, that is, it is larger than profit-maximising output *OA* but smaller than the total revenue-maximising output *OC*. Thus, in Prof. Baumol's model, oligopolistic firm will be in equilibrium at output *OB* and will be earning profits *BE* (or *OM*).

It should be carefully noted that the objective of total revenue (or sales) maximisation subject to the minimum profit constraint leads to a greater output and lower price than does profit maximisation. Price will be lower under revenue maximisation because the output under it, as seen above, is greater and given that demand or average revenue curve is sloping downward, the price will be less when the output is larger. To quote Prof. Baumol "The profit-maximizsing output *OA* will usually be smaller than the one which yields either type of sales maximum, *OC* or *OB*. This can be proved with the aid of the standard rule that at the point of maximum profit marginal cost must equal marginal revenue. For marginal cost is normally a positive number (we can't usually produce more of a good for nothing). *Hence marginal revenue will also be positive when profits are at a maximum*, *i.e.* a further increase in output will increase total sales (revenue). Therefore, if at the point of maximum profit the firm earns more profit than the required minimum, it will pay the sales maximizer to lower his price and increase his physical output."[2]

The price charged at output OB will be equal to $\frac{\text{total revenue}}{\text{output}}$, that is, $\frac{BR_1}{OB}$

Now suppose the minimum acceptable profits are equal to AH (which are maximum possible profits under the given cost-revenue situation), then even under total revenue maximisation objective subject to the minimum profit constraint, the firm will produce the profit-maximising output OA. But it will produce output OA not to maximise profits but to maximise total revenue, given the minimum profit constraint AH. Now, suppose the minimum acceptable profits for an entrepreneur are larger than AH, then it is obvious from the figure that given the cost-revenue situations depicted in the figure that he cannot earn profits greater than AH. Therefore, in this situation the entrepreneur must either lower his minimum acceptable profit level or go out of the industry.

Emphasis on Non-price Competition

Another important feature of sales-maximisation theory of the firm of Baumol is its emphasis on non-price-competition in oligopoly as compared to the price competition. It has been observed by many economists that oligopolists are often very much reluctant to use price cutting to promote their sales. Baumol rightly argues that this reluctance on the part of the oligopolists to use price as a competitive weapon should not be explained merely by that they want to live in *quiet life*. This is because when competition under oligopoly does become more intense and vigorous, it may not be in terms of price cutting but in terms of non-price weapons, that is, in the form of more advertising expenditure, product modification, introduction of special services for the customers etc.

This greater propensity to indulge in non-price competition under oligopoly can be better explained with sales-maximisation objective rather than with profit-maximisation objective. This is because extra expenditure on advertising etc., increases the physical volume of sales, it must also increase the total revenue, whereas the effect of price cutting on the total revenue is doubtful. This is because, "a price reduction is a double-edged sword which, while it serves as an influence to increase total revenue in that it usually adds to the number of units which can be sold, simultaneously it also works in the opposite direction by reducing the revenue on each unit sold. In other words, as the economists know so well, depending on whether demand is or is not elastic, *price cutting is an uncertain means for increasing dollar sales*."[3] The effect of price cutting on profits is more uncertain because if it fails to raise total revenue, it will most probably reduce profits because the increase in output as a result of reduction in price, will increase total costs. On the other hand, while the profitability of advertising, product modification, improved service is doubtful, their favourable effect on the sales is quite certain. Thus, according to Baumol, "the effect of advertising, improved services, etc., on sales is fairly sure while, very often, their profitability may be quite doubtful. Thus, *sales maximization makes for greater presumption that the businessman will consider non-price competition to be more advantageous alternative*."[4]

We now turn to explain that, according to Baumol's sales maximisation model, how much advertising expenditure a firm will undertake.

Sales Maximisation Model: Optimal Advertising Expenditure

We know that firms in oligopolistic market conditions compete not only in terms of price but also in terms of advertising expenditure, product variation and special services offered to the buyers. We shall discuss here the question of optimal advertising expenditure to be incurred by an oligopolist and the conclusions reached in this connection will apply equally to the questions of optimal product adjustment and the optimal amount of special services to be provided by an oligopo-

2. William J. Baumol, *Economic Theory and Operations Analysis*, 3rd. ed., pp. 326-297.
3. Baumol, *op. cit.*, p.266 (*italics added*)
4. *Ibid*, p. 266-67 (*italics added*)

list when he chooses to maximize sales (total revenue).

The important question in regard to the advertising is how much advertising expenditure a firm will make so as to achieve its objective. How much advertising outlay will be incurred by a firm is greatly influenced by the objective of the firm as to whether it seeks to maximise sales or profits. This optimal advertising expenditure from the viewpoints of both sales maximisation and profit maximi-sation is illustrated in Fig. 30.2 in which advertising outlay is measured along the X-axis and total cost, total revenue and total profits on the Y-axis. Baumol takes an important assumption in connection with the effect of advertising outlay on total revenue or sales. He assumes, and he quotes empirical evidence for this, that the increase in advertising outlay by a firm will always raise the physical volume of sales, though after a point these sales will increase at a diminishing rate.

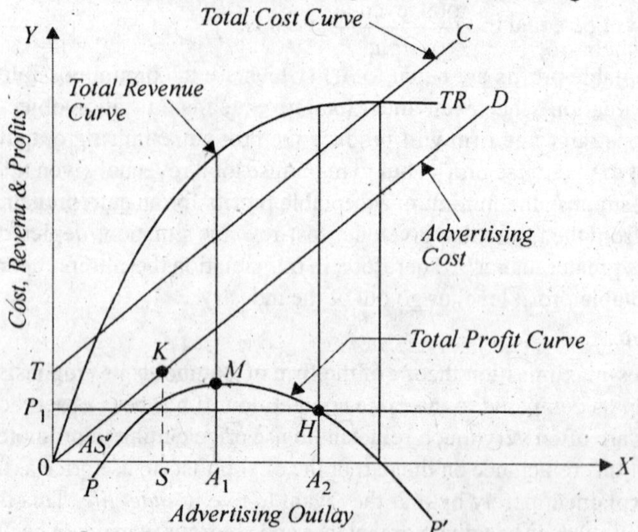

Fig. 30.2. *Optimal Advertising Outlay with Sales Maximisation and Profit Maximisation*

Now, given the price of product, the total revenue (*i.e.*, monetary value of the sales) will increase in proportion to the increase in the physical value of sales as a result of the increase in advertising outlay. Therefore, the increase in advertising outlay will always cause the total revenue to increase, though after a point diminishing returns are likely to set in. In Fig. 30.2, *TR* is the total revenue curve which represents the change in total revenue as the advertising outlay is raised, given the price of the product. Curve *OD* represents the advertising cost and has been so drawn as to make 45° angle with X-axis. This is because we have simply transferred the advertising outlay shown on the X-axis to the vertical axis as advertising cost, (for instance $OS = SK$). The *other costs* of the firm incurred on fixed and variable factors are taken to be independent of the amount of advertising outlay. Therefore, by adding a fixed amount of other costs (equal to *OT*) to the advertising curve *OD*, we obtain the total cost curve *TC*. Finally, by taking out the difference between total revenue curve (*TR*) and total cost curve (*TC*) we draw the total profit curve *PP'*.

Now, it will be seen from Fig. 30.2 that if the firm seeks to maximise its profits, it will incur advertising outlay equal to OA_1, at which the profit curve reaches its maximum point M. On the other hand, if OP_1 is the minimum profit constraint and the firm chooses to maximize its total revenue with OP_1 as the minimum profit constraint, it will spend OA_2 on advertisement which is greater than OA_1. We thus see that objective of constrained revenue maximization leads to a greater level of advertising outlay than the objective of profit maximization. In this connection, it should be noted that here there is no possibility of *unconstrained sales or revenue maximum*, as is there corresponding to output *OC* in the previous Fig. 30.1. This is because, unlike a reduction in price, *increase in advertising outlay always raises total revenue or sales* (by assumption). As a result, Baumol concludes that "it will always pay the sales maximizer to increase his advertising outlay until he is stopped by the profit constraint—until profits have been reduced to the minimum acceptable level. This means that sales maximizer will normally advertise no less than, and usually more than, do profit maximizers. For, unless the maximum profit level A_1M is not greater than the required minimum OP_1, it will be possible to increase advertising somewhat beyond the profit-maximizing level OA_1 without violating the profit constraint. Moreover, this increase will be desired since, by assumption, it will increase physical sales, and with them, dollar sales will rise proportionately."[5]

Critical Appraisal of Sales Maximisation Theory

Implication of sales maximisation theory of Baumol is that price would be lower and output greater under sales maximisation than under profit maximization. This is because total revenue is maximised at the price-output level where marginal revenue is zero, while at the profit-maximizing level of output marginal revenue is positive, given that marginal costs are positive. We have explained above that even under sales maximisation with a minimum profit constraint, output will be greater and price lower than under profit-maximization objective. If this is true that oligopolists seek to maximise sales or total revenue, then the greater output and lower-price will have a favourable effect on the welfare of the people.

As explained above, another implication of sales maximisation objective is more advertising expenditure will be incurred under it. Further, under sales maximisation objective of oligopolists, price is likely to remain sticky and the firms are more likely to indulge in non-price competition. This is what actually happens in oligopolistic market situations in the real world. Another significant implication of Baumol's model is that "there may be a conflict between pricing in the long and short run. In a short-run situation where output is limited, revenue would often increase, if prices were raised: but in the long-run it might pay to keep price low in order to compete more effectively for a large share of the market. This price policy to be followed in the short run would then depend on the expected repercussions of short-run decisions on long-run revenue."[6]

But sales maximisation model has not been without its critics. Shepherd[7] has asserted that an oligopolist confronts kinked demand curve and that if the kink is quite large, total revenue (*i.e.*, sales) and total profits would be maximised at the same level of output. But Hawkins[8] has shown that Shepherd's conclusions are invalid if the oligopolistic firms indulge in any form of non-price competition such as advertising, product variation, improvement in service, etc. and normally in the real world they do so.

An important and convincing criticism against sales maximisation model has been made by Hawkins.[9] As has been noted above, according to Baumol, sales-maximising firm will generally produce and advertise more than the profit-maximising firm. But Hawkins has shown that this conclusion is generally invalid. According to him, in case of single-product firms as compared with profit maximizing firm, whether a sales maximising firm will produce greater, smaller or same output and incur a greater, smaller or same advertising outlay depends upon the responsiveness of demand or total revenue to advertising expenditure as compared with the responsiveness of demand or total revenue to price cuts. As regards multi-product firms, which are generally found these days in the real world, in the *static model*, both sales maximisation and profit maximisation arrive at the same conclusion regarding choice of output and input combinations.[10] But besides a static model, Baumol has also developed a growth model[11] of a sales maximising firm which, as has been shown by Williamson, that different results follow as compared with profit maximisating firm.

In spite of the above cirticisms, the present author is of the view that Prof. Baumol's sales maximisation model is a significant alternative to profit maximisation and brings us closer to reality,

5. *Op. cit.*, p.262
6. A. Silberston, Price Behaviour of Firms, *Economic Journal*, 1970
7. W.G. Shepherd, On Sales Maximising and Oligopoly Behaviour, *Economica*, 1962
8. C.J. Hawkins, 'On the Sales Revenue Maximization Hypothesis, *Journal of Industrial Economics*, April 1970.
9. C.J. Hawkins, "The Revenue Maximisation Oligopoly Model", Comment, *American Economic Revew*, March, 1971
10. Sec C.J. Hawkins, On the Sales Revenue Maximization Hypothesis', *Journal of Industrial Economics*, April 1970

for in many cases as we brought out above in the explanation of the model, it explains the business behaviour in the real world better than profit maximisation. Even if in certain cases, sales and profit maximisation yield same or similar results, even then by providing intersting insight into managerial motivation in these days of manager-dominated big business corporations Baumol has made an important contribution to the theory of firm. Further, by explicitly incorporating advertising and other forms of non-price competition in his model, Baumol has made a significant contribution to our price theory.

QUESTIONS FOR REVIEW

1. "In corporate form of business organisation managers are more interested in maximising sales rather than profits" Discuss.

2. Why is sales maximisation a more realistic objective in today's world than the objective of profit maximization ? Explain *D.U., B.Com (Hons.) 2007*

3. What is meant by sales-maximisation ? Explain how, a firm determines optimal price and output when it pursues the goal of sales maximisation.

4. Explain Baumol's sales maximisation model using a suitable diagram. Campare it with profit, maximisation objective of the firm. *D.U. B.Com (Hons.) 2001.*

5. What is meant by non-price competition ? Explain that sales maximisation objective brings out that businessmen will consider non-price competition to more advantageous than price competition. Show, through sales maximisation model, the optimal amount of advertising expenditure.

6. If a price making monopolist firm wants to maximise its sales revenue, it should —

(*a*) set the highest price it can get.

(*b*) set the lowest price it can get.

(*c*) choose a selling price at which the elasticity of demand for its product is unity.

(*d*) choose a selling price where the extra revenue received from the last unit sold exceeds the extra cost of making that unit.

(Tick the right answer) *D.U. B.A.(Hons.) Economics*

[**Hint.** (C) is correct. This is because total revenue is maximum at the point on a demand curve at which price elasticity of demand is equal to unity.

7. Assuming that a firm pursues the objective of sales maximisation. How much advertising expenditure it will incure to maximise value of sales subject a minimum profit constraint. Compare it with the amount of advertising expenditure incurred for maximising profits.

8. A firm faces a demand curve given by $Q = 100 - 2P$. Marginal and average costs for the firm are constant at Rs. 10 per unit. What output level should the firm produce to (*i*) maximise profits, and (*ii*) maximise sales revenue ? What are the respective profits of each output level ?

Note. For the solution of this problem see solved numerical problem 3 in chapter 22.

CHAPTER 31

THEORY OF GAMES AND COMPETITIVE STRATIGY

Introduction

So far we have discussed those models of oligopoly which assume profit maximizing behaviour on the part of the oligopolists. There are other models of oligopoly which explain the price and output under oligopoly by assuming objectives other than profit maximization. One such model is to be found in the application of the theory of games to the oligopoly problem. Professors Neumann and Morgenstern in their book "*The Theory of Games and Economic Behaviour*" which was first published in 1944 provided a *new approach to many problems involving conflicting situations*. The game theory has been applied not only to the oligopoly but also to other economic questions like demand when uncertainty is present. Not only that, the game theory has been applied to the problems of subjects other than economics such as business administration, sociology, psychology, political science, military planning. The theory of games examines the outcome of a situation of interactions between the parties when they have *conflicting* interests. Basically, the game theory seeks to explain what is the rational course of action for an individual who is faced with an uncertain situation, the outcome of which depends not only upon this his own actions but also upon the actions of others who too confront the same problem of choosing a rational strategic course of action. We shall describe below how the game theory explains his fundamental question. We shall confine ourselves only to the oligopoly problem. According to professors Neumann and Morgenstern,[1] in an oligopolistic market situation, individual oligopolists is faced with a problem of choosing a rational course of action which is often called a strategy, keeping in view the possible reactions of his rivals whose reactions in turn would affect him. Thus, he confronts a problem similar to that of the player of any other game.

In a simple form of the game theory, the player has to choose among many possible courses of action which are called strategies. *A strategy is thus a course of action or a policy which a player or a participant in a game will adopt during the play of the game*. There are many possible strategies open to an individual among which he has to choose one at a time. In the case of oligopoly, the various alternative possible strategies which are relevant are : (*a*) changing the price, (*b*) changing the level of output, (*c*) increasing advertisement expenditure, and (*d*) varying the product. Changing the price may itself be divided into three strategies : (1) lowering the price, (2) raising the price, and (3) keeping the price unchanged. Similarly, the strategy of output may be (1) to increase the level of output, (2) to decrease output, and (3) to keep output constant. Likewise, increasing advertisement expenditure may further be divided into various strategies depending upon the various forms of advertisement, for instance, advertisement on radios, on television, in newspapers, in magazines, through handbills, through posters etc. Likewise, varying the product can be subdivided into various strategies depending upon the nature of the product to be chosen such as whether the colour of the package or the type of the package, or the quality of the product should be changed.

A basic feature of oligopoly is that each firm must take into account of its rival's reactions to its own actions. For example, Maruti Udyog cannot ignore the effect of an increase in price of its product

1. John Von Neumann and Oskar Morgenstern, *Theory of Games and Economic Behaviour*, 3rd ed., New York-Wiley, 1964.

on the prices and profits of its rival firms and how they will respond to its move of rise in price of its product. Thus, it is clear that oligopolistic behaviour has some of the characteristics of a game where a player must know how his move will affect his rival and how, assuming that he is rational, will react to his move.

Game theory highlights that, in an oligopolistic market, a *firm behaves strategically,* that is, it adopts *strategic decision-making which means that while taking decisions regarding price, output, advertising etc. it takes into account how its rivals will react to its decisions and assuming them to be rational it thinks that they will do their best to promote their interests and take this into account while making decisions*. Game theory shed new light on some of the important issues faced in explaining decision-making by firms operating in oligopolistic markets. It explains why an individual firm decides to cheat on a cartel agreement. Further, it explains why and how firms operating in oligopolistic markets prevent the entry of new firms in the industry.

Cooperative and Non-Cooperative Games

Games which firms play can be either cooperative or non-cooperative. A game is cooperative if the firm (*i.e.* players in the game) can arrive at an enforceable or *binding contract* that permits them to adopt a strategy to maximise joint profits. Suppose making of a carpet costs Rs 500 but the buyers value it at Rs 1000. Fixation of price between Rs 500 and 1000 per carpet will yield profits. In this case, two firms producing carpet can cooperate with each other and adopt a joint price strategy to maximise their joint profits rather than competing with each other. *If the two firms can sign a binding contract to share the profits between them from the production and sale of carpets, the game is called a cooperative game.*

On the other hand, a non-cooperative game is one where because of *conflict of interests* two firms cannot sign a binding contract. In most of the oligopolistic market situations binding contract, that is, contract that are enforceable cannot be negotiated. Therefore, in oligopoly in most cases we find examples of non-cooperative games. *In a situation of non-cooperative games while the competing firms take each other's actions into account but they take decisions independently and adopt strategies* regarding pricing, advertising, product variation to promote their interests.

It should be noted that a basic difference between a cooperative and non-cooperative game lies in the possibility of negotiating an enforceable contract. In cooperative games, negotiating binding or enforceable contracts are possible, in non-cooperative games they are not. In this chapter while explaining firms' decisions regarding pricing, advertising, we will be concerned mostly with non-cooperative games.

Note that there are games where the players move simultaneously. Each firm chooses a strategy before observing any action or strategy chosen by the rival firms. Not all games are of this type. In some games one player goes first and after which the other player reacts.

DOMINANT STRATEGY

How can firms decide about the optimal choice of a strategy? Some strategies may be successful (that is, more profitable) if competitors make a *particular* choice, that is, take a *certain* decision but will not be successful if competitors make *other* choices. On the other hand, *a dominant strategy is one which will be successful or optimal for a firm regardless of what others do, that is, no matter what strategy the rival firms adopt.*

Let us illustrate the dominant strategy in case of duopoly in the choice of whether to '*Advertise*' *or not*. In this case, deciding in favour of advertising by a firm to promote its sales and hence profits or deciding not to advertise are the two strategies. Thus, '*Advertising*' or '*Not Advertising*' are the two strategies between which each firm has to make a choice. We assume there are two firms, *A* and *B* which have to make a choice between the two strategies. The outcome (or profits made) from the various combinations of two strategies chosen by the two firms are presented in the following table in the form of payoff matrix. It should be noted that outcome or profits made by a firm by adopting a strategy is influended by the choice of a particular strategy by the rival firm.

Table 1 : **Payoff Matrix for Advertising Game**

(in Rs. Crores)

		FIRM B	
		Advertising	*Not Advertising*
FIRM A	*Advertising*	A : 10 B : 5	A : 15 B : 0
	Not Advertising	A : 6 B : 8	A : 10 B : 2

It will be seen from the payoff matrix that if *both firms* adopt the strategy of '*Advertising*', the firm *A* will make profits of 10 crores and firm *B* will earn profits of 5 crores. If firm *A* decides to advertise and firm *B* decides not to advertise, profits of firm *A* are 15 crores and of firm *B* are zero. Similarly, if firm *A* decides not to advertise but firm *B* decides in favour of advertising, firm *A* makes profits of 6 crores and *B* of 8 crores. Further, if both firms go in for '*not advertising*' profits of *A* are 10 crores and of *B* are 2 crores.

Now, the question is what strategy each firm should choose. It is assumed that each firm is rational and will adopt a strategy which will ensure it more profits. Let us first consider choices and their outcome available for firm *A*. If the firm *B* adopts a strategy of '*Advertising*', profits of firm *A* are 10 crores if it also chooses the strategy of advertising but only 6 crores if it chooses not to advertise. On the other hand, if firm *B* adopts strategy of '*Not Advertising*', profits of firm *A* are 15 crores if it opts for 'Advertising' and profits of 10 crores if it also chooses strategy of '*Not Advertising*'.

It is thus clear from the payoff matrix, choice of strategy of '*Advertising*' by firm *A* is better or optimal since it ensures more profits whether firm *B* adopts strategy of '*Advertising*' or the strategy of '*Not Advertising*'. Thus, in the present payoff matrix, whatever strategy firm *B* adopts, for firm *A* strategy of '*Advertising*' is optimal. *When payoff matrix of a game is such that a choice of one strategy is better regardless of what ever strategy the other firm chooses, the strategy is known as dominant strategy.* In the present case choice of strategy of '*Advertising*' is a dominant strategy for firm *A*.

From the payoff matrix of the advertising game given in the Table 1, the similar conclusion can be drawn for the optimal strategy to be adopted by firm *B*. Let us state the choices that are open to firm *B*. If firm *A* adopts strategy of 'Advertising', the firm *B* makes profits of 5 crores if it also chooses strategy of 'Advertising' and zero if it chooses strategy of 'Not Advertising'. Thus, choice of strategy of 'Advertising' by firm *B* is better, if firm *A* opts for the strategy of 'Advertising'. On the other hand, if firm *A* chooses strategy of 'Not Advertising', profits of firm *B* are 8 crores if it chooses strategy of 'Advertising' and 2 crores if it adopts strategy of 'Not Advertising'. Thus, in this case too, choice of strategy of 'Advertising' by firm *B* is optimal whatever strategy the firm *A* adopts. Thus, strategy of '*Advertising*' is a dominant strategy for firm *B*.

Since it is assumed that both firms behave rationally each of them will choose the strategy of 'Advertising' and the outcome will be profits of Rs 10 crores for firm A and Rs 5 crores for firm B.

It is important to note that all games do not have a dominant strategy for each player. To make it clear we make some changes in the payoff matrix and present them in Table 2. The payoff matrix in Table 2 differs from the previous payoff matrix in that profits shown in the bottom right hand corner are different, they are Rs 20 crores for firm *A* and Rs 2 crores for firm *B* in case both adopt the strategy of 'Not Advertising'.

Table 2. **Payoff Matrix for Advertising Game**

		FIRM B	
		Advertising	*Not Advertising*
FIRM A	*Advertising*	A : 10 B : 5	A : 15 B : 0
	Not Advertising	A : 6 B : 8	A : 20 B : 2

Note. *Numbers in the above table represent profits and are in Rs. crores.*

As will be seen from payoff matrix in Table 2, if firm *B* chooses strategy of 'Advertising' profits of firm *A* are Rs 10 crores if it also opts for strategy of 'Advertising' and are Rs 6 crores if it opts for strategy of 'Not Advertising'. Clearly, choice of strategy of 'Advertising' by firm *A* yields more profits and is therefore optimal if firm *B* adopts strategy of 'Advertising'. Now, if firm *B* chooses strategy of 'Not Advertising', profits of firm *A* are Rs 15 crores, if it decides in favour of 'Advertising' strategy and its profits are Rs 20 crores if it too adopts strategy of 'Not Advertising'. Thus, in this case given that firm *B* chooses stragegy of 'Not Advertising' choice of strategy of 'Not Advertising' by firm *A* is optimal.

It follows from above that in the payoff matrix presented in Table 2, *optimal strategy for firm A depends on which strategy the firm B adopts.* Choice of strategy of 'Advertising' is optimal for firm *A*, given that the firm *B* adopts the strategy of 'Advertising'. On the other hand, choice of strategy of 'Not Advertising' by firm *A* is better, given that the *B* adopts strategy of 'Not Advertising'. Thus, in this case there is no dominant strategy for firm *A*. The choice of an optimal strategy by firm *A* in the present case, that is, when dominant strategy does not exist, will be easier if firm *B* adopts a strategy before the firm *A* has to make its choice. But how a firm makes an optimal decision regarding choice of strategy if both firms must choose their strategies simultaneously, that is, at the same time. This is explained below.

Choice of an Optimal Strategy in the Absence of A Dominant Strategy

To decide about the optimal strategy by firm *A* when the choice of strategy by it depends on what strategy the other firm *B* adopts, the *firm A must put itself in firm B's place.* For this the firm *A* has to know what strategy is the best from firm *B's* point of view and further that it should assume that the firm *B* is rational and will therefore adopt the best strategy. From the payoff matrix given in Table 2, it will be seen that given that the firm *A* chooses strategy of 'Advertising' the firm *B* will make profits equal to Rs. 5 crores if it adopts strategy of advertising and its profits will be equal to zero if it opts for 'Not Advertising' strategy. Further, if firm *A* chooses strategy of 'Not Advertising' profits of firm *B* will be Rs 8 crores if it decides to advertise and only Rs 2 crores if it decides not to advertise. Thus, for firm *B*, strategy of 'Advertising' is better no matter firm *A* adopts strategy of 'Advertising' or 'Not Advertising' and therefore the firm *A* can safely conclude that firm *B* will adopt this strategy of 'Advertising'.

Now, given that firm *B will adopt strategy of 'Advertising'* the firm *A* will choose its strategy. If from *A* adopts strategy of 'Advertising' its profits will be Rs 10 crores and if its adopts strategy of 'Not Advertising', its profits will be Rs 6 crores. Thus, given the firm *B's* strategy of 'Advertising', the optimal strategy of firm *A* is that of 'Advertising' too. In this way both firms will reach the equilibrium *state by choosing strategy of 'Advertising' and will have no incentive to deviate form it.* It is quite logical outcome of the game because firm *A* is choosing the best strategy it can, given firm *B's* strategy, and firm *B* is choosing the best strategy, given firm *A's* strategy.

The Nash Equilibrium

We may refer here to the concept of Nash equilibrium which has been already explained in connection with Cournot's duopoly equilibrium. Nash equilibrium is named after John F. Nash, an American mathematician and economist. We have explained above that in many games we do not have dominant strategies, but still the firms achieve equilibrium in the adoption of their strategies. The application of the concept of Nash equilibrium is quite relevant here. Nash equilibrium is a more general concept of equilibrium that is widely applicable and highly appealing. In the second advertising game whose payoff matrix is given in Table 2 and in which firm *A* has no dominant strategy we reached the conclusion that the equilibrium state is reached when firm *A* adopts strategy of 'Advertising' *given that the firm B will choose the strategy of 'Advertising'.* That is, firm *A* is making the best choice, given the choice by its rival firm *B* and *B* is choosing the best strategy, given the strategy of firm *A*. Therefore, they have no incentive to change their strategies. Hence, there exists an equilibrium, called Nash equilibrium.

Nash equilibrium describes a set of strategies where each player believes that it is doing the best it can, given the stragy of the other playe or players.

In our above example of game 2 of advertising where firm *A* has no dominant strategy, each firm promotes its own interests and makes a best choice of strategy, given the other firm's strategy. In the above game, both firms *A* and *B* adopt strategy of 'Advertising' which is optimal for them. Since each is doing the best, given other's strategy and no one has a tendency to change it unilaterally, there exists Nash equilibrium. As no one has a tendency to deviate from the Nash equilibrium state, strategies chosen by them *are stable.*

Dominant Strategy and Nash Equilibrium. It is important to compare Nash equilibrium and equilibrium reached where each firm has a dominant strategy. Whereas a *dominant strategy equilibrium describes an optimal or best choice regardless of what strategy the other player adopts,* in Nash equilibrium each player adopts a strategy that is the best or optimal, *given the strategy the other player adopts.* However, it may be noted that in some games we do not have Nash equilibrium and that in some we have more than one Nash equilibrium.

NEUMANN–MORGENSTERN GAME THEORY

There is a fundamental assumption in the Neumann - Morgenstern game theory which is worth mentioning. According to their game theory, *an oligopolist while choosing his strategy will assume that his rivals will adopt a strategy which will be worst for him,* that is, the rivals will adopt the policy which will be unfavourable to him. That is to say, an oligopolist will adopt the policy of "*playing it safe*". Given this assumption, from among strategies which provide him various *minimum* gains, an oligopolist will select that one which is maximum in those minimum gains.

In order to discuss the solution of oligopoly problem suggested by Neumann-Morgenstern's theory of game, we suppose that an oligopolist knows the complete set of strategies open to him as well as those available to his rivals in the industry. Further, it is assumed that the struggle between the oligopolists is of the nature of "*strictly adversary game*". A strictly adversary game is one in which the outcome which is favourable from the viewpoint of one, is unfavourable to the other. Lastly, we take a *constant-sum game,* in which the outcomes to the two players, *i.e.,* oligopolits always add up to the same constant amount. Thus, in a constant sum game, one player's gain is always another player's loss. Thus, if the constant sum is profits of Rs. 10 which is to be shared between the two sellers, then if *A* receives Rs. 8, then *B* will be get Rs. 2, and if *A* gets Rs. 3, then *B* will obtain Rs. 7 and so on. In our explanation of the game theory below, we shall describe the behaviour of a pair of duopolists *A* and *B* who compete for a given total profits of Rs. 10. when in a game aggregate of gain (+) and loss (–) is zero, the constant-sum game becomes a *zero sum game.* In the oligopolistic market situation, if advertising compaign launched by a firm for promoting the sales of its product merely causes a *fixed number of consumers* to switch from other brands of the product to his brand without adding to the total demand of the product, it would be an example of a zero sum game.

Maximum and Minimax Strategies

Let us suppose that three strategies are open to *A* and three strategies are open to *B*. It is assumed that the duopolists are able to quantify the outcomes of the various combinations of different strategies. The various different strategies open to the duopolists and the effect on the profits of the various combinations of strategies are depicted in Table 3 which is called '*Payoff Matrix*'. The payoff matrix of a game represents the profits to each player for each combination of strategies that are chosen. In the table given below *A's* strategies such A_1, A_2 and A_3 are represented in a column, and *B's* strategies such as B_1, B_2 and B_3 are represented in a row. *A's* payoff matrix in Table 3 *shows the amount of profits which accrue to A* as a result of the strategies adopted by him and his rival *B*.

Table 3. **A's Payoff Matrix**

		B's Strategies			
		B_1	B_2	B_3	*Row Minima*
	A_1	2	8	1	1
A's Strategies	A_2	4	3	9	3
	A_3	5	6	7	5
Coumn maxima		5	8	9	

Thus, if *A* adopts strategy A_1 and *B* adopts strategy B_1, then the profits to *A* are Rs. 2. The profits to *B* will be the given constant sum (*i.e.* the profits of Rs. 10) minus the amount of profits which go to *A*. Therefore, in the above case (when *A* adopts strategy A_1 and *B* adopts strategy B_1) the profits of *B* will be Rs. 10 – 2 = Rs. 8. The profits of *B* are not shown in the Table 3 though they can be shown in a separate but the same type of table. In the table given above when *A* plays strategy A_1 and *B* plays strategy B_2 the profits to *A* will be Rs. 8. Likewise, if *A* selects A_2 and *B* selects strategy B_3, the profits to *A* will be Rs. 9. Again, if *A* adopts strategy A_3 and *B* adopts strategy B_1, then the profits to *A* will be Rs. 5. Similarly, each of the other profits figures for *A* in the Table 3 corresponds to a particular combination of strategies chosen by *A* and *B*.

Now, given the payoff matrix of *A* in the above table, which strategies will be selected by *A* and *B* and what will be the outcome? Suppose *A* has to choose his strategy before *B* chooses. As pointed out above, *A will choose his strategy keeping in mind that B will adopt the most unfavourable strategy for him, that is, B will play that strategy which will provide minimum possible share of profits to A. That is, if A decides to choose strategy A_1, then B can either choose strategy B_1 or B_2 or B_3. With A having* adopted strategy A_1, if *B* adopts B_1, the profits to *A* will be 2; if he adopts B_2 the profits to *A* will be 8; if he adopts B_3, the profits to *A* will be Re. 1. It is clear that when *A* has adopted strategy A_1, *B* will cause *A* to get minimum profits (Re. 1) if he plays strategy B_3. Likewise, if *A* decides to select strategy A_2, then *B* would play strategy B_2 and will give in this way minimum possible profits (Rs. 3) to *A* in this case. Again, if *A* adopts strategy A_3, then *B* will adopt strategy B_1 so as to cause minimum possible profits (Rs. 5) to *A* in this case. It is now obvious that *A* will choose strategy A_3 so that if *B* plays most unfavourable strategy even then he gets profits of Rs. 5 which is greater than the other minimum profits of Re. 1 and Rs. 3 in case of the selection of strategies A_1 and A_2 respectively. In other words, *A* will choose maximum of the minimum profits he gets in three strategies. For the sake of convenience, minimum profits in each row are written in a new column entiteld '*Row Minima*'. Thus while selecting his strategies *A* will look at the column of '*Row Minima*'. *A* will choose maximum of the row minima, that is, *A* will choose strategy A_3 which gives him maximum (Rs. 5) of the minimum profits (Rs. 1, 3 and 5). It is thus clear that *A* will follow a *maximin strategy*.

When *A* has selected strategy A_3 and *B* comes to know of it, then *B* will adopt strategy B_1 because by doing so he will cause minimum possible profits (Rs. 5) to *A* and will ensure maximum possible profits to himself. With *A* having adopted strategy A_3, if *B* adopts strategy B_2 or B_3, *A's* profits will be Rs. 6 or 7 respectively, that is, more than when he adopts strategy B_1. Thus when *A* has selected strategy A_3, *B* will select strategy B_1. With *A* having selected strategy A_3, with *B's* strategy B_1, *A* will get profits of Rs. 5 as is seen from his Payoff Matrix in the above table and *B* will get profits of Rs. 10

– 5 = Rs. 5 (Here, by chance, the shares of the profits of the two are equal, they need not be necessarily equal in all cases.)

Now suppose that *B* has to choose his strategy first before *A* chooses his strategy. While making his choice of a strategy, *B* will also keep in mind that *A* will adopt the strategy which will be most undesirable for him (*B*). *A's* worst strategy for *B* will be one which will provide him (*A*) maximum possible profits and therefore reduces the share of profits to *B* to the minimum possible. The same table which shows profits or payoff to *A* can be made use of to explain the strategy to be adopted by *B*.

It will be seen from *A's* payoff Matrix that if *B* decides to choose strategy B_1, then if *A* chooses strategy A_1, the profits to him will be Rs. 2 (and to *B* will be Rs. 8); if he chooses strategy A_2 the profits to him will be Rs. 4 (and to *B* will be Rs. 6); if he chooses strategy A_3, profits to him will be Rs. 5 (to *B* they will also be Rs. 5). It is thus clear that with *B* having decided to select strategy B_1, *A* will choose strategy A_3, because in this way, it will be getting maximum possible profits (Rs. 5) and will be rendering the share of profits to *B* to the minimum possible. Now, if *B* selects strategy B_2, then *A's* worst strategy for *B* will be A_1, in which case share of profits to *A* will be Rs. 8 as seen from the Table 3 the remaining Rs. 2 will go to *B*. Likewise, if *B* selects strategy B_3, *A* will select strategy A_2 so as to cause maximum possible profits (Rs. 9) to him and minimum possible profits (Re. 1) to *B*.

Given the above reaction pattern of *A*, what strategy will be selected by *B*, that is, whether *B* will adopt strategy B_1 or B_2 or B_3. If he adopts strategy B_1, worst possible for him will be profits to *A* of Rs. 5 which are maximum in the given column. Similarly, if he adopts strategy B_2 worst possibility for him will be profits to *A* of Rs. 8 which is maximum in the new column. Further, if *B* adopts strategy B_3, worst possibility for him will be profits to *A* of Rs. 9 which is maximum in the column under B_3. In the above table various maxima of the columns have been written in a new row entitled '*Column Maxima*'. The best course of action for *B* will be to choose *minimum of these maxima of columns,* since by doing so he will ensure minimum possible profits to *A* and hence maximum possible profits to him. Thus, given the situation as depicted in the above table, *B* will select strategy B_1 which provides to *A* profits of Rs. 5 which is minimum of the maxima of the column maxima. It follows therefore that *B* will follow a *minimax strategy*. When *B* has chosen strategy B_1 and announces it, *A* will examine his possible strategies and will naturally strategy A_3 since it gives him greater possible profits than A_1 or A_2.

We explained above the choice of strategies by *A* and *B* separately in two cases, first, when *A* chooses first before *B* makes a choice, and secondly when *B* has to choose first before *A* chooses. It has been seen above that, given *A's* pay-off matrix, as shown in the table, in both cases *A*'s choice is strategy A_3 and *B*'s choice is strategy B_1. It should be noted that in the *actual game in the real world, neither A nor B has to choose first, they choose simultaneously.* But the foregoing argument nevertheless applies. Given the assumption that each expects worst from his rival, when both have to choose simultaneously, *A* will look at the row minima of his payoff matrix and will select maximum of the row minima, and *B* will look at the column maxima of *A*'s payoff matrix and will choose minimum of the column maxima. Given the *A*'s payoff matrix, *A* will play *maximin strategy* and *B* will play *minimax strategy*. Thus even when both choose their strategies simultaneously, *A* will choose strategy A_3 because it is his maximin strategy and *B* will choose strategy B_1 because it is his minimax strategy. It is therefore clear that the *result is the same whether A chooses first, B chooses first or both choose simultaneously.*

Equilibrium (Saddle) Point

In payoff matrix in the above table the maximum of the row minima and the minimum of the column maxima are the same, that is, *A*'s maximin strategy coincides with *B*'s minimax strategy. When it happens so, the payoff matrix is said to possess an equilibrium point or, what is also technically called '*saddle point*'. In *A*'s pay off matrix in the Table 3 pay-off 5 is an equilibrium or saddle point because the maximum of the row minima is 5 and minimum of the column maxima is also 5. Thus, *A* by choosing strategy A_3 and *B* by choosing strategy B_1 are in equilibrum, that is, they will have no incentive to change their strategies. When a payoff-matrix possesses an equilibrium point, then the maximin strategy is the most advantageous strategy open to one firm, *if the other employs a minimax strategy.* Actually, it is because of this that the coincident pay-off entry (5, in our table above) of the maximin and minimax strategy combination is called an equilibrium point. In other words, when one firm employs a maximin strategy, the other is motivated to employ minimax strategy because that is how it can obtain the largest possible share of the profit. Conversely, if one firm plays minimax strategy, the other is motivated to employ the maximin strategy for the reason just mentioned above. In the words of Prof. Baumol, "*Equilibrium points therefore possess an element of stability in that if one player adopts a strategy consistent with the attainment of such a point, the other player is also motivated to do so.*"[2]

It is worth mentioning that when the maximum of row minima is not equal to the minimum of column maxima, that is, when there is no equilibrium or saddle point in the pay-off matrix, then stable equilibrium would not be attained. In such cases, it matters a great deal who plays first and also it is helpful to know rival's strategy in advance. Various methods have been developed to provide solution in such a pay-off matrix which does not contain equilibrium or stable point. One of these methods is to permit the players to employ mixed strategies. A mixed strategy is a combination of two strategies with the probabilities assigned to these strategies. The technique of solving games involving mixed strategies is too complicated and is therefore not attempted here.

Critical Appraisal of Neumann-Morgenstern Maximin or Minimax Strategy

The maximin game theory as applied to the oligopoly problem has been questioned on some grounds. First, the fundamental assumption underlying the game theory, namely, that an oligopolist believes that his rival will do worst and adopt his strategy keeping this in view has been questioned. It is pointed out that in essence this assumption about the behaviour of the entrepreneur (oligopolist) implies that he minimizes the chance of the maximum loss, that is, his policy is to "play safe." But such a behaviour on the part of the oligopolist, it is said, is very pessimistic as well as conservative. In the real world, the entrepreneurs do not adopt such a cautions and pessimistic approach. They seek to increase their profits and share of the market and for that they often take risks. Professors Ferguson and Kreps rightly remark : "The game theory may very well describe the type of the entrepreneur who is primarily intent upon maintaining solvency. It is a much less accurate description of the dynamic businessman who is constantly in quest of profit."[4]

Secondly, it is pointed out that the entrepreneurs in the real world do not possess the amount of knowledge assumed in the game theory. The entrepreneurs do not know even all the various strategies open to them, much less those open to their competitors. Moreover, the real world involves a good deal of uncertainty which has not been incorporated and also cannot be easily incorporated in the game theory.

In the third place, it is said that the oligopoly game is not a strictly adverse game, nor a zero sum game as considered in the theory of games. Contrary to these assumptions, the reduction in price by an oligopolist leads to the increase in the total quantity demanded and not a mere shift of customers from others. Besides, oligopolists do not fight over a lot of profits of a fixed size.

There is another flaw in the game theory. For the game theory to provide a definite solution, both the duopolists must be prudent, that is to say, both should play their maximin or minimax strategies. When one of the duopolists does not possess an adequate knowledge or is not very prudent or is prepared to take risks, then for any of these reasons he will not play minimax strategy. If this is so, then the adoption of maximin strategy by others will be unprofitable. In our example above, if B chooses strategy B_2 for any of the above reasons, then the selection of maximin strategy A_3 by A will not give him maximum possible share of the profits. With B having selected non-minimax strategy B_2, A will get maximum possible share of the profits if he plays strategy A_1. It is thus clear that when one of the duopolists is not prudent, the game theory cannot provide a solution. In the words of Professor Baumol "*the prudent maximin strategy is only guaranteed to be good when playing against another prudent man*"[5]

It is evident from the above criticism that the game theory does not provide a complete and all

3. William J. Baumol, *Economic Theory and Operations Analysis.*
4. C. E. Ferguson and J. M. Kreps, *Principles of Economics*, p. 531.

agreed solution to the oligopoly problem. To quote Professors Ferguson and Kreps again, "We can reasonably say that while the game theory points out some of the crucial aspects of competitive situations, it is not a model that offers a complete solution to the oligopoly problem".[6] When John von Neumann and Oskar Morgenstern published their book '*Their of Games and Economic Behaviour*' in 1944, it was widely hoped that their new theory would greatly improve the approach to the solution of oligopoly problem. But these great expectations have not been realised. Thus Prof. Donald Watson says, "Although game theory has been developed since 1944, its contribution to the theory of oligopoly has been a vast disappointment".[7] Professor H. H. Liebhafsky of the University of Texas makes similar remarks, "So far, the great hopes which have been held for the application of the game theory in this area of analysis have not been realized. Indeed, its principal value seems to lie in the fact that it provides a fertile field wherein the imagination may roam in analyzing oligopoly probelms."[8]

THE PRISONERS' DILEMMA AND OLIGOPOLY THEORY

The firms working in oligopolistic markets make decisions in the face of uncertainty about how their rivals will react to their moves. As explained above, game theory is a mathematically technique of analysing the behaviour of rival firms with regard to changes in prices, output and advertisement expenditure in the situations of conflicts of interest among individuals or firms. An important game model that has significant implications for the behaviour of the oligopolists is popularly known as prisoner's dilemma. Model of prisoner's dilemma explains how rivals behaving selfishly act contrary to their mutual or common interests. We have explained prisoner's dilemma in connection with th instability of a cartel.

Now, under these circumstances what choice will be made by two prisoners, say Ranga and Billa, when they cannot communicate with each other and have to choose between the two alternatives independently. *The model of Prisoners' Dilemma suggests that both behaving selfishly and working in self-interest confess to the crime and cheat each other.* Since both confess, each will get maximum imprisonment under the lew. Why do they make this choice and confess can be shown as under. Take Ranga first, most probably, he would confess when he does not know how his co-accused will act. Ranga would reason like this : If I don't confess it is very likely that I will be imprisoned for 10 years as the other prisoner will most probably confess. If I confess, I will get 5 years imprisonment if the other one also confesses, and only one year imprisonment if he does not confess. So in the presence of uncertainty about the other person's choice, and behaving in self-interest, Ranga is likely to confess. Billa too reasoning similarly would confess. As a result, both prisoners would be sentended for 5 years, though they would have received a lighter sentence of only one year if both of them had not confessed and remained loyal to each other. However, *it is self-interest which leads prisoner to confess and prevents them from attaining the best solution* for themselves (1 year imprisonment) if both do not confess to the crime and remain loyal to each other. But the decision of each prisoner in favour of confession is quite rational because each person works in self-interest and tries to make the "*best*" of the "*worst outcomes*" in an uncertain situation.

Similarly, in case of a cartel we have seen that to increase their own profits the member firms have incentive to cheat by trying to produce and sell more at the agreed price. It is due to the working of inner pressures and promotion of self-interest by cartel members that accounts for the instability of cartel arrangements.

REPEATED GAMES AND TIT-FOR-TAT STRATEGY

In our analysis of Prisoner's Dilemma it was assumed that games was played just once. While applying prisoner's dilemma type game to the case of a cartel we concluded that oligopolists like the prisoners lacking trust in each other and behaving selfishly cheated each other. This resulted in bad outcome (*i.e.* lower or no profits) for them. However, the firms facing prisoner's dilemma can increase

5. William J. Baumol, *Economic Theory and Operations Analysis*, p. 352.
6. *Op. cit.*, p. 531.
7. Donald S. Watson : *Price Theory and Its Uses*, 1663, p. 356.
8. H. H. Liebhafsky, *The Nature of Price Theory*, 1963, p. 280.

their profits if they coopeate with each other. But *such cooperation is unlikely to occur in a prisoners' dilemma game played only once.* In this game of prisoners' dilemma the players have only a single opportunity to play a game (*i.e.* to confess or not). But in the real world oligopolists have to *play games repeatedly* as they have to set price and output over and over again.

In the case of working of a cartel at every point of time each firm has to decide whether to cheat or not. Behaving selfishly and having no trust in others, all member firms of a cartel cheat (that is, undercut price) and as a result make only small profits. However, in case of repeated games the oligopolists may adopt a cooperative behaviour which enables them to earn large profits. Thus when oligopolists play a repeated game, the analysis of prisoners' dilemma type game played only once may not be correct.

In case of a game played repeatedly the players come to know how the others react to their moves and this in turn changes their strategic behaviour. Thus in case of a repeated game, one firm has the opportunity to penalise the other for his previous bad behaviour. In this context it has been suggested that **tit-for-tat strategy** is the optimal strategy that will ensure cooperative behaviour of the players participating in a game.[9] Let us suppose an oligopolist firm *A* adopts a cooperative behaviour and charges a high price. Tit-for-tat strategy means that firm *A* will continue to charge high price so long as its rival firm *B* will also continue to do so (*i.e.* adopts cooperative behaviour). But if firm *B* cheats and undercuts its price in a round, then in the next round firm *A* will retaliate and will also set a low price. Thus the firm *B* knowing that the firm *A* is adopting a tit-for-tat strategy will have to take into account the possibility of the rival firm *A* retaliating in the next round. In case of a repeated game, this tit-for-tat strategy results in cooperative behaviour among oligopolists.

However, whether tit-for-tat strategy will be viable depends on whether the repeated game is played indefinitely or infinite number of times. Let us first explain the outcome when repeated game is played indefinitely. We assume that there are two oligopolistic firms *A* and *B* and there are two possible strategies, namely, (1) charging a high price, and (2) charging a low price. The firms adopt a tit-for-tat strategy. It may be mentioned again that, according to tit-for-tat strategy, what one firm does in the current period, the other firm will do in the next period. In the case of game of prisoners' dilemma which is played only once, if one firm cheats the retaliation by the other firm in the next period does not arise as the game is over in the first round itself. However, in case of a repeated game, the other player (firm in our case) can penalise the other firm in the next period for any cheating by any player in the current period. It is assumed that a firm knows that its rival firm is adopting tit-for-tat strategy.

How tit-for-tat strategy is an optimal strategy and will result in cooperative behaviour on the part of the oligopolists is illustrated in payoff matrix given in Table 4.

Table 4 : **Pay-off Matrix**

(*Figures in millions*)

		FIRM B' Strategy	
		Low Price	*High Price*
Firm A's Strategy	*Low Price*	A's Profits : 10 B's Profits : 10	A's Profits : 100 B's Profits : –50
	High price	A's Profits : –50 B's Profits : 100	A's Profits : 50 B's Profits : 50

If game is played only once as in the above case of Prisoners' Dilemma, both firms will cheat and charge low price and as will be seen from payoff matrix each firm will earn profits of only Rs. 10 million (see top left side box), while if they had cooperated and charged high price they could have earned Rs 50 million each (see bottom right side box). Under tit-for-tat strategy in case of repeated game played for an indefinite period, suppose firm *A* starts with charging a high price and decides to

9. See R. Axelord, "*The Evolution of Cooperation*" (New York : Basic Books, 1984).

continue charging the high price so long as the other firm also does likewise. But when the firm *B* cheats, that is, charges a low price, *B*'s profits rises to 100 millions in that round while the firm *A*'s profits have become negative (–50 million). Now, under the tit-for-tat strategy, the firm *A* will retaliate in the next round and set a low price. When both charge low price profits of each are 10 million (see upper left box of Table 4). As the game is repeated indefinitely, round after round, the cumulative loss of profits suffered by firm *B* will outweight his gain of profits in the round when it undercut price. Thus cheating (*i.e.* undercutting price in the present example) when the rivals are pursuing tit-for-tat strategy is not a profitable proposition. In this way the firms will learn that cooperative behaviour is the best course of action when each firm is pursuing the tit-for-tat strategy.

When both cooperate and charge a high price, each firm will earn profits of Rs 50 million in each round (see bottom right hand box in payoff matrix of Table 4). Thus, Hal Varian writes, "The tit-for-tat strategy does very well because it offers an immediate punishment for defection. It is also a forgiving strategy. It finishes the other player only once for each defection. If he falls into line and starts to cooperate, then tit-for-tat will reward the other player with cooperation. It appears to be a remarkably good mechanism for the efficient outcome in a prisoner's dilemma that will be played an indefinite number of times."[10]

Let us now consider the case when the game is repeated a *finite number of times*, say in 10 rounds. Both players know that the game will be played 10 times and also that each is pursuing tit-for-tat strategy. Let us first consider the 10th round which by assumption is the last round when the game will be played between the two firms. Whether they will cooperate, each charging a high price or cheat each charging a low price. If firm *B* believes that its rival firm is rational will reason like this: Even knowing that the firm *A* is playing tit-for-tat strategy, the firm *B* will think that since 10th round is the last round of playing the game and after that since the game is over, the firm *A* will have no chance to retaliate. Therefore, firm *B* will charge the high price for the first nine rounds but will choose to cheat, that is, will charge the the low price and make a large profits in the last 10th round (this is shown in the bottom left-side box of the payoff matrix of Table 4).

However, firm *A* will also reason likewise and will charge high price in the first 9 rounds but will plan to cheat (charge low price) in the last 10th round and will hope to make a large profits in the last 10th round thinking that firm *B* will have no chance to retaliate thereafter. Thus, both thinking rationally will decide to charge a low price in the last 10th round and will not cooperate with each other Hall Varian rightly writes "Players cooperate because they hope that cooperation will induce further cooperation in the future. But this requires that there will always be the possibility of future play. Since there is no possibility of future play in the last round, no one will cooperate then".[11]

But what about next to the 10th round, that is, 9th round. Firm *B* will reason that it should charge low price in this next to the last round because in any case there will be no cooperation between the two in the last round. But of course, the firm *A* being equally rational will also reason likewise and will plan to charge the low price in the 9th round (*i.e.* next to the last round). The same reasoning can be repeated by both the firms for undercutting price, that is, for charging a low price in the 8th earlier rounds as well, that is, for the rounds 8th, 7th, 6th etc. till the first round. *Thus, when the game is played a finite number of times, even while pursuing tit-for-tat strategy the two firms will opt for non-cooperative behaviour*. Thus, even with tit-for-tat strategy in case of repeated games to be played a finite number of times, we are stuck in prisoners' dilemma without the outcome of the cooperative behaviour.

But cooperative outcome can come about even when the game is to be played finite number of time if a firm has a doubt about its competitor's rationality in pursuing tit-for-tat strategy and its ability to reason out the logical implications of a finite time horizon as explained above. Thus, if competing firms have doubts about whether the other firm is playing tit-for-tat or playing tit-for-tat

10. Hal R. Varian, *Intermediate Microeconomics : A Modern Approach* (New York : W.W. Norton & Co., Fourth Edition, 1997), p. 487.
11. Hall R. Varian, op. cit., p. 486

blindly, this will make cooperative behaviour a good strategy. Besides, in the case of finite number of times the game is to be played, cooperative behaviour can be regarded as a good strategy by the competing firms if the time is long enough and the firms are uncertain about how long they will be competing. Most managers don't know how long they and their firms will be competing with their rivals and this also serves to make cooperative behaviour a good strategy. Although the number of months that the firms compete is probably finite, managers are unlikely to know just what the number is. As a result, the unravelling argument that begins with a clear expectation of undercutting in the last month no longer applies. As with an infinitely repeated game it will be rational to play tit for tat".[12] Thus in view of the fact that in most oligopolist markets the game is in fact repeated over a long period and uncertain length of time and managers have doubts about how rationaly their competitors behave in case of the repeated game for a finite number of times, the prisoners' dilemma can have cooperative outcome.

STRATEGIC MOVES

In the earlier sections it has been emphasised that oligopolists must realise that their own profits depend not only on their own decision and behaviour but also on the decision and behaviour of their rivals. This shows the importance of strategic moves by the oligopolists to enhance their profits. By making certain strategic moves an oligopolist can gain competitive advantage in the market. Thomas Schelling of Harvard University who has make an important contribution to the theory of strategic decision making defines the concept of strategic move in the following words ; "*A strategic move is one that influences the other person's choice in a manner favourable to one's self, by affecting the other person's expectations on how one's self will behave*"[13]. For example, if Maruti Udyog threatens to retaliate by cutting the price of their cars to a level that would cause losses to its rival firms which reduce their prices, thise move of Maruti Udyog is a strategic move. This is because this threat is intended to ensure that the rival firms do not cut the prices of their cars.

Threat, Commitment and Credibility

For the strategic move of giving threat to be successful, there msut be commitment that the firm making a threat will definitely carry it out. Only when there is commitment to carry out a threat that it becomes credible. If there is no commitment to carry out the threat, it will be an empty threat and will therefore not have the desired effect on the behaviour of the rivals. If a firm can convince its rival firms that it is committed to a particular move that it is making, then the rivals may cooperate without retaliating because they may think that they would lose more than they would gain from a long period of conflict with the firm making a move.

When a threat is credible is illustrated in the payoff matrix of firms *A* and *B* given in Table 5 where the profits of the two firms making different brands of cars are shown when they charge low price or high price for their cars. This payoff matrix shows that charging a high price is a dominant strategy for firm *A*, that is, whatever strategy (whether of charging a high price or low price) the rival firm *B* pursues, the strategy of charging a high price is optimal for firm *A*. Thus, if firm *B* charges a low price, the firm *A* will earn profits of Rs 20 lakhs if it charges a low price and Rs 30 lakhs if it charges a high price. On the other hand, if the firm *B* charges a high price, the firm *A* will earn Rs 20 lakhs if it charges a low price and Rs 50 lakhs if it charges a high price. Thus, whether the firm *B* plays a low price strategy or a high price strategy, for firm *A* high price strategy is the optimal strategy to adopt. It will be seen from the payoff matrix of Table 5 that when the firm *A* will charge a high price, the firm *B* will opt for charging a low price and in this way will earn Rs 40 lakhs instead of Rs 30 lakhs if it charges a high price.

---

12. See Pindyck and Rubenfeld, op. cit., p. 466. This result is based on the original research work done by David Kreps, Paul Milgrom, John Roberts, and Roberts Wilson, "Rational Coopeation in the Finitely Repeated Prisoners, Dilemma, *Journal of Economic Theory*, 1982, pp. 245 - 252.
13. Thomas C Schelling, *The Strategy of Conflict*, (New York : Oxford University Press, 1960). Another work is M. Porter, *Competitive Strategy* (New York : Free press, 1980)

Table 5 : **Payoff Matrix for Pricing Game**

(in lacs)

		FIRM B	
		Low Price	*High price*
FIRM A	*Low Price*	20, 20	20, 10
	High Price	30, 40	50, 30

(**Note** : *The first number in the pair shows profits of firm A, the second number shows profits of firm B*)

Under these circumstances if firm *A* threatens firm *B* that it will charge a low price, this threat will be incredible or empty because the firm *B* knows that by charging a low price, the firm *A* will cause its profits to fall to Rs 20 lakhs. Being an incredible threat the firm *B* will not take it seriously. As explained above, one way to make the threat credible is to make it binding and irreversible. Thus, if a firm threatens to enter a particular market it can make its threat credible if the potential firm buys a plant rather than lease it or enters into a long-term contract for buying raw materials. This shows that the firm which gives a threat to enter has made an irreversible commitment and will therefore enter the market, come what way, and this makes the threat credible. Take another example. If a firm commits to a price reduction then if its rival firm lowers its price, then to make its commitment credible, it can make a verbal or written agreement with the customers that it will match any price cut by its rival. On the other hand, if a particular firm has the image that it will easily ignore its particular commitment that it makes, then the commitment is not credible and its competitors will not pay much attention to the commitment made by it.

Another way to make the threat credible is to build a reputation of irrationality for carrying out its threat even if it has to lose some profits or even incur losses. This irrational reputation is developed when a firm has actually carried out its threat several times in the past (even at the expense of its profits). Thus, the threat of a firm with reputation of irrationality is a credible threat and its rivals will take serious note of it. Consider payoff matrix of Table 5 again. If the firm *A* is charging a high price and the firm *B* is charging the low price, they are earning profits of Rs 30 and 40 lakhs respectively (see bottom left hand corner of Table 5), then if the firm *A* has a reputation for irrationality and gives a threat to lower its price to carry out its threat to lower price, then *B* will be induced to charge high price and as a result both firms will be charging high price and firm *A*'s profit will rise to Rs 50 lakhs, but profit of the firm *B* will fall to Rs. 40 lakhs (see bottom right hand corner). It is important to note though profits of the firm *B* has fallen because under threat from the firm *A* it has decided to cooperate, it is still greater than profits of Rs 20 lakhs that it would have earned if firm *A* had actually carried out its threat and both charged the low price.

In addition to what has been said above about credible commitment, it may be noted that for a threat to be credible, the firm's commitment must be backed up with assets, skills and expertise, financial and technological powers to carry out its commitment. Besides, a firm's commitments are more credible if it has a reputation and a long history of adhering to its commitments.

However, for tit-for-tat strategy to be successful certain conditions must be fulfilled. First, a reasonably stable set of players (that is, firms) is required for the successful working of tit-for-tat strategy. If the players (firms) change quite frequently, cooperative behaviour between them is not likely to develop. Second, in tit-for-tat strategy for cooperative behaviour to be achieved, there must be a small number of players (firms). In case of a large number of competing firms, it is difficult to know what each firm is doing. As a result, cooperation cannot be enforced and generally breaks down when there are many firms confronting each other. Third, for the success of tit-for-tat strategy to induce cooperative behaviour it is assumed that each firm can quickly detect cheating by others and is able and willing to retaliate if rivals do cheating. Fourth, the demand and cost conditions must remain stable for the success of tit-for-tat strategy. The failure to cooperate is quite often the result of changing demand or cost conditions. Uncertainties about demand or costs make it difficult for the firms to arrive at an implicit understanding of what cooperative behaviour requires. Lastly, tit-for-tat strategy to induce cooperative behaviour, the game is to be played either indefinitely or for a long uncertain number of times.

ENTRY DETERRENCE

The existing firms, expecially the monopolists try to prevent the entry of new firms as the entry of new firms reduce the profits of the existing firms. An important strategy for the existing firm to deter the entry of new firms in the market is giving threat to lower price and thereby inflict loss on the potential entrant. However, such a threat by the existing firm will work only if it is credible. To illustrate whether threat is credible or not consider the payoff matrix shown in Table 6. From this payoff matrix in Table 6 it follows that the threat by the existing firm *A* that if the potential firm *B* enters the market it will lower the price and impose loss on *B*, is not credible. It will be seen from the payoff matrix of Table 6 that before entry of firm *B* the firm *A* is charging high price and is making profits of Rs 10 lacks. (see bottom right hand corner). Now, on entry by firm *B* in the market, *if the existing firm charges* a higher price, the profits of the existing firm *A* are 7 lakhs and of the new firm *B* are 2 lakhs and on the other hand, if the existing firm *A* lowers the the price to carry out its threat, profits of firm *A* are 4 lakhs and the new firm *B* incurs a loss of 2 lakhs. This shows that despite the entry of new firm *B*, it is profitable for the existing firm to charge a high price and earn profits of Rs 7 lakhs which are greater than of Rs 4 lakhs[14] in case he lowers the price in accordance with the threat held out. This shows that threat is not creditable. And since the potential entrant knows this, the threat will not work and will not prevent firm *B* from entering the market. Unless the firm *A* is irrational, it will not lower the price on the entry of new firm *B*.

Table 6 : Payoff Matrix

(Profits in lakhs)

		Firm B (Potential Entrant)		
		Enter	*Stay out*	
Firm A (Existing firm)		Low Price	4, –2	6, 0
	High Price	7, 2	10, 0	

To make the threat credible the existing firm has to commit itself to resist the entry of the new firm *B* even at the loss of its profits. One way to make a credible commitment to resist the entry of the potential firm is the expansion of its capacity by the existing firm before it is needed, that is, by building excess capacity.[15] Since for building of excess capacity, the existing firm will incur costs, there will be a change in the payoff matrix. The new payoff matrix given in Table 7.

Table 7 : **Payoff matrix with credible commitment**

		Firm B (Potential entrant)	
		Enter	*Stay out*
Firm A	Low Price	4, –2	6, 0
(the existing firm)	High Price	3, 2	5, 0

Table 7 is the same as the previous Table 6 except that after building excess capacity, firm *A*'s profits are Rs 3 lakhs if it continues to charge high price and Rs 4 lakhs if it lowers the price. The profits of the existing firm *A* are now smaller even with the high price charged because of the costs incurred on building new capacity and sharing of the market with the new entrant. On the other hand,

14. Note that fall in profits of the existing firm *A* is due to (1) the market will now be shared between the two firms, and (2) lowering of price of the product to deter entry.

in case of low price being charged on the entry of new firm the profits of firm *A* are the same, namely, 4 lakhs as in the previous payoff in Table 6. This is because at the low price, the sales of the existing firm will increase resulting in greater revenue and as a result it will be able to utilise a part of the extra capacity built. Thus, with low price the increase in revenue may cancel out the increase in costs due to the addition of extra capacity and therefore profits of the existing firm *A* remains the same by charging a low price. However, charging a low price by firm *A* will cause losses of Rs 2 lakhs to the new entrant (see upper left hand corner). Thus realising that by entering the market it will suffer a loss, the firm *B* will not enter the market and stay out. Thus building of excess capacity before it is needed the existing firm commit itself to lowering price if the firm *B* dares to enter the market and this makes its threat credible and deters the entry of the potential firm. Having built excess productive capacity, the existing firm *A* will charge a low price and make a profit of Rs 4 lakhs instead of Rs 3 lakhs if it charges a high price. Since the new firm *B* on entry will have to sell the product at the low price, it will suffer a loss Rs 2 lakhs if it entered the market. Therefore, the firm *B* would not enter the market and stay out. Thus, the existing firm *A* has succeeded in deterring entry by holding out a credible threat.

An alternative to buidling excess capacity is creating a reputation of irrationality for preventing entry of potential firms in the market even if its causes decline in profits of the existing firms for quite a long time. Thus, when a firm has good reputation for behaving irrationally then, even given the payoff matrix of Table 6, it will succeed in deterring entry. The reputation of irrationality of the existing firm creates a credible threat of price warfare if the potential firms enter the industry. As a matter of fact, in the real world it is reputation for irrationality that seems to work in the real word in deterring entry.

QUESTIONS FOR REVIEW

1. Distinguish between cooperative game and non cooperative game. Give examples.
2. Explain a dominant strategy. How is stable equilibrium reached when a firm pursues its dominant strategy ?
3. What is Nash Equilibrium? Does equilibrium in a Prisoners' Dilemma game represent Nash Equilibrium ?
4. What is prisoners' dilemma? How is it used to explain the instability of a cartel ?

   OR

   How can prisoners' dilemma be used to explain the behaviour of firms in a Cartel under oligopoly

   D.U., B. Com (Hons.) 2007
5. Explain Neumann-Morgenstern theory of game? On what grounds has it been criticised ?
6. What is a tit-for-tat strategy ? Why is it a rational strategy when Prisoners, Dilemma type game is infinitely repeated ?
7. Explain the Prisoners' Dilemma game when it is repeated 15 times and both players are rational. Is tit-for-tat strategy optimal in this case?
8. What is a "strategic move"? What are the conditions required for strategic move to be successful?
9. What is a credible threat? How can a threat be made credible?
10. How does an incumbent firm succeed in detering entry into the market by potential competitors?
11. Can a threat of a price war deter entry by new firms? What actions might a firm take to make this threat credible ?
12. What is Prisoners' Dilemma ? Why do oligopolistic firms find themselves in prisoners' dilemma ?

    D.U., B. Com (Hons.) 2009

---

15. For an elaborate analysis of the use of excess capacity to prevent entry, see J. Tirole, "*The Theory of Industrial Organisation* (Cambridge, MA : MIT Press, 1988)

PART – V

FACTOR PRICING AND INCOME DISTRIBUTION

- Factor Pricing and Income Distribution : A General View
- Labour Supply and Wage Determination
- The Theories of Rent
- Alternative Theories of Interest
- The Theory of Profits
- Applications of Factor Pricing Theory

PART V

FACTOR PRICING AND INCOME DISTRIBUTION

- Factor Pricing and Income Distribution: A General View
- Labour Supply and Wage Determination
- The Theories of Rent
- Alternative Theories of Interest
- The Theory of Profits
- Applications of Factor Pricing Theory

CHAPTER 32

FACTOR PRICING AND INCOME DISTRIBUTION : A GENERAL VIEW

FUNCTIONAL VS. PERSONAL DISTRIBUTION

So far we have discussed how the prices of products are determined in different market forms. The pricing of factors of production is the subject matter of this part. The theory of factor of prices is popularly known as the *theory of distribution.* The distribution may be functional or personal. The distribution theory with which we are concerned in this book is the theory of functional distribution. The concept of functional distribution should be carefully distinguished from that of personal distribution. *Personal distribution* of national income or what is also known as '*size distribution of incomes*' means the distribution of national income among various individuals or persons in a society. As is well-known, national income is not equally distributed among various individuals in the country. Some are rich, while others are poor. In fact, there are large inequalities of income between various individuals. Thus the theory of personal distribution studies how personal incomes of individuals are determined and how the inequalities of income emerge. On the other hand, in the theory of *functional distribution* we study how the various factors of production are rewarded for their services or functions performed in the production process.

Factors of production have been classified by economists under four major heads, *viz.*, land, labour, capital and entrepreneur. Thus in theory of functional distribution we study how the relative prices of these factors of production are determined. The prices of land, labour, capital and entrepreneurship are called rent, wages, interest and profit respectively. Thus in the theory of functional distribution we discuss how the rent of land, wages of labour, interest on capital and profits of entrepreneur are determined. To be brief, *theory of functional distribution means the theory of factor pricing.* To conclude, in the words of Professor Jan Pen, "in functional distribution, we are no longer concerned with individuals and their individual incomes, but with factors of production : Labour, capital, land and something else that may perhaps best be called "entrepreneurial activity." The theory of functional distribution examines how these factors of production are remunerated. It is primarily concerned with the price of a unit of labour, a unit of capital, a unit of land, and being an extension of price theory it is sometimes called the theory of factor prices."[1]

The question that now arises is : Is it not the functional distribution that determines the personal distribution of national income. Personal distribution of income *only partly* depends upon functional distribution. How much income an individual will be able to get depends not only on the *price* of a particular factor he has but also on the *amount* of that factor he owns as well as the *prices* and *amounts* of other productive factors which he may possess. Thus the personal income of a landlord depends not only on the rent but also on the amount of land he owns. Given the rent per acre, the greater quantity of land he owns, the greater will be his income. Further, the landlord may have lent some money to others for which he may be earning interest. The total income from interest on money will also add to his personal income. Thus, as mentioned above, a person may be getting income from several sources *i.e.*, from the earnings of various factors of production. The earnings

---

1. Jan Pen, *Income Distribution*, Penguin Books, 1971, p. 16.

from all the sources will constitute his personal income. Thus if our landlord does not do any other work and owns no other factor of production, his personal income will depend on the rates of rent and interest and also on the amount of land he owns which he has given on rent and the amount of money he has lent out. Thus, "*personal distribution* (or the size distribution of incomes) relates to individual persons and their income. The *way in which* that income has been acquired often remains in the background. What matters is how much one earns, not so much whether income consists of wage, interest, profit, pension or whatever."[2] Thus, total income from rent and interest will make up his personal income. Theory of personal distribution of income has, therefore, to explain not only that how prices or rewards for factors such as rent of land, interest on capital are determined but also *how various people happen to own different quantities of these productive factors*. The theory of functional distribution, or the theory of factor prices, as it is often called, is thus only a part of the theory of personal distribution which covers the former. In this book we are primarily concerned with functional distribution of income or the pricing of factors of production.

Before we proceed further we would like to remove one confusion. It is that when we say how the prices of factors are determined, we do not really mean the prices of the factors *themselves* . By the prices of the factors, we mean the prices of their *services or use* for a period of time. Thus in factor pricing we do not study how the price or value of land as such is determined, instead we study how the *price for the use of land*, which is called rent, is determined. Similarly, in the theory of factor prices, we do not explain how the price of labourer as such is determined (the labourer does not sell himself, he sells only his labour or *service* for a period), and we study how the price for the use or service of labour for a period which is called the wage rate is determined. It is only for the sake of convenience and brevity that we speak of pricing of factors while we actually mean the pricing of their *services* or *uses*.

Functional Theory of Income Distribution : Micro and Macro

Even the 'functional distribution' of income can be studied from two viewpoints *viz*. micro and macro. The theory of micro distribution explains how the *rates of reward* for various factors of production are determined. In other words, the theory of micro distribution deals with the determination of *relative prices* of productive factors. It thus studies how the wage rate of labour, rate of rent on land, rate of interest on capital are determined. On the other hand, the theory of maco distribution deals with the problem of the determination of *aggregate rewards* of various factors in national income. In other words, the macro distribution means the relative shares of various factors in national income. Therefore, the theory of macro-distribution is also known as the *theory of distributive shares*. Thus the theory of macro-distribution or distributive shares tells us as to how the share of labour in the national income (*i.e.* the total amount of all wages of all labourers in the country) is determined. Similarly, the macro theory of distribution explains how the share of profits in the national income (*i.e.*, total amount of profits earned by all entrepreneurs as a ratio of national income of the country) are determined. To quote Professor Jan Pen again, "The theory of distributive shares attempts to explain the share of the total national income that each factor of production receives. It enquires into the percentage that labour receives of the whole, and also into the shares of interest, rent and profit. Now individual income recipients disappear beyond the horizon".[3]

As noted above, specific individuals may derive their personal income from various sources such as wages for labour or work done and from ownership of property or assets such as rent from land, interest on bank deposits and dividends (*i.e.*, profit from investment in shares of corporate companies. But in the functional distribution of income, we are not concerned with the personal distribution of income and what factors determine it. In the functional macro distribution of income, we attempt to explain the total contribution a factor of production makes to the total national product, that is, national income. In the neoclassical theory of distribution with which we are

2. *Op. cit. p.* 15.
3. Jan Pen, *Op. cit. p.* 18.

concerned in this book attempts to explain this with the supply and demand curves of factors. The supply and demand curves of factors are used to explain unit price of a factor and multiplying the unit price of a factor with the amount of factor employed gives us its total contribution to national income or its total factor share in the national product.

A graphical representation of neoclassical macro theory of functional distribution is illustrated in Fig. 32.0. In this we have assumed that there are two factors of production with labour as a variable factor of production and capital as a fixed factor of production. In Fig. 32.0, D_L is the demand curve of labour which is sloping downward to the right. We will explain later in this chapter that, given the competitive market conditions, demand for labour is determined by its value of marginal product (VMP_L). Given the competitive market conditions, the firms employ the amount of labour at which the wage rate is equal to the value of its marginal product. Due to the operation of diminishing marginal returns to a variable factor, demand curve of labour D_L slopes downward to the right. On the other hand, supply curve of labour *SL* is generally assumed to be sloping upward to the right. The demand and supply curves of labour intersect at point *E* and determines *OW* as the equilibrium wage rate and *ON* as the level of employment of labour. Now, given the two-factor production function, the value of output (that is, national product or national income) is given by the sum of values of marginal products from *O* to *N* amount of labour employed (is Σ*VMP* upto point *N*) which equals the area *OHEN*. With *OW* as wage rate (*i.e.*, wage per unit of labour) and *ON* as the amount of labour employed, the total wage payment, that is, share of labour in national income will be equal to the area *OWEN*. With *OWEN* as share of labour and *OHEN* as the total national product or national income, the area *WHE* will be the total profits share in national income which is return to the owners of physical capital[4] used in the production process under competitive conditions in the economy. With linear homogeneous production function when each factor gets paid equal to the value of its marginal product, the total factor shares (in the present case of two-factor production function, the total share of labour, that is total wage payments and the share of profits on capital) will exhaust the total national income. To quote Todara and Smith, "*Income is distributed by functions – labourers receive wages, owners of land receive rent and capitalists obtain profits. It is neat and logical theory in that each and every factor gets paid only in accordance with what it contributes to national output - no more no less*".[4a] This is neoclassical theory of macro functional distribution of income. We will discuss the product-exhaustion theorem later in this chapter.

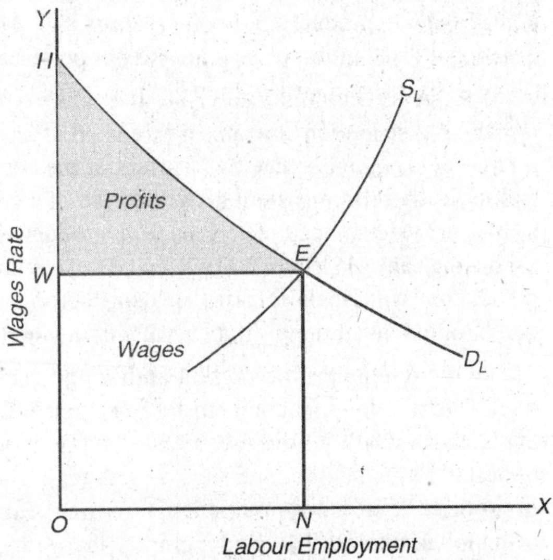

Fig. 32.0. *Macro Theory of Functional Distribution*

THEORY OF DISTRIBUTION AS A SPECIAL CASE OF THE THEORY OF PRICE

It is worth mentioning here that in modern economic theory, theory of distribution is only a special case of the theory of price. As the prices of products are explained with the interaction of the

1. It is worth noting that in the two-factor (i.e., labour and capital) production function reward for physical capital is generally deseribed as profits which go the capitalists who own it.

4a. Michael P. Todaro, and Stephen C. Smith, *Economic Development*, Pearson Education (Singapore) Pvt. Ltd. 110092 p. 204.

demand for and supply of them, similarly distribution is conceived as the determination of prices of the factors which are also explained with interaction of demand for and supply of them. The income which a factor will obtain depends on the price determined by market, *i.e.* demand and supply and the amount that will be used or employed of that factor. In other words, it is the forces of free market, that is, demand and supply that go to determine the prices and incomes of various factors and not any institutional framework such as ownership of property. Further, the association of various factors with particular social classes, such as land with land-owning class, capital with capitalists, and labour with the working class is also not emphasised. In fact, the factors are conceived merely as productive agents and distribution of income among them as merely functional rewards for their contribution to production. In other words, the contemporary theory of distribution merely explains functional distribution of income and not personal distribution of income.

Prof. A.K. Das Gupta describes the nature of contemporary distribution theory very clearly. He remarks, "distribution appears an extension of the theory of value *being just a problem of pricing of factors of production.* The two aspects of the economic problem are then integrated into a unified and logically self-consistent system. Value of a commodity is derived in the ultimate analysis from utility, and value of factors derived from productivity imputed by the commodities which they help in producing. The old tripartite division of factors into land, labour and capital is retained but their old association with social classes is lost. Factors are conceived as just productive agents independently of the institutional framework within which they operate."[5]

In the opinion of the present author, the contemporary theory of distribution is on the wrong track. Distribution of income, that is, who gets what share of the national cake in a society cannot be explained merely by the mechanism of the impersonal forces of the market, by the equilibrium between the demand for and supply of factors. The production relations governed by the ownership of property or means of production, power structure in the society play a vital role in the distribution of national income. The contemporary theory by asserting that every body or every factor under conditions of perfect competition is remunerated according to the value of its marginal product (that is, what it contributes to general output of industry) is tacit approval of the present distribution of income as just and right. But this is far from truth, since the present-day highly skewed distribution of income found in the capitalist countries (including India) has been greatly determined by the uneven ownership of property, production relations based on it and the power structure in the society. This is not to say that marginal productivity as a determinant of incomes is quite unimportant but the importance of the institutional factors just mentioned above cannot be glossed over.

MARGINAL PRODUCTIVITY THEORY OF DISTRIBUTION

We now turn to the question as to what determines the prices of factors of production A theory which tries to answer this question and which has been fairly widely held by professional economists is known as *marginal productivity theory of distribution.* It may, however, be pointed out that in recent years its popularity has somewhat declined due to bitter criticisms levelled against it. The essence of this theory is that price of a factor of production depends upon its marginal productivity. It also seems to be very fair and just that price of a factor of production should get its reward according to the contribution it makes to the total output, *i.e.*, its marginal productivity.

Marginal productivity theory was first put forward to explain the determination of wages, *i.e.*, reward for labour but later on prices of other factors of production such as land, capital *etc.* also were explained with marginal productivity. The origin of the concept of marginal productivity can be traced to Ricardo and West. But both Ricardo and West applied the marginal productivity doctrine only to land. The concept of marginal productivity is implicit in the Ricardian theory of rent. But the idea of marginal productivity did not gain much popularity till the last quarter of 19th century, when it was re-discovered by economists like J.B. Clark. Jevons, Wicksteed, Walras and later Marshall and

5. A.K. Das Gupta, *Tendencies in Economic Theory*, Presidential Address to the 43rd Annual Conference of the Indian Economic Association, held at **Chandigarh, December, 1960.**

J.R. Hicks popularised the doctrine of marginal productivity. Since marginal productivity theory has been mainly evolved for the determination of reward for labour, we shall discuss below its application to wage determination. But it should be understood to apply equally to the rewards of other factors of production.

Clark's Version of Marginal Productivity Theory

J.B. Clark, an American economist who developed marginal productivity theory of distribution in a number of articles and later on presented it in a complete form as an explanation for "*The Distribution of Wealth*". In order to bring out the fundamental factors at work in the mechanics of income distribution Clark assumed a *completely static society*, free from the disturbances caused by economic growth or change. In other words, assumed a constant population, a constant amount of capital and unchanging techniques of production. Besides the assumption of a static economy, he also assumed perfect competition in the factor market and perfect mobility on the part of both labour and capital. Further, it was assumed by him that the total stock of capital remains constant. Clark also supposed that the *form* of capital can be varied at will. In other words, physical instruments of production can be adapted to varying quantities and abilities of available labour. Further, he treats labour as a homogeneous factor by taking identical labour units and discusses how the wage rate of labour is determined.

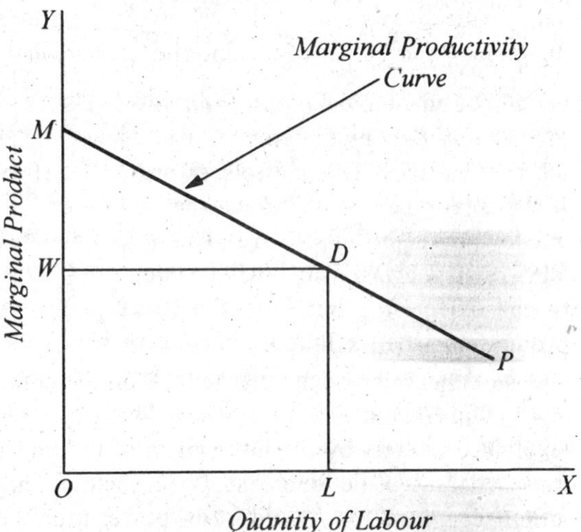

Fig. 32.1. *Wage rate is equalised with marginal productivity of labour by a firm.*

Every rational employer or entrepreneur will try to utilise his fixed amount of capital so as to maximise his profits. For this he will hire as many labourers (labour units) as can be profitably put to work with a given amount of capital. For an individual firm or industry, marginal productivity of labour will decline as more and more workers are added to the fixed quantity of capital. He will go on hiring more and more labour units as long as the addition made to the total product by an extra labour unit is greater than the wage rate he has to pay for it. The employer will reach equilibrium position when the wage rate is just equal to the marginal product of labour.

Just consider Fig. 32.1 where units of labour are represented on the *X*-axis and the marginal product of labour on the *Y*-axis. Then the *MP* curve shows the diminishing marginal product of labour. If the prevailing wage rate which an employer must pay is equal to *OW*, then it will be profitable for the employer to go on employing additional workers until the marginal product of labour becomes equal to the prevailing wage rate *OW*. It will be evident from Fig. 32.1 that if the prevailing wage rate is *OW*, then the employer will employ *OL* units of labour since the marginal product of labour is equal to *OW* at *OL* employment of labour. He would not employ more than *OL* amount of labour as the marginal product of labour falls below the wage rate *OW* and he would therefore be incurring losses on the employment of additional workers beyond *OL*. Thus, an employer would be maximising his profits by equalising the marginal product of labour with the wage rate *OW*. Since perfect competition is assumed to be prevailing in the labour market, an individual firm or industry will have got no control over the wage rate. An individual firm or industry has, therefore, to determine only the number of factor units (labour in the present case) to which it has to give employment at the prevailing wage rate. Thus at micro level (*i.e.* for individual firm or industry) marginal productity theory is the theory of employment.

A marginal-product schedule or curve shows a particular wage-employment relationship. Since Clark has assumed a stationary state, he takes the total supply of labour available for employment in the whole economy as given and constant. In other words, *in Clarkian analysis, aggregate supply curve of labour has been assumed to be perfectly inelastic.* Given the total supply of labour in the economy, the wage rate will be determined by the marginal product of the available amount of labour assuming that all labour get employment. Given the aggregate amount of labour that is seeking employment, the wage rate that the labourers will get will be equal to the *addition made to the total product* by the employment of the marginal unit of labour. In other words, if the total quantity of labour seeking employment is '*n*' units, then each unit of labour will get wage which will be equal to the difference between the total production when *n* labour units were employed and that when *n* – 1 labour units were employed. In other words, in the competitive labour market the wage rate is *determined by the marginal product of a given quantity of labour force.*

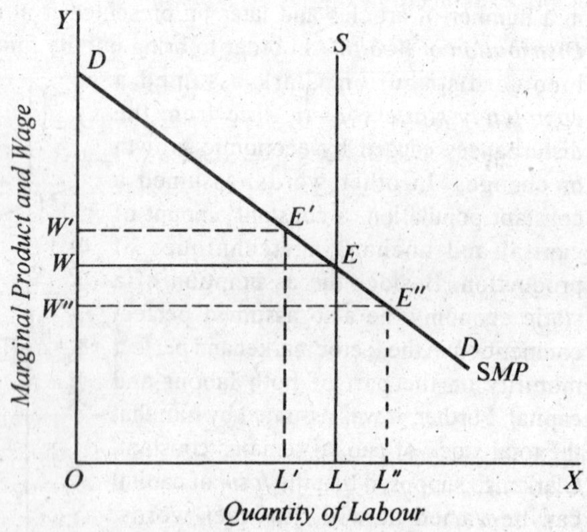

Fig. 32.2. *Wage rate is determined by marginal productivity.*

If the labourers compete with each other for obtaining jobs, they will bid down the wage rate if some of them find themselves unemployed. The employers will bid the wage rate up if the prevailing wage rate is smaller than the marginal product of available labour force. This is so because at the wage rate lower than marginal product the employers' demand for labour force will be more than the available number of labourers. Consider Fig. 32.2. In this figure *DD* curve represents the demand curve for labour by all employers and has been obtained by summing up horizontally marginal product curves (Σ *MP*) of all employers demanding labour. Marginal product of labour diminishes as more units of labour are employed in the economy, *assuming the quantities of other factors used as unchanged.* Now, if the available supply of labour force is *OL* in the whole economy, the marginal product of *OL* quantity of labour is *LE*. The wage rate will be determined by this marginal product *LE* and therefore equilibrium wage rate which will settle down in the market will be equal to *LE* or *OW*. At a higher wage rate *OW'* the employers will employ *OL'* amount of labour leaving *LL'* amount of labour unemployed. Unemployed workers in their attempt to get employment will bring the wage rate down to the level *OW* (=*LE*) at which all are employed.

On the other hand, at a lower wage rate than *OW*, say *OW''*, the employers will demand *OL''* amount of labour since at this their profits will be maximium but the available of labour is *OL*. Thus, at a lower wage rate than *OW* the demand for labour by the employers will be greater than the available quantity of labour. In their bid to get more labour, competition among employers will push the wage rate up to *OW* at which the employers' demand for labour is just the same amount of labour which is actually available.

Thus given the quantity of labour in the country, wage rate is *determined* by marginal productivity of labour. *One assumption which is implicit in the Clarkian marginal productivity theory as applied to the economy as a whole is that of full employment of labour and further that the supply curve of labour is perfectly inelastic at this full-employment level.* In other words, it is assumed that all the existing number of workers in the economy are employed. To sum up, in Clark's presentation, the marginal productivity of a given quantity of available labour determines its wage rate when we consider the market as a whole. In the disaggregated picture, however, where a single employer finds the wage level determined by the forces beyond his control the marginal product of labour determines the level of employment.

Thus, with a given fixed supply of labour in the market the wage rate will be determined by the marginal product of labour.

Marshall-Hicks' Version of Marginal Productivity Theory

Alfred Marshall who was contemporary of J.B. Clark gave a different version of the marginal productivity theory. Marshall's version has been called by many as the marginal productivity theory. Marshall differed with those like Clark who held that wage rate (or for that matter, the price of any other factor) is determined by the marginal product of labour. Marshall said it was wrong to regard the marginal productivity concept with regard to wage determination as a *wage theory. This is because he believed that wage rate (or any factor price) is determined by both demand for and supply of labour*. Marginal productivity concept explains only the demand side of the problem. That is, given the wage rate, a rational employer will employ as many units of labour as will equalise the wage rate with the marginal product of labour. At different wage rates, the employer will employ different amounts of labour units depending upon the corresponding amount of the value of the marginal product. Thus, according to Marshall, the relationship between the wage rate and the marginal productivity of labour provides us with the demand curve of labour. In a complete theory for an *explanation of wage determination, the upward-sloping supply curve of labour has also to be introduced into the analysis*. The wage rate at which the supply curve of labour cuts the demand curve of labour (governed by the marginal productivity) will be *determined. However, the wage rate thus determined by demand and supply will be equal to the value of marginal product of a factor*.

It is clear from above that Marshall considered marginal productivity principle as one of the two forces that *determine* wages, the other force being the supply of labour. Marshall and Hicks believed that wages would tend to be equal to the marginal product, but they emphasised several times that the *wages are not determined* by marginal product, since like all other marginal quantities, marginal product, *together with the price* (wage) is determined by the interaction of demand and supply. Further, *they considered the supply curve of labour as upward sloping to the right.*

Furthermore, Marshall pointed out that the marginal productivity doctrine plus the competitive conditions in the labour market would in the long run tend to make the *wages of labour in different industries or uses equal to each other* and to the marginal product of labour (assuming of course that labour is homogeneous). Further, Marshall drew the distinction between the marginal productivity principle which determines the demand for a factor and the marginal productivity theory as a complete theory of determination of factor prices. Thus, according to Marshall, *price of a factor such as wage rate of labour, rent of land are determined by demand for and supply of the factor and is equal to the marginal productivity of the factor*. While the marginal productivity principle determines the demand for a factor, namely, how much quantity of the factor is demanded at its various prices, the marginal productivity theory explains how through the interaction of demand and supply, price of a factor, say wage rate of labour, is determined.

It may however be noted that in our view the difference between Clark's Version and Marshall-Hicks version of marginal productivity theory is not that whereas Clark considered the demand side (*i.e.* marginal productivity) of a factor and ignored the supply of labour, Marshall and Hicks considered the roles of both of them as the determinants of wage rate. The real difference in our view is that ***while Clark considered supply curve of labour as perfectly inelastic at full-employment level, Marshall and Hicks considered it as upward-sloping*** to the right indicating as wage rate (*i.e.* price of the factor) rises, its quantity supplied increases. This is how we have explained above Clark's version of marginal productivity theory.

A detailed analysis how wage rate (and also prices of other factors) are determined by demand for and supply of the factor will be explained in detail in the next chapter.

CRITICAL EVALUATION OF MARGINAL PRODUCTIVITY THEORY

Marginal productivity theory has been a pillar in the traditional theory of distribution and till today it continues to be an important factor in modern analysis of factor pricing. We discuss below the various objections raised against marginal productivity theory.

1. It has often been argued that *marginal productivity theory takes too many assumptions which are quite unrealistic*. Therefore, it is concluded that theory has no validity. The theory of marginal productivity (Clarkinan version) assumes a stationary state, perfect competition, perfect mobility of factors, equal bargaining power of buyers and sellers, and perfect knowledge which are all far away from the actual conditions of the real world. World is not static. Instead, developments are continually taking place making the actual world a dynamic one. Competition is not perfect; instead there are large imperfections in the factor markets which make any analysis of factor pricing based on the assumption of perfect competition quite useless. Bargaining powers of buyers and sellers of factor services, for instance, of employers and labourers are not equal and thus make the exploitation of the weaker party possible.

2. Another significant criticism levelled against marginal productivity theory (both Clarkian and Marshall-Hick's versions) is that being based upon the assumption of perfect competition both in product and factor markets, *it is unable to explain the determination of factor process under conditions of imperfect competition in the factor and product markets*. As we shall see later in this chapter, following the developments of imperfect and monopolistic competition theories by Joan Robinson and Chamberlin, there emerged two concepts of marginal productivity, namely, marginal revenue product (*MRP*) and value of the marginal product (*VMP*). Thus, when there prevails imperfect competition in the product market (assuming perfect competition in the factor market) a factor of production would not get remuneration equal to the value of the marginal product as is asserted in marginal productivity theory. Under imperfect competition in the product market, a factor of production is remunerated according to a different principle, namely, marginal revenue product (*MRP*) which is less than the value of marginal product (*VMP*). According to Joan Robinson[6], a factor is exploited if it is paid less than value of its marginal product, whereas in marginal productivity theory, as it was presented in neo-classical economic thought, there is just and fair distribution of total product; every factor getting equal to its contribution to the total production.

If imperfect competition or *monopsony prevails in the factor market, a factor will not even get its reward equal to its marginal revenue product*. Under imperfect competition or monopsony or oligopsony in the factor market, the firm to be in equilibrium, will equate marginal wage of labour with the marginal revenue product of labour and, as shall be seen later, this marginal wage is greater than the average wage rate which will be paid to labour. We are therefore of the view that in the context of imperfect competition in the product markets and factor markets marginal productivity theory needs to be modified.

3. Another serious shortcoming of marginal productivity theory is that it cannot explain the rewards of the factors which are to be used in *fixed proportions*. Marginal productivity theory takes it granted that a good degree of elasticity of substitution exists between the factors of production so that increase in one factor, keeping other factors constant, leads to the increase in the addition to the total product, that is, it has a positive marginal productivity and therefore gets positive reward for its contribution to production. But when the factors are used in fixed proportions, increase in one factor

6. Joan Robinson, *Economics of Imperfect Competition*. p. 283.

keeping the others constant, will not lead to any increase in total production at all. That is to say, *in case of fixed proportions or fixed relations between the factors, marginal productivity of the factors is zero.* In view of their zero marginal productivity, then according to the marginal productivity theory, their rewards or prices should also the zero. But this is quite absurd, for the factors of production, even when they have fixed relations with each other obtain positive rewards.

4. Still another serious drawback of marginal productivity theory is that, in its original and rigid version, *trade unions or collective bargaining cannot raise the wages of labour without creating unemployment.* Thus, according to this theory, trade unions are superfluous and collective bargaining by them is a futile activity. Given the downward sloping nature of the marginal productivity curve, at a higher wage secured by the union, the employer will demand or employ less number of workers than before so that some labour will be rendered unemployed. But, as we shall see in a later chapter, increase in wage rate by the union does not always cause unemployment. Indeed, we shall study there that under conditions of monopsony in the labour market the increase in the wage rate by the union may be accompained by the increase in employment rather than the creation of unemployment. As noted above, under conditions of imperfect competition in the product and factor markets, labour (or any other factor) is exploited, that is paid less than the value of its marginal product or less than its marginal revenue product. In this context trade unions can play a useful role of removing the exploitation of labour by getting the wage rate raised to the level of value of marginal product or marginal revenue product.

5. Marginal productivity theory also *ignores the positive interrelation between rewards of the factors and their productivity, especially between wages and efficiency or productivity of labour.* It has been pointed out that rise in wages has a favourable effect on the efficiency and productivity of labour. With higher wages workers can afford to have better standard of living and better health which will raise their productivity and efficiency. This positive relationship between wages and labour efficiency especially holds good in case of the developing countries like India where wage rates in many industries are even below the minimum subsistence level. With wages even below the subsistence level, workers remain underfed and undernourished and, as a result, unhealthy and inefficient. If, following the rise in wages, efficiency and productivity of labour improve, then it may be worthwhile from the viewpoint of employers to raise wages. It has therefore sometimes been asserted that "*higher wages are economical*" or there is a '*economy of high wages*'. But, as mentioned above, marginal productivity theory completely ignores this favourable effect of higher wages on productivity of labour.

Now, if the favourable effect of higher wages on labour productivity is recognised, then the unique level of wage-equilibrium arrived at in the marginal productivity theory is not valid. With evey rise in the wage rate there will be a different curve of marginal productivity of labour and a different wage-employment equilibrium. Thus, there are various possible positions of wage-employment equilibrium depending upon the productivity and efficiency and there is a choice for a firm or the industry to select among them. That there is a *unique* wage equilibrium, as has been asserted by the strict and rigid version of marginal productivity theory, is therefore not acceptable.

6. Like the neo-classical theory of pricing of products, marginal productivity theory of distribution. which has been developed by neo-classical economists is also a *marginalist approach* to the problem and therefore *assumes that the entrepreneurs or employers seek to maximise profits.* It is only if the entrepreneurs are maximisers of profits that they will equate wage with marginal product of labour. If they do not seek to maximise profits, then they may employ the amount of labour at which marginal product of labour stands higher than the wage. Likewise, they may employ the number of workers at which the marginal product lies below the wage rate. Just as Hall and Hitch have criticised the marginalist approach as it applies to product pricing on the ground that

entrepreneurs do not maximise profits. R.A. Lester [6], an American economists has criticized the marginal productivity theory of distribution on the ground that entrepreneurs do not behave as maximisers of profits and therefore wages in the real world will differ from the marginal product of labour. Lester has provided empirical evidence in support of his view. But Machlup[7] and Pen [8] have defended the marginal productivity theory of distribution and the profit maximization assumption on which it is based. To quote Pen, "It is not necessary for every entrepreneur to be able to find the exact point of equilibrium, some will overshoot the equality of wage and marginal product, others will remain below it. However the *trend is towards equality*. In this sense the theory gives only a rough approximation of equality, but as such it is probably not bad."

7. Another basic objection that has been raised against marginal productivity theory is that various factors are jointly demanded for the production of a commodity. That is, production of a commodity is the end result of co-operation of various factors and their *individual productivities cannot be estimated separately*. Labour without the assistance of capital goods can produce almost nothing and capital without the assistance of labour will not produce anything at all. Now, when one cannot speak of the individual productivities of the factors at all or when we cannot calculate their individual productivities at all, then the question of rewarding the factors according to their marginal product cannot arise at all. This argument was forcefully advanced by English literary figures such as Bernard Shaw and Bertrand Russel. Bernard Shaw writes, "When a farmer and his labourers sow and reap a field, no body on earth can say how much of the wheat each of them has grown."[9] Likewise, Bertrand Russel writes, "In an industrial system a man never makes the whole of everything, but makes the thousandth part of a million things. Under these circumstances it is totally absurd to say that a man has the right to the produce of his own labour. Consider a porter on a railway whose business it is to shunt goods trains. What proportions of the goods carried can be said to represent the produce of his own labour? The question is wholly insoluble."[10]

It may however be noted that may economists believe that there exists a good degree of elasticity of substitution between the factors and therefore one factor can be varied by a small amount keeping the other factors constant. In this way they argue that marginal products of various factors can be estimated separately.

8. A controversial problem concerning the marginal productivity theory is that if the various factors are remunerated in accordance with their marginal products, whether the total product would be just exhausted. Suppose there are two factors of production, labour and capital which are required for production of a commodity (ignore other factors). Now the question is when wages of the labour are paid equal to its marginal product, whether the remaining total product would be equal to capital's marginal product or it will be less or more than it. This difficulty is called the *adding up problem or product exhaustion problem* of the marginal productivity theory of distribution. Whether payment to factors equal to their marginal products does or does not exactly exhaust the total product depends on the form of the production function. If the production function is homogeneously linear, or in economic terms, constant returns to scale prevail, then with the aid of Euler's theorem of mathematics it has been proved that payments to factors equal to their marginal products would just exhaust the total product. But, "The practical question is whether constant returns to scale do or do not occur in reality; once again, that differs entirely for the different branches of industry. At some places, something will be left. That too shows that the marginal productivity theory gives only a

---

6. R.A. Lester, Shorcomings of Marginal Analysis for Wage Employment Problems, *American Economic Reivew*. 1946.
7. F. Machlup, Marginal Analysis and Empirical Research, *American Economic Review*, vol. 36, 1946.
8. J.Pen, *Income Distribution*, Penguin Books, 1971.
9. Bernard Shaw, *Intelligent Woman's Guide to Socialism*, p. 21, quoted by Dennis Robertson, *Principles of Economics*, The Fontana Library Edition, p. 186.
10. Bernard Russel, *Prospects of Industrial Civilisation*, p. 146, quoted, by Dennis Robertson, *op. cit.*, 186-87.

rough approximation of reality.[11]

9. Another important criticism of marginal productivity theory of distribution is that it does not explain the remuneration of entrepreneurs, that is, profits. Marginal productivity of a factor can be known if it can be varied by keeping other factors fixed. But the entrepreneur in a firm is only one and a fixed factor and variation in it is not possible. Therefore, marginal productivity of entrepreneur from the viewpoint of a firm is meaningless. If the single entrepreneur is withdrawn from the firm, keeping all other factors constant, the whole production process of the firm will collapse. And there is no meaning of adding one entrepreneur to a firm. The new entrepreneur will mean the establishment of altogether a new firm. It is because of this that in the neo-classical theory of distribution profits are shown as surplus or residual income and not as determined by marginal productivity.

10. Finally, the marginal productivity theory of distribution *does not give any importance to the power structure, social conventions, social status, and prestige of a group of workers in the determination of remuneration of various groups or classes of labour force*. Professor Pen rightly writes that marginal productivity theory based on perfect competition "does not explain discrimination between men and women, between races and between social classes; it does not make it clear why top executives earn as much as they do and why unions can push up wages"[12]. According to Pen, the high salaries drawn by the top executives of the firm cannot be explained by marginal productivity theory, since the concept of marginal productivity in their case is utterly vague and further that their remunerations can be explained only by the power structure. To quote him again, "remuneration of executives and staff workers are fixed in another way: social conventions, the power structure, considerations of prestige and status play a much larger part than marginal productivity. And that also holds good for the remuneration of the people not working in industry: of teachers, for instance (what is the marginal productivity of a contribution to the knowledge of economics ?) and doctors (what is the marginal productivity of a human life?). These are the sectors in which other laws apply than the derivatives of production. Economists often forget this".[13]

Conclusion

We have discussed above the various criticisms levelled against marginal productivity theory of distribution. Marginal productivity theory of distribution does not explain fully the determination of all factor prices. *But marginal productivity of a factor is the most important economic factor governing the prices of factors*. Other factors such as power structure, social conventions, status and prestige do play a part in fixation of remunerations but the economic factor of marginal productivity does exercise an important influence on the determination of factor rewards.

CONCEPTS OF FACTOR PRODUCTIVITY

Before turning to the detailed study of the various determinants of factor prices, it will be helpful for the proper understanding of the subject if we first explain the various concepts of productivity. The knowledge of these various concepts will greatly help in understanding the modern theory of factor prices. At the very outset it is desirable to make it clear why economists are interested at all in the productivity of a factor. *We are concerned with productivity since the price which a factor will be able to get depends upon its productivity*. Why? This is because the factors are demanded not because they directly satisfy the wants. The factors are purchased to put them to work for producing consumer goods which satisfy human wants. Other things being equal, the greater the contribution made to the production of goods by a factor unit, the greater the price which it will be able to command in the market. Thus productivity is an important determinant of the price of a factor.

---

11. J.Pen, *Op. cit.*, p. 85.
12. *Ibid* p. 80.
13. *Ibid* p. 86.

We have already explained the concepts of average physical productivity and marginal physical productivity in a previous chapter. To repeat here *average physical product of a factor is the total production divided by the number of units of a factor employed.*

$$\text{Average physical product } (APP) \text{ of a factor} = \frac{\text{Total output}}{\text{Total No. of units of a factor used}}$$

Marginal physical product (MPP) of a factor is the increase in total output caused by employing an additional unit of the factor, quantity of other factors remaining fixed. The fixed factors are, however, conceived to be adjusted or adapted in such a way that increased amount of the variable factor can be used with them.

Before the development of the theory of product pricing under imperfect competition (monopoly and monopolistic competition) by Joan Robinson and Chamberlin, the assumption of perfect competition in the product market was usually made while discussing the pricing of factors. Under perfect competition in the product market conversion of the marginal physical product into money terms merely involves multiplying the marginal physical product with the price of the product since the price of the product of an individual firm under perfect competition is a given and constant quantity. Money value of the marginal physical product under perfect competition thus means the marginal physical multiplied by the price of the product. However, with the development of imperfect competition theory in explaining product prices the two distinct concepts of marginal productivity have been evolved. They are :

(*i*) Marginal Revenue Product (*MRP*)

(*ii*) Value of Marginal Product (*VMP*)

Marginal Revenue Product (MRP)

Marginal revenue product is the increment in the total value product caused by employing an additional unit of a factor, the expenditure on other factors remaining unchanged. In other words, marginal revenue product is the marginal physical product of the factor multiplied by the marginal revenue

$$MRP = MPP \times MR$$

It is the marginal revenue product which is often termed as marginal product or marginal productivity.

TABLE 32.1

Value of Marginal Product (VMP) and Marginal Revenue Product (MRP) when there is Perfect Competition in the Product Market

I	II	III	IV	V	VI	VII
Units of a Factor	*Total output (Q)*	*Marginal Physical Product (MPP)*	*Price of Product (P)*	*Value of Marginal Product (VMP)*	*Total Revenue (PQ)*	*Marginal Revenue Product (MRP)*
1	25	25	2	50	50	50
2	70	45	2	90	140	90
3	110	40	2	80	220	80
4	145	35	2	70	290	70
5	172	27	2	54	344	54
6	191	19	2	38	382	38
7	199	8	2	16	398	16
8	199	0	2	0	398	0

Value of Marginal Product (VMP)

It means the marginal physical product of the factor multiplied by the price of the product (*i.e.* average revenue).

$$VMP = MPP \times \text{Price (or } AR)$$

Since under perfect competition the demand curve of the product facing an individual firm is perfectly elastic and therefore price and marginal revenue are equal, the value of marginal product (*VMP*) and marginal revenue product (*MRP*) will be equal to each other as is shown in Table 32.1 and Fig. 32.3. But since in monopoly or imperfect competition in the product market, average revenue (or demand curve) is falling downward and marginal revenue curve lies below the average revenue curve, price is not equal to marginal revenue. Therefore, in monopoly or in other forms of imperfect competition in the product market, marginal revenue product will not be equal to the value of marginal product. Since price is higher than marginal revenue under monopoly or monopolistic competition in the product market, the value of marginal product (*VMP*) will be larger than the

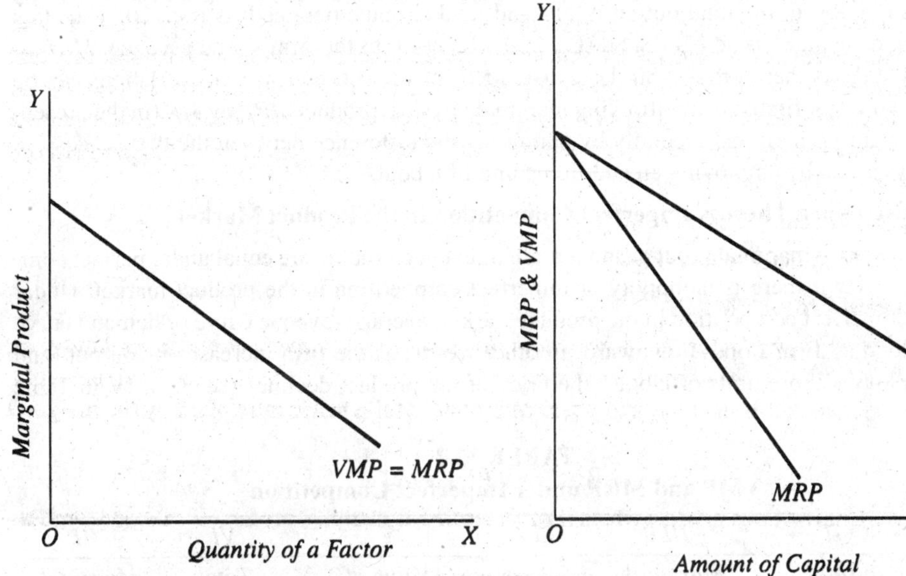

Fig. 32.3. *VMP and MRP under Perfect Competition in the Product Market*

Fig. 32.4. *VMP and MRP under Imperfect Competition in the Product Market.*

marginal revenue product (*MRP*) and the marginal revenue product (*MRP*) curve will lie below the value of marginal product (*VMP*) curve as is shown in Fig. 32.4. Thus, in perfect competition *MRP* and *VMP* have identical meaning but in monopoly and imperfect competition in the product market they diverge.

The distinction between Marginal Revenue Product (*MRP*) and the Value of Marginal Product (*VMP*) can be better understood from Table 32.1. In the above Table 32.1 perfect competition has been assumed to be prevailing in the product market. Therefore, price of the product (Rs. 2) for an individual firm remains the same whatever the level of its output. As more units of labour are employed, total output is increasing but at a diminishing rate. That is to say, marginal physical product of the factor is declining (law of diminishing marginal returns has been assumed to be operating). Since *VMP* is equal to *MPR* × Price, *VMP* (Col. V) can be found by multiplying Col III by Col. IV. Thus when one labour unit is employed the marginal physical product is 25. Since the price of the product is Rs. 2, the value of marginal product (*VMP*) will be equal to 25 × 2 = 50 and so for the subsequent units of labour. It shall be noticed from Col V that value of marginal product is declining as more units of labour are employed after the second unit. This is so because marginal physical product is declining due to the operation of law of diminishing returns.

Since when there is perfect competition in the product market *MR* is equal to price (*P*), Marginal Revenue Product (*MRP*) also can be found out by multiplying the Col. III by Col. IV. Thus under perfect competition value of marginal product (VMP) will be equal to marginal revenue product (*MRP*) (compare Co. VII with Col. V). Since marginal revenue product (*MRP*) of a factor can also be defined as the increment in the total revenue of a firm by employing an additional unit of a factor, it can also be directly found out from Col. VI which shows the total revenue at the various levels of output.

MRP can be obtained by taking out the difference between the two successive total revenues. The difference in the two successive total revenues occurs due to the employment of an extra unit of a factor. Thus when two units of labour are employed, total revenue is Rs. 140 which is obtained by selling 70 units of output produced by 2 units of labour at price of Rs.2 per unit. When another labour unit is employed, the total output is 110 and total revenue obtained is Rs. 220. Thus this additional unit of labour has added Rs. 80 (Rs. 220 – Rs. 140) to the firm's total revenue, *MRP* of labour at this stage is therefore Rs. 80. Likewise, *MRP* of the subsequent units of labour can be found out in two ways: firstly, by multiplying marginal physical product *MPP* by *MR* (in the present case *MR* is equal to price); and secondly by taking out the difference between the two successive total revenues caused by employing an additional unit of labour.

VMP and MRP When There is Imperfect Competition in the Product Market

Whereas value of marginal product and marginal revenue product are equal under perfect competition, they differ if there is monopoly or imperfect competition in the product market. Under monopoly or imperfect competition in the product market, average revenue curve or demand curve facing an individual firm slopes downward. In other words, as the firm increases its output (and sales) by employing more units of labour, the price of the product declines (see Col. IV in Table 32.2). Since

TABLE 32.2
VMP and MRP under Imperfect Competition

I	*II*	*III*	*IV*	*V*	*VI*	*VII*
Units of Labour	*Total output (Q)*	*Marginal Physical Product (MPP)*	*Price of Product (P)*	*Value of Marginal Product (VMP)*	*Total Revenue (II × IV) (Q.P.)*	*Marginal Revenue Product (MRP)*
1	25	25	2.00	50.00	50	50
2	70	45	1.80	81.00	126	76
3	110	40	1.50	60.00	165	39
4	145	35	1.30	45.50	188.50	23.50
5	172	27	1.20	32.40	206.40	17.90
6	191	19	1.15	21.85	219.65	13.25
7	199	8	1.13	9.04	224.87	5.22
8	199	0	1.13	0.00	224.87	0.00

the average revenue curve (*i.e.* price curve) falls downward under monopoly and imperfect competition in the product market, *MR* curve will lie below it. In other words, *MR* will be less than *AR* (*i.e.*, price) of output. Since *VMP* is equal to *MPP* × Price and *MRP* is equal to *MPP* × *MR*, the two will not be equal to each other when monopoly or imperfect competition prevails in the product market.

VMP at various levels of labour employment which is shown in Col. V of Table 32.2 is obtained by multiplying *MPP* (Col. III) with price of the product which goes on falling (Col. IV). Thus when two units of labour are engaged, marginal physical product (*MPP*) is 45 and price of the product is Rs. 1.80. By multiplying 45 with Rs. 1.80 we get *VMP* equal to Rs. 81 which we write in Col. V corresponding to two units of labour. Likewise, *VMP* for other levels of labour employment can be found out.

In order to obtain *MRP*, we have first to find out the total revenue at various levels of employment. The total revenue (Col. VI) is obtained by multiplying total output (Col. II) with price of product (Col. IV). By finding out the the difference between two successive total revenues, *MRP* can be obtained. Thus when two units of labour are employed, total revenue is Rs. 126 and when 3 units of labour are employed the total revenue is Rs. 165. Increment in total revenue caused by the third unit of labour is thus equal to Rs. 165–126 = Rs. 39. Thus *MRP* of labour when three units of it are employed is Rs. 39. Similarly, *MRP* of other levels of labour employment is found out and recorded in Col. VII. By comparing Col. V and Co. VII, it will be clear that *VMP* and *MRP* are not the same and further that *MRP* is less than *VMP*. This is so because, as explained above, price and *MR* are not equal (*MR* is less than the price) for a firm working under monopoly or imperfect competition in the product market. To sum up, *under monopoly or imperfect competition in the product market, MRP and VMP will diverge and MRP curve will lie below VMP curve.*

A COMPETITIVE FIRM'S EQUILIBRIUM REGARDING FACTOR EMPLOYMENT : GENERAL CONDITIONS

In the previous parts we have discussed the conditions of firm's equilibrium in the product market in order to show what level of output it will produce so as to maximise its profits. In other words, we have explained there firm's equilibrium in regard to the level of output it has to produce. At the present moment, we are concerned with the firm's equilibrium in the factor market. That is, we are here concerned with the equilibrium of the firm with respect to the amount of a factor it has to employ. Of course, we explained in a previous chapter firm's equilibrium in regard to factor combination and found that in order to produce a given level of output at the minimum cost possible with given factor prices, a firm will be in equilibrium when it is combining the various factors in such a way that marginal rate of technical substitution between any two factors is equal to their price ratio $\left(MRTS_{ab} = \frac{P_a}{P_b}\right)$. In terms of marginal products of factors we can say that a firm is in equilibrium in regard to the usage of factors so that

$$\frac{MP_a}{P_a} = \frac{MP_b}{P_b} = \frac{MP_c}{P_c}$$

where *a*, *b* and *c* stand for various factors of production, *MP* for marginal products of the factors and *P* for factor prices.

We shall explain below how a firm determines the absolute amount of a single variable factor it has to use or employ and what factors govern its decision about this. There can be various possible situations in both the factor and product markets in which a firm may find itself. In the present analysis we assume a firm is facing perfect competition in both the factor and product markets. Further, in our analysis we assume that the entrepreneur who has to hire other factors of production is rational, *i.e.* he tries to maximise his profits. In deciding about the number of units of a factor which will be employed, the rational entrepreneur will be guided by the change in cost as a result of employment of a factor unit and the change in revenue made by the sale of the additional product produced by that factor unit. The entrepreneur will compare the change in revenue with the change in cost of utilising an extra unit of a factor. If the change in revenue resulting from the employment of an additional factor unit exceeds the change in cost of hiring it, it will be profitable for the firm to employ that unit. Change in revenue resulting from the employment of an extra unit of the factor is called *Marginal Revenue Product* (*MRP*) and the change in cost brought about by hiring an extra unit of the factor is called *Marginal Factor Cost* (*MFC*). *The firm will go on employing more and more units of a factor as long as marginal revenue product of the factor exceeds the marginal factor cost of it.* The firm will not employ an extra unit of a factor if its marginal factor cost is greater than its marginal revenue product, because it will not be profitable for the firm to do so. The profits of the entrepreneur will be maximum when it is employing such a number of units of a factor that its marginal revenue product equals its marginal factor cost. Therefore, the firm will achieve equilibrium in the employment of a factor when the following condition is satisfied:

Marginal Revenue Product = Marginal Factor Cost

$$MRP = MFC$$

The equality of *MRP* with *MFC* of the factor is necessary but not a sufficient condition of firm's equilibrium with regard to the employment of the factor. For the firm to be in equilibrium position a second order condition must also be fulfilled. This second order condition is that the *marginal revenue curve must cut the marginal factor cost curve from above at the point of equilibrium*. In other words, this second order condition states that for employment greater than the equilibrium level, marginal revenue product must be less than marginal factor cost; and for employment less than the equilibrium level, the marginal revenue product must be greater than the marginal factor cost. Thus, for the equilibrium level of employment the following two conditions must be fulfilled:

(1) $MRP = MFC$

(2) *MRP* curve must cut the *MFC* curve *from above*

OR

For employment greater than the equilibrium one, $MRP < MFC$, and

for employment less than the equilibrium one, $MRP > MFC$

When there is perfect competition in the product market, an individual firm cannot influence the price of the product by changing its output level and therefore it has to take the ruling price of the product in the market as given and only adjusts its output level so as to maximize its profits. Since for a perfectly competitive firm in the product market the price in the market as given and constant the average revenue curve facing it is a horizontal straight line and marginal revenue curve coincides with it. For it, Price = *MR*. Therefore, a firm which is working under conditions of perfect competition in the product market the marginal revenue product of the factor (*MRP*) will be equal to the value of marginal product of the factor (*VMP*). Thus under perfect competition in the product market, *MRP* and *VMP* curves will be the same.

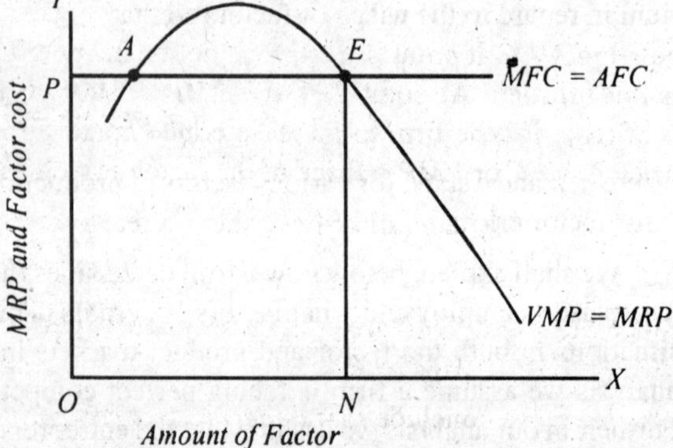

Fig. 32.5. *Employment of a Factor : Profit Maximising by a Firm*

Perfect competition prevails in the factor market when :

(1) the factor is homogeneous and buyers are identical from the sellers[14] point of view;

14. In the factor market, the buyers are the entrepreneurs of firms who have to buy the factors for producing goods, and the sellers are the owners of factors who have to supply these factors to the entrepreneurs. Workers supply labour, landords supply land and so forth.

(2) both buyers and sellers possess perfect information regarding the current bids in the market;
(3) the number of buyers and sellers is very large; and
(4) both buyers and sellers are free to enter or leave the market.

When a firm is confronting perfect competition in the factor market, it cannot affect the price of the factor by varying its level of factor employment. A single firm's demand for the factor is so small compared with the total demand for the factor that any change in its demand for the factor will not affect its price. It has to take the price of the factor as given and constant for it. The firm can employ as many number of factor. Therefore, *the supply curve of the factor for a single firm under perfect competition in the factor market will be perfectly elastic (horizontal straight line) at the level of the prevailing price of the factor.* As a result, for a firm working under perfect competition in the factor market, the extra cost of hiring an extra unit of the factor will be equal to the price of the factor which remains unchanged. Thus marginal factor cost under perfect competition in the factor market is equal to the price of the factor ($P_F = MFC$). This is shown in Fig. 32.5. In this figure, ruling price of the factor in the market is *OP*, which the firm has to accept as given and constant. Supply curve of the factor (or *AFC* curve) is a horizontal straight line and *MFC* curve coincides with it.

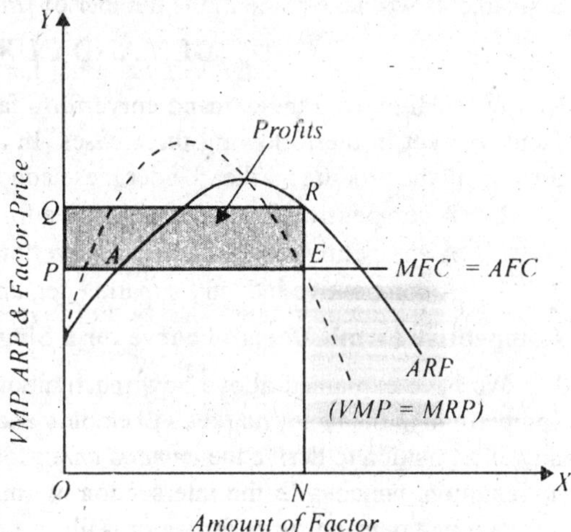

Fig. 32.6. *Employment of a Factor Under Conditions of Perfect Compeition*

As explained above, the firm will continue employing more units of a factor as long as the marginal revenue product is greater than marginal factor cost and will achieve equilibrium position where marginal revenue product is equal to marginal factor cost. As in the present case when perfect competition prevails in both the factor and product markets, *MRP* is equal to *VMP* and *MFC* = *P*., we can state that a firm which is working under conditions of perfect competition will attain equilibrium at the level of factor employment where *VMP* is equal to the price of the factor. In Fig. 32.5 the firm is in equilibrium at *ON* level of employment (or at point *E*) at which *VMP* (or *MRP*) is equal to the price of the factor (or *MFC*). At point *E*, the second order condition is also satisfied since the *VMP* (or *MRP*) curve is cutting *MFC* curve from above. It will be noticed from the Fig. 32.5 that marginal revenue product (*MRP*) is also equal to *MFC* at point *A*. But *A* cannot be the position of equilibrium since second order condition is not fulfilled. At point *A*, *VMP* or *MRP* curve is cutting *MFC* curve from below and it will be profitable for the firm to increase employment further. Thus, *E* is the point of equilibrium where *MRP* = *MFC* or *VMP* = Price of the factor as well as *MRP* curve is cutting *MFC* curve from above.

To sum up, in equilibrium under perfect competition in both the factor and product markets :

$$MRP = MFC = P_F$$

Since MRP and VMP are equal when there is perfect competition in the product market, therefore, $MRP = VMP = MFC = P_F$

Thus, we conclude that *under perfect competition in both the markets, a factor of production will get the price equal to the marginal revenue product of the factor which under perfect competition in both the factor and product markets is equal to value of its marginal product.*

In order to know whether the firm is earning profits or losses we have also to draw average revenue product curve (*ARP*) as is shown in Fig. 32.6. It will be seen from this figure that when the firm is an equilibrium at *ON* level of employment (*i.e.* at point *E*) average revenue product which is equal to *RN* is greater than average factor cost (*AFC*) which is equal to *EN*. Therefore, *ER* is the profit per unit of the factor. Rectangle *PERQ* is the total profit earned by the firm. Thus, with factor price *OP* and equilibrium at *E*, the firm is making super-normal profits by employing *OM* of the factor. Firm can earn such supernormal profits in the short run. But this cannot happen in the long run since by lure of these profits other firms in the long run will be attracted into the industry which is using that factor.

To sum up, while in the short run, the firms may make supernormal profits, but in the long run adjustments will take place in the number of firms so that only normal profits are being earned.

DEMAND CURVE FOR A FACTOR

We shall explain the demand curve for a factor under condition of perfect competition in the factor market in the following three cases. In all three cases we assume that perfect competition prevails in the product market. Under these conditions, *MRP* and *VMP* of the factors are equals.

1. A competitive firm's demand curve for a single variable factor.
2. A competitive firm's demand curve for a factor when other factors are also variable
3. A competitive industry's market demand curve for a factor.

Competitive Firm's Demand curve for a Single Variable Factor

We have explained above how much amount of a factor a firm, under conditions of perfect competition in the factor market will employ and demand both in the short run and long run. We are now in a position to derive the *demand curve* for a factor of production under conditions of perfect competition, which with the intersection of supply curve of that factor determines its price. The derivation of demand curve for factor is illustrated in Fig. 32.7. It always pays an entrepreneur to go on hiring more and more units of a factor until its marginal revenue product equals its marginal factor cost. If there is a perfect competition in the factor market, then marginal factor cost (*MFC*) of the factor will be equal to the market price of the factor which remains unaltered. As already explained, a perfectly competitive buyer in the factor market will employ a factor of production to a point where its *MRP*, which is equal to *VMP*, equals its market price. In doing so, he will be maximising his profits and will thus be in equilibrium position. Thus, in Fig. 32.7, if the market price of a factor is *OP*, then the employer will hire or employ *ON* units of the factor since at *ON* units *MRP* of the factor is equal to its price *OP*. Thus, at market price *OP*, *ON* amount of the factor will be demanded by the producer. If now the market price of the factor falls to *OP'* the amount demanded of the factor will rise to *ON'* where marginal revenue product of the factor is equal to the new market price *OP'* . If the factor price further falls to *OP''* , the *ON''* quantity of the factor will be demanded by the firm.

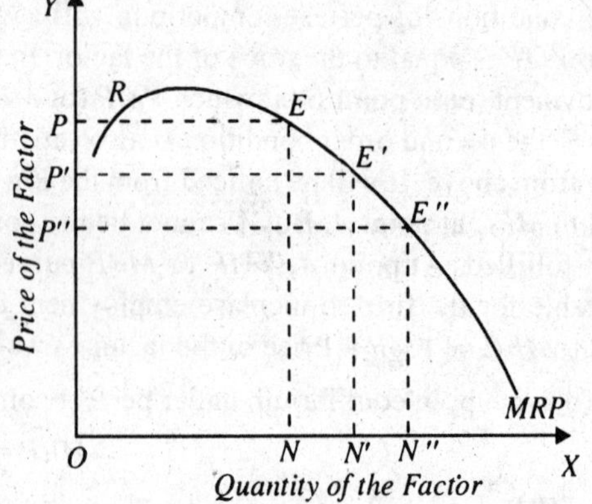

Fig. 32.7. *Marginal revenue product curve constitutes the demand curve for a single variable factor*

It is thus obvious that given the market price of the factor, we can read the quantity demanded of the factor by the firm from the marginal revenue product curve of the factor. The marginal revenue product curve of a variable factor usually first rises upward to a point and then slopes downward. But it should be noted that only the downward-sloping portion of the *MRP* curve forms the demand curve for that factor. This is so because the entrepreneur cannot be in equilibrium at the rising part of the *MRP* curve. For instance, with market price *OP*, the entrepreneur will not be in equilibrium at point *R*, since at *R*, marginal revenue product curve is cutting marginal factor cost curve (which is here same as factor price curve) from below. The firm will be in equilibrium at point *E* where *MRP* curve is cutting the factor price curve from above and will employ or demand *ON* amount of the factor. We thus conclude *that, under perfect competition in the factor market, downward sloping part of the marginal revenue product curve of the factor is the demand curve for that factor.*

We have derived the demand curve for the factor of an individual competitive firm. We now turn to derive the demand curve for the factor of the whole competitive industry. To make our analysis simple, if we assume that the price of the product does not change as the industry employs more of the factor and thus expands its output. If this assumption holds, the demand curve for the factor of production of the whole competitive industry would be obtained by the lateral summation of the *MRP* or *VMP* curves of the firms (*i.e.* demand curves of the firms) in the industry.

Firm's Demand Curve for a Factor : With all Factors (inputs) Variable

In showing value of marginal product (*VMP*) curve as a firm's demand curve for labour we assumed that quantities of other factors such as capital, raw materials fixed. Thus when wage rate declines and as a result more labour is employed, a firm moves along the given *VMP* or demand curve. However, a fall in the price of a variable factor, such as wage rate of labour generally leads to the increase in employment not only of that factor but also of other factors as well, at least in the long run. Note that the two factors are said to be complementary if increase in the amount of one raises the marginal productivity of the other. Thus, when due to the decline in wage rate the employment of labour is increased, it also leads to the increase in the quantity of capital.[15] Further, this increase in the quantity of capital will in turn raise the marginal productivity of labour. As a result of this adjustment in capital, value of marginal product (*VMP*) curve of labour will shift to the right. Thus when we consider that a firm can vary several factors, the firm's demand curve for a factor is no longer its value of marginal product (*VMP*) curve. This is because a change in price of a factor will result in change in the quantities of other factors. Thus, when several other factors such as capital, raw materials are variable, (and wage rate of labour) falls, it will not only lead to the increase in the demand for labour but will also require adjustment in the amounts of other factors such as capital, raw materials in the production process. Considering that the two factors, labour and capital are complementary to each other, when there is increase in the employment of labour consequent to a fall in wage rate, it would bring about increase in the quantity of capital (and other factors), at least in the long run.

Thus, the demand for labour following the reduction in the wage rate will be determined by the equality of the lower wage rate with the new value of marginal product of labour corresponding to the new amount of capital employed. How the long-run demand curve of a factor when capital is also variable is derived is illustrated in Figure 32.8, where to begin with the value of marginal product of labour (*VMP*) has been drawn with a given amount of capital equal to K_1. It will be seen from the figure that at wage rate *OW*, the firm demands ON_0 amount of labour ($OW = VMP$ at ON_0 amount of labour). Now, if the wage rate falls to *OW'* the firm will demand labour equal to ON_1 at the wage rate *OW'* provided the capital stock had remained constant at K_1. How-

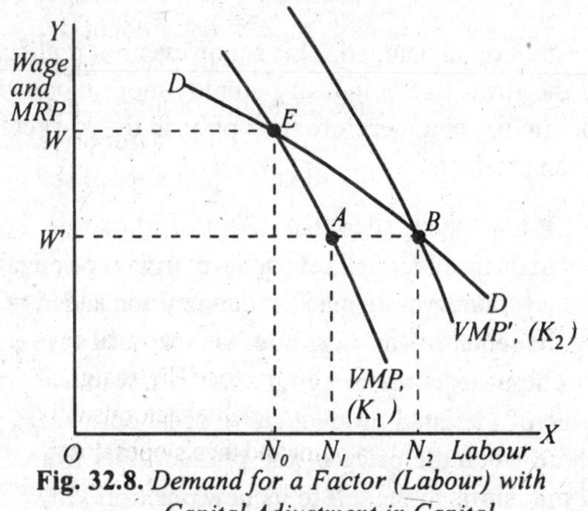

Fig. 32.8. *Demand for a Factor (Labour) with Capital Adjustment in Capital*

15. We are here assuming that labour and capital are complementary to each other.

ever, as explained above, the increase in the quantity demanded of labour at the lower wage rate OW would raise the marginal product of capital and therefore in the long run the firm would adjust the amount of capital. Suppose that by adjusting the amount of capital the firm raises it to the new level K_2. The increase in capital to K_2 in the production process causes a shift in the value of marginal product (VMP) curve of labour to the new position VMP'. With this new marginal value product curve of labour, VMP' obtained after adjusting the amount of capital to the level K_2, at the lower rate OW' the firm will demand ON_2 quantity of labour. Thus by joining points like E and B, we obtain the firm's demand curve EB for labour when capital is also variable and adjusted appropriately. It will be seen from the Figure 32.8 that firm's demand curve for labour EB obtained when other factors such as capital are varied is more elastic than either of the two VMP curves.

COMPETITIVE INDUSTRY'S DEMAND CURVE FOR A FACTOR

We now turn to explain competitive industry's demand curve for labour. In a previous section we obtained the competitive industry's demand curve for labour by the horizontal summation of the VMP curve (*i.e.* demand curves) of the factor of all firms assuming that price of the product remains

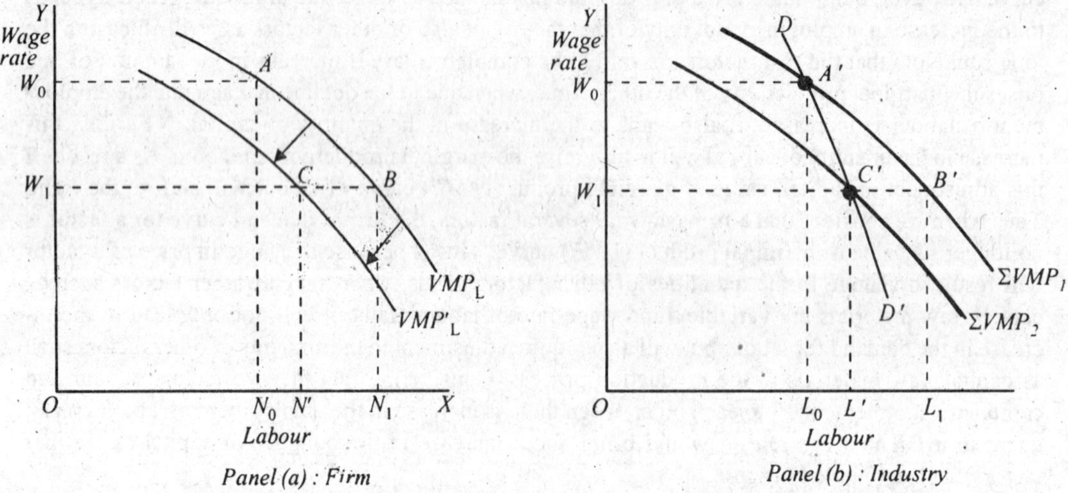

Fig. 32.9. *The Competitive Industry (Market) Demand Curve for Labour*

constant or unchanged. This is however not realistic. When following the reduction in the wage rate all the firms in the industry employ more labour in the production of a commodity, the output of commodity and therefore its supply in the market increases. This would result in lowering the price of the product.

It may be recalled that the value of marginal product (VMP_L) of labour under perfect competition in the product market equals marginal physical product (MPP) of labour multiplied by the price of the product (under perfect competition $MRP_L = VMP_L = MPP_L \times$ Price of Product). Now, following the reduction in wage rate, as more labour is employed by all the firms in the competitive industry output expands bringing about a fall in the price of the product. This will cause a shift in the value of marginal product curve of labour (VMP_L) to the left as shown in Panel (*a*) of Figure 32.9 where when the price of the product falls from P_0 to P_1, the value of marginal product curve of labour shifts to the left to its new position VMP'_L and as will be seen from panel (*a*) of Figure 32.9 that at the lower wage rate W_1 the firm demands and employs labour ON' rather than ON_1 amount of labour which it would have demanded at the lower wage rate W_1 if the product price had remained constant at P_0. This represents the *product price effect* on the demand for labour. It will be seen that when this price effect is taken into account, with the reduction in the wage rate from W_0 to W_1 the firm's demand for labour increases from ON_0 to ON' and not to ON_1.

Having explained how a firm's demand for labour is affected by the change in price of the product following the reduction in the wage rate, we can now derive the market demand curve for labour of the competitive industry. This is illustrated in panel (*b*) of Figure 32.9. At the wage rate OW_0, a competitive firm employs ON_0 amount of labour by equating wage rate OW_0 with the value of marginal product of labour (VMP_L), price of the product equal to P_0 being given. (See panel (*a*) in Figure 32.9). At the wage rate OW_0 the demand for labour of the industry as a whole can be obtained by the horizontal summation of the quantity demanded of labour by the given number of firms. Suppose there are 100 firms in the industry. By adding up horizontally the quantity demanded of labour by all the firms in the industry, that is, 100 ON_0, given the price of the product equal to P_0, we get a point A' in panel (*b*) on ΣVMP_1 curve which shows that at wage rate OW_0 the industry demand for labour will equal OL_0 (*i.e.*, $OL_0 = ON_0 \times 100$). Now, when the wage rate falls to W_1 and with expansion in output or supply, price of the product falls to P_1 and consequently VMP curve of labour shifts to the left to the new position VMP_L, a firm demands ON' quantity of labour. With this, the horizontal summation of the VMP'_L curves to obtain the industry's demand curve for labour would also shift to the left to the new position ΣVMP_2 with the price of the product equal to P_1. As will be seen from the figure that at the wage rate OW_0 the industry will demand OL_0 amount of labour and at the wage rate OW_1, the industry would demand OL' amount of labour rather than OL_1. Thus by joining points like A' and C', we obtain the demand curve DD' of labour showing the quantity demanded of labour by the competitive industry at different wage rates when product price effect of the change in the wage rate has been taken into account. It will be seen from the Figure 32.9 that the industry's demand curve for labour DD' is *steeper or less elastic* than the marginal value product curves of labour of the firms.

THE SUPPLY OF FACTORS

We now turn to the second determinant of factor prices. As said above, the supply of factors also exercises an important influence on the prices of factors. The Clark's version of marginal productivity theory takes full employment of productive factors as given and assumes that the supply of factors is perfectly inelastic. Therefore, in Clark's marginal productivity theory, demand for a factor plays an active and dominant role in the determination of factor prices. As pointed out earlier, the Clark's marginal productivity theory was one-sided and viewed factor-price determination mainly from demand side alone. But following Marshall and Hicks, in the modern explanation of pricing of factors role of both the demand and supply of factors is given equal importance. We have discussed above the nature of demand for factors and the factors determining it and its price elasticity of demand. In what follows we shall spell out the nature of supply of various factors. It is worth mentioning at the very outset that, unlike the demand for factors, the nature and behaviour of supply of various factors is not uniform. We shall explain in detail the nature of supply of various factors when we make analysis of the price determination of each factor separately. Here we shall indicate only the broad features of their supply.

It may be noted that the supply represents the different quantities of that factor which are offered for sale at various alternative prices. From the viewpoint of the nature of supply, factors may be divided into two classes : *original and produced factors*. Produced factors are the inermediate physical inputs such as capital equipment (*i.e.* machinery, tools, components etc.), steel, cement, fertilizers, fuels which are themselves produced in some industries and are used as inputs or productive factors in other industries for production of other products. So far as the supply curve of these produced factors is concerned it is governed by the same laws of production which apply to the the production and supply of goods produced by various industries. Therefore, the supply curves of produced inputs (factors) depend upon the changes in marginal cost of production. So long as marginal cost rises as output is expanded in industries such as machine-making steel, fertilizers, marginal cost curve slopes upward and therefore the supply curve of these material inputs slopes upward. However, if the industries producing certain intermediate physical inputs experience decreasing costs as their outputs expands, their supply curve will be sloping downward.

Supply of Land

Land and labour are called original or primary factors of production as they are not produced in the industries. Land is a free gift from nature and therefore its quantity is fixed by nature. More land cannot be produced in response to greater demand for it. Whatever the rent, high or low, for the use of land, its supply to the economy as a whole remains unchanged. In other words, the supply of land to the entire economy does not depend on the price *i.e.*, rent for its use. Hence, from the standpoint of the whole economy, the supply of land (which includes natural resources) is *perfectly inelastic*. Since supply of land is a free gift from nature and not a produced factor, cost of production has no relevance for its supply. For the society as a whole, land has got no cost of production, since society did not produce it; it got it free from nature.

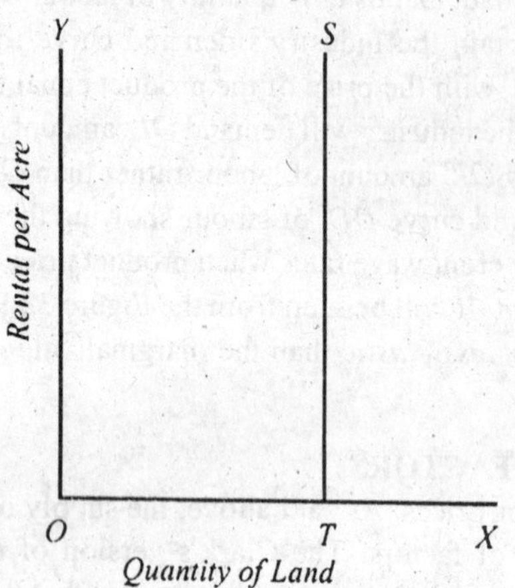

Fig. 32.10. *Perfectly Inelastic Supply Curve of Land for the Economy as a Whole*

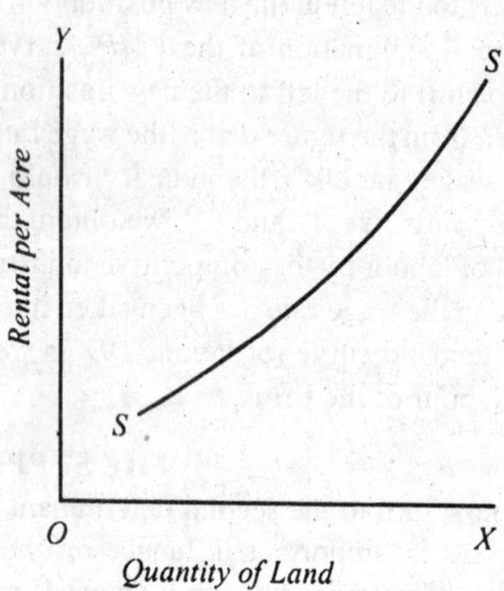

Fig. 32.11. *Somewhat Elastic Supply Curve of Land for a Particular Crop or Industry*

But the supply of land to a *single use or to a particular* industry is not perfectly inelastic. The supply of land to a particular use or industry can be increased by shifting of land from other uses or industries. By offering attractive rents, the supply of land for a particular use can be increased by taking it away from other competitive uses.

The supply of land for a particular crop or industry can be better explained with the help of the concept of *transfer or alternative earnings. The transfer earnings of a factor may be defined as the earnings in the next best alternative use.* Thus the transfer earnings of a piece of land under wheat is the amount of money earned by it if it is put to the cultivation of cotton, assuming that, after wheat, growing of cotton is the next best use of that piece of land. If that piece of land earns Rs. 500 under wheat and Rs. 400 under cotton, then Rs. 400 is the transfer earnings of that piece of land. Now, a piece of land will be supplied to a particular use if at least its transfer earnings are paid to it. In our present example, if the earnings of the prices of land fall below Rs. 400, then the price of land (*i.e.* rent) increases in one particular use, the land from other uses would be attracted towards it, so that the supply of land to the particular use in question would increase. Therefore, the *supply curve of land to a particular use, crop or industry is elastic and slopes upward from left to right.* This is shown in Figure 32.11.

Supply of Capital

We now turn to the supply of capital which is a produced factor and occupies these days a paramount place in the productive process. Here a distinction must be made between *real or physical capital i.e.,* capital goods on the one hand and *financial capital* or *money capital* on the other, since the nature of their supply is quite different. Capital goods are produced factors as compared to the primary factors like land and labour which are not produced. Capital goods are produced by firms on the same basis as consumer goods. The nature of supply of consumer goods has been discussed in part IV. The supply of capital goods is determined by the same factors as those which determine the supply of consumer goods. Since capital goods are reproducible, the cost of production exercises a significant influence over their supply. If the industry producing a capital good is subject to increasing costs, the supply curve of that capital good will be upward sloping indicating that more of it will be supplied at a higher price. And if the industry producing a certain captial good is working under constant cost conditions, the more of that capital good will be supplied at the same price and therefore its supply curve will be a horizontal straight line. However, once the durable capital goods have been produced, their supply is independent of their cost. But, over a period of time, cost is, no doubt, a determining factor of their supply.

As regards financial capital, the nature of its supply is very complex. The supply of financial captial depends upon the money supply in the economy, the savings of the people, their willingness to lend it or buy shares and bonds (*i.e.* their liquidity preference) and the ability as well as willingness of the banks to lend money to businessmen. An increase in the rate of interest has an important effect on the willingness of the people to save more and to accumulate more financial capital. Moreover, increase in the rate of interest exercises a strong effect in inducing the people to part with the money capital and lend it to businessmen or buy shares and bonds of companies. In other words, the rise in the rate of interest induces people to surrender liquidity, and lend it to others. We will discuss the supply of financial capital or saving in detail in chapter, 44 which explains intertemporal choice between present consumption and future consumption.

Supply of Labour

The supply of labour can be viewed as supply of labour (working hours) of an individual, the supply of labour for an industry or occupation, and supply of labour for the economy as a whole. We begin with the analysis of supply of labour (working hours) by an individual. As explained in Chapter 33, supply of labour by an individual depends on his choice between work and leisure. Alternative or opportunity cost of working for a period is the sacrifice of leisure by the individual for that time period. It should be noted that leisure is a desirable object which provides satisfaction to the individuals. On the other hand, work provides income to the individual with which he can buy goods and services to satisfy his wants. How much leisure an individual will be willing to sacrifice, that is, how many hours of work he will do depends on the wage rate. We discuss in the next chapter their choice between work (income) and leisure and therefore the supply of labour in detail with the help of indifference curves.

DETERMINATION OF FACTOR PRICES UNDER PERFECT COMPETITION

According to the neo-classical theory, under conditions of perfect competition in the factor and product markets, it is both demand for and supply of factors which determine their prices. It is therefore essential to understand first the nature of demand for factors of production. Demand for a factor differs in certain respects from the demand for consumer goods or products. Products or consumer goods are demanded because they satisfy the wants of the people directly. People demand food to satisfy the pangs of their hunger, they demand clothes to satisfy their want of providing a cover to their bodies and so forth. These products possess utility which directly satisfy the desires of the people and who are therefore willing to pay price for these products.

Derived Demand

But unlike the products, the factors of production do not satisfy the wants of the people directly.

The factors of production are demanded not because they directly satisfy the wants of the people who wish to buy them. Instead, they are demanded because they can be used to produce consumer goods which then directly satisfy human wants. Therefore, demand for factors of production is called *derived demand*. It is derived from the demand for the product they help to make. Thus, the demand for a factor ultimately depends upon the demands for goods it helps to produce. The greater the demand for goods a particular type of factor helps to make, the greater the demand for that type of factor. Just as demand for a consumer good depends upon its utility, the demand for a factor depends upon the marginal revenue productivity of the factor. In fact, as has beem explained earlier, the marginal revenue productivity curve of the factor is the demand curve for that factor. The entrepreneur's demand for a factor of production is governed by the marginal productivity of the factor.

Determination of a Factor Price

According to Marshall-Hicks'version of marginal productivity theory of distribution, price of a factor is determined by demand and supply of a factor. Marshall and Hicks held that the price of a factor of production is determined by both the demand for and supply of the factor, but is be equal to the marginal revenue product of the factor. Thus, in their view, price of the factor is not *determined* by the marginal revenue product but is, in equilibrium, *equal* to the marginal revenue product of the factor. We will discuss below the various determinants of the demand for a factor of production. Further, we have seen above how the demand for a factor of production depends upon its marginal revenue product. We have also derived the demand curve for a factor of production of an industry. The supply curve of a productive factor is given by the curve showing the amounts of factor offered by the owners of the factor at various factor prices and it slopes upward to the right. The supply curve of a factor for an industry depends upon the transfer earnings of the various units of the factor. *The price of a factor is determined by the intersection of these demand and supply curves of the factor*. In other words, given the demand and supply curves of a factor, the price of the factor will adjust to the level at which the amount of the factor supplied is equal to the amount demanded. This is shown in fig. 32.12, where *DD* is the demand curve and *SS* is the supply curve of the factor. Only at price *OP*, quantity demanded is equal to the quantity supplied. The price *OP* is thus determined. The price of a factor cannot be determined at a level higher than or lower than price *OP*, *i.e.*, other than the price where amount demanded is equal to the amount supplied. For example, the price cannot be established at the level *OP'*, since at price *OP'* the quantity offered to supply (*P' H*) of the factor is greater than the quantity demanded (*P'S*) of it. As a result, the competition between the owners of the factor will force down the price to the level *OP* where the quantity supplied is equal to the quantity demanded. Likewise, the price of the factor cannot be determined at the level *OP''*, since at price *OP''* the quantity demanded of the factor is greater than the quantity offered to supply of it. Consequently, the competition among the producers or entrepreneurs demanding the factor of production will push up the price to the level *OP*.

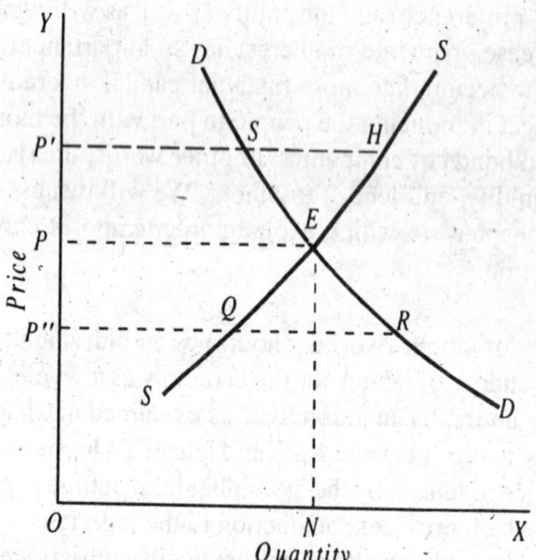

Fig. 32.12. *Equilibrium between demand for and supply of a factor determines its price.*

Though price of a factor is determined by demand for and supply of the factor, it is equal to the marginal revenue product of the factor. This is illustrated by Fig. 32.13. It will be seen from Fig. 32.13(*a*) that equilibrium price *OP* of the factor is determined in the market and *ON* is equilibrium quantity demanded and supplied of the factor. An individual producer or firm who demands that factor will take the factor price *OP* as given. It will now be seen from Fig. 32.13 (*b*) which depicts the position of a single firm or entrepreneur that at price *OP* the firm will employ or use *OM* quantity of the factor. This is so because in order to maximise its profits, the firm will equalise the price of the factor with the *MRP* of the factor, and at *OM*, the price of the factor is equal to the marginal revenue product of the factor. If the firm employs fewer than *OM* units of the factor, then the *MRP* of the factor will bc greater than the price of the factor which will imply that there is still a scope for earning more profits by increasing the use of the factor. If, on the other hand the, firm employs more than *OM* units of the factor, *MRP* of the factor will be less than the price paid for it. As a result, the firm will incur losses on the marginal units and it will therefore be to the advantage of the firm to reduce the employment of the factor. Thus, the firm maximises its profits and is in equilibrium when it is employing *OM* amount of the factor at which *MRP* of the factor is equal to the price of the factor. *To sum up, price of a factor is determined by the demand for and supply of the factor and is equal to the marginal revenue product of the factor.*

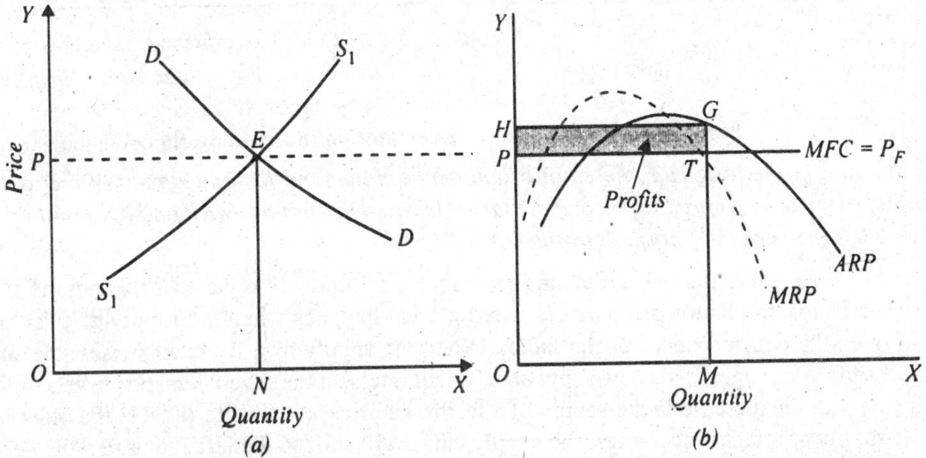

Fig. 32.13. *Factor price which is determined by demand for and supply of the factor is equal to marginal revenue product of the factor.*

As is evident from 32.13, at price *OP*, the firm is earning super-normal profits, since in equilibrium *ARP* of the factor is greater than the price of factor. This can happen in the short run, but not in the long run. If firms are earning super-normal profits, more entrepreneurs will enter the market in the long run to purchase that particular factor to produce the products made by that particular type of the factor. Entry of more entrepreneurs to the factor market will compete away the super-normal profits. As a result, the demand for factors will rise and the demand curve for the factor in Fig. 32.13(*a*) will shift outward to the right. This shift in demand curve due to rise in demand for the factor is shown in Fig. 32.14. With this increase in demand, the price of the factor willl rise to *OP'*. It is evident from Figure 32.14 that with factor price *OP '*, the firm will be in equilibrium at *H* when it is employing *OM'* amount of the factor. At *OM'* amount of the factor the price of the factor is equal to *MRP* as well as *ARP* of the factor. Since at *OM '* the price of the factor *OP'* is equal to *ARP* of the factor, the firm is neither making super-normal profits, nor having losses. It is earning only normal profits.

If, in the short run, firms are having losses, some entrepreneurs will leave and stop purchasing the factor. As a result, the demand for the factor will decrease. The demand curve will shift downward and to the left so that the price of the factor will fall to a level at which price the firms earn only normal profits. Thus, in the long run, under perfect competition in the factor market, price of the factor is equal to both *MRP* and *ARP* of the factor.

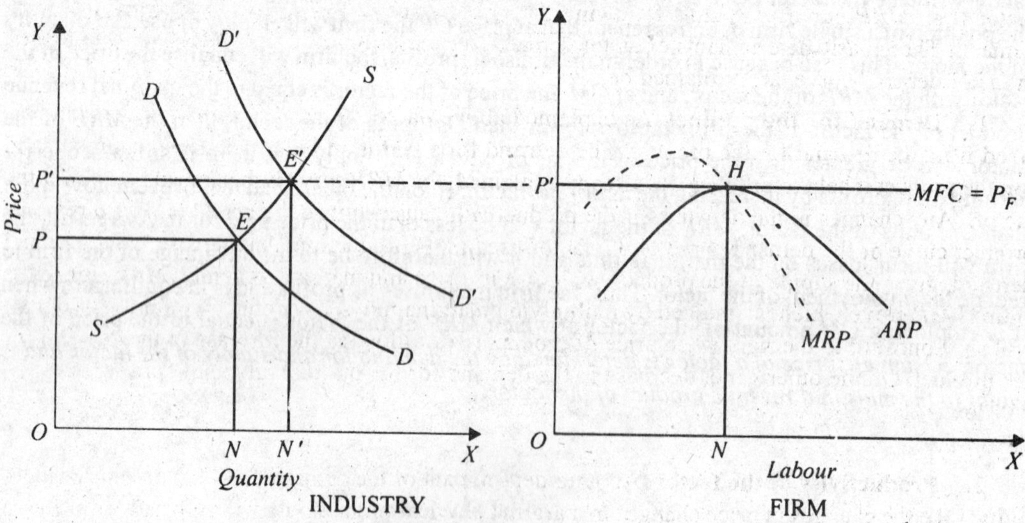

Fig. 32.14. *Factor Price Determination in the Long Run*

To sum up, in the long run, the equilibrium between demand for and supply of the factor is established at the level where the price of the factor is equal to both the MRP and ARP of the factor and thus the firms earn only normal profits.

We have seen above that when demand for a factor of production increases, given the supply curve of the factor, the factor price will rise. Now, what happens when the supply of a factor increases, given the demand curve of the factor. When the supply of a factor increases, the supply curve will shift to the right. This new supply curve will intersect the given demand curve at a lower price. Thus, with the increase in the supply of a factor, its price will tend to fall. On the other hand, when the supply of a factor decreases, the supply curve will shift to the left and, given the demand curve, the price of the factor will rise.

As regards the policy of factor owners, two results follow from our analysis. First, if the owners of a factor want to raise the price of the service of their factor, they should try to increase the demand for their factor service. The demand for a factor will rise if demand for and price of the product rise, or the price of the substitute factor rises, or there is increases in the productivity of the factor due to the improvement in technology. Second, if factor owners want to maintain the price of their factor service, *i.e.*, to prevent the price from falling, they should not allow their supply to increase.

The above modern theory of factor pricing under conditions of perfect competition is based upon Marshall-Hicks' version of marginal productivity theory. In this, marginal productivity of a factor is an important economic force which determines the price of the factor. Therefore, this is subject to many criticisms which have been levelled against the marginal productivity theory and which we have already discussed above in the present chapter.

DETERMINANTS OF THE DEMAND FOR FACTORS

We shall now explain those causes which bring about changes in the factor demand. In other words, we shall discuss those factors which cause shifts in the whole *MRP* curve or demand curve of the factor. These shifts or changes in factor demand are caused not by the change in the price of the factor itself but by other influences which work upon factor demand. These changes or shifts in *MRP* curve or demand curve for a factor are effected by the changes in the basic determinants of factor demand. Just as the demand curve of a product changes or shifts as a result of changes in income or changes in tastes or preference of the consumers, similarly the demand curve for the factor (*i.e., MRP* curve) will shift following the changes in the basic determinants of the factor demand. These basic determinants of factor demand, the variations in which will bring about shifts in factor demand curve, are explained below :

1. **Demand for the product**. As explained above, factor demand is a derived demand, derived from the demand for the product. The demand for a factor, therefore, depends upon demand for the product it help to produce. As already explained, the *MRP* curve is the demand curve for the factor. Any changes in the demand for the product will cause shift in the whole marginal revenue product curve or the demand curve of the factor used in its production. An increase in the product demand, given the supply of the product, will raise its price and marginal revenue (*MR*). Hence the entire *VMP* curve which is obtained by multiplying marginal physical product with price of output will shift outward to the right when price of product rises following the increase in the demand for the product. On the other hand, decrease in the demand for the product, given the product supply, will lower its price. As a result, the *VMP* or demand curve of the factor will shift to the left (*i.e.* downward).

2. **Productivity of the factor**. Another determinant of the demand for a factor is its productivity. Like the changes in price changes in marginal physical productivity will also cause a shift in the entire *MRP* or factor demand curve. For instance, increase in marginal physical productivity of labour will shift the *MRP* or demand curve of labour to the right (*i.e.* outward). It may also be pointed out that historically we have experienced only *increase* in the physical productivity of the factors. *Decrease* in physical productivity, except under exceptional circumstances, has not been noticed. There are mainly three ways in which the marginal physical productivity of the factor can be increased. First, the *quality of the factor* may be improved. For instance, the labour productivity can be increased by making labour more educated and more skilful. Thus any improvement in the quality of the factor by enhancing its marginal productivity will cause outward shift in the factor demand curve.

Secondly, the marginal physical product of any factor depends upon the *quantity of the fixed co-operating factors used* with it. For example, the position of *VMP* or *MPP* curve of labour is dependent on the *quantity of capital* used with it. The greater the quantity of fixed capital used with labour, the higher the level of marginal physical product curve of the factor. Thus increase in the marginal physical productivity of a factor as a result of increase in the quantity of capital (likewise, other fixed factors) will raise the *MRP* or factor demand curve outward to the right.

Thirdly, the marginal physical productivity is increased by the *advancement in technology*. The technological progress raises productivity by bringing about improvement in techniques of production. Hence as a result of advance in technology, *MRP* curve or the demand curve of the factor will shift to the right.

3. **Prices of other Factors**. Just as the demand for a commodity depends upon the prices of other related commodities, demand for a factor also depends upon the prices of other related factors. But the effect of the changes in the price of related factors on the demand for a given factor would have different effects depending upon whether these related factors are substitutes or complements for the given factor. We first take the case of substitutes.

Suppose two factors, labour and machinery, are used in production of a commodity. Now, labour and machinery are largely substitutes. We want to consider the effect on the demand for labour as a result of change in the price of machinery. If the price of machinery falls so that machinery becomes relatively cheaper than labour, there would be large substitution of machinery for labour. Since machinery is now relatively cheaper than labour, it will pay the employer to use more machinery and less labour. Therefore, as a result of change in the price of machinery, demand for labour will fall and machinery would be used in place of labour. Thus the change in the price of machinery will have, what is called *substitution effect* on the demand for labour. As a result of the substitution effect of the fall in the price of machinery, the demand curve for labour will shift to the left. The extent to which the demand for labour will fall depends upon the extent to which it is possible to substitute machinery for labour. Since machinery and labour are close substitutes, such substitution takes place on a large scale.

But the change in the price of factor has not only a substitution effect but also *expansion or output effect*. The prices of factors govern the cost and price of the product. When, in our above example, the price of machinery falls, the cost of production of the product will decline and hence there would be fall in the price of the product. With the fall in the price of the product, more of it will be demanded. In response to greater demand, more output of the product would be made. The fall in the price of the machinery will thus lead to greater output of the product. To produce more output, more of labour as well as more of other factors including machinery will be required. This expansion in output due to the fall in the price of machinery, that is, output effect, would tend to increase the demand for labour. Thus the fall in price of machinery has two opposite effects: first, substitution effect which tends to reduce the demand for labour: and second, output effect (expansion effect) which tends to increase the demand for labour.

The net effect on the demand for labour would depend upon the relative strengths of these two opposite effects. But in the present case, substitution effect would outweight the output effect and, therefore, there would be a net decrease in the demand for labour as a consequence of fall in the price of machinery.

But the change in the price of a complementary factor would have a different effect on the demand for a given factor. Suppose two factors A and B are being used in the production of a commodity. Further suppose that factors A and B bear complementary relation to each other. We are interested to know what happens to the demand for factor A, when the price of factor B changes. If the price of factor B falls, its quantity demanded will rise. Since B is complementary to A, when B will be used more due to fall in its price, it will necessitate more employment of factor A also. Thus the demand for factor A will rise as a consequence of the fall in the price of its complementary factor B. But this is not all. *Output effect will also exercise its influence*. When the price of B falls, cost of production will decline. As a result, the price of the product will fall which will bring about an increase in the quantity demanded of the product. Consequently, output of the product would be expanded. This increase in output will require more of both factors A and B. Thus the demand for factor A will rise due to not only complementary effect but also output effect in the case of complementary factors which work in the same direction, thereby reinforcing each other.

EULER'S THEOREM AND PRODUCT EXHAUSTION PROBLEM

As soon as it was propounded that the factors of production are paid equal to their marginal products, a difficult problem cropped up over which there has been a serious debate among the famous economists. The difficult problem which has been posed is that if all factors were paid rewards equal to their marginal products, would the total product be just exactly exhausted ? In other words, if each factor is rewarded equal to its marginal product, the total product should be disposed of without any surplus or deficit. The problem of proving that the total production will be just exhausted if all factors are paid rewards equal to their marginal products has been called "*Adding-up Problem*" or *Product Exhaustion Problem*.

The two solutions to the problem of product exhaustion have been put forward. First, important solution was put forward by P.H. Wicksteed who assumed the operation of constant returns to scale

in production (that is, the first degree homogenous production function) and applied Euler theory to prove the product exhaustion problem. The second important solution has been provided by J.R. Hicks and P.A. Samuleson who used perfect competition model of determination of product and factor prices to prove the product exhaustion problem. We discuss below these solutions of product exhaustion problem.

Wicksteed's Solution of Product Exhaustion Problem with Euler's Theorem

Philip Wicksteed was one of the first economists who posed this problem and provided a solution for it. Wicksteed applied a mathe-matical proposition called Euler's Theorem[18] to prove that the total product will be just exhausted if all the factors are paid equal to their marginal products. Let Q stand for the total output of the product, a stands for the factor labour and b stands for the factor capital and c stands for land. Assuming that there are only three factors employed for production. Then, the adding up problem implies that,

$$Q = MP_a \times a + MP_b \times b + MP_c \times c$$

That is, the marginal product of factor a multiplied by the amount of factor a plus the marginal product of factor b multiplied by the amount of factor b plus the marginal product of factor c multiplied by the amount of factor c equals the total product of the firm. Marginal products of various factors can be expressed as partial derivatives. Thus, the marginal product of labour (*i.e.* factor a) can be expressed as $\frac{\partial Q}{\partial a}$, and the marginal product of capital (factor b) as $\frac{\partial Q}{\partial b}$, and the marginal product of land (factor c) as $\frac{\partial Q}{\partial c}$, then for the adding-up problem (*i.e.* product exhausion problem) to be fulfilled, the following equation must hold good:

$$Q = a\frac{\partial Q}{\partial a} + b\frac{\partial Q}{\partial b} + c\frac{\partial Q}{\partial c},$$

where $a\frac{\partial Q}{\partial a}$ represents share of the total product going to labour.

$a\frac{\partial Q}{\partial b}$ represents share of the toal product going to capital

$a\frac{\partial Q}{\partial c}$ represents share of the total product going to land.

Now, Euler's Theorem states that if production function is a homogenous function of the first degree, that is, if in $Q = f(a, b, c)$ for any increase in the variables a, b and c by the amount n, the output Q also increases by n, then Q will be equal to the total sum of the partial derivatives of production function with respect to various factors multiplied by the amounts of the factors respectively. The homogeneous function of the first degree or linear homogeneous function is written in the following form :

$$nQ = f(na, nb, nc)$$

Now, according to Euler's theorem, for this linear homogeneous function :

$$Q = a\frac{\partial Q}{\partial a} + b\frac{\partial Q}{\partial b} + c\frac{\partial Q}{\partial c}$$

Thus, if production function is homogeneous of the first degree, then according to Euler's theorem the total product is :

18. This is after the name of its author 'Leonhard Euler' (1707-1783), a Swis mathematician.

$$Q = a\frac{\partial Q}{\partial a} + b\frac{\partial Q}{\partial b} + c\frac{\partial Q}{\partial c}.$$

where Q represents the total product and $\frac{\partial Q}{\partial a}, \frac{\partial Q}{\partial b}, \frac{\partial Q}{\partial c}$ are partial derivatives of the production function and therefore represent the marginal products of labour, capital, and land respectively. It follows therefore that if production function is homogeneous of the first degree (that is, where there are constant returns to scale), then, according to Euler's Theorem, if the various factors a, b and c are paid rewards equal to their marginal products, the total product will be just exhausted, with no surplus or deficit.

Cobb-Douglas Production Function and Product Exhaustion Problem

Let us demonstrate product exhaustion problem with Euler's theorem by taking an example of a specific linear homogeneous production function. We take Cobb-Douglas production function which is an important type of linear homogenous production to prove the product exhaustion problem with Euler theorem. Two factor Cobb-Douglas production function is written as

$$Q = AL^a K^b \quad \text{... (1)}$$

This function is homogeneous of first degree when $a + b = 1$

To study the distribution of total product we require to determine the marginal products of the two factors. We can determine these by differentiating the production function (1) with respect to labour and capital respectively. Thus

$$MP_L = \frac{\partial Q}{\partial L} = Aa\,L^{a-1} K^b \quad \text{... (2)}$$

$$MP_K = \frac{\partial Q}{\partial K} = Ab\,L^a K^{b-1} \quad \text{... (3)}$$

Euler theorem as applied to product exhaustion problem implies that if each factor is rewarded equal to the marginal product per unit of the factor the total incomes paid to factors would add up to the total product produced. The total payment made to each factor is given by the reward per unit of a factor multiplied by the number of units of the factor employed . Thus

$$Y_L = \frac{\partial Q}{\partial L}.L = Aa\,L^{a-1} K^b .L$$

$$= Aa\,L^a K^b \quad \text{... (4)}$$

where Y_L stands for the total payment made to labour in real terms. From equation (1), we know that $AL^a K^b$ is the total product Q. Thus

$$Y_L = a\,Q$$

Similarly, for capital we obtain

$$Y_K = \frac{\partial Q}{\partial K}.K = Ab\,L^a K^{b-1}.K$$

$$= Ab\,L^a K^b$$

$$Y_K = bQ$$

Since the total payment to factors is the sum of the payments made to each factor, we have

$$Y = Y_L + Y_K = aQ + bQ$$

or

$$Y = (a + b)\,Q \quad \text{... (5)}$$

Now, in case of Cobb Doughas production with homogeneous of first degree, $a + b = 1$, from equation (5) we have

$$Y = Q$$

This implies that total product is just exhausted if each factor is paid a reward per unit equal to its marginal product. This is what was required to be proved.

We thus see that Euler's Theorem is able to explain product exhaustion when production function is homogenous of the first degree. In this way, Wicksteed assuming constant returns to scale and applying Euler's Theorem, proved the adding-up problem, that is, demonstrated that if all factors are paid equal to their marginal products, the total product will be just exactly exhausted.

A Critique of Euler's Theorem and Wicksteed's Solution

Wicksteed's solution was critcized by Walras, Barone, Edgworth and Pareto. It was asserted by these writers that production function was not homogeneous of the first degree, that is; returns to scale are not constant in the actual world. Thus Edgeworth satirically commented on Wicksteed's solution, "there is a magnificence in this generalisation which recalls the youth of philosophy. Justice is a perfect cube, said the ancient sage ; and rational conduct is a homogeneous function, adds the modern savant". Critics pointed out that production function is such that it yields a U-shaped long-run average cost curve. The U-shape of the long-run average cost curve implies that up to a point increasing returns to scale occur and after it diminishing returns to scale are obtained. In case a firm is still working under increasing returns to scale, then if all factors are paid equal to their marginal products, the total factor rewards would exceed the total product. On the other hand, if a firm is working under diminishing returns to scale, and if all factors are paid equal to their marginal products the total factor rewards would not fully exhaust the total product and will therefore leave a surplus. It follows that Euler's Theorem does not apply and therefore the adding-up problem does not hold good when either there is increasing returns to scale or decreasing returns to scale.

Another drawback pointed out in Wicksteed's solution is that when there is constant returns to scale, the long -run average cost curve of the firm is a horizontal straight line which is incompatible with perfect competition. (Under horizontal long-run average cost curve, the firm cannot have a determinate equilibrium position). But perfect competition was essential to the marginal productivity theory and therefore to Wicksteed's solution. Thus Wicksteed solution leads us to two contradictory things.

Wicksell, Walras and Barone's Solution of Production Exhaustion Problem

After Wicksteed, Wicksell, Walras and Barone, each independently, advanced more satisfactory solution to the problem that marginally determined factor rewards would just exhaust the total product. These authors assumed that the typical production function was not homogeneous of the first degree, but was such that yielded U-shaped long-run average cost curve. They pointed out that in the long-run under perfect competition, the firm was in equilibrium at the minimum point of the long-run average cost curve. At *the minimum point of the long-run average cost curve, the returns to scale are momentarily constant*, that is, returns to scale are constant within the range of small variations of output. Thus the condition required for the marginally determined rewards to exhaust the total product, that is, the *operation of constant returns to scale, was fulfilled at the minimum* point of the long-run average cost curve, where a perfectly competitive firm is in long-run equilibrium. Thus in the case of perfectly long-run equilibrium, Euler Theorem can be applied and if the factors are paid rewards equal to their marginal products, the total product would be just exactly exhausted.

Hicks-Samuelson's Solution to the Product Exhaustion Problem

After Wicksell, Walras and Barone, J.R. Hicks[19] and P.A. Samuelson[20] provided more

19. John R. Hicks, *The Theory of Wages.*
20. Paul A. Samuelson, *The Foundations of Economics.*

satisfactory solution to the problem of product exhaustion problem. The basic point to note in their solution is that it is the market conditions of perfect competition with its important feature of zero economic profits in the long run and not the first degree-homogeneous production function that ensure that if factors are paid rewards equal to their marginal products, total value product would be just exhausted.[21]

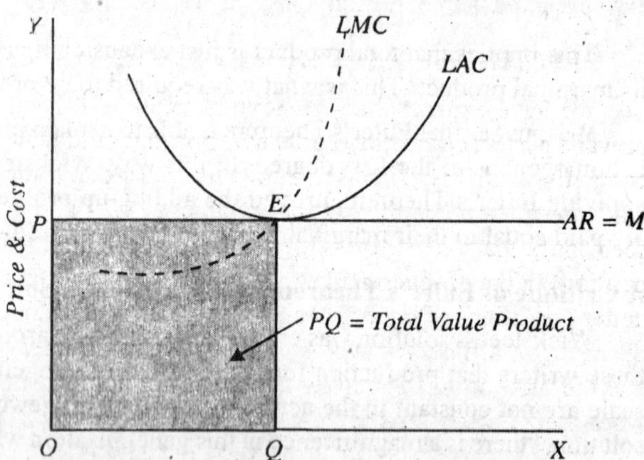

Fig. 32.15. *Hicks–Samuelson Solution to Product Exhausion Problem.*

In a perfectly competitive market structure, firms make neither economic profits, nor make losses. Thus the solution of product exhaustion problem in case of the firms working in competitive factor markets where factors are paid equal to their marginal products, the existence of perfect competition in the product markets will ensure zero economic profits in the long run Consider Figure 32.15 where a perfectly competitive firm is in long-run equilibrium at the minimum point of the long-run average cost curve *LAC* producing level of output *OQ* at price *OP*.

The total value product produced by the firm in this long-run equilibrium is equal to the area *OPEQ*. Since price *OP* is equal to average cost (*AC*) at this long-run equilibrium output with zero pure profits, total value product (*P.Q*) will be equal to the total cost (*TC*). Thus

In long-run competitive equilibrium

$$\text{Total Value Product } (P.Q.) = w.L + K.r. \qquad \text{...(1)}$$

Now, marginal productivity theory of distribution requires that

$$w = VMP_L = P.\ MPP_L \qquad \text{... (2)}$$

$$r = VMP_K = P.\ MPP_K \qquad \text{... (3)}$$

where w and r are prices of labour and capital respectively and MPP_L and MPP_K are marginal physical products of labour and capital respectively and P is the price of the product.

Substituting the values of w and r into equation (1) we have

$$P.Q = L.\ (P.\ MPP_L) + K.\ (P.\ MPP_K)$$

Dividing both sides by P we have

$$Q = L.\ MPP_L + K.\ MPP_K$$

That is, if labour and capital are paid equal to their marginal physical products, total output will be just exhausted.

It is important to note that in contrast to the solutions of Wicksteed and of Wicksell, Walras and Barone, the solution furnished by Hicks and Samuelson proves the product exhaustion theorem without assuming constant returns to scale (*i.e.* first-degree-homogeneous production function) and without using Euler theorem. They prove it by just assuming conditions of perfect market structure.

The merit of the Hicks-Samuleson solution is that it highlights when conditions of perfect competitive market do not hold, that is, when there is either monopoly or imperfect competition in

21. According to Hicks in long-run competitive equilibrium, with zero profits, entrepreneur has no function of decision making to perform and hence his economic profits are zero.

the product market or monopsony or imperfect competition in in the factor market, the hired factors do not get rewards equal to the value of their marginal products and are therefore exploited by the entrepreneurs who may enjoy large economic profits.

PRICING OF FACTORS IN IMPERFECTLY COMPETITIVE MARKETS

We have explained above how the price of a factor of production is determined when there prevails perfect competition both in the product and factor markets. Before the theories of imperfect competition and monopolistic competition were introduced in economic theory no distinction was made between value of marginal product (*VMP*) and marginal revenue product (*MRP*). We have seen above that when there is imperfect competition (*i.e.* monopoly, oligopoly or monopolistic competition) in the product market, marginal revenue differs from the price of the product. As a result, under conditions of imperfect competition in the product market, *marginal revenue product* (*MRP*) of the factor differs from *value of the marginal product (VMP)*. This affects the demand for a factor and the price it will get under conditions of imperfect competition Determination of Factor Price when there exists Monopoly (or Imperfect Competition in the Product Market but Perfect Competition in the Factor Market or monopoly in the product.

Determination of Factor Price when there is Imperfect Competition in the Product Market and Perfect Competition in Factor Market

In what follows we will explain the determination of prices and employment of factors under imperfect completition in the product and factor markets in general. In the next chapter, we will explain in detail the determination of wages and employment of labour under conditions of imperfect competition and monophony in the labour market.

We will explain below the employment of a factor by a firm and the price it will pay to a factor when the firm is working under conditions of imperfect competition or monoply in the product market. *However we assume in this section that as far as factor market is concerned perfect competition prevails in it.* Since perfect competition is assumed to be prevailing in the factor market, price of the factor will be determined by demand for and supply of the factor of production, as explained above. But now the demand for the factor of production is determined not by the value of the marginal product (*VMP*) but by the marginal revenue product (*MRP*) of the factor. As we will see below, in this case price of the factor, which is determined by demand for and supply of the factor, will be equal to the marginal revenue product, but will be less than the value of the marginal product (*VMP*) of the factor.

The conditions of firm's equilibrium in factor market developed above will also apply in the present case. The firm working under *perfect competition in factor market but monopoly or imperfect competition in the product market* would also be in equilibrium position where $MRP = MFC$, and *MRP* curve cuts *MFC* curve from above. But there are some differences between this case and the case explained above.

Since in this case, as in the previous, the firm is working under perfect competition in the factor market it will not be able to affect the price of the factor and factor-cost line will be a horizontal straight line. Therefore, the firm will be in equilibrium, that is, will be maximising profits when $MRP = MFC =$ Price of the factor. But because the firm in the present case is working under conditions of monopoly or imperfect competition in the product market, it will be able to exercise some influence or control over the price of the product. *AR* curve for it will slope downward and *MR* curve will be below it. Consequently, *MRP* which is equal to $MPP \times MR$ will not be equal to *VMP* which is equal to $MPP \times$ price of the product. Since *MR* is less than the price of the product under monopoly or imperfect competition, *MRP* would be less than *VMP*. In symbolic terms:

$$MRP = MPP \times MR$$

$$VMP = MPP \times \text{Price of the product}$$

Since, under imperfect competition or monopoly in the product market, $MR <$ Price of the product, therefore

$$MRP < VMP$$

In equilibrium in the factor market, the firm will make

$$P_F = MRP$$

Therefore, $$P_F = MRP < VMP$$

It is, therefore, concluded that *under conditions of monopoly or imperfect competition in the product market, assuming perfect competition in the factor market, the factor will get price less than the value of its marginal product.*

The equilibrium of the firm when it is working under conditions of perfect competition in the factor market and monopoly or imperfect competition in the product market is shown in fig. 32.16. Since *VMP* is greater than *MRP* when there is imperfect competition in the product market, *VMP* curve will be above *MRP* curve (for the sake of convenience, we have drawn only the downward-sloping portions of *MRP* and *VMP* curves). The firm will be in equilibrium at *E*, where *MRP* = *P*. The equilibrium employment of the factor is *ON*. It will be noticed from the figure that the price of the factor *OP* is, in equilibrium, equal to marginal revenue product *EN* but is less than its value of marginal product which is equal to *RN*. Therefore, factor gets *RE* less than the value of its marginal product.

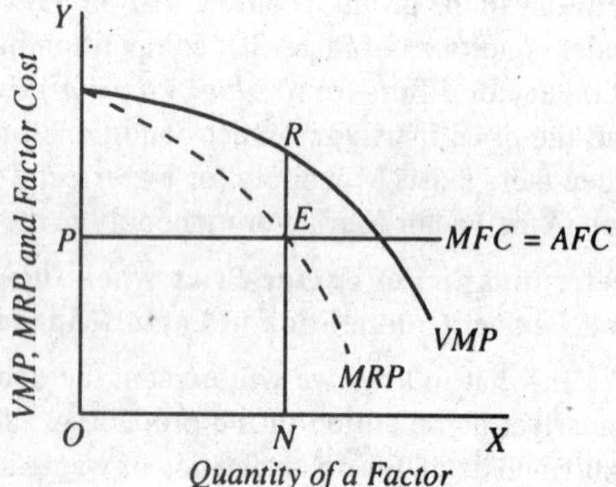

Fig. 32.16. *Employment of a Factor by a Firm under Conditions of Perfect Competition in the Factor Marketand Monopoly or Imperfect Competition in the Product Market.*

Meaning of Factor Exploitation

It follows from above that *price of a factor will be less than the value of the marginal product of the factor under conditions of monopoly and imperfect competition in the product market.* According to Joan Robinson[16] *a factor is exploited when it is paid less than the value of its marginal product (VMP).* Therefore, according to Joan Robinson, when imperfect competition prevails in the product market, labour and other factors, (*i.e.*, factors other than the entrepreneur) are exploited by the entrepreneur. But many economists, especially E.H. Chamberlin, do not agree with Robinson's definition of exploitation of labour. According to Chamberlin, a factor is exploited only when it is paid less than the marginal revenue product (*MRP*). As explained above, when there prevails imperfect or monopolistic competition (including monopoly and oligopoly) with perfect competition in the factor market, price of a factor is equal to the marginal revenue product, though it is less than the value of the marginal product. Therefore, according to Chamberlin, there is no any exploitation of labour or any other factor by the entrepreneur when imperfect competition exists in the product market if there is perfect competition in the factor market. We shall discuss this question of exploitation of labour in detail in the next chapter.

DETERMINATION OF FACTOR PRICES UNDER MONOPSONY

What is monopsony ? Monopsonist means a single buyer. There can be a single buyer in the product market as well as in the factor market. *Where there is a single buyer of a product, he is monopsonist in the product market.* However, we are concerned here with monopsonist in the factor market. *Monopsony in the factor market is said to exist when there is a single buyer of a specific*

16. See Joan Robinson, *Economics of Imperfect Competition* p. 283.

factor of production. For instance, when in a particular area, there is only one employer of specific type of labour, he is monopsonist of that labour. Monopsony in the labour market also comes into existence when various employers of labour in an area form a collusion so far as recruitment of labour is concerned. While monopsony is very rare in product markets, it is more often found in factor markets.

While a monopolist in the product market faces a downward sloping demand curve and can influence the price of the product by varying the level of his output, *a monopsonist in the factor market faces an upward sloping supply curve of the factor and can affect the price of the factor by varying the level of its employment*. By restricting employment it can lower the price of the factor. And if he wants to buy more amount of the factor, he will have to raise its price. Therefore, *the supply curve of the factor or average cost (AFC) curve of the monopsonist will be rising upward to the right*. This average factor cost curve or supply curve of an input is also called *average expense on input*. As the *AFC* curve will be rising, marginal factor cost (*MFC*) curve will be above it. This marginal factor cost is also called *marginal expense of an input (MEI)*. *MRP* curve, as usual, will have an inverted U-shape. As we are assuming that perfect competition prevails in the product market, the value of marginal product (*VMP*) and marginal revenue product (*MRP*) would be equal. The *AFC* and *MFC* curves and *MRP* or *VMP* curves under these conditions are shown in Fig. 32.17.

Firm's Equilibrium when there is Monopsony in Factor Market and Perfect Competition in Product Market.

The general condition for the firm' equilibrium also applies to this case. The firm will be in equilibrium when *MRP* is equal to *MFC* and *MRP* curve cuts *MFC* curve from above. But here there is an important difference. Under monopsony in the factor market *MFC* and *AFC* (or P_F) will not be equal, the former being greater than the latter. *MFC* curve lies above the *AFC* curve. Therefore, in equilibrium when *MRP* is equal to *MFC*, it is greater than the *AFC*, that is, price of the factor.

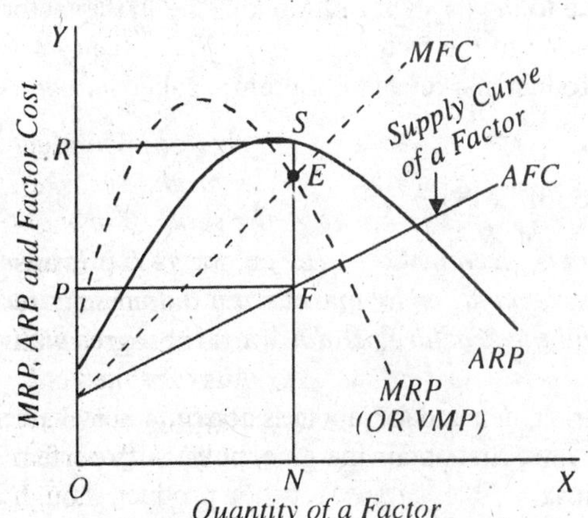

Fig. 32.17. *Determination of Price and Employment of a Factor under Monopsony when there is Perfect Competition in Product Market*

The equilibrium of the firm under monopsony in a factor market assuming perfect competition in the product market is presented in fig. 32.17. The firm is in equilibrium at point *E* (or at *ON* level of employment) where *MRP* = *MFC*. But the *AFC* at *ON* level of employment is *NF*. In other words, the factor is being paid *NF* (or *OP*) price, while its marginal revenue product is *NE*. The difference *EF* between the marginal revenue product (*NE*) and the price paid to the factor of production (*NF*) is called **monopsonistic exploitation of factor** *because this has arisen due to the monopsony in the factor market*. *EF* is monopsonistic exploitation per unit of the factor. *The degree of monopsony power can be measured as the difference between MRP and price of the factor (AFC) at the equilibrium employment*. This is similar to measuring monopoly power as the difference between the price of the product and marginal cost of the product at the equilibrium output. It should be noted that in Fig. 32.17, the firm is making profits equal to *PFSR* which is the difference between the total revenue product and the total factor cost.

When the firm is working under perfect competition in the factor market, $MFC = P_F$ so that in equilibrium $MRP = MFC = P_F$. But if the firm is a monopsonist, $MFC > P_F$ so that in equilibrium.

$$MRP = MFC > \text{Price of the factor } (P_F)$$

Thus a factor under conditions of monopsony will get less than its *MRP*. As we are assuming perfect competition in the product market, *VMP* will be equal to *MRP*. Therefore, we can write complete condition for firm's equilibrium in the present case.

$$VMP = MRP = MFC > \text{Price of the factor}$$

Firm's Equilibrium when there is Monopsony in Factor Market and Monopoly or Imperfect Competition in Product Market.

The same general equilibrium conditions will also apply when there is monopsony in the factor market and monopoly in the product market. Under these conditions, as in others the firm will be in equilibrium where *MRP* = *MFC*. But since there is monopoly in the product market, *MRP* and *VMP* will not be equal; the latter will be greater than the former. *MFC* curve will be above *AFC* curve, because the firm has monopsony in the factor market. Equilibrium of a monopolist-monopsonist firm is shown in Fig. 32.18. The firm's profits will be maximized at *E* (or at *ON* level of employment) where *MRP* = *MFC*. But the price which is paid to the factor of production by the firm is *FN* which is less than both *MRP* and *VMP*. Thus the conditions of firm's equilibrium can be stated as :

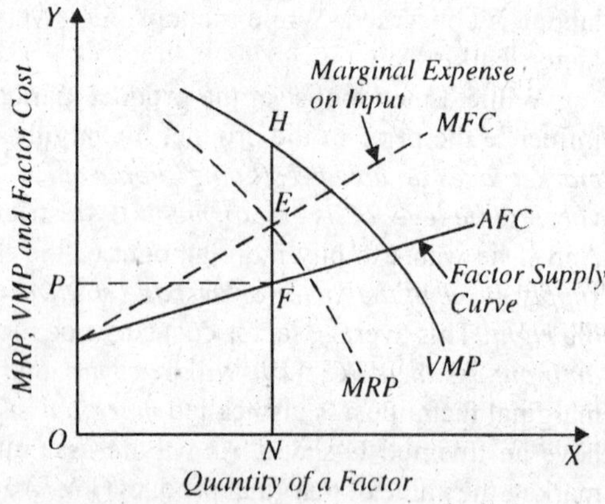

Fig. 32.18. *Determination of Price and Employment of a Factor under Monopsony.*

$$VMP > MRP = MFC > P_F$$

The factor is, therefore subject to double exploitation under conditions of monopoly-monopsony. The gap *EF* between *MRP* and *AFC* or P_F is due to the existence of monopsony in the factor market and is therefore called *monopsonistic exploitation* of the factor. The gap *HE* between *VMP* and *MRP* is due to the existence of monopoly in the product market and is therefore called *monopolistic exploitation* of the factor.

NUMERICAL PROBLEMS

Problem 1. *Suppose a firm's production function is given by $Q = 12L - L^2$ where L is labour input per day and Q is output per day. Derive firm's demand for labour curve if output sells for Rs. 10 in a competitive market. How many workers will the firm hire per day when the wage rate is Rs.30 per day ?*

Solution. For a firm working in a competitive market, demand for labour is determined by value of its marginal product (*VMP*). Since $VMP_L = P \times MP_L$, we first obtain marginal physical product of labour (MP_L) from the given production function. Thus,

$$Q = 12L - L^2$$

$$MP_L = \frac{dQ}{dL} = 12 - 2L$$

$$VMP = P \times MP_L = 10(12 - 2L)$$

$$VMP = 120 - 20L$$

Thus, demand for labour is given by

$$L_d = 120 - 20L$$

The firm will hire labour per day at which $VMP_L = w$. Using this and given that w = Rs. 30, we have

$$120 - 20L = 30$$

$$20L = 120 - 30 = 90$$

$$L = \frac{90}{20} = 4.5$$

The firm will hire 4.5 hours of labour per day.

Problem 2. *The demand for labour by a competitive industry is given by the following demand function :*

$$L_d = 1200 - 10w$$

where L_d is the labour demand per day and w is wage rate.

If labour supply curve is given by $L_s = 20w$, how much labour will be hired by the industry and what wage rate will it pay? Also find out how much economic rent will be earned by labour employed.

Solution. In a competitive labour market equilibrium wage rate and labour employment are determined by the intersection of labour demand and labour supply curves. Therefore equating demand for and supply of labour functions we have

$$1200 - 10w = 20w$$

$$30w = 1200$$

$$w = \frac{1200}{30} = 40$$

Substituting $w = 40$ in labour demand function we have

$$L_d = 1200 - 10w$$
$$= 1200 - 10 \times 40$$
$$= 800$$

Thus, 800 workers will be hired per day and wage rate of Rs. 40 per day will be paid to them.

Economic Rent. The economic rent earned by the quantity of a factor employed is its surplus earnings over and above its transfer earnings. Note that the transfer earnings of the units of a factor employed can be measured by the area under the supply curve of the factor. The total earnings of 800 workers employed at wage rate of Rs. 40 is

$$L.w = 800 \times 40 = \text{Rs. } 3200$$

As is demonstrated in the accompanying diagram, the economic rent earned by 800 workers employed is given by half of the total earnings of workers (In Fig. 52.33 the total earnings of workers employed are given by the area of the rectangle *OLEW* and the economic rent of the workers is given by half of this area).

Economic Rent earned by 800 workers employed $= \frac{1}{2}(3200)$

= Rs. 1600 per day.

(*Note: The diagram need not be drawn. We have drawn it to make it clear that in the present case of linear demand and supply curves, economic rent will be half of the total earnings of the workers employed.*)

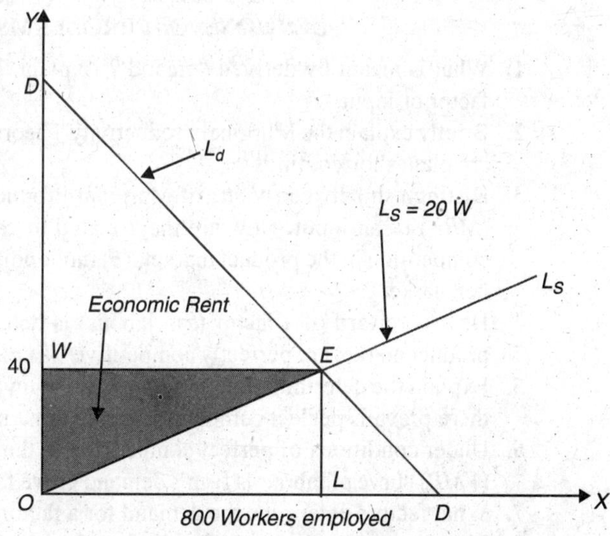

Fig. 32.33. Economic Rent

Problem 3. *Consider the following short-run production function (where X = variable input, Q = output).*

$Q = 10X - 0.5X^2$

Suppose the competitive firm sells its output for Rs 10 per unit and it can obtain the variable input X at Rs 20 per unit as much as it needs.

(*a*) *Determine the marginal revenue production function.*

(*b*) *Determine the marginal factor cost function.*

(*c*) *Determine the optimal value of X, given that the objective of the firm is to maximise profits.*

Solution. (*a*) Marginal revenue production function (*MRP*) is the first derivative of the total revenue function. Total revenue function can be obtained by multiplying the production function with price of output which is Rs 10 per unit. Thus,

$$TR = PQ = 10(10X - 0.5X^2)$$

$$= 100X - 5X^2$$

$$MRP_X = \frac{dTR}{dX} = 100 - 10X \quad ...(1)$$

(*b*) Marginal factor cost function is the addition to total cost by using an extra unit of input. It is the first derivative of the total cost function $\left(MFC = \frac{dTC}{dX}\right)$. Since in the question, the price of the variable factor (*X*) is given and constant, *MFC* will be equal to the price of the variable input which is equal to Rs 20 per unit). Thus,

$$MFC = 20 \quad ...(2)$$

(*c*) A firm which seeks to maximise profits will be making optimal use of the variable input when it is using its so much quantity at which its $MRP_x = MFC_x$. Thus, we can obtain the optimum value of the variable factor by equating the marginal revenue product function (equation 1) with marginal factor cost function (equation 2). Thus,

$$MRP_x = MFC_x$$

$$100 - 10X = 20$$

$$10X = 100 - 20 = 80$$

$$X = 8$$

Use of 8 units of the variable input *X* is optimal for the firm.

QUESTIONS AND PROBLEMS FOR REVIEW

1. What is meant by derived demand ? Explain the factors which determine demand for a factor or input.
2. Briefly explain the Marginal Productivity Theory of factor pricing (*i.e.*, distribution). What are main shortcomings? *D.U. B.A (Hons.), 1984*
3. Distinguish between Value of Marginal Product (*VMP*) and Marginal Revenue Product (*MRP*) of an input. How are they related to each other when there prevails (*a*) perfect competition in the product market, (*b*) monopolistic competition or monopoly in the product market ?
4. How is reward of a factor (say labour) is determined when both the factor market and product market are perfectly competitive ? Explain. *D.U. B.Com (Hons.) 2002*
5. Explain the determination of optimal use of a variable input (*e.g.*, labour) by a firm when there prevails perfect competition in the input market.
6. Under conditions of perfect competition in the labour market value of marginal product (*VMP*) curve of labour is firm's demand curve for it. Explain.
7. What factors determine the demand for a factor input ? Explain.
8. The economy-wide demand curve for a factor will be more elastic, the greater the elasticity

of the consumer demand for goods in the production of which the factor is employed. Explain

9. A Theory of factor pricing is only a special case of general theory of pricing. Discuss.
10. How can the demand curve of labour be derived when labour is not the only variable factor of production in case of perfect competition in both product and input market ?
D.U., B.Com (Hons.) II Year 2008

OR

Derive the demand curve for labour when several variable inputs are used under conditions of perfect competition in both the product and input markets.
D.U., B. Com (Hons.) II Year 2007

11. Derive the demand curve of a firm for *a single variable factor* under conditions of perfect of competition in both product and factor markets. *D.U. B.Com (Hons.) II Year 2006*
12. A perfectly competitive firm can hire labour at Rs. 50 per day. The firm's production function is given below :

Number of days/labour	*Number of units of output*
0	0
1	16
2	30
3	42
4	52
5	60

If the output is sold at price Rs. 5 per unit, how many labour days should the firm hire ? [**Hints:** From the production data, we have to find out marginal physical product of labour days (MPP_P). We then multiply marginal physical products by price of output (= Rs. 5) to obtain VMP_L at different levels of labour use. The firm will hire the number of labour days at which $VMP_L = 50$.]

13. Wages under perfect competition in labour market are equal to the marginal revenue product; but under imperfect competition (*e.g.* monopsony) in labour market wages are not equal to the marginal revenue product of labour. Explain with the help of diagrams.
14. Derive graphically the competitive firm's demand curve for a variable factor when several variable factors are used. *D.U. B.A. (Hons.) 1998*
15. How is market demand for a variable factor of production derived from the demand of individual firms ?
16. A monopolist's demand curve for labour will be downward sloping even if marginal physical product of labour is constant. Explain. *D.U. B.A. (Hons.) 1997*

CHAPTER 33

WAGE DETERMINATION IN COMPETITIVE AND IMPERFECTLY COMPETITIVE MARKETS

Introduction

In the previous chapter we have explained the determination of prices of factors in general. In the present chapter we shall explain in the detail how wages are determined under conditions of perfectly and imperfectly competitive markets. It is here worth noting some *special characteristics of labour* First, unlike land and capital, labour (that is, workers) are usually found to be combining together to form trade unions for demanding higher wages and better working conditions from the entrepreneurs. Second, labour cannot be separated from labourer himself, whereas land and capital are distinct from their owners (*i.e.*, landlords and capitalists). Thirdly, workers are, within certain limits, free to choose whether or not they will work on a particular day as they can take leave or abstain from work. Fourthly, unlike other factors, workers can decide whether or not to increase their supply by working a large number of hours per week.

Nominal and Real Wages

While nominal wage is wage in terms of money, the real wage is measured in terms of goods and services it will purchase. When prices in the economy rise, the same money wage will buy less goods and services. Therefore, the rise in prices, money wage remaining constant, will lead to the fall in real wages. Thus, *real wages are obtained after adjusting for inflation, that is, for rise in prices in the economy.* Thus real wage is equal to money wage divided by the price level, that is, $W_r = \frac{W}{P}$ stands for real wage, W for money wage rate and P for the general price index number.

The term real wage is also sometimes used to mean the *money wages plus the non-monetary benefits* which workers receive in some jobs. Thus college professors with equal qualifications and skill may prefer lower money wage rates as compared to the persons employed as business executives in private firms because the teaching in a university or college offers some *non-monetary benefits* such as flexible working hours, pleasant surroundings, opportunities for advancement etc. Thus real wages of a college professor will be his money salary plus the above mentioned non-monetary benefits which he gets in the teaching profession.

Like the prices of other factors of production, wage rate depends on demand for and supply of labour. For explanation of wage determination it is therefore essential to understand first the nature of demand for labour. Demand for labour like other factor prices differs in certain respects from the demand for consumer goods. Consumer goods are demanded because they satisfy the wants of the people directly. People demand food to satisfy the pangs of their hunger, they demand clothes to satisfy their want of providing a cover to their bodies and so forth. These products possess utility which directly satisfies the wants of the people who are therefore willing to pay price for these products.

Demand of labour is a derived demand. But, unlike the goods, the labour does not satisfy the wants of the people directly. The labour is demanded not because it directly satisfies the wants of the people who wish to buy them. Instead, labour is demanded because it can be used to produce consumer goods which then satisfy human wants. Therefore, demand for labour, like that of other factors of production, is called derived demand. It is derived from the demand for the products it helps to produce. Thus, the *demand for labour ultimately depends upon the demand for goods it helps to produce.* The greater the demand for goods which a particular type of labour helps to make, the greater the demand for that type of labour. Just as demand for goods depend upon their utility, the *demand for labour depends upon marginal revenue product of labour.* In what follows we first explain supply of labour.

SUPPLY OF LABOUR : CHOICE BETWEEN WORK AND LEISURE

It is important to know how many hours a worker will be willing to work at different wage rates or in other words, how much work-effort a worker will supply at various money wage rates. Normally, the work-effort put in by the workers will vary in response to the changes in wage rates. We assume that the worker makes a contract with the employer to work for a certain wage rate per hour and that he is free to choose the number of hours he has to work in a week. This assumption, it may be pointed out, is not entirely realistic, because generally the workers are employed for a fixed number of hours in a week. The number of work-hours in a week may be fixed by law or by an agreement between the workers as a whole (or their trade unions) and the employer. Therefore, in actual practice, the worker may not be free to vary the number of hours he has to work. Even then, it may be pointed out that the workers can vary the number of hours to work in a week to some extent by choosing whether or not to work overtime, by taking leave on false pretexts, and by making similar other adjustments. This is the case with the workers who are employed on the basis of wages or salaries. Then, there are self-employed people such as farmers, business proprietors, independent professionals, etc. who can choose the number of hours they have to work in a week and their choice will depend upon the money rewards they are able to obtain for their work. In order to enunciate a general principle in regard to the supply of work-effort or labour by an individual worker we assume that the worker is completely free to vary the number of hours he has to work in a week.

Consider the workers' demand for income in exchange for the work-effort of labour he puts in. More income a worker has, more better off he will be. But, given the wage rate, more money income he can earn only by supplying more work-effort (or labour), that is, only by putting in more hours of work in a week. But more hours of work mean more sacrifice of leisure. It is, therefore, clear that given these circumstances a worker can have more income only by the loss of more leisure. And leisure, it should be noted, is a thing which provides satisfaction to the individual as other goods of consumption. Therefore, the gain in satisfaction which a worker obtains as a result of earning more income by doing work has to be balanced against the loss of satisfaction he experiences as a result of the sacrifice of more leisure. It, therefore, follows that *when the wage rate rises, whether or not a worker will offer to work more hours in a week depends upon his preference for leisure vis-a-vis income.* It is important to note here that in this chapter we will be considering only the *real wage* which is equal to *nominal wage* divided by the price level. Thus, real wage = $\frac{W}{P}$ where W stands for nominal wage and P for the price level.

It needs to be emphasised that leisure does not necessarily mean 'doing nothing'. During the period of leisure, the worker may play with his children, do his gardening, listen radio or watch television, eat goods, visit the cinema, *etc*. Most of the consumption goods are enjoyed during the period of leisure. In fact "*Most of the good things of life must be enjoyed during leisure if they are to be enjoyed at all.*"[1]. Having leisure strictly means '*not working for income*'. Income is demanded for spending on ordinary consumers' goods. But, as explained above, leisure is also a thing that yields satisfaction to the worker. Therefore, a worker has to decide how much hours of work he should do and thereby earn income for spending on the consumption of ordinary consumers' goods and how much leisure he should have. The standard of living of the worker depends upon the quantity and quality of the consumers' goods he consumes as well as the amount of leisure he is able to enjoy.

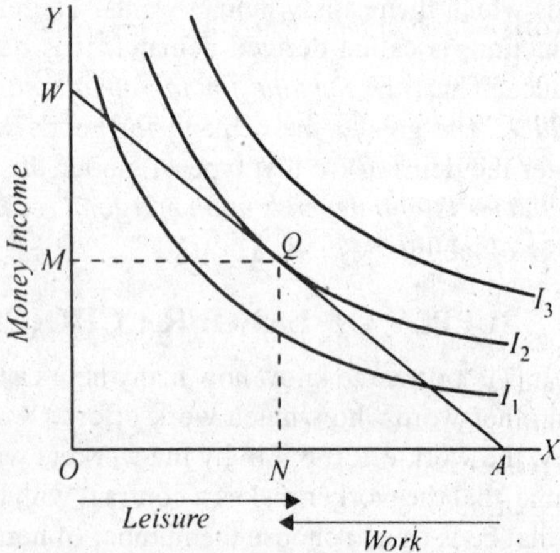

Fig. 33.1. *Equilibrium regarding Work Effort and Leisure*

When the wage rate rises whether or not a worker will feel induced to work a larger number of hours depends upon his attitude towards income and leisure. In modern economic theory, relative preference between income and leisure are represented by indifference curves, with income represented on one axis and leisure on the other. In Chapter 11 (*Applications of Indifference curves*) of this book we made a detailed analysis of an individual's equilibrium regarding work and leisure using indifference curve analysis. For the convenience of the students we reproduce in Figure 33.1 individual's equilibrium regarding work and leisure

Fig. 33. 1 depicts an indifference map representing an individual's desires for money income and leisure and his relative preference between different combinations of them. Suppose the real wage rate is Rs. 25 per hour and the corresponding wage line is *AW*. The slope of the wage line *AW* represents the wage rate (that is, $\frac{OW}{OA}$ = wage rate = Rs. 25 per hour).

We assume the individual to be rational, that is, we assume that the individual will choose the combination of income and leisure so as to maximise his satisfaction. But in his attempt to maximize satisfaction, the individual is restricted by the time available with him and by the real wage per hour which shows the rate at which time can buy money income. Given these constraints, the consumer will try to reach the highest possible indifference curve. Thus, in Fig. 33.1, given the wage line the individual will be in equilibrium position (that is, will be maximising his satisfaction) at a point on line *AW* which lies on the highest possible indifference curve. Such point is *Q* at which the wage line *AW* is tangent to the indifference curve I_2. In this equilibrium position *Q*, the individual is having *ON* leisure and *OM* money income. Further, he is working for *AN* hours of work. It is by working *AN* hours of work that he makes income equal to *OM*. It is, therefore, clear from the figure that at the given wage rate, he supplies *AN* amount of work-hours in a week.

1. Stonier and Hague, *op, cit*., p. 305

Effect of Wage Increase on Work Effort (Labour Supply) : Income Effect and Substitution Effect

When the real wage rate rises, the wage line will shift upward and individual will be in equilibrium at a higher indifference curve. An important question which arises is: whether in the new equilibrium position reached as a result of the increase in the real wage rate, the individual will offer to work for larger number of hours than before or not.

When the real wage rate increases, the individual will be pulled in two opposite directions. As mentioned above, the real wage rate is the relative price of leisure which has to be given up for doing work to earn income. As real wage rate rises, leisure becomes relatively more expensive (in terms of income foregone) and this induces the individual to substitute work (or income) for leisure. This is called *substitution effect* of the rise in real wage and induces the individual to work more hours (i.e. supply more labour) to earn more income.

But the increase in the real wage rate also makes the individual richer, that is, his income increases. This increase in income tends to make the individual to consume more of all commodities including leisure. This is called *income* effect of the rise in wage rate which tends to increase leisure and reduce number of work hours (*i.e.* reduce labour supply. The economists generally believe that substitution effect of a rise in real wage is larger than its income effect and therefore individuals work for more hours (that is, supply more labour) at a higher wage rate. However, beyond a certain higher real wage and number of hours worked, leisure becomes more desirable and income effect outweights substitution effect, and as a result supply of labour decreases beyond a certain higher wage rate. In what follows we shall explain how we derive a supply curve of labour of an individual and of the economy as a whole in all these circumstances.

It is clear from above that whether an individual will supply more work-effort or less as a result of the rise in the wage rate depends upon the relative strengths of the income and substitution effects.

SUPPLY CURVE OF LABOUR

We now turn to explain the changes in the work-effort or labour supplied by an individual worker due to the changes in the wage rate. Consider Fig. 33.2(*a*) To begin with, the wage line is AW_1; the slope of the wage line indicates the wage rate per hour. With wage line AW_1, the individual is in equilibrium at point Q on indifference curve I_1 and is working AL_1 hours in a week. Suppose the wage rate rises so that the new wage line is AW_2 With wage line AW_2, the individual is in equilibrium at point R on the indifference curve I_2 and is now working AL_2 hours which are more than before. If the wage rate further rises so that the new wage line is AW_3, the individual moves to the point S on indifference curve I_3 and works AL_3 hours which are more than AL_1 or AL_2. Suppose the wage rate further rises so that the wage line is AW_4. With wage line AW_4, the individual is in equilibrium at point T and works AL_4 hours. If points Q, R, S and T are connected, we get that is called *wage offer curve, which shows the number of hours that an individual offers to work at various wage rates*. It should be noted that the wage offer curve, strictly speaking, is not the supply curve of labour though it provides the same information as the supply curve of labour. The supply curve of labour is obtained when the wage rate is directly represented on the Y-axis and labour (*i.e.* work effort) supplied at various wage rates on the X-axis reading from left to right. In Fig. 33.2(*b*) the supply curve of labour has been drawn from the information gained from Fig. 33.2(a). Let the wage line AW_1 represent the wage rate equal to P_1, wage line AW_2 represenst wage rate P_2, wage line AW_3 represents wage rate P_3, and wage line AW_4 represent wage rate P_4. It will be seen that as the wage rate rises from P_1 to P_4 and as a result the wage line shifts from AW_1 to AW_4 the number of hours worked, that is, the amount of labour supplied increases from AL_1 to AL_4. As a result, the supply curve of labour in Fig. 33.2(*b*) is upward sloping. *The indifference map depicted in Fig. 33.2(a) is such that the substitution effect of the rise in the wage rate is stronger than the income effect of the rise in the wage rate so that the work-effort supplied increases as the wage rate rises.*

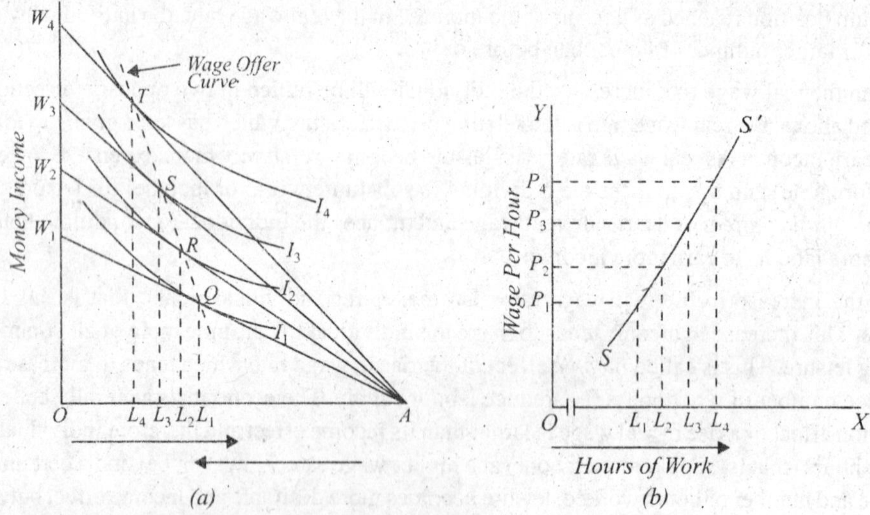

Fig. 33.2. *Upward Sloping Supply Curve of Labour*

Backward-Sloping Supply Curve of Labour

But the supply curve of labour is not always upward sloping. When an individual prefers leisure to income, then the supply of labour (number of hours worked) by an individual will decrease as the wage rate rises. This is because in such a case income effect which tends to reduce the work effort overweighs the substitution effect which tends to increase the work effort. In Fig. 33.3 such an indifference map is shown which yields a backward sloping supply curve of labour which indicates that the number of hours worked per week decreases as the wage rate rises. AW_1, AW_2, AW_3 and AW_4 are the wage lines when the wages rates are P_1, P_2, P_3 and P_4 respectively. Q, R, S and T are the equilibrium points with the wage lines AW_1, AW_2, AW_3 and AW_4 respectively. It will be noticed from Fig. 33.3(*a*) that when the wage rate rises and as a consequence the wage line shifts from AW_1 to AW_4. the number of hours worked per week decreases from AL_1 to AL_4. In Fig. 33.3(*b*) supply curve of labour is drawn with *Y*-axis representing the hourly wage rate and *X*-axis representing number of hours worked per week at various wage rates. It will be seen from Fig. 33.3(*b*) as the wage rate rises from P_1 to P_4 the supply of labour (*i.e.*, number of hours worked per week) decreases from OL_1 to OL_4. In other words, the *supply curve of labour slopes backward,* that is, *slopes upward from right to left.* It should be noted that it is the nature or pattern of indifference curves between income and leisure that yields backward sloping supply curve. A glance at Fig. 33.2(*a*) and Fig. 33.3(*a*) will reveal that the nature of indifference curves in the two is different. As said above, the nature of indifference curves depend upon the relative preference between income and leisure. In Fig. 33.3(*a*) *indifference curves between income and leisure are such that the individual's preference for leisure is relatively greater than for income. In this case, when the wage rate rises, the individual enjoys more leisure and accordingly reduces the number of hours worked per week.*

But it sometimes happens that as the hourly wage rate rises from a very low level to a reasonably good level, the number of hours worked per week rises and as the hourly wage rate rises further, the number of hours worked per week decreases. This may be the case of an individual who has some more or less fixed minimum wants for goods and services which he can satisfy with a certain money income. When the wage rate is so low that he is not earning sufficient money income, then to satisfy his more or less fixed minimum wants for goods and services, his preference for income will be relatively greater than that for leisure and, therefore, when the wage rate rises the individual will work more hours per week. When the wage rate has risen to a level which is sufficient to yield a sufficient money income for satisfying his fixed minimum wants, then for further increases in wage rate the number of hours worked per week will decrease because now the individual can afford to have more leisure and also earn an income sufficient to meet his minimum wants for goods and services.

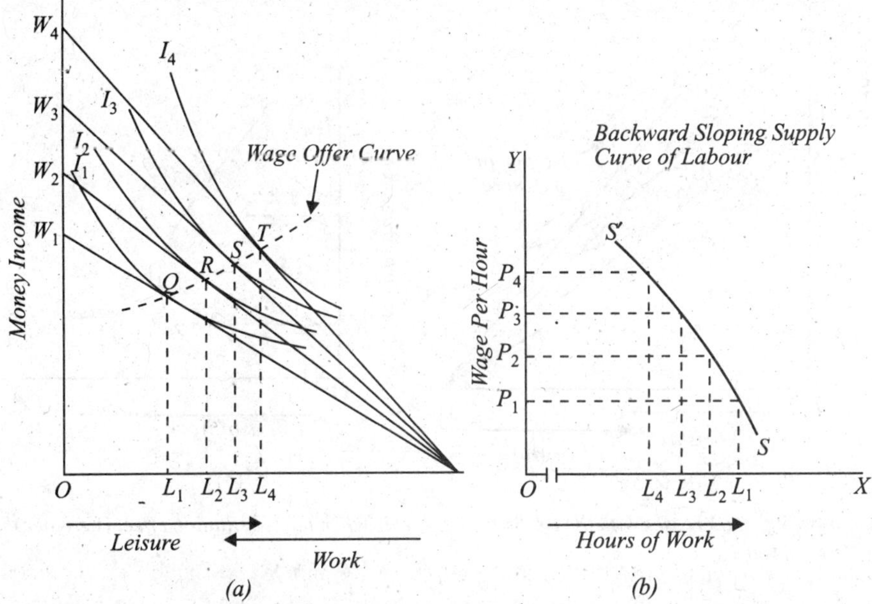

Fig. 33.3. *Backward Bending Supply Curve of Labour*

It follows from above that up to a certain wage rate the supply curve will slope upward from left to right and then for further increases in the wage rate the supply curve of labour will slope backward.

In Fig. 33.4(*a*) an indifference map along with a set of wage lines AW_1, AW_2, AW_3, AW_4 (showing wage rates P_1, P_2, P_3, P_4 respectively) are shown. As the wage rate rises to P_2 and hence the wage line shifts to AW_2 the number of hours worked by the individual per week increases but when the wage rate further rises to P_3 and P_4 and hence the wage line shifts to AW_3 and AW_4, the number of hours worked by the individual decreases. From Fig. 33.4(*b*) it will be explicitly seen that the supply curve of labour slopes upward to the wage rate P_2 (that is, point *K*) and beyond that it slopes backward.

Supply Curve of Labour for the Economy as a Whole

The supply curve of labour of a group of individuals or of the whole working force in the economy can be derived by summing up horizontally the supply curves of individuals. It may be noted that the supply curve of labour for the economy as a whole will be upward sloping or backward sloping depending upon whether the relative number of individuals having upward sloping supply curves is greater or less than those having backward sloping supply curves of labour. Further, different individuals will have backward sloping portion in their supply curve at different wage ranges, which creates difficulties in finding the nature of supply curve of the whole work force. It is generally found that when the wage rate rises from the initially low level to a sufficiently good level, the total supply of labour to the economy as a whole increases (that is, supply curve for the economy as a whole slopes upward to a certain wage rate) and for further increases in the wage rate, the total supply of labour to the economy as a whole decreases (that is, beyond a certain wage rate the total supply curve of labour slopes backward). Thus, the total supply curve of labour for the economy as a whole is generally believed to be the shape depicted in Fig. 33.4(b).

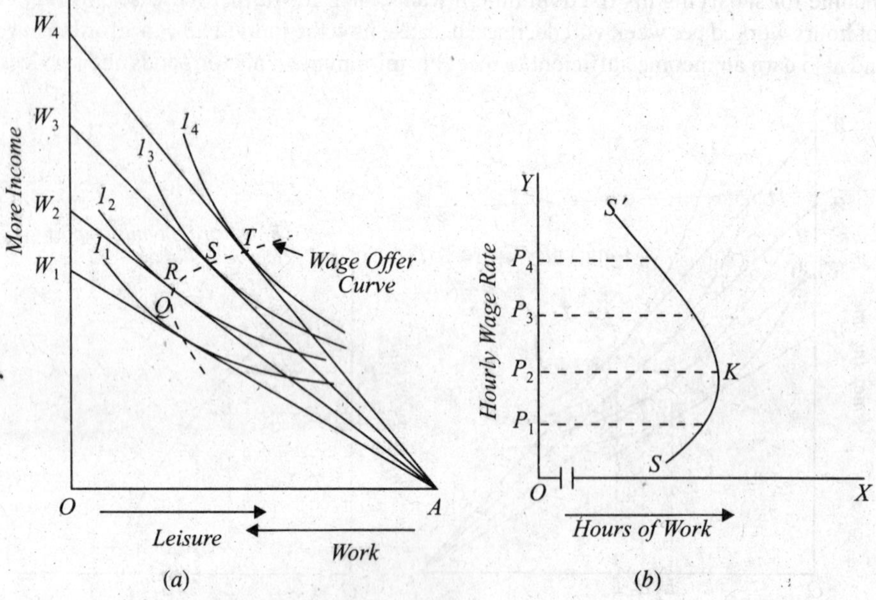

Fig. 33.4. *Work effort increases with the rise in the wage rate when the substitution effect is greater than the income effect.*

WAGE DETERMINATION UNDER PERFECT COMPETITION IN THE LABOUR MARKET

We have explained in the Chapter 32 how the price of factor is determined under conditions of perfect competition in the factor market. The analysis of wage determination under conditions of perfect competition is exactly the same as given there. In the case of wage determination, it should be remembered that average factor cost (AFC) becomes average wage (AW) and marginal factor cost becomes marginal wage (MW). As explained there, when there prevails perfect competition in the labour market, wage rate is determined by the equilibrium between the demand and supply of labour. Demand for labour is governed by marginal revenue product of labour (MRP). Wage rate determined by demand for and supply of labour is equal to the marginal revenue product of labour. Thus, under perfect competition in labour market, a firm will employ the amount of labour at which wage rate = MRP of labour.

As regards the supply of labour, it may be pointed out that supply of labour to the whole economy depends upon the size of population, the number of workers available for work out of a given population, the number of hours worked, the intensity of work, the skills of workers and their willingness to work. The size of population is not influenced in any significant manner by the changes in the current wage rates. The advocates of the subsistence theory of wages believed that the size of population rises or falls with a rise or fall respectively in the wage rate, and from this they had deduced a law called "Iron Law of Wages". But the history has shown that rise in the wage rate may have just the opposite effect on the size of population from what the subsistence theory of wages conceives.

Moreover, the historical experiences have revealed that the size of population is dependent upon the great variety of social, cultural, religious and economic factors among which wage rate plays only a minor determining role. However, the willingness to work may be influenced greatly by the changes in the wage rate. On the one hand, as wages rise, some persons will do not work at lower wages may now be willing to supply their labour. But, on the other hand, as wages rise, some persons may be willing to work fewer hours and others like women may withdraw themselves from labour force, since the wages of their husbands have increased. Thus there are two conflicting responses to the rise in wages and therefore the exact nature of supply curve of labour is difficult to ascertain. *It is, however, generally held that the total supply curve of labour rises up to a certain wage level and after that it slopes backward.* This is shown in Fig. 33.5. As wage rate rises up to *OW*, the total quantity supplied of labour rises, but beyond *OW*, the quantity supplied of labour decreases as the wage rate is increased.

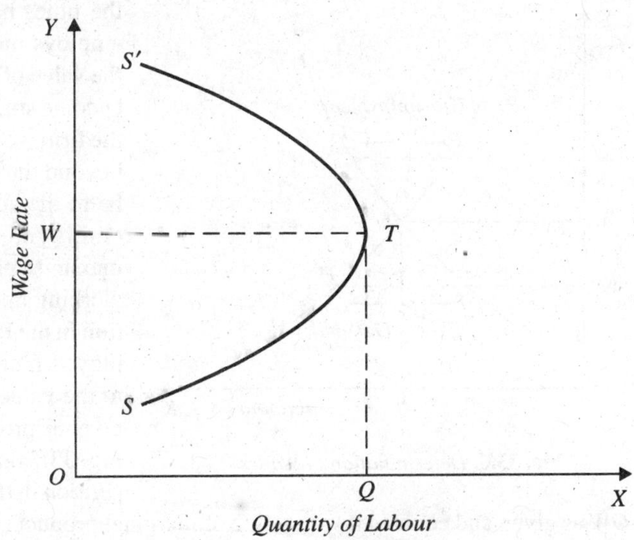

Fig. 33.5. *Beyond a certain wage rate, supply curve of labour is backward sloping.*

But so far as supply of labour to a particular industry is concerned it slopes upward. As the wages in an industry are increased labourers from other industries will shift to this industry. The elasticity of the supply curve of labour to an industry will also depend upon the transfer earnings of labourers. Similar is the case of supply of workers to a particular occupation. If wages in one occupation go up, some persons from other similar occupations would be attracted to it and thus the supply of labour to that occupation will increase. Thus because of occupational shifts, the supply curve of labour to a particular occupation is elastic and rises upwards. The long-run supply curve of labour is more elastic than the short-run supply curve since, in the long-run, besides the occupational shift in the labour force, new entrants in the labour market (who are now children) can also adopt the occupation by getting training for it in the very first instance.

How the wage rate is determined by demand for and supply of labour is shown in Figure 33.6 where *DD* represents the demand curve for labour and *SS* represents its supply curve. The two curves intersect at point *E*. This means that at wage rate *OW*, quantity demanded of labour is equal to quantity supplied of it. Thus, given the demand for and supply of labour wage rate *OW* is determined and at this wage rate labour market is cleared. All those who are willing to work at the wage rate *OW* get employment. This implies that there is no involuntary unemployment and full employment of labour prevails. It is important to note that there will be no equilibrium at any wage rate higher or lower than *OW*. For example, at a higher wage *OW′*, supply of labour exceeds quantity demanded of it and as a result involuntary unemployment equal to *UT* emerges. Given the competition among labourers, this unemployment would push down the wage rate to *OW*. On the other hand, at a lower wage rate *OW″*, the demand for labour exceeds the amount of labour which people are willing to supply. In view of the excess demand for labour, the wage rate will go up to *OW* where the demand for labour equals the amount supplied of it. Thus wage rate *OW* will finally settle in the labour market.

Though wage rate is determined by demand for and supply of labour, it is equal to the value of marginal product of labour. This is so because in order to maximise its profits, a firm will equalise the wage rate with the value of the marginal product (*VMP*) of labour. If the firm stops short of this equality, the value of the marginal product (*VMP*) will be greater than the wage rate which would imply that there was still scope for earning more profits by increasing the employment of labour. On the other hand, if the firm goes beyond and employs more labour than the equality point, the value of the marginal product of labour will become smaller than the wage rate. As a result, the firm will incur losses on workers employed beyond the equality point and it will therefore be to the advantage of the firm to reduce the employment of labour. Thus in order to maximise profits and be in equilibrium the firm working under conditions of perfect competition in the factor and product markets will employ so much labour that the wage rate is equal to the value of marginal product (or marginal revenue product) of labour. It will be seen from Fig. 33.7 that the *firm* working in perfect competition in the labour market will take the wage rate *OW* as given and equates it with value of marginal product (*VMP*) and employs *OM* labour. To sum up, *the wage rate is determined by demand for and supply of labour, but is equal to the value of marginal product (or marginal revenue product) of labour.*

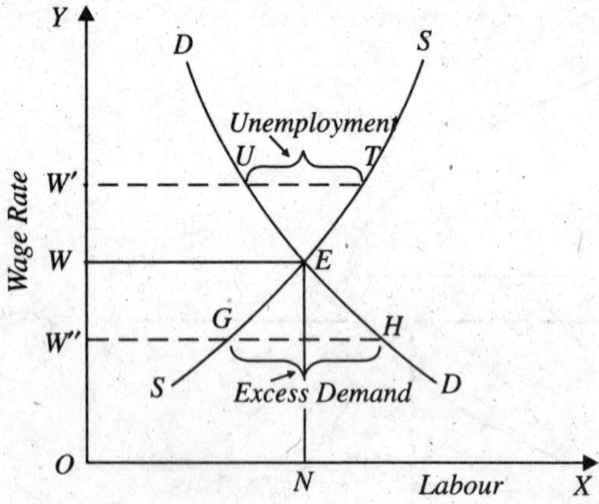

Fig. 33.6. *Determination of Wages*

It is worth mentioning that when the firms are in equilibrium by equating value of marginal product of labour to the wage rate, they may be making profits or losses in the short run. Consider Figure 33.7 which depicts the equilibrium position of the firm in the short run. It will be seen from Fig. 33.7 that at the wage rate *OW*, the firm is in equilibrium when it is employing *OM* amount of labour. It will be further seen that the firm is making super-normal profits since in equilibrium employment *OM*, average revenue product of labour (*ARP*) which is equal to *RM* is greater than the wage rate *OW*

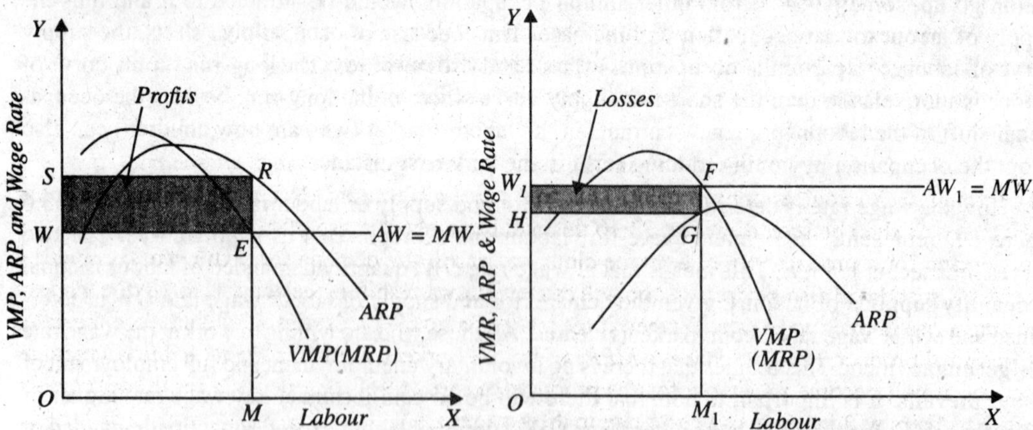

Fig. 33.7. *Equilibrium of the Firm with Super-Normal Profits*

Fig. 33.8. *A firm will not employ labour at wage rate OW_1.*

(=*ME*). This can happen in the short run, but not in the long run. When firms are earning super-normal profits in the short run more entrepreneurs will enter the market in the long run to purchase labour to produce the products made by it. Entry of more entrepreneurs to the labour market will compete away the super-normal profits. As a result, the demand for labour will rise and the demand curve for labour will shift outward to the right, which will raise the wage rate and will eliminate the profits.

It should be carefully noted that a firm will not employ labour if wage rate exceeds average product of labour. Unlike machines labour is a variable factor and if its employment is not sufficient to recover its wages, it will be laid off even in the short run. Consider Fig. 33.8 at wage rate OW_1, a firm will be incurring losses if it employs ON_1 amount of labour at which wage rate $OW_1 = VMP = MRP$ Therefore, at wage rate OW_1, the firm will not employ labour.

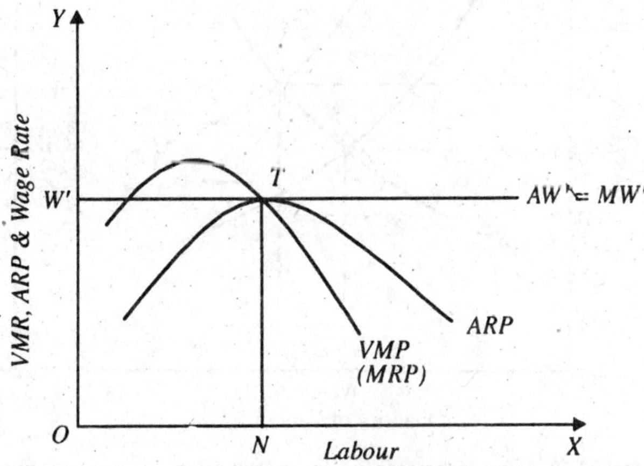

Fig. 33.9. *Long-Run Equilibrium of the Firm*

To sum up, in the long run, the equilibrium between demand for and supply of labour is established at the level where the wage rate of labour is equal to both the VMP (MRP) and ARP of labour and thus the firms earn only normal profits. The long-run equilibrium position of the firm working under perfect competition is depicted in Fig. 33.9 where it will be seen that the firm is in equilibrium at *ON* level of employment (*i.e.*, at point *T*) at which wage rate is not only equal to value of marginal product but also average revenue product of labour. Given the *ARP* and *VMP* curves, if the wage rate is lower than *OW'* (= *N.T.*), the number of firms employing labour will change causing changes in demand for labour. As a result of this, the wage rate will ultimately settle at the level *OW* or *NT*.

Changes in Equilibrium Wage Rate

We have explained above how through interaction of demand for and supply of labour determines the market wage rate. Now, if any of the factor causes a shift either in demand curve or in supply curve of labour, the equilibrium will be disturbed causing a change in the wage rate. Both demand for and supply of labour can shift.

Shift in Demand Curve for Labour. Demand for labour increases if its productivity increases, say through technological improvement. This will cause a rightward shift in the demand curve for labour and as shall be seen from Fig. 33.10 this will bring about a rise in the wage rate. Similarly, if the demand for a product, say of a textile cloth, increases, the demand for textile workers being a derived demand will also go up. This too will cause an upward shift in the demand for textile workers causing a rise in their wage rate. Further, if the price of a textile cloth rises, it will increase the value of marginal product, (*VMP* = *Price* × *MPP*) of textile workers. With this higher value of marginal product, it will become profitable for the producer to hire more workers. As a result, demand for textile workers will increase causing a rise in their wage rate.

Conversely, if the demand for a product decreases or its price falls, it will induce a reduction in the demand for labour. Given the supply curve, decrease in demand for labour will bring about reduction in wage rate.

Shift in Labour Supply Curve. If the factors determining labour supply undergo a change, the supply curve of labour will shift causing a change in the equilibrium wage rate. The supply of labour to a given occupation or industry will decrease *if the wages in alternative occupations or industries go up*. In this case at every wage rate less labour will be offered to a given occupation or industry.

This will cause a shift in the supply curve of labour to the left and, given the demand curve for labour, result in rise in the wage rate. This is shown in Figure 33.11.

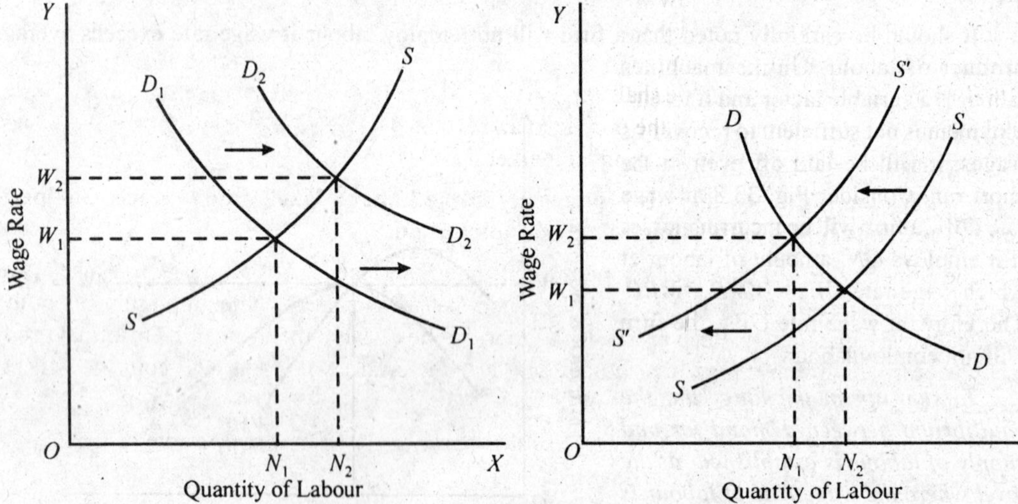

Fig. 33.10. *Effect of Increase in Labour Demand on the Wage Rate*

Fig. 33.11. *Effect of Decrease in Labour Supply on Wage Rate*

Similarly, if workers valuation of their leisure time changes, the supply curve of labour will shift. If most workers start attaching a higher value to their leisure time spent with their families, the less labour will be supplied to an occupation or industry. This will cause a shift in the labour supply curve to the left resulting in higher wage rate as is illustrated in Fig. 33.11.

Conversely, if for any reason, the wage rate in alternative occupation fall or workers' preferences for leisure declines, supply of labour to a given occupation or industry will increase at every wage rate. This will cause a shift in the supply curve of labour to the right and result in fall in the wage rate.

WAGE DETERMINATION UNDER MONOPSONY

Monopsony in the labour market is said to exist when there is a single buyer of labour. Under monopsony in the labour market, a single buyer faces a large number of workers who are unorganised and whose geographical mobility of labour is very much limited. Monopsony may prevail when a big employer hires a proportionately very large number of a given type of labour so that he is in a position to influence the wage rate or it may prevail when various employers have an understanding not to compete for labour and thus act as one in hiring labour. Thus, in the actual world, monopsony exists in the labour market when a large single employer or, various employers acting as one confronts a large number of workers who are unorganised (*i.e.*, non-unionized) and who lack geographical mobility.

It should be noted that non-organisation of labourers into unions is an essential condition for the existence of monopsony, for when the labourers organise themselves into trade union, then the supply of labour is channelled through the trade union and the trade union therefore becomes a sole seller of labour. When a single buyer-the employer, faces a single seller—the trade union, the market situation is one of bilateral monopoly and not of monopsony. Thus monopsony will prevail when the workers are not organised into trade unions. Likewise, immobility of labour is also an essential condition for the existence of monopsony in the labour market. If the workers are sufficiently mobile so that they will move to places or industries where wages are higher, then the single employer in a local market will not possess a determining influence in hiring labour.

It is clear from above that non-organisation of workers and lack of mobility on their part are the essential conditions on the side of the workers for the existence of monopsony in the labour market. We shall now explain how wage rate is determined in a monopsonistic market situation. In a proper analysis of the same, we must know what type of market situation is confronted by the monopsonist in selling the product produced by the labour employed by him. We shall first explain the wage determination in the case where monopsony in the labour market is found with perfect competition in the product market. After this we shall explain wage determination when monopsony in the labour market is found with monopoly in the product market, that is, where the monopsonist in the labour market is also the monopolist in the product market.

Wage Determination when there is Monopsony in the Labour Market but Perfect Competition in the Product Market : Monopsonistic Exploitation

The demand curve of labour of the monopsonist, as of perfect competitor, is given by the curve of marginal revenue productivity. It should be noted that when perfect competition prevails in the product market, marginal revenue product of labour will be equal to the value of its marginal product. Therefore, in this case, the curve of marginal revenue product of labour will coincide with its curve of value of the marginal product.

What will be the nature of supply curve of the monopsonist? The supply curve of labour to a monopsonist is usually drawn as a rising curve, as S_L curve in Fig. 33.12 which indicates that to get more labour the monopsonist must pay higher wages. It should be noted that the supply curve of labour S_L in Fig. 33.12 is the same as the average factor cost (*AFC*) curve described in chapter 32. As wage rate rises, the greater quantity of labour is supplied. Therefore, the supply curve of labour S_L is sloping upward. Since when wage rate rises and more labour is hired, marginal factor cost of labour (*MFC*) of labour is greater than average factor cost. Therefore, marginal factor cost curve of labour (MFC_L) lies above *AFC* of labour (*i.e.* the labour supply curve S_L). Note that marginal factor cost curve MFC_L is also called marginal expenditure curve.

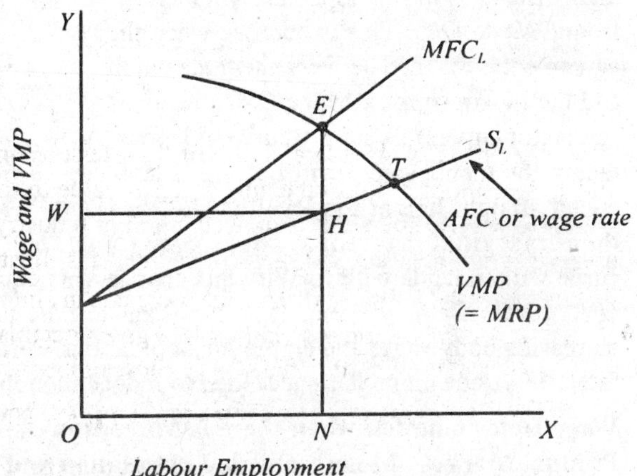

Fig. 33.12. *Wage Determination under Monoposony*

Now, the monopsonist will be maximising his profits and therefore will be in equilibrium where the marginal factor cost of labour (MFC_L) is equal to its marginal revenue product. It will be seen from Fig. 33.12 that the corresponding to the point *E* at which marginal revenue product curve of labour cuts the marginal factor cost curve (MFC_L) the level of labour employment is ON_0. *Further, it is evident from the figure that ON* amount of labour is forthcoming at *NH* or *OW* wage rate. Thus the monopsonist, in equilibrium, will employ *ON* amount of labour and will pay *OW* wage rate to the labourers. It is clear from the figure that the wage rate *NH* (= *OW*) determined under monopsony is smaller than the value of marginal product (*VMP*) which is equal to the *NE*. Thus each worker gets *EH* less than the value of its marginal product. According to Joan Robinson, to pay a worker less than his value of marginal product (*VMP*) is to exploit him.[2] Therefore, in Fig. 33.12 exploitation of each worker done by the monopsonist is equal to *EH*. Because this exploitation is due to the existence of monopsony in the labour market, Joan Robinson calls it as '*monopsonistic exploitation*[2].

2. Joan Robinson, *Economics of Imperfect Competition*

It should be noted that monopsony results in a lower wage rate and lower level of labour employment than under perfect competition in the labour market. Given Fig. 33.12 if there was perfect competition in the labour market, the equilibrium would have been at the point *T* where the demand curve or *VMP* curve for labour intersects the supply curve, S_L. Therefore, under perfect competition in the labour market, the higher wage rate and larger employment would have been determined.

A very important conclusion can be derived from the above analysis of wage-employment equilibrium under monopsony in the labour market. It is that *under conditions of monopsony in the labour market, trade unions can raise the wage rate without creating unemployment.* In fact, it can be shown that a wage increase secured by trade unions under such circumstances may result in greater employment. Thus, in Fig. 33.13 if the wage rate is raised to OW_1 as a result of trade union's bargaining with the monopsonist, the employment offered by the monopsonist will increase from ON_0 to ON_1. This is because when the agreement is reached between the trade union and the monopsonist at wage OW_1, the average factor curve (*i.e.*, supply curve of labour) facing the monopsonist will become a horizontal straight line at the level of OW_1 and the marginal factor cost (*MFC*) curve will coincide with it. With this change, his equilibrium will be at point *C* corresponding to ON_1 level of employment. It is important to note that in this case trade union has succeded is increasing both wages and employment of labour. Further, with the success in getting a higher wage rate OW_1, trade union has succeded to reduce monopsonstic exploitation of labour.

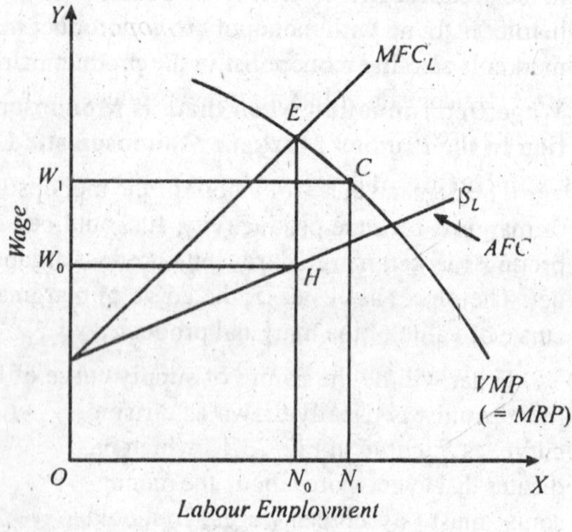

Fig. 33.13. *Effect of Increase in Wages by Trade Union*

Wage Determination when there is Monopsony in the Labour Market but Monopoly in the Product Market : Monopsonistic Exploitation and Monopolistic Exploitation.

Where there is monopoly in the product market, the curve of marginal revenue product will differ from the curve of the value of marginal product. The marginal revenue product curve (*MRP*) will lie below the curve of the value of marginal product (*VMP*), for the marginal revenue is less than the average revenue when there is monopoly in the product market. The supply curve of S_L labour (average factor cost curve *AFC*), as in the above case, slopes upward and the marginal factor cost curve lies above it. The equilibrium of the monopsonist will be where the marginal revenue product of labour equals marginal factor cost of labour (*MFC*) . In Fig. 33.14 the equilibrium of the monopsonist is at point *E* according to which wage *NH* or *OW* is determined and labour *ON* is employed. It will be seen from Fig. 33.14 that wage rate *NH* is not only less than marginal revenue product (*NE*) but is also less than the value of the

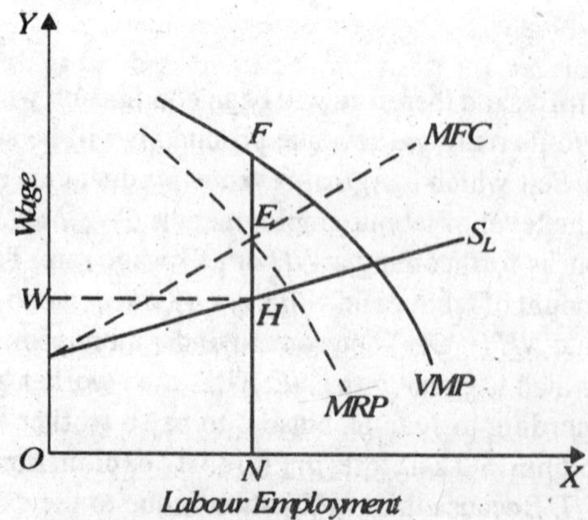

Fig. 33.14. *Wage Determination under Monopsony in Labour Market and Monopoly in the Produt Market*

marginal product (*NF*). The difference *EH* between marginal revenue product *NE* and the wage rate *NH* is due to the existence of monopsony in the labour market and has, therefore, been called by Joan Robinson as *monopsonistic exploitation*. But the difference *FE* between the value of the marginal product (*VMP*) which is equal to *NF* and the marginal revenue product (*MRP*) which is equal to *NE* is due to existence of monopoly in the product market. The worker get *FE* amount less than his value of the marginal product because of the fact of monopoly in the product market and has, therefore, been designated as '*monopolistic exploitation*' by Joan Robinson. Under monopsony-monopoly market situation, the worker is subjected to double exploitation; because of monopoly he gets less than value of its marginal product and because of monopsony he gets less than his marginal revenue product.

Exploitation of Labour

We have explained above that labour is exploited when there prevails imperfect competition in the product market as well as when there is imperfect competition or monopsony in the labour market. In the former case it is called monopolistic exploitation and in the latter it is called monopsonistic exploitation. In our above analysis we have followed Joan Robinson's approach to the exploitation of labour. However, Robinson's definition of exploitation of labour is not accepted as valid by some economists, especially Chamberlin. It is, therefore, useful to discuss the concept of exploitation of labour and various meanings and interpretations of exploitation of labour that have been provided.

It should be noted that Pigou-Robinson concept of exploitation of labour, namely, labour being paid less than the value of its marginal product (*VMP*), assumes perfect competition as the 'ideal' and the wage rate determined under it as just, fair and proper. Any deviation from this perfectly competitive wage is regarded as exploitation. Thus, according to Rothschild, "Professor Pigou, and following him Joan Robinson have made the *ideal of perfect competition* their starting point. Under the system the worker would get, as we saw, a wage equal to the value of the marginal physical product. Every deviation from this is regarded as exploitation."[3]

The above concept of exploitation can be looked at from two viewpoints. Firstly, it can be viewed as a *purely technical way* of describing the wage payments which are less than those which would have prevailed under conditions of perfect competition. In this purely technical viewpoint of exploitation, any evil design or sinister motive of the entrepreneur is not implied. Secondly, the Pigou-Robinson's concept of exploitation can be viewed as the *concept which regards perfect competition wages as the just, fair or right wages which ought to be paid by the entrepreneur to the labour*. In this second sense emotional colouring is given to the concept of exploitation and sinister motive on the part of the entrepreneur is implied. Further, it is also implied in this second sense of exploitation that market price of a product reflects its social value. Pigou and to somewhat lesser extent Robinson regarded exploitation in the second sense, that is, from the viewpoint of emotional colouring and ethical standard. In the opinion of present author to regard "deviations from perfect competition" as unethical is unjustified and unwarranted. We, therefore, agree with Rothschild who writes: "this usage of exploitation....may be regarded as an implicit assumption that perfect competition wages are the 'right' or 'proper' wages of labour. There can be no doubt that such a moral understone is part of Professor Pigou's definition, who stood under the influence of the newly developed marginal productivity theory; and to a lesser extent this is probably also true of Joan Robinson. It should be clear, however, that there is *no any scientific reason to warrant such an assumption*. By calling deviations from the perfect-competition equilibrium 'exploitation', it does not follow that *this equilibrium has any superior ethical or political qualities*."[4]

3. K.W. Rothschild, *The Theory of Wages*, Augustus M. Kelley, New York, 1966
4. *Op. cit.*, p. 103

How can Labour Exploitation be Removed ?

We have discussed above the two concepts of exploitation and also highlighted the conditions under which labour exploitation arises. Now, an important question is how this labour exploitation can be removed. That is, whether trade unions or Government can remove exploitation by raising the wages of workers or some other steps have to be taken to remove exploitation.

As far as *monopolistic exploitation* depicted in Fig. 33.14 by *EF* which has arisen due to the imperfect competition in the product market, is concerned, it cannot be removed by raising wages by the trade unions. This is because, in this situation, if the trade unions succeed in raising wages, the employer will employ smaller amount of labour so as to equate the new high wage rate with the marginal revenue product (*MRP*) of labour. But the important point to note is that with lower employment and higher wage rate, labour would still be exploited, for in this new wage position also, value of the marginal product (*VMP*) will be greater than the marginal revenue product (*MRP*) with which new higher wage will be equated by the employer. We thus see that *monopolistic exploitation of labour* as conceived by Joan Robinson cannot be removed through raising wages by trade unions or government. Monopolistic exploitation can only be removed by *creating the conditions of perfect competition in the product market*. The government can take measures for removing monopolistic conditions or imperfections from the product market.

But so far as monopsonistic exploitation of labour is concerned it can be, as explained above, removed by raising wages through trade unions or government. We have already explained this in this chapter.

ROLE OF TRADE UNIONS AND COLLECTIVE BARGAINING IN RAISING WAGES

For a long time economists believed that trade unions and collective bargaining could not play an important role in raising the wages of workers or effecting improvements in their economic conditions. In other words, they thought that trade unions as an instrument to raise wages of workers or to improve their overall economic conditions are *ineffective and superfluous* and thus the collective bargaining by them is a *futile undertaking*. Therefore, in the leading nineteenth century wage theories such as subsistence theory of wages and wage fund theory. the role played by trade unions and collective bargaining in the determination of wages was entirely neglected.

According to the Marginal Productivity Theory of Wages with its assumptions of perfect competition and the given supply of labour, trade unions cannot succeed in raising wages or cannot succeed in raising wages without creating unemployment. According to this theory, marginal revenue productivity (*MRP*) curve is the employers' demand curve. Consider Fig. 33.15 where *MRP* is the marginal revenue productivity curve of labour. If *ON* is the available supply of labour, *OW* is the equilibrium wage rate. Now, if the wage rate is increased to *OW'* by the collective bargaining of trade unions, *NN'* amount of workers would be rendered unemployed. If these unemployed workers are free to compete, they would press down the wage back to *OW*. If these *NN'* workers are, for one reason or the other, not

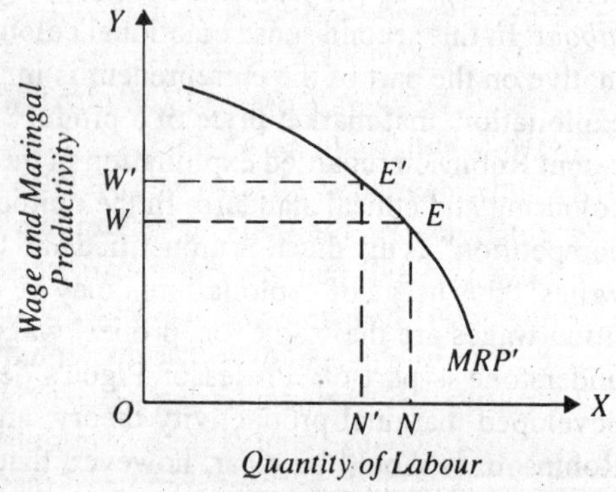

Fig. 33.15. *Marginal Productivity Theory: Trade unions cannot enhance wages without creating unemployment.*

free to compete, they will continue to remain unemployed. It is thus clear that, even according to marginal productivity theory, trade unions are unable to raise wages without creating unemployment.

It is evident from above that in the *static* marginal productivity theory there was no room for trade unions and collective bargaining in fixing and improving wages of the workers. The view about the futility of trade union also prevailed in the early twentieth century, even though many theorists expressed doubts about the correctness of this view. It was only in the 'thirties' of the 20th centuary that role of trade unions and collective bargaining was introduced into the economic theory and significant place was accorded to them in fixing wages of the workers. The realisation of the fact that perfect competition only prevailed in some exceptional cases in the real world led to the reconsideration of whole price and wage theory. Though the marginal productivity approach to the wage fixation was maintained; it was however extended to the conditions of imperfect competition wherein scope for trade unions and collective bargaining in raising wages was shown.

Moreover, there has been the emergence of two kinds of theories known as *institutional and psychological theories of wage determination under trade unions*. These theories do not try to reconcile the marginal productivity approach with the role of collective bargaining in the context of imperfect competition, but instead assign an eminent role to trade unions and collective bargaining in the wage determination, regardless of the marginal productivity doctrine. Thus in these institutional and psychological theories, trade unions and collective bargaining do not enter through the back door but occupy a central place right from the beginning in the determination of wages. In recent years there has been a due recognition of the role which the trade unions and collective bargaining play in the fixation of wages and various theories of bargaining have been advanced. Rather than being alternative explanations of wage determination under collective bargaining, these different bargaining theories of wages in fact bring out various factors which play a determining role in the bargaining process; different theories laying stress on different factors.

Bargaining Approach to Wages and Trade Unions

As explained above, there was not much room for the bargaining by trade unions in the marginal productivity theory in its earliest static versions. First of all, a bargaining approach to wages was developed which indicated a scope for collective bargaining within the framework of marginal productivity theory. This was done by giving up some of the assumptions of marginal productivity theory which had been essential parts of its earlier versions. Then, with the emergence of the theories of imperfect competition, monopsony and oligopoly, *bargaining approach within the framework of marginal productivity principle was considerably widened.*

Rise in Wage Rate and Labour Efficiency. To begin with, static assumptions of marginal productivity theory have been dropped. It is accepted that marginal productivity curve is employer's demand curve and that, given the marginal productivity curve, the increase in the wage rate by trade-union power will lead to the creation of unemployment. But it is pointed out that when the wage increase is achieved through a successful bargaining, the marginal productivity curve may not remain the same but may shift above due to the rise in efficiency of workers brought about by the higher wage. When the efficiency and therefore the marginal productivity curve rises due to the increase

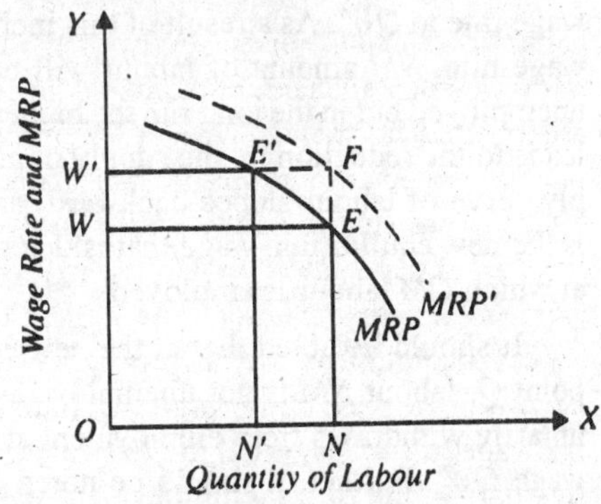

Fig. 33.16. *Increase in Marginal Revenue Productivity or Efficiency as a result of Rise in Wage Rate*

in wages of the workers the unemployment may not be created as a result of the increase in the wage rate secured by the trade union. This is shown in Fig. 33.16. Initially the marginal productivity curve is *MRP* and the equilibrium wage is *OW* and employment is *ON*. Now suppose the wage is raised to *OW'* by the successful collective bargaining of the trade union. If the marginal productivity curve *MRP* remains unchanged, then at *OW'* wage rate, *ON'* men will be employed, which means that *NN'* number of men will be rendered unemployed. But if the rise in wage brings about a sufficient increase in efficiency and productivity so that the marginal productivity curve shifts upward to the dotted position, then unemployment will not be created. It will be seen from the Fig. 33.16 that with the marginal revenue productivity curve *MRP'*, *ON* men are employed at the higher wage rate *OW'*.

We thus see that if we consider the effect of the wage bargain on the increase in efficiency or marginal productivity, then the trade unions can succeed in raising wages without creating unemployment. Again, the increase in wages may force the employers to improve the efficiency of production process in which case also the marginal productivity curve shifts upward and as a result at the increased wage rate the same men may be employed. Again, the marginal revenue productivity curve may also be shifted above, if the increase in the wage rate brought about by collective bargaining is passed on to the consumers in the form of higher price of the product. In this case also the danger of unemployment being created will not be very much there and the higher wage rate will become the equilibrium wage rate equal to the new higher marginal revenue productivity. Therefore, the supporters of bargaining approach to wage fixation maintain that it is not so much the movements along the marginal productivity curve as it is the shifting of this curve that has to be considered when the impact of a wage bargaining is to be known.

Impact of Wage-hike on Labour Supply. Similarly, when the wage rate is raised by collective bargaining, the supply of labour may fall so that the increased wage becomes the equilibrium of wage without involuntary unemployment. Supply of labour can fall because when men are earning higher wage their women can stop working (that is, women withdraw themselves from labour force and stay at home) and children can be kept at school for a longer time. Further, at higher wages individuals may work less hours in a week or smaller number of days in a month or year. Because of the reduction in the supply of labour at the higher wage rate, the higher wage rate may become the 'equilibrium' wage rate. Consider Fig. 33.17 where *SS'* is the supply curve of labour and *DD'* is the demand curve for labour. Suppose the initial equilibrium is at point *P* where *ON* labour is employed at the wage rate *OW* or *NP*. Suppose the trade union through collective bargaining succeeds in raising the wage rate to *OW'*. As a result of this increase in the wage rate, *NM* amount of labour will be rendered unemployed but in the long run the higher wage rate leads to the reduction in the supply of labour (supply curve of labour slopes backward) so that *OW'* is the new equilibrium wage that is determined and at which *OM* labour is employed.

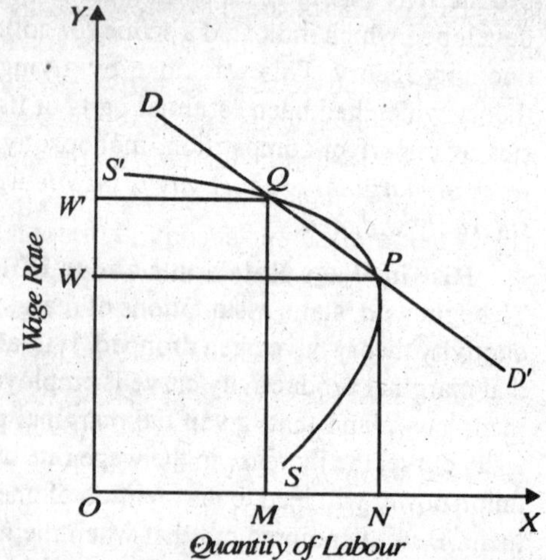

Fig. 33.17. *A higher wage secured by the union can become an equilibrium wage without involuntary unemployment if a part of the supply of labour withdraws itself from the labour force.*

It should be noted that at the new equilibrium point *Q*, labour *NM* is not unemployed, it has voluntarily withdrawn from employment at the higher wage *OW'*. Further, it should be noted at the new higher-level equilibrium where the supply of labour is less than before, the workers would get a large proportion of the new higher national income and enjoy higher standards of leisure and education. (The national income will increase if the increase in output due to higher productivity at the increased wage rate is greater than the loss in output due to the reduction in the supply of labour.)

It is clear from above that when the increase in wage rate is attained by trade unions through collective bargaining, there are such changes in the factors determining wage employment situation that the increased wage becomes the equilibrium wage without creating unemployment. Prof. Rothschild rightly remarks, "*The imposition of a higher wage may lead initially to some unemployment but may then produce such a change in the determinants of the wage-employment situation that the unemployment disappears and the higher wage rate becomes an equilibrium wage*".[4]

Role of Trade Unions in Raising Wages Under Monopsony. It is evident from above that under perfect competition and in the framework of the marginal productivity theory conceived in dynamic terms, there is a good room for collective bargaining to raisc wages. Further, the realisation that it is not the perfect competition, but the market forms of imperfect competition, oligopoly, monopoly, monopsony, oligopsony, *etc.* which mostly prevail in the real world, opened up new vistas for combining the marginal productivity analysis with the bargaining approach to the wage determination. The most striking case in these various forms of imperfect markets is of monopsony when there is a single buyer of labour. The monopsonist, as explained before, working on the marginal productivity principle equates marginal revenue product of labour with the marginal wage to be in equilibrium posit labour. In such a situation wage rate (*i.e.*, average wage) determined is less than the marginal revenue productivity. It will be seen from Fig. 33.18 that, under monopsony, wage rate *OW* and employment *ON* is determined. Under such circumstances if workers organise themselves into trade unions, they can achieve increase in the wage rate without creating unemployment, indeed the employment will increase for some increases in the wage rate.

When the trade unions come into existence, the supply of labour is channelled through it and the bargaining with the employer is on the basis of '*all or nothing*' at a particular wage rate demanded, that is, no supply of labour will be offered below the demanded and/or mutually agreed wage rate and the whole supply of labour will be offered at the mutually agreed wage. This means, in other words, that the supply curve of labour under trade union becomes perfectly elastic at the demanded or mutually agreed wage rate. It will be seen from Fig. 33.18 that if the trade union succeed in getting higher wage rate *OW'*, the supply curve of labour becomes horizontal or prefectly elastic shape at the agreed wage level *OW'*, the new supply supply curve of labour will coincide with the marginal factor cost curve. It will be seen that, given the wage rate equal to *OW'* and the labour supply curve *W' F*, the employer's equilibrium will be at point *F*, at which employment *ON'*, which is greater than *ON*, will be offered by the employer.

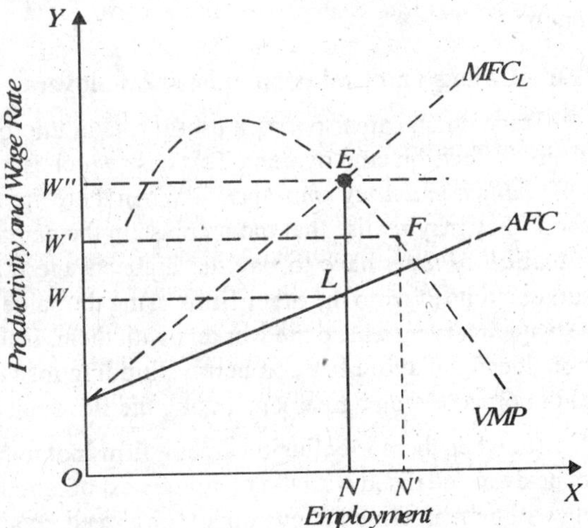

Fig. 33.18. *When there is monopsony in the labour market, increase in the wage rate can be secured by the labour union without creating unemployment.*

It should be carefully noted that a powerful trade union can raise the wage rate even

4. K.W. Rothschild, Approaches to the Theory of Bargaining, published in *The Theory of Wage Determination*, edited by J.T. Dunlop, p. 284

up to OW'', that is equal to the marginal value product NE at the original level of employment ON. When the wage rate OW'' is fixed under collective bargaining and as a consequence the supply curve of labour or margunal factor cost curve $W''E$ becomes perfectly elastic at the level OW'', the employer's equilibrium will be at ON, the original level of employment. Thus, under conditions of monopsony, a strong trade union can raise the wage rate to the level of value of marginal product NE without the fear of creating unemployment. In the absence of trade union, the monopsonist would exploit the workers to the extent of LE or WW''. It is, therefore, clear that the workers by organising themselves into trade unions and thereby collectively bargaining with the employer, can raise the wage rate to remove monopsonistic exploitation by the monopsonist.

Trade Unions and Monopsonistic Discrimination

The role of trade union to improve the lot of the workers is also important when there prevails the conditions of *monopsonistic discrimination.* Monopsonistic discrimination is said to prevail when the monopsonist pays different wages to the different workers. Monopsonistic discrimination is quite common in the actual world where workers are unorganised and where due to fear of unemployment they have to accept the essential minimum wage. Under such circumstances, if the workers organise themselves into strong trade unions, they can force the monopsonist to stop discrimination and pay the same wage to all the workers of a given type and thereby can reduce his excess profits earned because of discrimination.

In developed countries and well established industries, the organisation of labourers into powerful trade unions and thereby bargaining collectively with the employers, perfect monopsonistic discrimination (that is, discrimination between individual and individual) has vanished. But "group discrimination" is still very common in all countries, developed as well as underdeveloped. By group discrimination is meant the discrimination between different, groups or sections of the population. Thus, for the same work women are generally paid lower wages than men in many countries. In some countries, coloured people are likewise paid less wages than white men for the same work. Boys are also sometimes paid smaller wages than men. The group discrimination can be ended if the discriminated sections organise themselves into powerful trade unions and also by governmental action.

Trade Unions and Collusion among Employers

Trade union can also play a useful role in improving the wages of the workers without causing adverse effects on employment. This case which is intensely associated with the idea of monopsony is of "*collusion among employers*". When there are few large firms competing for the same kind of labour they may realise that the increase in the demand for the labour by one firm may raise wages so that *all of them* have to pay the higher wage rate. If one firm offers a higher wage to attract workers to itself from the other firms using the same type of labour the others too will have to raise the wage in order to keep the workers with them. Under such circumstances the firms will develop a strong desire to avoid any competitive bidding for labour and spoiling the labour market. This may lead to open or tacit agreement among the firms not to raise wages.

But when there is collusion among firms not to raise wages, then the marginal productivity will not be even equalised with the marginal cost of labour. Under collusion among employers, the wage rate will be maintained at customary or agreed level even though the marginal revenue product of labour will stand higher than the wage rate paid. Although the firm can increase its profits by expanding employment to the point where the marginal revenue product equals marginal cost of labour, but in doing so the firm will have to increase the wage rate which is prohibited under collusion. Under such conditions of collusion, the formation of trade union by workers can force the employers to pay the wage rate equal to the marginal revenue product of labour. Such a rise in the wage rate to the level of marginal productivity under pressure of trade union would not create any unemployment, because such a rise in the wage rate will only fill up the gap between the marginal revenue productivity and marginal cost of labour, and will not raise the latter above the former.

Trade Unions and Oligopoly in Product Market

Furthermore, even in the case of oligopoly in the product market which so extensively prevails in the capitalist countries, the increase in the wage rate by the trade union may be achieved without creating unemployment. It is generally believed that the oligopolist confronts a 'kinked' demand curve (having a kink at the prevailing price of the product), corresponding to which the marginal revenue curve has a discontinuous or broken portion vertically below the kink. In such a case, when the increase in the wage rate occurs due to the collective bargaining by the trade union, the marginal cost curve will shift above, but for a moderate increase in the wage rate it will still cut the marginal revenue curve through its discontinuous portion, indicating thereby that the output remains unchanged despite the increase in the wage rate and consequently the rise in cost. No change in output as a result of the increase in the wage rate means that the employment will remain the same, provided the employer does not substitute machinery for labour.

It follows, therefore, that in this case too the collective bargaining can succeed in raising the wage rate without adversely affecting the employment level. The oligopolistic market situation imposes a certain price and output policy on the employer due to which he is forced to swallow the whole increase in the wage bill following a moderate increase in the wage rate. Thus in the oligopolistic market situation the trade union can succeed in raising wages by making inroads into the profits of the capitalist employer.

Conclusion

It is clear from the above analysis that trade unions are not superfluous and collective bargaining by them not a futile activity. In fact, the trade union can play a useful role in raising the wage of workers and can save them from the exploitation of the employers. Indeed, in many cases, the trade unions can raise wages without creating unemployment.

WAGE DETERMINATION UNDER BILATERAL MONOPOLY WHEN MONOPSONIST BUYER FACES A MONOPOLIST SELLER

Collective bargaining by trade union with an employer or, if it is industry-wide bargaining, with the employers' association *represents a situation where a single seller (i.e., monopolist) faces a single buyer*. Trade union of the firm or industry acts as a single voice representing the workers so that trade union becomes a single seller of labour to the employer. In other words, trade union has the monopoly of selling labour. On the other hand, the employer, if he is monopsonist, or the employers' association is a single buyer of labour. Thus in such a bilateral monopoly a single buyer of labour faces a single seller of labour. Therefore, we are confornted here with a special case of bilateral monopoly and wage determination under trade unions. In this case collective bargaining becomes a special case of price determination under bilateral monopoly. *Analysis of wage determination under bilateral monopoly as of product under bilateral monopoly does not theoretically lead us to a certain particular wage at which agreement will be reached.* Analysis of bilateral monopoly only brings out two limits—the upper limit sought by the union and the lower limit set by the employer—within which range the wage will be fixed. Actual wage rate fixed in a bilateral monopoly will lie within that range and whether it will be more nearer to the upper limit or to the lower limit depends upon the relative bargaining strengths of the union and the employer. Apart from pointing to the range within which the wage will be determined, economic theory cannot lead us to conclude at which particular wage the agreement will be reached. Theoretically, the wage determination under bilateral monopoly or collective bargaining within the range between upper and lower limits is indeterminate; wage may be set at any level within the range between the two limits.

However, it is useful to analyse the two limits or the range within which wage rate will be fixed under collective bargaining. A difficulty which crops up in the beginning of the analysis is in regard to the union behaviour. Just as economists have built up many models of oligopoly depending upon the assumptions in regard to the behaviour of the oligopolists, similarly many models of collective bargaining have been constructed depending upon the different assumptions in regard to the goal and behaviour of the union. A basic question in this regard is whether the trade unions are economic or political or politico-economic institutions. Again, even if aims of trade unions are purely economic, what economic goal will they pursue or what quantity will they seek to maximise. Thus, will the trade union may seek a wage rate which could *maximise the incomes of its members* or will the trade union try to seek the wage which will *maximise the number of its members* ? Again, will the trade union strive to increase the wage rate to as high a level as possible without regard to the employment effect of its action, or will it seek some optimum combination of wage rate and employment. These are the different alternative objectives of trade unions which imply different patterns of their behaviour in their negotiation or bargaining with the employer.

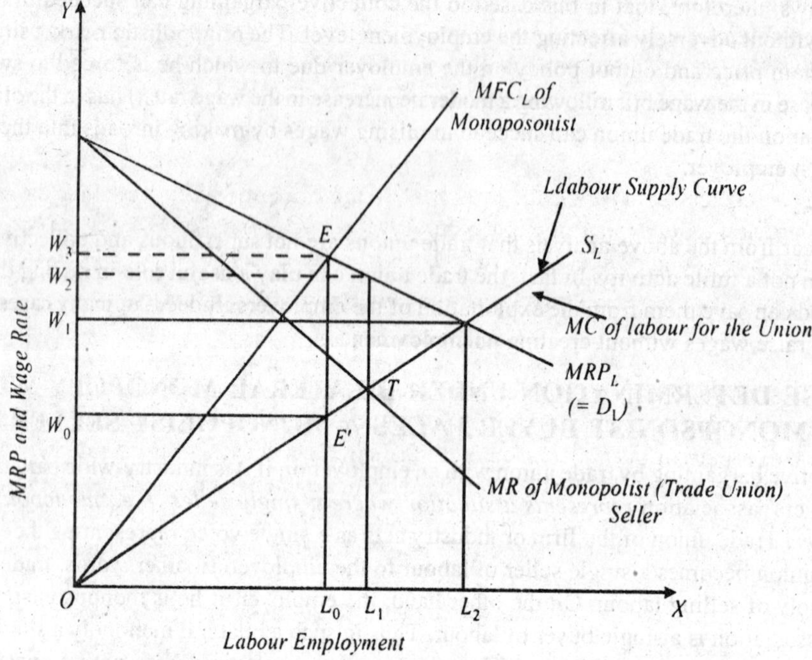

Fig. 33.19. *Indeterminacy of Wage Determination in Bilateral Monopoly*

In modern economic theory wage determination under collective bargaining is explained in terms of bilateral monopoly model. *Bilateral monopoly is a market form where a monopolist, the single seller of a product or service, sells to the monopsonist who is a single buyer of that product or service.* In the present case the trade union is a single seller of labour, whereas the firm, if it is a monopsonist is a single buyer of labour. The range of wage rates within which a particular wage rate will be settled can be easily explained with the Figure 33.19 where the bargaining about wage rate between a trade union and a single employer is explained. It will be seen from this figure that the employer (monopsonist) would maximise his profits where marginal factor cost (*MFC*) on labour equals marginal revenue product (MRP_L) of labour. As will be seen from Figure 33.19 that the employer will be maximising his profits by setting wage rate equal to OW_0 and employing OL_0 labour. Note that marginal factor cost (*MFC*) curve of labour intersects the marginal revenue product curve (*MRP*) of labour at point *E* and accordingly wage rate OW_0 will be paid by him. Thus, OW_0 is the minimum limit below which wage rate cannot fall.

The trade union (that is, the single seller of labour – a monopolist) faces *MRP* curve of labour which acts as a demand curve (D_L) for labour. This is because, given a wage rate, the monopsonist (*i.e.* employer) will equate the wage rate with marginal revenue product (*MRP*) of labour. The downward sloping *MRP* curve of labour means that as the number of workers employed increases, wage rate falls. In fact, the trade union has to choose a point on the MRP_L curve ($= D_L$) of labour. Since the wage rate paid to workers falls as more workers are hired, marginal revenue (*MR*) curve which describes the additional wages obtained by the union for its workers as the number of workers hired increases lies below MRP_L (*i.e.* D_L) curve of labour. On the other hand, the supply curve of labour S_L represents the minimum wage necessary to induce the union workers to offer their labour to the buyer. Therefore, the trade union views the supply curve S_L of labour as the marginal cost of labour. *If the labour union aims at maximizing net revenue or economic rent (i.e. revenue over and above the opportunity costs of labour) it will press for wage rate equal to* W_2 at which OL_1 quantity of labour will be employed. It should be noted that this economic rent or surplus is maximised at the level of employment L_1 (in Figure 33.19) at which supply curve of labour (S_L) representing marginal opportunity costs of workers intersects the marginal revenue curve (*MR*) of the union. Note that if trade union wants to maximise employment of labour, it will agree to wage rate W_1 corresponding to which supply curve of labour S_L intersects the MRP_L (*i.e.*, D_L) curve of labour and at which employment is OL_2.

Thus W_2 is the upper limit or the wage rate sought by the union whereas W_0 is the lower limit. At which wage rate and employment, settlement will be reached between the two parties depends on their bargaining powers and strategies. If the union can make a strong threat to strike, it might succeed in achieving a wage closer to W_2. On the other hand, if the employer makes a credible threat to declare lockout or hire non-union labour, it might secure a wage rate closer to W_0. The result which depends on the relative bargaining powers of the two parties is indeterminate.

HICKSIAN ANALYSIS OF WAGE DETERMINATION UNDER COLLECTIVE BARGAINING

In pure economic theory wage determination through collective bargaining has been treated as price determination in the framework of a ***bilateral monopoly*** and was explained so by Edgeworth[5] as the result of bargaining between trade unions and employer or entrepreneur. Edgeworth explained that final settlement between labour union and employer may take place at a point on the contract curve which is the *locus* of the points of tangency of the indifference curves of the two parties. Since the final settlement between the trade union can occur at *any point* on the contract curve, there was a large range of indeterminacy about wage fixation. Whether the final settlement reached at a point on the contract curve between the two parties is favourable to the trade union or to the employer depends on their relative bargaining strength.

How the bargaining between the trade union and employer takes place and final settlement is reached has been explained by J.R. Hicks[6] through what he calls *employer's concession curve and union's resistance curve* which are drawn in Figure 33.20. Along the vertical axis we measure wage rate and along the horizontal axis we measure length of strike. Suppose *OW* is the wage rate in the market which the employer is willing to pay prior to trade union's pressure and bargaining with the employer. The trade union will demand higher wage rate. The instrument used by trade union of workes to get their demand conceded is the strike. Hicks uses two special curves to explain wage determination under collective bargaining. They are an *employer's concession curve and union's resistance curve.* Hicks asked the question to what extent can trade union pressure or force the employer to pay higher wages than they would have obtained if there would have been no such pressure. The instrument of pressure, as mentioned above, is strike. To get its demand for higher wages conceded trade union threatens the employer that it will go on strike for a longer period.

---

5. See Edgeworth, *Mathematical Psychics*, London 1932.
6. J.R. Hicks, *The Theory of Wages*, London 1932

The employer would compare the cost of the higher wage and cost to him of the strike. The cost of the strike to the employer will depend on its expected duration, the size of his inventories and the state of the product market. If the employer thinks that the union is weak and the strike will fizzle out soon, the concession in terms of wage increase he will be inclined to offer will be small. The concession will rise as the expected staying power of the union and expected length of the strike rises. The employer's concession curve will rise, that is, it will slope upward and then flatten out at the maximum wage the employer is willing to pay rather than shut down his business.

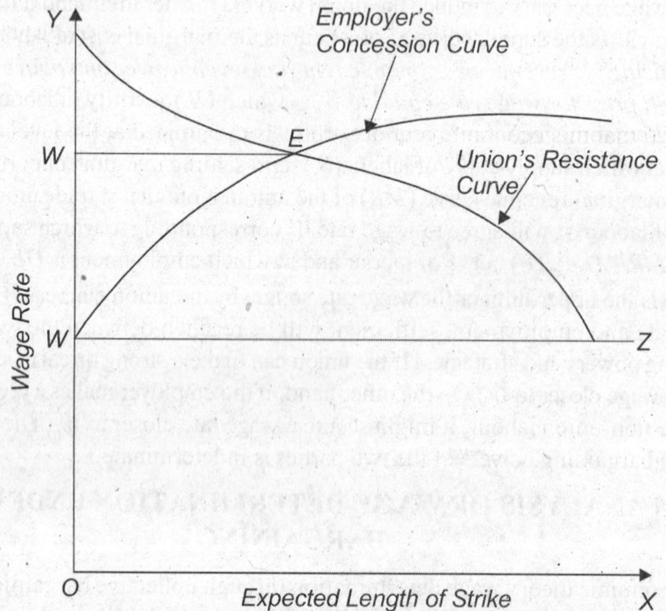

Fig. 33.20. *Hicks's Approach to Wage determination under Collective Bargaining*

On the other hand, the union's resistence curve slopes downward from the maximum wage demanded. As the strike proceeds further, union will get more information about the nature of employer's concession curve. The downward-sloping union's resistance curve will ultimately cut the *WZ* line when members become desperate and are not willing to strike for any more period. According to J. R. Hicks, the equilibrium will be reached at point *E* where employer's concession curve and union's resistance curve intersect each other and corresponding wage rate is *OW* . It will be seen from Fig. 33.20 that the new negotiated wage rate *OW* as result of collective bargaining by the trade union is higher than the wage rate *OW* in the absence of trade union's pressure and collective bargaining by it. Since wage rate *OW* is greater than *OW*, it means the collective bargaining by labour union has succeeded to achieve a higher wage rate for its member workers.

However, it is important to note that point *E* or new wage rate *OW* is only one possible point of equilibrium and not *the* equilibrium. In fact, *OW* represents just one point on the Edgeworthian contract curve. Even initial wage rate *OW* represents another point on the contract curve. Likewise, there are other possible points more or less away from the initial wage rate *OW*, depending on the shape and location of the employer's concession curve and union's resistance curve. Thus, though with the help of the given union's resistence curve and employer's concession curve Hicks was able to pinpoint the wage rate at which equilibrium will the reached, the wage rate under bilateral monopoly model and collective bargaining is indeterminate as it depends on the shape and location of the two curves which can differ as they depend on the relative strengths of the two parties.[7]

An interesting result follows from the Hicksian model of collective bargaining. "The degree of concession that labour union is likely to secure from the employer, given the expected length of the strike depends upon who the employer is. If it is the government, the concession curve is likely to be relatively low, it is easier for the Government to shift the prospective loss due to stoppage of work on to tax payers than it is for private industry to shift it on the consumers."[8]

WHY WAGE RATES DIFFER

Under conditions of perfect competition the identical workers doing the same type of jobs would get same wages. However, in the real world it is seen that different wages are paid to workers because of the following three factors:

1. *Workers differ* in quality, skill and training.
2. *Jobs differ*; some jobs are dangerous and others pleasant, some require more education and training than others.
3. Some institutional factors cause imperfections in labour markets such as discrimination against some workers, such as black race in America, women in many parts of the world, Scheduled Castes and Scheduled Tribes in India.

It should be noted that differences in wages of workers do not make demand–supply analysis of wage determination invalid. It is differences in demand and supply conditions in various labour markets that cause differences in wage rates. In other words, there is not one labour market but many—each with its different demand-supply conditions and therefore different equilibrium wage rates. Wages of the workers for whose services demand is relatively high and supply is relatively small are high. On the other hand, wages of workers whose supply is large but demand relatively weak are low. Several factors operate to cause the differences in demand and supply conditions of different types of workers. We explain below these different factors.

1. Differences in Abilities, Skill and Training

The first important factor that causes differences in workers and therefore wages earned by them is that *various workers differ in abilities, skill and training*. An example will make this clear. Let us consider the wages of computer engineers and unskilled workers. To become computer engineers one

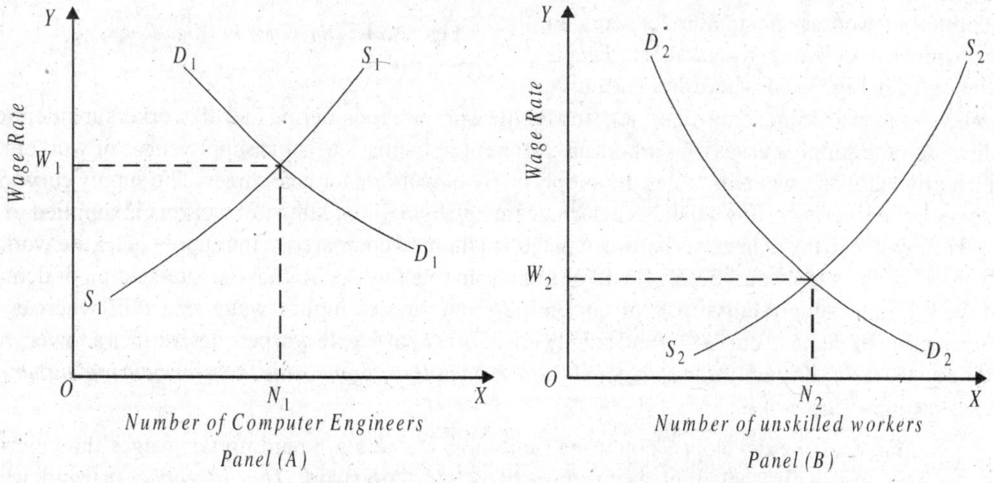

Fig. 33.21. *Difference in Wage Rates*

7. A.K. Dasgupta, *A Theory of Wage Policy* (New Delhi; 1976), Oxford University Press.
8. *Ibid.*

requires a lot of education and training to acquire the skill. On the other hand, unskilled workers do not have to spend time and money for obtaining education and training. The result is that not only demand for computer professionals is high but also their supply is relatively small. This is illustrated in Fig. 33.20. In panel (*A*) of this figure determination of wages of computer engineers is shown. In this panel (*A*) demand for computer engineers D_1D_1 is high and supply S_1S_1 relatively small. As is seen from Fig. 33.20 the wage rate of computer engineers determined by these demand and supply curves is OW_1 which is much higher than the wage rate OW_2 of unskilled workers shown in panel (*B*). In panel (*B*) the demand curve D_2D_2 represents the demand for unskilled workers which is low and supply for them depicted by S_2S_2 is relatively large. Therefore, wage rate OW_2 of the unskilled workers is low. It should be noted again that demand for unskilled workers is small because due to lack of skill, education and training their marginal productivity is low and their supply is large because those who cannot spend time and money in acquiring education and training can get employment as unskilled workers. It is thus clear that the difference in wages can be explained through demand-supply analysis.

2. Differences in Jobs or Occupations : Compensating Wage differentials

The second important factor that causes differences in wages is the differences in the nature of jobs. Some jobs are more dangerous, risky and dirty than others. For example, jobs of miners in coal mines is quite dangerous; a blast or some other accident can cause even one's life. The workers working in coal mines are therefore paid higher wages than in a manufacturing industry, say in the textile industry, where there does not exist much risk of life. In the U.S.A. coal miners are generally paid 25 per cent more wages than textile workers. It should be noted that the reason for the differences in wages in this case lies on the supply side. At each wage rate, the quantity supplied of workers is smaller for work in coal mines than in a textile industry. This is illustrated in Fig. 33.21 where demand curve *DD* is assumed to be the same for miners and textile workers, considering that all workers are identical. However, the supply curves of workers are different in them. S_1S_1 is the supply curve of workers for the textile industry, whereas S_2S_2 is the supply curve of workers for coal mines. The supply curve S_2S_2 for coal mine workers shows that at each wage rate, the smaller quantity of workers is supplied to the coal mines due to the dangerous nature of the job in them as compared to the supply of textile workers depicted by the supply curve S_1S_1. It will be seen from this Fig. 33.21 that the intersection of demand curve *DD* and supply curve S_2S_2 of coal miners determines higher wage rate OW_2 whereas the intersection of demand curve *DD* and supply curve of S_1S_1 of textile workers determines a lower wage rate equal to OW_1. *Higher wage rate paid to coal miners is to compensate them for bearing higher risk for working in coal mines.*

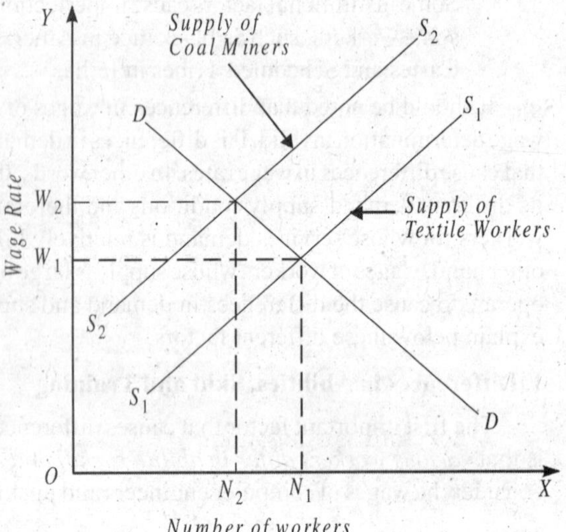

Fig. 33.21. *Difference in Wage Rates*

Similarly, in the developed countries sanitation workers are paid higher wages than clerical workers because of dirty and unpleasant nature of the sanitation work. *The differences in wages which arise due to the differences in jobs arising due to more dangerous, more dirty, more harsh climate, higher cost of living are called compensating wage differentials.* Thus compensating wage differentials show higher wages that must be paid to the workers to compensate them for undesirable job characteristics.

3. Institutional Factors Causing Imperfect Labour Market Conditions

Institutional factors such as discrimination on the basis of sex, race, colour of skin etc. make labour market imperfect and give rise to differences in wages. In the U.S.A. black workers (Negros) are generally paid less wages than the white workers for the same type of work on account of discrimination practiced between them. In many countries, including India, women are paid less wages than men for the same work. Therefore, demand for equal pay for equal work both for men and women has been raised in recent years. Similarly, in several parts of India, rural workers belonging to Scheduled Caste and Scheduled Tribes are paid less than high caste workers.

We have explained above only some of the factors causing differences in wage rates. *The differences in natural abilities, differences in non-monetary benefits such as job satisfaction, pleasant atmosphere, freedom to choose one's work* schedule as in case of a college professor and some other factors account for differences in wage rates.

NUMERICAL PROBLEMS

Problem 1. *Suppose a firm is a monopsonist in the market for labour it hires. The firm can hire the quantity of labour at $W = 10+4L$. If MRP of labour $= 100 - L$, how many number of workers the firm will hire and what wage rate will it pay?*

Solution. To maximise profits the firm will hire labour until $MFC_L = MRP_L$. Therefore, we have to find out marginal factor cost of labour (MFC_L) from the given wage function (*i.e.*, labour supply function)

Thus, $W = 10 + 4L$ ... (*i*)

To find total cost of labour we multiply (*i*) by the quantity of labour (*L*). Thus

$$TFC_L = W \cdot L = 10L + 4L^2$$

$$MFC_L = \frac{d(TFC)}{dL} = 10 + 8L$$

For profit maximisation :

$$MFC_L = MRP_L$$
$$10 + 8L = 100 - L$$
$$9L = 90$$
$$L = 10$$

Thus the 10 workers will be employed.

To find wage rate paid ,we substitute *L* in the wage function (*i*). Thus,

$$W = 10 + 4L = 10 + 4 \times 10$$
$$= ₹\ 50$$

The wage rate of ₹ 50 will be paid by him.

Problem 2. *A firm has a monopsony in labour market. Its MRP of labour is $14 - L$ and the wage rate is $W = 2 + L$.*

(*a*) *How much labour will the firm hire and what wage rate it will pay?*

(*b*) *Calculate the amount of monopsonistic exploitation of labour.*

(*c*) *How much labour will it hire and use if a minimum wage of ₹ 10 is imposed on it.*

Solution. (*a*) The firm will hire labour until $MFC_L = MRP_L$

The supply curve of labour is :

$W = 2 + L$ ... (*i*)

To obtain *TFC* of labour we multiply (*i*) by *L*

$$TFC = W \cdot L = 2L + L^2$$

$$MFC_L \quad \frac{d(TFC_L)}{dL} \quad 2.\ 2L$$

and the given MRP_L 14 0L

Equating MFC_L and MRP_L we have

$$2 + 2L = 14 - L$$
$$3\,L = 14 - 2 = 12$$
$$L = 4$$

Thus 4 units of labour will be employed. To obtain wage rate (w) we substitute $L = 4$ in equation (i). Thus

$$W = 2 + L = 2 + 4 = 6$$

Wage rate of ₹ 6 will be paid.

(b) The difference between the marginal revenue product (MRP) of labour and wage rate (i.e. average wage) at the equilibrium employment level measures monopsonistic exploitation of labour. Therefore, for measuring monopsonistic exploitation of labour we have to calculate MRP (which in the present case equals VMP because of perfect competition in the product market) at the equilibrium level of employment which, as found above, is equal to 4. Therefore, substituting labour employment (L) in the given demand for labour function (i.e., MRP function) we have:

$$MRP = 14 - L$$
$$= 14 - 4 = 10$$

Thus while marginal revenue product of labour (MRP) in equilibrium is equal to ₹ 10, it is paid wage equal to ₹ 6. Therefore exploitation of labour per unit is ₹ 4.

(c) When the minimum wage rate of ₹ 10 is imposed on it, it will equate MRP of labour with this minimum wage rate. Thus

$$10 = 14 - L$$
$$L = 14 - 10 = 4$$

Thus at the minimum wage rate of ₹ 10, 4 units of labour input will be hired. (Note that by imposing minimum wage rate of ₹10, the government has succeeded in removing labour exploitation without adversely affecting employment).

Problem 3. *The demand for computer engineers in the local market is given by* $D_e = 760 - 0.1\,Q_e$ *and their supply curve* $S = 60 + 0.04\,Q_e$ *where* Q_e *is the quantity of engineers.*

(a) *Calculate wage and employment levels that would prevail if market for engineers is perfectly competitive.*

(b) *If the engineers organise themselves into a power union, then what wage and employment the union will demand to maximise the total income of its members.*

Solution. (a) (Note that both the given demand and supply functions of engineers are inverse demand and supply functions. Therefore, the given inverse demand function can also be written as $W = 760 - 0.1Q_e$ and the given inverse supply function can be written as $W > 60$, $0.04Q_e$). To obtain wage and employment in a competitive market for engineers we have to equate the demand and supply functions. Thus

$$760 - 0.1Q_e = 60 + 0.04Q_e$$
$$760 - 60 = 0.04\,Q_e + 0.1\,Q_e$$

or $$0.14\,Q_e = 700$$

$$Q_e = 700 \times \frac{100}{14} > 5000$$

To obtain the equilibrium wage rate at this level (*i.e.* 5000) of employment we substitute $Q_e > 5000$ in the supply function. Thus

$$S_e \text{ or } W = 60 + 0.04\, Q_e$$

$$W = 60 + 0.04 \times 5000$$

$$= 60 + 200 = 260$$

Thus the competitive level of employment of engineers is 5000 and wage rate is ₹ 260.

(*b*) When the engineers organise themselves into a powerful union, there comes into existence monopoly in respect of sale of engineers' services. It will be remembered that a monopolist revenue is maximum when he sells the quantity of output corresponding to unit elasticity point of the demand curve facing him (that is, at the output level where *MR* is zero). Now, the labour union's marginal revenue function can be derived from the labour (demand function (W 760 00.1 Q_e) by first obtaining from its total revenue function and, then taking its first derivative.

$$\text{Total revenue } (TR) = Q_e(760 - 0.1\, Q_e)$$

or $$TR = 760\, Q_e - 0.1\, Q_e^2$$

Differentiating it with respect to Q_e we have

$$MR = \frac{dTR}{dQ_e} > 760\,.\ 0.2\, Q_e$$

Now, total revenue (i.e. income) of the labour union will be maximum at the level of employment (Q_e) *at which* $MR = 0$. Therefore, setting *MR* function equal to zero we have

$$760 - 0.2\, Q_e = 0$$

$$760 = 0.2\, Q_e$$

$$Q_e = 760\ \frac{10}{2} > 3800$$

To obtain the wage rate corresponding to employment of 3800 engineers we substitute $Q_e > 3800$ in the given inverse demand (*i.e.* wage) function for engineers, namely,

$$W = 760 - 0.1\, Q_e$$

$$= 760 - 0.1 \times 3800$$

$$= 760 - 380$$

$$= ₹\ 380$$

Thus, to maximise income (*i.e.* wage bill) of its members the union will try to raise wage rate to ₹ 380 at an employment of 3800 engineers

QUESTIONS FOR REVIEW

1. Explain the effect of increase in wage rate on supply of labour (*i.e.*, work effort) by an individual in terms of income effect and substitution effect.
2. Derive the supply curve of labour using indifference curves between income and leisure. Why does supply curve of labour generally slope upward? When is the supply curve of labour effort backward bending? Explain. *D.U., B.Com. (Hons)* 1999
3. "Will an increase in the wage rate always lead to an increase in the number of hours worked"? Explain. *D.U., B.A. (Hons)* 2002
4. How is wage rate determined in a perfectly competitive labour market? Show that the wage rate determined in such a market is equal to the value of marginal (*VMP*) of labour.
5. Show that wage rate in a perfectly competitive labour market will be equal to both the value of marginal product and average revenue product of labour in the long run.
6. How are wages determined in a perfectly competitive labour market? If in such a market trade unions succeed in getting wage rate higher than the competitive equilibrium wage rate, what will be its consequences?
7. A trade union enforces a floor on minimum wage which lies above the market clearing wage. What are economic implications?
8. What is monopsonistic exploitation of labour? How can collective bargaining by trade unions help in increasing wages and employment both? Explain with the help of diagrams. *D.U. B.Com. (Hons.)* 2002
9. Given the following production function of a firm, where *L* is the number of workers hired per day (the only variable input) and *Q* is the quantity of a commodity produced per day and the constant commodity price of *P* = ₹ 5.00 is assumed.

L	0	1	2	3	4	5
Q	0	10	18	24	28	30

(*a*) Find the marginal revenue product of labour.

(*b*)How many workers per day will the firm hire, if the wage rate is ₹ 40.00 ?

[**Hints.** First find the *Total Revenue* by multiplying output (*Q*) with price (₹ 5). Then find the successive differences in *TR* to find *MRP* of labour. Firm will employ labour where MRP_L = ₹ 40. (**Ans.** 2 workers).

10. (a) For a monopsonist what is the relationship between the supply of labour and marginal expense input curve ? Show how equilibrium wage rate and employment are determined ? What is monopsonistic exploitation of labour. *D.U., B. Com (Hons.) 2nd Year 2006, 2007*

[**Hint :** Note that, marginal factor cost (*MFC*) curve is also called marginal expense input curve and average factor cost (*AFC*) is the supply curve of input.

11. Differentiate between monopolistic and monopsonistic exploitation. Show that monopolistic exploitation consists of a part attributable to monopoly in the product market and a second part uniquely attributable to monopsony. Explain *D.U., B.Com (Hons.) 2nd Year 2007*
12. Distinguish between monopolistic and monopsonistic exploitation of labour and illustrate diagrammatically. *D.U. B.A. (Hons.)*, 1996
13. How far are labour unions successful in raising wages and employment under monopsonistic conditions ? Explain *D.U.B.A. (Hons.)* 1989, 1997
14. "Trade unions can eliminate the portion of total monopsonistic exploitation that is uniquely attributable to monopsony in the labor market; however the portion attributable to monopoly can in no way be eliminated by trade union activity." Explain the statement with the help of diagram. *D.U., B.Com (Hons.) 2009*

15. What is monopsony ? Explain how wages and employment are determined in a monopsonistic labour market.
16. What is meant by exploitation of labour ? Show how labour is exploited under monopsony in a labour market. *D.U. B.Com. (Hons.)* 2000
17. What would be the effect of increase in wage rate secured by labour union in monopsonistic labour market? Would it lead to unemployment? *D.U. B.Com. (Hons.)* 2000
18. Discuss the circumstances under which a trade union can raise wages in an industry without affecting level of employment adversely. *D.U. B.A. (Hons)* 1986., *B.Com. (Hons.)* 1996
19. Explain why trade unions do not always to promote the interest of all workers when labour market is perfectly competitive. *D.U., B. Com (Hons.) 2nd Year 2007*
20. Explain the role of trade unions in raising wages of labour. Does it necessarily lead to unemployment ? Explain.
21. Is it possible for a labour union to raise wages without reducing employment under conditions of :
    (*i*) Perfect competition in the labour market.
    (*ii*) Monopsony in the labour market.
22. Explain the alternative union strategies for raising wages of labour.
    [**Hints:** There are mainly four strategies which trade unions can adopt to improve wages of workers. First, *using its monopoly power over supply of labour*, trade union can raise wages, without bothering about employment. Secondly, the union can raise wages by *increasing labour demand* through raising productivity or efficiency of labour and also by promoting the demand for the product which labour helps to produce. Thirdly, it can improve wages by restricting the supply of labour. Fourthly, when it faces a monopsonist it can remove exploitation by raising wages without any adverse effect on employment]
23. If a trade union of labour faces a single buyer of labour, how would the wage rate and level of employment is determined ? Explain. *D.U. B.A. (Hons.)* 1994
24. Wages and employment are indeterminate when a monopsonistic employer faces a monopolistic union. Explain. *D.U. B.A. (Hons.)*, 1998
25. Explain the role of trade unions in raising wages in competitive labour market. Does raising wage necessarily lead to unemployment of labour ?
26. Define and contrast 'equalising' and non-equalising differences in wages. Which concept is involved when high wages contained 'pure economic rent'? *D.U. B.A. (Hons.)* 1988
27. If wages are determined by marginal productivity, trade unions are superfluous. Do you agree? Discuss.
28. If the government wants to intervene in a monopsonistic labour market, at what level would you suggest the minimum wages be fixed ? Why. *D.U. B.A. (Hons.) 2000*

APPENDIX TO CHAPTER 33

An Application of the Theory of Wages

In the previous chapters we have explained the determination of prices of factors. Thus we have explained the determination of wages of labour,under conditions of perfect competition and monopsony in labour market. In the present chapter we will discuss an important application of the theory wages, namely, fixation of minimum wages.

FIXATION OF MINIMUM WAGES

The way in which labour market works greatly influences the distribution of income in a society. Some workers, especially unskilled ones are poor because they are paid low wages. The skilled workers are relatively rich because they receive high wages. Therefore, the objective of fixation of minimum wages by the Government is to remove the poverty of the unskilled workers by fixing a minimum wage rate at a level higher than the one determined by the working of free labour market. However, it has been argued by some economists that fixation of minimum wages of the unskilled workers by the Government may not improve the economic conditions of the unskilled workers as a whole. The consequences of fixation of minimum wages by the Government is illustrated in Figure 33A.1 where determination of wages of unskilled workers is shown. *DD* and *SS* are demand and supply curves of labour respectively. It will be seen from the figure that in the free-market equilibrium wage rate is determined at the level OW_0 where quantity demanded of labour is equal to its quantity supplied. If this free-market wage rate OW_0 is considered to be too low, the Government may intervene and fix the minimum wage at a higher level OW_1. As a result of the imposition of minimum wage legislation, the employers cannot pay wage rate below this minimum wage rate OW_1.

It is important to note that minimum wage rate is fixed *above the equilibrium wage rate* so as to enable unskilled workers to earn a decent living. The fixation of minimum wage below the free-market equilibrium rate will not serve any purpose and will also have no effect on labour market. When the minimum wage rate is fixed at a level higher than the equilibrium wage rate OW_0, that is, at OW_1 in Figure 33A.1, although it will increase the wage rate of low-wage workers, it will have other important effects on the labour market and on the economic conditions of the working class. We discuss below the various important effects of fixation of minimum wages.

1. Labour Employment. An important effect of the minimum wage rate is on the level of labour employment which can be easily seen from Fig. 33A.1. When the minimum wage rate is fixed at the level OW_1, that is, higher than the equilibrium wage rate OW_0, the producers will reduce the quantity demanded of labour to ON_1. This means the number of workers equal to N_0N_1 who were already employed will now be rendered unemployed. In addition to this, as will be seen from Fig. 33A.1, at the higher minimum wage rate OW_1, the quantity supplied of labour increases to ON_2 (or W_1L). This means at the higher minimum wage rate OW_1, the additional N_0N_2 workers offer themselves for work, that is, seek employment. With this total number of workers equal to N_1N_2 or KL ($N_1N_2 = N_0N_1 + N_0N_2$) will become unemployed at the higher minimum wage rate OW_1. It may be emphasised again that the labour surplus or unemployment of workers has come into existence because the minimum wage rate OW_1 has been fixed at a level higher than the equilibrium rate (employers employ or demand smaller amount of labour ON_1) and, secondly, because, at the higher wage rate OW_1, the additional number of workers are now willing to work and therefore add to the number of employment seekers who are unable to find jobs.

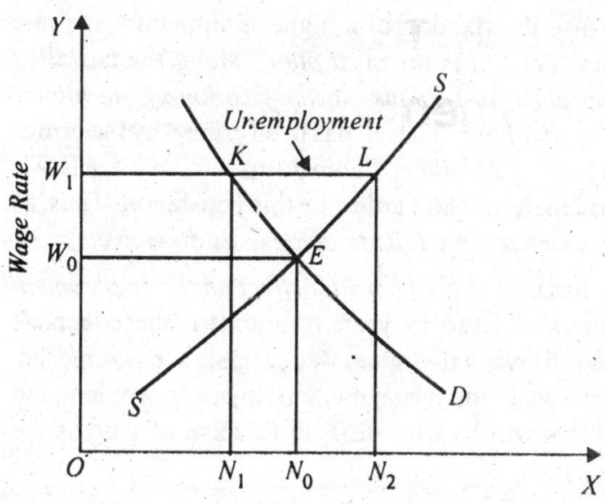

Fig. 33A.1. *Fixation of Minimum Wages*

Since fixation of minimum wages has resulted in the emergence of surplus labour, there will be pressure for wage cutting because the workers who are rendered unemployed will be willing to offer their labour at lower wages than the legally fixed minimum wage rate OW_1. However, an important point to note is that, *unlike the case of maximum price control, this case of minimum price fixation will not lead to the emergence of a group of black-market operators who buy at the controlled price (i.e., minimum wage rate) and sell at the lower free-market equilibrium price (i.e., wage rate OW_0) because nothing will be gained by this.*

From the above analysis of the effect of minimum wage rate on employment of labour in case perfect competition prevails in the labour market we reach the following conclusions:

1. The fixation of minimum wage rate will reduce employment of labour (by the amount N_0N_1 in Fig. 33A.1)

2. The fixation of minimum wage will create labour surplus or unemployment. Some workers will be willing to obtain employment but cannot get it.

3. Some workers who are rendered unemployed will be tempted to evade the law and offer to supply their labour at the wage rate below the legally fixed one.

4. The fixation of minimum wages will not lead to the emergence of black marketers who buy labour at the controlled wage rate and sell it in a black market.

Effect on Income of Workers. If the minimum wage law is effectively enforced, it will raise the incomes of those workers who remain employed. But an important question is to understand to what extent the minimum wage legislation benefits the workers as a whole group. The workers who are able to retain their employment when the minimum wage rate is fixed will definitely become better off. They receive higher wages because minimum wage rate is fixed at a level higher than the market determined wage rate. But those unskilled workers who lose their jobs because at a higher minimum wage rate, employers reduce employment of labour and are unable to find new employment will become worse off as a result of minimum wage legislation. It has been argued by some economists that if the total income of the unskilled workers as a whole group increases, then the whole group of unskilled workers gain from the fixation of minimum wages. But even this cannot be said with certainty. This is because the *total income of the unskilled workers as a group will increase only when the demand for unskilled workers* is *inelastic.* In Fig. 33A.1 with the free market determined wage rate OW_0 and employment of unskilled workers ON_0 at this wage rate, the total income of the workers equals the area OW_0EN_0. With the higher minimum wage rate OW_1 and reduced employment equal to N_1, the total earnings of the workers will be OW_1KN_1 which will be greater if the elasticity of demand for labour is less than unity. On the contrary, if the demand for labour is *elastic,* the employment of labour falls greatly with the result that the new total income OW_1KN_1. of the workers as a group will decrease.

However, even if the demand for unskilled labour is inelastic and they as a whole group gain from fixation of minimum wage rate, the fact remains that a good number of workers who are rendered unemployed as a result will individually suffer a loss.

Another important thing to note is that all unskilled workers are not identical. Some unskilled workers earn wages only slightly lower than the minimum wage rate fixed while others earn much less than the minimum wage rate fixed. The employment of those unskilled workers will decline most who are initially paid very low wages because the fixation of a higher minimum wage rate sharply increases the cost of hiring these workers. Thus, *it is the most poor among the unskilled workers who are likely to lose their employment when, in response to the fixation of the higher minimum wage rate, employers reduce employment of labour*. Thus, it has been argued by the critics of minimum wage fixation that some of the poor low-wage workers whom the minimum wage law is intended to help find themselves out of jobs and are therefore hit hardest by this legislation. Thus, as *an anti-poverty measure, fixation of minimum wage miserably fails to achieve its objective.*

Fixation of minimum wage rate in the U.S.A. has also caused *harmful effect on the employment of teenage workers,* that is, employment of workers of 10 to 19 years of age. It is these teenage workers, who are less productive also, mostly lose jobs when minimum wage legislation is imposed. Therefore, Professors Banmol and Blinder observe that "the teenage unemployment problem and especially the black teenage unemployment problem will be very difficult to solve as long as the minimum wage remains effective."[1]

Besides, fixation of minimum wages may have particularly *more harmful effects on those who are the victims of discrimination.* In America employers discriminate against blacks, in India employers often discriminate against workers belonging to schedule castes and schedule tribes. When minimum wages are imposed, the employers of unskilled workers have more applicants seeking jobs than the available employment opportunities. As a result, the employers pick and choose among the applicants and often discriminate against blacks in the U.S.A. and against Schedule castes and tribes in India. It is worth nothing that it is the workers belonging to these weaker sections who because of the past discrimination have not been able to acquire skills required for being employed in higher-paid jobs. In case of the USA, most economists believe that the fixation of minimum wage has contributed greatly to the increase in unemployment of black teenage workers.

It is important to understand as to who bears the cost of fixing higher minimum wages. It is generally assumed that the cost of paying higher minimum wages are borne by the employers, that is, the capitalist class. However, this is not true. When higher minimum wages are imposed, the employers often pass on these higher wages to the consumers in the form of higher prices of goods produced by them. Moreover, the employers often try to shift the cost of higher wages to the suppliers of other inputs which are complementary factors of labour in the form of lower prices paid for these inputs. It follows, therefore, that the costs of higher minimum wages are more widely spread through the society as a whole and not exclusively borne by the employers or business class.

An important effect of fixation of minimum wages is worth mentioning. In our above analysis we have assumed that all workers are covered by minimum wage law. This is however not correct. Minimum wage law does not apply to or cover all jobs or industries. For example, in case of the USA, it has been estimated that 15 per cent of workers are not covered by the minimum wage legislation. In India, the percentage of uncovered workers or jobs is much greater. This has an important consequence. When the minimum wage law is imposed in some sectors or industries and as a result employment of workers is reduced in these covered sectors, supply of labour to the uncovered sectors or jobs increases which depresses wages in these uncovered sectors. This means the workers who remain employed in the covered sectors benefit at the expense of the workers employed in the uncovered jobs. Therefore, whether workers as a group will receive net gain from minimum wage legislation depends on how large is the uncovered sector.

Another potential effect of minimum wage is *the reduction* in *the fringe benefits enjoyed by the*

---

1. Baumol and Blinder, *Economics, Principles and Policy*, Fifth edition, 1992, p.774

workers. Fringe benefits are the non-monetary benefits such as medical insurance, sickness benefits, pensionary benefits which workers receive in addition to the money wage. As a matter of fact, real wage rate is money wage plus these fringe benefits. Now, when as a result of minimum wage law, employers have to pay highestmoney wage rate, they may reduce fringe benefits offered to their workers so that real wages may not rise much. To the extent the employers are able to reduce the fringe benefits and real wages do not rise as much as money wages, the fall in employment as a result of fixation of minimum wages will be less. Since fixation of minimum wages creates unemployment of labour, workers cannot resist reduction in their fringe benefits.

Lastly, the fall in employment of labour as a result of minimum wage may not fully reflect itself in the reduced number of workers employed but in the form *of reduction in the number of hours worked per day or per week by each worker.* In other words, as a result of reduccd employment opportunities, instead of two out of ten workers becoming unemployed, all workers remain employed but each worker now works 80 per cent of the hours which he worked before the fixation of minimum wages. It has however been pointed out by some economists quoting some empirical evidence that since hiring each worker is associated with increase in some overhead costs, the employers prefer to cut back on employment of workers rather than to reduce hours per worker.

Conclusion. The analysis of adverse effect of minimum wage fixation leads us to the conclusion that it cannot be said with certainty that fixation of minimum wages benefits the workers as a whole. Fixation of minimum wages reduce employment opportunities and thereby lead to unemployment of labour, especially of the teenage and young workers. Further, it reduces the fringe benefits of workers and promote discrimination against the blacks, women, Schedule castes and tribes. Of course, some workers who retain employment benefit from minimum wages. But the main objective of minimum wage legislation is to provide decent living to the low-wage or poor workers. It is believed by many Western economists that *minimum wage fails to achieve its objective of removal of poverty of these workers.*

Case for Minimum Wage

In the opinion of the present author, the above analysis of the adverse effects of minimum wage legislation is based upon the assumptions of wage determination by demand for and supply of labour in a competitive labour market. Further, the above analysis assumes static conditions. If we remove these assumptions, the beneficial effects of the fixation of minimum wage legislation can be easily shown and the unfavourable effect of increase in unemployment of the fixation of minimum wage rate can be prevented. This is because *fixation of higher minimum wage rate may increase labour productivity.* The increase in labour productivity will cause a shift in the labour demand curve to the right. This will prevent the increase in unemployment which fixation of higher minimum wage rate may create. But the pertinent question is how the fixation of higher minimum wage rate for unskilled workers can result in increase in labour productivity. First, it is argued that *higher minimum wage for low-wage unskilled workers may produce shock effect upon employers.* It has been generally observed that firms using low-wage unskilled workers tend to be inefficient in the use of labour. The imposition of higher minimum wage will provide a shock to them, that is, prompt them to improve labour efficiency so that it is profitable for them to keep employing them. Second, it has been pointed out that the *fixation of higher minimum wages leads to the increase in real incomes of these unskilled workers who with their higher wages may improve their health and vigour by meeting their basic needs.* This is true especially in the case of poor and developing countries like ours where unskilled workers are paid very low wages which are quite inadequate even to meet basic needs. Besides, the higher real income *may increase the motivation of these workers* to do more work. The improved health, greater vigour and higher motivation to do more work resulting from higher minimum wages may result in rise in their efficiency or productivity. This will cause a shift in the demand curve for labour to the right which will tend to offset the tendency to reduce labour employment when the higher minimum wage is imposed. This is generally referred to as *economy of high wages.*

In the case of the existence of monopsony in the labour market, workers are exploited by the employees by restricting employment of labour and paying low wages. *Under the monopsonistic conditions in labour market, imposition of minimum wages can lead to the increase in wage rate without creating unemployment.* As a matter of fact, fixation of higher minimum wage can lead to the increase in employment of labour by doing away with monopsonistic employer's motive of restricting employment. This is illustrated in Fig. 33A.2 where the curve *VMP* represents value of marginal product of labour. *SL* is the supply curve of labour and *MW* is marginal wage or marginal factor cost curve of labour of the monopsonist. The monopsonist is in equilibrium when he employs *OL* labour and pays *OW* or *LK* wage rate which is less than the value of marginal product of labour *LE*. Thus, he is exploiting labour by restricting employment.

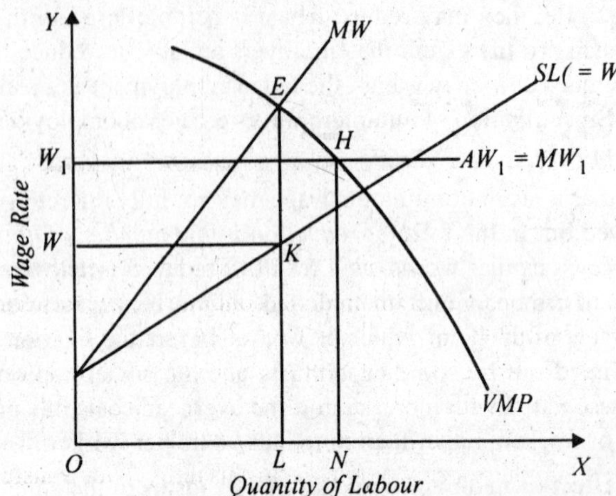

Fig. 33A.2. *Effect of Minimum Wage in Case of Monopsonistic Labour Market*

Now, if minimum wage rate OW_1 is fixed, the monopsonist must pay wage rate OW_1 since payment of wage rate below it will not be permitted by law. With the given minimum wage rate OW_1 the supply curve of labour will now become horizontal straight line and marginal wage curve will coincide with it. With the wage rate OW_1, the monopsonist will maximise profits by employing *ON* labour which is greater than *OL*. Thus, it is clear that in monopsonistic labour market, fixation of minimum wage rate has led to the increase in employment of labour. What is true of monopsonistic labour market generally applies to oligopsonistic labour market.

Conclusion

Two opposite views regarding effects of minimum wages have been explained above. Whether or not fixation of minimum wage by the Government has a net beneficial or adverse effect on unskilled workers cannot be decided on the basis of theoretical grounds alone. This 'is primarily an empirical issue which can be clinched by undertaking research studies. A large number of research studies concerning the effect of minimum wages have been made in the case of the developed countries such as USA. These studies generally conclude that minimum wage legislation causes some increase in unemployment of unskilled workers, especially of teenage workers and black ones.

QUESTIONS FOR REVIEW

1. Explain what is the effect of the fixation of minimum wages in a competitive labour market. Does it necessarily lead to unemployment of labour ? *D.U. B.A. (Hons) 2000*
2. As an anti-poverty measure fixation of minimum wages fails to achieve its objective. Do you agree ? Discuss.
3. What is meant by *economy of high wages* ? How would you explain the beneficial effect of fixation of minimum wages on the basis of the hyphothesis of economy of high wages.
4. Show that the fixation of minimum wages in a monopsonistic labour market may lead to the increase in both wages and employment of labour. *D.U. B.Com Hons)*
5. Explain the effect on empoyment if a minimum wage is applied to a monopsonic labour market. *D.U. B.A. (Hons) 2001*
6. "Rent Control of houses reduces the availability and quality of houses in the long run" Discuss

CHAPTER 34
THE THEORY OF RENT

CONCEPTS OF RENT

Having discussed the determination of reward for labor, we now turn to explain the determination of rent which is the price paid for the use of land. However, in modern economic theory, the term rent is used not only in the sense of reward for the use of land, but also in the sense of surplus earnings of the factors over their transfer earnings. In fact, in the later sense the concept of rent has been generalised so that it applies to *surplus return over and above the transfer earnings of all factors of production*, so that it is no longer peculiarly associated with land. We shall first discuss the determination of land rent and will then explain the concept of rent as surplus return over transfer earnings of the factor.

A distinguishing feature of land is that no human effort or sacrifice has been necessary to make it available to the society. Land to society is a free gift of nature. Society has not incurred any cost to obtain the land. Further, since land is not producible by man, *its supply is absolutely inelastic*, although its productivity can be increased by various improvements such as clearing, draining, introduction of irrigation facilities etc. These improvements are made by the efforts of man and therefore constitute capital goods. As the quantity of land available for use is scarce relative to demand, a price must be paid for its use. This price for the use of land, or what is commonly called *land rent*, is obtained by those people in the society in whom the ownership of land is vested. Since these private owners of land have not incurred any real cost to bring land into existence, the rent which they obtain is a surplus payment to them. The whole of the earnings of land *i.e.*, land rent (excluding, of course, the return on capital investment in the form of improvements made on land by the owners) are *surplus*, since land is there in any case and does not require any costs or human efforts to be made to bring it into existence. Thus, the term rent which was originally employed for the price paid for the use of land came to be used for *the surplus earnings of any factor of production in excess of the cost incurred to obtain its service*. Since the land in its entirety to the whole society, being free gift of nature, does not require any cost to be paid in order to make it available to the society for use in production, the whole earnings of land are regarded as surplus. Thus, the whole earnings of land from the view point of the society become economic rent. We shall discuss this concept of economic rent in greater detail when we take up the explanation of the concept of rent as a surplus over transfer earnings to all factors of production.

It should be noted that rent as a payment to the landlord for hiring or use of land by the tenant and the concept of economic rent as surplus over transfer earnings which applies to all factors of production are altogether different concepts and therefore should not be confused with each other. Modern economists generally call payment for hiring of land as *land rent* and surplus over transfer earnings of the factors as *economic rent*.

It is worthwhile to note here that Marshall extended the concept of rent to cover the earnings (net of depreciation and interest charges) of fixed capital equipment like machinery in the short run. The distinguishing characteristic of land is the fact that its supply is perfectly inelastic and therefore its earnings depend mainly upon the demand for it. But, in the short run period, fixed capital equipment like machinery is likewise perfectly inelastic in supply and cost of production is not relevant once it has been installed for production. Thus, in the short period, the earnings of fixed capital equipment depend mainly upon the demand conditions and are thus similar to land rent and have therefore been called rent by Marshall. Since these capital equipments are not permanently in fixed supply like land, and instead their supply is very much elastic in the long run. Marshall preferred to call their earnings in the short period as *Quasi-Rent rather than rent*.

Now we propose to discuss the above three concepts of rent as mentioned above. We start with the Ricardian theory of rent which discusses the problem of payment for the use of land and other natural resources.

RICARDIAN THEORY OF RENT

The Ricardian theory of rent follows from the views of classical writers about the operation of law of diminishing returns in agriculture. Classicical authors, West, Torrents, Malthus and Ricardo, each of them independently formulated the theory of differential rent. However, the classical theory of rent in the form presented and elaborated by David Ricardo has become more popular, though the ideas of all of them concerning the land rent is fundamentally same. Ricardo gave credit to West and Malthus as his forerunner in the development of the theory of rent.

Ricardo defined rent as follows : "*Rent is that portion of the produce of earth which is paid to the landlord for the use of the original and indestructible powers of soil.* "It should be noticed that land rent, according to Recardian definition, is a payment for the use of only land and is different from contractual rent which includes the return on capital investment made by the landlord in the form of hedges, drains, wells and the like. When return on the capital investment made by the land owner is deducted from the contractual rent, what is left is pure land rent which is the price for the use of only land or "*the original and indestructible powers of the soil*".

Assumptions of Ricardian Theory

It will greatly help in the understanding of the Ricardian model of rent determination, if we clearly state the various assumptions made by him. Firstly, Ricardo considers the supply of land from the viewpoint of the whole society and takes the quantity of land as completely fixed. No amount of higher price for the use of land can call forth an increased supply of it. Thus the total supply of land is perfectly inelastic and unresponsive to any changes in rent. Secondly, *he does not take into account the various alternative uses to which land can be put*. He assumes the land to be used for growing a single composite crop 'corn'. Thus land has been taken to be completely specific to one crop, *i.e.*, corn. In this way, in Ricardian model, either land is to be used for growing of corn or alternatively it has be left idle. There are only two alternative uses of land: its use for growing of corn or no use at all. Thus *he takes the transfer earnings of land as zero*. No land owner would like to leave the land idle and therefore every land owner will be would prepared to give it for any rent however little it may be provided that perfect competition prevails.

Thirdly, *he assumes that land differs in quality*. There are various grades of land, differing from each other in respect of fertility and location. Some pieces of land are more fertile than others and, as compared to others, some are more well located or near to the market centres.

Fourthly, *he assumes that there is perfect competition in the market for land*. In other words, there are many land owners who are to give their land on rent and there are many farmers who are to get land on rent for the purpose of growing corn. Further, each individual land owner and farmer has no influence over rent *i e.*, the price for the use of land.

Given the above assumptions, according to the Ricardian theory, rent arises due to two reasons. Firstly, if land is homogeneous, *i.e.*, of uniform quality and same location, the scarcity of land relative to demand will give rise to rent. Ricardo calls it a *scarcity rent*. Second, when land differs in quality, *i.e.*, in fertility and location, the scarcity of superior grades of land will give rise to *differential rents*.

We shall discuss below the emergence of scarcity and differential rents, as conceived in the Ricardian theory.

Scarcity Rent

The emergence of land rent in the classical theory can be easily explained by imagining that a new island is discovered and some people come to settle there. We suppose that all land in this island is completely homogeneous or is of uniform quality. In other words, all pieces of land in this island are equally fertile and equally well-situated. The quantity of land available for cultivation on this island is fixed and is therefore completely inelastic to changes in the price for its use. Land is to be used for the cultivation of a single crop "*corn*". Land is assumed to be having no other alternative uses. When the people come to settle on this island, they will use the land for producing corn by applying labour and capital on it. When all the available land is not yet put in use, the price of the corn will be equal to the *average cost of output incurred on labour and capital*, with the farmers working at the minimum point of the average cost (exclusive of land rent). The price of the corn must at least be equal to the average cost (exclusive of land rent) in the long run if the use of labour and capital is to be worthwhile. Since we are assuming perfect competition in the market for corn, the farmer's equilibrium will be established at the lowest point of long-run average cost curve (exclusive of rent).

As long as some land is idle, the production of corn will be increased by bringing new land under cultivation. Thus until land is not scarce, *i.e.*, some land is yet idle, the price of corn cannot rise *permanently* above the average cost of labour and capital cost. Since the price of corn is, in long-run equilibrium, equal to the average cost of only labour and capital, as long as all land is not yet in use, *there will be no surplus left to be earned as rent on land*. In other words, it means that so long as there is some available land which is not yet brought into use, farmers will not have to pay any rent to the landlords for the use of their land.

Provided the competition among landlords is perfect (as is the case we are assuming here), the rent will not arise when there is still surplus land for use because the demand for land is relatively less than the supply of it. In other words, land is yet not scarce relative to demand. Price of any things arises only when it is scarce in relation to demand. If any landlord tries to charge any rent when there is still some land lying idle with other landlords, farmers will go to take up that land for cultivation. The landlord need not be paid rent for the use of land since its only alternative use is keeping it idle. To sum up, so long as land is not scarce, rent cannot arise, since price will equal minimum average (labour and capital) cost. Suppose that the population continues increasing so that the demand for corn becomes so large that all available land is brought under cultivation. If the population of the island further increases beyond this, it will raise the demand for the product which will bring about rise in the price level above the minimum average (labour and capital) cost per unit of output giving rise to rent on land. Since it

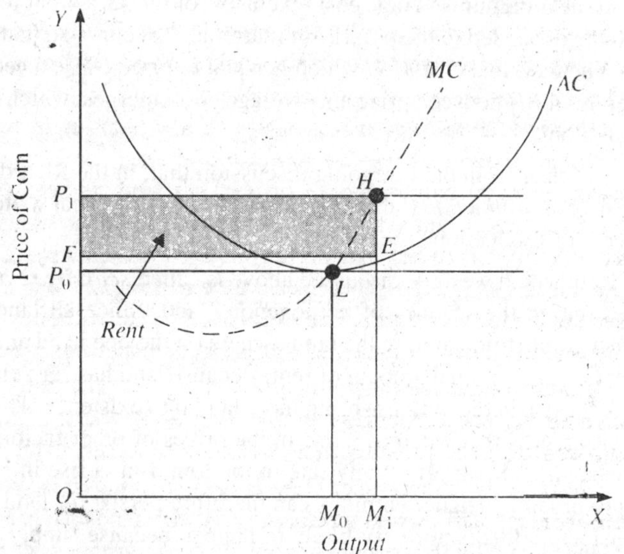

Fig. 34.1. *In Ricardian theory scarcity rent arises as surplus over cost of production.*

has arise in due to scarcity of land, it has been called scarcity rent.

Recardian concept of scarcity rent is illustrated in Fig. 34.1. Where *AC* and *MC* curves show average and marginal cost per unit output of corn incurred on labour and capital. Price of corn must be equal to OP_0 if land is to be cultivated at all. Note that price OP_0 is equal to the minimum average cost per unit of corn output on labour and capital. At price OP_0 there is no surplus over cost of production and therefore no rent accrues to the land. In other words, supply of land is not scarce in relation to demand for it upto price of corn equal to OP_0.

Now, if due to the expansion in population, demand for corn increases and as a result price of corn rises to OP_1 land will be more intensively cultivated. With price of corn equal to OP_1, the equilibrium of the farmer is at point *H* or at output OM_1 as price of corn is equal to marginal cost at output level OM_1. It will be seen that with price OP_1, surplus over cost of production equal to P_1HEF (shaded area) has emerged. This surplus over cost will be given to the landlord. The price of corn rises abvoe the minimum average cost of production only when the demand for corn has greatly increased and as a result land has become scarce in relation to the derived demand for it. Since all pieces of land are homogeneous, the same amount of rent will accrue on all pieces of land.

It is evident from Fig. 34.1 that a difference between the price of the corn and the average cost on labour and capital has arisen. In other words, farmer earns more than the labour and capital cost incurred by him. While the average labour and capital cost incurred by him is M_1E, the price of the corn is $M_1H(= OP)$. Thus the differential *EH* between the price and the average labour and capital cost has arisen. This *EH* is the rent per unit of output which will be paid by the farmer to the landlord. Total rent to be paid by the farmer to the landlord will be $FEHP_1$. This rent (difference between price and cost) cannot be competed away by the entry of more farmers in production since all land is already being employed for production. This rent has arisen because of the scarcity of land. In other words, rent arises due to the niggardliness of nature; nature has not provided land large enough to meet the level of demand by producing on the minimum level of average cost. The demand for corn has increased so much that the required output cannot be produced with total available supply of land at the minimum average cost (exclusive of rent). In order to meet the increased demand, output has to be expanded to the point *H* of marginal cost curve so that the new price OP_1 equals marginal cost. The marginal cost M_1H which is equal to price OP_1 exceeds average cost M_1E by *EH*. Thus a differential *EH* between price and average cost emerges, which is rent of land required to be paid to the landlord.

It is clear from the foregoing discussion that, in the Ricardian theory, *rent emerges as surplus over cost of production* (labour and capital cost). Classical writers did not consider rent as a part of the cost of production.

Rent which we have discussed above is called *scarcity rent.* It is called scarcity rent because it arises due to the scarcity of homogenous land. Since all land is homogeneous and there exists perfect competition among the land owners on the one hand and among the tenants on the other all farmers will pay equal amount of rent. Because land has zero elasticity of supply *i.e.*, its quantity is fixed, the rise in rent will not bring more land into existence. Therefore, the essential feature of pure scarcity rent is that whereas a rise in the prices of other factors of production will bring about an increase in their supply, at any rate in the long run, a rise in rent cannot cause an increase in the supply of land. "Higher earnings can therefore persist for land even in the long run, whereas with other factors this is not very likely to happen because supply will increase to meet the increased demand. *It is the fixity of its supply which distinguishes homogeneous land and its scarcity rent from other factors of production and their prices. Scarcity rent is essentially the result of the fact that land is in inflexible supply.*"[1]

1. Stonier and Hague, *A Textbook of Economic Theory*, 4th edition, 1972, p.283

Differential Rent

In the discussion of scarcity rent above, we have assumed that all land is homogeneous, *i.e.*, equally well fertile and equally well-situated. This is, however, not a realistic assumption. In fact, Ricardo was most interested in showing the emergence of rent when the land differs in quality *i.e.*, in fertility and situation. Some pieces of land are more fertile than others. Again, some pieces of land are more favourably situated than others. That is, they are located near to the market centres where produce has to be sold, than others.

Fertility of tracts of land varies primarily because of the differences in the nature of the soil , temperature, rainfall and other climatic factors. With a given application of labour and capital, some pieces of land will yield more output per acre than others. Thus the differences in fertility will bring about differences in the costs of production (exclusive of rent) of various farmers operating on the different grades of land. The farmers working on the superior or more fertile grades of land will have their average cost curve at a lower level than those working on the inferior or less fertile grades of land. Likewise, differences in location cause differences in costs of various farmers because of the differences in transportation costs. In practice, land will be of numerous grades, shading off gradually from the best to the poorest. To simplify our analysis, we however, assume that in our island there are three grades of land. Land *A* being the superior most and *C* the poorest, *B* grade of land lies between *A* and *C*.

When people first come to island, they will take up the best grade land *A* for the production of corn. So long as some of grade *A* land is yet lying idle, there will be no rent. When with the increase in the population of the island or with the development of the island, the demand for corn increases, the whole of the grade *A* land will be put into use for the production of corn. At this stage each of the many farmers who will be using the grade *A* land will work at the lowest point of the average cost curve as shown in Fig. 34.2(*a*). When once the whole of grade *A* land is brought into use and the demand for corn still further increases due to either growth of population or the development of the island, *two courses of action will be adopted*. First, grade *B* land will also be taken up for cultivation. Secondly, grade *A* land will be *more intensively used i.e.*, more doses of labour and capital will be applied to the pieces of grade *A* land.

Now, the grade *B* land can be taken for use only when the price sufficiently rises so that it covers the average cost of production on grade *B* land. In other words, price must be high enough to cover the minimum average cost (exclusive of rent) on grade *B* land, otherwise it will not be worthwhile to cultivate it. In other words, if the price is lower than the lowest average cost on grade *B* land, its cultivation will not pay back even the labour and capital cost incurred and therefore it will not be

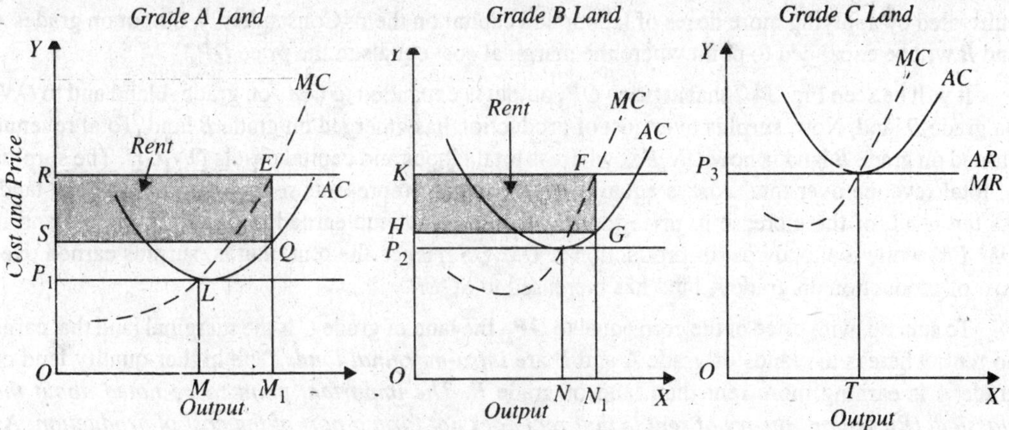

Fig. 34.2. *Differential Rent*

brought under cultivation. It is evident from Fig. 34.2 (*b*), that price must rise to OP_2 if the grade *B* land is to be taken up for production. Now suppose that demand for corn has risen so much that price of corn is OP_2 and therefore grade *B* land has been brought under cultivation. Thus, margin of cultivation has been extended to grade *B* land. In other words, grade *B* land is now on the *margin of extensive cultivation*. Every farmer cultivating the grade *B* land will operate on the lowest point of average cost curve *AC* in Fig. 34.2(b). Since the price of OP_2 is equal to average labour and capital cost on grade *B* land, there is no surplus over cost of production and hence grade *B* land does not earn any rent. But because price OP_2 stands higher than the lowest average cost on grade *A* land, surplus over cot of production would appear on grade *A* land. This surplus is rent which will be paid to the landlord of grade A land.

It should be noticed that besides extending the margin of cultivation to grade *B* land, there will also be side by side more intensive cultivation of grade *A* land by applying more does of labour and capital on it. In other words, *margin of intensive cultivation* will also be pushed forward. In terms of Fig. 34.2, it will mean that the farmers operating on grade *A* will not produce at the lowest average cost, they will also expand output to meet the increased demand. With the expansion in output, the marginal costs on farms of grade *A* land will rise. The price must rise to cover this increase in marginal cost, if the extra costs incurred on additions to capital and labour for expanding output are to be recovered. In Fig. 34.2(*a*) when the farmers of grade *A* land extend the margin of their intensive cultivation in response to increased demand, their new equilibrium position will be where the marginal cost is equal to new higher price OP_2.

It should be noticed that rent on grade *A* land would have arisen even if no more intensive cultivation was done and the output was restricted to *OM* level since the price OP_2 stands higher than the lowest average cost *ML* on grade *A* land. But, in practice, both the extensive and intensive margins are pushed further in order to meet the increase in demand and the surplus over cost of production *i.e.*, land rent on intra-marginal lands arises because of both the more extensive and intensive cultivation. At this stage grade *B* land is *marginal land* which earns no rent and grade *A* land is *intra-marginal land*, which will earn rent.

Now suppose that population of the island further increases which brings about further increases in demand for the produce of land so that the price of corn further rises to the level OP_3. As a result of this, the grade *C* land will also be brought under cultivation and lands of grade *A* and *B* will be more intensively cultivated. Price OP_3 is equal to the minimum average cost on grade *C* land. There will be no surplus earned over cost of production on grade *C* land and hence grade *C* land does not earn any rent. Grade *C* land is now on the margin of extensive cultivation. Thus, grade *C* land is the *marginal land*. Besides, at price OP_3, lands of grade *A* and *B* will be more intensively cultivated by applying more doses of labour and capital on them. Consequently, output on grades *A* and *B* will be expanded to point where the marginal cost equals to the price OP_3.

It will be seen Fig. 34.2 that at price OP_3 output is expanded to OM_1 on grade *A* land and to ON_1 on grade *B* land. Now, surplus over cost of production has emerged on grade *B* land. Total revenue earned on grade *B* land is now ON_1FK, whereas total labour and capital cost is ON_1GH. The surplus of total revenue over total cost is equal to *HGFK* which represents rent earned by grade *B* land. As the result of the increase in price to OP_3, the total revenue earned in case of grade A land is OM_1ER, while the total cost of production is OM_1QS. Hence the rent, that is, surplus earned over cost of production on grade *A* land has increased to *SQER*.

To sum up, with price of the corn equal to OP_3, the land of grade *C* is the marginal land that earns no rent, whereas the lands of grade *A* and *B* are *intra-marginal lands*. The higher-quality land of grade *A* is earning more rent than land of grade *B*. *The important point to be noted about the classical (Ricardian) theory of rent is that rent does not form a part of the cost of production.* As seen above, rent on land is the earnings over and above the cost of production. As rent does not enter into cost of production, it therefore does not determine price. Price of corn (or produce of the land) must be equal to the minimum average cost of production of the marginal land, but the marginal land earns no rent. It is thus clear that in Ricardian Theory, rent is not *price determining*. In fact, in this theory rent is price determined, that is, it is price of corn which determines rent, and not other way around. The quote Ricardo, "*Corn is not high because a rent is paid, but a rent is paid because corn is high.*"

CRITICAL EVALUATION OF RICARDIAN THEORY OF RENT

So far as the determination of land rent is concerned and the forces which influence it, modern economists agree with Ricardian theory of rent. Like Ricardo, modern economists are also of the view rent of land arises because of its scarcity. Although Ricardo explained the determination of land rent through a '*differential return' approach* and not the basis of *direct* demand for and supply of land, and accordingly did not employ demand and supply curves to depict the determination of land rent, yet in Ricardian theory it is the forces of demand for and supply of land which determine the rent of land. Like modern economists, Ricardo too believed that demand for land is derived demand, it is derived from the demand for the produce of land, that is, what Ricardo called 'corn'.

In the Ricardian theory with its differential approach, increase in the population of a country raises the demand for the corn and brings about rise in the land rent. In the modern approach based on direct interaction of demand and supply, the increase in population will shift the demand curve for land to the right and thereby will push up the rent. Thus *the demand-supply approach (or in other words, marginal productivity approach) of the modern economists and differential return approach of Ricardo are alternative explanation of the same phenomenon and are in no sense contradictory*; in both approaches forces of demand and supply play a crucial role in determination of rent. But the use of Ricardian differential approach does not provide any better understanding of the nature of rent than that of modern approach based on the use of direct demand and supply concepts. However, the adoption of Ricardian differential approach often leads to misunderstanding, for its suggests that rent of land requires a special theory for its explanation, that is, it may lead one to conclude that whereas rent of land can be explained with differential principle, the other factor rewards of labour, interest on capital, etc. can be explained with demand and supply or marginal productivity theory. Obviously, such a conclusion would not be correct. We thus see that whereas there is not contradiction between differential theory of rent propounded by Rciardo and the modern theory based on direct use of demand and supply and the marginal productivity principle, there seems to be a little reason for the special theory of rent (*i.e.*, differential theory). Unity of economic thought and similarity of treatment requires that land rent should also be explained directly with demand and supply curves as other factor prices. We shall explain later in this chapter how rent of land is determined by demand for and supply of land.

Ricardian theory has also been cirticised by some modern economists for its laying undue emphasis on the "*original and industructible powers of the soil*". According to them, fertility of the soil gets destroyed after a few years of continuous cultivation. Further, fertility of soil can be greatly improved by using modern techniques of production. Thus, according to Stonier and Hague, "In these days of nuclear physics and atomic energy it is very dangerous to assert that anything is indestructible..... It is not reasonable to regard the powers of the land as indestructible."[2] They further write "it seems more reasonable to attribute the payment of rent not to the original and indestructible powers of the soil but rather to the fact that land is a factor of production which is in almost completely inelastic supply to changes in its price."[3]

Briggs and Jordan criticise the Ricardian differential theory of rent as a mere truism. According to them, it just seeks to prove that a superior grade land would earn more than an inferior land. They

2. Stonier and Hague, A Textbook of Economic Theory, 4th edition, p.276
3. Ibid, p.267

thus write "Fundamentally, all that the Ricardian theory of rent amounts to is the truism that the better article will always command the higher price. A more fertile acre will be worth more than less fertile one simply because they are different things." However, in our view, criticism of Briggs and Jordan is misplaced. Through his defferential theory of rent Ricardo tried to show that productivity of land like the marginal productivity of other factors is an important factor in determining demand for land and therefore rent for its use.

Another disagreement of modern economists with Ricardo relates to the role of rent in determining price of product (*i.e.*, corn in Ricardo's case). As seen above, Recardo was of the view that rent is a surplus over cost of production and therefore does not enter into cost of producing corn and hence does not determine its price. In fact, according to him, *rent is price-determined and not price determining*. Thus, according to him, price of corn determines rent of land and not the other way around. As we shall explain late in detail, from the point of view of an individual firm or individual industry rent of land or at least transfer earnings of land is a necessary part of the cost of production and therefore contributes to the determination of the price of corn or product of land. Thus modern economists do not agree with Ricardo that land rent does not determine price of corn.

Land's Share in National Income and Stagnation of Economic Growth. Another aspect of Ricardian theory with which modern economists do not agree is the prediction by Ricardo, on the basis of his rent theory, that process of economic growth would come to an end and there will be economic stagnation. He argued that as the population increased, the demand for land would also increase. As a result, both the extensive and intensive margins would be pushed further and due to this rent of land will go up. According to him, in this process, share of land rent in the toal national product will go up and share of profits will decline. Decline in profits means not much money will be available for financing the industry. Further, decline in the rate of profit will discourage inducement to invest. Consequently, further investment and growth process would come to a halt. But in actual practice things have not worked out in accordance with the prediction of Ricardo. To quote Jan Pen again, "the grandiose theory developed by D. Ricardo at the beginning of the nineteenth century.... amounts to the fact that population growth and shortage of land will force up the share of land rent, as a result of which no money will be left for the financing of industry. Ricardo predicted stagnation of economic growth, but this prediction did not work out, nor has the increase in the share of rent of land occurred.... There is in fact a clear shortage of land at many places, and especially in the cities this may lead to high prices and rents. This situation is not without it problems, but it is nothing like Ricardo's predictions

EXPLAINING DETERMINATION OF LAND THROUGH DEMAND AND SUPPLY

Ricardian differential approach, demand and supply of land determine rent, through they are not directly shown to do so. The Ricardian theory can be expressed and explained directly in terms of demand for and supply of land. In the Ricardian treatment of rent, the supply of land for the economy as a whole is fixed, and the demand for land is derived from the demand for the "corn" produced by land. Thus, according to Lipsey, "The modern student of Economics will recognize in the Ricardian arguments the idea of derived demand. Landlords, Ricardo was saying, cannot just charge any price they want for land; the prices they get will depend on demand and supply. The supply of land is pretty well fixed and the demand depends on the price of corn. The higher the price of corn, the more profitable will it be to grow corn, higher will be the demand for corn land, and the higher will be the price for its use."[4]

In the Ricardian model, it is assumed that land has only one use, that is, of growing corn on it. Therefore, no price is required to be paid to prevent land from transferring itself to other uses, that is, to uses other than growing corn. Further, the land has been considered for the economy as a whole.

4. *Op. cit.*, p. 349

Therefore, the supply of land is a given and fixed quantity. Given these assumptions, supply curve of land is *perfectly inelastic*. Scarcity rent will arise only when the available quantity of land is scarce in relation to demand for it, which is derived from the demand for the corn. The Ricardian model of the determination of scarcity rent through demand and supply curves has been illustrated in Fig. 34.3 where *SS'* is the supply curve of land with *OS* as the available quantity of land. It is assumed that all land is homogeneous and therefore no differences in fertility or location exist. It will be seen from the Fig. 34.3 that various demand curves such as D_0D_0, D_1D_1, D_2D_2, D_3D_3 and D_4D_4 for land depend upon the various levels of demand for the product *i.e.*, corn.

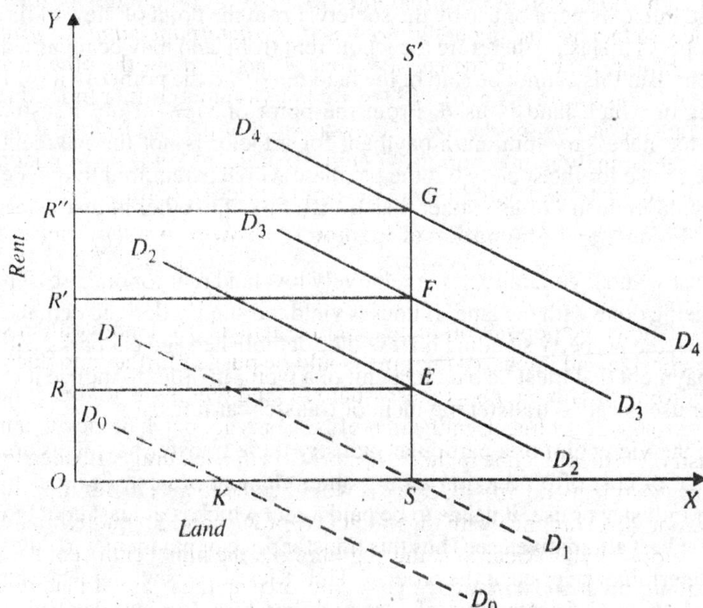

Fig. 34.3. *Ricardian Model: Determination of Land Rent through Demand and Supply Curves*

It should be noted that aggregate demand curves for land have been obtained by summing up the marginal revenue product curves of all farmers cultivating the land. Thus, as the demand for other factors, demand for land, is also determined by its marginal revenue productivity. If, to begin with, demand curve for land is given by the curve D_0D_0, *then no rent on land will be charged* on hiring it. This is because with D_0D_0 as the demand curve, the available land *OS* is abundant in relation to the demand for it. With D_0D_0 as the demand curve, various farmers will use *OK* amount of land and as a result *KS* amount of land will remain idle or uncultivated. If the demand for land increases to D_1D_1, even then the rent of land will be nil, but now the whole amount of available land *OS* will be cultivated. If the demand for land increases to D_2D_2, the demand for and supply of land will be in equilibrium at point *E* and rent *OR* is determined. With the increase in demand for land to D_3D_3, rent rises to *OR'* and with the further increase in demand for land to D_4D_4, rent rises to *OR''*, whereas the supply of land remains fixed at *OS*. Demand for land can increase as a result of population growth which raises the consumption of corn or agricultural produce. This increased demand for corn or agricultural produce causes the demand curve for land to shift upward and thereby brings about a rise in the rent of land.

We thus see that Ricardian model of determination of land rent can be better explained with demand and supply curves. Therefore, there is no need for the adoption of special differential return theory of rent, while other factor prices are explained on the demand and supply basis and marginal productivity principle.

Demand Supply Analysis and Differential Rents. With demand-supply approach we can also explain differential rents arising on different kinds of lands between which there are differences of fertility and location. In our above analysis of rent determination through demand and supply, we have assumed that all land is homogeneous. Therefore, a single uniform rent is determined. When there are differences in land, each kind of land would have its own separate demand and supply curves and consequently different rents depending on their demand and supply will be determined.

Thus, on demand and supply basis, even differential rents on different grades of land in respect of fertility and location can be explained.

LAND RENT, COST AND PRICE

Ricardo explained the determination of land rent from the standpoint of the economy as a whole. He did not consider the question of rent payment from the point of view of a single industry or use. He did not consider the *various different uses or industries* for which land can be used. Since he confined himself to the whole land and a single use of it, he concluded that whole land rent is a surplus, superfluous and unnecessary payment. It is a surplus or unnecessary payment in the sense that it is not required to bring land into existence or use by the society. From the point of view of the economy as a whole, the total supply is inelastic, therefore the whole rent from land may be regarded as surplus or unnecessary payment. But this cannot be said of the land rent from the point of view of the individual industries or uses in which land is used. From the point of view of an industry producing a particular product, the necessary minimum payment for a factor is not the payment which will bring it into existence or use for the society but the payment which is required to induce that factor to remain in that particular industry or use rather than transfer itself to other industries or uses.

If land has various possible uses, and it generally has, a relatively low land rent for one use of it will lead to something different being done with the land. If houses yield too small a derived demand for land, and car parks a higher one, the property standing on it will be demolished and car parks will appear.[5] The minimum price or payment that must be paid to a unit of a factor in order to induce it to work in the particular industry or use is called transfer payment or transfer earnings.

It should be noted that from the viewpoint of a particular industry these transfer payments are as much a part of the supply price or cost of production as any other element of cost. In order to obtain the land for any particular industry or use, it needs to be paid a rent which is at least equal to the income it could earn in the next best alternative use. Thus this transfer price or payment will enter into cost of production and will determine the price of the product. Thus Ricardo was wrong when he asserted that rent does not enter into cost of production of corn and therefore does not determine the price of the corn. Thus, according to modern economists, at least that part of land rent which is the transfer cost or transfer earnings enters into the cost of production of the commodity produced by land and therefore determines the price of the commodity as any other element of cost. Prof. Robertson expresses the modern viewpoint in regard to the land rent entering into the cost of production of a commodity in the following words: "the old phrase about rent not entering into cost . . . . conjures upto my mind a stately temple labelled costs of production with poor Rent standing disconsolately on the mat outside . . . . from the point of view not only of the individual firm but of the individual industry the price paid for the use of land is exactly on all fours with the price paid for the use of the other factors of production."[6]

That the land rent enters into the cost of production and thus determines price of a commodity for the production of which land is used is quite evident if we consider the supply of land from the viewpoint of the individual farmer or any other individual uses of land. For an individual farmer, the supply of land is perfectly elastic at the given rate of land rent. If an individual farmer does not pay this land rent, the land will get transferred to other farmers who will be ready to pay the current rate of land rent. It is therefore quite clear that for the individual farmer the whole of land rent is a necessary payment and he therefore must include it in his cost of production on the basis of which price of the commodity will be determined. Jan Pen rightly writes: "Ricardo was right when he wrote: corn is not high because a rent is paid, but a rent is paid because corn is high. But that 'right' must

5. Jan Pen, *Income Distribution*, Penguin Books, 1971, p.128
6. D.H. Robertson. *Lectures on Economic Principles*, Fontana Library Edition, p. 204.

be interpreted solely in the sense of inelastic supply curves that are confronted with a derived demand. If the latter is at a high level because end-product is expensive, a high land rent results from the market, that rent is not a cause but a consequence. However, *one may not deduce from this that rent for the individual farmer is not a part of the costs.* Not a single farmer would believe that, and rightly so. He simply has to pay for the land as for labour and for capital."[7]

We therefore see that Ricardo's view that rent of land does not enter into cost of production and therefore does not take part in the determination of the price of corn is quite wrong. He formed this view by considering land from the point of view of the whole society for which land is completely inelastic and has zero transfer cost. As a result, from the point of view of the society as a whole, the whole land rent is surplus and unnecessary payment. But, as Chamberlin writes, "Although rents may be surpluses from certain points of view or for certain purposes, or subject to certain interpretation, they are to the individual producer no different from any other money expense. They do not arise as a surplus from his own operations; they are a cost rigidly imposed upon him by the competition of his rivals for the use of rent-yielding property. They figure in the same way as do the wages of labour and the interest of capital in his computations ."[8]

To sum up, from the point of view of the individual industry and farmer or producer, land rent enters into cost of production and therefore determines price. Ricardo was wrong in holding an opposite view that rent does not enter into cost of production and therefore does not determine price.

MODERN THEORY OF RENT

Economic Rent as a Surplus over Transfer Earnings

In the modern theory of rent the concept of economic rent has been generalised and extended to the surplus payments made to other factors of production besides land. As we saw above, Ricardo regarded land as a free gift of nature and considered the whole earnings of land as the economic rent. Later on, this Ricardian concept of rent has been extended to designate a part of earnings of other factors of production—labour, capital and entrepreneurial ability—over and above the minimum necessary income required to induce the factors to do their work. Thus, in accord with Ricardo's concept, from the social point of view Joan Robinson say, "The essence of the conception of *rent* is the conception of a surplus earned by a particular part of a factor of production over and above the minimum earnings necessary to induce it to do work."[9]

According to Benham, economic rents are "the sum paid to the factors which need not be paid in order to retain the factors *in the industry*."[10] Likewise, according to Boulding, economic rent is the payment to a factor "in excess of the minimum amount necessary to keep that factor in *its present occupation*."[11] Joan Robinson also discusses the question of surplus or economic rent from the viewpoint of individual industries or uses. She thus say, "from the point of view of an industry producing a particular commodity the necessary minimum payment for a factor is not the payment which will cause that factor to exist, but the payment which will cause it to take service in that particular industry rather than in another."[12] And "the difference between the earnings actually received by a certain unit of a factor and its transfer price is its rent from the point of view of the industry."[13]

7. Jan Pen, *op, cit.* p. 128 (*italics added*)
8. E.H. Chamberlin, *The Theory of Monopolistic Competition*, 1950
9. *Economics of Imperfect Competition* (London 1948), p.102.
10. Fredrick Benham, *Economics*, 6th edition (London), p. 227.
11. K.E. Boulding, The Concept of Economic Surplus, *American Economic Review*, Vol. 35 December 1945.
12. *Economics of Imperfect Competition*,p.104.
13. *Op. cit.*, p.110.

Likewise, according to George Stigler, the rent of a factor is "the excess of its return in the best use over its possible return in other uses."[14]

It is clear from above that other factors of production, labour, capital, entrepreneur may also be found to be earning economic rent when they are getting payment greater than what is required to induce them to work in the present industry occupation or use. Thus, in modern economic theory, *economic rent is not merely confined to land, it also refers to the surplus payments made to some units of other factors over and above what is necessary to keep them in the present industry or use.* Thus, the units of other factors may also earn economic rent.

ECONOMIC RENT ARISES WHEN THE SUPPLY OF A FACTOR IS LESS THAN PERFECTLY ELASTIC

Boulding[15] and Joan Robinson[16] emphasized that whenever the supply of factor units to an industry or economy is not perfectly elastic, a part of the earnings of a factor will consist of surplus or economic rent, since the full price they get are not necessary to make all the factor units available. If the supply is not perfectly elastic, some factor units will be available at a price lower than the price they will actually receive, the difference between the actual price and the one necessary to make them available is surplus or economic rent. We shall now explain below the concept of economic rent with special reference to land and will bring out the conditions under which it arises.

As explained above, in the Ricardian theory, the rent was conceived as a payment made to a factor of production whose total supply was completely inelastic or fixed. When the total supply of a factor is completely fixed or inelastic, no price is needed to be paid in order to induce it to be available for production. Land is the main example of the factor of production whose total supply is fixed and completely inelastic to the economy as a whole. This is because land is a free gift of nature and is non-reproducible. Thus supply of land cannot be increased when the demand for it and hence the price for its use rises. On the contrary, even if the price of its use falls to zero, the total supply of land will remain unaffected. Land is there in any case and does not require to be paid any price in order to exist and become available for production. To put it in other words, the transfer earnings of land for the economy as a whole are zero. Thus, to Ricardo and other classical economists, the whole earnings of land are functionless surplus, that is, whatever price the land happens to earn is not required to be paid for it in order to keep it in existence or to make it available to the society. Therefore, they regarded the whole price or earnings for land as *economic rent defined as the surplus payment over and above what is required to be paid to make it available to society*. Thus the term rent which in ordinary usage means the price or payment for hiring land came to be used by economists as the *title for the surplus earnings which the land receives.*

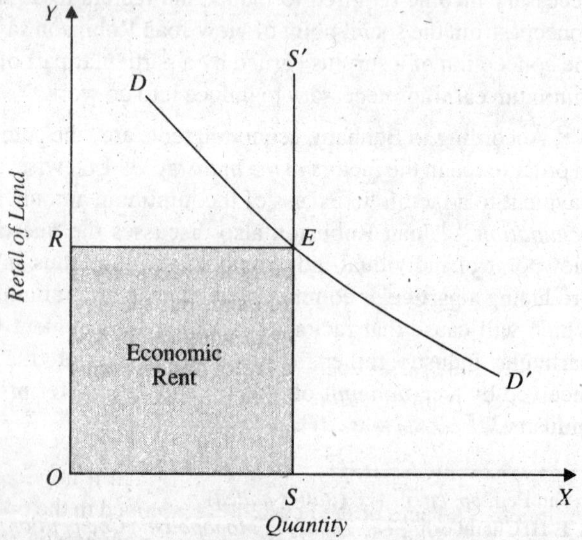

Fig. 34.4. *Whole Earnings are Economic Rent.*

14. George Stigler, *The Theory of Price*, 2nd edition p.99
15. K.E. Boulding. The Concept of Economic Surplus, *American Economic Review*, vol. 35, Dec. 1945.
16. *Economics of Imperfect Competition*, Ch. 8.

Since the whole price or payment made to land is surplus earnings in the sense defined above, therefore the rent as a price for the use of land and rent as surplus earnings of land have often been used interchangeably, though they are conceptually different. Figure 34.4 illustrates that whole of the earnings of land are economic rent from the viewpoint of the society. Suppose *OS* is the amount of land available to the society. The society then confronts a perfectly inelastic supply curve *SS′* of land. This perfectly inelastic curve *SS′* indicates that even if the price for the use of land falls to zero, its supply remains *OS*. This is because the transfer earnings of land for the society are zero. Curve *DD′* represents the demand for land of the society as a whole. As a result of the intersection of demand and supply curves of land, the rental *OR* per unit for the use of land is determined. Since transfer earnings are zero, the whole rental *OR* will be the economic rent earned per unit of land. The total earnings of land will be *ORES* and whole of these earnings of land will represent economic rent, since the transfer earnings are zero.

The whole earnings of a factor can be surplus only if its supply is perfectly inelastic. Land is such a factor because of its being a free gift of nature and society having incurred no cost to make it available for production. Therefore, *economic rent has also been defined as a payment for any factor whose supply is perfectly inelastic*. Thus, economic rent refers to the payment for the use of land and other natural resources since it is the supply of land and other natural resources which are permanently in fixed supply.

According to the modern economists, it is only from the standpoint of the economy as a whole that land has perfectly inelastic supply. The supply of land for a particular use or industry is not perfectly inelastic. There are various uses or industries competing for the use of land. A unit of land being employed to produce a particular crop will be transferred to the production of other crops, if its earnings in the present use fall below the possible earnings in the production of any other crop. It is therefore clear that from the viewpoint of a particular use or industry a payment has to be made for a unit of land so as to prevent it from being transferred to some other use or industry.

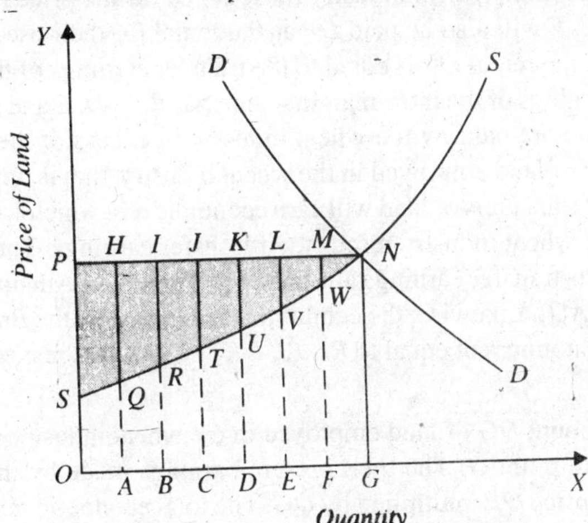

Fig. 34.5. *When the supply curve of a factor is less than perfectly elastic, a part of the earnings is economic rent and a part transfer earnings.*

The payment of price which is necessary to keep a unit of factor (land in the present case) in a certain use or industry is called transfer earnings or transfer price, because a payment of a price below this will cause it to be transferred elsewhere. Thus, ***transfer earnings are the minimum earnings which must be paid to a unit of factor in order to induce it to remain in the present use or industry.*** The transfer earnings of a unit of a factor may also be defined as the amount of earnings which it can obtain in the ***next best alternative use, occupation or industry.*** This is because reduction in the earnings of a unit of factor below its earnings in the next best alternative use will cause it to transfer itself from the present use to its next best use. For instance, if a wheat-growing industry has to keep land with it, then it must pay for the land at least its transfer earnings. Suppose, an acre of land currently employed in the production of wheat has its next best alternative of being used for the production of potato where it can earn Rs. 500. Thus the transfer earnings of this acre of land is Rs. 500. Then, in order to keep this particular acre of land in the wheat industry it must be paid at least Rs. 500, otherwise it will transfer itself to the potato-growing industry. Now, if actually this acre of land is being paid Rs. 600 in the wheat industry, it will be earning economic rent of Rs. 100 which is the difference between actual earnings of Rs. 600 in the present use and its transfer earnings of Rs. 500.

As the wheat industry uses more land, it will draw into it the land with successively higher supply price (*i.e.* transfer earnings). Thus, in Fig. 34.5, *A*th unit of land has a supply price equal to *AQ*. In other words, *AQ* must be paid to the *A*th unit of land in order to keep it in the wheat industry. Thus *AQ* represents the transfer earnings of *Ath* unit of land. Similarly, *B*th unit of land must be paid *BR* if it is to be attracted into or retained in the wheat industry. *BR* is therefore the transfer earnigs of the *Bth* unit of land. Likewise, transfer earnings of *Cth, Dth, Eth, Fth* and *G*th units of land are *CT, DU, EV, FW* and *GN* respectively. Demand curve *DD* of wheat industry for land and supply curve *SS* of land intersect at point *M* and thus determine *OP* as price for the use of land.

Suppose all units of land are equally productive in respect of wheat production. Then all acres of land will get the same price as determined by demand for land for wheat production and supply of land to it. But if various units of land are different in respect of other uses, they will have different supply prices to the wheat industry, that is, they need to be paid different prices to attract them to the wheat industry. The units of land having larger earnings in other uses will need to be paid higher prices to attract them to the wheat industry and those with smaller earnings in other uses will be required to be paid relatively smaller prices to draw them into the wheat industry. Under such conditions, therefore the supply curve of land to the wheat industry will be upward sloping, as is shown by the curve *SS* in Fig. 34.5 where price for the use of land determined is *OP* and equilibrium amount of land employed in the wheat industry is *OG*.

It will be seen from Fig. 34.5 the *G*th is the marginal unit of land employed in the wheat industry and further that the rental *OP* per unit of wheat land is equal to transfer earnings *GN* of the marginal unit *G*th of land. But, since we are assuming that all units of land are identical, *i.e*., equally productive in respect of wheat, every unit of land employed in the wheat industry must get *OP* as the price for its use. Thus intra-marginal units, *A, B, C, D, E, F* will also be paid *OP* as the rental for their use in wheat industry. But it will be seen that whereas the rental *OP* is equal to the transfer earnings of the marginal unit *G*, it is greater than the transfer earnings of the intra-marginal units, *A, B, C, D, E* and *F*. That is to say, these intra-marginal units of land are paid by the wheat industry in excess of their transfer earnings. Thus, while the marginal unit of land employed in the wheat industry, that is, unit *G* does not earn any economic rent, the intra-marginal units of land will earn economic rent which will be equal to the price or earnings they get in the wheat industry minus their transfer earnings. Thus *A*th unit of land obtains price ($AH = OP$) while its transfer earnings are only *AQ*. Therefore, Ath unit of land earns *QH* as economic rent ($QH = AH - AQ$). Likewise, the economic rent earned by the *Bth, Cth, Dth, Eth* and *Fth* units of land will earn economic rent equal to *RI, TJ, UK, VL* and *WM* respectively.

The total transfer earnings of the whole amount *OG* of land employed in the wheat industry is *OSNG* — the area under the supply curve up to point *G*. The total present earnings made by the whole amount *OG* of land is *OPNG*, that is, the price *OP* multiplied by *OG*. The total economic rent earned by the whole amount *OG* of land employed in the wheat industry is, therefore, the area *SNP* which is equal to the whole earnings *OPNG* minus the transfer earnings *OSNG*. It is now clear that *whereas in the case of society as a whole, the whole earnings of land represents a surplus or economic rent, from the viewpoint of a single industry or use, a part of the earnings are transfer earnings (which must be paid in order to retain the land in the given use or industry) and only the remaining amount of earnings (i.e., surplus over transfer earnings) represents economic rent.*

A careful study of Fig. 34.5 will reveal that economic rent as a surplus over transfer earnings is different from the rent as price for the use of land. In Fig. 34.5 whereas the price (per unit) for the use of land is *OP* and the total price (that is, the total rent for the use of land) of the whole land employed in the given industry is the area $OPNG$, the total economic rent (*i.e.*, the total rent as surplus over transfer earnings) earned is the area SNP.

Furthermore, Fig. 34.5 makes it clear that all units of land do not earn equal amounts of economic rent; different units of land earn different amounts of economic rent depending upon their transfer earnings. Thus, economic rent earned by *A*th unit is QH, *B*th unit is RI, Cth unit is TJ and so on. It should be noted that these differences in economic rent earned by different units of land are not due to the differences in their productivity in respect of wheat but due to the differences in their ability to earn in their next best uses.

When the supply of a factor is perfectly elastic, no economic rent is earned

Now, suppose that all units of land used in the wheat industry are not only identical in respect of wheat production but are also identical in respect of all other uses. In such circumstances, each unit of land employed in the wheat industry will have the same transfer earnings and therefore the supply curve of land for the wheat industry will be perfectly elastic as shown by SS curve in Fig. 34.6. In this, therefore, the transfer earnings of every unit of land employed in the wheat industry is OS. In other words, every unit of land needs to be paid equal to OS in order to retain it in the wheat industry. It will be seen in Fig. 34.6 that price per unit for the use of land in the wheat industry as determined by demand for and supply of land is also OS. Thus, every unit of land in the wheat industry gets OS and its transfer earnings are also OS. Therefore, in this case no unit of land in the wheat industry earns more than its transfer earnings, i.e., no unit of land in the *wheat industry earns any economic rent. It is, therefore, clear that when the supply of any factor is perfectly elastic to an industry, no unit of this factor will earn any economic rent*. Further, it has been seen above, that whereas to the economy or society as a whole, the supply of land is perfectly inelastic and, therefore, the whole of its earnings are *economic rent*, the supply of land to an industry (the wheat industry in the above case) may be perfectly elastic and earns no economic rent at all.

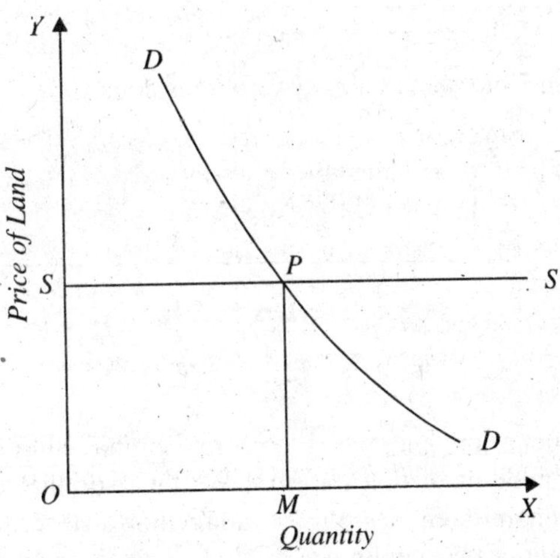

Fig. 34.6. *No economic rent is earned when the supply of a factor is perfetly elastic.*

Economic Rent can accrue to all factors

We have seen above that under certain circumstances some units of land from the viewpoint of industry may earn economic rent, *i.e.*, earnings in excess of their transfer earnings, and under some other conditions, land may not earn any economic rent at all. The same kind of analysis can be made for other factors as well. As pointed out above, the concept of *economic rent is not merely confined to land, it applies to other factors of production as well. Thus labour, capital and entrepreneurs may also be earning economic rent when their supplies are less than perfectly elastic.* Now, consider the supply of a particular kind of workers in a given industry, all of which are being paid a certain uniform wage rate by the industry. But all these workers may be heterogeneous from the point of view of the other industries. As a result of this, they would have different transfer earnings and the supply curve of this kind of workers will be upward sloping (*i.e.*, less than perfectly elastic). Since all are getting the same wage rate in the given industry which is determined by demand and supply. Now, workers whose transfer earnings are less than the wage rate will be getting economic rent or surplus. It will be seen from Fig. 34.7 that only the marginal worker (*i.e.*, *L*th worker) employed would not be obtaining any economic surplus or rent. In Fig. 34.7 the total economic rent earned by all the intra-marginal workers is equal to *WES*.

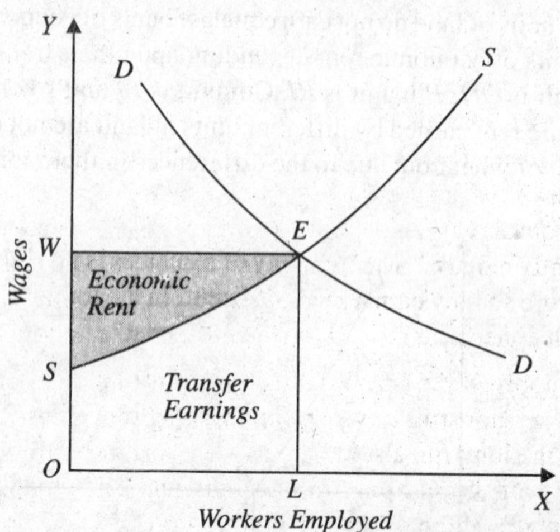

Fig. 34.7. *Economic Rent of Workers*

Likewise, entrepreneurs may be able to earn different amounts of profits in different industries. An entrepreneur will work in the industry in which he is able to get greater amount of profits and if his profits fall below a certain level, he will shift himself to the next best industry. But the additional amount of profits which he is able to earn in an industry over and above his transfer earnings (that is, the profits in the next best profitable industry) are surplus or economic rent from the point of the given industry.

Similarly, a particular kind of capital equipment is not equally efficient from the viewpoint of all industries. It will earn higher income for which it is best suited and will earn over and above the necessary income that is required to keep that in the industry. This additional income, which owner of capital equipment will get, will be the economic rent from the standpoint of that industry. We thus see that all factors under certain circumstances may earn economic rent. But this economic rent will be different if we consider their supply from the standpoint of the economy as a whole than from the standpoint of the individual industry.

QUASI RENT

The concept of quasi rent was introduced in economic theory by Marshall Marshall's concept of quasi-rent is the extension of the Ricardian concept of rent to the short run earnings of the capital equipment (such as machinery, building etc.) which are in inelastic supply in the short run. The distinguishing characterisitc of land is the fact that its supply is perfectly inelastic to changes in its price and therefore its earnings depend mainly upon the demand for it. But, in the short run, the fixed capital equipment such as machinery is likewise perfectly inelastic in supply and cost of its production is not relevant once it has been produced. During the short period, the earnings of specialised capital equipment depend mainly upon the demand conditions and are thus similar to land rent and have therefore been called rent by Marhsall. Since the capital equipment is not permanently in fixed supply like land and instead their supply is very much elastic in the long run. Marshall preferred to call their earnings in the short period as Quasi rent rather than rent.

The *quasi-rent is only temporary surplus* which is enjoyed by the owner of the capital equipment in the short run due to the increase in demand for it and this will disappear in the long run due to the increase in the supply of capital equipment in response to the increased demand. In the short run, specialised machinery has no alternative use and therefore its supply will remain fixed in the short run even if its earnings fall to zero. Thus, the transfer earnings of the capital equipment or machinery in the short run are zero. Therefore, the *whole of the earnings of the machinery in the short run are surplus over transfer earnings and therefore represent rent*. It may, however, be pointed out that some maintenance costs are required to be incurred in the short run to keep the machinery in the running order. Therefore, more precisely, the quasi rent may be defined as *the short run earnings of a machine minus the short run cost of keeping it in running order.*

There is every reason to believe that quasi rents will be generally earned in the short run by the capital equipment like machinery, building etc. This is because, however keen the competition between entrepreneurs may be, the supply of capital equipment cannot be increased in the short run.

Consequently, when very high earnings are being made from capital equipment they will not be competed away in the short run. But in the long run the position regarding the supply of capital equipment (*e.g.*, machines) is quite different. Capital equipment are man-made instruments of production and therefore their supply can be increased in the long run to meet the increased demand for them. Thus, as a result of the increase in the supply of machines in the long run their excessive earnings will be competed away. In the long run, therefore, the competitive equilibrium is reached when the earnings from the capital equipment are just sufficient to maintain them in running order and provide only normal profits to entrepreneur. Thus in the long run no surplus over cost of production is earned by the machines. Therefore, quasi rent will disappear in the long-run competitive equilibrium. Professors Stonier and Hague rightly remark, "The supply of machines is fixed in the short run whether they are paid much money or little so they earn a kind of rent. In the long run this rent disappears for it is not a true rent, but only an ephemeral reward—a 'quasi-rent".[17]

But the case of land is quite different. The supply of land being a free gift of nature and non-reproducible, its supply is perfectly inelastic in the short run as well as in the long run. Thus the surplus earnings or rent earned by land persist in the long run also. It is thus clear that the earnings of land and of capital equipment (machines etc.) are similar only in the short run. The analogy between the two does not hold in the long run because of the difference in the nature of their long-run supply. To quoto Professors Stonier and Hague again, "In the long period, machines will stand on a very different footing from land or natural ability. For machines are produced by human effort while land or human ability are gift of nature. In the long run, therefore, the supply of land will not respond to an increase in demand for it, the supply of machines will. In the long-run, therefore, land will earn rent but machines will, assuming competition, earn only just enough to make their existence worthwhile".[18]

Quasi Rent as Surplus over Variable Costs

Production of a good is possible when a fixed factor is combined with some variable factors. The amount of variable factors used depends upon the level of output produced, while the quantity of the fixed factor remains unchanged during the short period. The variable costs must be recovered in the short run, otherwise the production would be stopped. Whatever excess earnings over and above the total variable costs are made are ascribed to the machines (*i.e.*, fixed factor). Therefore, quasi-rent has also been defined as the excess of total revenue in the short run over and above the total variable costs. Thus,

Quasi Rent = Total Revenue Earned –Total Variable Costs

Since in long run, all costs are variable and, in long run competitive equilibrium, total receipts are equal to total costs (including normal profits to the entrepreneur), no excess earnings over and above the costs will accrue to the machines

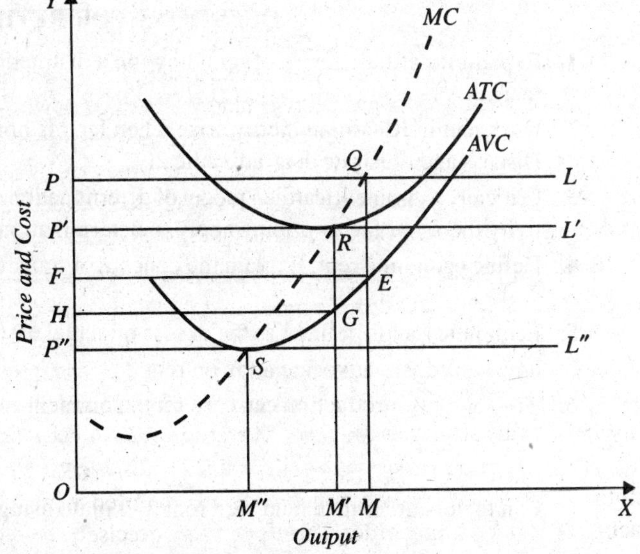

Fig. 34.8. *Quasi rent*

17. A.W. Stonier and D.C. Hague: *A Textbook of Economic Theory*, Fourth edition, 1972, p. 329.
18. *Op. cit.*, p.329

and therefore no quasi rent will be earned by the machines. The earnings of quasi rent in the short run and its disappearance in the long run is illustrated in Fig. 34.8 wherein, as usual, output is measured on the *X*-axis and price and cost are measured on the *Y*-axis. *ATC* and *AVC* represents the average total cost and average variable cost curves respectively in the short run. It should be noted that the average variable cost, *AVC* includes the cost incurred per unit of output on the variable factors such as labour, raw materials etc. as well as the cost per unit of output for keeping the machinery in the working order during the short period. (As said above, the cost of maintaining the machinery in the working order during the short period is a part of variable costs).

Now suppose that the demand for the product is such that the price *OP* the is determined. With price of the product *OP* the price line faced by an individual entrepreneur is *PL* which represents the marginal revenue as well as the average revenue. With price line *PL*, the entrepreneur is in equilibrium at point *Q* and is producing *OM* level of output. It will be seen from the figure that the total revenue earned is *OMQP*, while total variable costs incurred is *OMEF*. The area *FEQP* represents the surplus of total revenue earned over the total variable costs (*FEQP* = *OMPQ* – *OMEF*). Thus *FEQP* is quasi rent, that is, the short-run earnings of the machinery.

If now the demand for the product declines so that the price for the product falls to *OP′*. With price *OP′*, the price line is *P′L′* and equilibrium of the entrepreneur is at point *R* with output *OM′*. Now, the total revenue earned is *OM′RP′* and the total variable cost is *OM′GH*. Thus the quasi rent earned by the machinery is now *HGRP′* (= *OM′R-P′* – *OM′GH*). If the demand for the product further declines and the price falls to *OP″*, the price line confronting the entrepreneur will be *P″L″* and he will be in equilibrium position at point *S* – the minimum point of the curve *AVC*. At point *S*, the total revenue earned is just equal to the total variable costs and quasi rent earned by the machinery has fallen to zero. The entrepreneur will close down production if the price falls below *OP″*, for at a price below *OP′*, it will not be realising fully even the variable costs. It is, therefore that clear the *quasi rent cannot be negative*. But in the long run all factors are variable and all costs including costs incurred on capital equipment such as machinery must be recovered if the firm is to stay in the industry. In the long run competitive equilibrium, price must equal long run average cost. Consequently no quasi rent is earned in the long run.

QUESTIONS FOR REVIEW

1. Explain Ricardian theory of rent drawing a distinction betwen scarcity rent and differntial rent.
2. Does rent in Ricardian theory arise when land is homogenous and equally well-situated ? Discuss and illustrate diagrammatically.
3. Critically examine Ricardian model of determination of land rent. Does not marginal productivity theory of factor pricing apply to determination of land rent.
4. Define economic rent. Explain the concept of transfer earnings ? How is it related to rent ?
   D.U. B.Com (Hons.) 2000
5. Economic rent is defined as the excess of actual earnings over transfer earnings. Explain how would you advocate a tax on rent ? *D.U. BA. (Hons.) 1991*
6. Any factor of production can earn rent. Comment *D.U. B.A. (Hons.) 2000*

   OR

   Can factors other than land earn rent ? Explain using diagrams.
   D.U. B.Com. (Hons.) 1997, 1998, 2001
7. (*a*) Distinguish between economic rent and quasi rent
   D.U. B.Com (Hons) 1999, B.A. (Hons. 1996, 1997, 2001

Can quasi rent be negative ? *D.U. B.A. (Hons) 1996*

(*b*) In case the supply function of labour is 45° line passing through the origin, what would be the percentage of economic rent in the toal earnings of a factor.*D.U. B.A. (Hons.) 2001*

[**Hints.** In figure given below *DD* and *SS* are the demand and supply curves of a factor and through their intersection determine *OP* or *NE* as the price of the factor and *ON* as the quantity employed of the factor. Total earnings of the factor are equal to the area *OPEN*. The shaded area *OPEN* represents economic rent as surplus over transfer earnings. Transfer earnings of the factor are equal to *OEN*. Since supply curve *SS* makes 45° angle with the *X*-axis, $\angle EON = \angle EOP$, both being equal to 45°. Further, $ON = PE$, both being equal to the quantity of the factor employed. Besides, $\angle ENO = \angle EPO$ both being right angles. Thus triangle *OPE* is congruent to the triangle *ONE* and therefore each would be half of the total earnings *OPEN*. Thus, economic rent *OPE* is half of total earnings *OPEN*]

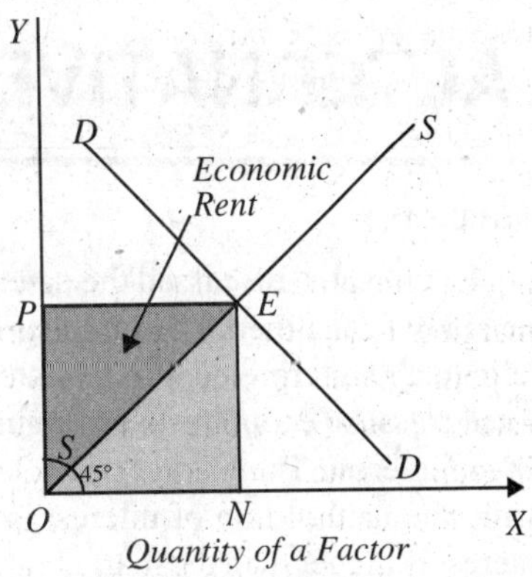

8. Is rent price determined or price determining ? Explain *D.U. B.Com (Hons) 2001*

OR

Explain the relationship between land rent, cost of production and price of the production of the land. Show that from the point of view not only of the individual firm but of the individual industry the price paid for the use of land is exactly on *all fours* with the price paid for the use of the other factors of production.

9. Explain the concept of Quasi rent. Must it always be non-negative.*D.U. B.A. (Hons) 1999*
10. What is economic rent ? Explain that economic rent arises when the supply of a factor is less than perfectly elastic.
11. The more elastic the supply curve the less the amount of payment to factors that is rent and the more that are transfer earnings. *D.U. B.A. (Hons.) 1999*
12. Division of a given factor payment between transfer earnings and economic rent depends on the type of transfer earnings considered. *D.U. B.A (Hons.) 1989*
13. Distinguish economic rent earned by a factor from the viewpoint of (1) the society as whole, (2) an individual industry and (3) the individual firm.
14. While the whole earnings of land are economic rent from the viewpoint of the society as a whole, an individual farmer earns no economic rent. Explain.
15. Explain the concept of economic rent. How is it related to transfer earnings ? Explain with the help of diagrams. *D.U. B.Com (Hons.) 2nd Year 2006, 2007*
16. Any excess that a factor earns over its reservation price is called its economic rent. Explain with the help of diagrams. *D.U., B.Com (Hons.) 2007, 2008*

[**Hint.** Note that reservation price of a factor is its transfer earnings].

CHAPTER 35
ALTERNATIVE THEORIES OF INTEREST

Introduction

Having now discussed the determination of rent of land and wages of labour, we now pass on to the study of the theory of interest. But what do we mean by interest ? Interest has been variously defined and interpreted. Firstly, interest is conceived by economists as the rate of return on capital. Some classical economists distinguished between the *natural or real rate* of interest and the *market rate of* interest. The market rate of interest is the rate at which funds can be borrowed in the market, while the natural rate of interest is rate of return on capital investment. When the natural rate of interest is higher than the market rate of interest, then there will be greater investment in capital with the result that the natural rate of interest (*i.e.*, the rate of return on capital) will fall. The equilibrium will be established when the natural rate of interest becomes equal to the market rate of interest.

Since physical capital has to be purchased with monetary funds, rate of interest becomes the rate of return over money invested in physical capital. But since money to be invested in physical capital has to be saved by some one, interest also becomes rate of return or saving. Thus, there are two concepts of interest which are related to each other. First, *the term interest is used to express a rate of return earned on capital as a factor of production. The second concept of interest refers to the price which is paid by the borrowers to lenders for the use of their saving funds*. When the borrowers are entrepreneurs or businessmen, who use the saving funds for investment in capital for them rate of return on physical capital is highly significant. However when we consider things from the viewpoint of lenders who save money to slnd it to others, the concept of interest as a price for borrowed funds is of crucial importance therefore, *interest is generally defined as price for the use of borrowed funds*.

It is also important to note the difference between the real rate of interest and nominal rate of interest. *The real rate of interest is the nominal rate of interest corrected for inflation* (*i.e.* rise in the general price level) in the economy. Thus

Real rate of interest = Nominal rate of interest – rate of inflation

In our analysis in this chapter we will be concerned with real rate of interest.

For explaining the determination of rate of interest, the three theories have been put forward. First theory of interest is *Classical Theory of Interest* which explains interest as determined by saving and investment. Secondly, neo-classical economists such as Wicksell, Ohlin, Haberler, Robertson, Viner developed what is known as *Loanable Funds or Neo-Classical Theory of interest*. These writers consider the interplay of monetary and non-monetary forces in the determination of the rate of interest. At their hands, interest theory ceased to be purely real or non-monetary theory. In their view, monetary factors along with the real factors determine the rate of interest. The loanable funds theory is partly a monetary theory of interest.

But monetary theory gained more recognition with the publication of *Keynes' General Theory*. According to Keynes, interest is a purely a monetary phenomenon and as such it is determined by the demand for money (*i.e.*, liquidity preference) and the supply of money. According to him, interest is a price not for the sacrifice of waiting or time preference but for parting with liquidity.

Since he emphasised the role of *liquidity preference* in the determination of the interest rate, his theory is known as liquidity preference theory of interest. Keynesian theory is a purely *monetary theory*.

It is worth noting that all these theories of interest seek to explain the determination of the rate of interest through the equilibrium between the forces of demand and supply. In other words, all these theories are *demand and supply theories*. The difference between the various theories of interest lies in the answer to the question : *demand for what and supply of what*. According to the classical theory, rate of interest is determined by *demand for savings to make investment and the supply of savings*. Loanable-funds theory seeks to explain the determination of the rate of interest through the equilibrium between *demand for and supply of loanable funds*. Besides savings, loanable funds consist of funds derived from other sources as well. Keynesian theory of interest explains the determination of interest through the equilibrium between *demand for and supply of money*.

Another point worth mentioning is that a theory of interest has to explain two things. First, why does interest arise ? Secondly, how rate of interest is determined ? All the three theories mentioned above explain both these aspects of interest.

CLASSICAL THEORY OF INTEREST

As mentioned above, this theory seeks to explain the determination of the rate of interest through the interaction of the demand for savings to make investment and the supply of savings. Since this theory explains the determination of the rate of interest by real forces such as thriftiness, time preference and productivity of capital, it is also called the *real theory of interest*. Various classical writers differ a good deal from each other in respect of their views about interest. Some of them laid emphasis on the forces governing the supply of savings. Thus they considered interest as a price for abstinence or waiting or time preference. Some others like J.B. Clark and F.H. Knight thought the marginal productivity of capital, which is a force that operates on the demand side of savings, determines the rate of interest.

Fisher and Bohm-Bawerk explained the interest with both types of factors. There is a basic assumption that is common to all classical writers. It is that all of them assume full employment of resources. In other words, in their models if more resources are to be devoted to investment, that is, to the production of capital goods, some resources have to be withdrawn from the production of consumers' goods. According to this theory, money which is lent out to the entrepreneurs for investment in capital goods is to be made available by those who save out of their incomes. By abstaining from consumption they release resources for the production of capital goods. In order to induce people to save and refrain from consuming a part of their incomes, they must be offered some interest as a reward. To persuade them to save more, the higher rate of interest has to be offered. So far the various classical economists agreed but they differed in detail about the nature of interest We shall discuss below the views of some of them.

Interest is a price for abstinence or waiting. It was Nasau Senior who first pointed out that saving involved a sacrifice of abstinence and interest is a price for this sacrifice. Any one who saves some money and is therefore able to lend it to others abstains from consuming a part of his income and in order to induce him to do so, he must be paid interest by the borrower. Thus, according to Senior, interest arises because of the abstinence involved in the act of saving. Without giving him the interest as compensation, the individuals will not like to undergo the sacrifice of abstaining from consumption. The idea of abstinence was criticised by some economists, in particular by Karl Marx, who pointed out that the rich people who are the main source of savings are able to save without making any real sacrifice of abstinence. They save because something is left over after they have indulged in consumption to their heart's desire. In order to avoid this criticism Marshall substituted the word *waiting* for "abstinence". According to him, when a person saves money and lends it to others, he does not abstain from consumption for all time ; *he merely postpones consumption*. But the individual who lends his savings has to wait until he gets back the money. Thus, the person who saves money and lends it to others undergoes the sacrifice of waiting. To induce people to save and wait some price has to be paid to them as compensation for making this sacrifice. According to this view, interest is a price for waiting.

Interest is paid because of time preference (Fisher's Theory). The views of Irving Fisher, an eminent American economist, are very popular among economists. According to him, enjoyment interst needs to be paid to the lenders because people prefer present enjoyment of goods to future of them. Fisher laid greater emphasis on time preference as a cause of interest. But along with time preference he also considered the role of marginal productivity of capital for which he used the term '*rate of return over cost*' as a factor that also determines interest.

Rate of interest arises because people prefer present satisfaction to future satisfaction. They are therefore impatient to spend their incomes in the present. According to Fisher, interest is a compensation for the time preference of the individual. The greater the impatience to spend money in the present, that is, the greater the preference of individuals for the present enjoyment of goods to future enjoyment of them, the higher will have to be the rate of interest to induce them to lend money.

The degree of impatience to spend income in the present depends upon the size of the income, the distribution of income over time, the degree of certainty regarding enjoyment in the future and the temperament and character of the individual. The people whose incomes are large are likely to have their present wants more fully satisfied. Therefore, these rich people will discount the future at a relatively lower rate of interest (that is, their time preference will be less) and will be required to be paid a relatively lower rate of interest. As regards distribution of income over time, three kinds of situation are possible. The income may be uniform throughout one's life or may increase with age or decrease with age. If it is uniform the degree of impatience to spend in the present will be determined by the size of the income and the temperament of the individual. If income increases with age, it means the future is well provided for and the degree of impatience to spend money in the present (that is, time preference) will be greater. On the other hand, if income decreases with age, the degree of impatience to spend money at present will be less.

As regards certainty of enjoyment in the future, if the individual is sure of enjoyment of income in the future, other things remaining the same, the impatience to spend money in the present will be less, that is, the degree of time preference will be smaller. Finally, the character and the temperament of the individual will also determine his time preference. A man of foresight will be less impatient to spend income in the present, that is, his rate of time preference will be less as compared to that of a spendthrift. The rate of time preference is also influenced by expectation of life. If a man expects to live long, his preference for spending income in the present will be comparatively low.

It is clear from the above analysis that Fisher, like Bohm Bawerk, regarded the rate of interest as an agio on the present goods exchanged for future goods of the same kind. Fisher based his explanation of the rate of interest on his concept of income. According to him, interest is the link between expected future income values and the present capital values based on them. The present capital value of the stream of expected income in future years depends on the rate interest (*i.e.*, rate of time preference) at which they have to be discounted. He says, "The value of the orchard depends upon the value of its crops and in this dependence lurks implicitly the rate of interest itself."

As said above, Fisher also regarded productivity of capital which he called *rate of return over cost*, as a determinant of interest. According to him, several different uses of capital which may yield different income streams are open to the owner of capital. The greater the expected income

1. Irving Fisher, *Rate of Interest*, (1907), p. 13.

stream from use of capital, the greater will be the rate of interest. Another point worth mentioning is that Fisher introduced risk and uncertainly in his explanation of interest. According to him, individual has a choice of any *one* of a number of uncertain income streams so that instead of a single rate of interest representing the rate of exchange between this year and next year we now find a great variety of rates according to the risks involved.

Determination of the Rate of Interest in the Classical Theory

According to the classical theory rate of interest is determined by the supply of savings and demand for savings to invest. We have explained above the forces working on the side of supply of saving. Some classical economists laid stress on the abstinence or waiting involved in the act of savings and supply of them and some others emphasised the role of time preference as a determinant of the supply of savings. According to this theory, the money which is to be used for purchasing capital goods is made available by those who save from their current income. By postponing consumption of a part of their income they release resources for the production of capital goods. It is assumed in this theory that *savings are interest elastic. The higher the rate of interest, the more the savings which people will be induced to make*. Besides, at higher rate of interest, savings would be forthcoming from those persons whose rates of time preference are more strongly weighed in favour of present satisfaction. The supply curve of savings will, therefore, slope upward to the right.

On the other hand, the demand for savings comes from the entrepreneurs or firms which desire to invest in capital goods. Capital goods are demanded because they can be used to produce further goods which can be sold to earn income. Thus capital goods have a revenue productivity like all other factors. For any given type of capital asset, *e.g.*, a machine , it is possible to draw a marginal revenue productivity curve showing the addition made to total revenue by an additional unit of a machine at various levels of the stock of that machine.

As said above, like other factors of production, capital has marginal revenue productivity. But the marginal revenue productivity of capital is a more complex concept than that of other factors because capital has a life of many years. A capital asset continues to yield returns for many years. But the future is quite uncertain. Therefore, the entrepreneurs have to judge the uncertainties of the future and estimate prospective yield or income from a capital asset after making allowance for

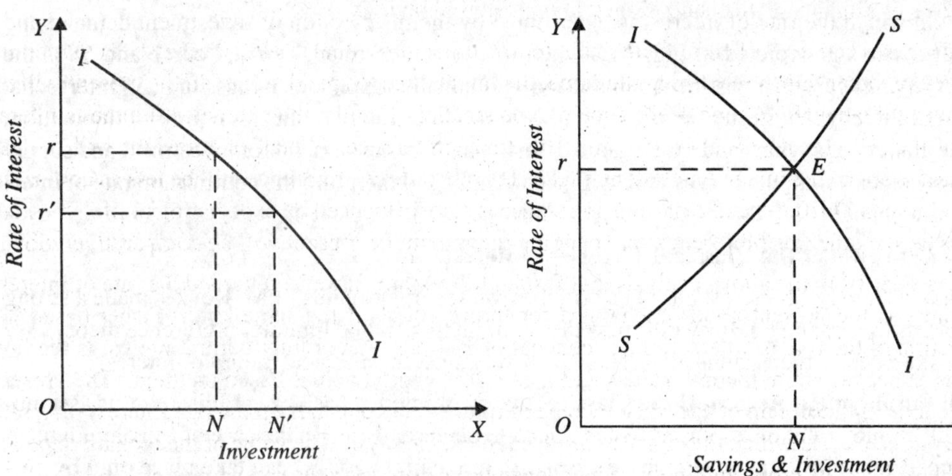

Fig. 35.1. *Investment Demand Curve*

Fig. 35.2. *Classical Theory: Determination of Interest*

maintenance and operating costs. In other words, they have to find out the *net expected return* of a capital asset. This net expected return is expressed as percentage of the cost of capital asset. The more capital assets of a giv · kind there are, the less income will be expected to accrue from a

marginal unit of it. Therefore, the marginal revenue productivity curve of capital slopes downward to the right.

We have seen in the previous chapters that a firm in a perfectly competitive factor market will hire a factor upto the point at which the price of that factor equals the marginal revenue product of the factor. Now, the marginal revenue product of a capital asset can be regarded as marginal revenue product of money invested in that capital asset. The *price* of money invested in capital assets is the rate of interest which a person has to pay on the borrowed funds. An entrepreneur will continue making investment in capital assets as long as the expected net rate of return, or in other words, marginal revenue produc of capital or investment is greater than the rate of interest. He will be in equilibrium position when marginal revenue product of capital (or expected rate of return) falls to the level of the rate of interest. Since the marginal revenue product curve of capital slopes downward, it will become profitable to purchase more capital goods as the rate of interest falls, *i.e.*, with the fall in the rate of interest more money will be demanded for investment. Thus, the investment demand curve connecting the rate of interest with the investment demand will be downward sloping. In other words, investment demand is assumed to be interest-elastic.

The way in which the investment demand increases as the interest falls is illustrated in Fig.35.1 where *II* is the investment demand curve showing the falling marginal revenue productivity of capital which, in other words, indicates the declining marginal net expected return as more investment is undertaken. When the rate of interest is *Or*, the entrepreneurs will make investment upto *ON* because the marginal net expected return is equal to *Or* rate of interest when *ON* investment is made. Now, it the rate of interest falls to *Or′*, then more capital projects will become profitable to be undertaken. Therefore, as a result of the fall in the rate of interest to *Or′*, investment increases to *ON′*

It is clear from the above analysis that investment demand curve slopes downward to the right. With the change in the rate of interest, investment will change.

Equilibrium between Demand and Supply. As seen above, according to the classical theory, the rate of interest is determined by the intersection of the investment demand curve and the supply of savings curve – the curves showing the relation of investment and savings to the rate of interest. The way in which the rate of interest is determined by the intersection of investment demand and supply of savings is depicted in Fig. 35.2 where *II* is the investment demand curve and *SS* is the supply of savings curve. Investment demand curve *II* and the supply of savings curve *SS* intersect at point *E* and thereby determine *Or* as the equilibrium rate of interest. In this equilibrium position, *ON* is the amount of savings and investment. If any change in the demand for investment and supply of savings comes about, the curves will shift accordingly and therefore the equilibrium rate of interest will also change.

Critical Appraisal of the Classical Theory of Interest

Classical theory of interest has been criticised on several grounds. J.M. Keynes made a strong attack on this theory and put forward a new theory of interest called liquidity preference theory. We shall consider below the various criticisms levelled against the classical theory of interest.

Full Employment Assumption. Classical theory of interest has been critcised for its assumption of full employment of resources which is said to be unrealistic. In the case of full employment of resources, more investment (*i.e.*, production of more capital goods) can take place only by curtailing consumption and there by releasing resources from the production of consumption goods. Therefore, when full employment of resources prevails, people have to be paid interest so as to induce them to abstain from consumption so that more resources should be devoted to the production of capital goods. But, when unemployed resources are found on a large scale there is no need for paying people to abstain from consumption or to postpone consumption and wait in order that more savings for undertaking investment should take place. More investment then can be undertaken by employing the unemployed or unutilised productive resources. Prof. Dillard rightly remarks : "Within the framework of a system of theory built on the assumption of full employment, the notion of interest as reward for waiting or abstinence is highly plausible. It is the premise that resources are typically fully employed that lacks plausibility in the contemporary world."[2]

Changes in Income Level Ignored. By assuming full employment the classical theory has ignored the changes in income level and their effect on savings and investment. Classical theory establishes a direct functional relationship between interest rate and the volume of savings. As the rate of interest goes up, more savings will take place. But at the higher rate of interest investment demand will be less with the result that interest will tend to fall to the level where savings and investment are in equilibrium. But this is not so realistic firstly, because the direct functional relationship between savings and the rate of interest is doubtful, and secondly, because when more savings take place as a result of the rise in the rate of interest, these more savings should lead to more investment, as according to classical theory investment is governed by savings. But, in the whole process of adjustment, change in income is not at all considered by the classical theory. As a matter of fact, when the rate of interest rises and investment shrinks as a consequence, income will decline. With the decline in income, the savings will decline. Therefore, the equality between savings and investment are brought about not so much through changes in the rate of interest but through changes in income.

Now, take the opposite case. If the rate of interest falls, according to classical theory, the investment demand will increase. But because of the lower rate of interest the greater supply of savings would not be forthcoming. Therefore, in classical theory more investment cannot take place even at lower rates of interest, because of the paucity of savings at lower rates of interest. But this is not what actually happens. At a lower rate of interest, more investment will be undertaken and increase in the investment will lead to the increase in income via multiplier. And out of increased income more would be saved. Again the tendency to equalise savings and investment is brought about by changes in income. Thus, the lower rate of interest through the increase in investment and income leads to the rise in savings. But this is quite contrary to the classical theory wherein at the lower rate of interest small savings are made.

From the above analysis it follows that by neglecting the changes in income the classical theory is led into the error of viewing the rate of interest as the factor which brings about he equality of savings and investment. The classical theory ignores the changes in income level because it assumes full employment of resources. When the resources are fully employed, income level will remain constant, production techniques being given. Now, it was Keynes who abandoned the assumption of full employment and, therefore, considered the change in the income level and its relation with savings and investment. Quoting Prof. Dillard again, *"The difference between the traditional theory of interest and Keynes' money theory of interest is a fundamental aspect of the difference between the economics of full employment and the economics of less than full employment."*[3]

Disincentive Effect of Lesser Consumption on Investment Ignored. According to the classical theory, more investment can occur only by cutting down consumption. More the reduction in consumption, the greater the increase in investment in capital goods. But as we know the demand for capital goods is a derived demand; it is derived from the demand for consumer goods. Therefore, the reduction in consumption, which means decrease in demand for consumer goods, will adversely affect the demand for capital goods and will thus reduce the inducement to invest. The disincentive effect of the fall in consumption on investment is glossed over by the classical theory.

As we shall see later, in Keynes' theory more investment does not occur at the expense of

---

2. D. Dillard, *Economics of J.M. Keynes*, p. 162.
3. *Op. cit.*, p. 160.

consumption. In Keynes' theory, in view of the unemployment of resources, more investment is possible by utilising the unemployed and under-employed resources. When investment increases, it leads to the increase in the income level. With the increase in incomes, people will consume more. Thus in Keynesian analysis more investment leads to more consumption, or in other words, investment and consumption go together. Keynesian analysis is more realistic in the context of unemployment of resources prevailing in the economy.

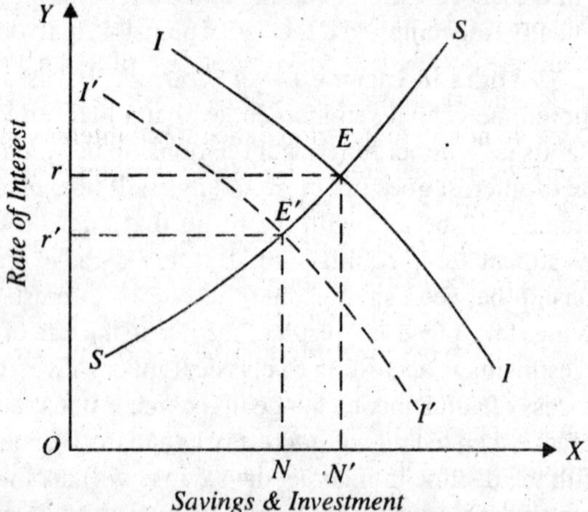

Fig. 35.3. *According to Classical Theory, investment schedule can change without affecting the savings schedule.*

Independence of Savings Schedule from Investment Schedule Assumed. Another implication of assuming full employment and constant level of income by classical theory of interest is that investment demand schedule can change without causing a change in the savings schedule. For instance, according to classical theory, if investment demand curve *II* shifts downward to the dotted position *I'*I *'* (Fig. 35.3) because the profit prospects have lessened, then according to classical theory, the new equilibrium rate of interest is *Or'* where the new investment demand curve *I'I'* intersects the supply curve *SS* which remains unaltered. But this is quite untenable. As a result of the fall in investment, income will decline. Since the supply curve of savings is drawn with a given level of income, when income falls, there will be less savings than before and as a result savings curve will shift to the left. But the classical theory does not take into account changes in the income level as a result of changes in investment and regards the savings schedule as independent of investment schedule which is not correct and realistic.

Indeterminateness. Finally, the classical theory, as pointed out by Keynes, is indeterminate. Position of the savings curve varies with the level of income. There will be different savings schedules for different levels of income. As income rises, the savings curve will shift to the right and as income falls the savings curve will shift to the left. Thus, we cannot know the position of the savings curve unless we already know the level of income, and if we do not know the position of the savings curve, we cannot know the rate of interest. It follows therefore that we cannot know what the rate of interest will be unless we already know what the income level is. But we cannot know the income level without already knowing the rate of interest because with the changes in the rate of interest investment will change which will in turn bring about changes in the income level. The classical theory, therefore, offers no determinate solution to the problem of interest rate determination and is indeterminate.

Savings out of current income is not the only source of supply of funds. As we have seen, the classical theory considered only savings out of current income as constituting the supply of funds in the market. But savings out of current income is not the only source of capital supply. People have usually past hoarded savings, which they may dishoard in a period adding to the supply of funds in the market. Further, now-a-days bank credit has become a very important source of investible funds which are also not taken into account by the classical theory.

We have critically explained the classical theory of interest. Some of the shortcomings of the classical theory were removed by the loanable funds theory which we now turn to discuss.

LOANABLE FUNDS THEORY OF INTEREST

Another school of thought developed what is called loanable funds theory of interest. Among the principal economists who contributed to the development of loanable funds theory mention may be made of Wicksell, Bertil Ohlin, Robertson, Myrdal, Lindahl, Viner, etc. According to this theory, real forces, such as thriftiness, waiting, time-preference and productivity of capital alone do not go to determine the rate of interest, monetary forces such as hoarding and dishoarding of money, money created by banks, monetary loans for consumption purposes also play a part in the determination of the rate of interest. Thus the exponents of the loanable funds theory saw the interplay of monetary and non-monetary forces in the determination of the rate of interest. We, therefore, see that loanable funds theory is a monetary theory of interest, although it is only partly monetary since it also recognises the importance of real forces such as thriftiness and productivity of capital in the determination of the rate of interest.

According to this theory, rate of interest is determined by demand for and supply of loanable funds. The supply of loanable funds consists of savings out of disposable income, dishoarding, money created by the banks and disinvestment (*i.e.*, disentangling of fixed and working capital). The demand for loanable funds is composed of the demand for investment, demand for consumption and demand for hoarding money. We shall discuss below in detail these several sources of supply and demand of loanable funds.

Supply of Loanable Funds

Savings. Savings by individuals and households constitute the most important source of the supply of loanable funds. In the loanable funds theory savings are considered in either of the two ways. Firstly, in the sense of *ex-ante* savings, that is, savings planned by individuals and households in the beginning of a period in the hope of expected incomes and anticipated expenditures on consumption, and secondly, in the sense of Robertsonian savings, that is, the difference between the income of the preceding period (which becomes disposable in the present period) and consumption of the present period. In both these senses of savings it is assumed that the amount of savings varies with rate of interest. More savings will be forthcoming at higher rates of interest and *vice versa*. It is granted that savings by individuals and households primarily depend upon the size of their income. But, given the level of income, savings vary with the rate of interest; the higher the rate of interest, the greater the volume of savings. Therefore, supply curve of savings slopes upward to the right.

Like individuals, business concerns also save. When the business is of the type of single proprietorship or partnership, a part of the income from the business is used for consumption purposes and a part is kept for further expansion of the business. When the business is of the type of joint stock company, a part of the earnings is distributed as dividends to the shareholders and a part of the earnings of the company is retained undistributed which constitutes the *corporate savings*. Business savings depend partly upon the current rate of interest. A higher rate of the interest is likely to encourage business savings as a substitute for borrowing from the loan market. These savings are mostly used for investment purposes by the business firms themselves and, therefore, most of them do not enter into the market for loanable funds. But these savings influence the rate of interest since they serve as substitute for borrowed funds and, therefore, reduce the market demand for loanable funds. In Fig. 35.4, the curve labelled as *S* indicates the supply curve of savings which slopes upward to the right.

Dishoarding. Dishoarding of the past accumulated savings constitutes another source of supply of loanable funds. Individuals may possess idle cash balances hoarded from the incomes of the previous periods which they may dishoard in a period. When people dishoard, the idle cash balances become active cash balances in the present period and thus add to the supply of loanable funds. People hoard money because of their preference for liquidity. When the rate of interest rises or when the prices of securities decline, they may like to take advantage of these market movements and thus dishoard money for lending it to others or for purchasing securities. At a higher rate of interest, the individuals possessing idle cash balances will be induced to dishoard more money. At very low rates of interest, their parting with liquidity will not be rewarded sufficiently and, therefore, they will hold on to money. It is evident that *dishoarding is interest-elastic and*, therefore, the curve of dishoarding slopes upwards to the right as is shown in Fig. 35.4 by curve *DH*.

Bank Money. The banking system is another important source of the supply of loanable funds. The commercial banks by creating credit money advance loans to the businessmen and industries for investment. Banks can also reduce the supply of loanable funds by contracting their lending. Banks also purchase and sell securities and thereby affect the supply of loanable funds. The supply curve of funds provided by banks is to some degree interest-elastic. Generally speaking, the banks would like to lend more money at higher rates of interest than at lower ones. Therefore, supply curve of bank money also slopes upward to the right as is shown by the curve *BM* in Fig. 35.4.

Disinvestment. Disinvestment is another source of the supply of loanable funds. Disinvestment means disentangling of the present fixed and working capital. Usually a good amount of depreciation reserves are kept so as to replace the fixed capital when it is completely worn out. When there is a declining tendency in certain industries due to some structural changes in the economy, the entrepreneurs may not like to remain tied to those industries and therefore they may allow the existing stock of machines and other equipment belonging to those industries wear out without replacement. As a result, they may bring the depreciation reserves in the market for loanable funds. Similarly, working capital invested in business may be withdrawn gradually and made available as loanable funds. When disinvestment is decided to be undertaken, then not only the depreciation reserves but also a part of the revenue earned from the sale of the output instead of going into capital replacement flows into the market for loanable funds. At higher rates of interest, the entrepreneurs will generally contemplate a greater amount of disinvestment. Prof. M.M. Bober rightly remarks, "Disinvestment is encouraged somewhat by a high rate of interest on loanable funds. When the rate is high, some of the current capital may not produce a marginal revenue product to match this rate of interest. The firm may decide to let this capital run down and to put the depreciation funds in the loan market."[4] It is, therefore, clear that disinvestment curve will also slope upward to the right, as is indicated by the curve *DI* in Fig. 35.4.

By lateral summation of the curves of savings (*S*), dishoarding (*DH*), bank money (*BM*) and disinvestment (*DI*) we get the total supply curve of loanable funds *SL* which slopes upward to the right showing that a greater amount of loanable fund will be available at higher rates of interest and vice versa.

Demand for Loanable Funds

Having now explained the sources of supply of loanable funds, we turn to explain the factors which determine the demand for loanable funds. Loanable funds theory also differs from the classical theory in its explanation of the demand for funds. Whereas the classical theory considers only the demand for funds for investment purposes, the loanable funds theory also considers the demand of loans for consumption and demand for hoarding money, apart from the demand of funds for investment. In considering the hoarding of money, loanable funds theory incorporates in itself the factor of liquidity preference on which Keynes later laid great stress as an important determinant of interest. We shall explain below these different sources of demand for loanable funds.

Investment Demand. Demand for investment constitutes an important factor working on the side of demand for loanable funds. Investment demand includes businessmen's borrowings for purchasing or making of new capital goods including the building up of inventories. The price of

4. M.M. Bober, *Intermediate Price and Income Theory* (1955), p. 371.

obtaining the loanable funds required to purchase or make in capital goods is obviously the rate of interest. It will pay businessmen to demand and undertake investment of loanable funds upto the point where the expected net rate of return on investment equals the rate of interest. In the loanable

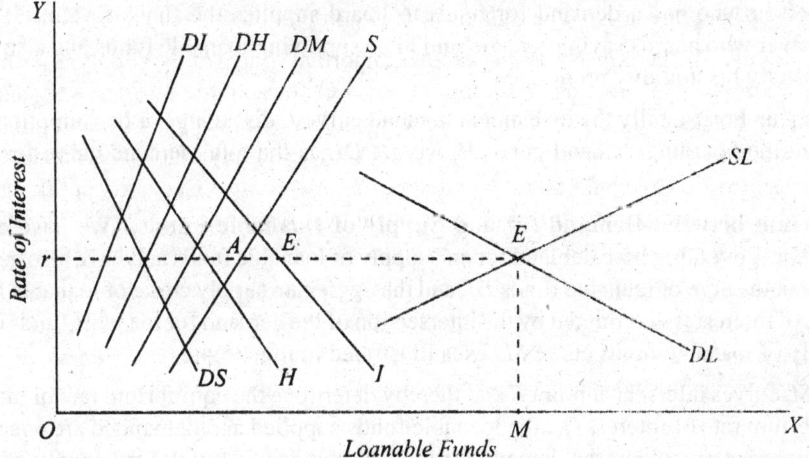

Fig. 35.4. *Determination of rate of interest*

funds theory, demand for investment depends upon the marginal revenue productivity of capital (or the marginal rate of return) in the same way as in the classical theory. When the rate of interest falls, businessmen will find it profitable to increase investment in capital goods with the result that their demand for loanable funds will rise. We thus see that demand of loanable funds for investment is interest-elastic ; at a low rate of interest, there will be greater investment demand and vice versa. Therefore, the curve of investment demand for loanable funds slopes downward to the right as is shown by the curve *I* in Fig. 35.4.

Consumption Demand. Another important source of demand for loanable funds are the loans desired to be taken by the people for consumption purposes. Loans for consumption purposes are demanded by the people when they wish to make purchases in excess of their current incomes and idle cash resources. The loans for consumption purposes are demanded generally for buying durable use goods such as houses, automobiles, refrigerators, television sets, air conditioners etc. Whereas a lower rate of interest will induce people to borrow more for consumption, the higher rates of interest will discourage borrowing for consumption. Therefore, consumption demand for loanable funds slopes downward to the right and is shown by the curve labelled as *DS* in Fig. 35.4.

Demand for Hoarding. Lastly, demand for money to hoard is another important factor determining demand for loanable funds. Demand for hoarding money arises because of people's preference for liquidity, *i.e.*, for cash balances. Hoarded money represents idle cash balances. People save money when they do not spend all their disposable income on consumption. Now the people can lend out their savings to others or purchase securities with their savings or invest their savings in real capital assets. *Another alternative use of income saved (i.e., income not spent on consumption) is to hoard them, that is, to hold them as idle cash balances.* People can also hoard money when they sell securities or assets owned by them and not spending the proceeds obtained therefrom. Now the question arises as to why people hoard money when they can earn some income by lending it to others or investing it in securities or capital assets. An important reason for the demand for hoarding money is that people like to take advantage of the changes in the rate of interest or changes in the prices of securities in the future. At higher current rates of interest, people will hoard less money because much of the money will be lent out to take advantage of the higher rates of interest, and people will hoard more money at lower rates of interest because loss suffered in hoarding money in this case will not be very much. It follows therefore that the curve of demand for hoarding money will slope downwards as is shown by the curve *H* in Fig. 35.4. An important point to be noted here is that the person who has a demand for funds to hoard supplies the funds to himself for that purpose. A saver who hoards savings can be said to be supplying loanable funds and also demanding them to satisfy his liquidity preference.

By adding up horizontally the investment demand curve *I*, dissavings or consumption demand curve *DS*, and the hoarding demand curve *H*, we get *DL* as the total demand curve for loanable funds.

Equilibrium between Demand for and Supply of Loanable Funds. We have explained above the factors governing both demand for and supply of loanable funds and have also derived the aggregate demand curve of loanable funds *DL* and the aggregate supply curve of loanable funds *SL*. Now, the rate of interest is determined by the intersection of the demand for loanable funds curve *DL* and the supply of loanable funds curve *SL*, as is illustrated in Fig. 35.4.

DL and *SL* curves intersect at point *E* and thereby determine the equilibrium rate of interest *Or*. At the equilibrium rate of interest *Or*, the loanable funds supplied and demanded are equal to *OM*. At any other interest rate either the demand for loanable funds will exceed the supply of loanable funds or the supply of loanable funds will exceed the demand for loanable funds and therefore there will be a change in the rate of interest until it reaches the level or where demand for and supply of loanable funds are equal.

It should be noted that *at the equilibrium rate of interest where aggregate demand for and supply of loanable funds are equal, planned savings and investment may not be equal*, as is the case in Fig. 35.4. It will be seen from this figure that at equilibrium rate of interest *Or*, while investment is equal to *rE*, the savings are equal to *rA*. As a result of investment being greater than savings, income will increase. With the increase in income, the savings curve *S* and therefore the aggregate supply curve *SL* will shift to the right. And this shift in the savings and supply of loanable funds curve *SL* will cause a change in the rate of interest. We thus see that the *rate of interest as determined by the demand for and supply of loanable funds will not be a stable one if there is inequality between savings and investment at that rate*. This inequality will bring about a change in the income and thereby a change in the savings and supply of loanable funds. As a result, the rate of interest will tend to change. A *stable equilibrium rate of interest will be achieved where intersection of the aggregate supply and demand curves of loanable funds determines the equilibrium rate of interest at which the savings and investment are also equal*. But in a single period, the rate of interest at which demand and supply of loanable funds are equal will prevail in spite of the inequality of savings and investment, although the equilibrium rate of interest in such a situation will tend to change over time through changes in income.

We have explained above the various components of demand for and supply of loanable funds and have shown how the equilibrium rate of interest is determined. We have taken the savings (*S*) on the supply side, dissavings (*DS*) on the demand side ; dishoarding (*DH*) on the supply side and hoarding (*H*) on the demand side ; investment (*I*) on the demand side and disinvestment on the supply side. We can further simplify our analysis of components of demand for and supply of loanable funds and bring out the conditions for the equilibrium rate of interest in a better way if we use *net of savings* (*i.e.*, savings *minus* dissavings), *net* of hoarding (*i.e.*, hoarding *minus* dishoarding) and *net* of investment (*i.e.*, investment *minus* disinvestment). This will become clear from the following :

We know that equilibrium rate of interest is determined where

Supply of loanable funds = Demand for loanable funds

or $S + DH + BM + DI = I + DS + H$

By taking DS to the left hand side and DH and DI to the right hand side we get

$(S - DS) + BM = (I - DI) + (H - DH)$

Or Net S + BM = Net I + Net H

Or, Net savings + Bank money = Net Investment + Net hoarding

Thus we see that the rate of interest will be at the equilibrium level where the supply of net savings and bank money will be equal to the demand for investment and net hoarding. This is the essence of the loanable funds theory of interest.

Critical Evaluation of Loanable Funds Theory

Loanable funds theory is superior to classical theory of interest. It has greatly improved our understanding of the forces working on the supply of and demand for loanable funds. It makes quite comprehensive analysis of the determination of the rate of interest and takes into consideration all the relevant factors which have a bearing on the rate of interest, namely, saving or thriftiness, investment demand, hoarding and bank credit. However, loanable funds theory has been criticised by Keynes and Keynesians.

First, it was asserted by Keynes that the concept of hoarding as used in loanable funds theory is quite dubious. This is so because hoarding simply cannot increase or decrease as long as the amount of money remains the same. Money in circulation in an economy has to be in somebody's cash balances at any time. According to him, if the quantity of money remains the same, then the total amount of cash balances in the beginning and at the end of a period will be the same ; the greater hoarding of money by one person must have been offset by the dishocarding of any other person. But this criticism of loanable funds theory is misplaced. As a matter of fact, the effective supply of money in a society does not merely depend upon the quantity of money, it also depends upon the velocity of circulation of money. And it is this velocity of circulation which changes as a result of hoarding or dishoarding and, therefore, involves the changes in the effective supply of money, although the amount of money in existence may have remained the same.

Thus, we see that the hoarding can occur even if the quantity of money in circulation remains constant during a period and, therefore, Keynes's objection against the loanable funds theory on this ground is not valid. As a matter of fact, Keynes himself introduced distinction between '*active*' and '*idle*' balances. Now, increase in idle balances at the expense of active balances is hoarding and results in a reduction in the velocity of circulation of money. If the time duration of idleness of money (*i.e.*, period of rest between the two transfers) increases, it will mean hoarding which will reduce the supply of loanable funds in the market and thus affect the determination of the rate of interest.

Keynes also criticised the loanable funds theory on the ground that like classical theory it *did not provide a determinate solution to the interest-rate determination* and involved what was called circular reasoning. According to him, since savings is an important constituent of the supply of loanable funds, the supply of loanable funds curve will vary with the level of income which determines savings. We, therefore, cannot know the rate of interest unless we know what the level of income is. And we cannot know the level of income unless we know the rate of interest since rate of interest affects investment which in turn determines the level of income. Following Keynes, Hansen also disapproves loanable funds theory and maintains that "the schedule of loanable funds is composed of savings plus net additions to loanable funds from new money and dishoarding of idle balances. But since the savings portion of the schedule varies with the level of disposable income, it follows that the total supply schedule of loanable funds also varies with income making the rate of interest indeterminate."[5]

5. A.H. Hansen, *Guide to Keynes*, p. 141.

Keynes was correct in criticising the classical theory for its ignoring the effect of changes in the level of income upon the supply of savings but his criticism against loanable funds theory is not valid. This is because *loanable funds theory seeks to explain the interest rate determination through period analysis with a lag of one period*, which makes the theory quite determinate. In loanable funds theory, the supply of savings is regarded as being determined by the income of the preceding period and savings so determined along with other components of supply and the demand for loanable funds determine the rate of interest in the current period. The current rate of interest so determined affects the level of income in the succeeding period through investment. Prof. Halm rightly maintains that "It is not circular reasoning to say that income is influenced by investment, investment by rates of interest, rates of interest by the supply of loanable funds, the supply of loanable funds by savings, and savings in turn, by the income received in the last period."[6] We, therefore, conclude that charge against loanable funds theory that it is indeterminate is untenable. In fact, it is Keynes's own liquidity preference theory of interest, as we shall see later, which is indeterminate.

Another charge against the loanable funds theory is that it is based upon the assumption of full employment level of income which does not hold in the real world. And the superiority of Keynes's theory is sought to be proved on the basis of its being based upon realistic assumption of less than full employment. But this is not correct interpretation of loanable funds theory. As we have seen above in the explanation of the loanable funds theory that it takes into account the increases in the level of income as a result of investment and their influence on savings. According to loanable funds theory, stable equilibrium regarding rate of interst will be reached at the level where not only demand for and supply of loanable funds are equal also saving and investment are equal. If the full-employment were income the assumption, how the income could increase ?

As a matter of fact, loanable funds theory is a synthesis between the classical theory and Keynes's liquidity preference theory since it takes into account the savings and investment demand of the classical theory as well as liquidity preference of Keynes's theory. By incorporating hoarding and dishoarding it considers the liquidity preference on which Keynes laid a great stress as an important factor determining the rate of interest. Besides, loanable funds theory has been described as dynamic. Thus Prof. H.G. Johnson[7] has suggested that the Keynesian theory is 'static' seeking only to explain the state of affairs in a short period equilibrium and how changes in circumstances will alter the equilibrium values, while the loanable funds theory is dynamic and seeks to explain precisely how interest and income move from one equilibrium level to another when circumstances have changed.

KEYNES'S LIQUIDITY PREFERENCE THEORY OF INTEREST

In his epoch-making book, "*The General Theory of Employment, Interest and Money*" J.M. Keynes gave a new view of interest. According to him, "*interest is the reward for parting with liquidity for a specified period*."[8] A man with a given income has to decide first how much he is to consume and how much to save. The former will depend on, what Keynes calls, the propensity to consume. Given this propensity to consume, the individual will save a certain proportion of his given income. He then has to make another decision. Should he hold his savings ? How much of his resources will he hold in the form of ready money (cash or non-interest-paying bank deposits) and how much will he part with or lend depends upon what Keynes calls his "*liquidity preference*". Liquidity preference means the *demand for money to hold or the desire of the public to hold cash*.

Demand for Money or Motives for Liquidity Preference

Liquidity preference of a particular individual depends upon several considerations. The ques-

6. G.N. Halm, *Monetary Theory* p.147 (italics added).
7. "Some Cambridge Controversies in Monetary Theory", *Review of Economic Studies*, Vol. XIX. No. 49 (1951-52).
8. Op. cit., p. 167.

tion is : Why should the people hold their resources liquid or in the form of ready money, when they can get interest by lending such resources ? The desire for liquidity arises because of three motives; (*i*) the transactions motive, (*ii*) the precautionary motive, and (*iii*) the speculative motive.

The **Transactions Motive.** The transactions motive relates to the demand for money or need for cash for the current transactions of individuals and businessmen. Individuals want to hold cash in order "to bridge the interval between the receipt of income and its expenditure". This is called the '*Income Motive*'. Most of the people receive their incomes by the week or the month, while the expenditure goes on day by day. A certain amount of ready money, therefore, is kept in hand to make current payments for goods and services to be purchased. This amount will depend upon the size of the individual's income, the interval at which the income is received and the methods of payment prevailing in the society.

The businessmen and the entrepreneurs also have to keep a proportion of their resources in ready cash in order to meet current needs of various kinds. They need money all the time in order to pay for raw materials and transport, to pay wages and salaries and to meet all other current expenses business. This Keynes calls the '*Business Motive*' for keeping money. It is clear that the amount of money held under this business motive will depend to a very large extent on the turnover (*i.e.*, the volume of trade of the firm in question). The larger, the turnover, the larger in general, will be the amount of money needed to cover current expenses.

Precautionary Motive. Precautionary motive for holding money refers to the desire of the people to hold cash balances for unforeseen contingencies. People hold a certain amount of money to provide for the danger of unemployment, sickness, accidents, and the other uncertain emergencies. The amount of money held under this motive will depend on the nature of the individual and on the conditions in which he lives.

Speculative Motive. The speculative motive relates to the desire to hold one's resources in liquid form in order to take advantage of market movements regarding the future changes in the rate of interest (or bond prices). The notion of holding money for speculative motive is a new typically Keynesian idea. *Money held under the speculative motive serves as a store of value* as money held under the precautionary motive does. But it is a store of money meant for a different purpose. The cash held under this motive is used to make speculative gains by dealing in bonds[9] whose prices fluctuate. If bond prices are expected to rise, which, in other words, means that the rate of interest is expected to fall, businessmen will buy bonds to sell when their prices actually rise. If, however, bond prices are expected to fall, *i.e.*, the rate of interest is expected to rise, businessmen will sell bonds to avoid capital losses. Nothing being certain in this dynamic world, where guesses about the future course of events are made on precarious basis, businessmen keep cash balances to speculate on the probable future changes in bond prices (*i.e.* the rate of interest) with a view to making profits.

Given the expectations about the changes in the rate of interest in future, less money will be held under the speculative motive at a higher current or prevailing rate of interest and more money will be held under this motive at a lower current rate of interest. The reason for this inverse relation between money held for speculative motive and the prevailing rate of interest is that at a lower rate of interest less is lost by not lending money or not investing it, that is, by holding on to money, while at a higher rate of interest holders of cash balances would lose more by not lending or investing.

Thus, the demand for money under speculative motive is a function of the current rate of interest, increasing as the interest rate falls and decreasing as the interest rate rises. Thus, demand for money under this speculative motive is a decreasing function of the rate of interest. This is shown in Fig.35.5.

---

9. All securities and other such papers that yield a fixed and known rate of interest over a period of time are known as bonds.

Along the X-axis is represented the speculative demand for money and along the Y axis the rate of interest. The liquidity preference curve LP is a downward sloping towards the right signifying that the higher the rate of interest, the lower the demand for speculative motive, and *vice versa*. Thus, at the high current rate of interest Or, a very small amount OM is held for speculative motive. This is because at a high current rate of interest much money would have been lent out or used for buying bonds and therefore less money will be kept as inactive balances. If the rate of interest falls to Or', then a greater amount OM' is held under speculative motive. With the further fall in the rate of interest to Or'', money held under speculative motive increases to OM''. It will be seen in Fig. 35.5 that the liquidity preference curve LP becomes quite flat *i.e.*, perfectly elastic at a very low rate of interest. It is horizontal line beyond point E'' towards the right. This perfectly elastic portion of liquidity preference curve indicates the position of absolute liquidity preference of the people. That is, at a very low rate of interest people will hold with them as inactive balances any amount of money they come to have. This *portion of liquidity preference curve with absolute liquidity preference is called liquidity trap by some economists.*

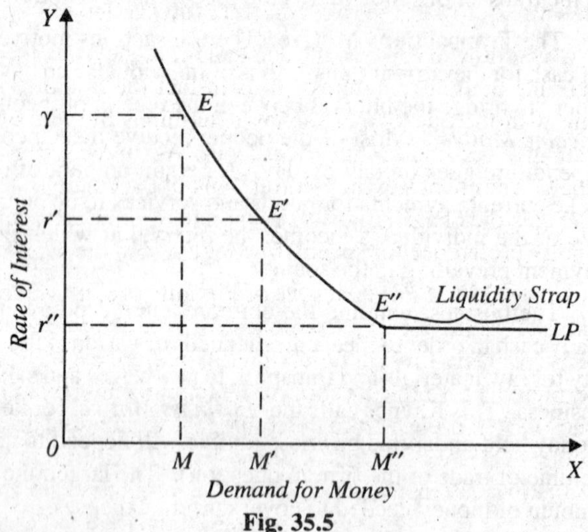

Fig. 35.5

But the demand for money to satisfy the speculative motive does not depend so much upon what the current rate of interest is, as on expectations of changes in the rate of interest. If there is a change in the expectations regarding the future rate of interest, the whole curve of liquidity preference for speculative motive will change accordingly. Thus, if the public on balance expect the rate of interest to be higher (*i.e.*, bond prices to be lower) in the future than had been previously supposed, the speculative demand for money will increase and the whole liquidity preference curve for speculative motive will shift upward.

If the total supply of money is represented by M, we may refer to that part of M held for transactions and precautionary motives as M_1 and to that part held for the speculative motive as M_2. Thus $M = M_1 + M_2$. According to Keynes, the money held under the transactions and precautionary motives, *i.e.* M_1, is completely interest-inelastic unless the interest rate is very high. The amount of money held as M_1, that is, for transactions and precautionary motive, is mainly a function of the size of income and business transactions together with the contingencies growing out of the conduct of personal and business affairs. We can write this in a functional form as follows :

$$M_1 = L_1(Y) \qquad \ldots (i)$$

where Y stands for income, L_1 for liquidity preference function, and M_1 for money held under the transactions and precautionary motive. The above function implies that money held under the transaction and precautionary motive is a function of income.

On the other hand, money demanded for speculative motives, *i.e.*, M_2, as explained above, is primarily a function of the rate of interest. This can be written as :

$$M_2 = L_2(r) \qquad \ldots (ii)$$

where r stands for the rate of interest, L_2 for liquidity preference function for speculative motive.

Since total supply of money $M = M_1 + M_2$, we get from (*i*) and (*ii*) above

$$M = L_1(Y) + L_2(r)$$

Determination of the Rate of Interest : Interaction of Liquidity Preference and Supply of Money

According to Keynes, the demand for money, *i.e.*, the liquidity preference and supply of money determine the rate of interest. It is in fact the liquidity preference for speculative motive which along with the quantity of money determines the rate of interest. We have explained above the speculative demand for money in detail. As for the supply of money, it is determined by the policies of the Government and the Central Bank of the country. The total supply of money consists of coins plus notes plus bank deposits. How rate of interest is determined by the equilibrium between the liquidity preference for speculative motive and the supply of money is shown in Fig. 35.6.

In Fig. 35.6, *LP* is the curve of liquidity preference for speculative motive. In other words, *LP* curve shows the demand for money for speculative motive. To begin with, *ON* is the quantity of money available for satisfying liquidity preference for speculative motive. Rate of interest will be determined where the speculative demand for money is in balance or equal to the fixed supply of money *ON*. It is clear from the figure that speculative demand for money is equal to *ON* quantity of money at *Or* rate of interest. Hence *Or* is the equilibrium rate of interest. Assuming no change in expectations, an increase in the quantity of money (say through open market operations by central bank of a country) for the speculative motive will lower the rate of interest. In Fig. 35.6, when the quantity of money increases from *ON* to *ON′*, the rate of interest falls from *Or* to *Or′* because the new quantity of money *ON′* is in balance with the speculative demand for money at *Or′* rate of interest. In this case we move down the curve. Thus, given the curve of liquidity preference for speculative motive, an increase in the quantity of money brings down the rate of interest.

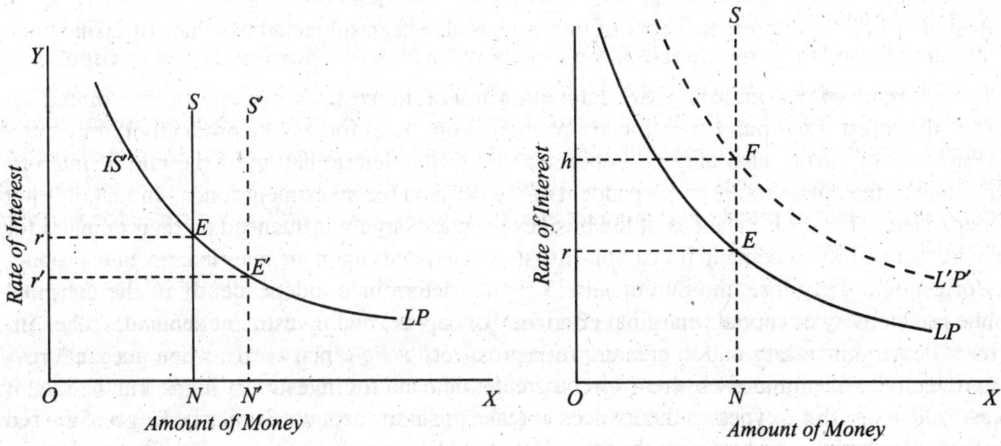

Fig. 35.6. *Determination of Rate of Interest and Effect of Expansion in Money Supply*

Fig. 35.7. *Effect of Increase in the Lignidity prefereance on Rate of Interest*

But the act of increase in the quantity of money may cause a change in the expectations of the public and thereby cause an upward shift in liquidity preference curve for speculative motive bringing the rate of interest up. But this is not certain. "New developments may only cause wide differences of opinion leading to increased activity in the bond market without necessarily causing any shift in the aggregate speculative demand for money[10].

10. Hansen, *A Guide to Keynes*, p. 133.

It is worth mentioning that shift in liquidity preference schedule or curve can be caused by many other factors which affect expectations and might take place independently of changes in the quantity of money by the central bank. Shifts in the liquidity function may be either downward or upward depending on the way in which the public interprets people a change in events. If some change in events leads the people on balance to expect a higher rate of interest in the future than they had previously supposed,theliquidity preference for speculative motive will increase which will bring about an upward shift in the curve of liquidity preference for speculative motive and will raise the rate of interest. In Fig. 35.7, assuming that the quantity of money remains unchanged at *ON*, the rise in the liquidity preference curve from *LP* to *L′*P′, the rate of interest rises from *Or* to *Oh* because at *Oh*, the new speculative demand for money is in equilibrium with the supply of money *ON*. It is worth noting that when the liquidity preference for speculative motive increases from *LP* to *L′P′*, the amount of money hoarded does not increase; it remains *ON* as before. Only the rate of interest rises from *Or* to *Oh* to equilibrate the new liquidity preference for speculative motive with the available quantity of money *ON*.

Thus we see that Keynes explained interest in terms of purely monetary forces and not in terms of real forces like productivity of capital and thriftiness times which formed the foundation-stones of both classical and loanable fund theories. According to him, demand for money for speculative motive together with the supply of money determines the rate of interest. He agreed that the marginal revenue product of capital tends to become equal to the rate of interest but the rate of interest is not determined by marginal revenue product of capital. Moreover, according to him, interest is not a reward for saving or thriftiness or waiting but for parting with liquidity. Keynes asserted that it is not the rate of interest which equalises saving and investment. But this equality is brought about through changes in the level of income.

Critical Appraisal of Keynes's Liquidity Preference Theory of Interest

Keynes Liquidity Prefernce theory of Interest has also been subjected to some criticism which we discuss below :

Keynes ignored real factors in the determination of interest. Firstly, it has been pointed out that rate of interest is not purely a monetary phenomenon. Real forces like productivity of capital and thriftiness or saving also play an important role in the determination of the rate of interest. Keynes makes the rate of interest independent of the demand for investment funds. In fact, it is not so independent. The cash-balances of the businessmen are largely influenced by their demand for capital investment. This demand for capital-investment depends upon the marginal revenue productivity of capital. Therefore, the rate of interest is not determined independently of the marginal revenue productivity of capital (marginal efficiency of capital) and investment demand. When investment demand increases due to greater profit prospects or, in other words, when marginal revenue productivity of capital rises, there will be greater demand for investment funds and the rate of interest will go up. But Keynesian theory does not take this into account. Similarly, Keynes ignored the effect of the supply of savings on the rate of interest. For instance, if the propensity to consume of the people increases, savings would decline. As a result, supply of funds in the market will decline which will raise the rate of interest.

2. **Keynesian theory is also indeterminate.** Now exactly the same criticism applies to Keynesian theory itself on the basis of which Keynes rejected the classical and loanable funds theories. Keynes's theory of interest is also indeterminate. According to Keynes, rate of interest is determined by the speculative demand for money and the supply of money available for satisfying speculative demand. Given the total money supply, we cannot know how much money will be available to satisfy the speculative demand for money unless we know how much the transactions demand for money is. And we cannot know the transactions demand for money unless we first know the level of income Thus the Keynesian theory, like the classical, is indeterminate. "In the Keynesian case the supply and demand for money schedules cannot give the rate of interest unless we already

know the income level; in the classical case the demand and supply schedules for saving offer no solution until the income is known. Precisely the same is true of loanable-fund theory. Keynes' criticism of the classical and loanable-fund theories applies equally to his own theory."[11]

3. **No liquidity without Savings.** According to Keynes, interest is a reward for parting with liquidity and in no way a compensation and inducement for saving or waiting. But without saving how can the funds be available to be kept as liquid and how can there be question of surrendering liquidity if one has not already saved money. Jacob Viner rightly maintains, "*Without saving there can be no liquidity to surrender*". Therefore, the rate of interest is vitally connected with saving which is neglected by Keynes in the determination of interest.

It follows from above that Keynesian theory of interest is also not without flaws. But importance Keynes gave to liquidity preference as a determinant of interest is correct. In fact, the exponents of loanable funds theory incorporated the liquidity preference in their theory by laying greater stress on hoarding and dishoarding. We are inclined to agree with Prof. D. Hamberg when he says, "Keynes did not forge nearly as *new* a theory as he and others at first thought. Rather, his great emphasis on the influence of hoarding on the rate of interest constituted an invaluable addition to the theory of interest as it had been developed by the loanable funds theorists who incorporated much of Keynes's ideas into their theory to make it more complete."[12]

QUESTIONS FOR REVIEW

1. **Define interest.** Distinguish between nominal rate of interest and real rate of interest
2. Critically examine the following views about why rate of interest arises (or is paid).
   (*a*) Interest is a reward for abstinence
   (*b*) Interest arises because of time preference
   (*c*) Interest is a reward for parting with liquidity
3. Explain how saving and investment are related to rate of interest. Critically examine the classical theory that rate of interest is determined by saving and investment.
4. Explain how Keynes showed that Classical theory of interest was indeterminate. The same criticism of indeterminacy has been made against Keynes' own theory of interest. Discuss
5. Explain the components of demand for and supply of loanable funds. Show that rate of interest is determined by demand for and supply of loanable funds. Show that rate of interest is determined by demand for and supply of loanable funds. Is the rate of interest determined through equality of demand for and supply of loanable funds stable ?
6. How does loanable funds theory of interest differ from (i) Classical theory, and (2) Keynes' theory of interest
7. Explain the Keynesian theory of interest. How is the Keynesian theory of interest different from the Classical theory. *D.U. B.Com (Hons) 1999.*
8. What is meant by liquidity preference ? How does it explain why interest is paid ?
9. Explain Keynes' liquidity preference theory of interest. Why is it considered to be indeterminate ? *D.U. B.Com (Hons) 1998*
10. In what ways is the Keynesian theory of interest a departure from the classical theory ? Discuss *D.U. B.A. (Hons), 1995*
11. Explain why demand for money is considered to be declining function of rate of interest. *D.U. B.A. (hons) 1999*
12. The deference between the classical theory of interest and Keynes' money theory of interest is a fundamental aspect of the difference between the economics of full employment and the economics of less than full employment (D. Dillard). Discuss.

---

11. Hansen, *Guide to Keynes*, p. 141.
12. D. Hamberg, *Business Cycles*, p. 183.

Chapter 36
THE THEORY OF PROFITS

Introduction

After having discussed the determination of rent of land, wages of labour and interest on capital, we now pass on to the study of profits which are said to be the reward for enterprise, the fourth factor of production. No doubt profits are associated with entrepreneur and his functions but the economists from time to time have expressed diverse and conflicting views about the nature, origin and role of profits. Till today, there is no complete agreement among economists about the true nature and origin of profits. As a matter of fact, there has been perhaps no topic in the whole economic theory which has been in such a confused and tangled state as the theory of profit.

A part of the confusion in the theory of profit is due to the lack of agreement among economists about the true or proper function of the entrepreneur. Some have held the view that the function of the entrepreneur is to organise and co-ordinate the other factors of production. According to them, entrepreneur earns profits for his performing this function. On this view, enterprise is a special type of labour and profits a special form of wages. Some others have described the entrepreneur as performing the functions of bearing risk and uncertainty as he controls the business and takes price and output decision. The entrepreneur earns profits because he bears risk and uncertainty because as his price and output policies may prove to be incorrect in view of the future business movements. Schumpeter has assigned to the entrepreneur the role of an innovator and profits as a reward for his introducing innovations. Lastly, F.H. Knight has emphasised uncertainty in the economy as a factor which gives rise to profits and bearing uncertainty is the task of the entrepreneur.

Besides, some economists have described profits as *non-functional income*. Thus, J.M. Keynes expressed the view that profits resulted from the favourable movements of the general price level. Joan Robinson, E.H. Chamberlin and M. Kalecki have associated profits with imperfect competition and monopoly. According to them, the greater the degree of imperfection or, in other words, the greater the degree of monopoly power, the greater the profits made by the entrepreneur. Thus, profits has been connected by F.H. Knight with uncertainty, by Schumperter with innovations, by Hawley with risk-bearing, and by Joan Robinson. E.H. Chamberin and M. Kalecki with the degree of monopoly power. As a matter of fact, profits arise from all these sources. Therefore, no single explanation or theory of profits is adequate; each omits some crucial factors and fails to bring out some important economic factors having a relation with profits. B.S Keristead, therefore, expresses the view that profits originate from monopoly, successful innovations and a correct estimate of uncertain future. He thus says, "Profits may come to exist as a result of monopoly or monopsony, as a reward for innovation, as a reward for the correct estimate of uncertain factors, either particular to the industry or general to the whole economy."[1]

Profits as a Residual Income

It is worth mentioning that profits are *residual income* left after the payment of the contractual rewards to other factors of production. The entrepreneur while engaging other factors of production enters into contract with them. He thus pays wages to the workers, rent on the land employed,

1. B.S. Keirstead, *Capital, Interest and Profits*, (1959), p. 6.

interest on the loans taken at the rates already fixed by contracts. In fact, the entrepreneur makes payment to these factors much in advance of the realisation of the values of output produced after sale of the product. What is left after paying the contractual rewards to other factors employed is the profits of entrepreneur. Thus profits are *non-contractual income* and therefore they may be positive or negative, whereas the contractual income of other factors such as wages, rent and interest are always positive and never negative. It should be further noted that *pure profits* of the entrepreneur are found by subtracting from the gross residual income the *imputed values* of rent and interest on self-owned land and capital employed by the entrepreneur and also the imputed *wages* for his work of routine management.

PROFITS AS A DYNAMICS SURPLUS : CLARK'S DYNAMIC THEORY OF PROFITS

A popular conception of profits is that they arise in a dynamic economy, that is, in an economy where changes are taking place. In a static economy where nothing changes there can be no profits. It was J.B. Clark who first propounded that profits are a dynamic surplus. He argued that in a stationary state where no changes in conditions of demand and supply are occurring, the prices paid to the factors on the basis of their marginal productivity would exhaust the total value product and therefore no profits would accrue to the entrepreneur. Profits result when selling prices of the goods exceed their cost of production. Now, in a competitive long-run equilibrium, price equals average cost of production (including normal profits which are in fact wages for routine supervision and management) and therefore no pure profits are made. Now, if no changes either in the conditions of demand or in the conditions of supply occur, competitive equilibrium will persist and therefore no pure profits will be earned by the entrepreneur.

On the contrary, if due to the changes in either demand or supply, price exceeds cost of production, profits will emerge. If due to these changes, price falls below the cost of production, negative profits, that is, losses will accrue to the entrepreneur. It is evident that changes distrub the long-run competitive equilibrium achieved and thereby give rise to profits. In other words, profits arise due to disequilibrium caused by the changes in demand and supply conditions. Prof. Stigler rightly says, "Firms in a competitive industry may receive profits....because of a state of disequilibrium....these profits can arise even if all entrepreneurs are identical, for *disequilibrium* can characterize a whole industry. If prices are higher, or costs lower than were anticipated, entrepreneurs will receive a return in excess of the alternative product of their resources. If prices were lower or costs higher than were anticipated, entrepreneurs will receive less than the alternative product of their resources *i.e.*, negative profits. Positive profits may persist for a long time if firms outside the industry are slow to enter the industry and negative profits can persist as long as specialised equipment yields more than when used in the industry that when used elsewhere, say as scrap."[2]

It should be noted that these disequilibrium profits arise from unanticipated changes in demand or cost conditions. If the changes could have been foreseen in advance, then suitable adjustments could have been made according to the anticipated changes so that forces of competition would have driven profits to zero.

The Types of Changes

Now, the question is what changes occur in the economy and give rise to profits. Clark mentioned five changes that occur in a dynamic economy and which give rise to profits. These five changes are: (1) The changes in the quantity and quality of human wants, (2) changes in methods or techniques of production, (3) changes in the amount of capital (4) changes in the forms of business organisation, and (5) the growth of population. These changes are constantly taking place and bring

2. G.J. Stigler. *The Theory of Price* (revised edition, 1952), p. 181.

about the divergence between price and cost and thereby give rise to profits, positive or negative. If the demand for a commodity increases due to the increase in population or increase in the incomes of the people or due to the increase in consumers' preferences for the commodity, the price of the commodity will rise, and if cost remains the same, profits would accrue to the entrepreneurs producing the commodity. On the other hand, cost of production may go down as a result of the adoption of a new technique of production, or as a result of cheapening of the raw material, and if price remains constant or does not fall to the same extent, the profits would emerge.

Apart from the five changes mentioned by Clark, there are other changes also which occur in the economy. All the changes which take place and as a result of which profits arise in a dynamic economy may be classified into two types: (1) *innovations* and (2) *external changes*. We explain below these changes in some detail. Innovations represent changes which are introduced by individual entrepreneurs themselves.

Innovations. The entrepreneur earns large profits from introducing innovations such as a new product, a new and cheaper method of production, a new method of marketing the product, a new way of advertisement. The innovational changes may either reduce cost or increase the demand for the product and thereby bring profits into existence. Those entrepreneurs who introduce successful innovations earn large profits. But as the innovation gets known to other entrepreneurs and they also adopt similar other innovations, profits which arise because of a particular innovation tend to disappear. But new innovations are being continuously introduced by the entrepreneurs and profits continue to arise out of them.

External Changes. External changes refer to those changes which are external to the firms or industries in an economy. These changes affect all firms in an industry or sometimes all industries in the economy. Examples of external changes are breaking out of wars, occurrence of sometimes periods of inflation and rising prices and sometimes business depression and falling prices, changes in the monetary and fiscal policies of government affecting favourably or unfavourably, changes in the technology of production, changes in tastes and preferences of the consumers, changes in income and spending habits of the people, changes in the availability of substitute products, alteration in the legislative and legal environment affecting the industries, and changes in preference between income and leisure. All these changes affect either the cost or demand for the products and give rise to profits, positive or negative as the case may be. For instance, during wars when prices of goods mount up, and costs lag behind, the entrepreneurs make a lot of profits. Similarly, when inflation occurs due to the increased demand for goods caused by the rising incomes, increasing population and expansion in the money supply, huge profits accrue to the firms. On the contrary, when period of depression comes due to the fall in effective aggregate demand, firms suffer huge losses and some may go into liquidation. During periods of depression all prices, rents, wages, and interest tend to fall but because of the non-contractual nature, profits fall sharply and may even become negative.

Knight's Views on Dynamic Theory

Here the views of Prof. F.H. Knight about dynamic changes giving rise to profits are worth mentioning. According to him, "Dynamic changes give rise to a peculiar form of income only in so far as the changes and their consequences are unpredictable in character....It cannot, then, be the change which is the cause of profits, since if the law of change is known, as in fact is largely the case, no profits can arise. The connection between change and profits is uncertain and always indirect. Change may cause a situation out of which profit will be made if it brings about ignorance of the future....It is not dynamic change, nor any change as such which causes profits, but divergence of actual conditions from those which have been expected and on the basis of which business arrange-

3. F.H. Knight, *Risk, Uncertainty and Profits*, pp. 37-38.

ments have been made. For a satisfactory explanation of profit we seem to be thrown back from the dyanmic theory to the *Uncertainty of the Future*."[3]

As far as unpredictable, unforeseen changes and uncertainty about the future giving rise to profits are concerned, there can be no disagreement with Prof. Knight. But with his assertion that dynamic changes as such are not the cause of profits, one can differ. Against Knight's view it may be pointed out if there is no change there will be no uncertainty about the future and therefore no profits. Thus the factor of change is fundamental in bringing profits into existence. Professors Stonier and Hague rightly maintain, "in an economy where nothing changes, there can be no profits. There is no uncertainty about the future, so there are no risk and no profits."[4]

SCHUMPETER'S INNOVATIONS THEORY OF PROFITS

Successful innovations as important dynamic changes and as source of profit have been, in brief, explained above. But since innovations have been singled out as a very important factor responsible for the occurrence of profits to the entrepreneurs it requires to be dealt with separately. It has been held by Joseph Schumpeter that the main function of the entrepreneur is to introduce innovations in the economy and profits are reward for his performing this function. Now, what is innovation ? Innovation, as used by Schumpeter, has a very wide connotation. Any new measure or policy adopted by an entrepreneur to reduce his cost of production or to increase the demand for his product is an innovation. Thus innovations can be divided into two categories.

First type of innovations are those which reduce cost of production, or in other words, which change the production-functions. In this first type of innovations are included the introduction of a new machinery, new and cheaper technique or process of production, utilisation of a new source of raw material, a new and better method of organising the firm, etc. Second type of innovations are those which increase the demand for the product, or in other words, which change the demand or utility function. In this category are included the introduction of a new product, a new variety or design of the product, a new and superior method of advertisement, discovery of new markets etc. If an innovation proves successful, that is, if it achieves its aim of either reducing the cost of production or enhancing the demand for a product, it will give rise to profit. Profits emerge because due to successful innovations either cost falls below the prevailing price of the product or the entrepreneur is able to sell more and at a better price than before. It should be noted that profits accrue not to him who conceives innovation, nor to him who finances it but to him who introduces it. Further, whenever any new innovation is to be introduced, it always calls for a new combination of factors or reallocation of resources.

It is here worth mentioning that *profits caused by a particular innovation are only temporary* and tend to be competed away as others imitate and also adopt that. An innvation ceases to be new or novel, when others also come to know of it and adopt it. When an entrepreneur introduces a new innovation, he is first in a monopoly position, for the new innovation is confined to him only. He therefore makes large profits. When after some time others also adopt it in order to get a share, profits will disappear. If the law allows and the entrepreneur is able to get his new innovation *e.g.*, new product patented, then he will continue to earn profits.

But in a competitive economy and without patent laws, the existing competitors or the new firms will soon adopt any successful innovation and profits would be eliminated. But in a competitive and progressive economy the entrepreneurs always continue to introduce new innovations and thus profits continue emerging out of them. Thus Prof. Stigler writes, "Unless one can construct a permanent monopoly, such profits as are realised by successful innovations are essentially transitional and will be eliminated by the attempts of other firms to share them. But these profits may exist for a

4. Stonier and Hague, *A Textbook of Economic Theory*, 2nd edition, p. 327.

considerable time because of the ignorance of other firms of their existence or because of the time required for the entry of new firms. More important, the successful innovator can continuously seek new disequilibrium profits since the horizon of conceivable innovations is unlimited."[5]

We have seen above that innovations are important source of profits. Obtaining profits is a necessary incentive for the entrepreneurs to conceive and introduce innovations which help the economic development of the country. Since innovations, if successful, yield profits and profits is also the motive to introduce innovations, *profits are both the cause and effect of innovations.*

RISK, UNCERTAINTY AND PROFITS : KNIGHT'S THEORY OF PROFITS

An important theory associates profit with risk and uncertainty. According to F.H. Knight, profit is a reward for uncertainty bearing. Even before Knight, F.B. Hawley and A.C. Pigou had pointed out that entrepreneurs earn profits because they have to bear the risks of production. But Knight has greatly developed the theory of profits based on uncertainty. He has distinguished between risk and uncertainty on the one hand and predictable and unpredictable changes on the other. According to him, dynamic changes give rise to profits only if changes and their consequences are of unpredictable character. Only those changes whose occurrence cannot be known before hand give rise to profits.

Profits, Unpredictable Changes and Uncertainly

As we have noted above, if there were no changes or if the changes were foreseen and predictable, there would have been no uncertainty about the future and therefore no profits. Profits arise because of the uncertainty of future. If the future conditions could be completely foreknown in the present, then competition would certainly adjust things to the ideal state where all prices would equal costs and profits would not emerge. Thus it is our ignorance about the future and uncertainty of it that give rise to profits. In other words, it is the divergence of actual conditions from those which have been expected and on the basis of which business contracts have been made that give rise to uncertainty and profits. Prof. A.K Dass Gupta rightly maintains, "uncertainty is thus a permanent feature of economic system. It is one of the limitations of human ingenuity that it cannot unearth the contents of the future. Trained insticts of businessmen coupled with statistical information may go a long way, but in so far as the course of nature (both physical and human) is any thing but rhythmical, the future would always remain more or less of mystery."[6] He further writes, "so long as entrepreneurs start operations with imperfect knowledge about the state of the market and so long as the anticipated marginal product of the hired factors deviates from their actual product, so long a surplus would persist."[7]

We thus see that entrepreneurs have to undertake the work of production under conditions of uncertainty. In advance they have to make estimates of the future conditions regarding demand for the product and other factors which affect price and costs. In view of their estimates and anticipations, they make contract with the suppliers of factors of production in advance at fixed rates of remuneration. They realise the value of the output produced by the hired factors after it has been produced and sold in the market. But a good deal of time is spent in the process of producing and selling the product. It follows, therefore, that a good time gap elapses between the contracts made by the entrepreneur with the factors of production at fixed rates and the realisation of sale proceeds from the output made by them. As mentioned before, these contracts are based upon anticipations about the future conditions. But between the times of contracts and sale of the output many changes may take place which may upset anticipations for good or for worse and thereby give rise to the

5. G.J. Stigler, *op. cit.*, p. 182.
6. A.K. Dass Gupta, *The Conception of Surplus in Theoretical Economics*, p. 188.
7. *Ibid.*, p. 188.

profits, positive and negative. Now, if the conditions prevailing at the time of sale of output could be known or predicted when the entrepreneurs enter into contractual relationships with the factors of production about their rates of remuneration, there would have been no uncertainty and, therefore, no profits. *Thus uncertainty, that is, ignorance about the future conditions of demand and supply, is the cause of profits.* It should be noted that positive profits accrue to those entrepreneurs who make correct estimate of the future or whose anticipations prove to be correct. Those whose anticipations prove to be incorrect will have to suffer losses.

We thus see that profit is a residual and non-contractual income which accrues to the entrepreneurs because of the fact of uncertainty. The entrepreneur is unhired factor; he hires others for work of production. It is, therefore, *entrepreneur who bears uncertainty and earns profits as a reward for that.* J.F. Weston who has been a prominent exponent and supporter of uncertainty theory of profit explains the emergence of profits in the following way: "Under uncertainity total product may not be equal to total costs (explicit and implicit) *because plans are not fulfilled.* How this occurs is briefly indicated. Two classes of owners of productive services are distinguished. First, those with rates of compensation fixed in advance of the determination of the results of operations, are called *hired factors* and receive contractural returns. Second, those with rates of compensation dependent upon the results of operation are referred to as unhired factors who receive non-contractual or residual returns. Whatever the basis upon which contractual relationships have been entered, actual results will not have been accurately foreseen because of uncertainty. Hence *whatever the basis upon which contractual commitments have been made events actually do not turn out that way.* This is the significance of economic profit. *It is not possible to plan in advance exactly what total product or total costs will be.*"[8]

What Causes Uncertainty ?

Now, the question is what changes cause uncertainty. As has been explained earlier, there are *two types of changes* which take place and are responsible for conditions of uncertainty. First type of changes refer to innovations (for example, introduction of a new product or a new cheaper method of production etc.) which are introduced by the entrepreneurs themselves. These innovations not only create uncertainty for the rivals or competitors who are affected by them but they also involve uncertainty for the entrepreneur who introduces them because one cannot be certain whether a particular innovation will be definitely successful. The second type of changes which cause uncertainty are those which are external to the firms and industries. These changes are: (1) changes in tastes and fashions of the people, (2) changes in Government policies and laws especially taxation, (3) wage and labour policies and laws, (4) movements of prices as a result of inflation and depression, (5) changes in income of the people, (6) changes in production technology etc. All these changes cause uncertainty and bring profits, positive or negative, into existence.

Insurable and Non-Insurable Risks

We have seen above that entrepreneurs work under conditions of uncertainty and that they bear uncertainty and earn profits as a reward for that. Here a distinction drawn by F.H. Knight between *insurable and non-insurable risk* is worth mentioning. Because of the changes that are continuously occurring in the economy entrepreneur has to face many risks. But all risks do not cause uncertainty and give rise to profits. It is only *non-insurable risks* that involve uncertainty and the entrepreneur earns profits for bearing these non-insurable risks. Now, the question arises as to what kind of risks are insurable and what non-insurable. The entrepreneur faces risks like fire, theft, accident etc. which may cause him huge losses. But these risks of fire, theft, accident etc. can be insured against on the payment of a fixed premium. Insurance premium is included in the cost of production. Thus no uncertainty arises due to insurable risks as far as individual entrepreneurs are

8. J. Fred Weston, 'A Generalized Uncertainty Theory of Profit', *American Economic Review*, XL (March 1950), (italics added).

concerned and therefore they cannot give rise to profits.

Now, only those risks can be insured the probability of whose occurrence can be calculated. Thus an insurance company knows by its calculation on the basis of past statistics that how much percentage of the factories will catch fire in a year. On the basis of this information, it will fix the rate of premium and is able to insure the factories against the risk. But there are risks which cannot be insured and therefore they have to be borne by the entrepreneurs. These non-insurable risks relate to the outcomes of the price-output decisions taken by the entrepreneurs. Whether it will pay him to increase output, reduce output and what will be the outcome in terms of profits or losses as a result of his particular output decision. Again, whether it will pay him to lower price or to raise it, and when he takes a particular price decision whether he would make profits or losses. Similarly, he has to face risks as a result of his decisions regarding mode of advertisement and outlay to be made on it, product variation to be made by him etc. For taking all these decisions he has to guess about demand and cost conditions and always there is risk of suffering losses as a result of decisions. No insurance company can insure the entrepreneurs against commercial losses which may emerge out of decisions regarding price, output, product variation and also against the losses which may fall upon the entrepreneurs due to the structural, cyclical and other exogenous changes which take place in the economy. It is, therefore, clear that it is non-insurable risks that involve *uncertainty and give rise to profits*. To quote Knight, "*It is 'uncertainty' distinguished from insurable risk that effectively gives rise to the entrepreneurial form of organisation and to the much condemned 'profit' as an income form.*"[9]

Role and Functions of Profits

Profits play an important role in a free market economy. Profits perform three important primary roles in such an economy. First, profits serve as a signal to change the rate of output or for the firms to enter or leave the industry. Second, profits play a critical role in providing incentive to introduce innovations and increase productive efficiency and to take risks. Third, profit serves as source of saving which can be invested in building up more productive capacity. Even corporate firms do not distribute all profits earned by them among shareholders as dividends but retain a good part of them as undistributed profits which are ploughed back into investment for expansion of their productive capacity by buying new machines, equipment and buildings. By serving as a source of saving and investment profits make a significant contribution to economic growth of a country.

As regards the first role, high economic profits being earned in an industry serve as a *signal* that consumers want more of the commodity being produced by that industry. These profits indicate to the firm to expened output of the commodity and for the new firms to enter the industry to gain a share of economic profits that exist in the industry. As a result, more resources will be allocated to the output of that industry. On the other hand, below normal profits in an industry serve as a signal that either less output of the industry is demanded by the consumers or inefficient production methods are being used by the firms. In response to the lower demand for the product the firms will reduce their output and also some firms will leave the industry. As a result, some productive resources will be released from that industry and made available for the production of other goods. If the lower profits are due to the inefficient production and organisation, this will induce firm to improve efficiency by changing the production methods or making organisational changes to reduce costs.

As explained above, profit motive drives a free-market economy. Although it has been observed that sometimes managers and entrepreneurs in a free market system are swayed by greed and avarice, and break laws to make money or profits by exploiting the consumers or workers but in general profits perform useful function of sending signals for changing levels of output of various products and for reallocation of resources among them.

9. Social Economic Policy, *Canadian Journal of Economic and Political Science*, (26 Feb. 1960), p.31

Secondly, above normal rate of profits in a free enterprise system is an essential reward for introducing innovations and taking risks. No entrepreneur will introduce new products or more efficient production methods or undertake investment in risky projects unless there is prospect of making profits. Some firms continue to earn above-normal rate of profit year after year as they are continually introducing new products, new production methods and providing good customer services.

In the economy changes in demand for the product often occur due to cyclical and structural changes. Besides, new strategies of rival firms also affect the demand for the product of a firm. All these uncertain and unanticipated changes involve a good deal of risk. An important function of economic profits is to reward entrepreneurs for taking these risks involved in making investment and organising factors for the production of products.

However, in some cases firms are also able to make supernormal profits by virtue of their having monopoly power. Their monopoly power may be due to some legal patent and license obtained from the government, the economies of large scale production, exclusive control over essential raw materials which prevent the other firms from producing the same product or service. These enable the monopoly firms to charge higher prices and thereby make large economic profits. Therefore, even in free-market economies steps are taken to prevent the emergence of monopolies through anti-trust laws or Competition Acts as recently enacted in India. Of course, monopolies are legally permitted if they are needed in public interest. For example, in several cities Government grants license to some private firms to provide public utility services such electricity, gas, telephone etc. In these cases of legal monopolies government regulates them and fix reasonable prices to be charged by them from the public but at the same time ensures fair return or normal profits to the private firms on their investment.

QUESTIONS FOR REVIEW

1. Profits arise due to innovations and entrepreneurs are rewarded for introducing innvations. Discuss
2. Profit is the reward for making innovations. Do you consider this as an adequate explanation for profits ? *D.U. B.A. (Hons) 1989.*
3. Profit is defined as a functional reward to the entrepreneur. *D.U. B.A (Hons) 1991.*
4. Explain why profits are zero in a competitive economy. *D.U. B.A. (Hons) 1995.*
5. "In a purely competitive static economy economic profits are eliminated" Discuss. *D.U. B.A. (Hons), 1993*

   OR

   "There can be no profits in the stationary state" Discuss *D.U. B.A. (Hons) 1986.*
6. Profits are a dynamic surplus. Discuss. *D.U. B.A. (Hons) 1987.*
7. Profits are a reward for uncertainity bearing. *D.U. B.A. (Hons) 1996.*
8. "Profits may come to exist as a result of monoposoly or monopsony, as a reward for innovation, as a reward for making a correct estimate of uncertain factors either particular to the industry or general to the economy as a whole" Discuss.
9. What is the role of profit in a free market economy ? Is there a conflict between profit earning and social welfare ? *D.U. B.A. (Hons) 1990.*
10. Distinguish between risk and uncertainty. What causes uncertainty in an economy ? Critically examine the view that entrepreneurs are rewarded in the form of profits for bearing uncertainity.

PART - VI

GENERAL EQUILIBRIUM ANALYSIS AND WELFARE ECONOMICS

- General Equilibrium Analysis
- Welfare Economics : An Introduction
- Economic Efficiency and Pareto Optimality
- Market Failures, Externalities and Public Goods
- New Welfare Economics : Compensation Principle
- Social Welfare Function

CHAPTER 37
GENERAL EQUILIBRIUM ANALYSIS

Partial Equilibrium Analysis and General Equilibrium Analysis

In the previous chapters we have focussed on explaining the determination of price and quantity of a commodity or a factor and the working of its market viewed in isolation of what happens to other commodities and factors. We have analysed how equilibrium price and quantity of a commodity or a factor is determined through demand and supply, assuming prices of other commodities and factors would remain the same when changes occur in the price of the commodity under consideration. That means the effect, if any, of the changes in price of a commodity on the demand for other commodities is ignored. *This type of analysis where we do not take into account the interrelationship or inter-dependence between prices of commodities or between prices of commodities and factors of production is called partial equilibrium analysis.* In this partial equilibrium analysis each product or factor market is considered as independent and self-contained for the proper explanation of the determination of price and quantity of a commodity or a factor.

However, *partial equilibrium analysis is not useful and relevant to apply when there is interrelationship between commodities or between factors.* Thus when markets for various commodities and factors are interdependent, that is, when changes in the price of a commodity or a factor have important repercussions on the demand for other commodities or factors, partial equilibrium analysis would not yield correct results. In such cases when there is significant inter-relationship between various markets or that the changes in one market would significantly affect others, we should employ general equilibrium analysis which considers *simultaneous equilibrium* of all markets taking into account all effects of changes in price in one market over others. It may be mentioned that both types of equilibrium analysis are useful, each being valuable in its own way. Partial equilibrium analysis is useful when the changes in conditions in one market have little repercussions on other markets. However, when the changes in conditions in one market have significant effects on other markets, general equilibrium analysis should be used. Thus, in partial equilibrium analysis when we consider the determination of market price of a commodity we assume that prices of other goods do not change.

For example, the rise in price of petrol following imposition of a tax on it would cause little effect on the prices of goods such as wrist watches, drapers, bowling balls, and in turn there would be negligible feedback effect of changes in prices of these goods on the demand and price of petrol. If prices of petrol and of only these commodities are to be considered and since there are little repercussions of changes in prices of petrol on these other commodities, the use of partial equilibrium analysis of price determination of petrol would be quite reasonable. However, when market for automobiles is considered, the rise in price of petrol would have an important effect on their demand and price. Therefore, the assumption of partial equilibrium analysis that prices of automobiles would remain constant, when the price of petrol changes would be seriously wrong. This is because petrol and automobiles being *complements* to each other, their markets are inter-related and mutually interdependent and changes in their prices would significantly affect each other. In such cases when there exist inter-relationship and inter-dependence of the markets for goods (whether they are complements or substitutes), the general equilibrium analysis should be used. In *general equilibrium analysis, all prices are considered variable and the analysis of simultaneous determination of equilibrium in all markets is made.*

In fact when we look at the economic system as a whole, there is a great deal of inter-relationship and inter-dependence among various markets for commodities and factors and there are a large number of decision making agents—consumers, producers, workers, (who supply labour) and other resource owners. All these agents are self-interested and would behave to maximise their goals; consumers would maximise their utility, and producers would maximise their profits. A comprehensive analysis of the economic system when prices and quantities of all commodities and factors are considered as variable and which would take into account all inter-relationships and inter-dependence could be made only through general equilibrium analysis. The general equilibrium would occur when markets for all commodities and factors and all decision-making agents, consumers, producers, resource owners are simultaneously in equilibrium.

To sum up, *partial equilibrium analysis focuses on explaining the determination of price and quantity in a given product or factor market when one market is viewed as independent of other markets. On the other hand, general equilibrium analysis deals with explaining simultaneous equilibrium in all markets when prices and quantities of all products and factors are considered as variables.*

Thus, in general equilibrium analysis inter-relationship among markets of all products and factors are explicitly taken into account.

In what follows we shall explain the conditions of general equilibrium of exchange and production in an economy. We shall concentrate on the conditions of general equilibrium with regard to the following three aspects :–

1. the distribution of goods and services for consumption among individuals in the society;
2. the allocation of productive factors to the production of various goods and services; and
3. the composition of production (or output mix) together with the distribution of consumption.

In this chapter, we shall discuss *whether a general equilibrium exists at all.* Although the question of existence of general equilibrium is an abstract one, it is very important because many propositions of economics rest on the existence of general equilibrium. We shall also explain that in case general equilibrium exists, whether it is *unique.*

GENERAL EQUILIBRIUM OF EXCHANGE AND CONSUMPTION : DISTRIBUTION OF GOODS BETWEEN INDIVIDUALS

First, we shall *explain general equilibrium in a pure exchange economy.* In this pure exchange system, we assume *that there is no production.* That is, we consider the case when two goods are provided to the individuals in the economy from outside the system. To keep our analysis simple we assume that there are (1) *two goods,* a specific bundles of which have been made available to the individuals for consumption; and (2) there are *two individuals* between which exchange of goods has to take place and equilibrium reached with regard to the distribution of the specific amounts of these two goods.

Edgeworth Box and General Equilibrium of Exchange. In this two goods, two individuals (2x2) model of pure exchange, the famous Edgeworth Box diagram has been employed to explain the general equilibrium of distribution of two goods between two individuals. In what follows we first explain the concept of Edgeworth Box and then analyse the general equilibrium in this pure exchange system. Consider Figure 37.1 where a box with a certain fixed dimensions has been drawn. Along the *X*-axis we measure the commodity *X* and along the *Y*-axis, the commodity *Y*. The total available amount of commodity *X* is OX_0 and of commodity *Y is* OY_0. The available amounts of the two commodities, OX_0 and OY_0 determine the dimension of the box. The quantity of *X* available with the individual *A* is measured from left to right along the *X*-axis with bottom left-hand corner O_A as the origin. And, quantity of commodity Y available with the individual A is measured along the Y-axis from bottom upwards with the origin O_A. For individual B, the top right hand corner O_B has been taken as the origin and with the given quantities of X and Y, the quantity of X available for consumption for individual B is measured, right to left, with the origin O_B and the quantity of Y available for B is measured, from top to bottom, from the origin O_B.

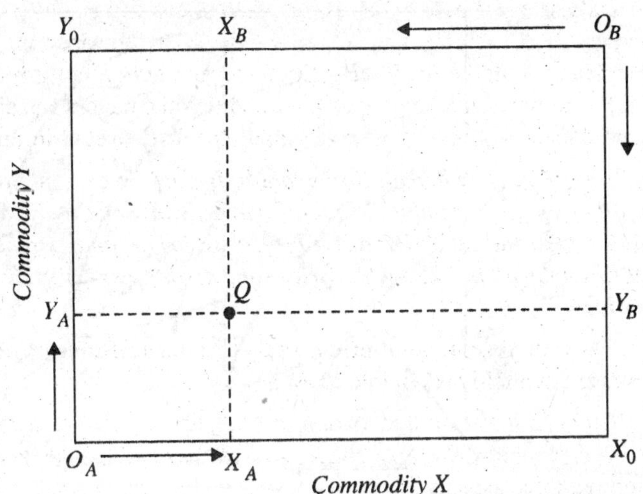

Fig. 37.1. *Edgeworth Box*

It follows from above that Edgeworth Box has fixed dimensions representing the maximum available quantities of X and Y to be distributed between the two individuals. We further assume that the two individuals between them will entirely consume all the available quantities of the two goods. It may be noted that a point in the Edgeworth Box represents a particular distribution pattern of two goods between the two consumers. This implies that if the two individuals trade goods with each other and accordingly move from one point in the Edgeworth Box to another, the quantities purchased and sold of each good would be equal. Thus, with trade or exchange of goods, it is the distribution or consumption of two goods of the two individuals that will change, the total quantities of the two goods remaining constant.

In the Edgeworth Consumption Box we also draw the indifference curves of the two individuals A and B depicting their scale of preferences between the two goods. As we move upward from bottom-left to top right, the satisfaction of individual A increases and that of B decreases, that is, A-moves to successively higher indifference curves and individual B to successively lower indifference curves.

We can now show that the *general exchange equilibrium would lie somewhere on the contract curve*, that is, the curve QT in Fig. 37.2 which passes through the tangency points of indifference curves of two individuals. At these tangency points of indifference curves, MRS_{xy} of individual A equals that of individual B. Thus, the general equilibrium of exchange will occur when the following condition holds good :-

$$MRS^{A}_{XY} = MRS^{B}_{XY}$$

Since a point on the contract curve lies within the Edgeworth box with the fixed quantities of the two goods, the equilibrium reached after exchange or trading between the two individuals implies that the distribution for consumption of the two goods between the two individuals would just exhaust the available quantities of the two goods.

From the above it cannot be known at which specific point or location of the contract curve, the general equilibrium of exchange will be reached. This is because the equality of MRS_{xy} of the two individuals exists at all points of the contract curve. However, if we know the initial distribution of two goods between the two individuals we can pinpoint the boundaries within which the general equilibrium of exchange would lie. Consider Figure 37.2. If the *initial distribution* of two goods between the two individuals is represented by point C where individual A has X_{AI} amount of good X and Y_{A1} amount of good Y. The remaining quantity of good X, that is, $X_0 - XA_1 = X_{BI}$ *would be allocated to* individual B and the remaining Y_{B1} amount of good Y would go to individual B. At this initial distribution of goods X and Y between the two individuals A and B the indifference curves of two individuals are intersecting. Now, this initial distribution at point C cannot be the position of

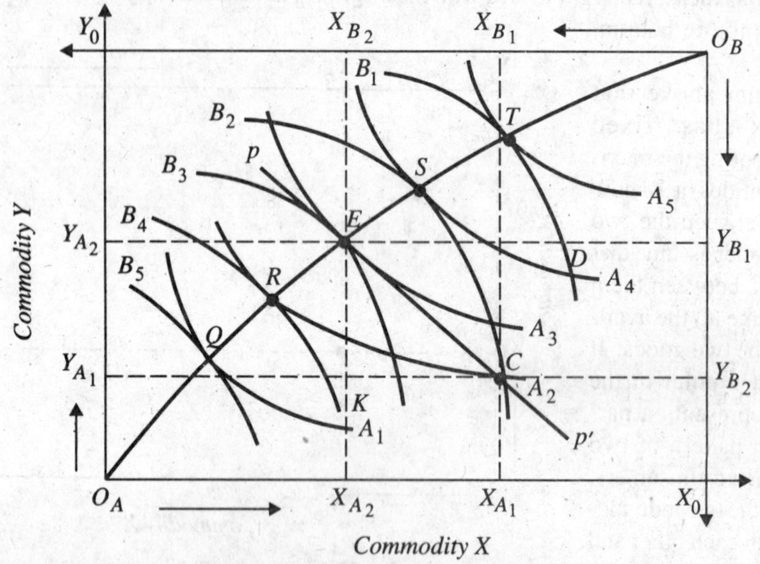

Fig. 37.2. *General Equilibrium of Exchange*

equilibrium for the two individuals, since the two individuals can gain in welfare or, in other words, can become better off if they exchange some amounts of the goods possessed by them and move to the contract curve. If the individuals think that they can benefit from trading or exchange, they will trade with each others. As long as they think there are possibilities of becoming better off, they will exchange goods and end up at the contract curve.

With the initial distribution of two goods as implied by point C, if the two individuals through exchange of goods between them move to the point R on the contract curve, individual B reaches on his higher indifference curve B_4 and therefore becomes better off and A is no worse off as he remains on the same indifference curve A_2 as on the initial distribution point C. On the other hand, if through exchange they move to point S on the contract curve, individual A becomes better off and individual B no worse off as compared to the initial position C. And if through exchange of goods they move to any point between R and S on the contract curve both the individuals will gain from exchange of goods as they will be reaching their respective higher indifference curves.

With initial distribution at point C and through exchange of goods nearer they move to point R on the contract curve, individual B will benefit more and nearer they move to point S on the contract curve, the individual A will gain more as compared to the initial distribution position C. *Where exactly on the contract curve, their equilibrium position of exchange will lie depends upon the bargaining power of each individual.* With their almost equal bargaining power, their equilibrium position of exchange on the contract curve may lie at point E where the two individuals gain almost equally as a result of exchange. Thus, if the initial distribution of two individuals is not on the contract curve, there will be tendency on the part of individuals to trade or exchange goods between themselves and to move to a point on the contract curve because in doing so they will be increasing their satisfaction.

It is evident from the foregoing analysis that the position of exchange equilibrium can be somewhere between R and S on the contract curve. *On all points between R and S, the exchange equilibrium can exist. Although equilibrium will exist at a point on the contract curve, there is no unique position of exchange equilibrium ; all points between R and S on the contract curve are possible equilibrium positions.* If point *E* on the contract curve is the position of exchange equilibrium actually reached, then individual *A* has exchanged the amount of commodity *X* equal to *CK* for the amount of commodity *Y* equal to *KE* Since point *E* lies on the contract curve which is the locus of the tangency points of indifference curves of the two individuals, marginal rate of substitution between the two goods (MRS_{XY}) of individual A equals marginal rate of substitution between the two commodities (MRS_{XY}) of individual *B*. Thus exchange of *CK* of commodity *X* for *KE* of commodity *Y* has been settled between them at the equilibrium position *E*. The general equilibrium of exchange attained at point *E* on the contract curve has the following important features :

1. Individuals maximise their satisfaction by equating their MRS_{XY} *subject to their initial endowments of goods.*
2. Since the equilibrium point *E* lies within the Edgeworth Box, drawn with the given amounts of two goods, the exchange of goods between the two individuals when they move to the equilibrium point *E* on the contract curve would imply that quantity sold of each good equals the quantity purchased of the good. That is, markets for the two goods would clear. This implies that on moving to the equilibrium position *E*, individual *A* relative to his initial endowment of goods is selling good *X* and buying good *Y*. The opposite is true of individual *B* who buys good *X* and sells good *Y*. The quantity sold and purchased of each good must equal each other. If this does not happen the two markets will not clear and shortages or surplus would emerge.
3. The general exchange equilibrium determines not only the final distribution of two goods between the individuals *but also a certain exchange rate (i.e. relative prices of the two goods)*. Thus at the equilibrium position *E*, the exchange rate *CK* of *X* for *KE* of *Y* has been settled between them. It is at this price ratio that exchange of goods takes place between the individuals.
4. The general equilibrium of exchange does not lead to the determination of *absolute prices* of goods but only *relative prices* of goods. This will be explained in detail later in this chapter.
5. The general equilibrium of exchange must lie on the contract curve, and given the initial distribution implied by point *C*, it must lie between the point *R* and *S* on the contract curve. *The general exchange equilibrium cannot be at a point in the Edgeworth Box which is not on the contract curve.* This is because at a point which is not on the contract curve, indifference curves of two individuals will intersect each other and therefore their MRS_{XY} will not be equal to each other.
6. The equilibrium can lie *anywhere* between *R* and *S* on the contract curve, that is, general equilibrium of exchange in this bargaining is *not unique*.

GENERAL EQUILIBRIUM OF PRODUCTION

We now extend our analysis of general equilibrium to the sphere of production. Production of goods requires the use of inputs or factors of production. The level of production of goods depends upon the allocation of resources to them. As emphasised in the beginning, the general equilibrium analysis takes into account the mutual inter-dependence of markets. In it, we are not only concerned with the mutual inter-dependence of markets for goods between themselves but also between product markets and factor markets. To keep our analysis simple we shall assume that two factors or inputs, labour and capital, are required for the production of two goods *X* and *Y*. This analysis of general equilibrium by taking two goods and two factors will enable us to capture the essential characteristics of the general equilibrium of production, Besides taking 2 × 2 model, we make the following assumptions :

1. All units of labour are homogeneous so that they receive equal remunerations for their contribution to the production of goods. So is the case with all units of capital.

2. The available quantities of the two factors, labour and capital, are fixed in the economy and both of them are fully employed and utilised.

3. There is smooth production function for each good so that production factors, labour and capital, can be freely transferred from one good to the other.

4. Technology is given which together with the factor endowments limits the production possibilities.

It may be mentioned here that there are four markets in the model considered here : two factor markets of labour and capital, and two product markets of goods *X* and *Y*.

With the above assumptions we shall analyse the general equilibrium of production under conditions of perfect competion in all the markets. It may be emphasised again that the various markets are inter-related. For example, if more labour is employed in the production of good *X*, then, given its fixed supply, some labour will have to be withdrawn from the production of good *Y*. Changes in labour allocation between the production of the two goods, would also have repercussions on the use of capital in the production of two goods. It is indeed the task of general equilibrium analysis to determine the pattern of relative prices and quantities of goods and factors at which all markets clear together, that is, prices and quantities at which demand and supply in each of the four markets are brought into equilibrium simultaneously.

Edgeworth Production Box and General Equilibrium of Production

As in case of general equilibrium of exchange or consumption, the general equilibrium of production can also be analysed with the help of Edgeworth Box diagram. In case of Edgeworth Production Box, dimensions of the box represent the available fixed quantities of the two factors, labour and capital. Thus, in the Edgeworth Production Box as shown in Figure 37.3, along the horizontal axis we measure the quantity of labour and along the vertical axis we measure the quantity

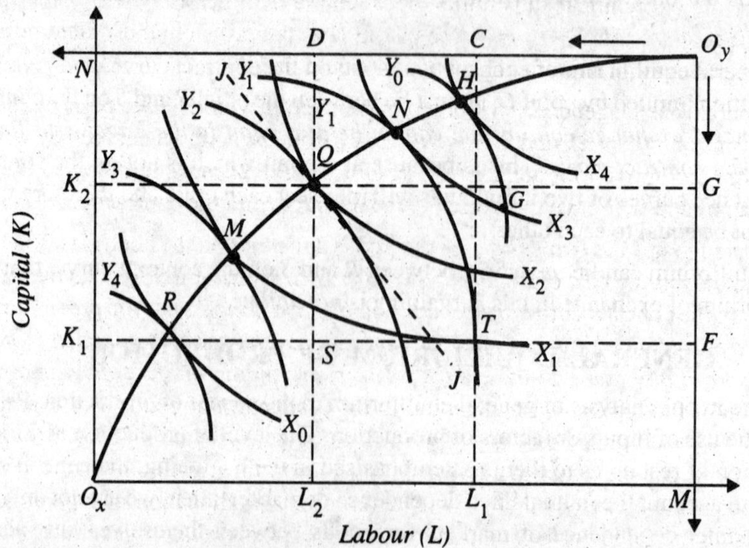

Fig. 37.3. *General Equilibrium of Production*

of capital. In this box various isoquants are also drawn for the products *X* and *Y*. For good *X*, various isoquants representing successively higher levels of output such as X_0, X_1, X_2 etc. are drawn with the bottom left hand corner O_x as their origin. For good *Y*, various isoquants such as Y_0, Y_1, Y_2 representing-successively higher levels of output of Y are drawn with top right hand corner O_y as the origin. The isoquant map of each good exhibits its production function. As constructed, isoquants for good X imply that the good X is relatively capital-intensive and isoquants for good Y imply that good Y is relatively labour-intensive. This means that for any given factor price ratio, that is, ratio of price of labour to the price of capital (w/r), minimisation of cost for *a given level of output* of good X requires higher capital-labour ratio (K/L) than that of good Y.

It is important to note that any point in the Edgeworth Box represents a *particular allocation of labour and capital* between the two industries, one producing good X and the other producing good Y. Various points in the box represent different alternative allocations of factors between the two commodities. For example, point T in the box shows that $O_x L_1$ (or $K_1 T$) amount of labour and $O_x K_1$ (or $L_1 T$) amount of capital are allocated to the production of X and the remaining amount of labour TF and the remaining amount of capital TC are allocated to the production of good Y. It will be seen from Figure 37.3 that the points M, Q, N etc. represent different allocations of factors from the point T.

Now, a smooth curve RH joining the tangency points of isoquants of X and Y has been drawn. This is called the *production contract curve.* It can be shown that the general equilibrium of production under competitive conditions in the factor markets would lie somewhere on this production contract curve. The allocation of factors implied by the point away from the contract curve such as point T cannot be the possible competitive equilibrium position. This is because from the point T where X-isoquant and Y-isoquant are intersecting, the economy can move by re-allocating resources between the two goods to a point M or N on the contract curve where the output of one good increases without the reduction in output of the other. And, if through reallocation of factors, the economy moves to any point between M and N on the contract curve, say to point Q the outputs of both the goods X and Y would be higher than at T. Thus, resource allocation implied by a point on the contract curve leads to greater output than those not on the contract curve. Since the production contract curve is the locus of the tangency points of the isoquants of X and Y, slopes of isoquants of the two goods are equal to each other at various points on it. Since slope of an isoquant measures marginal rate of technical substitution between the two factors (MRS_{LK}), on the various points on the contract curve, $MRTS^{X}_{LX} = MRTS^{S}_{LK}$. It is at the production efficient points of the contract curve that general equilibrium of production would lie.

Now, what ensures that the general equilibrium of production would lie at a point on the contract curve. If the two firms or industries find themselves away from the contract curve, they will trade or exchange the factors and move to a point on the contract curve because in doing so they will be increasing their output and will have therefore incentive to move to the contract curve.

It should be noted that if the firms produce the goods at a point on the contract curve, one firm can increase output only at the cost of output of the other firm. Thus, if in Fig. 37.3 the firms move from point M to N on the contract curve, the production of good X increases, the production of good Y decreases. It is worth mentioning that *point of general equilibrium of production is not unique because it may occur at any point on the contract curve, depending on the starting point*, that is, the initial allocation of factors (labour and capital to the production of goods. For example, if the initial allocation of factors is denoted by point T in Fig. 37.3, then with reallocation through trading of factors, the two firms can move to and attain general equilibrium at any point on the segment MN of the production contract curve. Further, with a different initial allocation of a given amount of factors, say point G in the Edgeworth Box, there will be a different point of general equilibrium of production anywhere on the segment HN of the contract curve.

Note that an initial point such as T or G shows not only the allocation of factors between the goods but also the amounts of the two goods produced. Further, it may also be noted that in the equilibrium situation *how much amount of goods are produced depends on the demands for them which in turn are determined by the initial ownership of the factors by the two individuals* and the factor prices together with their preferences of the two goods. Ownership of the factors and factor prices determine the income of the people which determine the demand for the two goods.

It will be observed from Fig. 37.3 that given the initial factor allocation point *T*, if the general equilibrium of production occurs at point *Q* on the contact curve *RH*, it will determine not only allocation of factors between the two goods but also the equilibrium amount of the two goods produced. Thus, if the general equilibrium of production occurs at point *Q*, it means that output X_2 of good *X* and output Y_2 of good *Y* are determined. Besides, the *general equilibrium of production determines ratio of factor prices (i.e. exchange rate of labour for capital*). It will also be seen from Fig. 37.3 that in moving from the starting point *T*, if the general equilibrium of production occurs at point *Q*, *TS* amount of labour has been exchanged for *QS* amount of capital.

The exactly at which point on the production contract curve the general equilibrium of production would lie depends upon the demand for goods *X* and *Y*. If the demand for good *X* is relatively higher than that of good *Y*, the equilibrium of production would lie on a some upper point such as *N* on the contract curve *RH* where a larger quantity of good *X* and smaller quantity of good *Y* are produced. On the other hand, the lower the demand for *X* and greater the demand for *Y*, the production equilibrium would lie at a lower point on the contract curve which indicates smaller output of *X* and larger output of *Y*. Thus, the exact point of equilibrium on the contract curve depends upon the specific consumer' demand for goods *X* and *Y*. And *individuals demand for good is determined by the initial ownership of factors and the factor price received for them.*

From the foregoing analysis it follows that the general equilibrium of production requires the *simultaneous equilibrium of the two factor markets determining* allocation of resources between the production of the two goods. For an economy with many goods and many factors, the general equilibrium of production requires that the marginal rate of technical substitution *between any pair of factors* is the same for all goods and all producers using the same pair of factors.

Transformation Curve and General Equilibrium of Production

In our above analysis we have shown the output of two goods *X* and *Y* through isoquants in the *factor space* of the Edgeworth Production Box. To bring outputs of two goods directly into the picture and to clearly show the equilibrium in markets for goods, we require to display outputs of the two goods in the *output space*. This is done through a familiar concept of *transformation curve* which is also known as production possibility curve. A transformation curve shows the alternative combinations of two goods that can be produced with the given fixed amounts of the factors. The transformation curve is derived from the contract curve of production in the space by mapping or plotting the various output combinations of two goods directly in *output space* corresponding to the various points of the contract curve. In Figure 37.4 A transformation curve has been drawn from the production contract curve in Figure 37.3. For example, corresponding to point *Q* on the contract curve *RH* in Figure 37.3 indicating X_2 level of

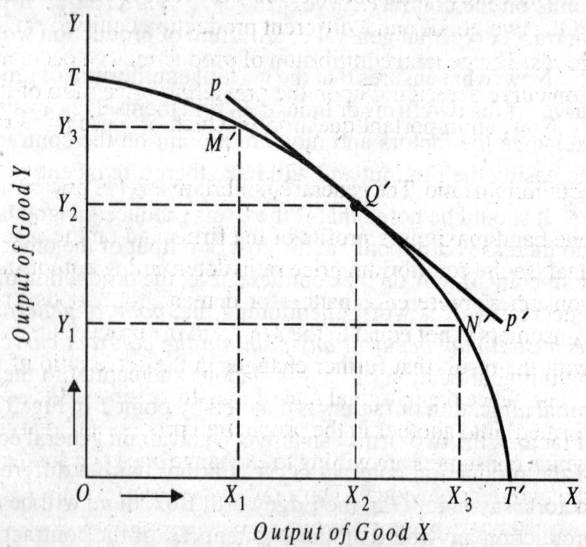

Fig. 37.4. *Transformation Curve*

output of good X and Y_2 level of output of good Y, we plot the point Q' in the output space of Figure 37.4. Likewise, point N' corresponding to point N on the contract curve, point M' corresponding to the point M of the contract curve are plotted and on joining such points as N', Q', M' we get the transformation curve TT'. A transformation curve shows how one good is transformed into another by transferring resources from the production of one good into the production of the other.

Three aspects of the transformation curve are worth noting. First, *it is concave to the origin* which implies that the amount of commodity Y which has to be given up or sacrificed in order to produce an additional unit of good X goes on increasing as we produce more of good X. This implies the operation of diminishing returns to scale in the production of X. In case returns to scale increase, the transformation curve obtained would be convex to the origin. We will get a straight line transformation curve when returns to scale are constant. Thus the shape of the transformation curve depends upon the nature of the production function of a commodity.

Secondly, the slope of the transformation curve at a point measures the marginal rate of transformation between the two goods. Marginal rate of transformation of good X for good Y ($MRTxy$) indicates the amount by which the production of good Y has to be reduced to produce one more unit of good X with the help of resources released from the reduction in output of good Y, that is, MRT_{xy} is the rate at which one good is transformed into another and is equal to the ratio of marginal costs of production of the two goods. Thus

$$MRT_{XY} = \frac{MC_X}{MC_Y}$$

Thirdly, every point on the production possibility or transformation curve is a point of general equilibrium of production. This is because we have derived the transformation curve by mapping the production contract curve from input space to output space.

GENERAL EQUILIBRIUM OF PRODUCTION AND EXCHANGE (CONSUMPTION)

There are several points on the transformation curve; each point will indicate a different price ratio of the two goods and a different production equilibrium indicating a different output-mix of the two goods. The general equilibrium of production can occur at any of the points on the given transformation curve depending upon the prevailing price ratio of the two goods.

Now, an important question is which of these price ratios of commodities or MRT_{xy} will be the equilibrium ratio. The general equilibrium level of price ratio $\left(\frac{P_X}{P_Y}\right)$ or MRT_{XY} will be one which on the one hand maximises profits of the firms and on the other maximises satisfaction of consumers. To analyse the equilibrium price ratio determining output-mix, we have to introduce in our analysis the consumers preference pattern or demand for goods. It can be easily shown that if MRS_{xy} of the consumers is not equal to the MRT_{xy} in the production, consumer satisfaction will not be maximised with the result that further changes in the price ratio of the two goods and output-mix will tend to occur. Since the marginal rate of transformation (MRT_{xy}) shows the rate at which one good is 'transformed' into another in the production process and marginal rate of substitution measures the rate at which consumers are willing to exchange one good for the other, equilibrium cannot be reached unless the two rates are equal. Thus, only when MRT_{xy} equals MRS_{xy}, planned pattern of production will be consistent with the preferences of consumers and ensure general equilibrium of production and exchange. This can be made clear with a simple numerical example. For instance, suppose at a given output-mix of two goods X and Y, MRT_{xy} of the producers of the economy is $3Y/1X$ and MRS_{xy} of consumers equals $2Y/1X$. Thus, in this case MRS_{xy} of consumers is less than MRT_{xy} of producers. That is, the economy can producer 3 units of Y by foregoing one unit of good X, while the consumers are willing to exchange or buy 2 units of *Y* for one unit of *X*. MRS_{xy} of consumers being less than MRT_{xy} of producers implies that relatively greater quantity of commodity *X* and the smaller quantity of commodity *Y* is being produced than desired by the consumers. Obviously, if the economy redues the

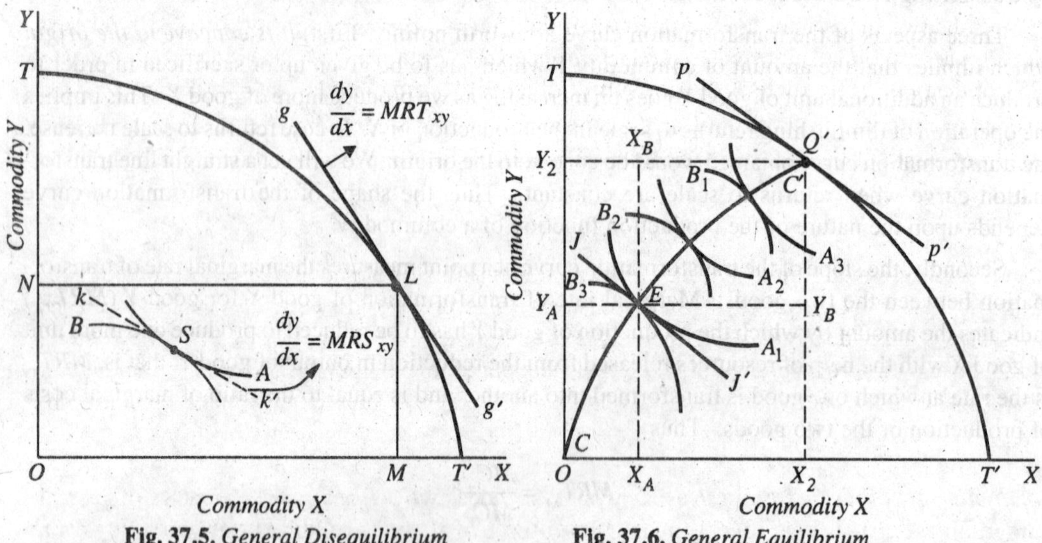

Fig. 37.5. *General Disequilibrium* **Fig. 37.6.** *General Equilibrium*

production of *X* by one unit and product 3 units more of *Y* and give them to the consumers, their satisfaction or welfare will increase as they are willing to get 2 units of *Y* for the sacrifice of one unit of *X*. Thus consumers' satisfaction can be raised by expanding the production of *Y* and reducing the production of *X* until the two rates, namely, MRS_{xy} of consumers and MRT_{xy} of producers become equal. General equilibrium will thus be reached if with adjustment in output-mix of the two commodities, MRS_{xy} equals MRT_{xy}. In a free market economy, forces of competition would ensure such adjustment which will bring about product-mix that will equate MRS_{xy} of consumers with MRT_{xy} of producers and thus ensuring maximum consumers' satisfaction.

The general equilibrium of production together with the general equilibrium of exchange (or consumption) requires that the marginal rate of transformation *(MRT_{xy})* be equal not only to marginal rate of substitution *(MRS_{xy})* of the consumers but also MRS_{xy} of the two consumers be equal to each other.

Thus, for the achievement of general equilibrium of production and exchange simultaneously we arrive at the following condition:

$$MRT_{XY} = MRS^{A}_{XY} = MRS^{B}_{XY}$$

The overall general equilibrium of production and exchange is illustrated in Figure 37.5 and 37.6. Consider Figure 37.5 where a transformation curve *TT'* has been drawn. Let us consider the point *L* on the production transformation curve *TT'* . At point *L* on it *OM* of good *X* and *ON* of good *Y* are being produced. With the given preference pattern and resource endowments of the two consumers, their indifference curves are tangent to each other at point *S* and their MRS_{xy} is indicated by the slope of the tangent line *kk'* . It will be seen from Figure 37.5 that MRS_{xy} of consumers is less than MRT_{xy} of producers indicating that production pattern is inconsistent with consumers preferences. Thus, the system is in disequilibrium indicating that relatively greater quantity of *X* and smaller quantity *Y* is being produced than desired by the consumers. In response to this disequilibrium situation and to maximise their profits producers would tend to produce more of *Y* and less of *X* and this process of adjustment in output mix will continue until the MRT_{xy} in production is brought into equality with MRS_{xy} of consumers. With this equality, general equilibrium of production and exchange (consumption) would be attained. This general equilibrium is shown in Figure 37.6 where at position Q' on the transformation curve TT', OX_2 level of output of X and OY_2 level of output of Yare being produced and MRT_{xy} at point equals MRS_{xy} at E (slopes of JJ' and PP' are equal). Note that there is general equilibrium of production at point Q' because all points of transformation curve corresponds to the points of the production contract curve. There is general equilibrium of exchange or consumption as MRS of, the two individuals are the same (their indifference curves being tangent to each other at point E). There is joint equilibrium of production and exchange as the MRT_{xy} in production is equal to MRS_{xy} of the two individuals at the consumption equilibrium point E. Thus, with point Q on the transformation curve TT' and point E on the consumption contract curve drawn in the Edgeworth Box made from point Q', the following condition of general equilibrium of production and consumption holds good:–

$$MRT_{XY} = MRS^{A}_{XY} = MRS^{B}_{XY}$$

General equilibrium of production determines total output X_2 of. commodity X and total output Y_2 of commodity. It is with OX_2 and OY_2 as the dimensions, Edgeworth Box has been drawn and indifference curves of two individuals depicting their scale of preferences are drawn with CC' as the contract curve. Consumption equilibrium point E reveals that out of total output X_2 of good X the amount X_A is being consumed by individual A and the remaining amount of X goes to individual B for consumption. Out of total output Y_2 of commodity Y, the amount Y_A is consumed by A and the remaining amount by the individual B.

Conclusion. It follows from above that in our two goods, two persons ($2 \times 2 \times 2$) model of general equilibrium, we arrive at the conclusion that the position of general equilibrium can exist. However, this general equilibrium position is *not unique*. There can be *several points* of general equilibrium on the production possibility curve IT' in Figure 37.6 and consumption contract curve in it depending upon the T', *distribution* of income which (among other things) is determined by ownership of resources. A general equilibrium position at point Q', on the production possibility curve IT' in Fig. 37.6 indicates that factor markers of labour and capital and product markets of goods X and Y are simultaneously in equilibrium and determine the following things :—

1. relative prices of factors (w & r) as indicated by the exchange rate of ST of labour for SQ of Y in Figure 37.3
2. Allocation of factors between products X and Y as indicated by point Q in Figure 37.3.
3. relative prices of products X and Y as measured by the slope of tangent PP' in Figure 37.6.
4. the product-mix, that is, the levels of output of goods X and Y as given by point Q' in Figure 37.6.
5. the distribution of goods X and Y between the two individuals as indicated by point E in Figure 37.6.

GENERAL EQUILIBRIUM AND PERFECT COMPETITION

In our foregoing analysis we have explained the general equilibrium of exchange and production by taking two individuals, two factors and two goods case (*i.e.* $2 \times 2 \times 2$ model) through the process of bargaining by the individuals. It was *emphasised that exactly at what point on the contract curve the equilibrium occurs depends on the bargaining strengths of the two individuals.* It was further pointed out that equilibrium arrived at through bargaining between the two parties is not unique, it can occur anywhere on the consumption contract curve or the production contract curve as the case may be. We shall now explain *how general equilibrium is established when perfect competition prevails in the product and factor markets.* In other words, we shall now show that competitive equilibrium is consistent with general equilibrium.

It may be noted that in perfectly competitive market there are many buyers and sellers of products and factors. If a buyer does not like the terms of exchange of one seller, he can look for another seller who is willing to exchange on better terms, Therefore, in competitive markets no individual buyer or seller of a product or factor is in a position to influence the price. They take the price prevailing in the market as given and constant and are therefore mere *price takers*. At the given price, they decide how much to buy or sell of a good or factor. We shall explain how general equilibrium of exchange and production, both separately and simultaneously, is achieved under perfect competition. It will be known from our analysis made below that *while in case of the bargaining between the two parties, the general equilibrium is indeterminate or not unique, under competitive conditions general equilibrium is unique*.

Perfect Competition and General Equilibrium of Exchange

We will explain first general equilibrium of exchange under competitive conditions. With perfect competition in the buying and selling of goods no individual can influence the prices of goods; he takes the prices as given and constant. Thus, with given prices of goods X and Y, consumer A maximises his satisfaction by equating his marginal rate of substitution (MRS_{xy}) with the given price ratio. Thus

$$MRS^{A}_{XY} = \frac{P_x}{P_y} \qquad \text{... }(i)$$

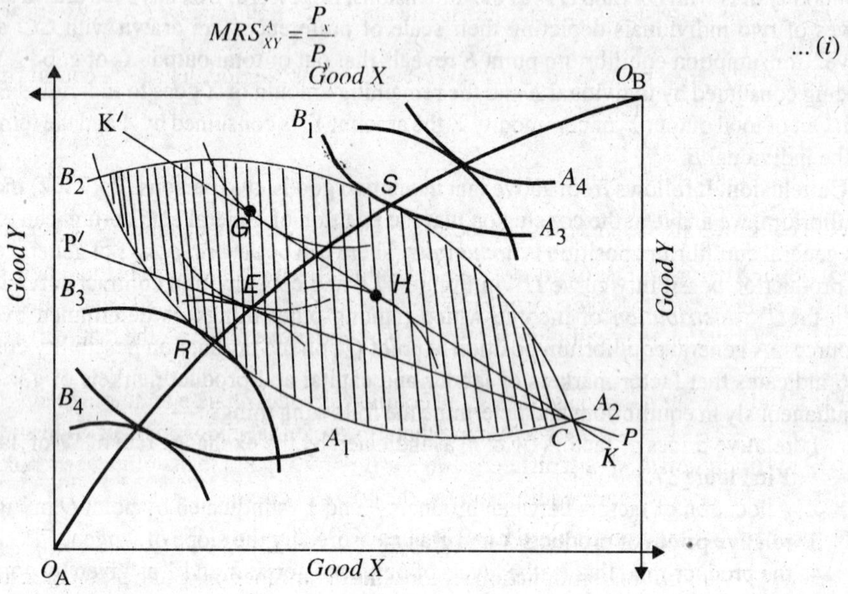

Fig. 37.7. *General Equilibrium of Exchange Under Perfectly Competitive Conditions*

Similarly, the individual B would be maximising his satisfaction when

$$MRS^{B}_{XY} = \frac{P_x}{P_y} \qquad \text{... }(ii)$$

Since under perfect competition both the individuals will be facing the same set of prices, from (*i*) and (*ii*) we get

$$MRS^{A}_{XY} = MRS^{B}_{XY} = \frac{P_X}{P_Y}$$

Now consider Figure 37.7. Suppose the initial endowments of individuals A and B is given by point C. Further suppose that the prevailing perfectly competitive price ratio $\frac{P_x}{P_y}$ is denoted by the slope of the price line PP' which is drawn through the initial endowment point C. In fact, the price line

PP' passing through initial endowment point C is the budget line for the two consumers. With the initial endowment of the two individuals represented by point C and the price-ratio line PP' the two individuals in their attempt to maximise satisfaction will trade goods with each other and move to a *unique point E* on the contract curve where their indifference curves are tangent to the given price line PP'. In this way, by adding the assumption of perfect competition in the sale and purchase of goods and starting from initial endowment point C we have reached the unique point E where the general equilibrium of exchange occurs on the segment RS of the contract curve.

With position C as the starting point and point E where they reach the equilibrium position, individual A has sold good X and purchased good Y, whereas individual B has purchased good X and sold good Y. Price ratio of the two goods is given by the slope of the budget line PP'. At equilibrium at E with the budget line PP' (*i.e.* the given price ratio) the quantity of good X demanded by B equals the quantity of good X supplied by A and, similarly, quantity demanded of good Y equals the quantity supplied of good Y. As a result, markets for the two goods are in equilibrium and therefore general equilibrium of exchange exists. Note that a *general equilibrium refers to a set of prices at which quantity demanded equals the quantity supplied.* We thus that *competitive equilibrium is consistent with perfect competition.*

However, it may be noted that not all prices are consistent with general equilibrium under perfect competition. For instance, price ratio of the two goods represented by the price line KK' which also passes through the initial endowment point C. With this price ratio or price line KK' individual A is in equilibrium at point G and individual B is in equilibrium at point H, the markets of goods X and Y are not in equilibrium as their MRS_{XY} of the two individuals are not equal to $\frac{P_x}{P_y}$ at the same point. While individual B demands less of good X, the individual A is willing to supply more of it, that is, surplus of good X emerges in the market. As regards good Y, with price ratio line KK', individual A demands more of Y, than individual B is willing to supply it Thus, with price line KK', the markets of two goods are not in equilibrium.

It should be emphasised again that the equilibrium of exchange on the segment RS of the contract curve in Fig. 37.7 is reached by assuming that C is the initial endowment of goods (i.e. initial income) of the two individuals. With a different initial endowment point in the Edgeworht box, we will obtain a different point of exchange equilibrium on the contract curve.

Perfect Competiton and General Equilibrium of Production

General equilibrium of production requires the determination of allocation of resources among the firms which use the factors for production of goods. We have seen above that general equilibrium of production occurs at a point on the production contract curve where the $MRTS_{LK}$ in the production of commodity X equals the $MRTS_{LK}$ in the production of commodity Y. With perfect competition prevailing in the factor markets factor-price ratio $\left(\frac{w}{r}\right)$ will be given for each firm. In order to minimise cost for producing a given output, a firm will be in equilibrium when $MRTS_{LK} = \frac{w}{r}$, where w stands for wage rate (*i.e.* price of labour and γ stands for rate of interest (*i.e.* price of captial).

Now, what ensures that the general equilibrium of production would occur at a point on the contract curve. As we are assuming factor markets are competitive, it is the competitive forces that would bring the economy in equilibrium at a point on the contract curve. If the two firms find themselves away from the contract curve, they will trade or exchange the factors and move to a point on the contract curve because in doing so they will be increasing their output and will have therefore incentive to move to the contract curve. To produce a given level of output of a commodity, each firm will minimise its cost of production by equating marginal rate of technical substitution between factors ($MRTS_{LK}$) with the *same factor price ratio* of labour and capital $\frac{w}{r}$ where w stands for the wage rate of labour and r for the rental price of capital. To conclude, under competitive conditions general equilibrium of production would occur at a point on the contract curve where the following condition holds :

$$MRTS_{LK}^{X} = MRTS_{LK}^{Y} = \frac{w}{r}$$

Consider Fig. 37.3 again, competitive forces will bring the economy to be in general equilibrium at point Q on the production contract curve in Figure 37.3. It should be noted that JJ' is the price line which passes through the initial endowment point T representing the given factor-price ratio $\left(\frac{w}{r}\right)$.

Perfect Competition and General Equilibrium of Production and Exchange

In the two factors, two goods and two persons (2 × 2 × model) with the exchange conducted through bargaining between the two persons. We have explained above that the simultaneous equilibrium of production and exchange occurs at a point where the following condition is fulfilled :

$$MRTS_{XY} = MRS_{XY}^{A} = MRS_{XY}^{B}$$

As explained earlier, marginal rate of transformation between two goods, MRT_{XY} is equal to the ratio of marginal costs of production of two commodities. Thus

$$MRT_{XY} = \frac{MC_X}{MC_Y}$$

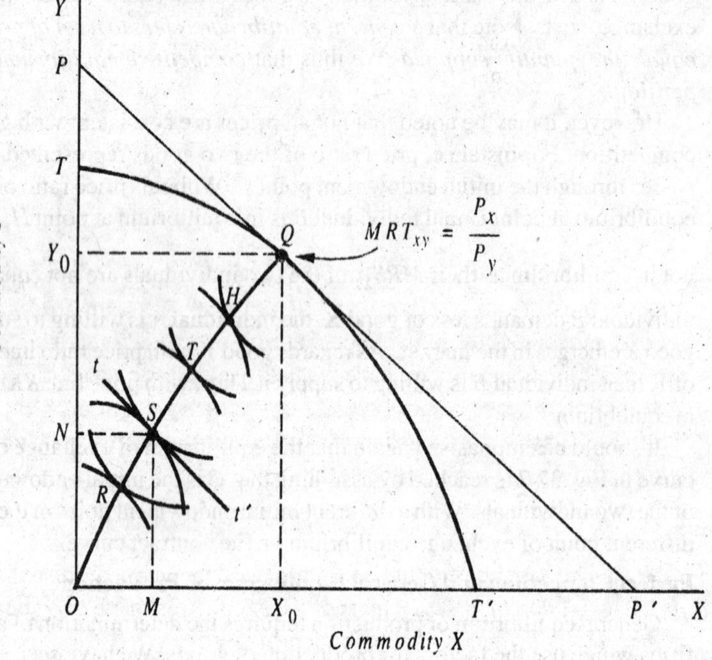

Fig. 37.8. *General Equilibrium of Production and Exchange*

Now, if perfect competition is prevailing in the goods markets, then the individual firms producing the goods would have no influence on their prices and will, therefore, equate the given price of each good with its marginal cost of production. Thus

$$MC_X = P_X \text{ and } MC_Y = P_Y$$

The slope of the production transformation curve measures the marginal rate of transformation (MRT_{xy}). Thus, given the market prices of goods for the firms as is the case under perfect competition, the general equilibrium of production will occur at a point on the production transformation curve at the point where marginal rate of transformation equals the ratio of prices of goods. Thus, in equilibrium under perfect, competition.

$$MRT_{XY} = \frac{MC_X}{MC_Y} = \frac{P_X}{P_Y} \quad \text{... (i)}$$

Such general equilibrium of production is represented by point Q on the transformation curve TT in Figure 37.8 where the price line PP' is tangent to it. Note that the slope of the price line PP'

measures the given ratio of competitive prices of the two goods $\left(\frac{P_x}{P_y}\right)$. This general equilibrium of production at point Q on the production transformation curve TT' determines the product mix; X_0 of good X and Y_0 of good Y.

It follows from above that, given the factor endowments of the economy and the nature of production function (*i.e.*, technology), under perfect competition the general equilibrium of production reaches a unique position on the transformation curve of the economy and a unique position on the corresponding contract curve in the Edgeworth Production Box.

Now, we have to see how in general equilibrium under perfect competition, this equilibrium product mix is to be distributed for consumption between the two individuals. We know that in order to maximise satisfaction, consumers equate their marginal rate of substitution between the two goods (MRS_{xy}) with the ratio of the given competitive prices of the two goods. Thus, in equilibrium under perfect competition.

$$MRS^A_{XY} = \frac{P_x}{P_y} \quad \text{and} \quad MRS^B_{XY} = \frac{P_x}{P_y} \qquad \text{... } (ii)$$

Since the consumers and producers (firms) *face the same price ratio of the two goods*, from conditions *(i)* and *(ii)* above we have

$$MRT_{xy} = MRS^A_{xy} = MRS^B_{xy} = \frac{P_x}{P_y}$$

This general equilibrium of production and exchange is shown in Figure 37.8 where from point Q at the transformation curve we have made Edgeworth Box with dimension X_0 of good X and Y_0 of good Y. It will be observed from Figure 37.8 that at its point S on the contract curve, the slope of the indifference curve of the two individuals measuring the marginal rate of substitution (MRS_{xy}) between two goods is equal to the slope of the price line PP'. Thus, *with perfect competition we are able to determine a unique position of general equilibrium of production and exchange at a point on the contract curve.*

It may however be emphasised again that even this position of general equilibrium depends on the *initial allocation of fixed amounts* of the two factors to the two goods which in turn is determined by the *initial* endowments or distribution of goods (*i.e.* distribution of real income) between the two individuals. With a different initial allocation of factors to the two goods or different initial endowments of the goods of the two individuals even with perfect competition, we would have reached a different position. of general equilibrium of production and exchange.

GENERAL EQUILIBRIUM DETERMINES ONLY RELATIVE PRICES

It is important to note that micro-economic theory is concerned with analysing the factors that determine *relative prices* and not *absolute prices.* Relative price means prices of a good as compared to the price of another good or a factor. In other words, by relative prices we mean the ratio of prices of goods. That micro-economic theory is concernsed with relative prices is made quite clear in the analysis of general equilibrium analysis. In our analysis of general equilibrium when we talked about the determination of factor prices, it was the ratio of factor prices (*i.e.*, the ratio of price of labour to the price of capital, $\frac{w}{r}$) as measured by slope of the tangent line JJ' to the relevant isoquants that was determined. In fact, we did not explain how absolute prices, namely, wage rate of labour, w and price of capital, r were determined (see Fig. 37.3). Likewise, in general equilibrium of exchange we did not concern ourselves with the determination of absolute price of good X (*i.e.*, P_x) and absolute price of good Y (*i.e.* P_Y) separately; we only showed how general equilibrium determine the *ratio of prices* of two goods *i.e.* $\left(\frac{P_x}{P_y}\right)$. as measured by the slope of prcie line PP' which is tangent to the indifference curces of the two individuals at point E (see Fig. 37.8). Thus we found that in Figure 37.6 general equilibrium is established at point Q on the transformation curve TT' where $MRT_{XY} = MRS^A{}_{XY} = MRS^B{}_{XY}$ and saw that this yields relative prices of goods X and Y, that is, the ratio $\frac{P_X}{P_Y}$ which is measured by the slope of the transformation curve at that equilibrium point Q' and not the absolute prices.

An important thing to note is that because it is the relative and not absolute prices that result from the general equilibrium analysis that doubling or halving of *all prices* so that relative prices remain the same would not bring any change in the equilibrium position. For example, suppose the relative prices of two goods X and Y *i.e.* $\frac{P_X}{P_Y}$ as measured by the marginal rate of transformation at point Q' in Figure 37.6 is 2/1 and the relative price of labour and capital (w/r) as measured by the slope of the isoquants at point Q in Figure 37.3 is 3/1. Further suppose price of good X is Rs. 20 and the price of good Y is 10, so that relative product prices are 20/10 = 2/1 and the price of labour (w) is Rs. 30 and the price of capital (r) is Rs. 10. So the relative factor prices $\frac{w}{r}$ equals 3/1. Now, if all prices are doubled, P_x = Rs. 40, P_y = Rs. 20, w = Rs. 60 and r = Rs. 20, then the relative prices of products $\frac{P_x}{P_y} = \frac{40}{20} = \frac{2}{1}$ and relative factor prices $\frac{w}{r} = \frac{60}{20} = \frac{3}{1}$ since all relative prices have remained the same despite the change in their absolute levels, the position of general equilibrium would remain unaltered. In real terms nothing would change. Consumers would have twice the payments or income but would buy exactly the same quantities of goods X and Y. Each firm would receive double the total revenue than before but would buy and employ the same amounts of factors at double the prices. Thus, *it is the relative prices that are significant* in determining the real outcome or production, employment of factors, income distribution and the distribution of goods between the individuals. That is why micro-economic theory lays stress on the determination of relative prices. To conclude, general equilibrium analysis yields relative and not absolute prices. If absolute prices of all products and all factors change by a same percentage, the real situation would remain unchanged.

QUESTIONS FOR REVIEW

1. Distinguish between partial and general equilibrium. What does the contract curve indicate in an Edgeworth Box diagram ?

   D.U. B.Com (Hons) 1996, 1999, 2000 D.U. B.A. (Hons) 19991, 1993.

2. In what way is general equilibrium analysis more useful ?

   B.Com. (Hons) D.U. 1999.

3. In an economy characterised by two consumers, two commodities show how general equilibrium of exchange is attained. State your assumption clearly.

   B.A. (Hons) Delhi 1992.

4. What is the marginal rate of transformation ? Explain why the marginal rate of transformation of one good for another is equal to the ratio of the marginal costs of producing the two goods. *D.U. B.A. (Hons) 2001*

5. Point out the inadequacies of partial equilibrium analysis. Under what conditions can the existence of a meaningful general equilibrium solution be guaranteed ?

B.A. (Hons.) D.U. 2001

6. What do you mean by contract curve for exchange ? How can it be used to explain General Equilibrium of Exchange ? *D.U., B.Com (Hons.) 2nd Year 2007*

7. Define a contract curve. What determines the final location of the two parties on the contract curve. In what sense is the contract curve a locus of optimal locations ?

8. With the help of the Edgeworth production Box diagram, explain the general equilibrium of production. What does the production contract curve indicate ?

D.U., B.Com (Hons.) 2nd Year 2007, 2008

9. Define and illustrate general equilibrium in an economy with perfectly competitive factor and product markets. State and explain clearly the conditions under which an equilibrium will exist for such an economy. *D.U. B.A. (Hons.) 1997*

10. "General equilibrium of exchange occurs at a point on the exchange contract curve." Explain. Can there be two such points ? *D.U. B.A. (Hons.) 1994*

11. "Absolute prices are indeterminate in a model of general equilibrium analysis" True or false ? Explain. *D.U. B.A. (Hons.) 1973*

12. "General equilibrium analysis is solely concerned with relative prices" Explain.

D.U. B.A. (Hons.) 1984, 1956

13. "For an economy composed of many consumers and many commodities, the general equilibrium of exchange occurs where the marginal rate of substitution between every pair of commodities is the same for all consumers consuming both commodities." Explain this statement with the help of Edgeworth Box Diagram. *D.U., B.Com (Hons.) 2nd Year 2009*

CHAPTER 38
WELFARE ECONOMICS : AN INTRODUCTION

WHAT WELFARE ECONOMICS IS ABOUT

So far we have been concerned with the analysis of what has been called positive economics which explains merely "how it is". That is, we have been concerned with explaining how prices of products and factors are determined and further on the basis of these prices how the allocation of resources is made in a free private enterprise economy. Now, in this part of the book we shall discuss whether any allocation of resources is efficient or not. *By efficiency in economics we mean whether any state or situation regarding resource allocation maximises social welfare.* In welfare economics attempt is made to establish criteria or norms with which to judge or evaluate alternative economic states and policies from the viewpoint of efficiency or social welfare. These criteria or norms serve as a basis for recommending economic policies which will increase social welfare. Thus the norms established by welfare economics are supposed to guarantee the optimal allocation of economic resources of the society. Putting it more specifically, Prof. Baumol writes, "Welfare Economics has concerned itself mostly with policy issues which arise out of the allocation of resources, with the distribution of inputs among the various commodities and the distribution of commodities among various consumers." And it may be emphas.sed again that allocation of resources is efficient or optimum when social welfare is maximum.

The inter-relationship among various parts of the economy means that certain particular change in one part of the economy affects resource allocation in all other parts of it. Thus, a central problem in welfare economics relates to whether a particular change in resource allocation will increase or decrease social welfare. However, an almost insurmountable difficulty which is faced in welfare economics is that it is not possible to measure social *welfare objectively*, for it involves making interpersonal comparison of utilities or welfares of different individuals comprising the society. In order to avoid making interpersonal comparison of utility, whose scientific nature has been challenged, among others, by Lord Robbins, economists have mostly used what is known as *Pareto-optimality criterion* for evaluating whether social welfare increases or decreases as a result of a specific change in economic state, situation or policy. According to Pareto criterion of optimality or efficiency, *any change that makes at least one individual better off without making any other worse off is an improvement in social welfare.* Of course, when a certain change makes every one in the society better off, social welfare will undoubtedly increase. On the other hand, social welfare will decrease if a certain change makes no individual better off while it makes at least one individual worse off. With the aid of this criterion we can define the state of maximum social welfare or what is known as *Pareto optimality or economic efficiency. Economic state or situation is said to be Pareto-optimal or efficient in which allocation of resources is such that by any rearrangement of them it is impossible to make any individual better off without making any other worse off.* This concept of Pareto-optimality or economic efficiency is the basis of welfare economics and has a large number of applications in applied economics. We shall explain the conditions which ensure Pareto optimality and also critically evaluate Pareto's welfare criterion in the next chapter at length.

Pareto criterion and the concept of Pareto optimality does not embrace those changes in eco-

1.W.J. Baumol, *Economic Theory and Operations Analysis*, 4th edition, 1978, p. 406.

nomic state which make some better off and others worse off. This involves interpersonal comparisons of utility which were ruled out by Pareto and his followers. Kaldor and Hicks propounded a welfare criterion, which is known as *compensation principle*, to judge those changes in situation which make some better off and others worse off. They have claimed that their welfare criterion does not involve interpersonal comparison of utility and value judgements. It is asserted that Kaldor and Hicks rehabilitated welfare economics from the damaging criticism of Lord Robbins and founded a "*New Welfare Economics*" free from value judgments or interpersonal comparison of utility. In the development of new welfare economics, Scitovsky and Little have also made significant contributions. The critical evaluation of "New Welfare Economics" forms the subject matter of a separate chapter.

After discussing new welfare economics we shall study the concept of the *social welfare function* propounded by Bergson and Samuelson. According to this social welfare concept, any attempt to establish propositions in welfare economics without the introduction of explicit value judgements is sterile. Bergson-Samuelson social welfare function as well as Arrow's analysis of how to obtain social welfare function from preferences of individuals shall be discussed at the end of this part. Welfare economics has been a controversial subject in recent years because it involves value judgements about which there is a sharp difference of opinion among economists.

Now-a-days the establishment of a welfare state is the fundamental objective of modern democratic Governments. In order to achieve this objective the State attempts to satisfy the wants of each and every individual of the society. Non-satisfaction of wants gives pain to a man and its satisfaction, a pleasure. The word 'pleasure' is associated with welfare. Some wants always remain unsatisfied and give pain to an individual whereas some are always satisfied or are in the process of being satisfied and thus give rise to welfare. The fact remains that the welfare is the result of the satisfaction of wants. It can be concluded from this fact that to increase the welfare of a man his wants must be satisfied. According to Prof. J.K. Mehta, if we compare the two periods of time, then "a given man has greater welfare in which a larger number of his wants have been satisfied. Conversely, we can say that the smaller the number of wants (of given intensities) that remain unsatisfied the greater is the welfare."[2]

Three Concepts of Social Welfare

Prof. Graff has distinguished three concepts of social welfare.[3] The first concept of social or group welfare is the *paternalist* one which describes the views of a paternalist authority or state and not of the individuals in the society. According to this concept, the preferences of the individual members of the society may be ignored and the state or a paternalist authority or a dictator uses its own ideas about social welfare; social welfare increases when that paternal authority or the dictator thinks it so.

The second concept of social welfare is one which has been used by V. Pareto and his followers. According to this *Paretian concept*, welfare of the society is simply the sum total of the welfare of different individuals comprising it. If some persons are made better off and none worse off, social welfare increases and if some are made worse off and none better off, it decreases. But if some are made better off and some worse off, then, according to Paretian concept, we cannot know what has happened to the welfare of the society. The Paretian concept of social welfare rules out interpersonal comparison of utility or welfare and rests only on a generally accepted ethical view that "it is good to make somebody better off while making nobody worse off". But since in most cases of changes in economic organisation and policy, at least some people are made worse off, the Paretian concept of social welfare is of limited value for most of the real world economic problems.

2. J.K. Mehta and Mahesh Chand, *A Guide to Modern Economics*, Somaiya Publications, Bombay, 1970, p. 180.
3. J. De V. Graff. *Theoretical Welfare Economics*, Cambridge University Press, 1957, pp. 7-11.

The third concept of social welfare involves interpersonal comparison of utility which is to be made by introducing explicit value judgements. This concept of social welfare has been propounded by Bergson and Samuelson in their now well-known theory of *social welfare function*. Thus they have described the utility functions of the various persons in the society with the help of a social welfare function. These economists are of the opinion that changes in social welfare cannot be assessed without making interpersonal comparisons of utility and therefore without making value judgements. It is because of this that this concept of social welfare is able to judge the welfare implications of even those changes in economic organisation and policies that make some people better off and others worse off.

Various concepts of social welfare have been referred to above. Economists generally do not accept the paternalist or dictatorial concept of social welfare. Some economists such as Robbins and his followers tried to separate economics from ethics but now-a-days there is consensus among economists that welfare economics cannot be separated from ethics. Bergson, Samuelson, Little, Arrow and others are of the opinion that value judgements are most important in welfare economics. But the fact remains that social welfare and changes in it cannot be measured accurately due to heterogeneity of the interests of the various individuals in a society.

ROLE OF VALUE JUDGEMENTS IN WELFARE ECONOMICS

It is important to explain the role of value judgements in welfare economics. Since welfare economics is concerned with the desirability or otherwise of economic policies, the value judgements play a crucial role. As mentioned above, by value judgements or values we mean the conceptions or ethical beliefs of the people about what is good or bad. These conceptions regarding values of the people are based on ethical, political, philosophical and religious beliefs of the people and are not based on any scientific logic or scientific law. There is a great controversy regarding whether value judgements should have any role to play in welfare economies. Robbins and his followers have been asserting that the inclusion of value judgements would make our subject unscientific and therefore, according to them, economists should refrain from making value judgements. On the other hand, majority of modern economists are of the view that economists should not fight shy of making value judgements if there is a wide consensus about them among the community. Using his knowledge of economics together with these value judgements he should comment upon the desirability or otherwise of economic policies and issues. Professor Paul Streeten rightly says, "Economists cannot and should not refrain from making value judgements if their studies are to be more than a purely formal technique of reasoning, an algebra of choice. The technique, the algebra, is important and ought to be as scientific as possible, but it is significant only as a means to study of wealth and welfare and of the way to improve them".[4]

It should be noted that as far as the welfare of individual is concerned, though difficult to measure in cardinal terms, economists can measure it in ordinal terms and by observing the act of choice of the individual. For instance, if an individual chooses *A* rather than *B*, it shows that his welfare is greater in *A* than in *B*. Thus, choice by an individual is an objective test for knowing and comparing his welfare in different economic states. Therefore, what promotes individual welfare or not can be tested and verified. However, when welfare economics has to judge the social welfare or group welfare, it encounters difficulties because the measurement of social welfare is not an easy task and involves value judgements and interpersonal comparisons of utility. This is because the society or group whose welfare we have to judge cannot be regarded as an organic whole, having its own mind. Therefore, social welfare, unlike individual welfare, is not something which resides in the mind of the society. We cannot derive propositions of social welfare from choice of individuals comprising the society, because individuals choose differently and, therefore, there is no unanimous

4. Paul Streeten, Economics and Value Judgements, *Quarterly Journal of Economics*, 1950, p. 595.

social choice. Individual choices differ because various individuals have different tastes, preferences and ethical beliefs and therefore different value judgements. The vital issues in welfare economics are concerned with social welfare and devising certain criteria to judge the social welfare. Therefore, welfare economics cannot be purely objective or free from value judgements.

It is worth noting that *Pareto evolved the concept of social welfare which is said to be free from any value judgements*, because it is not based upon any interpersonal comparison of utility. According to Pareto, the social welfare depends upon the welfare of the individuals comprising the society and, according to him, if at least one individual is made better off by certain economic reorganisation and no one being made worse off, the social welfare increases, that is, if any economic reorganisation increases the welfare of one without reducing the welfare of any other, then the social welfare increases. When such an economic state is reached *that through any reorganisation it is not possible to make at least one individual better off with no other being worse off, this is called the state of maximum social welfare or Pareto optimum.* However, Paretian concept of social welfare is confined to only limited issue of welfare economics. Generally, when any economic reorganisation increases the welfare of some, it would reduce the welfare of some others and therefore, in this case, *Pareto criteria* will not apply. Following Robbins some economists object to making inter-personal comparison of utility to derive welfare propositions, since, according to them, inter-personal comparison of utility is based upon value judgements.

However, Kaldor and Hicks by propounding a compensation principle laid the foundations of *New Welfare Economics* which is supposed to be free from value judgements. According to this compensation principle, if a change in economic organisation increases the welfare of some and reduces the welfare of others, but those who gain in welfare are able to compensate the losers and still be better off than before, then the change in economic organisation will increase the social welfare. However, Kaldor-Hicks welfare criterion has been subjected to swvere criticisms. The claim of Kaldor and Hicks that their criterion is free from value judgements or ethical assumptions has been contested. To quote Professor Baumol, "*Both the Kaldor and the Scitovsky tests operate on the basis of an implicit and unacceptable value judgement. By using a criterion involving potential money compensation, they set up a concealed inter-personal comparison on a money basis*."[5] He further writes, "It is no answer to this criticism to say that these criteria are just designed to measure whether production, and hence, potential welfare, are increased by a policy change that these criteria disentangle the evaluation of a production change from that of the distribution change by which it is accompanied. Consider a change in *production* which increases gin output but reduces the output of whiskey. If *X* likes highballs but *Y* prefers martins, the question whether this is an increase in production is inextricably tied in with the question of the distribution of these beverages between *X* and *Y*."[6]

In the end we may note that Professor Bergson has pursued a different line of approach to welfare economics. He has propounded the concept of social welfare function in which a set of value judgements is *explicitly* introduced and with this social welfare function, the economists can judge the desirability of certain economic reorganisations or policy changes. *These value judgements, according to Bergson, "must be determined by its compatibility with the values prevailing in the community the welfare of which is being studied*."[7] Followers of Bergson like Samuelson and I.M.D. Little are of the view that welfare economics cannot be separated from value judgements, because any statement about increase or decrease of social welfare necessarily involves value judgements. On the rightness of Bergson's social welfare function, and his introduction of explicit value judgements in it, Prof. Baumol writes, "*Essentially the Bergson criterion must be judged right, if not very*

5. Nicholas Kaldor, Welfare Propositions in Welfare Economics, *Economic Journal*, 1939 and J.R. Hicks, Foundations of Welfare Economics, *Economic Journal*, 1939.
6. Op. cit., p. 403-4.
7. A. Bergson, On the Concept of Social Welfare, *Quarterly Journal of Economics*, 1954.

helpful. To decide whether B is better than A, we must certainly employ some value judgements, and unless these judgements are explicit they must be treated with suspicion."[8] Likewise, Professor K. E. Boulding writes: "One must admit that the task of making value judgements explicit is very important. It is obviously preposterous to suppose that one can set up criteria for judgement which are somehow independent of ethical norms".[9]

Thus, according to several modern economists such as Samuelson, Little, Boulding welfare economics cannot be purged of value judgements. In fact, the study of welfare economics has been developed to make policy recommendations to promote social welfare. And for doing so economists cannot escape from introducing ethical norms or value judgements since we all take interest in the question concerning happiness and welfare of the society. "*Welfare economics and ethics cannot, then, be separated.* They are inseparable because the welfare terminology is a value terminology.....*Getting rid of value judgements would be throwing the baby away with the bath water.* The subject is one about which nothing interesting can be said without value judgements for the reason that we take a moral interest in welfare and happiness".[10]

It should not be gathered from above that the explicit introduction of value judgements makes the study of welfare economics unscientific. In spite of the explicit introduction of value judgements in welfare studies, the economist's approach can still be scientific in the sense that he scientifically deduces the welfare propositions from the given value judgements.

QUESTIONS FOR REVIEW

1. In welfare economics attempt is made to establish criteria or norms to judge the social desirability of economic policies. Explain.
2. What is meant by social welfare ? Is it possible to measure social welfare without interpersonal comparison of utility ?
3. What is meant by economic efficiency ? Is it right to ignore equity in distribution when it clashes with the objective of economic efficiency ?
4. What is new welfare economies ? Explain its approach to social welfare.
5. Explain three concepts of social welfare mentioning in each case the approach to the interpersonal comparision of utility.
6. What is meant by value judgements ? Explain their role in welfare economics
7. "Welfare economics and ethics cannot be separated.... Getting rid of value judgements would be throwing the baby away with the bath water" (I.M.D. Little) Examine critically.
8. "Wheras the normal way of testing a theory in positive economics is to test its conclusions, the normal way of testing a welfare proposition is to test its assumptions" (J. de. V. Graaff) Discuss
9. "The interest attaching to a theory of welfare depends almost entirely upon the realism and relevance of assumptions".

---

8. *Op.cit.*, p.404
9. K.E. Boulding, 'Welfare Economics' in B.E. Haley (ed) A.E.A., *A Survey of Contemporary Economics*, Richard D. Irwin 1952
10. I.M.D. Little, *A Critique of Welfare Economics*, Oxford University Press, 2nd Edition, 1957. (*Italic added*)

CHAPTER 39
ECONOMIC EFFICIENCY AND PARETO OPTIMALITY

Notion of Pareto Optimality and Economic Efficiency

We saw in the previous chapter that neo-classical and earlier economists defined social welfare as a sum total of cardinally measurable utilities of different members of the society. An optimum allocation of resources was one which maximised the social welfare in this sense. V. Pareto was the first to part with this traditional approach to social welfare in two important respects. First, he rejected notion of cardinal utility and its additive nature and, second, he detached welfare economics from the inter-personal comparisons of utilities. Pareto's concept of maximum social welfare which is based upon ordinal utility and is also free from value judgements occupies a significant place in modern welfare economics. Pareto optimum may not be sufficient condition for attaining maximum social welfare but it is a necessary condition for it. We have already explained the concept of Pareto optimality in chapters in 38. To repeat, *Pareto optimum (often called Economic Efficiency) is a position from which it is impossible to make anyone better off without making someone worse off by any reallocation of resources or distribution of outputs*. Thus, in the Pareto "optimum position the welfare of any individual of the society can not be increased without decreasing the welfare of another member. Before explaining the conditions of achieving Pareto optimality, we shall explain Pareto criterion of evaluating changes in social welfare because the concept of Pareto optimality or maximum social welfare is based upon Pareto criterion of welfare.

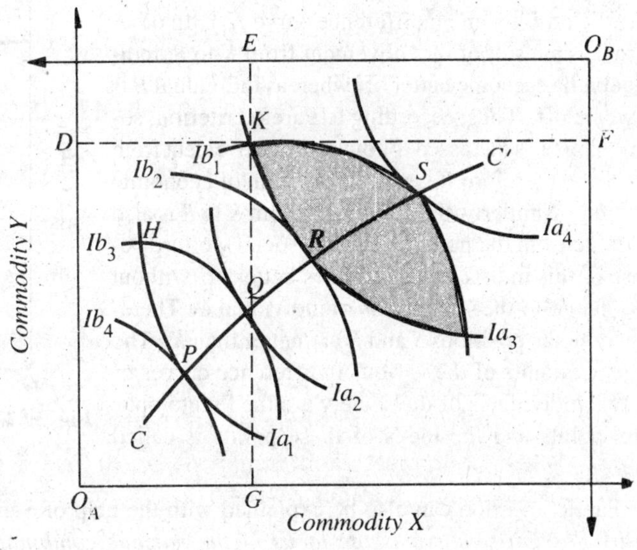

Fig. 39.1 *Pareto Criterion and Pareto Optimality.*

Pareto Criterion of Social Welfare

The concept of Pareto optimum or economic efficiency stated above is based on a welfare criterion put forward by V. Pareto. Pareto criterion states that if any reorganisation of economic resources does not harm anybody and makes someone better off, it indicates an increase in social welfare. If any reorganistaion or change makes everybody in a society better off, it will, according to Pareto, undoubtedly mean increase in social welfare. Thus, in the words of Prof. Baumol "any change which harms no one and which makes some people better off (in their own estimation) must be considered to be an improvement."[1] Parto criterion can be explained with the help of Edgeworth Box diagram which is based on the assumptions of ordinal utility and non-interpersonal comparison of utilities. Suppose two persons *A* and *B* form the society and consume two goods *X* and *Y*. The various levels of their satisfaction by consuming various combinations of the two goods have been represented by their respective indifference curves.

In Figure 39.1 O_a and O_b are the origins for the utilities of two persons *A* and *B* respectively. I_{a1}, I_{a2}, I_{a3}, I_{a4} and I_{b1}, I_{b2}, I_{b3}, I_{b4} are their successively higher indifference curve. Suppose the initial distribution of goods *X* and *Y* between the members of the society, *A* and *B*, is represented by point-*K* in the Edgeworth Box. Accordingly, individual *A* consumes O_AG of $X + GK$ of *Y* and is at the level of satisfaction represented by indifference curve I_{a3}. Similarly, individual *B* consumes *KF* of $X + KE$ of *Y* and gets the satisfaction represented by indifference curve Ib_1. Thus the total given volume of goods *X* and *Y* is distributed between *A* and *B*. In this distribution, individual *A* consumes relatively larger quantity of good *Y* and individual *B* of good *X*. Now, it can be shown with the aid of Pareto's welfare criterion that a movement from the point *K* to a point such as *S* or *R* or any other point in the shaded region will increase social welfare.

Any movement from *K* to *S* through redistribution of two goods between two individuals increases the level of satisfaction of *A* without any change in the satisfaction of *B* because as a result of this *A* moves to his higher indifference curve I_{a4}, and *B* remains on his same indifference curve I_{b1} (*K* and *S* lie on *B*'s same indifference curve I_{b1}). In other words, as a result of the movement from *K* to *S*, individual *A* has become better off whereas individual *B* is no worse off. Thus, according to Pareto criterion, social welfare has increased following the movement from *K* to *S* and therefore *K* is not the position of economic optimum. Similarly, the movement from *K* to *R* is also desirable from the point of view of social welfare because in this individual *B* becomes better off without any change-in-the satisfaction of individual *A*. Therefore, both the positions *S* and *R* are better than *K*. The tangency points of the various indifference curves of the two individuals of the society are the Pareto optimum points and the locus of these points is called '*contract curve*'.

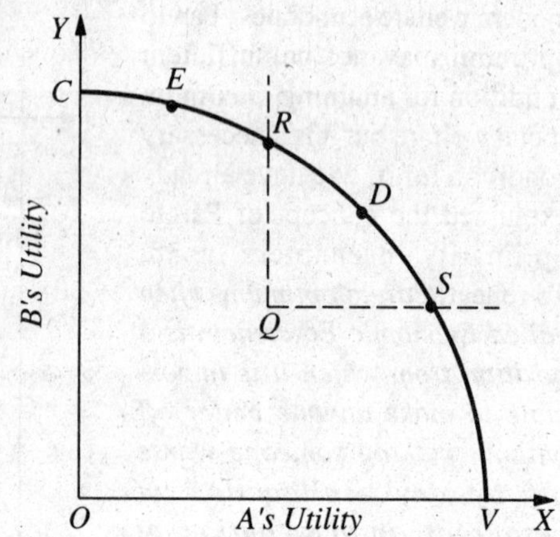

Fig. 39.2. *Pareto Criterion Explained with Utility Possibility Curve*

Pareto criterion can also be explained with the help of Samuelson's utility possibility curve. *Utility possibility curve is the locus of the various combinations of utilities obtained by two persons from the consumption of a particular bundle of goods.* In Figure 39.2, *CV* is a utility possibility curve which shows the various levels of utilities obtained by two individuals *A* and *B* of the society resulting from the redistribution of a fixed bundle of goods and its consumption by them. According to Pareto criterion, a movement from *Q* to *R*, or *Q* to *D*, or *Q* to *S* represents the increase in social welfare because in such movements the utility of either *A* or *B* or both increases. A movement from *Q* to *R* implies that the utility or welfare of *B* increases, while that of *A* remains the same. On the other hand, a movement from *Q* to *S* implies that while *A* has become better off, *B* is no worse off. And a movement from *Q* to *D* or any other point on the segment between *R* and *S* will mean increase in welfare or utility of both the individuals. Thus points *R*, *D* and *S* are preferable to *Q* from the point of

1. W.J. Baumol, *Economic Theory and Operations Analysis*, Prentice Hall, 4th edition,1978, p. 527.

view of social welfare. But unfortunately Pareto criterion does not help us in evaluating the changes in welfare if the movement as a result of redistribution is from the point Q to a point outside the segment RS; such as point E on the utility possibility curve CV. As a result of the movement from point Q to E, the utility of A decreases while that of B increases. In such circumstances, Pareto criterion can not tell us as to whether social welfare increases or decreases.

MARGINAL CONDITIONS OF PARETO OPTIMALITY

Pareto concluded from his criterion that competition leads the society to an optimum position but he had not given any mathematical proof of it, nor he derived the marginal conditions to be fulfilled for achievement of the optimum position. Later on, Lerner and Hicks derived the marginal conditions which must be fulfilled for the attainment of Pareto optimum. These marginal conditions are based on the following important assumptions :

1. Each individual has his own ordinal utility function and possesses definite amount of each product and factor.
2. Production function of every firm and the state of technology is given and remains constant.
3. Goods are perfectly divisible.
4. A producer tries to produce a given output with the least-cost combination of factors.
5. Every individual wants to maximise his satisfaction.
6. Every individual purchases some quantity of all goods.
7. All factors of production are perfectly mobile.

Given the above assumptions various marginal conditions (first-order conditions) required for the achievement of Pareto optimum or maximum social welfare are explained below :

1. The Optimum Distribution of Products among the Consumers : Efficiency in Exchange

The first condition relates to the optimum distribution of the goods among the different consumers composing a society at a particular point of time. The condition says : "*The marginal rate of substitution between any two goods must be the same for every individual who consumes them both.*"[2] The marginal rate of substitution of one good for another so as is the amount of one good necessary to compensate for the loss of a marginal unit of another so as to maintain a constant level of satisfaction. So long as the marginal rate of substitution (*MRS*) between two goods is not equal for any two consumers, they will enter into an exchange which would increase the satisfaction of both or of one without decreasing the satisfaction of the other.

This condition can be better explained with the help of the Edgeworth Box diagram. In Figure-39.3, goods X and Y, which are consumed by two individuals A and B composing a society are represented on the X and Y axes respectively. O_A and O_B are origins for A and B respectively. I_{a1}, Ia_2, Ia_3 and Ib_1, Ib_2, Ib_3 are the indifference curves showing successively higher and higher satisfaction of consumers A and B respectively. CC' is the contract curve passing through various tangency points Q, R, S of the indifference curves of A and B. The marginal rates of substitution (*MRS*) between the two goods for individuals A and B are equal on the various points of the contract curve CC'. Any point outside the contract curve does not represent the equality of *MRS* between the two goods for two individuals A and B of the society.

Let us consider point K where indifference curves I_{a1} and I_{b1} of individuals A and B respectively intersect each other instead of being tangential. Therefore, at point K marginal rate of substitution between two goods X and Y (MRS_{xy}) of individual A is not equal to that of B. With the initial

---

2. M.W. Reder, *Studies in the Theory of Welfare Economics*, Columbia University Press, New York, 1947, p. 24.

distribution of goods as represented by point K, it is possible to increase the satisfaction of one individual without any decrease in that of the other or to increase the satisfaction of both by redistribution of the two goods X and Y between them. A movement from K to S increases the

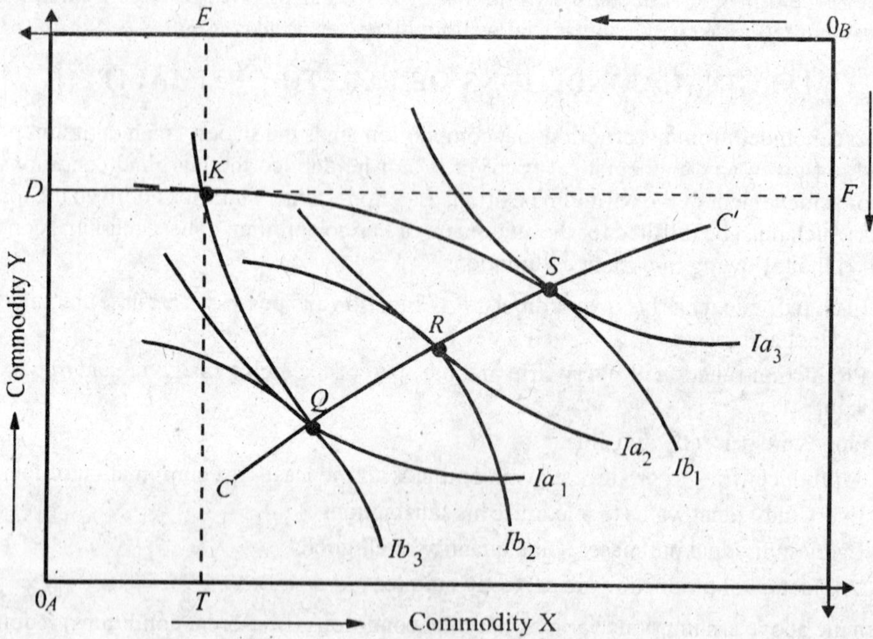

Fig. 39.3. *The Optimum Distribution of Goods.*

satisfaction of A without any decrease in B's satisfaction. Similarly, a movement from K to Q increases B's satisfaction without any decrease in A's satisfaction. The movement from K to R increases the satisfaction of both because both move to their higher indifference curves. Thus, a movement from K to Q or to S or to any other point on the segment SQ of the contract curve will, according to Pareto criterion, increase the level of social welfare.

From above it follows that movement from any point away from the contract curve to a point on the relevant segment of the contract curve will mean increase in social welfare. At any point away from the contract curve in the Edgeworth box, the indifference curves of the two individuals will intersect which will mean that MRS_{xy} of two individuals is not the same. And, as explained above, this indicates that through exchange of some units of goods between them, they can move to some point on the contract curve where the social welfare (that is, welfare of two individuals taken together) will be higher.

Since the slope of an indifference curve represents the marginal rate of substitution (MRS_{xy}) at any point of the contract curve, which represents tangency points of the indifference curves, MRS_{xy} of the two individuals are equal. Therefore, points on the contact curve represent the maximum social welfare. However, a movement along the contract curve in either direction will make one individual better off and the other worse off since it will put one individual on his successively higher indifference curves and the other on his successively lower indifference curves. Thus, every point on the contract curve denotes maximum social welfare in the Paretian sense but we can not say anything about the best of them with the help of Pareto criterion.

2. The Optimum Allocation of Factors : Pareto Efficiency in Production.

The second condition for Pareto optimum requires that the available factors of production should be utilised in the production of products in such a manner that it is impossible to increase the output of oen firm without a decrease in the output of another or to increase the output of both the goods by any re-allocation of factors of production. *This situation would be achieved if the marginal technical rate of substitution between any pair of factors must be the same for any two firms producing two different products and using both the factors to produce the products.*[3]

This condition too can be explained with the help of Edgeworth Box diagram relating to production. This is depicted in Fig. 39.4. Let us assume two firms *A* and *B* producing the same product by

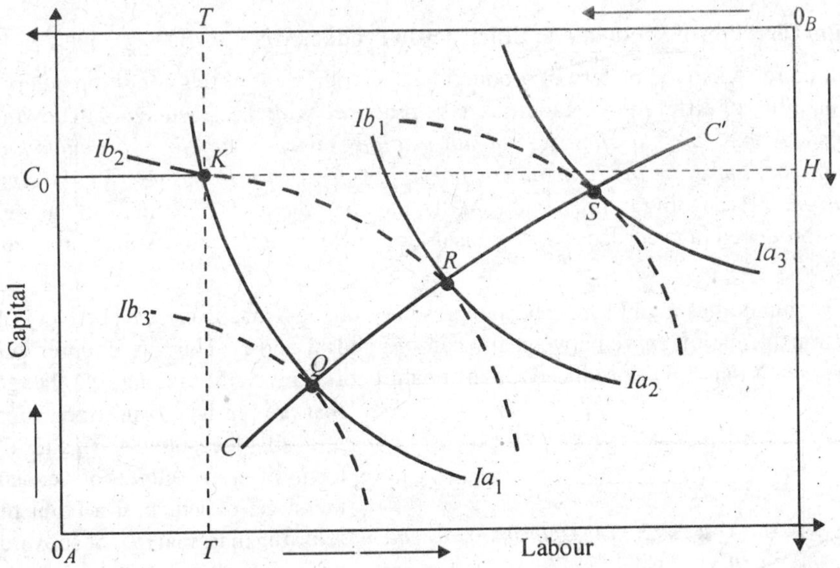

Fig. 39.4. *The Optimum Allocation of Factors.*

using two factors labour and capital. The available quantities of labour and capital are represented on *X* and *Y* axes respectively. O_A and O_B are the origins for firms *A* and *B* respectively. Isoquants I_{a1}, I_{a2}, I_{a3} and I_{b1}, I_{b2}, I_{b3} of firms *A* and *B* respectively represent successively higher and higher quantities of output which they can produce by different combinations of labour and capital. The slope of the iosquants, which are convex to the origin, represents the marginal rate of technical substitution (*MRTS*) between two factors. *MRTS* of one factor for another is the amount of one factor necessary to compensate for the loss of the marginal unit of another so that the level of output remains the same. So long as the *MRTS* between two factors for two firms is not equal, total output of a product can be increased by transfer of factors from one firm to another. In terms of the above diagram any movement from *K* to *S* or to *Q* raises the output of one firm without any decrease in the output of the other. The total output of the two firms increases when through redistribution of factors between the two firms, a movement is made from the point *K* to the point *Q* or *S* on the contract curve. A glance at Figure 39.4 will reveal that movement from point *K* outside the contract curve to the point *R* on the contract curve will raise the output of both the firms individually as well as collectively. Therefore, it follows that corresponding to a point outside the contract curve there will be some points on the contract curve production at which will ensure greater total output of the two firms. As the contract curve is the locus of the tangency points of the isoquants of two firms, the marginal rate of substitution of the two firms is the same at every point of the contract curve *CC'*. It, therefore, follows that on the contract curve at every point of which *MRTS* between the two factors

3. M.W. Reder, *op. ci*, p. 29.

of two firms is the same, the allocation of factors between the two firms is optimum. When the allocation of factors between the two firms is such that they are producing at a point on the contract curve, then no re-allocation of factors will increase the total output of the two firms taken together.

But it is worth mentioning that there are several points on the contract curve and each of them represents the optimum allocation of labour and capital as between the two firms. But which one of them is best cannot be said on the basis of Pareto criterion because movement along the contract curve in either direction represents such factor reallocation which increases the output of one and reduces the output of another firm.

3. Optimum Direction of Production : Efficiency in Product Mix

This condition relates to the pattern of production. The fulfilment of this condition determines the optimum quantities of different commodities to be produced with the given factor endowments. This condition states that "*the marginal rate of substitution between any pair of products for any person consuming both must be the same as the marginal rate of transformation (for the community) between them.*"[4] According to this condition, for the attainment of maximum social welfare goods should be produced in accordance with consumer's preferences. Let us explain this with the help of Fig. 39.5

In Fig. 39.5 commodities *X* and *Y* have been represented on the *X* and Y axes respectively. *AB* is a community's transformation curve between any pair of goods *X* and *Y*. This curve represents the maximum amount of *X* that can be produced for any quantity of *Y*, given the amounts of other goods that are produced and fixed supplies of available resources. IC_1 and IC_2 are the indifference curves of a consumer the slope of which at a point represents the marginal rate of substitution between the two goods of the consumer. The MRT_{xy} of the community and MRS_{xy} of the consumer are equal to each other at point *R* at which the community's transformation curve is tangent to the indifference curve IC_2 of a representative consumers, Point *R* represents optimum composition of production in which commodities *X* and *Y* are being produced and consumed in *OM* and *ON* quantities. This is because of all the points on the community's transformation curve, point *R* lies at the highest possible indifference curve IC_2 of the consumer. For instance, if a combination of goods *X* and *Y* represented by *S* is being produced and consumed, the consumer would be at a lower level of welfare because *S* lies on his lower indifference curve IC_1 which intersects the community's transformation curve instead of being tangential to it. As a result, at point *S*, MRS_{xy} of the consumer is not equal to the MRT_{xy} of the community. With the situation at *S* there is a possibility of moving the consumers to a higher indifference curve by changing the direction (*i.e.* composition) of production *i.e.* by increasing the production of *X* and reducing the production of *Y*. Thus, the optimum direction of production is

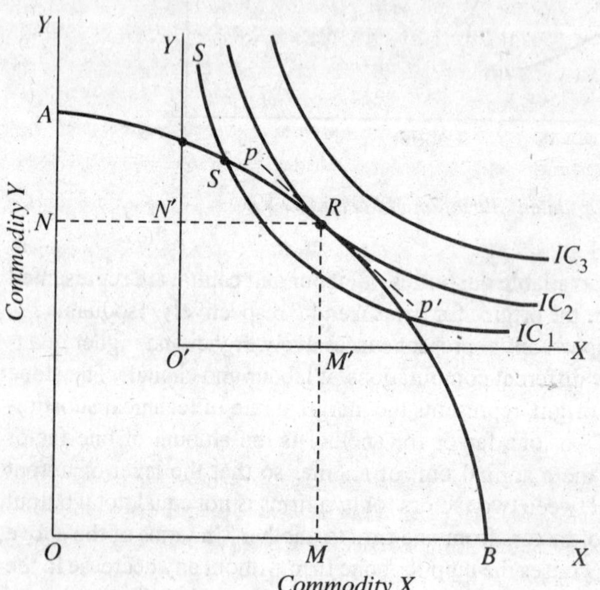

Fig. 39.5. *Optimum Direction of Production :Optimum Product Mix.*

4. Reder, *op. cit.*, p. 30.
5. Reder, *op. cit.*, p. 37.

established at point R where community's transformation curve is tangent to the indifference curve of a consumer in the society.

The Second-Order and Total Conditions of Pareto Optimality

The marginal or the first order conditions explained above are '*necessary*' but not sufficient for the attainment of maximum social welfare because the marginal conditions by themselves do not guarantee maximum welfare. The marginal conditions can be fulfilled even at the level of minimum welfare. To attain the maximum social welfare position second-order conditions together with the marginal conditions must be satisfied. *The second order conditions require that all indifference curves must be convex to the origin and all transformation curves concave to it in the neighbourhood of any portion where marginal conditions are satisfied.*

But even the satisfaction of both (first and second order conditions) does not ensure the largest maximum welfare because even when marginal conditions (first and second order) are fulfilled, it may still be possible to move to a position where social welfare is greater. To attain the maximum social welfare, another set of conditions which are called by J.R. Hicks as the '*total conditions*' must also be satisfied. The total conditions state, "that if welfare is to be a maximum, it must be impossible to increase welfare by producing a product not otherwise produced or by using a factor not otherwise used."[5] If it is possible to increase welfare by such activities the optimum position is not determined by marginal conditions alone.

Therefore, welfare will be really maximum if the marginal as well as total conditions are satisfied. *But such a social optimum too is not a unique one. It is one of a large number of optima.* The whole analysis of conditions of Pareto optimality *assumes a given distribution of income.* With a change in the distribution of income Pareto optimality will be achieved with different output-mix of various products and different allocation of various factors among products. Thus, a new optimum will emerge due to redistribution of income and there are no criteria to judge whether the new optimum is better or worse than the previous social optimum. This can be known only with the help of some value judgements regarding income distribution which has been ruled out by the Pareto criterion.

A CRITICAL EVALUATION OF PARETO CRITERION AND PARETO OPTIMALITY

Pareto criterion and the concept of Pareto optimality and maximum social welfare based on it occupies a significant place in welfare economics. To judge the efficiency of an economic system, the notion of Pareto optimality has been used. It has also been used to bring out the gains of trading or exchange of goods between individuals. But even Pareto criterion which rules out comparing those changes in policies which make some worse off has been a subject of controversy and has been criticised on several grounds.

First, it has been alleged that *Pareto criterion is not completely free from value judgements.* The supporters of Pareto criterion claim that it provides us with an 'objective' criterion of efficiency. However, this has been contested. Against Pareto criterion it has been said that to say that a policy change which makes some better off without others being worse off increases social welfare is itself a value judgement. This is because *we recommend such changes which pass Pareto criterion.* The implication of this assertion will become obvious when the persons who gain as a result of policy change are the rich and those who remain where they were before are poor. Therefore, to say on the basis of Pareto criterion that whenever any policy change which, without harming anyone, benefits some people regardless of whoever they may be, increases social welfare is a value judgement which may not be accepted by all.

Second, an important limitation of Pareto criterion is that *it cannot be applied to judge the social desirability of those policy proposals which benefit some and harm others.* Such policy changes are quite rare which do not harm at least some individuals in the society. Thus, Pareto criterion is of limited applicability as it cannot be used to pronounce judgements on a majority of policy proposals which involve a conflict of preferences of two individuals. Thus, according to Prasanta K. Patnaik, "Pareto criterion fails seriously when it comes to comparing alternatives. *Whenever there is conflict of preferences of two individuals with respect to two alternatives, the criterion fails to rank those two alternatives no matter what the preferences of the rest of individuals in the society might be*".[6] To evaluate social desirability of those policy changes which benefit some and harm others, we need to make interpersonal comparison of utility which Pareto criterion refuses to do. Thus, "Pareto criterion works by sidestepping the crucial issue of inter-personal comparison and income distribution, that is, by dealing only with cases where no one is harmed so that the problem does not arise".[7]

Another shortcoming of Pareto criterion and notion of maximum social welfare based on it is that *it leaves a considerable amount of indeterminacy in the welfare analysis* since every point on the contract curve is Pareto-optimal. For instance, in Fig. 39.1, every point such as *P*, *Q*, *R*, *S* on the contract curve is Pareto-superior to any point such as *K* and *H* which lies outside the contract curve. Movement from one point on the contract curve to another as a result of change in economic policy, that is, through re-allocation of resources that makes one individual better off and the other worse off, that is, one gains at the expense of the other. This means that on the basis of Pareto criterion, social alternatives lying on the contract curve cannot be compared since with any movement on the contract curve one individual gains and the other loses, that is, it involves redistribution of income or welfare. Therefore, to compare various alternatives lying on the contract curve and to choose between them, inter-personal comparison and value judgements regarding proper distribution of income need to be made. However, Pareto refused to make value judgements and sought to put forward a value-free or objective criterion of welfare.

It, therefore, follows that on the basis of Pareto criterion where the change from an alternative lying outside the contract curve to an alternative on the contract curve is judged to increase social welfare but this cannot be said of the change from one position on the contract curve to another on it. But as there are infinite number of points on the contract curve all of which are Pareto optimal, no choice can be made out of them on the basis of Pareto criterion. To remove this indeterminacy and to choose among the alternatives lying on the contract curve one needs to make some additional value judgements beyond what is implied in the Pareto criterion. Henderson and Quandt hold a similar view when they assert, "*The analysis of welfare in terms of Pareto optimality leaves a considerable amount of indeterminacy in the solution : there are infinite number of points which are Pareto optimal.*" They further remark that, `The indeterminacy is the consequence of considering an increase in welfare to be unambiguously defined only if an improvement in one individual's position is not accompanied by a deterioration of the position of another. The indeterminacy can only be removed by further value judgements."[8]

Above all, *a chief drawback of Pareto-optimality analysis is that it accepts the prevailing income distribution and no attempt is made to find an optimal distribution of income*, since it is thought that there does not exist any objective, value-free and scientific way of finding optimal distribution of income. Thus, Pareto optimality analysis remains either silent or biased in favour of status quo on the issue of income distribution. Further, Pareto optimality analysis may lead to recommend the prevailing income distribution where a majority of the population lives on the subsistence level or below the poverty line while a few live a life of affluence. Thus, "Ultimately, the Paretian approach can be considered the welfare economists' instrument par excellence for the

---

6. Prasanta K. Patnaik, Some Aspects of Welfare Economics, *The Indian Economic Journal*, Conference Number, 1974, p. 68C.
7. W. J. Baumol, *Economic Theory and Operations Analysis*, 4th edition, 1977 Prentice Hall, p.527.
8. J. M. Henderson, and R. E. Quandt, *Microeconomic Theory*, 2nd edition, 1971, p. 265.
9. Baumol, *op.cit.* p. 503.

circumvention of the issue of income distribution."[9]

It may also be mentioned that for any initial distribution of income (that is, for any given distribution of goods) between the individuals, there will be several Pareto optimal positions. Consider Figure 39.1. Corresponding to point, *K*, the points on the segment *RS* on the contract curve *CC′* will all represent Pareto optimal positions. Likewise, corresponding to a given distribution of income (*i.e.* distribution of goods) as represented by point *H*, the points on the segment *PQ* of the contract curve *CC′* will be Pareto-optimal. Thus corresponding to a different distribution of income, there will be different Pareto optima. In the Paretian analysis there is no way of evaluating whether one pattern of income distribution is better than the other.

Prof. Amartya Sen's Critique of Pareto Optimality

Further, criticising Pareto criterion Prof. Amartya Sen has pointed out that the success that the criterion of Pareto optimality has achieved in judging the desirability of a social state or a policy change is very limited. To quote him, "A Social state is described as Pareto optimal if and only if no-one's utility can be raised without reducing the utility of someone else. This is a very limited kind of success and in itself may or may not guarantee much. *A state can be Pareto optimal with some people in extreme misery and others rolling in luxury, so long as the miserable cannot be made better off without cutting into the luxury of the rich.*"[10] So, according to him, this is not a good and adequate criterion for juding social welfare.

Further, Prof. Sen has criticised Pareto optimality on the basis that *it identifies well-being with utility* and captures the efficiency aspects only of utility-based accounting. It may be noted that utility is interpreted in two ways, Firstly, it is said to mean '*happiness*'. Secondly, it is interpreted in the sense of '*desire-fulfilment*'. He is of the view that utility does not always reflect well-being. To quote him, "*To judge the well-being of a person exclusively in metric of happiness or desire-fulfilment has some obvious limitations.* These limitations are particularly damaging in the context of interpersonal comparison of well-being. Since the extent of happiness reflects what one would expect and how the social 'deal' seems in comparison with that."[11] He is of the view that *people living a life of great misfortune with little hope and opportunities may get more utility or happiness even from small gains.* But that should not be interpreted that there is a significant improvement in their well-being. The measure of utility in the sense of happiness may not reveal the true picture about the state of his deprivation. He thus writes The hopeless beggar, precarious landless labourers, the dominated housewife, the hardened unemployed or the over-exhausted coolie may all take pleasure in small mercies, and manage to suppress intense suffering for the necessity of continued survival, but it would be ethically deeply mistaken to attach correspondingly small value to the loss of their well-being because of their survival strategy."[12]

According to Prof. Sen, even in case of desire-fulfilment, the same problem arises, because "*the hopelessly deprived lack the courage to desire much, and their deprivations are muted and deadened in scale of desire-fulfilment.*" The sum and subsistence of Sen's criticism is that the concept of utility used in for indjudging Pareto optimality whether it is interpreted in terms of happiness or desire-fulfilment is seriously inadequate and insufficient for judging a person's well-being. To quote him, well-being is ultimately a matter of valuation, and while happiness and fulfilment of desire may well be valuable for the person's well being, they cannot on their own or even together adequately reflect the value of well-being."[13]

---

10. Amartya Sen, *On Ethics and Economics*, Oxford University Press, 1990, pp. 31-32
11. *Ibid*
12. Amartya Sen, *op, cit., pp.* 45-46
13. *Ibid.*, p. 46

It is thus clear that welfare or well-being of individuals depends on a wide range of variables that those associated with utility which is derived from the consumption of goods and services and amount of leisure enjoyed. *Welfare or well-being also depends on such variables as political and environmental factors, personal and political freedom individuals enjoy, disposition of their neighbours.* For an adequate measure of well-being these variables cannot be ignored. "In comparing different economic systems or comparing different ways of organising a given economy, the possibility that some of these variables might be affected cannot be ignored. Thus, *a reorganisation that gives everyone more income and leisure might not improve the welfare of the community if at the same time it limits individual freedoms or requires the abandonement of cherished cultural traditions.*"[14]

In the end, it may be pointed out that Pareto criterion is not altogether unless. It is useful in the sense that, "by throwing out the Pareto inoptimal alternatives, it reduces the range within which socially best alternatives are to be looked for, and therefore does serve as a useful first step. The trouble arises if one gets so fascinated with this first step that one does not try to go any further, but that can hardly be called a defect of Pareto criterion."[15] Moreover, as has been pointed out above, Pareto analysis has been used to bring out the gains from trading or exchange of goods between the two individuals.

PERFECTLY COMPETITIVE EQUILIBRIUM AND PARETO OPTIMALITY

In our above analysis we have explained the various marginal conditions of attaining Pareto optimality or, in other words, optimum allocation of resources. It has been claimed by several economists that perfect competition is an ideal market form which ensures the attainment of Pareto optimality or maximum social welfare as it fulfils all the marginal conditions required for the purpose. In what follows we shall show how perfectly competitive equilibrium satisfies all the marginal conditions required for the achievement of Pareto optimum. We shall further explain what are the major obstacles in the way of maximising social welfare or achieving Pareto optimality.

Perfect Competition and Optimal Distribution of Goods or Efficiency in Exchange

The condition for Pareto optimality with regard to the distribution of goods among consumers requires that the marginal rate of substitution (*MRS*) between any two goods, say *X* and *Y*, must be the same for any pair of consumers. Let *A* and *B* be the two consumers between whom two goods *X* and *Y* are to be distributed. Under perfect competition prices of all goods are given and same for every consumer. It is also assumed that consumers try to maximise their satisfaction subject to their budget constraint. Now, given the prices of two goods, consumer A will maximise his satisfaction when he is buying the two goods *X* and *Y* in such amounts that:

$$MRS^{A}_{XY} = \frac{P_X}{P_Y} \quad \ldots (i)$$

Likewise, the consumer *B* will also be in equilibrium (maximise his satisfaction) when he is purchasing and consuming the two goods *X* and *Y* in such amounts that:

$$MRS^{B}_{XY} = \frac{P_X}{P_Y} \quad \ldots (ii)$$

Since this is essential condition of perfect competition that prices of goods are the same or uniform for all consumers, the price ratio of the two goods $\left(\frac{P_x}{P_y}\right)$ in equations (*i*) and (*ii*) above will

14. Else, P. Curwen, *Principles of Microeconomics*, Unwin, Hyman, London, 1990, p. 324.
15. Prasanta K. Patnaik, *Op.cit.*

be the same for consumers A and B. It, therefore, follows from equations (i) and (ii) above that under conditions of perfect competition marginal rate of substitution between two goods X and Y will be equal for the two consumers. That is,

$$MRS_{XY}^{A} = MRS_{XY}^{B}$$

This result will hold good between any pair of goods for any pair of consumers.

Perfect Competition and Optimal Allocation of Factors : Production Efficiency

The second marginal condition for Pareto optimality relates to the optimal allocation of factors in the production of various goods. This condition requires that for the optimal allocation of factors marginal rate of technical substitution (*MRTS*) between any two factors, say labour and capital, must be the same in the production of any pair of products. This condition is also satisfied by perfect competition. For a producer working under perfect competition prices of factors he employs are given and constant and he is in equilibrium (that is, minimises his cost for a given level of output) at the combination of factors where the given isoquant is tangent to an iso-cost line. As is well known, the slope of the isoquant represents marginal rate of technical substitution between the two factors and the slope of the iso-cost line measures the ratio of the prices of two factors. Thus, under perfect competition, a cost-minimising producer producing goods will equate *MRTS* between labour and capital with the price ratio of these two factors. Thus under perfect competition :

$$MRTS_{LK}^{X} = \frac{P_L}{P_K} \qquad \ldots (i)$$

where P_L and P_K are the prices of labour and capital respectively and and $MRTS_{LK}^{x}$ is the marginal rate of technical substitution between labour and capital in the production of good X. Similarly, producer B producing good Y and working under perfect competition will also equate his marginal rate of technical substitution between the two factors with their price ratios. Thus

$$MRTS^{Y}{}_{LK} = \frac{P_L}{P_K} \qquad \ldots (ii)$$

Since, under perfect competition, prices of factors are the same for all the producers, each producer will adjust the use of factors in such a way that his marginal rate of technical substitution (*MRTS*) between labour and capital in the production of goods is equal to the same factor price ratio. In other words, $\left(\frac{P_L}{P_K}\right)$ will be the same for all of them and to this $MRTS_{LK}$ of the producers will be made equal. It, therefore, follows from (i) and (ii) above that under perfect competition :

$$MRTS_{LK}^{X} = MRTS_{LK}^{Y}$$

We thus see that perfect competition ensures optimal allocation of resources as between different firms using these resources for production of commodities.

Perfect Competition and Optimum Direction of Production (Product-mix) : Allocative Economic Efficiency

The most important condition for the attainment of Pareto optimum is one which refers to the optimum direction or composition of production. In other words, this condition requires how much amounts of different goods should be produced and resources allocated accordingly. This refers to the general condition for optimum allocation of resources which has also been called the condition for *General Economic Efficiency* and *General Pareto Optimum*. This condition states that marginal rate of substitution between any two commodities for any consumer should be the same as the marginal rate of transformation for the community between these two commodities.

Under conditions of perfect competition, each firm to be in equilibrium produces so much output of a commodity that its marginal cost is equal to the price of the commodity. Thus, for firms in perfect competition, $MC_x = P_x$, $MC_y = P_y$, where MC_z and MC_y are marginal costs of production of commodities X and Y respectively and P_x and P_y are prices of commodities X and Y. Therefore, it follows that firms working in perfect competition will be in equilibrium when they are producing commodities in such quantities that

$$\frac{MC_x}{MC_y} = \frac{P_x}{P_y} \qquad \ldots (i)$$

The ratio of marginal costs of two commodities represents the marginal rate of transformation between them. Therefore, for firms producing under perfect competition :

$$MRT_{xy} = \frac{MC_x}{MC_y} = \frac{P_x}{P_y} \qquad \ldots (ii)$$

When there prevails perfect competition on the buying side, each consumer maximises his satisfaction and is in equilibrium at the point where the given budget line is tangent to his indifference curve. In other words, each consumer is in equilibrium when :

$$MRS_{xy} = \frac{P_x}{P_y}$$

Since, under perfect competition, *the ratio of prices of two commodities* $\left(\frac{P_x}{P_y}\right)$ *is the same for a consumers and producers* it follows from (i) and (ii) above that

$$MRS_{xy} = MRT_{xy}$$

Likewise, this will hold good for any other pair of commodities. Thus, perfect competition satisfies the marginal condition required for the Pareto optimal composition or direction of production.

We thus see that all first order marginal conditions required for the attainment of Pareto-optimality or maximum social welfare are fulfilled under perfect competition. It is in this sense that perfect competition represents economic optimum from the viewpoint of social welfare.

Fundamental Theorem of Welfare Economics and Its Critique

It has been shown above that *perfectly competitive equilibrium is Pareto optimal*. This is called fundamental theorem of welfare economics. This is also called the **invisible hand theorem**. The belief that competitive market economy provides an efficient means of allocating scarce resources goes back to Adam Smith who argued in his famous book "*Wealth of Nations*" that *individuals who pursue their self-interest, they operating through market promote the welfare of others and welfare of the society as a whole*. Thus individual consumers seek to maximise their own satisfaction and producers pursue to maximise their own profits. Even though promoting the interests of the society as a whole is not a part of their intention but they are led by the invisible forces of market system to promote the interest of the society as a whole.

We have proved above that perfect competition in the market satisfies Pareto's optimum condition of exchange, that is (1) MRS_{xy} of any pair of individuals under it is the same, (2) Pareto's optimum condition of production, that is, $MRTS_{LK}$ of any pair of firms using the two factors for producing products under it is the same, and (3) Pareto's condition for optimal direction of production (*i.e.* optimum product mix), namely, MRT_{xy} in production equals MRS_{XY} of consumers (For details regarding proofs of these and other conditions see the above section).

However, the conditions under which a perfect competitive market system achieves Pareto-optimality or what is also called *economic efficiency* are quite restrictive. One important condition for the achievement of Pareto optimality is that the *general competitive equilibrium exists*. This requires that all markets concerned are in equilibrium simultaneously. If one market is not in equilibrium for some reason, the condition for Pareto optimality would be violated which would leave unutilised the opportunities for Pareto improvement.

The second important requirement for the validity of the fundamental theorem of welfare economics is that *second order conditions for equilibrium must be fulfilled*. This implies that consumer preferences (or indifference curves) are convex and also producers' production sets (i.e. isoquants) are convex. This implies that consumers' marginal rate of substitution and producers' marginal rate of technical substitution ($MRTS_{LK}$) must be diminishing at or near the equilibrium point. Further, the second order condition also requires *that production transformation curves must be concave in the relevant region*. The existence of perfect competition does not guarantee that these second order conditions will be fulfilled. In this context it may be noted that many areas of production there prevail *increasing returns* to scale. In case of increasing returns to scale equilibrium of competitive firms is not possible. This would ensure that general competitive equilibrium will not exist which will lead to the violation of the condition.

The third condition required for the fulfilment of fundamental theorem of welfare economics is that externalities in production and externalities in consumption do not exist. The assumption of the absence of production externalities implies that consumption production choices by any firm do not affect the production possibilities of other firms. Similarly, the assumption of the absence of consumption externalities implies that consumption decisions of a consumer do not affect the consumption possibilities of the other consumers. In case these externalities in production and consumption exist, the competitive equilibrium will not achieve Pareto-optimality from the social point of view. How externalities prevent the achievement of Pareto optimality and lead to loss of social welfare will be explained in detail in a later chapter.

Lastly, it is important to note that the competitive equilibrium under the conditions mentioned above ensures Pareto optimality or efficiency in use and allocation of resources. It has nothing to do with desirable distribution of welfare. In other words, *it ensures Pareto efficiency not justice*. Pareto optimality analysis assumes the initial factor endowment as given. Initial inequalities in the ownership of assets or factor-endowments causes inequalities which leads to non-optimal distribution of goods and services and therefore loss of social welfare.

Further, it may be noted that perfectly competitive equilibrium achieves Pareto optimality when the second order conditions of equilibrium are satisfied. These second order conditions require that at or near the equilibrium point indifference curves of consumers and isoquants of producers are convex and production transformation curves are concave to the origin. However, *perfect competition does not guarantee that second order conditions required for the achievement of Paret optimality will also be fulfilled*. Besides, when externalities, that is, external economies and diseconomies in production and consumption are present, perfect competition will not lead to Pareto optimality. When external economies and diseconomies either in production or consumption are present, social marginal cost (or benefit) will diverge from private marginal cost (benefit). Now, *perfect competition only ensures the equality of price of a product with the private marginal cost and not with the equality of price with the social marginal cost*. Thus, the existence of externalities will prevent the achievement of Pareto optimality or efficient allocation of resources even when perfect competition prevails in the economy. How the occurrence of externalities obstructs the achievement of maximum social welfare will be explained at length in a later chapter.

Further, even if the above two factors, namely, non-fulfilment of the second order conditions and the existence of externalities are not actually found, the perfect competition will not lead to economic efficiency or Pareto optimality (that is, optimum allocation of resources) if the given distribution of income is not optimal from the viewpoint of social welfare. As mentioned before, nalysis of Pareto optimality accepts the prevailing income distribution which may be far from the optimum distribution. There is nothing in perfect competition which ensures optimum distribution of income. That the distribution of income is an important factor determining social welfare is now widely recognised by the economists.

Finally, there is another factor which prevents the achievement of Pareto-optimality or maximum social welfare even when perfect competition prevails in the economy. This factor relates to the employment or utilisation of available resources. *Pareto-optimality will not be attained if the available resources are not fully employed or utilised.* This is because if some of the available resources are unemployed or unutilised, then the society could produce more of a commodity by employing the unemployed resources and therefore without cutting down the production of any other commodity. Now, when it is possible to produce more of a commodity without reduction in the output of another, then the society could make either all individuals better off or at least some better off without making *others worse off.*

If the economy is operating at a point inside its transformation curve (*i.e.* production possibility curve), it would not then he employing or utilising its resources fully and it would then be possible to increase the output of both commodities (represented on the two axes) or to increase the output of one commodity without reducing the output of the other. Thus, any position of working inside the transformation or production possibility curve cannot be a position of Pareto optimality. Therefore, for the economy to achieve Pareto-optimality it must work at some point on the given production possibility curve implying full employment of resources. Full employment of available resources is therefore a necessary condition for the attainment of Pareto optimality. But it is important to note that perfect competition does not guarantee full employment of resources and therefore does not necessarily lead to the achievement of Pareto-optimality.

It follows from above that *perfect competition though a necessary condition is not a sufficient condition for Pareto-optimality.* Therefore, that a free enterprise economy characterised by perfect competition ensures efficient allocation of resources or maximum social welfare cannot be accepted without some qualifications. And these qualifications are : (1) the second order conditions are satisfied, (2) the externalities in production and consumption are absent, (3) prevailing distribution of income is optimal from the social point of view, and (4) available resources are fully employed. It may also be noted that in present-day free enterprise capitalist economies perfect competition is an exception rather than the rule. In the present-day capitalist economies, it is monopolies, oligopolies and monopolistic competition which largely prevail and, as shall be demonstrated in the next chapter, these market forms serve as a great obstacle for the achievement of Pareto-optimality or optimum allocation of resources.

QUESTIONS FOR REVIEW

1. Define economic efficiency ? Explain Pareto's three conditions for achievement of economic efficiency
2. State Pareto's Criterion of Social welfare. Explain Pareto's Criterion of social welfare using Edgeworth Box diagram.
3. Explain the concept of utility possibility curve. How would you explain Pareto's. criterion of social welfare with utility possibility curve ?
4. What is Pareto Optimality ? State the conditions of Pareto optimality regarding (1) distribution of goods between individuals, (2) allocation of resources between firms and (3) direction of production.
5. Pareto Critierion does not give us a sufficient basis for ordering states from the viewpoint of social welfare. Examine critically *B.A. (Hons) D.U. 1984*
6. State and explain Pareto optimality criterion. How far is it useful in suggesting policies that will make the community better off ? *B.A. (Hons) D.U. 1986.*

7. Perfect Competition will tend to yield an optimal allocation of resources. Discuss.
B.A. (Hons.) D.U. 1986

8. State and explain diagrammatically the marginal conditions for a Pareto-optimal distribution of goods and resources in a two factors, two commodities, two consumers model.
B.A. (Hons.) D.U. 1987

9. Explain conditions of economic efficiency in competitive markets.
D.U., B.Com (Hons.) 2nd Year 2006.

10. State the conditions of Pareto optimality. How are these conditions affected in the presence of (*i*) social costs and (*ii*) public goods. Explain *B.A. (Hons.) D.U. 1988, 1999, 1991*

[**Hints** (*i*) *Social Costs* are brought about when productive activities of private firms generate external diseconomics and external economies. In case of the emergence of external diseconomies, marginal social cost will be higher than marginal private cost which will lead to more output of a product to be produced under conditions of perfect competition than is socially desirable from the viewpoint of Pareto Optimality. (For details see next chapter)

(*ii*) *Public goods* will also not be produced in a competitive market conditions in optimal quantities as required by Pareto optimality. Public good are not rival in consumption. A person using a public good (say enjoying a walk in a public park) does not affect the utility derived by other persons. Similarly, in case of public goods it is not possible to exclude from their consumption those persons who do not pay for it. If the production of the public goods is left to be produced by the market driven private firms, they will not be produced in Paretian optimal quantities (for details see the next chapter).

11. "Pareto criterion works by sidestepping the crucial issue of interpersonal comparison and income distribution" (Baumol) Discuss.

12. Pareto's analysis leaves a considerable amount of indeterminacy in maximisation of social welfare. Discuss

13. Pareto optimality is necessary but not a sufficient condition for social welfare maximisation. Discuss. *B.A. (Hons.) (D.U.), 1991.*

14. The collapse of the communist regime in Eastern Europe and Soviet Union can be attributed to economic inefficiencies. Discuss. *B.A. (Hons.) D.U. 1992.*

15. With the help of Edgeworth consumption box diagram explain efficiency in exchange of two goods between two consumers. What does contract curve for exchange indicate.
D.U., B.Com (Hons.) II year 2006

16. Show that a general competitive equilibrium is also Pareto optimal.
B.A. (Hons.) (D.U.) 1994

17. There is only one Pareto-optimal allocation in an economy. True or false ? Explain
B.A. (Hons.) D.U. 1998

18. When perfectly competitive markets are in equilibrium, all the three conditions for economic efficiency are also satisfied *B.A. (Hons.) D.U. 1999.*

19. Show how a perfectly competitive market leads to Pareto optimality in exchange, production and product-mix. *D.U., B.Com (Hons.) II year 2008.*

20. Perfect competition is an ideal market form as it ensures the attainment of Pareto optimality. Examine critically.

21. What is fundamental theorem of welfare economics ? What are the conditions required for it to be valid ? Examine critically.

22. Perfect competition is a necessary but not a sufficient condition for Pareto optimality. Discuss.

CHAPTER 40
MARKET FAILURES, EXTERNALITIES AND PUBLIC GOODS

We have explained in the previous chapter conditions for the achievement of pareto optimality or maximum social welfare. We have also briefly discussed that with some qualifications perfect competition ensures the achievement of Pareto optimality or maximum social welfare. Now, the pertinent question is what are the factors which hinder the attainment of pareto-optimality and maximum social welfare. The main obstacles are :

1. the existence of monopoly or imperfect competition;
2. the presence of externalities, *i.e.* external economies and diseconomies in production and consumption; and
3. the consumption of Public Goods, and

We shall explain below these obstacles at some length.

MONOPOLY (MARKET POWER) AS AN OBSTACLE TO THE ATTAINMENT OF PARETO OPTIMALITY

An important complaint against monopoly (and as a matter of fact against all forms of imperfect competition) is that it causes misallocation of productive resources and thus hinders the achievement of maximum social welfare. The crucial condition required for Pareto optimality is that marginal rate of transformation (*MRT*) of the community between any two commodities should be equal to the marginal rate of substitution (*MRS*) between these commodities of every consumer. We saw above that perfect competition satisfies this condition of Pareto optimality. But under monopoly (or any other form of imperfect competition such as oligopoly or monopolistic competition) the marginal rate of transformation of the community between two commodities is not equal to the marginal rate of substitution between them of the consumers. Consequently, monopoly does not ensure optimum allocation of resources and serves as an obstacle to the attainment of maximum social welfare. The reason for this is that a monopolist does not equate price of his product with marginal cost of production; he restricts output and charges higher price than marginal cost.

Assume that there are two commodities, X and Y, and further that the commodity X is being produced under conditions of monopoly whereas the commodity Y is being produced under conditions of perfect competition. Since the commodity X is being produced under conditions of monopoly, the price (P_x) of commodity X will be grater than marginal cost (MCx) of its production. Thus $P_x > MC_x$. But since the commodity Y is being produced under conditions of perfect competition, price (Py) of commodity Y will be equal to the marginal cost (MC_y) of production. That is, $P_y = MC_y$. It therefore follows that :

$$\frac{MC_x}{MC_y} < \frac{P_x}{P_y}$$

Since the ratio of marginal costs of two commodities represents the marginal rate of transformation (MRT_{xy}) between them, therefore,

$$MRT_{xy} < \frac{P_x}{P_y}$$

But the consumers in order to be in equilibrium will equate their marginal rate of substitution between two commodities (MRS_{xy}) with the price ratio of the two commodities $\left(\frac{P_x}{P_y}\right)$. This is because each individual consumer will take the prices of commodities as given and constant for him. Thus, for consumers,

$$MRS_{xy} = \frac{P_x}{P_y} \qquad \ldots (ii)$$

From (*i*) and (*ii*) above it follows that under conditions of monopoly in the production of X

$$MRT_{xy} < MRS_{xy}$$

or

$$MRS_{xy} > MRT_{xy}$$

That is, when monopoly exists in the production of a commodity marginal rate of substitution between commodities will be greater than the marginal rate of transformation. In other words, consumers would like the commodity under monopoly production to be produced more but monopolists would not be producing the desired quantity of the commodity and will, therefore, be causing loss of satisfaction and misallocation of resources.

That monopoly causes loss of welfare and misallocation of resources will become very clear by considering Figure 40.1. It will be seen from this figure that the transformation curve of the community AB is tangent to the community indifference curve IC_3 at point E. Therefore, at point E marginal rate of transformation (MRT_{xy}) of the community between two commodities is equal to the marginal rate substitution (MRS_{xy}) of the community. Thus E represents maximum possible level of social welfare and the combination of two commodities being produced (*i.e.* OM of X and ON of Y) represents optimum allocation of resources.

But when the commodity X is being produced under conditions of monopoly, the equilibrium will

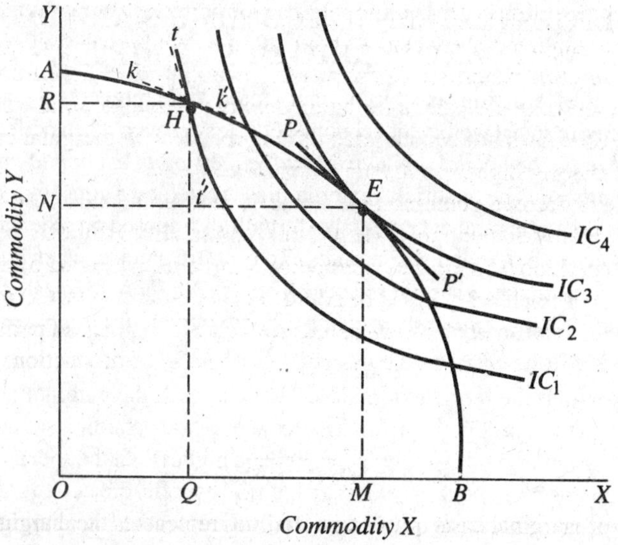

Fig. 40.1. *Monopoly as an Obstacle to Maximisation of Social Welfare.*

not be at point *E*, but instead it will be at point *H*. This is because, under monopoly, producers would be equating marginal rate of transformation (*MRT*) or ratio of marginal costs $\left(\frac{MC_x}{MC_y}\right)$ with the ratio of marginal revenues $\left(\frac{MR_x}{MR_y}\right)$ and not with the ratio of prices of two goods $\left(\frac{P_x}{P_y}\right)$. Since consumers would be equating marginal rate of substitution (MRS_{xy}) with the price ratio of two goods, the marginal rate of transformation in the equilibrium position at point *H* will not be equal to the marginal rate of substitution. This is quite obvious from Figure 40.1 where at point *H* transformation curve *AB* and consumers' indifference curve IC_1, are intersecting each other. This implies that slopes of transforma-tion curve at point *H*, which indicates marginal rate of transformation, and the slope of consumers' indifference curve IC_1, which indicates marginal rate of substitution, are not the same. It will be observed from Figure 40.1 that at point *H* marginal rate of substitution between two goods (*MRSxy*) is greater than the marginal rate of transformation (*MRTxy*) between them as tangent *tt′*, *drawn at point H* on the indiffrence curve IC_1 is greater than the slope of the langent *kk′* drawn at point *H* on the transformation curve *AB*. This means that consumers' preferences require that good *X* should be produced more but because of the existence of monopoly in the production of commodity *X*, it is not being produced equal to the desired quantity. As a result, the level of satisfaction or welfare of the consuming community is at a lower level than possible under the given production conditions. Consuming community's satisfaction will be greater at point *E* which lies on indifference IC_3 but under conditions of monopoly in the production of *X*, equilibrium is at point *H* which lies on the lower indifference curve IC_1.

Thus monopoly causes loss of satisfaction or welfare. This loss of satisfaction or welfare is due to the fact that monopoly is not optimally allocating its resources between the production of two commodities according to the consumers' preferences. Given the transformation curve and consum-ing community's indifference map, the optimal production pattern is represented by the point *E* where *OM* amount of commodity *X* and *ON* amount of commodity *Y* are being produced. But under condi-tions of monopoly in the production of *X*, the equilibrium is established at point *H* where smaller quantity *OQ* of commodity *X* and larger quantity *OR* of commodity *Y* are being produced. Thus *monopoly has caused misallocation of resources.*

EXTERNALITIES (EXTERNAL ECONOMIES AND DISECONOMIES) AND PARETO OPTIMALITY

The existence of externalities is an important factor which prevents the achievement of Pareto-optimality (or maximum social welfare or economic efficiency) even when perfect competition prevails. *Externalities refer to the beneficial and detrimental effects of an economic unit (a firm, a consumer or an industry) on others.* The beneficial externalities created by a consumer or a firm for others are known as external economies and detrimental externalities imposed on others by a productive firm or a consumer are known as external diseconomies. To be more precise, *when an economic unit creates benefits for others for which he does not receive any payment, there exist external economies. On the other hand, external diseconomies occur when an economic unit inflicts costs on others for which he is not required to pay.*

It is noteworthy that the term "externalities" covers both the external economies and external diseconomies. When for a productive firm there exist external economies, that is, beneficial external effects, then the private marginal cost of the firm will be higher than the social marginal cost, since the firm will not take into account benefits external to it (*i.e.* benefits created for others). And the market price fixed on the basis of private marginal cost will not reflect the social marginal cost which will be lower when external economies occur. Similarly, when with the expansion of a firm external diseconomies occur, then the private marginal cost will be lower than the social cost, since the firm will not take into account the disadvantages caused to others by its activity. Thus, when external diseconomies occur, price fixed on the basis of private marginal cost will be lower than that determined on the basis of social cost.

It follows from above that *in the absence of externalities*, all costs incurred and all benefits received by producers and consumers will be reflected in market prices and that there will not be any divergence between private and social costs (or benefits). But, *when externalities (external economies and diseconomies) occur, market prices determined on the basis of private costs and benefits will not truly reflect social costs and therefore divergence is caused between private and social costs (or benefits).*

It follows from above that externalities arise primarily due to the fact that the effects regarding costs, output, employment, labour skills, technological capabilities of the activities of a producer or consumer on others or society as a whole are not reflected in market prices and therefore *market prices do not truly reflect social costs.* We shall give below a few examples of externalities, that is, external economies and diseconomies in production and consumption. The basic idea behind the belief that a competitive price system is optimal is based on the fact that a producer benefits himself only by benefitting the society because he makes available certain goods and services to the society. In other words, by promoting his own interests he promotes the interests of society as well. But there are so many cases in production and consumption "when members of the economy do things which benefit others in such a way that they can receive no payment in return or where their actions are detrimental to others and involve no commensurate cost to themselves."[1] Thus, due to externalities there arises the divergence between social and private costs and benefits.

External Economies and Diseconomies in Production

1. External Economies

As the firm expands its scale of production, it becomes possible for the firm to produce a unit of product at a relatively lower cost due to internal economies of large-scale production. On the other hand, external economies occur when the expansion of a firm's output creates benefits, part of which goes to others. A firm may create external benefits for others in two ways : (*a*) By expanding its production, the firm may render a direct service to others such as training the labourers by its manpower training programme and thus benefit the other firms by making available skilled and trained labourers when they have to pay no cost or only nominal cost. (*b*) By expanding its production a firm may make the supply of some inputs cheaper for all the firms in the industry.

For example, an expansion in the production of an engineering firm may increase the demand for steel. And if the steel production is subject to internal economies of large-scale production, the expansion of steel industry following the increase in its demand will lower its cost and price. Another example of external economies is provided by the construction of a bridge or a highway which reduces transport cost and increases the land values in the neighbouring areas. Still another example of external economies of production is provided by the pumping of water from a mine. If a firm pumps out water from mine '*A*', it will lower the cost of pumping water from mine '*B*' owned by another firm. Similarly, bees of producers of honey create benefits for the owners of nearby orange groves, for the bees help pollinate oranges in the groves. On the other hand, orange groves create external economies for the honey producers since the orange groves provide nectar for the bees producing honey.

In all these cases, a firm incurs cost in its expansion but the benefits arising out of it are also reaped by others who pay no price for them.

External Diseconomies. Let us explain some external diseconomies of production. There are a good number of external diseconomies which may be created by the productive activity of a firm. *The*

---

1. W.J. Baumol, *op. cit.* p.517

pollution of air by the factories through emitting smoke and the wastes of factories poured into streams or ocean create health hazard for men, especially those who live in the surrounding areas. For these external harms caused to the other members of the society, the firms are not required to pay any price. A factory owner pays nothing to the residents of the neighbouring colony who happen to be the victims of pollution by the factory. Another example of external diseconomies is provided by a firm or industry which has to keep more trucks on the road to do its business. This will overcrowd the road which will increase the transportation costs of other firms or industries which had to carry their own goods by trucks. The expanding firm or industry does not pay any price for the higher transport cost incurred by others.

External Economies and Diseconomies in Consumption

External economies in consumption arise when the consumption of a person creates beneficial effects on others. Many examples of external economies can be given. For example, the satisfaction of a telephone owner increases with the increase in the number of telephone owners because he can now contact a larger number of persons on telephone. Likewise, if a person maintains a beautiful garden or lawn, he not only increases his own satisfaction but also that of others, especially his neighbours who also enjoy the look of his garden or lawn. Similarly, when a person maintains his car in such a way that it is quite safe to drive it and also does not emit any smoke, it will also improve others' safety and health and therefore welfare. In this category, we may also include the expenditure incurred by the parents on educating their sons. This will not only benefit them and their sons but also other members of the society. This is because the education makes a person civilised and a better citizen and therefore whoever comes in contact with him, derives satisfaction from him. Thus in the presence of external economies in consumption the social utility exceeds the private utility and therefore divergence between social and private benefits is caused when external economies in consumption prevail.

On the contrary, external diseconomies of consumption occur when a person's consumption creates unfavourable impact on other consumers. A good example of it is provided by the *conspicuous consumption* of a person who through demonstration effect causes a lot of dissatisfaction to friends and neighbourers who now feel themselves inferior to him. Likewise, when a person purchases candy bars for his children, it will make his neighbour's children unhappy because their parents cannot afford. Likewise, loud music played by your neighbour may disturb you and cause a lot of dissatisfaction. Also falls in this category the purchasing of a new Maruti Esteem by your friend because now your Maruti car 800 in your own eyes becomes outdated. More examples of such external diseconomies of consumption can be given.

The existence of external economies and diseconomies explained above plays a significant role in determining the activities of production and consumption in the economy. A pertinent question is how these externalities can lead to the misallocation of resources and thereby act as on obstacle to the attainment of Pereto optimality or maximum social welfare. When externalities in production and consumption prevail and as a result divergence is caused between private and social costs and benefits, the economy guided by the market prices alone, even in the presence of perfect competition, will fail to achieve optimum allocation of resources (or, in other words, maximum social welfare). When external economies of production occur private marginal cost will be greater than the social marginal cost and when external diseconomies in production are present, private marginal cost will be lower than social marginal cost.

Under these circumstances, therefore, a firm which creates external benefits for others will not produce *its product* to the extent social interest requires. This is because equating price with the private marginal cost, which is higher than the social marginal cost, will result in *under-production of the product*. Thus in this case of the existence of external economies in production, output of the product determined on the basis of private marginal cost will be less than the socially optimal level of output. This is illustrated in Figure 40.2 where *SS* represents the supply curve for the product of the industry which has been obtained by summing up the private marginal cost curves of firms. Due to the existence of external economies, social cost will be smaller than the private costs. Therefore, the supply curve *S′ S′* (dotted) of the product reflecting social cost will be lower than the supply curve *SS* based on private marginal cost. The supply curve reflecting social cost is lower because it takes into account external economies generated by the production in the industry, while private cost does not take into account these external economies. It will be seen from the Figure 40.2 that the given demand curve and the supply curve *SS*, based upon the private cost of production, intersect at point *E* and thus determine *OQ* as the actual amount of the product produced. But the socially optimum output is *OM* at which the supply curve *S′S′* reflecting social cost intersects the given demand curve. It is thus evident that the product is being produced in smaller quantity than the socially optimum output *OM*. Thus, *the existence of external economies results in under-production and loss of social welfare equal to the area EKT.*

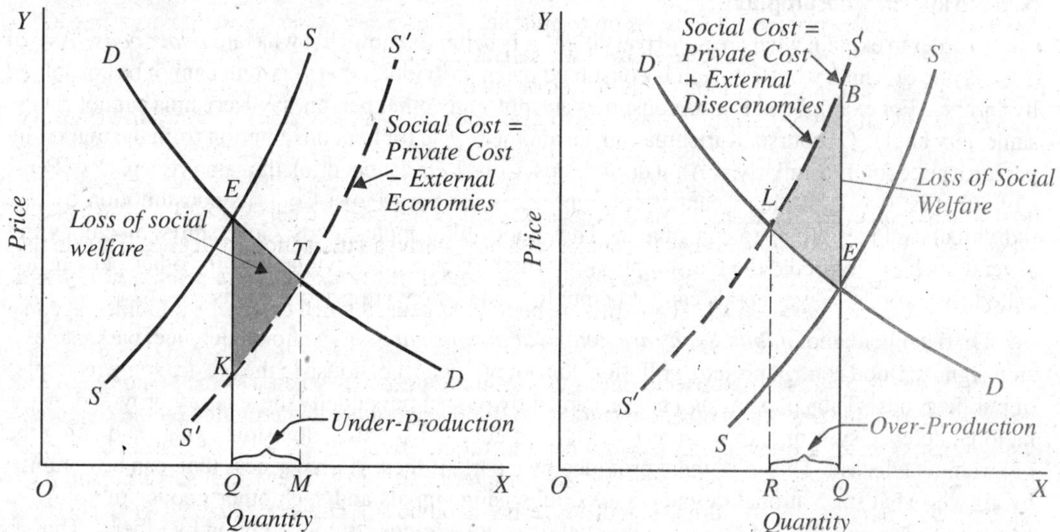

Fig. 40.2. *Under-Production in Case of External Economies*

Fig. 40.3. *Over-Production in Case of External Diseconomies*

On the other hand, when there exist external diseconomies in production, private marginal cost will be lower than the social marginal cost, since the former will not take into account costs or harms imposed on others. Therefore, when external diseconomies are present, equating price with marginal cost will result in over-production of the product, that is, more than socially optimum output will be produced. This is illustrated in Figure 40.3. It will be seen that the supply curve *SS* based on private marginal costs intersects the demand curve at point *E* and thus determines *OQ* amount of output. Supply *S′ S′*) (dotted) which takes into account external diseconomies and therefore reflects social cost lies at a higher level and intersects the demand curve at point *L* and therefore socially optimum output will be *OR*. Thus, it follows *when external diseconomies are present, equating price with private marginal cost will result in over-production of the product, that is, more than socially optimum output will be produced and will cause a loss of social welfare equal to the area ELB.*

When there are external economies in consumption, then the demand curve for the product determined on the basis of private marginal utility will be lower than that based on social marginal utility, because the former will fail to reflect the external economies in consumption being generated. Therefore, in this case too, output determined on the basis of private marginal utility and demand will result in lower output than the socially optimum level. On the other hand, when there exist external diseconomies in consumption the private marginal utility will be higher than the social marginal utility, since the former will not take into account the external diseconomies. As a result, when external diseconomies in consumption are present, the output determined on the basis of private marginal utility (benefit) will be more than the socially optimum level.

PUBLIC GOODS AND MARKET FAILURE

The existence of public goods provides us another important source of market failure. It should be noted that public goods are not necessarily produced by the public sector. It is due to the possession of certain properties that some goods are called public goods and has nothing to do with whether they are produced in the public sector or private sector. It is thus very nature of some goods that makes it difficult if not impossible for the markets to achieve Pareto optimality or economic efficiency. Two essential characteristics of public goods are that they are *non-rival* and *non-exclusive* in consumption. Let us explain these characteristics of public goods in some details.

Non-Rivalry in Consumption

In order to explain what are non-rival goods, it is better to know first what are *rival goods*. A rival good is one of which when one unit is consumed by an individual, that very unit cannot be consumed by another. For example, if Rekha consumes an apple, any other person, say Karishma cannot eat the same very apple. Of course, Karishma can get another apple for her consumption from the market by paying a price for it. Similarly, if Amit drinks Pepsi Cola, Bela cannot drink the same very pack of Pepsi Cola, that is, two individuals cannot consume the same very Pepsi Cola; its consumption by one individual excludes others to consume it. Thus goods like, apples, Pepsi Cola, shirts, machines and several such other goods, the consumption of which reduce their availability for other persons are called rival goods. Rival goods cannot be public goods, they are private goods.

On the other hand, *public goods are non-rival in consumption*. National defence, parks, television signals, flood control project, pollution control project, light house in the sea are some examples of public goods. Thus persons of a nation can enjoy (consume) equally the security provided by the national defence system. All persons of a city can benefit from the television signals and enjoy the programme telecast. The enjoyment provided by a park, if there is free access to it, can be obtained by all who visit it. National defence, parks, television signals and such other goods are non-rival goods as their consumption by one individual does not exclude its consumption by others. That is, the consumption of a non-rival good by an individuals does not reduce its amount available for others to consume. To conclude, public goods are non-rival.

Non-Excludiability

The other essential characteristic of a public good is non-excludiability in distribution of their consumption benefits. This non-exclusive nature of a public goods implies that it is difficult if not impossible to exclude those from consuming them who are not willing to pay for them. In case of private rival goods such as shirts, cars, Pepsi Cola, apples those who do not pay for them can be easily prevented from consuming them or receiving benefits from them because the producer or seller simply does not provide them these goods, if they do not pay price for them. On the contrary, in case of public goods, either it is not possible or it is very costly to prevent those people from consuming them who do not pay for these goods. We will explain later that it is due to the feature of non-excludiability of public goods that accounts for the failure of market in case of these goods to ensure Pareto efficiency.

For example, national defence is a public good and is provided to all members of a society and its benefits are available to all equally irrespective of whether some people pay for it or not. It is difficult if not impossible to exclude those people from receiving benefits of security provided by national defence system who do not pay for it. Likewise, if a lighthouse is constructed in a sea, it provides light for all the ships whether any one of them pays for it or not and it is not possible to prevent those who do not pay from receiving light from the light house. This inability to exclude those who do not pay from receiving benefits also applies in case of other public goods such as television signals, pollution control project to provide clear air, flood control projects, parks etc.

Free - Rider's Problem and Public Goods

It is easy to show how non-excludiability of a public good can lead to the market failure, that is, failure of market to achieve pareto efficiency. As explained above, non-excludiability of public goods arises because producers are not able to prevent those from consuming these or enjoying benefits from these who do not pay their share of cost. There is a problem called a *free-rider's problem* which states that because people cannot be excluded from consuming public goods or enjoying benefits from them, there is incentive for persons in these situations to free ride and try to enjoy benefits from reduced pollution, parks, television signals, light house without paying for them. These persons want to get something for nothing and rely on others to make payment for public goods whose benefits they will also automatically get.

Due to this free-rider problem or inability of the producers of public goods to prevent those who do not pay from receiving benefits from them, that a profit-maximising firm will either not produce a public good or produce too little of it. This creates economic inefficiency or Pareto non-optimality. Let us take an example of this free rider's problem in case of public goods leading to economic inefficiency. Suppose the construction of a dam to check floods which cause a lot of damage in a city is required. This dam when built will protect equally all people of the city from the damages due to floods. However, some people of the city would not like to pay for the dam with the hope that others would pay for it and they because of non-excludiability would also enjoy its benefits. But in view of this incentive to free ride, adequate revenue to cover costs of building the dam cannot be provided, and therefore, no private entrepreneur would consider it worthwhile to construct the dam to control floods. Similarly, the production of other public goods such as lighthouse, television signals, pollution abatement projects would not be extended to the socially desirable level in view of the non-excludiability and incentive to free ride.

Public Goods and Pareto - Efficiency

Before explaining further how the free-rider problem results in less than socially optimal production of public goods, it is important to understand how Pareto optimal level of production of public good is determined. Because public goods are non-rival in consumption, some modifications are required in formulation of Pareto optimality conditions. To illustrate the conditions of Pareto - optimality in case of public goods we take the case of a society composed of two persons A and B and the public good is the pollution control project aimed to clean air which if produced would benefit both of them. But the two persons may not perceive to receive the same amount of marginal benefits from this pollution control measure. In other words, they may have different evaluation of the marginal benefits of pollution control measure. Each person will place some value on the pollution control. The marginal benefits they obtain or values they place on the different quantities of pollution abatement are depicted in Figure 40.4. Due to differences in tastes or perceptions of two individuals, the curve showing marginal benefits from the pollution-free air are different, the curves MB_A and MB_B depict the marginal benefits obtained by individual A and B respectively from the varying quantities of pollution-free air. *The marginal benefit curve can also be interpreted as the price which the individuals are willing to pay for the different quantities of pollution free air.* Thus, it will be seen from the marginal benefit curves that individual A will be willing to pay price Q_1A_1 for OQ_1 quantity of pollution-free air, whereas individual B is willing to pay Q_1B_1 for the same OQ_1 quantity of the pollution-free air. Similarly, for OQ_2 quantity of the pollution-free air, the individual A is wiling to pay price equal to Q_2A_2 and individual B is willing to pay price equal to Q_2B_2. Therefore, the marginal benefit curves can be interpreted as the demand curves of the individuals for pollution-free air. It should also be noted that the marginal benefits or the price which the individuals are willing to pay depend on the values they place on the different quantities of the pollution-free air.

In order to determine the Pareto-optimal quantity of pollution-free air we need the total market demand curve or the aggregate marginal benefit curve of the individuals comprising the society. Market demand curve for a public good cannot be obtained in the way market demand curve is obtained in case of private goods. Since a private good is rival in consumption, the market demand curve of it is obtained by adding up sideways (*i.e.* horizontal addition) of the demand curves (*i.e.* marginal benefit curves) of the two individuals. But, as explained above, public goods are non-rival in consumption, that is, in case of public goods same units of output can be consumed by various people at the same time. Therefore, different individuals can pay for the same units of a public good at the same time. Thus, a pollution control project renders the air of a town free of pollution to some degree from which everybody in the town is benefited and should pay for it. Consider Figure 40.4, where it will be seen that individual A is prepared to pay price Q_1A_1 for OQ_1 quantity of pollution-free air and the individual B is prepared to pay price Q_1B_1 for the same OQ_1 quantity of pollution-free air which he enjoys or consumes at the same time as individual A. Thus, for OQ_1 quantity of clean air, the total price which the two individuals are willing to pay equals $Q_1A_1 + Q_1B_1 = Q_1M$. Similarly, for the same OQ_2 quantity of pollution-free air, individual A is prepared to pay price equal to Q_2A_2, and individual B is prepared to pay price equal to Q_2B_2. Thus, the total price which the individuals together are willing to pay for the same OQ_2 quantity of the good is equal to the sum of these two prices, *i.e.* $Q_2A_2 + Q_2B_2 = Q_2N$. It therefore follows that in case of a public good market demand curve is derived by *summing up vertically* the demand curves of the individuals because each individual consumes the same units of the good at the same time.

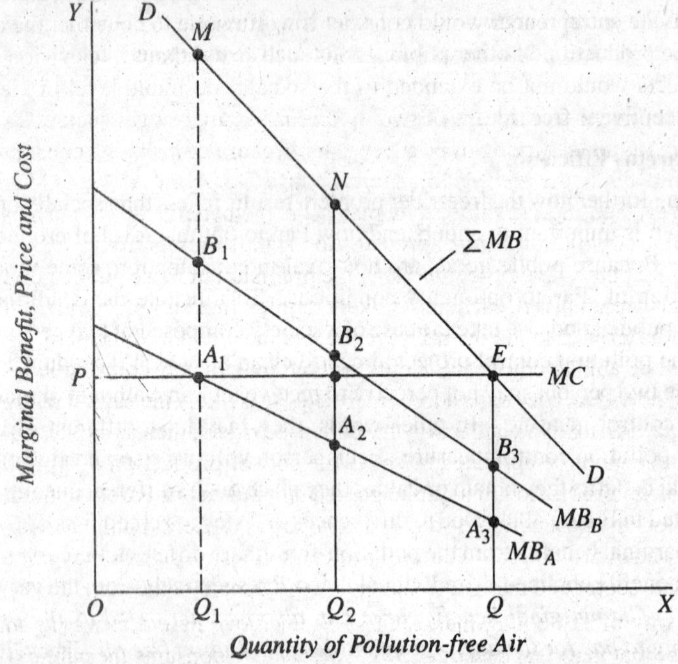

Fig. 40.4 *Public Goods and Pareto Optimality*

Having now obtained the market demand curve of a public good we can now show what will be the Pareto-efficient output of a public good. In this connection it should be noted that a society has to bear the costs it incurs on labour and materials to produce pollution-free air. Pareto efficient level of output is determined at which the price, which the individuals together are willing to pay for the good (that is, aggregate benefit), equals the marginal cost of production. Suppose the marginal cost of production is equal to *OP* per unit and remains constant. In Figure 40.4, with *OP* as the constant marginal cost, *MC* is the marginal cost curve. It will be observed from the figure that price which the two individuals together are willing to pay equals marginal cost (*MC*) at *OQ* quantity of pollution free air. As said above, price which the persons are willing to pay indicates the aggregate marginal benefit. Thus, aggregate marginal benefit and marginal cost of production are equal at *OQ* level of output of pollution-free air. If resources are allocated to the pollution control project to the extent that *OQ* quantity of pollution-free air is produced at which price (marginal benefit) equals marginal cost incurred the social welfare (*i.e.*, the aggregate benefits of the two individuals) will be maximum. Thus *OQ* is Pareto-efficient level of output of the public good.

Public Goods and Market Failure

But a private firm will produce Pareto optimum output *OQ only if each individual pays a price equal to the marginal benefit.* At *OQ* output marginal benefit of pollution free air is QA_3 for individual *A* and QB_3 for individual *B*. If both are willing to pay prices equal to these marginal benefits, the aggregate price per unit which they together will pay for Pareto efficient quantity *OQ* amounts to *OP* or $QE = QA_3 + QB_3$. In this way total revenue collected by the private firm will cover the cost of pollution control project which cleans the air and therefore will be worthwhile for the private firm to undertake the pollution control project.

But, as explained above, due to inability of the producer of a public good to exclude those who do not pay and want to be free-riders, the costs of optimal level of output cannot be covered by a private producer. Therefore, in this situation too little or even none of the public good will be produced though the marginal benefits of additional units (*i.e.*, the value the individuals place on these additional units) exceeds the social marginal costs of producing these units. Thus, private production and functioning of market in case of public goods do not lead to Pareto efficiency in the provision of public goods.

It may be further noted that in case of two individuals composing a society, there may not be much problem for an individual trying to be a free rider because of his being constantly watched and pressured by the other, but in the real world a society consists of *many* persons. There is incentive to the persons for misrepresenting the values they place (*i.e.* the benefits they receive) on public goods such as national defence, pollution control project, flood control programme, television signals, and apparently claiming that they have little interest in the provision of these public goods. Since a large number of individuals are involved, each one is likely to think that his not paying for the public good will not make much difference to the overall revenue and the amount of the public good that will be produced and he will be able to enjoy its benefits without making any contribution. This, of course, would be true if one individual tries to be a free rider. But, as is likely the case, if many individuals and may even all of them thinking in a similar way try to be free riders, then as explained above in Figure 40.4, enough revenue cannot be collected to cover the cost of production of a public good. In this situation there will be no production of a public good at all, at least its Pareto optimal quantity would not be produced. Thus the production of highly important and useful public goods such as national defence, pollution control project, flood control project, television signals may not be undertaken at all if we rely on private sector and market. This is glaring example of the market failure.

An interesting way of explaining market failure to achieve Pareto efficiency in case of public goods is to emphasise that marginal cost of allowing a person to consume the public good is zero *once it is produced*, even if it is possible to prevent him from consuming the commodity. Thus, parks, television signals, flood control projects etc. having been produced, the cost of letting additional consumers to consume these goods or their services is zero. For example, within good limits a visitor to a public park who has not paid is not to affect the enjoyment of the park by those who have paid for it, and it costs the society or a private producer nothing for this additional person visiting the park and enjoying (consuming) it. In fact he would be made better off and no one would be worse off because no more resources of the society are used when the additional person is allowed to enjoy the park (i.e. marginal cost is zero). Now, if the marginal cost of permitting additional persons to consume the good is zero, then Pareto-efficiency requires that price of the public good should be zero. But the total cost of production of public goods is not zero; to produce public good is indeed very expensive. To meet these total costs of production private producer sets a positive price to cover cost. Consequently, price set will be higher than marginal cost and less than Pareto-optimal quantity will be consumed. *Thus production of a public good by the private sector does not lead to Pareto-optimality in allocation of the good.* In other words, market fails to achieve Pareto efficiency in the production of public goods.

FAILURES OF MARKET AND ROLE OF GOVERNMENT

We have explained above the various concepts of economic efficiency and have seen how a perfectly competitive markets succeeds in achieving exchange efficiency, production efficiency and allocative efficiency. As a result, competitive market achieves maximum possible well-being of the people of a society. In an economy characterised by perfectly competitive markets, government performs only its basic functions, namely, to maintain law and order in the economy, to enforce property rights and contracts made by the people while making market transactions.

There is a good deal of difference of opinions among economists regarding whether markets in the actual world can be relied upon to achieve economic efficiency, prosperity of the people and acceptable distribution of resources and incomes. On the one extreme, there are economists like Fredrich von Hayek of Austria and Milton Friedman of the United States who believe that markets in the real world are highly competitive and free market economies are quite successful in achieving economic efficiency, prosperity and desirable distribution of income. They think that wherever there are departures from ideal of perfectly competitive markets, intervention of government will not improve the working of the economy.

However, the dominant view among main stream economists is that though perfectly competitive markets are ideal and serve as useful benchmark with which the outcome of actual markets can be compared, there are significant failures of market system. According to them, government intervention can bring about improvements in the allocation of resources and distribution of incomes.

Imperfect Competition and Monopoly. When there prevails monopoly or imperfect competition (that is, monopolistic competition and oligopoly) in the product markets, output of products is lower than the optimal level and price is greater than marginal cost. As a result, such markets do not produce most efficient product-mix.

Many markets in the economy are not sufficiently competitive and there are firms which wield great market power and restrict output of goods and raise their prices. Government can intervene and regulate them, especially natural monopolies where competition is non-viable. Besides, government can take measures to check monopolistic and restrictive trade practices to encourage competition in the economy. Through passing laws government can declare illegal the mergers such as a cartel which lead to monopolies.

Price of a good reflects marginal utility of the good for the consumers and marginal cost is the opportunity costs of factors used in the production of goods. In imperfect competitive markets for goods prices of goods charged by the producers exceeds marginal cost and therefore consumers are exploited and their satisfactions are not maximised. Thereforc, prices charged in imperfect competitive markets are imperfect guide for resource allocation and therefore do not lead to the achievement of economic efficiency or Parete optimality. This requires intervention by the Government to fix prices, at least of essential goods at appropriate levels so as to ensure economic efficiency in resource, allocation. This is quite evident in case of *natural monopolies* such as public utilities engaged in electricity distribution, gas and water distribution when due to substantial economies of scale marginal cost goes on declining and prices charged on the basis of marginal costs are not viable for private production. Therefore the Government undertakes their production itself or regulate the prices if their production is permitted by the private sector.

In factor markets also market imperfection also prevail as when there are monopsonies, oligopsonies and other types of less than perfect factor markets. Factor prices fixed under such imperfect factor markets do not reflect the *true opportunity cost* to the society. Due to these imperfections wages of labour may be fixed above their opportunity cost to the society and therefore used too little resulting in unemployment. On the other hand under imperfect market conditions, capital and foreign exchange may be fixed above their true opportunity costs the society. This also requires government intervention so that market system does not lead to economic inefficiency or Pareto non-optimality from social point of view. The government should intervene to *remove these factor price distortions* of social optimum or economic efficiency is to be restored.

Further, there is *existence of externalities*, both positive and negative. Both these externalities cause deviation of production goods and as a consequence allocation of resources from those which are economically efficient. The existence of externalities cause difference between social marginal cost (*SMC*) and private marginal cost (*PMC*). When positive externalities exist private marginal cost exceeds social marginal cost ($PMC > SMC$) which leads to *under-production of goods* from the socially optimum levels.

On the contrary, when *negative externalities* exist, for example, when industries create pollution of environment which harms the society but the producers do not pay for it. In case of these negative externalities social marginal cost exceeds private marginal cost ($SMC > PMC$) resulting in *over-production of goods* by private enterprise guided by the market forces.

In case of both types of externalities the Government should intervene to correct market failures. The Government can curb negative externalities by levying indirect taxes on them so that private marginal cost (*PMC*) inclusive of tax corresponds to social marginal cost (*SMC*) and therefore socially optimum production is made by the private enterprise. Alternatively, Government can regulate the private enterprises to ensure optimum levels of output of goods is produced.

Equally important is the intervention by Government is case of industries or sectors creating positive externalities as they are highly essential for accelerating economic growth. The example of positive externalities are infrastructure facilities such as power generation, transport facilities including highways and ports, irrigation facilities and so forth as well as social capital such as education and health care facilities. In case of both the physical and social infrastructure facilities social benefits exceed private benefits as they have large positive or beneficial externalities. As a result, there will be *under-production of them* by private enterprises compared to their socially optimum levels.

To induce the private enterprises to produce socially optimum output, the government should provide subsidies on their production or alternatively undertake itself provision or production of them so as to ensure socially optimum levels of their production.

Some economists lay emphasis on failures of market which arise due to **imperfect information** that prevails in the real world. In perfectly competitive markets, it is assumed that both the firms and buyers have perfect information about the quality of workers, and return which they will receive from investment. However, in the real world firms do not have perfect information about the quality of workers hired by them. Firms do not have perfect information on the likely returns from different types of investment made by them. Further, individuals do not have perfect information about the quality of products, especially the second-hand products.They may turn out to be '*lemons*'

Some form of misinformation can be corrected by the government by enforcing rules preventing false advertising. In some cases government provides information to the people regarding jobs available, government can ban the sale of spurious drugs and control the prices of drugs so that buyers cannot be overcharged.Government can set up consumer information services for providing right information.

Besides, there are **public goods** which are collectively consumed by the members of a society and it is not possible to exclude anyone who does not pay for them from consuming them or enjoying their services. The important examples of public goods are national defence, law and order, light houses. Since people who do not pay for them because they cannot be excluded from consuming them or enjoying their services, it is not profitable for private firms to produce them. Therefore, government has to provide these public goods.

Another significant failure of market is the **existence of unemployment** which exists on a large scale in the free market economies. The existence of unemployment implies that some resources, especially labour, are lying idle and putting them to use will enable us to poduce more of some goods without reducing the production of any other.

Equity in Income Distribution. Last but not the least, the government should intervene to bring about equitable distribution of income, especially in developing countries, it should take appropriate measures to eradicate poverty. It may be recalled that Pareto optimality takes the *distribution of income in a society as given* and explain how socially optimum resource allocation is achieved. It does not go into the question of optimum distribution of income in a society. With a different income distribution, there will be different Pareto optimum. As a matter of fact, any government policy affects the distribution of income. This issue was even raised by classical economits Adam Smith and Ricardo who advocated for free trade which benefits some and harm other members of the society. N. Kaldor and J.R. Hicks provided a welfare criterion according to which if as a result a government policy those who gain can compensate the losers and still remain better a off, the new situation would represent an improvement over the existing one. However, the serious drewback of this criterion is that the *compensation visualised is potential and not real*. Let us take the example of the Indian Government's foreign direct policy (FDI) in retail trade. This will benefit those who get these giant retail shops and the consumers who get cheaper consumer goods. But it can harm others such retail traders many of which may be rendered unemployed as a result of big giant retailers such as Wal-Malt. Besides, some producers of goods will also suffer losses as giant retailers are likely to bring cheaper Chinese goods for sale in India. Therefore, unless the compensation is real or actual which is generally not contemplated in many cases of policy changes the equitable distribution of income is not ensured.

Removal of absolute poverty and gross inequality is not only an ethical and political issue as it creates social unrest, but an economic issue as well as it may create eonomic instability in the economy which may adversely affect investment and growth. Joseph E. Stiglitz, a Nobel Laureate, in his recent book, "*The Price of Inequality*" points out that there is clear association between inequality and economic instability. According to him, in the US the people in top income-groups save a lot and relatively spend little, whereas the people in low and middle income groups save very little and spend all or most part of their incomes. This is the result of highly skewed income distribution and this reduces an aggregate consumption demand in a society which tends to reduce the level of GDP and thus causes economic instability. However, in case of India when the problem is more on supply-side though large saving by the rich is good as it makes large investment and growth possible but to rely on greater income inequalities to generate higher saving and investment is not the right approach. Many East Asian countries such as Singapure, Malysia, Taiwan, South Korea which achieved higher rate of GDP growth from the mid-sixties to the mid-nineties were not associated with increase in income inequalities and they were able to achieve high rates of economic growth with active participation of Government in their economies. Writing about growth miracle of East Asian Countries, Joseph Stiglitz writes, "*Their economic model included a strong role for the public sector. They clearly did not believe in free and unfettered markets but government played a critical role. Governments acted* as catalyst which helped markets by providing the requisite physical and institutional infrastructure by remedying market failures and by promoting saving and technology"[4].

Further, he writes,contrary to what has happened in In India, "East Asian countries proved that the initial stages of development did not have to be associated with an increase in inequality. Instead the new prosperity was widely shared among the population and millions were lifted out of poverty. For example, in Malysia and Thailand, the incidence of poverty declined from almost 50 per cent in the 1960s to less than 20 per cent by the end of the century"[5].

Inequality is bad partly due to the fact that for any given average per capita income, the higher the inequality a *larger number of people lack the collateral to get loan from banks* or any other source that is, they are not credit-worthy. With low incomes, the people cannot educate their children and cannot spend adequately on their health care. As a result, their children remain uneducated and under-nourished. Besides, in case of India due to large income inequalities as in other developing countries, the people in high income-brackets such as big capitalists, landlords, high salary persons spend lavishy on imported goods, luxury cars, palatial houses, gold and jewellery etc. which have *demonstration effect* on the middle-income group people and tend to lower overall saving rate of the society by increasing their propensity to consume. It is thus evident that income inequalities are bad for economic growth.

Conclusion. We have explained above the cases when markets do not perform well and therefore government intervention is needed to improve economic efficiency. However, it does not *necessarily* mean that Government intervention will definitely improve economic efficiency. *Just as there are market failures there are Government failures too.* However, in our view if there is no corruption among bureaucrats and ministers and MPs, role of government is essential in the economy to achieve social objectives of efficiency, improvement in distribution of income, reducing unemployment, provision of public goods and correcting market failures arising due to existence of externalities.

COMMON PROPERTY RESOURCES

Common property resources are the resources to which every one has *free access*, that is, anyone can use the property without making any payment. Park, rivers, ocean, fisheries, public roads and highways are examples of common property resources. For example, anyone can have a free entry into the India Gate parks in Delhi and enjoy there. However, *each person's use of common property reduces its value to others and thus creates negative externality*. We explain this below.

Since people do not have to pay for the use of common property resources, they tend to be overused or overexploited. For example, parks with free entry often become overcrowded which result in lowering of enjoyment of parks by everybody. Further, the use of rivers, Ganga and Yamuna, in India is quite free and have become so much polluted because factories dump their waste products into them without paying any cost. Even people in general throw all sorts of their wastes (even dead bodies, and their remains) into these rivers. Similarly, costless use of public common land for grazing of cattle, or hunting result in overuse of these common property resources. **This *overuse* of common property resources where there is free access to them is often referred to as the tragedy of commons.**

An important common property resource is fisheries in which no fee is charged for catching fishes from them. Each fisherman wants to catch fish before others do the fishing. *This results in overfishing which may ultimately* leads to the destruction of stock of fish in the fisheries for use in future years.

---

4. Joseph E. Stiglitz, *Free Trade for All* (New York: Oxford University Press, 2005), p.15
5. Joseph E. Stiglitz, *Op. cit.* pp. 14-15.

It is worth noting that **lack of property rights over the common resources** *leads to their overuse. Fishermen when they have costless access to the use of common property resources have incentive to catch more fish than they would if the fisheries were private property, whose owner would charge fee or price for catching fishes by fishermen.* Suppose now each fishery has been given exclusive private property right to a lake where fishes are caught by fishermen. Now, since there exist well-defined property rights, there are no externalities. Therefore, each owner of lake would not allow overfishing in any year so as to maintain the stock (*i.e.*, the number) of fish for the future years.

On the other hand, most *ocean fisheries* are common property to which fishermen have free access. As in case of private manufacturers who create external diseconomy by polluting air or water, fishermen operating in ocean fisheries take into account only their *private costs*. Thus in calculating their costs they include in them the cost of boats, other complementary equipment, a crew etc. *They do not take into account the costs they impose on future generation as their fishing in the present leads to the decrease in the stock of fish in the ocean in the future years.* Thus professor Perloff writes, "The fewer fish there are, the harder it is to catch any, so reducing the population of fish today raises the cost of catching fish in the future. As a result, fishers do not forego fishing now to leave fish for the future. *The social cost is the private cost plus the externality cost from reduced future population of fish*"[6]. It may be emphasised again that it is the lack of clearly defined property rights of fisheries that leads to overfishing. Fishermen have an incentive to catch more fish than they would if the fishery was private property.

Roads and Highways. Let us take another case of common property resources : roads and highways. Every one has access to them for driving their cars and other vehicles. Since owner of a car has no exclusive right, to use the highway on which he drives, he cannot exclude others from driving on the same highway and must share it with others. This leads to the too many drivers using the highway for driving their vehicles which leads to congession and often jams (*i.e.*, a negative externality). This slow down driving on the highway. Thus this is another example of overuse of the common property resource.

Diagrammatic Illustration of Overuse of Common Property Resources.

Let us illustrate diagrammatically *how in case of common property resources, there is overuse of them which is often referred to as 'tragedy of commons'.* Let us take the case of a lake which is the common property of nearby town and this lake is used for fishing. Every fisherman has free (*i.e.*, costless) access to catch fishes from the lake and then sell it in the market. But by catching fish from the lake, fishermen reduce the population of fish in the lake and thereby raise the cost of catching fishes for others. That is, by catching fishes from the lake, fishermen create external diseconomy for other fishermen.

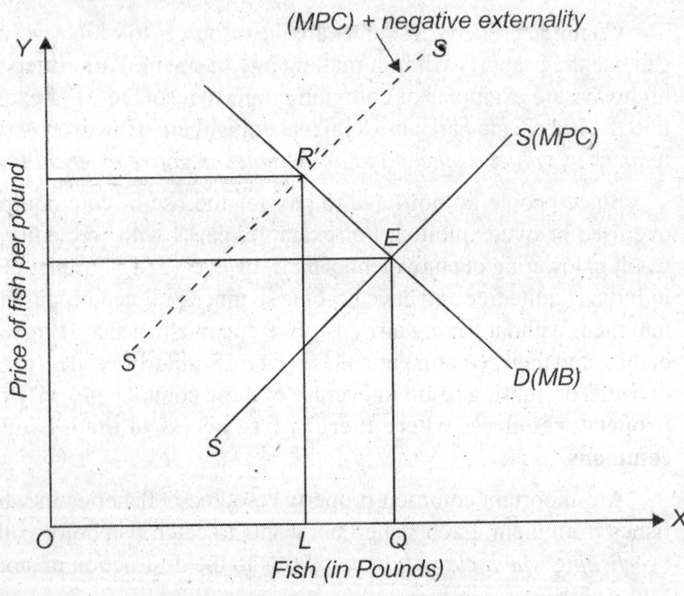

Fig. 40.5. *Overuse of Common Property Resources*

6. Jeffrey M. Perloff, *Microeconomics*, Addison - Wesley, 1998, p. 679.

In Figure 40.5 we have drawn a demand curve *DD* for fish (in pounds) in the market which reflect consumer's marginal benefits (*MB*) from fish and *SS* is the market supply curve of fish based on marginal private cost (*MPC*) of fishermen. If there is free access to lake, the number of fish caught and supplied in the market is *OQ* pounds. Since fishermen do not take into account the negative externality they create, the fishermen's marginal private costs (therefore the supply curve *SS* based on them) will be less than the marginal social cost (*MSC*). Therefore, the supply curve *S* #*S* #epresenting the marginal social costs intersects the market demand curve (*i.e.*, marginal benefit curve) at point *R* and thus determine the *OL* quantity of fish caught and sold. (Note that the marginal social cost (*MSC*) equals marginal private cost (*MPC*) plus the negative externality created). Thus *OL* quantity of fish (in pounds) is the *socially optimum* output. But as fishermen do not take into account the external diseconomy or social marginal cost and operate on the basis of their marginal private cost (*MPC*), they catch more fish equal to *OQ* which thus *leads to the overuse of the fishery*. This is therefore called tragedy of commons.

Assigning Property Rights and Coase Theorem

We have explained above that common property resources tend to be overused and therefore there is economically inefficient use of them. R. Coase,[7] a Nobel Prize Winner of 1991, has proposed a solution for this problem to ensure economically efficient use of common property resources. According to Coase, if costs of negotiating between the parties is quite small, the parties that create negative externality and the victim of their activity negotiate, they can arrive at a price which properly takes into account the negative external effect and thus ensure economic efficiency in the use of common property resources. For example, if *downstream water users* are assigned the property right *to obtain water of a particular quality*, a firm that wants to pollute the stream will be prepared to give compensation to them (*i.e.*, to downstream water users who have been given rights to obtain water of certain specified quality). Since the firm will now have to give compensation to the downstream water users, it will not find it worthwhile to pollute the stream beyond the economically efficient point. This is the gist of Coase theorem and its importance lies in its suggestion that assignment of well-defined property rights might help to promote economic efficiency.

It may be emphasised that Coase theorem assumes that transaction costs, that is, costs of negotiating and contracting by the interested parties are very small. For instance, in our above example, the downstream water users join together and then effectively negotiate with the polluting firm without much cost about the price to be charged from the latter for polluting the stream. Besides, even if the transactions costs are small, negotiations with the polluting firm may not be practical because *it is difficult to measure precisely the external cost* (*i.e.*, negative externality) of pollution imposed by the polluting firm on the downstream water users. Further, if the number of interested parties in negotiating a deal is large, it may not be possible to get unanimity required to make the negotiation effective. To conclude in the words of Edwin Mansfield, Coase theorem suggests that "the assignment of well-defined property rights might help to promote economic efficiency. For example, to get around the difficulties caused by external diseconomies arising from waste disposal, society might find it useful to try to establish more unambiguous property rights for individuals and firms with respect to environment quality. Then, assuming that the relevant negotiations are feasible, the interested parties in a particular area might try to negotiate to determine how much pollution will occur."[8]

---

7. R. Coaso, *The problem of Social Choice.*

8. Edwin Mansfield, *Microeconomics*, Seventh Edition, 1991, p. 472

QUESTIONS FOR REVIEW

1. What is meant by optimum allocation of resources ? Show that monopoly leads to misallocation of resources.
2. What are the major sources of competitive market failure ? Explain briefly in each case why the competitive market does not operate efficiently. *B.Com (Hons) D.U. 1998*
3. (*a*) In the case of production externalities the optimal pattern of production is independent of the assignment of property rights.

   (*b*) What are public goods ? What limits the possibility of the private supply of public goods ? *B.A. (Hons) D.U. 1998*
4. (*a*) What are the characteristics of a pure public good ?

   (*b*) What do you understand by the *free rider problem*
5. What is public good ? What are the economic implications of public good ? Explain *B.Com (Hons) D.U. 2002.*
6. Why private markets will fail to provide public goods efficiently
7. Why are externalities likely to lead to an inefficient allocation of resources ? Can the effect of externality (external cost) be corrected with the help of taxation. *D.U. B. Com (Hons.) II Year 2009*
8. Competitive markets fail due to market power, incomplete information, externalities and presence of public goods. Explain these concepts in support of your answer ? *B.Com (Hons) D.U. 1998*
9. Explain the role of externalities in the failure of competitive markets. Can the effects of externality be corrected with the help of taxation and subsidies ? (Use suitable diagram) *D.U. B.Com (Hons) II Year 2006*
10. What are external costs and benefits ? How can the presence of such externalities lead to the failure of competitive markets ? *D.U. B.Com (Hons.) II Year 2007*
11. When external costs are associated with the production of some goods, should the outputs of the goods on efficiency grounds are limited to a level at which the external costs are zero? Why or why not *B.A. (Hons) D.U. 1997*
12. Show that when there is externality in consumption, the equality of marginal rate of substitution across individuals may not provide a Pareto optimum outcome. *B.A. (Hons) D.U. 1996*
13. What do you understand by market failure ? Explain the role of monopolys and asymmetric information in causing market failure.
14. What role government can play to correct market failures to maximise social welfare.
15. Explain the role of government in the (*a*) Provision of Public Goods (*b*) Correcting market failures arising out of externalities (*c*) Promoting Economic Growth (*d*) Improvement in Income Distribution.

CHAPTER 41
NEW WELFARE ECONOMICS : COMPENSATION PRINCIPLE

Pareto laid the foundation of the modern welfare economics by formulating the concept of social optimum which is based on the concept of ordinal utility and is free from interpersonal comparisons of utilities and value judgements. He aimed at formulating a value-free objective criterion designed to test whether a proposed policy change increases social welfare or not. Pareto critrion states simply that an economic change which harms no one and makes someone better off indicates an increase in social welfare. Thus, this criterion does not apply to those economic changes which harm some and benefit others. In terms of Edgeworth box diagram Pareto criterion fails to say as to whether or not social welfare increases as movement is made in either direction along the contract curve because it rejects the notion of interpersonal comparison of utility. As we have seen in the previous chapter, every tangency point of the two indifference curves on the contract carve represents a Pareto optimum. There is thus no any unique optimum position. This criterion does not tell us about changes in the level of social welfare if one moves on the contract curve from one tangency point to another because such movement harms one and benefits the other. Thus, the analysis of welfare in terms of Pareto optimality leaves a considerable amount of indeterminacy, for there are numerous Pareto optimum points on the contract curve.

Kaldor-Hicks Welfare Criterion : Compensation Principle

Economists like Kaldor, Hicks and Scitovsky have made efforts to evaluate the changes in social welfare resulting from any economic reorganisation which harms somebody and benefits the others. These economists have sought to remove indeterminacy in the analysis of Pareto optimality. They have put forward a criterion known as the '*compensation principle*' on the basis of which they claim to evaluate those changes in economic policy or organisation which makes some individual better off and others worse off. The 'compensation principle' is based on the following assumptions.

Assumptions

1. The satisfaction of an individual is independent of the others and he is the best judge of his welfare.
2. There exist no externalities of consumption and production.
3. The tastes of the individuals remain constant.
4. The problems of production and exchange can be separated from the problems of distribution. Compensation principle accepts the level of social welfare to be a function of the level of production. Thus it ignores the effects of a change in distribution on social welfare.
5. Utility can be measured ordinally and interpersonal comparisons of utilities are not possible.

Given the above assumptions, a criterion of compensation principle can be discussed. Kaldor, Hicks and Scitovsky have claimed to formulate a value-free objective criterion of measuring the changes in social welfare with the help of the concept of 'compensating payments'.

Nicholas Kaldor was the first economist to give a welfare criterion based on compensating payments. Kaldor's criterion helps us to measure the welfare implications of a movement in either direction on the contract curve in terms of Edgeworth box diagram. According to Kaldor's welfare criterion, if a certain change in economic organisation or policy makes some people better off and others worse off, *then a change will increase social welfare if those who gain from the change could compensate the losers and still be better off than before.* In the words of Prof. Baumol, "Kaldor's criterion states that a change is an improvement if those who gain evaluate their gains at a higher figure than the value which the losers set upon their losses."[1] Thus, if any policy change benefits any one section of the society (gainers) to such an extent that it is better off even after the payment of compensation to the other sections of the society (losers) out of the benefits received, then that change leads to increase in social welfare. In Kaldor's own words, *"In all cases.... where a certain policy leads to an increase in physical productivity and thus of aggregate real income.... it is possible to make everybody better off without making anybody worse off. It is quite sufficient.... to show that even if all those who suffer as a result are fully compensated for their loss, the rest of the community will still be better off than before."*[2]

Prof. J.R. Hicks supported Kaldor for employing compensation principle to evaluate the change in social welfare resulting from any economic reorganisation that benefits some people and harms the others. This criterion states that, "if *A* is made so much better by the change that he could compensate *B* for his loss and still have something left over, then the reorganisation is unequivocal improvement."[3] In other words, *a change is an improvement if the losers in the changed situation cannot profitably bribe the gainers not to change from the original situation.* Hicks has given his criterion from the losers' point of view, while Kaldor had formulated his criterion from gainers' point of view. Thus the two criteria are really the same though they are clothed in different words. That is why they are generally called by a single name 'Kaldor-Hicks criterion'.

Kaldor-Hicks criterion can be explained with the help of the utility possibility curve. In Fig. 41.1 ordinal utility of two individuals *A* and *B* is shown on *X* and *Y* axes respectively. *DE* is the utility possibility curve which represents the various combinations of utilities obtained by individuals *A* and *B*. As we move downward on the curve *DE*, utility of *A* increases while that of *B* falls. On the other hand, if we move up on the utility curve *ED*, utility of *B* increases while that of *A* falls.

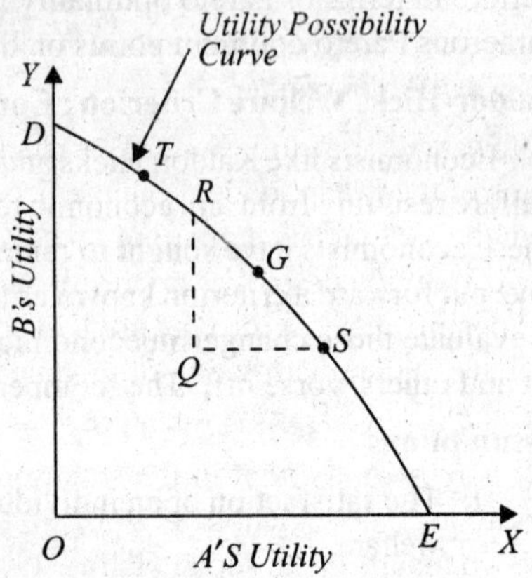

Fig. 41.1. *Kaldor-Hicks Criterion Explained with Utility Possibility Curve*

Suppose the utilities obtained by *A* and *B* from the distribution of income or output between them are represented by point *Q* inside the utility possibility curve *DE*. Let us assume that as a result of some change in economic policy, the two individuals move from point *Q* to point *T* on the utility possibility curve *DE*. As a result of this movement, utility of individual *B* has increased while the utility of *A* has declined, that is, *B* has been become better off and *A* has become worse off than before. Therefore, this movement from point *Q* to point *T* cannot be evaluated by means of Pareto criterion. Of course, points such as *R*, *G*, *S* or any other point on the segment *RS* of utility-possibility curve *DE* are socially preferable to point *Q* on the basis of Pareto criterion.

1. W. J. Baumol, *Economic Theory and Operations Analysis*, 3rd Ed. 1972, p. 402.
2. N. Kaldor, "Welfare Propositions of Economics and Interpersonal Comparison of Utility", *Economic Journal*, Sept. 1939.
3. J.R. Hicks, The Foundations of Welfare Economics, *Economic Journal*, Vol. XIX, December 1939.

However, the compensation principle propounded by Kaldor-Hicks enables us to say whether or not social welfare has increased as a result of movement from *Q* to *T*. According to Kaldor-Hicks criterion, we have to see whether the individual *A* who gains with the movement from position *Q* to position *T* could compensate the individual *A* who is loser and still be better off than before. Now, it will be seen from Figure 41.1 that utility possibility curve *DE* passes through points *R*, *G* and *S*. This means that by mere redistribution of income between the two individuals, that is, if individual *B* gives some compensation to individual *A* for the loss suffered, they can move from position *T* to the position *R*. It is evident from the figure that at position *R* individual *A* is as well off as at the position *Q* but individual *B* is still better off as compared to the position *Q*. It means due to a policy change and consequent movement from position *Q* to position *T*, the gainer (individual *B*) could compensate the loser (individual *A*) and is still better off than at *Q*. Therefore, according to Kaldor-Hicks criterion, social welfare increases with the movement from position *Q* to position *T*, because from *T* they could move to the position *R* through mere redistribution of income (*i.e.* compensation).

It is noteworthy that, according to Kaldor-Hicks criterion, compensation may not be actually paid to judge whether or not social welfare has increased. It is enough to know whether the gainer *could* compensate the loser for the loss of welfare and still be better off. Whether redistribution of income (that is, payment of compensation) should be actually made following the change in policy is left for the Government to decide. If it is *possible* for the gainer to compensate the loser and still be better off, the economists can say that social welfare has increased. It may be noted that gainer can compensate the losers and still be better off only when the change in economic policy leads to the increase in output or real income. That is why Kaldor and Hicks claim that they have been able to distinguish between *change* in output from *change in distribution*. When their criterion is satisfied by a change in the situation, it means that the economy has moved to a potentially more efficient position and as a result social welfare can be said to have increased. Now, whether redistribution of income is actually made through payment of compensation by the gainers to the losers, according to them, is a different matter.

Now, the implications of Kaldor-Hicks criterion become more clear if through redistribution the position of the two individual changes from *T* to *G* (see Fig. 41.1). It is quite manifest that at position *G* both the individuals *A* and *B* are better off than at the position *Q*. Thus, the position *T* to which the two individuals moved as result of a certain change in economic policy is superior to the initial position *Q* from the viewpoint of social welfare, since from position *T* movement can be made merely through redistribution of income to position *G* where both are better off as compared to the position *Q*.

It may be noted that in the situation depicted in Figure 41.1, the change in economic policy brings about a movement from a position *inside* the utility possibility curve to a *point on it*. Now let us see what happens to social welfare if as a result of the adoption of a certain economic policy the utility possibility curve moves outward and the two individuals move from a point on a lower utility possibility curve to a point on a higher utility possibility curve. It can be shown that, according to Kaldor-Hicks criterion, such a movement causes an improvement in social welfare. Consider Figure 41.2. *UV* is the original utility possibility curve and *Q* represents the position at which the two individuals are initially placed. Now, suppose utility possibility curve shifts outward to the new position, *U′V′*, and the two individuals are placed at point *R* on it. In movement from *Q* on the utility possibility curve *UV* to point *R* on the utility possibility curve *U′V′* the utility of *A* has increased and that of *B* has declined. But position *R* denotes greater social welfare on the basis of Kaldor's criterion when compared to the position *Q* on the original utility possibility curve *UV* because with *U′V′* as the utility possibility curve it is possible to move through mere redistribution of income from position *R* to position *S* where the individual *B* has been fully compensated for his loss of utility, the individual *A* is still better off as compared to position *Q*. To conclude, any change in the economy that moves the individuals from a position on a lower utility possibility curve to a position on a higher utility possibility curve increases social welfare.

Scitovsky Paradox

Scitovksy pointed out an important limitation of Kaldor-Hicks criterion that it might lead to contradictory results. He showed that, if in some situation, position *B* is shown to be an improvement over position *A* on Kaldor-Hicks criterion, it may be possible that position *A* is also shown to be an improvement over *B* on the basis of the same criterion. For getting consistent results when position *B* has been revealed to be preferred to position *A* on the basis of a welfare criterion, then position *A* must not be preferred to position *B* on the same criterion. According to Scitovsky, Kaldor-Hicks criterion involves such contradictory and inconsistent results. Since Scitovsky was the first to point out this paradoxical result in Kaldor-Hicks criterion, it is known as '*Scitovsky Paradox*'.

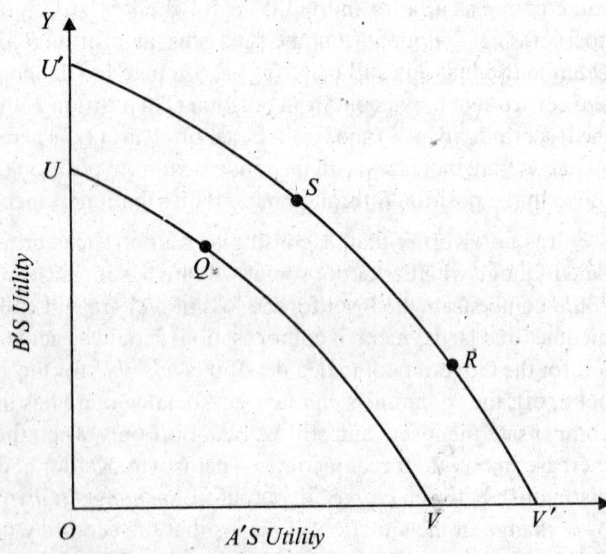

Fig. 41.2. *Kaldor-Hicks Welfare Criterion*

How Kaldor-Hicks criterion may lead to contradictory results in some situation is depicted in Figure 41.3. In this figure *JK* and *GH* are the two utility possibility curves which intersect each other. Now suppose that the initial position is at point *C* on *JK*. Further suppose that due to a certain policy change, utility possibility curve changes and takes the position *GH* and the two individuals find themselves at position *D*. Position *D* is superior to position *C* on the basis of Kaldor-Hicks criterion because from position *D* movement can be made through mere redistribution to position *F* at which individual *B* has been fully compensated but individual *A* is still better off as compared to the original position *C*. Thus movement from position *C* to position *D* satisfies Kaldor-Hicks criterion.

But, as has been pointed out by Scitovsky, reverse movement from position *D* on the new utility possibility curve *GH* to the position *C* on the old utility possibility curve *JK* also represents an improvement on Kaldor-Hicks criterion, that is, *C* is socially better than *D* on the basis of Kaldor-Hicks criterion. This is because from position *C* movement can be made by mere redistribution of income to position *E* on the utility possibility curve *JK* on which position *C* lies and which also passes through the position *E*. And, as will be observed from Fig. 41.3, that at position *E* while *A* is as well of as at position *D*, the individual *B* is still better off than at *D*. We thus see that the movement from position *C* to the position *D* due to a policy change is passed by the Kaldor-Hicks criterion and also the movement back from position *D* to position *C* is also passed by the Kaldor-Hicks criterion. This implies that *D* is socially better than *C* on this criterion and *C* is also socially better than *D* on the same crite-

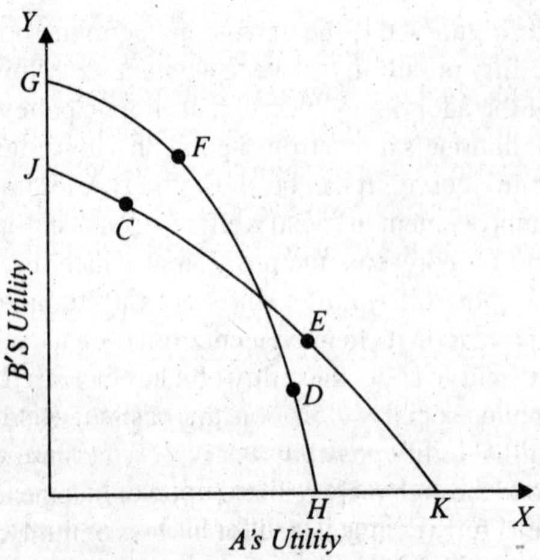

Fig. 41.3. *Scitvosky Paradox*

rion. So Kaldor-Hicks criterion leads us to contradictory and inconsistent results. It is mentionworthy that these contradictory results are obtained by Kaldor-Hicks criterion when following a policy change new utility possibility curve intersects the former utility possibility curve. After bringing out the possibility of contradictory results in Kaldor-Hicks criterion Scitovksy formulated his own criterion which is generally known as Scitovsky's Double Criterion.

Scitovsky's Double Criterion of Welfare

To rule out the possibility of contradictory results in Kaldor-Hicks criterion Scitovsky formulated a double criterion which requires the fulfilment of Kaldor-Hicks criterion and also the fulfilment of the reversal test. It means that a change is an improvement if the gainers in the changed situation are able to persuade the losers to accept the change and simultaneously losers are not able to persuade the gainers to remain in the original situation. Scitovsky's double criterion can also be explained with the help of utility possibility curve. In Figure 41.4, *CD* and *EF* are the two utility possibility curves which do not intersect each other at any point. Suppose there is a change from position *Q* on the utility possibility curve *CD* to the position *G* on the utility possibility curve *EF* as a result of the adoption of a new economic policy. Such a movement is an improvement on Kaldor-Hicks criterion because *G* lies on the utility possibility curve *EF* passing through point *R*. From the position *G*, movement can be made to the position *R* simply by redistributing income between the two individuals. And *R* is better than *Q* because the utility of both the individuals is greater at *R* as compared to the position *Q*. Thus the Kaldor-Hicks criterion is satisfied and therefore change from *Q* to *G* will increase social welfare.

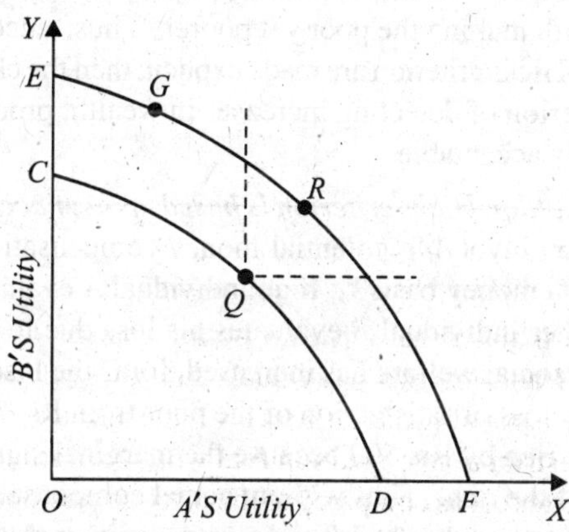

Fig. 41.4. *Scitovsky's Double Criterion*

Now, let us see, what happens to the reversal test. It must also be satisfied, if the Scitovsky double test is to be fulfilled. That is, a movement from the position *G* back to the original position *Q* *must not be* passed by Kaldor-Hicks criterion if Scitovsky's reversal test is to be satisfied. It is evident from Figure 41.4 that from position *R* we cannot move to any position on the utility possibility curve *CD* merely through redistribution of income which is socially better than *G* (that is, which raises utility of either *A* or *B*, the utility of the other remaining constant or which raises the utility of both). We thus see that while movement from position *Q* to *G* is passed by Kaldor-Hicks criterion, reverse movement from position *G* to position *Q* is not passed by Kaldor-Hicks criterion. Hence, in Figure 41.4 the movement from the position *Q* to *G* satisfies Scitovsky's criterion. Thus when the two utility possibility curves are non-intersecting and change involves movement from a position on a lower utility possibility curve to a position on a higher utility possibility curve, the change raises social welfare on the basis of Kaldor-Hicks-Scitovsky criterion. This happens only when a change brings about increase in aggregate output or real income.

A CRITIQUE OF THE COMPENSATION PRINCIPLE

The compensation principle as developed by Kaldor, Hicks and Scitovsky, has been a topic of much discussion in welfare economics since 1939. Prof. Kaldor was the first to give a criterion to judge the changes in social welfare when an economic change benefits some people and harms the others. Later Hicks also supported this criterion in 1940, though he put it in different words. Scitovsky tried to improve the Kaldor-Hicks criterion by formulating his own double criterion. These welfare economists have claimed that they have succeeded in developing a welfare criterion based on ordinal concept of utility and also which is free from any value judgements. But compensation principle has been bitterly criticised by the various welfare economists.

First, Little has pointed out that Kaldor did not formulate a new welfare criterion at all because he assumed welfare to be a function of increase in production or efficiency irrespective of the changes in distribution. Thus, according to Little, Kaldor has given only a definition of 'increase in wealth' or 'increase in efficiency'. Kaldor himself has interpreted the compensation principle in this sense as he says that, "when the production of wealth goes up, some income distribution could be found which makes some people better off, and no one worse off than before". However, as *desired income distribution via compensation is only hypothetical, therefore, according to Little, it is not a welfare test but a definition of 'economic efficiency' in terms of over-compensation*.

Second, compensation principle is *not free value judgements* as is claimed by its propounders. It involves, implicit value judgements. Prof. Baumol and Little are of the opinion that the contention of Prof. Kaldor that the changes which enable the gainers to compensate the losers and still be better off are good changes, is itself a value judgement. According to Little, to say that a policy which meets the Kaldor-Hicks criterion increases the output or "efficiency" of society is, in effect, to recommend it. According to him, Kaldor and Hicks have coined a *definition of* "efficiency" whose implicit ethical implications or value judgements will hardly find favour with many people. Compensation is after all only hypothetical; it is consistent with making the poor yet poorer. Thus, according to Little, if the value judgements implicit in Kaldor-Hicks criterion are made explicit, then the claim of Kaldor and Hicks that they have discovered a criterion of detecting increases in wealth, production or efficiency free from value judgements is hardly acceptable.

Third, likewise, Baumol is also of the view that *Kaldor-Hicks criterion is based upon unacceptable implicit value judgements*. "By using a criterion involving potential money compensations, they set up a concealed interpersonal comparison on a money basis"[4]. If an individual *A* evaluates his gain from a change worth Rs. 500 whereas another individual *B* evaluates his loss due to that economic change at Rs. 75, we cannot conclude that social welfare has increased; for if the loser is poor and the gainer a rich one, it may be possible that loss of satisfaction of the poor from Rs. 75 is far greater than the addition to the satisfaction of the rich by Rs. 500 because the marginal significance of one rupee to a poor is far greater than that of the rich. Thus without actual compensation, the change would mean a major loss of welfare to the poor individual *B* and a trivial gain of welfare to the rich individual *A* even if it passes the Kaldor criterion with flying colours. To quote Baumol again, "*The Kaldor and Scitovsky criteria have thus ducked the basic problem of the interpersonal comparison required to evaluate a policy change which harms X but aids Y. They duck it by saying implicitly that the recommendation should be based on X's and Y's relative willingness and ability to pay for what they want*".[5]

Fourth, *Kaldor-Hicks* have claimed that through compensation principle they have been able to separate a production change from the distribution change by which it is accompanied. For instance, as a result of a policy change output of Coca-Cola increases and that of whisky decreases. Now, if individual *X* prefers Cola Cola but *Y* prefers whisky, the question whether there has occurred any increase in production is inseparably connected with the distribution of these beverages between *X* and *Y*. In many cases it is, therefore, difficult to say whether or not production has increased without considering how the output or real income is being distributed.

Moreover, Kaldor and Hicks think that the *level of production is the main determinant of social welfare and the distribution a secondary one*. But this is quite untenable. A lower total output equitably distributed ensures greater social welfare than larger output, inequitably distributed. They

4. Baumol, *op. cit*, p. 530.
5. *Op.cit.* p.530

essentially accept the existing distribution of income and wealth and ignore its impact on individual utilities and well-being.

Fifth. Prof. Baumol, Little and Arrow point out another major flaw in compensation principle that it does not envisage social welfare. This principle proves the sociol desirability of change in the social state on the basis of the criterion that gainers *could compensate* the losers and still be better off than before. These critics are of the opinion that policy changes which would increase social welfare when accompanied by actual compensation need not lead to improvement in social welfare if compensation is not actually made. Dr. Rothenberg has given a very good example to illustrate this. He supposes an initial social state in which a firm adopts a new invention and as a result the cost of production of the firm is reduced but it throws the competitors out of industry and the workers become unemployed. Let us suppose that the gainer firm from the invention can compensate the losers out of its increased income and still be better off. If the compensation is not actually made in the changed situation, social welfare will decrease as the welfare loss suffered by the workers rendered unemployed will be very large indeed. As a matter of fact, there is no guarantee that compensation will be actually made in such cases. Thus, so long as compensation is hypothetical a change might make the rich richer and the poor yet poorer and therefore reduce social welfare.

It follows from above that a basic flaw in Kaldor-Hicks compensation principle is that it refers to *potential welfare* rather than *actual welfare* since it does not envisage that compensation should be actually made. In the absence of actual compensation one cannot say whether or not actual social welfare has increased as a result of a certain policy change unless one is prepared to make some value judgements. Therefore, making value judgements, especially that concerning distribution of income or welfare, is quite indispensable in welfare economics. And economists should not fight shy of making those value judgements which are widely accepted by the people.

It may also be noted that if compensation is actually made then Kaldor-Hicks criterion is quite unnecessary, for in that case only Pareto criterion will be sufficient to judge the effect of a policy change on social welfare.

Sixth, compensation principle does not take into account the external effects on consumption and production. The exponents of compensation principle are of the opinion that an individual's welfare depends solely upon his own level of production and consumption and is not affected by the production and consumption activities of the others. But this is not a realistic assumption because a person's level of satisfaction (or dissatisfaction) depends to a large extent upon the consumption of goods and services by other persons. A person is more satisfied as his *relative economic* position in the society is improved. Thus, if an economic change leaves a person where he was before but makes some other individuals better off, he will not feel as well off as in the original situation, that is, his level of welfare will fall. The gains by some individuals from a policy change have usually unfavourable external effects on the welfare position of those whose position is said to have remain unchanged.

Bergson Social Welfare Criterion

Bergson pointed out that for comparing utility levels of different individuals resulting from changes in economic policy, making interpersonal comparison of utility cannot be avoided. But he stressed that these comparision of interpersonal utilities should be made explicit. Thus Bergson put forward a social welfare criterion in which he incorporates explicitly such comparison as utility of individual *A* from Re 1= utility of individual *B* from Re 0.20. On the basis of such explicit value judgements or interpersonal comparison of utilities he gives ranking to alternative social states from the viewpoint of social welfare. Bergson along with Samuelson developed the concept of social welfare function which incorporates explicit value judgements for evaluating the welfare implications of policy changes and also finding out a unique social optimum. We shall discuss Bergson – Samulson's social welfare function in the next Chapter.

QUESTIONS FOR REVIEW

1. What is compensation principle of judging change in social welfare brought about by the adoption of an economy policy ? In compensation considered in this principle real or hypothetical.
2. State Kaldor-Hicks criterion of judging social welfare. Explain with the help of utility possibility curve how it judges the social welfare impact of an economic policy which makes some better off and others worse off.
3. Show how Kaldor-Hicks criterion helps in solving the problem of indetermincy involved in Pareto's analysis of maximisation of social welfare.
4. "Pareto criterion does not give us sufficient basis of ordering states. The Kaldor-Hicks – Scitovsky criteria do not carry us much further" Examine critically. *B.A. (Hons) D.U. 1984*
5. Does Kaldor-Hicks-Scitovsky criterion give us sufficient basis for ordering states from the viewpoint of social welfare ? Give reasons for your answer. *B.A. Hons (D.U) 1993*
6. In proposing compensation criterion Kaldor and Hicks claimed that they succeded in giving a welfare criterion which was free from value judgements. Do you agree ? Discuss.
7. In what way is Scitovsky criterion an improvement over Kaldor-Hicks criterion ? Do you agree with the view that Scitovsky criterion does not remove all the weaknesses of Kaldor - Hicks criterion ? Discuss. *B.A. (Hons) D.U. 1996*
8. How far can Kaldor - Hicks Scitovsky criteria be considered an improvement over Pareto's criterion of social welfare ? Discuss.
9. Show that alternative *A* being better than *B* on Kaldor-Hicks criterion does not rule out the possibility that alternative *B* is better than *A* on Kaldor - Hicks criterion.
10. The Kaldor and Scitovsky criteria have ducked the basic problem of the interpersonal comparison of utility required to evaluate a policy change which *harms X* but aids *Y*" (Baumol). Do you agree ? Discuss.
11. It is generally felt that a rupee means more to a poor man than to a rich man. Hence an economic system that merely reacts to the number of rupees spent in different directions is grossly unsatisfactory in the optimal allocation of resources and goods. Discuss in the context of Kaldor-Hicks-Scitovsky compensation principle.

CHAPTER 42
SOCIAL WELFARE FUNCTION

The concept of 'Social Welfare Function' was propounded by A. Bergson in his article '*A Reformulation of Certain Aspects of Welfare Economics*' in 1938. Prior to it various concepts of social welfare had been given by different welfare theorists but they failed to provide a satisfactory solution to the problem of maximisation of social welfare and measurement. Bentham talked of welfare in terms of '*the greatest happiness of the greatest number.*' Neo-Classical welfare theorists discussed the problem of social welfare on the basis of cardinal measurability of utility and interpersonal comparison of utility. Analysis of Pareto optimality maximises social welfare by satisfying various marginal conditions of production, distribution and allocation of resources among products. But unfortunately they are not fulfilled due to the existence of various externalities and imperfections in the market. Moreover, Pareto optimality analysis fails to measure the changes in welfare resulting from any change which benefits one section of society and harms the other. Compensation principle as given by Kaldor-Hicks-Scitovsky attempts to measure the changes in social welfare resulting from such economic changes which harm some and benefit others through hypothetical compensating payments. Compensation theorists claimed to give a value-free objective criterion based on ordinal concept of utility but, as seen in a previous chapter, this is based upon implicit value judgements and does not evaluate changes in social welfare satisfactorily.

By providing the concept of social welfare function Bergson and Samuelson have attempted to provide a new approach to welfare economics and have succeeded in rehabilitating welfare economics. They have put forward the concept of social welfare function that considers only the ordinal preferences of individuals. They agree to Robbins' view that interpersonal comparison of utility involves value judgements but they assert that without making some value judgements, economists cannot evaluate the impact of changes in economic policy on social welfare. Thus, according to them, welfare economics cannot be separated from value judgements. According to them, welfare economics is essentially a normative study. But the approach to study it must be scientific despite the fact that the use of value judgements in it is unavoidable.

BERGSON-SAMUELSON SOCIAL WELFARE FUNCTION

Social welfare function is an ordinal index of society's welfare and is a function of the utility levles of all individuals constituting the society. Bergson-Samuelson social welfare function can be written in the following manner :

$$W = W(U_1, U_2, U_3 \ldots\ldots, U_n)$$

where W represents the social welfare $U_1, U_2, U_3, \ldots\ldots, U_n$ represent the ordinal utility indices of different individuals of the society. The ordinal utility index of an individual depends upon the goods and services he consumes and the magnitude and kind of the work he does. The important thing to note about social welfare function is that in its construction *explicit value judgements* are introduced. Value judgements determine a form of the social welfare function; with a different set of value judgements, the form of social welfare function would be different. Value judgemtns are essentially ethical notions which are introduced from outside economics. The value judgements required to construct a social welfare function may be obtained through democratic process with voting by individuals or it may have to be imposed on the society in a dictational manner. Whatever the case may be, the form of social welfare function depnds upon the value judgements of those who decide about them since it expresses their views regarding the effect which the utility level of each individual has on the social welfare. In the worlds of Prof. Scitovsky. "The social welfare function can be thought of as a funtion of each individual's welfare which in turn depends both in his personal well being and on his appraisal of the distribution of wlefare among all members of the community".[1]

Since the value judgements requaired for the formation of social welfare function are not of the economist himself and instead they are introduced from outside economics they are not obtained through any scientific method. It has been claimed that social welfare function has solved the basic problem of welfare economics, since it thinks unnecessary for the economists themselves to make value judgements concerning what is a desirable distribution of welfare as between indindividuals constituting the society. In other words, economist need not himself decide about what is the most desirable distribution of wlefare. He can take value judgements regarding distribution as given from outside economics.

Bergson's social welfare function is supposed to be dependent on changes in economic events that have a direct effect on individual welfares. The ordinal utility level of an individual is a function of his own consumption of goods and services and not of others. Morever, the utility level of an individual depends on his own value judgments regarding the composition of different goods and services consumed which depends upon his tastes. An individual may derive more utility from the consumption of liquor whereas another individual may derive very nominal utility or no utility at all from it.

Social Welfare Function and Value Judgements

So far we have been mainly concerned with the value judgements of individuals regarding their utility levels. From the view point of social welfare function, the value judgements regarding the welfare of the society as a whole are relevant. The formulation of a welfare function for the society as a whole is a very difficult task because utility being a mental phenomenon cannot be measured or estimated accurately by any person or institution entrusted to furnish value judgements regarding the changes in social welfare, Moreover, addition and substraction of utilities of different individuals by an authorised person or institution too is a very difficult task.

The social welfare function and its form depends upon the value judgements of the person or institution whom the society has authorised to decide. The authorised person or institution may be any body but for true value judgements regarding the social welfare *he must be unbiased* because changes in social welfare will depend upon his value judgements. "These judgements as to what constitutes justice and virtue in distribution may be those of the economist himself or those set up by the legislature, by some other governmental authority or by some other unspecified person or group."[2] A social welfare function can be attained by common consensus or it may be forced upon the society by a dictator.

Since the forms of social welfare functions are known by value judgements about social welfare, therefore there arises the problem of finding an authority who could give purely unbiased value judgemtents. Bergson and Samuelson have assumed a "Superman" who provides a value judgements about changes in social welfare. Superman alone can take decisions about the solution of various problems of the economy. What goods and services should be produced and supplied in the society ? How much of various goods should be produced ? What should be the quality and kind of goods ? What should be capital intensity of producing a particular type of good ? What should be

1. T. Scitovsky, *The State of Welfare Economics*, printed in his *Papers on Welfare and Growth*, George Allen and Unwin Ltd., 1964, p.184
2. W. J. Baumol, *Economic Theory and Operations Analysis*, p. 531.

the pattern of distribution of national income among different sections of the society ? Which wants should be satisfied at present and which at a future date and so on. All these questions can be answered by the superman alone in accordance with his views about the determinants of social welfare. The society would have to accept the solutions of all these questions provided by him assumpting that he will give any value judgements which aim to achieve maximum social welfare rather than maximum self-interest. Thus we are free from the addition, substraction, measurement and interpersonal comparisons of utilities by assumpting the existence of a superman.

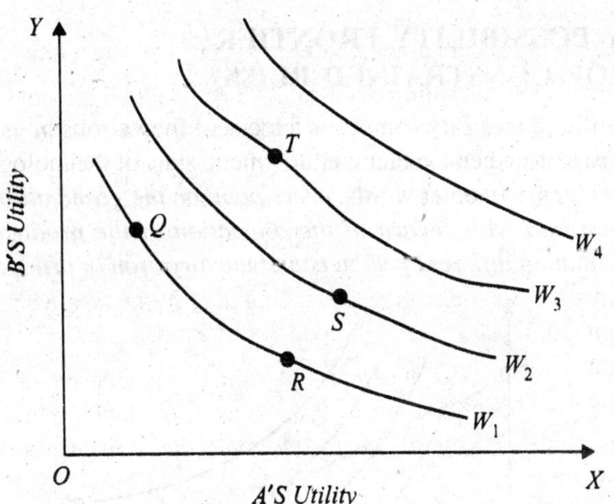

Fig. 42.1. *Social Indifference Curves depicting Social Welfare Function*

In modern age of democratic governments people elect their representatives who constitue the Government. The political party in majority forms the Government and rules the country. The representatives' Government formed by the majority rule formulates various policies on the basis of value judgements and it is expected that all the policy decisions by the Government will aim at maximising social welfare rather than maximising the welfare of an individual or a particular section of the soceity.

Bergson and Samuelson expressed the view that *all value judgements used to construct the social welfare function must be consistent which implies* that if in a given situation *A* is perferred to *B* and *B* is preferred to *C* then *A* must be preferred to *C*. This is nothing new to the students of economics as this is the well know assumption of transitivity in social choice among various alternatives. We can explain the social welfare function wilth the help of *social indifference curves or welfare frontiers*. Let us assume a society of two persons. In such a case social welfare function can be represented with the help of social indifference curves.

In Fig. 42.1 the utilities of individuals *A* and *B* have been represented on the horizontal and vertical axes respectively. W_1, W_2 and W_3 are the social indifference curves representing successively higher levels of social welfare. A social indifference curve is a locus of various combinations of utilities of *A* and *B* which result in an equal level of social welfare. The properties of social indifference curves are just like that of individual consumer's indifference curves. Given a family of social indifference curves, the effect of a proposed change in policy on social welfare can be evaluated. In terms of Fig. 42.1 any policy change that moves the economy from *Q* to *T* is an improvement. Similarly, a movement from *Q* to *S* or from *R* to *S* also represents an improvement in social welfare, and a movement from *T* to *Q* or *T* to *S* represents a decrease in social welfare. A movement along the same social indifference curve represents no change in the level of social welfare.

Analysis of Pareto optimality failed to provide a 'unique optimum solution' which represents maximum social welfare. There are a large number of solutions which are optimum on the basis of Pareto criterion. In terms of Edgeworth-box diagram every point on the contract curve represents the optimum position. In terms of Grand Utility Possibility Frontier, all points on it are Pareto optimal or economically efficient. But Pareto criterion does not tell us the best of them. Thus, Paretian analysis leaves us with a lot of indeterminacy in the choice of maximum social welfare point. Now, the significance of social welfare function is that it enables us to obtain a unique optimum position regarding social welfare. This unique optimum position is best of all the Pareto optima and therefore ensures the maximum social welfare. By including the concept of grand utility possibility frontier along with Bergson-Samuleson social welfare function we are able to obtain a unique optimum position or maximum social welfare position which is expiained below.

GRAND UTILITY POSSIBILITY FRONTIER AND POSITION OF CONSTRAINED BLISS

As shall be explained below, a grand utility possibility forntier is a locus of the vairous physically attainable utility combinations of two persons when the factor endowment, state of technology and preference orders of the individuals are given.[3] In other words, *every point on the grand utility posibility curve represents the optimum position with regard to the allocation of the products among the consumers, allocation of factors among different products and the direction of production.* Thus every point on the grand utility possibility curve represents a Pareto optimum and as we move from one point to another on it the utility of one individual increases while that of the other falls.

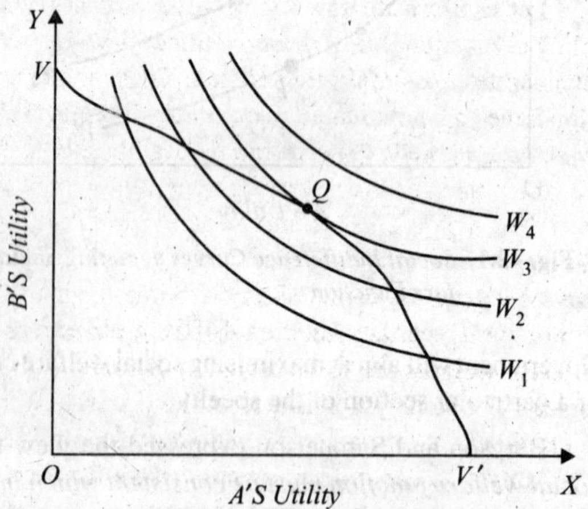

Fig. 42.2. *Social Welfare Function and Position of Constrained Bliss.*

Now, let us superimpose grant utility possibility curve on the social indifference curves representing social welfare function to find a unique optimum position of social welfare. In Fig. 42.2 social indifference curves W_1, W_2, W_3 and W_4 representing the social welfare function have been drawn along with the grand utility possibility curve VV'. Social indifference curve W_3 is tangent to the grand utility possibility curve VV' at point Q. Thus, point Q represents the maximum possible social welfare given the factor endowments, state of technology and preference scales of the individuals. Point Q is known as the point of **constrained bliss** since, given the constraints regarding factor endowments and the state of technology. Q is the highest possible state of social welfare which the society can attain. Social welfare represented by the social indifference curve W_4 is higher than social indifference curve W_3 passing through Q but it is not possible to attain it, given the technology and factor endowment. Thus, from among a large number of Pareto optimum points on the grand utility possibility curve, we have a unique optimum point Q at which the social welfare is the maximum. The point of constrained bliss represents the *unique* pattern of production of goods, *unique* distribution of goods between the individuals and unique combination of factors employed to produce the goods.

The following features of the Bergson-Samuelson Social Welfare function are worth noting :

1. The Bergson-Samuelson social welfare function is based on explicit value judgements and involves interpersonal comparisons of utility in ordinal terms.
2. Bergson-Samuelson social welfare function, the maximum social welfare position is completely determined as a result of the introduction of value judgements regarding distribution of welfare among individuals.
3. The social welfare function is not based on any unique value judgements. Instead, any set

3. How Grand Utility Possibility Curve is derived see Author's book *Advanced Economic Theory*, 14th edition, S. Chand & Co.

of value judgements can be used by a welfare economist to construct a social welfare function. Thus, it is not any unique function but changes with the change in value judgements.

4. Once the social welfare function has been decided upon by value judgements, the maximisation technique is used to obtain the maximum social welfare position at which allocation of resources is Pareto optimum and also the distribution of goods and services is equitable. Thus, both efficiency and equity are achieved so that social welfare may be maximised.
5. Used along with the Pareto optimality analysis the concept of social welfare function enables us to find a unique optimum solution which combines economic efficiency with distributive justice.

Mathematical Illustration of Social Welfare Function

Let us illustrate how social welfare function is constructed to determine which is the optimum policy choice regarding resource allocation. Let a Government policy or choice of a project under consideration has multiple benefits. These multiple benefits of a policy or project under consideration have to be evaluated to construct a social welfare function. Suppose a Government has three objectives, namely, (1) maximum possible growth in GDP, (2) the growth of adequate employment for labour and (3) the reduction in income inequalities. These objectives are measured in different units : growth in GDP is measured in terms of percentage growth in value of real national output (that is, at constant rupee prices, the growth in employment may be measured in man-days of employment generated and reduction in income inequalities in terms of Gini coefficient. For construction of social welfare function different objectives are required to be measured in single units and different weights are to be assigned to various objectives depending on the value judgements of a society. The society will like to achieve a certain rate of GDP growth, a certain amount of man days of employment and a certain reduction in Gini-coefficient (which measures the extent of income inequality). To construct a social welfare function all objectives are first weighted and then transformed into a common unit of account.

Assume B_1, B_2, B_3 represent the levels of social welfare or benefits from three objectives mentioned above. However, as noted above, these objectives are originally measured in different units. If the government on behalf of a society on the basis of value judgements considers benefit W_1 units of benefit B_1 are equivalent to W_2 units of benefits from objective B_2, W_3 units of benefits from objective B_3, we can the write total social welfare function as :

$$SW = W_1B_1 + W_2B_2 + W_3B_3 \quad \ldots (1)$$

One of these benefits an be chosen as a common unit of account, generally called a *numerare* and total social welfare or benefits from these objectives can be measured in terms of this common unit of account, say in terms of benefit B_1. Depending upon the value judgements, then total social welfare or benefit in terms of B_1 can be obtained by dividing each term in the equation (1) above by weight W_1 of benefit B_1, then social welfare or total social benefit can be written as

$$SW = \frac{W_1B_1}{W_1} + \frac{W_2B_2}{W_1} + \frac{W_3B_3}{W_1} \quad \ldots (2)$$

Now, instead of writting social welfare function in terms of three social benefits, we can generalise the social welfare function stated in (2) above as under

$$SW = \sum_{i=0}^{n} = k_i B_i$$

where k_i measures the weights at which a society can substitute one benefit for another. Thus

$k_1 = 1$, $k_2 = \frac{w_2}{w_1}$, $k_3 = \frac{w_3}{w_1}$ and so on. It may be noted that weights assigned to various objectives or benefits may change over time. Thus, in view of the increase in unemployment in a society, weight assigned to the employment objective (*i.e.* B_2) may be given a higher weight as compared to that of growth in GDP.

Let us give a numerical example of measuring social welfare from aggregating benefits or utilities of various objectives. Suppose one unit of GDP growth is equivalent to 5 times the additional unit gain of employment (*i.e.* B_2) and 4 times reduction in income inequality as measured by Gini coefficient. Taking GDP growth as a unit of account of measurement of social welfare, then equation (2) above can be written as

$$SW = B_1 + \frac{1}{5}B_2 + \frac{1}{4}B_3 \qquad \ldots (3)$$

It is thus evident if a society wants to have 50 units of additional GDP, 30 units of extra employment, and 2 units of reduction in Gini coefficient (i.e. income inequality) then the specific social welfare function described in (3) above can be written as

$$SW = 50 + \frac{30}{5} + \frac{2}{4} \qquad \ldots (4)$$

The mathematical form of social welfare function is generally used in the appraisal of public projects.

A CRITICAL EVALUATION OF BERGSON-SAMUELSON SOCIAL WELFARE FUNCTION

The main aim of welfare economics has been to find an acceptable social welfare function which could measure the changes in social welfare resulting from a change in economic and non-economic variables. Bergson and Samuelson solved this problem by formulating a social welfare function which is based on explicit value jdugements. This function can incorporate the various economic and non-economic determinants of the welfare of individuals. In this function utility or welfare is conceived and measured in ordinal terms. Preferences or utilities of different individuals of the society and decisions about them are taken through a democratic method or by an authorised institution on the basis of its own value judgements. Even according to its bitter critic Little, the *concept of social welfare function is a brilliant theoretical construct which completes the formal mathematical system of welfare economics.*

Pareto optimality analysis does not help us in providing a unique solution to the problem of maximising social welfare. As seen above, with the help of social welfare function we can measure the changes in social welfare even when one individual becomes better off and another worse off by making some distributional value judgements in the form of social welfare function. The Bergson-Samuelson's social welfare function incorporating explicit value judgements is an improvement over earlier attempts such as compensation principle advanced by Kaldor, Hicks and Scitovsky. However, economists have pointed out some important drawbacks in the concept of social welfare function.

Limited Practical Significance. Little, Streeten and Baumol have pointed out that social welfare function is of limited practical significance. According to Little, the social welfare function can neither be used in a democratic state, nor even in a totalitarian one because in them there would be as many vague social welfare functions as there are individuals. Social welfare function, to quote Little is only "a formal device necessary to a perfectly general abstract system of 'welfare', which is devoid of any practical significance."[4]

4. I.M.D. Little, *A Critique of Welfare Economics*, p. 122

Likewise, Paul Streeton also thinks that *social welfare function is a highly formal concept which has hardly any relation with the important facts of social life and choice.* To quote him, "No political programme or individual value standard would fit the model of a social welfare function of the required type"[5] Prof. Baumol is also of the opinion that the concept of social welfare is of limited practical value as it does not tell us how to get the value judgements which it requires for its construction. Though Bergson criterion of social welfare function, writes Baumol, "provides us with a highly useful frame of reference, unfortunately it does not come equipped with a kit and a set of instructions for collecting the welfare judgements which it requires. Thus it still leaves us with the difficult part of the job unsolved"[6]

Welfare depends on a wider range of variables than those associated with utility. Social welfare function approach is based on the utility which an individual derives from economic variables such as consumption of goods and services. Apart from these economic variables, welfare or well-being of individuals depends on a whole range of political and environmental variables such as enjoyment of human rights, political freedom, pollution-free environment. Thus, "in comparing different economic systems or in comparing different ways of organising a given economy, the possibility that some of these variables might be affected cannot be ignored. Thus a reorganisation that gives everyone more income and leisure *might not improve the welfare of the community if at the same time it limits individual freedom or requires the abandonment of cherished cultural traditions.*"[7]

Prof. Amartya Sen's Critique : Judging welfare or well-being in terms of utility is of limited significance.

Prof. Amartya Sen has criticised modern welfare economics covering both Pareto efficiency and social welfare function on the ground that utility is not a true indicator of well-being. To quote him, "A difficulty witn welfarism arises from the particular interpretation of well-being that utility provides. To judge the well-being of a person exclusively in the metric of happiness or desire-fulfilment has some obvious limitations. These limitations are particularly damaging in the context of interpersonal comparisons .of well-being."[8] He further adds, "A person who has had a life of misfortune, with very little opportunities, and rather little hope, may be more easily reconciled to deprivations than others reared in more fortunate and affluent circumstances. *The metric of happiness may, therefore, distort the extent of deprivation, in a specific and biased way*. The hopeless beggar, the precarious landless labourer, the dominated housewife, the hardened unemployed or the over-exhausted coolie may all take pleasures in small mercies and manage to suppress intense suffering for the necessity of continuing survival, but *it would be ethically deeply mistaken to attach a correspondingly small value to the loss of their well-being because of the survival strategy*".[9]

It follows from above that Amartya Sen has criticised the concept of social welfare based on utility which means psychological reactions of individuals to goods and services which they consume. Further, Prof. Sen shifts the focus on promoting *positive freedoms* of individuals for assessing the change in their welfare following a change in organisation or public policy. He defines freedom as '*capabilites to function*' as to what persons can do or cannot do. It is capabilities to function that reflect freedom in the positive sense and determine well-being or welfare of the people.[10]

---

5. Paul Streeton, Appendix to Gunnar Myrdal's *The Political Elements in the Development of Economic Theory*, p. 216.
6. Baumol, *op. cit.*, p. 531.
7. P. Else and P. Curwin, *Principles of Microeconomics*, Unwin Hyman, London, 1990. p. 324 (Italics added).
8. Amartya Sen, *On Ethics and Economics*, Oxford University Press, Delhi, 1990. pp. 45-46. (italics added).
9. *Ibid.*
10. See his well-known article, "*The Concept of Well-Being*" a Silver Jubilee Lecture at Institute of Economic Growth, Delhi University.
11. K.J. Arrow, *Social Choice and Individual Values*.

Impossibility of Constructing a Social Welfare Function from Individual Preferences. A highly damaging drawback of social welfare function has been pointed out by K.J. Arrow who has shown that social welfare function cannot be constructed on the basis of value judgements arrived at through democratic process of majority rule in group decision-making. Arrow has proved that the *majority rule leads to contradictory results or intransitivity of social choices when individuals are asked to make a choice from among more than two alternatives available to them.* Therefore, Prof. Arrow concludes that a social welfare function which is based on mere ordinal preferences cannot in principle be constructed from the preferences of all the individuals comprising a society. Of course, social welfare function can be set up on the basis of value judgements of an individual who can impose his will on the society but that will reflect the aims and aspirations of an absolute dictator.[11]

QUESTIONS FOR REVIEW

1. Show diagramtically how socially optimum allocation of consumption and resources can be obtained from the *Bliss Point*. What is the underlying assumption? *B.A. (Hons) D.U. 2001*
2. How is Grand Utility Possibility Frontier derived ? Examine its significance in the attainment of maximum social welfare. *B.A. (Hons) D.U. 1990*
3. What is social welfare function ? It is analogous to an individual's utility function ?
4. What is Bergson-Samuelson's social function ? How does it incorporate value judgements to evaluate changes in social welfare ?
5. Explain how Bergson-Samuelson's concept of Social welfare function helps us to solve the problem of indeterminacy of optimality found in Pareto's analysis of social welfare ?
6. How would you express social welfare function in mathematical form incorporating value judgements. In what types of studies it is generally used ?

CHAPTER 43
MARKETS WITH ASYMMETRIC INFORMATION

Introduction

So far in our study of markets we have assumed that sellers and buyers were perfectly and equally informed about the quality of goods being sold in the market. This assumption is valid if it is either quite easy to verify the quality of a goods or it is not costly to ascertain which goods arc of high quality and which goods are of low quality. In view of the known differences in qualities of various goods, the different prices of the goods will then reflect the quality differences between them.

When it is not easy to know about the quality of goods or it is costly to get information about them and the buyers and sellers of goods are not equally informed about the quality of goods, then there is asymmetric information. Thus, *asymmetric information means the market situation when the buyers and sellers have a different information while making a transaction.*

The various examples of markets with asymmetric information can be given. An important example of asymmetric information is of the market for used cars. In this case the sellers are better informed than the buyers about quality of the goods that are being sold. The theory of lemons was first developed in connection with the sale of used cars. Some used cars are of bad or low quality (*i.e.* they are lemons) and others are of good quality. While the sellers know whether the cars they are selling are 'lemons' or of good quality but the buyers do not know about whether they are lemons or of good quality. The other examples of markets with asymmetric information are provision of insurance service and labour market. The customer is better informed than the insurance company about the probability of his getting ill. In case of labour market, different workers have different productivities and it is difficult for the employer to know the productivity of the workers and employees.

The problem about the asymmetric information is that it leads to market failure, that is, failure to achieve Pareto efficiency. We shall discuss the markets with asymmetric information and the problems it gives rise to.

The Market for Lemons

The important example of market with asymmetric information is the market for lemons. In the market for lemons, the buyers and sellers have different information about the quality of the goods being bought and sold. The word lemon is used to describe a defective or low quality product[1]. Let us consider the market for used cars. We assume that the used cars are of different qualities; some of them are of good quality while others are just lemons. The bad quality cars (*i.e.* lemons) quite often break down and require a lot of repairs. However, while the sellers of used cars fully know the quality of their used cars, the buyers are uncertain about their quality due to lack of information. Therefore, the market for used cars is an important example of asymmetric information. It is important to note that though some of the used cars available for sale are of bad quality, but all sellers of used cars, whether of good quality or bad quality, claim that their car is of good quality. The buyers of course

1. Nobel Laureate George Akerlof was the first economist who discussed the problem posed by asymmetric information in market for lemons. See his paper, "The Market for Lemons": Qualitative Uncertainty and the Market Mechanism" *The Quarterly Journal of Economics,* August 70, pp. 488-500

cannot know which of the used cars are of good quality and which are just lemons. Therefore, *the price of the used car in the market depends on the average quality of the used car offered for sale.* This is because the buyers being uninformed about the quality of the used cars will not be willing to pay more than what an average quality used car is worth. This means that the owners of bad quality cars will get price for their used cars more than what they are worth. This has an important consequence. Since the owners of good quality used cars will not be able to get the price for their better quality cars since the price determined in the market for used cars will be equal only to what average quality used cars are worth. As a result, the owners of good quality used cars will withdraw their cars from the market. This will reduce the number of used cars available for sale in the market. With this the average quality of used cars offered for sale will also go down and so also the price of the used cars. This will cause some more car owners whose used cars are relatively of good quality to go out of the market for used cars. This process of withdrawing from the market for used cars will go on until only bad quality used cars, that is, lemons are left for sale in the market. This phenomenon is called *adverse selection as due to asymmetric information on the part of sellers and buyers the bad quality products drive out the good quality products from the market.*

Graphic Illustration of Lemons Problem*

The lemon problem is illustrated in Fig. 43.1[2]. It is assumed that two types of used cars—high quality cars and low quality cars are available for sale in the market. *To begin with, we assume* that *both the sellers and buyers know which cars are high quality cars and which are low quality cars.*

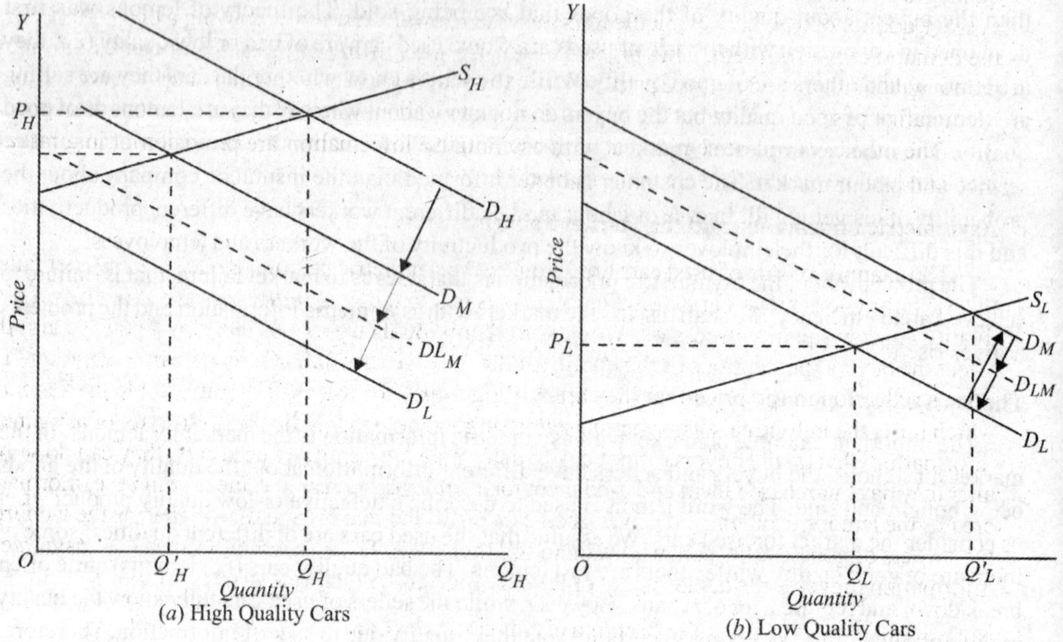

Fig. 43.1. *The Problem of Lemons*

This means there will be two markets, one for high quality cars and the other for low-quality cars. In panel (*a*) of this figure S_H is the supply curve of high quality used cars and D_H is the demand curve for them. It will be seen from Fig. 43.1 that the supply curve S_H of the high-quality used cars

* The students may skip over this graphic illustration of the problem as it does not add much to the understanding of the problem.

2. This figure has been adapted from *Microeconomics* (3rd ed.) by Robert S. Pindyck and Daniel L. Rubinfeld, published by Prentice Hall of India.

(panel (*a*)) lies at a higher level than supply curve S_L of the low-quality used cars. This is because sellers of high-quality used cars will be willing to supply their product at a relatively higher price as compared to the low quality product. Similarly, demand curve of high-quality used car D_H is higher than that of low-quality used cars.

It will be seen from Fig. 43.1 that P_H is the price of high-quality used cars and Q_H is the quantity of high-quality used car bought and sold. On the other hand, in panel (*b*) the price of used cars determined is P_L and the quantity transacted is Q_L. It will be seen from Fig. 43.1 the $P_H > P_L$ and $Q_H = Q_L$.

Since sellers of the used cars have better information about the quality of their products than the buyers of them, there is the problem of asymmetric information. In the first instance the buyers might think that there are 50 per cent chance of their getting high-quality cars. Therefore, when deciding to buy the used cars, the buyers would consider all cars to be of medium quality represented by D_M curve in both the panels of Fig. 43.1. The demand curve D_M is lower than the demand curve D_H in panel (*a*) but higher than D_L in panel (*b*). This means that now greater quantity Q'_L of the low-quality used cars will be transacted than the high-quality used cars whose equilibrium quantity sold has now declined to Q'_H. Thus, in the market for used cars the quantity of low quality cars has increased. As a result, the buyers of the used cars will think that the most of the used cars are of low quality, they would be willing to pay lower price for them. This will cause the demand curve for used cars to shift below in both the panels, say to D_{LM} representing demand for lower medium used cars. Given their supply curves, and the demand curves D_{LM}, in the composition of the used cars quantity of low-quality cars will further increase. As a result, the buyers of used cars will soon expect that the average quality of used cars available for sale will be lower than before causing a downward shift in the demand curve for them. This process of downward shifting of the demand curves in both the panels will continue and average price will continue falling until, given their supply curves, only the low-quality cars (*i.e.* lemons) are sold in the market and the high quality cars are completely driven out of the market. It will be seen that at the price P_L of the low-quality car (*i.e.* lemon) no high-quality used cars will be offered for sale in the market.

Asymmetric Information and the Market Failure

The example of sale of used cars brings out how asymmetric information leads to market failure, that is, failure to achieve Pareto efficiency. This is due to the *externality* between the seller of high-quality and low-quality used cars. When some individuals try to sell their low-quality cars, they affect the buyers' perceptions of the quality of the average car available for sale in the market. This causes reduction in the price that they are willing to pay for the used cars available in the market which hurts the individuals who want to sell their good or high-quality cars. Because of asymmetric information, that is, the buyers cannot easily determine the quality of used cars; they can do so only after they have purchased them and used them for a while. As seen above, the asymmetric information creates the lemons problem and drives good cars out of the market and thereby harms the welfare of the owners of good quality cars who want to sell their cars. Thus, externality created by asymmetric information prevents the achievement of Pareto efficiency and creates market failure.

Measures Adopted to Solve the Problem of Adverse Selection

The lemons problem arises because the sellers of good used cars are not able to inform accurately to the buyers about the quality of their cars. To solve this problem, some institutions have been developed to deal with the problem. The first institution that has come about into existence is of *used car dealers* who provide *guarantees* for the cars they sell. The well-reputed dealers who want to keep their goodwill in the market give assurance for the quality of cars bought through them. Besides, there are *automobiles service centres* that check the quality of used cars for a certain fee. The buyers of used cars can thus get information about the quality of the used cars from these testing centres.

Some other devices that have been developed to solve the problem of quality uncertainty are the use of brand names, the practice of providing franchisees (such as Apollo Hospitals, franchisees of NIIT etc.), Chain stores etc. These brand names and franchisees of some reputed companies also provide assurance about the good quality of goods or service being provided. As we shall see below with regard to insurance market, the devices of *coinsurance* and the *deductibles* have been adopted to tackle the problem of moral hazard that arises due to asymmetric information.

The Insurance Market and Adverse Selection

After Akerlof who first analysed the lemons problem created by asymmetric information in the market for used cars, his analysis has been extended to the markets for insurance, financial credit and labour employment. These other markets are also characterised by asymmetric information. In this section we will study how Akerlof's analysis has been applied to the insurance market.

In the case of insurance, the insurance company has less information about the state of health of the individuals who want to get their life insured or want insurance for sickness or in case of general insurance about the accident proneness of their cars, etc. Let us take the case of insurance against illness. Suppose there are two groups of individuals who want to ensure for the risk of illness. One group of individuals belong to high risk group. There are H number of individuals who constitute the high risk group. The second group is of low risk individuals and there are L number of them. The possibility of their becoming ill and therefore becomes entitled to claim insurance money is P_H and P_L respectively. The individuals belonging to both these groups get themselves insured and the insurance company is not able to distinguish between them. While insurance company does not know the true state of their health, the individuals,that is, the buyers of insurance, are fully informed about the likelihood of their becoming ill. Thus, this is a case of asymmetric information. The weighted average probability of their becoming ill is

$$\bar{P} = P_H \cdot \frac{H}{H + L} + P_L \cdot \frac{L}{H + L}$$

where $\bar{P}$ stands for the weighted average probability of illness. Obviously, $P_H < \bar{P} < P_L$. Suppose the cost of insurance is C. If the insurance company is to recover at least the cost of insuring them against illness, then the insurance premium to cover both the high-risk and low-risk individuals which we denote by I is given by

$$I = C\bar{P}$$

As the individuals know their risk of becoming ill, as is being assumed here, while the individuals with low risk (P_L) may not be willing to buy the insurance, given the above insurance premium, the individuals with high risk will be very much eager to buy it. This is because $\bar{P} < P_L$, the insurance premium will be much greater than CP_L in case of low-risk individuals. Therefore, the low-risk individuals are likely to drop out and in that case to recover the insurance cost of high-risk individuals, the insurance company will have to raise the rate of insurance premium. As a result, only the high risk individuals will buy the insurance and the *individuals with low risk* of illness will *go without insurance.* Thus, as in case of used cars, the problem of adverse selection also arises in case of insurance market. In fact, the term adverse selection was first used in case of health insurance because the insurance company *do not get unbiased selection of individuals who buy insurance policy and it is only the high-risk individuals who purchase it.* In such a situation the insurance claims will *mostly* be made by the individuals with high risk and as a result the insurance company *who charges premium rate on the basis of average risk* of both kinds of individuals with high-risk and low risk of illness will go bankrupt.

However, the various measures have been proposed to overcome the problem of adverse selection. First, the insurance company can offer the low-risk individuals to get *coinsurance* (under the coinsurance scheme the individuals share a portion of the loss with the insurance company) or get some *deductibility scheme* (that is, get some amount deducted from the claim for the loss suffered). The insurance company can offer various individuals to make a choice among different schemes with different rates of coinsurance, the amounts of deductibles, length of contract etc. From the choices made the insurance company can know the risk characteristics of various individuals willing to buy insurance and adjust the insurance premium accordingly.

From above it follows that some schemes have been devised to tackle the problem of adverse selection in connection with health insurance. But one thing is certain from above that there *cannot be a single insurance premium policy.* There can be at least two insurance policies, one for high-risk individuals who get complete insurance and the other for low-risk individuals who get insurance with a large deductible. In this case the low-risk individuals get only partial insurance. However, given the fact that there is not only two groups of individuals with either high risk or low risk but a continuum of individuals with several probabilities, there can be no equilibrium in the insurance market that ensures market efficiency.[3]

It may be emphasized that the problem of adverse selection in health insurance arises because insurance company cannot fix their rates of premium on the *average incidence* of illness in the population. Therefore, to solve the problem of adverse selection, *compulsory purchase plan of insurance* by a group of people containing both high-risk and low-risk individuals and an insurance company fixing its premium rate on the basis of *average incidence* of health problem has been adopted in some cases. In such a situation it is claimed that each of the individuals comprising compulsory purchase group can be made better off. The high-risk individuals are better off because they buy insurance at a rate that is relatively lower than the risk they face and the low-risk individuals can purchase insurance at a rate less than the rate that would be prevailing *when only high-risk people purchased it.* Such compulsory insurance plans with some variation have been extensively adopted. For example, all teachers of a college or university can be brought under the compulsory health insurance plan with the insurance company fixing its premium rate on the basis of average risk of health problem faced by the teachers. Similarly, all employees of a factory can be asked to participate in the compulsory insurance plan. But the scheme of compulsory purchase plan is repugnant to most of the economists who lay stress on 'free choice' as a means of achieving Pareto efficiency. But a compulsory purchase plan of insurance restricting choice of individuals ensures Pareto efficiency by tackling the adverse conseques of the existence of externality between the low- risk and high-risk individuals. In this connection, it may be noted that some employers offer health insurance plans to their employees as *a part of the package of fringe benefits*. As a set of all employees with low-risk and high-risk of illness participate in the health plan the insurance company can fix its premium rate on the basis of average risk and also the problem of adverse selection is eliminated. But in this case cost of insurance plan is borne by the employer and the employees get it as an incentive to work for the employer.

The Problem of Moral Hazard

Another problem that often arises in the insurance market is that of moral hazard. The moral hazard refers to a person or firm's behaviour which may change after buying insurance so that *it increases the probability of theft, fire, illness or other accident.* This is because when a person buys insurance, the loss from an accident, fire or getting ill is shifted from the person to the insurance company. Therefore, when insured against risk, a person takes less care or take fewer precautions to

3. See M Rothschild and J. Stiglitz, "Equilibrium in Competitive Insurance Markets : An Essay on the Economics of Imperfect Information, *Quarterly Journal of Economics*, November 1976"

avoid accident, fire, illness or any other disaster. As a result, the probability of the accident, illness or any other disaster which is insured increases. And when the accident, illness or any other insured disaster occurs, the person or firm inflates the loss suffered. This behaviour of the insured person raises the cost of insurance of the insurance company. For example, if a person gets his car insured for theft and accident. Knowing that the loss occurred as a result of an accident will be borne by the insurance company, he will drive the car more carelessly after buying insurance and thus increasing the probability of accident taking place.

Take another example, say of medical insurance involving moral hazard. After buying medical insurance, individuals usually spend less on health care which increases the probability of their getting ill. Besides, they are likely to spend more on treatment when fall ill than if they had no insurance. This behaviour on the part of individuals increases the amount payable by the insurance companies on account of mediclaim.

Similarly, in case of fire insurance, the firms are likely to take fewer precautions such as installation of fire detector system and thereby increasing the probability of a fire and in addition, the firms inflate the loss of property damaged if fire actually occurs. In fact, the probability of fire rises very much, if the property is insured for an amount greater than its true value.

It is worth nothing that if the care taken by an individual who buys insurance is observable, then there is no problem. In case care is observable, the insurance company can fix its premium on the basis of the amount of care taken by the person or firm. Thus, in real life the insurance companies usually charge different rates from firms which have a fire sprinkler system in their building; or to charge smokers higher premium rates than non-smokers for health insurance. In these cases the firms try to discriminate among those who buy insurance depending on the care or choices they make that affect the probability of damage.

But the problem of moral hazard arises because the insurance companies cannot observe all the relevant actions regarding care the individuals take after buying insurance. If the problem of moral hazard is not reduced, it could lead to the very high insurance costs and premium rates which would defeat the very purpose of insurance. The purpose of insurance is to distribute the given risks of a large monetary loss among many individuals or firms participating in an insurance programme. But if the facility of available insurance increases the total risks and claimed losses, then insurance does not prove to be efficient and it may not be even possible to provide insurance.

Insurance companies have tried to reduce or overcome the problem of moral hazard. One method generally adopted by the insurance companies is *specifying the precautions that individuals or firms buying insurance must take to be eligible for making a claim.* For example, the insurance company might require that individual must get medical check-up annually to continue enjoying health insurance. Similarly, the insurance companies may charge higher premium from drivers involved in accidents, may require the installation of fire detector system by the firms as a condition for providing insurance to them. By specifying these conditions, the insurance company attempts to reduce the probability of illness, accident or fire and thereby reduce the possible claims on it.

Another method often adopted by the insurance companies to reduce the problem of moral hazard is that of *coinsurance.* In coinsurance the individual or firm shares a good portion of a potential loss with the insurance company. That is, in case of coinsurance, the insurance company insures only a part of the possible loss or value of property insured. The idea behind such a proposal is that when the individual or firm shares a good part of potential loss with the insurance company, the individual or firm will take more care and precautions to avoid losses.

A similar proposal to overcome the problem of moral hazard is the provision made in the insurance policy that includes a large "*deductible*" under which the insured individual or firm has to pay a part of the claim. This also ensures that the insured individual will have incentive to take some amount of care.

Moral Hazard and Allocative Inefficiency

Moral hazard is not only a problem for insurance companies. It also affects the ability of the market to achieve efficient resource allocation. This is illustrated in Fig. 43.2 where we have shown the demand curve driving in kilometers per week. The demand curve *D* is sloping downward to the right. This is because at the higher cost of driving, the individuals switch over to other means of transportation. To begin with, let us suppose the *cost of driving per kilometer* includes the cost of insurance and the insurance company can *measure correctly* the number of kilometers driven. Thus in this case the problem of moral hazard does not arise. The owner-driver knows the more driving by him will increase his insurance premium and therefore his total cost of driving will increase. For example, as will be seen from Fig. 43.2 when the cost of car driving is ₹ 15 per kilometer, (including ₹ 5 per kilometer of insurance cost), the driver will do car driving 200 kilometers per week. Since there is no problem of moral hazard, marginal utility of car driving for 200 kilometers is equal to marginal cost of driving (₹ 15) per kilometer. 200 kilometers car driving is socially efficient level.

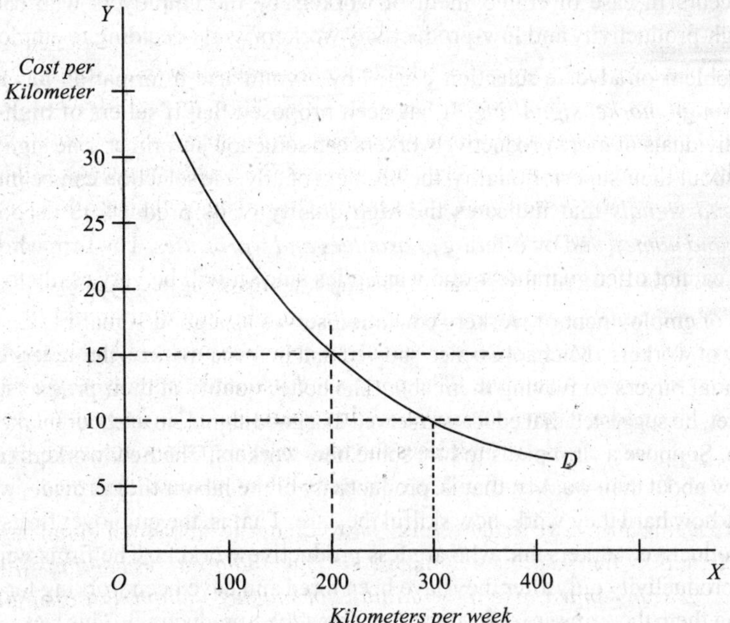

Fig. 43.2. *Moral Hazard and Allocative Inefficiency*

However, the problem of moral hazard arises because it is very difficult for an insurance company to monitor driving habits of individuals and further that insurance premium does not depend on the number of kilometers driven. Once a car owner buys a car insurance policy he has to pay a given insurance premium for a week, month or a year. Therefore, the owner-driver thinks that any additional accident cost will be borne by the insurance company and further that since the *insurance premium does not vary with the number of kilometers driven*, he will have therefore incentive to drive car more kilometers than without insurance. Without the insurance premium of ₹ 5 per kilometer, the cost of driving per kilometer will now be ₹ 10 (that is, ₹ 15 – 5 = 10). It will be seen that from Figure 65.2 that at the cost of driving ₹ 10 per kilometer, the owner-driver will drive 300 kilometers per week which is more than the socially efficient number of 200 kilometers. Thus it is clear that the problem of moral hazard leads to socially inefficient kilometers of driving activity.

MARKET SIGNALLING

In the earlier section of this chapter we have explained how asymmetric information leads to the lemons problem. Since sellers know more about the quality of their products than the buyers, the buyers assume that products offered for sale are of low quality. This results in fall in price of the product and ultimately only low-quality products are sold in the market, the good quality products having been driven out of the market. This is called the adverse selection which is the consequence of asymmetric information. Similarly, in case of insurance market we have seen that since the insurance companies cannot know who are high-risk individuals and who are low-risk individuals in order to provide insurance at an appropriate rate of insurance premium the result is again of adverse selection, that is, only high-risk individuals buy insurance at high premiums. In the extreme case such high rates of insurance premiums may come about that no one is willing to buy insurance and the insurance market even ceases to exist. Similarly, as shall be explained at length below, the problem of adverse selection occurs in case of employment of workers by the employers who can not distinguish between high-productivity and low-productivity workers while deciding to employ them.

The problem of adverse selection caused by asymmetric information has been sought to be resolved through *market signalling.* It has been proposed that if sellers of high-quality products, low-risk individuals or more productive workers can somehow inform or send signals to the potential customers about their superior quality, the problem of adverse selection can be mostly overcome. A firm *can send signals* that indicates the high quality of its products to its potential buyers by adopting *brand names*, and by offering *guarantees and warranties*. The firm whose products are of low quality cannot offer guarantees and warranties since it will be very costly to do so.

In case of employment of workers education serves as a good signalling device regarding the productivity of workers. Michael Spence showed that in some markets the sellers could send signals to the potential buyers conveying them about the better quality of their products. In the context of labour market, he suggested that education served as a good signal[4] in a labour market with asymmetric information. Suppose a firm plans to hire some new workers. The new workers (*i.e.* sellers of their labour) know about their quality, that is, productivity of the labour they provide, whereas the buyers do not know how hard they work, how skilful they are. That is, the employer firms do not know who are more productive workers and who are less productive workers. The firms will be able to know about their productivity only after they have been hired and have been working for some time. At the time of hiring them the firms are quite uncertain about their productivity. This lack of information may lead to the adverse selection explained earlier in the context of market for used cars and insurance market.

A pertinent question is why don't firms first hire workers, observe them for some time to know how well they work and terminate the services of those workers who have low productivity and retain only those who are actually more productive. However, this is not a practical proposition because labour laws in many countries do not permit the firing of workers who have worked for more than 6 months in a firm. Besides, firms have to invest a lot of money on providing on the job training to workers. If they are fired at a later time, the resources spent on their training will go waste. Therefore, it is much better for the firms if they know about the potential productivity of the workers

4. See Michael Spence, *Market Signalling* (Cambridge, MA Harvard University Press, 1974).

before hiring them.

Spence has claimed that education of workers is a good signal that can be used by the employers to distinguish between high-productivity workers and low-productivity workers. A person's education level can be easily measured by the number of years of schools, the degrees obtained, the college or university where he studied, the grade or marks obtained etc. The education undoubtedly can raise one's productivity. But as has been stressed by Spence in his model of signalling that *even if education does not improve one's productivity, it will still be a useful signal of productivity* because it is easier and less costly for more productive persons to obtain a higher level of education as compared to the low-productivity persons. More productive persons are more intelligent, highly motivated, more hard-working and are therefore likely to obtain a higher level of education which can be used as a signal of their higher productivity to enable them to get highly lucrative jobs. For all these reasons firms are also right in thinking that education is a signal of productivity.

Spence in his important contribution regarding education as a signal emphasized that education is a good signal if cost of acquiring it is less by a more productive worker as compared to the low productive worker. We explain below his model of signalling in some detail.

Spence Model of Signalling

Suppose P_H represents the productivity of high-quality workers and they are H in number and P_L represents the productivity of low-quality of workers whose number is L. The total number of workers seeking jobs are therefore $H + L$. If H workers are paid wages equal to their marginal productivity P_L and L workers are paid wages equal to their marginal productivity Q_1, then there will be efficient use of labour. But, since the employers are unable to distinguish between high-productivity P_L workers and low productivity workers it is not possible to achieve Pareto efficiency in labour use. The *weighted average* productivity of workers which we represent by $\bar{P}$ is given by

$$\bar{P} = P_H \cdot \frac{H}{H+L} + P_L \cdot \frac{L}{H+L}$$

$$P_H < \bar{P} < P_L$$

In view of the fact that it is not possible for the employers to distinguish between high and low productivity workers, they may pay each worker equal to their *average* marginal productivity $\bar{P}$ as obtained above. Paying workers equal to their average marginal productivity rather than their own marginal productivity would violate the conditions of achieving Pareto efficiency.

Let us suppose as Spence does that though education does not cause increase in productivity of workers, it *costs less* for more productive workers (H) to acquire education as compared to the less productive workers. Using education as a signal of their higher marginal productivity, the educated workers are able to get jobs and are paid high wages. On the other hand, low-quality workers are unable to get education because it is either not easy for them to get education or is very costly for them to acquire education which can serve as signal to get employment.

Spence showed that a number of conditions must be fulfilled if education is to serve as a good signalling device in the job market and equilibrium is achieved that ensures market efficiency in the sense that more productive workers in fact get employment and are paid equal to the value of their marginal products.

The conditions stipulated by Spence in his signalling model can be stated as under. Let C_H the cost of education for high-productivity workers and C_L the cost of education of the low-productivity workers.

1. The first essential condition of Spence's model of education as a successful signalling device for higher productivity is $C_H < C_L$, that is, it costs less for high-productivity workers to acquire education.
2. The second condition is : $C_L > P_H - P_L$, that is, it costs more for low-productivity workers to acquire education for using as a necessary signal than the differential in productivity and therefore the differences in wages paid to the two types of workers.
3. $C_H < P_H - P_L$, that is it *costs less* to high productivity workers to invest in education so as to use it as a signal than the differential in productivity that is *perceived* to result from possessing that signal.

Those having acquired education to use it as a signal are paid a wage $W_H = P_H$ and those who have not acquired educational signal are paid a wage $W_L = P_L$. The following equilibrium condition follows from the above conditions :

$$C_H : (P_H + P_L) : C_L \qquad ...(i)$$

According to the above equilibrium condition, since $C_H : (P_H + P_L)$, *high productivity workers find it worthwhile to invest in acquiring education as a signal and get job at the wage rate equal to their high productivity,* P_H, *and, on the other hand, since* $(P_H + P_L)$ C_L or $C_L < (P_H + P_L)$, *the low productivity workers do not find it worthwhile to invest in acquiring education as a signal for perceived high productivity and are satisfied with accepting the low wage rate equal to* P_L.

The above equilibrium condition (*i*) is called *separating equilibrium.* It shows how the two groups of workers separate themselves for acquiring education as a signal, to get jobs. However, the equilibrium condition (*i*) is a *necessary but not the sufficient condition* for the success of education as a signalling device. For example, suppose that the equilibrium condition (*i*) is satisfied but *all* workers before they invest in acquiring education are paid a wage equal to their average productivity $\bar{P}$. Because, as stated above, $C_L < P_H + P_L$, it does not pay the low-productivity workers to invest in acquiring education to serve as signal to get high-paid jobs. However, even though $C_H : P_H + P_L$ but at the same time $C_H < P_H + \bar{P}$, then even high-productivity workers would not find it sufficient to induce them to invest in acquiring education. Hence in view of being presently paid wage equal to the average productivity $\bar{P}$, the wage differential $(P_H + \bar{P})$ is considered by the high-productivity workers being not worthwhile to invest in acquiring education as a signal to earn wage rate equal to P_H. Under these circumstances, both the low-productivity workers and high-productivity workers would have no incentive to acquire education as signal. Hence the equilibrium condition (*i*) derived above is a necessary but a sufficient condition for the success of education as a signal.

Spence's model of treating education as a mere signalling device has been criticised on the ground that it represents a social waste of resources. Based on the assumption that acquiring education does not lead to the increase in true productivity and merely serves as a signal of *perceived* productivity, high productivity workers are induced to spend a lot of time (even years) simply to invest in acquiring education to act as successful signal of high *perceived* productivity. Thus, commenting on Spence's model, Griffiths and Wall write, "The *efficiency gain is* that of more appropriate allocation of high-productivity employees after the educative signal is acquired; the *efficiency loss* is the resources used up by society in providing some individuals with educational opportunities merely to serve as a non-productive signalling device and; of course, the *opportunity cost* of work foregone by high-productivity workers during the educational process."[5]

---

5. Allan Griffiths and Stuart Wall, *Intermediate Microeconomics, Theory and Applications* (London, Addison Wesley Longman Ltd 1996).
6. See E.F. Fauna, "Agency problems of the Theory of the Firm" in *Journal of Political Economy,* April 1980.

THE PRINCIPAL-AGENT PROBLEM

In the modern corporate companies there is a separation of ownership from control between shareholders who are the owners and the managers who actually organise and control the working of the companies. The owners (shareholders in case of corporate companies) are often referred to as *principals* and the managers who organise, manage and control the business firm are called *agents*. In this case of separation of ownership from control of the business firms, the *principal-agent problem* arises. The principal-agent problem refers to the situation when the managers pursue their goals such as high salaries, power, prestige, perquisites even at the cost of the owners (*i.e.* their principals)[6]. Whereas the shareholders want to maximise their profits or present value of the net worth of their companies managers who pursue their own goals often take decisions which are contrary to the goal of the owners.

Asymmetric information plays a role in this principal-agent relationship. The managers, that is, agents possess information which is not available to the owners. The owners could acquire information through research activity and extensive and costly monitoring of the managers. Since it is very costly and also not possible to gather all the required information to fully overcome the asymmetry in information, it is quite unlikely that the owners (*i.e.*, principals) will undertake such costly activity. As a result, due to the lack of adequate information by the owners, the managers (*i.e.* agents) have ample freedom to behave discretionally and take decisions to promote their own interests rather than the interests of the owners. It is important to note that the principal-agent problem exists not only in private corporate enterprises but also in public enterprises. We briefly explain below this agency relationship problem in both the sectors.

The Principal-Agent Problem in Private Sector

In large private corporate enterprises, an individual or an institution holds a relatively very small part of the share capital in the enterprise. This fact makes it difficult to obtain adequate information about how efficiently the managers are working. Theoretically, an important function of the owners or their representatives is to monitor the managers' functioning. But, as noted above, it is very costly for an individual shareholder to gather sufficient information to monitor the decision-making by the managers.

But managers can pursue which objectives which conflict with the interests of their principals (*i.e.* owners). First, it has been pointed out that managers try to maximise the growth or sales of the firm rather than profits or net worth of the firms. The more rapid growth in output or sales or increase in market share provide larger cash flows which help the managers to get more perks or perquisites. The other objective that is often said to be pursued by the managers is maximisation of their utility by them. As Williamson has suggested that the utility which a manager gets from his job depends not only on salaries, but also on respect from the peers, power to control the corporation, the large subordinate staff they have, the fringe benefits and other perks they enjoy and a long tenure of the job.

However, in a private corporate enterprise there are limitations to managers' ability to pursue objectives which conflict with the maximisation of owners' profits or net worth of the firms. First, shareholders can raise objections when they find that managers are not working efficiently and as a result they are not getting adequate dividend or when the value of the stock of the firm is not increasing. They can in extreme cases can get the managers dismissed, of course with the help of the board of directors who monitor managerial activities.

7. See R. Morck, A Shliefer and R Vishny, "Manaagement Ownership and Corporate Performance", *Journal of Financial Economics,* March 1988.

But what are the ways to overcome this principal-agent problem so as to improve the efficiency of the business organisation.

Takeover by other owners. If a business firm is poorly managed and its owners are unable to properly control and monitor the managerial actions, it may be taken over by other firms who are quite tough and adept in controlling management. When a firm is poorly managed, the old owners are happy to sell out to the new firms. There is every possibility that the new firms dispense with the services of the existing managers. Therefore, the threat of takeover often induce the management to improve its performance to avoid being taken over. Thus one way in which the performance of poorly managed companies may be improved is through the threat posed by potential takeover.

Long-Term Contracts. An important way of dealing with the principal agent problem to enter into long-term contracts such as *profit-sharing contracts* with managers so that they have the incentive to pursue the objective of profit maximisation in their own interest. It may however be noted that the objective of owners' contract is to promote managers' effort and work, but the payment scheme under the contract must be based on measured output of his efforts, that is, profits. The other examples of long-term contracts are *many years' service contracts with CEO and other senior managers.* These long period service contracts enable managers to take a long-term view and devise such strategies that ensure large profits over a long period of time.

Providing Part-Ownership. A more popular way of coping with the principal-agent problem is to *give the managers a financial stake in the better performance of the firm*. Many corporate companies in India and abroad have stock purchase plans whereby managers can buy equity shares of the company at less than market price. These partial ownership plans provide incentive to managers to maximise firm's profits and to act in accordance with the interests of the firm's owners. An important research study has found that if managers own between 5 and 10 per cent of the stock of a firm, the firm is likely to perform better in terms of profitability than if they own less than 5 per cent.[7]

Incentive Pay. Incentive Pay Schemes are quite common method of coping with principal-agent problem. In these incentive pay schemes, management salaries and bonuses are related to company's profitability or high salaries or bonuses are given to the managers who succeed in meeting profit targets set for them. It has been found that markets for managers come into existence. Those managers who secure high profits for the firms because of their better performance earn high salaries. Thus profit-linked salaries give incentive to managers to maximise profits or net worth of the firms which is consistent with the interests of the owners. Thus, to quote Pindyck and Rubinfeld, "*When it is impossible to measure effort directly, an incentive structure that rewards outcome of high levels of effort can induce agents to aim for the goals that the owners set.*"[8]

Despite the above measures that may be taken to cope with the principal-agent problem, the means by which the shareholders can control and monitor management functioning are limited and imperfect. The principal-agent problem exists not only between owners and managers of firms but also between *owners and workers.* The workers, like managers, may pursue their own interests rather than maximising profits or net worth of the firm. Some incentive schemes, similar to those for managers, such as bonus payment to the workers and profit-sharing arrangement with them as a reward for putting in a high level of work-effort, have often been adopted to induce workers to show better performance. In this connection efficiency wage theory has been offered which explains that better paid workers would put in large effort to create more output and profits for the owners. We will explain this wage efficiency theory in a later section.

---

8. R.S. Pindyck and D.L. Rubinfeld, *Microeconomics*, Prentice Hall of India, 1995, p. 613.

THE EFFICIENCY WAGE THEORY

Efficiency wage theory is a recent development in the analysis of determination of wages and employment. As shall be explained below, an interesting feature of this theory is that it helps to explain that whereas wage rate remained at above the competitive equilibrium rate, substantial unemployment of labour prevails in a competitive economy. Given the competitive labour market the existence of such unemployment could not be expected if unemployed workers were willing to work for a lower wage than that received by the employed workers. The question that arises is that under such circumstances why firms do not lower wages and increase employment and thereby raise their profits and eliminate involuntary unemployment. Efficiency wage theory makes a different assumption than the simple competitive model of wage determination which is based on the assumption that productivity of labour is independent of wage rate paid to labour. On the contrary the *efficiency wage theory assumes that productivity or efficiency of labour, that is, output per hour or per day depends on the level of wage rate paid to it.*

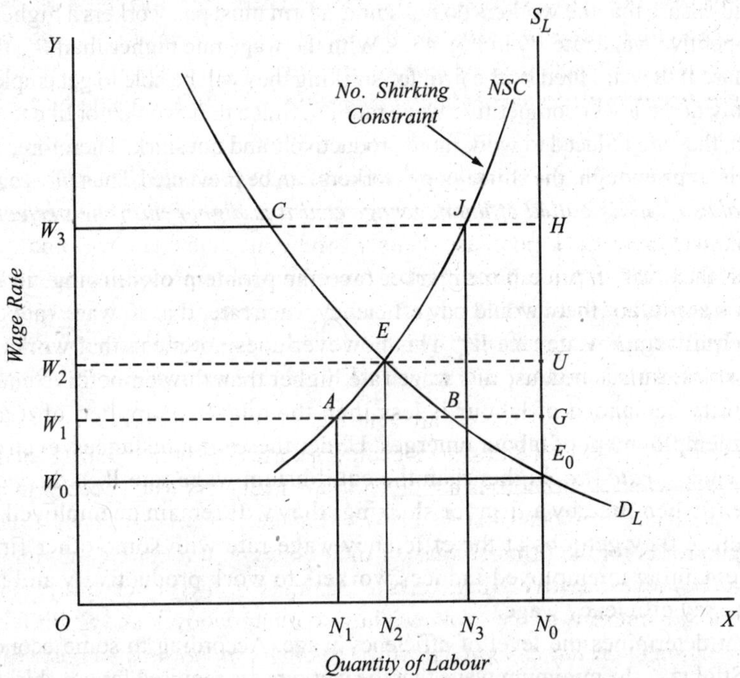

Fig. 43.3. *Efficiency Wage and Unemployment in a Non-Shirking Model*

According to the efficiency wage theory *it is difficult for the firms to accurately know about workers' productivity* and therefore the workers can shirk work and do not put in their best efforts in raising their productivity. As a result, since the firms cannot monitor workers' productivity, they also encounter principal-agent problem arising from asymmetric information between the owners of the firms and the workers. Therefore, the efficiency wage theory suggests that the firms willingly pay higher than the equilibrium competitive wage rate in order to provide incentive to workers not to shirk work (*i.e.* not to slack off). But since firms have limited or imperfect information about worker's productivity, the workers who shirk cannot be fired for shirking.

Let us illustrate the efficiency wage theory with a diagram. The shirking model assumes that perfectly competitive labour market prevails and all workers are equally productive and get the same wage. But once they are employed they can either work productively or shirk. But, as mentioned above, the firms employing them have imperfect information about their true productivity, they are not likely to be fired for shirking. The model works as follows.

D_L curve in Fig. 43.3 represents the demand for labour and S_L is the supply curve of labour which for sake of simplicity is assumed to be perfectly inelastic at ON_0 number of workers. Given the competitive market, wage rate is determined at the level of W_0 corresponding to which demand curve D_L of labour intersects the supply curve S_L. If the firm pays its workers the competitive wage rate W_0, the workers will have incentive to shirk. This is because firm's managers having limited information about workers' productivity are unable to detect workers who are shirking and even if they are able to detect those who are shirking and fire them, these workers can readily get employment elsewhere at the current wage rate as there does not exist any unemployment at this wage rate. As a result, the workers have little incentive to put in their best work-effort to become more productive and are likely to shirk.

In order to ensure that the workers do not shirk, a firm must pay workers a higher wage than the perfectly competitive wage rate W_0 in Fig. 43.3. With the wage rate higher than W_0, the workers will not shirk because if they are fired by the firm for shirking they will be able to get employment in some other firms only at the lower competitive wage rate W_0. Since they would not like to give up present higher pay job, they are induced to work more productively and not shirk. Therefore, if the difference in wage rates is large enough, the shirking by workers can be prevented Thus *the wage rate at which no shirking takes place is called efficiency wage and it is higher than the perfectly competitive equilibrium wage rate.*

But since all firms in the labour market face the problem of shirking, in order to avoid shirking by workers all of them would pay efficiency wage rate, that is, wage rate higher than the competitive equilibrium wage rate W_0. This however does not mean that workers will now be motivated to shirk. This is because at a wage rate higher than the competitive equilibrium wage rate W_0, quantity demanded of labour is less than the quantity supplied of it and as a result involuntary unemployment of labour emerges. Under these circumstances, even when *all firms pay efficiency wage rate* (*i.e.* higher than the equilibrium wage rate W_0), the workers will not shirk because if when fired by a firm for shirking, they will remain unemployed (perhaps for a long time) before they get jobs at the efficiency wage rate with some other firms. Thus, the prospect of remaining unemployed induces workers to work productively and not shirk even when all firms pay efficiency wage.

Now, what determines the level of efficiency wage. According to some economists such as J. Yellen[9], J. Stiglitz[10], the minimum wage that the workers are required for not shirking is inversely related to the level of unemployment. For example, in Fig. 43.3 if wage rate is W_1, the level of unemployment equal to AG (which is equal to N_1N_0) must be there to induce workers not to shirk. If wage rate is W_2, then the unemployment level of $EU(=N_2N_0)$ is required to prevent shirking by the workers. Further, if wage rate is W_3, then $JH(=N_3N_0)$ must be the level of unemployment needed to prevent shirking by workers. Thus, the no-shirking constraint curve is upward sloping that indicates the efficiency wage rate (that is, the wage rate that must be paid to prevent shirking) is higher, the smaller the level of unemployment. It may be noted that as efficiency wage is higher, the non-shirking constraint (*NSC*) curve gets nearer and nearer the given vertical supply curve S_L of labour but never crosses it.

---

9. J. Yellen, "Efficiency Wage Models of Unemployment, *American Economic Review*, May 1984.
10. J. Stiglitz, "The Causes and Consequences of the Dependence of Quality of Price, *Journal of Economic Literature*, March 1987.

The equilibrium efficiency wage rate is determined at the level where non-shirking constraint (*NSC*) curve intersects the demand curve D_L of labour. It will be seen from Fig. 43.3 that W_2 is the equilibrium efficiency wage rate because corresponding to this wage rate non-shirking constraint curve (*NSC*) intersects the demand for labour curve D_L at point *E*. Why W_2 is the equilibrium efficiency wage rate? At the wage rate W_2, the actual demand or employment of labour is W_2E or ON_2 and therefore actual unemployment will be *EU* which is the level of unemployment required to induce workers not to shirk. On the other hand, if wage rate is W_1, actual unemployment will be equal to *BG* whereas level of unemployment equal to *AG* is required to prevent shirking by workers. Therefore, efficiency wage rate will tend to rise.

If wage rate is W_3, the actual unemployment *CH* is higher than the level of unemployment *JH* required to prevent shirking. As a result, efficiency wage rate falls. Thus equilibrium is reached at the efficiency wage rate W_2 at which actual unemployment equals the level of unemployment required to avoid shirking by workers. Therefore, W_2 is the equilibrium efficiency wage rate at which unemployment equal to *EU* (that is, N_2N_0) prevails. Note that equilibrium efficiency wage rate W_2 is higher than competitive equilibrium wage rate W_0 at which all who want employment are in fact employed and therefore there is no unemployment. Thus, no shirking model or efficiency wage model explains why higher than competitive wage rate is paid to the workers while there exists substantial unemployment in a competitive economy.

Application. Although efficiency wage model is highly simplified, it helps to explain a number of real world phenomenon. The chief example of application of efficiency wage theory was by Henry Ford, who has been a major producer of automobiles in the United States. In 1914 Henry Ford took a famous decision to raise the minimum daily wage from \$2.34 to \$5 a day for labour. Besides, he reduced the length of the working day from 9 to 8 hours. This was a unprecedented decision as it was quite unusual for a firm to announce that it, would double the wage rate it pays to his workers.

Although Henry Ford was criticised by other producers for his policy of paying higher wages to his labour, it paid him good dividends. Henry Ford not only succeeded in maintaining a stable labour force but also could hire workers who were on an average more productive. According to the evidence available, productivity in Ford's factory increased by 51 per cent and absenteeism had been halved. The higher wages resulted in fewer layoffs and discharges, and workers worked hard and more productively. As a result his average cost declined and profitability greatly increased. Ford's profits increased from \$ 30 million in 1914 to \$ 60 million in 1916. Ford himself later said that his decision to raise wage rate "was one of the finest cost-cutting moves we ever made."[11] According to modern economists, what Ford did was to pay an efficiency wage.[12]

To what extent the efficiency wage theory is applicable to developing countries like India, I leave it for the readers to think about it. However the present author is of the view that Indian industrialists do not have such progressive and innovative outlook as Henry Ford had. It may be noted that apart from the efficiency wage theory explained above, in India and other developing countries the productivity of workers depends on the wage rate for nutritional reasons as well. If poor Indian workers are paid better wages, they would afford to purchase more and better food which would make them healthier and more productive than at present.

---

11. Henry Ford, *My Life and Work,* 1922, p. 147.
12. See D. Raff and L Summers, "Did Henry Ford Pay Efficiency Wages", *Journal of Labour Economics, 1987*

QUESTIONS FOR REVIEW

1. What is asymmetric information ? Explain why asymmetric information between buyers and sellers leads to market failure when a market is otherwise perfectly competitive.
2. Explain why Lemons in the used cars market drives out good quality used cars?
3. Explain the lemons problem in the market for used goods. How can this problem be overcome?
4. Adverse selection is the direct result of asymmetric information. Explain. How can the problem of adverse selection be overcome? *D.U. B.Com (Hons.) IInd Year 2009*
5. Explain the Principal-Agent, Problem. How are incentive pay and profit-sharing payment schemes likely to resolve principal agent problem?
6. What is an efficient wage ? Why is it profitable for the firm to pay an efficiency wage?
7. Explain the efficiency wage theory. Is it relevant in case of India?
8. Explain how imperfect information can result in fall in quantity demanded when the price of a commodity falls. *(D.U., B.A (Hons.) Ist Year 2007)*
9. Explain the problem of *adverse selection* by the consumer when he cannot judge the true quality of a product in the presence of imperfect information. What are the solution to the adverse selection problem? *D.U., B.A. (Hons.) Ist Year 2009*
10. What is market signalling? How can it be used to solve the problem of adverse selection resulting from asymmetric information ? *D.U., P ~om (Hons.) II year 2008*
11. What is asymmetric information? How can the problem of adverse selection resulting from asymmetric information be resolved by market signalling. *D.U. B.Com (Hons.) II Year 2007*

CHAPTER 44
CHOICE UNDER RISK AND UNCERTAINTY

Introduction

So far in our analysis of consumer's behaviour we have assumed that while making a choice the consumers do not face any uncertainty. For example, when consumers buy goods they know with certainty what they are getting and how much utility they will get from their consumption. However, in the real world situations this assumption of certainty is not valid. This is due to three factors. First, some goods that individuals buy are in the nature of *games or lotteries* for which outcome is quite uncertain. For example, in case of some games such as horse racing, buying insurance, playing gambles outcome is quite uncertain. You may view a gamble and get a certain amount of money which will increase your utility. On the other hand, you may lose the game which will reduce money with you and cause a loss of utility. Buying of such goods such as gambles does not guarantee an individual any particular outcome with certainty.

Secondly, individuals who make investment in assets face uncertainty as the outcome (*i.e.*, return) from the assets or from any combination (*i.e.*, portfolio) of assets cannot be known with certainty. This is because cost conditions and future prices can vary and cannot be known with certainty. Therefore, the individuals have to make a choice of assets or investment portfolio of assets in uncertain and therefore risky situation.

The third case in which the individuals face uncertainty is when there is lack of information about the quality of goods they buy for example, while buying cars, colour TVs, refrigerators, the individuals are not quite sure the carm refrigerator or colour TV they buy will offer best quality for money. The problem of uncertainty arising out of lack of information is more true when individuals buy used or second-hand cars or second-hand bikes.

Of the above three cases of uncertainty we will be concerned with individual choice in the first two cases of uncertainty of outcomes. Choice or decision making in case of uncertainty date to lack of information on the part of buyers will be analysed in the last part of the book.

In what follows we first explain the concept of risk and how to measure it. We will then explain the different preferences toward risk. Risk is considered to be undesirable. Many individuals are risk averse and like to avoid risks, but some others are willing to bear risk if it yields them sufficient return. We also explain why some people gamble. In the end we will explain the ways such as diversification, insurance, gathering of information by which risk can be reduced.

The Concept of Risk

The risk refers to a situation when the outcome of a decision is uncertain but when the probability of each possible outcome is known or can be estimated. The analysis of decision making and choice involving risk or uncertainty requires that the individual knows all the possible outcomes and also have some idea of the probability of occurrence of each possible outcome. For example, in tossing a coin there is equal or 50-50 chance of getting either a head or tail. Likewise, when an individual invests in the shares of a company, the probability of outcome (that is, how much dividend it will yield and how much its price will rise in a year) can be estimated from the past experience. The outcome can vary a good deal. The greater the variability of possible outcome, the greater the risk involved in making the investment decision. Therefore, in the theory of choice or decision making under uncertainty it is necessary to know the meaning of probability of outcome and its variability.

It is important to mention the distinction between risk and uncertainty. *The uncertainty refers to the situation when there is more than one possible outcome of a decision but where the probability of occurrence of each particular outcome is not known or even cannot be estimated.* This may be due to lack of sufficient past information or the great instability of the variables involved that determine the outcome. In some extreme cases even outcomes themselves are not known. For example, in case of drilling for exploration of oil in an *unproven field*, investor does not know either the probability of oil being struck or the possible output of oil from it. Though the distinction between risk and uncertainty is theoretically significant the two terms are generally used interchangeably in decision making analysis.

In decision making involving risk or uncertainty the three terms are quite often used. They are : (1) *strategy*, (2) *state of nature* and (3) *outcome*. A strategy refers to one of several alternative courses of action or plans that can be implemented to achieve the desired goal. For example, a manager may be considering the following three strategies aimed at increasing profits of the firm.

(*i*) Building a new technologically more efficient plant so as to reduce the cost of production.

(*ii*) Launching of a new advertising and marketing campaign to increase sales.

(*iii*) Redesigning of the product so as to lower the cost of production and to increase in demand for it by getting greater consumer acceptance.

A state of nature refers to the conditions that prevail in future and which have a significant effect on the success or failure of the strategy. For example, in case of building a technologically superior plant the different states of nature that may exist in some future years are (a) boom, (b) recession, or (c) normal conditions. It is worthwhile to note that the decision maker has little or no control over the state of nature. For example, whether economic conditions of boom or recession will exist in future is beyond the control of the decision maker.

Finally, ***outcome*** refers to the results which are usually in the form of profits that come about as a result of implementation of a strategy. A *payoff matrix* lists the outcomes associated with combinations of each strategy and state of nature. It is important to note that *risk refers to the amount of variability in the outcome as a result of the adoption of a particular strategy*.

Measuring Risk: Probability of an Outcome

We have seen above that risk refers to the situation when there is more than one possible outcome of a decision and the probability of each outcome is either known or can be estimated. Therefore, to measure the degree of risk we need to know the probability of each possible outcome of a decision. *The probability means the likelihood of occurring of an event.* Thus, if possibility of an outcome occurring is $\frac{1}{4}$ or 0.25, this means that there is 1 chance in 4 for the outcome to occur. For example, suppose a person is considering to invest in a company which is engaged in the new exploration of offshore oil. If the exploration is successful, the price of company's stock will rise to ₹ 50 per share and if its exploration meets with a failure, the company's stock will fall to ₹ 10 per share. Given these two possible outcomes, namely, ₹ 50 per share price and ₹ 10 per share price, if the past information reveals that the chance of oil exploration being successful is $\frac{1}{4}$ and chance of its failure is $\frac{3}{4}$, then we say the probability of success of oil exploration is $\frac{1}{4}$ and the probability of its failure is $\frac{3}{4}$ (The success and failure are the two possible outcomes). Thus, *probability is a number that indicates the likelihood of an event or outcome occurring.*

These are two concepts of probability depending on how it is measured. The first is the frequency concept of probability. If past information or data is available regarding occurrence of outcomes or events, the probability is defined as the proportion of times an outcome occurs if the situation is repeated in the long run over and over again. In general, if a situation is repeated over a large number of times, say *M*, and if outcome, say *X*, occurs *m* times, then

$$P(X) > \frac{m}{M}$$

Thus, in our example if we know from the past data of oil exploration that rate of success is 25 per cent, then the probability of getting success is $\frac{1}{4}$ or 0.25. The measurement of probability based on the past experience is generally known as the ***objective measure of probability.***

But in many cases there are no similar past situations which helps us in measuring probability. In that case the ***concept of subjective probability*** is used. The subjective probability is an individual's personal view about the chance of an outcome to occur and is based on his personal judgement, experience or knowledge about the subject and not on the frequency with which outcome actually took place in the past. Obviously, when probability is subjectively determined and not based on the past data, the different individuals will attach different probabilities to the occurrence of various outcomes and therefore they will make different choices. In whatever way the probability is arrived at, it helps us to measure two important concepts, namely, *expected value and variability of outcome.* With the use of these two concepts we compare the profitability of various strategies involving risk and uncertainty which helps us to make a choice among them.

Expected Value and Expected Utility. In the theory of making a choice under risk and uncertainty an individual will make a decision on the basis of **expected utility of outcome** rather than **expected money value.**[1] Let us explain these two concepts. Suppose a vegetable vendor who moves around in the streets of a town to sell his vegetables. How much vegetables he will be able to sell and earn income depends on weather, namely, whether it rains or not. If it does not rain he will be able to sell more and earn more income or profits, say equal to ₹ 700 and if it rains he will not be able to sell much and his earnings or profit will be ₹ 100. Weather forecast is that there is 50 per cent chance of raining. Now in this situation what is the expected money value, *E*(*V*) or expected money earnings. Now, the expected money value or earnings is the sum of values of each possible outcome times the probabilities of those outcomes.

Thus,

$E(V) = P_r$(Earnings if it rains) $+ P_r$ (Earnings if it does not rain)

where P_r stands for probability

1. Daniel Bernoulli provided a convincing explanation of behaviour of a rational individual in deciding on the basis of expected utility of outcome and is known as **Bernoulli hypothesis**.

or $E(V) > \frac{1}{2}(700), \frac{1}{2}(100)$

$$= 350 + 50 = 400$$

Note that the expected value represents the amount of earnings on an average per day if the above sale by the vendor is repeatedly made for several days. Now, in order to find the expected utility of outcome of the above event of sale we have to know the utility function of the individual. With the information of utility function the individual's expected utility $E(U)$ is found as under :

$E(U) = P_r$(no rain) × U(Earnings in case of no rain) + P_r(rain) × Earnings in case of rain)

Since probability (P_r) of both raining and not raining is $\frac{1}{2}$. $P_r = \frac{1}{2}$ in both cases. Suppose from the utility function of the individual we know that the utility of the earnings of ₹ 700 in case of no rain is 140 and expected utility of earnings of 100 (in case of no rain) is 70, then expected utility is given by

$$E(U) > \frac{1}{2}\ U(₹700),\ \frac{1}{2}\ U(₹100)$$

$$> \frac{1}{2}\ 140,\ \frac{1}{2}\ 70$$

$$= 70 + 35 = 105$$

Now, it is important to know that utility function of an individual depends on his attitude toward risk as to whether he is risk averter, risk lover or risk neutral. Now the choice in the risky and uncertain situation depends the individual's attitude towards risk.

It may be further noted that risk is mainly measured in two ways. First, by using the concept of variance or standard deviation. Second, by using utility function approach. In this chapter, we adopt utility function approach to measure risk.

ATTITUDES TOWARD RISK

We analyse the problem of investment choice to describe how people makes a choice among alternative investments involving different degree of risk involved. But the underlying principles of making a choice in risk and uncertain situation, namely, expected return and the degree of risk involved apply equally well to other choices. In this section, we focus on examining individual's choices in the face of risk. In the theory of consumer's behaviour we saw that in making choices among commodity bundles when there is no risk and uncertainty, the consumer maximises his utility. We will analyse below how an individual maximises his expected utility when risk or uncertainty is present.

People's preferences toward risk greatly differ. Most individuals generally prefer the less risky situation (that is, the situation with less variability in outcomes). In other words, most individuals seek to minimise risk and are called ***risk averter*** or ***risk averse.*** However, some individuals prefer risk and are therefore called *risk seekers* or *risk lovers.* Some other individuals are indifferent toward risk and are called ***risk neutral.*** But it is important to note that these different preferences toward risk depend on whether for an individual *marginal utility of money diminishes or increases or remains constant as his income or wealth increases.* As shall be explained below, *for a risk averse individual marginal utility of money diminishes* as he has more money, while *for a risk seeker marginal utility of money increases as money with him increases.* In case of *risk neutral individual marginal utility of money remains constant as he has more money.*

Risk Averter. To explain the preference toward risk we will consider a single composite commodity, namely, money income. An individual's money income represents the market basket of goods that he can buy. It is assumed that the individual knows the probabilities of making or gaining money income in different situations. But the outcomes or payoffs are measured in terms of utility[2] rather than rupees.

In Fig. 44.1 we have drawn a curve *OU* showing utility function of money income of an individual who is risk-averse. It will be seen from this figure that the slope of total utility function *OU* decreases as the money income of the individual increases. Note that we measure money income on the *X*-axis and utility on the *Y*-axis. It will be seen from Fig. 44.1 that as money income of the individual increases from 10 to 20 thousand rupees, his total utility increases from 45 to 65 units (that is by 20 units) and when his money increases from 20 thousand to 30 thousand rupees, his total utility increases from 65 to 75 units (that is, by 10 units). Thus in this **concave utility function** depicted in Fig. 44.1 marginal utility of money of an individual decreases as his money income decreases and therefore it represents the case of risk-averse individual.

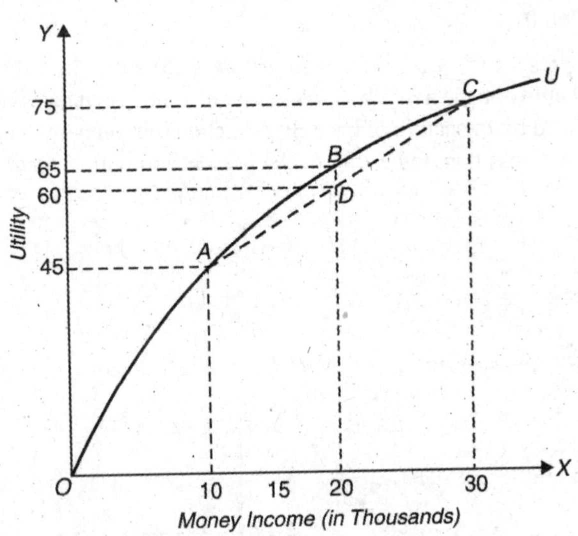

Fig. 44.1. *Utility Function of a Risk Averter*

Suppose the individual is currently employed on a fixed monthly salary basis of ₹ 20,000. There is no uncertainty about the income from this present job on the fixed salary basis and hence no risk. Now, suppose that the individual is considering to join a new job of a salesman on a *commission basis*. This new job involves risk because his income in this case is not certain. This is because if he proves to be a successful salesman, his income may increase to ₹ 30 thousand per month but if he does not happen to be a good salesman his income may go down to ₹ 10 thousand per month. Suppose in this new job there is 50-50 chance of either earning ₹ 30 thousands or ₹ 10 thousands (that is, each has a probability of 0.5). When there is uncertainty, the individual does not know the actual utility from taking a particular action. He has to decide on the basis of expected utility. *Given the probabilities*

2. *Neumann and Mrgenstern in their important contribution. "**The Theory of Games and Economic Behaviour**" suggested a way of measuring utility in quantitative terms in situations involving risk and uncertainty. They construct index numbers, termed as N-M Index Numbers, to measure utility. However, to simplify our analysis we just assume that utility can be measured in some units.*

of alternative outcomes, we can calculate his expected utility. Whether the individual will choose the new risky job or retain the present salaried job with *a certain* income can be known by comparing the expected utility from the new risky job with the utility of the current job. It will be seen from the utility function curve *OU* in Fig. 44.1 that the utility of his current certain money income of ₹ 20.000 with *certainty* is ₹ 65. Further, in case of new risky job if he is proved to be a successful salesman and his income rises to ₹ 30 thousands, his utility from ₹ 30 thousands is 75, and if he fails as a good salesman, his income falls to ₹ 10 thousands which yields him utility of ₹ 45. (Note that in the new risky job, the *expected value of income* is 20,000 which is given by $E(V) = 0.5 \times 10{,}000 + 0.5 \times 30{,}000$ = ₹ 20,000). It will be seen from the utility function in Fig. 44.1 that utility of ₹ 10,000 is 45 and that of ₹ 30,000 is 75. Given that the probability of success or failure as a salesman is 0.5, the expected utility of the new job is given by

$$E(U) = 0.5\ U(10{,}000) + 0.5\ U(30{,}000)$$
$$= 0.5 \times 45 + 0.5 \times 75$$
$$= 22.5 + 37.5$$
$$= 60.0$$

Thus with the present job with a fixed salary of ₹ 20,000 with no uncertainty utility is 65, whereas the expected utility of the new job as salesman on commission basis is 60. Since, the individual is risk averse as revealed by the nature of his utility function of money income, and since the expected utility of the risky job is less than the utility of the present job with a *certain* income, he will reject new risky job.

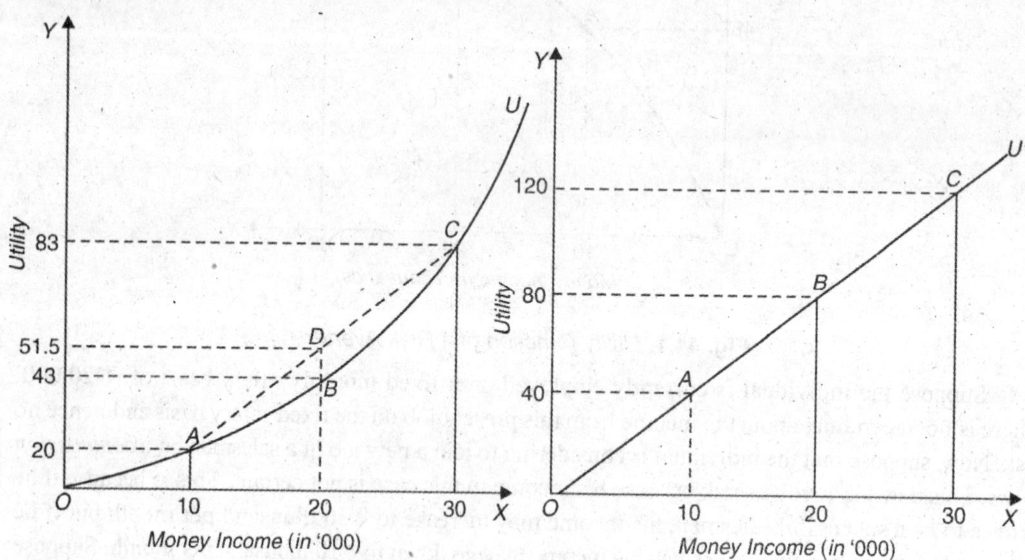

Fig. 44.2. *Utility Function of a Risk Seeker or Risk lover* **Fig. 44.3.** *Utility Function of a Risk Neutral*

Note again that in Fig. 44.1 we are considering the choice of a risk-averse individual for whom marginal utility of money declines as he has more of it. We are now in a position to provide a precise definition of risk-averse individual. Precisely speaking, *a person who prefers a certain given income to a risky job with the same expected income is called risk averter or risk averse.* Risk aversion is the most common attitude toward risk.

Risk Seeker. On the other hand, *a person is risk seeker or risk lover who prefers a risky job with the same expected income to a certain income*. In case of a risk loving individual, marginal utility of income to the individual increases as his money income increases as shown by the **convex total utility function curve** *OU* in Fig. 44.2. Suppose this risk-seeking individual has a present job with a certain income of ₹ 20 thousands. It will be seen from Fig. 44.2 that the utility of ₹ 20 thousands is 43 units to this individual. Now, if he is offered a risky job with his income of ₹ 30 thousands if he happens to be highly efficient and ₹ 10 thousands if he happens to be not so efficient in the new job with the equal probability of 0.5 in these two jobs, then the expected utility from the new is given by

$$E(U) = 0.5\ U(10{,}000) + 0.5\ U(30{,}000)$$

It will be seen from Fig. 44.2 that the utility of ₹ 10 thousands to this individual is ₹ 20 while utility of ₹ 30 thousands to him is 83. Therefore,

$$\begin{aligned} E(U) &= 0.5\ (20) + 0.5\ (83) \\ &= 10 + 41.5 \\ &= 51.5 \end{aligned}$$

Since the expected utility from the new risky job is 51.5 which is greater than the utility of 43 from the present job with a certain income of ₹ 20 thousands, the *risk-loving individual will prefer the new risky job even though the expected income in the new risky job is also ₹ 20,000* as (0.5 × 10,000) + 0.5 (30,000) = ₹ 20,000). But expected utility of 51.5 in the new risky job is greater than 43 in the present job with certain income of ₹ 20,000.

As mentioned above, most of the individuals are risk averse but there is a good deal of evidence of people who are risk seekers or risk lovers. It is risk-loving individuals who indulge in gambling, buy lotteries, engage in criminal activities such as robberies, big frauds even at risk of getting heavy punishment if caught.

Risk Neutral. *A person is called risk neutral, if he is indifferent between a certain given income and an uncertain income with the same expected value. An individual will be risk neutral if his marginal utility of money income remains constant with the increase in his money*. The total utility function of a risk neutral person is shown in Fig. 44.3. It will be seen from this figure that utility of a *certain* income of ₹ 20 thousands to him is 80. Now, in a risky job when income increases to ₹ 30 thousands if he proves to be a successful salesman, the utility of ₹ 30 thousands is 120 units. On the other hand, if in a new risky job, he proves to be a bad salesman, his income goes down to ₹ 10,000 whose utility to the individual is 40 units. We assume that there is equal probability of high and low income in the new risky job. Note that expected value of income in the new job with an uncertain income is 20,000 as (0.5 × 10,000 + 0.5 (30,000) = 20,000). The expected utility of the new risky job is given by

$$\begin{aligned} E(U) &= 0.5\ U(10{,}000) + 0.5\ U(30{,}000). \\ &= 0.5\ (40) + 0.5\ (120) \\ &= 20 + 60 \\ &= 80 \end{aligned}$$

It is seen from above that in *case of risk-neutral person expected utility of an uncertain income with the same expected value* (₹ 20,000 *in the present case*), is equal to utility of an assured or a certain income of the same amount. That is, risk-neutral person is indifferent between them.

INSURANCE AND RISK PREMIUM

Our foregoing analysis shows why most people buy insurance when they are faced with a risky and uncertain situation. As mentioned above, most people are risk averters and therefore they buy insurance to avoid risk. Now an important question is how much money or premium a risk-averse individual will pay to the insurance company to avoid risk and uncertainty facing him. Suppose the individual buys a house which yields him income of ₹ 30 thousands per month. But if the house catches fire and due to the damage caused, his income from it falls to ₹ 10 thousands per month and thus he suffers a loss of income. For the sake of simplifying analysis suppose there is 50 per cent chance of the house catching fire. Then the expect value of income in this risky and uncertain situation is

$$E(V) = 0.5 \times 30{,}000 + 0.5 \times 10{,}000$$
$$= 15{,}000 + 5{,}000$$
$$= 20{,}000$$

The utility function *OU* with a diminishing marginal utility of money income of a risk-averse individual is shown in Fig. 44.4. With money income of ₹ 30 thousands, his utility is 75 and with his lower income of ₹ 10 thousands his utility is 45. Given that there is probability of 0.5 for each outcome, expected utility of the two outcomes is given by

$$E(U) = 0.5\,U(30{,}000) + 0.5\,U(10{,}000)$$
$$= 0.5 \times 75 + 0.5 \times 45$$
$$= 37.5 + 22.5$$
$$= 60$$

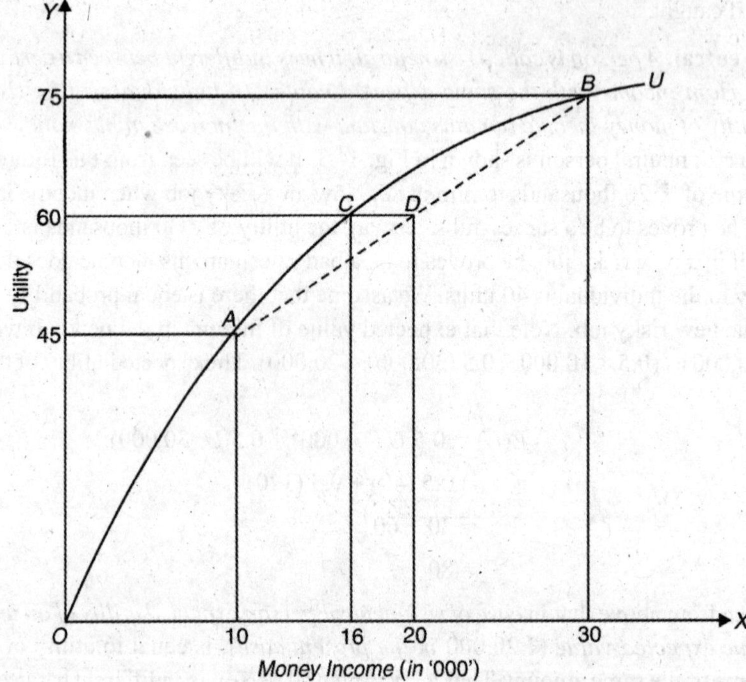

Fig. 44.4. *Insurance and Risk Premium*

It will be seen from Fig. 44.4 that we have drawn a straight line *AB* joining the utilities of 75 and 45. It is on this straight line *AB* that the amount of expected utility will be corresponding to the expected value of income in the present risky and uncertain situation. It will be seen from Fig.44.4 that on this straight line *AB* and corresponding to the expected value of income of ₹ 20 thousands, the expected utility is 60 which corresponds to point *D* on the straight line *AB*. But it will be seen from the individual's utility function *OU*, that utility of 60 is associated with *an assured and certain income* of ₹16 thousands. Thus the individual with an uncertain income of ₹ 20 thousands will be willing to forego ₹ 4 thousands (or *DC*) to get a certain or guaranteed income of ₹ 16 thousands as the expected utility of *uncertain expected income* of ₹ 20 thousands is equal to the utility of a *certain income* of ₹ 16 thousands. This means that if the individual gives up ₹ 4 thousands (20 – 16 = 4) from his uncertain expected income he will get the same utility of 60 as with a certain income of ₹ 16 thousands. ₹ 4 thousands equal to the distance *DC* is called the *risk premium*. Therefore, *the risk premium is the maximum amount of money that a risk-averse individual will be willing to pay to avoid the risk.* By paying the risk premium the individual can insure himself against a large loss from a fire and to get an assured or certain income.

It is clear from above way people buy insurance for fire, accident, ill health and even life.

RISK LOVER AND THE GAMBLING

Now, we explain how a risk lover responds to a fair gamble. It may be noted that a risk lover is one who prefers a gamble with the same expected value of income to the equivalent income with certainty. In Fig. 44.5 the utility curve of a risk lover has been drawn and, as it will be seen, it is *convex*. The convexity of the utility curve implies that marginal utility of money income of the person increases as his income increases. Now, suppose that present income of the individual is ₹ 3,000 and is offered a gamble with 50:50 chance of winning or losing ₹ 1,000. Therefore, if he wins, his money income will rise to ₹ 4,000, and if he loses his income will fall to ₹ 2,000. The expected money value of the gamble will therefore be equal to 1/2(4000) + 1/2(2000) = ₹ 3,000. And the expected utility from the expected value of income of ₹ 3,000, as it will be seen from Fig. 44.5 will be M_2D or OU_2 which is more than utility M_2C or OU_1 of income of ₹ 3,000 with certainty.

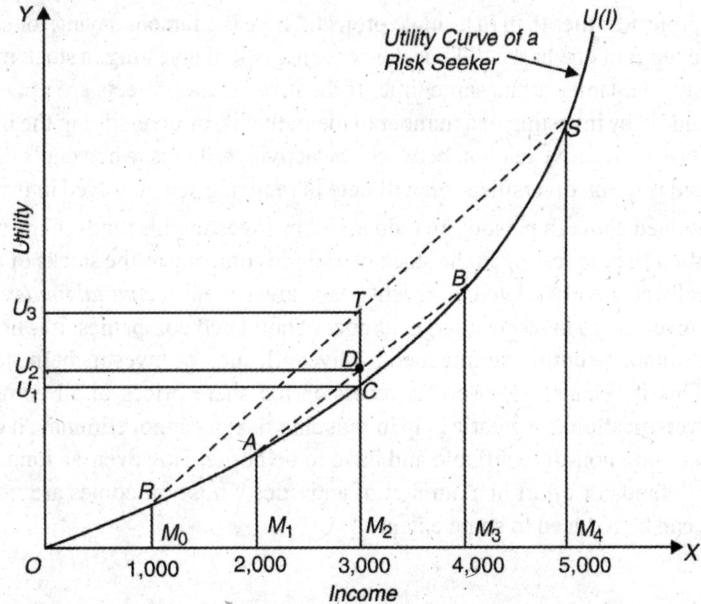

Fig. 44.5. *The Utility Curve of a Risk-Lover and his Preference for Gambling*

Since his expected utility from the gamble is greater than that from his income with certainty, he will accept the gamble. Further, it can be shown that risk lover, a person whose marginal utility of money increases with increase in his income, will prefer a gamble having greater risk, that is, the gamble which has a larger variability of outcome to a gamble with less risk (that is, with smaller variability of outcome). Suppose a person with increasing marginal utility of income is offered two fair gambles: One with 2,000 chance of winning or losing ₹ 1,000 and the other with a 50:50 chance of winning or losing ₹ 2,000 as outcome of the gamble. Given his present income of ₹ 3,000, the expected value of the two gambles is the same.

$E(V)$ of the Gamble I = 1/2 (4000) + 1/2 (2000) = 3000

$E(V)$ of the Gamble II = 1/2 (5000) + 1/2 (1000) = 3000

However, it will be seen from Fig. 44.5 that the expected utility of the two gambles differs; the expected utility of the second gamble, as will be seen from the straight-line segment *RS*, is equal to M_2T or OU_3 which is greater than M_2D or OU_2 of the first gamble with less variability (or risk) of outcome. It therefore follows that the risk lover will prefer the second gamble with greater risk and variability of outcome.

MANAGEMENT OF RISK : REDUCING RISK

We have seen above that though some individuals are risk seekers, most of the individuals are risk averse and try to reduce risk or uncertainty they face. There are three methods by which individuals or consumers can reduce risk. They are:

1. Diversification
2. Insurance
3. Gathering more Information.

We discuss below these methods.

Diversification

An important way of reducing risk is diversification, that is, spreading the risks. For example, an investor can reduce risk involved in investment by investing his investible funds in a number of independent projects rather than in a single project. There is a famous saying for safe investment, "Do not put all your eggs in one basket." Thus, for reducing risk in investing in stock market is to purchase shares of many companies at the same time. If the investment projects are not closely related, then risk can be reduced by investing in a number of them, that is, by diversifying the investment portfolio. If there is inverse or negative relation between two activities, that is, when one's demand is strong, the other's demand is weak, diversification will help in reducing risk involved in investment or activity.

As mentioned above, a person can reduce risk by investing his funds in the stock of a number of companies rather than investing in the stock of a single company as the stocks of different companies are not generally positively related. In recent years, investment in *mutual funds* are preferred as they enable small investors to invest in a large number of unrelated companies. It is however important to note that risk cannot be entirely eliminated by diversification of investment in stocks of a number of companies. This is because in case of a recession the share prices of all companies tend to fall. Therefore, diversification can greatly help in reducing risk; it cannot eliminate it completely. Risks of *systemic nature* are non-diversifiable and have to be borne. However, as long as you can allocate your investible funds or effort in a number of activities whose outcomes are not closely positively related, risks can be reduced to some extent.

Insurance

Insurance is another important method of reducing risk. We have explained above that risk-averse individuals are willing to give up some income to avoid risk. *The maximum price which an individual is willing to forego or pay for insurance is called risk premium.* Therefore, if the cost of insurance is equal to the amount of *risk premium* which they are prepared to give up to assure themselves a certain income in a risky and uncertain situation, they will buy the insurance policy. For example, if an individual owns a house worth ₹ 20 lakhs and faces a probability of 0.01 *i.e.*, one per cent chance of his house getting burnt down, then the expected value of loss is $\frac{1}{100} \times 20{,}00{,}000 = 20{,}000$. If a fire insurance policy is offered to the house owner for ₹ 20,000, he will definitely buy it. Such an insurance premium is fairly priced as it is equal to the expected loss that may assure to the individual in case his house is burnt down due to catching fire. In fact, a risk-averse individual may be willing to pay more than this depending on the degree of his risk aversion as measured by the risk premium he is prepared to pay.

The individuals generally buy insurance from the companies which specialize in the insurance business. These insurance companies work on the basis of *a law of large numbers.* The insurance companies not only insure against the loss suffered by the individuals but also earn profits for them. For example, from the past information, the insurance companies know that 1 per cent houses will catch fire. To provide insurance cover they pool a large number of policies. It insures against the expected loss to 100 policy holders, they will actually pay the loss to one policy holder if the probability of houses catching fire is one per cent. They fix such an amount of insurance premium that they are not only able to compensate the loss to the individuals but also earn profits for themselves.

Obtaining More Information

Collecting more accurate information is one important way in which individual can reduce risk while making a choice under conditions of uncertainty. More information will enable them to increase expected value and expected utility. With more information about the new good you want to purchase or about the new job you are offered will reduce the possibility of suffering a loss. For example, by buying a car or refrigerator of a company many individuals seek information from friends, read reviews of the car or refrigerator in the newspapers or on television to know how frequently a particular brand is likely to break down and require repairs more often. By gathering such information you can reduce the possibility of making a wrong decision.

NOTES

NOTES